AUTOMOTIVE MECHANICS

AUTOMOTIVE MECHANICS

TENTH EDITION

WILLIAM H. CROUSE
AND
DONALD L. ANGLIN

GLENCOE
McGraw-Hill

New York, New York   Columbus, Ohio   Mission Hills, California   Peoria, Illinois

ACKNOWLEDGMENTS

Special thanks are owed to the following organizations for information and illustrations they supplied: AC Spark Plug Division of General Motors Corporation; AC Rochester Division of General Motors Corporation; AC-Delco Division of General Motors Corporation; Airpax Corporation; American Suzuki Motor Corporation; American Honda Motor Company, Inc.; ATW; Audi of America, Inc.; Bear Manufacturing Company; Belden Automotive Wire & Cable; Bendix Corporation; Black & Decker Inc.; Blackhawk Automotive Inc.; BMW of North America Inc.; Bridgestone Tire; British Leyland, Limited; Brush Research Manufacturing Company, Inc.; Buick Division of General Motors Corporation; Cadillac Division of General Motors Corporation; California Bureau of Automotive Repair; Champion Spark Plug Company; Chevrolet Division of General Motors Corporation; Chicago Pneumatic Tool Company; Chrysler Corporation; Concept Technology, Inc.; Dana Corporation; Deere & Company; Delco Moraine Division of General Motors Corporation; Delco-Remy Division of General Motors Corporation; Dow Corning Corporation; EPIC Technologies, Inc.; Federal Mogul Corporation; Fel-Pro Inc.; Fiat Motors of North America, Inc.; Firestone Rubber Company; Ford of Europe, Inc.; Ford Motor Company; Ford Motor Company of Germany; General Electric; General Motors Corporation; George Olcott Company; GM Hughes Electronics Corporation; Goodyear Tire & Rubber Company; Gould Corporation; Gunk Laboratories, Inc.; Hunckler Products, Inc.; Hunter Engineering Company; Hydra-Matic Division of General Motors Corporation; Intercont Products Inc.; Jenny Division of Homestead Industries; John Fluke Manufacturing Company, Inc.; Johnson Bronze Company; Kent-Moore Division of SPX Corporation; Kwik-Way Manufacturing Company; Leroi Division of Dresser Industries, Inc.; Lincoln St. Louis Division of McNeil Corporation; Lisle Corporation; Loctite Corporation; LuK, Inc.; Maremont Corporation; Mazda Motors of America, Inc.; McQuay-Norris Manufacturing Company; Mercedes-Benz of North America, Inc.; Michelin North America, Inc.; Mitsubishi Motor Sales of America, Inc.; Monroe Auto Equipment Company; Moog Automotive, Inc.; Motor Vehicle Manufacturers Association; National Institute for Automotive Service Excellence; Neway Manufacturing, Inc.; Nilfisk of America, Inc.; Nissan Motor Corporation; Oldsmobile Division of General Motors Corporation; OTC Tool & Equipment Division of SPX Corporation; Peugeot Motors of America, Inc.; Phillips Temro, Inc.; Pontiac Division of General Motors Corporation; Proto Tool Company; Robert Bosch Corporation; Rochester Products Divison of General Motors Corporation; Rockwell International; Saab Cars USA, Inc.; Saturn Corporation; Schwitzer Division of Wallace-Murray Corporation; Sealed Power Corporation; Sioux Tools Inc.; Snap-on Tools Corporation; Standard Motor Products, Inc.; Subaru of America, Inc.; Sun Electric Corporation; Sunnen Products Company; The L. S. Starrett Company; The Reynolds & Reynolds Company; 3M Automotive Trades Division; Tire Industry Safety Council; Tomco, Inc.; Toyota Motor Sales, U.S.A., Inc.; Trico Products Corporation; TRW Inc.; United Tool Processes; United States Safety Service Company; Vendredi II; Volkswagen of America, Inc.; Volvo Cars of North America; Walker Manufacturing Division of Tenneco, Inc.; Warner Electric Brake and Clutch Company; ZF of North America, Inc.

William H. Crouse and Donald L. Anglin

Cover Photograph: Thunderbird Super Coupe, Neil Nissing/FPG International. **Part Opener Photographs:** Part 1, Courtesy of Saturn Corporation; Parts 2, 3, 5, and 8, Courtesy of Ford Motor Company; Parts 4, 6, 7, and 9, Courtesy of General Motors Corporation.

Library of Congress Cataloging-in-Publication Data
Crouse, William Henry, (date)
Automotive mechanics / William H. Crouse and Donald L. Anglin.— 10th ed.
p. cm.
Includes index.
ISBN 0-02-800943-6
1. Automobiles. 2. Automobiles—Maintenance and repair.
3. Automobiles—Maintenance and repair—Examinations, questions,
etc. I. Anglin, Donald L. II. Title.
TL205.C86 1993
629.28'72—dc20   92-36588
                                                          CIP

Automotive Mechanics, Tenth Edition

Imprint 2003

Send all inquiries to:
Glencoe/McGraw-Hill
8787 Orion Place
Columbus, OH 43240-4027

ISBN 0-02-800943-6

Printed in the United States of America.

13 14 15 042/046 03

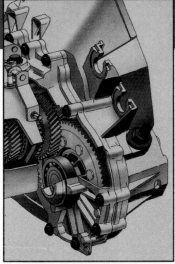

CONTENTS

PART 3 Automotive Engine Systems 184

PART 4 Automotive Electrical and Electronic Equipment 338

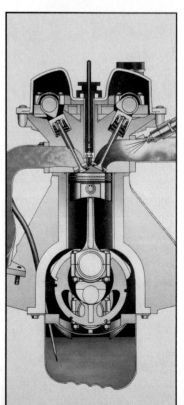

PART 8 Automotive Chassis 656

PART 9 Automotive Heating and Air Conditioning 764

PREFACE

This is the tenth edition of *Automotive Mechanics*. Since the publication of the ninth edition, tremendous changes have taken place in the automotive industry. Two powerful forces have been at work. One is the challenge of foreign automotive manufacturers. The other is the effect of the Federal laws passed by Congress covering *automotive air pollution, automotive safety, and automotive fuel economy.*

These two forces, acting on both American and foreign automotive manufacturers, have caused the manufacturers to develop new generations of light, fuel-efficient vehicles. This is an ongoing, evolutionary process. Each year, automotive manufacturers bring out new models that improve on fuel efficiency and performance, with less air pollution.

The competition among manufacturers has resulted in many innovations that are being widely adopted. A few of these include *antilock braking systems (ABS), traction-control systems (TCS); four-wheel steering; four-wheel drive (4WD) and all-wheel drive (AWD); electronically-controlled and active suspension systems; supplemental restraint systems (air bags); electronic automatic transaxles and transmissions; electronic engine control and management; distributorless ignition systems; sequential port fuel injection; supercharging and turbocharging; variable engine-valve timing and lift; onboard diagnostics;* and a host of other innovations.

Now undergoing tests by automotive manufacturers are two-cycle engines that do not produce excessive air pollution. If these become successful, and automobiles with two-cycle engines are built, there will be further changes in automotive production and service.

This new edition of *Automotive Mechanics* covers the latest developments in automotive design, construction, operation, diagnosis, and service. The entire text has been rewritten to integrate the new with the old. Rewriting has simplified explanations, shortened sentences, and improved readability. Hundreds of new illustrations have been added to cover new developments. Many chapters now end with vocabulary words and "think-type" review questions, in addition to the ASE-type multiple-choice questions. These all serve to make the pages, concepts, and practices more interesting and understandable to the student.

However, the objective of *Automotive Mechanics* remains the same: to provide the student with the basic principles of all automotive components and systems. This includes how they are constructed, how they operate, what troubles they might develop, and possible causes of these troubles. Typical specifications and sample service procedures are included. These introduce the student to the way automotive manufacturers, service instructors, and master technicians recommend that diagnosis and service procedures be performed. Every effort was made to incorporate the use of the vehicle's onboard diagnostics, scan tools, service-bay diagnostic computers, and the latest in computerized automotive testing and servicing equipment.

The ancillary materials for use with *Automotive Mechanics* have also been revised. These include a *Study Guide,* a *Workbook,* and a combined *Instructor's Planning Guide and Testbook.* These materials along with the textbook provide the instructor with a flexible teaching package that should fit any type of teaching situation. The instructor's planning guide explains how the materials can be used to meet any teaching requirements. It also has the answers to the multiple-choice questions in the textbook, ASE practice tests, transparency masters, and handouts that will be helpful to the automotive instructor.

The *Automotive Mechanics* program covers in depth the subjects tested by the National Institute for Automotive Service Excellence (ASE). These tests are used to certify master automotive technicians as well as automotive-service technicians working in specific areas of specialization under the ASE voluntary testing and certification program. For schools seeking program certification by the National Automotive Technicians Education Foundation (NATEF), every attempt has been made to include the *high priority* items from their diagnosis, service, and repair task lists. At least 80 percent of these items must be included in the curriculum to meet the minimum standards for certification.

During the planning and preparation of this new tenth edition of *Automotive Mechanics,* the authors and publisher had the advice and assistance of many people—educators, researchers, artists, editors, and automotive industry service specialists. Special thanks must go to these reviewers: James Majernik, Tommy Smith, and Richard Rogers.

William H. Crouse
Donald L. Anglin

ABOUT THE AUTHORS

WILLIAM H. CROUSE

Behind William H. Crouse's clear technical writing is a background of sound mechanical engineering training as well as a variety of practical industrial experience. After finishing high school, he spent a year working in a tinplate mill. Summers, while still in school, he worked in General Motors plants, and for three years he worked in the Delco-Remy Division shops. Later he became Director of Field Education in the Delco-Remy Division of General Motors Corporation, for which he prepared service bulletins and educational literature.

Mr. Crouse has contributed numerous articles to automotive and engineering magazines, and has written many books about science and technology. He was the first Editor-in-Chief of the 15-volume *McGraw-Hill Encyclopedia of Science and Technology.* In addition, he has authored more than 50 technical books, including *Automotive Mechanics,* which has sold over a million copies. His books have been widely translated and used in automotive mechanics training throughout the world.

William H. Crouse's outstanding work in the automotive field has earned for him membership in the Society of Automotive Engineers and in the American Society of Engineering Education.

DONALD L. ANGLIN

Trained in the automotive and diesel service field, Donald L. Anglin has worked both as a technician and as a service manager. He has taught automotive courses in high school, trade schools, community colleges, and universities. Interested in all types of vehicle performance, he has served as a racing-car mechanic and as a consultant to truck fleets and others on failure analysis, maintenance problems, and trade practices in the automotive service industry.

Currently, he devotes full time to automotive and technical writing. Together with William H. Crouse, he has coauthored a number of magazine articles on automotive education, as well as more than 100 automotive books published by McGraw-Hill and Glencoe.

Donald L. Anglin is a certified Master Automobile Technician, Master Heavy-Duty Truck Technician, Body Repair Technician, and Engine Machinist. He is also certified in refrigerant recovery and recycling, and holds other licenses and certificates in automotive education, service, and related areas. He is a member of the American Society of Mechanical Engineers and the Society of Automotive Engineers. In addition, he is a member of the Board of Trustees of the National Automotive History Collection.

TO THE STUDENT

Automotive Mechanics was designed with you, the student, in mind. It was put together to help you learn, in the quickest and easiest way possible, all about automotive vehicles and the automotive service industry. By the time you have finished studying this book, and have done the related shopwork, you will be ready to enter the world of automotive servicing as a wage earner.

Various special materials have been developed to make learning easier. These materials include a study guide and a comprehensive, yet practical, shop workbook. Each of these was prepared with one thought in mind—to help you learn all about automobiles.

Your major job now is to study this book and to do your shopwork. Studying is usually a challenge for everyone. It takes willpower to sit down and read this technical material. But if you follow the suggestions listed below, you will find studying much easier.

1. The first thing to do when you pick up your textbook to study your assignment is to turn the pages one by one. Look at the pictures. Read the numbered section headings. Study each section heading carefully. This will give you an idea of what the assignment is about.
2. If you are starting a new chapter in the textbook, read the objectives that tell you what you should know and be able to do after you have studied the chapter. This emphasizes what you should learn from the chapter.
3. Read the first section in your assignment. Then read the first section again slowly and carefully so that you make sure you understand it.
4. Continue studying the pages assigned to you. Read each section carefully.
5. If you come to a word you don't know, first look for the definition in the text. You can also look up the word in the Glossary at the back of the book, and check in the Index. Many of the words are in the dictionary in the school library or that you use for other classes. With today's rapidly changing technology, an up-to-date dictionary can be a valuable learning tool for an automotive technician.
6. If you read a sentence that you don't understand, read it again aloud. Think about it. If this does not help, write the sentence on a piece of paper. When you have a chance, ask your instructor to explain the sentence.
7. Don't hesitate to admit that something puzzles you. Everybody gets stuck once in awhile. Your instructor is there to help you understand.
8. Don't worry about not understanding everything the first time you read it. Many students read and reread their lessons several times. Each time you will understand and retain more.

William H. Crouse
Donald L. Anglin

William H. Crouse died in March, 1991, while working on the manuscript for this book, the tenth edition of *Automotive Mechanics*. Bill's distinguished career as an internationally acclaimed automotive author spanned six decades. With an Introduction by Charles F. Kettering, the first edition of *Automotive Mechanics* and the many other "Crouse books" that followed became synonymous with clear technical writing and excellence in automotive education. Bill's longtime publishing associate and coauthor, Donald L. Anglin, will continue to prepare the new editions of *Automotive Mechanics* and other titles in the Crouse-Anglin Automotive Technology Series.

Introduction by Charles F. Kettering to the first edition of *Automotive Mechanics* by William H. Crouse

The automobile has become a trusted and valuable servant of the American people. Engineering design and manufacturing skill have made the modern motor car simple to operate and economical to maintain. To achieve utmost simplicity of operation, and thus ensure greatest utility, engineers have made many design improvements and have added new devices from time to time. The electric self-starter, for example, was added to eliminate the uncertain and sometimes dangerous job of hand-cranking the engine, and brought along with it battery ignition and electric lights for the automobile. Automatic oil pressure and engine temperature gauges were added to enable the driver to detect troubles before they developed to the point of actual failure. The syncro-mesh transmission has simplified gear-shifting, while automatic gear-shifting mechanisms have done away with hand gear-shifting altogether. Many other instances could be mentioned.

Manufacturing skill, combined with improved designs, has effected great savings so that economical transportation has become available to many millions. At the same time, improvements in manufacturing methods have made it possible to use better materials and closer tolerances so that car life has been tremendously increased.

This increasing complexity of the machine, plus the improving skill with which it is manufactured, has extended a challenge and provided an opportunity for automotive mechanics who, in garages and service stations all over the country, do their part to keep America's cars rolling. Automotive mechanics have kept pace with the automobile industry; their record has been outstanding. Aiding them in achieving their record have been factory service publications and educational programs, trade and technical school activities, trade magazines, and such books as *Automotive Mechanics*. All these help, too, in training the new mechanic entering the automotive service field.

The *Automotive Mechanics* book, in particular, should prove of value to those interested in the subject. Its author has been identified with the automotive industry for many years in manufacturing, engineering, and field service activities. He is at present a field service engineer for an automotive electrical equipment manufacturer and is responsible for the service publications issued by that company. His experience gives authenticity to the book; maintenance, testing, and repair procedures are based on practices approved by car and equipment manufacturers. The book is practical in approach, and pertains to the construction, theory of operation, testing, adjustment, repair and maintenance of automobiles. Anyone desiring to improve their knowledge along these lines should find the book helpful. The simple treatment and arrangement of the textual matter makes the book especially suitable for use in school courses in the subject of automotive mechanics.

C. F. Kettering
Dayton, Ohio
1946

PART 1

AUTOMOTIVE SERVICE AND SHOP WORK

Part 1 of *Automotive Mechanics* gives you a historical view of the automobile. Its basic construction, operation, and regulation are described. Job opportunities are discussed. Shop work and working safely are introduced, along with how to use and take care of the various tools used in the shop.

There are eight chapters in Part 1:

CHAPTER 1

INTRODUCTION TO THE AUTOMOBILE

After studying this chapter, you should be able to:

- Define *motor vehicle, automobile, truck,* and *bus.*
- Describe how front-wheel drive, rear-wheel drive, and four-wheel drive differ.
- List the support systems an engine needs to run, and describe each.
- Explain how a basic control system works.
- Review the three areas of federal legislation and how each has affected the automobile.

➢ 1-1 DEFINING THE AUTOMOBILE

The automobile (Fig. 1-1) is a self-propelled vehicle that travels on land. It usually has four wheels. An *engine* provides the power to move the vehicle. The automobile, or *car,* carries people primarily for their personal transportation.

There are many different styles of cars. Some people prefer a *sports car* like the Chevrolet Corvette (Fig. 1-2). It seats only two, has limited luggage space, and is expensive. But the Corvette has distinctive body styling and outstanding performance.

For most people, a sports car is not the best family vehicle. Parents with young children want additional space and seating inside the vehicle. A small *van* (Fig. 1-3) may fill this need. It may serve as a car, and often is similar in construction.

Regardless of style, the automobile is a type of *motor vehicle.* This is the name given to any self-propelled vehicle that does not run on rails. Two other types of motor vehicles are the *truck* and the *bus.* A truck primarily transports goods and cargo. A bus is a motor vehicle that may carry many passengers. Motor vehicles are also called *automotive vehicles.*

Fig. 1-1 People use a variety of cars primarily for personal transportation. *(Ford Motor Company)*

INTRODUCING THE AUTOMOBILE

➢ 1-2 HISTORY OF THE AUTOMOBILE

The automobile has been around for more than 100 years. The first automobiles were basically horse-drawn buggies and carriages powered by gasoline-fueled engines instead of horses. They were called *gas buggies* and *horseless carriages*. The early engines had one cylinder that could produce only one or two horsepower. A *horsepower* is roughly the power of one horse.

The first automobile was a gas buggy built by Karl Benz in Germany in 1885 and 1886. It had three wheels, one in the front and two in the rear. That year another German, Gottlieb Daimler, mounted an engine in a wooden bicycle. The next year he also built a four-wheel gas buggy.

Two brothers, Charles and Frank Duryea, built the first

Fig. 1-3 A small van with additional space and seating may serve as a car, and often has similar construction. *(Pontiac Division of General Motors Corporation)*

Fig. 1-4 An early Ford car built in 1896. *(Ford Motor Company)*

automobile in the United States in 1893. By 1895, Henry Ford, Ransom Olds, and others were building cars in this country. Figure 1-4 shows a car built by Ford in 1896. The early cars were crude compared to today's cars. But they ran—most of the time.

By 1900, several factories in Detroit and elsewhere were making automobiles. Most manufacturers were building cars that kept getting bigger and more expensive. Ford wanted to make cars as cheaply as possible so more people could buy them. By 1908, he had the car in production that put America on wheels. This was the *Model T Ford* (Fig. 1-5), manufactured on the first modern assembly line. During the next 20 years, 15 million Model T Fords were sold.

Today, the automotive industry is one of the biggest in the world. In the United States, about 12 million people work in the automotive industry and its related businesses. This is one out of every seven workers. The job of about a million of these men and women is to service automotive vehicles and keep them running.

Fig. 1-5 Model T Fords coming off the assembly line in 1914. The first assembly-line production of the automobile was achieved by Henry Ford. *(Ford Motor Company)*

➤ 1-3 CONSTRUCTION OF THE AUTOMOBILE

About 15,000 separate parts are put together to make an automobile. These parts are grouped into several *systems*. Each system is made up of two or more parts that work together to perform a specific job. Examples are such jobs as braking and steering.

Automotive vehicles are produced in a large variety of sizes and shapes (Fig. 1-6). All have the same basic parts and systems (Fig. 1-7). Today, many of these systems are controlled electronically by one or more *electronic control modules* (ECM). Sometimes an ECM is called a *computer*.

The basic parts and systems in an automobile are the major *components*. These include:

- An engine, or *power plant*, that produces power to move the vehicle.
- A *power train*, to carry the power from the engine to the drive wheels.
- A *suspension system*, that absorbs the shock of the tires and wheels meeting bumps and holes in the road.
- A *steering system*, so the driver can control the direction of vehicle travel.
- A *braking system*, so the driver can slow and stop the vehicle.
- An *electrical system*, to provide electricity for cranking the engine, charging the battery, and powering the lights and other electrical equipment.
- A *body*, that provides enclosures or compartments for the engine, passengers, and luggage or cargo.

Fig. 1-6 Various body styles of automotive vehicles. *(Chevrolet Division of General Motors Corporation)*

Fig. 1-6 *Continued.*

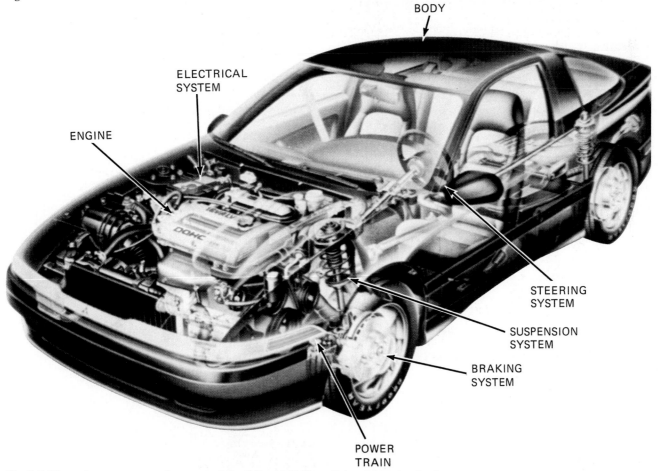

Fig. 1-7 The major components of an automobile. *(Mitsubishi Motor Sales of America, Inc.)*

➤ 1-4 UNDER THE HOOD

The *engine compartment* is usually at the front of the vehicle. When you raise the hood, you see the engine and some of the parts attached to it (Fig. 1-8). These may include the *air-conditioning compressor, alternator, power-steering pump, starting motor,* and *supercharger* or *turbocharger.* Other parts, such as the *battery* and *power-brake booster,* are near the engine. They are connected to it by *electric wiring* and *hose* or *tubing.*

5

Fig. 1-8 Engine compartment of a car that has a supercharger mounted on a V-6 engine. *(Buick Division of General Motors Corporation)*

In the car, the engine mounts either longways or sideways (Fig. 1-9). An engine mounted longways (Figs. 1-2 and 1-9A) has *longitudinal* mounting. The *transmission* attaches to the rear of the engine. A long *driveshaft* connects the transmission, through the rear *drive axle* and *differential*, to the rear wheels.

An engine that mounts sideways has *transverse* mounting (Figs. 1-7, 1-8, and 1-9B). With this arrangement, the car is more *compact*. The engine compartment requires less space. Instead of a transmission, a *transaxle* attaches to one end of the engine. The transaxle combines the *trans*mission and many parts of the rear drive

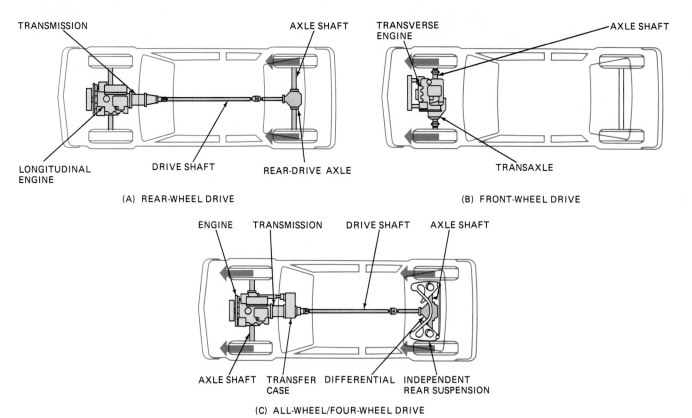

Fig. 1-9 The three basic automotive power trains or drive trains. *(ATW)*

axle into a single assembly. Short *axle shafts* or *half shafts* connect the transaxle to the front wheels.

➤ 1-5 IDENTIFYING THE DRIVE WHEELS

The way the engine mounts usually tells you which wheels are the *drive wheels*. These are the wheels that move the car. If the engine mounts longitudinally, the car usually has *rear-wheel drive* (RWD). Engine power flows through the transmission and driveshaft to the rear wheels. However, some rear-wheel-drive vehicles may also drive the front wheels (Fig. 1-9C). These vehicles usually have a *transfer case*. It can send or *transfer* some of the engine power to the front wheels. This is called *four-wheel drive* (4WD) or *all-wheel drive* (AWD).

If the engine mounts transversely at the front of the vehicle, the vehicle has *front-wheel drive* (FWD). Engine power flows through the transaxle to the front wheels (Fig. 1-9B). To get four-wheel drive, the rear wheels are also driven.

➤ 1-6 THE SOURCE OF POWER

The automotive engine (Fig. 1-10) is an *internal-combustion engine*. *Internal* means inside and *combustion* means burning. Power is produced by burning a mixture of air and fuel inside *cylinders* in the engine. Most automotive engines have four, six, or eight cylinders. Each cylinder is like a tin can in which a round *piston* slides up and down. This movement is carried through gears and shafts to rotate the wheels and move the car. Later chapters explain how this works.

To continue running, an engine must have four support systems. These are the fuel, ignition, lubricating, and cooling systems.

SUPPORTING ENGINE OPERATION

➤ 1-7 THE FUEL SYSTEM

The *fuel system* (Fig. 1-11) mixes gasoline or similar fuel with air to make a mixture that will burn in the engine cylinders. Some fuel systems use a *carburetor* (Fig. 1-12). It sits on top of the engine *intake manifold*. The carburetor mixes the air and fuel into a combustible mixture.

Instead of a carburetor, most engines have *electronic fuel injection* (EFI). An electronic control module (ECM) or computer controls one or more *fuel injectors* (Fig. 1-13). When the engine needs fuel, a signal from the ECM opens the injector. Fuel then sprays into the air on its way to the engine cylinders. This provides the air-fuel mixture the engine needs for combustion.

Fig. 1-10 An internal-combustion engine burns a mixture of fuel and air inside cylinders in the engine. *(Cadillac Division of General Motors Corporation)*

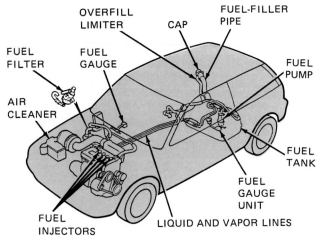

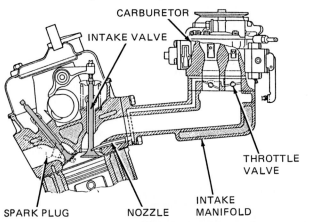

Fig. 1-11 The basic parts of a fuel system, with a fuel injector located in the intake port for each cylinder. *(Chrysler Corporation)*

Fig. 1-12 The carburetor sits on top of the engine intake manifold. *(American Suzuki Motor Corporation)*

There are two basic types of electronic fuel injection. *Throttle-body injection* (TBI) has only one or two injectors. These are in the *throttle body* above the intake manifold (Fig. 1-13). *Port injection* (Fig. 1-14) has a fuel injector in the intake port for each cylinder.

➤ 1-8 THE IGNITION SYSTEM

After the air-fuel mixture enters the engine cylinder, the piston moves up the cylinder. This compresses the trapped mixture. Then electric sparks at the *spark plug* (Fig. 1-15) ignite the mixture. The resulting combustion produces the power to move the car. The *ignition system* provides the sparks.

Today all ignition systems are electronic, operated by an electronic control module. Many use an ignition *distributor* (Fig. 1-15) to "distribute" the sparks to the proper engine cylinders. Other engines have a *distributorless ignition system* (Fig. 1-13).

➤ 1-9 THE LUBRICATING SYSTEM

The *lubricating system* (Fig. 1-16) keeps all moving parts inside the engine coated with layers of oil. This reduces wear on the parts. It also allows the parts to move freely with little power lost in making them move.

An *oil pan* at the bottom of the engine holds several quarts [liters] of oil. The engine drives an *oil pump* that picks up oil from the oil pan and sends the oil through the engine.

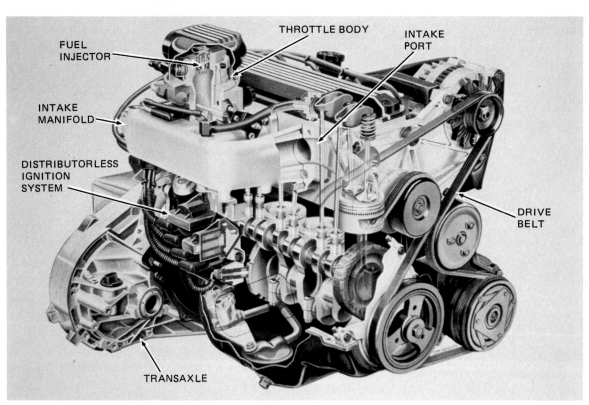

Fig. 1-13 A four-cylinder engine with throttle-body injection. A fuel injector is located above the intake manifold in the throttle body. *(Chevrolet Division of General Motors Corporation)*

Fig. 1-14 A V-6 engine with port injection. A fuel injector is located in the intake port for each cylinder. *(Pontiac Division of General Motors Corporation)*

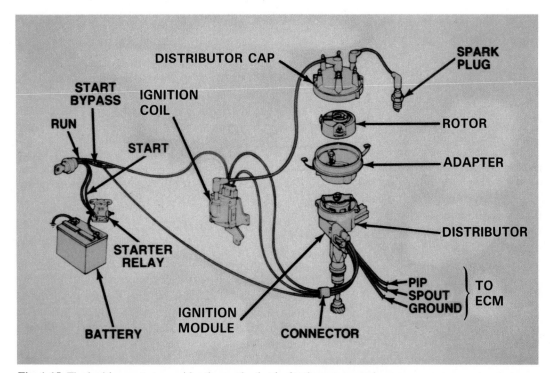

Fig. 1-15 The ignition system provides the sparks that ignite the compressed air-fuel mixture in the engine cylinders. *(Ford Motor Company)*

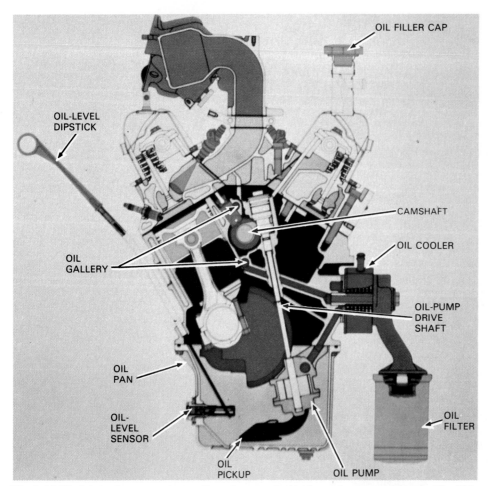

OIL FILLER CAP

OIL-LEVEL
DIPSTICK

CAMSHAFT

OIL COOLER

OIL
GALLERY

OIL-PUMP
DRIVE
SHAFT

OIL
PAN

OIL-
LEVEL
SENSOR

OIL
FILTER

OIL
PICKUP

OIL PUMP

Fig. 1-16 The lubricating system keeps all moving parts inside the engine coated with oil. *(Ford Motor Company)*

➤ 1-10 THE COOLING SYSTEM

Burning fuel inside the engine cylinders produces heat. If some of the heat is not removed, metal engine parts will melt. Some of the heat helps push the pistons down the cylinders. This is the useful heat. Some of the heat escapes in the hot burned gases that leave the engine cylinders. This is wasted heat. And some of the heat is removed by the engine *cooling system* (Fig. 1-17). This is also wasted heat.

The cooling system removes just enough heat so the engine runs at the proper temperature. A *water pump* circulates liquid called the *coolant* between the engine and the *radiator*. Cooler outside air flows through the radiator. The air picks up and carries away the excess heat. A *thermostat* helps keep the coolant at the proper temperature. A *fan* helps keep air moving through the radiator.

GETTING POWER TO THE WHEELS

➤ 1-11 THE POWER TRAIN

The drive train or power train carries power from the engine to the drive wheels (Fig. 1-18). Major power-train

parts may include the *clutch,* transmission or transaxle, transfer case, driveshaft, and *differential.* Figure 1-9 shows the layout of these parts for front-wheel drive, rear-wheel drive, and four-wheel drive.

Transmissions and transaxles may be either *manual* or *automatic.* Automatic transmissions and transaxles automatically shift from one *gear ratio* to another. The driver takes no action. Manual transmissions and transaxles are shifted by hand. To shift from one gear ratio to another, the driver depresses the *clutch pedal* and moves the *shift lever.*

> **NOTE** Sometimes references are made to the "transmission" in a vehicle that has a transaxle. This usually refers to the *transmission section* of the transaxle.

➤ 1-12 THE CLUTCH

Vehicles with a manual transmission or transaxle have a *clutch* (Fig. 1-19). It is between the engine and the transmission or transaxle. Before shifting, the driver depresses the foot-operated clutch pedal. This disconnects the engine from the transmission or transaxle. Parts in these *units* may be damaged by trying to shift while under load.

> **NOTE** In the automotive trade, an assembly such as a transmission or transaxle is called a *unit.*

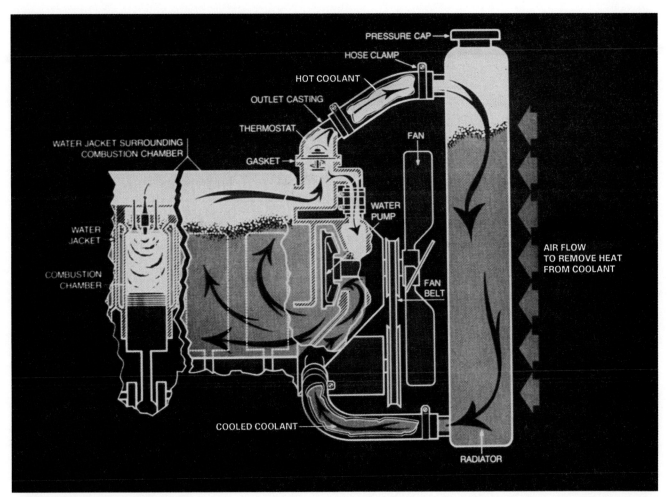

Fig. 1-17 The engine cooling system.

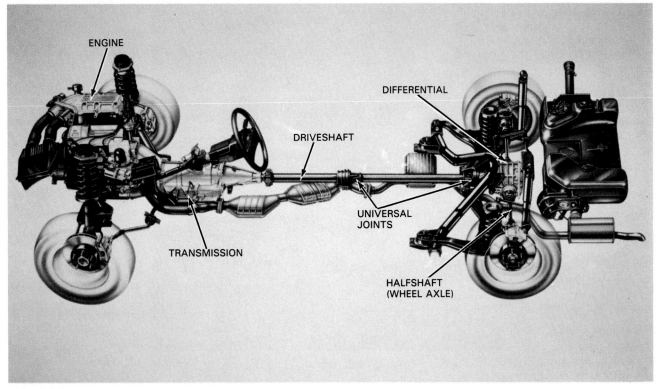

Fig. 1-18 The drive train or power train carries the power from the engine to the wheels that turn to move or drive the vehicle. *(Ford Motor Company)*

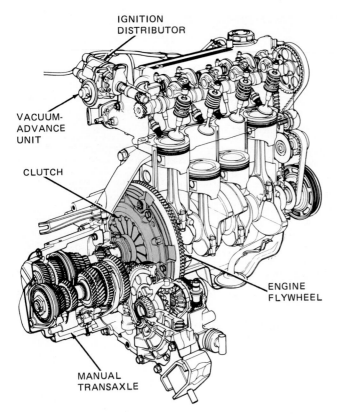

IGNITION
DISTRIBUTOR

VACUUM-
ADVANCE
UNIT

CLUTCH

ENGINE
FLYWHEEL

MANUAL
TRANSAXLE

Fig. 1-19 Location of the clutch between the engine and the transaxle. *(Mazda Motors of America, Inc.)*

➤ **1-13 TRANSMISSIONS AND TRANSAXLES**

Transmissions and transaxles look different. Figure 1-20 shows a six-speed *manual transmission*. Figure 1-21 shows a four-speed *automatic transaxle*. They are similar in some ways. Both are *gear boxes* made up of a metal case containing gears and shafts. The case is filled with oil.

The transmission or transaxle provides several different forward *gear ratios* between the engine and the drive wheels. Gear ratio is the difference in rotating speed between the transmission or transaxle input shaft and output shaft (➤43-4). Other positions are *reverse* and *neutral*. Reverse allows the vehicle to move backward. Neutral disengages all gears for starting and running the engine without moving the vehicle.

When an engine is turning slowly, it cannot produce enough power to get the vehicle moving. The transmission gear ratios provide the necessary increase in engine *torque*. Torque is twisting or turning force. It is the torque supplied by the engine that turns the wheels to move the car.

➤ **1-14 AUTOMATIC TRANSMISSIONS AND TRANSAXLES**

Most cars have an automatic transmission or transaxle (Fig. 1-22). It shifts automatically to match the driving conditions. For example, when the car is going up a steep

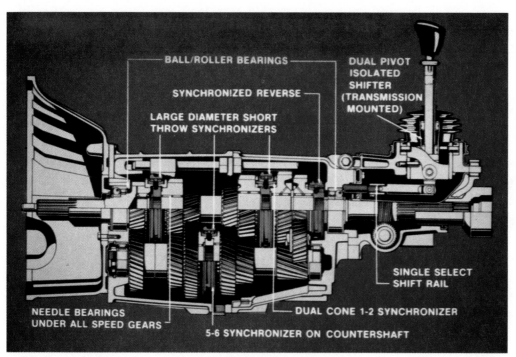

Fig. 1-20 A six-speed manual transmission. *(Chevrolet Division of General Motors Corporation)*

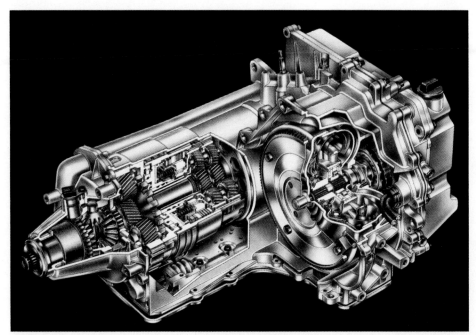

Fig. 1-21 An electronically-controlled four-speed automatic transaxle. *(Cadillac Division of General Motors Corporation)*

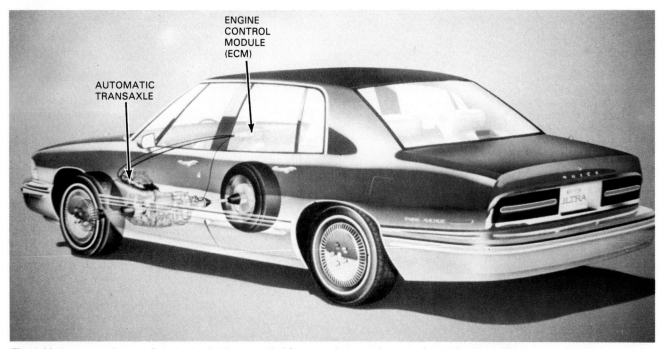

AUTOMATIC
TRANSAXLE

ENGINE
CONTROL
MODULE
(ECM)

Fig. 1-22 Layout on the car of an electronically-controlled four-speed automatic transaxle and the electronic control module (ECM). *(Buick Division of General Motors Corporation)*

hill, the transmission or transaxle will *downshift*. This allows the engine to turn faster and produce more power.

Automatic transmissions and transaxles are controlled primarily by devices that react to vehicle speed and engine load. Many newer units are computer-controlled (Figs. 1-21 and 1-22). An electronic control module (ECM) controls when and how the transmission shifts.

CONTROLLING RIDE AND HANDLING

> ## 1-15 THE SUSPENSION SYSTEM

Springs, shock absorbers, and related parts between the wheels and the car body make up the suspension system

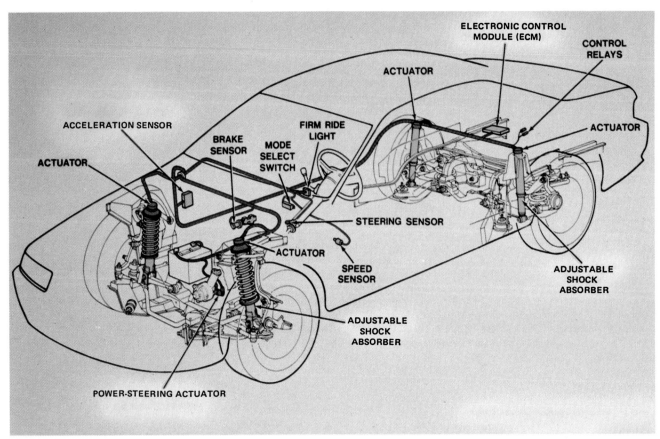

Fig. 1-23 An automotive suspension system. Springs support the weight of the vehicle while allowing the wheels to move up and down. The electronic ride control automatically changes the firmness of the shock absorbers. *(Ford Motor Company)*

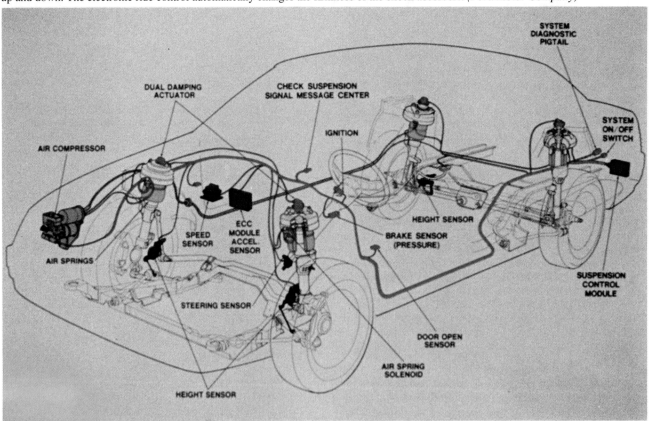

Fig. 1-24 An electronically-controlled air suspension system using rubber air springs instead of metal springs. *(Ford Motor Company)*

(Fig. 1-23). A spring at each wheel supports the weight of the vehicle and the load it is carrying. The springs allow the wheels to move up and down as they meet holes and bumps in the road. As the wheels do this, the springs absorb most of the motion. Little up-and-down movement reaches the body. A shock absorber at each wheel helps limit spring travel and wheel bounce.

Automobile suspension systems use four types of springs. These are *coil springs* (Fig. 1-23), *leaf springs, torsion-bar springs,* and *air springs* (Fig. 1-24). Some cars have *electronic ride control* (Fig. 1-23). It automatically changes the firmness of the shock absorbers to suit road conditions. Other cars have an electronic *air suspension* system (Fig. 1-24). It is similar to electronic ride control. However, rubber bags filled with air ("air springs") replace the metal springs.

The steering system (Fig. 1-25) enables the driver to turn the front wheels left or right. This changes the direction of vehicle travel. Steering starts at the *steering wheel* in front of the driver. As it is turned, shafts and gears act on linkage which connects to the front wheels. The wheels swing to the right or left. The vehicle then follows the direction in which the front wheels point.

A few vehicles have *four-wheel steering*. When the front wheels swing to one side for steering, the rear wheels also swing slightly. This can make parking easier and improve high-speed stability. Four-wheel steering is controlled either mechanically or electronically. However, the rear-wheel steering movement is very small compared to that of the front wheels.

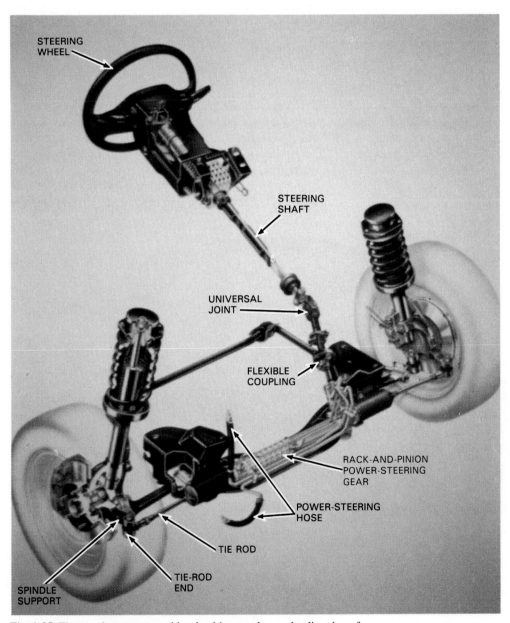

Fig. 1-25 The steering system enables the driver to change the direction of vehicle travel by turning the steering wheel. *(Ford Motor Company)*

To apply the brakes, the driver pushes down on the *brake pedal* (Fig. 1-26). This sends fluid under pressure to a *brake assembly* at each wheel. In the brake assembly, the fluid forces a stationary part against a rotating part. The *friction* between the two parts slows or stops the rotating part and the wheel. This slows and stops the car.

The car has two kinds of brakes at the wheels: *drum* or *disc*. Figure 1-26 shows a car with front disc brakes and rear drum brakes. The drum attaches to the inside of the wheel. When braking, curved *brake shoes* are forced against the inside of the rotating drum. The disc also rotates with the wheel. Flat shoes called *disc-brake pads* nearly touch the two sides of the disc. Braking action forces the pads against the rotating disc.

Many vehicles have an electronic *antilock brake system* (ABS). It prevents the wheels from locking during braking (Fig. 1-26). A locked wheel is not very effective in stopping the vehicle. The tire skids and loses much of its braking ability. The antilock brake system automatically reduces the pressure on the fluid at each wheel that is about to lock. This provides the most effective braking.

Some vehicles with ABS have a *traction-control system* (TCS). This is also shown in Fig 1-26. It acts when one or both drive wheels try to spin during heavy acceleration. Then the system rapidly applies and releases the brake at that wheel. This prevents wheel spin and improves tire contact with the road.

NEED FOR ELECTRICITY AND ELECTRONICS

The engine provides the power to move the car. However, *electricity* powers most devices on the car (Fig. 1-27). The starting motor requires electricity to crank the engine. The ignition system requires electricity to deliver sparks to the cylinders. The fuel-injection system needs electricity to provide fuel. The lights, horns, radio, and air conditioner all require electricity to operate.

The car has two sources of electricity. One is the *battery*. The other is the alternator in the *charging system*. The battery supplies electricity while the engine is off and for cranking the engine. After the engine starts, the alternator recharges the battery and supplies power for the electrical load.

Many devices and systems on the car require an electronic *control system* for safe and proper operation. They include electronic control of automatic transmissions and trans-axles, suspension and steering, and antilock-brake and traction-control systems.

A basic control system has three parts. These are the *inputs*, the *control unit*, and the *outputs*. The inputs are

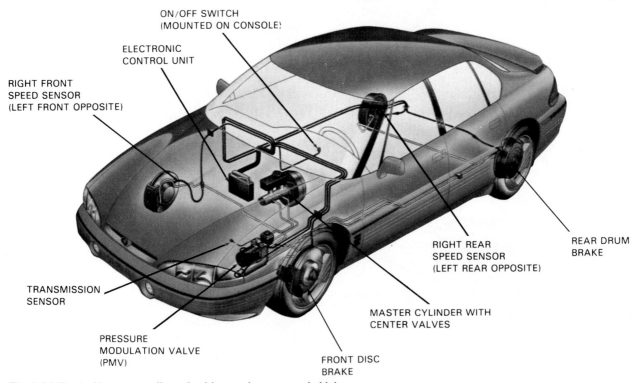

Fig. 1-26 The braking system allows the driver to slow, stop, or hold the vehicle by pushing down on the brake pedal. *(Pontiac Division of General Motors Corporation)*

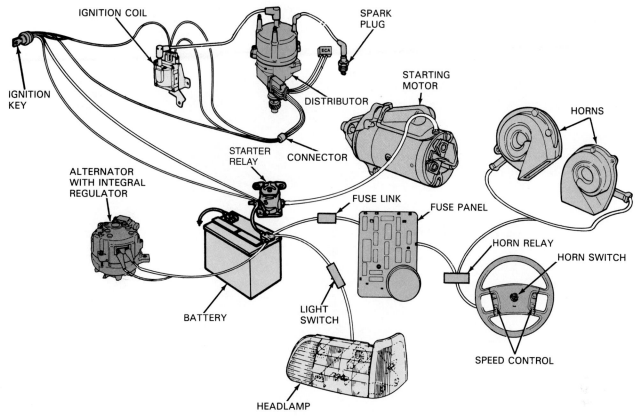

Fig. 1-27 The electrical system, which provides electricity to power most devices on the vehicle. *(Ford Motor Company)*

switches and *sensors*. They provide information to the electronic control module (ECM). It then decides how much change to make, if any. Then the ECM signals the output devices or *actuators* to take the required action.

On most engines, an *electronic engine control system* (EEC) controls the ignition and fuel-injection systems (Fig.1-28). In the EEC system, the electronic control module usually has a *self-diagnostic* capability. This means a *memory* stores information about faults or *malfunctions* that have occurred and perhaps disappeared. A malfunction is an improper or incorrect operation. When recalled from the memory, this stored information helps the technician diagnose and repair the vehicle.

BODY DESIGN AND CONSTRUCTION

➤ 1-20 BODY STYLES

There are many body styles (Fig. 1-6). Although they may look different, all body shapes should slip through the air with minimum resistance. This is the goal of *aerodynamic* styling, or *streamlining*.

Engine power and fuel are required to push a car through the air. At 90 miles per hour (mph) [145 km/h], it takes up to 75 percent of the power that reaches the wheels to overcome air resistance. This is the *drag* of the air on the car. A car with a low *coefficient of drag* (C_d) is more fuel efficient. It can travel as many as 2.5 miles farther on a gallon of gasoline than a comparable car with a higher C_d. This is one reason that car bodies have smooth curves and sloping surfaces.

➤ 1-21 BODY CONSTRUCTION

The body encloses the passenger compartment. This helps protect the passengers while providing for their comfort and safety. There are three main types of body construction:

1. Body-and-frame
2. Unitized body or *unibody*
3. Space frame

Today few cars have a separate body and frame. Figure 1-29 shows a pickup truck with this type of construction. The body is shown above the *chassis*, which usually includes everything *except* the body.

The *unitized body* does not have a separate frame (Fig.1-7). The body panels are welded together. A short *stub frame* or engine *cradle* fastens under the bottom front of the body. This provides the needed strength and mounting

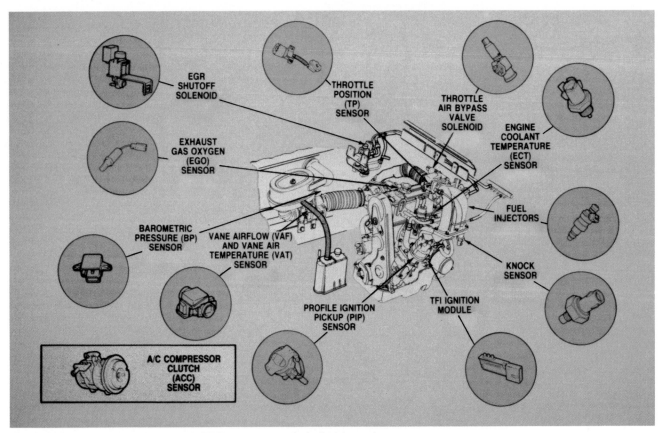

Fig. 1-28 The electronic engine control (EEC) system controls the ignition and fuel-injection systems, and usually has a self-diagnostic capability. *(Ford Motor Company)*

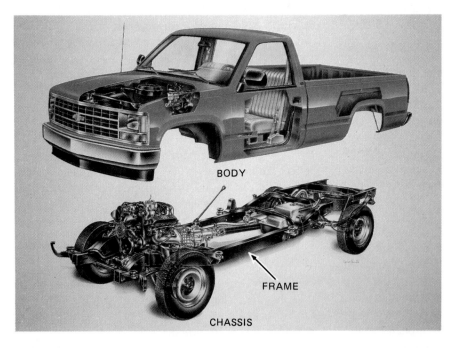

Fig. 1-29 Construction of a pickup truck that has a separate body and frame. The body is shown above the chassis. *(Chevrolet Division of General Motors Corporation)*

points for the engine, suspension, and steering parts. Some cars have a short stub frame at the rear. Figures 1-23 and 1-24 show front and rear stub frames with steering and suspension parts attached. The cradle and subframe must be properly positioned to avoid a wheel-alignment problem.

A third type of body construction is the *space frame* (Fig. 1-30). It is made of steel stampings welded together. This is similar to the tube chassis and *roll cage* in a race car. Plastic panels fasten to the space frame to complete the body.

Most bodies are sheet steel, shaped and then welded together. Some body parts and panels such as the hood are *aluminum,* a light metal. Other panels, and even complete bodies, are *fiberglass* or plastic.

REGULATING THE AUTOMOBILE

➤ 1-22 FEDERAL LEGISLATION

The United States Congress has passed a series of laws that affect the construction, operation, and service of automobiles. These laws cover:

- Automotive air pollution.
- Automotive safety.
- Automotive fuel economy.

Each law and its effects are briefly described below.

➤ 1-23 AUTOMOTIVE AIR POLLUTION

The automobile discharges or *emits* substances that pollute the air, especially while the engine is running. These substances are *emissions.* In 1963 Congress passed the *Clean Air Act.* The act and its amendments order the United States *Environmental Protection Agency* (EPA) to set automotive emission standards. These standards require *emission-control devices* that control engine and fuel-system operation. Later chapters cover automotive emission controls.

➤ 1-24 AUTOMOTIVE SAFETY

During the early 1960s, traffic deaths in the United States were nearly 50,000 a year. In 1966 Congress passed the *National Traffic and Motor Vehicle Safety Act.* It requires that all new motor vehicles sold in the United States comply with *Federal Motor Vehicle Safety Standards* (FMVSS).

Safety items fall into three classes:

1. Crash avoidance (such as the high-mounted rear stoplight).
2. Occupant protection (such as the padded dash and locking seat backs).
3. Post-crash protection (such as roll bars and air bags that deploy almost instantly after a crash begins).

Some safety devices added weight to the vehicle. This encouraged auto manufacturers to make parts from lighter, stronger material.

➤ 1-25 AUTOMOTIVE FUEL ECONOMY

To help reduce our dependence on imported oil, Congress passed the *Energy Policy and Conservation Act* in 1975. It set up *Corporate Average Fuel Economy* (CAFE) standards. The new cars produced each year by each automotive manufacturer must deliver the required average *miles per gallon* (mpg).The standards have increased almost every year. The CAFE requirement for 1980 was 20 mpg. In 1990, the CAFE requirement was 27.5 mpg. Failure to meet the standard can result in the manufacturer paying a large fine.

In 1978, Congress passed the *Energy Tax Law*. It places a "gas guzzler tax" on cars that do not meet the minimum EPA standards. The tax ranges from $500 for fuel economy of 22.4 mpg to $3,850 for fuel economy of 12.4 mpg or below.

➤ 1-26 EFFECTS OF FEDERAL LAWS

To reduce air pollution, improve automotive safety, and increase fuel economy, the automobile continues to undergo major changes. Each year, design improvements reduce weight. Bodies become more aerodynamic. Friction and power losses in the engine and power train decrease.

Many cars use fuel-efficient three- and four-cylinder engines instead of larger engines with six and eight cylinders. A small car with a three- or four-cylinder engine can get 50 mpg [22 kilometers per liter, or km/L] or more. This contrasts with the eight-cylinder big cars of the 1970s which could get only 12 to 15 mpg [5 to 6 km/L].

An electronic engine control system manages the electronic ignition and fuel-injection systems. This improves fuel efficiency and reduces exhaust emissions. Some engines have a supercharger (Fig. 1-8) or turbocharger. It forces more air-fuel mixture into the engine cylinders. This allows a smaller engine to produce more power. Automotive electronics have spread from engine management to almost every major system of the car. The average car is now smaller and lighter, or *downsized*. This allows it to go farther and pollute less while burning a gallon of fuel.

Many of these changes would have occurred eventually without the federal laws. But the effects of the laws forced more rapid change.

➤ 1-27 FUTURE AUTOMOTIVE ISSUES

The purpose of the car is to provide people with personal transportation. Today, people in and out of government want improvement in the way the car does this. Almost every city has problems with traffic jams and a shortage of parking spaces.

One proposed solution is development of *intelligent vehicle/highway systems* (IVHS). This includes improvements in traffic management, driver information, and vehicle control methods (Fig. 1-31). These improvements are possible because of advances in computers, electronics, and *telecommunications*. The goal of IVHS is to make vehicle traffic safer, more energy

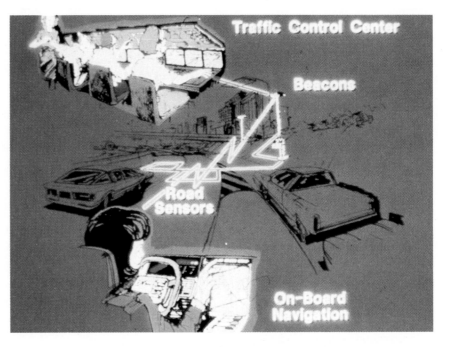

Fig. 1-31 Components of an intelligent-vehicle-and-highway system (IVHS). *(General Motors Corporation)*

efficient, and more productive. The ideal system will accomplish this while not harming the earth's environment.

➤ 1-28 FUTURE POWER PLANTS AND ELECTRIC VEHICLES

Regulating the automobile may continue to change the vehicle as we know it today. By the end of the 19th century (➤ 1-2), the automobile with its internal-combustion engine was beginning to replace the horse and carriage. Some people now predict that by the end of the 20th century, the automobile and its gasoline-burning engine itself will be on the way out (Fig. 1-32).

A driving force behind further changes to our personal-

Fig. 1-32 An electric-powered concept car, with styling and technical features that may be found on cars of the future. *(Ford Motor Company)*

transportation vehicles is a new approach to controlling automotive emissions. The Clean Air Act (➤1-23) has not produced sufficient improvement in air quality. So automotive manufacturers are looking at cleaner burning fuels to replace gasoline. They are also looking again at the electric vehicle. Abandoned years ago, by legal definition the electric vehicle is a *zero emission vehicle* (ZEV). This is because it has no direct emissions.

Whatever the future brings to the automotive vehicles of tomorrow, the change will probably evolve over a number of years. There is not likely to be an overnight revolution in automotive design, construction, diagnosis, and service. The changes that will be made will be based on proven and accepted design and engineering principles. And these have provided the vehicles, engines, and systems covered in this book.

TRADE TALK

aerodynamic	downsized	malfunction	unit
chassis	drive axle	pollution	
control system	longitudinal	transverse	

MULTIPLE-CHOICE TEST

*Select the **one** correct, best, or most probable answer to each question.*
You can find the answers in the section indicated at the end of each question.

1. The purpose of the automobile is primarily to (➤1-1)
   a. transport goods and cargo
   b. carry many passengers
   c. carry people for their personal transportation
   d. run on rails and tracks
2. To keep running, the engine needs the (➤1-6)
   a. power train, suspension system, and steering system
   b. fuel, ignition, lubricating, and cooling systems
   c. braking system, electrical and electronic systems, and body
   d. battery, starting motor, and vacuum-brake booster
3. All the following provide different gear ratios *except* (➤1-12 and 1-13)
   a. manual transmission
   b. automatic transaxle
   c. manual transaxle
   d. clutch

4. Most devices on the car are powered by (➤1-18)
   a. the engine
   b. electricity
   c. electronics
   d. vacuum
5. In an electronic control system, the devices that provide information are (➤1-19)
   a. sensors
   b. outputs
   c. actuators
   d. control units

REVIEW QUESTIONS

1. Name the basic parts and systems in a car. Describe the primary purpose of each. (➤1-3)
2. Explain how to identify the drive wheels on a car. (➤1-5)
3. Name the two basic types of electronic fuel injection, and describe the basic difference between them. (➤1-7)

4. Describe how the antilock brake system acts when a wheel starts to lock up. Describe how the traction control system acts when a wheel starts to spin. (➤1-17)
5. List the three areas of federal legislation that affect the automobile. Discuss the importance of each. (➤1-22 to 1-27)

CHAPTER 2

YOUR JOB IN AUTOMOTIVE SERVICE

After studying this chapter, you should be able to:

- Describe five types of businesses that perform automotive service.
- Explain the differences among *domestics, exports, imports,* and *transplants.*
- Discuss predelivery service, warranty service, and periodic service.
- Explain what a recall is, and who pays for it.
- Define *automotive technician certification,* and describe how to become certified.

INTRODUCTION TO AUTOMOTIVE SERVICE

➤ 2-1 AUTOMOTIVE SERVICE

There are about 190 million automotive vehicles on the streets and highways of the United States (Fig. 2-1). All these vehicles require service periodically. More than one million men and women work at servicing vehicles.

Each year thousands of jobs become available in automotive servicing. After you finish your automotive courses, you may decide to enter this field. Here are some of the places that employ trained automotive mechanics and technicians.

- Dealerships that sell and service vehicles.
- Independent garages that service all types of automotive vehicles.
- Service stations where vehicles get fuel, oil, and related products and services.
- Service facilities set up by large retail stores.
- Specialty shops that handle brakes, tuneup, transmission repair, and wheel alignment.
- Fleet garages operated by the government or private companies to service their own vehicles.

➤ 2-2 THE AUTOMOTIVE INDUSTRY

A business that produces or assembles automotive vehicles is an *automotive manufacturer.* There are three major

domestic manufacturers—the "big three"—in the United States. These are the Chrysler Corporation, Ford Motor Company, and General Motors Corporation. They sell the cars and trucks they build through their own franchised dealers (Fig. 2-2). "Franchised" means there is a written agreement between the dealer and the manufacturer.

Vehicles built here and shipped to other countries are *exports.* Vehicles built in other countries and shipped here

Fig. 2-1 About 190 million automotive vehicles operate on the streets and highways of the United States. *(ATW)*

Fig. 2-2 An automotive dealership where new and used cars and trucks are sold and serviced. *(ATW)*

are *imports*. Several Japanese companies have their own automotive manufacturing plants in the United States. These companies and their products are *transplants*. The "big three" dealers sell some imports and transplants.

However, most imports and transplants are sold through their own franchised dealers.

➤ 2-3 CAREER OPPORTUNITIES IN AUTOMOTIVE SERVICE

A variety of jobs are available in automotive service. To get your first job, you should know the basics. This includes how automotive parts work and how to service them when they do not work properly.

The automotive mechanic or technician is a respected, well-paid worker. He or she may earn as much as workers in other skilled jobs. Many service managers, dealers, and independent garage owners were once automotive mechanics. Walter Chrysler, Henry Ford, and Ransom Olds all started as automotive mechanics.

Learn all you can from studying this book. In the shop, learn what to do and how to do it. Complete this course in

automotive mechanics. Take any other automotive courses you can. They all provide you with knowledge and skill. And they become important entries on your employment application.

AUTOMOTIVE SERVICE FACILITIES

➤ 2-4 AUTOMOTIVE DEALER

There are about 25,000 new-car dealers in the United States (Fig. 2-2). The automotive manufacturer supplies the dealer with vehicles at wholesale prices. The dealer marks up the prices to the retail selling price. This gives the dealer a profit on each car.

The dealer must prepare and service each car before delivery to the customer. These steps are the *predelivery service* (Fig. 2-3). Sometimes trouble develops in the car after the sale. Then the dealer must fix the car under *warranty*. This is repair work that, if required, the manufacturer will pay for. The warranty covers these repairs only for a specified time or mileage after the date of sale.

Sometimes the manufacturer has a *recall* of certain vehicles. This means the manufacturer asks the owner to return the vehicle to the dealer. Something needs inspection and possibly repair. The manufacturer pays for any parts or service required. Never allow the vehicle owner to ignore a recall. It is usually safety-related.

New-car dealers have a *used-car department* that sells the used vehicles taken in trade when a customer buys a new vehicle. After inspection and reconditioning, the dealer sells the trade-in with a *limited warranty*. This protects the buyer if a defect shows up shortly after the sale. Sometimes dealers sell used vehicles "as is." Then the buyer does not receive a warranty of any kind.

The dealership has a *service department* (Fig. 2-4). This is a properly equipped shop staffed with trained technicians. They do warranty work and work for which the customer pays. Diagnostic equipment, special tools, and

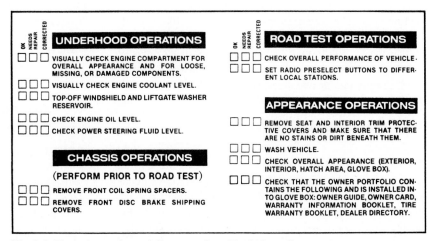

Fig. 2-3 Typical steps in predelivery service. *(Ford Motor Company)*

Fig. 2-4 A service department in a car dealership. *(ATW)*

Fig. 2-5 A service station, which may sell only fuel, oil, and other automotive fluids. *(ATW)*

parts must be available. Some service departments are small. They may employ only one to five technicians. Larger dealer shops may employ 100 or more people.

Many dealerships have a computer in the service department. It is *online* with the vehicle manufacturer. This means the small computer at the dealership connects to the manufacturer's big computer. A telephone line or satellite link makes the connection. If a car has a new or difficult problem, the technician can use the computer to help find out what is wrong. The big computer shows the technician how to locate the problem. It also tells where and how to make the repair. The screen may display the parts needed, their prices, and if the parts are *in stock*. If not, the computer may order the parts.

➤ 2-5 AUTOMOTIVE REPAIR SHOP

There are about 150,000 non-dealership automotive repair shops in the United States. These are the *independent garages*. Some are one-person specialty shops. Others are general repair shops that employ many master automotive technicians. The larger shops often operate like a dealership service department.

The master automotive technician works in all areas of automotive service. Specialist automotive technicians may work in only one or two areas, such as brakes or air conditioning.

➤ 2-6 SERVICE STATION

There are about 115,000 service stations in the United States (Fig. 2-5). This includes about 25,000 convenience stores with gasoline pumps. At one time, many service stations performed some repair and maintenance jobs. Today, most service stations sell only fuel, oil, and other

automotive fluids. No service work is done. In many service stations, you must pump your own fuel. They are "self-service" and not "full-service" service stations.

➤ 2-7 FLEET SHOP

A *fleet* is usually five or more vehicles operated by a single owner. Automotive dealers and independent repair shops maintain some fleet vehicles. However, there are about 39,000 fleet shops or garages in the United States. Companies that prefer to do their own maintenance and repair work operate these shops. They include bus and trucking companies, and taxicab and delivery fleets.

The technician in a fleet shop usually works for the same company that owns the vehicles. Often, the work is done on a preset schedule. This is *periodic maintenance*, or *preventive maintenance*. It helps *prevent* failure.

The driver checks some items daily before taking the vehicle out on the road. Then, at scheduled intervals, the vehicle enters the shop. The technician checks the fluid levels. If necessary, fluids and filters are changed. A visual inspection determines the condition of tires and other parts. Meters and gauges show the condition of the battery and electrical system. A road test checks vehicle performance. Any problems found are corrected.

➤ 2-8 SPECIALTY SHOP

A variety of specialty shops provide "trade services" for the automotive-service industry. These include wheel alignment shops and radiator repair shops. Small repair shops often take their *machine work* to an automotive machine shop. This includes such jobs as refinishing brake drums and rotors, and engine flywheels. The machine shop may also repair cracks in cylinder blocks and heads, and *bore* and *sleeve* engine cylinders.

> **NOTE** If a dealer removes a leaking radiator and sends it to a radiator repair shop for repair, this is a *sublet repair*. In some states, the customer must consent to a sublet repair.

➤ 2-9 PARTS STORE

An automotive parts store (Fig. 2-6) may be both a *wholesaler* and a *retailer*. As a wholesaler, the store sells parts at a discount to other automotive service businesses. This is the *automotive trade*. As a retailer, the parts store sells parts to people who service their own vehicles. For these sales, there is no "trade discount."

Fig. 2-6 Parts stores stock and sell automotive parts. *(Lisle Corporation)*

Fig. 2-8 A microfiche has hundreds of pages reduced to almost microscopic size. *(ATW)*

The primary job of the *parts counter person* is to identify the needed part in a *parts catalog*. Then the price is found on a *price list*. Parts catalogs may contain hundreds of pages. They include illustrations, *part numbers*, and related information (Fig. 2-7).

Many manufacturers have replaced their paper catalogs with *microfiche* (Fig. 2-8). Each *fiche* (pronounced "fish") is a sheet of film about the size of a postcard. It has hundreds of parts-catalog pages reduced to almost microscopic size. To find a part number, select the proper fiche. Place it in the *microfiche reader* (Fig. 2-8). The controls

on the reader shift the fiche to bring the desired page onto the screen. To get a printed copy of the page on the screen, place the fiche in a *microfiche printer*. It works like a microfiche reader, with a copier built in.

Electronic parts catalogs are replacing paper catalogs and microfiche. A computer *terminal* (screen and keyboard) displays the illustrations, part numbers, prices, and other information (Fig. 2-9). The computer also checks the *inventory* and reports if the part is in stock. Some shops have a computer terminal in or near the service bays. The technician can use it to check on parts availability or to order parts.

BECOMING A PROFESSIONAL

➤ 2-10 AUTOMOTIVE TECHNICIAN CERTIFICATION

You have probably heard or read about the *National Institute for Automotive Service Excellence* (ASE). Many

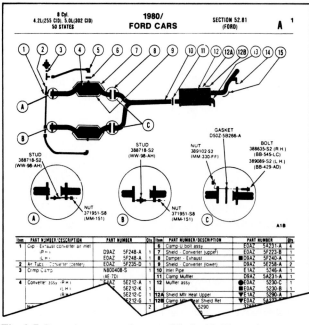

Fig. 2-7 Pages in parts catalogs are filled with illustrations, part numbers, and related information. *(Ford Motor Company)*

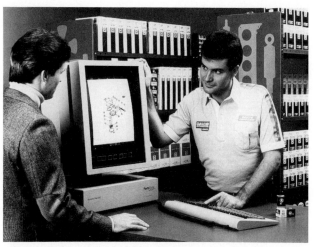

Fig. 2-9 Electronic parts catalogs display illustrations, part numbers, prices, and other information on a computer screen. *(The Reynolds & Reynolds Company)*

shops display their sign (Fig. 2-10). This organization provides voluntary testing and certification for automotive technicians. ASE gives tests in each of eight specialty areas (Fig. 2-11) twice a year. ASE also offers three tests for *engine machinist*.

To earn the ASE certification in any service area, you must pass a written test for that specialty. The test covers practical problems of diagnosis and repair. To become certified as a *master automobile technician*, you must pass all eight tests.

To become certified, you must also show that you have the required practical experience. For certification, ASE requires two or more years of full-time "hands-on" work

Fig. 2-10 The ASE sign which shows that the shop employs certified automotive technicians. *(National Institute for Automotive Service Excellence)*

Automobile Tests
A1 Engine Repair
A2 Automotive Transmission/Transaxle
A3 Manual Drive Train and Axles
A4 Suspension and Steering
A5 Brakes
A6 Electrical/Electronic systems
A7 Heating and Air Conditioning
A8 Engine Performance

Fig. 2-11 The eight specialty areas in which automotive-technician certification tests are given twice yearly by the National Institute for Automotive Service Excellence *(ASE)*.

experience. Sometimes your school training can substitute for work experience.

There are two very important benefits of becoming an ASE-certified technician. First, many employers hire only certified technicians. Second, certified technicians may receive higher pay. For more information about certification, ask your instructor or write a letter to ASE. Request a *Registration Book*. The address is:

National Institute for Automotive Service Excellence
13505 Dulles Technology Drive
Herndon, Virginia 22071-3415

You may also call ASE for a *Registration Booklet*.

➤ 2-11 LEARNING ABOUT AUTOMOTIVE SERVICE

There are two parts to learning about automobiles and how to service them. One is to study this book and complete the classroom work. The other part is going into the shop. There you will work on the components and do the jobs you study about.

Some classes use the *Workbook for Automotive Mechanics*. Follow the step-by-step procedure in the Job sheet covering the service procedure you are doing. Another aid you may have is the *Study Guide for Automotive Mechanics*. It gives you key points and quick reviews of the chapters in the *Automotive Mechanics* textbook. Also, your instructor may be using tests from the *Instructor's Planning Guide and Testbook for Automotive Mechanics*. These tests help you find out what you know. They also show you what you don't know. This helps prepare you to take the ASE certification tests.

➤ 2-12 KEEPING A NOTEBOOK

Start now to keep a notebook. It can help you in many ways. It will be a record of your progress in your studies. It will become a storehouse of valuable information you will refer to time after time. And it will help you organize your training program to do you the most good.

Get a large 8 1/2 × 11 inch [216 × 279 millimeters] three-ring notebook.

NOTE In this textbook, metric equivalents of United States customary measurements follow in brackets [ ].

Place a set of notebook dividers or index tabs in your notebook. Then organize it into the same 9 parts as in this textbook. The 9 parts are:

1. Automotive service and shop work.
2. Automotive engines.
3. Automotive engine systems.
4. Automotive electrical and electronic equipment.
5. Engine performance and driveability.
6. Automotive engine service.

7. Automotive drive trains.
8. Automotive chassis.
9. Automotive heating and air conditioning.

Study each textbook assignment with your notebook open in front of you. Start with a fresh notebook page. Write the assignment number or textbook pages and date at the top of the page. As you study the assigned pages, write down the chapter title, section headings, and key points.

In the shop, you may not want to carry your big notebook with you while working on a car. Put a small scratch pad or a few index cards in your pocket. You will need paper anyway to write down part numbers, measurements, and specifications. Always have a pencil or pen with you. As you complete each job, write down the steps covered. Make a note about any special conditions or problems you found. Later, use these notes as reminders. Write on a separate page for your notebook a description of the job. Include the procedures, special tools, and equipment you used.

Make sketches for your notebook. These may be anything more easily described by a sketch rather than words. They include wiring or hose diagrams, or the position and location of parts before removal.

Save articles and illustrations from newspapers and automotive magazines. Tape small items to blank notebook paper. Three-hole punch magazine pages. Then file all of the information in your notebook. Other important information to save includes the instructions you find with service parts. For example, a set of piston rings has an instruction sheet showing how to install the rings. File this in the *Automotive Engine Service* section of your notebook.

Your notebook can become one of your most valuable possessions. It will be a permanent record of how you became a trained, qualified, and certified automotive technician. So, *keep a notebook!*

MULTIPLE-CHOICE TEST

*Select the **one** correct, best, or most probable answer to each question.*
You can find the answers in the section indicated at the end of each question.

1. The big three domestic manufacturers in the United States are (➤2-2)
   a. Honda, Suzuki, and Toyota
   b. Chevrolet, Dodge, and Lincoln
   c. Chrysler, Ford, and General Motors
   d. American Motors, Chrysler, and General Motors
2. If a vehicle develops trouble while under warranty, the cost of repair is paid by the (➤2-4)
   a. dealer
   b. manufacturer
   c. technician
   d. customer
3. A vehicle *recall* means that the manufacturer is (➤2-4)
   a. asking owners to return the vehicle to the dealer for inspection and possible repair
   b. repossessing the vehicle
   c. shortening the warranty period
   d. sending the owner a bill for the work

4. The purpose of preventive maintenance is to (➤2-7)
   a. help schedule breakdowns
   b. eliminate routine service work
   c. force the driver to use self-service service stations
   d. help prevent failure
5. A parts catalog may be (➤2-9)
   a. printed on paper
   b. on microfiche film
   c. displayed on a computer screen
   d. all of the above

REVIEW QUESTIONS

1. Explain what a franchise is.   (➤2-2)
2. Describe the steps performed during a predelivery service.   (➤2-4)
3. How does a dealership service department differ from an independent garage?   (➤2-4 and ➤2-5)

4. Who does the technician work for in a dealership, independent garage, and fleet shop?   (➤2-4, ➤2-5, and ➤2-7)
5. What are the advantages of becoming an ASE-certified automotive technician?   (➤2-10)

CHAPTER 3

SHOP WORK AND SERVICE INFORMATION

After studying this chapter, you should be able to:

- List the six steps in automotive repair and explain each.
- Explain the purpose of the VIN and its location on the car.
- Describe the flat-rate manual and its use.
- Discuss how automotive technicians are paid.
- List the various sources of service information.

➤ 3-1 THE AUTOMOTIVE SERVICE PROCEDURE

When something is wrong with a car, the technician must perform four basic steps to find and correct the problem. These are:

1. *Inspection,* which answers the question "Is something wrong?" or "Is there a problem?" The answer is usually a "yes" or "no."
2. *Diagnosis,* also called *trouble-diagnosis* and *trouble-shooting.* This answers the question "What is wrong?" or "What caused or is causing the problem?"
3. *Repair,* which includes the steps necessary to fix the problem or repair both the problem and its cause.
4. *Quality check,* or performing step 1 again. If the proper repair has been made, the original problem no longer exists.

➤ 3-2 THE SIX STEPS IN AN AUTOMOTIVE REPAIR JOB

Servicing jobs vary from simple to difficult. No repair job requires more than six steps. These are:

1. Measuring
2. Disassembling
3. Machining
4. Installing new, rebuilt, or serviced parts
5. Reassembling
6. Adjusting

Some jobs require fewer steps. Many require removal of a part from the vehicle, and then reinstalling it or a new or rebuilt part. The various steps may require hand tools, measuring tools, and power tools. Following chapters describe tools and their uses.

> **NOTE** There is a difference between *reinstall* and *replace.* When you reinstall a part, you put back the same part you removed. When you replace a part, you discard the part you removed. Then you install a new or different part. These are the definitions used in the automotive-service business and in this book.

1. MEASURING You often start a service job by taking measurements. These could be *linear* measurements – those made in a straight line. They could also be *angular* measurements made in degrees. You measure the level of engine oil in the crankcase with a dipstick. You use special instruments to make other measurements. These include alternator output, engine compression, and wheel-alignment angles.

2. DISASSEMBLING Compare the measurements with the vehicle-manufacturer's specifications. An "out of specs" condition may mean trouble. Such indicators are low pressure or excessive clearance. You may have to disassemble, or *tear down,* a component to fix a trouble. This is done carefully, part by part.

3. MACHINING This requires a special machine that removes metal from a part by cutting or grinding. Machining a part removes its irregularities. For example, *boring* or *honing* an engine cylinder removes the taper caused by wear at the top of the cylinder.

4. INSTALLING NEW OR SERVICED PARTS If parts are so worn that they can no longer do their job, discard them. Install new or rebuilt parts.

5. REASSEMBLING After repair, the removed parts are either reinstalled or replaced. This is *reassembly*. You put the parts back together to make the complete assembly.

6. ADJUSTING As a vehicle runs, its parts wear. They may require adjustments periodically. Adjustments also are often needed after service work. For example, after replacing drum-brake shoes, adjust the clearance between the lining and the drums.

FINDING AND USING AUTOMOTIVE SERVICE INFORMATION

➤ 3-3 VEHICLE IDENTIFICATION NUMBER (VIN)

Most diagnosis and repair work on a vehicle requires you to have the *service specifications* (➤3-4). You must first positively identify the vehicle to know which specifications to use.

The *vehicle identification number* (VIN) is the number assigned to each vehicle by its manufacturer. The VIN is mainly for registration and identification purposes. On domestic cars, the number is on a plate located on the top left side of the instrument panel. The plate is close to the windshield and readable from outside the vehicle (Fig. 3-1).

Since 1981, the VIN has 17 numbers and letters called *characters* or *digits*. Each digit has a special meaning. To find the model year of the vehicle, read the tenth digit from

the left. Another digit is the *engine code*. It identifies the original engine in the vehicle. On Chrysler, Ford, and General Motors vehicles, the engine code is the eighth digit on the VIN plate (Fig. 3-1). On American Motors vehicles, the engine code is the fourth digit. Figure 3-2 shows the meaning of each digit in a typical General Motors VIN.

➤ 3-4 SERVICE SPECIFICATIONS

The vehicle manufacturer sets the service specifications, or *specs*. These are the measurements necessary for each part to operate properly. Some automotive manufacturers print the specifications in the vehicle *service manual* (➤3-5). Other vehicle manufacturers publish *Service Specifications* books each year. Figure 3-3 shows a page of specifications for a Ford four-cylinder engine. Later chapters explain the terms and units of measurement.

A new car or truck may have more than 30 labels and decals. They list emission and safety certification, identification numbers, and fluid capacities. Others list cautions for your protection, service instructions, and specifications.

The engine compartment contains the *Vehicle Emission Control Information* (VECI) label (Fig. 3-4). It is the most important label in the engine compartment. The label has engine performance specifications and tuneup instructions. The VECI label also includes a *schematic* or line drawing showing the proper routing of the emission-system vacuum hose. Sometimes the VECI label shows drive-belt routing and location of the ignition-timing marks.

Modern electronic testers such as engine analyzers and wheel aligners have a built-in computer with a memory. It holds service information and specifications for most modern vehicles. For example, the computerized 4-wheel aligner (Fig. 3-5) can display vehicle specifications on its screen. Step-by-step instructions and vehicle adjustment graphics also display. The technician does not need to "look up the specs" in a book or on a wall chart.

➤ 3-5 SERVICE MANUALS AND SHOP MANUALS

Manufacturers issue a *service manual* or *shop manual* for each year and body-style of vehicle (Fig. 3-6). The manual may actually be one or more books. Sometimes the manual covers a series of similar models. Service manuals provide trouble-diagnosis charts and service procedures. The infor-

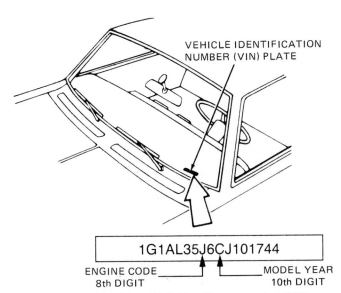

Fig. 3-1 Location of the vehicle identification number (VIN) plate. The VIN number shown is for a General Motors car. *(Champion Spark Plug Company)*

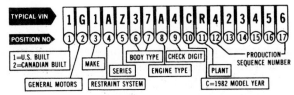

Fig. 3-2 The meaning of each digit in a typical General Motors VIN. *(General Motors Corporation)*

Powertrain — Gasoline Engine, 2.3L HSC/HSO I-4

SERVICE SPECIFICATIONS

General Specifications	
DISPLACEMENT	2.3L (2309 cc)
NUMBER OF CYLINDERS	4
BORE AND STROKE	
Bore	93.53mm (3.68 in.)
Stroke	84mm (3.30 in.)
FIRING ORDER	1, 3, 4, 2

Cylinder Head and Valve Train	
COMBUSTION CHAMBER VOLUME (cc)	62.8-59.8
VALVE GUIDE BORE DIAMETER	
Intake & Exhaust	8.720-8.745mm (.3433 in.)
VALVE SEATS	
Width	
Intake	1.53-2.03mm (.080 in.)
Exhaust	1.78-2.28mm (.090 in.)
Angle	44°-45°
Runout (T.I.R.)	
Seat with Respect to Guide	025mm (.001 in.)
INTAKE AND EXHAUST MANIFOLD	
Joint Face Flatness	12mm Overall (.08mm) in Any 150mm
Cylinder Head	
Joint Flatness	18mm Overall (.08mm) in Any 150mm
VALVE STEM TO GUIDE CLEARANCE	
Intake	.047mm (.0018 in.)
Exhaust	.0595mm (.0023 in.)
VALVE HEAD DIAMETER	
Intake	43.76-44.37mm (1.72-1.74 in.)
Exhaust	37.9-38.3mm (1.49-1.50 in.)
VALVE FACE ANGLE	44°45°
VALVE STEM DIAMETER (STANDARD)	
Intake	8.677-8.694mm (.3415-.3422 in.)
Exhaust	8.664-8.682mm (.3411-.3418 in.)
Oversize	
Intake	9.058-9.075mm (.3566-.3572 in.)
Exhaust	9.045-9.063mm (.3561-.3568 in.)
Oversize	
Intake	9.439-9.456mm (.3716-.3722 in.)
Exhaust	9.045-9.063mm (.3561-.3568 in.)
VALVE SPRINGS	
Compression Pressure (N @ Spec. Length)	
Loaded (Without Damper)	805 ± 32N @ 27.63mm
Unloaded (Without Damper)	333.6 ± 17.8N @ 38.1mm
Free Length (approximate)	46.99mm (1.85 in.)
Assembled Height	38.1mm (1.49 in.)
Service Limit	10% Pressure Loss @ Spec. Length
ROCKER ARM	
Ratio	1.568
VALVE TAPPET, HYDRAULIC	
Diameter (STANDARD)	22.200-22.212mm (.874-.8744 in.)
Hydraulic Leakdown Rate	10-50 seconds
Collapsed Tappet Gap (Nominal)	
Intake	1.80-4.34mm (.070-.170 in.)
Exhaust	1.80-4.34mm (.070-.170 in.)
DISTRIBUTOR SHAFT BEARING BORE DIAMETER	
Tappet Bore Diameter	22.230-22.268mm (.875-.876 in.)
CAMSHAFT BORE INSIDE DIAMETER	
No. 1	56.013-55.987mm (2.205-2.204 in.)
No. 2	55.613-55.587mm (2.189-2.188 in.)
No. 3	55.613-55.587mm (2.189-2.188 in.)
No. 4	58.013-55.987mm (2.205-2.204 in.)

77

mation covers most customer complaints, troubles, and service jobs. Service manuals also give the specifications and special tools needed.

Study service manuals issued by the various automotive manufacturers. Notice the arrangement of the manuals into sections. Figure 3-7 is the section index from a Chevrolet service manual. Each section covers a major part of the car, including diagnosis and servicing of individual components. Some service manuals are available only on microfiche (Fig. 2-8).

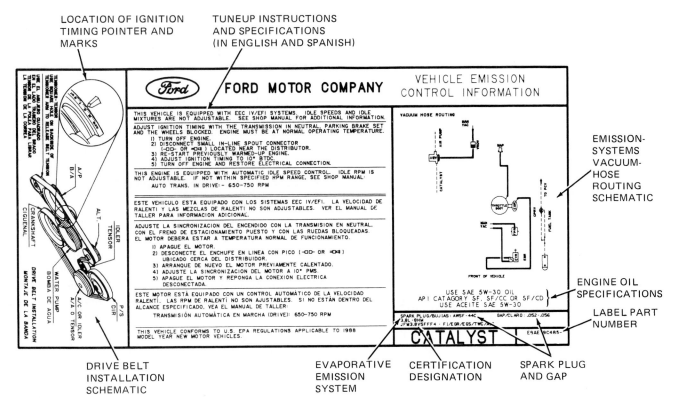

LOCATION OF IGNITION
TIMING POINTER AND
MARKS

TUNEUP INSTRUCTIONS
AND SPECIFICATIONS
(IN ENGLISH AND SPANISH)

EMISSION-
SYSTEMS
VACUUM-
HOSE
ROUTING
SCHEMATIC

ENGINE OIL
SPECIFICATIONS

LABEL PART
NUMBER

DRIVE BELT
INSTALLATION
SCHEMATIC

EVAPORATIVE
EMISSION
SYSTEM

CERTIFICATION
DESIGNATION

SPARK PLUG
AND GAP

Fig. 3-4 The Vehicle Emission Control Information (VECI) label
is the most important label in the engine compartment. *(Ford
Motor Company)*

Fig. 3-5 A computerized four-wheel aligner that can display the
vehicle specifications, step-by-step instructions, and vehicle
adjustment graphics. *(Hunter Engineering Company)*

Fig. 3-6 Automotive manufacturers' service manuals or shop
manuals furnish detailed diagnosis and servicing information.
(Chrysler Corporation)

Manufacturers also issue *Service Bulletins* or *Technical
Service Bulletins* (TSBs). These may be a single page or
booklets of several pages. They update and inform technicians about engineering, production, and warranty-repair
changes. They also alert technicians to recalls (➤2-4).
Other TSBs include revised or new repair and diagnostic
procedures. At the end of a model year, some manufacturers publish the service bulletins for that year as a bound
book. Changes made by the manufacturer during the
model-year production are called *running changes*.

If you work on a variety of cars, buying the service

TABLE OF CONTENTS		
SECTION NAME		SECT.
GENERAL INFORMATION		0
0A.	General Information	
0B.	Maintenance & Lubrication	
HEATING AND AIR CONDITIONING		1.
1A.	Heating and Ventilation	
1B.	Air Conditioning	
1D2.	HR-6 A/C Compressor Overhaul	
1D3.	V-5 A/C Compressor Overhaul	
FRAME AND BUMPERS		2.
2A.	Frame (Cradle) and Mounts	
2B.	Bumpers	
2C.	Chassis Sheet Metal	
STEERING, SUSPENSION, WHEELS AND TIRES		3.
3.	Diagnosis	
3A.	Wheel Alignment	
3B2.	Manual Rack and Pinion	
3B4.	Steering Wheels/Columns	
3C.	Front Suspension	
3D.	Rear Suspension	
3E.	Tires and Wheels	
FINAL DRIVE		4.
4D.	Drive Axle	
BRAKES		5.
5.	Brakes	
5A3.	Composite Master Cylinder	
5B4.	48H Front Caliper	
5B10.	48H Rear Caliper	
5D2.	Tandem Diaphragm Booster	
5F.	Specifications	
ENGINE		6.
6.	Engine General Information	
6A.	General Engine Mechanical	
6A1.	2.5 Liter L4	
6A2.	2.8 Liter V6	
6B.	Engine Cooling	
6C.	Engine Fuel	
6D.	Engine Electrical	
6D1.	Battery	
6D2.	Cranking System	
6D3.	Charging System	
6D4.	Ignition System	
6D5.	Engine Wiring	
6E.	Driveability and Emissions — Gen Info	
6E2.	Fuel Injection TBI	
6E3.	Emissions — PFI	
6F.	Engine Exhaust	
TRANSMISSION		7.
7A.	Automatic Transaxle/Transmission — Diagnosis and General Service	
7A1.	Automatic Transaxle — On-Car Service	
125C.	Automatic Transaxle — Hydraulic Diagnosis	
125C.	Automatic Transaxle — Unit Repair	
7B2.	5-Speed Isuzu Manual Transaxle — On-Car Service	
7B2A.	5-Speed Isuzu Manual Transaxle — Unit Repair	
7B3.	Muncie 282 5-Speed Manual Transaxle — General Description, Diagnosis, On-Car Service	
7B3A	Muncie 282 5-Speed Manual Transaxle — Unit Repair	
7C.	Clutch	
CHASSIS ELECTRICAL		8.
8A.	Electrical Diagnosis	
8B.	Chassis Electrical	
8C.	Instrument Panel, Gages & Console	
8E2.	Wiper and Washer System	
ACCESSORIES		9.
9A.	Radio	
9B.	Cruise Control	
9E.	Engine Block Heater	
9F.	Miscellaneous Accessories	
BODY SERVICE MANUAL		END OF MANUAL

Fig. 3-7 Section index from a Chevrolet service manual. *(Chevrolet Division of General Motors Corporation)*

manuals for each make and model every year is expensive. Instead, many technicians use an *Auto Repair Manual* (Fig. 3-8). Book companies such as Chilton, Motor (Hearst), and Mitchell publish these every year. Typically, the manual covers all domestic cars, trucks, or imports and transplants (➢2-2) for the past six to eight years. The manual includes service specifications, key steps, and illustrations. These are for the most frequently performed mechanical repairs. No coverage is included of body repair or painting.

➢ 3-6 FLAT-RATE MANUALS

Every year the automotive manufacturers publish a manual called the *Labor Time Guide* (Buick), *Service Labor Time Standards* (Ford), or *Flat Rate Manual* (Isuzu). It lists all the service jobs on the different models sold that year by the vehicle manufacturer. Each job is an *operation* with its own *operation number*. The estimated time that a technician should require to do that job is also listed. This is *factory time* or manufacturer's *flat-rate time*.

In the shop, the work performed by the technician is *labor*. The *labor rate* is how much the shop charges the customer in dollars for an hour of the technician's time. For warranty work, the "customer" is usually the vehicle manufacturer. The car owner or driver is the customer for other service work.

The labor rate multiplied by the flat-rate time gives the *labor charge* that the customer pays.

$$\text{Labor Rate} \times \text{Flat-Rate Time} = \text{Labor Charge}$$

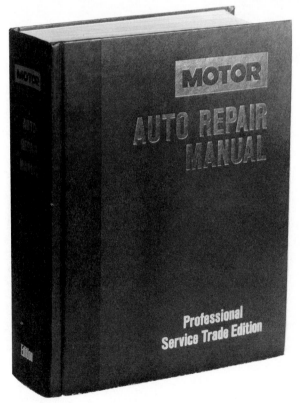

Fig. 3-8 An auto repair manual. *(Hearst Corporation)*

For example, suppose the shop labor rate is $50.00 per hour. The flat-rate time for adjusting a parking brake is 0.3 hour. Then the shop receives $15.00 as the labor charge for the job:

$$\$50.00 \times 0.3 = \$15.00$$

Manufacturers send flat-rate manuals to their dealers. Independent shops do not normally receive them. The same book companies that publish auto repair manuals (➤3-5) also publish flat-rate manuals. These are called *Labor Guide and Parts Manual*. They usually cover the past five to seven model years. The manuals include current prices of the parts needed for each job. The prices are often on the same or facing page. Using this information, you can prepare an *estimate* of the total cost of parts and labor to do a job.

NOTE | In some states, the law requires that the customer receive a written estimate. The customer must then agree to the estimate. Service work cannot begin until after the shop receives the customer's authorization.

➤ 3-7 HOW AUTOMOTIVE TECHNICIANS ARE PAID

In the past, there were two basic ways that an automotive mechanic was paid. One was a weekly, biweekly, or monthly *salary*. This is a fixed amount paid on a regular basis. The other was by *flat rate* (➤3-6). The mechanic typically received 50 percent of the labor rate. The shop kept the other half. Due to high shop operating costs, today few technicians receive 50 percent.

Some technicians still get either a salary or flat rate. Others are *hourly* workers. They receive an hourly rate for each hour worked. In some shops, the skill level required of the technician and the complexity of the job affect the labor rate. It is higher for complicated jobs that require greater skill. Another arrangement is to pay technicians a guaranteed salary plus a commission on labor. This provides the security of a minimum income, with a reward for being more productive. Total earnings depend on the amount of work completed.

In some shops, the technician may receive additional income in two ways. One is a percentage or commission on the parts sold to the customer during the service work. The other is a *bonus*, or cash reward. It is based on factors such as productivity and ASE certification.

➤ 3-8 OTHER SOURCES OF AUTOMOTIVE SERVICE INFORMATION

The most important booklet for the car owner and driver is the *Owner's Manual*. It contains the operating, safety, and maintenance instructions for the car. The booklet should remain in the glove compartment or *glove box*. If you cannot identify a marking or indicator on the instrument panel, look in the Owner's Manual (Fig. 3-9). It provides information on how to operate the car and its accessories.

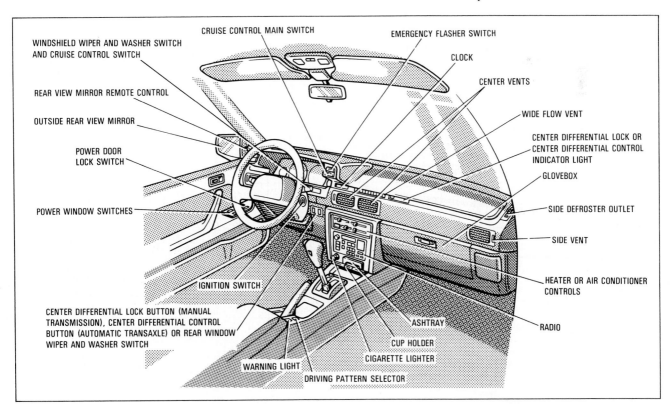

Fig. 3-9 The Owner's Manual provides the vehicle owner with information on how to operate the vehicle and its accessories. *(Toyota Motor Sales, U.S.A., Inc.)*

In a new car, starting instructions may be on a band slipped over the driver's sun visor. Safety notices may be on the instrument panel. The glove box may contain the Owner's Manual, warranty booklets, and tire and battery pamphlets. The new owner also may receive a maintenance schedule, service-record log, and consumer information sheets with the car. These papers and pamphlets are not primarily service information. However, familiarity with them may help you recognize problems caused by the driver. For example, the driver may be using an improper starting procedure.

A label on the driver's or passenger's doorjamb or glovebox cover supplies tire size and inflation information. On many vehicles, the sticker also has other information.

In a new-car dealership, access to the latest service bulletins may be through a computer that is online with the manufacturer (➤2-4). Each new bulletin electronically becomes part of the computer's memory, or *database*. This is a collection of information or *data* arranged for quick recall by the computer. Other shops may receive a new computer disk periodically through the mail. The new disk contains the updated database.

The computer may have several different databases stored in its memory. It may access others when it is online with the host or main computer. For example, the *electronic service bulletins* form one database. Service specifications may be another.

An advantage of the computer is that it can quickly search the service-bulletin database for *keywords*. The number of each TSB containing a keyword displays on the screen. You can then scan through the TSBs. When you find the bulletin you need, the computer's printer can provide a paper copy.

There are many automotive-service magazines, or *trade magazines*. They contain information on vehicle servicing and articles on specific service jobs. The magazines include "shop tips" about how to make hard jobs easier. Parts manufacturers and tool-and-equipment manufacturers also publish booklets and manuals. These cover how to install their parts and use their equipment. These publications are *Installation Instructions*, *Operating Instructions*, or *Operator's Manuals*. After you complete a job, add the parts-installation instructions to your notebook (➤2-12).

AUTOMOTIVE SERVICE MANAGEMENT AND TRAINING

➤ 3-9 CONTROLLING SERVICE OPERATIONS

The phone rings in the shop. Someone with car trouble wants to bring the car in. The person at the shop consults the work schedule or appointment sheet for tomorrow. Then he or she tells the caller to bring the car in tomorrow morning at 10:00. This is noted on the appointment sheet.

When the car arrives the next morning, a *service writer* or *service advisor* greets the customer. The driver explains the problem. The service advisor writes the customer's complaint on a *repair order*. Also entered are the labor instructions and any notes to the technician (Fig. 3-10). The

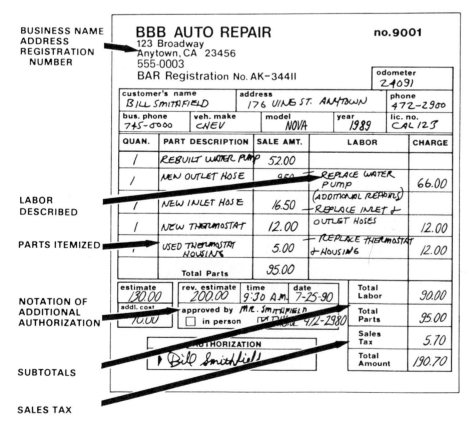

Fig. 3-10 Service advisors write labor instructions on the repair order that tell the technician what to do. *(California Bureau of Automotive Repair)*

hard copy of the repair order is *dispatched* or given to the technician who is to do the job. The technician gets the car and follows the labor instructions on the repair order.

> **NOTE** The repair order is a multiple-part form. It serves as the control document in most shops. The last copy is made of stiff paper, about like an index card. This is the "hard copy" given to the technician. The rest of the repair order goes to the parts department. When the job is completed, the cashier "closes out" the repair order. The parts and labor costs are totaled. Taxes are added. Then the amount due is collected from the customer.

The parts department provides any new parts needed. The technician presents the hard copy to the parts counter person. He or she issues the parts. The price of each part is entered in the parts column of the repair order. The labor

charge may be flat-rate time or *clock time*. This is the actual time it took the technician to do the job.

Sometimes the technician performs a warranty repair (➤2-4). The car owner may first have to furnish proof of proper maintenance. The specified time or mileage is given in the *maintenance schedule* (Fig. 3-11). This is the list of required lubrication and maintenance services. It also shows when they should be done. The maintenance schedule may be a separate pamphlet, included in the Owner's Manual, or in the manufacturer's Service Manual.

➤ 3-10 COMPUTERIZED SERVICE OPERATIONS

Some shops use a computer to increase shop efficiency. Large shops write more than 100 repair orders a day. The

---

CUSTOMER MAINTENANCE ## SCHEDULE B

Follow maintenance **Schedule B** if, generally, you drive your vehicle on a daily basis for more than 10 miles (16 km) and **NONE OF THE DRIVING CONDITIONS SHOWN IN SCHEDULE A APPLY TO YOUR DRIVING HABITS.**

PERFORM AT THE MONTHS OR DISTANCES SHOWN, WHICHEVER OCCURS FIRST								
MILES (000)	7.5	15	22.5	30	37.5	45	52.5	60
KILOMETERS (000)	12	24	36	48	60	72	84	96
EMISSION CONTROL SYSTEMS								
Change engine oil and oil filter — **every 6 months** or 7500 miles, whichever occurs first — If equipped with Vehicle Maintenance Monitor (VMM) change oil and filter when indicted by VMM but do not go beyond 7500 miles or 6 months whichever occurs first	X	X	X	X	X	X	X	X
SUPERCHARGED ENGINES — Replace spark plugs (platinum plugs)								X
(3.8L only) **Change oil and filter** when indicated by Vehicle Maintenance Monitor (VMM) but <u>do not</u> go beyond.	EVERY 5,000 MILES (8 km) OR 6 MONTHS, WHICHEVER OCCURS FIRST							
Replace spark plugs				X				X
Inspect accessory drive belt(s)				X				X
Replace PCV valve — 5.0L engine		(X)		(X)		(X)		X
Change crankcase filter (1)				X(1)				X(1)
Replace air cleaner filter (1)				X(1)				X(1)
Check/clean choke linkage (5.8L only)				X				X
Replace engine coolant (every 36 months) OR				X				X
Check engine coolant protection, hoses and clamps	ANNUALLY							
GENERAL MAINTENANCE								
Inspect exhaust heat shields				X				X
Lubricate steering and/or suspension		X		X		X		X
Lubricate steering linkage (inner-outer tie rod ends both sides, pitman arm socket) Crown Victoria/Grand Marquis		X		X		X		X
Inspect disc brake pads and rotors (front) (2)				X(2)				X(2)
Inspect brake linings and drums (rear) (2)				X(2)				X(2)
Inspect and repack front wheel bearings				X				X
Rotate tires	X		X		X		X	

(1) If operating in severe dust, more frequent intervals may be required. Consult your dealer.
(2) If your driving includes continuous stop-and-go driving or driving in mountainous/hilly areas, more frequent intervals may be required.

(X) This item not required to be performed, however, Ford recommends that you also perform maintenance on items designated by an (X) in order to achieve best vehicle operation. Failure to perform this recommended maintenance will not invalidate the vehicle emissions warranty or manufacturer recall liability.

Fig. 3-11 A vehicle maintenance schedule. *(Ford Motor Company)*

computer can schedule these jobs. It can also organize the flow of work and parts through the shop. The computer:

1. Matches the right technician with the job.
2. Tracks each vehicle through its maintenance or repair.
3. Continually estimates how long it will be before the vehicle is ready for pickup by the customer.

The computer may also pinpoint specific areas on the car that require service. Later chapters cover computerized trouble diagnosis.

Figure 3-12 shows a computer that helps customers accurately and fully describe repair problems to the service advisor. The computer asks the customer a series of questions. These include the nature and location of the problems. The customer touches the appropriate answers displayed on the screen. Then the computer prints out a description of the problem and its possible causes.

Sometimes the shop is not open when the car is left for service. Then the customer can use the computer to prepare the repair order.

➤ 3-11 AUTOMOTIVE SATELLITE TELEVISION NETWORK (ASTN)

Paper and computers are not the only ways that automotive service information and training are available. Dealers and independent shops may subscribe to the *Automotive Satellite Television Network* (ASTN). It broadcasts only automotive news, information, and training. Programming, six hours a day, five days a week includes sales, finance, business management, and parts and service programs.

Short series of special training programs for technicians provide product and service information. This includes how to diagnose and service new features, such as computers and electronic fuel injection. The programs may be videotaped for playback at other times. The tapes become part of the shop reference library.

➤ 3-12 QUALITY OF REPAIR

When the job is not done right the first time, the unhappy customer brings the car back to the shop. This is a *shop comeback*. A dissatisfied customer rates the shop *quality of repair* as poor. To stay in business, a shop needs satisfied customers.

In most shops, the defective job "comes back" to the technician who worked on the car the first time. There are three causes of a shop comeback. These are:

1. Defective parts.
2. Faulty workmanship.
3. Poor communication.

A defective part usually fails soon after installation. This is a "no cost" repair for the car owner. However, the technician may get paid for making the repair.

Fig. 3-12 A computer helps customers accurately and fully describe repair problems to the service advisor. *(General Motors Corporation)*

Faulty workmanship by the technician is also a "no cost" repair for the car owner. The technician who made the mistake usually is not paid for correcting it. This is an important reason for you to *do the job right the first time.*

Poor communication between the driver and the technician causes many shop comebacks. To correct the driver's complaint, you have to fix the right problem. Be sure you know what the driver is talking about.

Road test the vehicle with the customer, if possible. When the problem is not obvious, ask the customer:

1. What is the problem?
2. When does it occur?
3. Where on the vehicle does it occur?
4. When did it start?

IDENTIFYING A RECALLED VEHICLE

➤ 3-13 NHTSA RECALL HOTLINE

To find out if a vehicle has been recalled (➤2-4), call the National Highway Traffic Safety Administration (NHTSA) toll-free *hotline.* It provides information and identification of recalled vehicles. To use the hotline, write down the make, model, and VIN (➤3-3) of the vehicle. Then make the call. You will be asked for the vehicle information and the problem. Then you will be told if there is a recall of the car for this or a related problem.

TRADE TALK

comeback	flat rate	replace	troubleshooting
diagnosis	hotline	spec	
dispatched	reinstall	specification	

MULTIPLE-CHOICE TEST

*Select the **one** correct, best, or most probable answer to each question.*
You can find the answers in the section indicated at the end of each question.

1. The steps in automotive repair service include (➤3-2)
   a. measuring and disassembling
   b. machining and installing
   c. reassembling and adjusting
   d. all of the above
2. To *reinstall* means to (➤3-2)
   a. repair a disassembled part
   b. put back the same part you removed
   c. reassemble a component
   d. remove and replace a part
3. To *replace* means to (➤3-2)
   a. put back a removed part
   b. discard the old part and install a new part
   c. reassemble a part
   d. adjust a replacement part

4. Service specifications are set by the (➤3-4)
   a. vehicle manufacturer
   b. technician
   c. service manager
   d. Society of Automotive Engineers (SAE)
5. *Flat rate* is the (➤3-6)
   a. rate in dollars required to do the job
   b. speed with which you can do a job, working flat out
   c. estimated time it takes to do a service job
   d. actual time it takes to do a service job

REVIEW QUESTIONS

1. What are the four basic steps in the automotive service procedure? (➤3-1)
2. What is the difference between *reinstall* and *replace?* (➤3-2)
3. Where is the VECI label located, and what information does it contain? (➤3-4)

4. A customer phones and wants to bring a car in for service. Describe the steps or service operations performed. (➤3-9)
5. What are the three basic causes of a shop comeback? (➤3-12)

CHAPTER 4

AUTOMOTIVE SHOP SAFETY

After studying this chapter, you should be able to:

- List the hazards due to faulty working conditions.
- List the hazards due to equipment defects or misuse.
- Describe the various types of fire extinguishers and how to use them.
- List the safety rules for working safely in the automotive shop.
- Define *hazardous material* and *hazardous waste,* and explain how to dispose of hazardous waste from your shop.

BASICS OF SHOP SAFETY

➤ 4-1 SAFETY IN THE SHOP

Safety means protecting yourself and others from possible danger and injury. You do not want to hurt yourself or someone else. To prevent this, follow the *safety rules* in the shop. *When everyone obeys the rules, the shop is a much safer place in which to work than your home!*

Safety is *your* job! In the shop, you are "safe" when you protect your eyes, fingers, feet—all of you—from danger. Just as importantly, you must look out for the safety of others around you.

➤ 4-2 SHOP LAYOUT

The term *shop layout* means the location of workbenches, vehicle lifts, machine tools, and other equipment (Fig. 4-1). Shop layouts vary. When you first go into a shop, find where everything is located. Many shops have lines painted on the floor to mark off work areas. These lines guide customers and workers away from danger zones around equipment. The lines also remind workers to keep their tools and equipment inside their work areas.

NOTE Many shops discourage customers from roaming around in the shop work areas. A customer can get into a dangerous spot without realizing it. Serious injury is possible. Most shops have a waiting room or lounge area where customers can wait in safety.

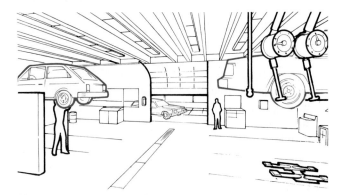

Fig. 4-1 A typical automotive-shop layout.

➤ 4-3 SIGNS

Signs posted around machinery and on the walls remind everyone to operate the machinery safely. Many of these are OSHA signs (Fig. 4-2). OSHA stands for *Occupational Safety and Health Administration.* This federal agency is responsible for studying and correcting conditions and equipment that may be hazardous to workers. Always follow the posted instructions. The most common cause of accidents in the shop is failure to follow instructions.

THINK
OSHA REQUIRES EMPLOYEES TO WEAR GOGGLES WHERE EYE INJURY HAZARDS EXIST & FACE MASKS WHEN PAINTING
ACT IN A SAFE MANNER

Fig. 4-2 Signs are posted in the shop to remind employees and others to obey the safety rules.

HAZARDS AND HOW TO AVOID THEM

➤ 4-4 SHOP HAZARDS

The *National Institute for Occupational Safety and Health* (NIOSH) is another federal agency. It studies working conditions and reports on potential hazards. The law requires that workplaces having hazards must eliminate them. Hazards are sometimes the fault of management and sometimes the fault of the workers. The following sections describe hazards due to faulty work habits, equipment defects or misuse, and faulty or improperly-used hand tools.

➤ 4-5 HAZARDS DUE TO FAULTY WORK HABITS OR CONDITIONS

Here are some major hazards. They are due to faulty work habits of the employees or unsafe working conditions.

1. *Smoking while handling dangerous materials such as gasoline or solvents (Fig. 4-3).* This can cause a fire or explosion.
2. *Careless or incorrect handling of gasoline, alcohol, solvents, or other flammable fluids.* Figure 4-4 shows the use of a *portable holding tank.* It can pump gasoline or diesel fuel out of the tank during repair or replacement of the tank or fuel gauge, and during other body and service work. The tank filters the fuel and stores it safely. A hand-operated valve controls whether pumping the handle pumps fuel in or out of the vehicle fuel tank. *Ground wires* prevent sparks that might jump between the tank or hose and the vehicle. This could cause an explosion and fire.

Fig. 4-3 Do not smoke or have open flames around combustibles such as gasoline and solvents.

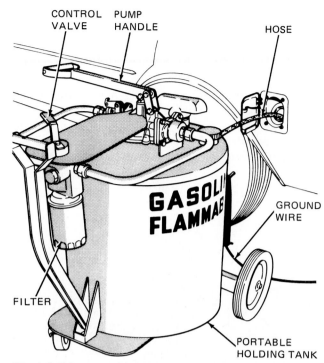

Fig. 4-4 Using a portable holding tank to hold gasoline from the vehicle fuel tank during fuel-system service or repair. *(Chrysler Corporation)*

There may be other flammable liquids in the shop. When pumping a flammable liquid from a large container into a smaller one, the larger container should be electrically grounded. Connect a *bond wire* from the large container to the small container. This prevents static electricity from causing a dangerous spark.

3. *Blocking exits.* Keep areas around exit doors and passageways leading to exits free of all obstructions. If there is an explosion and fire, a blocked exit could mean serious injury or death!
4. *Spilled oil or antifreeze not cleaned up.* Serious injury can result if someone slips and falls in the shop.
5. *Lack of shop exhaust system, or failing to connect the system to the tail pipe of a vehicle with a running engine.* This is a hazard to everyone in the shop. Exhaust gas contains carbon monoxide (CO) and other poisonous materials.
6. *Allowing dangling hair, ties, sleeves, or jewelry to fall into the engine fan, drive belt, or other moving part.* Injury may occur.

➤ 4-6 HAZARDS DUE TO EQUIPMENT DEFECTS OR MISUSE

Here are common hazards in the shop due to faulty equipment or its improper use.

1. *Incorrect safety guarding of moving machinery.* Ventilating fans should have proper guards and no

exposed blades. Guards should be placed around the belts and pulleys on the shop air compressor (Fig. 4-5).

2. *Asbestos dust from brake and clutch lining.* If the vehicle has asbestos brake lining, asbestos dust collects in the brake mechanisms at the wheels. Remove the dust before working on the brakes. Use a special vacuum cleaner with a *High Efficiency Particulate Air* (HEPA) filter (Fig. 4-6). An ordinary shop vacuum cleaner will not filter out asbestos fibers. They can remain floating in the air for days if not trapped by the HEPA filter. There is more on controlling asbestos dust in Chaps. 42 and 53 on clutch and brake service.

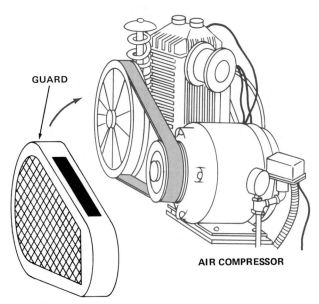

GUARD

AIR COMPRESSOR

Fig. 4-5 Belts and pulleys on shop equipment must always be protected with guards.

Fig. 4-6 A special vacuum cleaner with a high efficiency particulate air (HEPA) filter, used to remove asbestos dust before brake and clutch service. *(Nilfisk of America, Inc.)*

3. *Misuse of compressed air.* Shop *air nozzles* or *blowguns* (Fig. 4-7) discharge compressed air to blow parts dry and clean. A *diffuser* on the blowgun reduces the discharge pressure to less than 30 psi [207 kPa]. Never point a blowgun at another person or use it to blow dust off your clothes. Compressed air can drive dust particles at high speed. These can penetrate the skin and eyes.

When drying rotating parts, such as a ball bearing, avoid spinning them. A ball bearing spinning at high speed can explode. The flying pieces may seriously injure you.

CAUTION!

High-pressure air directed at an open wound can send air into the bloodstream. This can cause death!

---

4. *Flexible electric cord with worn or frayed insulation.* Do not use an electric cord that is worn or spliced. Flexible cord should not run through holes in the wall or be tacked onto the wall. Any of these could cause fire, shock, or electrocution.

5. *Compressed-gas cylinders improperly stored or misused.* Do not store gas cylinders near room heaters or other heat sources. Never store cylinders in unventilated lockers or closets. Have at least 20 feet [6.1 meters (m)] between stored oxygen and acetylene cylinders. They must not stand free. A chain or lashing must secure the cylinders. Never use cylinders as supports or rollers to move an object. The cylinder could explode.

6. *Hand-held electric tools not properly grounded.* They must have a separate ground lead (Fig. 4-8) or double insulation to guard against electric shock.

7. *Automotive lifts (Chap. 8) not properly used.* Never raise a vehicle with passengers in it. To prevent damage, first close the doors, hood, and trunk lid. If the lift has a mechanical locking device, engage it before you go under the vehicle. Do not use a hydraulic lift that jumps, jerks, or settles slowly when it should not.

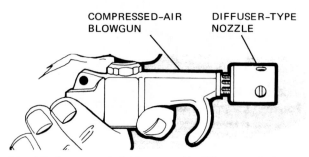

COMPRESSED-AIR BLOWGUN

DIFFUSER-TYPE NOZZLE

Fig. 4-7 Compressed-air blowgun with diffuser nozzle that reduces discharge air pressure to 30 psi [207 kPa] or less. *(Ford Motor Company)*

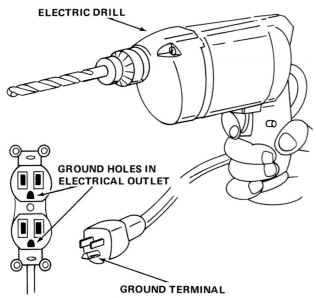

ELECTRIC DRILL

GROUND HOLES IN
ELECTRICAL OUTLET

GROUND TERMINAL

Fig. 4-8 Electric drill with three-wire cord. The third wire and terminal ground the drill motor.

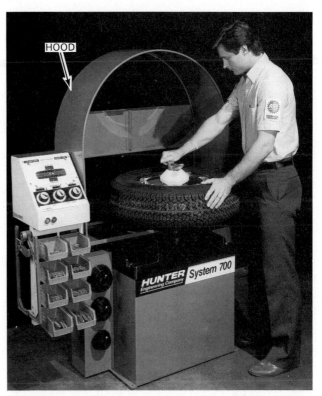

HOOD

HUNTER System 700

Fig. 4-9 A computer wheel balancer with safety hood that lowers over the tire to protect the technician from objects thrown from the tread. *(Hunter Engineering Company)*

Also, do not use a lift that works slowly or leaks oil from the exhaust line or packing gland.

8. *Jacks or safety stands improperly placed.* Vehicles and their major components are heavy. Always place jacks and safety stands so they support the vehicle or component. If a jack or safety stand slips out, damage or injury may result.

9. *Using a wheel-and-tire balancer without the hood in place (Fig. 4-9).* OSHA regulations require all *dynamic* (spinner type) wheel balancers to have a hood. It protects you if a stone or other object flies out of the spinning tire tread.

10. *Letting tester leads fall into the engine fan.* This can damage the leads, topple the tester, and injure you.

11. *Sudden startup of the electric fan (Fig. 4-10) for the engine cooling system.* These fans can run even if the ignition key is off. To protect yourself, disconnect the fan-lead connector before you work around the engine. Otherwise, if the engine is still hot, the fan could start running and injure you.

12. *Leaving a running power tool unattended.* If you must leave it, turn it off. Otherwise someone might come along and, not realizing it is running, get hurt.

13. *Playing with a fire extinguisher.* Some people have thought it was fun to play with a fire extinguisher. But the liquid or spray discharge made the floor slick. Then someone was injured by a slip and fall. Other people have had eye damage from being hit by the discharge. Never play with a fire extinguisher. The discharge may cause an injury. Also, this leaves the extinguisher empty and useless if needed for a fire. Chapter 8 describes other precautions to take when working with power tools.

➤ **4-7 HAND-TOOL HAZARDS**

Keep hand tools clean and in good condition. Greasy and oily tools are difficult to hold and use. Wipe tools clean before and after using them. Do not use a hardened hammer or punch on a hardened surface. Hardened steel is brittle and can shatter from heavy blows. Slivers may fly out and enter a hand or an eye.

There are other hand-tool hazards to watch out for. These include hammers with broken or cracked handles, chisels and punches with mushroomed heads, and broken or bent wrenches. Never use a tool that is in poor condition or not right for the job. Chapter 7 describes and illustrates the proper use and care of hand tools.

FIRES AND HOW TO PREVENT THEM

➤ **4-8 FIRE PREVENTION**

Gasoline is very dangerous if not handled properly. Sometimes people forget that, because gasoline is so common in the shop. A spark or lighted match in a closed place filled with gasoline vapor can cause an explosion. Even the spark from a light switch can set off an explosion. Here are some safety rules.

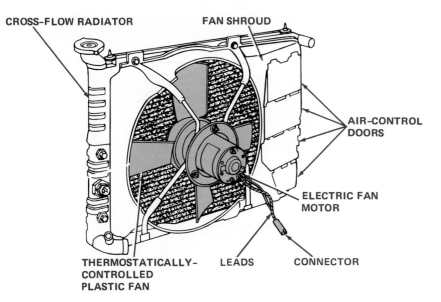

CROSS-FLOW RADIATOR
FAN SHROUD
AIR-CONTROL DOORS
ELECTRIC FAN MOTOR
THERMOSTATICALLY-CONTROLLED PLASTIC FAN
LEADS
CONNECTOR

Fig. 4-10 Disconnect the lead to an electric fan before working under the hood. The fan can start running even with the ignition key off. *(Chrysler Corporation)*

1. *Do not smoke or light cigarettes around gasoline or other flammable liquids.*

2. *Leaking or spilled gasoline quickly vaporizes.* Keep the shop doors open and the ventilating system running. Wipe up the spilled gasoline at once. Put the rags or towels outside to dry.

3. *Sometimes you must work on a vehicle that is leaking gasoline.* Be very careful. Catch the leaking gasoline in a container or on rags. Put the soaked rags outside to dry. Do not make sparks, such as by connecting a test light to the battery.

4. *Store gasoline in an approved* **safety container** *(Fig. 4-11).* Never store gasoline in a glass jug. The glass could break. An explosion and fire could result.

5. *Oily rags can catch fire, without a spark or flame, by* **spontaneous combustion.** To prevent this, always store oily rags and waste in a fireproof safety container (Fig. 4-12). Do not overfill the safety container. The lid should close completely.

➤ 4-9 FIRE EXTINGUISHERS

A *fire extinguisher* (Fig. 4-13) is a portable container filled with chemicals which can be discharged in a stream to put out small fires. The most common shop fire extinguisher is the multipurpose *dry chemical* type. It can be used to fight ordinary combustible fires, flammable-liquid fires, and electrical fires.

Note the location of the fire extinguishers in the shop (Fig. 4-13). Make sure you know how to use them. Figure 4-14 shows different types of fires and the type of extin-

GASOLINE SAFETY CONTAINER

Fig. 4-11 Always store gasoline and all flammable liquids in approved safety containers. *(ATW)*

OILY RAG SAFETY CONTAINER

Fig. 4-12 Safety container for the storage of oily rags.

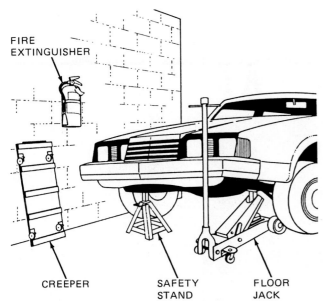

FIRE EXTINGUISHER

CREEPER   SAFETY STAND   FLOOR JACK

Fig. 4-13 Know where the nearest fire extinguisher is located. *(ATW)*

guisher to use for each. The quicker you begin to fight a fire, the easier it is to control. Use the right kind of fire extinguisher, and use it correctly (Fig. 4-15). Ask your instructor any questions you have about reporting a fire, the use of the building fire-alarm system, and fire extinguishers and their use.

CAUTION!

Never spray water over a flammable liquid or gasoline fire. Because the burning liquid floats, the water will only spread the fire.

WORKING SAFELY

➤ 4-10 SHOP SAFETY RULES

Some people say, *"Accidents will happen!"* But safety experts disagree. They say, *"Accidents are caused. They are caused by careless actions. They are caused by inattention to the job. And they are caused by using damaged or incorrect tools."* Fewer accidents occur in shops that are neat and clean.

To help prevent accidents, follow these safety rules.

1. Work quietly and give your full attention to the job you are doing.
2. Keep your tools and equipment under control.
3. Keep jack handles out of the way (Fig. 4-13). Stand the *creeper* against the wall when not in use.

4. Never indulge in horseplay or other foolish action. You could cause someone to get seriously hurt.
5. Never put screwdrivers or other sharp objects in your pocket. You could cut or stab yourself. Or you could damage the upholstery in a car.
6. Make sure your clothes are right for the job. Dangling sleeves or ties can get caught in machinery and cause serious injury. Do not wear sandals or open-toe shoes. Wear full leather shoes with nonskid rubber heels and soles. Steel-toe safety shoes are best for shopwork. Keep long hair out of machinery by wearing a cap.
7. Do not wear any rings, bracelets, or watches when working around moving machinery or electrical equipment. Jewelry can catch in moving machinery with very serious results. Also, a ring or bracelet can accidentally create a short circuit of the battery. Then the metal of the ring or bracelet may become white hot in an instant. This will severely burn you.
8. Wipe oil and grease off your hands and tools. You need a good grip on tools and parts.
9. If you spill oil, grease, or any liquid on the floor, clean it up. Help prevent injury from slips and falls.
10. Never use compressed air to blow dirt from your clothes. Never point a compressed-air blowgun at another person. See item 3 in ➤4-6 above.
11. Always wear eye protection when liquid spray or particles are flying about. Safety glasses, safety goggles, or a face shield (Fig. 4-16) should always be available. Always wear eye protection when using a grinding wheel (Fig. 4-17).
12. Watch out for sparks flying from a grinding wheel or a welding job. The sparks can set hair or clothes on fire.
13. When using solvents or other chemicals, wear goggles to protect your eyes. If you get a chemical in your eyes, flush them with water at once (Fig. 4-18). Then go to the school nurse, a doctor, or a hospital emergency room.
14. When using a *floor jack* (Fig. 4-13), position it properly. It must not slip out. Never lift a vehicle while someone is working under it! People have been killed when the jack slipped and the vehicle fell on them. Always put safety stands in place before going under a vehicle (Fig. 4-19).
15. Always use the right tool for the job. The wrong tool could damage the part you are working on or could hurt you.
16. Keep your hands away from the engine fan and accessory *drive belts* (Fig. 1-13) when the engine is running. Your hand could get caught in the fan or between a belt and pulley. You could be badly cut or even lose fingers.
17. Do not stand directly in line with the engine fan when it is turning or the engine is running. Some fans, especially fans with flexible blades, have thrown off a blade while spinning. A flying fan blade may injure or kill anyone it strikes.

EXTINGUISHERS

FIRES	TYPE	USE		OPERATION
A CLASS *A* FIRES ORDINARY COMBUSTIBLE MATERIALS SUCH AS WOOD, PAPER, TEXTILES AND SO FORTH. REQUIRES...COOLING-QUENCHING	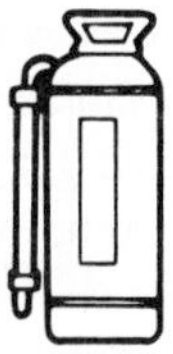 **FOAM** SOLUTION OF ALUMINUM SULPHATE AND BICARBONATE OF SODA	OK FOR	**A B** **C** (NOT FOR)	*FOAM*: DON'T PLAY STREAM INTO THE BURNING LIQUID. ALLOW FOAM TO FALL LIGHTLY ON FIRE 
	 **CARBON DIOXIDE** CARBON DIOXIDE GAS UNDER PRESSURE	NOT FOR / OK FOR	**A** (NOT FOR) **B C** (OK FOR)	*CARBON DIOXIDE*: DIRECT DISCHARGE AS CLOSE TO FIRE AS POSSIBLE. FIRST AT EDGE OF FLAMES AND GRADUALLY FORWARD AND UPWARD 
B CLASS *B* FIRES FLAMMABLE LIQUIDS, GREASES, GASOLINE, OILS, PAINTS AND SO FORTH. REQUIRES...BLANKETING OR SMOTHERING	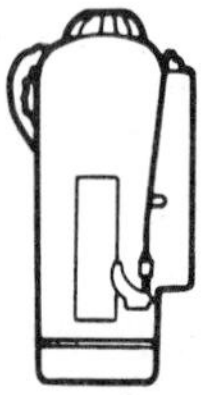 **DRY CHEMICAL**	MULTI-PURPOSE TYPE: OK FOR **A B C**	ORDINARY BC TYPE: NOT FOR **A** / OK FOR **B C**	*DRY CHEMICAL*: DIRECT STREAM AT BASE OF FLAMES. USE RAPID LEFT-TO-RIGHT MOTION TOWARD FLAMES 
C CLASS *C* FIRES ELECTRICAL EQUIPMENT, MOTORS, SWITCHES AND SO FORTH. REQUIRES...A NONCONDUCTING AGENT	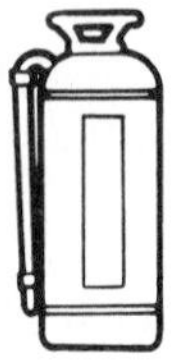 **SODA-ACID** BICARBONATE OF SODA SOLUTION AND SULPHURIC ACID	OK FOR / NOT FOR	**A** (OK FOR) **B C** (NOT FOR)	*SODA-ACID*: DIRECT STREAM AT BASE OF FLAME 

Fig. 4-14 Chart showing types of fire extinguishers, the classification of fires, and which extinguisher to use. *(Ford Motor Company)*

Fig. 4-15 Know how to use the shop fire extinguisher. The quicker you begin to fight a fire, the easier it is to control. *(ATW)*

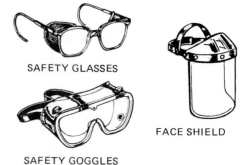

SAFETY GLASSES

SAFETY GOGGLES

FACE SHIELD

Fig. 4-16 Always wear safety glasses, safety goggles, or a face shield when liquid spray or particles are flying or falling around you. *(United States Safety Service Company)*

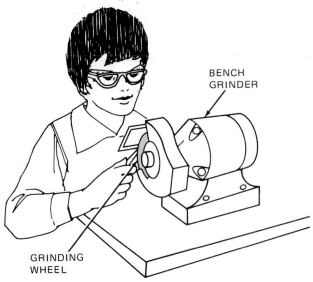

Fig. 4-17 Always wear eye protection when using a grinding wheel.

Fig. 4-18 If solvent or some other chemical splashes in your eyes, immediately wash them out with water.

CAUTION!

Never run an engine in a closed garage that does not have a ventilating system. The exhaust gases contain carbon monoxide (CO). This is a colorless, odorless, tasteless, poisonous gas. Enough carbon monoxide to kill you can collect in only 3 minutes from a running engine in a closed one-car garage!

➤ 4-11 USING POWER TOOLS

In the automotive shop, you use many types of power tools. Study the operating instructions for any power tool or piece of shop equipment before using it. Chapter 8 describes shop equipment and power tools, and how to use them safely.

➤ 4-12 WHAT TO DO IN EMERGENCIES

If there is an accident and someone gets hurt, tell your instructor at once. The instructor will know what to do. It may be to give first aid, phone for the school nurse, a doctor, or an ambulance. Be careful in giving first aid. Trying first aid on an injured person can do more harm than good if it is done wrong. For example, improperly moving a person with a serious back injury could make the injury worse. However, quick mouth-to-mouth resuscitation may save the life of a person who has suffered an electric shock. Ask your instructor any questions you have about first aid.

➤ 4-13 HAZARDOUS MATERIAL

A *hazardous material* is anything corrosive, explosive, flammable, radioactive, reactive, or toxic (poisonous). These materials may endanger human health or pollute the environment if improperly handled. Many materials used in automotive service can be hazardous if not handled

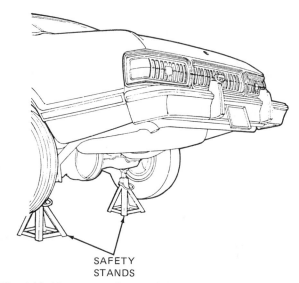

Fig. 4-19 Always put safety stands in place before going under a vehicle. *(Ford Motor Company)*

properly. Examples include air-conditioning refrigerant, antifreeze, brake fluid, gasoline, and engine oil. Other hazardous materials are asbestos dust (➤4-6), parts-cleaning solvent, grease, paint, and shop adhesives (glue and cement).

To protect workers from unsafe exposure to hazardous materials on the job, OSHA issued the *Hazard Communication Standard*. This is often called the "right to know" law. It requires the shop owners to inform people who work there of the risks. The workers must receive information and training on how to protect themselves. The shop must also maintain a file of *Material Safety Data Sheets* (MSDS) in a place that is accessible to all employees.

Many types of automotive service work create hazardous waste. This is any material that could pose danger to

CHAPTER 5

MEASURING SYSTEMS AND MEASURING TOOLS

After you have studied this chapter, you should be able to:

- Describe the basic differences between the metric system and the USC system.
- Explain the relationship among linear measurements, weight, and volume in the metric system.
- Explain how to convert measurements from one system into the other (metric into USC or USC into metric).
- List and describe the measuring tools discussed in the chapter.
- Demonstrate how to use measuring tools in the shop.

MEASUREMENTS AND MEASURING SYSTEMS

➤ 5-1 MEASUREMENTS

You make many kinds of measurements in the automotive shop. These measurements tell you if parts are worn or damaged. They also tell you if the parts are out of adjustment or out of specs (➤3-4), and by how much. Sometimes you measure engine vacuum or power, alternator output, or battery voltage. Alignment specialists measure angles in the front-suspension system. But for much service work, you measure length, diameter, or clearance. For example, in engine work you often measure the *bore* or *diameter* of the engine cylinders (Fig. 5-1).

You make these measurements either in inches or in *millimeters* (mm). Which units you use depends on whether you are measuring in the *United States Customary* (USC) system or in the *metric* system. Figure 5-2 compares the two systems. Markings along the upper edge of the rule or steel scale are in *centimeters* and millimeters (metric). The markings on the lower edge are in inches and fractions of inches (USC system).

➤ 5-2 USC AND METRIC SYSTEMS

In the United States, we have grown up with the USC system. It uses inches, feet, miles, pints, quarts, and gallons. We all know the meaning when someone says a piston measures 3 inches in diameter. In the metric system, this is 76.2 millimeters (mm). One inch equals 25.4 mm.

The metric system is used for the measurements in all imported cars and most cars made in the United States. In this book, the USC measurements are given first. The metric equivalent follows in brackets. For example, 1 inch [25.4 mm].

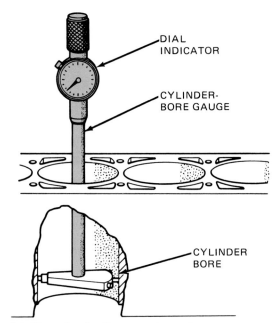

Fig. 5-1 Measuring the diameter or bore of a cylinder with a cylinder-bore gauge. *(Chrysler Corporation)*

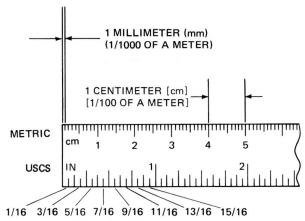

Fig. 5-2 Rule or steel scale marked in both the metric and the USC systems.

➤ 5-3 REASONS FOR GOING METRIC

Every other major country in the world uses the metric system. There are only three basic measurements. These are *meter* (m) for length, *liter* (L) for volume, and *gram* (g) for weight. The system is based on multiples of 10, just like our money system. Ten cents equals one dime and ten dimes equals one dollar. In the same way, 10 mm equals

10 millimeters (mm)	=	1 centimeter (cm)
10 centimeters	=	1 decimeter (dm) = 100 millimeters
10 decimeters	=	1 meter (m) = 1000 millimeters
10 meters	=	1 dekameter (dam)
10 dekameters	=	1 hectometer (hm) = 100 meters
10 hectometers	=	1 kilometer (km) = 1000 meters

Fig. 5-3 Complete list of metric linear measurements. To convert from one unit of measurement to another, move the decimal point.

1 centimeter (cm), 10 cm equals 1 decimeter (dm), and 10 dm equals 1 meter (m) (Fig. 5-3). One thousand meters equals 1 *kilometer* (km), which is 0.62 mile.

The system works because prefixes like *milli-, centi-,* and *kilo-* have special meanings. For example,

Kilo- means 1000 (one thousand).
Deci- means 0.10 (one-tenth).
Centi- means 0.01 (one-hundredth).
Milli- means 0.001 (one-thousandth).

Compare this with our USC system:

12 inches = 1 foot.
    3 feet = 1 yard, or 36 inches.
1760 yards = 1 mile, or 5280 feet, or 63,360 inches.

➤ 5-4 USING THE USC SYSTEM

When making small measurements in the USC system, you deal with small fractions of an inch (Fig. 5-2). For example, 1/4, 1/8, 1/16, 1/32, and 1/64. Sometimes these may not be small enough. Many automotive measurements are in thousandths and sometimes ten-thousandths of an inch. For example, 1/64 inch is 0.0156 inch. A bearing clearance may be 0.002 inch (two thousandths of an inch). To convert fractions of an inch into decimal fractions, you may need a table of decimal equivalents (Fig. 5-4). In the metric system, just move the decimal point (Fig. 5-3).

➤ 5-5 WEIGHT AND VOLUME IN THE METRIC SYSTEM

The metric unit of mass, or weight, is the gram. It is the weight of 1 cubic centimeter (cc) of water at its temperature of maximum density. A cubic centimeter is a cube that measures 1 cm [1/100 m] on a side (Fig. 5-5). One

Inches			Inches			Inches		
Fraction	Decimal	mm	Fraction	Decimal	mm	Fraction	Decimal	mm
1/64	0.0156	0.3969	23/64	0.3594	9.1281	11/16	0.6875	17.4625
1/32	0.0312	0.7938	3/8	0.3750	9.5250	45/64	0.7031	17.8594
3/64	0.0469	1.1906	25/64	0.3906	9.9219	23/32	0.7188	18.2562
1/16	0.0625	1.5875	13/32	0.4062	10.3188	47/64	0.7344	18.6531
5/64	0.0781	1.9844	27/64	0.4219	10.7156	3/4	0.7500	19.0500
3/32	0.0938	2.3812	7/16	0.4375	11.1125	49/64	0.7656	19.4469
7/64	0.1094	2.7781	29/64	0.4531	11.5094	25/32	0.7812	19.8438
1/8	0.1250	3.1750	15/32	0.4688	11.9062	51/64	0.7969	20.2406
9/64	0.1406	3.5719	31/64	0.4844	12.3031	13/16	0.8125	20.6375
5/32	0.1562	3.9688	1/2	0.5000	12.7000	53/64	0.8281	21.0344
11/64	0.1719	4.3656	33/64	0.5156	13.0969	27/32	0.8438	21.4312
3/16	0.1875	4.7625	17/32	0.5312	13.4938	55/64	0.8594	21.8281
13/64	0.2031	5.1594	35/64	0.5469	13.8906	7/8	0.8750	22.2250
7/32	0.2188	5.5562	9/16	0.5625	14.2875	57/64	0.8906	22.6219
15/64	0.2344	5.9531	37/64	0.5781	14.6844	29/32	0.9062	23.0188
1/4	0.2500	6.3500	19/32	0.5938	15.0812	59/64	0.9219	23.4156

Fig. 5-4 Table for changing common fractions (in inches) to their decimal or metric equivalent.

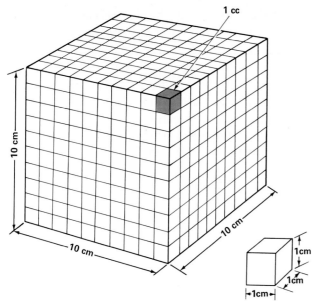

Fig. 5-5 A cubic centimeter is a cube measuring 1 cm on a side. A liter is 1000 cc. Since the gram is the weight of 1 cc of water, a liter of water weighs 1000 g, or 1 kg.

thousand grams is 1 *kilogram* (kg). This is equal to 1000 cc (Fig. 5-6).

The metric unit of volume for fluid (liquid) measurement is the liter [L]. It is slightly larger than a quart. The liter is the volume of a cube that measures 10 cm on a side (or 1000 cc). This is the same measurement for weight or mass. One liter of water weighs 1 kg [1000 g]. One kg equals 2.2 pounds.

➤ 5-6 WEIGHT AND VOLUME IN THE USC SYSTEM

There is no direct relationship among linear measurements, weight, and volume in the USC system. The relationship among inches, feet, yards, and miles is given in ➤5-3. These are linear measurements.

In measuring liquid volume in the USC system:

16 fluid ounces (fl oz) = 1 pint (pt)
2 pints = 1 quart (qt)
4 quarts = 1 gallon (gal)

In weight measurements in the USC system:

16 ounces (oz) = 1 pound (lb)
2000 pounds = 1 ton

➤ 5-7 CONVERTING USC MEASUREMENTS TO METRIC

Sometimes you must convert USC measurements to metric measurements, or from metric to USC. One way is to use *conversion tables,* which your instructor may give you as a handout for your notebook. These relate the various measurements in one system to measurements in the other system. Another way is to use a hand-held *calculator.*

Length		
1 km	= 1000 m	= 100,000 cm
1 m	= 100 cm	= 1000 mm (millimeters)
Capacity and Volume		
1 kL (kiloliter)	= 1000 liters	= 100,000 cL (centiliters)
1 L (liter)	= 1000 cc (cubic centimeters)	= 1000 mL (milliliters)
Mass and Weight		
1 kg	= 1000 g	= 100,000 cg (centigrams)

Fig. 5-6 Metric measurements for length, capacity and volume, and mass and weight.

LINEAR MEASUREMENT TOOLS

➤ 5-8 RULES

The simplest tool used for measuring linear distances is the 6-inch-long *steel scale,* or *rule* (Fig. 5-2). The *tape measure* is another type of steel rule. However, neither is accurate enough for most automotive service work.

➤ 5-9 THICKNESS GAUGES

Thickness gauges, or *feeler gauges,* are strips or blades of metal of various thicknesses (Fig. 5-7). They are used to measure small gaps or distances such as the clearance between two parts. Many thickness gauges are dual-dimensioned. For example, the "3" and "0.08 mm" on the first blade in Fig. 5-7 means it is 0.003 inch or 0.08 mm thick.

Stepped thickness gauges have a tip that is thinner than the rest of the blade. The top blade in Fig. 5-8 is 0.004 inch [0.10 mm] thick at the tip. The rest of the blade is 0.006 inch [0.15 mm] thick.

Figure 5-9 shows a thickness gauge being used to check the clearance between the rocker arm and valve stem in an engine. On some engines, turning the adjusting nut changes

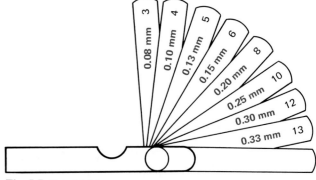

Fig. 5-7 Set of thickness gauges.

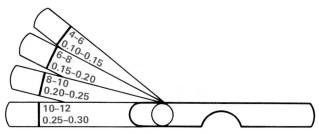

Fig. 5-8 Set of stepped thickness gauges.

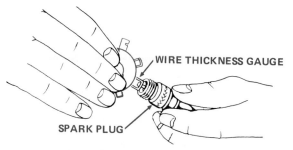

Fig. 5-10 Measuring spark-plug gap with a wire thickness gauge.

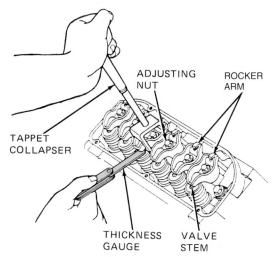

Fig. 5-9 Using a thickness gauge to check the clearance between an engine rocker arm and valve stem. *(Ford Motor Company)*

the clearance. The adjustment is correct when the specified-thickness blade fits the gap snugly, without binding.

Stepped thickness gauges are used for fine adjustments. For example, suppose the specifications call for a valve clearance of 0.005 inch [0.13 mm]. Select the 0.004 to 0.006 inch [0.10 to 0.15 mm] stepped gauge. Then make the adjustment. Clearance is correct when the 0.004-inch [0.10-mm] end enters the gap but the thicker part does not. Stepped thickness gauges are called *go no-go* gauges.

Most thickness gauges are made of steel. However, sometimes you need a *nonmagnetic thickness gauge*. Brass thickness gauges are available for use near permanent magnets. One example is measuring the air gap in an electronic ignition distributor (➤33-23). The permanent magnet that is part of the pickup coil in the distributor will attract the steel gauge. This prevents an accurate measurement. Brass or plastic gauges are unaffected by magnetism.

➤ 5-10 WIRE GAUGES

Wire gauges are precisely-sized pieces of round wire (Fig. 5-10). The diameter is usually marked on the handle or holder. Spark-plug gaps and other openings are measured with wire gauges. The specified gauge should fit into the gap snugly, without binding.

➤ 5-11 MICROMETERS

The *micrometer* or *"mike"* is a hand-held precision measuring instrument. In the USC system, it measures thicknesses in thousandths or ten-thousandths of an inch. Metric measurements are in hundredths of a millimeter. The two types of micrometer are the *inside micrometer* (Fig. 5-11) and *outside micrometer* (Fig. 5-12). The outside micrometer is used most in the automotive shop.

To be sure of accurate measurements, *calibrate* the micrometer regularly. "Calibrate" means to check for accuracy. Check the outside micrometer by first cleaning the contact faces. Then close them lightly against the standard bar or test gauge from the micrometer set. Follow the procedure in the manufacturer's operating instructions, or as explained by your instructor. A micrometer can be damaged by improper use.

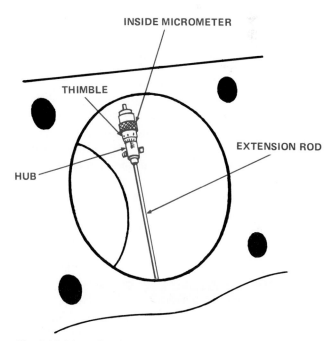

Fig. 5-11 Measuring the cylinder diameter or bore with an inside micrometer. *(ATW)*

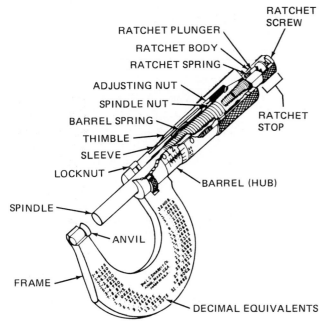

Fig. 5-12 Principle parts of an outside micrometer. *(The L.S. Starrett Company)*

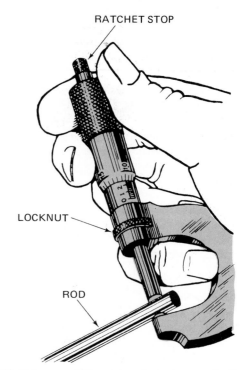

Fig. 5-13 Using an outside micrometer to measure the diameter of a rod.

➤ 5-12 OUTSIDE MICROMETER

The outside micrometer (Fig. 5-12) has a frame and a movable spindle. To measure an object, place it between the spindle and the anvil. Turning the thimble moves the spindle toward or away from the anvil. The thimble has precision screw threads. These cause the spindle to move as the thimble is turned.

Careful! Improper use can damage a mike. Use it properly. After each use, wipe it clean with a clean shop towel. Then return the mike to its case. Never drop a mike or treat it roughly. This could destroy its accuracy.

Figure 5-13 shows how to measure the diameter of a rod. Hold the rod against the anvil. Turn the ratchet stop until the spindle touches the rod. The ratchet stop prevents you from applying excessive force on the mike. When the spindle touches the rod, the ratchet stop clicks and slips. Now take the reading.

CAUTION!

Never try to measure a rotating shaft or other moving part. The mike might jam on the part and start spinning around with it. You could be hit by the mike, or by flying particles if the mike breaks. Serious injury could result.

➤ 5-13 READING THE USC MICROMETER

The USC or "inch micrometer" reads in thousandths of an inch. Some read in ten-thousandths. To read the mike, look at both the revolution line and the thimble position (Fig. 5-14). Every revolution of the thimble moves it exactly one marking on the revolution line. Each marking means twenty-five thousandths (0.025) of an inch. The markings on the thimble run from 0 to 24. There are 25 markings on the thimble. When the thimble is turned enough for its next mark to align with the revolution line, the spindle has moved 0.001 inch. This is the measurement, for example, if the thimble moves from 24 to 23. When the thimble turns one complete revolution, it moves the spindle 25 markings

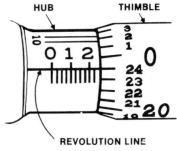

Fig. 5-14 Hub and thimble markings on a inch micrometer which measures in thousandths (1/1000) and ten-thousandths (1/10,000) of an inch.

(0.025 inch). This is the distance between the revolution-line marks.

To read the mike setting shown in Fig. 5-14, notice that you can see the "2." You can also see one of the in-between markings on the revolution line. This means that the distance between the spindle and anvil is 0.2 inch plus 0.025 inch, or 0.225 inch—plus something more. That something more is the amount the thimble has turned away from the 0.225 reading on the revolution line. This is 24, or 0.024 inch. So add 0.024 to the 0.225 to get the total reading of 0.249 inch. Figure 5-15 shows other micrometer readings. Practice using the micrometer.

➤ 5-14 METRIC MICROMETERS

The metric micrometer reads in hundredths of a millimeter. You read directly from the revolution or reading line on the barrel, and the thimble. Millimeter marks are above the reading line and half millimeter marks are below. In Fig. 5-16, the thimble is backed off to show the 10 (10 mm)

mark on the reading line, plus one of the upper markings (1.0 mm). This makes 11 mm. To this, add the thimble marking of 45 (0.45 mm). The total reading is 11.45 mm. One complete revolution of the thimble moves it along the reading line 0.50 mm.

Some micrometers provide direct readings in millimeters (Fig. 5-17) or in inches. As you adjust the thimble, a counter inside the mike shows the measurement in numbers or *digits*. Therefore, these mikes are metric (or inch) *digital micrometers.*

➤ 5-15 MEASURING INSIDE DIAMETER WITH OUTSIDE MICROMETER AND TELESCOPE GAUGE

An outside mike and a telescope gauge can measure inside diameters (Fig. 5-18). Adjust the telescope gauge to the diameter. Then measure the telescope gauge with the outside mike.

Fig. 5-17 A metric digital micrometer adjusted to a reading of 7.00 mm. *(The L.S. Starrett Company)*

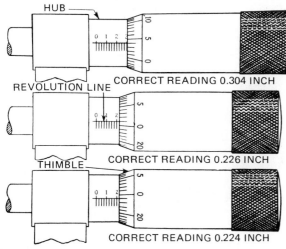

HUB
REVOLUTION LINE
CORRECT READING 0.304 INCH
CORRECT READING 0.226 INCH
THIMBLE
CORRECT READING 0.224 INCH

Fig. 5-15 Reading the micrometer.

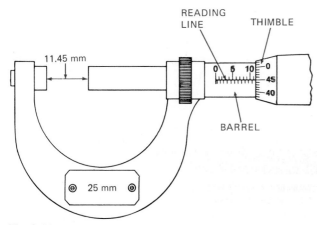

READING LINE
THIMBLE
11.45 mm
BARREL
25 mm

Fig. 5-16 Metric micrometer adjusted to a reading of 11.45 mm.

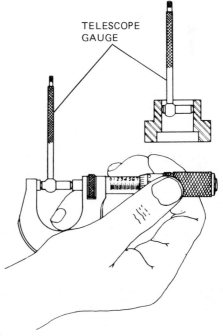

TELESCOPE GAUGE

Fig. 5-18 Using a telescope gauge and an outside micrometer to measure the diameter of a small cylinder. *(The L.S. Starrett Company)*

➤ 5-16 MACHINE-TOOL MICROMETER ADJUSTMENTS

Many machine tools in the automotive shop have micrometer adjustments. The machines have knobs or dials with markings similar to those on mikes. This enables the technician to set the machine precisely.

➤ 5-17 DIAL INDICATORS

The *dial indicator* has a dial face and a needle to register measurements (Fig. 5-19). The needle moves in relation to movement of a movable arm or plunger. As the plunger moves, the needle shows the distance or variation. The reading may be in thousandths of an inch or hundredths of a millimeter.

The dial indicator can measure end play in shafts or gears (Fig. 5-20). To take the measurement, push the plunger against the part you are measuring until the needle moves. Tighten the clamp screw (Fig. 5-19). Rotate the

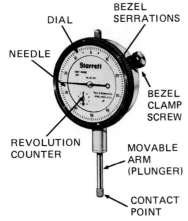

Fig. 5-19 A dial indicator that has a range of 1.000 inch. Each mark around the dial represents 0.001 inch. *(The L.S. Starrett Company)*

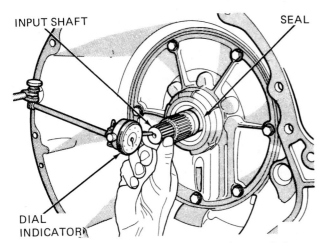

Fig. 5-20 Checking the endplay of an automatic-transmission input shaft with a dial indicator. *(Chrysler Corporation)*

bezel, or grooved rim, until the needle aligns with the 0 mark. Then move the part back and forth. Read the amount of needle movement on the dial. The *total* distance that the needle moves—to the left and to the right—of the 0 mark is the *total indicator reading* (TIR).

Figures 5-1 and 5-21 show how to check an engine cylinder with a *cylinder-bore gauge.* It is basically a dial indicator in a special holder. The gauge is moved up and down and then around the cylinder bore. Needle movement shows surface variation. This is the wear, taper, and out-of-round in the cylinder.

A cylinder-bore gauge and an outside micrometer together can measure the diameter of the cylinder. Place the gauge in the cylinder and note the needle position. Remove the gauge from the cylinder. Then measure the same reading with an outside micrometer (Fig. 5-22).

➤ 5-18 VERNIER CALIPER

A *vernier caliper* (Fig. 5-23) can take both inside and outside measurements. These may be in either thousandths of an inch or hundredths of a millimeter. On the USC vernier caliper shown in Fig. 5-23, marks on the frame

Fig. 5-21 A cylinder-bore gauge can measure cylinder wear, taper, and out-of-round.

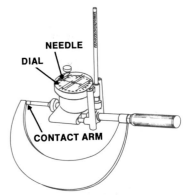

Fig. 5-22 Measuring the reading of the cylinder-bore gauge to find the diameter of an engine cylinder.

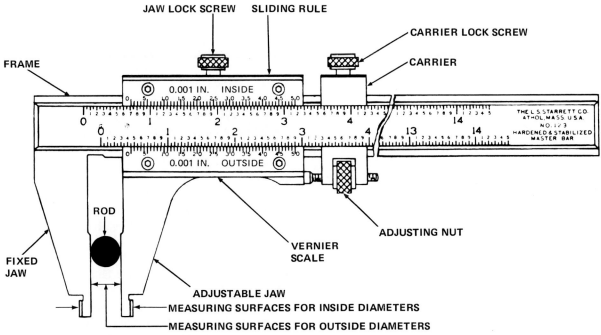

Fig. 5-23 Measuring the diameter of a rod with a vernier caliper. *(The L.S. Starrett Company)*

show twentieths (0.050) of an inch. Every other mark is numbered to represent one-tenth (0.100) inch. The vernier scale is divided into 50 parts and numbered by fives from 0 to 50. The 50 divisions on the vernier scale occupy the same space as 49 divisions on the frame. The difference is 1/1000 (0.001) inch.

Read the vernier caliper (Fig. 5-23) by noting how far the 0 mark on the vernier scale is from the 0 mark on the frame. Do this by adding up how many inches, tenths (0.100), and twentieths (0.050) there are between the two marks. Then add the number of divisions on the vernier scale from 0 to the line which aligns exactly with a line on the frame. Each of these lines represents 0.001. There are also *dial calipers* which combine a vernier caliper with a dial indicator. The dial makes reading small measurements easier and more accurate.

➤ 5-19 DEPTH GAUGE

The *depth gauge* (Fig. 5-24) is a type of micrometer. It measures the depth of grooves or holes. You can insert different length measuring rods after unscrewing the ratchet stop. Rods that measure depths up to 9 inches [228.6 mm] are available.

On some vernier and dial calipers (➤5-18), a thin blade attaches to the adjustable jaw. As the jaw moves, the blade extends from the other end of the frame. This extension can serve as a depth gauge.

➤ 5-20 SMALL-HOLE GAUGE

The *small-hole gauge* (Fig. 5-25) measures the diameter of small holes. Figure 5-25 shows how to measure the wear in an engine *valve guide* (➤14-9). Adjust the gauge until you

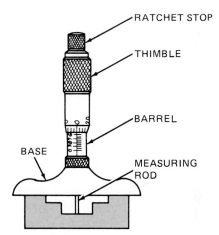

Fig. 5-24 Using a depth gauge to measure the depth of a slot. *(The L.S. Starrett Company)*

feel a slight drag as the split ball slides in the hole. Remove the gauge. Then measure the distance between the two sides of the split ball with an outside micrometer.

PRESSURE AND VACUUM MEASUREMENTS

➤ 5-21 PRESSURE GAUGE

A *fluid* is a substance that has no rigidity. A liquid or gas is a fluid. Squeezing or compressing causes it to exert equal force in all directions. This force applied to each unit of surface area is *pressure*.

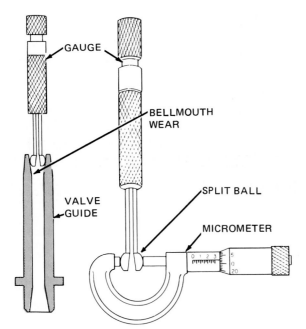

Fig. 5-25 Using a small-hole gauge to measure the size of a small hole.

You measure many pressures on the car. These include pressure in the automatic transmission, cylinder compression pressure, fuel-pump pressure, power-steering pump pressure, and tire pressure. In the USC system, pressure is measured in *pounds per square inch* (psi). This is the pounds of force applied to each square inch of surface. In the metric system, pressure is measured in *kiloPascals* (kPa).

$$1 \text{ psi} = 6.895 \text{ kPa}$$

For quick conversions in the shop, use 1 psi equals 7 kPa.

Figure 5-26 shows a *cylinder-compression tester*. It measures the pressure in the engine cylinder at the end of the compression stroke. If the compression pressure is low, there is trouble in the engine. Later chapters explain the possible causes.

To convert a compression pressure of 120 psi to its metric equivalent:

$$120 \text{ psi} \times 7 = 840 \text{ kPa}$$

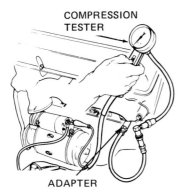

Fig. 5-26 Using a cylinder compression tester. *(Sun Electric Corporation)*

Atmospheric pressure is 14.7 psi at sea level. When the pressure is less than atmospheric, the reduced pressure is a *vacuum*. The engine is a sort of vacuum pump. The intake strokes create a vacuum that causes the air-fuel mixture to enter the cylinders. The amount of vacuum the engine develops is a measure of its condition. Suppose the engine is running at a steady idle speed. Normal vacuum in the *intake manifold* should be from 15 to 22 "inches of mercury."

If the engine cannot produce normal vacuum, something is wrong. Improper vacuum may affect braking, fuel economy, and exhaust emissions. It may also affect the shifting of the automatic transmission, and the operation of the heater and air conditioner.

Figure 5-27 shows a *vacuum gauge* connected to the intake manifold to read manifold vacuum. The gauge measures vacuum in *inches of mercury*. There is no mercury in the gauge. The reading only indicates how high the vacuum would raise a column of mercury in a *barometer* (➤9-16). This is an instrument for measuring atmospheric pressure. In Fig. 5-27, the needle shows a reading of "20 inches," or "20 inches Hg." Hg is the chemical symbol for mercury.

In the metric system, vacuum is measured in *millimeters of mercury*. To convert inches of vacuum to millimeters of vacuum:

$$1 \text{ inch Hg} = 25.4 \text{ mm Hg}$$

For shop use, 1 inch Hg = 25 mm Hg is usually accurate enough.

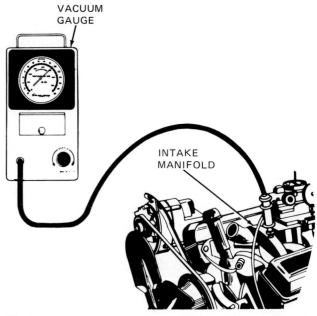

Fig. 5-27 Vacuum gauge connected to measure the vacuum in the engine intake manifold. *(Sun Electric Corporation)*

TRADE TALK

barometer   digit   kilogram   total indicator reading
bore   fluid   millimeter   vacuum
calibrate   pressure

MULTIPLE-CHOICE TEST

*Select the **one** correct, best, or most probable answer to each question.*
You can find the answers in the section indicated at the end of each question.

1. Measurements will tell you if parts are (➢5-1)
   a. worn
   b. out of adjustment
   c. out of specs
   d. all of the above
2. The bore of an engine cylinder is 3.000 inches. In the metric system the bore is (➢ 5-2)
   a. 76.2 m
   b. 76.2 cm
   c. 76.2 mm
   d. 76.2 km
3. A fuel tank holds 21 gallons. How many liters does it hold? (➢ 5-5)
   a. 7.9 L
   b. 79 L
   c. 79 cc
   d. 79 kL
4. The spark-plug gap for an imported car engine should be 2.03 mm. What is this in the USC system? (➢ 5-4)
   a. 0.050 inch
   b. 0.060 inch
   c. 0.080 inch
   d. 0.080 mm
5. Connecting-rod-bearing clearance for an imported car engine is given as 0.051 mm. What is this in the USC system? (➢ 5-4)
   a. 0.0002 inch
   b. 0.002 inch

   c. 0.020 inch
   d. 0.200 inch
6. The USC micrometer reads in (➢5-13)
   a. thousandths of an inch
   b. hundredths of an inch
   c. hundred-thousandths of an inch
   d. hundredths of a millimeter
7. The metric micrometer reads in (➢5-14)
   a. thousandths of an inch
   b. hundredths of an meter
   c. hundredths of a centimeter
   d. hundredths of a millimeter
8. A cylinder-bore gauge will measure cylinder (➢5-17)
   a. wear
   b. taper
   c. out of round
   d. all of the above
9. A vernier caliper is accurate to the nearest (➢5-18)
   a. thousandth of an inch or hundredth of a millimeter
   b. hundredth of an inch or thousandth of a millimeter
   c. hundredth of an inch or hundredth of a centimeter
   d. ten-thousandth of an inch or hundredth of a centimeter
10. A specification given in kiloPascals is a measurement of (➢5-21)
    a. vacuum
    b. force
    c. pressure
    d. mercury

REVIEW QUESTIONS

1. Explain why measurements are necessary in the automotive shop, and what can they tell you.   (➢5-1)
2. Describe the relationship of weight and volume in the metric system.   (➢5-5)
3. What is a dual-dimensioned thickness gauge?   (➢5-9)
4. Explain how to use and read a USC micrometer.   (➢5-13)
5. Explain how to read a metric micrometer.   (➢5-14)

CHAPTER 6

AUTOMOTIVE FASTENERS, GASKETS, AND SEALANTS

After studying this chapter, you should be able to:

- Explain how bolt heads are marked to indicate their strength.
- Describe four ways that nuts and bolts can be prevented from loosening.
- Explain the difference between a *prevailing-torque fastener* and a *torque-to-yield fastener.*
- Describe the functions of a gasket, and list four places in the engine they are used.
- Define *aerobic sealant* and *anaerobic sealant,* and describe typical uses of each.

MECHANICAL FASTENERS

➤ 6-1 FASTENERS

Fasteners hold automotive parts together. Examples are screws, nuts, and studs (Fig. 6-1). Others are rivets, snap rings, and cotter pins. Most fasteners are removable so the assembly can be taken apart. There are also permanent ways of fastening parts together, such as soldering and welding. Metal parts and panels are welded together to form the car body (➤1-21).

➤ 6-2 SCREW THREADS

A fastener that has a spiral ridge, or *screw thread,* on its surface is a *threaded fastener* (Fig. 6-1). This includes bolts, screws, studs, and nuts. *Bolts* and *screws* are lengths of rod with a head on one end and threads on the other. A *stud* looks like a headless bolt with threads on one or both ends. Bolts, screws, and studs have external (outside) threads. Nuts and threaded (or *tapped*) holes have internal (inside) threads (Fig. 6-1).

Screws, bolts, studs, nuts, and tapped (threaded) holes are manufactured with either US customary (USC) or metric screw threads. They are not interchangeable. A USC screw will not fit a metric tapped hole. And a metric screw will not fit a USC tapped hole. Some cars have metric fasteners. Others have USC fasteners. Some have

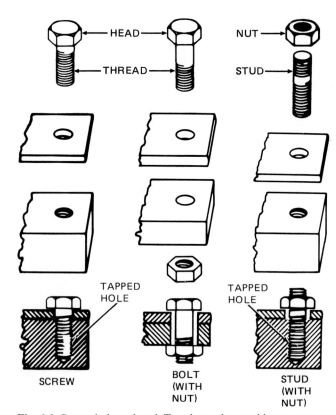

Fig. 6-1 Screw, bolt, and stud. Top shows the attaching parts separated but aligned for assembly. Bottom shows the parts together.

both. To work on a variety of cars, you need new fasteners of both types available. In addition, your tools must include both USC and metric sockets and wrenches. Chapter 7 covers shop hand tools.

➤ 6-3 USC SCREW THREADS

Five ways of describing USC screw threads are:

1. By size (Fig. 6-2).
2. By threads per inch or *pitch* (Fig. 6-2).
3. By thread series, which is the coarseness or fineness of the thread (Fig. 6-3).
4. By thread class (closeness of fit).
5. By right-hand or left-hand direction of the threads. All threads are right-hand unless otherwise noted. If the bolt tightens as the head is turned clockwise, the bolt has right-hand threads.

Figure 6-4 is a table of USC screw-thread sizes and pitches. When you are doing a service job, you must use the correct screw, bolt, or nut. A 1/4-inch screw can have 20, 28, or 32 threads per inch. You cannot use a 20-thread (coarse) screw in a 28-thread (fine) hole.

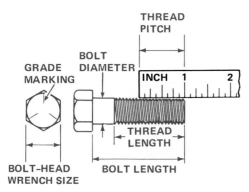

Fig. 6-2 Various measurements of a bolt. *(ATW)*

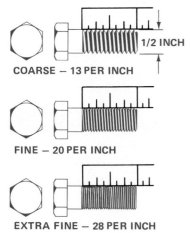

Fig. 6-3 Thread series of a 1/2-inch bolt. *(ATW)*

		Threads per Inch		
Size	Diameter (Decimal)	Coarse (UNC or NC)	Fine (UNF or NF)	Extra-Fine (UNEF or NEF)
0	0.0600		80	
1	0.0730	64	72	
2	0.0860	56	64	
3	0.0990	48	56	
4	0.1120	40	48	
5	0.1250	40	44	
6	0.1380	32	40	
8	0.1640	32	36	
10	0.1900	24	32	
12	0.2160	24	28	32
¼	0.2500	20	28	32
⁵⁄₁₆	0.3125	18	24	32
⅜	0.3750	16	24	32
⁷⁄₁₆	0.4375	14	20	28
½	0.5000	13	20	28
⁹⁄₁₆	0.5625	12	18	24
⅝	0.6250	11	18	24
¾	0.7500	10	16	20
⅞	0.8750	9	14	20

Fig. 6-4 Thread series for various USC sizes of screw, bolt, stud, and nut.

Figure 6-2 shows one way to determine pitch (threads per inch). Count how many threads there are to an inch. Figure 6-5 shows how to use a *thread gauge* to determine pitch. Simply find the blade that fits the threads. Blades are marked with the pitch, or number of threads per inch.

➤ 6-4 OTHER USC THREAD DESIGNATIONS

Thread series and class are among other USC thread designations.

1. THREAD SERIES The three series are coarse, fine, and extra fine (Fig. 6-4). The difference is in the number of threads per inch.

2. THREAD CLASS This designates the closeness of fit. Class 1 is the loosest fit. It is easily removed and installed, even if it has dirty and battered threads. Class 2 is a tighter

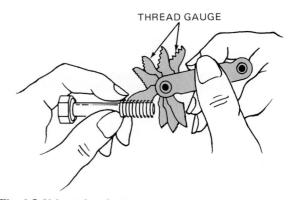

Fig. 6-5 Using a thread gauge.

fit. Class 3 has a very close fit. It is used where maximum strength and holding power are required.

3. A AND B DESIGNATIONS External threads, as on screws and bolts, are *A threads*. Internal threads, as in nuts and tapped holes, are *B threads*.

4. COMPLETE THREAD DESIGNATION A complete thread designation is by size, pitch, series, and class. For example, a 1/4-20 UNC-2A bolt is 1/4 inch in diameter. It has coarse threads of 20 threads per inch. The thread is an external, class 2 thread.

> **Careful!** For screws, bolts, nuts, and threaded holes to match, they must match in size, pitch, series, and class. Using the wrong screw or nut could be dangerous. Even if you could force a fit, the damaged threads will be weak and may fail. Start a threaded fastener by hand to be sure it fits. This avoids cross-threading.

5. LENGTH The length of a bolt or screw is the length from the bottom of the head to the end of the threads (Fig. 6-2). However, the threads do not always extend from the end to the head of the bolt or screw.

6-5 METRIC SCREW THREADS

Metric bolts, screws, and threads are measured in millimeters. Figure 6-6 shows the designation of a metric bolt. Thread pitch is the distance between individual threads. A pitch may run from 1 to 2 mm as the diameter of the threads increases. A bolt with a basic thread diameter of 6 mm has a pitch of 1 mm. A bolt with a thread diameter of 16 mm has a pitch of 2 mm.

6-6 BOLT AND SCREW STRENGTH

The type of material from which the bolt or screw is made determines its strength. Markings on USC and metric screw and bolt heads show their strength (Fig. 6-6). Common metric-fastener bolt-strength markings are 9.8 and 10.9. On metric fasteners, the higher number indicates greater strength.

Figure 6-7 is a table showing the markings on USC screw and bolt heads. The table also shows typical applications for bolts or screws of different strength. The *minimum tensile strength* is the pull in pounds that a round rod with a cross section of 1 square inch can stand before it breaks apart. Higher-strength bolts and screws are more expensive. They are used only where the added strength is needed.

6-7 SCREW AND BOLT HEADS

Vehicles have a great variety of screw and bolt heads. Figure 6-8 shows several, along with the screwdrivers and wrenches required to turn them. Most bolts have *hex heads*. This means the heads are *hexagonal*, or six-sided.

6-8 NUTS

Figure 6-9 shows several nuts. The hex nut is the most common in the automotive shop. The slotted hex and the castle nut are used with a *cotter pin* (Fig. 6-10). To install

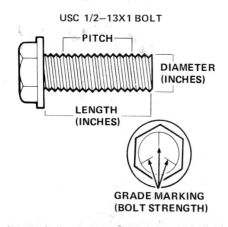

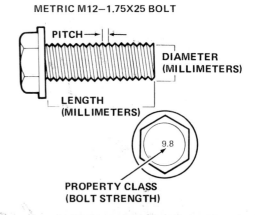

INCH				
½	—	13	X	1
Thread major diameter in inches		Number of threads per inch		Length of bolt in inches

METRIC				
M12	—	1.75	X	25
Thread major diameter in millimeters		Distance between threads in millimeters		Length of bolt in millimeters

Fig. 6-6 Basic measurements of a USC bolt compared with a metric bolt.

USAGES IN VEHICLES	SOME USED	MUCH USED	FOR SPECIAL EQUIPMENT	CRITICAL POINTS	COMPETITION MAXIMUM REQUIREMENTS
TYPICAL APPLICATIONS	FENDERS	CLUTCH HOUSINGS	HEAD BOLTS	BEARING CAPS	RACE CARS
MINIMUM TENSILE STRENGTH, PSI	64,000	105,000	133,000	150,000	160,000
MATERIAL	LOW-CARBON STEEL	MEDIUM-CARBON STEEL	MEDIUM-CARBON STEEL	ALLOY STEEL	SPECIAL ALLOY STEEL
QUALITY	INDETERMINATE	MINIMUM COMMERCIAL	MEDIUM COMMERCIAL	BEST COMMERCIAL	BEST QUALITY
HEAD MARKINGS					

Fig. 6-7 Meaning of USC bolt-head markings.

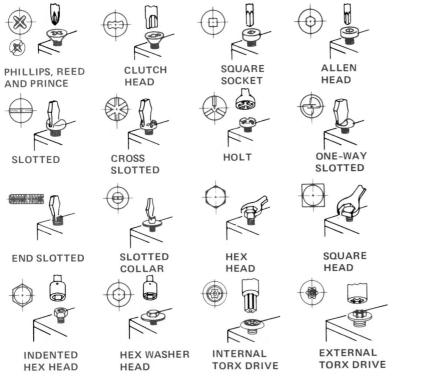

PHILLIPS, REED AND PRINCE   CLUTCH HEAD   SQUARE SOCKET   ALLEN HEAD

SLOTTED   CROSS SLOTTED   HOLT   ONE-WAY SLOTTED

END SLOTTED   SLOTTED COLLAR   HEX HEAD   SQUARE HEAD

INDENTED HEX HEAD   HEX WASHER HEAD   INTERNAL TORX DRIVE   EXTERNAL TORX DRIVE

Fig. 6-8 Screwdrivers and wrenches required to drive various types of screws and bolts. *(ATW)*

WING   HEX

SLOTTED HEX   CASTLE

ACORN   SPEED

SELF-LOCKING   PALNUT

Fig. 6-9 Several common nuts. *(ATW)*

it, tighten the nut. Then insert the cotter pin through a hole in the bolt and two slots in the nut. Bend the ends of the pin around the nut. This prevents the nut from loosening. To remove a cotter pin, straighten the bent ends. Then pull the pin out. Another way to lock a nut on a bolt or stud is to tighten a second nut against the first. The second nut is a *jam nut* or *Palnut* (Fig. 6-9).

The *acorn nut* (Fig. 6-9) covers the end of a screw or bolt. This gives the assembly a neat appearance. The *speed nut* has little holding power. However, it installs quickly by

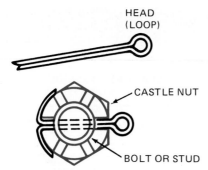

Fig. 6-10 A cotter pin before installation (at top) and after installation (at bottom). *(ATW)*

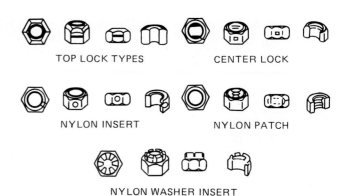

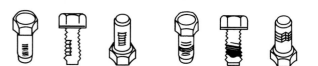

Fig. 6-12 Prevailing-torque nuts. *(General Motors Corporation)*

pushing it over the threads. The speed nut provides a light clamping force when fast assembly is needed.

➤ 6-9 LOCK WASHERS

A *lock washer* under a nut or bolt head helps lock the fastener in place (Fig. 6-11). The sharp edges of the lock washer bite into the metal. This helps prevent the bolt or nut from turning.

➤ 6-10 PREVAILING-TORQUE FASTENERS

Some nuts and bolts have a continuous resistance to turning, even if not tightened down. This is because the threads have an *interference fit*. They do not need cotter pins or lock washers to keep them from loosening. This type of fastener is a *prevailing-torque fastener*.

All-metal nuts usually have the top threads distorted to provide interference (Fig. 6-12). Some nuts are distorted at the center of a hex flat. Other nuts have a nylon patch on the threads, a nylon washer insert at the top of the nut, or a nylon insert through the nut. The distorted threads and nylon inserts help prevent the nut from loosening.

Bolts may have some of the threads distorted to provide interference (Fig. 6-13). Other bolts have a nylon strip or patch, or a dry adhesive coating, on the threads. Any of these methods helps prevent unwanted loosening.

Fig. 6-13 Prevailing-torque bolts. *(General Motors Corporation)*

➤ 6-11 REUSE OF PREVAILING-TORQUE FASTENERS

Sometimes you can reuse clean, unrusted prevailing-torque fasteners. Here is the procedure:

1. Clean any dirt from the bolt or nut.
2. Inspect the fastener for cracks, stretching, or other signs of overtightening or misuse. Discard damaged nuts and bolts. If in doubt about quality or condition, install a new prevailing-torque fastener of equal or greater strength.
3. Lightly lubricate the threads and assemble the parts.
4. Start the bolt or nut by hand. Then use a torque wrench (➤7-11) to tighten it. Before the fastener seats, it should develop the specified prevailing torque. This is the resistance to turning given in Fig. 6-14. If the fastener turns too easily, discard it.
5. Tighten the fastener to the torque specified in the manufacturer's service manual.

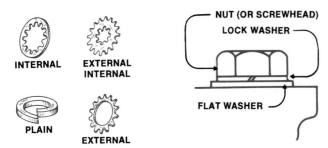

Fig. 6-11 Lock washers (left), and plain lock washer installed between a flat washer and a nut or bolt (right).

Careful! For certain jobs, manufacturers recommend discarding prevailing-torque fasteners after removal. Then install new prevailing-torque fasteners on reassembly or installation.

PREVAILING TORQUE FOR METRIC FASTENERS

	Millimeters	6 & 6.3	8	10	12	14	16	20
Nuts and all-metal bolts	N-m	0.4	0.8	1.4	2.2	3.0	4.2	7.0
	in-lb	4.0	7.0	12	18	25	35	57
Adhesive- or nylon-coated bolts	N-m	0.4	0.6	1.2	1.6	2.4	3.4	5.6
	in-lb	4.0	5.0	10	14	20	28	46

PREVAILING TORQUE FOR USCS FASTENERS

	Inch	¼	5/16	3/8	7/16	½	9/16	5/8	¾
Nuts and all-metal bolts	N-m	0.4	0.6	1.4	1.8	2.4	3.2	4.2	6.2
	in-lb	4.0	5.0	12	15	20	27	35	51
Adhesive- or nylon-coated bolts	N-m	0.4	0.6	1.0	1.4	1.8	2.6	3.4	5.2
	in-lb	4.0	5.0	9.0	12	15	22	28	43

Fig. 6-14 Torque specifications for prevailing-torque nuts and bolts. *(General Motors Corporation)*

➤ 6-12 TORQUE-TO-YIELD BOLTS

Some bolts should be discarded anytime they are loosened or removed, and new bolts installed. These bolts, called *torque-to-yield bolts,* are used for engine cylinder-head bolts and in other parts of the car. Tightening the bolt during installation permanently stretches it. Reuse may cause further stretching. Then breakage or stripping may occur. If these are head bolts in the engine, the cylinder-head gasket (➤6-22) will quickly fail.

To install torque-to-yield bolts, tighten each bolt in the proper sequence to the specified *initial torque,* or *threshold torque.* This lightly seats the bolt head against the surface. Repeat the tightening sequence, turning each bolt through the specified angle (usually 90 degrees). A second sequence of turning each bolt through another specified angle may be required. The result is a more accurate clamping force and fewer gasket failures. A *torque-angle gauge* (➤7-12) accurately measures how much the bolt turns.

➤ 6-13 THREAD-LOCKING CHEMICAL

Another way to prevent nuts and screws from loosening is to coat the threads with a thread-locking chemical before installation. The chemical locks the threads so the nut or screw will not loosen under normal conditions. Chemical thread-locking is discussed further in ➤6-26.

➤ 6-14 ANTISEIZE COMPOUND

Sometimes you must install a steel bolt in an aluminum part such as a cylinder head or engine block. First coat the bolt threads with an *antiseize compound* (Fig. 6-15). Without the compound the steel threads may seize or lock in the

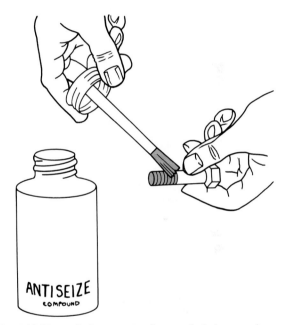

Fig. 6-15 Use antiseize compound on any bolt that goes into aluminum threads. *(ATW)*

aluminum threads. Then removing the bolt may damage or pull out the aluminum threads. Coating the bolt threads with antiseize compound helps prevent this. Bolts that get extremely hot, such as exhaust-manifold bolts, should also be coated with antiseize compound.

➤ 6-15 THREAD INSERTS

Installing a *thread insert* replaces damaged or worn threads in a threaded hole (Fig. 6-16). To install one type of thread insert, drill out the old threads. Rethread the hole with the special thread-cutting tool or *tap* (➤7-23) from the *thread*

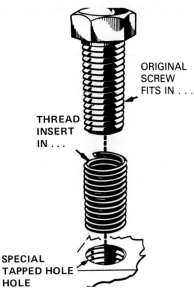

Fig. 6-16 Installing a thread insert in a tapped hole.

repair kit. Then install the thread insert in the tapped hole. This restores the threads in the hole to their original size.

➤ 6-16 SETSCREWS

A *setscrew* (Fig. 6-17) secures a collar or gear on a shaft. Tightening the screw "sets" the collar or gear into place.

➤ 6-17 SELF-TAPPING SCREWS

Self-tapping screws cut their own threads when turned into drilled holes (Fig. 6-18). One type also drills the hole. These screws are usually used where a light clamping force and fast assembly are required.

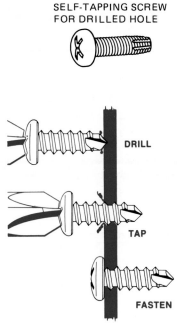

Fig. 6-18 Self-tapping screws. The lower one drills and then taps the hole.

➤ 6-18 SNAP RINGS

There are two types of *snap rings*—external and internal (Fig. 6-19). External snap rings fit on shafts to prevent gears or collars from sliding on the shaft. Internal snap rings fit in housings to keep shafts or other parts in position. Some snap rings have holes which make it easier to install and remove them (Fig. 6-20). Other snap rings have prongs or *tangs* instead of holes. If necessary use matching *snap-ring pliers* to avoid damaging the snap ring during removal or installation.

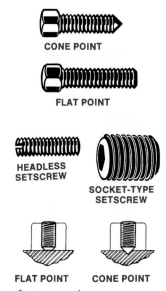

Fig. 6-17 Types of setscrew points.

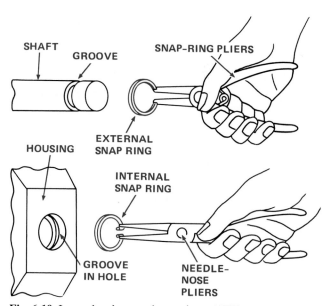

Fig. 6-19 Internal and external snap rings. *(ATW)*

64

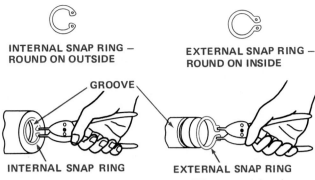

INTERNAL SNAP RING –
ROUND ON OUTSIDE

EXTERNAL SNAP RING –
ROUND ON INSIDE

GROOVE

INTERNAL SNAP RING

EXTERNAL SNAP RING

Fig. 6-20 Installing internal and external Truarc retaining rings or snap rings. *(ATW)*

6-19 KEYS AND SPLINES

Keys and splines lock gears, pulleys, and hubs to shafts. Then they rotate with the shaft. Figure 6-21 shows a typical key installation. The wedge-shaped key fits into slots called *keyways* in the shaft and hub.

Splines are external and internal teeth cut into the shaft and the installed part (Fig. 6-22). The shaft and installed part turn together. In many devices, the splines fit loosely. This allows the installed part to slide freely along the shaft while they turn. Splines may be straight or curved.

6-20 RIVETS

Rivets (Fig. 6-23) are metal pins used to fasten parts together. One end has a head. After the rivet is in place, use a driver (or hammer and rivet set) to form a head on the other end. To remove a rivet, cut off the rivet head with a chisel and hammer. Then use a punch and hammer to drive the rivet out of the hole.

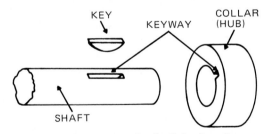

Fig. 6-21 A key locks parts together by fitting into slots or keyways.

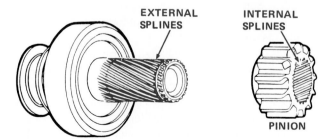

Fig. 6-22 External and internal splines.

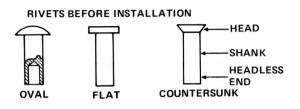

RIVETS BEFORE INSTALLATION

HEAD
SHANK
HEADLESS END

OVAL   FLAT   COUNTERSUNK

RIVETS AFTER INSTALLATION

OVAL   COUNTERSUNK

Fig. 6-23 Rivets before installation (top) and after installation (bottom).

6-21 BLIND RIVETS

A *blind hole* is a hole where you cannot reach the end to form a head. Install a *blind rivet* in a blind hole. Figure 6-24 shows the installation of a blind rivet.

GASKETS AND SEALS

6-22 GASKETS

A *gasket* is a thin layer of soft material such as paper, cork, rubber, copper, synthetic material, or a combination of these. The gasket is *preformed* or *precut* to the desired shape and thickness. Clamping the gasket between two flat surfaces makes a tight seal.

The clamping force that results from the tightening of the fasteners squeezes the gasket. The soft material then fills any small irregularities in the mating surfaces. This prevents leakage of fluid, vacuum, or pressure from the joint. Holes through the gasket allow it to seal in fuel, oil, or coolant. The gasket material keeps dirt, water, and air out of the passages. Sometimes the gasket serves as a shim to take up space.

The automobile uses many types of gaskets, especially in the engine. The *head gasket* seals between the cylinder head and the cylinder block (Fig. 6-25). Figure 6-26 shows a complete *engine-overhaul gasket set* for a V-8 engine.

6-23 OIL SEALS

Cars and light trucks may have up to 15 *oil seals,* or *shaft seals.* The seal closes or seals the space between stationary and moving parts. It protects the bearings, retains the lubricant, and seals out contaminants. The oil seal may act as a separator that prevents two different substances from mixing.

Most oil seals are *radial lip seals* (Fig. 6-27). A metal case holds the flexible sealing lip against the rotating shaft. Some seals have a *garter spring* that helps hold the lip in

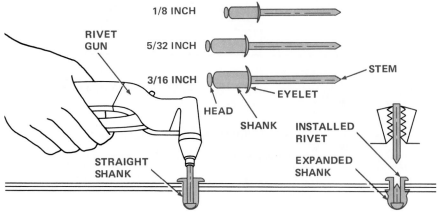

Fig. 6-24 Installing a blind rivet. *(ATW)*

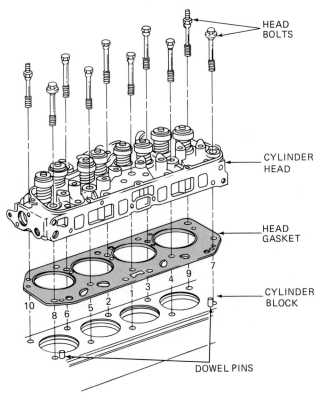

Fig. 6-25 A head gasket is placed between the cylinder head and the cylinder block to seal the joint. *(Chevrolet Division of General Motors Corporation)*

contact with the sealing surface. Seals of this type include the front and rear crankshaft seals and the camshaft seal on overhead-camshaft engines. Front-wheel *grease seals* are similar to oil seals. Lip seals are also used on the steering-gear input shaft and the power-steering-pump shaft (Chap. 50).

The automobile and engine use a variety of seals. They include *O-ring seals* and *packing seals*. These often serve as gaskets to seal between two nonmoving parts.

SEALANTS

➤ 6-24 FORMED IN-PLACE GASKETS

Instead of being preformed (➤6-22), some gaskets are *formed in place*. You squeeze a bead of plastic gasket material or *sealant* from a tube onto one of the mating surfaces (Fig. 6-28). Typical surfaces include valve covers, thermostat housings, water pumps, and differential covers. Follow the instructions on the tube when using this material.

There are two types of plastic gasket material, *aerobic* (➤6-25) and *anaerobic* (➤6-26). Aerobic material hardens in the *presence* of air. Anaerobic material hardens in the *absence* of air. These materials are not the same. Do not use them interchangeably.

➤ 6-25 SILICONE-RUBBER SEALANT

Aerobic material is called *self-curing* or *room-temperature-vulcanizing* (RTV) silicone-rubber sealant. When squeezed from the tube, it "vulcanizes" at room temperature. This means it cures when exposed to air. RTV sealant is used either with or without a preformed gasket. On a preformed gasket, apply the sealant to both sides and assemble immediately. If the bead of RTV sealant is to be the gasket, apply the sealant to one surface (Fig. 6-28). Then wait to allow a skin to form. This takes about 15 minutes after exposure to air, depending on humidity. It takes less time with high humidity. Some technicians put wet rags around the surface (not on the surface) to speed up skin forming. After the skin forms, assemble the parts. Tightening the fasteners squeezes the bead. It then flattens to form the seal.

RTV sealant can be used on surfaces that flex or vibrate slightly, such as the engine valve cover. Never use RTV sealant around high temperatures and pressures, such as for head gaskets. The mating surfaces must be thoroughly clean before RTV or anaerobic sealant (➤6-26) is applied. Sealants cannot seal to dirty, greasy, or oily surfaces.

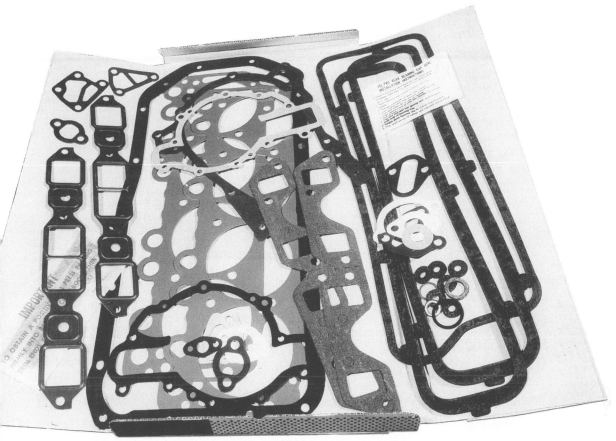

Fig. 6-26 Engine-overhaul gasket set for a V-8 engine, showing all gaskets and seals used in the engine. *(Fel-Pro Inc.)*

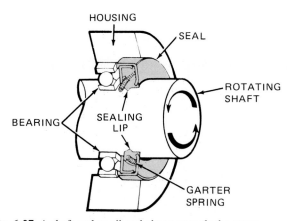

Fig. 6-27 A shaft seal or oil seal closes or seals the space between stationary and moving parts. *(Federal Mogul Corporation)*

Fig. 6-28 Using a tube of RTV silicone rubber to make a formed-in-place gasket. *(Dow Corning Corporation)*

NOTE On engines with an *oxygen sensor* (➤19-17), use only RTV sealant that says "sensor safe" on the label. Fumes from some RTV sealant can damage the oxygen sensor. This may cause excessive exhaust emissions and poor fuel economy.

➤ **6-26 ANAEROBIC SEALANT**

Anaerobic material hardens only in the *absence* of air. One way to remove the air is to squeeze the material between two surfaces. It can be used as an adhesive, a sealer, and a locking cement. It serves as a chemical thread-locker on bolts, nuts, screws, and bushings (Fig. 6-29). Do not use anaerobic material on parts that flex.

Figure 6-29 shows anaerobic sealant being applied to the outside of a bushing. When the bushing is installed, the anaerobic sealant fills the small spaces between the outside of the bushing and the hole. Deprived of air, the material hardens. This locks the bushing in place. Anaerobic sealant is used on some vehicles to seal between the clutch housing and manual-transmission case (Chap. 42). It is also used on some engines to seal the engine front cover (Chap. 39), cylinder liners (➤41-20), exhaust-gas recirculation (EGR) valve (➤36-11), water pump (➤26-17), and various plugs and fasteners.

Sometimes you must remove a screw locked in place with anaerobic material. Soften the material by heating the area around the screw with a *soldering iron* (➤8-7). Do not use a torch or open flame. Sometimes applying fresh anaerobic material will soften the old material.

Fig. 6-29 Applying an anaerobic material to the outside of a bushing. *(Loctite Corporation)*

TRADE TALK

aerobic sealant	blind rivet	oil seal	torque-to-yield bolt
anaerobic sealant	gasket	prevailing-torque fastener	
antisieze compound	hex head	thread insert	

MULTIPLE-CHOICE TEST

*Select the **one** correct, best, or most probable answer to each question.*
You can find the answers in the section indicated at the end of each question.

1. Pitch in USC threads is (➤6-3)
   a. distance between individual threads
   b. number of threads per inch
   c. depth of the threads
   d. thread class

2. Pitch in metric threads is the (➤6-5)
   a. thread class
   b. number of threads per inch
   c. depth of the threads
   d. distance between individual threads

3. Technician A says the more lines there are on the head of a USC bolt, the stronger the bolt. Technician B says the higher the number on the head of a metric bolt, the stronger the bolt. Who is right? (➤6-6)
   a. A only
   b. B only
   c. both A and B
   d. neither A nor B

4. Nuts and bolts that have a continuous resistance to turning are (➤6-10)
   a. prevailing-torque fasteners
   b. torque-to-yield fasteners
   c. used with a cotter pin
   d. self-tapping setscrews

5. Bolts that are tightened by measuring how much the head is turned are (➤6-12)
   a. prevailing-torque fasteners
   b. torque-to-yield fasteners
   c. used with a cotter pin
   d. self-tapping setscrews

6. Before installing a bolt in an aluminum part, coat the bolt threads with antiseize compound to (➤6-14)
   a. lock the bolt in place
   b. prevent thread damage when removing the bolt
   c. turn the bolt with less torque
   d. none of the above

7. Use thread inserts to repair damaged (➤6-15)
   a. external threads
   b. studs
   c. internal threads
   d. nuts

8. Technician A says internal snap rings are used on shafts. Technician B says external snap rings are used in housings. Who is right? (➤6-18)
   a. A only
   b. B only
   c. both A and B
   d. neither A nor B

9. Before the soft material of a gasket can fill any small irregularities in the mating surfaces, the gasket must be (➤6-22)
   a. coated with antiseize compound
   b. coated with RTV silicone rubber
   c. soaked in water before installation
   d. squeezed by the tightening of fasteners

10. Technician A says to use RTV silicone rubber to make an engine valve-cover gasket. Technician B says to make the valve-cover gasket from a bead of anaerobic sealant. Who is right? (➤6-25)
   a. A only
   b. B only
   c. both A and B
   d. neither A nor B

REVIEW QUESTIONS

1. If two bolts look like they have the same diameter, how can you tell if the threads are exactly the same? (➤6-3)

2. Describe five ways to lock a nut in place. (➤6-8, 6-9, 6-10, and 6-26)

3. List the five steps that must be followed to reuse a prevailing-torque fastener. (➤6-11)

4. Explain what *initial torque* or *threshold torque* means in the installation of a torque-to-yield bolt. (➤6-12)

5. What are three jobs of an oil seal, and how does it prevent leakage? (➤6-23)

CHAPTER 7

SHOP HAND TOOLS

After studying this chapter, you should be able to:

- Describe the four types of basic hand tools used in the automotive shop, and give two examples of each.
- Explain the difference between a torque wrench and a torque-angle gauge, and demonstrate their use.
- Show how to remove a broken bolt or stud.
- Demonstrate how to select, set up, and use a pressure-screw puller and a slide-hammer puller.
- Show how to cut threads on a rod and in a hole using a tap-and-die set.

➤ 7-1 HAND TOOLS AND POWER TOOLS

Automotive service work requires a great variety of tools. The proper tools properly used enable you to do a job with safety, speed, and efficiency. You need two main types of tools in the shop. These are *hand tools* and *power tools*.

This chapter covers hand tools (Fig. 7-1). Your hand supplies the energy to use them. They include striking, turning, gripping, and cutting tools. They also include tube bending and flaring tools.

Power tools or *machine tools* use an energy source other than your muscle power. Chapter 8 describes these tools which are powered by electricity, compressed air, or hydraulic pressure.

STRIKING TOOLS

➤ 7-2 HAMMERS

A *hammer* is a hand tool used for striking. The *ball-peen hammer* (Fig. 7-2) is the one used most in the shop. Grip the hammer on the end of the handle. Swing it so the hammer face strikes the object or surface squarely. Avoid hitting the object at an angle. Use rawhide, plastic, brass, and rubber hammers to strike easily marred surfaces. A *dead-blow hammer* has a hollow head partially filled with small metal shot (Fig. 7-2). This reduces rebounding.

TURNING TOOLS

➤ 7-3 SCREWDRIVERS

Use the proper *screwdriver* to drive or turn screws. Screwdrivers are made in a variety of sizes, shapes, and special-purpose designs. The most common type has a single flat blade for driving screws with slotted heads (Fig. 7-3). There are also Torx-head and Phillips-head screwdrivers (Fig. 7-3). Figure 6-8 shows other types.

Always select a screwdriver of the proper type and size for the job. When using a single-blade screwdriver, the blade should completely fill the screw slot. This helps prevent damage to the screw head.

➤ 7-4 WRENCHES

A *wrench* is a long-handled tool with fixed or adjustable jaws. You use a wrench to turn bolts, nuts, and screws (Fig. 7-4). To work on both USC and metric fasteners, you need both USC and metric wrenches. A 3/8- to 1-inch USC set and a 6- to 19-mm metric set will handle most jobs. You need these sizes in sets of open-end, box, and combination wrenches.

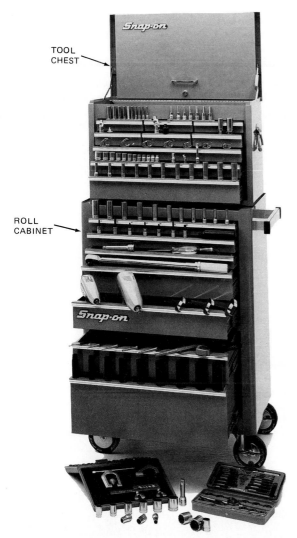

Fig. 7-1 A set of hand tools used by the automotive technician. *(Snap-on Tools Corporation)*

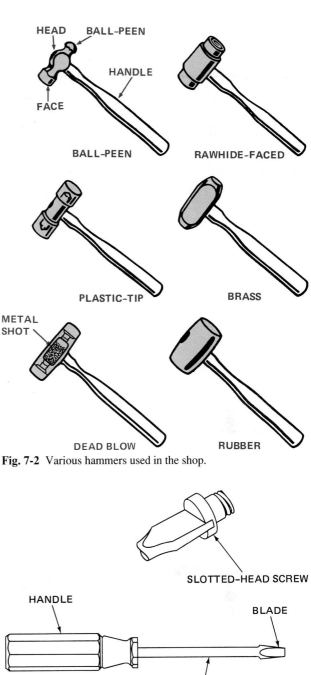

Fig. 7-2 Various hammers used in the shop.

➢ **7-5 OPEN-END WRENCH**

The *open-end wrench* usually has the jaw opening at a 15-degree angle to the handle (Fig. 7-4). Turn the bolt or nut as far as the space permits. Then flip the wrench over for further turning of the fastener.

An open-end wrench has a different size on each end. Make sure the wrench fits snugly against the *flats*. These are the sides of a nut or bolt head. A loose fit may break or spring the jaws of the wrench. Springing jaws spread apart and round off the corners of the hex. This makes use of the proper wrench more difficult.

Careful! Never use an open-end wrench to final-tighten a fastener or to free a frozen fastener. The jaws may spread enough to allow the wrench to slip. Use a box wrench (➢7-6) or a socket wrench (➢7-10) for these jobs.

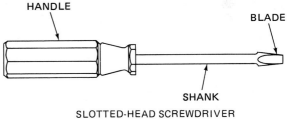

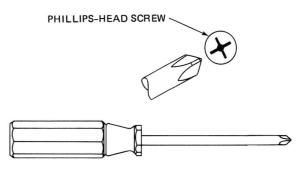

Fig. 7-3 Slotted-head screwdriver (top) and Phillips-head screwdriver (bottom).

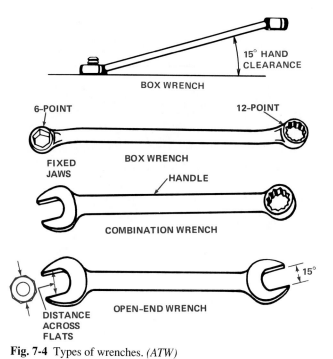

Fig. 7-4 Types of wrenches. *(ATW)*

than on other wrenches. This helps prevent slipping and rounding off the points on soft-metal *tube fittings*. The six-point box end has one of the flats cut out (Fig. 7-5). The opening is large enough to slip over the tube.

Figure 7-5 shows the second wrench in back of the first. Most flare nuts attach to a *coupling nut* (Fig. 7-6). Hold the coupling nut while turning the flare nut.

Careful! Do not turn the flare nut without holding the coupling nut. This will usually twist and break the metal tube.

➤ 7-9 ADJUSTABLE WRENCH

An *adjustable wrench* (Fig. 7-7) has a movable jaw that you adjust to fit nuts and bolt heads of various sizes. Figure 7-7 shows how to use it. Tighten the jaws against the flats of the nut or bolt before applying a turning force. Adjustable wrenches are normally used only when applying relatively light torque. They are not always as strong as fixed jaw wrenches and may be damaged if excessive torque is applied.

➤ 7-10 SOCKET WRENCH

Socket wrenches (Fig. 7-8) are the most widely used tools in the shop. They are like box wrenches except that the

➤ 7-6 BOX WRENCH

The *box wrench* opening surrounds or "boxes in" the nut or bolt head (Fig. 7-4). An advantage is that the box will seldom slip off. However, you must lift the box wrench completely off and then place it back on for each swing. The wrench-head is thin for use in tight places. The head usually sets at a 15-degree angle to the body. This provides hand clearance for swinging the wrench.

The most common box wrench has 12 notches or "points" in the head (Fig. 7-4). This allows turning the fastener if the wrench can swing 30 degrees. A six-point box wrench holds better on a nut or bolt but needs a greater swing. The box wrench has different-size openings on each end.

➤ 7-7 COMBINATION WRENCH

The *combination wrench* has a box on one end and an open end on the other (Fig. 7-4). The two ends are usually the same size. The box end is more convenient for breaking loose or final-tightening a nut or bolt. But you must lift the box completely free after each swing. The open end is more likely to slip off. However, once the fastener is loose, the open end can turn it faster.

➤ 7-8 FLARE-NUT WRENCH

A *flare-nut wrench* is a special type of combination or box-end wrench. It is used to attach or loosen a *flare nut* or *tubing nut*. The ends of the flare-nut wrench are thicker

Fig. 7-5 Using a flare-nut wrench on a tubing nut or flare nut. *(Chrysler Corporation)*

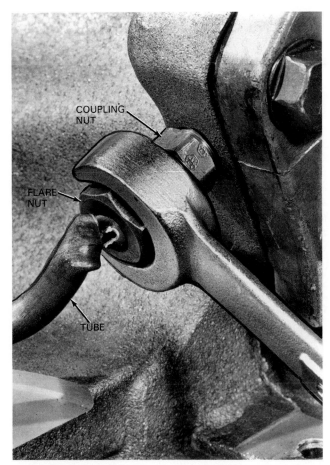

Fig. 7-6 If the flare nut is turned without holding the coupling nut, the metal tube will usually twist and break. *(Chrysler Corporation)*

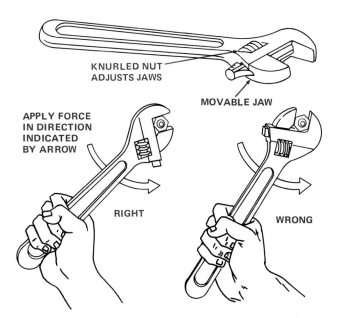

Fig. 7-7 How to use an adjustable wrench. *(Ford Motor Company)*

head or socket is detachable from the handle. You assemble the socket wrench you need from the socket set in your toolbox.

First, select the handle or driver. Figure 7-8 shows the *nut spinner, ratchet, speed handle,* and other *drivers.* Then select the *socket* to fit the bolt head or nut. There are several kinds of sockets (Fig. 7-9). The *12-point socket* is the most common. Attach the socket to the driver (Fig. 7-10). If you need an *extension* or *universal joint,* attach it to the driver first. Then attach the socket.

The drive end of the socket snaps onto the driver (Fig. 7-10). The *drive lug* is square and always sized in fractions of an inch. Common drive-lug sizes are 1/4, 3/8, 1/2 inch.

1. SOCKETS The 12-point socket (Fig. 7-9) allows you to turn a bolt or nut in tight spots. However, if a bolt head or nut has rounded corners or excessive resistance to turning, the 12-point socket may slip. Use a *six-point socket* for these. The *eight-point socket* is for turning square heads. These include drain plugs, fill plugs, and pipe plugs.

Deep sockets reach nuts on bolts or studs that are too long for the standard socket to reach. You remove and install spark plugs with a *spark-plug socket.* This is a six-point deep socket with a rubber insert. The insert holds the plug to prevent it from falling out of the socket.

2. HANDLES Figure 7-8 shows several handles. The ratchet handle has a mechanism that permits free motion in one direction but lockup in the other. You select the direction for lockup by moving the reversing lever (Fig. 7-10).

Extensions of various lengths provide access to hard-to-reach bolts or nuts. The universal joint allows you to turn a nut or bolt while holding the driver at an angle. *Adapters* allow you to use a driver with a socket having a different drive size. Also, various kinds and sizes of screwdrivers, Torx drives, Allen wrenches, and flare-nut wrenches will fit the drivers and adapters.

NOTE To work on a variety of domestic and imported cars, you need both USC and metric socket sets.

➤ 7-11 TORQUE WRENCH

A *torque wrench* (Fig. 7-11) is basically a special handle for a socket (➤7-10). An indicator on the torque wrench measures the *torque* or twisting force. This is the amount of force applied to a nut or bolt while tightening it. Vehicle service manuals and auto repair manuals give the torque specifications for most fasteners. A typical specification might be to tighten a bolt to "20 lb-ft." This means to apply a 20-pound pull at a distance of 1 foot from the bolt.

To use the torque wrench, attach the proper socket. Place the socket on the nut or bolt head. Then pull on the wrench handle. When the torque wrench indicates the specified torque, the bolt or nut is properly tightened. However, the threads must be clean and in good condition. Dirty or damaged threads put a drag on the threads as the bolt or nut is tightened. This gives a false reading on the torque wrench. It can also result in not enough tightening.

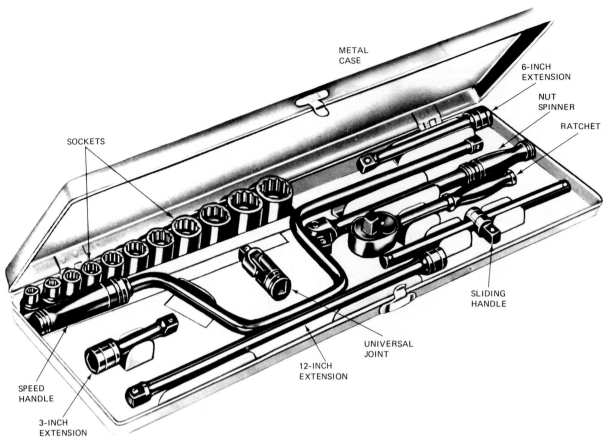

Fig. 7-8 Set of sockets with handles, extensions, and universal joint. *(Snap on Tools Corporation)*

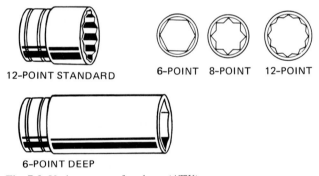

Fig. 7-9 Various types of sockets. *(ATW)*

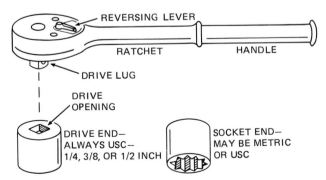

Fig. 7-10 How a socket attaches to a ratchet handle. *(ATW)*

Many torque wrenches read in pound-feet (lb-ft). Some read in pound-inches (lb-in). Use these where you need to accurately apply a small torque. Twelve pound-inches equals one pound-foot.

The scale on metric torque wrenches is in kilogram-meters (kg-m), kilogram-centimeters (kg-cm), or newton-meters (N-m). Newton-meters is the preferred unit. To convert from USC to newton-meters, multiply pound-feet by 1.35.

➤ 7-12 TORQUE-ANGLE GAUGE

Tighten *torque-to-yield bolts* (➤6-12) to an initial torque with a torque wrench (➤7-11). Then final-tighten the bolts by turning them through a specified angle with a socket wrench (➤7-10).

You can easily see a 90-degree turning angle by watching how far a ratchet handle or *breaker bar* moves. For other angles, use a *torque-angle gauge* (Fig. 7-12). It accurately measures the turning angle in degrees. The gauge attaches to the socket driver. The socket attaches to the gauge. As the handle turns, the degree indicator remains at the greatest angle reached.

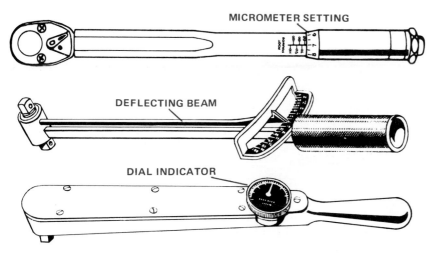

MICROMETER SETTING

Fig. 7-11 Types of torque wrenches.

DEFLECTING BEAM

DIAL INDICATOR

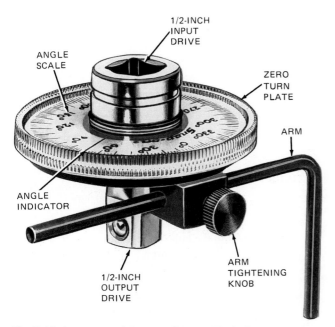

1/2-INCH INPUT DRIVE

ANGLE SCALE

ZERO TURN PLATE

ARM

ANGLE INDICATOR

1/2-INCH OUTPUT DRIVE

ARM TIGHTENING KNOB

Fig. 7-12 A torque-angle gauge. *(Snap-on Tools Corporation)*

➤ 7-13 REMOVING FROZEN NUTS AND BOLTS

Sometimes a nut or bolt is *frozen*. It will not break loose with normal turning force. Try applying *penetrating oil* around the threads. Give the penetrating oil time to soak in. Then try loosening the fastener again. Tapping lightly on the nut or bolt with a hammer may help. Use a chisel (➤7-18) or a *nut cracker* or *splitter* to split off a frozen nut.

GRIPPING TOOLS

➤ 7-14 PLIERS

Pliers are hand tools with a pair of adjustable pivoted jaws for cutting or gripping (Fig. 7-13). There are many styles

and sizes of pliers. Combination slip-joint pliers may have cutting edges at the back of the jaws for wire cutting. *Tongue-and-groove* or *groove-and-land* pliers such as *Channellock pliers* have the tongues or lands on one jaw. The grooves are on the other. Shifting the tongues or lands to different grooves changes the distance the jaws can open. The jaws remain parallel at any setting.

Locking pliers such as *Vise-Grip pliers* (Fig. 7-13) have locking jaws. This makes them useful as pliers, wrenches, clamps, and small vises. Lock the jaws by turning a screw in the end of the handle. This adjusts the size of the opening. Closing the handles then locks the jaws into place. To release the jaws, pull the release lever.

Figure 7-14 shows how to adapt combination pliers for use as hose-clamp pliers by drilling holes in the jaws. You can then use the pliers to remove and install spring-wire hose clamps.

Careful! Never use gripping pliers on hardened steel surfaces. This dulls the pliers' teeth. Never use pliers on nuts or bolt heads. The pliers may slip and round off the edges of the hex. Then a wrench or socket will not fit on the fastener properly.

➤ 7-15 REMOVING BROKEN BOLTS AND STUDS

Excessive torque applied to a bolt or stud may cause it to break. For example, suppose a bolt or stud is damaged, rusted, or stretched. Then the bolt or stud may break as you apply the specified torque.

When a threaded fastener breaks, approach the problem logically. You must remove the broken part. Be patient, and be careful not to create an even bigger problem. Removal methods to try depend on where the break occurred on the fastener.

1. BREAK ABOVE SURFACE When the break is above the surface, you may be able to file flats on two sides.

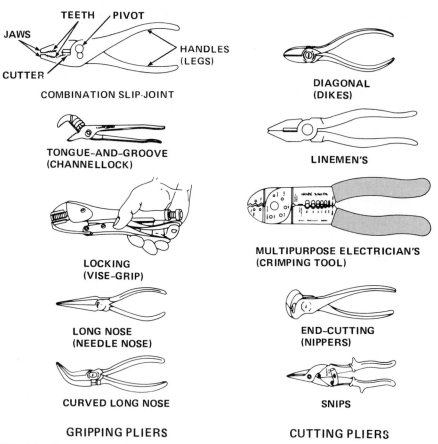

Fig. 7-13 Various types of gripping pliers and cutting pliers. *(ATW)*

Then use a wrench to back out the broken part. Sometimes you can cut a slot in the bolt. Then remove it with a screwdriver. Another way is to attach locking pliers to the threads. Then turn the bolt out.

2. BREAK CLOSE TO SURFACE If the break is close to the surface, try removing the bolt with a center punch. Place the point of the punch on the bolt, but off center. Then tap the punch lightly with a hammer. By moving the punch and tapping it, the bolt may back out.

3. BREAK BELOW SURFACE Sometimes the break is near or below the surface. Try removing the broken bolt with a *bolt* or *stud extractor* (Fig. 7-15). Center-punch the

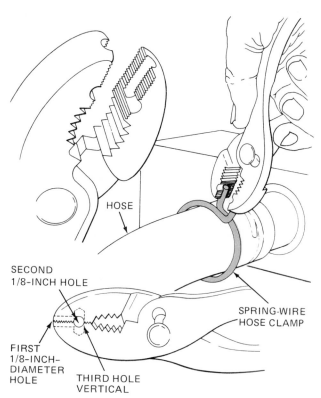

Fig. 7-14 How to adapt combination pliers so they can handle spring-wire hose clamps.

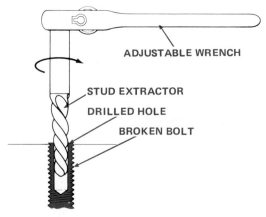

Fig. 7-15 Using a stud extractor to remove a broken stud.

broken bolt and then drill it. Use a drill that makes a hole almost as large as the inside diameter of the threads. Then use an extractor of the proper size to remove the bolt.

Careful! Extractors are hard and brittle. Excessive force will break the extractor. A broken extractor can be more difficult to remove than the broken bolt. If a reasonable turning force on the extractor does not turn the bolt, remove the extractor. Drill out the hole to remove the rest of the bolt. Then retap the hole (➤7-23) or install a thread insert (➤6-15).

➤ 7-16 PULLERS

Pullers remove parts assembled with an interference fit. This includes removing gears and hubs from shafts, and bushings from blind holes. Pullers also remove seals from bores and cylinder liners from engine blocks.

A *puller set* (Fig. 7-16) has many pieces that can fit together to form the puller needed for the job. There are three basic types of pullers. These are *pressure screw* (Fig. 7-17), *slide hammer* (Fig. 7-18), and *combination*.

CUTTING TOOLS

➤ 7-17 CUTTING TOOLS

Cutting tools remove metal. They include chisels, hacksaws, files, punches. Drills, taps, and dies are also cutting tools. *Power cutting tools* include grinders, hones, lathes, and boring machines. Later chapters cover these.

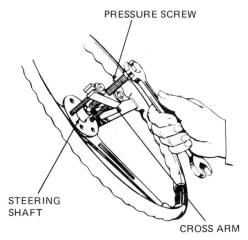

Fig. 7-17 Using a pressure-screw puller to remove a steering wheel. *(Lisle Corporation)*

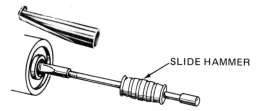

Fig. 7-18 Removing an axle seal with a slide-hammer puller. *(Proto Tool Company)*

➤ 7-18 CHISELS

The *chisel* (Fig. 7-19) is a cutting tool with a single cutting edge. There are various sizes and shapes of chisels. Striking the chisel with a hammer makes the chisel cut

Fig. 7-16 A puller set. *(Snap-on Tools Corporation)*

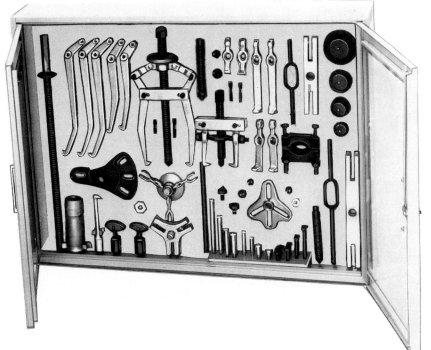

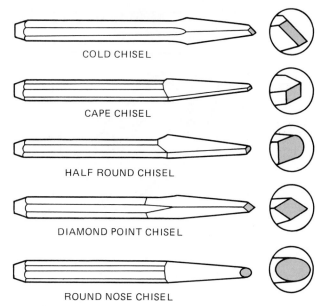

Fig. 7-19 Various types of chisels.

metal (Fig. 7-20). Hold the chisel with one hand and the hammer in the other. Hit the end of the chisel squarely. Holding the chisel in a *chisel holder* or smooth-jaw locking pliers will protect your hand.

The cutting edge of the chisel may chip and get dull after use. The head may "mushroom" (Fig. 7-21). Chapter 8 describes how to grind the cutting edge and head on a grinding wheel. Keep the chisel sharp. A sharp chisel cuts better.

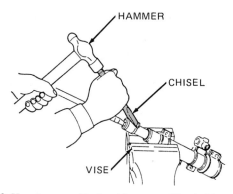

Fig. 7-20 How to use a chisel and hammer. *(Mazda Motors of America Inc.)*

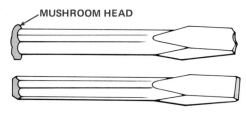

Fig. 7-21 Top, a chisel with a mushroom on head and chipped cutting edge. Bottom, chisel with mushroom on head ground off and cutting edge sharpened.

➤ 7-19 HACKSAW

A *hacksaw* is basically an adjustable metal frame that holds a steel saw blade (Fig. 7-22). The blade is replaceable and has from 14 to 32 teeth per inch. Cutting occurs on the forward stroke as you push the blade across the metal. The teeth act like tiny chisels and cut off fine shavings or chips.

Use a long steady forward stroke. Apply enough downward force so the teeth cut rather than slide. Lift the down force on the return stroke. This helps prevent dulling the teeth. A light drag may help clear chips from the teeth.

Select a blade with the proper number of teeth per inch for the job. The teeth must be close enough so at least two teeth are cutting. Teeth that are too close together clog and stop cutting. The hacksaw blade for general cutting has 18 teeth per inch.

➤ 7-20 FILES

Files (Fig. 7-23) are used for cutting and shaping metal. They have many cutting edges or teeth. There are many types of files with various "cuts" (Fig. 7-24). When the cuts are far apart, there are only a few per inch. This is a *rough-* or *coarse-cut* file. When the cuts are close together, the file is a *smooth* or *dead-smooth* file. A *single-cut* file

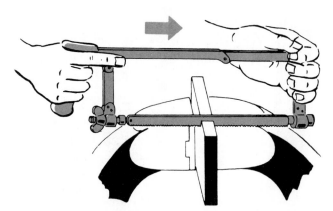

Fig. 7-22 Using a hacksaw.

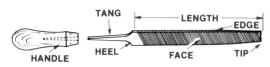

Fig. 7-23 The parts of a file.

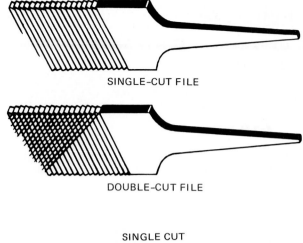

SINGLE-CUT FILE

DOUBLE-CUT FILE

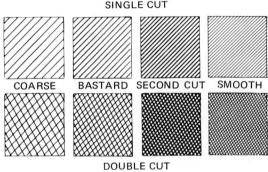

SINGLE CUT

COARSE BASTARD SECOND CUT SMOOTH

DOUBLE CUT

Fig. 7-24 Types of files and file cuts.

has a series of sharp blades. A *double-cut* file has a second series cut at an angle to the first. This creates a series of sharp teeth. Various sizes and cuts of round, half-round, flat, and triangular files are used during automotive service work.

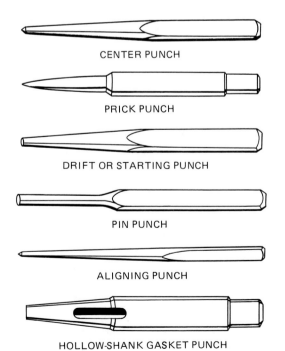

CENTER PUNCH

PRICK PUNCH

DRIFT OR STARTING PUNCH

PIN PUNCH

ALIGNING PUNCH

HOLLOW-SHANK GASKET PUNCH

Fig. 7-25 Various types of punches.

Always use a handle with a file. Tapping the end of the handle on the bench tightens the file in the handle. Keep the file teeth clean with a *file card*. It has short stiff-wire bristles that remove chips and dirt from the teeth.

➤ 7-21 PUNCHES

Punches (Fig. 7-25) are used to knock out rivets and pins. They also align parts for assembly. To remove a rivet, grind off the rivet head. Or cut it off with a chisel. Then use the starting punch and pin punch as shown in Fig. 7-26.

Mark spots where holes are to be drilled with a center punch. The punch mark keeps the drill bit centered as it starts cutting (Fig. 7-27). You can use the center punch to mark parts before they are disassembled. Align the punch marks to reassemble the parts in the same position.

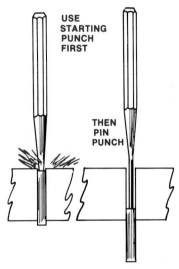

USE STARTING PUNCH FIRST

THEN PIN PUNCH

Fig. 7-26 Using a starting and a pin punch.

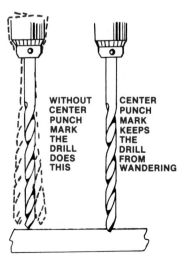

WITHOUT CENTER PUNCH MARK THE DRILL DOES THIS

CENTER PUNCH MARK KEEPS THE DRILL FROM WANDERING

Fig. 7-27 Center-punching a hole location will keep the drill from wandering.

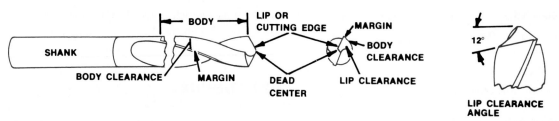

Fig. 7-28 The parts of a twist drill.

➤ 7-22 TWIST DRILLS

Drill bits or *twist drills* (Fig. 7-28) are tools for making holes. The material being drilled determines the preferred shape of the cutting edges that form the point. The grooves along the body carry the chips out of the hole. A hand-held air or electric drill motor, or a drill press, drives the drill bit. These are described in Chapter 8.

➤ 7-23 TAPS AND DIES

Most shops have *tap-and-die sets* for cutting USC and metric threads. *Taps* cut inside threads (Fig. 7-29). To tap a hole, determine the thread size needed. Refer to a *tap drill chart* (Fig. 7-30) and select the size of drill bit required. The hole made by the specified *tap drill* will be the proper diameter for tapping.

Dies cut outside threads on rods (Fig. 7-31). A *diestock* holds the die. *Chamfer* or *bevel* the rod end so the die starts easily. The basic procedure is the same for both taps and dies. Apply cutting lubricant to the surface. Then begin thread cutting. After every two turns, back off the tap or die and apply more lubricant.

NOTE

You can use taps and dies to clean and straighten damaged threads. However, a *thread chaser* is the preferred tool for this job.

THREAD SIZE AND THREADS PER INCH	DRILL*		THREAD SIZE AND THREADS PER INCH	DRILL*	
	SIZE	NO.		SIZE	NO.
1-64	0.0595	53	10-32	0.1610	20
1-72	0.0595	53	12-24	0.1770	16
2-56	0.0670	82	12-28	0.1800	15
2-64	0.0700	50	¼-20	0.1990	8
3-48	0.0781	⁵⁄₆₄	¼-24	0.2090	4
3-56	0.0810	46	¼-32	0.2187	⁷⁄₃₂
4-40	0.0890	43	⁵⁄₁₆-18	0.2570	F
4-48	0.0935	42	⁵⁄₁₆-24	0.2720	I
5-40	0.0995	39	⁵⁄₁₆-32	0.2812	⁹⁄₃₂
5-44	0.1040	37	⅜-16	0.3125	⁵⁄₁₆
6-32	0.1065	36	⅜-24	0.3320	Q
6-40	0.1130	33	⅜-32	0.3437	¹¹⁄₃₂
8-32	0.1360	29	⁷⁄₁₆-20	0.3906	²⁵⁄₆₄
8-36	0.1360	29	⁷⁄₁₆-28	0.4162	¹³⁄₃₂
10-24	0.1470	26	½-20	0.4531	²⁹⁄₆₄

*Drill sizes are designated in four ways—by numbers (Nos. 80 to 1, or from 0.135 to 0.228 in), by letters (A to Z, or from 0.234 to 0.413 in), by fractions (¹⁄₆₄ to 3½ in), and by millimeters (in the metric system). The drill sizes indicated in the table are based on approximately 75 percent thread depth; that is, the tap will not give a full thread when it is run down into the hole but will give a 75 percent thread. This means that the top 25 percent, or one-fourth of each thread crest is absent. However, the remaining 75 percent is sufficient for most commercial purposes. For special precision applications, a fuller thread may be desirable. The fuller thread increases the thread strength only slightly (perhaps 5 percent) but makes the tapping job much harder; many more taps are broken.

Fig. 7-30 Tap drill sizes.

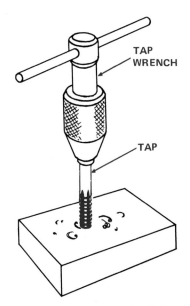

Fig. 7-29 Tap being used to cut threads in a hole. *(ATW)*

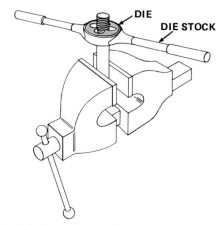

Fig. 7-31 Die being used to cut threads on a rod. *(ATW)*

➤ 7-24 TUBE CUTTING, BENDING, AND FLARING

Metal pipes or tubes are sometimes called lines. They carry pressurized fluid or vacuum from one place to another on the car. The *fuel line* carries gasoline from the fuel tank to the engine compartment. A *vapor-return line* sends fuel vapor from the carburetor back to the fuel tank. *Brake lines* and flexible hose carry brake fluid from the master cylinder to the brakes at the wheels. Other lines are part of the air conditioner, automatic transmission, fuel-injection system, and power-steering system.

Steel lines may be copper-coated to protect against rust and corrosion. The tube ends usually have either a *double flare* (Fig. 7-32) or the metric International Standards Organization (ISO) flare. Flaring the ends of the tube helps prevent leakage. Tube nuts or flare nuts (➤7-8) fasten the tube to a coupling nut or other fitting.

A damaged tube must be replaced. Make the new line by cutting, bending, and flaring a length of new tubing. It must be of the proper length and material.

Careful!   Never replace steel tube with aluminum or copper tube. These soft metals may fail from high pressure or excessive vibration.

Figure 7-33 shows how to use a *tube cutter* to cut and *ream* the tubing. Reaming removes any burrs created on the inside of the tube during cutting. Place fittings or nuts on the tube and flare the ends of the tube with a *flaring tool* (Fig. 7-34). Use a *tube bender* (Fig. 7-35) to bend the tube to the desired shape.

BUILDING YOUR TOOL SET

➤ 7-25 APPRENTICE'S TOOLBOX

To get a job as an automotive technician you usually must have your own hand tools. This means you must also have a toolbox, tool chest, or roll cabinet to store your tools in.

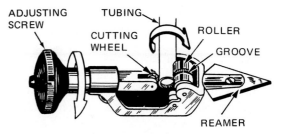

CUTTING THE TUBING

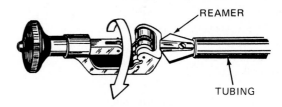

REAMING THE TUBING

Fig. 7-33 Using a tubing cutter to cut and ream metal tubing. *(Gould Inc.)*

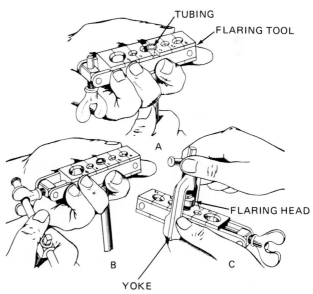

Fig. 7-34 Using a flaring tool to flare the end of a tube. *(Gould Inc.)*

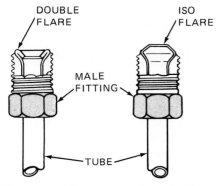

Fig. 7-32 Two types of flares on ends of metal tubing. *(Bendix Corporation)*

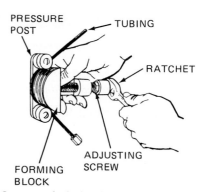

Fig. 7-35 One type of tube bender. *(Lisle Corporation)*

Figure 7-1 shows a complete set of technician's hand tools in a *tool chest* sitting on a *roller cabinet*.

You may not need a complete tool set to get your first job. However, most employers want you to continually expand and upgrade your tools. Your school may supply you with the tools you need in this course. But it is important for you to start working now on building up your own set of tools.

If possible, buy a tool every week or so. Get tools as you need them. Many technicians start by keeping their tools in a toolbox with a top tray. Ask your instructor's advice on the toolbox and tools you need. Figure 7-36 is a suggested list of tools that provides a basic tool set to build on in the future.

- 16-ounce [0.45-kg] ball-peen hammer.
- Plastic hammer.
- Five-piece screwdriver set (two Phillips).
- Standard pliers.
- Needle-nose pliers.
- Channellock pliers.
- Diagonal pliers.
- Spark-plug ratchet (⅜-inch drive with break-over handle).
- Spark-plug sockets (⅝ and ¹³⁄₁₆ inch)
- Set of combination wrenches, ¼ through ⅞ inch.
- Set of metric combination wrenches, 6 mm thru 22 mm.
- Flashlight (one that works, with new batteries).
- Short jumper wires. (You can make these, and more as needed.)
- 12-volt continuity light.
- Tape measure.
- 6-inch [152.4-mm] scale (metric on one side, inches on the other).
- Screw starter with magnet on one end.
- Tire-pressure gauge.
- Thickness-gauge set (can be go no-go type). Buy combination thickness gauges, marked with both inches and millimeters.

- Spark-plug gauge set (round wire).
- Point file.
- Center punch.
- Set of ⅜-through ¹¹⁄₁₆-inch flare nut wrenches.
- ½-inch drive socket set.
- Ratchet.
- Speed handle.
- Breaker bar.
- 4-inch [100-mm] extension.
- 8-inch [200-mm] extension.
- U-joint.
- Set of sockets, ⅜ through ⅞ inch (12 point).
- Set of metric sockets, 6 mm through 22 mm (12 point).

Optional
- Vise-Grip pliers.
- Insulated pliers.
- Small adjustable wrench.
- Large adjustable wrench.

Fig. 7-36 Suggested list of tools for the apprentice or beginning automotive technician.

TRADE TALK

bolt extractor	flats	torque	twist drill
dead-blow hammer	puller set	torque-angle gauge	
flare-nut wrench	spark-plug socket	Torx-head screwdriver	

MULTIPLE-CHOICE TEST

*Select the **one** correct, best, or most probable answer to each question.*
You can find the answers in the section indicated at the end of each question.

1. An open-end wrench should fit the flats snugly to avoid (➤7-5)
   a. springing the jaws
   b. breaking the jaws
   c. rounding off the corners of the hex
   d. all of the above

2. Use a flare-nut wrench when working on (➤7-8)
   a. metal tubing and fittings
   b. adjustable nuts
   c. thread cutting
   d. Phillips-head screws

3. When using a ratchet, the handle will (➤7-10)
   a. turn freely in both directions
   b. turn freely in one direction and drive the socket in the other
   c. drive the socket in both directions
   d. none of the above
4. Technician A says the scale on USC torque wrenches reads in either foot-pounds (ft-lb) and inch-pounds (in-lb). Technician B says the scale on metric torque wrenches reads in either meters-kilogram (m-kg) and meters-newton (m-N). Who is right? (➤7-11)
   a. A only
   b. B only
   c. both A and B
   d. neither A nor B
5. Vise-Grip pliers have (➤7-14)
   a. jaws that remain parallel at any setting
   b. a tongue-and-groove design
   c. a screw in the end of the handle to adjust jaw opening
   d. all of the above
6. To remove a bolt that breaks below the surface (➤7-15)
   a. center punch the broken bolt
   b. drill it
   c. remove the drilled piece with a stud extractor
   d. all of the above
7. Three basic types of pullers are (➤7-16)
   a. Channellock, screw, and Vise-Grip
   b. pressure screw, pusher, and twister
   c. pressure screw, slide hammer, and combination
   d. adjustable, socket, and combination
8. Put the blade into the hacksaw so it cuts on (➤7-19)
   a. the forward stroke
   b. the back stroke
   c. both strokes
   d. lifting pressure
9. When a file has two cuts made at an angle with each other, the file is a (➤7-20)
   a. smooth file
   b. two-cut file
   c. double-cut file
   d. coarse-cut file
10. To knock out rivets and pins, use a (➤7-21)
   a. pin punch and aligning punch
   b. drill punch and center punch
   c. center punch and pin punch
   d. starting punch and pin punch

REVIEW QUESTIONS

1. Explain where the energy comes from to operate hand tools and power tools.   (➤7-1)
2. Describe the proper jaw to use to turn and then final-tighten a bolt using a combination wrench.   (➤7-7)
3. If a 12-point socket slips on a hex nut, explain why you cannot tighten the nut with an eight-point socket. (➤7-10)
4. When is a torque-angle gauge used?   (➤7-12)
5. Describe the tools you now own, and what your next purchases will be.   (➤7-25)

CHAPTER 8

SHOP EQUIPMENT AND POWER TOOLS

After studying this chapter, you should be able to:

- Define power tools and shop equipment, and explain when to use each type.
- Demonstrate the use of the electric drill, drill press, and grinding wheel.
- Show how to use the air hammer, air impact wrench, air drill, and air ratchet.
- Demonstrate the use of the hydraulic jack, shop crane, hydraulic press, and automotive lift.
- Explain when and how to use the various types of parts cleaners.

➤ 8-1 POWER TOOLS AND SHOP EQUIPMENT

Tools powered by electricity, compressed air, or hydraulic pressure are *power tools*. They include electric drills, drill presses, air impact wrenches, air drills, and air ratchets. When you are doing any automotive service job, use the proper power tool whenever possible. This saves time and increases productivity. That may increase your income (➤3-7). Hand tools are too slow to meet or beat most time allowances in the flat-rate manuals (➤3-6).

The shop furnishes some equipment the technician uses in diagnosis and repair. This is *shop equipment*. It includes power tools and machine tools, cranes and lifts, air compressors, and testers and analyzers. Also included are work benches, holding fixtures (➤8-2), cleaning equipment, and welding equipment.

This chapter is divided into four parts, *electric tools, pneumatic tools, hydraulic tools,* and *cleaning equipment.* Later chapters cover specialized power tools and shop equipment.

➤ 8-2 BENCH VISE

The *bench vise* (Fig. 8-1) is a holding device mounted on a workbench. The vise has flat steel jaws that you can close to grip an object. Then the object does not move while you

work on it. Turning the handle of the vise moves the movable jaw toward or away from the stationary jaw. Sometimes you must protect the surface of a part. Cover the steel jaws with caps of soft metal, or *soft jaws*. Some vises have *pipe jaws* below the flat jaws. The pipe jaws are less likely to damage a pipe or other round object while holding it more securely than the flat jaws.

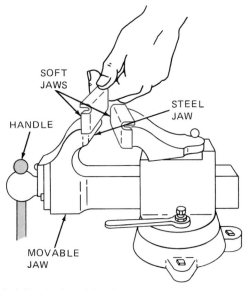

Fig. 8-1 A bench vise with soft jaws being put on the vise jaws.

There are three types of power tools: electric, pneumatic, and hydraulic. *Electric tools* have electric motors. Examples are the electric drill (➤8-4) and drill press (➤8-5). The word *pneumatic* means "of or pertaining to air." Pneumatic tools operate by compressed air. They include air hammers, air impact wrenches, air ratchets, and air jacks.

The word *hydraulic* means "of or pertaining to a fluid or liquid." Hydraulic tools work because of pressure on a liquid. These tools include hydraulic jacks, shop cranes, hydraulic presses, and automotive lifts.

Following sections cover these various types of power tools.

CAUTION!

Never use any power tool or piece of shop equipment until after you have received instruction on when and how to use it. Also, your instructor must give you permission to begin.

ELECTRIC TOOLS

➤ **8-4 ELECTRIC DRILL**

The electric drill (Fig. 8-2) has an electric motor that drives a *chuck*. This is a device with adjustable jaws that holds a tool in a machine. The chuck jaws are opened and a drill bit inserted (Fig. 8-3). Turning a *chuck key* closes the jaws. They tightly grip the shank of the drill bit. Chapter 7 describes drill bits or twist drills.

Observe the following cautions when using an electric drill:

1. Drill must be properly grounded (Fig. 4-8) through the third blade or ground terminal in the plug. Some drills are double-insulated instead.

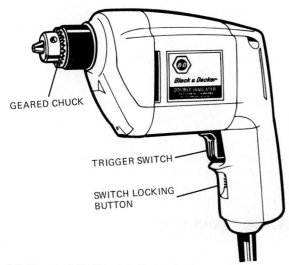

Fig. 8-2 Electric drill. *(Black & Decker Inc.)*

GEARED CHUCK

TRIGGER SWITCH

SWITCH LOCKING BUTTON

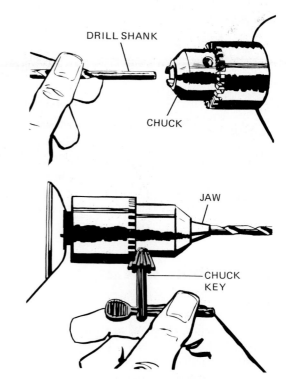

Fig. 8-3 Installing a twist drill in a drill chuck.

DRILL SHANK

CHUCK

JAW

CHUCK KEY

2. Do not drag the drill by its cord. Do not kink the cord, step on it, or run a vehicle or machine over it. This could damage the insulation. Then someone could get a dangerous electric shock.

3. Keep your hands and clothes away from the rotating chuck and drill bit.

4. Keep a firm grip on the drill. Be ready to shut it off if the drill bit jams.

5. If the bit jams, do *not* try to break it free by turning the drill on and off. This can damage the drill. Pull the drill back to free it.

6. When you finish with the drill, disconnect it. Wipe it clean and put it away. Most drills have preoiled bearings which do not require periodic lubrication.

➤ **8-5 DRILL PRESS**

A *drill press* (Fig. 8-4) is a vertical drilling machine powered by an electric motor. Clamp the piece you are drilling to the table of the drill press. Place the drill bit (➤7-22) in the chuck. Pull down on the hand-operated *feed lever*. This moves the chuck down and forces the drill bit into the workpiece.

Adjustments on the drill press set the hole depth and cutting speed. You usually control the feed. The drill press cuts holes more accurately than a hand-held electric drill (➤8-4).

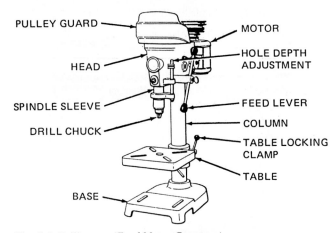

Fig. 8-4 Drill press. *(Ford Motor Company)*

➤ 8-6 GRINDING WHEEL

The *grinder* (Fig. 8-5) mounts on a bench or pedestal. It may have one grinding wheel and one wire wheel, or two grinding wheels. Figure 8-6 shows the use of a grinding wheel to sharpen a chisel (➤7-18). The grinding wheel also removes the mushroom from the head of a chisel or punch (➤7-21).

Observe the following CAUTIONS when using a grinding wheel:

1. Do not hammer on the grinding wheel or apply excessive force against it.
2. Do not grind on the side of the wheel.
3. Do not adjust the tool rest while the grinder is running.
4. Watch for sparks. They are hot and can burn you or set your clothing on fire.
5. Do not touch the rotating wheel. It removes skin on contact.
6. Adjust the light to see clearly what you are doing.
7. When grinding a tool, do not overheat it. This will "draw the temper." The tool will get soft and not hold

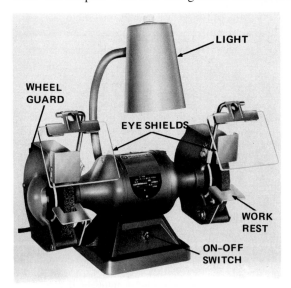

Fig. 8-5 Bench grinder. *(Rockwell International)*

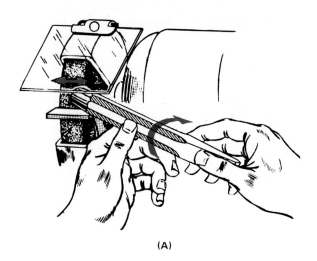

(A)

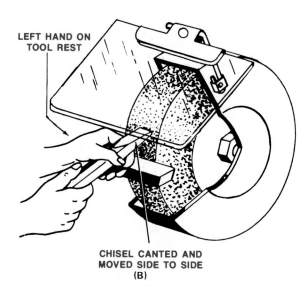

Fig. 8-6 (A) Grinding the mushroom from the head of a chisel. (B) Grinding the cutting edge of a chisel.

an edge. To prevent overheating, dip the tool in water repeatedly while grinding it.

8. Always wear eye protection even if the wheel has an eye shield.
9. Always make sure the safety guards and shields are in place and correctly adjusted. Never operate a grinder that has any safety device removed.

➤ 8-7 SOLDERING GUN

Soldering is a semi-permanent metal joining process. Heat from the tip of an electric *soldering iron* or *gun* (Fig. 8-7) melts *solder*. This is a soft metal *alloy* or mixture of tin and lead. It melts at a relatively low temperature.

The shop solder is usually a spool of hollow wire containing a liquid flux. This cleans the surfaces being joined. Use *rosin-core solder* for electrical work. This type of flux prevents a coating forming from the heat. The coating prevents a good electrical connection.

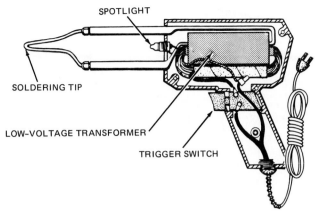

Fig. 8-7 An electric soldering gun. *(Ford Motor Company)*

A variety of shop jobs require soldering. These include replacing brushes and diodes in the alternator, and repairing a broken wire. After you connect or *splice* two wires together, solder the splice. Then wrap the splice and any bare wires or terminals with three layers of *electrical tape*. Later chapters cover the precautions for working on automotive electrical systems and components.

➤ 8-8 CORDLESS TOOLS

All the electric tools described above require a cord connected to a shop electrical outlet. Sometimes outlets are not available. Or you may not want a cord in the way. Then use a battery-powered *cordless tool*. These include the cordless soldering gun (➤8-7), drill (➤8-4), and screwdriver. The chuck on the cordless drill is the same as on the electric drill (➤8-4). It takes the same drill bits and other tools.

Cordless tools are not capable of continuous operation. As the battery discharges, the tool lacks power and slows down. Some tools have a replaceable battery pack. Remove it and put it in a charging stand for charging. Or install a spare battery back that is kept charged. Other tools recharge when placed on their storage stand.

PNEUMATIC TOOLS

➤ 8-9 AIR COMPRESSOR AND AIR-SUPPLY SYSTEM

The *air compressor* produces compressed air. The *air supply system* distributes the compressed air throughout the shop (Fig. 8-8). The air-compressor assembly is usually an air tank with an electric motor that drives a two-cylinder air compressor. When the pressure in the tank falls below a preset limit, the motor automatically starts running. The compressor then forces more air into the air tank to rebuild the pressure. This reserve of compressed air is ready to power the air-operated tools and equipment in the shop.

Flexible air hose connects from the *quick disconnect* on the shop air line to the air tool. Air hose also supplies compressed air to inflate tires and for blowguns (Fig. 4-7).

➤ 8-10 AIR TOOLS

Pneumatic tools or *air tools* give either rotary or reciprocating (back and forth) motion. You need rotary motion to turn nuts and bolts, and to spin a drill bit. You need reciprocating motion to drive a cutting or hammering tool. These include a cutter, chisel, hammer, or punch.

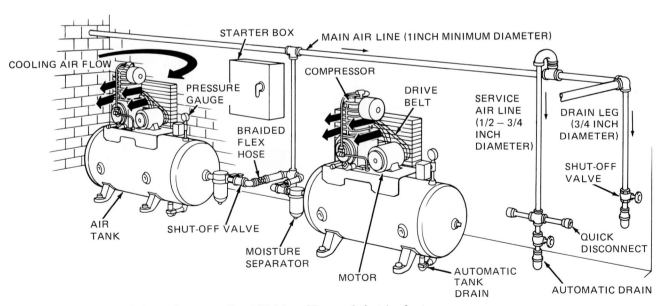

Fig. 8-8 Compressors and air-supply system. *(Leroi Division of Dresser Industries, Inc.)*

➤ 8-11 CAUTIONS ON OPERATING AIR TOOLS

Air tools operate on compressed air supplied by the shop air system (Fig. 8-8). Observe the following CAUTIONS when using an air tool:

1. Air nozzles or blowguns (Fig. 4-7) should have a diffuser. It reduces the outlet pressure to less than 30 psi [207 kPa]. This safety device is required by law and helps reduce the risk of personal injury.
2. Never use the blowgun to blow dust off your clothes and never point it at anyone. The air pressure can drive dust particles at high speed. They can penetrate the flesh or eyes. High-pressure air hitting an open wound can force air into the blood stream. This can result in death!
3. Never look into the air outlet of a pneumatic tool.
4. Never operate an air hammer without a bit installed. This can damage the tool.
5. Never blow-clean brake or clutch parts. This could put asbestos dust into the air. Use a vacuum cleaner with a HEPA filter (➤4-6).

➤ 8-12 AIR HAMMER

The *air hammer* (Fig. 8-9) produces a reciprocating (back and forth) motion to drive a hammering or cutting tool. Figure 8-9 shows a chisel splitting a frozen nut. Many different types of bits and tools attach to the air hammer. These include chisels, cutters, punches, and separators.

➤ 8-13 AIR IMPACT WRENCH

The *air impact wrench* (Fig. 8-10) produces a high-torque rotary (spinning) motion. This pounding or impact force loosens or tightens nuts and bolts. Moving a reversing button or lever changes the direction of rotation. The most common impact wrenches have a 1/2-inch or 3/8-inch drive lug. Hand-tool sockets (➤7-10) will fit, but only heavier *impact sockets* should be used.

| NOTE | Some impact wrenches are electric. Attach only impact sockets to either type of impact wrench. |

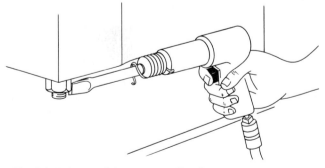

Fig. 8-9 Using an air hammer to split a frozen nut.

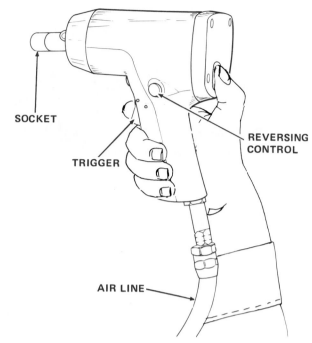

Fig. 8-10 Using an air impact wrench. *(ATW)*

Observe the following CAUTIONS when using an impact wrench:

1. Always use impact sockets of the correct size. Hand-tool sockets will "pound out" and may break.
2. Hold the impact wrench so the socket fits squarely on the nut or bolt. Apply a slight forward force to hold the socket in place.
3. Once a nut or bolt tightens, never impact it beyond an additional one-half turn.
4. Use a torque wrench (➤7-11) or torque-angle gauge (➤7-12) for final tightening.
5. Soak rusty nuts or bolts with penetrating oil before impacting them.

➤ 8-14 AIR DRILL

An *air drill* (Fig. 8-11) does the same job as an electric drill (➤8-4). However, the air drill has an air motor. This makes the tool lighter than an electric drill. Repeated stalls

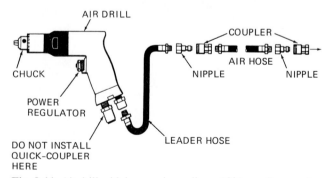

Fig. 8-11 Air drill with hose and couplings. *(Chicago Pneumatic Tool Company)*

and overloads do not overheat or damage the air motor. The same drill bits are used in air drills as in electric drills.

➤ 8-15 AIR RATCHET

Air ratchets (Fig. 8-12) are similar to hand-tool ratchets (➤7-10), but operate faster. They are available in 1/4-, 3/8-, and 1/2-inch drive. Air ratchets apply less force than an impact wrench. This allows them to use hand-tool sockets.

➤ 8-16 CARE OF AIR TOOLS

Never drag around an air tool by its hose. Never drop an air tool on the floor or otherwise abuse the tool. When not in use, disconnect the air tool from the air hose. Put the tool away in its storage place. Lubricate the air tool every day before using it. Apply three or four squirts of air-tool oil into the nipple closest to the tool (Fig. 8-11). Then connect the air hose to the nipple and operate the tool. This lubricates the internal parts. It also flushes out dirt and moisture.

CAUTION!

Do not flush air tools around an open flame. The mist coming out is flammable. Always point the air exhausting from the tool away from your body.

➤ 8-17 PNEUMATIC JACKS AND END LIFTS

There are many types of *pneumatic jacks* and *end lifts*. They use compressed air to raise one corner, end, or side of the car. Some lift under the front or rear bumper (Fig. 8-13, top). Others lift under the axle housing or other lift

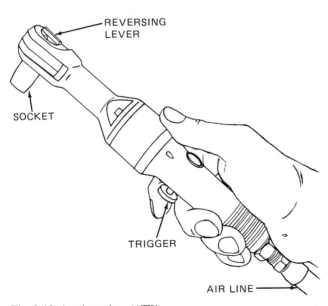

Fig. 8-12 An air ratchet. *(ATW)*

points (Fig. 8-13, bottom). Opening the *air valve* sends compressed air into the pneumatic cylinder. This causes the ram to extend and raise the vehicle. Reversing the lever exhausts the air. Then the vehicle settles back to the floor.

CAUTION!

Never work under a vehicle supported only by a jack. Always support the vehicle on safety stands before going under it (Figs. 4-13 and 4-19). A jack could slip or release. Then the vehicle would fall on you. Serious injury or death could result.

HYDRAULIC TOOLS

➤ 8-18 HYDRAULIC JACKS

The automotive shop uses a variety of hydraulic jacks. One type is the portable *floor jack* (Fig. 8-14). Pumping the handle increases the pressure in the hydraulic cylinder.

Fig. 8-13 A pneumatic end lift (top) and a pneumatic undercar lift (bottom). *(Blackhawk Automotive Inc.)*

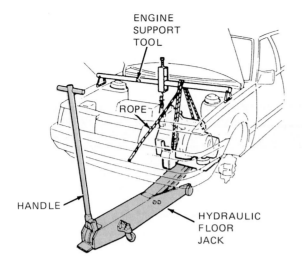

Fig. 8-14 Hydraulic floor jack and engine support tool. *(Mazda Motors of America Inc.)*

This causes the ram to extend and raise the lifting saddle. Turning the top of the handle or moving a lever on the handle releases the pressure. Then the saddle and load settle back down.

Always lift at the proper *lift point* (➤8-21) under the vehicle. If in doubt, refer to the vehicle manufacturer's service manual. Lifting at the wrong points can cause vehicle damage. Follow the CAUTION in ➤8-17.

➤ 8-19 SHOP CRANE

The hydraulic *shop crane* (Fig. 8-15) lifts and transports heavy objects. One use is removing the engine from the vehicle. The crane operates hydraulically by pumping the handle.

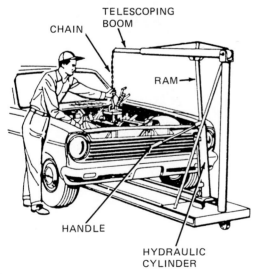

Fig. 8-15 Hydraulic shop crane. *(Kwik-Way Manufacturing Company)*

CAUTION!

Stand clear of the crane while an engine or other heavy component is suspended. This prevents injury if it falls off, the boom collapses, or the crane topples over. Never work on a suspended assembly. Lower it onto a workbench or holding fixture.

➤ 8-20 HYDRAULIC PRESS

To operate the *hydraulic press*, pump the handle on the hydraulic cylinder up and down (Fig. 8-16). This increases the pressure on the ram. It then exerts a much greater force against the part it is touching. This force can straighten bent parts or remove and install press-fit parts. These include bushings, bearings, brake-drum studs, piston pins, and rivets. The press can do many other jobs requiring a high and steady force.

Some shops have an *arbor press*. It is a hand-operated press that applies only a light force.

CAUTION!

Always wear eye protection when using a press. Place a *safety shield* between you and the workpiece in the press.

➤ 8-21 AUTOMOTIVE LIFTS

Automotive lifts are *in-ground lifts* or *surface lifts*. In-ground lifts may be single-post or double-post (Fig. 8-17). Both types require excavation of the ground for installation of hydraulic cylinders. Surface lifts bolt to the shop floor (Fig. 8-18). If a lift has movable arms, position the *lift pads*

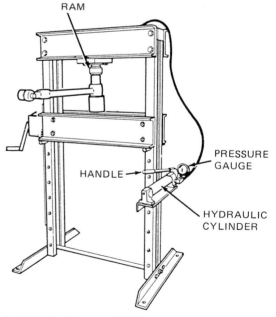

Fig. 8-16 Hydraulic press. *(ATW)*

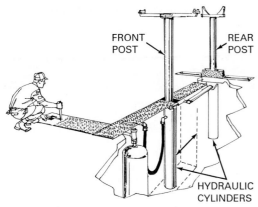

Fig. 8-17 A double-post in-ground lift. *(Lincoln St. Louis Division of McNeil Corporation)*

Fig. 8-18 A surface lift bolted to the shop floor. *(Vendredi II)*

before raising the vehicle. Vehicle service manuals show the lift points on the underbody, frame, and suspension (Fig. 8-19).

Many models of in-ground and surface lifts are available. Refer to the lift manufacturer's operating instructions for information about the lift you are using. Some surface lifts are the drive-on type. You drive the ve-

hicle onto two metal tracks. Moving the lift control causes an air or electric motor to operate a hydraulic pump. It sends liquid under pressure to the hydraulic cylinder. As the ram or post extends from the cylinder, the vehicle goes up.

CAUTION!

Some cautions to observe when using an automotive lift are described in number 7 of ➤4-6. Never overload the lift. A *name-plate* attached to the lift gives its rated capacity.

CLEANING EQUIPMENT

➤ **8-22 VACUUM CLEANER**

Many shops have a shop *vacuum cleaner* (Fig. 8-20). Its uses include cleaning floors and vehicle interiors after service work. Never use this vacuum cleaner to clean

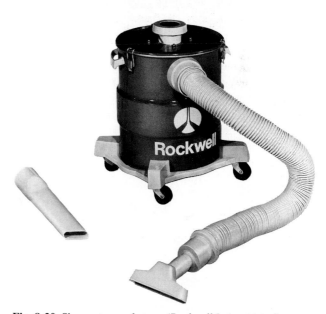

Fig. 8-20 Shop vacuum cleaner. *(Rockwell International)*

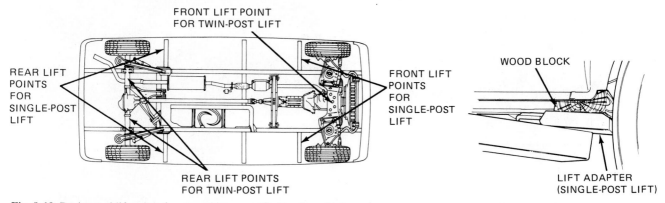

Fig. 8-19 Designated lift points for one vehicle, specified by the vehicle manufacturer. *(Ford Motor Company)*

clutch and brake assemblies. The filter will not trap asbestos dust on clutch and brake parts. For this, use a special vacuum cleaner with a *High Efficiency Particulate Air* (HEPA) filter (Fig. 4-6). Chapter 53 and number 2 of ➤4-6 describe hazards of working around asbestos dust.

➤ **8-23 PARTS CLEANERS**

Servicing automobiles requires clean parts. Even an experienced technician cannot always tell if a dirty part is defective. Also, if the parts are dirty, the dirt may ruin a rebuild or overhaul job. Parts cleaning is so important that many technicians will not let anyone else clean the parts they are working on. It is during the cleaning process that clues to the cause of the trouble often show up.

Following sections describe cleaning equipment used in automotive shops.

➤ **8-24 SOLVENT TANK**

Remove old gaskets and thick deposits on parts with a *putty knife, scraper,* and *wire brush.* Then final-clean by washing and degreasing the part in the *solvent tank* (Fig. 8-21). It contains *solvent* which is a cold liquid cleaner. Brush or spray the solvent on the dirty part. An electric pump in the tank provides the spray. For soaking, place parts in a tray or basket and lower it into the solvent. This loosens and dissolves some deposits. Strainers, filters, and sediment trays help keep the solvent clean.

Always remove thick deposits before placing the dirty part in the tank. Then use solvent along with a bristle brush

and scraper to remove the remaining deposits. Wash and rinse off the parts with the spray from the nozzle.

CAUTION!

Some parts-cleaning solutions and solvents are *toxic* and *caustic.* This means they are poisonous and will burn your eyes and skin. They should be used only in well-ventilated areas. Always wear eye protection while using shop cleaning equipment. Wear gloves (➤4-14), if necessary, and avoid overexposure of your skin to cleaning solutions. Afterwards wash your hands, arms, and other contacted areas with soap and water. This helps prevent skin irritation.

Dirty solvent may be hazardous waste (➤4-13). Dispose of it properly. Some shops have a *solvent reclaimer* or *recycler.* It heats the dirty solvent. The solvent evaporates into another container leaving the contaminants in the recycler. As the vapor cools, it condenses and becomes clean liquid solvent. Other shops use a *parts-cleaner service.* These companies provide the shop with fresh solvent regularly. They pick up the dirty solvent and recycle or dispose of it.

➤ **8-25 SPRAY WASHERS**

Engine blocks and transmission cases are too large to clean in a solvent tank (➤8-24). These and other large parts may be cleaned in a *spray washer* (Fig. 8-22). Place the part on the turntable and close the washer. Cleaning occurs as the pressurized spray of hot cleaning solution hits the rotating part. Washing, rinsing, and drying cycles are automatically controlled.

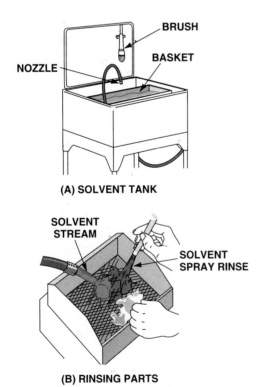

(A) SOLVENT TANK

(B) RINSING PARTS

Fig. 8-21 Solvent tank. *(Ford Motor Company)*

Fig. 8-22 Spray washer. *(Intercont Products Inc.)*

MULTIPLE-CHOICE TEST

*Select the **one** correct, best, or most probable answer to each question.*
You can find the answers in the section indicated at the end of each question.

1. Power tools are powered by (➤8-1)
   a. electricity, compressed air, or hydraulic pressure
   b. muscles, liquids, or gases
   c. breaker bars, ratchets, or speed handles
   d. mechanical power, animal power, or electrical power

2. An electric drill and a drill press both require (➤8-4)
   a. an electric motor
   b. a chuck and chuck key
   c. both A and B
   d. neither A nor B

3. A tool will get soft and not hold an edge if you (➤8-6)
   a. draw the temper of the tool while grinding it
   b. overheat the tool while grinding it
   c. fail to dip the tool in water while grinding it
   d. all of the above

4. Technician A says air tools give either rotary or reciprocating motion. Technician B says to tighten nuts and bolts with an air hammer. Who is right? (➤8-10 and 8-12)
   a. A only
   b. B only
   c. both A and B
   d. neither A nor B

5. Technician A says to lubricate an air tool every day before using it. Technician B says air tools are preoiled and never need lubrication. Who is right? (➤8-16)
   a. A only
   b. B only
   c. both A and B
   d. neither A nor B

6. To lift one end of a car, you can use (➤8-17, 8-18, and 8-21)
   a. a hydraulic press, shop crane, or arbor press
   b. a pneumatic jack, end lift, or hydraulic jack
   c. a single-post lift, surface lift, or shop crane
   d. all of the above

7. Use the shop crane to (➤8-19)
   a. lift the car to change oil
   b. lift the engine out of the car
   c. suspend parts so you can work on them
   d. all of the above

8. Technician A says surface lifts may be the drive-on type. Technician B says a nameplate attached to the lift shows the rated capacity. Who is right? (➤8-21)
   a. A only
   b. B only
   c. both A and B
   d. neither A nor B

REVIEW QUESTIONS

1. Explain the difference between *power tools* and *shop equipment*. (➤8-1)
2. List six Cautions to observe when using an electric drill. (➤8-4)
3. Describe when and where you could use cordless tools in automotive service work. (➤8-8)
4. List five Cautions to observe when using an air tool. (➤8-11)
5. Discuss the importance of finding and using lift points when raising a vehicle.   (➤8-18 and 8-21

PART 2

AUTOMOTIVE ENGINES

Part 2 of *Automotive Mechanics* describes the construction and operation of automotive engines. This includes "four-valve" engines with single- and double-overhead camshafts, and variable valve timing and lift. Also included is an introduction to electricity and electronic engine controls. Later chapters describe the engine systems that are necessary to make the engine run.

There are seven chapters in Part 2:

CHAPTER 9

FUNDAMENTALS OF ENGINE OPERATION

After studying this chapter, you should be able to:

- Explain the combustion process in the engine.
- Describe how pollutants form in the engine.
- List and explain the two rules relating pressure and temperature.
- Explain the difference between a thermometer and a thermostat. Describe how each works.
- Describe how temperature, humidity, and atmospheric pressure affect combustion.

FROM ATOMS TO POWER

➤ 9-1 ATOMS

Atoms are the basic "building blocks" of the world. They are very small. A single drop of water contains about 100 billion billion atoms. There are about a hundred varieties of atoms. Each has a special name: gold, silver, iron, aluminum, oxygen, hydrogen, nitrogen, and so on. The copper or other metals in a penny are made-up of billions of one kind of atom. Any substance made of only one kind of atom is an *element*.

➤ 9-2 CHEMICAL REACTIONS

Atoms of different elements can connect with each other. The process is a *chemical action* or *reaction*. Chemical reactions go on around us all the time. The burning of fuel (gasoline) in an automobile engine is a chemical reaction. This reaction is called *combustion*.

➤ 9-3 COMBUSTION IN THE ENGINE

Automotive fuels such as gasoline are made mostly of two elements: *hydrogen* and *carbon*. They have the chemical symbols H and C. This type of fuel is a *hydrocarbon* (HC) fuel. During complete combustion in the engine, these two elements unite with a third element, the gas *oxygen* (O). Oxygen, usually in the form of *free oxygen* (O_2), makes up about 20 percent of the earth's *atmosphere*. This is the *air* we breathe.

During combustion, each oxygen atom unites with two hydrogen atoms (Fig. 9-1). Each carbon atom unites with two oxygen atoms. Oxygen uniting with hydrogen produces H_2O, or *water*. Carbon uniting with oxygen produces CO_2, or the gas *carbon dioxide*. (*Di*oxide because there are *two* oxygen atoms to each carbon atom.)

NOTE	Figure 9-1 shows only a few atoms. Actually, billions of atoms unite every second in a running engine.

During combustion of the fuel, the burning gases get very hot. Their temperature may go as high as 6000°F [3316°C]. This high temperature produces pressure in the engine that makes it run and produce power.

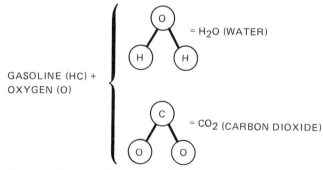

GASOLINE (HC) + OXYGEN (O)

= H_2O (WATER)

= CO_2 (CARBON DIOXIDE)

Fig. 9-1 When gasoline burns (combines with oxygen in the air), the result of perfect combustion is water and carbon dioxide.

With perfect combustion, all the hydrogen and all the carbon in the gasoline would unite with oxygen. The exhaust gas would contain only harmless H_2O (water) and CO_2 (carbon dioxide). But combustion is not perfect in the engine. Some of the gasoline (HC) does not burn. Also, some only partly burns. This produces *carbon monoxide* (CO). (*Mon*oxide because there is only one oxygen atom for each carbon atom.) The unburned gasoline (HC) and partly burned gasoline (CO) exit from the engine through the tailpipe. Once in the air, they cause *atmospheric pollution*. Another group of *atmospheric pollutants* from the engine is *nitrogen oxides* (NO_x). About 80 percent of the atmosphere is the gas *nitrogen* (N). The high temperatures in the engine cause some of the nitrogen to unite with oxygen. This forms the nitrogen oxides.

Automobiles have antipollution devices called *emission controls*. These reduce the amount of the pollutants (HC, CO, and NO_x). Chapters 35 and 36 describe emission controls and their service.

➤ 9-4 ESSENTIALS FOR ENGINE OPERATION

The automobile engine has three or more cylinders. A piston moves up and down in each cylinder (Fig. 9-2). Figure 9-3 shows the piston and cylinder in a four-cylinder engine. The car moves because the pistons move.

Before the pistons move up and down, the engine must have fuel available. *Gravity, atmospheric pressure,* and *vacuum* make it possible for the fuel to get into the engine cylinders. There the fuel burns to produce power.

➤ 9-5 GRAVITY

Gravity is the attractive force between the earth and all other objects. When you release a stone from your hand,

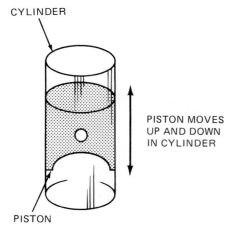

Fig. 9-2 In a piston engine, each piston moves up and down in a cylinder.

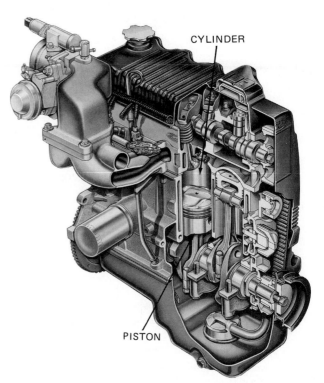

Fig. 9-3 A four-cylinder spark-ignition engine with overhead camshaft. (*Ford Motor Company*)

the stone falls downward. When you drive a car up a hill, part of the engine power is used to raise the car against gravity. A car coasts down a hill with the engine not running and the brakes off. Gravity pulls the car downward.

➤ 9-6 ATMOSPHERIC PRESSURE

Gravity also pulls the air toward the earth. At sea level and average temperature, a cubic foot of air weighs about 0.08 pound or about 1.25 ounces [0.035 kilograms]. This is very little. But the blanket of air—our atmosphere—is many miles thick. It is like many thousands of cubic feet of air, stacked one on top of another, all adding their weight (Fig. 9-4). The total weight or downward push of all this air is about 15 pounds per square inch (psi) [103 kPa]. This is at sea level.

The human body has a total surface area of several square feet, or several hundred square inches. The total weight of the air on your skin amounts to several tons! This pressure does not crush you because pressures inside you balance these outside pressures.

➤ 9-7 VACUUM

A *vacuum* is the absence of air. When a piston moves down in a cylinder (Fig. 9-2), the piston creates a partial vacuum. Atmospheric pressure then pushes air into this vacuum.

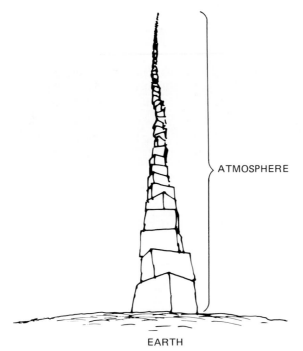

Fig. 9-4 Atmospheric pressure results from miles and miles of cubic feet of air, stacked up on top of one another.

> ## 9-8 THE ENGINE CYLINDER

The same actions take place in all cylinders. Figure 9-5 shows one cylinder of an engine. The piston slides up and down in the cylinder (Fig. 9-2). There are at least two openings or *valve ports* at the top of the cylinder. Valve ports are internal passages in the *cylinder head.* This is the engine part that encloses the top of the cylinder.

There is a *valve* centered in each port. A valve is a device that can be opened and closed to control the flow of a liquid or gas. The engine valve is a plug with a round

head on a long stem (Fig. 9-6). It is moved up and down at the proper time by the *valve train,* as explained in Chap. 14. This closes the port so no air-fuel mixture or exhaust gas can enter or leave the cylinder.

Two valves are shown in Fig. 9-7. One is the *intake valve.* When it is down or open (Fig. 9-7A), air-fuel mixture can flow into the cylinder. The other valve is the *exhaust valve.* When it is down or open (Fig. 9-7D), the burned gases remaining from combustion (➤9-3) can flow out of or *exhaust* from the cylinder.

> ## ➤ 9-9 ACTIONS IN THE ENGINE CYLINDER

Figure 9-7 shows what happens in one cylinder when the piston moves up and down, and the valves open and close. In Fig. 9-7A, the piston is moving down and the intake valve is open. Atmospheric pressure pushes air past the open intake valve and into the engine cylinder where there is a partial vacuum. On the way, the fuel system mixes fuel vapor with the air.

The intake valve closes after the piston passes its bottom position and starts to move up again (Fig. 9-7B). The bottom position is called *bottom dead center* or *BDC*.

As the piston moves up (Fig. 9-7B), it compresses the air-fuel mixture into a small space called the *combustion chamber.* Then, as the piston nears its top position (called *top dead center* or *TDC*), the spark plug *fires.* The spark plug has an air gap of about 0.040 inch [1 mm]. The *ignition system* produces and delivers a spark that jumps this gap at the right time (Chaps. 31 and 32).

The spark sets fire to or *ignites* the compressed air-fuel mixture (Fig. 9-7C). The temperature of the burning air-fuel mixture goes up as high as 6000°F [3316°C]. The result is a high pressure in the cylinder which can be as much as 600 psi [4140 kPa]. The pressure pushes down on the piston with a force of up to 4000 pounds [17,792

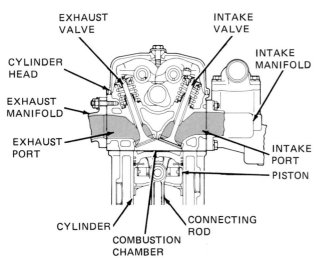

Fig. 9-5 One cylinder in an engine, showing the ports, valves, piston, and cylinder. (*Chrysler Corporation*)

Fig. 9-6 An engine valve is a long metal stem with a round head. (*ATW*)

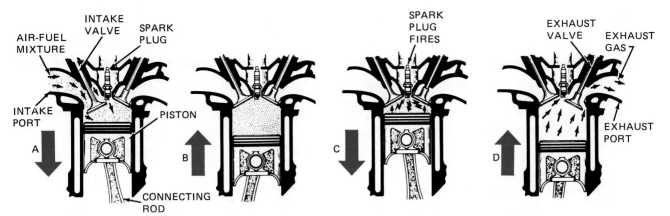

Fig. 9-7 The actions in a cylinder as the piston moves up and down.

newtons (N)]. This pushes the piston down. The downward movement, carried through the connecting rod, rotates the crankshaft. It turns gears and shafts to move the car. Chapter 11 describes this series of actions.

As the piston approaches BDC, the exhaust valve moves down. This opens the exhaust port. When the piston moves through BDC and starts upward, the burned gases leave the cylinder (Fig. 9-7D). They enter the exhaust port and pass through the tailpipe into the atmosphere.

BASIC PHYSICS

➤ 9-10 EXPANSION OF SOLIDS WITH HEAT

Understanding engine operation requires knowing some basic physics and chemistry. They help explain how increasing temperature of the burning air-fuel mixture produces high pressure. And this high pressure produces piston movement. One fundamental is the expansion of solids with heat.

Any solid, such as the metal in an engine piston, expands and gets larger when its temperature goes up. However, the piston must be free to move up and down in the cylinder, even if it gets very hot (Fig. 9-8). A piston that expands too much will stick in the cylinder. This damages the engine. The piston is designed to expand very little as it gets hot.

➤ 9-11 EXPANSION OF FLUIDS WITH HEAT

Fluids are substances that can flow. Examples are water and air. Both expand when heated. One cubic foot of water [0.0283 cubic meter] at 32°F [0°C] becomes 1.01 cubic foot [0.0286 cubic meter] when heated to 100°F [37.8°C]. One cubic foot of air [0.0283 cubic meter] expands to 1.14 cubic foot [0.0323 cubic meter] when heated to 100°F [37.8°C]. This occurs *without a change of pressure*.

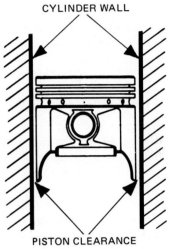

Fig. 9-8 The piston is designed so that even if it gets very hot, it will not expand enough to stick in the cylinder.

NOTE | The pressure will go up if the air is heated in a closed container and cannot expand.

➤ 9-12 INCREASE OF PRESSURE WITH TEMPERATURE

Something different happens when air is heated in a closed container that will not allow the air to expand. Heating a cubic foot of air from 32°F to 100°F [from 0 to 37.8°C] increases its pressure about 10 percent. This means a beginning pressure of 15 psi [103 kPa] will increase to a pressure of 17 psi [117 kPa] as the air heats up.

This is the first rule: *Pressure increases with increasing temperature.*

➤ 9-13 INCREASE OF TEMPERATURE WITH PRESSURE

When the piston moves up in a cylinder (Fig. 9-7B) or closed container, the piston compresses the trapped air or air-fuel mixture. Then the air or mixture gets hot.

This is the second rule: *Temperature increases with increasing pressure.*

Both rules are at work in the engine cylinders. *Compressing the mixture (increasing its pressure) increases its temperature.* Igniting and burning the mixture raises its temperature still further. This further increases its pressure. *Increasing the temperature increases the pressure.* This high pressure then pushes the piston down which moves the car.

9-14 THE THERMOMETER

The *thermometer* (Fig. 9-9) is a hollow tube partly filled with a liquid such as mercury. The liquid expands as its temperature increases. This forces some of the liquid to move up in the hollow tube. The higher the temperature, the more the liquid expands, and the farther up it rises in the tube. Degree marks on the tube indicate the temperature.

9-15 THE THERMOSTAT

Different metals expand different amounts when heated. For example, aluminum expands about twice as much as iron. One type of *thermostat* uses this difference in expansion of metals. The *coil thermostat* (Fig. 9-10) is made of two different metals, such as brass and steel, welded together. Heating the coil makes one metal expand more than the other. This causes the coil to wind or unwind. The motion of the coil then controls the flow of a fluid or electricity.

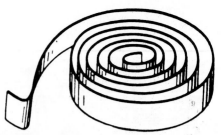

Fig. 9-10 A coil thermostat that winds up or unwinds as its temperature changes. This motion can be used to operate a control.

9-16 PRODUCING A VACUUM

A vacuum is an absence of air (➤9-7). The engine produces vacuum as the piston moves down during the intake stroke (Fig. 9-7A). This is how a *vacuum pump* produces vacuum. Other devices produce vacuum or operate by it. To control or use the vacuum, sometimes we need to know how strong it is. The barometer and vacuum gauge provide this information. They *read* vacuum.

1. BAROMETER The *barometer* uses vacuum to measure atmospheric pressure. You can make a barometer by filling a long tube with mercury (Fig. 9-11). Then cover the end to seal it closed. Turn the tube upside down and put the end into a dish of mercury (Hg). Now remove the seal to open the end.

Any increase in atmospheric pressure acts on the mercury in the dish. This forces some of the mercury up the tube. Any decrease in atmospheric pressure allows some of the mercury to flow out of the tube. If this happens, the barometer is "falling." It usually indicates stormy weather.

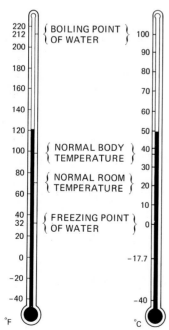

Fig. 9-9 Fahrenheit and Celsius thermometers.

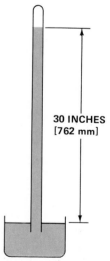

Fig. 9-11 In a barometer, the mercury will rise in the tube to about 30 inches [762 mm] above the surface of the mercury in the dish when the atmospheric pressure is 15 psi [103 kPa].

2. VACUUM GAUGE The *vacuum gauge* (Fig. 9-12) is a type of *pressure gauge*. It measures the pressure in a closed space and compares it with atmospheric pressure. A partial vacuum exists if the pressure in the closed space is less than atmospheric pressure. The vacuum gauge (➤5-22) reads in *inches of mercury*. However, there is no mercury in the gauge.

When connected to a running engine, the vacuum gauge shows how much vacuum the engine is developing. This is an indication of engine condition. For example, a low or unsteady reading indicates engine trouble. A later chapter describes using the vacuum gauge in engine diagnosis.

The vacuum gauge has a bellows or diaphragm linked to a needle on the dial face. Applying a vacuum moves the bellows or diaphragm. This causes the needle to move to show the amount of vacuum. Instead of a needle and dial face, some vacuum gauges have a digital display.

Many vacuum gauges have a small chamber with a nearly perfect vacuum. The gauge compares its reading with this vacuum to get *absolute vacuum*.

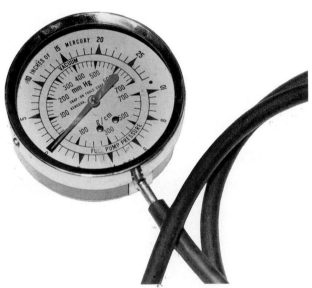

Fig. 9-12 A vacuum gauge.

➤ 9-17 HUMIDITY

Most air has some water vapor (evaporated water) in it. When the air is carrying a lot of water vapor, the air is *humid*. Air around bodies of water has high humidity. Air over deserts has low humidity.

Humidity is measured as a percentage. Zero percent humidity means the air has no water vapor. One-hundred percent humidity means the air is holding all the water vapor it can hold. A reading of 50 percent humidity means the air is holding half as much water vapor as it could.

Humidity affects engine performance. An engine develops less power in hot, dry air than in cool, moist air. The cool air is denser (atoms are closer together) so more air enters the engine. This means more power. The moisture displaces some of the oxygen from the air. This richens the air-fuel mixture. Then the engine runs more smoothly.

➤ 9-18 ATMOSPHERIC CONDITIONS AFFECTING COMBUSTION

Changes in temperature, humidity, and atmospheric pressure affect combustion in the engine. They change the way the fuel burns and the amount of power the engine produces. Chapter 19 describes how air pressure and temperatures are measured. Proper engine operation depends on the engine computer continuously receiving this information.

➤ 9-19 ELECTRICITY FOR ENGINES

Engines need electricity for starting and running (➤1-18). An electric current cranks the engine to start it. Electric current also provides the sparks at the spark plugs (➤9-9) and may operate the fuel system. In addition, electricity operates the electronic engine control system on modern engines. Therefore, an understanding of how engines operate and are controlled requires a basic knowledge of electricity. Chapter 10 explains basic electricity, electronics, and engine controls.

TRADE TALK

atmospheric pollution	chemical reaction	gravity	vacuum
atmospheric pressure	combustion	pressure	
bottom dead center (BDC)	element	top dead center (TDC)	

MULTIPLE-CHOICE TEST

*Select the **one** correct, best, or most probable answer to each question.*
You can find the answers in the section indicated at the end of each question.

1. During combustion of gasoline in the engine (➤9-3)
   a. oxygen unites with carbon to form carbon dioxide
   b. hydrogen unites with oxygen to form water
   c. some carbon unites with oxygen to form carbon monoxide
   d. all of the above

2. Which of these statements about a closed container is correct? (➤9-12 and 9-13)
   a. temperature increases with increasing pressure
   b. pressure increases with increasing temperature
   c. both a and b
   d. neither a nor b

3. Pollutants produced by the engine include (➤9-3)
   a. water, carbon dioxide, carbon monoxide, and NO_x
   b. carbon monoxide, carbon dioxide, HC, and NO_x
   c. carbon monoxide, HC, and NO_x
   d. water, HC, and NO_x

4. Atmospheric pressure is produced by (➤9-6)
   a. vacuum
   b. gravity
   c. humidity
   d. temperature

5. During burning of the air-fuel mixture in the cylinder, the force pushing the piston down may be as high as (➤9-9)
   a. 600 tons
   b. 600 psi
   c. 4000 pounds
   d. 1814 pounds

6. As the piston moves up the cylinder, the air-fuel mixture is compressed and the (➤9-13)
   a. temperature increases
   b. pressure increases
   c. air-fuel mixture gets hot
   d. all of the above

7. The device that provides control based on temperature changes is the (➤9-15)
   a. thermometer
   b. thermostat
   c. vacuum gauge
   d. pressure gauge

8. The atmosphere is (➤9-3)
   a. 80 percent O_2 and 20 percent N
   b. 20 percent O_2 and 80 percent N
   c. 20 percent O_2 and 80 percent HC
   d. 20 percent N and 80 percent HC

9. The vacuum gauge compares a vacuum source with (➤9-16)
   a. atmospheric pressure
   b. a nearly perfect vacuum
   c. either a or b
   d. neither a nor b

10. An engine develops more power when the air is (➤9-17)
    a. hot and dry
    b. hot and moist
    c. cool and dry
    d. cool and moist

REVIEW QUESTIONS

1. How are CO_2 and CO formed in the engine cylinders? (➤9-3)
2. How does gravity help the engine run? (➤9-5 and 9-6)
3. Explain what pushes the piston down. (➤9-9)
4. What are the two rules relating temperature and pressure? (➤9-12 and 9-13)
5. Explain how barometric pressure is measured. (➤9-16)

CHAPTER 10

ELECTRICITY AND ELECTRONIC ENGINE CONTROLS

After studying this chapter, you should be able to:

- Explain electricity in terms of electrons, and what makes electrons move.
- Define *voltage, current,* and *resistance* and explain how they are related.
- Explain the basic operation of diodes and transistors.
- Describe RAM, ROM, and PROM and explain what they do.
- Explain how the ECM controls engine operation.

ELECTRICITY

➤ 10-1 ELECTRICITY AND THE ENGINE

The *electric ignition system* supplies the sparks that ignite the compressed air-fuel mixture in the engine cylinders (➤9-9). This makes the engine run and produce power to move the car. To get the engine running, the *electric starting motor* must crank the engine until it starts. The *battery* supplies the power for cranking.

The engine also has *electronic controls* that time the sparks so they get to the spark plugs at the right instant. This is just before the pistons reach top dead center (TDC) on their compression strokes (Fig. 9-7). On most engines, the electronic controls also time the opening of the *fuel injectors* (Chap. 19). They open at the proper time to allow the fuel and air to mix as it enters the engine cylinders. The electronic controls determine how much fuel to deliver. The engine needs more fuel if the driver is depressing the accelerator pedal for acceleration and higher speed.

The following sections describe electricity, magnetism, electronics, and electronic engine controls. An understanding of these subjects, as explained here and in later chapters, helps you understand engine operation. Also, many times you will need this background to successfully diagnose and correct various engine and electrical troubles.

➤ 10-2 ELECTRICITY AND ELECTRIC CURRENT

Electric current is a flow of electrons. Just like water flows in a pipe, *electrons* flow in a wire. The electrons come from atoms (Fig. 10-1). Everything in the world is made of atoms (➤9-1). There are about a hundred different kinds of atoms. Atoms of one kind grouped together

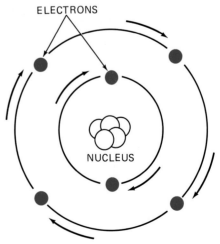

Fig. 10-1 An atom consists of a nucleus with electrons circling around it.

are called an *element*. The atoms of certain elements join together in *chemical reactions* such as *combustion* (➤9-2).

One basic difference among the atoms is the number of electrons that circle the center or *nucleus* of the atom (Fig. 10-1). For example, an atom of the gas hydrogen has only one electron circling its nucleus. The copper atom has 29 electrons circling its nucleus.

Atoms are very small. Electrons are even smaller. It takes a hundred thousand billion (100,000,000,000,000) electrons, side by side, to measure a single inch.

➤ 10-3 ELECTRICAL CHARGES

Electrons carry a *negative* charge (written "minus" or "−"). The nucleus of an atom has a *positive* charge (written "plus" or "+"). The electrons circle or *orbit* the nucleus. They are held in their orbits by the attraction between opposite *electrical charges*.

Figure 10-2 shows how *unlike electrical charges attract* and *like electrical charges repel*. In the automotive electrical system (Fig. 10-3), the *battery* and the *alternator* supply electrons (electrical current). They mass electrons at their negative (minus or −) terminal. They take electrons away from their positive (plus or +) terminal.

Connecting a wire from one terminal to the other completes the *electric circuit*. The electrons flow through the wire (Fig. 10-4). This is caused by the repelling force among the electrons at the negative terminal and the attracting force at the positive terminal. (It has a shortage of electrons.) This *difference of potential* causes electrons to flow from the negative terminal to the positive terminal. The flow of electrons is an *electric current*. It will power a light bulb or other electrical device connected in the circuit (Fig. 10-4).

➤ 10-4 MEASURING ELECTRICITY

Electricity is measured in two ways:

1. By the amount of current (electrons) flowing. This measurement is in *amperes* (or *amperage*).

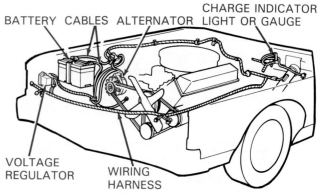

Fig. 10-3 Components of the automotive electrical system in the engine compartment. (*Chrysler Corporation*)

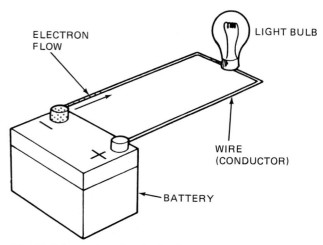

Fig. 10-4 A complete electric circuit. (*Ford Motor Company*)

2. By the electrical pressure (difference of potential) between two points that makes the electrons move. This measurement is in *volts* (or *voltage*).

Amperage is measured by an *ammeter*. Voltage is measured by a *voltmeter*. Figure 10-5 shows an ammeter

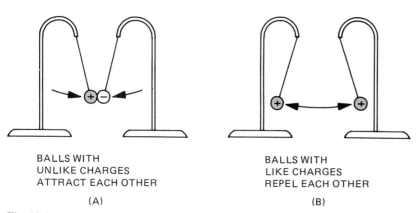

BALLS WITH UNLIKE CHARGES ATTRACT EACH OTHER

(A)

BALLS WITH LIKE CHARGES REPEL EACH OTHER

(B)

Fig. 10-2 In electricity, opposite charges attract each other. Like charges repel each other.

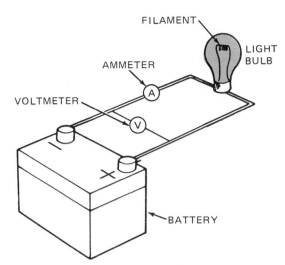

Fig. 10-5 How an ammeter and a voltmeter are connected in an electric circuit. (*Ford Motor Company*)

and a voltmeter connected into a circuit. The ammeter is connected *into the circuit* to measure the current (amperage) flowing. The voltmeter is connected *across the circuit*. It measures the electrical pressure (voltage) that is forcing the current to flow.

Current flowing through a wire creates a *magnetic field* around the wire. The strength of the magnetic field increases or decreases with the amount of current flowing. To avoid "breaking" the circuit to connect an ammeter, an *inductive ammeter* is used (Fig. 10-6). It has an *inductive pickup* that clamps around the wire. The pickup senses the strength of the magnetic field. Using this information, the digital multimeter can then display the amount of current flowing.

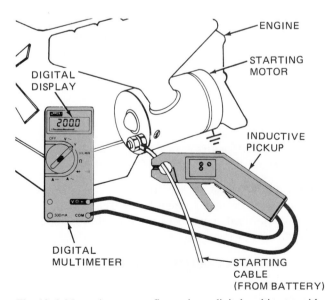

Fig. 10-6 Measuring current flow using a digital multimeter with an inductive pickup. (*John Fluke Manufacturing Company, Inc.*)

A *multimeter* (or *multitester*) is often used to make electrical measurements. In effect, the multimeter is two or more test instruments combined in a single case. A meter with a pointer or needle is an *analog* meter. A *digital* meter (Fig. 10-6) displays numbers.

➤ 10-5 CONDUCTORS AND INSULATORS

Conductors allow current to flow. *Insulators* prevent current from flowing. In the electrical system, conductors carry (*conduct*) current to devices that run on electric current. There are various sizes of conductors, usually covered with *insulation* (Fig. 10-7). The conductors are wires of copper or similar metal twisted together to make *cables*. A cable is more flexible than a single wire of the same size.

The insulation covering the cables prevents the current from flowing in the wrong direction. If the insulation fails, current could take a shortcut through the metal of the car body or frame. This is a *short circuit*. It can cause trouble and damage (➤27-11).

➤ 10-6 CONDUCTOR RESISTANCE

Conductors (wires and cables) offer very little resistance to the flow of electric current through them. The amount of resistance depends on the diameter (size) of the cable (Fig. 10-8) and the length of the cable. Resistance is measured in *ohms*. The symbol for ohms is Ω.

For example, number 10 gauge cable is about 0.100 inch [2.54 mm] in diameter (Fig. 10-8). A 1000-foot [305-m] length of this cable has a resistance of 1 ohm. A 2000-foot [610-m] length has a resistance of 2 ohms. With twice the length, there is twice the resistance.

If the cable is "heavier" (larger in diameter), it has less resistance. A number 4 gauge cable (Fig. 10-8) is 0.200 inch [5 mm] in diameter. A 1000-foot [305-m] length of this cable has a resistance of only 1/4 ohm.

The longer the cable, the farther the electrons (current) have to travel. This means a higher resistance to the current flow. However, the larger the cable diameter, the larger the path in which the electrons move. Its resistance to current flow is lower.

➤ 10-7 TEMPERATURE EFFECT

With most materials, such as copper, the resistance goes up as its temperature increases. The size of the cables used in automotive electrical circuits is large enough to carry the required current without overheating. The *starting cable* (Fig. 10-6) carries the high current needed to operate the starting motor. This cable is much larger than the ignition cable which carries only a small current. Compare the size of these cables in Fig. 10-7.

The heating effect is used to advantage in most light bulbs. They have a coil of *tungsten wire* called a *filament*

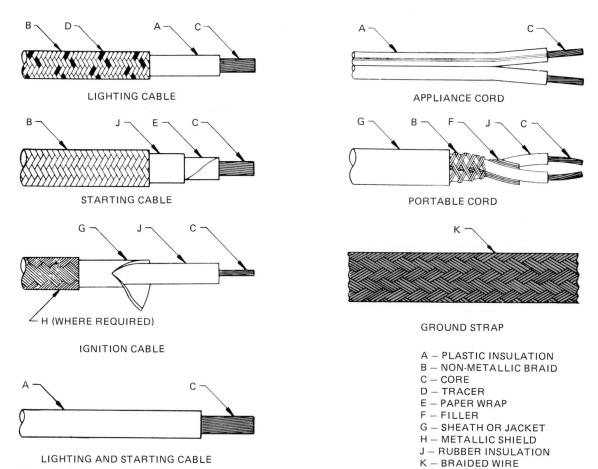

Fig. 10-7 Various types of insulation used on wire and cable. (*General Motors Corporation*)

A – PLASTIC INSULATION
B – NON-METALLIC BRAID
C – CORE
D – TRACER
E – PAPER WRAP
F – FILLER
G – SHEATH OR JACKET
H – METALLIC SHIELD
J – RUBBER INSULATION
K – BRAIDED WIRE

LIGHTING CABLE

STARTING CABLE

IGNITION CABLE

H (WHERE REQUIRED)

LIGHTING AND STARTING CABLE

APPLIANCE CORD

PORTABLE CORD

GROUND STRAP

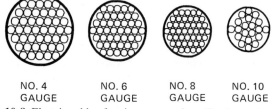

NO. 4 GAUGE   NO. 6 GAUGE   NO. 8 GAUGE   NO. 10 GAUGE

Fig. 10-8 Electric cable of various gauge sizes. The larger the diameter of the cable, the less its resistance.

(Fig. 10-5). When current flows through the filament, it gets so hot that it glows and gives off light.

A few materials have an opposite effect. Their resistance decreases as they get hot. For example, the *sensor* or *sensing unit* (➤25-19) in the engine for the coolant-temperature indicator loses resistance as its temperature increases. It then passes more current to a gauge or light in the instrument panel, which alerts the driver to engine overheating. This type of sensor is a *thermistor*.

NOTE A sensor is a device that receives and reacts to a signal such as a change in temperature, pressure, or voltage. A variety of sensors is used in the automobile.

10-8 OHM'S LAW

Ohm's law relates the current, voltage, and resistance in a circuit. The law says that *current flow is directly proportional to the voltage and inversely proportional to the resistance*. This means that if pressure (voltage) increases, more current (electrons) will flow. If resistance (ohms) increases, less current will flow. This is shown in the formula:

$$I = E/R$$

Where

I is current, in amperes
E is *electromotive force* (voltage), in volts
R is resistance, in ohms

A common cause of electrical trouble is excessive resistance. Not enough current flows. This may be due to loose or corroded connections, broken wires in the cable, or a defective switch.

10-9 ONE-WIRE SYSTEM

The electrons must have a complete circuit through which to flow (Fig. 10-5). They leave the negative terminal, go through the circuit and electrical device, and return to the positive terminal. The return path is *ground*. It is shown in wiring diagrams as ⏚ or ⏛.

To reduce the amount of wiring in the vehicle, the metal engine, chassis, and body parts serve as the return circuit (Fig. 10-9). This is a *one-wire* or *ground-return* system. Only one wire or cable connects to the electrical device. Attaching the case of the device to a grounded part of the car completes the circuit. This is a *case ground*. It is used in starting motors (Fig. 10-6) and other automotive electrical equipment.

Most automotive electrical circuits can be divided into two parts for diagnosis and testing. These are the *insulated circuit* and the *ground circuit*. The insulated circuit is from the battery positive terminal to the light or electrical device (Fig. 10-9). The ground circuit is from the light or device back to the battery negative terminal.

MAGNETISM

➤ 10-10 MAGNETISM

Two types of *permanent magnets* are *bar magnets* and *horseshoe magnets* (Fig. 10-10). Magnets have *poles* (*N* for *north* and *S* for *south*). Unlike poles attract (Fig. 10-11). North attracts south. South attracts north. However, like poles repel each other (Fig. 10-12). North repels north. South repels south.

These actions between magnetic poles make many electrical devices work. For example, the starting motor develops high *torque* (twisting force) so it can crank and start the engine. This torque comes from the attraction between unlike magnetic poles and the repulsion between like magnetic poles.

➤ 10-11 ELECTROMAGNETISM

Most permanent magnets are not strong enough to repel and attract with sufficient force to crank the engine. The

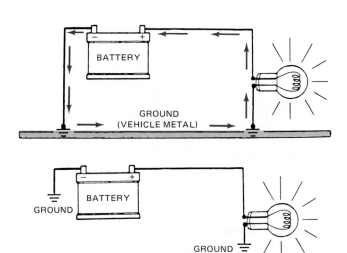

Fig. 10-9 Top, ground-return or one-wire electrical system used in cars and trucks. Bottom, how the ground-return system is shown in electrical diagrams. (*ATW*)

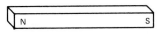
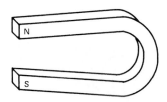

Fig. 10-10 Two types of permanent magnets.

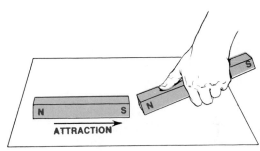

Fig. 10-11 Unlike magnetic poles attract each other.

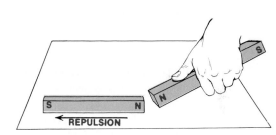

Fig. 10-12 Like magnetic poles repel each other.

magnetism must be greatly strengthened by an electric current (flow of electrons). Electrons have charges of negative electricity which carry a very small magnetic field with them. A single electron has too little magnetism to be noticeable. However, when billions of electrons start flowing in an electric circuit, their magnetism adds up. This effect is *electromagnetism*.

A coil of wire wound on a tube (Fig. 10-13) and connected to a battery becomes a magnet—an *electromagnet*. One end of the coil becomes a north pole, the other end a south pole. The poles can be reversed by reversing the connections to the battery. Sending the current through the coil in the opposite direction reverses the magnetism.

All these actions are used in the motors, alternators, relays, and *solenoids* in the automobile. For example, the solenoid is a coil of wire with a hollow center (Fig. 10-14).

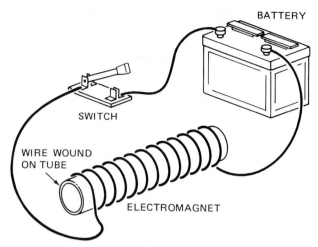

Fig. 10-13 When the switch is closed and current flows from the battery through the circuit, the windings become an electromagnet.

When connected to a battery, the solenoid coil produces a magnetic field. The iron core is pulled into the solenoid by the magnetic field (Fig. 10-14A).

However, if the iron core is magnetized as shown in Fig. 10-14B, the similar poles (S to S) oppose each other. Then the magnet is pushed out of the solenoid coil.

ELECTRONICS

➤ 10-12 INTRODUCTION TO ELECTRONICS

Electronic means "of or pertaining to electrons or electronics." This includes any device operated by electrons. It also includes *semiconductor* devices such as *diodes* and *transistors*.

Electronic systems follow the rules of electricity. Wires must connect the various parts into complete circuits and

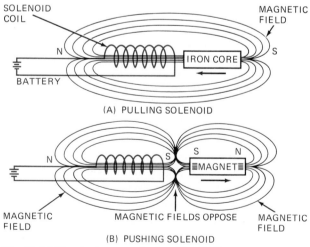

(A) PULLING SOLENOID

(B) PUSHING SOLENOID

Fig. 10-14 Two basic types of solenoid. (*ATW*)

voltage must be available. However, there is a difference. Electrical systems primarily use electric power to produce heat, light, or motion. Electronic systems usually include an *electronic control module* (ECM) with much greater capability (➤10-16). It may *receive* signals, *process* them, make *decisions*, and then send *commands* that control other devices.

➤ 10-13 SEMICONDUCTORS

Materials through which electrons (current) can flow are conductors (➤10-5). Insulators are materials through which electrons (current) cannot flow. There is a third kind of material called a semiconductor. Under some conditions, it can be either a conductor or an insulator.

Semiconductors are used to make *solid-state* devices. They are called "solid-state" because they are solid and have no moving parts except electrons.

➤ 10-14 DIODE

The *diode* is a widely-used semiconductor device. It acts as a one-way check valve for electricity. For example, the alternator in the electrical system (Fig. 10-3) produces electrical current. However, this current is *alternating current* (ac). It alternates, or flows first in one direction and then in the other. The automotive electrical system cannot use ac. It must have *direct current* (dc).

The diode *rectifies* or changes the ac to dc (Fig. 10-15). When the current from the alternator tries to flow in the wrong direction, the diode stops it. The diode lets the current through only when it flows in the other direction. This is the battery-charging direction. Most diodes are combined with other semiconductor devices into an *integrated circuit* (IC) or *computer chip* (➤10-16).

➤ 10-15 TRANSISTOR

The transistor is a semiconductor used to control the flow of an electric current. A transistor can act as a *switch* and stop current flow, or it can act as an *amplifier*. When

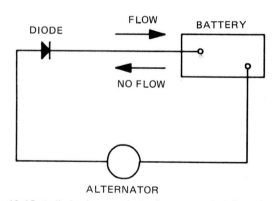

Fig. 10-15 A diode changes alternating current (ac) from the alternator to direct current (dc) for charging the battery.

supplied with a varying small current, the transistor then allows a varying larger current to flow. Like diodes (➤10-14), transistors can be very small.

Figure 10-16 shows how the transistor controls a circuit. When the switch to the transistor is closed (Fig. 10-16A), a 0.35-ampere current flows to the transistor *base*. This turns the transistor into a conductor and allows 4.5 amperes to flow through. When the switch opens (Fig. 10-16B), no current flows to the transistor base. The transistor then switches off the current that was flowing through it.

➤ 10-16 ELECTRONIC CONTROL MODULE (ECM)

Figure 10-17 shows a typical *electronic control module* (ECM). It is also called an *electronic control unit* (ECU), *microprocessor, computer, controller* and other names. The ECM serves as the processor or decision-maker in an electronic control system. The two main parts are the IC chips that contain the *microprocessor* (➤10-17) and the *memory* (➤10-18). The diodes, transistors, and other devices that makeup the chips are often too small to be

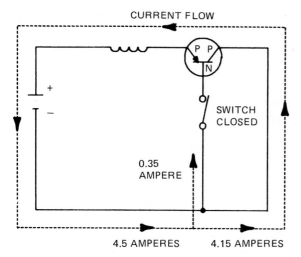

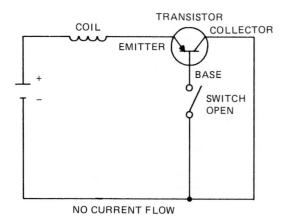

Fig. 10-16 Actions of a transistor to control current flow in a circuit.

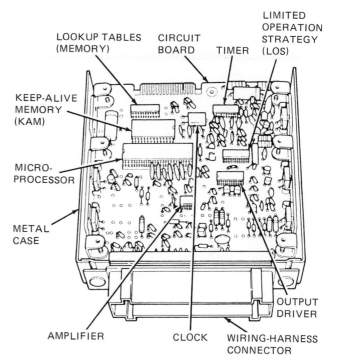

Fig. 10-17 Internal components of an electronic control module (ECM). (*Ford Motor Company*)

easily seen. Many thousands are put together to form a single chip. These chips are the basic components of electronic controls.

➤ 10-17 MICROPROCESSOR

The microprocessor (Fig. 10-18) is also called the *central processing unit* (CPU). It is the solid-state device that controls information flow in a computer. A set of instructions, called a *program*, is designed into the microprocessor to tell it what to do. By following the program, the microprocessor does the calculations and makes the decisions to solve a problem. The problem may be complicated and have many parts. However, the microprocessor solves it quickly, often in thousandths of a second or less.

The microprocessor *chip* is sealed in a protective package or *carrier* (Fig. 10-18). *Pins* connect the various circuits of the microprocessor to the input and output devices (➤1-19). Their signals are received and sent through connections or *terminals* in the ECM wiring-harness connector (Fig. 10-17).

➤ 10-18 MEMORY

The microprocessor cannot store information or *data*. To do its job, the microprocessor needs access to a great variety of information such as specifications and formulas. This information is stored in an electronic storage device called a *memory*.

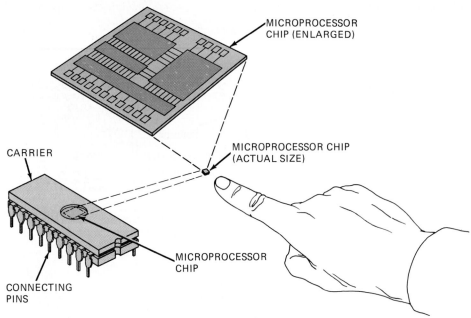

Fig. 10-18 The microprocessor chip is sealed in a carrier and connected through pins to other electronic devices. (*Ford Motor Company*)

The memory stores information (data) for recall later. Computers and microprocessors use two types of memory, *read only memory* (ROM) and *random access memory* (RAM). The microprocessor can "read" the information in a ROM memory, but cannot change it. A *programmable read-only memory* or *PROM* is a removable memory chip. Some types of PROM can be reprogrammed by another program or computer.

The microprocessor can read information from the RAM and change or "write" new information into it. Random-access memories may be *volatile* or *nonvolatile*. A volatile memory stores information temporarily, as long as battery power is available. Disconnecting the battery erases all the stored data. The information stored in a nonvolatile memory is not lost by disconnecting the battery.

Figure 10-17 shows two types of memory chips in an ECM. The *lookup tables* contain data about the car or conditions that are permanently stored on the chip. This is a nonvolatile memory. Disconnecting the battery does not affect it.

The *keep-alive memory* (KAM) (Fig. 10-17) is a volatile memory. Some of the data stored in it includes *trouble codes* if a failure occurs in the system. The keep-alive memory may also make changes in how the vehicle is operating. This is partly based on information from the lookup tables.

If the battery is disconnected, all information in the keep-alive memory is lost. However, nothing is lost from the nonvolatile lookup tables. After reconnecting the battery and starting the engine, the KAM goes to the lookup tables for the needed information. This enables the keep-alive memory to relearn all the information that was stored in it previously.

As long as the battery is connected, a small current flows from the battery to the keep-alive memory. This is called *key-off current drain* (➤30-16). It may eventually discharge the battery unless the engine is started and the battery is charged.

ELECTRONIC ENGINE CONTROLS

➤ 10-19 CONTROLLING THE ENGINE

Most engine systems and devices require some type of management or regulation. Otherwise an "out of control" condition may exist. This could damage the vehicle or engine, especially if the driver fails to correct or control the condition.

Some engine controls are mechanical. An example is the "gas pedal" or *accelerator pedal*. As the driver pushes the pedal down, linkage to the engine opens the *throttle valve*. This allows more air-fuel mixture to flow into the engine cylinders, increasing engine speed and power output. When the driver relaxes the accelerator pedal, the throttle valve partly closes. Less air-fuel mixture enters the engine so it produces less power.

Other engine controls are *electromechanical*. They provide mechanical action when fed an electric current. An example is the solenoid (➤10-11).

➤ 10-20 ELECTRONIC ENGINE CONTROLS

The basic parts of a *control system* (➤1-19) are the inputs, the control unit or decision-maker, and the outputs. The input devices are *sensors*. The output *actuators*. In the car, the decision-maker or controller may be one of three types:

1. The driver of the car.
2. A mechanical governor.
3. An electronic microprocessor.

Most automotive vehicles have an *electronic engine control* (EEC) system (➤10-12). It usually controls the fuel, ignition, and emissions systems (Fig. 10-19). This allows the engine to operate as fuel-efficient as possible. Engine exhaust emissions are minimized while the engine can still produce maximum power if necessary.

Many other components and systems in the car may be controlled by the engine ECM or by a separate microprocessor or computer. These include most components that operate under varying conditions, such as the charging system, transmission or transaxle, suspension, brakes, air conditioning, and driver information systems. Later chapters describe these components and systems.

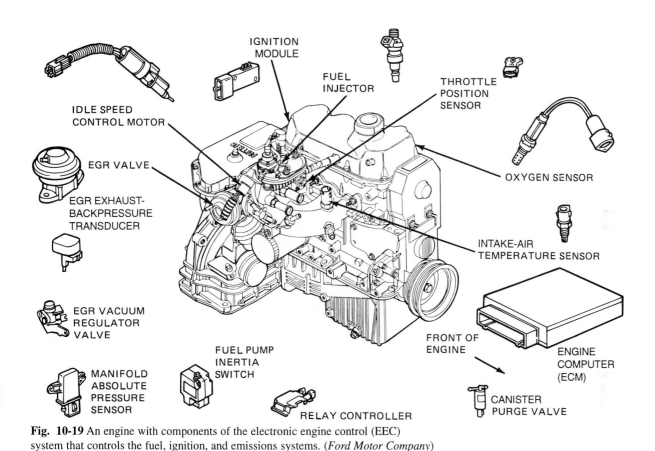

Fig. 10-19 An engine with components of the electronic engine control (EEC) system that controls the fuel, ignition, and emissions systems. (*Ford Motor Company*)

TRADE TALK

current	electrons	resistance	voltage
diode	microprocessor	thermistor	
electromagnet	PROM	transistor	

MULTIPLE-CHOICE TEST

*Select the **one** correct, best, or most probable answer to each question.*
You can find the answers in the section indicated at the end of each question.

1. Electrons flowing in the same direction are called (➤10-2)
   a. a nucleus
   b. magnetism
   c. voltage
   d. electric current

2. Voltage is (➤10-4)
   a. current flow
   b. resistance to current flow
   c. electrical pressure
   d. amperes flow

3. All of the following are true about resistance in a cable EXCEPT (➤10-6 and 10-7)
   a. resistance decreases with increasing temperature
   b. resistance decreases with larger diameter
   c. resistance increases with increasing length
   d. resistance increases with increasing temperature

4. Technician A says according to Ohm's law more current will flow if the voltage increases. Technician B says more current will flow if resistance increases. Who is right? (➤10-8)
   a. A only
   b. B only
   c. both A and B
   d. neither A nor B

5. All of the following are true about the ground-return system EXCEPT (➤10-9)
   a. uses the metal engine, chassis, and body parts as the return circuit
   b. uses two insulated wires to each electrical device
   c. uses one wire and a case ground
   d. uses electrons that leave the negative terminal

6. Technician A says a solenoid with a magnet core is a pull-in solenoid. Technician B says a solenoid with an iron core is a push-out solenoid. Who is right? (➤10-11)
   a. A only
   b. B only
   c. both A and B
   d. neither A nor B

7. Technician A says the diode is a one-way check valve for electric current. Technician B says the diode changes ac to dc. Who is right? (➤10-14)
   a. A only
   b. B only
   c. both A and B
   d. neither A nor B

8. The solid-state device that can act as a switch or an amplifier is a (➤10-15)
   a. diode
   b. transistor
   c. conductor
   d. resistor

9. All of the following are true about the microprocessor EXCEPT (➤10-17)
   a. controls information flow
   b. follows the instructions in its program
   c. performs calculations and makes decisions to quickly solve a problem
   d. permanently stores large amounts of data in its memory

10. The small electric current that flows, with the ignition key off, from the battery to a volatile memory (➤10-18)
    a. is called "key-off current drain"
    b. is also needed by the nonvolatile memory
    c. will discharge the battery overnight
    d. will always set a trouble code

REVIEW QUESTIONS

1. Describe how an inductive ammeter measures current flow.   (➤10-4)
2. Explain the advantages of using a case ground. (➤10-9)
3. What makes solid-state devices "solid state?" (➤10-13)
4. Describe the construction of a computer chip and the two main types of chips in the ECM.   (➤10-16 to 10-18)
5. List the three parts of a control system. Describe the job the EEC system performs in controlling engine operation.   (➤10-20)

CHAPTER 11

PISTON-ENGINE OPERATION

After studying this chapter, you should be able to:

- Explain the basic difference between spark-ignition and diesel engines.
- Describe the two types of piston rings and explain what they do in the engine.
- Name the two types of engine valves and explain the purpose of each.
- Describe the four piston strokes of a spark-ignition engine and explain what happens during each stroke.

➤ 11-1 INTERNAL COMBUSTION ENGINES

An *engine* (Fig. 11-1) is a machine that converts heat energy into mechanical energy. The heat from burning a fuel produces *power* which moves the vehicle. Sometimes the engine is called the *power plant.*

Automotive engines are *internal-combustion* (IC) *engines* because the fuel that runs them is burned *internally,* or inside the engines. There are two types: reciprocating and rotary (Fig. 11-2). *Reciprocating* means moving up and down, or back and forth. Most automotive engines are reciprocating. They have pistons that move up and down, or reciprocate, in cylinders (Fig. 11-3). These are *piston engines.*

Rotary engines have rotors that spin, or rotate. The only such engine now used in automobiles is the *Wankel* engine (➤12-17).

PISTON-ENGINE BASICS

➤ 11-2 TWO KINDS OF PISTON ENGINES

The two kinds of piston engines are the *spark-ignition engine* and the *compression-ignition* (diesel) *engine.* The differences between them are:

- The type of fuel used.
- The way the fuel gets into the cylinders.
- The way the fuel is ignited.

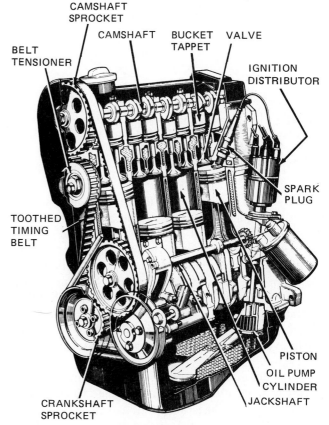

CAMSHAFT SPROCKET

CAMSHAFT BUCKET VALVE
TAPPET

BELT TENSIONER

IGNITION DISTRIBUTOR

SPARK PLUG

TOOTHED TIMING BELT

PISTON
OIL PUMP
CYLINDER
JACKSHAFT

CRANKSHAFT SPROCKET

Fig. 11-1 An inline four-cylinder spark-ignition engine with overhead camshaft. (*Chrysler Corporation*)

The spark-ignition engine usually runs on a liquid fuel such as gasoline or an alcohol blend. The fuel must be highly *volatile* so that it vaporizes quickly. The fuel vapor

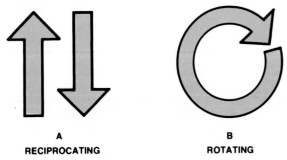

A
RECIPROCATING

B
ROTATING

Fig. 11-2 Reciprocating motion is up-and-down or back-and-forth motion as contrasted with rotary (rotating) motion.

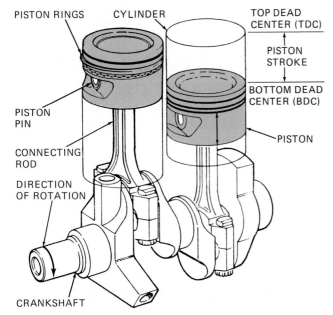

PISTON RINGS
CYLINDER
TOP DEAD CENTER (TDC)
PISTON STROKE
BOTTOM DEAD CENTER (BDC)
PISTON
PISTON PIN
CONNECTING ROD
DIRECTION OF ROTATION
CRANKSHAFT

Fig. 11-3 The two limiting positions of the piston are top dead center and bottom dead center. A piston stroke occurs when the piston moves from BDC to TDC or from TDC to BDC. (*Chevrolet Division of General Motors Corporation*)

mixes with air before entering the engine cylinders. This forms the highly combustible *air-fuel mixture* that burns easily. The mixture then enters the cylinders and is compressed. Heat from an electric spark produced by the ignition system sets fire to, or *ignites,* the air-fuel mixture. As the mixture burns *(combustion),* high temperature and pressure are produced in the cylinder (➤9-9). This high pressure, applied to the top of the piston, forces it to move down the cylinder. The motion is carried by gears and shafts to the wheels that drive the car. The wheels turn and the car moves.

In the diesel or compression-ignition engine, the fuel mixes with air *after* it enters the engine cylinders. The piston compresses the air to as little as 1/22 of its original volume. Compressing the air this much raises its temperature to 1000°F [538°C] or higher. A light oil called *diesel fuel* is then sprayed or *injected* into the hot air. The hot air or *heat of compression* ignites the fuel. The method of ignition — by heat of compression — gives the diesel engine the name compression-ignition engine.

114

Spark-ignition and compression-ignition piston engines are similar in construction. Both have pistons that move up and down in cylinders. The same action takes place in each cylinder, usually at equally-spaced intervals of crankshaft rotation.

Figure 11-1 shows a four-cylinder spark-ignition engine. Each cylinder is about 4 inches [102 mm] in diameter. The *cylinder head* covers the top of the cylinder. The bottom of the cylinder is open. As the engine runs, the pistons (Fig. 11-3) slide up and down in the cylinders.

Figure 11-4 shows the actions in the cylinder of a spark-ignition engine. In (A), the piston is at its lower limit of travel, or *bottom dead center* (BDC). The space above the piston is filled with air-fuel mixture. Next, the piston moves up the cylinder toward *top dead center* (TDC) (Fig. 11-4B). This compresses the mixture. As the piston nears TDC, an electric spark ignites the mixture (Fig. 11-4C). The mixture burns, creating high temperature and a resulting pressure that pushes the piston down the cylinder. This downward movement produces the power that moves the car. The actions are the same in all cylinders and continue as long as the engine runs.

➤ **11-4 PISTONS AND PISTON RINGS**

Pistons (Fig. 11-5) are made of aluminum *alloy* (aluminum mixed with other metals). They weigh about 1 pound [0.454 kg]. The piston is slightly smaller than the cylinder, which allows the piston to slide up and down. This is a *sliding fit.*

Because the pistons are slightly smaller, there is a small gap or *piston clearance* between the piston and the cylinder wall (Fig. 11-6). This gap must be closed.

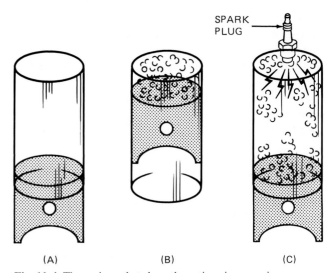

SPARK PLUG

(A)   (B)   (C)

Fig. 11-4 Three views that show the actions in an engine cylinder. (A) The piston is a metal plug that fits snugly into the cylinder. (B) When the piston is pushed up into the cylinder, air-fuel mixture is trapped and compressed. (C) When the compressed air-fuel mixture is ignited by a spark at the spark plug, the high pressure pushes the piston down in the cylinder.

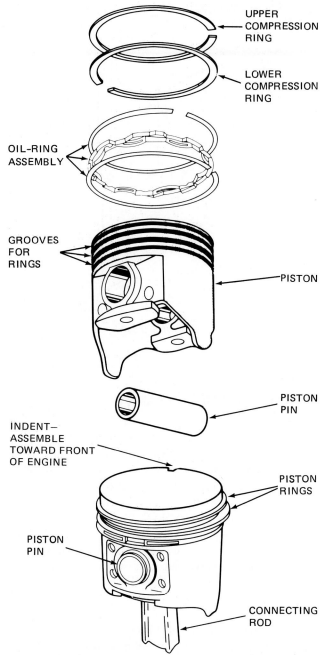

UPPER
COMPRESSION
RING

LOWER
COMPRESSION
RING

OIL-RING
ASSEMBLY

GROOVES
FOR
RINGS

PISTON

PISTON
PIN

INDENT—
ASSEMBLE
TOWARD FRONT
OF ENGINE

PISTON
RINGS

PISTON
PIN

CONNECTING
ROD

Fig. 11-5 Piston and piston rings. Top, rings separated and above the piston. Bottom, piston rings installed in grooves in the piston. Piston is attached to the connecting rod by the piston pin. Only the upper part of the connecting rod is shown.

Otherwise, some of the compressed air-fuel mixture leaks past the pistons and into the crankcase. This leakage is *blowby*. Excessive blowby reduces engine power, wastes fuel, and pollutes the air.

To prevent excessive blowby, *piston rings* are installed on the pistons (Fig. 11-5). The rings are split at one point. This allows them to be expanded slightly, slipped over the head of the piston, and into *ring grooves* cut in the piston.

There are two types of piston rings:

1. *Compression rings* These form a sliding seal between the piston and the cylinder wall.
2. *Oil-control rings* (or *oil rings*) These scrape off most of

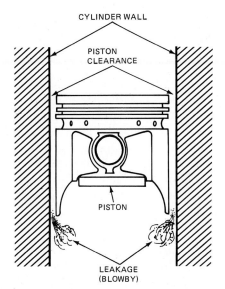

CYLINDER WALL

PISTON
CLEARANCE

PISTON

LEAKAGE
(BLOWBY)

Fig. 11-6 The clearance between the cylinder wall and the piston must be filled. Otherwise, compressed air-fuel mixture or high-pressure combustion gas will "blow by" the piston.

the lubricating oil splashed on the cylinder wall, and return the oil to the crankcase. Chapter 24 describes the engine lubricating system.

➤ 11-5 RECIPROCATING TO ROTARY MOTION

The reciprocating motion of the piston (Fig. 11-4) must be changed to rotary motion to turn the drive wheels. A *connecting rod* and a *crank* on the crankshaft (Fig. 11-7) make

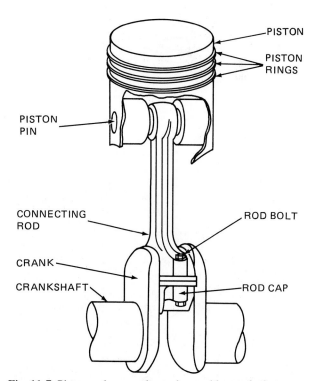

PISTON

PISTON
RINGS

PISTON
PIN

CONNECTING
ROD

ROD BOLT

CRANK

CRANKSHAFT

ROD CAP

Fig. 11-7 Piston-and-connecting-rod assembly attached to a connecting-rod journal on the crankshaft. The piston is partly cut away to show how the piston pin attaches the piston to the connecting rod.

115

this conversion. The connecting rod connects the piston pin in the piston to a *connecting-rod journal,* or *crankpin,* on the crankshaft (Figs. 11-7 and 11-8). The piston pin allows the connecting rod to tilt back and forth.

The connecting-rod journal is an offset part of the crankshaft (Figs. 11-7 to 11-9). It swings in a circle as the crankshaft rotates. A rod cap and bolts attach the connecting rod to the connecting-rod journal. They hold a split bearing (two halves), or *connecting-rod bearing,* in place in the cap and rod (Fig. 11-8). A slight clearance allows the connecting-rod journal to turn inside the bearing. The clearance is normally filled with oil to prevent metal-to-metal contact.

| NOTE | The crankshaft end of the connecting rod is the rod *big end.* The piston end is the *small end.* |

As the piston moves up and down, the rod journal moves in a circle and the crankshaft rotates. Figure 11-10A shows the action as the piston moves down. The connecting rod swings to one side so its lower end follows the rod journal. After the piston reaches BDC and starts up (Fig. 11-10B), the rod tilts to the other side. As the piston moves up and down, the connecting rod tilts back and forth. This allows the big end of the connecting rod to follow the rod journal as it swings in a circle around the crankshaft (Fig. 11-9). The action changes the reciprocating motion of the piston to rotary motion of the crankshaft.

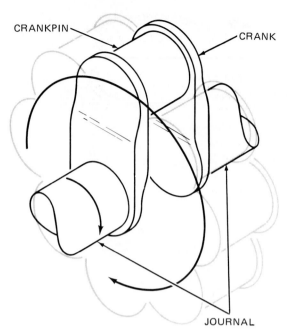

Fig. 11-9 As the crankshaft rotates, the rod journal or crankpin swings in a circle around it.

> ## 11-6 ENGINE VALVES

Most engines have two holes, or *ports* (Fig. 11-10), in the upper enclosed end of the cylinders. (Some engines have more than two ports.) One port is the *intake port.* The other is the *exhaust port.* Air-fuel mixture flows into the cylinder through the intake port. Burned gases leave the cylinder through the exhaust port.

The two ports are open only part of the time. The rest of the time they are closed by the intake and exhaust *valves* (Fig. 11-11). The valves are plugs with long stems that open and close the ports in the cylinder head (Fig. 11-12). When a valve moves up into its port, the valve seals tightly against a *valve seat.* In this position, the valve is closed, sealing the port. When a valve is pushed down off its seat, the port is open. Then the air-fuel mixture or exhaust gas can pass through the port.

The opening and closing of the valves are controlled by the *valve train* (➤11-12). Chapter 14 describes the major valve trains used in piston engines.

HOW THE ENGINE OPERATES

> ## 11-7 ENGINE OPERATION

The actions in the spark-ignition engine can be divided into four parts. Each part consists of a *piston stroke* (Figs. 11-3 and 11-10). This is the movement of the piston from BDC to TDC, or from TDC to BDC. The complete *cycle* of events in the engine cylinder requires four piston strokes. These are *intake, compression, power,* and *exhaust* (Fig. 11-10). The crankshaft makes two complete revolutions to

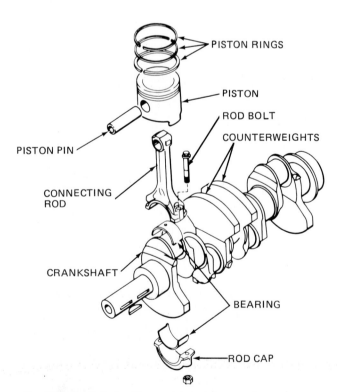

Fig. 11-8 Crankshaft with one piston-and-connecting-rod assembly, showing how the piston attaches through the connecting rod to the rod journal on the crankshaft.

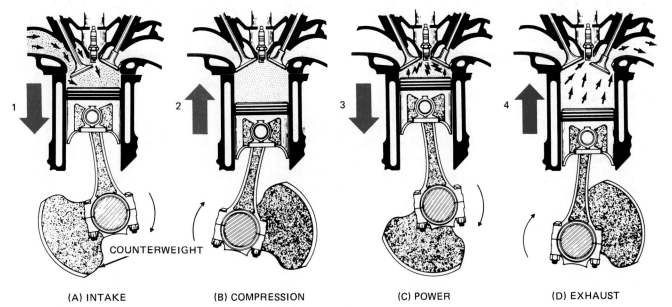

(A) INTAKE	(B) COMPRESSION	(C) POWER	(D) EXHAUST

Fig. 11-10 The four piston strokes. (A) Intake stroke. The intake valve (at left) has opened. The piston is moving downward, allowing the air-fuel mixture to enter the cylinder. (B) Compression stroke. The intake valve has closed. The piston is moving upward, compressing the mixture. (C) Power stroke. The ignition system has delivered a spark to the spark plug that ignites the compressed mixture. As the mixture burns, it creates a high pressure that pushes the piston down. (D) Exhaust stroke. The exhaust valve has opened. The piston moves upward as the burned gases escape from the cylinder.

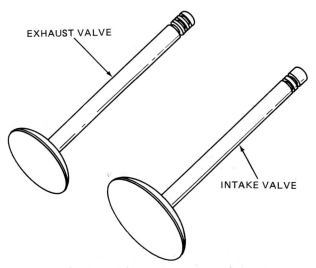

Fig. 11-11 Intake and exhaust valves for one cylinder of an engine. As in many engines, the intake valve is larger.

complete the four piston strokes. This makes the engine a *four-stroke-cycle* engine. It is also called a *four-stroke* or four-cycle engine. The word *cycle* means a series of events that repeat themselves.

➤ 11-8 INTAKE STROKE

During the intake stroke of a spark-ignition engine (Fig. 11-10A), the piston is moving down. The intake valve is open. Air-fuel mixture flows through the intake port and into the cylinder. The fuel system (Chap. 17) supplies the mixture.

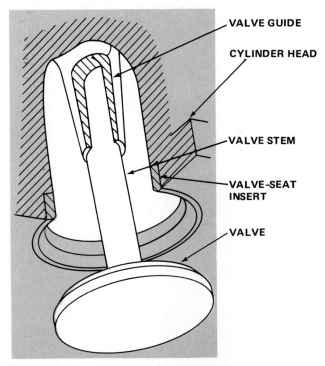

Fig. 11-12 Valve and valve seat in a cylinder head. Some engines have valve-seat inserts for the exhaust valves.

NOTE As the piston moves down, air-fuel mixture enters the cylinder. This is because the piston creates a partial *vacuum* above it. (A vacuum is a space with nothing in it.) With the intake valve open, *atmospheric pressure* forces the air-fuel mixture into the cylinder to fill the vacuum.

As the piston passes through BDC, the intake valve closes. This seals off the upper end of the cylinder.

➤ 11-9 COMPRESSION STROKE

After the piston passes BDC, it starts moving up (Fig. 11-10B). Both valves are closed. The upward moving piston compresses the air-fuel mixture into a smaller space, between the top of the piston and the cylinder head. This space is the *combustion chamber*. The mixture is compressed into 1/8 or less of its original volume. This is like taking a quart of air and squeezing it into about half a cup (Fig. 11-13). The amount that the mixture is compressed is the *compression ratio*. It is the ratio between the original volume (A in Fig. 11-14) and the compressed volume in the combustion chamber (B in Fig. 11-14). If the mixture is compressed to 1/8 of its original volume, then the compression ratio is 8 to 1 (written 8:1). Section 15-10 further describes compression ratio.

➤ 11-10 POWER STROKE

As the piston nears TDC at the end of the compression stroke, an electric spark jumps the gap at the spark plug (Fig. 11-10C). The heat from the spark ignites the compressed air-fuel mixture. The air-fuel mixture then burns rapidly, producing high temperatures of up to 6000°F [3316°C]. These high temperatures cause very high pressure which pushes down on the top of the piston (➤9-9). The connecting rod carries this force to the crankshaft, which turns to move the drive wheels.

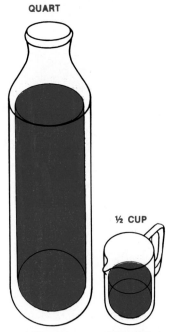

Fig. 11-13 With a compression ratio of 8:1, the air-fuel mixture is compressed to one-eighth of its original volume. This is like compressing a quart of air into half a cup. There are eight half-cups in a quart.

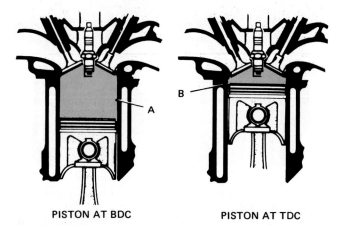

PISTON AT BDC   PISTON AT TDC

Fig. 11-14 Compression ratio is the volume in the cylinder at BDC divided by the volume with the piston at TDC, or A divided by B. A is the air volume. B is the clearance volume.

➤ 11-11 EXHAUST STROKE

As the piston approaches BDC on the power stroke, the exhaust valve opens. After passing through BDC, the piston moves up again (Fig. 11-10D). The burned gases escape through the open exhaust port. As the piston nears TDC, the intake valve opens. When the piston passes through TDC and starts down again, the exhaust valve closes. Another intake stroke begins (Fig. 11-10A) and the whole cycle — intake, compression, power, and exhaust — repeats. This goes on continuously in all engine cylinders as long as the engine runs.

➤ 11-12 VALVE ACTION

In many engines, each cylinder has two valves. One is an intake valve, the other is an exhaust valve. These are shown in Fig. 11-10 and described in ➤11-8 to 11-11. Some engines have more than two valves. These are *multivalve engines*. They have three, four, five, or six valves per cylinder. For example, an engine with four valves in each cylinder is a *four-valve engine*.

The *valve train* is the series of parts that open and close the valves. The action starts at the *camshaft* (Fig. 11-15).

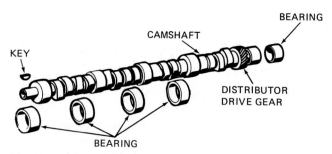

Fig. 11-15 Camshaft and bearings removed from an overhead-valve V-8 engine.

The crankshaft drives the camshaft through *gears, sprockets and chain, or sprockets and a toothed timing belt.* Chapter 14 covers camshaft drives. Most camshafts have a cam for each valve in the engine. Each cam is a round collar with a high spot or *lobe* (Fig. 11-16).

Figure 11-17 shows one of the simpler valve trains. The camshaft mounts overhead, on top of the cylinder head. The *bucket tappet* sits on top of the valve stem. Underneath the tappet is a *valve spring* that holds the tappet up against the cam. When the rotating cam brings the cam lobe down against the top of the bucket tappet, the lobe pushes the tappet down. This compresses the spring and pushes the valve down off its seat. The valve opens. As the cam continues to rotate, the lobe moves away from the tappet. The spring pushes the tappet and valve up until the valve seats. Figure 11-1 shows the alignment of the camshaft, bucket tappets, and valves in an engine.

Chapter 14 describes other valve trains.

➤ 11-13 MULTIPLE-CYLINDER ENGINES

A single-cylinder four-cycle engine has only one power stroke every two crankshaft revolutions. The engine delivers power only one-fourth of its running time. This is during the power stroke. During the other three strokes the piston is not delivering power to the crankshaft.

For a more even flow of power, automotive engines are *multiple-cylinder engines.* They have three or more cylinders. In general, the more cylinders in an engine, the smoother it runs. With six or more cylinders, the power impulses follow each other so closely that they overlap. The more even power flow results in a smoother running engine.

➤ 11-14 FLYWHEEL AND DRIVE PLATE

Even when the power impulses overlap (➤11-13), the flow of power from the pistons to the crankshaft is not smooth. Each power stroke delivers a sudden power impulse to the

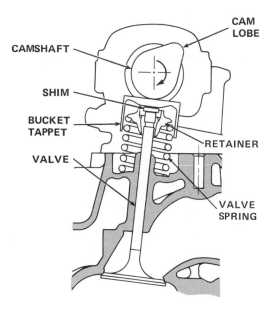

VALVE CLOSED

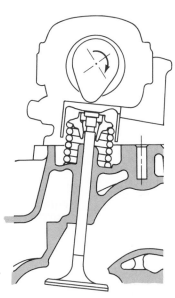

VALVE OPEN

Fig. 11-17 Operation of a cam on an overhead-camshaft engine as the camshaft rotates. Top, the cam lobe is away from the bucket tappet and the valve is closed. Bottom, the cam lobe is pushing the tappet and valve down, opening the valve.

crankshaft. This causes the crankshaft to try to speed up. During the other three piston strokes, the crankshaft tries to slow down. A weight on each end of the crankshaft, a *damper* (➤13-15) on the front and a *flywheel* on the rear, helps keep it turning smoothly.

On vehicles with a manual transmission, the heavy metal flywheel (Fig. 11-18) helps smooth out the power flow. It resists any sudden change in the crankshaft's speed of rotation. Vehicles with an automatic transmission or transaxle have a light *drive plate* (or *flex plate*) with a

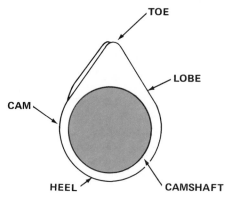

Fig. 11-16 Cam on a camshaft. Note locations of the toe and heel.

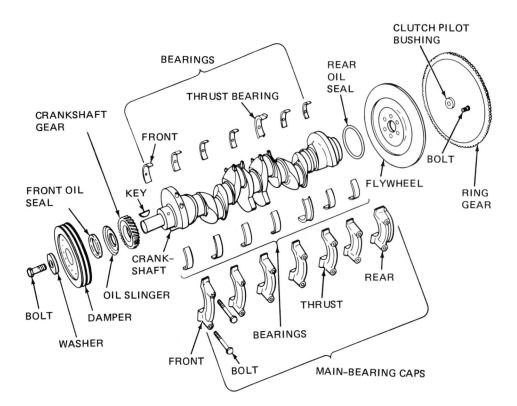

Fig. 11-18 Crankshaft and related parts for an inline six-cylinder engine. The flywheel is to the right. (*Ford Motor Company*)

fluid-filled *torque converter* attached to the crankshaft (Chap. 47). This acts the same as the flywheel to smooth power flow.

The flywheel also serves as the driving member of the clutch in cars with a manual transmission. In addition, the flywheel (and also the drive plate) has a ring of teeth on its outer rim (Fig. 11-18). A small *pinion* gear on the starting motor meshes with these *ring-gear* teeth when the starting motor operates (Chap. 29). This rotates the flywheel and crankshaft to start the engine.

Some engines have a *dual-mass flywheel* or *tandem-mass flywheel* (Fig. 11-19). This is basically two separate

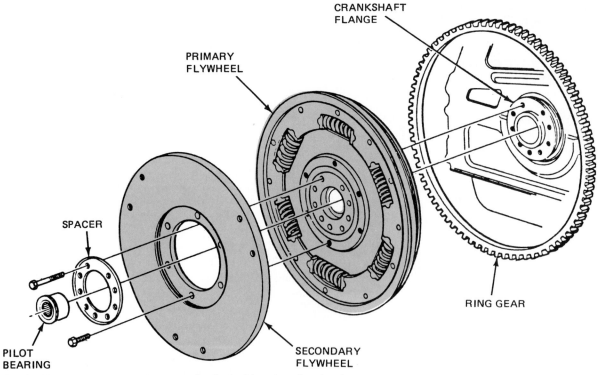

Fig. 11-19 A dual-mass or tandem-mass flywheel with springs that absorb crankshaft torsional vibration. This reduces drive-train noise and vibration. (*Ford Motor Company*)

flywheels — a *primary flywheel* and a *secondary flywheel*. The primary flywheel attaches to the crankshaft flange. As the crankshaft rotates, engine power is transmitted from the primary flywheel, through *torsional springs*, to the secondary flywheel. This arrangement allows the springs to absorb the crankshaft *torsional vibration* (➤13-15) caused by the engine power impulses. The result is a smoother power flow and reduced drive-train noise and vibration.

SUPPORTING ENGINE OPERATION

➤ 11-15 BASIC ENGINE SYSTEMS

A spark-ignition engine requires four basic systems to run (➤1-6). A diesel engine requires three of these systems. They are:

1. Fuel system.
2. Electric ignition system (except diesel).
3. Lubricating system.
4. Cooling system.

Each system is described below. Later chapters cover their operation in detail.

➤ 11-16 FUEL SYSTEM

The *fuel system* supplies gasoline (or similar fuel) or diesel fuel to the engine. The fuel mixes with air to form a *combustible mixture*. This is a mixture that readily burns. Each engine cylinder fills repeatedly with the mixture. Then the mixture is compressed, ignited, and burned (➤11-7 to 11-11).

Figure 11-20 shows one type of fuel system used with spark-ignition engines. The fuel tank holds a supply of fuel. A *fuel pump* sends fuel from the tank to the *fuel injectors*. These are valves controlled by an *electronic control module* (ECM), or computer.

1. FUEL TANK The fuel tank is made of sheet metal, fiberglass, or plastic. It has two main openings. Fuel is pumped in through one opening and out through the other.

2. FUEL PUMP Figure 11-20 shows the fuel pump inside the fuel tank. This is the arrangement used in most vehicles with electronic fuel injection. An electric motor operates the fuel pump.

3. FUEL INJECTORS Fuel injectors, or *fuel-injection valves,* are fluid-control valves. They are either open or closed. The fuel pump sends fuel under constant pressure to the injectors. On the system shown in Fig. 11-20, each cylinder receives fuel from its own injector. This is a *port injection system*. At the proper time for fuel delivery, the ECM turns on each injector. This opens the valve in the end of the injector. The pressurized fuel then sprays out into the air entering the cylinder.

Fuel delivery continues as long as the valve is open. The time is computed and controlled by the ECM. When the proper amount of fuel has sprayed out, the ECM turns off the injector. The valve closes and fuel delivery stops.

Another fuel-injection system uses one or two injectors located above the throttle valve (Fig. 1-13). They feed the proper amount of fuel to the air entering the intake manifold. This is *throttle-body injection* (TBI).

In the past, *carburetors* (Chap. 21) were part of most fuel systems. Carburetors are mixing devices. Air passing through the carburetor picks up and mixes with the fuel to provide a combustible mixture. Most vehicles now have fuel-injection systems.

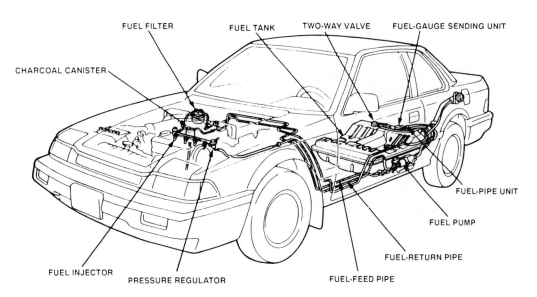

FUEL FILTER FUEL TANK TWO-WAY VALVE FUEL-GAUGE SENDING UNIT

CHARCOAL CANISTER

FUEL-PIPE UNIT

FUEL PUMP

FUEL-RETURN PIPE

FUEL INJECTOR PRESSURE REGULATOR FUEL-FEED PIPE

Fig. 11-20 Fuel-injection system on a car. This is a port-injection system, with a separate fuel injector for each cylinder. (*American Honda Motor Company, Inc.*)

The fuel system delivers a combustible mixture to each cylinder. The upward movement of the piston compresses the mixture. Then the *ignition system* (Fig. 11-21) delivers an electric spark to the spark plug in that cylinder. The spark ignites the compressed air-fuel mixture and combustion follows.

The ignition system takes the low *voltage* of the battery (12 volts) and steps up the voltage as high as 47,000 volts (or higher) in some systems. This high voltage produces sparks that jump the gaps in the sparks plugs. The hot sparks ignite the compressed air-fuel mixture.

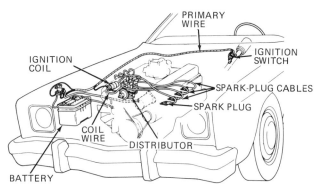

Fig. 11-21 Engine ignition system that uses a distributor. (*Ford Motor Company*)

The engine has many moving metal parts. When metal parts rub against each other, they wear rapidly. To prevent this, engines have a *lubricating system* that floods moving

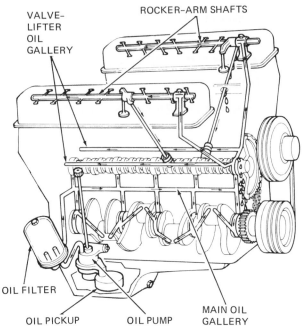

Fig. 11-22 Engine lubricating system, showing how the oil flows to moving engine parts.

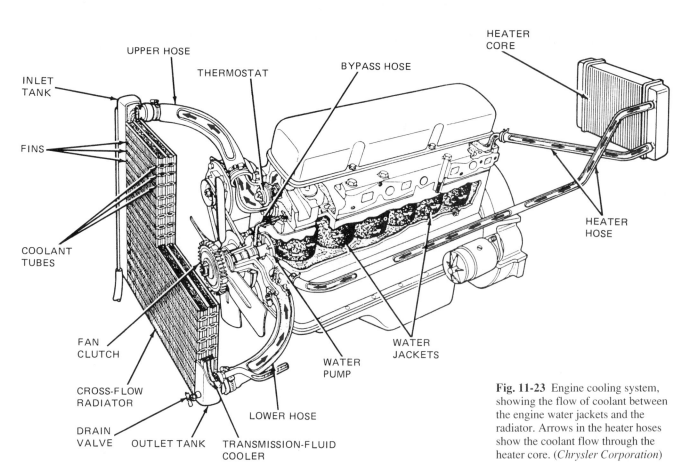

Fig. 11-23 Engine cooling system, showing the flow of coolant between the engine water jackets and the radiator. Arrows in the heater hoses show the coolant flow through the heater core. (*Chrysler Corporation*)

parts with oil (Fig. 11-22). The oil gets between the moving metal parts so they slide on the oil and not on each other.

The lubricating system has an *oil pan* at the bottom of the engine that holds several quarts (liters) of oil. An *oil pump,* driven by the engine, sends oil from this reservoir through the engine. After circulating through the engine, the oil drops back down into the oil pan. The oil pump continues to circulate the oil as long as the engine runs.

➤ 11-19 COOLING SYSTEM

Where there is fire (combustion), there is heat. Burning the air-fuel mixture raises the temperature inside the engine cylinder several thousand degrees (➤9-9). Some of this heat produces the high pressure that causes the pistons to move.

Some heat leaves the cylinders in the *exhaust gas.* This is the remains of the air-fuel mixture after it burns in the cylinders. The exhaust strokes clear out the exhaust gas. The lubricating oil also removes some heat. The oil gets hot as it flows through the engine. Then the oil drops into the oil pan and cools off.

The engine *cooling system* (Fig. 11-23) removes the rest of the heat. The engine has open spaces or *water jackets* surrounding the cylinders. A mixture of water and *antifreeze,* called *coolant,* circulates through the water jackets. The coolant picks up heat and carries it to the *radiator* at the front of the car. Air passing through the radiator picks up the heat and carries it away. This action prevents the engine from getting too hot or *overheating.*

➤ 11-20 OTHER ENGINE SYSTEMS

An engine will run with the four basic systems described above — fuel, ignition, lubricating, and cooling. For use in the car, the engine requires three other related systems. These are the *exhaust system,* the *emission-control system,* and the *starting system.*

The exhaust system reduces the noise of the burned gases leaving the cylinders. Also, it carries the exhaust gases and excess heat safely away from the passenger compartment.

The emission-control system reduces the air pollution from the vehicle and the engine. The *starting system* cranks and starts the engine. A battery provides the electric power to operate the starting motor and the ignition system during cranking. Later chapters describe these systems.

TRADE TALK

blowby	diesel engine	heat of compression	port injection
cooling system	fuel injector	ignition system	
cycle	fuel system	lubricating system	

MULTIPLE-CHOICE TEST

*Select the **one** correct, best, or most probable answer to each question.*
You can find the answers in the section indicated at the end of each question.

1. The two basic types of internal-combustion engines are the (➤11-1)
   a. piston and reciprocating
   b. reciprocating and rotary
   c. reciprocating and pushrod
   d. rotary and spark-ignition
2. The two basic types of piston engines are the (➤11-2)
   a. rotary and reciprocating
   b. pushrod and reciprocating
   c. spark-ignition and compression-ignition
   d. gasoline and spark-ignition

3. The engine produces power by the (➤11-10)
   a. rotation of the crankshaft
   b. valve action
   c. combustion pressure pushing on pistons
   d. up-and-down movement of pistons
4. Technician A says some piston rings control blowby. Technician B says some pistons rings control oil. Who is right? (➤11-4)
   a. A only
   b. B only
   c. both A and B
   d. neither A nor B

5. The two kinds of piston rings are (➤11-4)
   a. pressure and sealing
   b. compression and oil control
   c. oil-scraper and blowby
   d. snap and sealing

6. To change reciprocating motion to rotary motion, the engine has (➤11-5)
   a. a crankshaft and a camshaft
   b. pistons and connecting rods
   c. camshafts and connecting rods
   d. connecting rods and a crankshaft

7. The engine flywheel (➤11-14)
   a. smoothes out the flow of power
   b. serves as part of the clutch on cars with manual transmissions
   c. has teeth that mesh with the starting-motor pinion
   d. all of the above

8. A piston stroke is piston movement from (➤11-7)
   a. BDC to TDC
   b. TDC to BDC
   c. both a and b
   d. neither a nor b

9. The correct order in which the four piston strokes occur in the engine is (➤11-7)
   a. intake, compression, power, exhaust
   b. intake, power, compression, exhaust
   c. compression, power, intake, exhaust
   d. exhaust, compression, intake, power

10. In the diesel engine, the air is compressed to as little as (➤11-2)
   a. 1/4 of its original volume
   b. 1/22 of its original volume
   c. 1/10 of its original volume
   d. 1/50 of its original volume

REVIEW QUESTIONS

1. What is the source of ignition in a diesel engine and in a spark-ignition engine? (➤11-2)
2. Describe the actions of the piston and the intake and exhaust valves during each of the four piston strokes. (➤11- 8, 11-9, 11-10, and 11-11)
3. Explain why automotive engines are multiple-cylinder engines. (➤11-13)
4. Describe how the valves are opened and closed in an overhead-camshaft engine using bucket tappets. (➤11-12)
5. Explain why the flow of power from the pistons to the crankshaft is not smooth. (➤11-14)

CHAPTER 12

ENGINE TYPES AND CLASSIFICATIONS

After studying this chapter, you should be able to:

- List the various ways in which engines are classified and explain what each classification means.
- Explain what *firing order* means, and its importance in engine design and operation.
- Describe the two basic types of valve trains.
- Explain the basic differences between the two-stroke and the four-stroke cycles.

➤ 12-1 ENGINE CLASSIFICATIONS

Automotive engines can be classified according to:

1. Number of cylinders.
2. Arrangement of cylinders.
3. Arrangement of valves and valve trains.
4. Type of cooling.
5. Number of strokes per cycle (two or four).
6. Type of fuel burned.
7. Method of ignition.
8. Firing order.
9. Reciprocating or rotary.

ENGINE TYPES

➤ 12-2 NUMBER AND ARRANGEMENT OF CYLINDERS

American passenger-car engines have four, six, eight, or ten cylinders. Imported cars offer a greater variety. They use engines with three, four, five, six, eight, and twelve cylinders. Cylinders can be arranged (Fig. 12-1):

1. In a row (in line).
2. In two rows or banks set at an angle (V type).

Fig. 12-1 Various ways of arranging engine cylinders. (*ATW*)

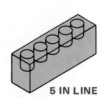
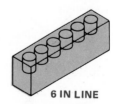
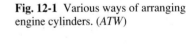

3 IN LINE   4 IN LINE   5 IN LINE   6 IN LINE

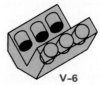
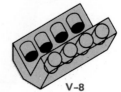

V–4   V–6   V–8

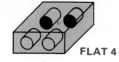
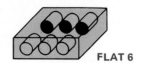

FLAT 4   FLAT 6

3. In two rows or banks opposing each other (flat, pancake, or horizontally-opposed type).

4. Like spokes on a wheel (radial type).

Only the first three are used for automobiles.

➤ 12-3 THREE-CYLINDER ENGINES

Two- and three-cylinder engines are popular in other countries. Several small cars with three-cylinder in-line engines are sold in the United States. Figure 12-2 shows a

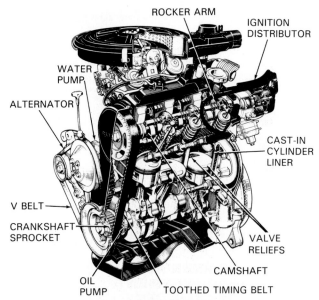

Fig. 12-2 An inline three-cylinder spark-ignition engine with overhead camshaft driven by a toothed belt. (*Chevrolet Division of General Motors Corporation*)

three-cylinder engine for a car manufactured in Japan and sold in this country. The engine has an overhead camshaft and produces 60 horsepower (hp) [45 kilowatts (kw)] at 5500 revolutions per minute (rpm).

To save weight, the camshaft and crankshaft are hollow. The cylinder block is aluminum alloy with cast-in cylinder liners of cast iron. (Cylinder liners are described in ➤13-6). The camshaft is driven from the crankshaft by a toothed timing belt. The ignition distributor is driven directly from one end of the camshaft. The oil pump is on the front end of the crankshaft. A V belt from the crankshaft drives the alternator and water pump.

➤ 12-4 FOUR-CYLINDER ENGINES

Four cylinders can be arranged:

1. In a line.

2. In a V (V-type).

3. Opposed (flat or pancake).

A V-type engine has the cylinders set in two rows (or *banks*) of two cylinders each. The two rows are at an angle to each other. For years, most V-type engines had the two rows of cylinders separated by 90 degrees. Many newer V-type engines separate the cylinder rows by only 60 degrees. This makes the engine narrower so it more easily fits the smaller engine compartments of downsized vehicles.

In an opposed-cylinder engine, two rows of two cylinders oppose each other. The rows are in the same plane, separated by 180 degrees.

1. FOUR-CYLINDER IN-LINE ENGINE Figure 12-3 shows a four-cylinder in-line engine. The camshaft in the

Fig. 12-3 An inline four-cylinder engine with the camshaft in the cylinder block, throttle-body injection, and distributorless ignition. (*Chevrolet Division of General Motors Corporation*)

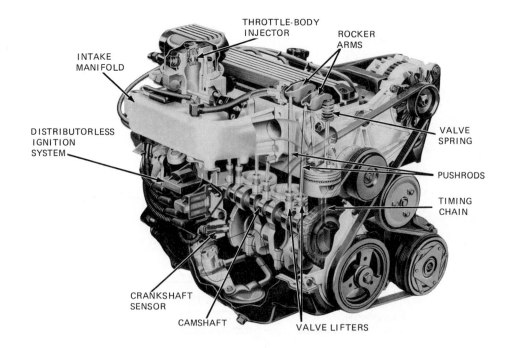

cylinder block is driven by a timing chain from the crankshaft. The valves in the cylinder head are operated through *valve lifters, pushrods,* and *rocker arms.* An engine with this type of valve train is often called an *overhead-valve* (OHV) *engine* or a *pushrod engine.* Chapter 14 describes valves and valve trains.

The engine shown in Fig. 12-3 does not have an ignition distributor. An electronic *distributorless ignition system* (Chap. 7) fires the spark plugs.

Figure 12-4 shows an engine using an *oil-pump drive shaft* to drive the oil pump. This engine has bucket tappets. The camshaft is driven by sprockets and a timing belt. A *bowl-in-piston* forms part of the combustion chamber.

Figure 12-5 shows the General Motors *Quad-4* engine. It has four valves per cylinder and bucket tappets. Sprockets

and a chain drive the two overhead camshafts. One camshaft operates the intake valves. The other operates the exhaust valves.

2. V-4 ENGINE The V-4 engine (Fig. 12-6) has two rows of two cylinders each, set at an angle to form a V. The crankshaft has only two connecting-rod journals. Connecting rods from opposing cylinders attach to the same journal. This type of engine is difficult to balance with counterweights on the crankshaft. To overcome the roughness and vibration, the engine has a *balance shaft.* It turns in the direction opposite the crankshaft.

3. OPPOSED FOUR-CYLINDER ENGINE The Volkswagen Beetle has an opposed (*flat* or *pancake*) air-cooled engine. It is mounted in the rear and drives the rear wheels. Figure 12-7 shows a flat-four engine used by Subaru. The liquid-cooled engine mounts at the front of the

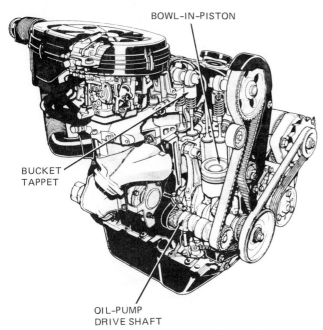

Fig. 12-4 An inline four-cylinder engine. (*Chrysler Corporation*)

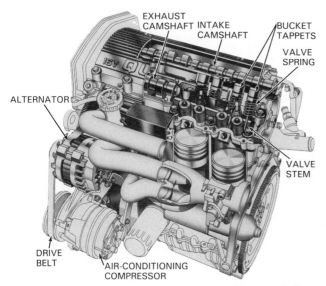

Fig. 12-5 A four-cylinder engine with two overhead camshafts and four valves per cylinder. (*Oldsmobile Division of General Motors Corporation*)

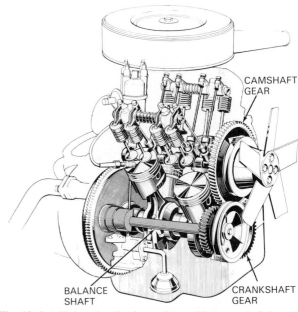

Fig. 12-6 A V-4 engine that has an internal balance shaft for smoother operation. (*Ford Motor Company of Germany*)

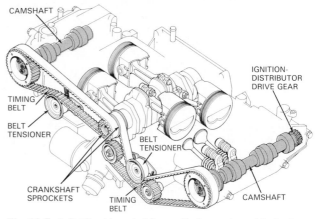

Fig. 12-7 A flat liquid-cooled four-cylinder engine with single overhead camshafts. (*Subaru of America, Inc.*)

car and drives the front wheels. Sprockets and toothed timing belts turn the two camshafts.

Chapter 25 describes air-cooled and liquid-cooled engines.

12-5 FIVE-CYLINDER ENGINES

Several manufacturers have made five-cylinder in-line engines. Mercedes makes a five-cylinder diesel engine. Figure 12-8 shows a five-cylinder spark-ignition engine used in a car with four-wheel drive. The engine mounts longitudinally. The transaxle sends power to both the front and rear drive axles.

Figure 12-9 shows a five-cylinder turbocharged spark-ignition engine. It mounts transversely and drives the front

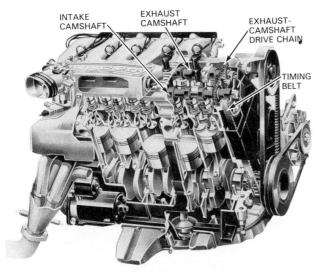

Fig. 12-8 A five-cylinder engine with double-overhead camshafts. (*Audi of America, Inc.*)

wheels. The engine produces 300 hp [220 kw] at 6500 rpm. A separate oil circuit supplies lubricating oil to the turbocharger bearings. Small nozzles direct a spray of cooling oil onto the underside of the pistons. This helps carry away (or *dissipate*) the heat produced by the high power output of each cylinder. A thermostatically-controlled *oil cooler* helps maintain the lubricating oil at the proper temperature. Chapter 18 describes turbochargers.

The five-cylinder engine in Fig. 12-8 has 20 valves—four valves per cylinder. Two camshafts in the cylinder head operate the valves through bucket tappets.

12-6 SIX-CYLINDER ENGINES

Six cylinders can be in line, in a V, or opposed. The valves may be operated by a camshaft in the cylinder block. Or they may be operated by one or two camshafts mounted in the cylinder head.

1. SIX-CYLINDER IN-LINE ENGINE Figure 12-10 shows a six-cylinder inline spark-ignition engine. The valves are operated by pushrods from the camshaft in the cylinder block. The oil pump mounts on the side of the block and is driven by a gear on the camshaft.

2. V-6 ENGINE The V-6 engine has two rows of three cylinders each, set at an angle. The angle between the banks is usually either 60 degrees or 90 degrees. Figure 12-11 shows a pushrod V-6 engine. Figure 12-12 shows a double-overhead-camshaft V-6 engine. The engine has four camshafts, two in each cylinder head. A timing chain turns the idler sprocket. It then drives the timing belt which rotates the four camshafts.

3. OPPOSED SIX-CYLINDER ENGINE Ferrari, Porsche, and Subaru make opposed six-cylinder engines with overhead camshafts (Fig. 12-13). The layout of the

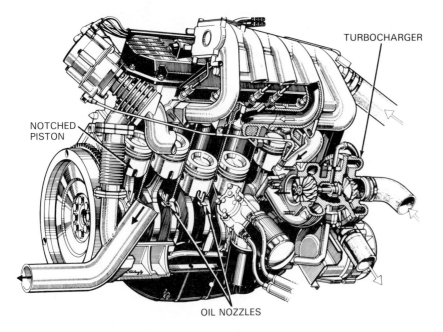

Fig. 12-9 A turbocharged five-cylinder engine with double-overhead camshafts and oil-cooled pistons. (*Volkswagen of America, Inc.*)

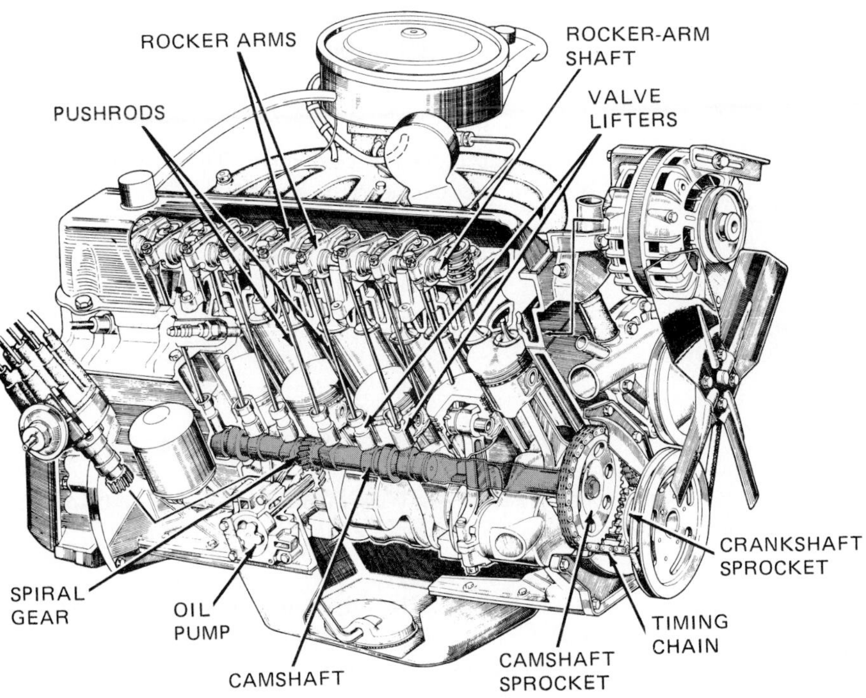

Fig. 12-10 An inline six-cylinder engine. The cylinders are slanted to permit a lower hood line. (*Chrysler Corporation*)

ROCKER ARMS

ROCKER-ARM SHAFT

PUSHRODS

VALVE LIFTERS

SPIRAL GEAR

OIL PUMP

CAMSHAFT

CAMSHAFT SPROCKET

TIMING CHAIN

CRANKSHAFT SPROCKET

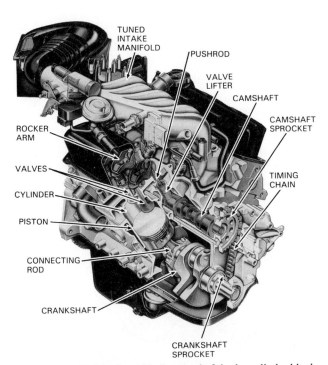

TUNED INTAKE MANIFOLD

PUSHROD

VALVE LIFTER

CAMSHAFT

CAMSHAFT SPROCKET

ROCKER ARM

VALVES

CYLINDER

PISTON

CONNECTING ROD

CRANKSHAFT

TIMING CHAIN

CRANKSHAFT SPROCKET

Fig. 12-11 A V-6 engine with the camshaft in the cylinder block and the valves operated by pushrods. (*Ford Motor Company*)

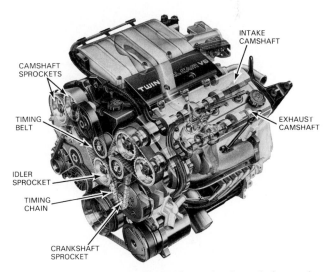

CAMSHAFT SPROCKETS

TIMING BELT

IDLER SPROCKET

TIMING CHAIN

CRANKSHAFT SPROCKET

INTAKE CAMSHAFT

EXHAUST CAMSHAFT

Fig. 12-12 A V-6 engine with double overhead camshafts, two in each cylinder head. (*Pontiac Division of General Motors Corporation*)

engines is similar to Fig. 12-7, with one more cylinder added to each bank.

➤ 12-7 V-8 ENGINES

The V-8 engine has two four-cylinder rows, or banks, set at a 90-degree angle. The engine is like two four-cylinder

engines mounted on a single crankcase and using a single crankshaft. The crankshaft has four crankpins. Connecting rods from opposing cylinders are attached to a single crankpin. Therefore, each crankpin has two connecting rods attached to it.

The V-8 engine shown in Fig. 12-14 has the camshaft in the cylinder block. Pushrods operate the valves. Figure 12-15 shows the double-overhead-camshaft V-8 engine used in the Chevrolet Corvette. There are four valves per cylinder, for a total of 32 valves in the cylinder heads. A chain from the crankshaft drives an *idler sprocket*. It drives the timing chain that turns the camshafts.

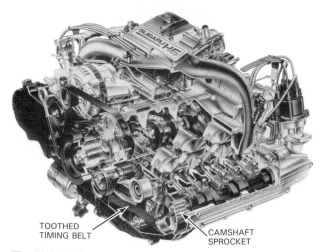

Fig. 12-13 A flat or opposed six-cylinder engine with a single overhead camshaft in each cylinder head. (*Subaru of America, Inc.*)

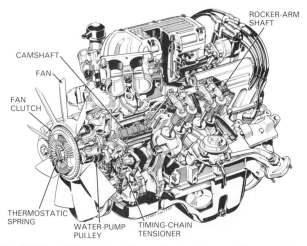

Fig. 12-14 A V-8 engine with overhead valves and the camshaft in the cylinder block. (*Ford Motor Company*)

➤ ## 12-8 TWELVE- AND SIXTEEN-CYLINDER ENGINES

These engines have been used in passenger cars, buses, trucks, and industrial equipment. The cylinders are most often in two banks (V or opposed). Some designs have three banks (W type) or four banks (X type). Passenger cars with a 12-cylinder engine sold in the United States include BMW, Ferrari, Jaguar, and Lamborghini. No new passenger cars with a 16-cylinder engine are now available.

ENGINE CLASSIFICATIONS

➤ ## 12-9 ARRANGEMENT OF VALVES AND VALVE TRAINS

Engine valves allow the engine to breathe (➤11-12). The intake valves open to admit air-fuel mixture (air only in diesel engines) to the engine cylinders. The exhaust valves open to allow burned gases to exit or exhaust from the engine cylinders. Cams on the rotating camshaft operate the valve train, which opens the valves.

There are several different arrangements of valves and valve trains. All are described in Chap. 14. Differences that affect engine classification include:

a. Location of the camshaft.
b. How the camshaft is driven.
c. Type of valve train.
d. Number of valves per cylinder.

1. CAMSHAFT LOCATION The camshaft (➤11-12) is either in the cylinder block (Fig. 12-14) or on the cylinder head (Fig. 12-15).

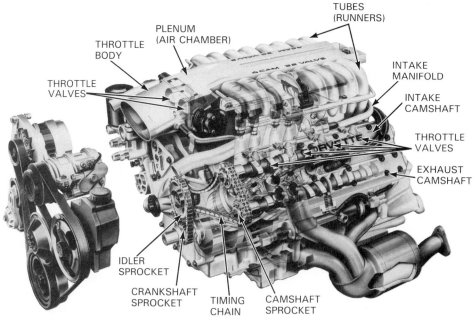

Fig. 12-15 A double-overhead camshaft V-8 engine used in the Chevrolet Corvette. The engine has four valves per cylinder and a total of 32 valves. (*Chevrolet Division of General Motors Corporation*)

2. TYPES OF CAMSHAFT DRIVE Camshafts are driven by *timing gears, sprockets and timing chain,* or *sprockets and toothed timing belt* (Fig. 12-16). Some engines use a combination of timing chain and timing belt to drive the camshafts (Fig. 12-12).

3. TYPES OF VALVE TRAIN Most automotive engines use one of two basic types of valve train (Fig. 12-17). These are *overhead camshaft* (Figs. 12-17A and B) and *camshaft in block* or *overhead valve* (Fig. 12-17C). In each type, the rotating cam lobe actuates the valve train to open the valve.

The camshaft in the cylinder block may also drive the ignition distributor (Fig. 12-18). A shaft from the distributor drives the engine oil pump. An eccentric on the camshaft operates the mechanical fuel pump (Chap. 17).

4. NUMBER OF VALVES PER CYLINDER Some engines have more than two valves per cylinder. Some have three, four, five, or even six valves in each cylinder. Figure 12-15 shows a *four-valve* or *multivalve* engine. The purpose of these added valves is to allow the engine to breathe more freely. The added valves allow more air-fuel mixture to enter and the burned gases to exit more freely.

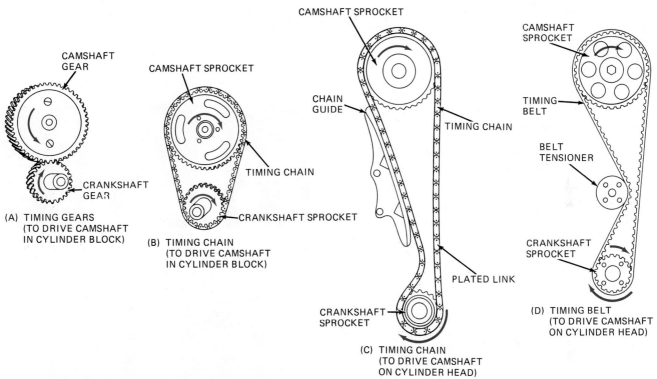

Fig. 12-16 Four methods of driving the camshaft. (*ATW*)

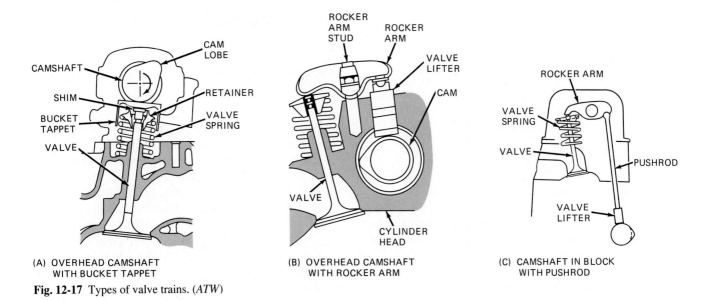

Fig. 12-17 Types of valve trains. (*ATW*)

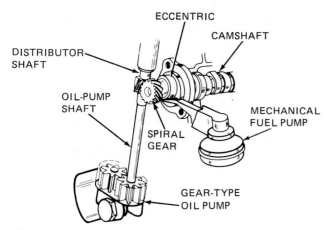

Fig. 12-18 Oil-pump, ignition distributor, and fuel-pump drives. The gear on the camshaft drives the oil pump and distributor. The eccentric (off-center) ring on the camshaft drives the fuel pump. (*Buick Division of General Motors Corporation*)

This improves *volumetric efficiency* (➤15-12) so the engine produces more power.

➤ **12-10 ENGINE ROTATION AND CYLINDER NUMBERING**

Most automotive engines, both spark-ignition and diesel, have *standard rotation*. This means that the crankshaft rotates in a counterclockwise direction, as viewed from the flywheel or output end of the engine. When you are looking at the front of the engine, the crankshaft rotates clockwise.

The cylinders in an engine are numbered (Fig. 12-19). In most engines, they are numbered in the sequence in which the connecting rods attach along the crankshaft. Cylinder number 1 is usually the cylinder farthest from the output end of the crankshaft. Using this method, the engine can be installed either longitudinally or transversely without affecting cylinder numbering.

In V-type or opposed-cylinder engines, the cylinders may be numbered in sequence in each bank. Cylinder number 1 is farthest from the output end of the crankshaft. Several different cylinder-numbering arrangements are used for V-6 and V-8 engines (Figs. 12-19B and C).

Service manuals often refer to *right-hand* or *left-hand* locations of parts that are near or on the engine. Cylinder bank and accessory locations are *right* or *left* when the engine is viewed from the output end.

➤ **12-11 FIRING ORDER**

The *firing order* is the sequence in which the cylinders deliver their power strokes. It is designed into the engine. The crankpin and camshaft arrangement determine the firing order. In most engines, the firing order evenly distributes the power strokes along the crankshaft (Fig. 12-20). Most engine designs avoid firing two cylinders, one after the other, at the same end of the crankshaft.

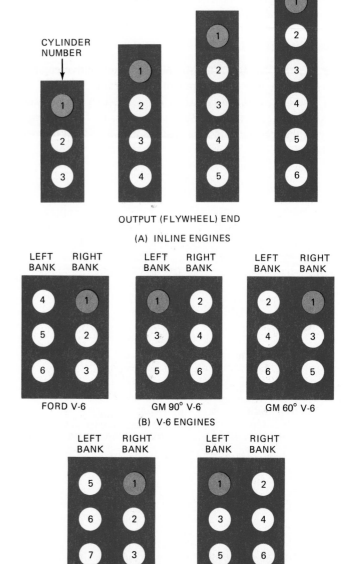

Fig. 12-19 Cylinder numbering for inline and V-type engines. (*ATW*)

Firing orders for the same type of engine may differ. Two firing orders for in-line four-cylinder engines are 1–3–4–2 and 1–2–4–3. In-line six-cylinder engines use 1–5–3–6–2–4 (Fig. 12-20). A Chrysler V-6 and two General Motors V-6 engines (Fig. 12-19) all have the same firing order of 1–2–3–4–5–6. Ford V-6 engines have fired 1–4–2–5–3–6 and 1–4–2–3–5–6. A firing order used on V-8 engines by Chrysler and General Motors is 1–8–4–3–6–5–7–2 (Fig. 12-20). Ford V-8 engines use 1–5–4–2–6–3–7–8 and 1–3–7–2–6–5–4–8.

Many engine service jobs require that you know the

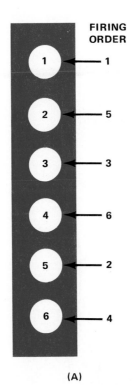

FIRING ORDER

1	1
2	5
3	3
4	6
5	2
6	4

(A)

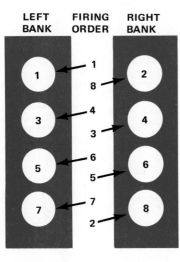

LEFT BANK	FIRING ORDER	RIGHT BANK
1	1 / 8	2
3	4 / 3	4
5	6 / 5	6
7	7 / 2	8

(B)

Fig. 12-20 Firing order related to cylinder numbering.

cylinder numbering and firing order. Some engines have cylinder-numbering identification, firing order, and direction of ignition-distributor rotation cast into or imprinted on the intake manifold. The information is also in the manufacturer's service manual.

The complete firing order of a four-cycle engine represents two complete revolutions of the crankshaft. This is 720 degrees of crankshaft rotation. Most engines are "even firing." This means, for example, that in an in-line six-cylinder engine a firing impulse occurs every 120 degrees of crankshaft rotation (720 ÷ 6 = 120). The firing order of this engine is 1–5–3–6–2–4. When piston number 1 is at TDC on the end of the compression stroke, piston number

6 is at TDC on the end of the exhaust stroke. To determine the two pistons that are moving up and down together (*piston pairs*), divide the firing order in half. Then place the second half under the first half:

$$\frac{1\text{--}5\text{--}3}{6\text{--}2\text{--}4}$$

The piston pairs for this inline six-cylinder engine are 1 and 6, 5 and 2, and 3 and 4.

➤ 12-12 CLASSIFICATION BY COOLING

Almost all automotive engines are liquid-cooled (Fig. 11-23). The liquid-cooled engine circulates coolant (➤11-19) between the engine and the radiator to remove excess heat. Chapter 25 describes engine cooling systems.

The Volkswagen Beetle engine, and some others, are air-cooled. They have metal fins on the cylinders to help carry away excess heat. The small one- and two-cylinder engines in power lawn mowers and similar equipment are air-cooled.

➤ 12-13 CLASSIFICATION BY CYCLES

Piston engines operate on either the *two-stroke cycle* or the four-stroke cycle. Automotive engines are four-stroke-cycle engines (Chap. 11). Every fourth piston stroke is a power stroke. In the two-stroke cycle, every other piston stroke is a power stroke. This provides a power stroke during each crankshaft revolution. Figure 12-21A shows the operation of the two types of engine.

The two-stroke-cycle engine produces twice as many power strokes at the same crankshaft speed (rpm) as the four-stroke-cycle engine. However, this does not make the two-stroke engine twice as powerful. In the two-stroke-cycle engine, the piston opens the transfer and exhaust ports (Fig. 12-21A). Then, there is always some mixing of the fresh air-fuel mixture with the exhaust gases. This reduces the amount of fresh air-fuel mixture that enters. Also, only part of the piston stroke is devoted to getting air-fuel mixture into the cylinder. This further reduces the amount of air-fuel mixture that enters. And finally, only part of the downward stroke (the power stroke) produces power.

Figure 12-21B shows a three-cylinder, two-stroke engine that Chrysler is developing for possible automotive use. The engine has no valve train and uses *direct injection* which injects the fuel directly into the cylinder. Some of the advantages of this engine include size and weight reductions, with a resulting improvement in fuel economy over other engines. However, before the two-stroke engine can be installed in new vehicles, it must meet the exhaust emissions standards and be as durable as a comparable four-stroke engine.

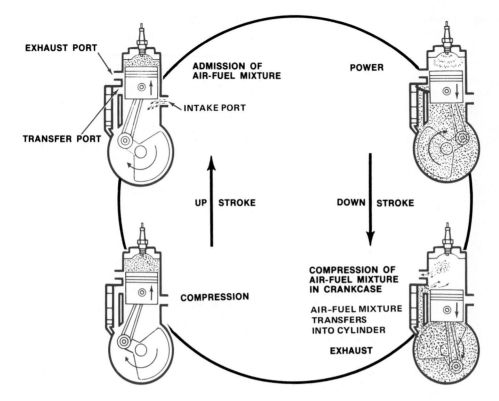

(a) TWO STROKES—ONE REVOLUTION

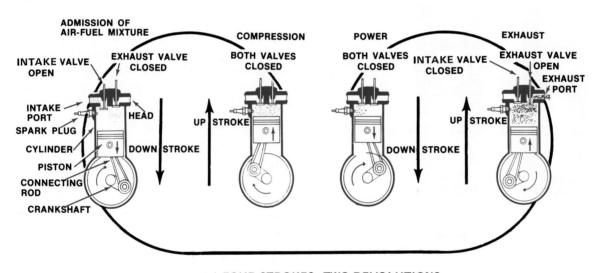

(b) FOUR STROKES—TWO REVOLUTIONS

Fig. 12-21A Comparison of the operation of a two-cycle engine with a four-cycle engine.

➤ **12-14 CLASSIFICATION BY FUEL**

Spark-ignition engines usually burn gasoline or *gasohol*. This is a blend of gasoline and alcohol. Some spark-ignition engines, especially in buses and trucks, burn *liquified petroleum gas* (LPG) or *compressed natural gas* (CNG). Diesel engines usually burn a light oil called *diesel fuel*. Flexible fuel vehicles (➤16-11) can burn gasoline or

alcohol-blend fuels. Chapter 16 describes engine fuels.

➤ **12-15 ADIABATIC ENGINES**

Adiabatic means "without loss of heat." In the standard piston engine, most of the heat energy in the fuel is lost. Instead of producing power, the heat leaves the engine

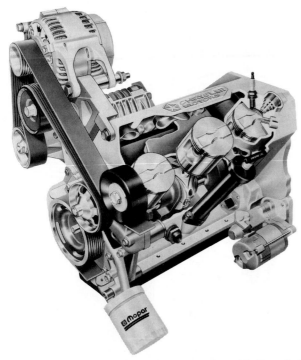

Fig. 12-21B A three-cylinder, two-stroke engine with direct fuel injection, being developed for possible automotive use. (*Chrysler Corporation*)

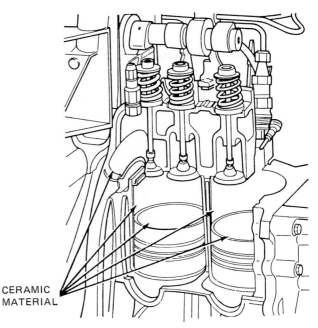

CERAMIC
MATERIAL

Fig. 12-22 Ceramic-coated parts in a diesel engine. (*Ford Motor Company*)

through the lubricating system, cooling system, and exhaust gas.

The hotter an engine runs, the higher its efficiency. More of the heat energy in the fuel is then used to move the car. However, simply raising the operating temperature of the piston engine will not work. The metal parts will melt or fail. Under development is the *adiabatic diesel engine* (Fig. 12-22). It uses parts made or coated with a *ceramic* material. This allows the engine to operate at a much higher temperature. Then more of the energy in the fuel produces power. Studies show that a small car with an adiabatic engine could get 100 mpg (42.5 km/L).

➤ 12-16 ROTARY ENGINES

In rotary engines, rotors spin to produce power. There are two types, only one of which is now used in passenger cars. The two are the *gas-turbine engine* and the *Wankel engine*. There has been much research on gas turbines, but so far no practical automotive engine has resulted. In the gas turbine, burning air-fuel mixture spins a power turbine that is geared to the car wheels.

The gas turbine is used successfully in airplanes, helicopters, and electric generating systems. In these installations, it operates mostly at constant speed. It does not do well in automotive vehicles. One reason is a noticeable delay in acceleration after the driver depresses the throttle. Also, the power-turbine section, which gets very hot and runs at very high speed, is made of expensive materials.

This makes the gas turbine cost more to manufacture than a comparable piston engine. However, a future oil shortage and the ability to operate on a variety of fuels could help make the gas turbine an important alternative powerplant.

➤ 12-17 WANKEL ENGINE

The Wankel engine (Fig. 12-23) has rotors that spin in oval chambers shaped like a fat figure 8. It is a *rotary-combustion* (RC) engine because the combustion chambers are in, and therefore rotate with, the rotors. The engine operates on the four-stroke cycle.

The four actions—intake, compression, power, and exhaust—are going on at the same time around each rotor while the engine is running. Figure 12-24 shows the action. Follow lobe A around, starting at the upper left Ⓘ. As it moves, the space between A and C expands. This causes air-fuel mixture to fill the space. Then, when lobe C passes the intake port, the space (A to C) is sealed off.

Meantime, the space between A and B has been greatly reduced. It has held air-fuel mixture (like 3 and 4 between lobes A and C). This mixture between A and B has been compressed. Now, a spark at the spark plug ignites the mixture. It burns and forces the rotor to turn. As lobe B passes the exhaust port, the burned mixture exhausts.

The "strokes" of intake, compression, power, and exhaust follow continuously in each rotor chamber. This occurs as long as the engine is running.

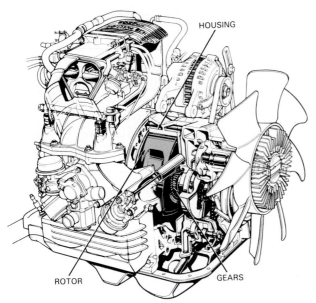

Fig. 12-23 A two-rotor Wankel engine. (*Mazda Motors of America, Inc.*)

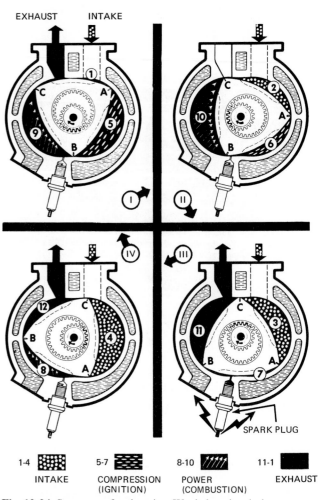

1-4	5-7	8-10	11-1
INTAKE	COMPRESSION (IGNITION)	POWER (COMBUSTION)	EXHAUST

Fig. 12-24 Sequence of actions in a Wankel engine during one complete revolution of the rotor. (*Mazda Motors of America, Inc.*)

TRADE TALK

adiabatic	horizontally-opposed engine	piston pairs	Wankel engine
firing order	overhead-camshaft engine	standard rotation	
four-stroke engine	overhead-valve engine	two-stroke engine	

MULTIPLE-CHOICE TEST

*Select the **one** correct, best, or most probable answer to each question.*
You can find the answers in the section indicated at the end of each question.

1. The three basic cylinder arrangements for automotive engines are (➤12-2)
   a. flat, radial, V
   b. in a row, in-line, opposed
   c. in-line, V, opposed
   d. V, double line, opposed

2. An engine with the camshaft in the block operates the valves through (➤12-4)
   a. valve lifters
   b. pushrods
   c. rocker arms
   d. all of the above

3. In the valve train using bucket tappets, the camshaft is (➤12-5)
   a. in the cylinder block
   b. directly above the tappet
   c. is operated by a pushrod
   d. is operated by a rocker arm
4. Six cylinders can be (➤12-6)
   a. in line, V, or opposed
   b. radially, opposed, and lined
   c. aligned, in a row, and overhead
   d. adjusted to improve volumetric efficiency
5. A V-8 engine has (➤12-7)
   a. two four-cylinder rows or banks
   b. a crankshaft with four crankpins
   c. two connecting rods attached to each crankpin
   d. all of the above
6. When you look at the flywheel end of an engine and see the crankshaft rotating counterclockwise, the engine has (➤12-10)
   a. reverse rotation
   b. clockwise rotation
   c. standard rotation
   d. standard firing order
7. The cylinder banks of an engine are identified as (➤12-10)
   a. right or left when viewed from the front of the engine
   b. right or left when viewed from the output end
   c. both a and b
   d. neither a nor b

8. The firing order is the (➤12-11)
   a. order in which the cylinders are numbered
   b. sequence in which the cylinders deliver their power strokes
   c. sequence in which the connecting rods attach along the crankshaft
   d. direction in which the crankshaft rotates
9. In an even-firing six-cylinder engine, a firing impulse occurs every (➤12-11)
   a. 60 degrees of crankshaft rotation
   b. 720 degrees of crankshaft rotation
   c. 30 degrees of crankshaft rotation
   d. 120 degrees of crankshaft rotation
10. The two-stroke-cycle engine (➤12-13)
   a. produces a power stroke every crankshaft revolution
   b. is twice as powerful as a similar four-stroke-cycle engine
   c. is used in most higher-priced cars
   d. produces a power stroke every other crankshaft revolution

REVIEW QUESTIONS

1. Describe two ways to drive the engine oil pump. (➤12-3 and 12-4)
2. Describe three ways of driving the engine camshaft. (➤12-9)
3. What are the two basic types of valve trains for automobile engines? (➤12-9)

4. In most engines, how are cylinders numbered and where is cylinder number 1 usually located? (➤12-10)
5. Give the firing order of an in-line six-cylinder engine, and list the piston pairs that travel together. (➤12-11)

CHAPTER 13

ENGINE CONSTRUCTION

After studying this chapter, you should be able to:

- Describe the construction of cylinder blocks and cylinder heads.
- Explain the purpose of intake and exhaust manifolds.
- Explain the purpose and operation of vibration dampers.
- Describe engine bearings, their purpose, requirements, and how they are lubricated.
- Discuss the purpose, construction, operation, and lubrication of pistons and piston rings.
- Describe the construction and operation of engine mounts and torque struts.

➤ 13-1 PISTON-ENGINE CONSTRUCTION

Spark-ignition and diesel engines are similar in construction. Both have cylinder blocks, cylinder heads, crankshafts, and bearings. Also, both have pistons, connecting rods, and valve trains (Chap. 14). The main difference between spark-ignition parts and diesel engine parts is that diesel parts are usually heavier and stronger. This is because the internal pressures are higher in diesel engines.

➤ 13-2 CYLINDER BLOCK

The cylinder block (Fig. 13-1) is the foundation of the engine. All other engine parts are assembled in or attached to the cylinder block (Fig. 13-2). Most blocks are cast from gray iron (*cast iron*) or iron mixed with other metals such as nickel and chromium. Some blocks are cast from aluminum alloy.

The block (Fig. 13-3) is a casting that has large holes for the cylinder bores. It also has *water jackets* and *coolant passages*. Water jackets are the spaces between the cylinder bores and the outer shell of the block. Coolant flows through these spaces to pick up heat and carry it away from the engine.

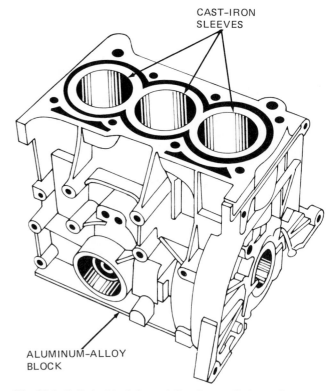

CAST-IRON SLEEVES

ALUMINUM-ALLOY BLOCK

Fig. 13-1 Cylinder block for an inline three-cylinder engine. (*Chevrolet Division of General Motors Corporation*)

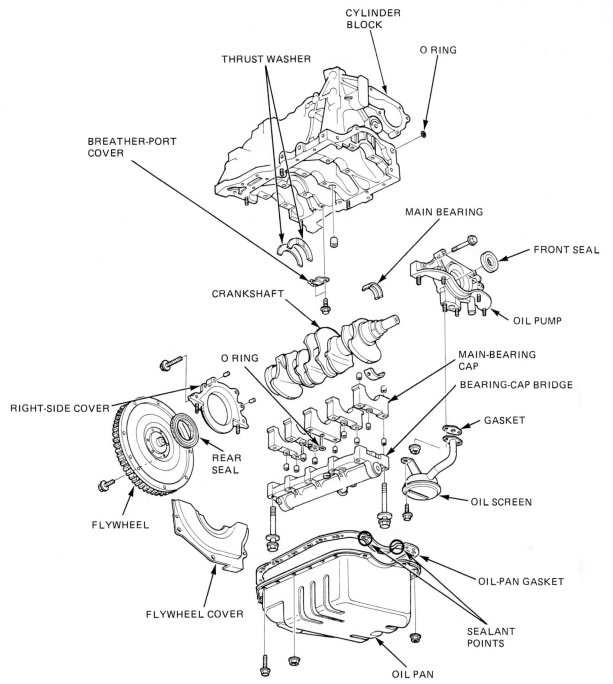

Fig. 13-2 Internal parts of a cylinder block for an inline four-cylinder engine. (*American Honda Motor Company, Inc.*)

The core *clean-out holes* (Fig. 13-3) allow removal of the cores that formed the water jackets. The cores are made of sand and shaped like water jackets. They are put into place and hot metal is poured around them. After the metal has cooled and hardened, the cores are broken up and removed through the clean-out holes. Then the holes are sealed with plugs. These are called *core plugs, freeze plugs,* or *expansion plugs.* If coolant in the block starts to freeze, the coolant expands and pushes the plugs out. This may provide some protection against a cracked block.

However, coolant that contains the proper amount of antifreeze is not likely to freeze.

➤ **13-3 MACHINING THE BLOCK**

After the cores are removed, the block is cleaned and machined. Then:

1. Holes are drilled for attaching various parts.
2. Cylinders are machined and finished.

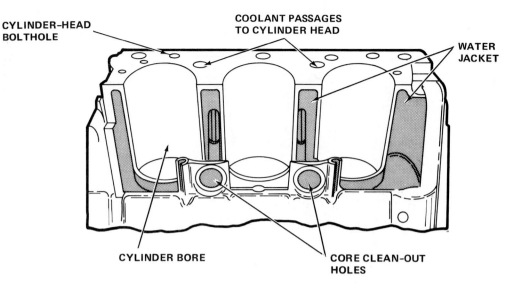

CYLINDER-HEAD BOLTHOLE

COOLANT PASSAGES TO CYLINDER HEAD

WATER JACKET

CYLINDER BORE

CORE CLEAN-OUT HOLES

Fig. 13-3 Internal construction of one bank of a V-6 cylinder block. (*General Motors Corporation*)

3. If the camshaft is to be in the block, camshaft-bearing holes are bored.
4. Surfaces to which parts attach are machined and finished.
5. Oil passages are drilled.
6. Valve-lifter bores are machined (pushrod engines).
7. Coolant passages are cleaned out.

➤ 13-4 PARTS ATTACHED TO AND INSTALLED IN BLOCK

1. The crankshaft, with main bearings, is attached to the bottom of the block (Fig. 13-2). (In the shop, the block is normally upside down while the crankshaft is installed.) The crankshaft fits into *bearings* in the *main-bearing caps* and block (Fig. 13-2).
2. The pistons, with rings installed and connecting rods attached, are installed (Fig. 13-4). (In the shop, the block is turned upright for this job.) The connecting rods, with *rod bearings,* are attached to the crankpins on the crankshaft (Fig. 13-2).
3. Other parts, as shown in Fig. 13-2, are installed.
4. The cylinder head with valves and camshaft (on OHC engines) is assembled (Fig. 13-5).
5. After bearing adjustments and installation of the head and oil pump, the oil pan is attached.

Lubricating oil is added to the engine. Then the engine is started and given a running test. Chapters 39, 40, and 41 describe how the engine is assembled in the shop.

When the internal engine parts shown in Fig. 13-2 have been installed, the assembly is a *short block*. A new or *remanufactured* short block is used if the old engine is beyond economical repair. Some parts from the old engine are installed on the short block. They include the cylinder head, oil pan, and front cover. Transferring these parts reduces the cost of the "new" engine.

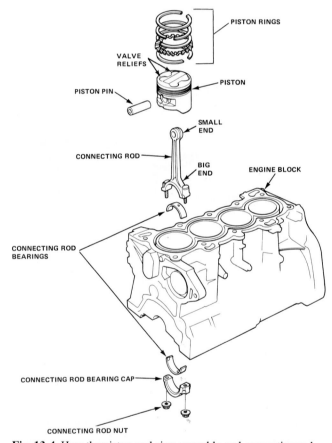

PISTON RINGS

VALVE RELIEFS

PISTON PIN

PISTON

SMALL END

CONNECTING ROD

BIG END

ENGINE BLOCK

CONNECTING ROD BEARINGS

CONNECTING ROD BEARING CAP

CONNECTING ROD NUT

Fig. 13-4 How the piston-and-ring assembly and connecting rod are installed from the top of the block. (*American Honda Motor Company, Inc.*)

➤ 13-5 OIL PAN

The *oil pan* (Fig. 13-2) is plastic or metal. It is shaped to fit on the bottom of the block. A gasket is installed between the pan and block to seal the joint and prevent oil leaks.

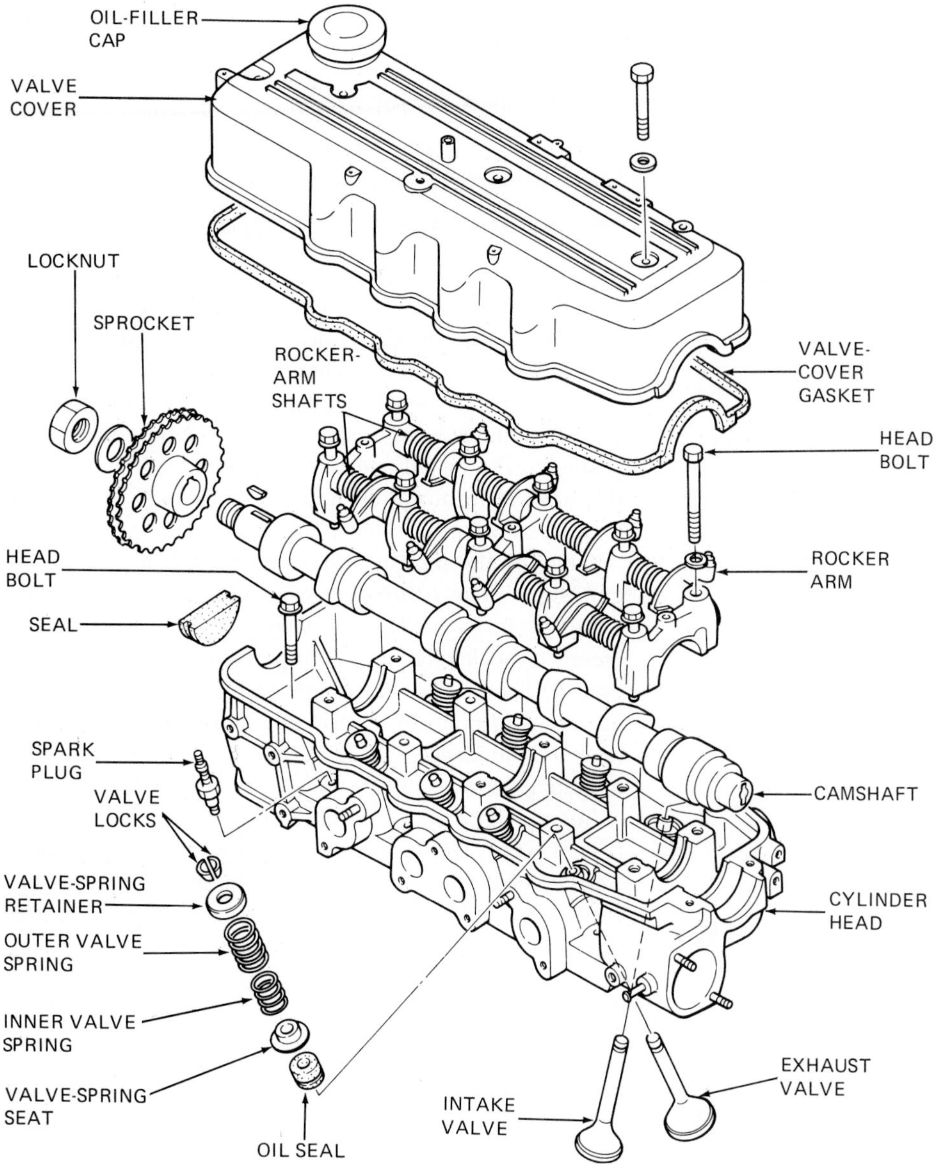

OIL-FILLER CAP

VALVE COVER

LOCKNUT

SPROCKET

ROCKER-ARM SHAFTS

HEAD BOLT

SEAL

SPARK PLUG

VALVE LOCKS

VALVE-SPRING RETAINER

OUTER VALVE SPRING

INNER VALVE SPRING

VALVE-SPRING SEAT

OIL SEAL

INTAKE VALVE

EXHAUST VALVE

CYLINDER HEAD

CAMSHAFT

ROCKER ARM

HEAD BOLT

VALVE-COVER GASKET

Fig. 13-5 Cylinder head for an OHC four-cylinder engine, with the major parts that are attached to and installed in the cylinder head. (*Mazda Motors of America, Inc.*)

The bottom of the block plus the oil pan form the *crankcase.* They enclose, or *encase,* the crankshaft.

The oil pan holds from 3 to 9 quarts [3 to 8 L] of oil, depending on the engine. An *oil pump* (Fig. 13-2) sends oil from the oil pan to the moving engine parts. Chapter 24 describes the engine lubricating system.

Some engines have an *acoustical* oil pan (Fig. 13-6). Pieces of plastic damping material and stamped-steel inserts attach to the flat surfaces inside the pan. When mechanical noise from the engine vibrates the steel pan, the plastic layer prevents the noise and vibration from reaching the passengers.

➤ 13-6 ALUMINUM CYLINDER BLOCK

Many engines have cylinder blocks made of aluminum alloy. Aluminum weighs much less and conducts heat more rapidly than cast iron. However, aluminum is too soft for use as cylinder-wall material. It would wear rapidly. Aluminum blocks have either cast-iron *cylinder liners* or are cast from an aluminum alloy containing silicon particles (➤13-7). Both types of cylinder blocks are used in automotive engines. This reduces vehicle weight and improves fuel economy.

Cylinder liners are sleeves that are either cast into the block or installed later. Cast-in cylinder liners are installed in the mold, and the aluminum is poured around them. They become a permanent part of the block. Two kinds of liners, *dry* and *wet,* can be installed later. Dry liners are pressed in. They touch the cylinder bore along their full length. Wet liners touch the cylinder block only at the top and bottom (Fig. 13-7). The rest of the liner touches only the coolant. Pressed-in dry liners and wet liners are replaced if they become worn or damaged.

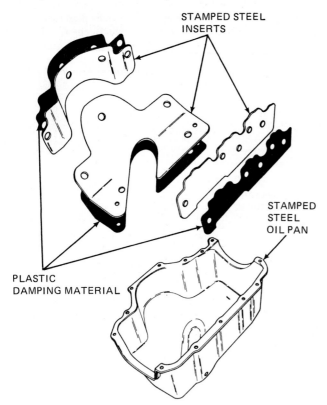

Fig. 13-6 An acoustic oil pan using layers of plastic that absorb engine noise and vibration. (*Chrysler Corporation*)

➤ 13-7 ALUMINUM CYLINDER BLOCK WITHOUT LINERS

Mercedes-Benz, Porsche, and others use aluminum blocks that have silicon particles in them. Silicon is a very hard material. After the block is cast, the cylinders are *honed*.

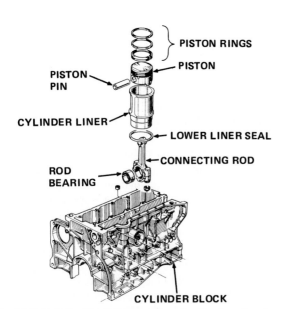

Fig. 13-7 Cylinder block for an automotive diesel engine that uses wet cylinder liners. (*Peugeot Motors of America, Inc.*)

This procedure uses rotating abrasive stones to enlarge the cylinders to their final finished size. Then the cylinders are treated with a chemical that eats away (or *etches*) the aluminum surface. This leaves only the silicon particles exposed (Fig. 13-8). The piston and rings slide on the silicon particles with minimum wear.

➤ 13-8 CYLINDER HEAD

Figures 13-5 and 13-9 show disassembled cylinder heads for OHC and pushrod engines. Heads are cast from cast iron or aluminum alloy. They are machined to take the various parts that are attached to or installed in the heads.

The cylinder head forms the top of the combustion chamber. The piston and rings form the bottom. Each of the basic combustion-chamber shapes (Fig. 13-10) produces a specific effect. The *wedge* increases the turbulence of the burning mixture, but has high exhaust emissions. The *hemispheric* provides relatively slow burning. The *cup* or *bowl-in-piston* improves turbulence in diesel, turbocharged, and high-performance engines. The cylinder head is flat. The height and shape of the *crescent* or *pent-roof* is easily varied to change the compression ratio and turbulence. Greater turbulence causes the air-fuel mixture to burn faster.

Some cylinder-head covers (*valve covers*) are *acoustic* (Fig. 13-11). They are stamped from three-layer sheets. The two outer layers are metal. The middle layer is plastic. Mechanical noise from the engine causes the inside metal layer to vibrate. However, the middle plastic layer prevents the noise and vibration from reaching the passengers.

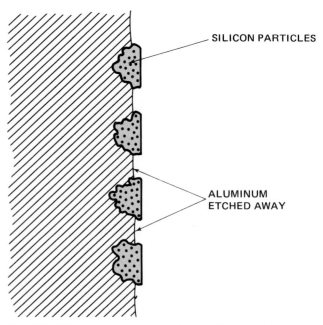

Fig. 13-8 Enlarged view of an aluminum cylinder wall. The aluminum is etched away, exposing the hard particles of silicon.

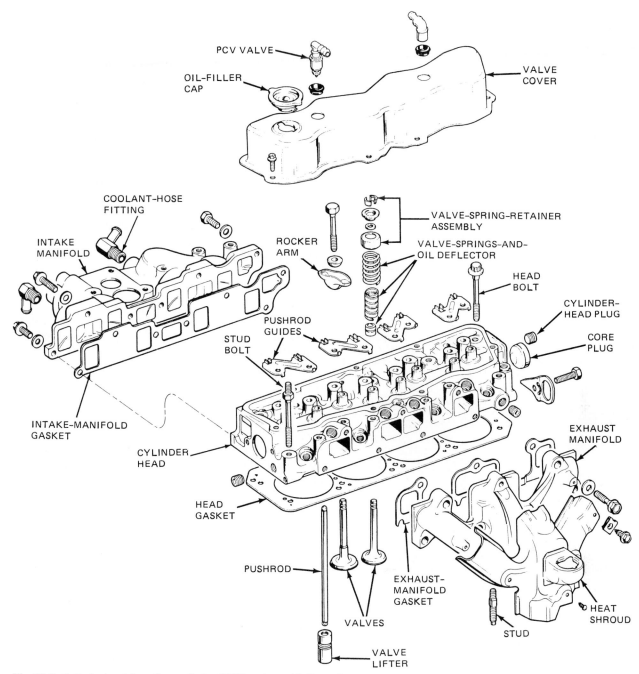

Fig. 13-9 Cylinder head for a four-cylinder OHV engine, with the major parts that are installed in and attached to the cylinder head. (*Chrysler Corporation*)

> **13-9 CYLINDER-HEAD GASKET**

A *head-gasket* seals the joint between the cylinder head and the cylinder block (➤6-22). The gasket is placed between the head and the block. Tightening the head bolts forces the soft material of the head gasket to fill any irregularity. This seals the joint. Head-gasket installation becomes extremely important in sealing between an aluminum head and a cast-iron block.

> **13-10 SWIRL-TYPE COMBUSTION CHAMBER**

Another way to improve turbulence is to use a *high-swirl* intake port and a masked intake-valve seat (Fig. 13-12). This arrangement causes the incoming air-fuel mixture to move rapidly in a circular pattern. Several other arrangements also produce high swirl and turbulence. One uses a small *jet valve*, or *auxiliary intake valve* (Fig. 13-

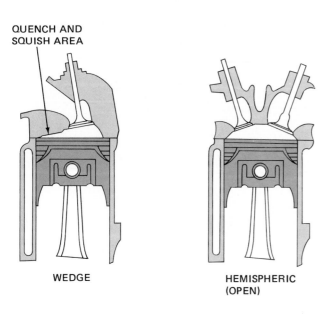

QUENCH AND
SQUISH AREA

WEDGE

HEMISPHERIC
(OPEN)

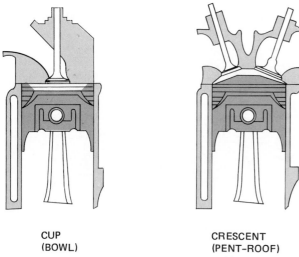

CUP
(BOWL)

CRESCENT
(PENT-ROOF)

Fig. 13-10 Shapes of combustion chambers. (*ATW*)

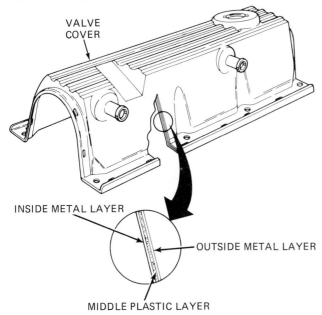

VALVE
COVER

INSIDE METAL LAYER

OUTSIDE METAL LAYER

MIDDLE PLASTIC LAYER

Fig. 13-11 An acoustic valve cover with a center plastic layer that absorbs engine noise and vibration. (*Chrysler Corporation*)

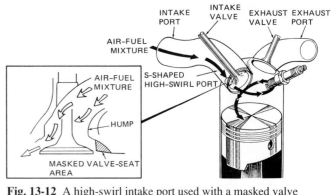

Fig. 13-12 A high-swirl intake port used with a masked valve seat to direct the mixture into the combustion chamber and increase turbulence. This allows the engine to run on a leaner mixture while reducing exhaust emissions. (*Mazda Motors of America, Inc.*)

13). It admits a jet or stream of air into the combustion chamber. This creates additional turbulence and reduces exhaust emissions.

➤ 13-11 PRECOMBUSTION CHAMBER

A *precombustion chamber* is a separate small combustion chamber where combustion begins (Fig. 13-14). A *primary intake valve* opens into the main combustion chamber. An *auxiliary intake valve* opens into the precombustion chamber. Both intake valves open at the same time. The auxiliary intake valve admits a rich mixture. The primary intake valve admits a lean mixture. The spark plug in the precombustion chamber ignites the rich mixture. It streams out and mixes with the lean mixture. This causes high turbulence and good combustion.

A spark-ignition engine using a precombustion chamber is a *stratified-charge* engine. "Stratified" means in layers. Ignition begins in a layer or pocket of rich mixture which is surrounded by a leaner mixture (or only air in a diesel engine). The leaner *average* air-fuel ratio provides greater fuel economy and less exhaust emissions. The diesel engine (Chap. 23) is a stratified-charge engine.

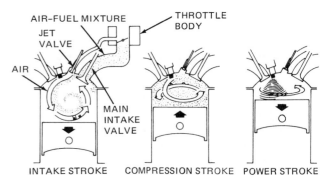

Fig. 13-13 Airflow through the auxiliary intake valve or jet valve creates a swirling action in the combustion chamber. (*Chrysler Corporation*)

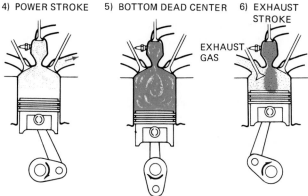

1) INTAKE STROKE   2) COMPRESSION STROKE   3) IGNITION

SPARK PLUG — RICH MIXTURE
LEAN MIXTURE

PRIMARY INTAKE VALVE

AUXILIARY INTAKE VALVE

4) POWER STROKE   5) BOTTOM DEAD CENTER   6) EXHAUST STROKE

EXHAUST GAS

Fig. 13-14 Sequence of actions in a stratified-charge spark-ignition engine using a precombustion chamber. (*American Honda Motor Company, Inc.*)

The *exhaust manifold* (Fig. 13-15) is a set of tubes. It carries exhaust gas from the cylinder head to the exhaust system. The manifold attaches to the head so the exhaust ports in the head align with the tube openings. An in-line engine needs one exhaust manifold. V-type and opposed-cylinder engines have two exhaust manifolds, one for each bank.

Figure 13-16 shows the exhaust system for a V-type engine using a single exhaust system. The two exhaust manifolds are connected through a *crossover pipe*. This forces the exhaust gas from both banks to flow through the *catalytic converter* and the *muffler*. The catalytic converter (Chap. 35) converts most of the pollutants in the exhaust gas to harmless substances. The muffler and the *resonator* (not used on all cars) reduce exhaust noise.

➤ **13-13 INTAKE MANIFOLD**

The *intake manifold* is also a set of tubes. These tubes carry air or air-fuel mixture from the throttle valves to the intake ports in the cylinder head. On in-line engines, the

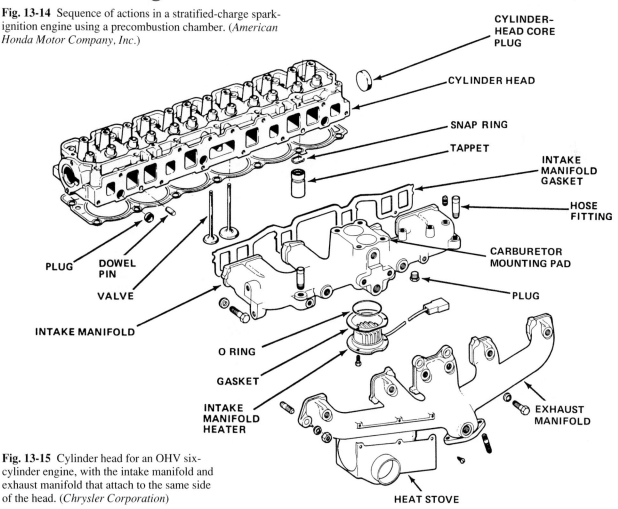

CYLINDER-HEAD CORE PLUG

CYLINDER HEAD

SNAP RING

TAPPET

INTAKE MANIFOLD GASKET

HOSE FITTING

CARBURETOR MOUNTING PAD

PLUG

EXHAUST MANIFOLD

PLUG

DOWEL PIN

VALVE

INTAKE MANIFOLD

O RING

GASKET

INTAKE MANIFOLD HEATER

HEAT STOVE

Fig. 13-15 Cylinder head for an OHV six-cylinder engine, with the intake manifold and exhaust manifold that attach to the same side of the head. (*Chrysler Corporation*)

intake manifold attaches to the side of the cylinder head (Figs. 13-9 and 13-15). On V-type engines, the intake manifold is between the two banks of cylinders (Fig. 12-11). Some in-line engines have the intake and exhaust manifolds on the same side of the cylinder head (Fig. 13-15). Other engines have the manifolds on opposite sides (Fig. 13-9).

Exhaust manifolds for some carbureted in-line engines have a *heat-control valve* (Fig. 13-17). It helps provide heat to the air-fuel mixture in the intake manifold while the engine is cold. This improves fuel vaporization for better cold-engine performance. Some V-type engines have an exhaust-gas passage that runs across the intake manifold under the carburetor mounting pad. When the engine is cold, the heat-control valve forces exhaust gas from one cylinder bank through the passage. This heats the air-fuel mixture entering the intake manifold. Section 21-22 describes heat-control valves.

➤ 13-14 CRANKSHAFT

The *crankshaft* (Figs. 13-2 and 13-18) is a one-piece casting or forging of heat-treated alloy steel. Counterweights placed opposite the crankpins (Fig. 13-19) balance the crankshaft. The crankshafts for some V-6 engines have spread out or *splayed* crankpins. A splayed crankpin is split into two parts (Fig. 13-19, top). Each connecting rod has its own crankpin. This reduces out-of-balance conditions.

The output end of the crankshaft has the flywheel or drive plate attached to it (Figs. 13-2 and 13-20). The front end has the gear or sprocket that drives the camshaft, the vibration damper (➤ 13-15), and the drive-belt pulley. Engines with a *distributorless ignition system* or an *electronic engine-control* (EEC) *system* have a notched plate or timing disc on the crankshaft. A *crankshaft sensor* (Fig. 12-3) signals the passing of the notches to the computer in the EEC system. The computer then uses this information to calculate engine speed (crankshaft rpm) and piston

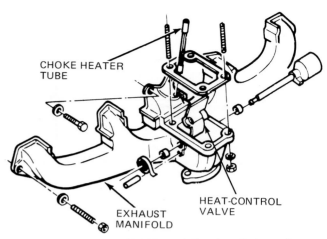

CHOKE HEATER TUBE

HEAT-CONTROL VALVE

EXHAUST MANIFOLD

Fig. 13-17 Exhaust manifold for an inline six-cylinder engine that uses a heat-control valve.

position. Chapters 19 and 32 describe electronic engine-control systems.

➤ 13-15 VIBRATION DAMPER

The power strokes tend to twist the crankshaft. Each power stroke applies a force that may exceed 4000 pounds [18,000 N] on the crankpin. This force tries to push the crankpin ahead of the rest of the crankshaft. Then, as the force on the crankpin recedes, the crankshaft untwists. This twist-untwist action repeats with every power stroke. The action tends to create an *oscillating* (back and forth) motion in the crankshaft. This is *torsional vibration*. It can break the crankshaft.

A *vibration damper* (or *harmonic balancer*) helps control torsional vibration. The damper mounts on the front end of the crankshaft (Fig. 13-20). This forms the hub to which the crankshaft pulley attaches. The inertia ring is bonded through the rubber ring to the pulley. The inertia ring has a damping effect which tends to hold the

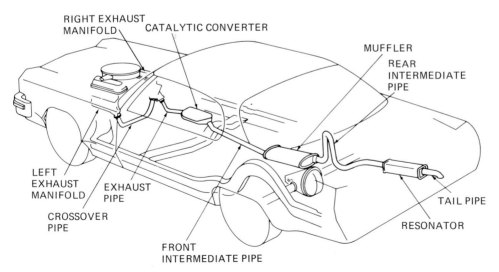

RIGHT EXHAUST MANIFOLD

CATALYTIC CONVERTER

MUFFLER

REAR INTERMEDIATE PIPE

LEFT EXHAUST MANIFOLD

EXHAUST PIPE

CROSSOVER PIPE

FRONT INTERMEDIATE PIPE

RESONATOR

TAIL PIPE

Fig. 13-16 Single exhaust system for a V-type engine that uses one catalytic converter. (*Oldsmobile Division of General Motors Corporation*)

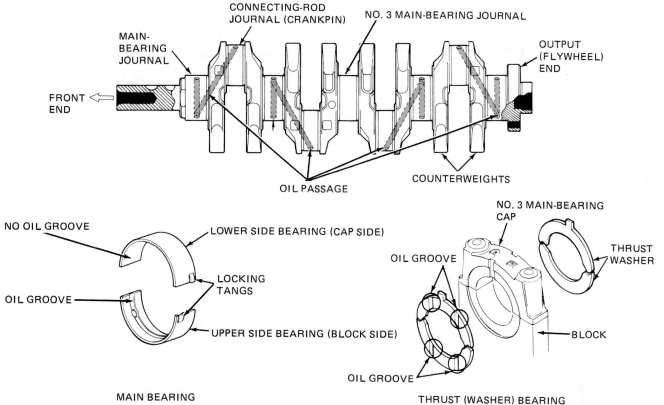

Fig. 13-18 The crankshaft has oil holes drilled through it to carry oil from the main bearings to the connecting-rod bearings. (*Toyota Motor Sales, U.S.A., Inc.*)

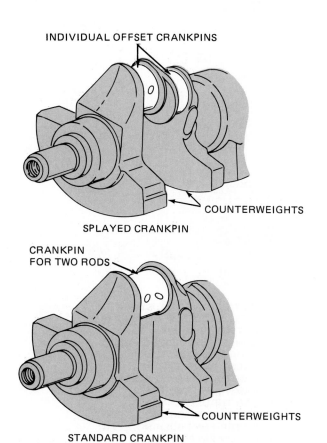

Fig. 13-19 Standard crankshaft for a V-6 engine compared with a V-6 crankshaft with splayed crankpins. (*Buick Division of General Motors Corporation*)

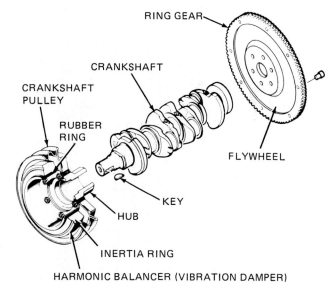

Fig. 13-20 The engine crankshaft has a vibration damper installed on the front end and a flywheel or drive plate attached to the rear. (*ATW*)

crankshaft to a constant speed. This cancels the twist-untwist action.

➤ 13-16 ENGINE BEARINGS

Bearings are placed in the engine where there is rotary motion between engine parts (Fig. 13-21). These bearings are usually *sleeve bearings* that fit like sleeves around the

147

rotating shafts. The part of the shaft that rotates in the bearing is a *journal*. Crankshaft and connecting-rod bearings are split into two parts (Fig. 13-22). One half of the connecting-rod bearing fits into the connecting rod. The other half fits into the rod-bearing cap (Fig. 13-4). One half of the crankshaft or *main bearing* fits into a semicircle machined in the cylinder block. The other half fits into the main-bearing cap (Fig. 13-23).

Each bearing half has a steel or bronze back with up to five linings of soft bearing material. The bearing wears, and not the more expensive crankshaft or other part. This reduces the cost of repair by allowing the reuse of the more expensive part.

> ## 13-17 THRUST BEARING

A *thrust bearing* (Figs. 13-18 and 13-22) limits crankshaft endplay. The thrust bearing is one of the main bearings that has flanges on its two sides. Flanges on the crankshaft fit close to the thrust-bearing flanges. This limits the forward and rearward movement of the crankshaft.

> ## 13-18 BEARING LUBRICATION

The engine oil pump sends oil onto the bearing surfaces. The rotating crankshaft journals are supported on layers of oil. The difference between the journal diameter and the

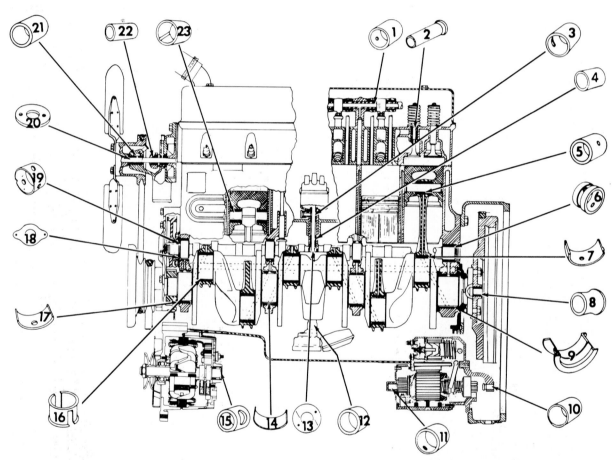

1. ROCKER-ARM BUSHING
2. VALVE-GUIDE BUSHING
3. DISTRIBUTOR BUSHING, UPPER
4. DISTRIBUTOR BUSHING, LOWER
5. PISTON-PIN BUSHING
6. CAMSHAFT BUSHINGS
7. CONNECTING-ROD BEARING
8. CLUTCH PILOT BUSHING
9. CRANKSHAFT THRUST BEARING
10. STARTING-MOTOR BUSHING, DRIVE END
11. STARTING-MOTOR BUSHING, COMMUTATOR END
12. OIL-PUMP BUSHING
13. DISTRIBUTOR THRUST PLATE
14. INTERMEDIATE MAIN BEARING
15. ALTERNATOR BEARING
16. CONNECTING-ROD BEARING, FLOATING TYPE
17. FRONT MAIN BEARING
18. CAMSHAFT THRUST PLATE
19. CAMSHAFT BUSHING
20. FAN THRUST PLATE
21. WATER-PUMP BUSHING, FRONT
22. WATER-PUMP BUSHING, REAR
23. PISTON-PIN BUSHING

Fig. 13-21 Bearings and bushings used in a typical OHV engine. (*Johnson Bronze Company*)

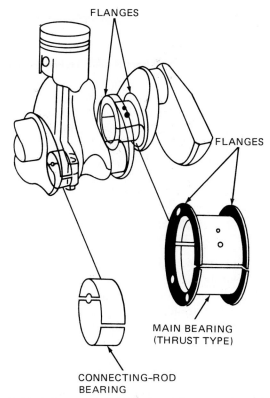

Fig. 13-22 A thrust-type main bearing and a connecting rod bearing, showing their positions on the crankshaft.

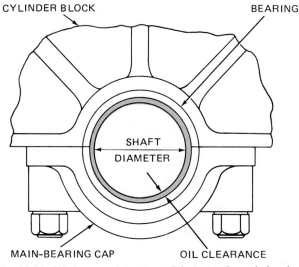

Fig. 13-23 Oil clearance (exaggerated) between the main bearing and the crankshaft journal. (*Gould Corporation*)

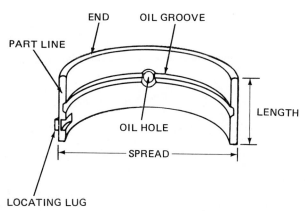

Fig. 13-24 Typical sleeve-type bearing half. (*McQuay-Norris Manufacturing Company*)

main bearings and carry it to the crankpins. From there, the oil flows into the bearing clearance.

The oil spreads through the bearing clearance to all bearing and journal surfaces. The oil is thrown off when it reaches the edges. The throwoff lubricates the cylinder walls, piston, and piston rings. Then the oil falls into the oil pan.

Heat is picked up by the oil as it circulates through the engine. By the time the oil leaves the oil pan, the oil is relatively cool. This is how the lubricating system helps keep engine parts cool. The oil also flushes and cleans the bearings. It carries dirt and grit particles back to the oil pan. They settle to the bottom or are filtered out by the oil filter when the oil is sent back through the engine.

➤ 13-19 BEARING OIL CLEARANCE

Oil clearance varies, with 0.0015 inch [0.04 mm] typical for new bearings. As bearings wear, oil clearance increases. Then more oil flows through and is thrown off on the cylinder walls. More oil works its way into the combustion chambers where it burns. This increases oil consumption. Excessive oil clearance causes some bearings to fail due to oil starvation. The pump can deliver only so much oil. Most of the oil passes through the "loose" bearings closest to the pump. Bearings farther away will not get enough oil.

➤ 13-20 BEARING REQUIREMENTS

Bearings must carry the loads imposed by high-compression, high-speed engines. The bearing surfaces must be soft enough to *embed* small particles that work their way onto the bearings (Fig. 13-25). However, the bearing must be hard enough not to wear too rapidly. If the bearing material is too hard, the particles lie on the surface and scratch the journal. Particles could also gouge out the bearing. With either condition, bearing failure results.

bearing diameter is the *oil clearance* (Fig. 13-23). In a running engine, the oil clearance is filled with oil.

Figure 11-22 shows an engine lubricating system. The oil pump sends oil through oil galleries in the cylinder block to the bearings. The upper main-bearing half has an oil hole in it (Fig. 13-24). Oil flows into the bearing through this hole. The crankshaft has oil passages drilled into it (Fig. 13-18). These passages pick up oil from the

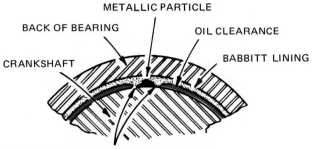

BABBITT DISPLACED BY PARTICLE AND
RAISED UP AROUND IT, GREATLY REDUCING OR
DESTROYING THE OIL CLEARANCE LOCALLY.

Fig. 13-25 Effect of a metal particle embedded in the bearing material. (*Federal Mogul Corporation*)

> ## 13-21 CONNECTING RODS

One end of the connecting rod attaches to a crankpin on the crankshaft (Figs. 13-4 and 13-7). The other end attaches to the piston pin. The end of the rod attached to the crankpin is the rod "big end." The other end is the rod "small end."

Figure 13-26 shows the two most common ways of attaching the rod to the piston. The most widely used is to *press-fit* the piston pin in the connecting rod (Fig. 13-26A). There is no bearing (or *bushing*) between the steel piston pin and the aluminum piston. The aluminum serves as the bearing surface. The other method uses a bushing in the connecting rod (Fig. 13-26B). The piston moves or floats freely in the rod and in the bushing. Snap rings prevent the pin from sliding out and striking the cylinder wall.

Oil scraped from the cylinder walls by the piston rings lubricates the piston pins in many engines. Some connecting rods with free-floating pins have oil passages drilled from the big end to the small end. Oil flows from the connecting-rod bearings through the drilled passages to the piston-pin bushings.

During manufacture, rod caps and rods are bolted together. Then the big-end bore is machined out. The result is that each cap fits only its own rod, and in only one position. Caps must not be interchanged during service work. If a cap is installed on the wrong rod, tightening the rod bolts may lockup the crankshaft. Sometimes a cap is lost or damaged. Then, most manufacturers recommend installing a new or reconditioned connecting-rod-and-cap assembly.

> ## 13-22 PISTONS

Pistons and piston rings (Fig. 13-27) are described in >11-4. During the power stroke, up to 4000 pounds [18,000 N] of force is suddenly applied to the piston head. This happens 30 to 40 times a second to each piston at highway speed. Temperatures above the piston head reach 4000°F [2204°C] or higher.

Pistons must be strong to take these stresses. They must also be light to reduce *inertia* loads on the bearings. Any object in motion resists any effort to change its speed or direction of motion. This is inertia. When a piston stops at TDC or BDC and starts to move in the other direction, it loads the bearings. Chapters 40 and 41 on engine service describe how this affects bearing wear.

Pistons are made of aluminum because it is a light metal.

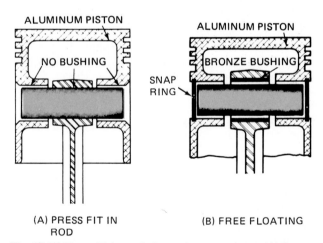

(A) PRESS FIT IN ROD   (B) FREE FLOATING

Fig. 13-26 Two widely used piston-pin arrangements. (A) Press-fit in the connecting rod. (B) Free floating. (*Sunnen Products Company*)

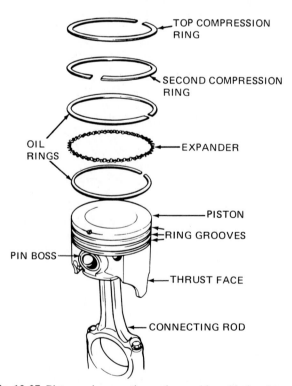

Fig. 13-27 Piston and connecting-rod assembly, with the piston rings above the piston. (*Buick Division of General Motors Corporation*)

Most automotive engines use full-slipper pistons (Fig. 13-28). The skirts are cut away to save weight and to make room for the counterweights on the crankshaft. Automotive pistons vary from 3 to 4 inches [76 to 122 mm] in diameter. They weigh about 1 pound [454 g]. To prevent excessive engine vibration, all pistons must be the same weight.

Many pistons are *plated*. They are given a thin coating of tin or other material. This helps prevent *scuffing* (➤13-31) during break-in.

Aluminum pistons are either *forged* or cast. Cast pistons are made by pouring molten aluminum into molds. Forged pistons are "hammered out" from slugs of aluminum alloy. The alloy, subjected to high forging pressure, flows (or *extrudes*) into dies to form pistons. Both cast and forged pistons are heat treated. The forged piston is denser, stronger, and has a better heat path so it runs cooler. Figure

13-29 compares the temperatures in a cast piston with those in a forged piston. High-performance engines use forged pistons.

➤ 13-23 PISTON CLEARANCE

Piston clearance (or *skirt clearance*) is the distance between the cylinder wall and the skirt (Fig. 11-6). The skirt is the lower part of the piston. The piston clearance is usually between 0.001 and 0.004 inch [0.025 and 0.10 mm]. In a running engine, the piston and rings move on films of oil that fill the piston clearance.

If the clearance is too small, there is loss of power from high friction and severe wear. Pistons can seize in the cylinders and lockup the engine. Excessive piston clearance causes *piston slap* (➤13-26). This noise is caused by the piston shifting from one side of the cylinder

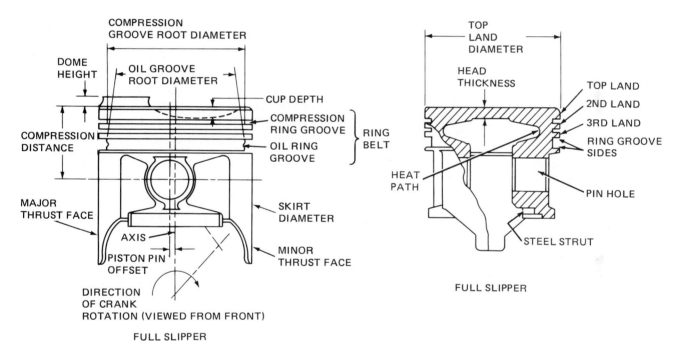

Fig. 13-28 Slipper piston with parts named.

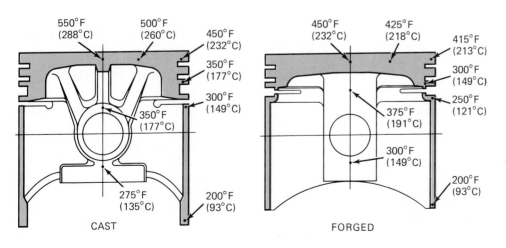

Fig. 13-29 Typical running temperatures in a cast piston compared with temperatures in a forged piston, (*TRW Inc.*)

151

to the other when the power stroke begins. Piston slap is usually a problem only in older engines with worn cylinder walls and worn or collapsed piston skirts.

➤ 13-24 EXPANSION CONTROL IN PISTONS

Aluminum expands more with increasing temperature than the cast-iron cylinder walls. Since the pistons run hotter than cylinder walls, the pistons expand even more. This expansion, especially in cast pistons, must be controlled to avoid loss of piston clearance.

One way to control piston expansion is to increase the amount of heat that leaves the piston head. This is done by increasing the thickness of the metal in the head (Fig. 13-28). More heat escapes so the head runs cooler. But if the head is too cool, the layers of air-fuel mixture next to it will not burn. Unburned air-fuel mixture escapes in the exhaust gas. This reduces engine efficiency and increases exhaust emissions (Chap. 35).

If the piston head is too hot, it can cause surface ignition or preignition. This can cause misfiring and engine damage, as explained in Chap. 16.

Many pistons are *cam-ground.* They are slightly oval in shape (Fig. 13-30). The pistons are finish-ground on a special machine. It uses a cam to move the piston toward and away from the grinding wheel as the piston revolves. When the piston is cold, it has normal clearance only in the areas 90 degrees from the pin holes (Fig. 13-30). As it warms up, the area of normal clearance increases. The head of the piston expands normally in all directions. However, the stiff piston-pin bosses move outward even more, causing the piston to assume a round shape.

Another way to control expansion is to use steel *struts* cast into the piston (Fig. 13-28). These carry the outward thrust of the expanding head toward the piston-pin bosses. The effect is similar to that in cam-ground pistons.

Some pistons taper slightly from bottom to top. The smaller head diameter allows more expansion space at the top.

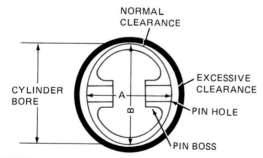

Fig. 13-30 As the cam-ground piston warms up, the expansion of the skirt distorts the piston from an elliptical to a round shape. This increases the area of normal clearance between the piston and the cylinder wall.

➤ 13-25 PISTON-HEAD SHAPES

Many engines use flat-top pistons (Fig. 13-29). But piston-head shapes vary according to engine design. They also vary according to the shape of the cylinder head (➤13-8) and combustion chamber (Figs. 13-10 and 13-28). Some piston heads have cups (Fig. 13-28) or reliefs (Fig. 13-4) into which the valves can move when they open. Other piston heads have a dome or other shape to improve turbulence in the combustion chamber (Fig. 13-10).

➤ 13-26 PISTON-PIN OFFSET

In many engines, the piston-pin holes are offset toward the *major thrust face* (Fig. 13-28). This is the piston face that bears most heavily on the cylinder wall during the power stroke. If the pin is centered, the minor thrust face remains in contact with the cylinder wall until the end of the compression stroke. Then, as the power stroke starts, the rod angle changes from left to right. This causes the piston to shift suddenly to the left. If there is too much clearance, the piston movement causes piston slap (➤13-23).

If the piston pin is offset slightly toward the major thrust face, combustion pressure causes the piston to tilt as it nears TDC. The lower end of the major thrust face makes first contact with the cylinder wall. Then, after TDC (when the reversal of side thrust occurs), the piston tilts. Full contact of the major thrust face occurs. This minimizes piston slap.

➤ 13-27 RING-GROOVE FORTIFICATION

The compression rings move up and down in their grooves. During the intake stroke, the compression ring moves up into contact with the upper side of the ring groove. Then, as the power stroke starts, the combustion pressure forces the top compression ring down hard against the lower side of the ring groove. These repeated impacts can cause wear in the top ring groove.

Some pistons have *top-ring-groove fortification.* A cast-iron or nickel-iron alloy ring is cast into the piston. In forged pistons, the ring-groove area is sprayed with molten metal having the proper wear resistance. Then the groove is machined to size.

➤ 13-28 LOW-FRICTION PISTONS

Some engines use *low-friction pistons* (Fig. 13-31). These pistons are made from aluminum alloy with silicon particles in it. After the pistons are cast, the surface is treated with a chemical which removes the surface aluminum. This exposes the silicon particles which provide a more durable surface than normal aluminum alloy. Aluminum cylinder blocks with silicon particles in them are described in ➤13-7.

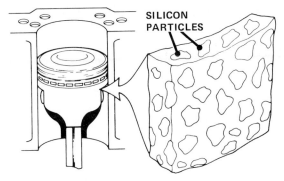

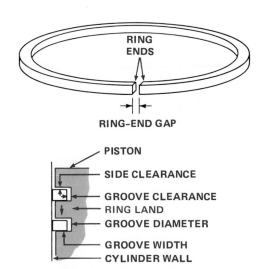

Fig. 13-31 Low-friction piston rings, made from aluminum alloy with silicon particles in it. (*General Motors Corporation*)

Fig. 13-33 Top, the ring end-gap in a piston ring with a butt joint. Bottom, clearance between the installed rings and the ring grooves in the piston. (*Sealed Power Corporation*)

➤ 13-29 PISTON RINGS

Pistons are fitted with piston rings (Fig. 13-27). The two types of piston rings are *compression rings* and *oil-control rings* (➤11-4). Compression rings seal compression and combustion pressures in the combustion chambers. Oil-control rings scrape oil from the cylinder walls.

Figure 13-32 shows a set of piston rings. Rings are slightly larger in diameter than the cylinder. The rings are compressed for installation. Then they remain somewhat compressed in the cylinder. This almost closes the *ring-end gap* (Fig. 13-33). The rings are under tension and press tightly against the cylinder wall. Figure 13-33 shows various compression-ring measurements. Piston and ring service includes checking some of these measurements.

➤ 13-30 COMPRESSION RINGS

Compression rings are usually made of cast iron (Fig. 13-32). Some diesel and high-performance engines use *ductile iron* rings. Compression rings also help control oil. As they move down on the intake stroke, they scrape all but a fine film of oil from the cylinder walls. On the exhaust stroke, the rings move upward and tend to skate over the oil film.

Compression rings have various shapes. *Reverse twist* and *barrel face* are two designs. Figure 13-34 compares

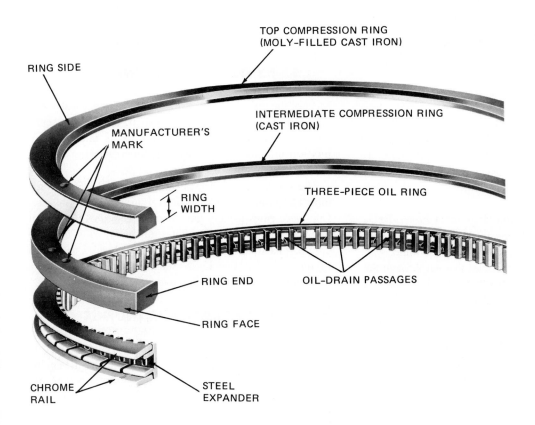

Fig. 13-32 Set of piston rings. The top ring is made of cast iron and filled with molybdenum. (*TRW Inc.*)

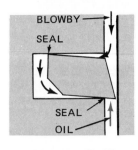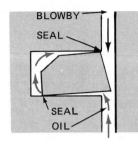

REVERSE TWIST   POSITIVE TWIST

Fig. 13-34 Action of a taper-face ring with (left) reverse twist and (right) positive twist. (*Chevrolet Division of General Motors Corporation*)

the action of the *reverse-twist ring* with the earlier *positive-twist ring*. Combustion pressures are highest at wide open throttle. Both compression rings are forced down flat against the lower side of the groove by the pressure. Compression rings do not flatten as much at part throttle, when pressures are lower.

During the intake stroke, vacuum above the piston tries to draw oil up the cylinder wall, past the rings. The reverse-twist ring prevents this (Fig. 13-34, left). The twist pushes the lower side of the ring against the ring groove to produce a seal. The positive-twist ring (Fig. 13-34, right) twists the other way so oil can work around the ring.

The *barrel-face ring* has a slightly rounded face. It has only a narrow line of contact with the cylinder wall so the force against the wall is relatively high. The ring rocks slightly at TDC and BDC when the piston changes directions. But the line of contact is not lost. The force of the ring on the cylinder wall is maintained. The rocking action reduces the formation of a *ring ridge* at the top of the cylinder (➤13-34).

➤ **13-31 COMPRESSION-RING COATINGS**

Coatings on compression rings help *wear-in* and reduce cylinder wall and ring wear. Wear-in means that when new, the rings and cylinder wall have slight irregularities so the fit is not perfect. After a time, these irregularities wear away so the fit improves. Relatively soft materials which wear rapidly, such as phosphate, graphite, and iron oxide, help wear-in. Also, they hold some oil which reduces *scuffing*.

The type of wear that piston rings meet in service is important in selecting ring coatings. At one time, *abrasive wear* was the most common type of ring and cylinder-wall wear. Abrasives are fine dust particles that get through the air filter and into the engine oil. Where abrasive wear is a problem, *chrome plating* helps. Chrome (or *chromium*) is a very hard metal. When finished to a smooth surface, it causes little cylinder-wall wear.

Abrasive wear is less important today because of better air filters. Now, *scuff wear* is more of a problem. Cylinder walls, rings, and pistons operate at higher temperatures. This increases the possibility that the moving metal surfaces will develop hot spots which reach the melting

point. Then, momentary welds form between rings and wall at TDC, when the rings are momentarily at rest. The welds break when the rings start down again. The broken welds leave rough, scuffed spots and surfaces. Rings, pistons, and walls are scratched and failure may occur.

To fight scuff wear, the cast-iron top compression ring may be filled with *molybdenum* (Fig. 13-32). Cast iron melts at about 2250°F [1233°C]. Chromium melts at about 3450°F [1898°C]. But molybdenum melts at about 4800°F [2449°C]. This allows molybdenum-filled rings to run at higher temperatures without scuffing.

NOTE Molybdenum (or "moly") is usually a filler, *not a coating*. Exposed edges of a molybdenum coating chip easily. Filling a groove or slot in the ring with molybdenum avoids this problem (Fig. 13-32).

➤ **13-32 NEED FOR TWO COMPRESSION RINGS**

At the start of the power stroke, combustion pressures may go as high as 1000 psi [6895 kPa]. A single compression ring usually cannot hold this much pressure. Therefore two compression rings are used. These are the *top compression ring* and the *lower* (or *intermediate*) *compression ring* (Figs. 13-27 and 13-32).

The two compression rings differ. Pressure gets behind the upper ring and pushes it out against the cylinder wall. The pressure also pushes the ring down against the lower side of the ring groove. This provides a seal at both places. The pressure that gets around the upper ring may not be enough to seal the lower ring at both places. The lower ring is often the twist type (Fig. 13-32) to improve sealing. Sometimes an expander or inner tension ring is installed behind the lower ring to improve sealing against the wall.

➤ **13-33 OIL-CONTROL RINGS**

Most of the time, more oil is thrown on cylinder walls than is needed to lubricate walls, pistons, and rings. If too much oil is left on the walls, some will work up into the combustion chambers. The oil will burn, leaving carbon deposits.

The oil-control rings (Figs. 13-32 and 13-35) scrape most of the oil off the walls so it returns to the crankcase. One-piece rings usually have expander springs in back of them for greater tension. The multipiece ring has two chrome-plated steel rails. An *expander* (Fig. 13-32) or an *expander-spacer* (Fig. 13-35) separates the rails and forces them upward, downward, and outward.

➤ **13-34 REPLACEMENT RINGS**

As cylinder walls wear, power is lost and oil is burned in the combustion chambers (➤24-17). Eventually the engine requires repair because it is losing so much power and burning so much oil. The cylinder head is removed to check the condition of the cylinder bores. If the *taper* (Fig.

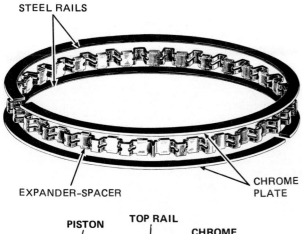

STEEL RAILS

EXPANDER-SPACER

CHROME PLATE

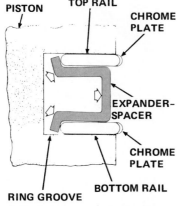

PISTON

TOP RAIL

CHROME PLATE

EXPANDER-SPACER

CHROME PLATE

BOTTOM RAIL

RING GROOVE

Fig. 13-35 Top, three-piece oil-control ring. Bottom, action of the expander-spacer. As shown by the white arrows, it forces the rails out against the cylinder wall and up and down against the sides of the ring groove. (*Dana Corporaton*)

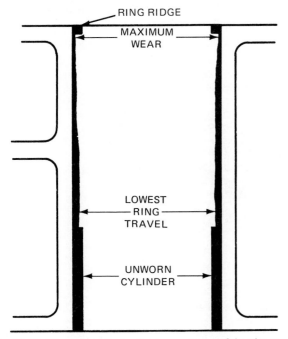

RING RIDGE

MAXIMUM WEAR

LOWEST RING TRAVEL

UNWORN CYLINDER

Fig. 13-36 Wear of a cylinder due to movement of the piston rings on the cylinder wall. The amont of taper is the difference between the cylinder diameter at the point of maximum wear and the diameter of the unworn part of the cylinder.

13-36) is not excessive, a set of new *standard-size piston rings* can be installed. If there is excessive taper or *out-of-round,* the cylinders are honed or bored. Then new *oversize piston rings* are installed. In engines with replaceable cylinder liners, new liners and rings are installed. Chapter 41 describes these procedures.

➤ 13-35 ENGINE MOUNTS

The engine bolts to the transmission or transaxle. This assembly then attaches at three or four places to the engine cradle or subframe. These attachments are *engine mounts.*

The mounts are located between mounting brackets on the engine-transmission assembly and the car frame or body (Figs. 13-37 and 13-38). They absorb engine noise

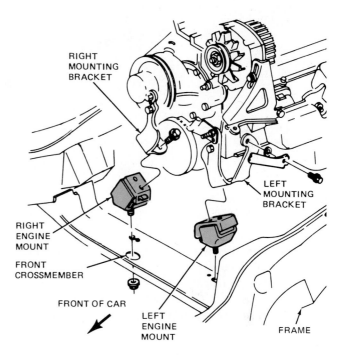

RIGHT MOUNTING BRACKET

LEFT MOUNTING BRACKET

RIGHT ENGINE MOUNT

FRONT CROSSMEMBER

FRONT OF CAR

LEFT ENGINE MOUNT

FRAME

(A) FRONT ENGINE MOUNTS

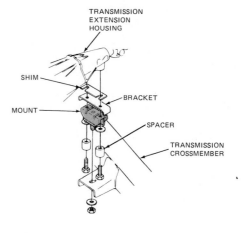

TRANSMISSION EXTENSION HOUSING

SHIM

BRACKET

MOUNT

SPACER

TRANSMISSION CROSSMEMBER

(B) REAR ENGINE (TRANSMISSION) MOUNT

Fig. 13-37 Engine mounts that attach a longitudinal engine-transmission assembly to the frame or body and absorb engine noise and vibration. (*Cadillac Division of General Motors Corporation*)

155

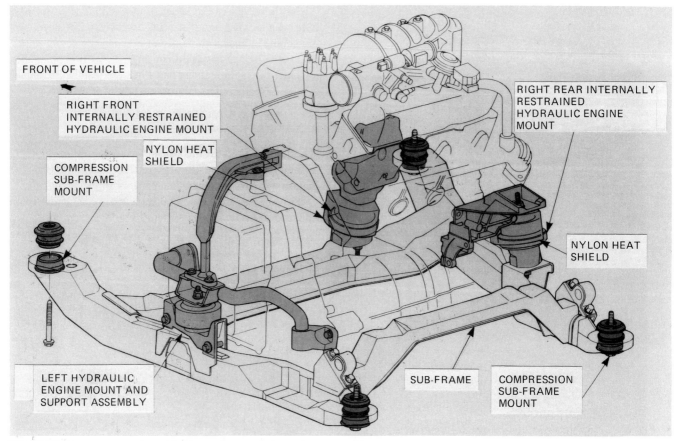

Fig. 13-38 A transverse engine with mounts that attach the engine to a cradle or sub-frame. (*Ford Motor Company*)

and vibration that would otherwise be felt by the passengers. The mounts also prevent damaging vibration from reaching the radiator, electronic controls, and other components.

Engine mounts are flexible to permit the car frame or body to twist. This occurs during normal operation. Many engine mounts are solid-rubber insulators (also called *dampers* or *isolators*). A longitudinal engine has one mount on each side (Fig. 13-37). A third mount is at the rear of the transmission.

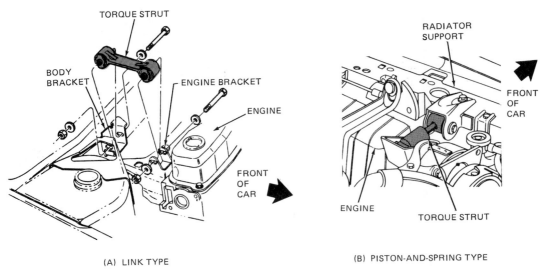

Fig. 13-39 A torque strut controls the tendency of a transverse engine to roll about its longtitudinal axis. (*Pontiac Division of General Motors Corporation; Moog Automotive, Inc.*)

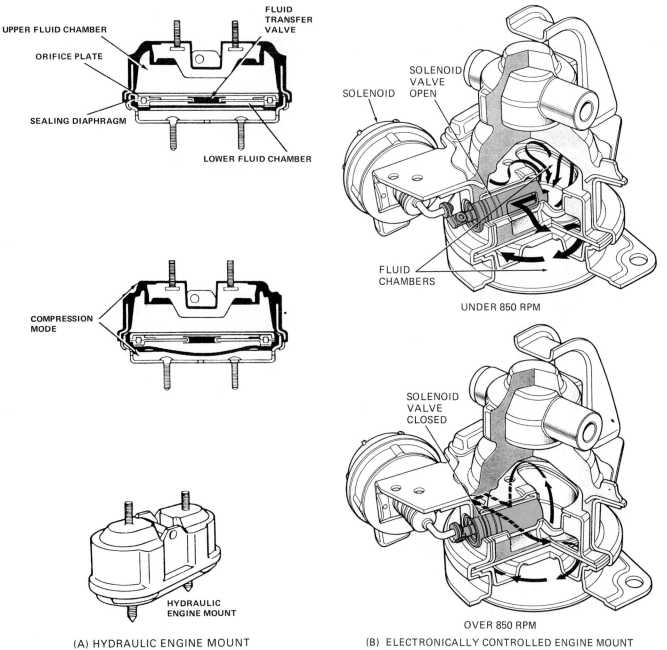

Fig. 13-40 Hydraulic engine mounts that (A) work automatically or are (B) electronically controlled. (*General Motors Corporation; American Honda Motor Company, Inc.*)

Figure 13-38 shows the mounts for a transverse engine. There are two engine mounts and a transaxle mount. The mounts attach the engine to a cradle or sub-frame that fastens to the body at four points.

Many cars with transverse engines also have a *torque strut* (Fig. 13-39). It controls the tendency of the engine to roll about on its long axis. One end of the torque strut mounts on a bracket on the engine. The other end attaches to the radiator support or other frame or body member. One type includes a hydraulic piston and spring (Fig. 13-39B). It acts like a shock absorber to prevent engine roll.

Some cars have liquid filled *hydraulic engine mounts* (Figs. 13-38 and 13-40). These have two fluid chambers, a fluid transfer valve, and an orifice plate. Fluid moves between the two chambers to damp vibration during engine operation. Some hydraulic mounts are electronically-controlled (Fig. 13-40B). At idle (below 850 rpm), the *mount control unit* signals the solenoid to open the valve. This allows fluid circulation between the two chambers. The valve closes at higher speed. This makes the mount firmer by limiting fluid flow. The result is that less vibration reaches the body.

TRADE TALK

cam-ground piston   engine mount   piston clearance   wear-in
compression ring   forged piston   thrust bearing
cylinder liner   oil-control ring   vibration damper

MULTIPLE-CHOICE TEST

*Select the **one** correct, best, or most probable answer to each question.*
You can find the answers in the section indicated at the end of each question.

1. The purpose of the core clean-out holes is to remove the cores that formed the (➤13-2)
   a. cylinder bores
   b. water jackets
   c. holes for the freeze plugs
   d. valve guides

2. A short block includes the (➤13-4)
   a. cylinder block
   b. crankshaft
   c. pistons and rods
   d. all of the above

3. The cylinder head forms the upper end of the combustion chamber. The lower end is formed by the (➤13-8)
   a. piston and rings
   b. connecting rods and crankshaft
   c. valves
   d. cams and camshaft

4. Technician A says turbulence causes the air-fuel mixture to burn more rapidly. Technician B says turbulence slows the spread of the flame so the mixture has more time to burn. Who is right? (➤13-8)
   a. A only
   b. B only
   c. both A and B
   d. neither A nor B

5. Technician A says the precombustion chamber improves turbulence. Technician B says it produces stratified charge. Who is right? (➤13-11)
   a. A only
   b. B only
   c. both A and B
   d. neither A nor B

6. The purpose of the heat-control valve in some exhaust manifolds is to (➤13-13)
   a. add heat to the air-fuel mixture
   b. improve fuel vaporization
   c. improve cold-engine performance
   d. all of the above

7. Excessive back-and-forth movement of the crankshaft is prevented by a (➤13-17)
   a. sleeve bearing
   b. shaft journal
   c. thrust bearing
   d. harmonic balancer

8. Piston pins are usually either a press fit in the rod or (➤13-21)
   a. locked to the rod with a bolt
   b. free-floating in the rod and piston
   c. locked to the piston with a bolt
   d. a press fit in the piston

9. Scuff wear is caused by (➤13-31)
   a. abrasive wear
   b. momentary welds at TDC
   c. momentary welds at BDC
   d. excessive oil in the combustion chamber

10. Technician A says worn cylinder walls cause the engine to loose power. Technician B says engine wear increases oil consumption. Who is right? (➤13-34)
   a. A only
   b. B only
   c. both A and B
   d. neither A nor B

REVIEW QUESTIONS

1. List the types of cylinder liners and identify the types that can be replaced. (➤13-6)

2. Define *stratified charge* and explain how it is used in spark-ignition engines. (➤13-11)

3. Explain why there is a notched plate on some crankshafts. (➤13-14)

4. Describe how expansion is controlled in pistons. (➤13-24)

5. Describe the different types of engine mounts and torque struts. Explain their locations and uses on longitudinal and transverse engines. (➤13-35)

CHAPTER 14

VALVES AND VALVE TRAINS

After studying this chapter, you should be able to:

- Explain the purpose, construction, and operation of engine valves.
- Describe the advantages, construction, and operation of overhead-camshaft valve trains.
- Define *camshaft timing, valve timing, variable valve timing,* and *variable valve timing and lift.*
- Describe the construction and operation of hydraulic valve lifters.
- Explain the purpose of valve rotators and how they work.

➤ 14-1 PURPOSE OF VALVES

Each engine cylinder has at least two valves: an intake valve and an exhaust valve (➤12-9). The intake valve opens just before the intake stroke begins. This allows the air-fuel mixture to enter the cylinder. (Air only in the diesel engine.) The exhaust valve opens just before the exhaust stroke begins so the burned gases can escape from the cylinder. Figure 11-10 shows these actions.

The valves are operated by a *valve train* (➤12-9). There are two basic types of valve trains (Fig. 12-17). These are *overhead camshaft with bucket tappets* or *rocker arms,* and *camshaft in block with pushrods.*

➤ 14-2 VALVES AND VALVE TRAINS

The valves may be arranged in various ways in the cylinder head or block (Fig. 14-1).

1. L-HEAD ENGINES The L-head engine has the valves and the camshaft in the cylinder block. This arrangement was once popular for automotive engines. Now it is used only in small engines for lawn mowers and similar equipment. These are applications where light weight and simplicity are important.

The L-head engine has two drawbacks for automotive use. First, it cannot be designed to have a high compression ratio (➤15-10). The higher the compression ratio, the more power the engine produces (➤15-11). Second, the L-head engine has excessive exhaust emissions. The exhaust gas contains too much unburned and partly burned

fuel. The reason is that the combustion chamber surfaces are large and relatively cool. This prevents combustion of the layers of air-fuel mixture close to those surfaces. Automotive manufacturers completed the switch to overhead-valve engines during the 1950s.

2. OVERHEAD-VALVE ENGINES In an overhead-valve or pushrod engine, the camshaft is in the cylinder block and the valves are in the cylinder head (Figs. 14-1 and 14-2). In-line engines usually have the valves in a single row. In V-type engines, the valves may be in single rows in each bank (Figs. 12-6 and 12-14), or in double rows in each bank. With double rows, one row is intake valves. The other row is exhaust valves.

Overhead-valve engines have higher compression ratios than L-head engines. Locating the valves directly over the piston permits the *clearance volume* to be smaller. This is the volume above the piston at TDC (B in Fig. 11-14). When the air-fuel mixture is compressed into a smaller space, the compression ratio is higher. This means more engine torque and power (➤15-13).

Some overhead-valve engines have *valve reliefs* cut into the piston heads (Figs. 13-4 and 14-2). The valve reliefs provide spaces into which the valves can open without striking the piston.

Figure 14-3 shows the valve action in an overhead-valve engine with the camshaft in the cylinder block. When the cam lobe comes up under the valve lifter, the lobe pushes the lifter up (Fig. 14-3, left). This pushes the pushrod up. Pushrod movement causes the rocker arm to rock on its pivot. As one end of the rocker arm moves up, the other

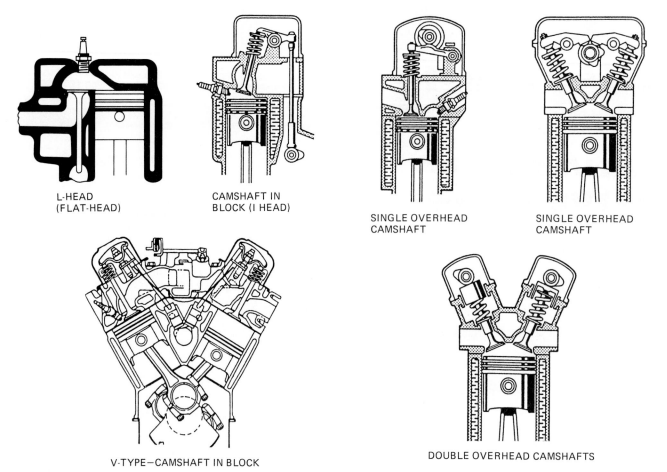

L-HEAD
(FLAT-HEAD)

CAMSHAFT IN
BLOCK (I HEAD)

SINGLE OVERHEAD
CAMSHAFT

SINGLE OVERHEAD
CAMSHAFT

V-TYPE—CAMSHAFT IN BLOCK

DOUBLE OVERHEAD CAMSHAFTS

Fig. 14-1 Various valve-train arrangements. (*ATW; Robert Bosch Corporation*)

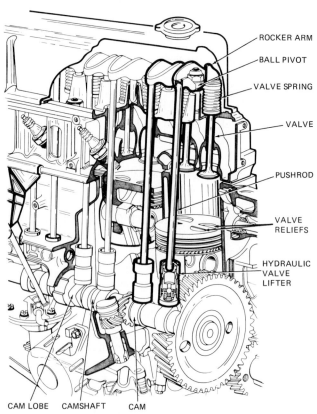

ROCKER ARM

BALL PIVOT

VALVE SPRING

VALVE

PUSHROD

VALVE
RELIEFS

HYDRAULIC
VALVE
LIFTER

CAM LOBE   CAMSHAFT   CAM

Fig. 14-2 Valve train in an overhead-valve engine. The camshaft is driven by gears from the crankshaft.

end moves down. The valve spring is compressed as the rocker arm pushes the valve stem down. This forces the valve off its seat to open the valve.

When the cam lobe passes out from under the valve lifter (Fig. 14-3, right), the valve spring expands. The spring forces the valve back up onto its seat. The stem end of the rocker arm goes up. As the other end goes down, it pushes the pushrod and valve lifter back down.

3. OVERHEAD-CAMSHAFT ENGINES Many newer engine designs place the camshaft (or camshafts) on the cylinder head. These are *overhead camshaft* (OHC) engines. One reason for the shift to OHC engines is that pushrods and rocker arms have *inertia*. This is a property of all objects. They resist changing speed and direction. Pushrod and rocker-arm inertia affects valve action. They resist moving until sufficient force is applied to them. As a result, the rocker arm and especially the pushrod bend or flex slightly before they open the valve.

Flexing has little effect at lower speeds. But flexing increases as speed increases, and with the length of the pushrod. This causes an increasing lag in valve action that tends to limit top speed. With the camshaft on the cylinder head, the cams can act directly on the bucket tappets or rocker arms. Valve action in an OHC engine using bucket tappets is described in ➤11-12 and shown in Fig. 11-17.

Many in-line OHC engines use one camshaft (Figs.

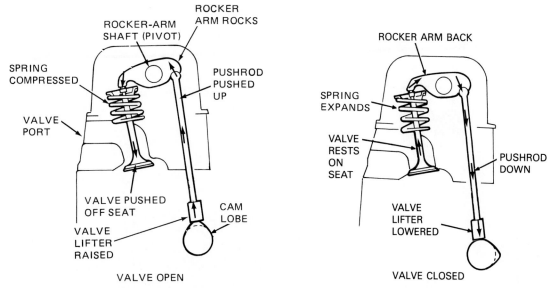

Fig. 14-3 Operation of the valve train in an overhead-valve engine.

11-1 and 11-17). These are *single overhead camshaft* (SOHC) engines. Other in-line engines use two overhead camshafts (Figs. 12-5 and 14-4). They are *double overhead camshaft* (DOHC) engines. One camshaft operates the intake valves. The other camshaft operates the exhaust valves. V-type engines may have one or two camshafts in each cylinder head.

4. MULTIVALVE ENGINES Engines have two, three, four, five, and even six valves per cylinder. Two valves and four valves per cylinder are the most common. For many years, most engines had two valves per cylinder. But to improve engine breathing and increase power output, many engines now have four valves per cylinder (Figs. 12-15 and 14-5).

Engines with more than two valves per cylinder are referred to as *multivalve engines*. The additional valves allow more air-fuel mixture to enter and the exhaust gas to escape more easily. This improves the volumetric efficiency (➤15-12) of the engine. Also, the valve-head diameter is smaller and the valves weigh less. This reduces the effects of inertia (➤15-5) and reduces the valve-spring

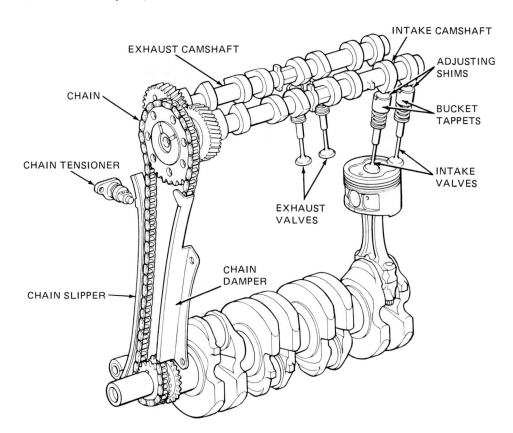

Fig. 14-4 Arrangement of the camshafts and valve train in a DOHC four-cylinder engine. The intake camshaft is chain-driven from the crankshaft. The exhaust camshaft is driven through a gear on the intake camshaft. (*Toyota Motor Sales, U.S.A., Inc.*)

161

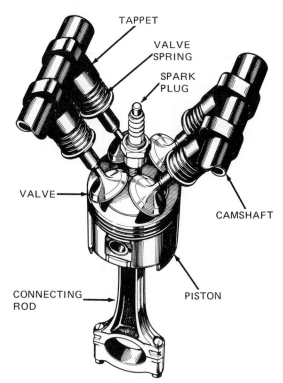

Fig. 14-5 Valve and canshaft arrangement for a four-cylinder DOHC engine with bucket tappets and four valves per cylinder (two intake and two exhaust). (*Nissan Motor Corporation*)

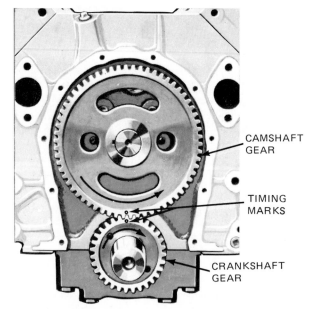

Fig. 14-6 Crankshaft and camshaft gears for a V-type OHV engine. The timing marks are on the gears. (*Chevrolet Division of General Motors Corporation*)

force needed to close a larger valve at high engine speed (➢14-2).

➢ 14-3 DRIVING THE CAMSHAFT

Figure 12-16 shows four basic ways in which the camshaft may be driven. The camshaft in the block is driven either by *timing gears* (Fig. 14-6) or by *sprockets and timing chain* (Fig. 14-7).

Sprockets are like gears, except that the teeth are shaped to fit into the chain links. A timing chain and sprocket usually run more quietly than gears. When the camshaft is driven by a timing chain, the crankshaft and camshaft rotate in the same direction. With gears, the camshaft rotates in the opposite direction.

A single overhead camshaft (SOHC) is driven by a timing chain and sprockets (Fig. 14-8), or by a toothed *timing belt and sprockets* (Fig. 14-9). Like a timing chain, the belt rotates the camshaft in the same direction as the crankshaft.

> **NOTE** The reason the gears are *timing gears* and the chains or belts are *timing chains* or *timing belts* is that they "time" the opening and closing of the valves (➢14-4).

Double-overhead camshafts (DOHC) are driven by a variety of methods. Figures 12-12 and 14-10 show a

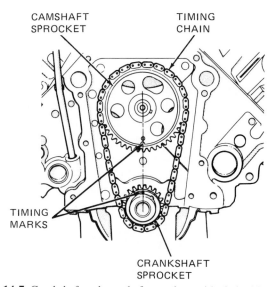

Fig. 14-7 Crankshaft and camshaft sprockets with chain drive for a V-type OHV engine. The timing marks are on the sprockets. (*Chrysler Corporation*)

DOHC V-6 engine using a single timing belt to drive all four camshafts. As in most V-type DOHC engines, the intake camshafts are toward the inside of the engine. The exhaust camshafts are toward the outside.

Figure 12-15 shows how the double overhead camshafts are driven in a Chevrolet Corvette V-8 engine. The crankshaft sprocket drives a timing chain which turns a center-mounted idler sprocket. The idler sprocket then drives a timing chain that rotates the camshafts on each bank.

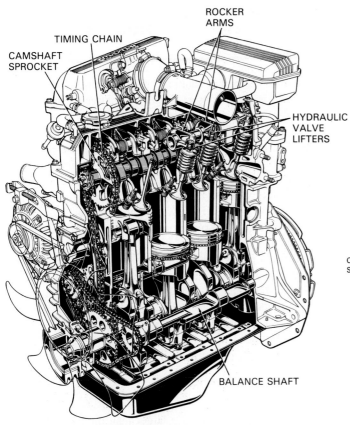

Fig. 14-8 A SOHC engine with the camshaft driven by a chain and sprockets. (*Mazda Motors of America, Inc.*)

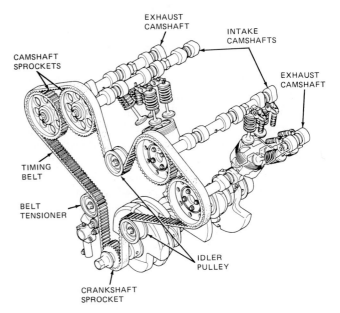

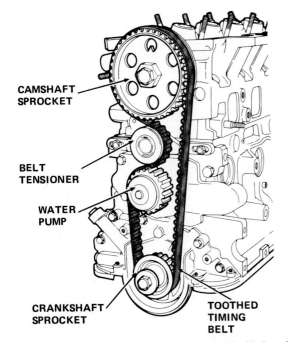

Fig. 14-9 Front end of an OHC engine using a toothed belt and sprockets to drive the camshaft. A belt tensioner is used to prevent the belt from jumping time. (*Ford Motor Company*)

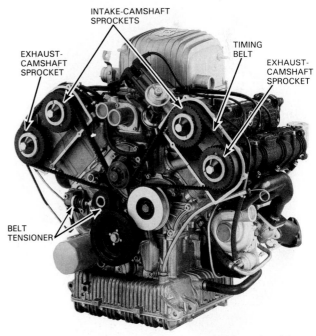

Fig. 14-10 Timing belt and sprocket arrangement used to drive the four camshafts on DOHC V-6 engines. (*Mazda Motors of America, Inc.; Maserati Automobiles Incorporated*)

163

> **NOTE** | An *idler pulley* or *idler sprocket* rests against a belt or chain to guide it or to take up slack.

Some DOHC engines use a timing belt at the front of the engine to drive the intake camshaft (Fig. 12-8). Sprockets and a chain at the front or rear of the intake camshaft then drive the exhaust camshaft. Figure 14-11 shows a DOHC V-6 engine that uses a timing belt to drive the intake camshafts. A drive gear on each intake camshaft meshes with a driven gear on each exhaust camshaft to rotate it. The Chevrolet Indy V-8 and the Ford Cosworth V-8 racing engines both use a gear train to drive all four camshafts.

➤ 14-4 CAMSHAFT TIMING

Camshaft timing is the relationship between the camshaft and the crankshaft. The camshaft is driven by the crankshaft. Anything that affects this relationship may greatly affect engine operation.

There are four strokes to the complete cycle of actions in the four-stroke-cycle engine (Chap. 11). The crankshaft must turn two times to turn the camshaft once, which opens each valve once. This 2:1 gear ratio is achieved by making the camshaft gear or sprocket twice as large as the crankshaft gear or sprocket (Figs. 14-6 and 14-10).

Fig. 14-11 A DOHC V-6 engine that uses a timing belt to drive the intake camshafts. Gears on the intake camshafts drive the exhaust camshafts. (*Toyota Motor Sales, U.S.A., Inc.*)

➤ 14-5 TIMING BELT AND CHAIN TENSIONERS

In most engines, the camshaft is driven by a timing belt or chain. As the belt or chain and the sprockets wear, the belt or chain becomes looser. This loose fit affects valve timing (➤14-18). Engine performance may suffer and exhaust emissions increase. However, the greatest danger is that a sprocket may "jump time." This occurs when the excessive slack in the belt or chain allows it to slip or jump to a different position on the sprocket. In some engines, this allows the valves to be so far out of time that they hit the tops of the pistons. Bent valves, cracked pistons, broken valve guides, and even more severe engine damage may result.

To help prevent the timing belt or chain from jumping time, many engines have a timing belt or chain *tensioner* (Figs. 14-10 and 14-11). It continually applies a slight force to the outside surface of the belt or chain. This takes up the slack. Some tensioners are spring-loaded. Others are hydraulic. These use oil pressure to keep the belt or chain stretched to the proper tension.

➤ 14-6 VALVES

The intake valve is usually larger than the exhaust valve (Fig. 14-12). The reason is that when the intake valve is open, the only force moving air-fuel mixture into the cylinder is atmospheric pressure.

> **NOTE** | Some engines have a *supercharger* or a *turbocharger* (Chap. 18). These are air pumps which increase the pressure in the intake manifold. Then, when the intake valves open, more air or air-fuel mixture is forced into the engine cylinders. This increases engine power.

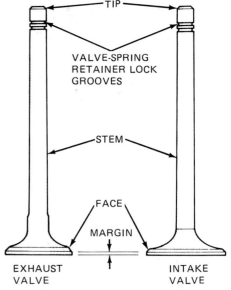

Fig. 14-12 Intake and exhaust valves. (*Chrysler Corporation*)

When the exhaust valve opens on the exhaust stroke, there is still high pressure in the engine cylinder. A smaller exhaust valve provides enough space for the high-pressure exhaust gases to get out of the cylinder. Some engines have three valves per cylinder (Fig. 14-13). Two valves are intake valves. One is an exhaust valve.

Most automotive engines run on unleaded gasoline. Lead was originally added to gasoline to permit higher compression ratios. But Federal regulations removed lead from most gasoline because the lead pollutes the atmosphere. Chapters 35 and 36 describe more about automotive air pollution.

Lead in gasoline forms a coating on the valve faces and seats. The coating acts as a lubricant. Without the lead, some faces and seats wear rapidly and *valve-seat recession* occurs. To prevent this, valves may have special coatings on their face. For severe service, the valve face is coated with *stellite* (a very hard metal).

Some valves have chrome-plated stems and a hard alloy tip welded onto the stem end (Fig. 14-14). This reduces wear on these two areas. Other valves have a hollow stem to reduce valve weight. Lighter valves reduce the effects of inertia (➤14-2). This increases engine power and responsiveness.

➤ 14-7 VALVE COOLING

The intake valve runs relatively cool. It passes only the air-fuel mixture. But the exhaust valve passes the very hot exhaust gases. The exhaust valve may become red hot in

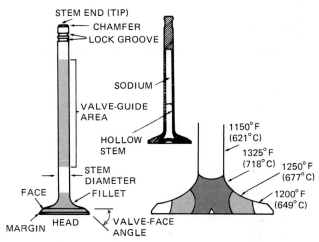

Fig. 14-14 Various parts and types of valves, with typical exhaust-valve temperatures. (*Chrysler Corporation*)

operation, with temperatures of up to 1600°F [871°C]. Figure 14-14 shows a typical temperature pattern for an exhaust valve. The valve stem is coolest. The area between the stem and the face is the hottest. The valve stem transfers heat to the valve guide to help cool the stem. The valve face transfers heat to the valve seat each time the valve closes. This helps cool the face.

The valve seat and stem are cooled by the engine cooling system. Coolant circulates through the water jackets or *coolant passages* around the valve seat and valve guide in the cylinder head (Fig. 14-15). Some heads have

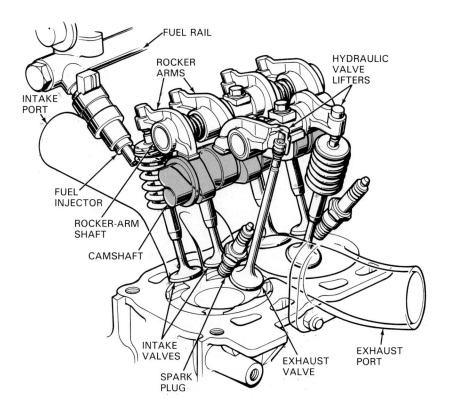

Fig. 14-13 Valve-train arrangement in engine using three valves per cylinder, two intake valves and one exhaust valve. The valves are operated by rocker arms with built-in hydraulic valve lifters. (*Ford Motor Company*)

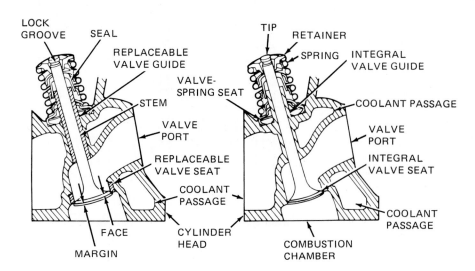

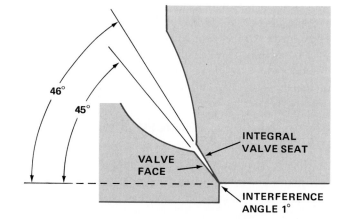

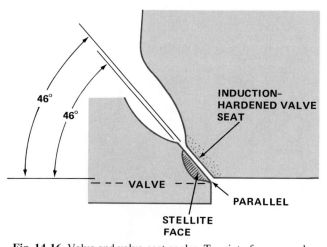

Fig. 14-15 Valves installed in cylinder head, showing the coolant passages and types of valve guides and seats. (*Ford Motor Company*)

nozzles that force coolant around the valve seats. Others use deflectors in the water jackets to improve coolant circulation around the seats.

To help cool exhaust valves, some have hollow stems partly filled with the metal *sodium* (Fig. 14-14). Sodium melts at 208°F [97.8°C]. When the engine is running, the sodium is a liquid. Valve movement throws the sodium up and down in the stem. This circulation takes heat from the valve head and carries it up to the cooler stem. A sodium-filled exhaust valve runs about 200°F [93.3°C] cooler than a nonfilled valve.

> **CAUTION!**
>
> Sodium is a dangerous and highly reactive metal. A piece of sodium dropped into water will burst into flame with explosive violence. If the sodium gets on your skin, it will cause deep and serious burns. Be careful when handling a sodium-cooled valve that has a cracked or broken stem. Escaping sodium could explode and severely injure you! Never cut into or try to open a sodium-cooled valve. Dispose of an old or damaged sodium-cooled valve as *hazardous waste* (➤4-13).

➤ 14-8 VALVE SEAT

The *valve seat* is the machined surface on which the valve face rests when the valve is closed. There are two types of valve seats: *integral* and *replaceable*. Most engines with cast-iron cylinder heads have integral valve seats (Fig. 14-15, right). These are ground into the combustion-chamber end of the valve ports in the cylinder head. To reduce wear, integral exhaust-valve seats are hardened by an electric heating process called *induction hardening* (Fig. 14-16). During manufacture of the cylinder head, the seat area is heated by an electrical device and then quickly cooled. A stellite coating may be spray-welded onto the valve face for use with an induction-hardened seat.

Replaceable valve seats are called *valve-seat inserts*

Fig. 14-16 Valve and valve-seat angles. Top, interference angle. Bottom, an induction-hardened valve seat. The valve shown is faced with stellite, which is resistant to heat and wear. The faces of the valve and valve seat (bottom) are parallel and have the same angle.

(Figs. 14-15 and 14-17). These rings of heat-resistant steel alloy are pressed into some cast-iron cylinder heads and all aluminum heads. Worn or damaged valve-seat inserts can be replaced. Sometimes a severely damaged integral valve seat is bored out and a valve-seat insert installed.

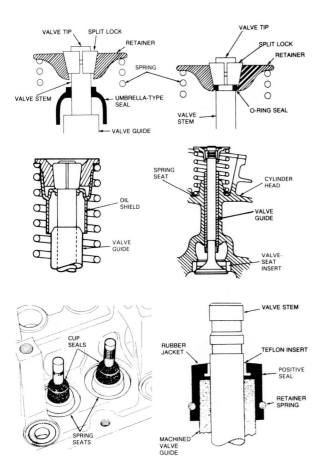

Fig. 14-17 Valve-spring attachments with various types of valve-stem oil seals. (*Chrysler Corporation*)

An *interference angle* (Fig. 14-16, top) between the valve and valve seat is recommended for many engines. The interference angle is produced by grinding the valve face at an angle slightly less than the valve-seat angle. For example, a typical interference angle of one degree is produced by grinding the valve seat to a 46-degree angle and the valve face to a 45-degree angle. The result is greater seating force at the outer edge of the valve seat. This helps the valve face cut through any deposits that form. The interference angle gradually disappears as the face and seat wear.

An interference angle is not always recommended. Stellite-faced valves and induction-hardened seats may be ground to the same angle (Fig. 14-16, bottom). Also, valves that have *valve rotators* (➤14-14) may not use an interference angle.

➤ 14-9 VALVE GUIDES

The valves slide up and down in *valve guides* in the cylinder head (Figs. 14-15 and 14-17). In some engines, the valve guides are replaceable metal tubes that are pressed or driven into the cylinder head (Fig. 14-15, left). Other engines use integral valve guides (Fig. 14-15, right). These are basically holes bored in the cylinder head.

Valve guides must provide a close fit with the valve stems. This prevents excessive oil from getting into the combustion chambers. However, there must be enough clearance between the guides and stems so the valves can move freely up and down.

➤ 14-10 VALVE-SPRING ATTACHMENT

On a cast-iron cylinder head, one end of the valve spring may press against a spring seat machined into the cylinder head (Fig. 14-17). In an aluminum cylinder head, the spring presses against a *valve-spring seat* (Fig. 14-15). This prevents excessive wear. The other end of the valve spring is attached to the valve stem with a *spring retainer* and *split locks* or *keepers* (Fig. 14-17).

The spring is installed by compressing it with the retainer above it. Then the locks are installed in the groove or grooves in the valve stem (Figs. 14-15 and 14-17). When the spring is released, the spring force wedges the tapered locks into the tapered hole in the retainer. This holds the locks and retainer in place.

➤ 14-11 ROCKER ARMS

A *rocker arm* is a pivoted lever that transfers cam or pushrod motion to the valve stem (Figs. 14-13 and 14-18). Many rocker arms are made of stamped steel (Figs. 14-2 and 14-18). Others are forged or cast aluminum (Figs. 14-19).

Some rocker arms are adjustable. One type of stud-mounted rocker arm (Figs. 14-18C and 14-20) is adjusted by turning the stud nut. Other rocker arms have an adjustment screw or nut in one end (Fig. 14-18B).

The pivot point of a rocker arm is usually offset from the center. This provides a *rocker-arm ratio* of about 1.5:1. In Fig. 14-21, an upward pushrod movement of 0.250 inch [6.35 mm] forces the valve stem down 1.5 times that distance. This is 0.375 inch [9.5 mm]. Because of the rocker-arm ratio, the cam lobe can be smaller. However, this places a greater load on the pushrod, valve lifter, and cam lobe.

Figure 14-22 shows a valve train in which the rocker arm floats between the valve stem and a *hydraulic tappet*. The tappet works like a *hydraulic valve lifter* (➤14-16). The center of the rocker arm rides on a cam on the cam shaft.

➤ 14-12 VALVE-STEM OIL SEALS

Various types of *valve-stem oil seals* (Fig. 14-17) keep excess oil out of the combustion chambers. The seals attach either to the valve stem or valve guide. When intake-valve seals fail, oil is drawn down between the valve stems and guides into the combustion chamber.

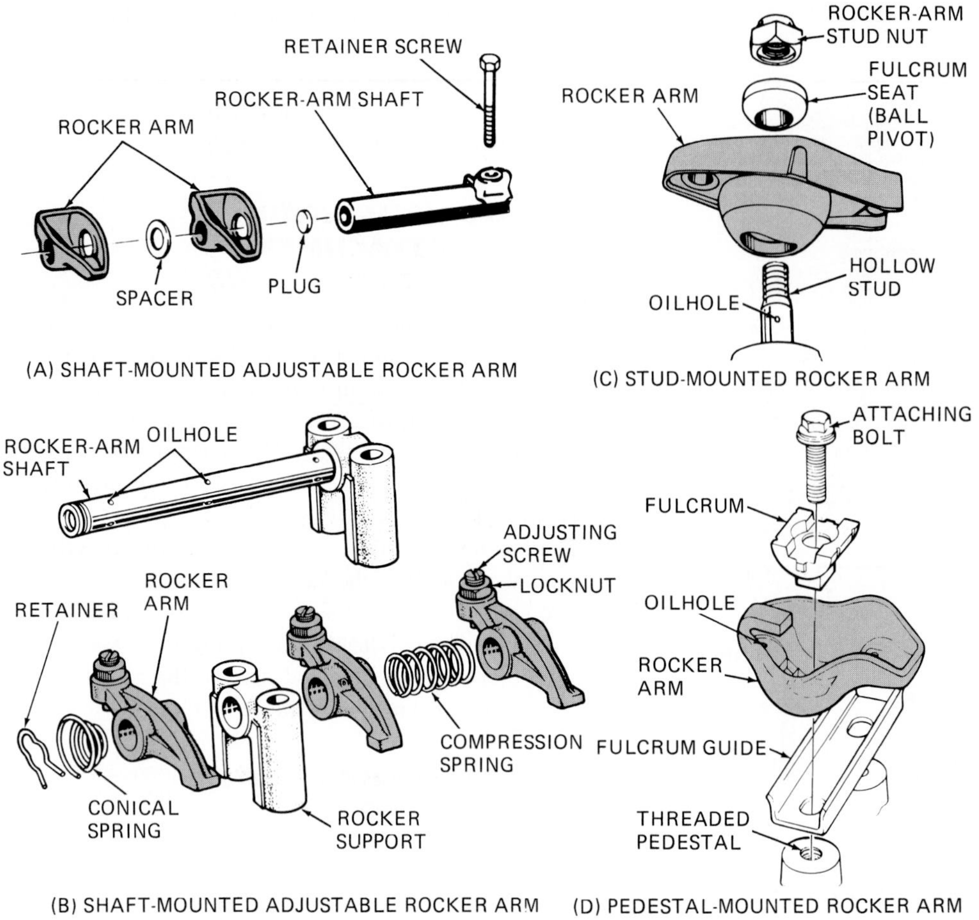

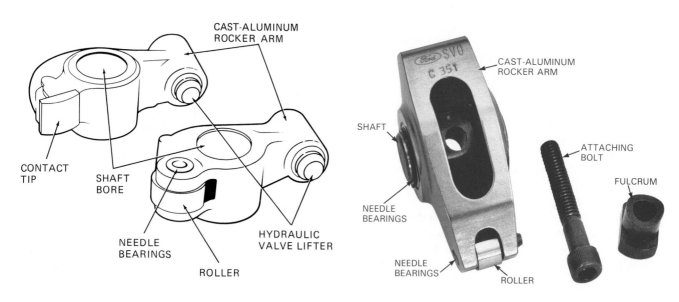

Fig. 14-18 Four types of rocker arms used in overhead-valve engines.

RETAINER SCREW

ROCKER-ARM SHAFT

ROCKER ARM

SPACER

PLUG

(A) SHAFT-MOUNTED ADJUSTABLE ROCKER ARM

ROCKER-ARM STUD NUT

FULCRUM SEAT (BALL PIVOT)

ROCKER ARM

HOLLOW STUD

OILHOLE

(C) STUD-MOUNTED ROCKER ARM

ROCKER-ARM SHAFT

OILHOLE

RETAINER

ROCKER ARM

CONICAL SPRING

ROCKER SUPPORT

ADJUSTING SCREW

LOCKNUT

COMPRESSION SPRING

(B) SHAFT-MOUNTED ADJUSTABLE ROCKER ARM

ATTACHING BOLT

FULCRUM

OILHOLE

ROCKER ARM

FULCRUM GUIDE

THREADED PEDESTAL

(D) PEDESTAL-MOUNTED ROCKER ARM

CAST-ALUMINUM ROCKER ARM

CONTACT TIP

SHAFT BORE

NEEDLE BEARINGS

ROLLER

HYDRAULIC VALVE LIFTER

(A) SHAFT-MOUNTED OHC ROCKER ARMS

CAST-ALUMINUM ROCKER ARM

SHAFT

NEEDLE BEARINGS

NEEDLE BEARINGS

ROLLER

ATTACHING BOLT

FULCRUM

(B) SHAFT-MOUNTED OHV ROCKER ARM

Fig. 14-19 Aluminum rocker arms for (left) OHC engines and (right) OHV engines. (*Mitsubishi Motor Sales of America, Inc.; Ford Motor Company*)

Failure of the exhaust-valve seals allows oil to enter the engine exhaust ports.

Figure 14-17 shows four types of valve seals. These are the *umbrella seal,* the *O-ring seal,* the *cup seal,* and the Teflon-insert *positive seal.*

➤ **14-13 VALVE ROTATION**

If the valve rotates as it opens, there is less chance of deposits causing the valve to stick partly open when it should be closed. Valve rotation also results in more even

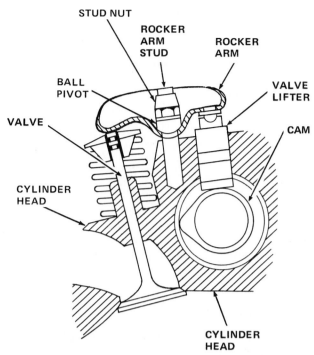

Fig. 14-20 Valve train for an OHC engine using a rocker arm. The valve-train clearance is adjustable by turning the nut on the rocker-arm stud.

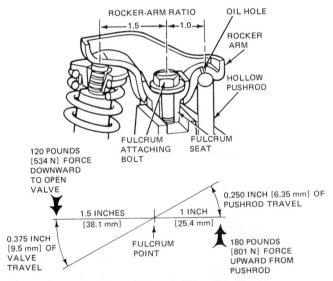

Fig. 14-21 Rocker-arm ratio in an OHV engine. Note the arrangement for oiling the valve train. The oil flows up through the hollow pushrod to the oil hole in the rocker arm. (*Ford Motor Company*)

valve-face temperature. Some parts of the valve seat may be hotter than others. If the same part of the valve face continues to seat on the hot spot, a similar hot spot develops in the valve face. It wears faster and the valve may burn. Valve rotation helps prevent hot spots on the valve face.

In many engines, rocker-arm contact with the valve stem

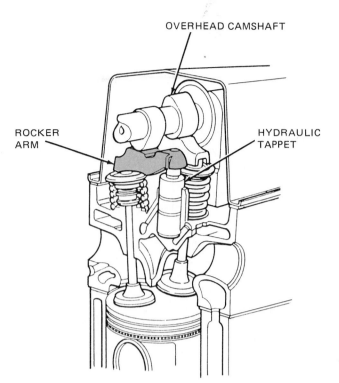

Fig. 14-22 An OHC valve train in which the rocker arm floats between the valve stem and a hydraulic tappet. The rotating cam lobe acts against the top of the rocker arm. (*Ford Motor Company*)

is slightly offset from the centerline of the valve. Every time the rocker arm presses against the valve stem, the off-center push rotates the valve slightly. This helps reduce valve seat and guide wear. It also prolongs valve life, helps remove carbon deposits, and improves combustion-chamber sealing.

➤ 14-14 POSITIVE VALVE ROTATOR

Some engines use *positive valve rotators* (Fig. 14-23) on the exhaust valves, or on all valves. The rotators are either above or below the valve springs. As the valve opens, small balls in the rotator are forced to roll up inclined grooves. This rotates the valve stem slightly.

➤ 14-15 VALVE LIFTERS (TAPPETS)

In pushrod engines, the *valve lifter* or *tappet* is the part that transmits cam-lobe movement to the pushrod (Figs. 14-2 and 14-3). The cam lobe raises the tappet which raises the pushrod. The pushrod causes the rocker arm to rock. This pushes the valve down, off its seat.

In some OHC engines, the cam-lobe motion is sent directly to the valve stems by bucket tappets (Figs. 14-4 and 14-5). Other OHC engines transmit cam-lobe motion through rocker arms to the valve stems (Figs. 14-20 and 14-22).

There are two types of valve lifters or tappets. These are *mechanical* (or *solid*), and *hydraulic* (➤14-16). The

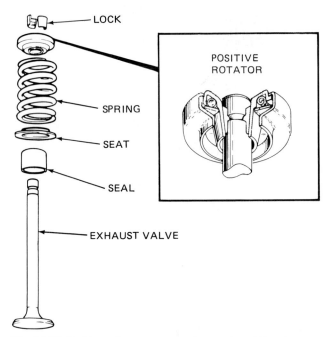

Fig. 14-23 Positive valve rotator on exhaust valve. (*Chrysler Corporation*)

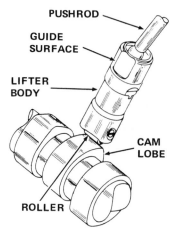

Fig. 14-25 A roller-type valve lifter or roller tappet has rolling contact with the cam lobe instead of sliding contact. (*Oldsmobile Division of General Motors Corporation*)

mechanical lifter is a solid or hollow cylinder. It rides on the cam (Fig. 14-24) and transmits cam-lobe motion directly to the valve stem through a bucket tappet (Fig. 14-5), or through a pushrod (Fig. 14-3) or rocker arm (Fig. 14-22). The face that rides on the cam lobe appears flat, although it usually is slightly *convex* (curved outward). The cam lobe makes off-center contact with the lifter face. This causes the lifter to rotate slightly each time it is raised.

Many engines use roller tappets (Fig. 14-25). These have a hardened steel roller turning on needle bearings. The roller rolls over the cam instead of sliding on it. This reduces friction and improves fuel economy.

Roller tappets must not rotate in their bores. This would cause the roller to turn sideways. To prevent rotation, the lifter has a flat *guide surface* on the body. The guide allows up-and-down motion while preventing lifter rotation.

> ## 14-16 HYDRAULIC VALVE LIFTER

The hydraulic valve lifter uses engine oil pressure to keep in contact with the cam lobe and, in pushrod engines, with the pushrod. In overhead camshaft engines with bucket tappets (Fig. 14-4), the tappet or lifter is between the cam lobe and the valve stem. The hydraulic lifter automatically adjusts to any normal variation in valve-train clearance. The clearance is caused by expansion or wear. Using hydraulic lifters reduces *tappet noise,* wear on valve-train parts, and the need for frequent valve-train clearance adjustments.

Figure 14-26 shows how a hydraulic valve lifter operates in a pushrod engine. Oil under pressure from the engine oil pump is fed into the lifter from an oil gallery. The oil gallery runs the length of the cylinder block. When

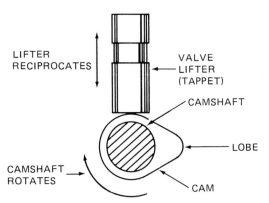

Fig. 14-24 Cam and lifter operation. As the cam rotates, the lifter moves up and down.

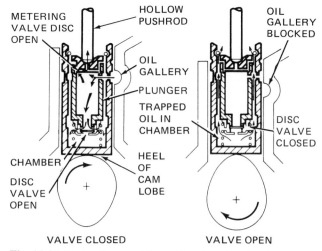

Fig. 14-26 Hydraulic valve lifter with valve closed and open. (*Chrysler Corporation*)

the valve closes, oil flows into the lifter through oil holes in the lifter body and the inner plunger (Fig. 14-26, left). The oil forces the disc valve to open. Oil then flows into the space below the plunger. This raises the plunger, which forces the pushrod up until all clearance in the valve train is eliminated. When the cam lobe raises the lifter, there is no tappet noise. The hydraulic lifter has taken up the clearance which creates the tapping sound.

Raising the lifter suddenly increases the oil pressure under the plunger (Fig. 14-26, right). This closes the disc valve, trapping the oil in the chamber. Now the hydraulic lifter acts as a solid lifter. It moves up, causing the valve to open. When the cam lobe moves out from under the lifter, the valve spring forces the valve closed. This action pushes the lifter back down, relieving the pressure in the chamber. If any oil has leaked out, more oil from the gallery now flows in to refill the chamber. Figure 14-27 shows how the hydraulic valve lifter can be combined with a roller mounted on needle bearings.

In many pushrod engines, oil from the lifter lubricates the rocker-arm pivot and contact faces. When the valve is closed, oil flows from the pushrod seat in the lifter up through the hollow pushrod (Figs. 14-21 and 14-26). In some OHC engines, the hydraulic valve lifter is built into the valve-stem end of the rocker arm (Fig. 14-13). Other OHC engines use hydraulic lifters built into the bucket tappets (Fig. 14-28).

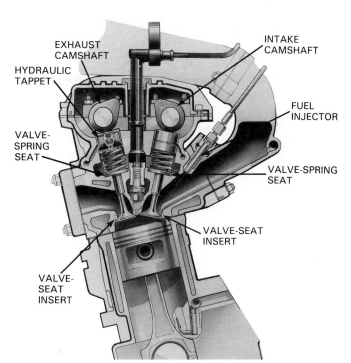

Fig. 14-28 A DOHC engine with hydraulic tappets. These are bucket tappets with built-in hydraulic lifters. (*Volkswagen of America, Inc.*)

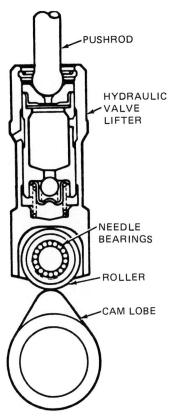

Fig. 14-27 Roller-type hydraulic valve lifter used in an OHV engine. (*Chevrolet Division of General Motors Corporation*)

➤ **14-17 LASH ADJUSTERS**

Some OHC engines use hydraulic valve lifters or tappets that only take up clearance in the valve train. These are *lash adjusters* (Figs. 14-19 and 14-29). They do not contact the cam lobe, and may not transmit cam-lobe movement. As in hydraulic valve lifters (➤14-16), engine oil pressure expands the lash adjuster to take up the clearance. Figure 14-19A shows an OHC rocker arm with a built-in lash adjuster ("hydraulic valve lifter") in one end.

➤ **14-18 VALVE TIMING**

Valve timing refers to when the valves open and close in relation to piston position. Figure 14-30 shows a typical valve-timing diagram. The specifications are given as degrees for *timing points* before or after TDC or BDC. The Society of Automotive Engineers (SAE) recommended practice is to measure the timing points at 0.006 inch [0.15 mm] valve lift. With mechanical lifters, the valves must first be adjusted to the specified clearance (Chap. 39).

In Fig. 14-30, the exhaust valve starts to open at 47 degrees before BDC on the power stroke. The valve stays open until 21 degrees after TDC on the intake stroke. This gives more time for the exhaust gases to leave the cylinder. By the time the piston reaches 47 degrees before BDC on the power stroke, the combustion pressure has dropped considerably. Little power is lost by giving the exhaust gas this extra time to exit.

171

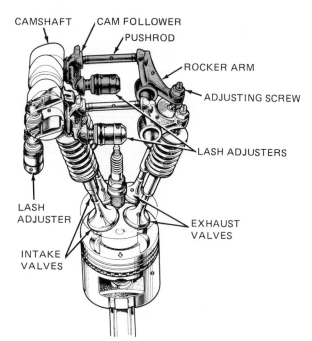

Fig. 14-29 An engine using a single overhead camshaft to operate four valves per cylinder. The valve train includes lash adjusters, rocker arms, and pushrods. (*American Honda Motor Company, Inc.*)

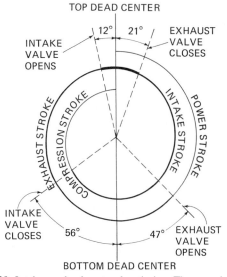

Fig. 14-30 Intake- and exhaust-valve timing. The complete cycle of events is shown as a 720-degree spiral, which represents two complete crankshift revolutions. Timing of valves varies for different engines. (*ATW*)

The intake valve (in Fig. 14-30) starts to open 12 degrees before TDC. It remains open for 56 degrees past BDC after the intake stroke ends. This gives additional time for air-fuel mixture to flow into the cylinder.

The exhaust valve closes 21 degrees after TDC (Fig. 14-30). This provides a *valve overlap* of 33 degrees. Valve overlap is the number of degrees of crankshaft rotation during which both the intake and exhaust values are

open. Valves do not open and close instantly. It takes several degrees of crankshaft rotation for the values to fully open or close after passing the timing points. Valve overlap helps *scavenge* or expel the remaining exhaust gases from the cylinder.

Valve timing is a function of cam-lobe shape, and the relationship between valve opening and closing and the position of the crankshaft. Changing the relationship between the driving and driven gears, or sprockets, changes valve timing. For example, suppose a worn timing belt or chain jumps time (➤14-5). This causes the camshaft to fall behind. The valves open and close later. This reduces engine performance and causes engine overheating. Timing gears and sprockets are marked so they can be properly aligned on reassembly (Figs. 14-6 and 14-7).

➤ 14-19 VARIABLE VALVE TIMING

The engine has a lower *volumetric efficiency* (➤15-12) at high speed. The intake valves are open a much shorter time so there is less time for the air-fuel mixture to enter the cylinders. If the intake valves opened earlier at high speed, the air-fuel mixture would start entering earlier so more would get in.

One way to open the intake valves earlier at high speed is to use a *variable-timing camshaft* (Fig. 14-31). It has a flexible connection between the camshaft sprocket and the camshaft. The connection includes a hydraulic piston operated by engine oil pressure and a solenoid-operated oil-control valve. When the electronic control module (ECM) signals the solenoid to close the valve, the oil pressure forces the piston forward (toward the camshaft in Fig. 14-31). As the piston moves, the internal teeth of the piston slide up the inclined teeth on the helical drive gear. This moves the camshaft ahead and advances camshaft timing about 10 degrees. The intake valves open earlier.

Another way to vary valve timing is being developed. Instead of a camshaft, electric *solenoids* (➤10-11) open the valves. Each solenoid is mounted so its plunger is against the end of the valve. Sensors send information on engine speed, load, and other variables to an electronic control module (ECM). The ECM then determines when and how long to open the valve. At the proper time, the ECM sends a voltage signal to the solenoid. This energizes the solenoid. Its plunger extends and opens the valve. At higher engine speeds, the ECM opens the valves earlier and may hold them open longer.

➤ 14-20 VARIABLE VALVE TIMING AND LIFT

Figure 14-32 shows an electronically-controlled *variable valve timing and lift system*. It can change both valve timing and valve lift. This gives the engine the smooth idle of a passenger-car engine and the high-speed performance of a racing engine.

The four-valve DOHC engine uses shaft-mounted rocker arms to transmit cam-lobe movement to the valve stems. The camshaft has three lobes for each pair of intake valves and exhaust valves. The third rocker arm is the *mid rocker arm* (5 in Fig. 14-32). It is between each pair of valves. Each rocker arm has a built-in hydraulic piston. Operation of the piston engages or disengages that rocker arm. The difference in performance occurs because each cam lobe is different. The center cam lobe is for high rpm. The primary and secondary cam lobes are for low rpm.

Sensors on the engine send information on engine speed, engine load, vehicle speed, and coolant temperature to the ECM. At a predetermined switch-over point, the ECM sends a voltage signal to a solenoid. As the solenoid opens and closes, engine oil pressure is sent to the pistons in the selected rocker arms. The rocker arms then engage or disengage. This changes which cam lobes are operating the valves. The change from the low lift of the outboard lobes to the higher lift and longer duration of the center lobe takes about 0.1 second. The system does not engage at low speed or when the engine is under no load.

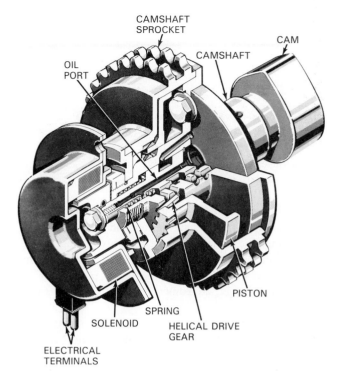

Fig. 14-31 A variable-timing camshaft which uses a solenoid controlled by the electronic control module (ECM) to open the intake valves earlier at high speed. (*Mercedes-Benz of North America, Inc.*)

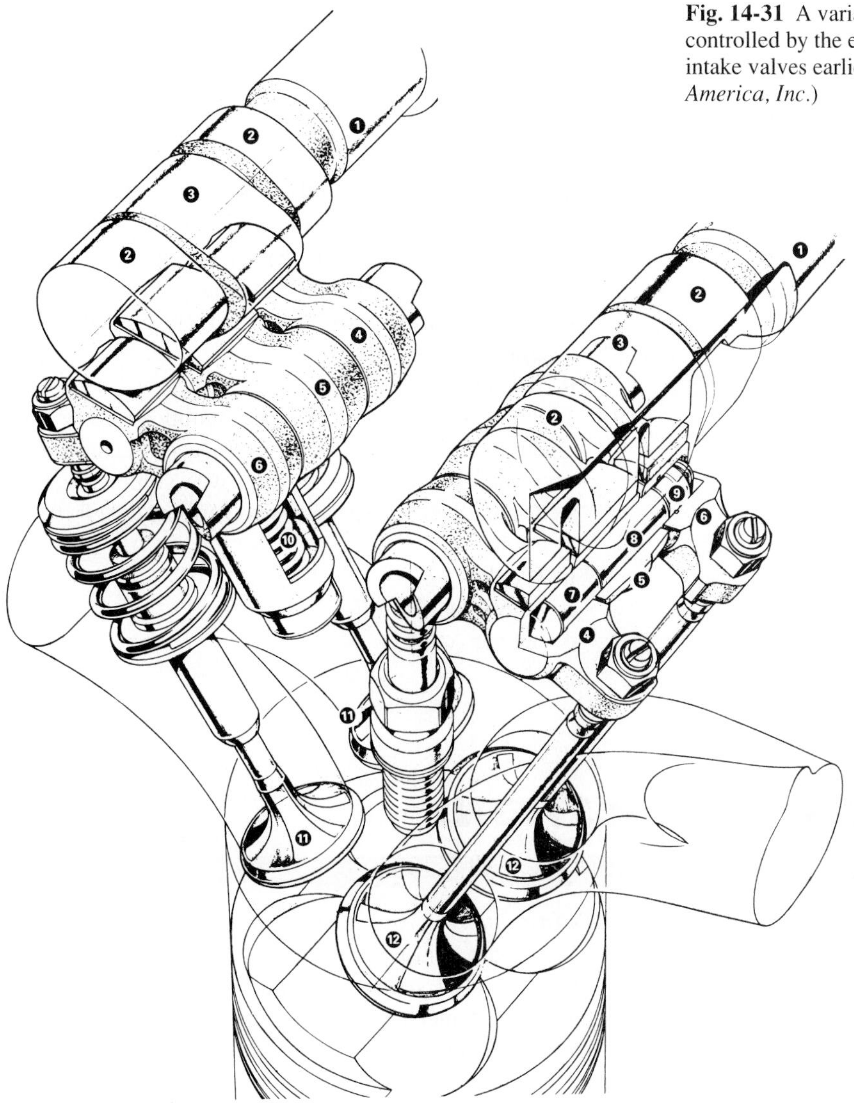

Fig. 14-32 Electronically-controlled variable valve timing and lift system. (*American Honda Motor Company, Inc.*)

① Camshaft
② Cam lobe for low rpm
③ Cam lobe for high rpm
④ Primary rocker arm
⑤ Mid rocker arm   ⑨ Stopper pin
⑥ Secondary rocker arm   ⑩ Lost-motion spring
⑦ Hydraulic piston A   ⑪ Exhaust valve
⑧ Hydraulic piston B   ⑫ Intake valve

173

MULTIPLE-CHOICE TEST

*Select the **one** correct, best, or most probable answer to each question.*
You can find the answers in the section indicated at the end of each question.

1. Two basic types of valve trains are (➤14-1)
   a. single-overhead camshaft (SOHC) and double-overhead camshaft (DOHC)
   b. pushrod and overhead valve
   c. camshaft in block and overhead camshaft
   d. fixed timing and variable timing

2. When the camshaft is in the cylinder block, the parts in the valve train include the cam and the (➤14-2)
   a. lifter, pushrod, rocker arm, and valve spring
   b. bucket tappet, adjustment screw, pushrod, and rocker arm
   c. roller tappet, adjustment screw, pivot, and roller rocker
   d. lifter, pushrod, lash adjuster, and valve spring

3. The camshaft is driven by sprockets and chain or toothed belt, or by (➤14-3)
   a. the distributor shaft
   b. an oil-pump gear
   c. timing gears
   d. a timing belt

4. Technician A says in an engine with one intake and one exhaust valve, the larger valve is the exhaust valve. Technician B says the larger valve is the intake valve. Who is right? (➤14-6)
   a. A only
   b. B only
   c. both A and B
   d. neither A nor B

5. When a valve-face angle is ground 1 degree less than the seat angle, it is called (➤14-8)
   a. sloppy workmanship
   b. a competition angle
   c. an interference angle
   d. induction hardening

6. Technician A says the valve rotates slightly as it opens. Technician B says the valve rotates slightly as it closes. Who is right? (➤14-13 and 14-14)
   a. A only
   b. B only
   c. both A and B
   d. neither A nor B

7. In the hydraulic valve lifter that rides on the camshaft, the oil that fills the chamber under the plunger (➤14-16)
   a. is pressurized by the engine oil pump
   b. flows through an oil gallery in the block
   c. enters the lifter through holes in the body and plunger
   d. all of the above

8. Technician A says *lash adjuster* is only another name for a valve lifter. Technician B says a lash adjuster does not contact the cam lobe. Who is right? (➤14-17)
   a. A only
   b. B only
   c. both A and B
   d. neither A nor B

9. Valve overlap is the number of degrees of crankshaft rotation during which (➤14-18)
   a. both intake and exhaust valves are closed
   b. both intake and exhaust valves are open
   c. the valves are moving from fully closed to the timing point
   d. the valves float

10. Technician A says variable valve timing improves volumetric efficiency at low engine speed. Technician B says variable valve timing improves volumetric efficiency at all engine speeds. Who is right? (➤14-19)
    a. A only
    b. B only
    c. both A and B
    d. neither A nor B

REVIEW QUESTIONS

1. Explain why tensioners are used with some timing belts and chains, and what can happen if a belt or chain jumps time. (➤14-5)

2. What is *valve-seat recession,* and what is done to prevent it? (➤14-6)

3. Describe the types of valve-stem oil seals, and how they prevent oil loss. (➤14-12)

4. Define *tappet noise,* and explain how a hydraulic valve lifter or lash adjuster prevents it. (➤14-16 and 14-17)

5. Describe how you would check valve timing on an engine with mechanical lifters, and on an engine with hydraulic lifters. (➤14-18)

CHAPTER 15

ENGINE MEASUREMENTS AND PERFORMANCE

After studying this chapter, you should be able to:

- Define *work, energy,* and *inertia.*
- Define *friction* and explain the three kinds of friction.
- Explain piston displacement and its relationship to compression ratio.
- Define *volumetric efficiency* and explain its relationship to torque and horsepower.
- Define *horsepower* and explain its relationship to volumetric efficiency and torque.
- Define *thermal efficiency* and *mechanical efficiency.*

➤ 15-1 WORK

Work is the moving of an object against an opposing force. The object is moved by a push, a pull, or a lift. For example, when lifting a weight, it moves upward against the pull of gravity. Work is done on the weight.

Work is measured in terms of distance and force. Suppose a 5-pound weight is lifted 5 feet (Fig. 15-1). The work done on the weight is 25 foot-pounds (ft-lb), or 5 feet times 5 pounds. *Distance times force equals work.*

In the metric system, work is measured in *meter-kilograms* (m-kg) or *joules* (J). For example, lifting a 5-kg weight [11 pounds] a distance of one meter [3.28 feet] requires 5 m-kg of work [36.08 ft-lb]. The joule is a unit of measure of energy (➤15-2). One joule is the energy required to lift one kilogram [2.2 lbs] a distance of 10 centimeters [3.9 inches]. One foot-pound equals 1.356 J.

➤ 15-2 ENERGY

Energy is the ability to do work. When work is done on an object, energy is stored in that object. Lifting a weight (Fig. 15-1) stores energy in it. The weight can do work if it is dropped. Work is done on a car when it is accelerating. Energy is being stored in it.

➤ 15-3 POWER

Work can be done slowly or it can be done rapidly. The rate at which work is done is called *power*. A machine that can do a large amount of work in a short time is a *high-*

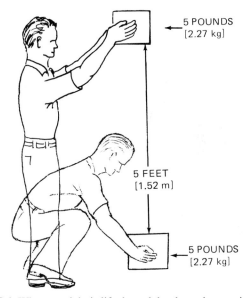

5 POUNDS [2.27 kg]

5 FEET [1.52 m]

5 POUNDS [2.27 kg]

Fig. 15-1 When a weight is lifted, work has been done on it.

powered machine. "Power" is the rate, or speed, at which work is done. Power requires motion. Something must be moving. Power is usually measured as *horsepower* [hp] or as *kilowatts* [kW] (metric). Later sections describe engine power measurements.

➤ 15-4 TORQUE

Torque is a twisting or turning force. You apply torque to the top of a screw-top jar when you loosen it (Fig. 15-2). You apply torque to the steering wheel when you steer a

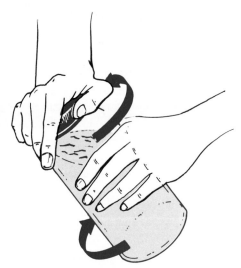

Fig. 15-2 Torque, or twisting force, must be applied to loosen and remove the top from a screw-top jar.

car around a curve. The engine applies torque to the car wheels so they rotate.

NOTE	*Torque* and *power* are not the same. Torque is turning force which *may or may not result in motion.* Power is the rate at which work is done (➤15-3). This means something *must be* in motion.

Torque is measured in pound-feet [lb-ft]. (Work is measured in foot-pounds [ft-lb]). For example, a 20-pound push on a 1 1/2-foot crank produces 30-pound-feet of torque (Fig. 15-3). The torque pushes on the crank whether it turns or not. The metric measurement of torque is made in *newton-meters* [N-m].

➤ 15-5 INERTIA

Inertia causes an object to resist any change of speed or direction of travel. A motionless object tends to remain motionless. A moving object tends to keep moving at the same speed and in the same direction.

When the automobile is standing still, its inertia must be

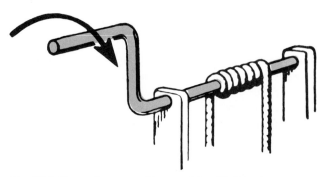

Fig. 15-3 Torque is measured in pound-feet (lb-ft) or in newton-meters [N-m]. It is calculated by multiplying the push by the crankshaft offset, or the distance of the push from the rotating shaft.

176

overcome by applying power to make it move. When the automobile goes around a curve, inertia tries to keep the car moving in a straight line. The tires must overcome this tendency. Otherwise inertia may cause the car to skid off the road.

➤ 15-6 FRICTION

Friction is resistance to motion between two objects in contact with each other. Suppose you put a book on a table and then pushed the book (Fig. 15-4). You find that it takes force to move the book. If you put a second book on top of the first book, you find it takes more force to move the two books. The *greater* the load, *the greater the friction.*

There are three classes of friction. They are *dry, greasy,* and *viscous.*

1. DRY FRICTION This is the resistance to motion between two dry objects. An example is a board being dragged across a floor. The automotive braking system uses dry friction to produce the braking action.

2. GREASY FRICTION This is the friction between two objects thinly coated with oil or grease. Greasy friction occurs in the engine when first starting. The oil may have drained away from the bearings, cylinder walls, piston rings, and pistons. The thin film that remains provides greasy friction. However, it is not enough to protect the engine from wear. This is why most engine wear occurs during initial starting and warm-up. The lubricating system quickly supplies oil as soon as the engine starts.

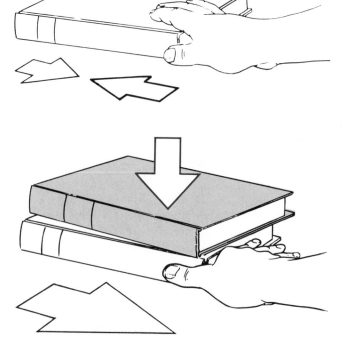

Fig. 15-4 Top, friction resists the push on the book. Bottom, increasing the weight or load increases the friction.

3. VISCOUS FRICTION *Viscosity* refers to the tendency of liquids such as oil to resist flowing. A heavy oil is more viscous and flows more slowly than a light oil.

Viscous friction is the resistance to motion between layers of liquid. In an engine bearing, layers of oil adhere to the stationary bearing and to the rotating shaft (Fig. 15-5). They wedge between the two. This lifts the shaft so the oil supports the shaft. There is no metal-to-metal contact. The only resistance to shaft rotation is the viscous friction between the layers of oil.

Figure 15-6 shows the three types of bearing surfaces in the engine. Oil protects these surfaces.

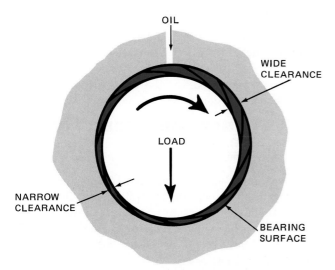

Fig. 15-5 Shaft rotation causes layers of clinging oil to be dragged around with it. The oil moves from the wide clearance and is wedged into the narrow clearance, thereby supporting the shaft weight on an oil film. The clearances are exaggerated.

ENGINE MECHANICAL MEASUREMENTS

➤ 15-7 ENGINE MEASUREMENTS

Earlier sections describe torque and power. Following sections describe engine *performance measurements* including volumetric efficiency. However, engine performance often depends on *mechanical measurements* of the engine. These include bore and stroke, piston displacement, and compression ratio. The mechanical measurements greatly affect engine torque and power. They also affect its *operating range,* or speed.

➤ 15-8 BORE AND STROKE

The size of an engine cylinder is given by its bore and stroke (Fig. 15-7). The *bore* is the diameter of the cylinder. The *stroke* is the distance the piston travels from BDC to TDC. The bore is always given first. For example, in a 4- by 3 1/2-inch cylinder, the bore is 4 inches and the stroke is 3 1/2 inches. These measurements are used to figure piston displacement (➤15-9). An engine with a larger bore than stroke is "oversquare." A "square" engine has a bore and stroke of equal size.

There are several reasons for square and oversquare engines. A shorter stroke has less friction loss. The pistons and rings move shorter distances. A shorter stroke reduces the load on the engine bearings. The shorter stroke also reduces engine height. The car can have a lower hood line.

Manufacturers have lengthened the stroke in some engines to reduce exhaust emissions. This gives a longer time for the air-fuel mixture to burn. The result is more complete combustion and cleaner exhaust gas.

Fig. 15-6 Three types of friction-bearing surfaces in an automotive engine.

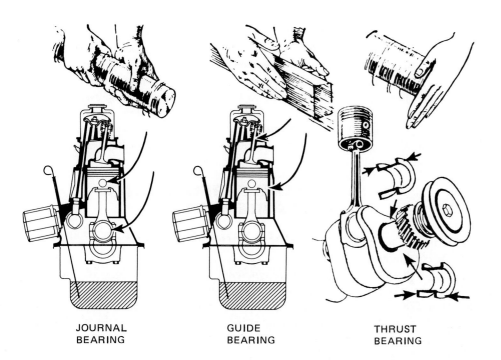

JOURNAL BEARING   GUIDE BEARING   THRUST BEARING

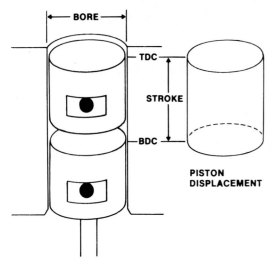

Fig. 15-7 Bore and stroke of an engine cylinder. Piston displacement is the volume the piston displaces as it moves from BDC to TDC.

> ## 15-9 PISTON DISPLACEMENT

Piston displacement is sometimes called "swept volume." This is the volume that the piston displaces or "sweeps out" as it moves from BDC to TDC (Fig. 15-7). For example, the piston displacement in a 4- by 3.5-inch [101.6 by 88.9 mm] cylinder is the volume in a cylinder 4 inches in diameter and 3.5 inches long. To find the piston displacement of this cylinder, use the formula

$$\frac{\pi \times D^2 \times L}{4} = \frac{3.14 \times 4^2 \times 3.5}{4}$$

$$= \frac{3.14 \times 16 \times 3.5}{4} = 43.96 \text{ cubic inches (in.}^3)$$

Suppose the engine has eight cylinders. The total displacement is 43.96 times 8, or 351.68 cubic inches. The engine is a 351.68 *cubic inch displacement* (CID) engine. The displacement is rounded off to "351."

Displacement is given in the metric system in *cubic centimeters* (cc) or *liters* (L). A 200 CID engine has a displacement of 3277.4 cc. This rounds off to 3280 cc or 3.3 L. One cubic inch equals 16.39 cc. One liter is 61.02 cubic inches.

The Wankel engine has rotors instead of pistons. Its displacement is the change in volume as the rotor moves from maximum volume to minimum volume (Fig. 15-8). This is the *single-chamber capacity.*

> ## 15-10 COMPRESSION RATIO

The *compression ratio* (CR) is the measure of how much the air-fuel mixture is compressed during the compression stroke. Compression ratio is found by dividing the volume of the cylinder and combustion chamber when the piston is at BDC by the volume when the piston is at TDC (Fig. 11-14). The volume with the piston at TDC is the

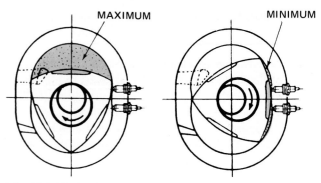

Fig. 15-8 Single-chamber capacity of a Wankel engine.

clearance volume. This is the volume that remains above the piston at TDC.

For example, one engine has a cylinder volume of 42.35 cubic inches [694 cc] at BDC. It has a clearance volume of 4.45 cubic inches [73 cc]. The compression ratio is 42.35 divided by 4.45 [694 ÷ 73]. This is 9.5:1. The air-fuel mixture is compressed to 1/9.5 of its original volume during the compression stroke.

> ## 15-11 INCREASING COMPRESSION RATIO

A higher compression ratio compresses the air-fuel mixture more during the compression stroke. After ignition, a higher combustion pressure results as the burning gas expands to a greater volume. This exerts more force on the piston for a longer part of the power stroke. Each power stroke produces more power.

In 1973, the Environmental Protection Agency (EPA) issued regulations requiring the removal of lead (*tetraethyllead* [TEL]) from gasoline (Chap. 16). Adding lead to gasoline allowed higher compression ratios. The lead prevented *spark knock* or *detonation.* This could seriously damage an engine. The lead left the engine in the exhaust gas and polluted the atmosphere. The lead also damaged some emission-control devices.

Removal of lead from gasoline began in 1975. This caused engine compression ratios to drop, which reduced engine power. Newer engine designs have increased compression ratios. The average engine compression ratio is about 8.9:1. This results from development of *lean-burn* and *fast-burn* combustion. Swirl-type combustion chambers (➤13-10) also allow higher compression ratios.

ENGINE PERFORMANCE MEASUREMENTS

> ## 15-12 VOLUMETRIC EFFICIENCY

Volumetric efficiency (VE) is the measure of how completely the cylinder fills with air-fuel mixture during the intake stroke. The cylinder fills completely (100 percent) when the mixture is drawn in slowly. In the running engine, the mixture must pass rapidly through narrow openings and bends in the intake manifold. The mixture also gets heated (from engine heat) and expands. The intake valve is open only a small fraction of a second (one hundredth of a second at high speed). The cylinders never get completely filled because the time is too short. The heat also has caused the mixture to expand (Chap. 17).

Good volumetric efficiency for an engine running at fairly high speed is 80 percent. The VE of some engines at high speed may drop to 50 percent. This means the cylinders are only half-filled. The decrease in VE is one reason that engine speed and power do not continue to increase.

Another action that affects VE is how quickly and easily the burned gases exhaust from the cylinder. Exhaust gases that remain in the cylinder after the intake stroke begins allow less air-fuel mixture to enter.

There are several ways to improve volumetric efficiency. One is to use larger intake valves. Another is to use more than one intake valve per cylinder (Fig. 14-5). The use of more than one exhaust valve improves the removal of the exhaust gas from the cylinder. Figure 14-5 shows the use of four valves—two intake and two exhaust—per cylinder.

Another way to improve engine performance is *forced induction*. A supercharger or a turbocharger (Chap. 18)

pressurizes the ingoing air or air-fuel mixture. This forces more air or air-fuel mixture into the cylinders. Increased engine power is the result.

Several design improvements can improve volumetric efficiency. One is to increase *valve lift* (➤14-20). This is the distance the valve moves down when it opens. Lift cannot be so great that the piston strikes the valve (➤14-2).

Tuned intake manifolds and *tuned exhaust manifolds* improve volumetric efficiency (Figs. 12-15 and 15-9). "Tuning" the passages or *runners* means to design their length and diameter for the desired performance. Then the runners in the intake manifold deliver the same amount of air or air-fuel mixture to each cylinder. Tuning the exhaust manifold in the same way can create a vacuum in the exhaust system. This helps draw the exhaust gas out of the cylinders and into the exhaust system.

➤ 15-13 ENGINE TORQUE

Torque is turning force (➤15-4). Engine torque results from combustion pressures pushing down on the pistons (Fig. 11-10). When a piston is moving down on the power stroke, this force acts through the connecting rod and becomes the crankshaft torque. The higher the volumetric ef-

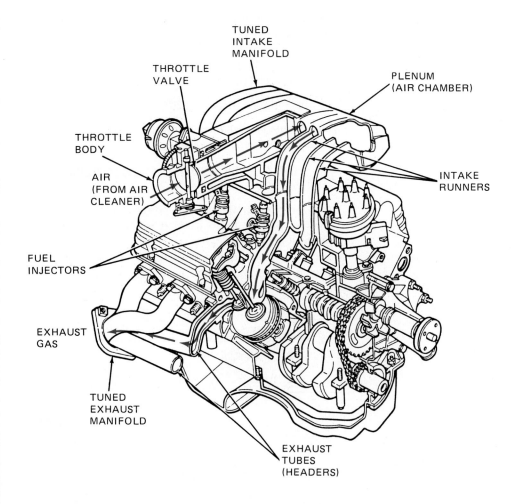

Fig. 15-9 Air and exhaust-gas flow through an engine with tuned intake and exhaust manifolds. (*Ford Motor Company*)

THROTTLE
VALVE

TUNED
INTAKE
MANIFOLD

PLENUM
(AIR CHAMBER)

THROTTLE
BODY

AIR
(FROM AIR
CLEANER)

INTAKE
RUNNERS

FUEL
INJECTORS

EXHAUST
GAS

TUNED
EXHAUST
MANIFOLD

EXHAUST
TUBES
(HEADERS)

ficiency (➤15-12) and the higher the combustion pressure, the greater the torque.

Figure 15-10 shows the relationship between combustion pressure and engine torque. The pressure in the cylinder drops rapidly as the piston begins to move down. In some racing engines, the exhaust valve opens as early as 92 degrees after TDC (88 degrees before BDC). This causes little power loss because little torque is being transmitted to the crankshaft.

Figure 15-11 compares the torque curves of a two-valve engine with a newer four-valve engine. The torque for the two-valve engine starts high and drops off as engine speed increases. The four-valve engine has a flatter or wider "torque band." It maintains a high torque output well past

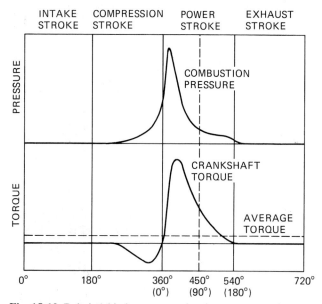

Fig. 15-10 Relationship between combustion pressure and engine torque. (*ATW*)

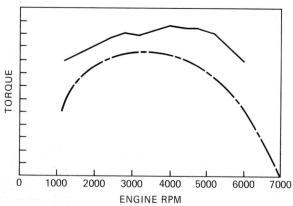

Fig. 15-11 Torque curve of a two-valve engine (dashed line) compared to the torque curve of a four-valve engine (solid line). The four-valve engine, with high volumetric efficiency, continues to produce high torque at high speeds. (*ATW*)

5000 rpm. This is because the four valves allow the engine to breathe freely even at high speed.

➤ **15-14 ENGINE POWER**

Engine power is the power available from the crankshaft to do work. The most common unit of measure for power is the horsepower [hp]. A horsepower is a measure of the rate at which a horse can work. This is 33,000 ft-lb of work per minute.

Figure 15-12 shows that a horse walks 165 feet in 1 minute lifting the 200-pound weight. The amount of work performed is 33,000 ft-lb (165 feet × 200 pounds). The time is 1 minute. A horse that did this work in 2 minutes would only be "half" working. It would be producing only 1/2 horsepower.

The formula for horsepower is

$$hp = \frac{\text{ft-lb per minute}}{33,000} = \frac{L \times W}{33,000 \times t}$$

Where

hp = horsepower
L = length in feet through which W is exerted
W = force in pounds exerted through distance L
t = time in minutes required to move W through L

In the metric system, engine power output is measured in kilowatts (kW). This is the amount of electricity an electric generator produces when driven by the engine. One horsepower is equal to 0.746 kW. One kW is equal to 1.34 hp.

You can calculate horsepower if you know engine torque and speed (rpm). The formula is

$$hp = \text{torque} \times \text{rpm} \div 5252$$

This formula is used when measuring engine performance with a chassis or engine *dynamometer* (➤15-15).

➤ **15-15 MEASURING HORSEPOWER**

Brake horsepower (bhp) is the power available from the engine crankshaft to do work. It is "brake" horsepower because it is measured with some type of brake. The brake places a load on the engine crankshaft. Today a *dynamometer* makes most engine power measurements. The

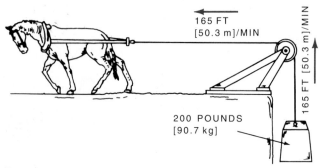

Fig. 15-12 One horse can do 33,000 ft-lb of work in one minute.

"dyno" has a built-in brake or *power absorber* to measure the power output of a running engine.

The *engine dynamometer* measures engine power when the engine is out of the car. The power absorber is usually an electric generator or a water brake that connects to the engine crankshaft. A varying load is placed on the engine by the power absorber. Instruments on the dynamometer measure brake horsepower and rpm, or torque and rpm. You then use these readings to calculate horsepower (➤15-14).

Emissions and fuel-economy testing require a *chassis dynamometer* (Fig. 15-13). It can also be used for trouble-diagnosis and performance testing. The chassis dyno measures engine power with the engine in the vehicle. The drive wheels are placed on rollers in the floor. The rollers attach to the power absorber. Instruments usually show either brake horsepower and rpm or torque and rpm. Some chassis dynos provide information on brake action and power-train operation.

➤ 15-16 GROSS AND NET HORSEPOWER

Gross horsepower is measured by testing a *basic* engine. This is an engine stripped except for the built-in items required to run it. These include the water pump, fuel pump, oil pump, and built-in emission-control devices.

Net horsepower is the power delivered by a fully-equipped engine. This includes air cleaner, cooling system, exhaust system, alternator, and all emission controls. Net horsepower is the power delivered to the transaxle or transmission.

Another horsepower rating is *road horsepower*. This is the power delivered to the vehicle drive wheels. It is much less than net horsepower. Power is lost through friction in the transaxle or transmission and power train. There is also power loss from driving the power-steering pump, air-conditioning compressor, and other accessories.

➤ 15-17 INDICATED HORSEPOWER

Indicated horsepower (ihp) is the power developed inside the combustion chambers during combustion. It is determined by measuring the pressures in the engine cylinder (Fig. 15-10). Indicated horsepower is always higher than brake horsepower. Some of the power developed in the cylinders is lost in overcoming the internal friction in the engine.

➤ 15-18 FRICTION HORSEPOWER

Friction horsepower (fhp) is the power required to overcome the friction of the internal moving parts. A major cause of friction loss is piston-ring friction. It can account for 75 percent of all friction losses in the engine. Pistons in the short-stroke oversquare engine do not move as far. This lowers ring friction. Some manufacturers further reduce friction by installing thinner and barrel-faced piston rings (Chap. 13).

➤ 15-19 RELATING BHP, IHP, FHP

Brake horsepower [bhp] is the power available to do work. Indicated horsepower [ihp] is the power developed in the engine cylinders. Friction horsepower [fhp] is the power lost in overcoming the internal friction. The relationship is:

$$bhp = ihp - fhp$$

➤ 15-20 ENGINE EFFICIENCY

The term *efficiency* means comparing the effort exerted with the results obtained. Engine efficiency is the relation between its actual power and its theoretical power. This is the power that would be available if the engine operated without loss. Two types of engine efficiency are its *mechanical efficiency* and its *thermal efficiency*.

1. MECHANICAL EFFICIENCY This is the relationship between bhp and ihp:

$$\text{Mechanical efficiency} = \frac{bhp}{ihp}$$

EXAMPLE: At one speed, the bhp of an engine is 116. The ihp is 135. The mechanical efficiency is 116/135 = 0.86, or 86

Fig. 15-13 Automobile in place on a chassis dynamometer. The drive wheels turn the dynamometer rollers, which measure the power available at the wheels. (*Ford Motor Company*)

percent. This means that 86 percent of the ihp is delivered by the engine. The remaining 14 percent is lost as fhp.

2. THERMAL EFFICIENCY *Thermal* means "of or related to heat." Engine thermal efficiency is the relation

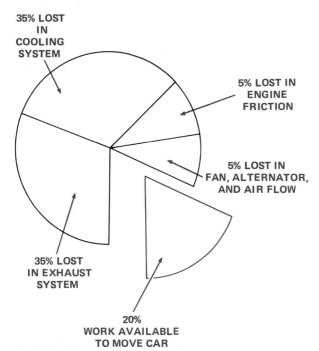

Fig. 15-14 Only about 20 percent of the energy in gasoline is available to move the car. (*Ford Motor Company*)

between the power produced and the energy in the fuel burned to produce that power.

Some of the heat produced by combustion is carried away by the engine lubricating and cooling systems. Some heat is lost in the hot exhaust gases as they leave the cylinder. These heat (thermal) losses reduce the thermal efficiency of the engine. The engine uses the remaining heat to produce power.

Thermal efficiencies of spark-ignition engines may be below 20 percent. They are seldom above 25 percent. Some diesel engines have thermal efficiencies of 35 percent or higher. Modern engine research is trying to develop adiabatic engines (➤12-15). These will use a greater percentage of the heat energy in the fuel. Increasing thermal efficiency 50 percent would about double fuel mileage.

➤ 15-21 OVERALL EFFICIENCY

Energy is lost at every step from combustion of the fuel to turning the drive wheels. Figure 15-14 shows that the vehicle is propelled by about 20 percent of the energy in the fuel. This energy is used up overcoming *rolling resistance* and *air resistance*.

1. ROLLING RESISTANCE This results from irregularities in the road and flexing of the tires.

2. AIR RESISTANCE This is the resistance of the air to the passage of the car body through it (➤1-20). Air resistance increases as car speed increases. At 90 miles per

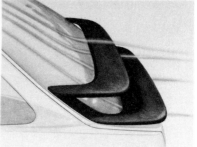

Fig. 15-15 Aerodynamic styling makes the car more "slippery" so it has less wind resistance. Top, the white lines show how the air moves up, over, and around the car. Bottom, how a cover has been applied so the underside of the car presents minimum air resistance. (*Ford Motor Company*)

hour (mph) [145 km/h], as much as 75 percent of the power that reaches the wheels is used to overcome air resistance. Even at lower speeds, air resistance is significant. The drag of the air reduces fuel economy.

Air resistance is measured as the *drag coefficient* (C_d). The lower the drag coefficient, the less fuel it takes to move the car through the air. An *aerodynamically* styled car (Fig. 15-15) has been *streamlined* or shaped to slip through the air more easily. It can go up to 2.5 miles farther on a gallon of gasoline than a similar unstreamlined car.

➤ 15-22 REVIEWING ENGINE PERFORMANCE

Several factors can influence engine performance.

1. Piston displacement is determined by the engine design.

Engine displacement is the volume of air or air-fuel mixture that the pistons displace as they move from BDC to TDC during one complete cycle of engine operation. The greater the displacement, the more mixture can enter, and the more powerful the power strokes.

2. Volumetric efficiency determines how much air-fuel mixture can enter the cylinder at any given speed.
3. The amount of mixture helps determine the pressure applied to the piston during the power stroke. Generally, the more mixture, the higher the pressure, and the more powerful the power stroke.
4. The pressure applied to the pistons (less internal friction) determines the engine torque (Figs. 15-10 and 15-11).
5. Torque and engine speed determine engine power.

MULTIPLE-CHOICE TEST

*Select the **one** correct, best, or most probable answer to each question.*
You can find the answers in the section indicated at the end of each question.

1. Distance times force equals (➤15-1)
   a. torque
   b. work
   c. power
   d. horsepower
2. The ability to do work is (➤15-2)
   a. torque
   b. energy
   c. power
   d. horsepower
3. The rate, or speed, at which work is done is (➤15-3)
   a. torque
   b. work
   c. power
   d. horsepower
4. The application of a twisting force, with or without motion, is (➤15-4)
   a. torque
   b. energy
   c. power
   d. horsepower

5. The three classes of friction are (➤15-6)
   a. dry, wet, and greasy
   b. journal, guide, and thrust
   c. dry, greasy, and viscous
   d. guide, thrust, and viscous
6. The size of an engine cylinder is given as (➤15-8)
   a. diameter and bore
   b. CID and efficiency
   c. displacement and ratio
   d. bore and stroke
7. The volume that the piston displaces as it moves from BDC to TDC is the (➤15-9)
   a. compression stroke
   b. compression ratio
   c. volumetric efficiency
   d. piston displacement

REVIEW QUESTIONS

1. Describe four types of engine mechanical measurements. (➤15-8, 15-9, and 15-10)
2. Explain volumetric efficiency and list three ways to improve it. (➤15-12)
3. What is a dynamometer and when is it useful? (➤15-15)

4. Define *indicated horsepower, friction horse-power,* and *brake horsepower,* and explain how they are related. (➤15-19)
5. What is the difference between mechanical efficiency and thermal efficiency? What are typical values of each? (➤15-20)

PART 3

AUTOMOTIVE ENGINE SYSTEMS

Part 3 of *Automotive Mechanics* describes the construction, operation, diagnosis, and servicing of automotive engine systems. These include electronic carburetor and fuel-injection systems, lubricating systems, and cooling systems. Also included are fueland exhaust systems, superchargers and turbochargers, and diesel-fuel injection systems.

There are eleven chapters in Part 3:

CHAPTER 16

AUTOMOTIVE ENGINE FUELS

After studying this chapter, you should be able to:

- Describe the composition of gasoline and the products that result from its combustion.
- Explain the characteristics that a good quality gasoline should have.
- Define *octane rating* and *volatility*, and explain how volatility affects engine performance.
- Describe the various types of abnormal combustion.
- Define *gasohol, methyl alcohol,* and *liquified petroleum gas* (LPG).
- Name three possible alternative fuels and their sources.

➤ 16-1 AUTOMOTIVE ENGINE FUELS AND COMBUSTION

Gasoline is the most widely used fuel for automotive engines. It is a *hydrocarbon* (HC), made up mostly of *hydrogen* (H) and *carbon* (C).

NOTE Gasoline is often called "gas." This is not the same as the gas burned in a gas stove or furnace. Gasoline is a liquid fuel. The gas you use at home is a vapor. So there is *gas* that is a vapor, and "gas" that is gasoline.

Air is about 20 percent *oxygen* (O) and 80 percent *nitrogen* (N). With "perfect combustion," the gasoline burns completely (Fig. 16-1, top). All the hydrogen in the gasoline unites with oxygen in the air (➤9-3). This forms *hydrogen oxide* (H_2O), or water vapor. All the carbon in the gasoline unites with oxygen in the air to form *carbon dioxide* (CO_2). Both of these are harmless gases.

However, incomplete combustion occurs in the automotive engine (Fig. 16-1, bottom). Some gasoline (HC) vapor does not burn or burns incompletely. It leaves the cylinder as part of the exhaust gas along with the *carbon monoxide* (CO) and *nitrogen oxides* (NO_x) that form. The engine exhaust gas always contains some HC, CO, and NO_x.

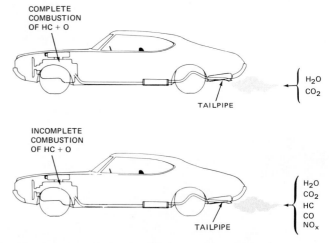

COMPLETE COMBUSTION OF HC + O

TAILPIPE

H_2O
CO_2

INCOMPLETE COMBUSTION OF HC + O

TAILPIPE

H_2O
CO_2
HC
CO
NO_x

Fig. 16-1 (Top) Perfect combustion produces only carbon dioxide (CO_2) and water (H_2O) from the tailpipe. (Bottom) With incomplete combustion, carbon monoxide (CO) is formed and unburned gasoline (HC) appears in the exhaust gas. Nitrogen oxides (NO_x) are also formed.

Carbon monoxide results from incomplete combustion. It forms when one atom of carbon combines with one atom of oxygen instead of two as in complete combustion. (*Mono* is a prefix meaning "one.") This lack of oxygen prevents the formation of carbon dioxide. Carbon monoxide is a poisonous gas that can cause death. Enough CO from a running engine can accumulate in a closed one-car garage in only three minutes to kill anyone in the garage.

Nitrogen oxides (NO_x) is a byproduct of high combustion temperatures in a running engine. High temperatures in the combustion chambers cause some of the nitrogen and oxygen to unite and form NO_x.

Here is what happens during combustion:

$$HC + N + O_2 = CO_2 + H_2O + CO + NO_x + HC$$

Notice that HC appears on the right side of the equation. This shows that some of the gasoline does not burn and comes out in the exhaust gas.

Carbon monoxide (CO), gasoline (HC), and nitrogen oxides (NO_x) are *air pollutants*. They pollute the air we breathe. Breathing polluted air is bad for humans and animals. Exposure to polluted air is bad for plants and trees.

There are four sources of air pollutants from the automobile. These are the engine crankcase, air cleaner or carburetor, fuel tank, and tailpipe. The amount of pollutants from each source is controlled by the vehicle *emission controls*. These are:

1. *Crankcase emission control system.* It sends blowby gases (➤11-4) back through the engine to be burned. This prevents their escape into the atmosphere.
2. *Evaporative emission control system.* It traps fuel vapors escaping from the air cleaner, carburetor (if used), and fuel tank. These vapors are then returned to the engine and burned.
3. *Exhaust emission control system.* It includes a variety of engine management and emission-control devices and systems. They all work to reduce the pollutants in the exhaust gas.

Chapter 35 describes automotive emission controls.

CAUTION!

Gasoline is a dangerous liquid if not handled properly. Gasoline vapor will rise from a gasoline leak in a vehicle or from an open container of gasoline. A spark, flame, or lighted cigarette will ignite the vapor. An explosion or fire can result.

➤ **16-2 SOURCES OF GASOLINE**

Gasoline is made or *refined* from crude oil (petroleum). The refining process also produces lubricating oil, diesel fuel, and other products. Several *additives* are put into gasoline during refining. These improve the characteristics of the gasoline.

A good quality gasoline should have:

1. Proper volatility, which determines how easily the gasoline vaporizes (turns to vapor).

2. Resistance to spark knock or detonation.
3. Oxidation inhibitors, which prevent formation of gum in the fuel system.
4. Antirust agents, which prevent rusting of metal parts in the fuel system.
5. Anti-icers, which retard icing in the throttle body and fuel-line freezing.
6. Detergents, which help keep the carburetor or fuel injectors clean.
7. Dye for identification, such as red dye which gives leaded gasoline a rust or orange color.

➤ **16-3 VOLATILITY**

Volatility is the ease with which a gasoline vaporizes. Gasoline must vaporize quickly after it is mixed with air in the throttle body or intake manifold. Otherwise, drops of liquid gasoline enter the cylinders. The drops wash oil off the cylinder walls. This increases wear of the cylinder walls, pistons, and rings.

Gasoline that does not vaporize will not burn. It leaves the cylinder in the exhaust gas and pollutes the air. This wastes gasoline and reduces fuel economy.

Volatility determines how quickly a gasoline vaporizes. A high-volatility gasoline vaporizes quickly. A low-volatility gasoline vaporizes slowly. Gasoline must have the right volatility for the climate in which it is used. The engine is hard to start if volatility is too low. Vapor lock results if volatility is too high. Then the gasoline in the fuel system turns to vapor. This prevents normal fuel flow. The engine stalls or will not start. Refiners adjust volatility seasonally to suit weather conditions. Gasoline is made more volatile in cold weather. This makes the engine start more easily at low temperatures.

➤ **16-4 ANTIKNOCK QUALITY**

How well a gasoline resists knocking (➤16-5) determines whether *normal combustion* or *abnormal combustion* occurs. Figure 16-2 compares normal combustion (top row) with abnormal combustion (lower row). During normal combustion, the flame front sweeps across the combustion chamber. This produces a smooth pressure rise.

The lower row of Fig. 16-2 shows abnormal combustion caused by *spark knock* or *detonation*. After the spark at the plug, the flame starts across the combustion chamber. However, before the flame reaches the far side, the last of the charge explodes. The two flame fronts meet, producing a very rapid, and high, pressure rise. The result is a high-pitch metallic rapping noise called *pinging*.

Detonation can ruin an engine. The heavy shocks on the pistons put great load on bearings and other engine parts. Pistons may chip and break. Severe detonation may lead to uncontrolled *preignition* (➤16-8). This can burn holes through the tops of the pistons.

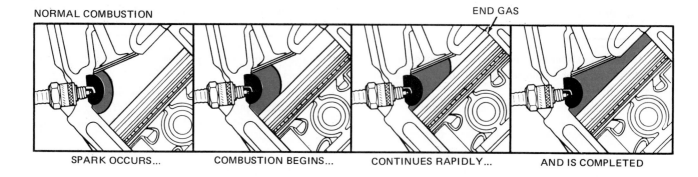

NORMAL COMBUSTION

END GAS

SPARK OCCURS...   COMBUSTION BEGINS...   CONTINUES RAPIDLY...   AND IS COMPLETED

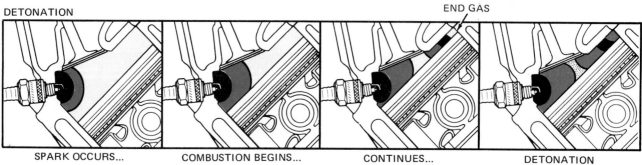

DETONATION

END GAS

SPARK OCCURS...   COMBUSTION BEGINS...   CONTINUES...   DETONATION

Fig. 16-2 Normal combustion without detonation is shown in the top row. The fuel charge burns smoothly from beginning to end, providing an even, powerful force on the piston. Detonation is shown in the bottom row. The last part of the fuel charge explodes, or burns almost instantly, to produce spark knock or detonation. (*Champion Spark Plug Company*)

➤ 16-5 OCTANE RATINGS

Octane number measures the antiknock quality (➤16-4) of a gasoline. The higher the octane number, the more resistant the gasoline is to knock. A 93-octane gasoline is more knock resistant than an 89-octane gasoline. Therefore, a gasoline that detonates easily is a *low-octane gasoline*. A gasoline that resists detonation is a *high-octane gasoline*.

Octane rating for any gasoline is determined by testing it in laboratory engines. The test results are used to calculate the minimum octane rating (Fig. 16-3). This is the number posted on the pumps at service stations.

High-compression engines require high-octane gasoline. Compression ratio is a measure of how much the air-fuel

mixture is compressed on the compression stroke (➤15-10). High-compression ratios are desirable because higher-compression engines can produce more power.

However, high compression increases the temperature of the air-fuel mixture. After the spark occurs, the high temperature may cause detonation. Part of the unburned air-fuel mixture explodes before normal combustion. Before 1975, adding tetraethyl lead to the gasoline solved this problem. The lead allowed higher compression ratios without detonation. (Another result of high combustion temperatures is excessive production of NO_x, described in ➤16-1).

Since 1975, Federal regulations have required that all new cars run on unleaded fuel. Lead added to gasoline does not burn. It leaves in the exhaust gas and pollutes the air. Lead is a poison. Breathing air containing lead may cause lead poisoning. This can cause illness and possibly death.

Lead in gasoline also is harmful to some emission-control devices. For example, the exhaust system includes a *catalytic converter*. It converts unburned gasoline (HC), carbon monoxide (CO), and nitrogen oxides (NO_x) into harmless gases. The lead prevents the catalytic converter from working (➤35-20 and 35-21).

➤ 16-6 TWO KINDS OF GASOLINE

Some service stations sell two kinds of gasoline, *leaded* and *unleaded*. By 1996, leaded gasoline should be phased

---

89
Minimum Octane Rating
(R + M) /2 Method

Fig. 16-3 Minimum octane rating posted on gasoline pumps at service stations. (*Ford Motor Company*)

out completely. Then only various grades of unleaded gasoline will be available.

Cars built since 1975 have catalytic converters. These cars must not be fueled with leaded gasoline. To prevent misfueling, a car with a catalytic converter has a smaller opening in the fuel-tank filler neck (Fig. 16-4). A gasoline pump dispensing leaded gasoline must have a nozzle that is too large to enter this opening.

➤ 16-7 OCTANE REQUIREMENTS

The engine design and compression ratio determines the octane it requires. However, this requirement changes with weather, driving conditions, and the mechanical condition

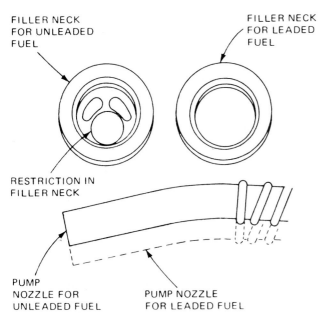

Fig. 16-4 Comparison of the filler neck and larger pump nozzle for leaded gasoline with the restricted filler neck and smaller pump nozzle for unleaded gasoline.

of the engine. Combustion-chamber deposits (Fig. 16-5) reduce clearance volume. They also increase octane requirements and the possibility of detonation. Reduced cooling efficiency, fuel system or ignition troubles, and failure of emission controls may also change octane requirements.

The way the driver operates the car also has an effect. Detonation is less likely to occur if the driver does not demand rapid acceleration and high-speed wide-open throttle operation. Then the octane requirement will be lower.

Automatic transaxles and transmissions also make a difference. There is little lugging or low-engine-speed full-throttle operation with an automatic. It simply shifts into a lower gear and engine speed increases.

With a manual transaxle or transmission, lugging can occur at full throttle at low engine speed. This can cause detonation even with a higher-octane fuel.

➤ 16-8 OTHER TYPES OF ABNORMAL COMBUSTION

Another type of abnormal combustion is *preignition* (Fig. 16-6). This is ignition of the air-fuel mixture before the spark occurs at the spark plug. The mixture "pre-ignites" from hot spots in the combustion chamber. Possible causes include a hot exhaust valve, spark plug, or carbon deposits. These surfaces can get so hot that they cause ignition. This is *surface ignition*.

Surface ignition can occur before or after the spark. It can cause engine *rumble,* rough operation, and mild to severe detonation. The characteristic sound of preignition is a dull thud (not a "ping"). Preignition can cause popback or backfire through the intake manifold and air cleaner.

Surface ignition, preignition, and rumble are usually service problems. They can be caused by installing the wrong spark plug, which runs too hot. Other possible causes are using the wrong fuel or oil, and deposits in the

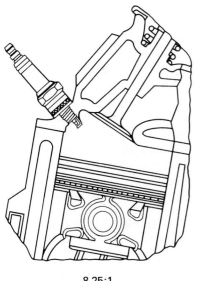
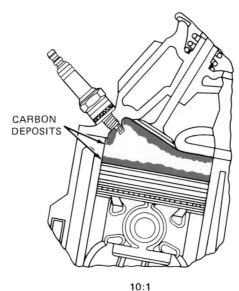

Fig. 16-5 Carbon deposits in the combustion chamber can raise the compression ratio from 8.25:1 (left) to as high as 10:1 (right). (*Chrysler Corporation*)

189

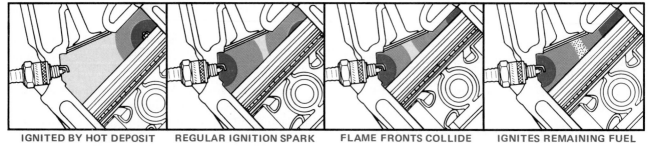

IGNITED BY HOT DEPOSIT   REGULAR IGNITION SPARK   FLAME FRONTS COLLIDE   IGNITES REMAINING FUEL

Fig. 16-6 One cause of preignition. The hot spot ignites the compressed air-fuel mixture before the spark occurs at the spark-plug gap. (*Champion Spark Plug Company*)

combustion chamber (Fig. 16-5). The deposits increase the compression ratio, so detonation results.

➤ 16-9 MECHANICAL FACTORS AFFECTING DETONATION

The shape of the combustion chamber has an effect on detonation. In the wedge chamber (Figs. 16-2 and 16-7, left), the flame front must travel across the chamber. The end of the wedge has a *squish-and-quench area*. This prevents detonation of the last part of the unburned air-fuel mixture or *end gas*. The squish occurs at the end of the compression stroke. The mixture is squeezed out (squished) so fast that it promotes turbulence. The turbulence improves combustion.

A hemispheric combustion chamber (Fig. 16-7, right) has a centrally-located spark plug. The flame front travels only a relatively short distance. There are no distant pockets of end gas that could detonate.

There are various shapes of combustion chambers and precombustion chambers (Figs. 13-10 and 13-14). These are used to promote turbulence and improve combustion.

➤ 16-10 GASOHOL

Gasohol is usually a mixture of 10 percent *ethyl alcohol* and 90 percent unleaded gasoline. Ethyl alcohol is made from sugar, grain, or other *organic* (living) material. Engines can run on gasohol without any change in the fuel system. Some people believe the use of gasohol will ease the demand for oil.

If more than 10 percent ethyl alcohol is added, the fuel

system must be reworked to supply a richer mixture. Straight ethyl alcohol requires an air-fuel ratio of about 9:1. The ideal air-fuel ratio for straight gasoline is 14.7:1.

➤ 16-11 METHANOL

Pure *methanol* or *methyl alcohol* is wood alcohol. It does not vaporize as readily as gasoline. Adding some gasoline makes cold starts easier and improves engine warm-up. A typical mixture called *M85* is 85 percent methanol and 15 percent gasoline.

Adding the gasoline makes the mixture safer. The gasoline vaporizes more readily. This enriches the vapor in the top of the fuel tank. As a result, the vapor is beyond the *flame point*. This is the temperature at which the vapor could ignite and burn. Pure methanol burns with an almost invisible flame. Adding gasoline gives the flame color. This is important in case of fire.

Methanol has about half the energy content of gasoline [15,900 kJ compared with 32,300 kJ]. An advantage to methanol is that it can be made from coal, oil shale, wood, manure, garbage, and other organic matter. Disadvantages are that methanol attacks aluminum, solder, plastics, and other material. A fuel system using methanol must be made of stainless steel and other metal and plastic parts resistant to methanol.

Methanol also attracts water. If water gets into the mixture or *blend,* the gasoline and alcohol can separate. Then the engine will stall because the fuel system can handle only the blend. To overcome this problem and give the vehicle the ability to operate on a variety of fuels, the fuel system includes a *variable fuel sensor* (Fig. 16-8). It determines the percentage of methanol in the fuel being used. The sensor sends this information to the electronic control module (ECM). The ECM then adjusts the ignition spark curve and fuel-injector timing to match the fuel. A vehicle with this type of fuel system is a *flexible-fuel vehicle,* or a *variable-fuel vehicle* (Fig. 16-8).

➤ 16-12 LIQUIFIED PETROLEUM GAS (LPG)

Liquified petroleum gas (LPG) is made from crude oil. LPG turns to liquid when put under pressure. When the

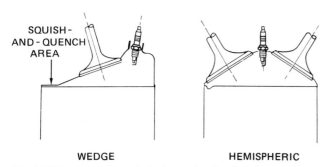

SQUISH-AND-QUENCH AREA

WEDGE   HEMISPHERIC

Fig. 16-7 Wedge and hemispheric combustion chambers.

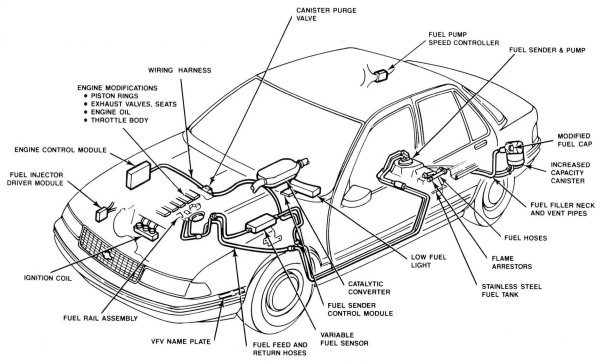

Fig. 16-8 Vehicle with a flexible-fuel system, or variable-fuel system, which can run on a blend of methanol and gasoline or on unleaded gasoline. (*General Motors Corporation*)

pressure is released, the liquid turns back to gas. The LPG used in many vehicles is *propane*. The vehicles require special fuel systems to handle LPG.

An advantage of LPG is that it has an octane rating of over 100. This means the engines can have a high com-

pression ratio for greater power and efficiency. LPG also burns cleanly. Little wear results. No fuel pump and little emission control equipment are required.

Figure 16-9 shows a vehicle that runs on *compressed natural gas* (CNG). Burning natural gas releases about 20

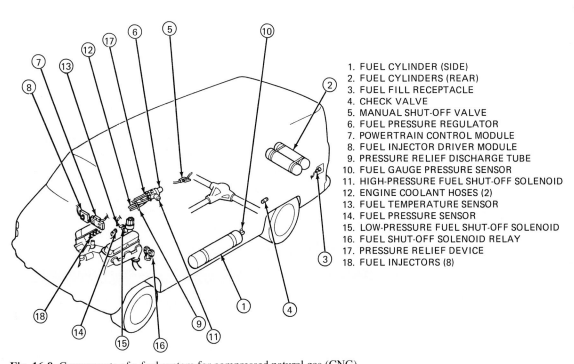

1. FUEL CYLINDER (SIDE)
2. FUEL CYLINDERS (REAR)
3. FUEL FILL RECEPTACLE
4. CHECK VALVE
5. MANUAL SHUT-OFF VALVE
6. FUEL PRESSURE REGULATOR
7. POWERTRAIN CONTROL MODULE
8. FUEL INJECTOR DRIVER MODULE
9. PRESSURE RELIEF DISCHARGE TUBE
10. FUEL GAUGE PRESSURE SENSOR
11. HIGH-PRESSURE FUEL SHUT-OFF SOLENOID
12. ENGINE COOLANT HOSES (2)
13. FUEL TEMPERATURE SENSOR
14. FUEL PRESSURE SENSOR
15. LOW-PRESSURE FUEL SHUT-OFF SOLENOID
16. FUEL SHUT-OFF SOLENOID RELAY
17. PRESSURE RELIEF DEVICE
18. FUEL INJECTORS (8)

Fig. 16-9 Components of a fuel system for compressed natural gas (CNG). (*Chrysler Corporation*)

percent less carbon dioxide (CO_2) than gasoline, but slightly more nitrogen oxides (NO_x). No charcoal canister (➤35-8) is needed for control of evaporative emissions. Vehicles using either LPG or CNG store the fuel in pressure cylinders.

➤ 16-13 THE SEARCH FOR ALTERNATE FUELS

Most fuels are forms of hydrocarbon (➤16-1). *Fossil fuels* are hydrocarbon fuels that are derived from living matter. These include oil (and fuel made from it, including gasoline), coal, and wood. Burning any hydrocarbon or fossil fuel produces carbon dioxide (CO_2).

Carbon dioxide is collecting in the earth's atmosphere because so much fuel is being burned. The carbon dioxide acts as a blanket. It allows heat from the sun to come in and prevents it from radiating away at night. As a result, the earth is warming up. This is the *greenhouse effect.*

The warming of the earth will produce many weather changes. Big stretches of land in the middle region of the United States and possibly elsewhere may become deserts. The polar ice caps will begin to melt. The sea level will rise. Then coastal cities such as New York and San Diego will be under water.

The threat has become so serious that major governments are working to reduce fossil-fuel burning. Scientists are trying to find alternate fuels. All hydrocarbon fuels produce CO_2 when burned. Some fuels, such as methanol, produce less CO_2 than others. Straight hydrogen gas and natural gas (➤16-12) are possible alternate fuels. But they still produce CO_2 when burned.

One possible solution is the electric car (➤1-28), perhaps combined with nuclear or solar energy. An electric car with a 200-miles-per-battery-charge would handle most travel needs. It would take us to school, the office, and shopping. At night, the car plugs into the home electrical system for battery recharge. However, with millions of electric cars in operation, the demand for electricity would increase. To supply this demand, more non-polluting atomic-energy or solar-energy power plants will be needed.

MULTIPLE-CHOICE TEST

*Select the **one** correct, best, or most probable answer to each question.*
You can find the answers in the section indicated at the end of each question.

1. Technician A says if combustion in an engine is not perfect, the exhaust gas will have HC and CO in it. Technician B says it will also have CO_2 and H_2O in it. Who is right? (➤16-1)
   a. Technician A
   b. Technician B
   c. both A and B
   d. neither A nor B
2. The ease with which gasoline vaporizes is called its (➤16-3)
   a. oxidation
   b. antiknock quality
   c. octane number
   d. none of the above
3. When the last part of the air-fuel mixture explodes before being ignited by the flame traveling from the spark plug, the result is (➤16-4)
   a. detonation
   b. preignition
   c. octane number
   d. stalling
4. Antiknock quality of gasoline is measured in (➤16-5)
   a. oxidation number
   b. vaporization number
   c. octane number
   d. detonation number
5. A gasoline that detonates easily is a (➤16-5)
   a. high-octane gasoline
   b. low-octane gasoline
   c. leaded gasoline
   d. blended fuel
6. Combustion-chamber deposits (➤16-7)
   a. reduce clearance volume
   b. increase octane requirements
   c. increase possibility of detonation
   d. all of the above
7. When the air-fuel mixture ignites before the spark takes place at the spark plug, this is (➤16-8)
   a. detonation
   b. preignition
   c. octane number
   d. stalling

REVIEW QUESTIONS

1. Describe seven characteristics that a good quality gasoline should have.   (➤16-2)
2. Explain the differences between spark knock (detonation) and preignition.   (➤16-4 and 16-8)
3. How do mechanical factors affect detonation? (➤16-9)
4. How does gasohol differ from M85 with methanol? (➤16-10 and 16-11)
5. What causes the greenhouse effect, and how will alternate fuels change it?   (➤16-13)

CHAPTER 17

ENGINE FUEL AND EXHAUST SYSTEMS

After studying this chapter, you should be able to:

- Locate each major component of the fuel system on the car. Describe the construction and operation of each.
- Explain the differences between carbureted and fuel-injected fuel systems.
- Locate each major component of the exhaust system on the car. Describe the construction and operation of each.
- Discuss the various devices used to reduce exhaust noise.
- Explain the operation of the various fuel-level indicators. Explain how each works.

➤ 17-1 INTRODUCTION TO FUEL AND EXHAUST SYSTEMS

The purpose of the fuel system is to supply the engine with a combustible mixture of air and fuel. This mixture is the *air-fuel mixture*. It is burned in the engine to produce power.

The fuel system is made up of two smaller systems or *subsystems*. These are the *fuel supply system* and the *fuel metering system*. The fuel supply system delivers fuel from the tank to the fuel metering system. The metering system uses either a *carburetor* or a *fuel-injection system*. It measures out or "meters" the amount of fuel needed by the engine. This is the fuel that mixes with the air entering the engine to form the air-fuel mixture. The air enters the engine through the *air-intake* or *air-induction system*.

The purpose of the exhaust system is to carry the burned gases — the *exhaust gases* — away from the engine. The exhaust gases discharge into the air at the rear of the car.

This chapter describes all the parts in the fuel system except the fuel-metering devices (the carburetor and fuel-injection systems). These are covered in Chaps. 19 and 21.

FUEL SUPPLY SYSTEM

➤ 17-2 TYPES OF FUEL SUPPLY SYSTEMS

There are two types of gasoline fuel systems: *fuel-injected* (Chap. 19) and *carbureted* (Chap. 21). They differ in how they measure or *meter* the fuel to produce the desired air-fuel ratio.

The carbureted fuel system uses a carburetor (Fig. 17-1). It is a mixing device that mixes fuel and air to form the air-fuel mixture. The fuel-injected fuel system uses a fuel-injection system with *fuel-injection valves* or *fuel injectors* (Fig. 14-13). They spray or "inject" fuel into the air to produce the combustible mixture.

Both types of fuel systems include the fuel tank, fuel-level indicator, fuel lines, fuel pump, fuel filter, air cleaner, throttle body, and intake manifold. Except for how the fuel is metered, both fuel systems basically operate the same way. The fuel tank holds a supply of fuel. The fuel pump delivers fuel from the tank through the filter and lines to the carburetor or fuel injectors. The air cleaner filters the air entering the engine. The throttle body regulates how much of the cleaned air enters the intake manifold. The intake manifold then carries the air (or air-fuel mixture) to the engine cylinders.

➤ 17-3 FUEL TANK

The fuel tank (Figs. 17-1 and 17-2) is made of metal or plastic. It is usually located at the rear of the vehicle. The fuel outlet line that supplies fuel to the engine attaches to a fuel *pickup tube*. It is usually part of the fuel-gauge sending unit (➤17-20) or an in-tank *electric fuel pump* (➤17-7). The tube extends almost to the bottom of the tank.

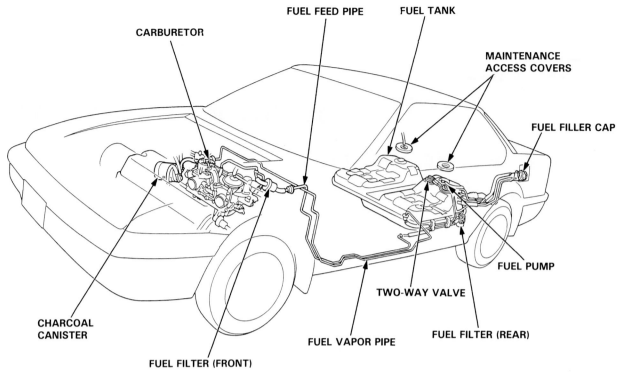

Fig. 17-1 Passenger car with a fuel system using a carburetor. (*American Honda Motor Company, Inc.*)

Fig. 17-2 Fuel tank with electric fuel pump and fuel-gauge sending unit. (*Toyota Motor Sales, U.S.A., Inc.*)

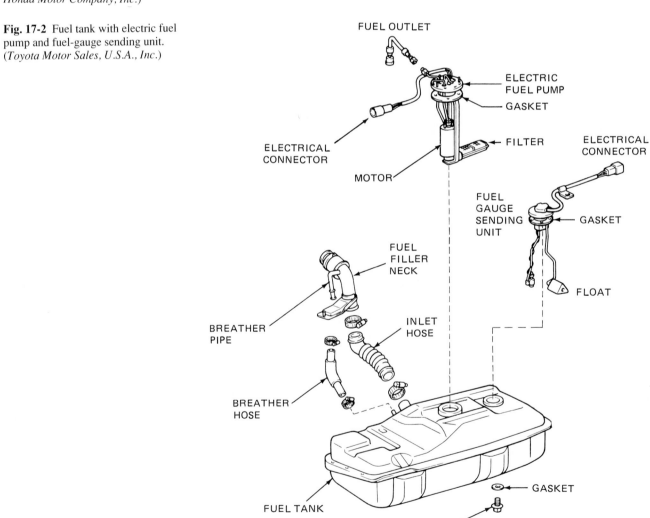

Fuel vapor (HC) escaping from the fuel tank causes air pollution. Cars made since 1970 have an *evaporative emission control system* (Chap. 35). A *fuel-vapor pipe* or line connects the fuel tank to a *charcoal canister* (Fig. 17-1). Charcoal in the canister traps any fuel vapor flowing through the pipe. The vapor in the canister is drawn into the intake manifold and then burned in the engine. Chapters 35 and 36 on emission controls describe more about the charcoal canister.

➤ 17-4 FUEL-TANK CAP

Most cars with an evaporative-emission-control system use a special cap on the fuel tank (Fig. 17-3). The cap has a *pressure-relief valve* and a *vacuum-relief valve*. The pressure-relief valve opens if pressure builds up in the

tank. The vacuum-relief valve opens to admit air if vacuum develops in the tank. Sometimes this occurs while the engine is running as fuel is pumped out.

Some caps include a *rollover check valve*. It closes the passages in the cap if the car rolls over. This prevents fuel leakage that could cause a fire during an accident.

➤ 17-5 FUEL PUMP

The fuel pump sends fuel from the fuel tank to the carburetor or fuel injectors. There are two types of automotive fuel pumps: *mechanical* and *electrical*.

Most carbureted fuel systems use a mechanical fuel pump (Fig. 17-4). It usually mounts on the side of the cylinder block. An eccentric on the camshaft operates the pump. The rotating eccentric (or a pushrod riding on it) rocks the rocker arm up and down (Fig. 17-5). This flexes a diaphragm to produce the pumping action.

Some overhead-camshaft engines have the mechanical fuel pump mounted on the side of the cylinder head. An eccentric on the overhead camshaft operates the fuel-pump rocker arm.

Electric fuel pumps are described in ➤17-7.

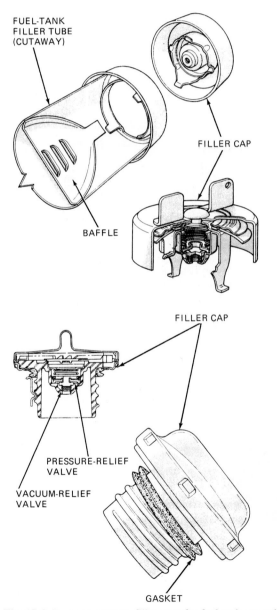

Fig. 17-3 Pressure-vacuum filler caps for fuel tanks on vehicles with evaporative-control systems. (*Chrysler Corporation*)

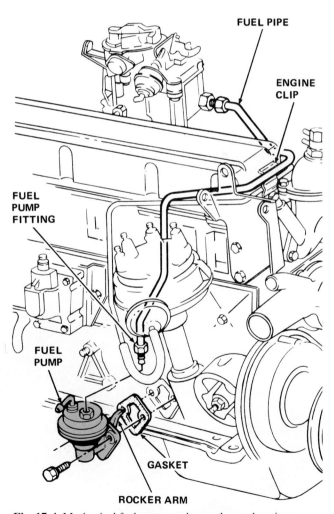

Fig. 17-4 Mechanical fuel pump used on carbureted engines. (*Chevrolet Division of General Motors Corporation*)

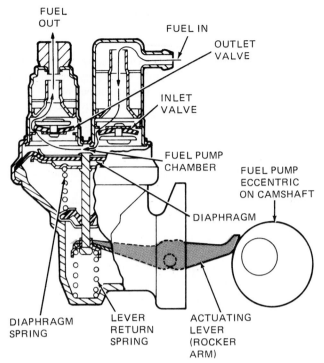

Fig. 17-5 Mechanical fuel pump operated by an eccentric that rotates with the camshaft. (*Chrysler Corporation*)

➤ 17-6 VAPOR-RETURN LINE

Many cars with a carburetor and a mechanical fuel pump have a *vapor-return line* (Fig. 17-6). It runs from the fuel pump or fuel filter to the fuel tank. The fuel pump can handle liquid only. Any vapor that forms in the pump returns to the tank through the vapor-return line. If the vapor is not removed, vapor lock occurs (➤16-3). This stops fuel delivery.

Some cars have a *vapor separator* between the fuel pump and carburetor. Vapor in the fuel flowing to the car-buretor rises to the top of the separator. The vapor then flows through the vapor-return line to the fuel tank. The fuel system in Fig. 17-6 uses a *filter separator*. It combines the fuel filter and the vapor separator into a single unit.

➤ 17-7 ELECTRIC FUEL PUMP

The *electric fuel pump* (Fig. 17-7) uses an electric motor or solenoid to provide the pumping action. There are two advantages to the electric fuel pump. First, fuel delivery can begin as soon as the ignition switch is turned on. Second, the electric fuel pump can always deliver more fuel than the engine needs.

The two types of electric fuel pumps are *in-line* and *in-tank*. An electric motor driving an impeller provides the pumping action (Fig. 17-7C). The fuel is pressurized from the pump to the engine. This helps prevent vapor lock. The in-line pump is *in the fuel line* between the fuel tank and the engine (Fig. 17-7A). The pump is usually located near the fuel tank at the rear of the vehicle. Most cars use the in-

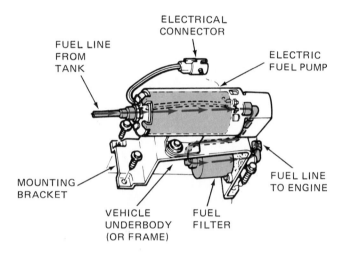

(A) IN-LINE FUEL PUMP

Fig. 17-7 Mounting and construction of electric fuel pumps. (*Ford Motor Company; Chrysler Corporation*)

Fig. 17-6 Transverse engine with a carbureted fuel system. (*Chrysler Corporation*)

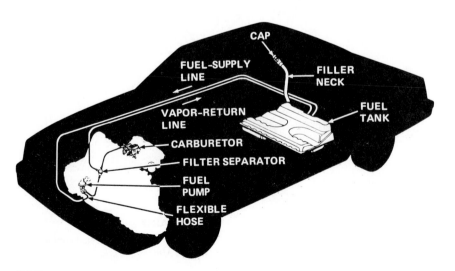

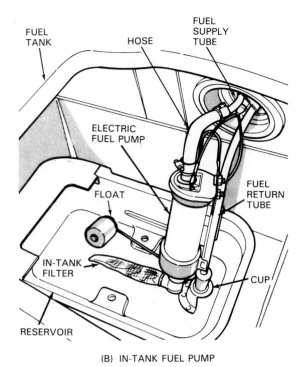

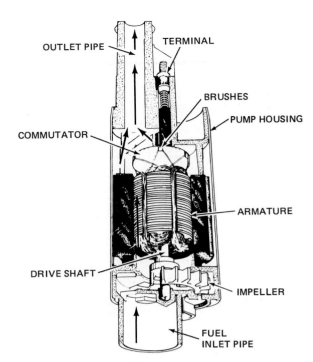

(B) IN-TANK FUEL PUMP

(C) ELECTRIC FUEL PUMP

Fig. 17-7 *(Continued)*.

tank pump (Fig. 17-7B) located *in the fuel tank*. Some vehicles use both.

Figure 17-8 is the wiring diagram for an in-tank fuel pump. The pump connects to the battery through contacts in the starting-motor relay. This allows the pump to start delivering fuel as soon as the starting motor begins to crank the engine. After the engine starts, the electrical circuit is maintained through the oil-pressure switch. The pump shuts off whenever the engine stops or the oil pressure drops. The pump also shuts off if the ignition

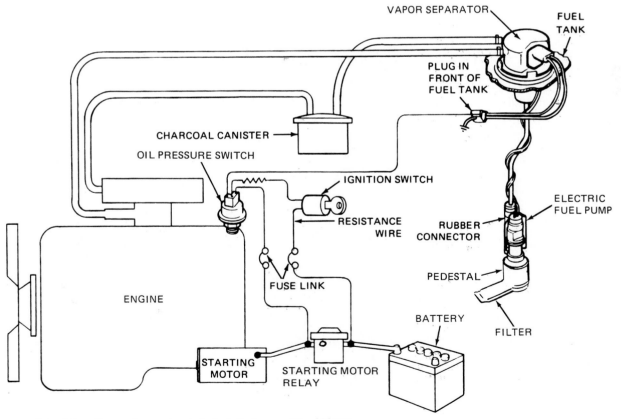

Fig. 17-8 Wiring diagram for an electric in-tank fuel pump. (*Ford Motor Company*)

197

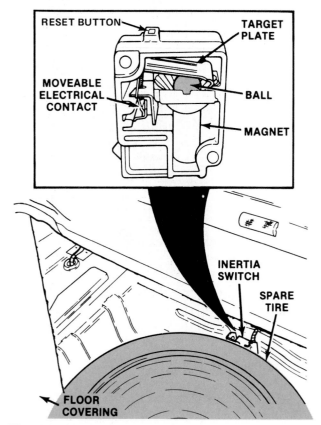

Fig. 17-9 Location and construction of the inertia switch for the electric fuel pump. (*Ford Motor Company*)

switch is turned off or if the ignition system stops working.

Some fuel-pump wiring circuits include an *inertia switch* (Fig. 17-9). If the car is in a collision or rolls over, the impact moves the ball in the inertia switch out of position. This opens the switch and shuts off the fuel pump, reducing the possibility of fire. The car may have a FUEL CUTOUT light in the instrument panel that comes on if the inertia switch opens.

Many electric fuel pumps are supplied with current through a *fuel-pump relay* (➤19-19). It is controlled by the engine computer or electronic control module (ECM).

➤ 17-8 FUEL FILTERS AND SCREENS

Fuel systems use filters and screens to prevent dirt from entering the fuel line and fuel pump. Most fuel systems have at least two filters. A filter screen or strainer attaches to the pickup tube in the bottom of the fuel tank (Fig. 17-7B). An in-line filter is between the fuel tank and the carburetor or fuel injectors (Fig. 17-10). Some filters thread into a tapped hole in the carburetor.

An in-line fuel filter may include a magnet to catch metal particles in the fuel (Fig. 17-10). The filter element is usually made of ceramic or paper. Fuel-filter service is covered in ➤20-19. Servicing fuel filters in carbureted fuel systems is covered in ➤22-14.

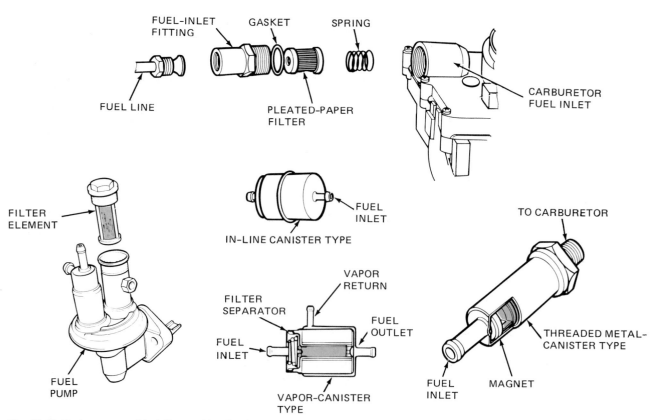

Fig. 17-10 Various types of fuel filters. (*Chrysler Corporation*)

AIR INTAKE AND MIXTURE DISTRIBUTION

➤ 17-9 AIR CLEANER

Air enters the engine through the air intake or air induction system. Induction means "to take into." As much as 100,000 cubic feet [2832 cubic meters] of air pass through the engine every 1000 miles [1609 km]. The grit and dust particles in this air must be removed before it enters the engine. If not, engine wear and damage can result.

The intake air passes through the air cleaner (Fig. 17-11) before entering the engine. The air cleaner has a ring or panel of filter paper or other material (Fig. 17-12). This traps dust and dirt as the air passes through.

Some engines mount the air cleaner directly on the carburetor or throttle body (Fig. 17-11A). Other engines use a *remote-mounted air cleaner* (Fig. 17-11B). It mounts elsewhere and connects by a hose or tube to the carburetor or throttle body (Fig. 17-13).

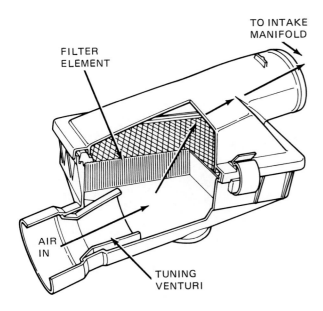

(A) RING-TYPE FILTER ELEMENT

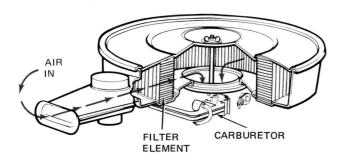

(B) PANEL-TYPE FILTER ELEMENT

Fig. 17-11 Air cleaners with (A) ring-type and (B) panel-type filter elements. (*Chrysler Corporation*)

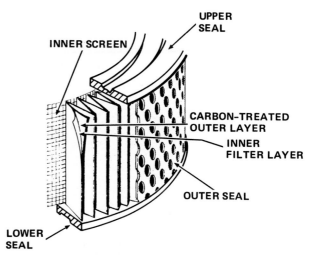

Fig. 17-12 Construction of a pleated-paper filter element made with two-ply paper. (*Chrysler Corporation*)

The air cleaner also muffles *induction noise*. This noise is caused by the intake air as the intake valves open and close. Some air cleaners have a *tuning venturi* inside the housing (Fig. 17-11B) to reduce induction noise. Others connect to a *resonator*. This is a tube or chamber that generates sound waves which cancel out the noise. The system is called a *tuned induction system*. The air cleaner also acts as a *flame arrestor* if the engine backfires through the air-intake system. The flame could erupt into the engine compartment and cause a fire without the air cleaner in place.

Some high-performance cars have used a *ram air cleaner*. A vacuum motor opens the ram-air valve under open-throttle or heavy-load conditions. This scoops additional air into the air cleaner for improved engine performance.

➤ 17-10 THERMOSTATIC AIR CLEANER

The *thermostatic air cleaner* (Fig. 17-14) is used with carbureted fuel systems and throttle-body fuel injection. It is not used with port fuel injection nor with supercharged or turbocharged engines (Chap. 18). Its purpose is to improve engine performance and driveability when the engine is cold. The system heats the air entering the throttle body or carburetor during cold-engine operation. This allows the engine to run on a leaner air-fuel mixture during warm-up.

A temperature-sensing spring (Fig. 17-15) in the thermostatic air cleaner reacts to the temperature of the air entering the air cleaner. Figure 17-16 shows the operation of the thermostatic air cleaner. When the air is cold, the spring holds the air-bleed valve closed (Fig. 17-16B). This applies intake-manifold vacuum to the *vacuum motor*. Atmospheric pressure pushes the diaphragm up. This raises the control-damper assembly (door or valve) which blocks off the snorkel tube. All air now has to enter through the hot-air pipe.

The hot-air pipe connects to the heat stove on the

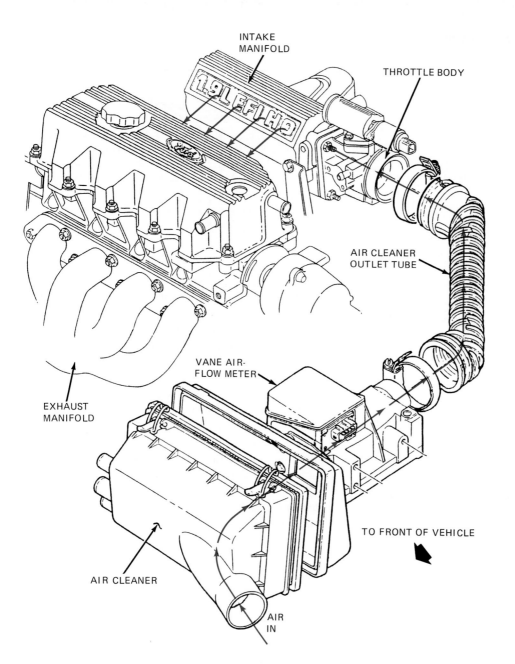

INTAKE MANIFOLD

THROTTLE BODY

Fig. 17-13 Air flow through a remote-mounted air cleaner. (*Ford Motor Company*)

AIR CLEANER OUTLET TUBE

EXHAUST MANIFOLD

VANE AIR-FLOW METER

TO FRONT OF VEHICLE

AIR CLEANER

AIR IN

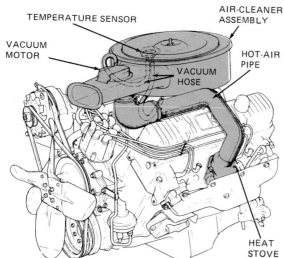

TEMPERATURE SENSOR

AIR-CLEANER ASSEMBLY

VACUUM MOTOR

HOT-AIR PIPE

VACUUM HOSE

HEAT STOVE

Fig. 17-14 Thermostatic air cleaner on a V-type engine. (*Buick Division of General Motors Corporation*)

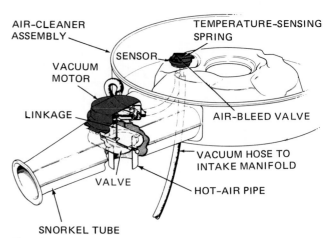

AIR-CLEANER ASSEMBLY

TEMPERATURE-SENSING SPRING

SENSOR

VACUUM MOTOR

LINKAGE

AIR-BLEED VALVE

VACUUM HOSE TO INTAKE MANIFOLD

VALVE

HOT-AIR PIPE

SNORKEL TUBE

Fig. 17-15 A temperature-sensing spring in the thermostatic air cleaner opens and closes the air-bleed valve to control the vacuum motor. (*Chevrolet Division of General Motors Corporation*)

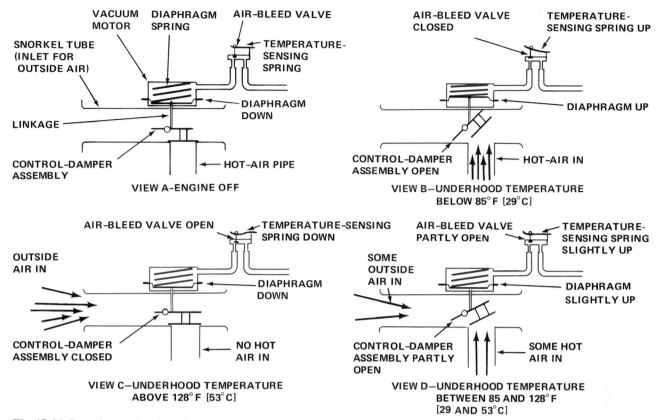

Fig. 17-16 Operating modes of the thermostatic air cleaner. (*Chevrolet Division of General Motors Corporation*)

exhaust manifold. The exhaust manifold heats up quickly after the engine starts. This sends heated air to the air cleaner. The heated air helps vaporize the fuel delivered by the carburetor or fuel injectors. This improves cold-engine performance.

Underhood temperature increases as the engine warms up. When the air gets hot enough, the temperature-sensing spring opens the air-bleed valve (Fig. 17-16C). This cuts off the vacuum to the vacuum motor. The diaphragm spring then pushes the diaphragm down. This lowers the control damper which closes off the hot-air pipe. All air entering the air cleaner now enters through the snorkel tube.

During warmup, the underhood temperature may not be hot enough to completely close the damper. Then the engine receives a blend of hot and cold air (Fig. 17-16D). Some cold underhood air enters the air cleaner along with some heated air from the heat stove.

NOTE Other engines use an electric heater under the carburetor or throttle body, or in the intake manifold, to preheat the intake air (➤21-24). The electric heater may be controlled by the engine computer or ECM.

➤ 17-11 THROTTLE BODY

The amount of air that enters a spark-ignition engine is primarily controlled by the driver moving the *accelerator pedal* (Fig. 17-17A). The foot-operated pedal connects through linkage or cable to the throttle valve in the *throttle body*. This is the air-control device for all spark-ignition engines — carbureted and fuel-injected.

Depressing the accelerator pedal opens the throttle valve (Fig. 17-17B). This allows fresh air from the air cleaner to enter the *intake manifold* (➤17-12). With a carburetor, the throttle valve controls the amount of air-fuel mixture that enters. The throttle valve controls only air if the engine has port (multipoint) or throttle-body injection.

Instead of a mechanically-operated throttle valve, some cars have an *electronic throttle control* or *drive-by-wire system*. It is used with *traction control* (Chap. 53). A sensor on the accelerator pedal signals its position to the electronic control module (ECM). The ECM computes the proper opening of the throttle valves. Signals then are sent to small motors on the throttle body which open and close the throttle valves as required. This prevents wheelspin during hard acceleration.

➤ 17-12 INTAKE MANIFOLD

The intake manifold (Fig. 17-18) connects the throttle body (➤17-11) with the intake ports in the cylinder head. The manifold has a set of passages or *runners* through which air or air-fuel mixture flows. With port fuel injection, only air flows through (Figs. 15-9 and 17-19). Fuel is injected into the air as it flows through the intake ports. With a carburetor (Fig. 17-18) or throttle-body injection (Fig. 17-20), fuel mixes with the air as it enters the intake manifold.

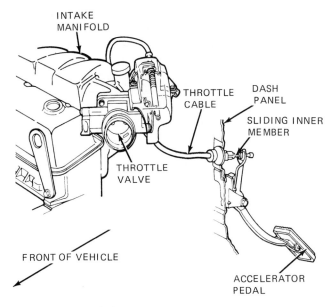

(A) THROTTLE LINKAGE

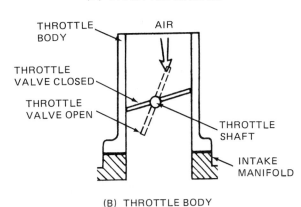

(B) THROTTLE BODY

Fig. 17-17 Depressing the accelerator pedal causes the throttle linkage to open the throttle valve in the throttle body. (*Ford Motor Company; ATW*)

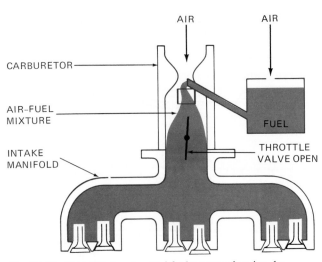

Fig. 17-18 Simplified carbureted fuel system showing the carburetor delivering air-fuel mixture to the intake manifold.

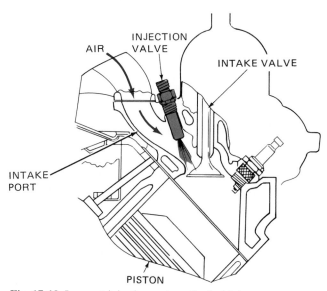

Fig. 17-19 In a port-injection system, the fuel injector or injection valve sprays fuel into the intake air just before it passes the intake valve and enters the cylinder.

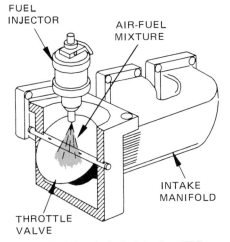

Fig. 17-20 Simplified throttle-body injection (TBI) system. (*Bendix Corporation*)

Figure 17-21 shows the intake manifold, cylinder head, and exhaust manifold for an in-line four-cylinder engine. The intake manifold is a one-piece casting of iron or aluminum alloy. The passages or runners carry air-fuel mixture. They are as short as possible and designed to avoid sharp corners.

When only air flows through the intake manifold, there are no distribution problems. The intake manifold can take on various shapes (Fig. 17-22) and the runners often are *tuned* (➤17-16). This means the length and size of the runners are selected to improve cylinder charging. Relatively long runners may improve volumetric efficiency (➤15-12).

Figure 17-22 shows a two-piece cast-aluminum intake manifold. When the throttle valve opens, air flows into the plenum or air chamber (Fig. 15-9). The air then flows through the primary runners and lower manifold to the intake ports in the cylinder head. In some engines, the plenum and runners (tubes) are separate parts (Fig. 12-15). They attach to the intake manifold.

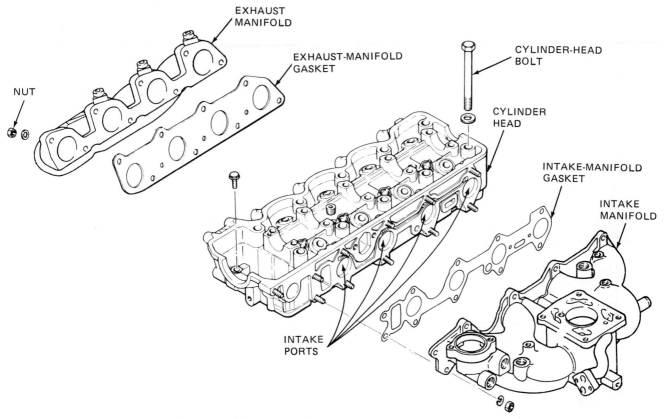

Fig. 17-21 Cylinder head for an overhead-camshaft engine with the intake and exhaust manifolds on opposite sides of the head. (*Chrysler Corporation*)

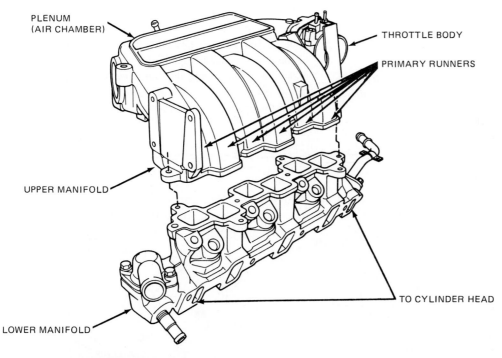

Fig. 17-22 Two-piece cast-aluminum intake manifold. Intake air flows through the plenum, primary runners, and lower manifold into the cylinder head. (*Chrysler Corporation*)

➤ 17-13 DISTRIBUTION OF AIR-FUEL MIXTURE

An intake manifold carrying air-fuel mixture (Figs. 17-18 and 17-21) may have a problem distributing it. Ideally,

each cylinder receives the same amount and richness of air-fuel mixture. Actually, the cylinders at each end of the manifold usually receive a richer mixture.

Air flows readily around corners and through variously shaped passages in the intake manifold. Unless the fuel vaporizes completely (Fig. 17-23), it contains some relatively heavy droplets of liquid fuel. Inertia (➤15-5) prevents these droplets from turning the corners as the mixture flows through the manifold. The droplets travel in a more or less straight line until they hit the end of the manifold. Then they collect in a puddle of liquid fuel (Fig. 17-23).

The air-fuel mixture flowing by the puddle of fuel into the end cylinder picks up some of the puddled fuel as it evaporates. This further enrichens the mixture flowing into the end cylinders. The center cylinders receive a leaner mixture. More even fuel distribution results after the intake manifold heats up. Then most of the fuel vaporizes.

EXHAUST SYSTEM

➤ 17-14 EXHAUST SYSTEM

The *exhaust system* (➤13-12) collects, quiets, and cleans the exhaust gases from the engine. The system carries the

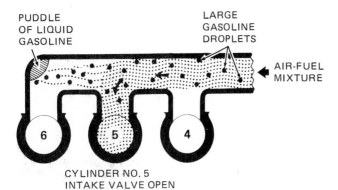

Fig. 17-23 Distribution pattern in an intake manifold. The gasoline particles tend to continue to the end of the manifold, enriching the mixture flowing into the end cylinders. (*Chevrolet Division of General Motors Corporation*)

gases to the rear of the car and discharges them into the air. The exhaust system (Fig. 17-24) includes the exhaust manifold, exhaust pipe, catalytic converter, muffler, resonator (on some cars), and tail pipe.

Each bank of cylinders in a V-type engine has an exhaust manifold. An *exhaust pipe* connects to each exhaust manifold. The two exhaust pipes may join and connect to a single catalytic converter (Fig. 13-16). Exhaust gas flows out of the catalytic converter through a muffler and resonator (if used). This is a *single exhaust system.*

Some cars with V-type engines have a *dual exhaust system* (Fig. 17-25). There are two separate exhaust systems, one for each cylinder bank. A *crossover pipe* connects the two inlet pipes to help reduce noise. The dual exhaust system improves engine breathing by allowing it to exhaust more freely. Increased engine power results.

➤ 17-15 EXHAUST MANIFOLD

The *exhaust manifold* (Figs. 17-13 and 17-26) is a set of passages or tubes (➤13-12). They carry the exhaust gas from the *exhaust ports* in the cylinder head to the exhaust pipe. The manifold collects the exhaust gas from each exhaust port (Fig. 13-15 and 17-24). Then the manifold merges the exhaust gas into a single flow. The exhaust pipe connects to the outlet from the exhaust manifold. A tube-type *header* exhaust manifold (Fig. 17-26) may merge the flow from two cylinders into one.

Some in-line engines have the intake and exhaust manifolds on opposite sides of the cylinder head (Fig. 17-21). Other in-line engines have the manifolds on the same side of the cylinder head (Fig. 13-15). The exhaust manifold is under the intake manifold. Some carbureted engines with this arrangement have a *heat-control valve* (➤21-22). When the engine is cold, it sends heat from the hot exhaust

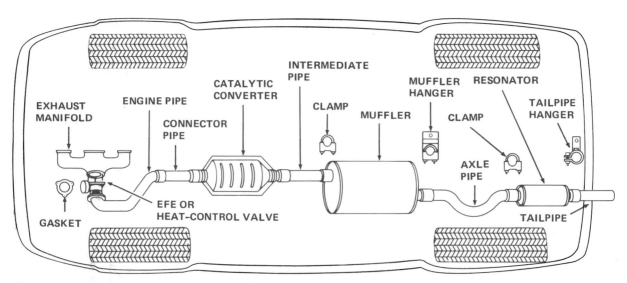

Fig. 17-24 Components of an exhaust system. (*Walker Manufacturing Division of Tenneco, Inc.*)

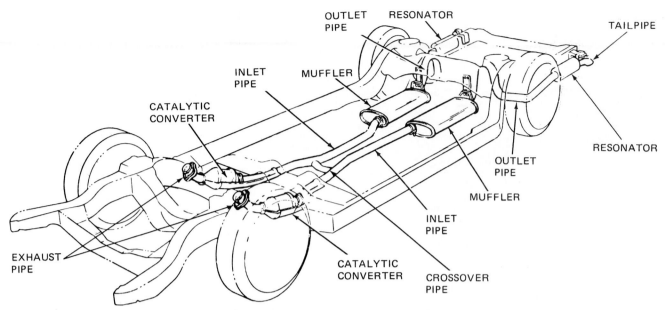

Fig. 17-25 A dual exhaust system for a V-type engine. Each bank of cylinders has its own exhaust system. (*Ford Motor Company*)

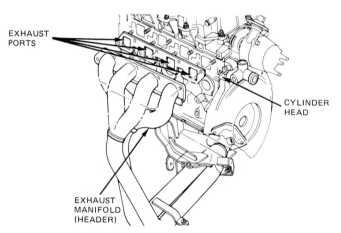

Fig. 17-26 Engine with a set of headers, which is a tube-type exhaust manifold. (*Ford Motor Company*)

gases to warm the intake manifold. This improves fuel vaporization for better cold-engine operation.

➤ 17-16 TUNED INTAKE AND EXHAUST MANIFOLDS

Tuning the intake and exhaust manifolds improves volumetric efficiency. The intake runners are the proper size and length to produce the highest possible pressure in the cylinder. The exhaust runners produce the lowest possible *backpressure* in the exhaust system. This is the pressure created in the exhaust manifold by any restriction to the exhaust gas flowing through. A tuned exhaust system has very little backpressure. The higher the exhaust backpressure, the lower the engine's volumetric efficiency (➤15-12).

The intake manifold takes advantage of the opening and closing of the intake valves to produce a "ram" effect. When an intake valve opens, the air or air-fuel mixture flows into the cylinder. The flow momentarily stops when the valve closes. However, the inertia of the air or mixture keeps it moving. This makes the air or mixture pile up or "ram" against the closed valve. If the valve opens while this is taking place, additional mixture is rammed into the cylinder. Greater engine power results.

Tuning of the intake manifold is most effective at high engine speed. To improve low-speed performance, some port-injected and four-valve engines have a *variable induction system*. Figure 17-27 shows this system on an in-line four-cylinder engine. It has two runners for each cylinder. The long runner or *primary runner* is tuned for low speed. The short runner or *secondary runner* is tuned for high speed. A computer-controlled throttle valve in each high-speed runner remains closed until engine speed is about 4000 rpm. Then the high-speed throttle valve opens and both runners deliver air-fuel mixture to the cylinders. This improves engine power and response. Figure 12-15 shows a V-8 engine with a similar system.

Tuning also works in the exhaust manifold. The length of the runners increases the speed of the exhaust gas. When an exhaust valve opens, the exhaust gas exits as a high-speed pulse. Following behind the pulse is a much lower pressure. When the exhaust valve opens again, the exhaust gas pulses into this lower pressure. With lower backpressure, the cylinder empties more completely. This allows more air or mixture to enter the next time the intake valve opens. An increase in engine power results. On some engines, the pulses in the exhaust system operate the *air-aspirator valve* (➤35-19).

205

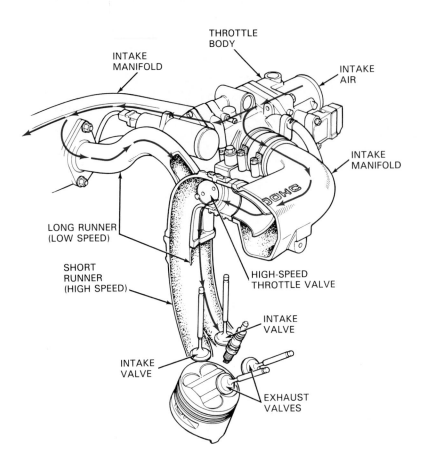

INTAKE
MANIFOLD

THROTTLE
BODY

INTAKE
AIR

INTAKE
MANIFOLD

LONG RUNNER
(LOW SPEED)

SHORT
RUNNER
(HIGH SPEED)

HIGH-SPEED
THROTTLE VALVE

INTAKE
VALVE

INTAKE
VALVE

EXHAUST
VALVES

Fig. 17-27 An electronically-controlled variable induction system which has two air paths, one for low-speed operation and another that opens for high-speed operation. *(Ford Motor Company)*

➤ 17-17 MUFFLER

The *muffler* (Fig. 17-28) is usually between the catalytic converter and the resonator or tail pipe. Its purpose is to quiet or "muffle" the noise of the exhaust. It has a series of holes, passages, and resonance chambers through which the exhaust gas passes. This damps out the noisy high-pressure surges resulting from the opening of the exhaust valves. Some exhaust systems use a smaller muffler-type resonator (Fig. 17-24) for further quieting (Fig. 17-25).

Some cars use *laminated* exhaust pipe. A two-ply laminated pipe is one layer of pipe inside another. A three-ply laminated pipe has a layer of plastic sandwiched between the two metal layers. Either pipe damps out exhaust-pipe "ring" which occurs in some exhaust systems.

A few high-performance sports cars have a *dual-mode muffler*, or *active exhaust system*. Moving a switch on the instrument panel from TOUR to SPORT opens a valve in the muffler inlet passage. This allows exhaust gas to flow through both the muffler and a bypass pipe. The larger total flow area reduces the restriction in the exhaust system. This improves fuel economy.

Electronic noise control systems are being developed. These can almost completely eliminate exhaust noise. The systems electronically produce sound waves that are the exact opposite of the exhaust sound waves. When the two sets of sound waves collide, they cancel each other. Some systems can cancel the sound of a running engine. The canceling sound waves are emitted by the sound-system speakers in the vehicle.

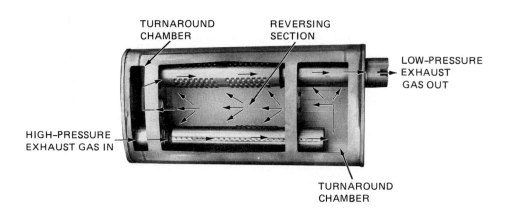

TURNAROUND
CHAMBER

REVERSING
SECTION

LOW-PRESSURE
EXHAUST
GAS OUT

HIGH-PRESSURE
EXHAUST GAS IN

TURNAROUND
CHAMBER

Fig. 17-28 Exhaust muffler cut away, with arrows showing the path of the exhaust gas as it flows through. *(Maremont Corporation)*

The catalytic converter cleans the exhaust gas by reducing the pollutants to harmless substances:

$$CO + HC + NO_x \text{ changes to } CO_2 + H_2O + N$$

The exhaust gases flow through the catalytic converter. *Catalysts* inside the catalytic converter cause these changes. Chapters 35 and 36 on emission controls describe how the catalytic converter works.

FUEL GAUGES AND DISPLAYS

➤ 17-19 FUEL-LEVEL INDICATORS

All cars have a *fuel-level indicator* (Fig. 17-29) located in the instrument panel or cluster. It keeps the driver informed about the amount of fuel remaining in the tank. The indicator is an electro-mechanical *fuel gauge* or electronic *fuel-level display*. Some cars also have a LOW FUEL light in the instrument panel. In addition, some cars have a *fuel computer*. It calculates and displays information about fuel consumption and fuel economy.

Electro-mechanical gauges (Fig. 17-29A) are *analog gauges*. They use a moving needle or pointer to show the reading. Electronic fuel-level displays often show the fuel level as bars on a bar graph (Fig. 17-29B). Some cars have a *digital fuel gauge*. The number displayed tells the gallons (liters) of fuel remaining in the tank.

There are two types of fuel gauges: *magnetic* (Fig. 17-30) and *thermostatic* (Fig. 17-31). Each has a *sending unit* in the fuel tank and a fuel gauge in the instrument cluster. The tank unit may be separate (Fig. 17-2) or combined with the electric in-tank fuel pump (Fig. 17-7B). As the fuel level in the tank changes, the float moves up and down. This changes the resistance of the sending unit which varies the current flow through the instrument-panel unit. The pointer then moves across the face of the gauge to indicate the fuel level in the tank.

1. MAGNETIC FUEL GAUGE Figure 17-30 shows the wiring circuit for a magnetic fuel gauge. The tank unit contains a *variable resistor*. Its resistance varies as the float moves up and down, moving the sliding contact. The instrument-panel unit has two coils. When the ignition switch is on, current from the battery flows through them. This produces magnetic fields that act on the armature. The gauge pointer attaches to the armature. When fuel level is high, the resistance in the sending unit is high. The FULL COIL magnetism pulls the armature and pointer to the right. As the tank empties, the resistance of the tank unit drops. More of the current passing through the EMPTY COIL flows to the tank unit instead of to the FULL COIL. This reduces the magnetism of the FULL COIL. The armature and needle move to the left. This shows a lower fuel level in the tank.

2. THERMOSTATIC FUEL GAUGE Figure 17-31 shows a thermostatic or *thermal fuel gauge*. When the fuel is low, the resistance in the tank unit is high. Little current flows through the instrument-panel unit. When the tank is filled, the float moves up. This reduces tank-unit resistance. More current flows through the instrument-panel unit.

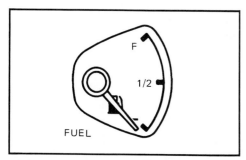

(A) ELECTRO-MECHANICAL FUEL GAUGE

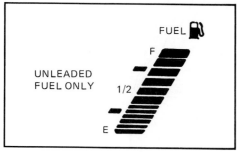

(B) ELECTRONIC FUEL-LEVEL DISPLAY

Fig. 17-29 Fuel-level indicators. (*Ford Motor Company*)

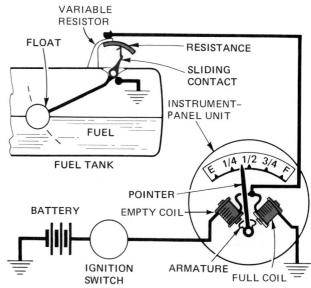

Fig. 17-30 Wiring diagram for a magnetic fuel gauge.

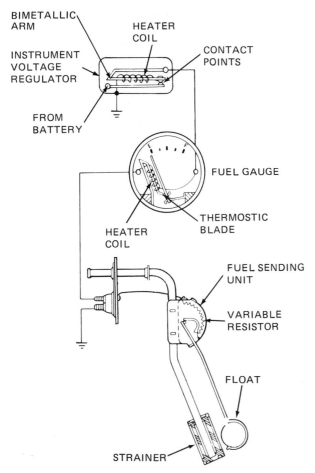

Fig. 17-31 Wiring diagram for a thermostatic fuel gauge, which uses a variable-resistance tank unit. (*ATW*)

The current flows through the heater coil wound around the thermostatic blade. The heat causes the blade to bend. As the blade swings to the right (in Fig. 17-31), the pointer moves toward the full mark.

NOTE *Fuel-tank sending units for magnetic and thermostatic gauges appear similar. However, the magnetic gauge uses a sending unit that has high resistance when the float is up and low when the float is down. The thermostatic gauge uses a sending unit that has low resistance when the float is up and high resistance when the float is down.*

➤ 17-21 INSTRUMENT-VOLTAGE REGULATOR

Figure 17-31 shows the *voltage limiter* or *instrument-voltage regulator* (IVR) used with thermostatic gauges (➤17-20). The IVR keeps the voltage to the gauges (or *instruments*) at about 5 volts. This prevents inaccurate gauge readings as the voltage varies during normal operation of the car. The current to the fuel gauge passes through a set of contact points and a bimetallic arm in the IVR. The current also flows through a heater coil around the arm. The arm bends as it warms up. This opens the contact points, allowing the arm to cool and close the contacts again. When the voltage is high, the contacts open and close so rapidly that they vibrate. The contacts vibrate at a slower rate when the voltage is lower.

NOTE *The vibrating contact points in the IVR may cause static in the radio. They also may affect the operation of the computer and other electronic devices. Magnetic gauges (➤17-20) avoid these problems because an IVR is not required.*

➤ 17-22 LOW-FUEL WARNING LIGHT

To help prevent the driver from allowing the vehicle to "run out of gas," many instrument panels include a *low-fuel warning light*. The light or a gas-pump symbol (Fig. 17-32) blinks when the remaining fuel drops to a preset

Fig. 17-32 An electronic instrument cluster that displays fuel level and other driver information. (*Ford Motor Company*)

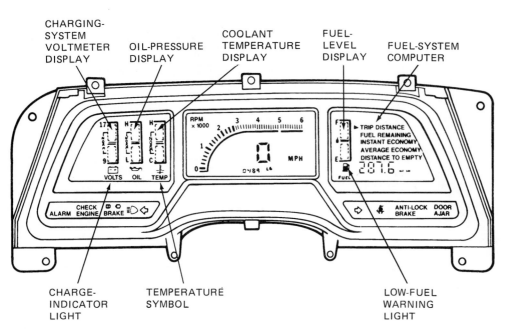

level. Some cars have an electronic *voice-alert system* that gives a spoken warning when fuel is low.

➤ 17-23 ELECTRONIC FUEL GAUGE

In many cars, the engine computer monitors the fuel system and other engine operating conditions. This allows the electronic instrument cluster to display fuel level (Fig. 17-32). It can also display other information related to fuel consumption and economy. Information available includes trip distance, fuel remaining, instantaneous fuel economy, average fuel economy, and distance to empty. Some cars have a fuel computer that provides similar information. An electronic fuel gauge may also alert the driver if the gauge-system itself malfunctions.

MULTIPLE-CHOICE TEST

*Select the **one** correct, best, or most probable answer to each question.*
You can find the answers in the section indicated at the end of each question.

1. The two fuel systems used with spark-ignition engines are (➤17-2)
   a. carbureted and diesel
   b. fuel injection and diesel
   c. port and throttle body
   d. fuel injected and carbureted
2. Technician A says the fuel-tank cap has a valve to prevent pressure buildup in the tank. Technician B says the cap has a valve to prevent vacuum buildup in the tank. Who is right? (➤17-4)
   a. Technician A
   b. Technician B
   c. both A and B
   d. neither A nor B
3. All of the following are true about the electric fuel pump EXCEPT (➤17-7)
   a. It may be mounted in-line or in-tank
   b. It mounts on the cylinder block or head
   c. It shuts off if the inertia switch opens
   d. It reduces the possibility of vapor lock
4. Technician A says the air cleaner cleans and cools the intake air. Technician B says the air cleaner acts as a flame arrestor and reduces exhaust noise. Who is right? (➤17-9)
   a. Technician A
   b. Technician B
   c. both A and B
   d. neither A nor B
5. The device that controls the amount of air entering the spark-ignition engine is the (➤17-11)
   a. throttle valve
   b. air cleaner
   c. intake manifold
   d. fuel injector
6. All of the following are true about the intake manifold EXCEPT (➤17-12 and 17-16)
   a. It has a set of passages called "runners"
   b. It carries either air or air-fuel mixture
   c. It mounts between the air cleaner and the throttle body
   d. It can be tuned to increase pressure in the cylinder
7. The crossover pipe in the dual exhaust system (➤17-14)
   a. increases engine power
   b. strengthens the pipes
   c. helps reduce noise
   d. feeds exhaust gas into the catalytic converter
8. An engine has a variable induction system. Technician A says the short runner is tuned for low speed and the long runner for high speed. Technician B says the throttle valves in the runners should open at about 4000 rpm. Who is right? (➤17-16)
   a. Technician A
   b. Technician B
   c. both A and B
   d. neither A nor B

REVIEW QUESTIONS

1. Discuss the problems that fuel vapor can cause in the fuel lines. (➤17-3 and 17-6)
2. Explain why the electric fuel pump stops if the engine stalls. (➤17-7)
3. Describe the parts and operation of the thermostatic air cleaner. (➤17-10)
4. Explain how the intake manifold can provide an improper air-fuel mixture to some cylinders. (➤17-13)
5. Describe the operation of the magnetic fuel gauge and sending unit. (➤17-20)

CHAPTER 18

SUPERCHARGERS AND TURBOCHARGERS

After studying this chapter, and with proper instruction and equipment, you should be able to:

- Explain how pressure differential affects the amount of air or air-fuel mixture that enters an engine.
- Describe the construction, operation, and controls of superchargers and turbochargers.
- Diagnose troubles in superchargers and turbochargers.
- Check boost pressure and wastegate operation.
- Service and repair superchargers and turbochargers.

➤ **18-1 NATURALLY-ASPIRATED ENGINES**

Suppose the engine is running with the throttle valve partly open (Fig. 18-1B). The amount of air that enters the intake manifold depends on the *pressure differential*. This is the difference in pressure on the air above and below the throttle valve (➤17-11). The air above the throttle valve is at atmospheric pressure. This is 14.7 psi [101.3 kPa]. The air below the partially-closed throttle valve is at less than atmospheric pressure. A pressure less than atmospheric is a *negative pressure*. It is commonly called a *vacuum* (➤9-16).

The vacuum below the throttle valve is created by the pistons during their intake strokes (➤5-22). As the pistons leave top dead center (TDC) and move down the cylinders, the space above the pistons gets larger (Fig. 11-10). This lowers the pressure in the intake manifold and creates the partial vacuum called *intake-manifold vacuum*.

Intake-manifold vacuum varies from "high" to "low," primarily depending on the position of the throttle valve. The engine may have a high vacuum of 22 inches [559 mm]

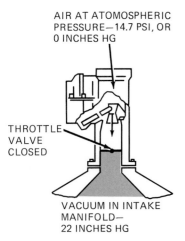

AIR AT ATOMOSPHERIC PRESSURE—14.7 PSI, OR 0 INCHES HG

THROTTLE VALVE CLOSED

VACUUM IN INTAKE MANIFOLD— 22 INCHES HG

(A) THROTTLE VALVE CLOSED

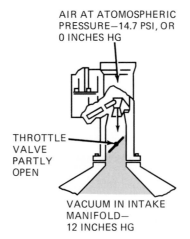

AIR AT ATOMOSPHERIC PRESSURE—14.7 PSI, OR 0 INCHES HG

THROTTLE VALVE PARTLY OPEN

VACUUM IN INTAKE MANIFOLD— 12 INCHES HG

(B) THROTTLE VALVE PARTLY OPEN

AIR AT ATOMOSPHERIC PRESSURE—14.7 PSI, OR 0 INCHES HG

THROTTLE VALVE FULLY OPEN

LITTLE VACUUM IN MANIFOLD. AIR AT NEARLY ATOMOSPHERIC PRESSURE—14.7 PSI, OR 0 INCHES HG

(C) THROTTLE VALVE FULLY OPEN

Fig. 18-1 Pressure differential above and below the throttle valve at various throttle positions. (*ATW*)

of mercury (Hg) when it is idling with the throttle-valve closed (Fig. 18-1A). As the throttle-valve opens (Fig. 18-1B), the vacuum decreases. At wide-open throttle (Fig. 18-1C), the air above and below the throttle valve is at nearly the same pressure — atmospheric pressure. Then intake-manifold vacuum is almost 0. (The restriction through the throttle body may cause a slight vacuum even at wide-open throttle.)

NOTE Figure 18-2 shows the relationship between vacuum and pressure. In the intake manifold, higher vacuum means lower pressure. Lower vacuum means higher pressure. Then the *absolute pressure* in the manifold — *manifold absolute pressure* (MAP) — is increasing. To convert from *pounds per square inch* (psi) to other pressure measurements:

inch Hg = psi × 2.036
mm Hg = psi × 51.71
kPa = psi × 6.9

In most engines, atmospheric pressure is the only force that pushes air into the intake manifold. These engines are *naturally aspirated* or *normally aspirated*. The air they "breathe" is at normal atmospheric pressure. The amount of fuel that can be burned in the cylinders is limited by the amount of air that the atmospheric pressure pushes in.

> ## 18-2 FORCED INDUCTION

An engine can produce more power at the same speed if more air-fuel mixture is forced into the cylinders. More air-fuel mixture means higher pressures during the power strokes and higher power output. Forcing additional air-fuel mixture into the cylinders is called *forced induction*. It is one way to improve volumetric efficiency (➤15-12). An engine with forced induction may produce 35 to 60 percent more power than a naturally-aspirated engine.

Forced induction may be provided by a *supercharger* (➤18-3) or by a *turbocharger* (➤18-7). These are air pumps or *blowers* that force more air-fuel mixture into the engine. Instead of a vacuum, there is a pressure in the intake manifold. The amount of pressure is the *boost pressure*. When boost is not needed, the engine runs almost

the same as a normally-aspirated engine. This allows a smaller engine to deliver good fuel economy during normal driving, and to have the power of a larger engine when needed.

The supercharger and turbocharger differ in construction and operation. One basic difference is in how they are driven. The supercharger is mechanically driven by a belt or chain from the engine crankshaft. The turbocharger is driven by the engine exhaust gas.

Following sections describe two types of superchargers and the turbocharger. Later sections cover trouble diagnosis and service of both.

SUPERCHARGERS

> ## 18-3 TYPES OF SUPERCHARGERS

Several older automotive engines used a supercharger, but its popularity faded. Most drivers complained about its noise and poor fuel economy. Because of the *turbo lag* (➤18-10) common to turbocharged engines, some manufacturers are installing a supercharger instead of a turbocharger on high-performance engines. The supercharger provides instant response when the accelerator pedal is depressed. It does not have to turn at high speed like the turbocharger. New designs have reduced noise and improved fuel economy.

Automotive manufacturers use two types of supercharger. These are the *Roots* type (➤18-4) and the *scroll* or *spiral* type (➤18-6).

> ## 18-4 ROOTS SUPERCHARGER

The most common type of supercharger is the *Roots supercharger* (Fig. 18-3). It has two long rotors which spin inside a housing. Each rotor has two or three lobes (Fig. 18-4) that are either straight or helical. The rotors are geared together and driven by a belt or chain from the

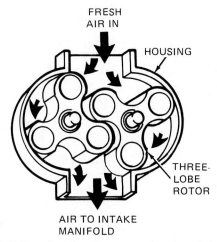

Fig. 18-3 Airflow through a Roots supercharger with three-lobe rotors. (*Ford Motor Company*)

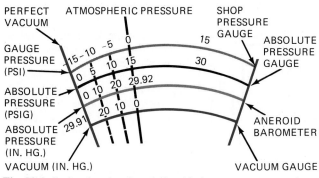

Fig. 18-2 Scales showing the relationship between vacuum and pressure. (*Ford Motor Company*)

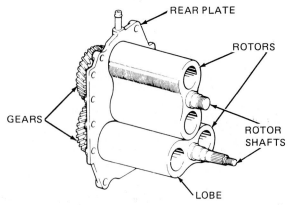

Fig. 18-4 Geared rotors for a Roots supercharger using straight two-lobe rotors. (*Toyota Motor Sales, U.S.A., Inc.*)

engine crankshaft. Supercharger speed is two to three times faster than engine speed.

The carburetor or throttle-body injection (TBI) unit usually mounts on the air-intake side of the supercharger (Fig. 18-5). The air-fuel mixture flows through the supercharger. Only air flows through when the engine has port fuel injection.

Figure 18-6 shows the intake-air flow through the Roots

supercharger for a port-injected engine. The air passes through the air cleaner and *air-flow meter* (Chap. 19). The air-flow meter signals the electronic control module (ECM) how much air is entering the engine. Then the air flows past the throttle valve and into the supercharger.

The air fills the spaces between the rotor lobes and housing (Figs. 18-3 and 18-6). The spinning rotors carry the trapped air around the housing to the discharge ports. Then the meshing rotors force the air out and into the intake manifold (Fig. 18-3) or *intercooler* (➤18-9). The *discharge air* or *boost air* (Fig. 18-7) compresses the air ahead of it. This creates the *manifold pressure* or boost pressure in the intake system.

The Roots supercharger is a *positive displacement* air pump. When the throttle valve is open, each revolution of the rotors forces the same volume of air into the intake manifold. This occurs regardless of engine speed. On one engine, maximum boost pressure of approximately 12 psi [82.8 kPa] is reached at about 4000 engine rpm (10,400 supercharger rpm).

| NOTE | Sometimes pressures are given as *bar* or *atm*. These refer to *bar*ometric pressure [bar] and *atm*ospheric pressure (atm). One bar or atm is about the same as 14.7 psi. For example, the boost pressure of 12 psi given above is the same as 0.8 bar or 0.8 atm. |

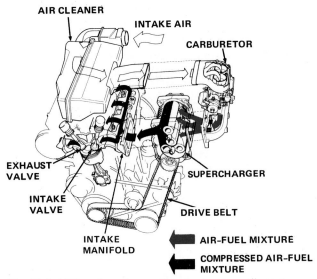

Fig. 18-5 Airflow through an engine that has the carburetor mounted on the air-intake side of a belt-driven Roots supercharger. (*Fiat Motors of North America, Inc.*)

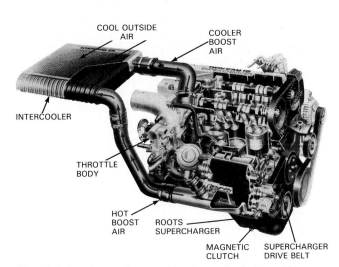

Fig. 18-7 Roots supercharger with a magnetic clutch and intercooler on a DOHC engine. (*Toyota Motor Sales, U.S.A., Inc.*)

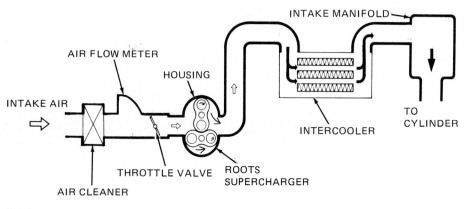

Fig. 18-6 Simplified intake-air flow through a Roots supercharger on a port-injected engine. After the air leaves the supercharger, the air passes through an intercooler before entering the intake manifold. (*Toyota Motor Sales, U.S.A., Inc.*)

➤ 18-5 REDUCING SUPERCHARGER DRAG

Driving the supercharger, especially at full load, takes power from the engine. This lost power or "drag" is called *parasitic loss*. To reduce parasitic loss, some superchargers have a *magnetic clutch* (Fig. 18-7). It is controlled by the ECM, and engages and disengages the supercharger as needed. The clutch is disengaged at light load (➤55-21).

Another way of reducing supercharger drag is with a *boost-control valve* (Fig. 18-8) or *bypass valve*. At part throttle, there is a vacuum in the intake manifold. Then the valve sends some discharge air back through the supercharger air intake. This improves performance and fuel economy. The bypass valve may be vacuum-controlled or operated by the throttle linkage. At idle (closed throttle valve), the bypass valve is wide open. At wide-open throttle, the bypass valve is closed.

➤ 18-6 SPIRAL (SCROLL) SUPERCHARGER

Another type of positive-displacement air pump is the scroll or spiral supercharger (Fig. 18-8). Volkswagen calls it a "G-charger" because the shape of the spirals resembles the letter G. In the housing, a *displacer* moves around inside the spirals to compress the air (Fig. 18-9). The displacer moves eccentrically. It does not rotate.

Two eccentric shafts are used. The *displacer drive shaft* (Fig. 18-9) supports and moves the displacer. The other shaft prevents the displacer from rotating. A small toothed timing belt keeps the two shafts turning in the proper relationship or in *phase*.

The displacer divides the intake airflow into an *inner chamber* and an *outer chamber*. As the displacer shaft

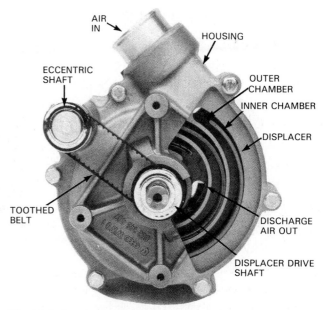

Fig. 18-9 Construction and drive of the spiral supercharger. (*Volkswagen of America, Inc.*)

rotates (Fig. 18-10), cams on the shaft move the displacer in a circular motion. This opens and closes the inner and outer chambers formed by the spirals. The action traps the air, compresses it, and forces it out through discharge ports near the center of the pump.

TURBOCHARGERS
➤ 18-7 TURBOCHARGER CONSTRUCTION AND OPERATION

The turbocharger (Fig. 18-11) is a centrifugal air pump driven by the engine exhaust gas. It forces an additional amount of air or air-fuel mixture into the engine. This

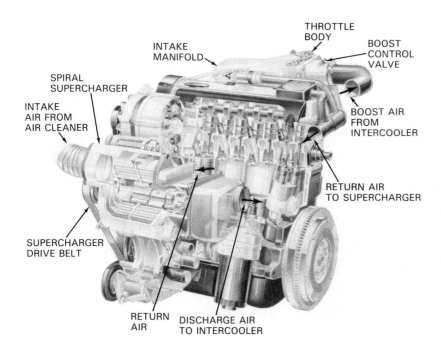

Fig. 18-8 Engine using a belt-driven scroll or spiral supercharger, called a "G-charger" by the manufacturer. (*Volkswagen of America, Inc.*)

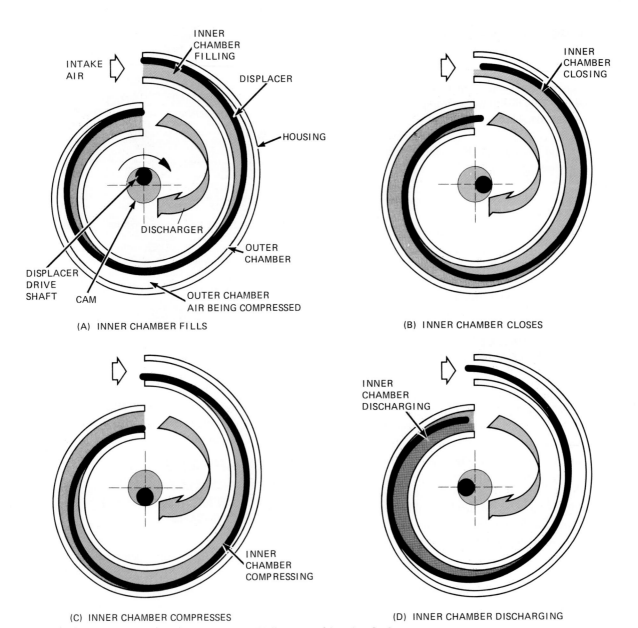

INTAKE AIR

INNER CHAMBER FILLING

DISPLACER

HOUSING

DISCHARGER

OUTER CHAMBER

DISPLACER DRIVE SHAFT

CAM

OUTER CHAMBER AIR BEING COMPRESSED

(A) INNER CHAMBER FILLS

INNER CHAMBER CLOSING

(B) INNER CHAMBER CLOSES

INNER CHAMBER COMPRESSING

(C) INNER CHAMBER COMPRESSES

INNER CHAMBER DISCHARGING

(D) INNER CHAMBER DISCHARGING

Fig. 18-10 Operation of the spiral supercharger. (*Volkswagen of America, Inc.*)

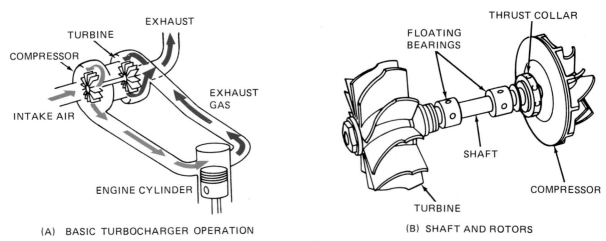

EXHAUST

TURBINE

COMPRESSOR

EXHAUST GAS

INTAKE AIR

ENGINE CYLINDER

(A) BASIC TURBOCHARGER OPERATION

THRUST COLLAR

FLOATING BEARINGS

SHAFT

COMPRESSOR

TURBINE

(B) SHAFT AND ROTORS

Fig. 18-11 Operation of a turbocharger. (A) Exhaust gases drive the turbine, which causes the compressor to spin. (B) The shaft-wheel assembly removed from the turbocharger. Note that the positions of the turbine and compressor are reversed from the way they are shown in A. (*Deere & Company*)

214

increases combustion pressure and engine power.

Figure 18-12 shows the air flow through the turbocharger. Two rotors or wheels — a *compressor* and a *turbine* — are mounted on the ends of a shaft (Fig. 18-11B). Together, the shaft and wheels make up the *shaft-wheel assembly*. When the engine is running, the exhaust gases flow into the turbine (Fig. 18-13). They strike the blades of the turbine, spinning it up to 120,000 rpm or higher. The compressor mounts on the same shaft and therefore spins at the same speed. As the compressor spins, it pulls fresh air in, compresses it, and then forces the compressed air out into the intake manifold.

The bearings supporting the shaft require special protection because of the high shaft speed. A steady flow of engine oil usually flows through the bearings (Fig. 18-13). This keeps the bearings cool and lubricated. On some engines, engine coolant flows through the bearing housing to help cool the bearings and lubricating oil.

➤ 18-8 TURBOCHARGER WASTEGATE

The turbocharger can raise boost pressure so high that detonation and engine damage occur. To limit boost pressure and prevent *overboost,* most turbochargers have a

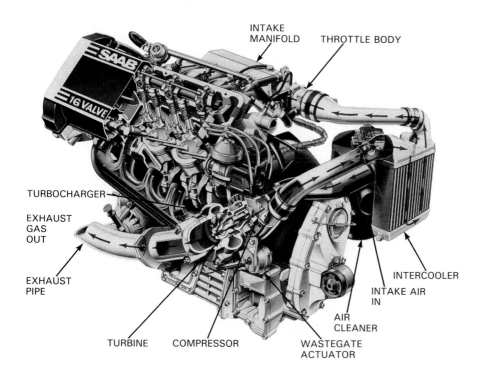

Fig. 18-12 Airflow through a turbocharged engine with intercooler. (*Saab Cars USA, Inc.*)

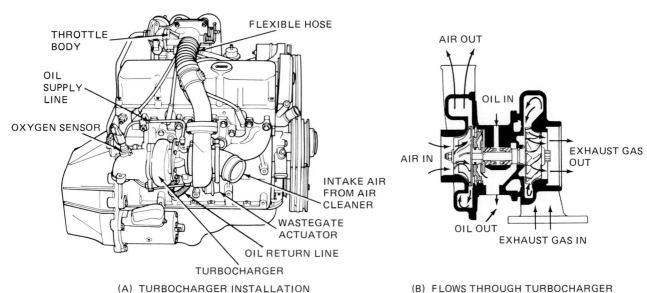

(A) TURBOCHARGER INSTALLATION

(B) FLOWS THROUGH TURBOCHARGER

Fig. 18-13 (A) Turbocharger installation on a four-cylinder engine. (B) Airflows and lubrication of the turbocharger. (*Ford Motor Company; Schwitzer Division of Wallace-Murray Corporation*)

wastegate (Fig. 18-14). It opens when boost pressure reaches a preset maximum. Then part of the exhaust gas bypasses the turbine and flows through the wastegate. This exhaust gas is "wasted" because it does not help spin the turbine.

The wastegate may be pneumatically- or computer-controlled. Figure 18-14 shows the operation of the *pneumatic wastegate*. (*Pneumatic* means operated by compressed air.) The actuator-diaphragm spring compresses when the boost pressure exceeds the spring force (Fig. 18-14B). This opens the *bypass passage* through the wastegate. No further increase in turbine speed is possible, which limits boost pressure.

Engines with a computer-controlled wastegate have a *pressure sensor* in the intake manifold (Fig. 18-15). The sensor signals the computer or ECM when the boost pressure goes too high. The ECM then signals a *solenoid valve* that controls the *wastegate actuator*. It opens the wastegate.

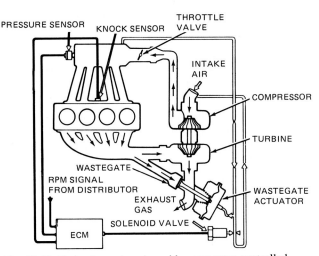

Fig. 18-15 Turbocharged engine with a computer-controlled wastegate. (*Saab Cars USA, Inc.*)

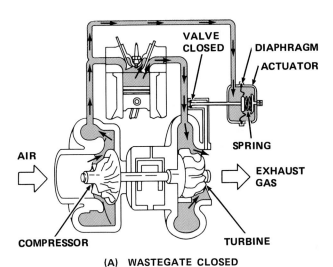

Fig. 18-14 Operation of the turbocharger wastegate, which limits boost pressure pneumatically. (*ATW*)

➤ 18-9 INTERCOOLER

Air gets hot when it is compressed. This causes the air to expand and become less dense. Heated air contains less oxygen to support combustion. To cool the air and increase its density, most turbocharged and supercharged engines have a *charge-air cooler* or *intercooler* (Figs. 18-7 and 18-12). This is a radiator-like *heat exchanger* that cools the air after it has been pressurized. Then air enters the engine cool and can take higher compression without detonation.

The intercooler shown in Figs. 18-7 and 18-12 is an *air-to-air intercooler*. It transfers heat from hot air to cool air. The hot compressed air flows through internal passages in the intercooler. Cooler outside air flows through fins that surround these passages. Some heat from the compressed air transfers to the cooler outside air.

Many turbocharged and supercharged engines have an electronic *detonation control system*. It includes a *detonation sensor* or *knock sensor* (Fig. 18-15). The sensor signals the ECM to retard the spark if detonation begins (➤16-4).

➤ 18-10 TURBOCHARGER LAG

During light load and cruising, the turbocharger is "idling." There is a vacuum in the intake manifold and little exhaust gas flows through the turbine. The compressor rotates too slowly to pressurize the intake air.

The throttle valve opens as the driver depresses the accelerator pedal for more power. More air (and fuel) enters the engine so there is less intake-manifold vacuum. Burning the additional air-fuel mixture increases the flow of exhaust gas. This speeds up the turbine and compressor until the compressor provides boost air.

Many drivers of turbocharged cars complain of "turbo

lag." This is the delay felt between the opening of the throttle valve and the turbocharger providing additional power. The lag is the time the idling turbine needs to reach boost speed. Plus, the time needed for the intercooler and tubing to fill as the change is made from a vacuum to a pressure. Total lag time may be a half second or more. This "turbo lag" is noticeable and objectionable to many drivers.

One partial solution is to make the rotating parts — the compressor and turbine wheels — as light as possible. Lighter parts pick up speed more quickly. Another solution is to use two smaller turbochargers instead of a larger single unit. The smaller and lighter rotating parts reduce lag time. Engines with two turbochargers are *bi-turbo* or *twin-turbo* engines.

➤ **18-11 VARIABLE-GEOMETRY TURBOCHARGING**

Variable-geometry turbocharging is another way to minimize turbo lag. The principle is to vary the angle at which the exhaust gas hits the turbine blades or vanes. This helps to increase boost at low speed and reduce turbo lag. No wastegate is needed with variable-geometry turbocharging. Moving the vanes controls both turbine speed and boost. Two types of variable-geometry turbocharging are the *variable-nozzle turbocharger* and *variable-area turbocharger*.

The *variable nozzle turbocharger* (VNT) has a series of 10 to 15 movable vanes around the turbine wheel (Fig. 18-16). An actuator controlled by the ECM positions the vanes. At low engine speeds, they are only partially open. This reduces exhaust restriction without producing

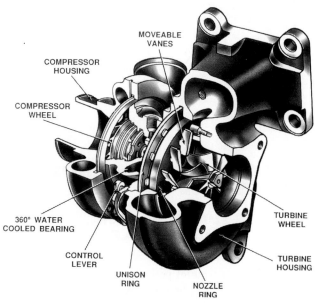

Fig. 18-16 Variable nozzle turbocharger. Computer-controlled movable vanes change position and turbocharger performance as the throttle valve opens. (*Chrysler Corporation*)

unneeded boost. When the throttle valve opens, the vanes open fully. The exhaust gases flow freely into the turbine blades. Then engine speed and power increase.

A variable-area turbocharger produces the same effect. The ECM controls one or more vanes in the turbine inlet. The vanes redirect the exhaust gas onto the turbine blades. This controls the velocity of the gas and therefore turbine speed. For acceleration, the vanes move to increase the velocity of the exhaust gas. This provides quicker boost.

SUPERCHARGER DIAGNOSIS AND SERVICE

➤ **18-12 SUPERCHARGER MAINTENANCE**

The supercharger requires little maintenance. Change the engine oil and filter as recommended in the vehicle maintenance schedule (➤3-9). The supercharger has its own oil supply and no oil change is required. At specified intervals, check the oil level in the supercharger. If low, add the specified oil. Inspect the drive belt and adjust or replace it if necessary.

Dirt and moisture must be prevented from entering the supercharger. Vacuum leaks pull dust into the supercharger and shorten its life. Pressure leaks reduce engine performance by lowering or preventing boost. To help prevent these problems, change the filter in the air cleaner as required. Clean any dirt and debris out of the intake system. Check all clamps and connections (Fig. 18-17) for tightness.

➤ **18-13 ROOTS-SUPERCHARGER TROUBLE DIAGNOSIS**

A vacuum leak in the intake system causes a normally-aspirated port-injected engine to run lean. More air enters the engine than is sensed by the throttle body or air-flow sensor and reported to the ECM (Chap. 19). This may cause rough idle and stalling. It may also set trouble codes for *system always lean* in the ECM memory (➤20-13). Always check the ECM memory for trouble codes. On a supercharged engine, these may indicate a supercharger-related problem. Chapter 20 describes how to get a trouble-code readout from the ECM.

Pressure leaks often cause a whistling sound while a supercharged engine is running with boost. Figure 18-18 is a trouble-diagnosis chart for a Roots supercharger. The chart lists various complaints, their possible causes, and the check or correction for the technician to make. Figure 18-17 shows the component locations on the engine. Complete diagnosis and service procedures are given in the vehicle service manuals.

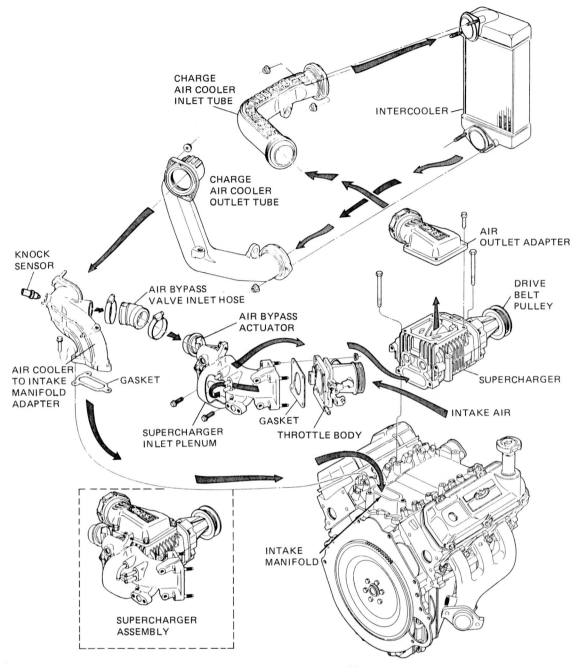

CHARGE
AIR COOLER
INLET TUBE

INTERCOOLER

CHARGE
AIR COOLER
OUTLET TUBE

AIR
OUTLET ADAPTER

KNOCK
SENSOR

DRIVE
BELT
PULLEY

AIR BYPASS
VALVE INLET HOSE

AIR BYPASS
ACTUATOR

AIR COOLER
TO INTAKE
MANIFOLD
ADAPTER

GASKET

SUPERCHARGER

INTAKE AIR

GASKET

SUPERCHARGER
INLET PLENUM

THROTTLE BODY

INTAKE
MANIFOLD

SUPERCHARGER
ASSEMBLY

Fig. 18-17 Airflow through the components of a Roots supercharger and inter-cooler on a V-type engine. (*Ford Motor Company*)

➤ 18-14 SUPERCHARGER SERVICE

No routine service is normally performed on the super-charger. Only cool intake air passes through it. This lengthens the life of the bearings and seals. Bearing lubrication is seldom a problem because of the relatively low speed of the rotors.

A supercharger needing repair is usually "serviced only as an assembly." This means that a defective supercharger is replaced with a new or rebuilt unit. A *supercharger assembly* is shown in the lower left of Fig. 18-17.

TURBOCHARGER DIAGNOSIS AND SERVICE

➤ 18-15 TURBOCHARGER MAINTENANCE

The turbocharger requires periodic maintenance to prevent early failure. Improper lubrication causes most tur-bocharger failures. The bearings must receive an adequate flow of clean lubricating oil. Damaged turbocharger bearings result if the oil is dirty or the flow is stopped.

COMPLAINT	POSSIBLE CAUSE	CHECK OR CORRECTION
1. Low boost	a. Air leak at intercooler, flanges, ducts, supercharger housing, supercharger outlet.	Locate and repair leak or replace damaged component.
	b. Contamination in system, blockage.	Remove obstruction.
	c. Supercharger not turning.	Check drive belt tension and condition.
		Check coupling for damage.
		Check for pulley slipping on shaft.
	d. Bypass not closing.	Check function of bypass actuator.
		Check bypass actuator stop adjustment.
		Check vacuum hose condition and installation.
	e. Insufficient flow from supercharger.	Check supercharger for incorrect clearances (wear from contamination).
		Check for correct pulley diameter.
2. High boost	Too much flow.	Check for exhaust restrictions or damage.
		Check for catalyst for damage.
		Check for correct pulley diameter.
3. Vehicle response too "touchy" and poor fuel economy	Bypass not opening.	Check function of bypass actuator.
		Check for stuck or restricted bypass valve.
		Check vacuum hose condition and installation.
		Check actuator diaphram for damage or leak.
4. Supercharger noisy	Mechanical damage to supercharger.	Replace supercharger.
5. Noise in air handling systems	Air leaks.	Check all flanges for proper fit and position.
		Check for proper isolation of components.
6. Oil on outside of supercharger	a. Leaking seals.	Replace supercharger.
	b. Loose fill plug.	Tighten fill plug.
	c. Input shaft damage at seal.	Replace supercharger.

Fig. 18-18 Supercharger trouble-diagnosis chart. (*Ford Motor Company*)

Special instructions may apply to changing oil in a turbocharged engine. Follow the procedure in the owners manual or service manual. Change the oil and filter whenever an engine bearing or the turbocharger is replaced. Clean the areas around the turbocharger before removal or disassembly. Cover all engine openings while the turbocharger is off.

➤ **18-16 TURBOCHARGER TROUBLE DIAGNOSIS**

A turbocharged engine must have proper filtering of the engine oil and intake air. Frequent causes of turbocharger failure are oil lag, restricted or no oil flow, and dirt in the oil. Sand and other particles or objects striking the blades will damage the compressor and turbine wheels (Fig. 18-19).

Sometimes a noise or a whistling sound may be heard while the engine is running. This may indicate an air leak between the compressor and the intake manifold (Fig. 18-12). Or it may indicate an exhaust leak between the exhaust manifold and the turbine.

When a turbocharged engine is not operating properly, make a visual inspection and diagnosis of the turbocharger. Check the ECM memory for trouble codes (➤20-13). These may indicate a turbocharger-related problem. If the turbocharger appears to be operating properly, proceed as though working on a non-turbocharged (normally-aspirated) engine. Chapter 38 covers engine trouble diagnosis.

> **CAUTION!**

The turbocharger gets very hot and takes a long time to cool. Be careful not to burn yourself or damage other parts, such as hoses and wiring, by touching the turbocharger. Allow the engine to cool before performing diagnosis or service work on a turbocharger.

To inspect the turbocharger on the engine, remove the pressure hose from the wastegate actuator. Then remove the inlet and exhaust tubing from the turbocharger. Inspect the compressor and turbine wheels for damage (Fig. 18-19) and the housings for rubbing marks. Rotate the shaft-wheel assembly by hand (Fig. 18-20) to check that it turns freely. There should be no oil leakage past the shaft seals. Push the shaft to one side while rotating it. The shaft should continue to turn freely and smoothly.

Service or replace the turbocharger if there is excessive drag or noise, or if the bearing clearance or shaft endplay is not within specifications. The turbocharger is not the probable cause of trouble if the shaft-wheel assembly rotates freely. However, there must be no wheel damage, binding, or rubbing of the wheels against the housings.

> **CAUTION!**

Never start or run a turbocharged engine unless all normally-installed tubing and filters are in place and connected. If not, you could be injured. Also, the turbocharger and engine could be damaged if an object enters the turbocharger.

Figure 18-21 is a trouble-diagnosis chart for a turbocharged engine. To find the cause of a turbocharger trouble in the chart, locate the problem at the left side of the chart. The black dots under each problem indicate the possible causes. After finding the causes, look in the right column under REMEDY for the action to take. Refer to the vehicle service manual for additional information and service procedures.

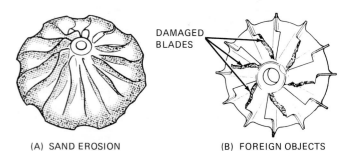

(A) SAND EROSION   (B) FOREIGN OBJECTS

Fig. 18-19 Damaged turbocharger compressor-wheel blades. (A) Blades damaged from sand erosion. (B) Blade damage from foreign objects.

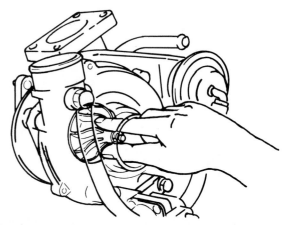

Fig. 18-20 When the engine is cool, check that the turbocharger shaft-wheel assembly turns freely and smoothly by rotating it by hand. *(Mazda Motors of America, Inc.)*

➤ 18-17 MEASURING BOOST PRESSURE

A defective wastegate may cause excessive boost pressure. To measure boost pressure, road test the vehicle with a *vacuum-pressure gauge* attached. Use a *T fitting* to connect the gauge hose into the pressure hose from the compressor to the wastegate actuator (Fig. 18-14).

Road test the vehicle on a dynamometer or in a safe area. Follow the procedure in the manufacturer's service manual. A typical procedure is to drive the vehicle at about 20 mph [32 kmph] in second gear with the engine running at about 1500 rpm. Then accelerate at wide-open throttle (WOT) to about 45 mph [72 kmph] while watching the vacuum/pressure gauge. Boost-pressure specifications are given in the manufacturer's service manual. Turbocharger *maximum boost pressure* is usually between 10 and 15 psi [69 and 103.5 kPa].

> **CAUTION!**

If you must road test the vehicle on the street or highway, you must first have a valid driver's license and your instructor's per-

Engine lacks power	Black exhaust smoke	Excessive engine oil consumption	Blue exhaust smoke	Turbocharger noisy	Cyclic sound from turbocharger	Oil leak from compressor seal	Oil leak from turbine seal	CAUSE	REMEDY
	•	•	•					Clogged air filter element	Replace element
	•	•	•	•	•			Obstructed air intake duct to turbo compressor	Remove obstruction or replace damaged parts as required
•	•			•				Obstructed air outlet duct from compressor to intake manifold	Remove obstruction or replace damaged parts as required
•	•			•				Obstructed intake manifold	Refer to engine mechanical section & remove obstruction
				•				Air leak in duct from air cleaner to compressor	Correct leak by replacing seals or tightening fasteners as required
•	•	•	•	•				Air leak in duct from compressor to intake manifold	Correct leak by replacing seals or tightening fasteners as required
•	•	•	•	•				Air leak at intake manifold to engine joint	Refer to engine mechanical section & replace gaskets or tighten fasteners as required
•	•	•	•	•	•			Obstruction in exhaust manifold	Refer to engine mechanical section & remove obstruction
•	•				•			Obstruction in exhaust system	Remove obstruction or replace faulty components as required
•	•				•			Gas leak in exhaust manifold to engine joint	Refer to engine mechanical section & replace gaskets or tighten fasteners as required
•	•			•	•			Gas leak in turbine inlet to exhaust manifold joint	Replace gasket or tighten fasteners as required
				•				Gas leak in ducting after the turbine outlet	Refer to engine mechanical section & repair leak
		•	•			•	•	Obstructed turbocharger oil drain line	Remove obstruction or replace line as required
		•	•			•	•	Obstructed engine crankcase ventilation	Refer to engine mechanical section, clear obstruction
		•	•			•	•	Turbocharger center housing sludged or coked	Change engine oil & oil filter, overhaul or replace turbo as required
•	•							Engine camshaft timing incorrect	Refer to engine mechanical section
•	•	•	•			•	•	Worn engine piston rings or liners (blowby)	Refer to engine mechanical section
•	•	•	•			•	•	Internal engine problem (valves, pistons)	Refer to engine mechanical section
•	•	•	•	•	•	•	•	Dirt caked on compressor wheel and/or diffuser vanes	Clean using a non-caustic cleaner & soft brush. Find & correct source of unfiltered air & change engine oil & oil filter
•	•	•	•	•	•	•	•	Damaged turbocharger	Analyze failed turbocharger, find & correct cause of failure, overhaul or replace turbocharger as required

Fig. 18-21 Turbocharged-engine trouble-diagnosis chart. (*Buick Division of General Motors Corporation*)

mission. Select a safe quiet area with little or no traffic. Have a helper ride with you to read the gauge or have the helper drive while you read the gauge. Never allow any testing to interfere with safe driving and control of the vehicle.

➤ 18-18 CHECKING THE WASTEGATE

The wastegate may stick either open or closed. When the wastegate valve sticks open, the turbocharger will develop little or no boost. When the valve sticks closed, overboost may occur. This causes detonation and engine damage. Most turbocharged cars have a *boost gauge* or *overboost indicator* in the instrument panel. It alerts the driver to the overboost condition. Overboost can cause detonation which will damage or destroy the engine.

To check the wastegate, first try to move the wastegate *actuator rod* (Fig. 18-22) by hand. If the rod moves freely, the actuator is defective. If the rod does not move, remove the pressure hose and connect a *hand air pump* to the actuator. Use the pump to apply the specified boost pressure to the wastegate actuator. The actuator rod should move. If not, the wastegate valve may be stuck.

Cleaning any deposits from the wastegate valve and seat

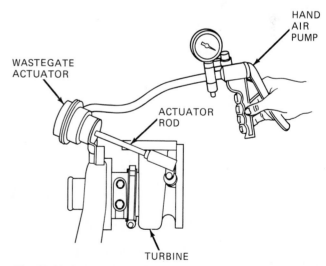

Fig. 18-22 Checking operation of the turbocharger wastegate with a hand air pump. (*Chrysler Corporation*)

may free the valve. Ford recommends replacing the *outlet elbow* (Fig. 18-23) which contains the wastegate valve. Others recommend replacing the turbocharger assembly.

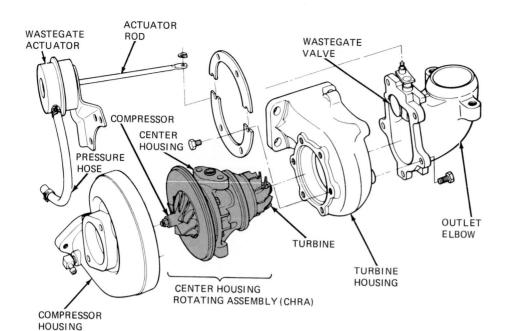

Fig. 18-23 Disassembled turbocharger, showing the replaceable center housing rotating assembly (CHRA). (*Ford Motor Company*)

Labels in figure: WASTEGATE ACTUATOR, ACTUATOR ROD, WASTEGATE VALVE, COMPRESSOR CENTER HOUSING, PRESSURE HOSE, OUTLET ELBOW, TURBINE, TURBINE HOUSING, CENTER HOUSING ROTATING ASSEMBLY (CHRA), COMPRESSOR HOUSING

➤ 18-19 TURBOCHARGER SERVICE

A damaged or defective turbocharger is usually replaced with a new or rebuilt unit. Some turbochargers can be rebuilt if the compressor and turbine housings (Fig. 18-23) are not damaged internally. Install a new or rebuilt *turbocharger cartridge* or *center housing rotating assembly* (CHRA). This complete assembly includes the *center housing,* shaft-wheel assembly, and bearings.

To rebuild the turbocharger, remove it from the engine (Fig. 18-24). Obtain a new or rebuilt turbocharger cartridge or a *turbocharger rebuild kit.* The kit includes the shaft-wheel assembly, bearings, and seals. Assemble the turbocharger following the installation instructions. Use *all* of the new parts. Then install the turbocharger on the engine. Before starting the engine after changing the oil and filter or other turbocharger service, disable the ignition. Crank the engine until the engine oil light goes out.

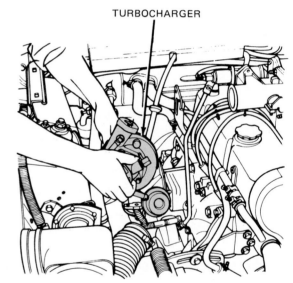

TURBOCHARGER

Fig. 18-24 Removing or installing the turbocharger on the engine. (*Ford Motor Company*)

TRADE TALK

blower	manifold absolute pressure	pressure differential	wastegate
boost pressure	naturally aspirated	supercharger	
intercooler	parasitic loss	turbocharger	

MULTIPLE-CHOICE TEST

*Select the **one** correct, best, or most probable answer to each question.*
You can find the answers in the section indicated at the end of each question.

1. The basic difference between the supercharger and the turbocharger is in (➤18-2)
   a. the way they are driven
   b. the size of the unit
   c. the number of wastegates
   d. the pressure they produce

2. An advantage of the supercharger is that it (➤18-3)
   a. provides instant response
   b. creates turbo lag
   c. uses less exhaust gas
   d. never needs an intercooler

3. The purpose of the wastegate is to (➤18-8)
   a. produce overboost
   b. use less power from the crankshaft
   c. prevent overboost
   d. cool the air-fuel mixture

4. The purpose of the intercooler is to (➤18-9)
   a. produce overboost
   b. cool the air after it has been pressurized
   c. allow higher engine speed
   d. reduce the amount of air that can enter the engine

5. Turbo lag may be reduced by all of the following EXCEPT (➤18-10 and 18-11)
   a. making the rotating parts lighter
   b. making the rotating parts smaller
   c. variable-geometry turbocharging
   d. using one large turbocharger

6. Technician A says a normally-aspirated port-injected engine with a vacuum leak will run lean. Technician B says a whistling sound while a supercharged engine is running with boost indicates a vacuum leak. Who is right? (➤18-13)

   a. A only
   b. B only
   c. both A and B
   d. neither A nor B

7. Bearing failure in a turbocharger may be caused by any of the following EXCEPT (➤18-15)
   a. dirty engine oil
   b. a clogged oil line
   c. adding oil to the turbocharger
   d. failure to change the engine oil filter

8. A turbocharged engine runs normally but has no boost. An inspection of the turbocharger shows no wheel or housing damage, and the shaft turns freely and smoothly. This indicates (➤18-16 and 18-18)
   a. the turbocharger is probably defective
   b. the turbocharger is probably OK
   c. the wastegate is probably OK
   d. the throttle valve is probably stuck open

9. Turbocharger maximum boost pressure is usually between (➤18-17)
   a. 1.0 and 1.5 psi [6.9 and 10.35 kPa]
   b. 10 and 15 psi [69 and 103.5 kPa]
   c. 100 and 150 psi [690 and 1035 kPa]
   d. cylinder compression pressure and combustion pressure

10. The turbocharger cartridge or center housing rotating assembly includes (➤18-19)
    a. compressor housing, compressor wheel, and center housing
    b. center housing, turbine wheel, and turbine housing
    c. wastegate, actuator rod, and center housing
    d. center housing, shaft-wheel assembly, and bearings

REVIEW QUESTIONS

1. Explain the changes in the absolute pressure in the intake manifold before and after the throttle valve opens on a supercharged engine. (➤18-1 to 18-3)

2. Describe how a boost-control valve or bypass valve works and the benefits of having it. (➤18-5)

3. What is turbo lag and how can it be reduced? (➤18-10)

4. Discuss how the wastegate controls boost pressure and describe how to measure it. (➤18-8 and 18-17)

5. Describe how to check the wastegate for proper operation. (➤18-18)

CHAPTER 19

ELECTRONIC FUEL-INJECTION SYSTEMS

After studying this chapter, you should be able to:

- Define *stoichiometric ratio* and explain why it is important.
- Explain the difference between a pulsed injection system and a continuous injection system.
- Describe three types of air-flow meters and explain how each works.
- List and explain the operation of the sensors reporting to the ECM.
- Describe the operation of a sequential electronic fuel-injection system.

➤ 19-1 INTRODUCTION TO GASOLINE FUEL-INJECTION SYSTEMS

Most 1980 and later cars have an *electronic engine control* (EEC) system (➤1-19). It controls the ignition and fuel-injection systems. The basic operation of electronic engine controls is described in Chap. 10.

The *fuel-injection system* supplies the engine with a combustible air-fuel mixture. It varies the richness of the mixture to suit different operating conditions. When a cold engine is started, the fuel system delivers a very rich mixture. This has a high proportion of fuel. After the engine warms up, the fuel system "leans out" the mixture. It then has a lower proportion of fuel. For acceleration and high speed, the mixture is again enriched.

There are two types of gasoline fuel-injection systems:

1. *Port fuel injection* (PFI) which has an injection valve or *fuel injector* in each intake port (Fig. 19-1).
2. *Throttle-body fuel injection* (TBI) in which one or two fuel injectors are located above the throttle valves (Fig. 19-2).

With either system, the electric fuel pump (➤17-7) supplies the fuel injectors with fuel under pressure. As soon as the injector opens, fuel sprays out (Fig. 19-3). An electric *solenoid* in the injector opens and closes the valve. The solenoid has a small coil of wire that becomes magnetized when a voltage is applied (Fig. 19-4). The magnetism lifts the armature which raises the needle valve or

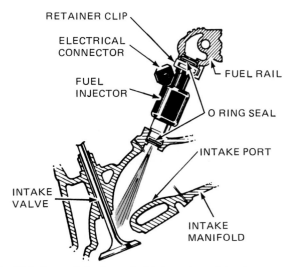

Fig. 19-1 In port injection, a fuel injector in each intake port sprays fuel into the intake air just before it passes the open intake valve and enters the cylinder. (*AC Rochester Division of General Motors Corporation*)

pintle off its seat. Fuel sprays out as long as the pintle is raised. When the voltage stops, the coil loses its magnetism. The closing spring pushes the pintle back down onto its seat. This stops the fuel spray. Each opening and closing of the injector pintle is an injector *pulse* (➤19-27).

| NOTE | Some injectors use a *ball valve* (➤19-8) instead of a needle valve. Operation of the ball-type injector is basically the same as described above. |

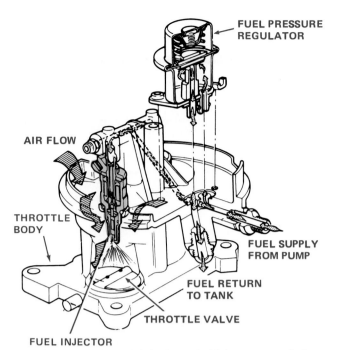

Fig. 19-2 In throttle-body injection, a fuel injector sprays fuel into the air passing through the throttle body. (*Ford Motor Company*)

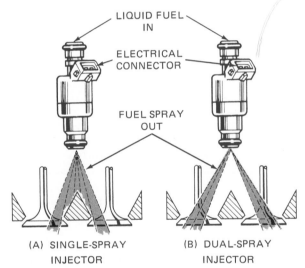

Fig. 19-3 When the fuel injector opens, fuel sprays out. The injector produces either a single spray or a dual spray. (*AC Rochester Division of General Motors Corporation*)

> ## 19-2 COMPARING PORT AND THROTTLE-BODY INJECTION

Port or multipoint injection provides more accurate control of the air-fuel mixture than does throttle-body injection. The same amount of fuel is delivered to each cylinder so the ratio is the same for all cylinders. This improves fuel economy and engine performance while reducing exhaust emissions.

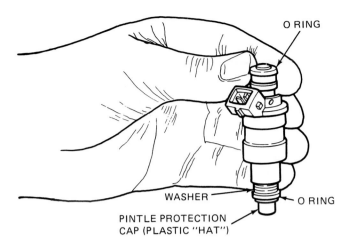

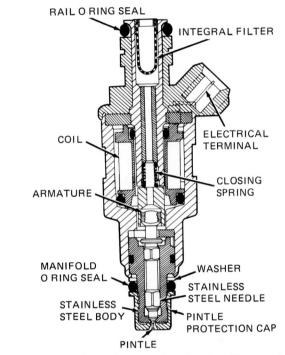

Fig. 19-4 Size and internal construction of a solenoid-operated fuel injector. (*Ford Motor Company*)

TBI requires fewer injectors and less fuel-line tubing and hose. It is not as accurate in balancing the air-fuel ratios among the cylinders. Fuel puddling may occur at the ends of the intake manifold as in a carbureted fuel system (Fig. 17-23). This tends to enrich the end cylinders.

> ## 19-3 ELECTRONIC FUEL INJECTION

Figure 10-19 shows the components of an *electronic fuel-injection* (EFI) system. Most fuel-injection systems are electronically controlled. The *controller* is an *electronic control module* (ECM) or *electronic control unit* (ECU). It is also called an "on-board *computer*" because it is "on board" the car.

Various components of the engine and fuel system send electric signals to the ECM (Fig. 19-5). The ECM continu-

225

ously calculates how much fuel to inject. It then opens the fuel injectors so the proper amount of fuel sprays out to produce the desired air-fuel ratio (➤19-4).

(➤19-4)

➤ 19-4 AIR-FUEL RATIO REQUIREMENTS

The fuel system must vary the *air-fuel ratio* as engine operating conditions change. The air-fuel ratio is the ratio of the air to the fuel *by weight*. Fifteen pounds of air to one pound of fuel is a ratio of fifteen to one. This is written as 15:1 and pronounced *"fifteen to one."* For example, 13:1 is a *rich* mixture. It has a larger percentage of fuel than 17:1 which is a *lean* mixture. It has a lower percentage of fuel.

Figure 19-6 shows air-fuel ratios required by one engine under different operating conditions. When starting cold, the mixture is rich (about 9:1). During idle, the mixture leans out to about 12:1. At medium speed, it leans out to around 15:1. If the driver "steps on the gas" to accelerate, the mixture is temporarily enriched as shown by the dashed lines. The mixture is also enriched at full throttle.

The purpose of varying the air-fuel ratio is so that a combustible mixture always reaches the engine cylinders. For example, when starting a cold engine, the mixture must be very rich. This is because only part of the fuel vaporizes at low temperatures. Then, enough of the extra fuel evaporates to provide the cylinders with a combustible air-fuel mixture.

➤ 19-5 STOICHIOMETRIC RATIO

The ideal air-fuel ratio is the *stoichiometric ratio*. This is 14.7:1 (Fig. 19-7). It is ideal because the ratio of the oxygen in the air to the hydrocarbons in the fuel is correct to produce the most complete combustion of the fuel. If the ratio is lower (14.0:1, for example), there is too much fuel for the available oxygen. If the ratio is higher (16.0:1, for example), there is an excess of oxygen.

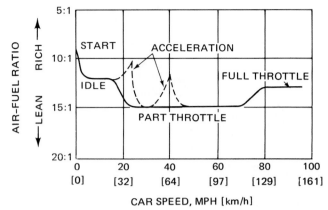

Fig. 19-6 Typical air-fuel ratios required by an engine under different operating conditions.

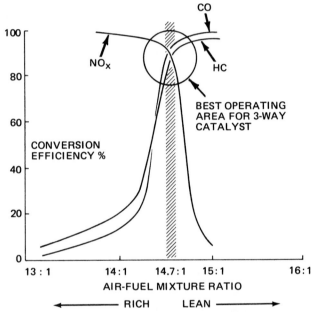

Fig. 19-7 The air-fuel-mixture ratio "window," within which the air-fuel ratio must remain if the three-way catalytic converter is to work efficiently. (*General Motors Corporation*)

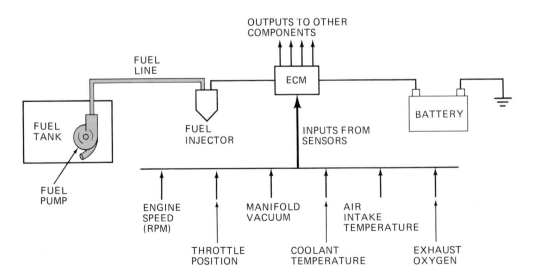

Fig. 19-5 Simplified electronic fuel-injection system. Sensors (bottom) provide information or input to the ECM. The ECM then determines the amount of fuel needed and opens the injectors to produce the desired air-fuel ratio.

Maintaining the stoichiometric ratio is important in vehicles using a catalytic converter (Chap. 35). It works best when the engine is running on the ideal air-fuel ratio of 14.7:1 (Fig. 19-7). Most engines have an ECM (Fig. 19-5). It keeps the air-fuel mixture at the stoichiometric ratio (at part throttle). Engines operate mostly at part throttle.

➤ 19-6 AIR AND FUEL METERING

The fuel system must accurately measure or *meter* the air and fuel entering the engine. This produces the proper air-fuel ratio to make a combustible mixture. A mixture that is too lean (not enough fuel in it) will not burn and produces excessive pollutants. A mixture that is too rich (excess fuel in it) will also produce excess pollutants. Figure 19-8 shows how mixture richness affects engine power. As the mixture becomes leaner, power falls off.

The electronic engine control system includes the ECM and various sensing devices or *sensors* that report to it. A sensor is a device that receives and reacts to a signal. This may be a change in pressure, temperature, or voltage. Some sensors report the amount of air entering. The ECM then calculates for how long to open the injectors (➤19-3).

➤ 19-7 OPERATION OF FUEL-INJECTION SYSTEMS

Sensors that report to the ECM include (Fig. 19-5):

- Engine speed.
- Throttle position.
- Intake-manifold vacuum or manifold-absolute pressure (MAP).
- Engine coolant temperature.
- Amount and temperature of air entering engine.
- Amount of oxygen in exhaust gas.
- Atmospheric pressure.

The ECM continuously receives all this information or *data*. The ECM checks this data with other data stored in *look-up tables* in its memory (➤10-18). Then the ECM decides when to open the injectors and for how long (Fig. 19-9). For example, when the engine is idling, the ECM might hold the injectors open for only 0.003 second each time they open.

The opening and closing of an injector is its *duty cycle*. How long the ECM signals the injector to remain open is the injector *pulse width*. Figure 19-9 shows how varying the pulse width varies the amount of fuel injected. Suppose more fuel is needed because the throttle has been opened for acceleration and more air is entering. Then the ECM increases the pulse width. This holds the injectors open longer each time they open to provide the additional fuel.

NOTE   The system described above is a *pulsed* fuel-injection system. The injectors open and close (pulse). The *continuous-injection system* (CIS) is another type of fuel-injection system. It is used in a

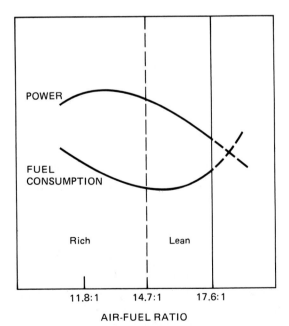

Fig. 19-8 Effect of mixture richness on engine power and fuel consumption. As the mixture goes lean, power drops off and fuel economy improves.

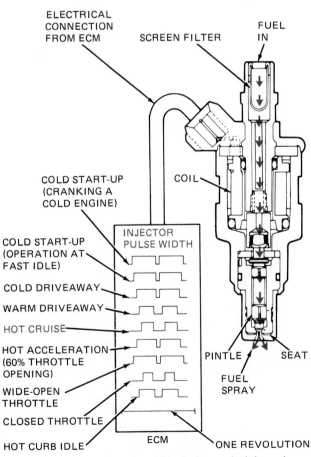

Fig. 19-9 The wider the pulse width, the longer the injector is open and the greater the amount of fuel that sprays out. (*Ford Motor Company*)

few vehicles. The injectors are open continuously. Changing the pressure applied to the fuel varies the amount of fuel injected.

19-8 TYPES OF FUEL INJECTORS

Two types of fuel injectors deliver fuel into the air entering the engine.

1. The *solenoid-operated fuel injector* (Fig. 19-4) is turned on and off by the ECM (Fig. 19-9). When the ignition key is ON, voltage is present at the injector. The solenoid is *energized* (turned on) when the ECM provides a ground. Then the injector opens and fuel sprays out. When the solenoid is *deenergized* (turned off) fuel spray stops. Pulsed port and throttle-body injection system use this type of injector.

Figure 19-10 shows another type of solenoid-operated fuel injector. Fuel enters through the fuel inlet along the side of the injector. A ball valve controls fuel spray from the nozzle. It has six small holes or *spray orifices*. Their angle gives the spraying fuel a whirling motion. This improves mixing of the fuel with air.

In many engines, the injector delivers fuel into an intake port that has only one intake valve (Fig. 19-1). Figure 19-3 shows two ways an injector can deliver fuel to engines with two intake valves. A *single-spray injector* (Fig. 19-3A) delivers a wide spray pattern through a single hole. A *dual-spray injector* (Fig. 19-3B) has two holes in the tip. The holes are positioned so the spray from each hole delivers fuel to one of the intake valves.

2. The *mechanical fuel injector* (Fig. 19-11) is used in continuous-injection systems. The injector is basically a fixed orifice with a mechanical needle valve operated

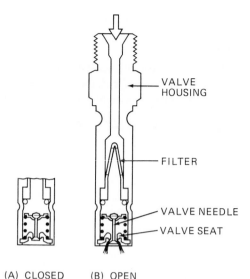

(A) CLOSED   (B) OPEN

Fig. 19-11 A mechanical fuel injector used in continuous-injection systems. (*Robert Bosch Corporation*)

by fuel pressure. The amount of fuel injected depends on the pressure applied to the fuel. Figure 14-28 shows a mechanical injector in a double-overhead-camshaft engine.

Figure 19-11 shows the open and closed positions of the valve needle and seat in the end of the mechanical injector. As fuel flows through, the passing fuel causes the needle to open and close rapidly. This chattering, which sometimes can be heard, helps atomize the fuel while the engine is running. When the ignition key is turned OFF, the electric fuel pump stops and the fuel pressure drops. Then the spring forces the needle valve to remain closed. This prevents any fuel from leaking or dribbling into the intake ports.

19-9 COLD-START VALVE

Some engines with electronic fuel injection have a *cold start valve* (Fig. 19-12). It supplies extra fuel for starting a cold engine. The valve is similar in construction and operation to the solenoid-operated fuel injector (➤19-8). A *thermo-time switch* (Fig. 19-13) limits the time the cold-start valve can inject fuel. This prevents the engine from receiving too much fuel or *flooding*. Figure 19-14 shows the location of the cold-start valve and the thermo-time switch in a fuel-injection system.

The thermo-time switch (Fig. 19-13) has a thermostatic blade, a pair of contacts, and a heating element. When the engine is cold, the blade is straight and the contacts are closed. The cold-start valve sprays fuel when the engine cranks. As the engine warms up, the thermostatic blade bends and the contacts separate. This opens the circuit to the cold-start valve and fuel-delivery stops. The heating element speeds this action. It reduces the time that the engine is operating on a very rich mixture.

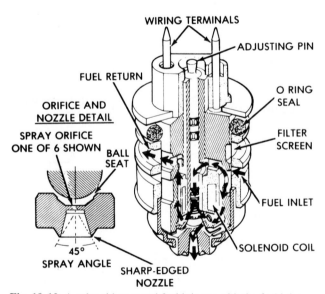

Fig. 19-10 A solenoid-operated fuel injector with the fuel inlet on the side and a ball-valve-and-seat controlling fuel delivery. (*Chrysler Corporation*)

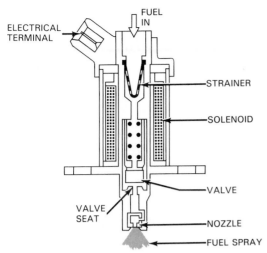

Fig. 19-12 A cold-start valve used in some electronic fuel-injection systems to supply extra fuel for starting a cold engine. (*Robert Bosch Corporation*)

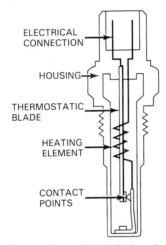

Fig. 19-13 The thermo-time switch limits how long the cold-start valve can inject fuel. (*Robert Bosch Corporation*)

| NOTE | Most pulsed systems do not require a cold-start valve. The ECM enriches the air-fuel mixture when the engine is cold by holding the injectors open longer each time they open. This delivers more fuel to produce the rich mixture needed for cold starting. |

SENSORS

➤ 19-10 THROTTLE-POSITION SENSOR

The throttle body (➤17-11) contains the throttle valve (Fig. 17-17B). The assembly usually mounts on the intake manifold (Fig. 19-15). The throttle valve connects by linkage to the accelerator pedal in the driver's compartment (Fig. 17-17A). Depressing the accelerator pedal opens the throttle valve. Then more air flows through and enters the engine.

The ECM must always know the position of the throttle valve. The ECM must match fuel flow with air flow to feed the engine the proper air-fuel mixture. A *throttle-position sensor* (TPS) on the throttle body continuously reports throttle position (Fig. 19-16) to the ECM.

The position of the throttle valve is also important in the control of idle speed and in the shift patterns of automatic transmissions and transaxles. On some engines, when the throttle valve closes during deceleration, the ECM shuts off fuel flow. This prevents an over-rich mixture during deceleration.

A rotary throttle-position sensor (Fig. 19-17) is a *variable resistor* or *potentiometer*. It has a coil of resistance wire in the form of a half circle. One end connects to ground. The other end connects to a 5-volt source from the ECM.

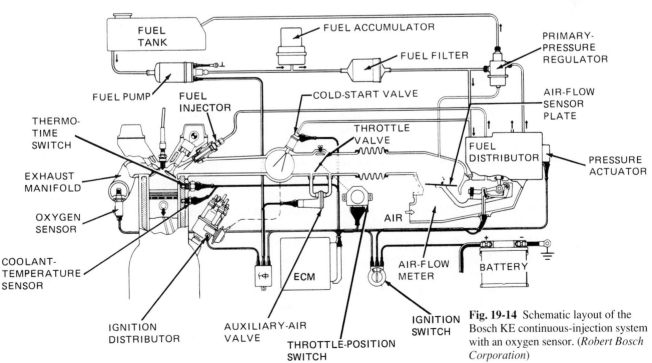

Fig. 19-14 Schematic layout of the Bosch KE continuous-injection system with an oxygen sensor. (*Robert Bosch Corporation*)

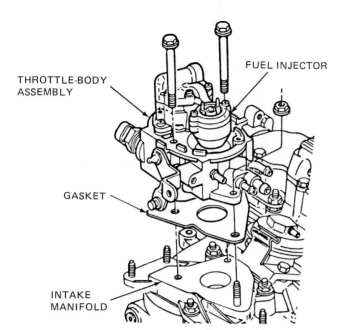

Fig. 19-15 Mounting of throttle body and fuel injector on intake manifold. (*Oldsmobile Division of General Motors Corporation*)

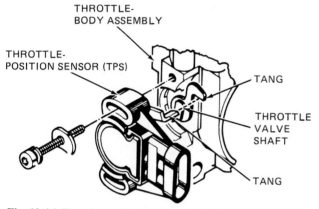

Fig. 19-16 Throttle-position sensor, showing how it mounts on the throttle-body assembly. (*Ford Motor Company*)

The wiper blade has a contact that rides on the coil and connects to the throttle-valve shaft. As the throttle-valve position changes, the wiper blade moves along the coil. When the throttle valve is closed, the blade is at the grounded end of the coil. Only a small voltage signal is sent to the ECM. As the throttle valve moves toward the open position, the wiper blade swings toward the 5-volt end of the coil. This sends an increasing voltage signal to the ECM. The voltage tells the ECM the exact position of the throttle valve.

Figure 19-18 shows two types of throttle-position sensors: rotary and linear. The resistance coil in the linear type is straight. The wiper blade moves along the coil to pick up the voltage signal (Fig. 19-18, lower right). Instead of a throttle-position sensor, some fuel-injection systems use a *throttle-position switch* (Figs. 19-14 and 19-21). The throttle-position switch (TPS in Fig. 19-21) signals the ECM when the throttle valve is closed, or when it is wide open.

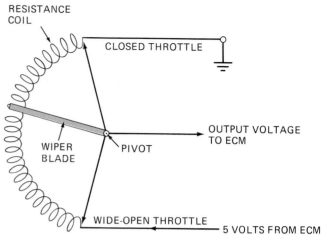

Fig. 19-17 Diagram of a rotary throttle-position sensor (TPS). As the throttle position changes, the wiper blade moves which changes the voltage signal to the ECM. This varies from about 5 volts at wide-open throttle to a fraction of a volt at closed throttle.

➤ 19-11 MEASURING INTAKE-AIR FLOW

The amount of air flowing into the intake manifold must be accurately measured. The ECM must have this information to calculate the amount of fuel to be injected. Air flow can be measured:

1. Indirectly using throttle position, engine speed, and intake-manifold vacuum or MAP (➤19-13).
2. Directly by vane, air-flow sensor plate, hot-wire induction, or heated film (➤19-14)

Following sections describe these methods.

➤ 19-12 INDIRECT MEASUREMENT OF AIR FLOW

Information about engine speed and engine load can tell the ECM how much air is entering the engine. Using this information to regulate fuel feed is called *speed-density metering*. It is used in fuel-injection systems that do not directly measure *mass air flow*. The *speed* is the speed of the engine. The *density* is the density of the air or air-fuel mixture in the intake manifold.

Throttle position (engine speed) and intake-manifold vacuum (engine load) measure air flow indirectly. Intake-manifold vacuum is continuously measured by a sensor that changes vacuum (or absolute pressure) into a varying voltage signal. The ECM combines this with the TPS signal to determine how much air is entering. Inputs from other sensors may cause the ECM to modify this calculation (Fig. 19-5). Engine speed (instead of throttle

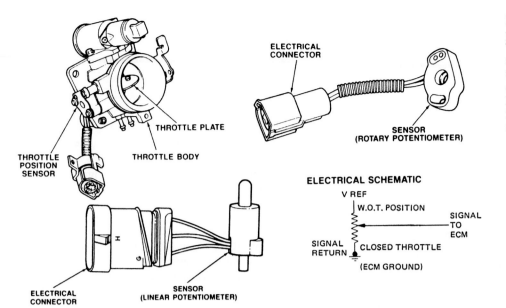

Fig. 19-18 Two types of throttle-position sensors, rotary and linear. The schematic in the lower right shows the operation of the linear type. The "V REF" means the reference voltage supplied by the ECM. In some systems, this is 5 volts. In others, it is 9 volts. (*Ford Motor Company*)

position) and intake-manifold vacuum can also tell the ECM how much air is entering the engine.

➤ 19-13 MEASURING INTAKE-MANIFOLD VACUUM (MANIFOLD ABSOLUTE PRESSURE)

Intake-manifold vacuum is measured in two ways (Fig. 19-19):

1. With a vacuum gauge (➤5-22).
2. With a manifold absolute-pressure (MAP) gauge.

The two gauges are basically the same. Both have a flexible diaphragm that separates the two chambers in the gauge. The difference is that one chamber of the vacuum gauge is open to the atmosphere. One chamber of the absolute-pressure gauge contains a vacuum (Fig. 19-19). The vacuum gauge compares atmospheric pressure with intake-manifold pressure. In a naturally-aspirated engine, manifold pressure is less than atmospheric pressure

(➤18-1). A vacuum gauge measures this partial vacuum in the intake manifold.

The manifold absolute-pressure (MAP) gauge compares the actual pressure in the intake manifold with a vacuum. This is more accurate than the vacuum gauge which compares intake manifold vacuum with atmospheric pressure. The vacuum gauge is less accurate because atmospheric pressure varies.

Vacuum and pressure sensors are not constructed exactly like the gauges described above. But their operation is basically the same. Most electronic-engine-control systems include a *manifold-absolute pressure* (MAP) *sensor* (Figs. 10-19 and 19-20). It senses the pressure (vacuum) changes in the intake manifold. This information is sent as a varying voltage signal to the ECM.

➤ 19-14 DIRECT MEASUREMENT OF AIR FLOW

Four methods of measuring air flow directly are *vane, air-flow sensor plate, hot-wire induction,* and *heated film.*

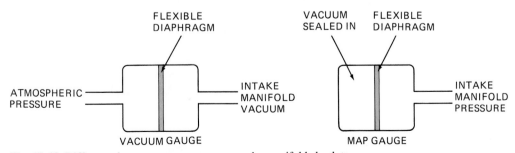

Fig. 19-19 Difference between a vacuum gauge and a manifold absolute-pressure (MAP) gauge. The vacuum gauge measures intake-manifold vacuum against atmospheric pressure (which varies). The MAP gauge measures intake-manifold vacuum against a sealed-in vacuum (which does not vary). Therefore, the MAP gauge is more accurate.

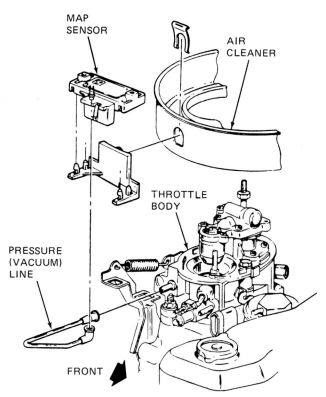

Fig. 19-20 A MAP sensor that attaches to the engine air cleaner. (*General Motors Corporation*)

Each continuously measures the actual amount of air flowing through the *air-flow meter* (Fig. 19-21). This information is then sent to the ECM.

1. VANE The vane type air-flow meter is used in some pulsed fuel-injection systems such as the Bosch L system (Fig. 19-21). The spring-loaded vane is in the air-intake passage of the air-flow meter. Air flowing through forces the vane to swing. The more air, the farther the vane swings. A *vane-position sensor* works like the rotary throttle-position sensor (➤19-10). Depending on its position, it sends varying voltage signals to the ECM. This tells the ECM how much air is flowing through. The ECM then adjusts fuel flow to match.

2. AIR-FLOW SENSOR PLATE The air-flow sensor plate is used in mechanical continuous-injection systems (Fig. 19-14). The plate is in the intake-air passage of the air-flow meter. As air flow increases, the plate moves higher. This lifts a control plunger in the fuel distributor to allow more fuel flow to the injectors. The added fuel flow matches the additional air flow.

3. HOT-WIRE INDUCTION A platinum wire is in the path of the incoming air through the air-flow meter. The wire is kept hot by an electric current flowing through it. However, the air flow cools the wire. The more air that

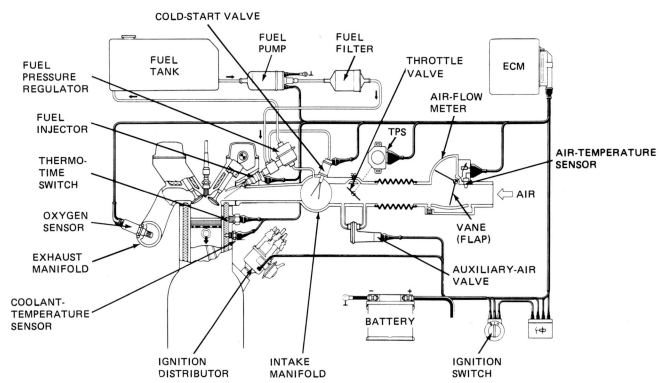

Fig. 19-21 The Bosch L electronic fuel-injection system uses a pivoted vane in the air-flow meter to signal the ECM how much air is entering the engine. (*Robert Bosch Corporation*)

passes through the air-flow meter, the more heat that is lost from the wire.

The system keeps the wire at a specific temperature by adjusting current flow. If more air flows through and takes more heat from the wire, the system sends more current through. This maintains the temperature. The amount of current required is therefore a measure of how much air is flowing through. The ECM reads this varying current as air flow.

4. HEATED FILM The heated film consists of metal foil or nickel grid coated with a high-temperature material (Fig. 19-22). Current flowing through the film heats it. Air flowing past the film cools it. Like the heated wire, the system maintains the film at a specific temperature. The amount of current required is a measure of air flow.

> ### 19-15 ATMOSPHERIC-PRESSURE AND AIR-TEMPERATURE SENSORS

Changing atmospheric pressure and air temperature change the density of the air. Air that is hot and at low atmospheric pressure is less dense. It contains less oxygen than an equal volume of cooler air under higher atmospheric pressure. When the amount of oxygen entering the engine varies, so does the amount of fuel that can be burned.

Some systems include an *atmospheric-pressure sensor*. It is also called the *barometric-pressure sensor* or *BARO sensor*. It is similar to the MAP sensor (➤19-13). However, the barometric-pressure sensor reads atmospheric pressure. The *air-temperature sensor* (Fig. 19-23) is a *thermistor*. Its electrical resistance decreases as its temperature increases. Figure 19-21 shows its location in the vane-type air-flow meter. Both types of sensors send varying voltage signals to the ECM so it knows the atmospheric pressure and air temperature.

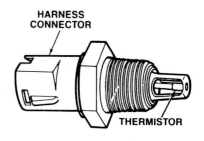

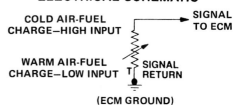

ELECTRICAL SCHEMATIC

COLD AIR-FUEL CHARGE—HIGH INPUT

SIGNAL TO ECM

WARM AIR-FUEL CHARGE—LOW INPUT

SIGNAL RETURN

(ECM GROUND)

Fig. 19-23 The air-temperature sensor uses a thermistor that loses resistance as it is heated. (*Ford Motor Company*)

> ### 19-16 COOLANT-TEMPERATURE SENSOR

The *coolant-temperature sensor* (CTS) is a thermistor that continuously reports engine coolant temperature to the ECM (Fig. 19-21). This is a varying voltage signal that the ECM uses in different ways. If coolant temperature is low, the ECM signals the fuel-metering system to supply additional fuel for cold-engine operation. The ECM also may alter ignition timing to suit engine temperature.

Most transverse engines use an electric engine-cooling fan (Fig. 4-10). When the engine is cold, no cooling is needed. The fan does not run. When the engine gets hot, the signal from the coolant-temperature sensor may cause the ECM to turn on the fan (➤19-19).

Fig. 19-22 Mass air-flow sensor using a heated film and an air-temperature sensor. (*Buick Division of General Motors Corporation*)

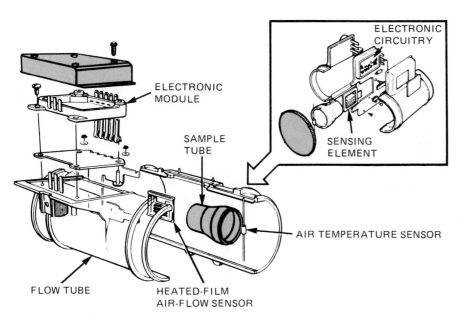

ELECTRONIC MODULE

SAMPLE TUBE

ELECTRONIC CIRCUITRY

SENSING ELEMENT

AIR TEMPERATURE SENSOR

FLOW TUBE

HEATED-FILM AIR-FLOW SENSOR

The *oxygen sensor* or O$_2$ sensor is installed in the exhaust manifold or exhaust pipe (Fig. 19-24). It measures the amount of oxygen in the exhaust gas. The oxygen sensor is about the size of a spark plug and produces a small voltage when exposed to oxygen. This varying voltage is sent to the ECM (Figs. 19-5 and 19-21). The voltage varies with the amount of oxygen in the exhaust gas.

Oxygen-sensor voltage is between 1.30 and 0.15 volt. When the voltage is close to 0.45 volt [450 millivolts], the air-fuel ratio is close to the ideal 14.7:1. If the voltage is higher than 0.45 volt [450 millivolts], the oxygen content is low. The air-fuel ratio is rich. If the voltage is less than 0.45 volt [450 millivolts], the oxygen content is high. The air-fuel ratio is lean.

The varying voltage tells the ECM whether the air-fuel mixture is rich or lean. The ECM then adjusts the duty cycle of the fuel injectors (Fig. 19-9). It turns them on for a longer or shorter time each time they open. This enriches or leans out the air-fuel mixture.

The oxygen sensor will not work unless it is hot. It must be between 392° and 1442°F [200° and 800°C]. The oxygen sensor will not produce a voltage signal when the engine is cold. While the engine is warming up, the electronic-engine-control system is in *open loop* "mode." (A *mode* is a certain method or set of operating conditions.) The ECM ignores any voltage signal sent by the oxygen sensor. Instead, the ECM uses data from the lookup table (➤10-18) to maintain an air-fuel ratio that allows the engine to run.

As soon as the engine and oxygen sensor reach operating temperature, the oxygen-sensor voltage signal is accepted by the ECM. The ECM switches to *closed loop* mode and begins using the oxygen-sensor signal to compute injector duty cycle.

Fig. 19-24 Construction and operation of an oxygen sensor. (*AC Spark Plug Division of General Motors Corporation*)

The engine may receive a rich mixture while running in open loop. This produces excessive pollutants in the exhaust gas. To reduce open-loop time, many oxygen sensors have an electric heating element inside. This causes the oxygen sensor to reach operating temperature more quickly.

If the engine idles too long, the oxygen sensor may cool off and stop producing a voltage signal. This puts the system in open loop. When engine speed increases, the oxygen sensor quickly reaches operating temperature. It again sends voltage signals to the ECM which switches to closed loop.

➤ **19-18 ENGINE-SPEED SENSOR**

The *engine-speed sensor* is usually a *crankshaft-position sensor* (➤32-11) that tells the ECM how fast the engine crankshaft is turning. The ECM uses this data to control fuel metering, ignition spark advance, and the shifting of electronic automatic transmissions and transaxles (Fig. 19-5).

Crankshaft-position sensors are either *Hall-effect sensors* (➤32-6) or *magnetic sensors* (➤32-11). Figure 19-25 shows a *Hall-effect switch* (➤32-6) used as the engine-speed sensor on a V-6 engine. To determine crankshaft speed, the ECM counts the number of crankshaft rotations per second. The crankshaft harmonic balancer carries three vanes. As the vanes pass between the permanent magnet and the *transducer,* the magnetic field acting on the transducer is repeatedly interrupted. (A transducer converts an input signal of one form into an output signal of a different form.) This turns the transistor OFF and ON, switching the signal voltage to the ECM from 12 volts to less than 1 volt. The ECM counts these voltage pulses to determine crankshaft speed.

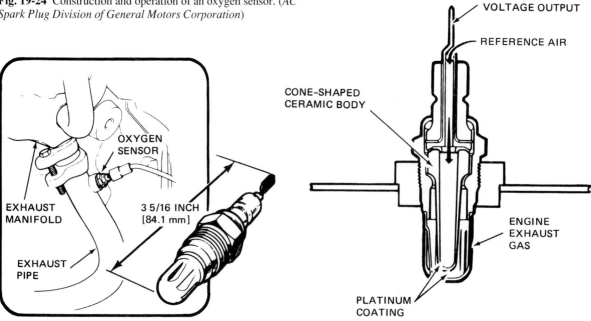

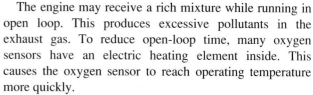

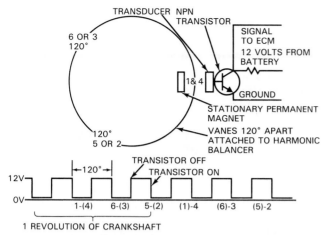

Fig. 19-25 Operation of a Hall-effect switch used as an engine-speed sensor, or crankshaft-position sensor. As the crankshaft rotates, vanes on the harmonic balancer cause voltage pulses which the ECM counts to determine crankshaft rpm. (*General Motors Corporation*)

Figure 12-3 shows a magnetic crankshaft sensor in the side of the block of an inline four-cylinder engine. A notched timing disc on the crankshaft causes voltage pulses in the sensor as the crankshaft rotates. These pulses are sent to the ECM. Another type of engine-speed sensor counts the voltage pulses from the ignition distributor. These trigger the high-voltage surges that produce the sparks at the spark plugs. Counting the number of pulses per second tells the ECM how fast the engine is running.

ACTUATORS

➤ 19-19 PURPOSE OF ACTUATORS

Sensors feed information into the ECM. The ECM then makes decisions and sends commands (outputs) to various *actuators*. These are the devices that operate automotive and engine components. Actuators are transducers (➤19-

18) that usually convert electrical signals from the ECM into mechanical motion. Figure 19-26 lists the ECM inputs and outputs for one car. Inputs are usually from sensors and switches. Outputs are usually to actuators which then operate switches, valves, and other devices.

➤ 19-20 MALFUNCTION-INDICATOR LIGHT

When certain troubles develop in the electronic control system, the ECM stores in its memory a number or *trouble code* for each fault. This turns on a *malfunction-indicator light* (MIL) in the instrument panel. A CHECK ENGINE, SERVICE ENGINE SOON, or similar light alerts the driver that service is needed.

If a single sensor fails, the ECM may substitute a value for the failed sensor. This allows the engine to appear to run normally. A fault that turns on the malfunction-indicator light may also put the engine into its *limp-in* mode. This means that the *limited operation strategy* (LOS) chip in the ECM (Fig. 10-17) has taken over. It provides basic instructions to the microprocessor if part of the electronic control system fails. The engine runs, but with fixed ignition timing and air-fuel ratio. The injector pulse width (➤19-7) does not change. This allows the vehicle to be driven but with greatly reduced performance. The vehicle can "limp in" for service instead of being towed.

The technician can retrieve the stored trouble code from the ECM memory. To use the code, the technician then finds the chart for that number in the vehicle service manual. The chart explains how to find and correct the fault.

➤ 19-21 IDLE-AIR-CONTROL VALVE

The *idle-air-control* (IAC) *valve* (Fig. 19-27) mounts on the throttle body. Its job is to maintain a steady idle speed and prevent engine stalling when the engine load is

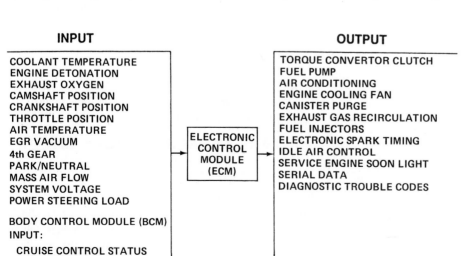

INPUT	OUTPUT
COOLANT TEMPERATURE	TORQUE CONVERTOR CLUTCH
ENGINE DETONATION	FUEL PUMP
EXHAUST OXYGEN	AIR CONDITIONING
CAMSHAFT POSITION	ENGINE COOLING FAN
CRANKSHAFT POSITION	CANISTER PURGE
THROTTLE POSITION	EXHAUST GAS RECIRCULATION
AIR TEMPERATURE	FUEL INJECTORS
EGR VACUUM	ELECTRONIC SPARK TIMING
4th GEAR	IDLE AIR CONTROL
PARK/NEUTRAL	SERVICE ENGINE SOON LIGHT
MASS AIR FLOW	SERIAL DATA
SYSTEM VOLTAGE	DIAGNOSTIC TROUBLE CODES
POWER STEERING LOAD	

ELECTRONIC CONTROL MODULE (ECM)

BODY CONTROL MODULE (BCM) INPUT:

CRUISE CONTROL STATUS
VEHICLE SPEED SENSOR
AC REQUEST

Fig. 19-26 ECM inputs and outputs in an electronic fuel-injection system. Since the ECM controls other components besides the fuel injectors, this is actually an engine management system. (*Buick Division of General Motors Corporation*)

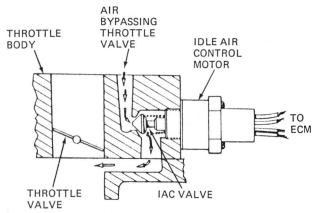

Fig. 19-27 Operation of the idle-air-control (IAC) motor that uses a conical valve to allow more or less air to bypass the throttle valve. The IAC motor is a "stepper" motor that can change the position of the conical valve in steps. (*Chevrolet Division of General Motors Corporation*)

suddenly increased. An example is what happens when parking a vehicle that has power steering. Turning the steering wheel with the vehicle stationary produces high hydraulic pressure in the steering system. This throws a momentary heavy load on the engine that could stall it. However, the high hydraulic pressure actuates the *power-steering switch* (Fig. 19-28). It sends a signal to the ECM. The ECM then signals the IAC valve to open so it passes more air around the throttle valve (Fig. 19-27). At the same time, the ECM causes the injectors to deliver more fuel to match the added air flow. This maintains idle speed.

The ECM also receives inputs from other sensors (Fig. 19-5). These include engine speed, throttle position, manifold vacuum, and coolant temperature. The ECM also uses these inputs to calculate how much air should bypass the throttle valve. For example, a cold engine may stall with a slow idle. The ECM therefore causes the IAC valve to bypass more air so the engine goes to fast idle. When the engine warms up, the ECM reduces the bypass air. The engine runs at slow idle.

There are two types of IAC valves. One has a conical

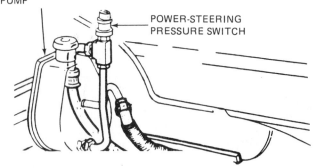

Fig. 19-28 The power-steering pressure switch signals the ECM to open the IAC valve and increase idle speed if the power-steering pressure goes high enough to stall the engine. (*Pontiac Division of General Motors Corporation*)

valve that opens varying amounts to allow more or less air to bypass (Fig. 19-27). The other has a needle valve that opens and closes at half-second intervals on command from the ECM (Fig. 19-29). If more air is needed, the valve stays open longer each time it opens. The diagram in the upper right of Fig. 19-29 shows the OFF-ON action. One OFF-ON is a duty cycle.

➤ 19-22 ELECTRONIC AIR-CONTROL VALVE

The *electronic air-control valve* (EACV) is another type of IAC valve (➤19-21). The valve has a solenoid controlled by the ECM. If there is a sudden added load on the engine, the ECM energizes the solenoid. Then the EACV bypasses more air around the throttle valve. At the same time, the ECM causes the fuel injectors to deliver more fuel. The added air-fuel mixture allows the engine to handle the added load without loss of speed.

FUEL INJECTION SYSTEMS

➤ 19-23 BOSCH FUEL-INJECTION SYSTEMS

Specific types of fuel-injection systems include throttle-body injection (TBI), port or multipoint injection, and the continuous injection system (CIS). Bendix and Bosch developed many of the gasoline fuel-injection systems. Most systems used today are either Bosch or based on Bosch designs. Various Bosch systems include:

1. *K- and KE-Jetronic fuel-injection systems* These are continuous injection systems. The K system is mechanical. It was later improved (KE) with the addition of a more powerful ECM and other refinements (Fig. 19-14).
2. *L-Jetronic fuel-injection system* This is a port, pulsed system (Fig. 19-21). It uses a vane-type air-flow sensor. It also uses a cold-start valve.
3. *Mono-Jetronic fuel-injection system* This is a throttle-body, pulsed injection system. It uses an oxygen sensor and other sensors with an ECM to provide control of the fuel system.
4. *Motronic fuel-injection system* This is a port, pulsed fuel-injection system. It controls the fuel and the ignition systems. Air intake is measured by a vane-type air-flow meter. No cold-start valve is required.

➤ 19-24 GENERAL MOTORS TBI SYSTEM

Figure 19-30 shows the basic fuel system used by General Motors with throttle-body injection. Figure 19-31 shows how a typical General Motors TBI system operates. On an in-line engine, a single fuel injector feeds all the cylinders. A *pressure regulator* maintains the correct fuel pressure to

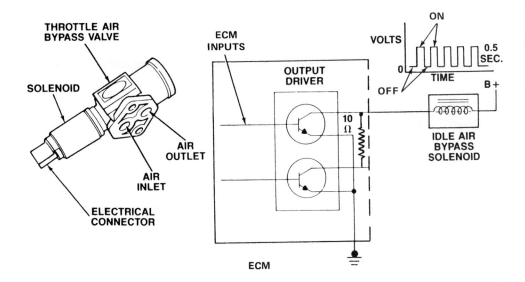

Fig. 19-29 Idle-air-control (IAC) valve controlled by an on-off solenoid. The schematic in the upper right shows the on-off (or duty) cycle. (*Ford Motor Company*)

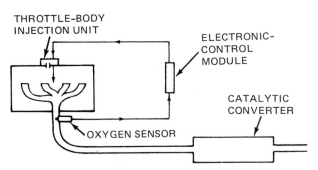

Fig. 19-30 Closed-loop operation of a throttle-body-injection system. (*Chevrolet Division of General Motors Corporation*)

the injector. The system (➤19-7) also uses an idle-air control valve and a throttle-position sensor (➤19-10).

Figure 19-32 shows a complete General Motors throttle-body assembly. Several versions are similar. Some V-type engines use a TBI assembly that has two fuel injectors (Fig. 19-33). Each injector supplies fuel to half the cylinders in the V-type engine.

Some General Motors V-6 engines have a *central port fuel-injection system* (Fig. 19-34). This system uses a single solenoid-operated fuel injector located in the intake manifold. When the ECM energizes the central fuel injector, it sends fuel through six nylon tubes to a mechanical injection valve in each intake port. This provides simultaneous port injection (➤19-27).

➤ 19-25 FORD TBI SYSTEM

Ford has a TBI system. It is similar in construction and operation to the TBI system described above (➤19-24).

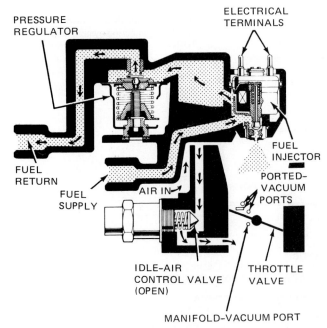

Fig. 19-31 Operation of the throttle-body assembly, showing the IAC valve open to admit air below the throttle valve. The pressure regulator returns some of the fuel to the tank if the pressure goes too high. (*Chevrolet Division of General Motors Corporation*)

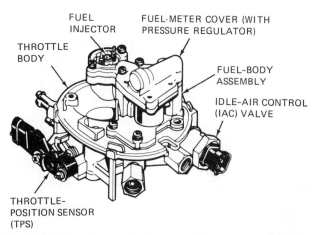

Fig. 19-32 Complete throttle-body assembly using a single fuel injector. (*Chevrolet Division of General Motors Corporation*)

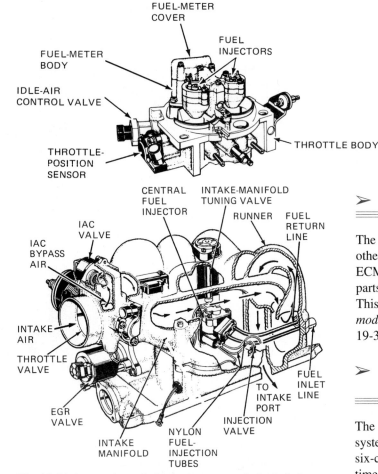

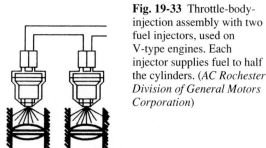

Fig. 19-33 Throttle-body-injection assembly with two fuel injectors, used on V-type engines. Each injector supplies fuel to half the cylinders. (*AC Rochester Division of General Motors Corporation*)

Fig. 19-34 A central port fuel-injection system. A single fuel injector sends fuel to six injection valves. (*Chevrolet Division of General Motors Corporation*)

➤ 19-26 CHRYSLER TBI SYSTEM

The Chrysler TBI system (Fig. 19-35) works the same as other systems. On earlier Chrysler engines, the job of the ECM or *engine controller* is performed by two separate parts. The *power module* handles larger electric currents. This protects the more sensitive circuitry in the *logic module*. Later systems have a single engine controller (Fig. 19-35).

➤ 19-27 ELECTRONIC PORT-INJECTION TIMING

The timing of the injection in an electronic port-injection system varies. Several methods are used. In some four- and six-cylinder engines, all fuel injectors open at the same time — once each crankshaft revolution. This arrangement of *simultaneous injection* simplifies the system. Each injector opens twice for each time its intake valve opens.

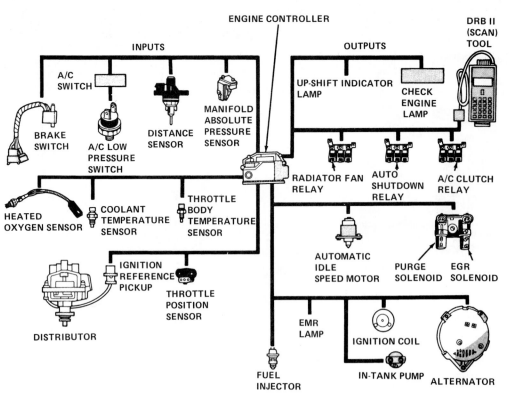

Fig. 19-35 Throttle-body-injection system with a single engine controller. Chrysler calls this TBI "single-point fuel injection." (*Chrysler Corporation*)

The intervals between injection and intake-valve opening are so short that there is little loss in efficiency.

Some systems open half of the injectors at the same time (Fig. 19-36 and 19-37). This is *group injection*. Other systems open each injector separately in firing-order sequence (Fig. 19-38). This is *sequential electronic fuel injection* (SEFI). It provides the most accurate fuel delivery and best engine performance while minimizing exhaust emissions.

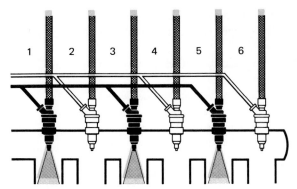

Fig. 19-36 Port injection for a six-cylinder engine with two groups of fuel injectors. One group, or half the injectors, open at the same time. (*Robert Bosch Corporation*)

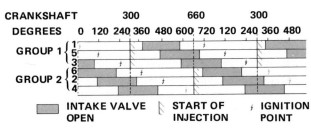

| | INTAKE VALVE OPEN | | START OF INJECTION | | IGNITION POINT |

Fig. 19-37 Injection timing for the two groups of injectors on a port-injected six-cylinder engine. (*Robert Bosch Corporation*)

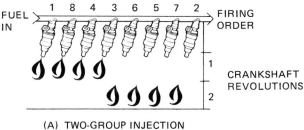

(A) TWO-GROUP INJECTION

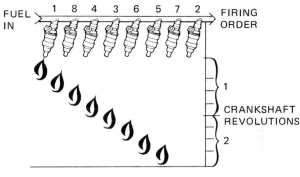

(B) SEQUENTIAL INJECTION

Fig. 19-38 Fuel delivery from two-group injection compared with sequential injection. (*Bendix Corporation*)

TRADE TALK

air-flow sensor plate
closed loop
hot-wire induction

idle-air-control (IAC) valve
limp-in mode
open loop

stoichiometric ratio
thermistor
transducer

trouble code

MULTIPLE-CHOICE TEST

*Select the **one** correct, best, or most probable answer to each question.*
You can find the answers in the section indicated at the end of the question.

1. In the pulsed electronic fuel-injection system, the (➤19-1)
   a. fuel injectors open by vacuum
   b. fuel injectors open and close
   c. fuel delivery is varied by varying the fuel pressure
   d. fuel is injected into the engine cylinders

2. The two locations for the fuel injectors are (➤19-1)
   a. in the cylinder and on the intake manifold
   b. in the throttle body and in the intake ports
   c. on the two sides of the air horn
   d. in the intake manifold and in the exhaust manifold

3. In the pulsed fuel-injection system, the amount of fuel injected depends on (➤19-7)
   a. how long the injectors stay open each time they open
   b. how far the injectors open
   c. how fast the injectors open
   d. the angle at which the injectors open
4. Technician A says the throttle-position sensor includes a potentiometer. Technician B says the TPS sends a varying voltage signal to the ECM. Who is right? (➤19-10)
   a. Technician A
   b. Technician B
   c. both A and B
   d. neither A nor B
5. Technician A says the indirect method of measuring air flow uses intake-manifold vacuum and throttle position. Technician B says the indirect method uses engine speed and intake-manifold vacuum. Who is right? (➤19-11)
   a. Technician A
   b. Technician B
   c. both A and B
   d. neither A nor B
6. Technician A says measuring manifold absolute pressure (MAP) is comparing intake-manifold vacuum with an absolute vacuum. Technician B says that measuring intake-manifold vacuum is comparing that vacuum with atmospheric pressure. Who is right? (➤19-13)
   a. Technician A
   b. Technician B
   c. both A and B
   d. neither A nor B

7. Three methods of directly measuring air flow are (➤19-14)
   a. vane, cold wire, hot wire
   b. vane, hot-wire induction, heated film
   c. vane, engine speed, hot wire
   d. vane, throttle position, and manifold vacuum
8. The oxygen sensor does all of the following EXCEPT (➤19-17)
   a. signals the ECM how much oxygen is in the exhaust gas
   b. helps adjust the mixture richness
   c. helps reduce pollutants in the exhaust gas
   d. signals the ECM the position of the throttle valve
9. The IAC valve does all of the following EXCEPT (➤19-21)
   a. maintains a steady idle speed
   b. prevents engine stalling when engine load is suddenly increased during idle
   c. bypasses varying amounts of air around the throttle valve
   d. sends idle-speed rpm to the ECM
10. In the typical throttle-body injection system on an in-line engine (➤19-24)
   a. one injector feeds all cylinders
   b. the secondary barrel feeds half the cylinders
   c. there is an injector for each cylinder
   d. varying pressure determines the amount of fuel injected

REVIEW QUESTIONS

1. Describe the construction and operation of the solenoid-operated fuel injector. (➤19-1)
2. Why does a throttle-body injection system have the same intake manifold problems as a carbureted fuel system? (➤19-2)
3. What is the difference between hot-wire induction and heated film in an air-flow meter? (➤19-14)
4. Describe two methods of measuring engine speed and tell how each operates. (➤19-18)
5. What are thermistors and transducers? Where are they used and how do they work in electronic fuel-injection systems? (➤19-15 and 19-18)

CHAPTER 20

FUEL-INJECTED FUEL SYSTEMS: DIAGNOSIS AND SERVICE

After studying this chapter, and with proper instruction and equipment, you should be able to:
- Relieve fuel-line pressure.
- Test fuel-pump pressure and capacity.
- Retrieve and interpret trouble codes.
- Diagnose sensor and ECM troubles.
- Clean fuel injectors and service fuel-system components.

➤ 20-1 FUEL-SYSTEM TROUBLE-DIAGNOSIS AND SERVICE

The fuel-injected fuel system (Fig. 20-1) requires little routine service other than filter changes. However, fuel pumps wear out, pressure regulators go bad, fuel injectors get dirty, sensors fail, and connectors separate or loosen and corrode.

When these problems occur in the fuel system, they often cause *driveability* complaints. Driveability means "vehicle operating characteristics that may concern the average driver." These include complaints such as hard starting, hesitation, missing, and surging.

This chapter covers trouble diagnosis and service of the fuel-supply and electronic fuel-injection systems. Diagnosis and service of carbureted fuel systems and carburetors are described in Chap. 22. Chapters 37 and 38 cover engine testing and driveability diagnosis.

➤ 20-2 FUEL-SYSTEM SAFETY CAUTIONS

Be careful while working on the fuel system to avoid personal injury and fire. Safety cautions for working around gasoline are described in Chap. 4. Below are other safety cautions that apply to gasoline fuel-injected and carbureted engines.

- *Caution 1:* Always have a Class B fire extinguisher (➤4-9) nearby and wear eye protection while working on the fuel system.

- *Caution 2:* The gasoline in the fuel lines may be pressurized. Before disconnecting a fuel line, relieve the pressure by following the instructions in ➤20-5 or in the manufacturer's service manual.

- *Caution 3:* Whenever you disconnect a fuel line, always cover the connection with a shop towel to soak up any gasoline that spurts out. Wipe up any fuel and put the towels outside to dry.

- *Caution 4:* Never prime an engine with the air cleaner off by pouring or squirting fuel into the air intake, carburetor, or throttle body. When cranked, the engine could backfire and cause an explosion or fire.

- *Caution 5:* Do not run the engine with the air cleaner off unless necessary for testing. On some engines, removing the air cleaner can lean out the air-fuel mixture enough to cause backfiring. Also, a malfunctioning engine can backfire.

FUEL-SYSTEM TROUBLE DIAGNOSIS

➤ 20-3 FUEL-SYSTEM VISUAL INSPECTION

When there is a driveability problem, check the malfunction-indicator light (➤19-20) in the vehicle instrument panel. If the light is not on, the first step in trouble diagnosis is to make a *visual inspection*.

With the engine off, check the engine compartment for possible fuel or air leaks (Fig. 20-2). A fuel odor indicates

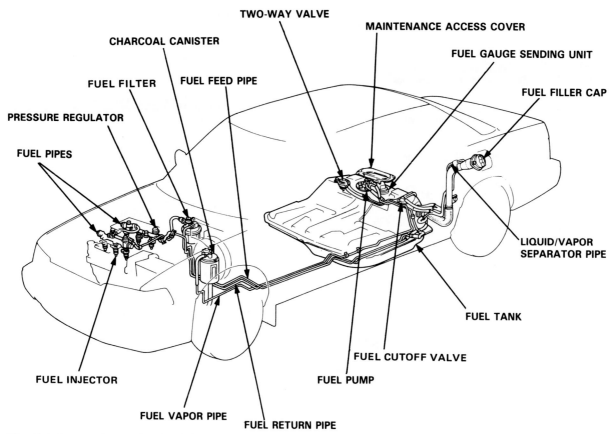

Fig. 20-1 Layout of a complete fuel-injected fuel system on the car.
(*American Honda Motor Company, Inc.*)

a leak. Examine all fuel-line connections from the fuel pump to the fuel injectors. An accumulation of dirt around a connection could mean a fuel leak. Dust sticks to the fuel residue. Install new seals as necessary and replace any defective hoses.

Air leaks in the air-intake system may allow air to enter the engine without passing through the air-flow meter (Fig. 19-21). This could result in a lean air-fuel mixture and poor engine performance. Vacuum leaks often make a hissing noise while the engine is running. Wiggling and pulling on a hose or tube that has a hole in it may make the noise change. Running a finger over the leak area may cover the hole and stop the noise. Spraying soapy water over a suspected leak area may temporarily seal the leak and cause an increase in engine speed. A stethoscope may also be used to locate a vacuum leak. Remove the sound drum and probe from the stethoscope. Then use the open end of the hose to find the leak. In addition, an *electronic leak detector* may be used.

Look for any obviously broken parts. Check for loose clamps, connectors, and fasteners. Determine that all leads, lines, and hoses are properly routed and securely attached (Fig. 20-3A). Correct hose routing is usually shown on the *vehicle emission control information* (VECI) label in the engine compartment (Fig. 3-4). Hoses must not be brittle or cracked. Look for signs of excess heat, leakage, and

rubbing. If possible, operate the system components by hand to check for full movement and smooth operation (Fig. 20-3B). When released, the components should return to their normal "at-rest" position.

If no cause of trouble is found during a visual inspection, check the ECM memory for stored trouble codes. Retrieving trouble codes is described later.

➤ 20-4 CHECKING FUEL INJECTORS

If the engine runs, you can usually make a quick check of TBI fuel-injector operation. Remove the air cleaner and start the engine. With the engine idling, you should see fuel spraying from the one or two injectors in the throttle body (Fig. 20-4). If not, disconnect the wiring-harness connector from the injector. Attach a special *injector test light* to the harness connector. Crank the engine while watching the light. If the test light flashes while cranking, the injector is receiving normal voltage pulses. The trouble is probably in the fuel system. If the light remains off or is on but not flashing, the trouble is electrical.

A quick check of each port injector can be made while the engine is running. Place a finger on the top of the injector. You should feel a vibration indicating the injector is opening and closing. Listen to the injector operation

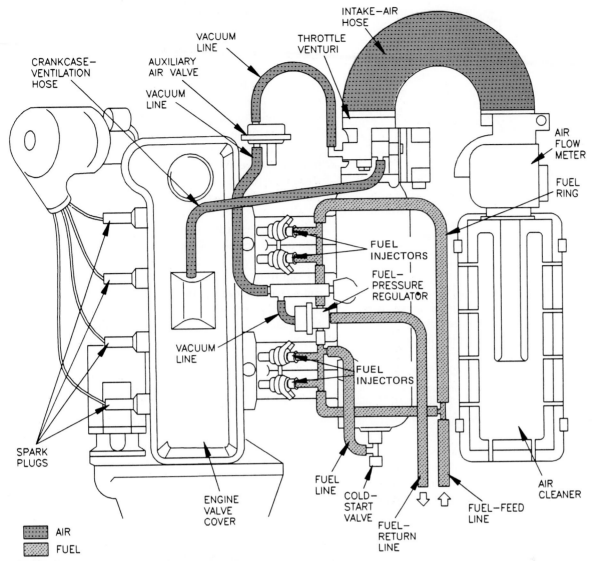

Fig. 20-2 Places to check on the engine for possible fuel leaks and air leaks. (*Robert Bosch Corporation*)

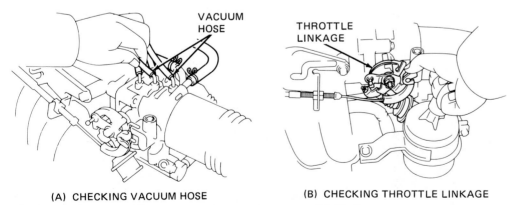

(A) CHECKING VACUUM HOSE

(B) CHECKING THROTTLE LINKAGE

Fig. 20-3 Making a visual inspection of a fuel-injection system. (A) Check that all vacuum hoses are in good condition, properly routed, and securely attached. (B) Operate the throttle linkage by hand and check for full movement and smooth operation. (*Toyota Motor Sales, U.S.A., Inc.*)

243

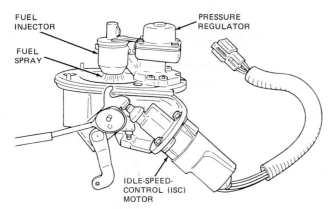

Fig. 20-4 Making a quick check of TBI fuel injectors. With the air cleaner removed and the engine idling, you should see fuel spraying from the one or two fuel injectors in the throttle body. (*Ford Motor Company*)

with an automotive stethoscope (➤38-19) or large screwdriver. A distinct clicking sound should be heard. If the sound is not clear, the injectors may need cleaning (➤20-23). No clicking sound indicates the injector is not working. It may be dirty or defective.

On systems with more than one injector, disconnect the wiring-harness connector from the injector while the engine is idling. If engine speed does not change, the injector is not working. If idle speed drops, the injector is probably okay.

If the injector is not working, it may not be receiving the voltage signal from the ECM. Check the wiring and connections between the ECM and the injector. If nothing appears wrong, check the *injector resistance* with an ohmmeter (Chap. 10). Remove the wiring-harness connector from the injector. Connect an ohmmeter lead to each of the injector terminals (Fig. 20-5). Replace the injector if the resistance is not within the manufacturer's specification.

NOTE Some cars have a continuous injection system (CIS). The fuel injectors used with this system are not solenoid-operated. They are usually removed from the engine for testing.

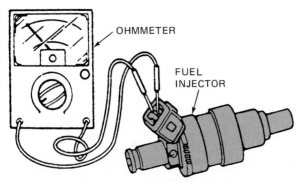

Fig. 20-5 Using an ohmmeter to measure injector resistance, which is the resistance through the solenoid windings. (*Ford Motor Company*)

➤ 20-5 RELIEVING FUEL-LINE PRESSURE

The fuel lines on fuel-injected engines carry a high fuel pressure. The fuel pressure must be relieved before disconnecting a fuel line. Many fuel systems use a *Schrader valve,* similar to a tire valve, as a *pressure-relief valve* (Fig. 20-6). The fitting can also be used to connect a pressure gauge. To relieve the fuel-line pressure, remove the cap from the valve. Wrap shop towels around the fitting to absorb the fuel. Then attach a pressure gauge and use the valve on it to relieve the pressure. Put the towels outside to dry.

Different procedures are used on vehicles without a pressure-relief valve. Follow the procedure in the manufacturer's service manual. Honda recommends removing the cap from the fuel tank and disconnecting the negative cable from the battery. Hold the hollow *banjo bolt* on top of the fuel filter with a flare-nut or open-end wrench. Place a box-end wrench on the *service bolt* (Fig. 20-7) that threads into the banjo bolt. Cover the service bolt and

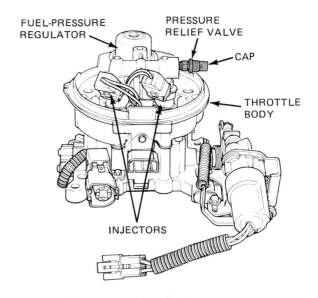

(A) THROTTLE-BODY INJECTION

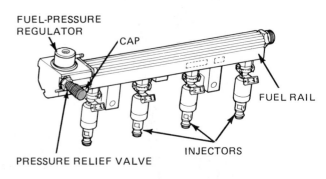

(B) PORT INJECTION

Fig. 20-6 Caps on the pressure-relief valves in (A) throttle-body injection and (B) port injection. (*Champion Spark Plug Company*)

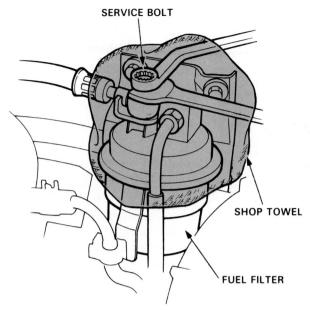

Fig. 20-7 To relieve fuel-line pressure, cover the wrench and service bolt on top of the fuel filter. Then slowly loosen the service bolt one turn to release the pressure. (*American Honda Motor Company, Inc.*)

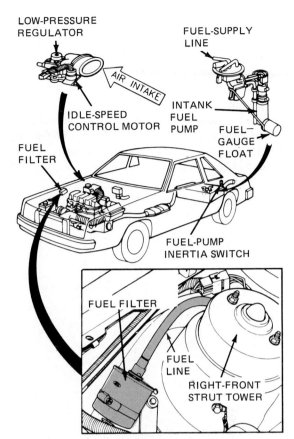

Fig. 20-8 If the electric fuel pump is not working, check for an open inertia switch in the fuel-pump wiring circuit. (*Ford Motor Company*)

wrenches with a shop towel. Then slowly loosen the service bolt one complete turn to release the pressure.

Another method is to remove the fuel-pump fuse. This works on port and TBI systems. Start the engine and run it until it stalls. Then crank the engine for five seconds to relieve any remaining fuel pressure.

Some TBI systems have a small hole or *orifice* in the pressure regulator. It bleeds off the pressure after the engine stops. Pressure relief is not required on these systems. However, always perform the procedure if there is any possibility of pressure in the fuel system.

CAUTION!

To prevent injury or fire, always relieve fuel pressure before disconnecting a fuel line. The fuel pressure in some fuel-injection systems may be 85 psi [586 kPa] or higher. This will cause fuel to spray out of any hole or loosened connection. The spray could hit you in the face or eyes, or strike a hot exhaust manifold or exhaust pipe. Always have a Class B fire extinguisher (➤4-9) nearby and wear eye protection while working on the fuel system.

➤ 20-6 CAUSES OF INOPERATIVE FUEL PUMP

Most electronic fuel-injection systems have an electric fuel pump mounted in the fuel tank (Fig. 20-8) or in the fuel line near the tank. Some vehicles have both (➤17-7). If the engine will not start, a fuel pump may not be working. This could be caused by a defective fuel pump, a blown fuse, an open or short circuit, or an open inertia switch (➤20-7). Any of these will open the electric circuit to the pump.

➤ 20-7 RESETTING INERTIA SWITCH

The inertia switch (Fig. 17-9) is a fuel-pump shutoff switch. It is in the trunk of many cars with electronic fuel injection (➤17-7). A severe bump or collision can cause the switch to open. This shuts off current to the fuel pump.

To reset the inertia switch, turn the ignition key to OFF. Check for fuel leakage. If you see or smell gasoline, correct the cause of the leak. If no fuel leakage is apparent, depress the *reset button* on top of the switch. This resets the switch. Immediately turn the ignition key to ON for a few seconds, then to OFF. This allows the fuel pump to pressurize the fuel system. Recheck for leaks. If no leaks are found, start the engine.

| NOTE | Not all fuel-injection systems include an inertia switch. If the vehicle has one, the location and reset procedure are shown in the owner's manual and manufacturer's service manual. |

➤ 20-8 TESTING FUEL-PUMP PRESSURE AND CAPACITY

If you suspect the fuel pump is not working properly, check its pressure and capacity (volume). Relieve the fuel-line pressure (➤20-5). Install the fuel-pressure gauge on the pressure-relief valve (Fig. 20-6). Or install the gauge between the fuel filter and the fuel inlet on the throttle body or fuel rail (Fig. 20-9). With the engine running, the pressure gauge shows the *injection pressure*. This is the pressure the pump is delivering to the fuel injectors. It should be within manufacturer's specifications.

Fuel-pump volume can be checked with the engine off. Place the *bypass hose* from the pressure gauge in a graduated container (Fig. 20-10). Open the drain valve on the gauge set and turn the ignition key to ON for 10 seconds. Fuel should discharge through the bypass hose into the container. Turn the ignition key to OFF and check

the amount of fuel in the container. It should be the specified volume.

NOTE *Some electric fuel pumps shut off if the engine is not running. Jump the test connectors specified in the manufacturer's service manual (C126 in Fig. 20-10). This allows fuel-pump operation with the engine off.*

Either high or low fuel pressure may be caused by a defective pressure regulator (➤20-9). High fuel pressure at idle may indicate low intake-manifold vacuum. Or the vacuum line to the pressure regulator is leaking or disconnected. High pressure also may indicate a kinked or restricted fuel-return line (Fig. 20-2).

When fuel pressure is low, install the pressure gauge between the fuel tank (or pump) and the fuel filter. Repeat the pressure test. If the gauge shows normal pressure, the fuel line is restricted or the fuel filter is clogged. A low reading indicates the intank fuel filter (Fig. 17-7B) is clogged or the fuel pump is defective. Another possibility in the tank is that the short hose between the pump and the fuel-supply tube is leaking.

Replace a fuel pump that does not deliver the specified pressure and volume when no other trouble is found. Some fuel systems have two electric fuel pumps (➤17-7). Test both pumps.

➤ 20-9 TESTING FUEL-PRESSURE REGULATOR

The pressure regulator on a port-injected fuel system should be checked for proper operation after checking fuel pressure (➤20-8). With the engine idling, remove the vacuum hose from the pressure regulator (Fig. 20-11). Plug the end of the hose and check fuel pressure. It should be within specifications.

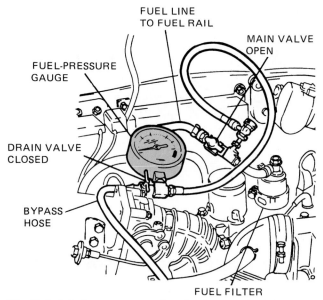

Fig. 20-9 A fuel-pressure gauge installed between the fuel filter and fuel inlet on the throttle body or fuel rail will show injection pressure when the engine is running. (*Ford Motor Company*)

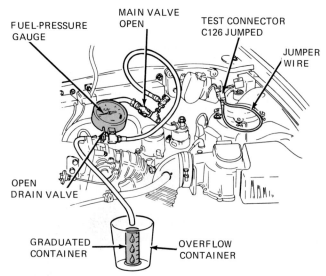

Fig. 20-10 Using the fuel-pressure gauge and drain valve to check fuel-pump volume with the engine off. (*Ford Motor Company*)

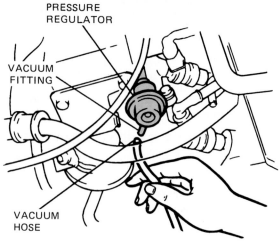

Fig. 20-11 Testing the pressure regulator on a port-injected fuel system. With the engine idling, remove and plug the vacuum hose. Fuel pressure should be within specifications. (*Ford Motor Company*)

Apply intake-manifold vacuum to the vacuum fitting on the pressure regulator. Fuel pressure should drop from 3 to 10 psi [21 to 69 kPa]. No change in fuel pressure indicates a defective pressure regulator. Replace it. Pressure regulators are not adjustable.

Pressure regulators in TBI systems (Fig. 20-6) do not have a vacuum fitting. If fuel pressure is not within specifications or the pressure regulator is leaking, replace it. Some TBI pressure regulators have a replaceable diaphragm.

➤ 20-10 TESTING FUEL INJECTORS

Three tests may be performed on a solenoid-operated fuel injector. These tests are for resistance (➤20-4), volume or flow, and leakage.

1. INJECTOR RESISTANCE Use an ohmmeter to check injector resistance as described in ➤20-4.

2. INJECTOR FLOW (VOLUME) Connect a *fuel-injector tester* (Fig. 20-12) to the fuel system. Follow the tester operating instructions. The procedure determines whether the volume of fuel flow through each injector is within specifications.

A similar test can be made with an *injector balance tester*. The test is made with the engine off, ignition key ON, and the pressure gauge connected to the fuel system. The tester opens each injector for the same length of time. The pressure gauge shows the amount of *pressure drop*. All injectors should have about the same pressure drop. A partially clogged injector has less pressure drop than a clean injector. Clean or replace any injector that fails this test.

3. INJECTOR LEAKAGE With the fuel system pressurized, check the tip end of each injector for leakage. No fuel should leak out. Some manufacturers allow one drop of fuel leakage after one minute. Clean or replace the injector if it leaks more than specified.

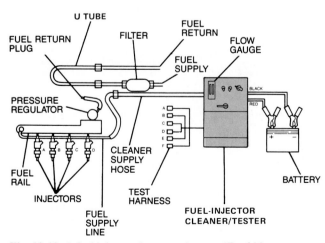

Fig. 20-12 A fuel injector cleaner and tester. (*Ford Motor Company*)

ON-BOARD DIAGNOSTICS

➤ 20-11 THE ROLE OF ON-BOARD DIAGNOSTICS

Electronic fuel-injection (EFI) systems are controlled by an electronic control module (ECM). Most ECMs store a trouble code (Fig. 20-13) if certain problems occur (➤19-20). However, a stored trouble code does not always pinpoint the cause of the problem. The code may only indicate trouble somewhere in a circuit or *subsystem*. Special diagnostic procedures and special testers may be required to locate the trouble.

To use trouble codes, you must first know how to retrieve them (➤20-13). Then you must understand and interpret what they mean (➤20-14). Knowing which circuits are *monitored* by the ECM and which are not is important to interpreting trouble codes.

➤ 20-12 MONITORED AND NON-MONITORED CIRCUITS

Monitor means "to keep track of." During engine operation, the ECM monitors the operation of many sensors and circuits. These input signals (Fig. 19-26) allow the ECM to determine if sensor voltage is within the proper range. The ECM also "senses" if the sensor or circuit is open or shorted. In addition, during closed-loop operation the ECM determines if the oxygen-sensor voltage is swinging between rich and lean. Most devices that provide an input to the ECM are part of the *monitored circuits*.

Non-monitored circuits are the devices and systems that are not directly monitored by the ECM. For example, the ECM usually does not monitor fuel pressure, spark-plug firing, or cylinder-compression pressure. The ECM also cannot directly detect:

- Dirty fuel injectors.
- Restricted air cleaner.
- Excessive oil consumption.
- Vacuum leaks.

Many of these problems could affect a monitored circuit. As a result, the monitored circuit may set a trouble code.

➤ 20-13 RETRIEVING TROUBLE CODES

Trouble codes are also called *fault codes* and *service codes*. On most cars with an on-board diagnostic system, there are three ways to retrieve stored codes. One way is to use the malfunction-indicator light (➤19-20) in the instrument panel. The light can display stored codes in a series of flashes representing numbers. The second and preferred way is to connect a *scan tool* or other diagnostic tester to the vehicle *diagnostic connector*. General Motors calls the diagnostic connector the *assembly-line diagnostic link*

Trouble Code	Circuit or Device Affected
12	No Reference Signal
13	Oxygen (O₂) Sensor Circuit (Open Circuit)
14	Coolant Temperature Sensor (CTS) Circuit (High Temperature Indicated)
15	Coolant Temperature Sensor (CTS) Circuit (Low Temperature Indicated)
21	Throttle Position Sensor (TPS) Circuit (Signal Voltage High)
22	Throttle Position Sensor (TPS) Circuit (Signal Voltage Low)
23	Intake Air Temperature (IAT) Sensor Circuit (Low Temperature Indicated)
24	Vehicle Speed Sensor (VSS) Circuit Fault
25	Intake Air Temperature (IAT) Sensor Circuit (High Temperature Indicated)
32	Exhaust Gas Recirculation (EGR) System Failure
33	Manifold-Absolute-Pressure (MAP) Sensor Circuit (Signal Voltage High-Low Vacuum)
34	Manifold-Absolute-Pressure (MAP) Sensor Circuit (Signal Voltage Low-High Vacuum)
35	Idle Air Control (IAC) Circuit
42	Electronic Spark Timing (EST) Circuit
44	Oxygen (O₂) Sensor Circuit (Lean Exhaust Indicated)
45	Oxygen (O₂) Sensor Circuit (Rich Exhaust Indicated)
51	Calibration Error (Faulty or Incorrect MEM-CAL)
53	System Over Voltage

Fig. 20-13 Trouble codes and the circuit or device affected. (*Chevrolet Division of General Motors Corporation*)

(ALDL) *connector*. A third way is to use the on-board self-diagnostics built into some cars.

1. MALFUNCTION-INDICATOR LIGHT Most General Motors cars have a 12-pin connector (Fig. 20-14) under the instrument panel near the steering column. To read stored trouble codes, turn the ignition key to ON but do not start the engine. Insert a *jumper wire* or *key* into terminal A (ground) and terminal B (the diagnostic terminal) of the diagnostic connector. The CHECK ENGINE or SERVICE ENGINE SOON light will flash code 12 (Fig. 20-15) three times. Then the light will flash each code stored in memory three times. All stored codes have been read when code 12 flashes again. Figure 20-13 is a partial list of trouble codes.

When there is more than one trouble code, correct the cause of the lowest code first unless otherwise directed by the service manual. Clear the codes from the memory after completing the repairs. With the ignition off, disconnect the fuse for the ECM for 30 seconds. Codes may also be cleared by removing the negative cable from the battery. However, this causes loss of data from other volatile memories (➤10-18). A stored code automatically erases if the trouble that caused it does not recur within 40 or 50 engine starts.

On many vehicles built by Chrysler, turning the ignition key ON-OFF-ON-OFF-ON within five seconds activates the readout. The light will then flash any stored codes. Refer to the service manual for the meaning of these codes.

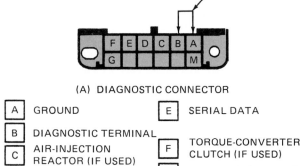

(A) DIAGNOSTIC CONNECTOR

A	GROUND	E	SERIAL DATA
B	DIAGNOSTIC TERMINAL		
C	AIR-INJECTION REACTOR (IF USED)	F	TORQUE-CONVERTER CLUTCH (IF USED)
D	SERVICE ENGINE SOON LAMP	G	FUEL PUMP (IF USED)
		M	SERIAL DATA (IF USED)

(B) TERMINAL IDENTIFICATION

Fig. 20-14 Typical General Motors diagnostic connector with the terminals identified. (*Cadillac Division of General Motors Corporation*)

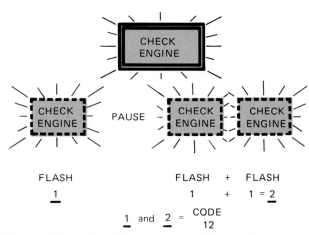

Fig. 20-15 Operation of the CHECK ENGINE light on General Motors vehicles. By jumping terminal A to terminal B in the diagnostic connector, the CHECK ENGINE light will start to flash. These flashes indicate a code (or codes). For example, a code 12 consists of one flash followed by a pause and then two more flashes. (*Rochester Products Division of General Motors Corporation*)

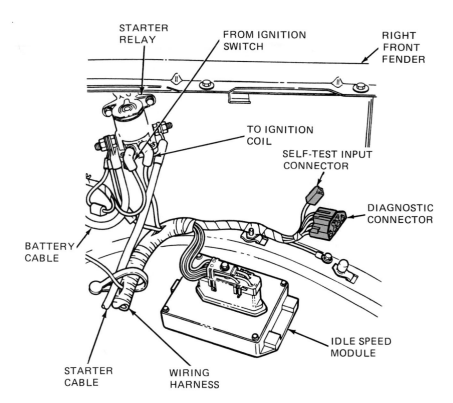

STARTER RELAY

FROM IGNITION SWITCH

RIGHT FRONT FENDER

TO IGNITION COIL

SELF-TEST INPUT CONNECTOR

DIAGNOSTIC CONNECTOR

BATTERY CABLE

IDLE SPEED MODULE

STARTER CABLE

WIRING HARNESS

Fig. 20-16 Diagnostic connector and self-test input connector in a Ford engine compartment. Connect a jumper wire from the self-test input connector to the signal return (top right) terminal in the diagnostic connector. The CHECK ENGINE light will flash the trouble codes. (*Ford Motor Company*)

Stored codes are retrieved from Ford vehicles with the ignition key ON and engine off. Locate the six-pin diagnostic connector (Fig. 20-16) and the single *self-test input* connector nearby in the engine compartment. With the ignition OFF, connect a jumper wire from the self-test input connector to the *signal return* terminal in the diagnostic connector. This is the top right terminal in the diagnostic connector shown in Fig. 20-16. Turn the ignition key ON. The CHECK ENGINE light will flash the trouble codes. Code 11 indicates normal operation.

2. SCAN TOOL Some automotive manufacturers require the use of a scan tool to perform system diagnosis. The hand-held scan tool (Fig. 20-17) is also called a *scanner* or a *readout box*. It connects to the diagnostic connector and can be read by the technician while road testing the car or working in the engine compartment. The scan tool pro-

vides information more quickly than the instrument-panel light. In addition, the tool displays numbers and words which are less likely to be misread than the series of flashes provided by the light.

The scan tool provides a variety of information that would otherwise be very difficult or impossible to obtain. It retrieves trouble codes and displays the PROM (➤10-18) identification number. It displays ECM data values which may indicate a problem even if no trouble code is set. It gives the status or condition of many input and output devices.

Typical values for *scan data* (Fig. 20-18) are given in the manufacturer's service manuals. These can be compared with the values read by the scan tool. The service-manual values are usually given for the engine idling, upper radiator-hose hot, throttle closed, transmission in PARK or NEUTRAL, closed-loop mode, and air conditioning OFF. Figure 20-19 shows scan values from a running engine.

Some scan tools have a one-line readout that displays trouble codes as numbers. Others have a four-line window that displays diagnostic data in words. This reduces the time spent in referring to charts in service manuals.

Replaceable test cartridges update the scan tool to cover new cars. Many scanners can be connected to a computer or a printer (Fig. 20-19). To help in finding *intermittents*, the scan tool can be observed while road testing the car. An intermittent is a trouble that comes and goes, and may or may not set a trouble code. Some scanners can take a *snapshot* or act as a *recorder* and store scan data during the road test. This is played back and analyzed after the vehicle returns to the shop.

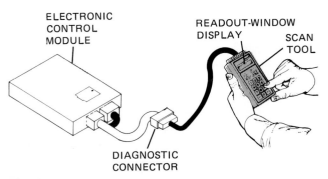

ELECTRONIC CONTROL MODULE

READOUT-WINDOW DISPLAY

SCAN TOOL

DIAGNOSTIC CONNECTOR

Fig. 20-17 Scan tool retrieving trouble codes through the diagnostic connector. (*OTC Tool & Equipment Division of SPX Corporation*)

249

SCAN Position	Units Displayed	Typical Data Value
Engine Speed	RPM	± 100 RPM from desired RPM (± 50 RPM in drive)
Desired Engine Speed	RPM	ECM idle command (varies with temperature)
Coolant Temperature	C°/F°	85°–109° (185°F–223°F)
IAT Temperature	C°/F°	10°–80° (50°F–176°F) depending on underhood temperature
MAP	kPa/Volts	29–48kPa (1–2 volts) depending on Vac & Baro Pressure
BARO	kPa/Volts	58–114kPa (2.5–5.5) depending on altitude & Baro Pressure
Throttle Position	Volts	0.29–0.98
Throttle Angle	0–100%	0
Oxygen Sensor	M/Volts	100–1000 and varying
Injection Pulse Width	M/Sec	1–4 and varying
Spark Advance	# of Degrees	Varies
Fuel Integrator	Counts	Varies
Block Learn	Counts	110–156
Open-Closed Loop	Open/Closed	Closed Loop (may go open with extended idle)
Block Learn Cell	Cell Number	0 or 1 (depends on Air Flow & RPM)
Knock Retard	Degrees of Retard	0
Knock Signal	Yes/No	No
EGR 1/EGR 2/EGR 3	Off/On	Off (On when commanded by ECM)
Idle Air Control	Counts (steps)	5–50
MPH/KPH	MPH/KPH	0
Torque Converter Clutch	On/Off	Off (on with TCC commanded)
Battery Voltage	Volts	13.5–14.5 volts
Fuel-Pump Voltage	Volts	13.5–14.5 volts
Crank Speed	RPM	Varies
A/C Request	Yes/No	No (Yes, with A/C requested)
A/C Clutch	On/Off	Off (On, with A/C commanded on)
A/C Pressure	psi/Volt	Varies (depends on temperature)
Fan (Fan if applicable)	On/Off	109°C (228°F) with A/C Off/106°C (223°F) with A/C On
Power Steering	Normal/High Pressure	Normal
Purge Duty Cycle	0–100	0%
Park Neutral	P/N and RDL	Park/Neutral (P/N)
2nd Gear	Yes/No	No (yes, when in 2nd, 3rd or 4th gear)
3rd Gear	Yes/No	No (yes, when in 3rd or 4th gear)
4th Gear	Yes/No	No (yes, when in 4th gear)
Prom ID	0–999	Varies
Time from Start	Hrs/Min	Varies

Fig. 20-18 Typical values for scan data in a General Motors vehicle. (*Oldsmobile Division of General Motors Corporation*)

3. ON-BOARD COMPUTER-SYSTEM DIAGNOSIS Some cars display trouble codes and scan data on the vehicle instrument panel (Fig. 20-20). With the ignition key ON, start the readout by pressing the OFF and WARMER buttons on the air-conditioning or *climate control panel*. Stored codes appear in place of the temperature. Many cars with this system have *digital fuel injection* (DFI). The scan tool may not be able to retrieve information through the diagnostic connector.

A car may have more than one electronic control module. A *body control module* (BCM) may control other electronic systems such as antilock-braking (ABS) and air conditioning. *Supplemental inflatable restraints* (SIR) or *air bags* have a separate electronic module. The electronic *instrument-panel cluster* (IPC) may have another module. Each module may store trouble codes. If these modules are linked to the ECM, all stored trouble codes can be displayed after entering DIAGNOSTICS (Fig. 20-20). Engine or powertrain trouble codes display first, followed by codes from the BCM, SIR, and IPC modules. A letter prefix identifies which module detected the fault.

The on-board computer-system diagnostics can also take a "snapshot" to help in diagnosis of intermittents. When the trouble occurs while driving, press HI on the climate-control panel until the message "ECM SNAPSHOT TAKEN" appears. This stores a set of scan data — all ECM values and output conditions — at that instant. The data can be retrieved and reviewed later in the shop.

➤ **20-14 INTERPRETING TROUBLE CODES AND SCAN DATA**

A vehicle may have a driveability or emissions problem that does not set a trouble code. This can occur even if the trouble is in a monitored circuit (➤20-12). An intermittent may set a code that is automatically erased before the car is brought in for service (➤20-13). Also, the code does not set because the ECM only monitors each circuit for faults under certain conditions. These relate to engine condition, temperature, and elapsed time. For example, a sensor may set a code only when one or more of the following conditions are met:

NO TROUBLE CODES

Tech 1 Data List

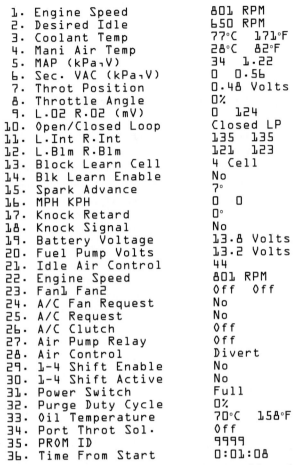

1.	Engine Speed	801 RPM
2.	Desired Idle	650 RPM
3.	Coolant Temp	77°C 171°F
4.	Mani Air Temp	28°C 82°F
5.	MAP (kPa,V)	34 1.22
6.	Sec. VAC (kPa,V)	0 0.56
7.	Throt Position	0.48 Volts
8.	Throttle Angle	0%
9.	L.O2 R.O2 (mV)	0 124
10.	Open/Closed Loop	Closed LP
11.	L.Int R.Int	135 135
12.	L.Blm R.Blm	121 123
13.	Block Learn Cell	4 Cell
14.	Blk Learn Enable	No
15.	Spark Advance	7°
16.	MPH KPH	0 0
17.	Knock Retard	0°
18.	Knock Signal	No
19.	Battery Voltage	13.8 Volts
20.	Fuel Pump Volts	13.2 Volts
21.	Idle Air Control	44
22.	Engine Speed	801 RPM
23.	Fan1 Fan2	Off Off
24.	A/C Fan Request	No
25.	A/C Request	No
26.	A/C Clutch	Off
27.	Air Pump Relay	Off
28.	Air Control	Divert
29.	1-4 Shift Enable	No
30.	1-4 Shift Active	No
31.	Power Switch	Full
32.	Purge Duty Cycle	0%
33.	Oil Temperature	70°C 158°F
34.	Port Throt Sol.	Off
35.	PROM ID	9999
36.	Time From Start	0:01:08

Fig. 20-19 Scan data printout. (*Chevrolet Division of General Motors Corporation*)

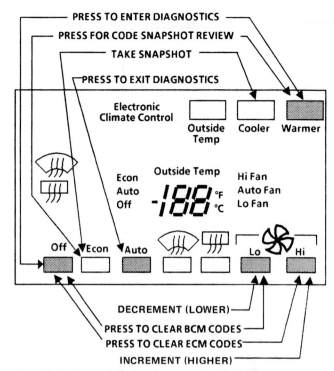

Fig. 20-20 Onboard diagnostic system that displays trouble codes and scan data on the air-conditioning control panel in the instrument panel. (*Cadillac Division of General Motors Corporation*)

> **NOTE** Step 3 in Fig. 20-21 asks, "Does *Tech 1* display ECM data?" The Tech 1 is the scan tool sold by General Motors to its dealers. The Chrysler scan tool or *data readout box* is the *DRB II.* The Ford tool is a *self-test automatic readout* or *STAR tester.* Other manufacturers sell similar tools under various names.

1. The engine is running at — or above or below — a specified speed.
2. The air or coolant temperature is higher or lower than specified.
3. The fault condition occurs for a specified time — at least two seconds to two minutes.

When a visual inspection (➤20-3) does not locate the trouble, use a scan tool to perform a *diagnostic circuit check* (Fig. 20-21). This is an overall self-test of the complete system. It determines if the diagnostics are working and if a trouble code is stored.

If a trouble code is found, go to the *code chart* for that code in the manufacturer's service manual. For example, suppose you are making a diagnostic circuit check (Fig. 20-21) on a General Motors V-6 engine with port fuel-injection. The scanner shows a code 21 (Fig. 20-13). This indicates the signal voltage from the throttle-position sensor (TPS) is high.

Turn to code chart 21 (Fig. 20-22) in the manufacturer's service manual. Follow the steps to locate the fault. You may be referred to other charts and wiring diagrams. But eventually you will find the trouble through the process of elimination. Repair the fault. Then confirm that the code does not reset.

Code charts are most useful when there are stored trouble codes and the CHECK ENGINE light is on. Trouble codes found stored in the memory when the CHECK ENGINE light is out were probably caused by an intermittent failure. These codes may or may not reset. However, such codes could be helpful in diagnosing the system. When a code is set by an intermittent, do not use a code chart for diagnosis. It could lead you to a false conclusion. Make a visual inspection of the related parts and system. If the

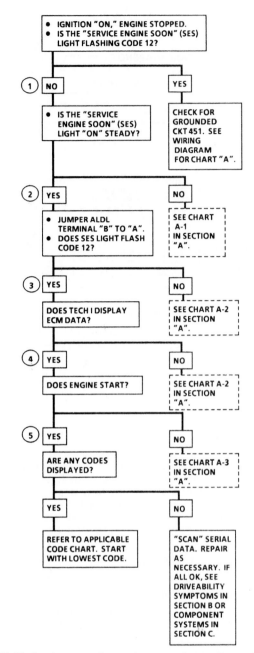

- IGNITION "ON," ENGINE STOPPED.
- IS THE "SERVICE ENGINE SOON" (SES) LIGHT FLASHING CODE 12?

① NO

- IS THE "SERVICE ENGINE SOON" (SES) LIGHT "ON" STEADY?

YES

CHECK FOR GROUNDED CKT 451. SEE WIRING DIAGRAM FOR CHART "A".

② YES

- JUMPER ALDL TERMINAL "B" TO "A".
- DOES SES LIGHT FLASH CODE 12?

NO

SEE CHART A-1 IN SECTION "A".

③ YES

DOES TECH I DISPLAY ECM DATA?

NO

SEE CHART A-2 IN SECTION "A".

④ YES

DOES ENGINE START?

NO

SEE CHART A-2 IN SECTION "A".

⑤ YES

ARE ANY CODES DISPLAYED?

NO

SEE CHART A-3 IN SECTION "A".

YES

REFER TO APPLICABLE CODE CHART. START WITH LOWEST CODE.

NO

"SCAN" SERIAL DATA. REPAIR AS NECESSARY. IF ALL OK, SEE DRIVEABILITY SYMPTOMS IN SECTION B OR COMPONENT SYSTEMS IN SECTION C.

Fig. 20-21 Service-manual procedure to perform a diagnostic circuit check on a General Motors vehicle, using a Tech I scan tool. (*Pontiac Division of General Motors Corporation*)

cause is not found, follow the diagnostic aids and intermittent procedure in the vehicle service manual.

When no trouble code is stored, compare the scan-tool readings with the typical scan data in the manufacturer's service manual. Other charts in the service manual provide test specifications and procedures for each device. *Symptom charts* provide checks for locating troubles such as intermittents and driveability problems that do not set a trouble code.

The most complete source of diagnostic information for any vehicle is the manufacturer's service manual (➤3-5). The publishers of auto repair manuals also publish separate *electronics* and *engine controls manuals*. These may also have charts, diagrams, and diagnostic aids.

Some *service-bay diagnostic computers* (Fig. 20-23) have the diagnostic charts and test procedures stored in memory. The information comes from a computer disk or other online computer (➤3-8). The technician connects the service-bay computer to the car. Then the stored trouble codes and scan data are retrieved and diagnosed. Test procedures, code and symptom charts, and diagnostic aids are displayed on the computer screen. After isolating the problem, the repair procedures and specifications may display. A paper printout can be made of any screen data.

➤ 20-15 SENSOR DIAGNOSIS

Five sensors largely determine the amount of fuel delivered by the fuel-injection system (Fig. 19-5). These are the engine-speed sensor, throttle-position sensor, manifold-absolute-pressure sensor, coolant-temperature sensor, and intake-air-temperature sensor. Other sensors and switches provide inputs to the ECM. It then adjusts the air-fuel mixture based on feedback from the oxygen sensor. Chapter 19 describes all of these sensors.

The ECM may substitute a value for a defective sensor (➤19-19). The result is little change in driveability. Other sensor failures cause immediate driveability problems and increase exhaust emissions. For example, a defective coolant-temperature sensor (➤19-16) will cause a warm engine to receive excess fuel. Then the exhaust gas contains a high level of carbon monoxide (CO) at idle.

Failure of a sensor or circuit may set a trouble code. The symptom or code chart directs you to test the switch or sensor (Fig. 20-22). Diagnostic aids and tips such as the normal condition, specifications, and typical values for the test are in the manufacturer's service manual.

Most sensors and switches can be checked with the scan tool or service-bay computer. Sensor voltage can be checked with a digital voltmeter. Throttle-position sensor (➤19-10) resistance can be measured with an ohmmeter. Figures 20-18 and 20-19 show typical scan-data values and settings for sensors and switches. When a defective switch or sensor is found, replace it.

Cars that have the on-board computer-system diagnostics described in ➤20-13 can also make self-tests of the sensors and switches. The readings appear on the climate-control display panel (Fig. 20-20).

➤ 20-16 ECM DIAGNOSIS

The ECM (Fig. 20-24) has a PROM (➤10-18) that may be a separate chip or combined in a chip that also performs other functions. These chips are called *calibration package* (CAL-PAK) or *memory-calibration* (MEM-CAL) chips. Each contains information based on vehicle weight, engine, transmission, drive-axle ratio, and other factors. By changing the chip, these values adapt the ECM for use in different vehicles. Therefore, the PROM stays with the vehicle. When a new ECM is being installed, transfer the PROM to it before installation.

Sometimes the PROM fails. Other times the information

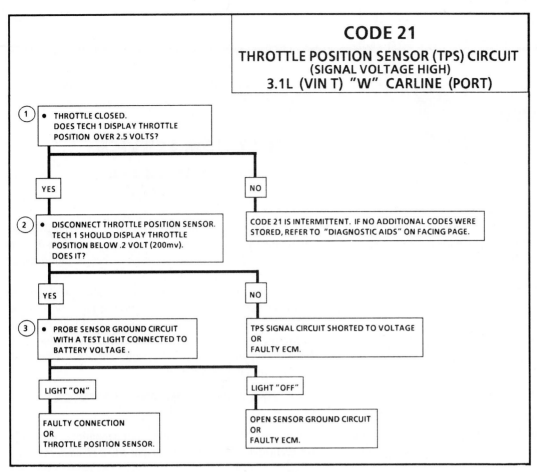

CODE 21

THROTTLE POSITION SENSOR (TPS) CIRCUIT
(SIGNAL VOLTAGE HIGH)
3.1L (VIN T) "W" CARLINE (PORT)

1 • THROTTLE CLOSED.
DOES TECH 1 DISPLAY THROTTLE POSITION OVER 2.5 VOLTS?

YES

NO

2 • DISCONNECT THROTTLE POSITION SENSOR. TECH 1 SHOULD DISPLAY THROTTLE POSITION BELOW .2 VOLT (200mv). DOES IT?

CODE 21 IS INTERMITTENT. IF NO ADDITIONAL CODES WERE STORED, REFER TO "DIAGNOSTIC AIDS" ON FACING PAGE.

YES

NO

3 • PROBE SENSOR GROUND CIRCUIT WITH A TEST LIGHT CONNECTED TO BATTERY VOLTAGE.

TPS SIGNAL CIRCUIT SHORTED TO VOLTAGE
OR
FAULTY ECM.

LIGHT "ON"

LIGHT "OFF"

FAULTY CONNECTION
OR
THROTTLE POSITION SENSOR.

OPEN SENSOR GROUND CIRCUIT
OR
FAULTY ECM.

Fig. 20-22 Code chart 21 in the vehicle service manual. The chart shows the steps to take to determine the cause of high signal voltage from the throttle-position sensor. (*Oldsmobile Division of General Motors Corporation*)

Fig. 20-23 A service-bay diagnostic computer, which has diagnostic charts and test procedures stored in memory. A paper printout can be made of any data displayed on the computer screen. (*Ford Motor Company*)

stored in the PROM must be changed because of a manufacturer's recall (➤2-4) or running change (➤3-5). This is a *calibration change*. Calibrate means "to determine the correct value of." The change is made by replacing the PROM, if an updated PROM is available. If not, the complete ECM is replaced. Some scan tools and service-bay diagnostic computers can reprogram the PROM. The new calibration values for the PROM are obtained online (➤3-8) from the vehicle manufacturer's main computer, or from an updated cartridge or disc.

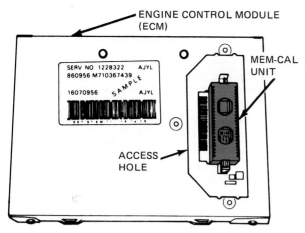

Fig. 20-24 Location of a PROM chip or memory-calibration (MEM-CAL) unit in the electronic control module. *(Cadillac Division of General Motors Corporation)*

Careful! Never touch the connector pins or soldered components on the circuit board of the ECM. Also, never touch the pins or leads of a replaceable PROM or other chip, or remove the chip from its carrier. This prevents possible damage from static electricity.

An improperly-seated or failed PROM will set a trouble code. Some failures in the ECM may not. Most failures blamed on the ECM are not ECM failures. They are dirty or intermittent connections in connectors or the wiring harness. The diagnostic charts and procedures help locate a trouble anywhere in the system through the process of elimination. When all other possible causes have been eliminated, only then is the recommendation made to replace the ECM.

FUEL-SYSTEM SERVICE

➤ 20-17 SERVICING THE FUEL SYSTEM

Review the *fuel-system safety cautions* in ➤20-2 before beginning any work on the fuel system. Then review ➤20-5 on *relieving fuel-line pressure* before loosening or disconnecting any connection.

Improper preparation and work habits may create problems that appear after completion of the service work. One major enemy is dirt. A trace of dirt in the wrong place in the fuel system or fuel injector can cause trouble later. Before beginning any fuel-system service, clean your hands, tools, and workbench.

➤ 20-18 AIR-CLEANER SERVICE

Air-cleaner (➤17-9) service recommendations vary with different manufacturers. The paper *filter element* (Fig. 17-

Fig. 20-25 Replacing the filter element in a remote-mounted air cleaner. *(Ford Motor Company)*

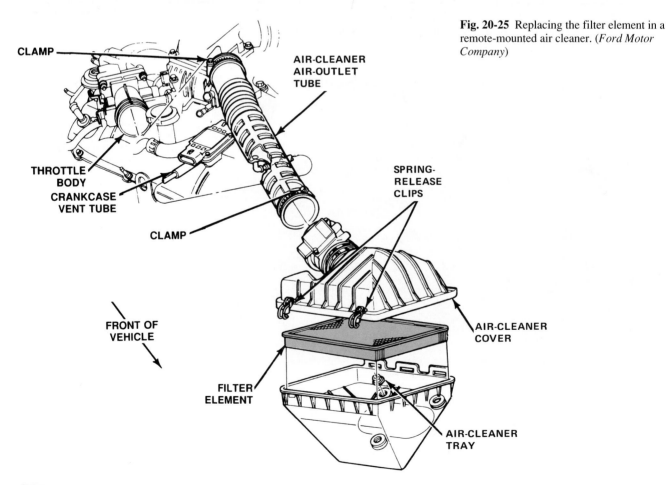

11) should be replaced periodically. Follow the manufacturer's recommendations. One recommendation is to replace the filter element every 52,500 miles [84,500 km] under normal driving conditions. For severe or dusty conditions, inspect and, if necessary, replace the filter element at least every 15,000 miles [24,000 km].

To replace the filter element, remove the cover from the air cleaner (Fig. 20-25). Lift out the filter element and check its condition. An oily filter element usually indicates the *crankcase-ventilating system* (Chap. 36) is carrying oil into the air cleaner.

Wipe all dust and oil out of the air-cleaner housing or tray. Make sure the plastic rings or seals on both sides of the element are smooth and fit properly, top and bottom. Install the filter element and cover.

➤ 20-19 FUEL-FILTER SERVICE

The fuel must pass through two filters (➤17-8) before reaching the fuel injectors. The *intank* or *fuel-pump filter* is on the fuel pickup in the fuel tank (Fig. 17-7B). It does not normally require service. The *inline filter* is in the fuel line between the tank and the injectors (Figs. 20-1 and 20-8). Replace this filter at periodic intervals as recommended by the vehicle manufacturer.

Filters may connect to the fuel lines (➤20-21) with *hose clamps* (Fig. 20-26) and *flare-nut fittings* (➤7-8). Others use *quick-connect couplings* which are not threaded. To disconnect the fuel line, wipe the connections at both ends of the filter. Blow out dirt from around the connections with a blowgun. Release the fuel pressure (➤20-5). Then disconnect the fuel lines from the filter. Some quick-connect couplings unlock by squeezing the plastic tabs and

pulling the connection apart. Others require a special tool to lock and unlock the connection (Fig. 20-27).

Some fuel-line connections are sealed with O-ring seals (Fig. 20-27). Replace any O ring that is cut, nicked, swollen, or distorted.

When installing the inline filter with a quick-connect coupling, put a few drops of clean engine oil on each end of the filter. This makes it easier to reconnect the lines.

➤ 20-20 ELECTRIC FUEL-PUMP SERVICE

Most fuel-injected engines have an electric fuel pump (➤17-7) in the fuel tank (Fig. 17-7B). The pump mounts on the same support as the fuel-gauge unit (Fig. 20-28). To remove the fuel pump, relieve the fuel pressure (➤20-5). Disconnect the electrical connector and fittings on the fuel and vapor lines. Then use a hammer and brass punch to remove the lock ring (Fig. 20-29). It holds the assembly in the tank. The gauge-and-pump assembly can now be removed. The complete assembly is usually replaced if the fuel pump is defective.

Careful! Be sure the fuel level in the tank is below the opening for the gauge-and-pump assembly before removing the fuel lines and lock ring. Liquid gasoline could run out and injure you, or cause an explosion or fire. Drain or pump the fuel in the fuel tank into a fuel safety container (Fig. 4-11) or portable holding tank (Fig. 4-4) if the level is too high. Wrap shop towels around the lines as they are removed to absorb any fuel that leaks out.

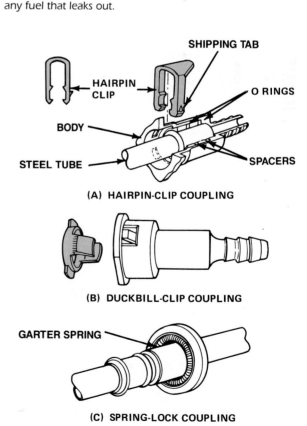

Fig. 20-27 Types of quick-connect fuel-line couplings. (*Champion Spark Plug Company*)

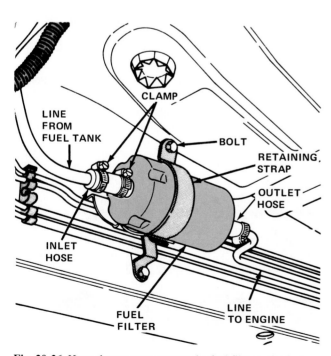

Fig. 20-26 Hose clamps may connect the fuel filter to the fuel line. (*Chrysler Corporation*)

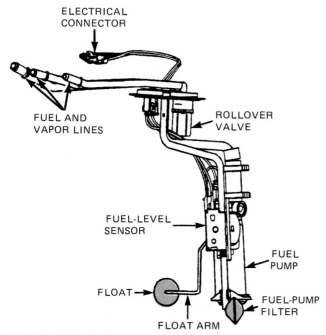

Fig. 20-28 Electric fuel-pump-and-gauge assembly, removed from the fuel tank. (*AC Rochester Division of General Motors Corporation*)

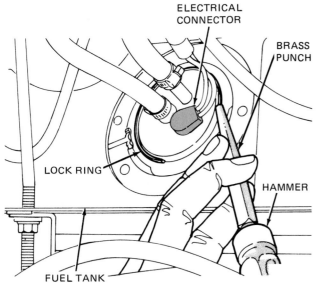

Fig. 20-29 Using a hammer and brass punch to remove the lock ring holding the electric fuel-pump-and-gauge assembly in the fuel tank. (*Chrysler Corporation*)

➤ 20-21 FUEL-LINE SERVICE

Fuel lines are also called *hose, tube,* and *pipe.* A hose is a flexible tube for carrying liquid or vapor. A tube or *tubing* may be flexible or rigid. Pipe is usually rigid. Flexible hose or tubing is called *flex hose* or a *flex line.*

Long fuel lines are usually rigid and made of nylon or steel. A damaged fuel line should be replaced. Quick-connect couplings are used on nylon and some metal lines. Figure 20-30 shows various types of threaded fuel-line

couplings used with metal lines. Use two wrenches to loosen or tighten the coupling without damaging the line (➤7-8). When installing a fuel line with flared ends, be sure the end has the matching *ISO (metric) flare* or a *double flare* (Fig. 7-32). These flares can be made in the shop using the proper flaring tool (Fig. 7-34). Fittings with an ISO flare or a double flare must not be interchanged.

The fuel lines must be well supported and must not rub against sharp corners. They should not be kinked or bent unnecessarily. Use a tube bender (➤7-24) if necessary to shape metal tube. Nylon fuel lines can be damaged by heat and high temperature. Protect or remove nylon lines from the vehicle if grinding, heating, or welding will be done nearby.

When replacing fuel hose, always use new fuel hose that meets or exceeds the vehicle manufacturer's specifications. If the wrong hose is installed, the high pressure in some fuel systems (➤20-5) could cause the hose to leak or split open. A fire or explosion could result.

➤ 20-22 FUEL-GAUGE SERVICE

If the fuel gauge (➤17-20) in the instrument panel is not registering correctly, substitute a new tank unit for the old one. This can be done without removing the old tank unit. Disconnect the tank-unit lead from the electrical connector (Fig. 20-29) and connect the lead to the terminal on the substitute unit. Connect a jumper wire from the metal frame of the substitute unit to a good ground on the car.

Turn the ignition key to ON. Move the float (Fig. 20-28) up and down on the substitute unit. If the instrument-panel unit works, the tank unit is defective. If the instrument-panel unit is defective, it will not register. Other methods of diagnosis may be found in the vehicle service manual.

FUEL-INJECTION SERVICE

➤ 20-23 CLEANING FUEL INJECTORS

Deposits that form on the tip of a fuel injector prevent proper fuel delivery and spray pattern. Driveability problems result such as rough idle, and loss of power and fuel economy. Figure 20-31 compares a dirty injector with

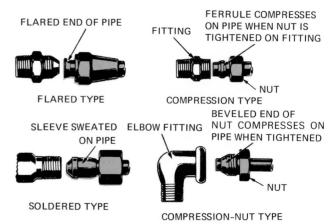

Fig. 20-30 Various types of threaded fuel-line couplings.

a clean injector. One reason deposits form is because heat affects some components of gasoline (Chap. 16). Other reasons include start-and-stop driving and injector design. Some injectors clog more easily than others.

Injectors can be cleaned by a flow of injector-cleaning solvent through them. The solvent removes gum, varnish, and other deposits. To clean the injectors, the engine should be at normal operating temperature. Relieve the fuel pressure (➤20-5) and disable the fuel pump. Remove and plug the vacuum hose at the pressure-regulator valve.

Follow the instructions for the injector-cleaning equipment you are using and connect a container of *injector cleaner* to the fuel rail (Fig. 20-32). The procedure may include first blocking off or clamping shut the fuel-return line to the fuel tank. Another step may be to set the pressure-regulator valve on the injector cleaner to the specified pressure. This will be slightly below the fuel-system pressure. These steps prevent the cleaner pressure from opening the vehicle fuel-pressure regulator and sending cleaner through the fuel-return line to the fuel tank.

Start the engine and let it idle until the container is empty and the engine stalls. This should take about 5 to 10 minutes. Then remove the container, restore the connections, and start the engine. The fuel-injector tester shown in Fig. 20-12 can also be used to clean injectors.

Careful! Injector cleaning uses a pressurized metal or other container filled with a highly volatile liquid. Do not allow the container to short across the battery, contact moving parts, or be exposed to heat exceeding 120°F [49°C]. Always wear eye protection and have a Class B fire extinguisher nearby. To avoid injury, damage, and fire, follow all safety cautions and operating instructions for the injector cleaner you are using. Do not allow any of the cleaner to spill on painted surfaces. Injector cleaner will damage the paint.

Fig. 20-32 Connect a container of fuel injector cleaner to the fuel rail to clean fuel injectors in the engine. (*3M Automotive Trades Division*)

(A.) DIRTY INJECTOR   (B.) CLEAN INJECTOR

Fig. 20-31 Comparing the tip end of a dirty fuel injector with a clean injector. (*3M Automotive Trades Division*)

➤ 20-24 CLEANING THROTTLE BODY

Carbon deposits may build up in the throttle-body bores. Even a small amount of carbon may be enough to limit air flow and set a trouble code. The engine may stall or idle slow and rough. The deposits can be cleaned out using an aerosol can of *carburetor-choke cleaner* (Fig. 20-33) or similar solvent. Disconnect the negative cable from the battery and the inlet-air duct from the throttle body. Cover the throttle-position sensor (TPS) and the idle-air-control

(IAC) valve with a shop towel. Plug the IAC air-inlet passage with a shop towel and block the throttle lever wide open.

Spray the cleaner around the throttle bores and on the back side of the throttle valves. Do not spray the throttle-shaft bearing surfaces. Use a nylon parts-cleaning brush to remove heavy deposits. Then release the throttle lever. Open and close the throttle lever several times to check for free movement.

NOTE | Do not spray rubber or plastic parts with the cleaner. Do not use any cleaner containing methyl ethyl ketone. The container label should read "sensor safe." Do not clean *sludge tolerant* throttle bodies. These are identified by a decal on the throttle body. Cleaning removes a special coating applied to the throttle bores during manufacturing.

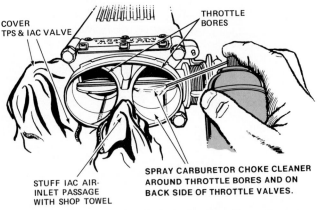

Fig. 20-33 Cleaning out throttle-body deposits with a spray can of carburetor-choke cleaner. (*AC Rochester Division of General Motors Corporation*)

➤ 20-25 THROTTLE-BODY-INJECTION SERVICE

Figure 20-34 shows a disassembled throttle-body-injection assembly. Several repair procedures can be performed with the unit on or off the car. Relieve the fuel pressure (➤20-5) and disconnect the negative cable from the battery. The fuel injector is replaced as a complete assembly. Install the injector using new O rings lubricated with clean engine oil. Do not reuse the O rings.

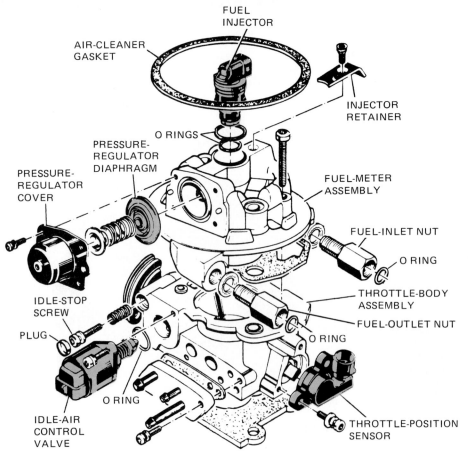

Fig. 20-34 Disassembled throttle-body-injection assembly. (*AC Rochester Division of General Motors Corporation*)

The pressure-regulator diaphragm, idle-air-control valve, and throttle-position sensor can also be replaced. Follow the procedures in the manufacturer's service manual.

➤ 20-26 PORT-INJECTION SERVICE

Figure 20-35 shows a disassembled fuel-rail assembly. Several components in the port-injection system can be serviced. Relieve the fuel pressure (➤20-5) and disconnect the negative cable from the battery. The fuel rail can be disassembled and cleaned or replaced. Some rails and injectors are difficult to reach and remove. Be careful to prevent damaging the electric terminals and spray tips on the injectors. Cap fittings and plug holes to prevent dirt or contaminants from entering components during servicing.

The rails can be cleaned with a special cleaner. Do not soak them in solvent or other liquid cleaner. When replacing injectors or the pressure regulator, use new O rings lubricated with clean engine oil. The throttle body can be cleaned and the throttle-position sensor and idle-air-control valve replaced. Refer to the manufacturer's service manual for procedures on how to perform these and other services.

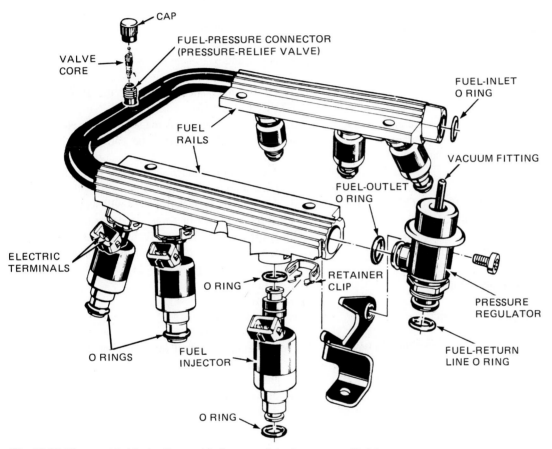

Fig. 20-35 Disassembled fuel-rail assembly for a port-injection system. (*Buick Division of General Motors Corporation*)

TRADE TALK

diagnostic connector	intermittent	scan tool	visual inspection
driveability	monitored circuit	symptom chart	
injection pressure	non-monitored circuit	trouble code	

MULTIPLE-CHOICE TEST

*Select the **one** correct, best, or most probable answer to each question.*
You can find the answers in the section indicated at the end of the question.

1. Technician A says with the air cleaner removed from a TBI unit and the engine idling, you should see fuel spraying from the injector. Technician B says a defective port injector vibrates and makes a clicking sound you can hear with a stethoscope. Who is right? (➤20-4)
   a. A only
   b. B only
   c. both A and B
   d. neither A nor B

2. One way to relieve fuel pressure is to remove the fuel-pump fuse and then (➤20-5)
   a. open the fuel line
   b. wait two hours
   c. run the engine until it stalls
   d. check for trouble codes

3. When the engine is running with a pressure gauge connected to the pressure-relief valve, removing the vacuum hose from the pressure regulator should cause (➤20-9)
   a. the engine to stall
   b. fuel pressure to rise 3 to 10 psi [21 to 69 kPa]
   c. fuel pressure to drop 3 to 10 psi [21 to 69 kPa]
   d. a trouble code to set

4. The ECM can detect all of the following EXCEPT (➤20-12)
   a. sensor voltage within proper range
   b. dirty fuel injectors
   c. oxygen sensor swinging between rich and lean
   d. closed-loop operation

5. Technician A says to get the CHECK ENGINE light to flash on a Ford, turn the ignition key OFF-ON-OFF-ON-OFF. Technician B says the light will flash in a Ford after placing a jumper wire from terminal A to terminal B in the diagnostic connector. Who is right? (➤20-13)
   a. A only
   b. B only
   c. both A and B
   d. neither A nor B

6. A car with an intermittent may NOT show a trouble code because (➤20-14)
   a. the code automatically erased after 50 restarts
   b. the trouble does not occur during monitored conditions
   c. the trouble occurs for too short a time
   d. all of the above

7. The throttle-position sensor can be checked with (➤20-15)
   a. a digital voltmeter
   b. an ohmmeter
   c. both a and b
   d. neither a nor b

8. The following statements about the PROM are true EXCEPT (➤20-16)
   a. A PROM cannot be damaged by static electricity
   b. The PROM stays with the car when the ECM is replaced
   c. A calibration change is made by replacing or reprogramming the PROM
   d. An improperly-seated PROM will set a trouble code

9. Technician A says fuel-injector deposits are caused by long trips on highways. Technician B says deposits form because some components of gasoline are affected by heat. Who is right? (➤20-23)
   a. A only
   b. B only
   c. both A and B
   d. neither A nor B

10. When replacing a fuel injector, coat the O rings with (➤20-25)
    a. gasoline
    b. silicone-rubber sealant
    c. gasket sealer
    d. clean engine oil

REVIEW QUESTIONS

1. Explain how to perform a visual inspection of the fuel system, and describe the indications of a fuel leak. (➤20-3)

2. What does pressure drop tell you about the condition of the pressure regulator and the fuel injectors? (➤20-9 and 20-10)

3. Explain how taking a snapshot or using a recorder helps to diagnose intermittents. (➤20-13)

4. On a car with digital fuel-injection, explain how to make an on-board computer-system diagnosis. (➤20-13)

5. How can the fuel-gauge tank unit be tested without removing it from the vehicle? (➤20-22)

CHAPTER 21

CARBURETORS

After studying this chapter, you should be able to:

- List and describe the operation of the six systems in the fixed-venturi carburetor.
- Explain the venturi effect, and the difference between the fixed-venturi and variable-venturi carburetor.
- Explain how the feedback carburetor works.
- Examine disassembled carburetors, identify the main parts, and explain the purpose of each.

➤ 21-1 PURPOSE AND TYPES OF CARBURETORS

The carburetor (Fig. 21-1) is a mixing device that supplies the engine with a combustible air-fuel mixture. Figure 21-2 shows the three basic parts of a *fixed-venturi* carburetor. These are the *air horn*, the *float bowl*, and the *throttle body* (➤17-11).

The *venturi* is a restricted space through which the air entering the engine must pass. The air movement produces a partial vacuum in the venturi. This is called *venturi vacuum*. The resulting *pressure differential* (➤18-1) causes fuel to discharge from the fuel nozzle into the intake air (Fig. 21-3). This produces the air-fuel mixture for the engine.

Some carburetors have a *variable-venturi*. These are described in ➤21-28.

CARBURETOR INTERNAL SYSTEMS

➤ 21-2 CARBURETOR OPERATION

The float bowl in the carburetor (Figs. 21-3 and 21-4) is supplied with fuel from the fuel tank by a fuel pump. Air passing through the venturi produces a vacuum. Because of the pressure differential, atmospheric pressure pushes fuel

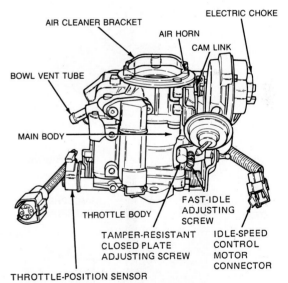

Fig. 21-1 A one-barrel carburetor with throttle-position sensor, idle-speed-control motor, and an electric choke. (*Ford Motor Company*)

from the float bowl up through the fuel nozzle. The fuel then spills out into the passing air.

The *throttle valve* (Fig. 18-1) is the basic control device. As the throttle valve opens, more air passes through which produces a greater vacuum. With a greater vacuum, more fuel discharges from the fuel nozzle. This relationship

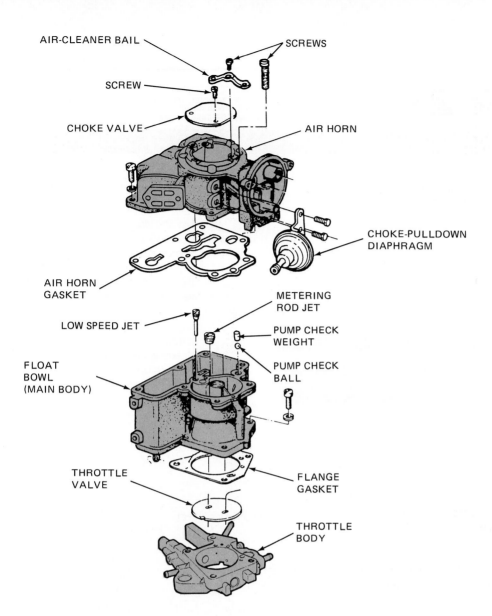

AIR-CLEANER BAIL

SCREWS

SCREW

CHOKE VALVE

AIR HORN

CHOKE-PULLDOWN
DIAPHRAGM

AIR HORN
GASKET

METERING
ROD JET

LOW SPEED JET

PUMP CHECK
WEIGHT

PUMP CHECK
BALL

FLOAT
BOWL
(MAIN BODY)

THROTTLE
VALVE

FLANGE
GASKET

THROTTLE
BODY

Fig. 21-2 The three main parts of a one-barrel carburetor. (*Ford Motor Company*)

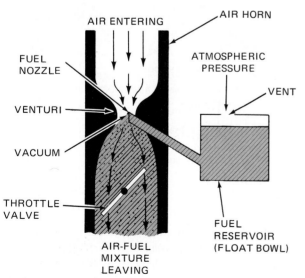

AIR ENTERING

AIR HORN

FUEL
NOZZLE

ATMOSPHERIC
PRESSURE

VENT

VENTURI

VACUUM

THROTTLE
VALVE

FUEL
RESERVOIR
(FLOAT BOWL)

AIR-FUEL
MIXTURE
LEAVING

Fig. 21-3 Actions in a carburetor. Air enters the air horn and picks up fuel from the fuel nozzle. The mixture then flows past the open throttle valve and into the intake manifold.

allows the carburetor to supply the amount of fuel to match the amount of air flowing through. This is the fundamental principle of fuel metering in all carburetors.

➤ 21-3 FIXED-VENTURI CARBURETOR SYSTEMS

The carburetor needs several special systems or *circuits* which change the air-fuel ratio to suit varying operating conditions. These internal systems include:

1. Float system.
2. Idle system.
3. Main metering system.
4. Power system.
5. Accelerator-pump system.
6. Choke system.

Carburetors also have several external devices. These include an idle solenoid, a speedup solenoid, a throttle-return check, and others. They are described in ➤21-25.

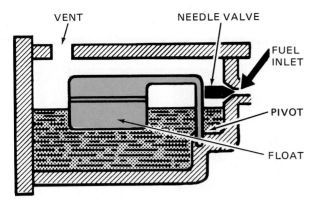

Fig. 21-4 Carburetor float bowl.

➤ 21-4 FLOAT SYSTEM

The float system includes a small fuel reservoir or float bowl with a float and needle valve (Fig. 21-4). The float and needle valve control the fuel level in the float bowl.

The fuel pump (➤17-5) sends fuel under pressure to the float bowl. As the fuel enters, the float rises. This pushes the needle valve toward its seat. As the fuel reaches the correct level, the needle valve shuts off the fuel supply.

When the carburetor withdraws fuel from the float bowl, the float falls. The needle valve moves off its seat so fuel from the fuel pump can enter. In operation, the float and needle valve take a balanced position. The same amount of fuel enters that is being withdrawn.

Improper float level causes the carburetor to deliver an improper air-fuel mixture. If the fuel level is too high, too much fuel will feed from the fuel nozzle. The air-fuel mixture will be too rich. If too low, not enough fuel will feed. The mixture will be too lean. Most carburetors have no external adjustments to change the air-fuel ratio for above-idle operations.

Floats may have many shapes. Figure 21-5 shows a carburetor with a dual float assembly. In some, the needle valve is vertical (Fig. 21-6). Some carburetors have an auxiliary fuel valve and inlet. During heavy loads or high speed, fuel may be withdrawn from the float bowl faster than it enters through the main fuel inlet. If this happens, the fuel level drops. Then, the end of the float lever presses against the auxiliary valve. It opens so more fuel can enter through the auxiliary inlet.

Some floats are hollow and made of brass. Others are made of a solid material that is lighter than gasoline.

➤ 21-5 FLOAT-BOWL VENTS

The float bowls are vented into the air horn at a point above the choke valve (top in Fig. 21-5, upper left in Fig. 21-6). The vent helps equalize the effects of a dirty air cleaner (➤17-9). A restricted air cleaner causes additional vacuum. This adds to the vacuum in the venturi. Then additional fuel flows, producing a rich mixture. The vent to the air horn or *internal vent* carries this same vacuum to the float bowl so the effect is canceled.

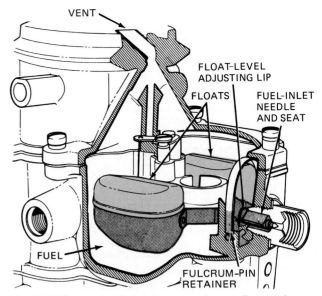

Fig. 21-5 Float system in a carburetor, using two floats and a single needle valve. (*Chrysler Corporation*)

The float bowl also has another vent (upper right in Fig. 21-6). This vent allows fuel vapors from the float bowl to flow into the *charcoal canister* (Chap. 35). After the engine is turned off, engine heat vaporizes some of the fuel in the float bowl. The charcoal canister traps these fuel vapors. This prevents them from escaping and causing air pollution.

➤ 21-6 HOT-IDLE COMPENSATOR VALVE

The internal vent to the air horn could pass enough fuel vapor from the float bowl during hot-idling to upset the

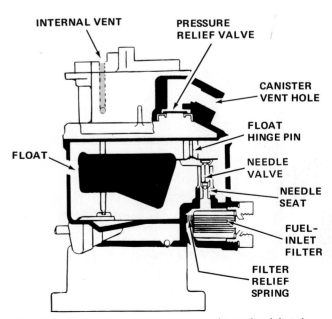

Fig. 21-6 Float system with two vents, one internal and the other to the charcoal canister. (*Chevrolet Division of General Motors Corporation*)

air-fuel ratio. This could excessively enrich the mixture. To prevent this, some carburetors have a *hot-idle compensator valve* attached to a thermostatic blade. When the temperature reaches a preset level, the blade bends enough to open the valve port. Then, additional air flows through the auxiliary air passage, bypassing the idle system. This leans the mixture enough to make up for the added fuel vapor from the float bowl.

➤ 21-7 IDLE SYSTEM

When the throttle valve is closed during idling, very little air passes through the venturi. This creates so little venturi vacuum (➤21-1) that no fuel discharges from the fuel nozzle.

The *idle system* (Fig. 21-7) supplies air-fuel mixture during closed-throttle operation. The high *intake-manifold vacuum* (➤18-1) is applied to the idle-system passages below the throttle valve. The vacuum causes air and fuel to discharge past the tapered point of the *idle-mixture screw*. This produces a very rich mixture, which is leaned out somewhat by the air that passes around the closed throttle valve. The screw usually is not adjustable unless the carburetor is partly disassembled or has been modified.

> **NOTE** The electronic-engine-control system controls idle richness and idle speed on many engines with feedback carburetors. This is explained later.

➤ 21-8 LOW-SPEED OPERATION

When the throttle valve opens slightly (Fig. 21-8 and 21-9), the edge of the throttle valve moves past the *low speed port* or *transfer port*. Additional fuel now feeds through this port. The fuel mixes with the additional air moving past the slightly opened throttle valve. The mixture has the proper richness for low-speed operation.

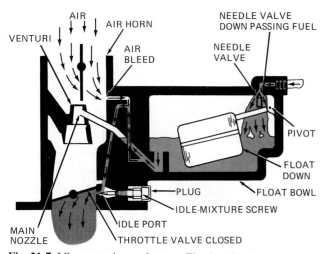

Fig. 21-7 Idle system in a carburetor. The throttle valve is closed so that only a small amount of air can pass. All fuel is being discharged past the idle-mixture screw.

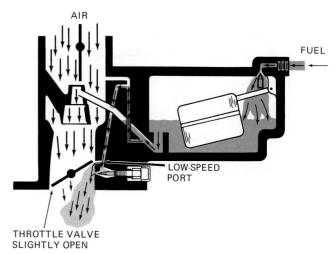

Fig. 21-8 Low-speed operation. The throttle valve is slightly open and fuel is being discharged through the low-speed port and the idle port.

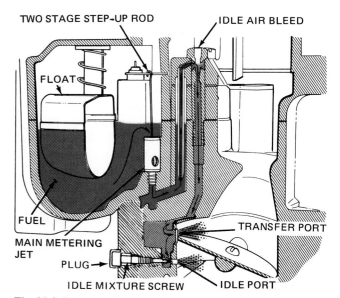

Fig. 21-9 Low-speed system in operation. The throttle valve is moving past the transfer port so additional fuel feeds through it. (*Chrysler Corporation*)

> **NOTE** This system is also called the *transfer system* because it transfers from idling to main-metering operation.

➤ 21-9 MAIN-METERING SYSTEM

When the throttle valve has opened enough so its edge is well past the low-speed port, there is little difference in vacuum between the upper and lower parts of the air horn (Fig. 18-1). Therefore, little air-fuel mixture discharges from the low-speed port.

However, as more air moves through the venturi, the venturi vacuum grows stronger. The fuel nozzle discharges fuel (Fig. 21-10) and the main-metering system takes over. The wider the throttle valve opens, the faster the air flows

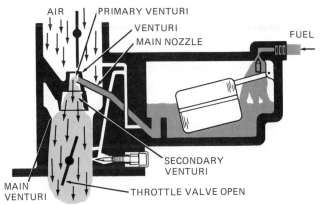

Fig. 21-10 Operation of the main-metering system. The throttle valve is open and the main (high-speed) nozzle is discharging fuel.

through and the greater the venturi vacuum. More fuel discharges from the main nozzle to maintain the proper air-fuel ratio.

| NOTE | Feedback carburetors (➤21-30) have electronic controls that accurately maintain the correct air-fuel ratio for the operating condition. |

➤ 21-10 POWER SYSTEM

For high-speed, full-power, wide-open throttle (WOT) operation, the air-fuel mixture must be enriched. The *power system* produces this enrichment. In older vehicles, power systems are operated mechanically or by intake-manifold vacuum. In newer vehicles with feedback carburetors (➤21-30), the power system is electronically controlled.

➤ 21-11 MECHANICALLY-OPERATED POWER SYSTEM

This system uses a *metering rod* and a *metering-rod jet*. A *jet* is an accurately drilled hole or orifice through which fluid flows. The metering rod has two or more steps of different diameters (Fig. 21-11). The metering rod attaches to the throttle linkage (Fig. 21-12). When the throttle is closed, the metering rod is down. The largest diameter is in the jet. This partly restricts fuel flow to the main nozzle. However, enough flows for part-throttle operation.

When the throttle opens, the rod lifts. This leaves a smaller diameter section of the rod in the jet. The jet is less restricted and more fuel flows for full-power performance.

➤ 21-12 VACUUM-OPERATED POWER SYSTEM

This system operates by intake-manifold vacuum. It includes a spring-loaded vacuum diaphragm linked to a metering rod (Fig. 21-13). When the throttle opens wide, there is little vacuum in the intake manifold. The spring then lowers the diaphragm and metering rod. This moves a

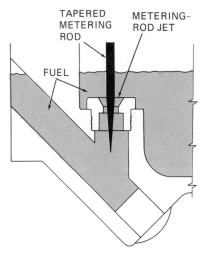

TAPERED METERING ROD

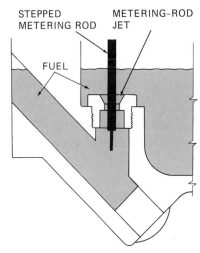

STEPPED METERING ROD

Fig. 21-11 Two types of metering rods that control fuel flow through the metering-rod jets in the power system.

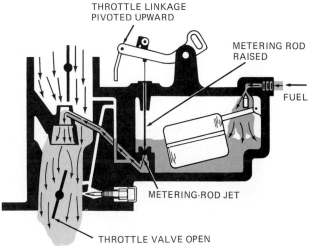

Fig. 21-12 Mechanically-operated power system. When the throttle valve is open (as shown), the metering rod is raised so that the smaller diameter of the rod is in the jet. This allows additional fuel to flow. *(ATW)*

265

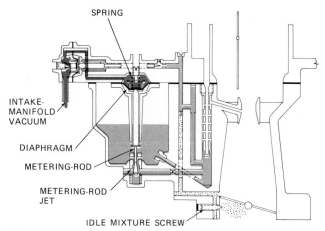

Fig. 21-13 Carburetor with metering rod operated by a vacuum diaphragm. (*Pontiac Division of General Motors Corporation*)

smaller diameter section of the rod into the jet. Now more fuel flows for full-power performance. Instead of a diaphragm, a *power piston* and spring may control the metering rod.

Some carburetors have a combination mechanical-and-vacuum system. The metering rod is linked to both the throttle and a vacuum diaphragm.

➤ 21-13 AIR-FUEL RATIOS WITH DIFFERENT SYSTEMS

Figure 21-14 shows air-fuel ratios with different carburetor systems operating. This is a typical curve only. Air-fuel ratios are different for other carburetors and operating conditions. The idle system supplies a rich mixture for starting. As engine speed increases, the mixture leans out. At intermediate speed, with the throttle valve only partly open, both the idle and main-metering system supply fuel. As the throttle opens wider, the main-metering system takes over completely. At full throttle and higher speeds,

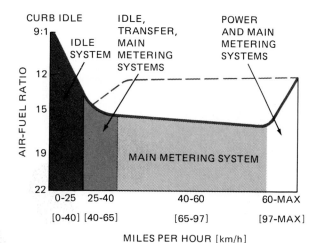

Fig. 21-14 Air-fuel ratios with different carburetor systems operating at different speeds. (*Chevrolet Division of General Motors Corporation*)

the power system comes on. It enriches the air-fuel mixture for full power.

➤ 21-14 AIR BLEED AND ANTISIPHON PASSAGES

All carburetor fuel-metering systems except the accelerator-pump system have small air passages. They allow air to enter or *bleed* into the system. This produces some pre-mixing of air and fuel and helps vaporize the fuel.

The air bleeds are also *antisiphon passages*. They prevent siphoning of fuel from the float bowl. When the engine is turned off, the intake manifold cools and a slight vacuum may form in it. The air bleeds allow air to flow through to satisfy the vacuum. This prevents the vacuum from drawing fuel through the idle system and emptying the float bowl.

➤ 21-15 ACCELERATOR-PUMP SYSTEM

When the throttle valve opens for vehicle acceleration, there is a sudden rush of air through the carburetor. This demands additional fuel. Without it, the engine will hesitate. This *flat spot* could cause the engine to backfire or stall.

The accelerator pump supplies the additional fuel needed for quick acceleration. Figure 21-15 shows one type. It has a pump plunger that is forced down by a pump lever linked to the throttle. When the throttle valve opens, the pump lever releases the *duration spring*. The spring forces the plunger down, sending a squirt of fuel from the pump jet into the air stream. This enriches the air-fuel mixture for quick acceleration.

The duration spring allows the accelerator pump to discharge fuel for about a second, or until the power system takes over. Another type of accelerator pump uses a diaphragm instead of a plunger. When the throttle opens, linkage pushes the pump diaphragm into a fuel-filled chamber. This forces fuel from the pump chamber out the pump jet.

➤ 21-16 FACTORY-ADJUSTED PART THROTTLE (APT)

This system (Fig. 21-16) allows the factory to correct the carburetor for any slight difference in fuel flow due to manufacturing tolerances. A pin in the power piston extends through a slot into a cavity containing the APT screw. Turning the screw raises or lowers the power piston and metering rod. The adjustment is made to minimize exhaust emissions and maximize engine performance.

➤ 21-17 ALTITUDE COMPENSATION

At higher altitudes, atmospheric pressure is lower and the air is less dense. This can cause the carburetor to produce a

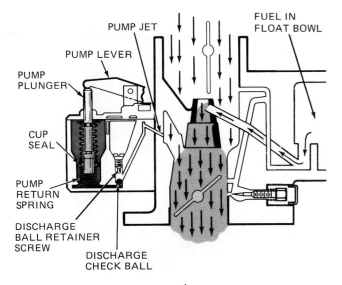

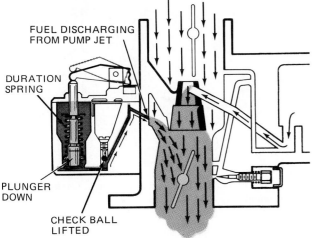

Fig. 21-15 Operation of the accelerator-pump system.

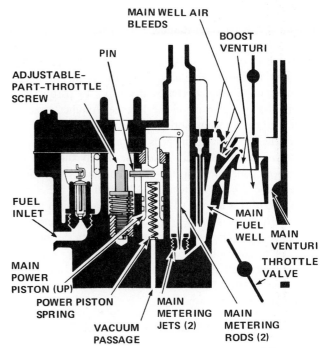

Fig. 21-16 Adjustable-part-throttle (APT) screw, used for making a factory adjustment of the metering rod. (*Chevrolet Division of General Motors Corporation*)

richer mixture with resulting poor engine performance and high exhaust emissions.

To correct for this, some carburetors have an *altitude compensator.* It automatically adjusts the air-fuel mixture for changes in altitude. One device is a small *aneroid barometer,* which is a sealed bellows with a partial vacuum inside it. The bellows expands with lower air pressure. This lowers a metering rod into a jet, reducing the amount of fuel that can flow through.

CARBURETOR CHOKES

➤ 21-18 CHOKE SYSTEMS

To start a cold engine, the carburetor must deliver a very rich mixture. With the carburetor and engine cold, only part of the fuel evaporates. Extra fuel is needed so enough will vaporize to produce a combustible mixture.

During cranking, air speed through the air horn is low. Venturi vacuum is too weak to cause the fuel nozzle or idle

system to deliver fuel. Closing the choke increases the vacuum in the air horn. Then the fuel nozzle delivers enough fuel so the engine can start and run.

The *choke valve* (Fig. 21-17) is a round plate shaped like the throttle valve in the top of the air horn. It is controlled mechanically or automatically.

When the choke valve is closed, it is almost horizontal (Fig. 21-17). Only a small amount of air can get through. The valve has "choked off" the air flow. When the engine cranks, a vacuum develops in the air horn. The vacuum

Fig. 21-17 When the choke valve is closed, little air can get past it. This produces a partial vacuum in the carburetor air horn when the engine is cranked. The partial vacuum causes the main nozzle to discharge fuel.

causes the main nozzle to discharge fuel. This provides the rich mixture needed for starting.

As soon as the engine starts, its speed increases. The engine needs more air and a leaner mixture. One method is to mount the choke valve off center. The vacuum produced by the running engine causes the valve to partly open against the spring in the choke linkage. Another arrangement is to have a small spring-loaded section in the choke valve. The partial vacuum opens it to admit more air.

Mechanically-operated chokes use a pull knob on the instrument panel. Pulling the knob out closes the choke valve. If the driver fails to push the knob in after the engine starts and warms up, the engine will continue to get a very rich mixture. This wastes fuel, causes poor engine performance, loads the combustion chamber with carbon, and pollutes the atmosphere.

To prevent all this, most carburetors have *automatic chokes* (➤21-19). They close when the engine is cold and open as the engine warms up.

➤ 21-19 AUTOMATIC CHOKES

Several types of automatic chokes are described below.

1. SEMI-AUTOMATIC CHOKE WITH AUTOMATIC RETURN This is a pull choke that closes when the choke knob is pulled out. A solenoid holds it closed until the engine warms up. Then a thermostatic switch opens. This turns off the solenoid allowing a spring to open the choke.

2. AUTOMATIC CHOKE The semi-automatic choke is not fast enough. Most carburetors have an automatic choke that works on exhaust manifold temperature and intake-manifold vacuum. These chokes open quickly. This reduces the time the engine gets a rich mixture which causes the exhaust gas to contain excessive HC and CO.

Figure 21-18 shows a carburetor with an automatic choke that works on exhaust-manifold heat and intake-manifold vacuum. It has a thermostatic spring and a vacuum piston. Both are linked to the choke valve. The thermostatic spring winds up or unwinds as temperature changes. The vacuum piston moves back and forth as intake-manifold vacuum changes.

When the engine is cold, the thermostatic spring has wound up so it closes the choke valve. As the engine warms up, the spring unwinds and the choke valve moves toward open. While the engine is cold, opening the throttle will cause the vacuum piston to close the choke valve. This enriches the mixture and prevents stumbling.

3. THERMOSTAT IN MANIFOLD Some V-type engines have the thermostat in a well in the intake manifold (Fig. 21-19). There the thermostat reacts quickly to engine heat as the engine warms up. Some inline engines have the thermostat well in the exhaust manifold.

4. COOLANT-OPERATED CHOKE Some carburetors use heat from the engine coolant to operate the thermostat.

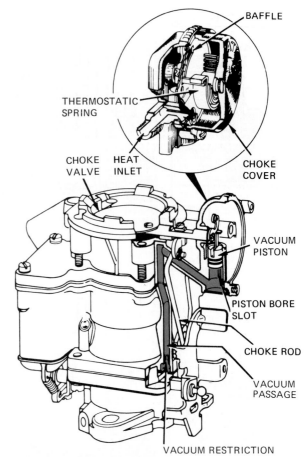

Fig. 21-18 Automatic choke on a carburetor. (*Chrysler Corporation*)

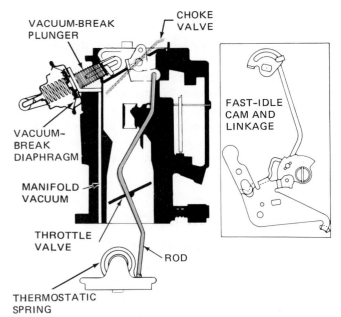

Fig. 21-19 Automatic choke with the thermostat in a well above the exhaust-gas crossover passage in the intake manifold of a V-type engine. (*Chevrolet Division of General Motors Corporation*)

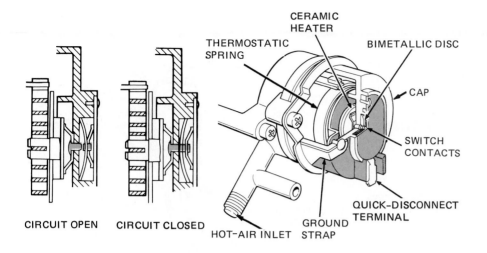

THERMOSTATIC SPRING

CERAMIC HEATER

BIMETALLIC DISC

CAP

SWITCH CONTACTS

QUICK-DISCONNECT TERMINAL

GROUND STRAP

HOT-AIR INLET

CIRCUIT OPEN   CIRCUIT CLOSED

Fig. 21-20 Operation of the electric-assist choke. At low temperatures, the ceramic heater turns on, adding heat so that the thermostatic spring acts more quickly to open the choke valve. (*Ford Motor Company*)

The thermostat housing has a passage through which coolant flows.

5. VACUUM DIAPHRAGM Instead of a vacuum piston, many automatic chokes use a vacuum-operated diaphragm (Fig. 21-19). The diaphragm is called a *vacuum-break* or *vacuum-kick diaphragm* because it can break loose a stuck choke valve. The linkage to the choke-valve lever rides in a slot in the vacuum-break plunger. During warm-up, changing vacuum causes the linkage to hit the end of the slot. This forces open the choke valve. The diaphragm can exert more force than the vacuum piston.

> **NOTE** The vacuum piston and vacuum diaphragm are *choke pulloffs*. When vacuum is applied to them, they pull the choke valve off the closed position.

6. ELECTRIC CHOKE Many carburetors use a choke which includes an electric heating element (Fig. 21-20). The extra heat opens the choke faster. Then the engine has a shorter time to produce excessive HC and CO because of the closed choke.

The electric current to the choke heating element feeds through the oil-pressure switch or a connection to the alternator stator (➤30-1). This prevents choke heating until after the engine starts. If the choke heats before the engine starts, the choke valve might open.

➤ 21-20 FAST IDLE

When a cold engine starts, it must run at fast idle or it will stall. The *fast-idle cam* (Fig. 21-21) is linked to the choke valve. Depressing the accelerator pedal before cranking allows the choke valve to close. At the same time, linkage rotates the fast-idle cam so its highest step is under the *fast-idle adjustment screw*. This holds the throttle valve partly open for fast idle after the engine starts.

As the thermostatic spring warms up and releases the choke, the cam rotates out from under the fast-idle adjustment screw. This may occur one step at a time. When the cam is completely out from under the screw, the engine idles at *slow idle* or *curb idle*.

> **NOTE** Many feedback carburetors have an idle-speed motor controlled by the ECM. It maintains idle speed as required by operating conditions. There is no adjustment.

➤ 21-21 CHOKE UNLOADER

If the engine does not start quickly when cranked with the choke closed, the intake manifold can be *flooded* or *loaded* with liquid gasoline. This makes it harder for the engine to start. However, if the accelerator pedal is pushed to the floor, linkage to the choke opens the choke valve. Then air flows through freely during cranking. The air will carry

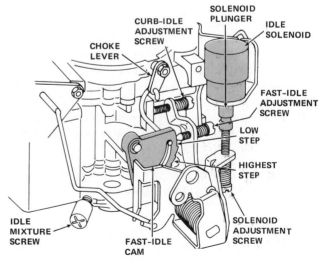

CURB-IDLE ADJUSTMENT SCREW

SOLENOID PLUNGER

IDLE SOLENOID

CHOKE LEVER

FAST-IDLE ADJUSTMENT SCREW

LOW STEP

HIGHEST STEP

IDLE MIXTURE SCREW

FAST-IDLE CAM

SOLENOID ADJUSTMENT SCREW

Fig. 21-21 Carburetor with an idle solenoid. The fast-idle cam is operated by the choke linkage. (*Chrysler Corporation*)

away or *unload* fuel that has collected in the intake manifold. This should allow the engine to start.

MIXTURE HEATING AND EXTERNAL DEVICES

➤ 21-22 MANIFOLD-HEAT-CONTROL VALVE

Fuel vaporizes poorly when the engine is cold. To improve fuel vaporization and cold-engine operation, some engines have a *manifold-heat-control valve*. It sends heat to the intake manifold when the engine is cold.

NOTE	Many engines have a thermostatic air cleaner (➤17-10). This system heats the intake air during cold-engine operation. These engines may not have a heat-control valve. On engines that use both, a vacuum motor operates the heat-control valve instead of a thermostatic spring. This is an *early fuel-evaporation* (EFE) *system* (➤21-23).

1. INLINE ENGINES Inline engines using a heat-control valve have the exhaust manifold under the intake manifold. The exhaust manifold has an opening to a chamber or oven that surrounds a portion of the intake manifold. A heat-control valve is in this opening (Fig. 21-22). A thermostatic spring controls the position of the valve.

When the engine is cold, the spring winds up so the valve is in the cold-engine position (Fig. 21-22, top). After the engine starts, hot exhaust gases circulate around the intake manifold. The heat helps vaporize fuel to improve cold-engine operation. As the engine warms up, the thermostatic spring unwinds and moves the valve to the hot-engine position (Fig. 21-22, bottom). Now the exhaust gases pass directly into the exhaust pipe.

2. V-TYPE ENGINES The intake manifold is between the two banks of cylinders in V-type engines. It has an *exhaust-gas passage* (Fig. 21-23) or *exhaust-crossover passage* through which exhaust gas can pass. One of the exhaust manifolds has a thermostatic valve that closes when the engine is cold. This causes exhaust gas from that manifold to flow through the passage. This adds heat to the intake manifold that improves cold-engine performance. When the engine warms up, the thermostatic valve opens. Exhaust gases then flow from both exhaust manifolds directly into the exhaust pipes.

➤ 21-23 EARLY FUEL EVAPORATION (EFE) SYSTEM

The EFE system uses a vacuum motor instead of a thermostatic spring to control the heat-control valve (Fig. 21-24). The vacuum comes from the intake manifold through a *thermal vacuum switch* (TVS). When the engine is cold, the thermal vacuum switch admits vacuum to the EFE

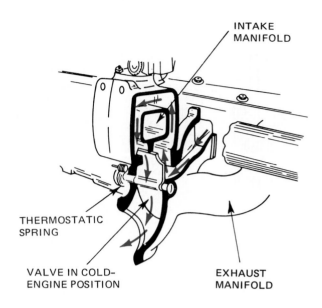

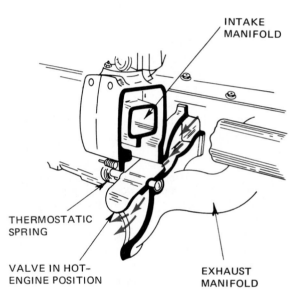

Fig. 21-22 Intake and exhaust manifolds on an inline engine that has a heat-control valve. Top, the valve is in the cold-engine (heat on) position. It is directing hot exhaust gas up and around the intake manifold (as shown by the arrows). Bottom, the valve is in the hot-engine (heat off) position. (*Ford Motor Company*)

motor. It then moves the heat-control valve to the cold-engine position (Fig. 21-22, top). When the engine warms up, the thermal vacuum switch closes. With no vacuum on the EFE motor, the heat-control valve moves to the hot-engine position (Fig. 21-22, bottom).

➤ 21-24 ELECTRIC INTAKE-MANIFOLD HEATER

Some engines use coolant temperature to control an *electric intake-manifold heater* or *grid heater* under the carburetor or throttle body (Fig. 21-25). When the ignition

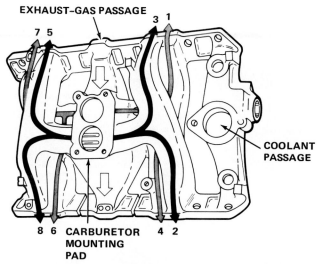

Fig. 21-23 Intake manifold for a V-8 engine. The arrows show the flow of air-fuel mixture from the two barrels of the carburetor to the eight cylinders in the engine. Exhaust gas flows through the crossover passage during engine warm-up. (*Pontiac Division of General Motors Corporation*)

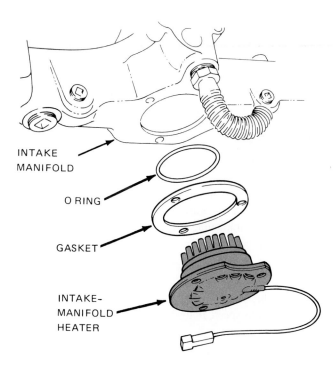

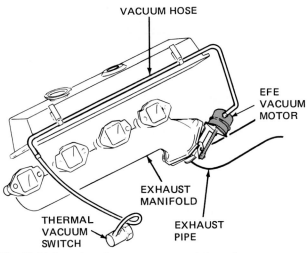

Fig. 21-24 Location of vacuum motor and thermal-vacuum switch in an early-fuel-evaporation (EFE) system. (*Cadillac Division of General Motors Corporation*)

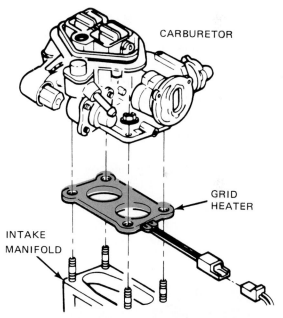

Fig. 21-25 Types of electric intake-manifold heaters. Top, a heater that mounts in the intake manifold. Bottom, a grid-type EFE heater that mounts between the carburetor and the intake manifold. (*Chrysler Corporation; Pontiac Division of General Motors Corporation*)

key is ON and the engine and coolant are cold, contact points close in the *heater relay*. This connects the heater to the battery. The heater begins to warm the intake manifold. This improves fuel vaporization and engine performance. As the engine warms up, the relay disconnects the heater from the battery. On many engines, operation of the electric heater is controlled by the engine computer or ECM.

➤ 21-25 EXTERNAL CARBURETOR DEVICES

Carburetors have several add-on devices that improve driveability and fuel economy. Some also help reduce air pollution.

1. IDLE SOLENOID Some engines *run-on* after turning the ignition key OFF. This is *dieseling* and results from incomplete closing of the throttle valve. It permits air-fuel mixture to feed through the idle system. Hot spots in the combustion chambers act like spark plugs. Dieseling or run-on can damage the engine.

To prevent dieseling, many carburetors have an *anti-dieseling* or *idle solenoid* (Fig. 21-21). When the engine is running, the battery connects to the solenoid and its plunger extends. The plunger serves as the *idle stop*. A "stop" is a device that halts or blocks movement. Turning the ignition key OFF disconnects the solenoid and the plunger retracts. The throttle valve closes completely, shutting off all air flow so run-on cannot occur.

Another arrangement shuts off fuel flow in the idle system when the ignition key is OFF. The engine cannot run without fuel.

2. ELECTRIC SPEEDUP SOLENOID Many air-conditioned vehicles have this solenoid. It looks like the idle solenoid. However, its purpose is to increase engine idle speed when the air conditioner is turned on. This prevents engine stalling at idle due to the extra load of the air-conditioning compressor.

3. IDLE SPEED-CONTROL MOTOR Many feedback carburetors have an *idle-speed control* (ISC) *motor* controlled by the ECM (Fig. 21-26). The ISC motor maintains the proper idle speed if load conditions change. It is not adjustable.

4. ELECTRIC SWITCHES Many carburetors have an electric switch that produces a signal or controls another device when the throttle position changes. For example, a *kickdown switch* (➤48-17) causes the automatic transaxle or transmission to downshift when the accelerator pedal is floored. A *cutout switch* (➤55-25) disengages the air-conditioning compressor at wide-open throttle (WOT). Then more engine power is available to move the car.

5. THROTTLE-POSITION SENSOR (TPS) If the engine has an electronic control system, the ECM must always know the position of the throttle valve. The TPS (Fig. 21-26) continuously reports this information to the ECM (➤19-10).

6. THROTTLE-RETURN CHECK If the throttle closes too fast after the driver releases the accelerator pedal, the air-fuel mixture can become momentarily too rich. This is

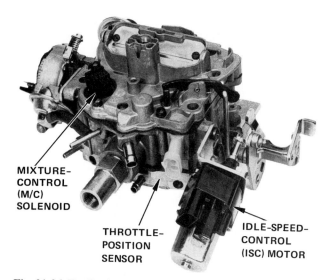

Fig. 21-26 Feedback carburetor that uses an idle-speed-control (ISC) motor to maintain idle speed. (*Pontiac Division of General Motors Corporation*)

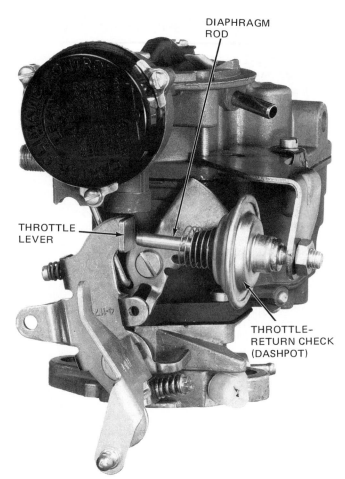

Fig. 21-27 Carburetor with a throttle-return check or dashpot. (*Carter Carburetor Division of ACF Industries*)

because the fuel nozzle continues to dribble fuel for a moment after the air flow is closed off. Also, the idle system may feed fuel. The engine may hesitate or stumble, and have high exhaust emissions of HC and CO. This is because the engine is running fast with the throttle-valve closed, causing high intake-manifold vacuum. Fuel droplets vaporize readily under low pressure (high vacuum).

Many carburetors have a *throttle-return check* or *dashpot* (Fig. 21-27) to prevent these problems. It slows throttle closing so the momentary excessive richness is avoided.

| NOTE | Carburetors with an idle solenoid (Fig. 21-21) do not require a throttle-return check. |

MULTIPLE-BARREL AND VARIABLE-VENTURI CARBURETORS

➤ 21-26 TWO-BARREL AND FOUR-BARREL CARBURETORS

Many small automotive engines use single-barrel carburetors (Fig. 21-2). However, two-barrel and four-barrel carburetors generally provide better engine performance. The added barrel or barrels improve engine breathing or volumetric efficiency (➤15-12), especially at high speed. Multiple barrels allow more air-fuel mixture to enter the engine. A single large-diameter barrel provides a venturi vacuum so weak it cannot be used to control the air-fuel ratios.

1. TWO-BARREL CARBURETOR This is basically two single-barrel carburetors in a single assembly (Fig. 21-28). The second barrel is used in two ways. One way has each barrel supplying the air-fuel mixture for half of the engine cylinders. For example, Fig. 21-23 shows the intake manifold for a V-8 engine using a two-barrel carburetor. One barrel supplies cylinders 2, 3, 5, and 8. The other barrel supplies cylinders 1, 4, 6, and 7. Each barrel has a complete set of systems. The throttle valves attach to a single shaft operated by the throttle lever, and open and close together.

The second design is a *staged carburetor* used on inline four and V-6 engines. The primary barrel supplies all cylinders until its throttle valve opens more than 45 degrees. Then linkage between the two throttle valves starts to open the secondary throttle valve. Further opening of the primary throttle valve opens the secondary throttle valve enough so it also begins to supply air-fuel mixture to all barrels. This imporves medium- to high-speed operation.

2. FOUR-BARREL CARBURETOR This is basically two two-barrel staged carburetors in a single assembly (Fig. 21-29). It is called a *Quadrajet* by General Motors. One pair of barrels makes up the primary side, the other two barrels make up the secondary side. The primary barrels handle all engine cylinders until the throttle valves move toward wide-open. Then the secondary barrels open. They supply additional air-fuel mixture for acceleration and full-power operation.

➤ **21-27 MULTIPLE CARBURETORS**

Some high-performance engines use more than one carburetor. An engine with two carburetors has *dual carburetors*. Three carburetors on an engine are *triple carbu-*

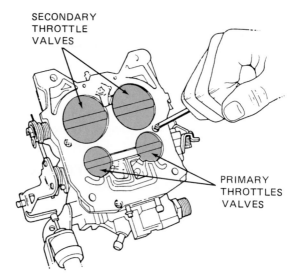

Fig. 21-29 Throttle body of a four-barrel carburetor, showing the locations of the four throttle valves. (*Oldsmobile Division of General Motors Corporation*)

retors. Many racing engines and motorcycles have a separate carburetor for each cylinder.

➤ **21-28 VARIABLE-VENTURI (VV) CARBURETORS**

This carburetor has a venturi that changes size in relation to changes in intake-manifold vacuum. Many imported cars and motorcycles have used the round-piston or *slide-valve* type (Fig. 21-30). The piston moves up and down in

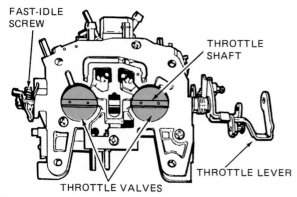

Fig. 21-28 Throttle body of a two-barrel carburetor, showing the locations of the two throttle valves. (*Oldsmobile Division of General Motors Corporation*)

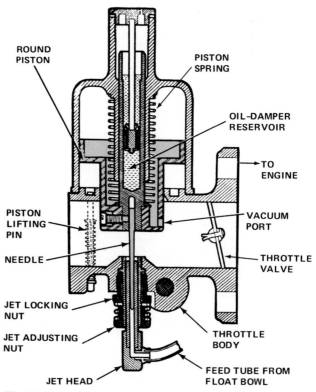

Fig. 21-30 Round-piston variable-venturi (VV) carburetor. (*British Leyland, Limited*)

its chamber as the vacuum between the throttle valve and piston changes. This causes the attached tapered needle to move in or out of the jet, controlling fuel flow.

The Ford rectangular venturi-valve carburetor (Fig. 21-31) was used in some Ford cars for several years starting in 1978. As intake-manifold vacuum changes, *venturi valves* move back and forth across the top of the carburetor. Metering rods attached to the venturi valves move in and out of *main jets* (Fig. 21-32) to control fuel delivery.

➤ 21-29 ELECTRONIC CONTROL OF AIR-FUEL RATIOS

The idle, low-speed, and power systems previously described depend on mechanical controls. These are not as accurate as emission-control laws require (➤16-1). Inaccurate fuel metering can cause the cylinders to receive a rich mixture. The result is excessive hydrocarbons (HC) and carbon monoxide (CO) in the exhaust gas as well as poor engine performance. An excessively lean mixture produces

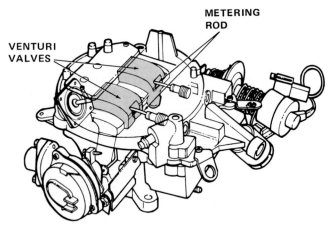

Fig. 21-31 Ford rectangular-piston variable-venturi (VV) carburetor. (*Ford Motor Company*)

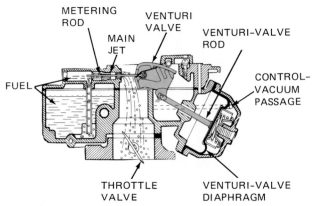

Fig. 21-32 The venturi valves slide back and forth across the top of the carburetor. This varies the size of the openings or venturis through which air enters the engine. (*Ford Motor Company*)

nitrogen oxides (NO_x) and poor engine performance.

For these reasons, more recent carbureted fuel systems are electronically controlled. The system is similar to the electronic fuel-injection system (Chap. 19). An oxygen sensor (➤19-17) monitors the amount of oxygen in the exhaust gas. The oxygen sensor sends a varying voltage signal to the electronic control module (ECM). The ECM then signals the carburetor, as necessary, to adjust the air-fuel mixture so it will provide the correct ratio for the operating conditions.

FEEDBACK CARBURETORS

➤ 21-30 ELECTRONICALLY-CONTROLLED CARBURETORS

Modern fuel systems, both fuel-injected and carbureted, are electronically controlled. Chapter 19 describes electronic fuel-injection systems. Operation of the carbureted electronic engine control system (Fig. 21-33) is very similar. The major difference is that the ECM sends pulses to a carburetor *mixture-control solenoid* (➤21-31) instead of to a fuel injector.

NOTE Ford has a similar electronically-controlled carburetor. It uses a vacuum-controlled metering valve instead of a mixture-control solenoid to vary the air-fuel ratio.

➤ 21-31 MIXTURE-CONTROL SOLENOID

A mixture-control solenoid (Figs. 21-26 and 21-34) controls mixture richness in many feedback carburetors (➤21-30). The solenoid replaces the vacuum- or mechanically-operated power system (➤21-10). A plunger extends from the solenoid. The tipped end acts like the metering rod (Figs. 21-12 and 21-13). It moves up and down to control fuel flow through the jet or *main-well passage*.

The ECM turns the solenoid on and off very rapidly by grounding and ungrounding the solenoid coil. This happens 10 times per second. When the solenoid is OFF, a spring holds the plunger up (Fig. 21-35, left). This allows more fuel to flow through the passage. The mixture is rich, with an air-fuel ratio of about 13:1. When the solenoid is ON, the plunger moves down. This restricts fuel flow (Fig. 21-35, right) and provides a lean air-fuel ratio of about 18:1.

The ECM tries to hold the air-fuel mixture at the stoichiometric ratio of 14.7:1. It does this by varying the *pulse width* (➤19-7). Figure 21-36 shows the relationship between pulse width and solenoid ON time. Fuel delivery (Fig. 21-35) depends on how long the plunger remains up or down during each *duty cycle*.

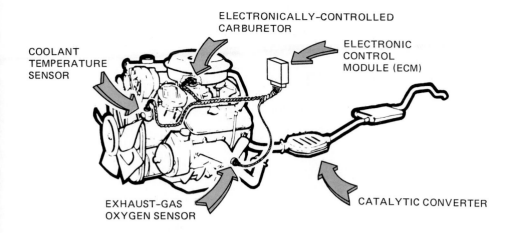

ELECTRONICALLY-CONTROLLED
CARBURETOR

ELECTRONIC
CONTROL
MODULE (ECM)

COOLANT
TEMPERATURE
SENSOR

EXHAUST-GAS
OXYGEN SENSOR

CATALYTIC CONVERTER

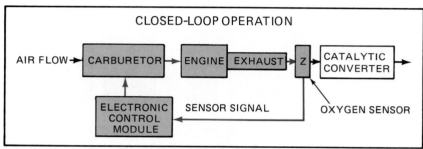

CLOSED-LOOP OPERATION

AIR FLOW → CARBURETOR → ENGINE → EXHAUST → Z → CATALYTIC CONVERTER →

ELECTRONIC CONTROL MODULE

SENSOR SIGNAL

OXYGEN SENSOR

Fig. 21-33 Electronic engine control system for a carbureted engine. Top, major components in the system. Bottom, diagram showing closed-loop operation. The oxygen sensor is reporting the exhaust-gas oxygen content to the electronic control module (ECM). The ECM then adjusts the carburetor to achieve the proper air-fuel ratio for the operating conditions. (*Rochester Products Division of General Motors Corporation*)

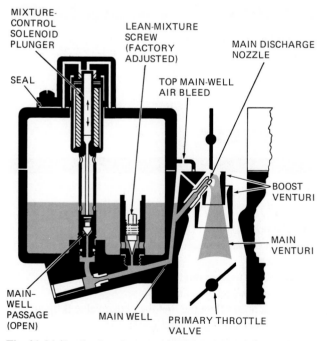

MIXTURE-
CONTROL
SOLENOID
PLUNGER

LEAN-MIXTURE
SCREW
(FACTORY
ADJUSTED)

MAIN DISCHARGE
NOZZLE

SEAL

TOP MAIN-WELL
AIR BLEED

BOOST
VENTURI

MAIN
VENTURI

MAIN-
WELL
PASSAGE
(OPEN)

MAIN WELL

PRIMARY THROTTLE
VALVE

Fig. 21-34 Feedback carburetor with the main-metering system controlled by a mixture-control solenoid. (*Chevrolet Division of General Motors Corporation*)

> **NOTE** To richen the mixture in a feedback carburetor, the ECM shortens the pulse width. To richen the mixture in a fuel-injected engine (➤19-7), the ECM widens the pulse width.

During closed-loop operation (➤19-17), the oxygen sensor reports to the ECM. If the oxygen content of the exhaust gas is high, the mixture is lean. The ECM then shortens the pulse width so the spring keeps the plunger raised longer (Fig. 21-36, left). If the oxygen sensor reports that the oxygen content is low, the mixture is rich. The ECM widens the pulse width to hold the plunger down longer (Fig. 21-36, right). This closes the main-well passage longer and leans the mixture.

Contact-point ignition systems (Chap. 31) use a *dwellmeter* (➤37-4) to measure *dwell*. This is the length of time that the contact points are closed and current flows in the primary winding of the ignition coil. A *high-impedance* dwellmeter that draws little current from the circuit can also be used to measure the duty cycle, or on and off time, of the mixture-control solenoid. If connecting the dwellmeter causes a change in engine performance, use a different dwellmeter.

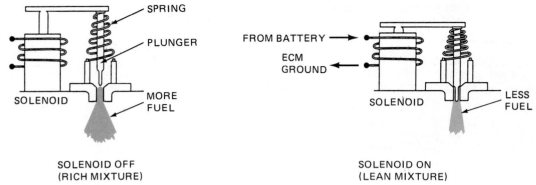

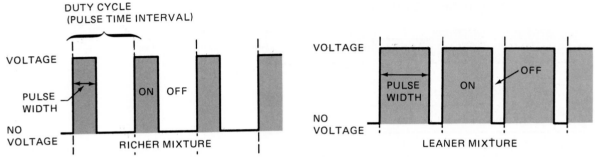

Fig. 21-35 How operation of the mixture-control solenoid affects fuel delivery. (*John Fluke Manufacturing Company, Inc.*)

Fig. 21-36 How the pulse width and solenoid ON time causes a richer or leaner mixture. (*John Fluke Manufacturing Company, Inc.*)

TRADE TALK

air bleed	feedback carburetor	manifold heat-control valve	venturi
altitude compensator	float bowl	mixture-control solenoid	
choke unloader	idle solenoid	variable venturi	

MULTIPLE-CHOICE TEST

Select the **one** *correct, best, or most probable answer to each question.*
You can find the answers in the section indicated at the end of the question.

1. The fuel in the float bowl is kept at a constant level by the action of the (➤21-4)
   a. float and needle valve
   b. pressure regulator
   c. opening of the throttle valve
   d. fuel pump

2. The transfer port comes into operation (➤21-8)
   a. as engine speed approaches a maximum
   b. during low-speed operation
   c. when the engine is idling
   d. after the engine is turned off

3. The power system (➤21-10)
   a. is operated mechanically, by vacuum, or electronically
   b. is not used in modern carburetors
   c. requires a solenoid
   d. increases the time that the choke valve is open

4. The accelerator pump has (➤21-15)
   a. a piston or diaphragm
   b. a duration spring
   c. linkage to the throttle
   d. all of the above

276

5. The automatic choke has (➤21-19)
   a. a vacuum piston or diaphragm
   b. a thermostatic coil
   c. linkage to the choke valve
   d. all of the above
6. The fast-idle cam is positioned by (➤21-20)
   a. the throttle valve
   b. adjusting the idle screw
   c. the automatic choke
   d. idle speed
7. The manifold heat-control valve (➤21-22)
   a. adds heat to the intake manifold when the engine is cold
   b. prevents overheating of the intake manifold
   c. improves high-speed performance
   d. all of the above

8. All the following are true about two- and four-barrel carburetors EXCEPT (➤21-26)
   a. Additional barrels improve high-speed performance.
   b. Primary barrels are for idling.
   c. Additional barrels improve low-speed performance.
   d. Secondary barrels are for acceleration and full power.
9. In the Ford variable-venturi carburetor, the position of the venturi valves and metering rods is controlled by (➤21-29)
   a. intake-manifold vacuum
   b. venturi vacuum
   c. fast-idle cam
   d. slow-idle cam
10. In a feedback carburetor, the mixture-control solenoid (➤21-31)
   a. opens wider to deliver more fuel
   b. controls fuel pressure by changing how far it opens
   c. is OFF longer to deliver more fuel
   d. controls air flow into the idle system

REVIEW QUESTIONS

1. Describe the actions that cause fuel to flow from the fuel nozzle into the air passing through the carburetor. (➤21-1)
2. Explain how a closed choke valve causes the carburetor to deliver a richer air-fuel mixture. (➤21-18)
3. How does the idle solenoid help prevent dieseling? (➤21-25)

4. What are the differences between a fixed-venturi carburetor and a variable-venturi carburetor? (➤21-1 and 21-28)
5. Explain how the mixture-control solenoid is controlled in a feedback carburetor. (➤21-30 and 21-31)

CHAPTER 22

CARBURETED FUEL SYSTEMS: DIAGNOSIS AND SERVICE

After studying this chapter, and with proper instruction and equipment, you should be able to:

* List the various troubles in carbureted fuel systems and describe their possible causes.
* Diagnose carbureted fuel system troubles.
* Test and replace fuel pumps.
* Adjust carburetor choke and idle settings.
* Rebuild, service, and adjust various carburetors.

➤ **22-1 CARBURETED FUEL-SYSTEM DIAGNOSIS AND SERVICE**

Carbureted fuel systems (Fig. 22-1) have many of the same problems and require many of the same procedures as fuel-injected fuel systems. Chapter 20 covers the diagnosis and service of fuel-injected fuel systems. Fuel-system safety cautions are described in ➤20-2. These apply equally to carbureted fuel systems. Chapter 4 describes safety cautions for working around gasoline. Review these and the safety cautions in ➤20-2 before beginning any diagnosis and service work on the fuel system or carburetor. Additional safety cautions are listed below.

* *Caution 1:* Never remove the carburetor from a hot engine. Spilled gasoline could ignite on hot engine parts and cause an explosion or fire.

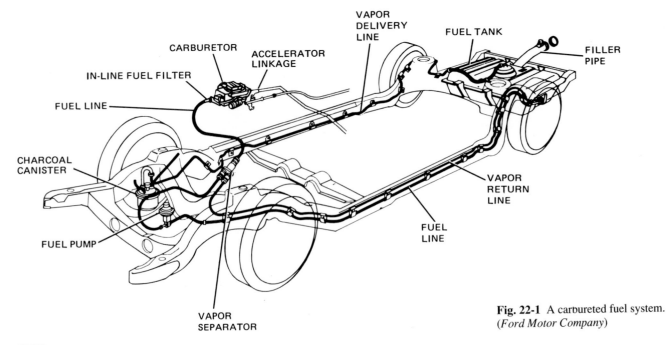

Fig. 22-1 A carbureted fuel system. (*Ford Motor Company*)

- *Caution 2:* Never stand in line with the engine fan while it is turning. A blade may break off and strike you, causing injury or death.

Air-cleaner service, relieving fuel-line pressure, fuel-line connections and service, and servicing fuel filters, electric fuel pumps, and fuel-gauge tank units are described in Chap. 20. Testing and servicing the thermostatic air cleaner (➤17-10) is covered in Chap. 36 on servicing emission-control systems.

CARBURETED FUEL-SYSTEM TROUBLE DIAGNOSIS

➤ 22-2 DIAGNOSING TROUBLES IN CARBURETED FUEL SYSTEMS

Much of the diagnostic information in Chap. 20 applies to carbureted fuel systems. This includes the general procedures for performing a visual inspection (➤20-3) and relieving fuel-line pressure (➤20-5). Using the on-board diagnostics, retrieving trouble codes, and interpreting the codes and scan data also apply to electronically-controlled carburetor systems. The use of the scan tool and service-bay diagnostic computer are similar. Code and symptom charts and other diagnostic aids are in the vehicle service manuals.

Computer-controlled or *feedback carburetor* systems (Fig. 22-2) have many of the same sensors as electronic fuel injection systems (Chap. 19). Both systems have an electronic-control module (ECM), throttle-position sensor, coolant-temperature sensor, manifold-absolute-pressure sensor, oxygen sensor, engine-speed sensor, and others. A major difference is that the ECM controls fuel delivery from the carburetor instead of from fuel injectors. Diagnosis and testing of sensors is described in ➤20-15. ECM diagnosis is covered in ➤20-16.

Many fuel-system and carburetor troubles are not caused by the electronic control system. They are caused by the filters, fuel lines, vacuum and vapor hose, and the fuel pump (➤17-5) and carburetor. These troubles and other driveability problems are described below.

➤ 22-3 MECHANICAL FUEL-PUMP TROUBLES

Listed below are fuel-system troubles that may be caused by the *engine-driven* or *mechanical fuel pump* (Fig. 22-1).

1. INSUFFICIENT FUEL DELIVERY This could result from low pressure due to any of the following conditions in the fuel pump:

a. Broken, worn-out, or cracked diaphragm.
b. Improperly operating fuel-pump valves.
c. Broken or damaged fuel-pump rocker arm.
d. Clogged fuel-pump filter or inlet screen.

Other conditions could prevent normal fuel delivery. These include a clogged vent in the fuel-tank cap, restricted fuel line or filter, air leaks into the fuel line, and vapor lock. In the carburetor, an incorrect float level, a

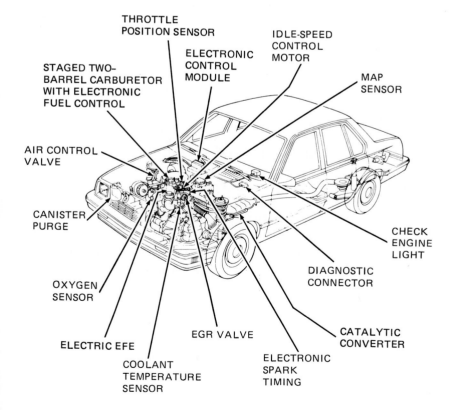

Fig. 22-2 Fuel system using a feedback carburetor, with the sensors and related devices. (*Chevrolet Division of General Motors Corporation*)

THROTTLE POSITION SENSOR
IDLE-SPEED CONTROL MOTOR
ELECTRONIC CONTROL MODULE
STAGED TWO-BARREL CARBURETOR WITH ELECTRONIC FUEL CONTROL
MAP SENSOR
AIR CONTROL VALVE
CANISTER PURGE
CHECK ENGINE LIGHT
OXYGEN SENSOR
DIAGNOSTIC CONNECTOR
ELECTRIC EFE
EGR VALVE
CATALYTIC CONVERTER
COOLANT TEMPERATURE SENSOR
ELECTRONIC SPARK TIMING

clogged inlet screen, or a malfunctioning needle valve prevents normal fuel delivery to the float bowl.

2. EXCESSIVE FUEL-PUMP PRESSURE High fuel-pump pressure causes delivery of too much fuel to the carburetor. The excessive pressure forces the needle valve off its seat, raising the fuel level too high in the float bowl.

3. FUEL-PUMP LEAKS Fuel-pump leaks allow gasoline to get into the engine oil pan faster than the crankcase ventilating system can remove it. Most fuel pumps are assembled by pinching or *crimping* the top and bottom together. An improper crimp may allow the diaphragm to leak around the edges, or the diaphragm may be damaged. If the fuel pump leaks, replace it. Leaks may also occur at loose fuel-line connections.

4. FUEL-PUMP NOISES A noisy pump is usually the result of worn or broken parts in the pump. These include a weak or broken rocker-arm spring, a worn or broken rocker-arm pin or rocker arm, or a broken diaphragm spring. In addition, a loose fuel pump or a scored rocker arm or cam on the camshaft may cause noise. Fuel-pump noise may sound like engine valve-tappet noise. It occurs at camshaft speed. A loud noise can be felt by touching the fuel pump with your hand (if this can be done safely). The noise may also be isolated using an automotive stethoscope. Tappet noise (➤38-19) is usually heard all along the engine.

➤ 22-4 TESTING MECHANICAL FUEL PUMPS

Mechanical fuel pumps are tested on the engine. Tests are made for pressure, volume, and vacuum. Connect the pressure gauge at the carburetor (Fig. 22-3). If the fuel pump has a vapor-return line (➤17-6), squeeze it closed. With the engine idling, the gauge shows fuel-pump pressure. Typical mechanical fuel-pump pressure is from 4 to 7 psi [27.6 to 48.3 kPa].

Place the end of the flexible hose in a graduated container. Open the hose restrictor for 30 seconds. With the engine idling, a good mechanical fuel pump delivers one pint [0.47 liter] or more of fuel in 30 seconds or less.

Stop the engine and connect a vacuum gauge to the fuel-pump fuel inlet or vacuum side. Then start the engine and let it idle on the fuel in the float bowl. A minimum vacuum reading is usually 10 inches [250 mm] mercury (Hg) at idle.

Replace the fuel pump if it does not meet the manufacturer's specifications for these tests. Sometimes the tests are made while cranking the engine instead of with it running.

➤ 22-5 CARBURETOR TROUBLES

Listed below are various engine troubles that can be caused by the carburetor. Many other conditions can also cause some of these troubles. Chapters 37 and 38 cover the testing and diagnosis of engines and related systems.

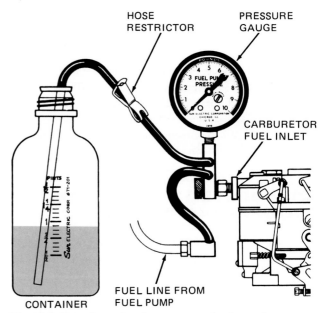

Fig. 22-3 Setup for testing the pressure and volume of a mechanical fuel pump. (*Sun Electric Corporation*)

1. Excessive fuel consumption can result from:
   a. High float level, or a heavy or fuel-soaked float.
   b. Sticking or dirty needle valve.
   c. Worn jets or nozzles.
   d. Stuck metering rod or power piston.
   e. Rich mixture or high fast idle.
   f. Stuck accelerator-pump check valve.
   g. Leaky carburetor.
   h. High fuel-pump pressure.
   i. Sticking or improperly-adjusted choke.
   j. Leaking power-valve diaphragm.
   k. Vacuum leaks.
   l. Faulty or improperly-adjusted throttle-position sensor.

2. Lack of engine power, acceleration, or high-speed performance can result from:
   a. The power step on the metering rod not clearing the jet.
   b. Dirt or gum clogging the fuel nozzle or jets.
   c. Stuck power piston or valve.
   d. Low float level.
   e. Dirty air filter.
   f. Stuck or non-operating choke.
   g. Air leaks into intake manifold.
   h. Throttle valve not open fully.
   i. Manifold heat-control valve stuck closed (Fig. 22-4).

3. Poor or rough idle can result from a leaky vacuum hose, stuck PCV valve, or retarded ignition timing. It could also be due to a clogged idle system or any of the causes listed in number 2 above.

4. Failure of the engine to start unless primed (by the accelerator pump) could be due to:
   a. No fuel in tank or carburetor.
   b. Wrong cap on fuel tank.
   c. Clogged fuel-tank vent.

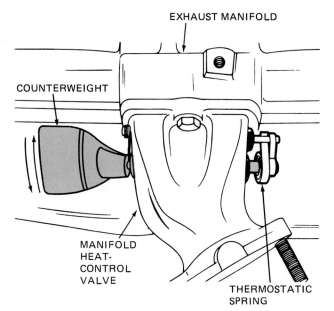

Fig. 22-4 Exposed parts of the manifold heat-control valve. (*Ford Motor Company*)

Labels in figure: EXHAUST MANIFOLD, COUNTERWEIGHT, MANIFOLD HEAT-CONTROL VALVE, THERMOSTATIC SPRING

  d. Air leaks into mechanical fuel pump due to poor connections or holes in flex hose.

  e. Clogged fuel line or carburetor jets.

  f. Choke not closing.

  g. Long delay between turning ignition key ON and cranking engine, allowing electric choke to release.

  h. Leaking float bowl.

5. Hard starting with engine warm could be due to a defective choke or closed choke valve, or the manifold-heat-control valve stuck closed (Fig. 22-4).

6. Slow engine warm-up could be due to a defective choke or manifold-heat-control valve stuck open.

7. Smoky, black exhaust gas is due to a very rich mixture. Carburetor conditions that could cause this are listed in number 1 above.

8. Engine stalling as it warms up could be due to an improperly-adjusted choke valve, defective choke pull-off, fast-idle speed too low, low fuel-pump capacity, or low float level in carburetor.

9. Engine stalling after high-speed driving could be due to a defective dashpot (➤21-26) or valve in the thermostatic air cleaner (Fig. 17-15).

10. Engine backfire can be caused by an excessively rich or lean mixture. If the backfire is in the exhaust system during deceleration, the cause is a rich mixture. Lean mixtures usually cause a popback in the carburetor. Backfiring may also be caused by the engine valves.

11. If the engine runs but misses, a vacuum hose may be off the intake-manifold fitting, causing the nearest cylinder to miss. Missing can also be caused by a leaking intake-manifold gasket. Also, the proper amount and ratio of air-fuel mixture may not be reaching the cylinders. This is possibly due to a worn carburetor jet or incorrect fuel level in the float bowl.

NOTE Some of the above conditions can be corrected by carburetor adjustment. Others require removal of the carburetor from the engine. Then the carburetor can be disassembled and repaired.

➤ 22-6 CARBURETOR QUICK CHECKS

A quick check can indicate if a carburetor system is working properly. More accurate diagnosis may require a vacuum gauge or *exhaust-gas analyzer* (➤37-9).

1. FLOAT-LEVEL ADJUSTMENT With the engine warmed up and idling, remove the air cleaner. Carefully look down the throat of the carburetor at the main nozzle (Fig. 21-7). If it is wet or dripping gasoline, the float level is probably too high. This can cause fuel to discharge from the nozzle while the engine is idling.

2. IDLE SYSTEM If the engine idles roughly after warm-up, the idle system could be at fault. Slowly open the throttle until the engine is running about 3000 rpm. If the speed does not increase evenly and the engine runs roughly through this speed range, the idle or main-metering system is probably defective.

3. ACCELERATOR-PUMP SYSTEM With the float-bowl full, the air cleaner off, and the *engine not running*, look down the throat of the carburetor. Open the throttle suddenly. You should see the accelerator-pump system discharge a squirt of fuel into each primary barrel (Fig. 22-5). The flow should continue for a few seconds after the throttle valve reaches the wide-open position. If not, the accelerator-pump system is defective.

4. MAIN-METERING SYSTEM With the engine warmed up and running at 2000 rpm, slowly cover part of the air horn with a piece of stiff cardboard (*not* your hand). The engine should speed up slightly. This restriction causes the main-metering system to discharge more fuel.

➤ 22-7 TESTING MIXTURE-CONTROL SOLENOID

If testing indicates the mixture-control solenoid (Fig. 21-26) may be defective, remove it from the carburetor.

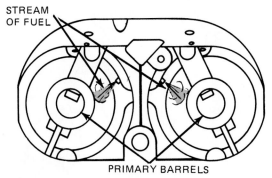

Fig. 22-5 To find out if the accelerator pump is delivering fuel, shut off the engine and remove the air cleaner. Look into the carburetor and quickly open the throttle valves. You should see a stream of fuel discharging into each venturi. (*Ford Motor Company*)

Repair or replace the solenoid if the connector or terminals are broken or bent. Replace the float-bowl seal (Fig. 21-34) if it is cracked, hard, or distorted.

Measure the solenoid resistance with a digital ohmmeter. The resistance of some solenoids should be about 26 ohms. Check for a grounded solenoid by placing one ohmmeter lead to a solenoid terminal and the other lead to the solenoid body. The ohmmeter should read maximum resistance or *infinity*. This shows no short to ground exists.

Using jumper wires, energize the solenoid by connecting it to battery voltage. Follow the polarity shown in Fig. 22-6. To further test a General Motors mixture-control solenoid, connect a hand-vacuum pump to the stem end of the solenoid (Fig. 22-6). Apply a vacuum of about 5 inches [17 kPa] Hg. A good solenoid should hold some vacuum for about 5 seconds. Apply the vacuum again and remove a jumper lead. The vacuum reading should drop to zero. If not, replace the solenoid. Stroke the vacuum pump rapidly. The gauge may move slightly, but must fall to zero before the next stroke. If not, the fuel-metering orifice is restricted. Replace the solenoid.

➤ 22-8 CHECKING THE CHOKE

Inspect the choke with the engine off. Remove the air cleaner. Hold the throttle half open, and open and close the choke valve several times (Fig. 22-7). If it sticks, spray the linkage and shaft with *carburetor choke cleaner*. Remove the carburetor for service if the choke does not operate freely.

Check the position of the choke valve. It should close completely when the throttle is opened slightly on a cold engine. Inspect the routing and condition of the vacuum hose to the vacuum break. The *vacuum-break plunger* (Fig. 21-19) should be fully extended with the engine off. If not, replace the vacuum break.

Install the air cleaner and start the engine. With the engine running at fast idle, remove the air cleaner. Measure the time in seconds it takes the choke valve to reach wide

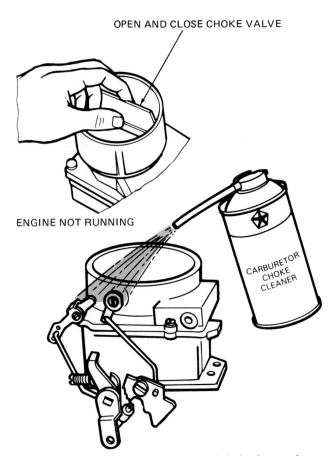

Fig. 22-7 Check the choke by opening and closing it several times. If it sticks, clean the linkage and shaft with spray carburetor choke cleaner. (*Chrysler Corporation*)

open. The electric choke should open within the specified time (for example, 90 seconds or less). If not, check the voltage at the choke heater (Fig. 21-20) with a voltmeter. Replace the heater if the voltage is 12 to 15 volts. If the voltage is low or zero, check the wiring, connections, oil-pressure switch, and fuse. The circuit has an improper or open ground.

A thermometer is needed to further check the operation of an electric choke. A typical procedure for a carburetor-mounted choke is to tape a bulb thermometer to the choke housing. Then start the engine. Note the temperature at which the choke opens and the time required. Specifications and test procedures vary. Refer to the vehicle service manual.

➤ 22-9 CHECKING THE IDLE SOLENOID

To check the idle solenoid (Fig. 22-8), turn the ignition key ON. Do not start the engine. Open the throttle to allow the solenoid plunger to extend. Hold the throttle wide open. Disconnect the electrical connector from the solenoid while feeling the end of the plunger. The plunger should retract into the solenoid. If not, connect a test light between the solenoid feed wire and ground. If the light glows,

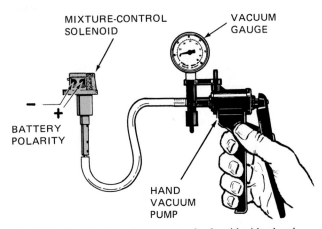

Fig. 22-6 Checking the mixture-control solenoid with a hand vacuum pump. (*Rochester Products Division of General Motors Corporation*)

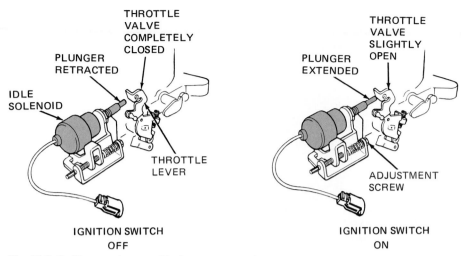

Fig. 22-8 Stalling may be caused by improper operation or adjustment of the idle solenoid. (*Ford Motor Company*)

replace the solenoid. When the light does not come on, there is an open in the wiring or connections.

> **NOTE** | All solenoids on carburetors do not operate this way. Refer to the manufacturer's service manual for the specified test procedure.

CARBURETOR ADJUSTMENTS

➤ **22-10 AUTOMATIC-CHOKE ADJUSTMENTS**

Many automatic chokes have an adjustable cover on the thermostatic spring (Fig. 21-18). Turning the cover one way or the other enriches or leans out the mixture. If the cover is riveted in place, remove the rivets to make the adjustment. Other automatic chokes are adjusted by bending a rod (Fig. 21-19) in the linkage.

Many carburetors have a *vacuum break* (➤21-19) that controls the opening of the choke valve. The amount the vacuum break opens the choke valve can be checked and adjusted. Remove the vacuum hose. Feel the end of the hose for vacuum. If there is vacuum, look for a small bleed hole in the vacuum break. Cover the hole with a piece of tape. Connect a hand vacuum pump to the vacuum break (Fig. 22-9). The vacuum-break plunger should move as vacuum is applied.

The amount that the vacuum break pulls the choke valve open is measured with a drill or plug gauge, or with a *choke-angle gauge* (Fig. 22-10). Place the gauge on the closed choke valve, center the leveling bubble, and set the degree scale to the specified angle. Then open the choke by applying vacuum with the hand vacuum pump. Adjust the linkage or the vacuum break to center the bubble. Specifications vary but typically range from 20 to 40 degrees. Carburetors with two vacuum breaks (Fig. 22-9) must have the choke-opening angle checked when vacuum is applied to each vacuum break.

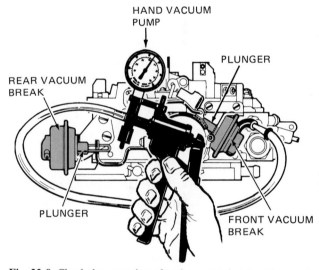

Fig. 22-9 Check the operation of each vacuum break with a hand vacuum pump. A bad or improperly adjusted vacuum break may cause a cold carbureted engine to stall shortly after starting. (*Rochester Products Division of General Motors Corporation*)

➤ **22-11 IDLE-MIXTURE SETTINGS**

Years ago, there were several adjustments that could be made on carburetors. Today emission-control laws limit the adjustments allowed. The only adjustment now recommended for late-model cars during tuneup is to adjust the idle speed (➤22-12).

The *idle-mixture screw* (Fig. 22-11) is preset at the factory. On some cars, a *limiter cap* prevents improper adjustment. Newer carburetors have the adjustment made at the factory. A steel plug (Fig. 21-7) is installed to prevent tampering.

The approved adjustment procedure is listed on the *vehicle emission control information* (VECI) *label* in the

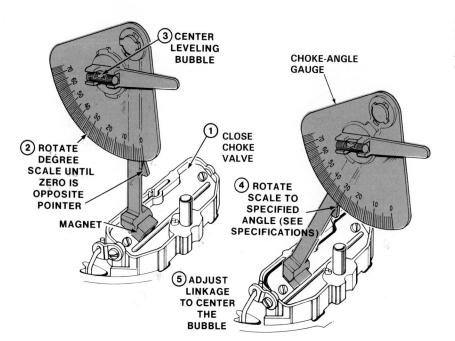

Fig. 22-10 Measuring the choke-valve angle with a choke-angle gauge. (*Rochester Products Division of General Motors Corporation*)

③ CENTER LEVELING BUBBLE

CHOKE-ANGLE GAUGE

② ROTATE DEGREE SCALE UNTIL ZERO IS OPPOSITE POINTER

MAGNET

① CLOSE CHOKE VALVE

④ ROTATE SCALE TO SPECIFIED ANGLE (SEE SPECIFICATIONS)

⑤ ADJUST LINKAGE TO CENTER THE BUBBLE

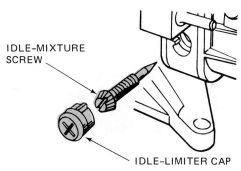

IDLE-MIXTURE SCREW

IDLE-LIMITER CAP

Fig. 22-11 Limiter cap on a carburetor idle-mixture screw.

engine compartment (Fig. 3-4). If the carburetor is disassembled for service, the caps or plugs can be removed and the mixture adjusted.

➤ 22-12 SETTING IDLE SPEED

First set the parking brake and block the wheels. Then follow the procedure on the VECI label. It includes the specifications and procedures for the vehicle on which it is located. A typical procedure follows.

1. Disconnect the evaporative purge hose from the charcoal canister.
2. Disconnect and plug the vacuum hose to the ignition distributor, and the vacuum hose to the exhaust-gas-recirculation valve (EGR valve).
3. Adjust the ignition timing at the specified engine speed. Disconnect the electrical lead to the idle solenoid (if used). Reconnect the hose to the distributor.
4. Adjust the idle speed to specifications. In earlier models, this was a screw in the throttle linkage. In later cars, the adjustment is in the solenoid (Fig. 22-8).
5. Reconnect the lead to the idle solenoid. Then extend the

solenoid plunger (Fig. 22-8) and adjust engine speed to specifications.

➤ 22-13 ADJUSTING IDLE MIXTURE

This adjustment is made only after major carburetor repair. A typical procedure follows.

1. With limiter caps off or steel plugs removed, turn the idle-mixture screws in until they lightly touch the seats. Then back them out two full turns.
2. Adjust the idle speed as described above (➤22-12).
3. Connect an exhaust-gas analyzer (➤37-9) to the exhaust system. With the engine idling at normal operating temperature, adjust the idle-mixture screws to get a satisfactory idle at the specified rpm. The carbon-

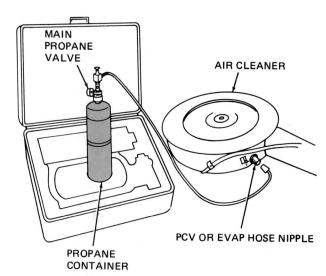

MAIN PROPANE VALVE

AIR CLEANER

PROPANE CONTAINER

PCV OR EVAP HOSE NIPPLE

Fig. 22-12 Setup for adjusting the carburetor idle mixture with propane. (*Ford Motor Company*)

monoxide (CO) reading must be below the specified allowable maximum. The engine should be running at normal idle. The automatic transmission or transaxle should be in DRIVE (D). A manual transmission or transaxle should be in NEUTRAL.

> **NOTE** | *Refer to the manufacturer's service manual for specific procedures and specifications. Some cars must have the idle mixture adjusted while the air-fuel mixture is being enriched with* propane *(Fig. 22-12). This is because the carburetors are set so lean. Adjusting the air-fuel mixture by any other method may be a violation of state and federal law.*

CARBURETED FUEL-SYSTEM SERVICE

➤ 22-14 CARBURETED FUEL-FILTER SERVICE

Figure 17-10 shows fuel filters used with the mechanical fuel pump. The fuel filter requires no service other than periodic replacement. On some cars, the filter is part of the fuel pump (Fig. 17-10, lower left). On others the filter attaches to the carburetor (Fig. 17-10, top and right). Replace this filter by unclamping and detaching the hose. Then remove and discard the filter. Be careful not to over-tighten or cross-thread the new filter when installing it. This can strip threads and cause a leak.

➤ 22-15 MECHANICAL FUEL-PUMP SERVICE

Most mechanical fuel pumps that fail are replaced. Wipe off any dirt or grease so it will not get into the engine. Then take off any heat shield and disconnect the fuel lines. Remove the attaching nuts or bolts and lift off the pump. If it sticks, work it gently from side to side or pry lightly under the mounting flange or attaching studs. Some engines use a *pushrod* (Fig. 22-13) to operate the fuel pump. Remove the rod and examine it for wear and sticking.

Make sure fuel-line connections are clean and in good condition. Connect the fuel lines to the pump before attaching the pump to the engine. Place a new gasket on the studs of the fuel-pump mounting pad or over the opening in the crankcase. The mounting surface on the engine should be clean. Insert the rocker arm of the fuel pump into the opening. Make sure that the arm goes on the proper side of the camshaft (Fig. 17-5) or that it centers on the pushrod (Fig. 22-13). Install the attaching nuts or bolts. Tighten the fuel lines, start the engine, and check for leaks.

➤ 22-16 CARBURETOR REMOVAL

To remove the carburetor, first disconnect the ground cable from the battery. Then:

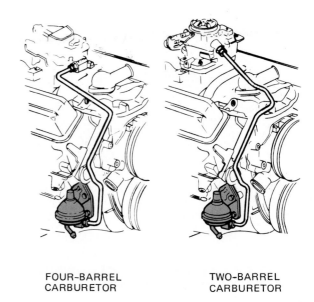

FOUR-BARREL CARBURETOR   TWO-BARREL CARBURETOR

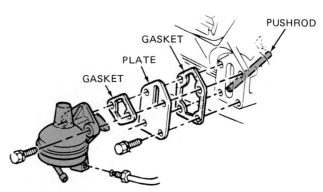

Fig. 22-13 Mounting of the mechanical fuel pump on a V-type engine with a pushrod between the fuel-pump rocker arm and the camshaft eccentric. (*Chevrolet Division of General Motors Corporation*)

1. Disconnect the air and vacuum lines.
2. Take off the air cleaner.
3. Disconnect the throttle and choke linkage.
4. Disconnect the hot-air tube to the choke (if used).
5. Disconnect the fuel line and vacuum-advance line from the carburetor. Use two wrenches (Fig. 7-5) to avoid damaging tubes or fittings.
6. Disconnect the wires from switches and electrical controls (where present).
7. Take off the carburetor attaching nuts or bolts and lift off the carburetor. Hold the carburetor level to avoid spilling fuel from the float bowl. Then pour the fuel into a safety container.
8. Put the carburetor in a clean place where dirt cannot get into it.
9. Cover the hole in the intake manifold with *masking tape* (Fig. 22-14). This avoids engine damage from loose parts dropped into the intake manifold. Anything in the manifold could get into the engine combustion chambers. Cranking the engine would then cause serious damage.

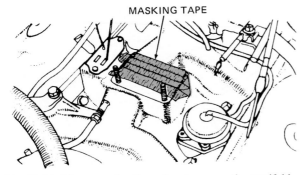

MASKING TAPE

Fig. 22-14 After removing the carburetor, cover the manifold holes with masking tape. This prevents loose parts falling into the intake manifold and damaging the engine.

➤ **22-17 CARBURETOR CLEANING AND REBUILDING**

Carburetor disassembly and assembly procedures vary. Follow the manufacturer's recommendations. The service procedures are in the vehicle service manuals. Similar *instruction sheets* are in every *carburetor kit* (Fig. 22-15). These are available for most carburetors. They contain all necessary parts such as jets, gaskets, washers, and gauges needed to rebuild the carburetor. Some carburetor adjustments may require the use of special carburetor tools and other measuring tools.

To clean or rebuild a carburetor, get the kit for the carburetor you are servicing. The *carburetor identification number* is on the carburetor or on a tag attached to it. Perform all steps in the instruction sheet. Do not use drills

or wires to clean out fuel passages or bleed holes in the carburetor or throttle body. This can enlarge the openings and upset the carburetor calibration. Clean these openings with chemical cleaner and blow them out with compressed air. General carburetor service procedures follow.

1. Empty any gasoline remaining in the carburetor into a safety container. Disassemble the carburetor, noting the position of each part as it is removed. Place the parts in small pans. Disassemble the carburetor only as necessary for cleaning.
2. Soak the metal castings and parts in *carburetor cleaner* (Fig. 22-16). Never soak the mixture-control

PARTS BASKET

INSTRUCTIONS AND CAUTIONS

Fig. 22-16 A shop-size container of carburetor cleaner. The basket has long handles so your hands do not get in the liquid cleaner. (*Gunk Laboratories, Inc.*)

GAUGE

IDLE-LIMITER CAPS

Fig. 22-15 Contents of a carburetor kit for a two-barrel carburetor. (*Standard Motor Products, Inc.*)

solenoid, accelerator-pump plunger, or any fiber, rubber, or plastic part. Wipe these parts clean with a shop towel.

3. After soaking in carburetor cleaner for the specified time, remove the parts. Follow the instructions on the cleaner container and rinse off each part. This may be in warm water or other liquid. Blow out all jets and passages in the castings with compressed air. These passages must be clean and open.

CAUTION!

Use the air hose with care. Wear eye protection while blow-drying parts or clearing out passages.

4. Replace any damaged or worn parts. Shake hollow floats to determine if they leak and have liquid inside. Weigh all floats (Fig. 22-17) to determine if they are fuel-soaked and too heavy. Replace scored or burred power pistons (Fig. 21-16). Check the bores for the choke shaft and throttle shaft for wear.

5. Replace the idle-mixture screws (Fig. 21-7) if they have burrs or grooves. Inspect the accelerator-pump well in the float bowl (Fig. 21-15) for wear and scoring.

6. Check the choke housing for deposits and corrosion. This indicates a defective choke heat tube in the exhaust manifold. Check the choke piston for free movement.

7. Inspect the venturi nozzle and cluster assembly (Fig. 21-7). Replace it if any parts are loose or damaged.

8. Replace any other parts that are worn, damaged, or excessively loose. Then assemble the carburetor following the steps in the instruction sheet. Be sure all filter screens are clean and in place.

9. Install all of the new gaskets and parts in the carburetor kit. This includes the small accelerator-pump inlet and discharge *check balls* (Fig. 21-15). Leaving out the inlet check ball may cause hard starting and hesitation when the throttle is opened suddenly. A missing discharge check ball allows air to enter the pump chamber when the accelerator pedal is released.

10. Before completing final assembly of the carburetor, set the *float level* and *float drop* (Fig. 22-18). Improper operation of the float system affects fuel delivery to all other systems.

11. Install a new fuel filter. Fill the float bowl with fuel before installing the carburetor. Operate the throttle lever until fuel discharges from the accelerator-pump jet (Fig. 22-5). After completing all other steps on the instruction sheet, the carburetor is ready for installation.

➤ 22-18 CARBURETOR INSTALLATION

Remove any tape placed over the intake-manifold openings (Fig. 22-14). Check that the mounting surface is clean and install the carburetor. Use a new gasket (Fig. 22-19) to assure a tight seal. Installation is the reverse of removal (➤22-16). Complete these steps and make any necessary on-car adjustments. Then start the engine and check for air, fuel, and vacuum leaks. Road test the car to check for proper operation and driveability.

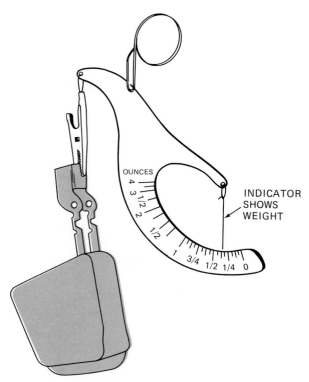

Fig. 22-17 Weighing a carburetor float on a float-weight scale shows if the float has absorbed fuel. (*Tomco, Inc.*)

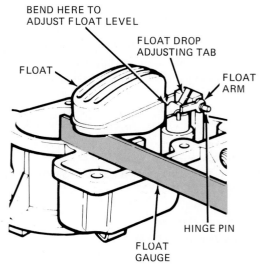

Fig. 22-18 Setting the float level and float drop. (*Ford Motor Company*)

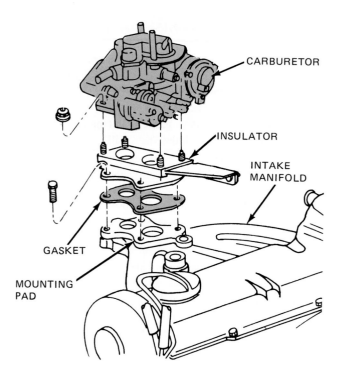

Fig. 22-19 Installing a carburetor.

CARBURETOR

INSULATOR

INTAKE
MANIFOLD

GASKET

MOUNTING
PAD

TRADE TALK

carburetor cleaner	feedback carburetor	fuel-pump vacuum	mixture-control solenoid
check balls	float level	idle solenoid	
choke-angle gauge	fuel-pump pressure	mechanical fuel pump	

MULTIPLE-CHOICE TEST

*Select the **one** correct, best, or most probable answer to each question.*
You can find the answers in the section indicated at the end of the question.

1. Technician A says a blown fuse will prevent a mechanical fuel pump from working. Technician B says to crank or run the engine while making pressure and vacuum tests on a mechanical fuel pump. Who is right? (➤22-4)
   a. A only
   b. B only
   c. both A and B
   d. neither A nor B

2. Excessive fuel consumption can be caused by all the following EXCEPT (➤22-5)
   a. a heavy float
   b. stuck power piston
   c. worn metering-rod jets
   d. low fuel-pump pressure

3. The driver complains that after turning the ignition key ON to listen to the radio, the cold engine is hard to start. On a car with an electric choke, this indicates (➤22-5)
   a. failure of the electric choke
   b. a stuck manifold-heat-control valve
   c. the throttle-valve not closing
   d. normal operation

4. Backfiring in the exhaust system is caused by (➤22-5)
   a. a rich mixture in the exhaust gas
   b. a lean mixture in the exhaust gas
   c. low fuel-pump capacity
   d. a disconnected air-cleaner vacuum hose

5. A digital ohmmeter reads "infinity" when connected to the mixture-control-solenoid terminals. This indicates (➤22-7)
   a. a normal reading
   b. a defective mixture-control solenoid
   c. a defective ohmmeter
   d. insufficient resistance
6. With the ignition key ON and voltage to the idle solenoid, the solenoid plunger does not move when the solenoid electrical lead is disconnected. This indicates (➤22-9)
   a. a defective solenoid
   b. an open in the wiring or connections
   c. a defective vacuum break
   d. the throttle is not wide open
7. Technician A says the vacuum break sets the fast-idle speed. Technician B says the vacuum break opens the choke valve. Who is right? (➤22-10)
   a. A only
   b. B only
   c. both A and B
   d. neither A nor B
8. To set idle speed, follow the specifications and procedures (➤22-12)
   a. in the owner's manual
   b. on the shop tachometer
   c. on the engine compartment VECI label
   d. indicated by the CHECK ENGINE light
9. All the following are true about adjusting the idle mixture EXCEPT (➤22-13)
   a. using propane may be the only legal method
   b. using propane is required because some carburetors are set so lean
   c. the CO reading must be below a specified maximum
   d. the automatic transaxle should be in neutral
10. Deposits in the choke housing indicate (➤22-17)
    a. a defective choke heat tube
    b. improper choke linkage adjustment
    c. a stuck piston in the choke housing
    d. improper vacuum-break operation

REVIEW QUESTIONS

1. Explain how a defective mechanical fuel pump can allow gasoline to get into the crankcase.   (➤22-3)
2. Name the three tests of a mechanical fuel pump and give typical specifications for each.   (➤22-4)
3. Describe the possible causes of engine stalling as it warms up and after high-speed driving.   (➤22-5)
4. Explain how to check and adjust the opening and closing of the automatic choke.   (➤22-10)
5. What happens if the accelerator-pump check balls are left out when assembling the carburetor?   (➤22-17)

CHAPTER 23

DIESEL FUEL-INJECTION SYSTEMS

After studying this chapter, you should be able to:

- Explain the difference in operation between diesel (compression-ignition) and gasoline (spark-ignition) engines.
- Describe the two basic types of fuel-injection pumps used on auto-motive diesel engines.
- Locate the components of diesel fuel-injection systems on cars and explain how each component works.
- Explain the difference between direct injection and indirect injection.
- Diagnose and service various automotive diesel fuel-injection systems.

DIESEL-ENGINE CONSTRUCTION AND OPERATION

➤ 23-1 DIESEL ENGINES

Diesel engines are similar to spark-ignition engines in construction. Both have pistons, with piston rings, moving up and down in cylinders. Both burn fuel in combustion chambers in the upper part of the cylinders. The high pressure produced by the burning fuel pushes the pistons down. This rotates the crankshaft and the rotary motion is carried through shafts and gears to the drive wheels. Diesel and spark-ignition engines are compared in ➤11-2.

➤ 23-2 DIESEL-ENGINE OPERATION

Figure 23-1 shows the four piston strokes in a four-stroke-cycle diesel engine.

1. INTAKE STROKE The diesel engine takes in air alone. No throttle valve impedes the airflow. In the spark-ignition engine, a mixture of air and fuel enters the engine cylinders on the intake stroke. The throttle valve controls the amount that enters.

2. COMPRESSION STROKE In the diesel engine, the upward-moving piston compresses air alone. On the other hand, in the spark-ignition engine, the piston compresses the air-fuel mixture.

3. POWER STROKE In the diesel engine, a light oil called *diesel fuel* is sprayed (injected) into the compressed and hot air. The *heat of compression* ignites the fuel. In the spark-ignition engine, a spark at the spark plug ignites the compressed air-fuel mixture.

4. EXHAUST STROKE The exhaust stroke is the same for both engines. The exhaust valve opens and the burned gases flow out as the piston moves up the cylinder.

➤ 23-3 DIESEL-ENGINE CHARACTERISTICS

The diesel engine has the following characteristics:

1. No throttle valve (except some engines with the *pneumatic governor* described in ➤23-12).
2. Compresses only air on the compression stroke.
3. Heat of compression ignites fuel as it sprays into the engine cylinders.
4. Has a high compression ratio (➤15-10) of 16:1 to 22:1.
5. Controls engine power and speed only by the amount of fuel sprayed into the cylinders. More fuel equals more power.
6. Has *glow plugs* or an electric intake-manifold heater to make starting easier (➤23-15).

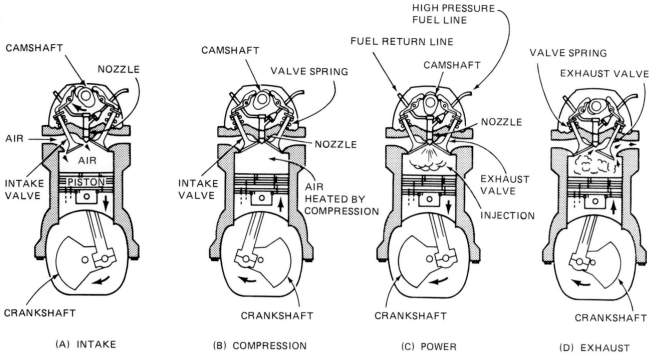

Fig. 23-1 The four piston strokes in a four-stroke-cycle diesel engine.

(A) INTAKE   (B) COMPRESSION   (C) POWER   (D) EXHAUST

DIESEL-ENGINE FUEL

➤ 23-4 DIESEL FUEL

Diesel engines burn *diesel fuel oil.* It is a light oil made from crude oil by the same refining process that produces gasoline. The oil must have the proper viscosity, volatility, and *cetane number* (➤23-5) for use as a diesel fuel.

1. VOLATILITY This is a measure of how easily a liquid evaporates. Gasoline vaporizes easily (➤16-3). It has high volatility. Diesel fuel has low volatility. It boils at a temperature of about 700°F [371°C]. There are two grades of diesel fuel for automotive diesel engines, *number 1 diesel* and *number 2 diesel.* Number 1 diesel is more volatile. It is used where temperatures are very low. Number 2 diesel is the recommended fuel in most automotive diesel engines for most driving conditions. The less-volatile fuel usually has a higher *heating value.* When it burns, more energy is available than from a fuel with higher volatility.

2. VISCOSITY This refers to a liquid's resistance to flow. The lower the viscosity the more easily the liquid flows. Diesel fuel must have a relatively low viscosity. It must flow through the fuel-system lines and spray into the engine cylinders with little resistance.

An oil with high viscosity will not break into fine particles when sprayed. Large particles burn slowly resulting in poor engine performance. If viscosity is too low, the oil will not lubricate the moving parts in the injection pump and injection nozzles. Damage may result.

Number 2 diesel has the right viscosity for most driving

conditions. Number 1 diesel has lower viscosity so it will flow and spray properly at low temperatures. The owner's manual gives the proper fuel or blend to use for the conditions.

➤ 23-5 CETANE NUMBER

The cetane number refers to the ease with which diesel fuel ignites. A high cetane number means the fuel is fast-burning and ignites easily at a relatively low temperature (Fig. 23-2). A low cetane number means the fuel is slower burning and requires a higher temperature to ignite.

Diesel fuel with a low cetane number takes a little longer to ignite. This may cause excessive *ignition lag.* During this slight delay, the fuel collects in the cylinder. When ignition does occur, all the fuel ignites at once. The pressure goes up quickly and combustion knock results. This is similar to spark knock or detonation in a spark-ignition engine (Fig. 16-2).

High cetane fuel ignites as soon as it enters the cylinder. There is no accumulation of fuel. The result is a smooth pressure rise so no combustion knock occurs.

DIESEL-ENGINE FUEL SYSTEMS

➤ 23-6 DIESEL-ENGINE FUEL SYSTEMS

Figure 23-3 shows a typical automotive diesel-engine fuel system. It uses *injection nozzles* or *injectors* similar to the

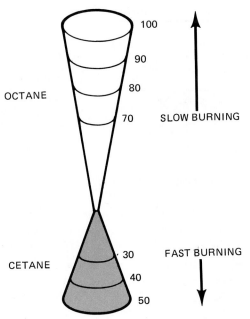

Fig. 23-2 The higher the cetane number of diesel fuel, the faster the fuel burns. The higher the octane number of gasoline, the slower it burns. (*Ford Motor Company*)

fuel injectors in gasoline fuel-injection systems (Chap. 19). The gasoline injectors are solenoid operated. Diesel injection nozzles are hydraulically operated. When high pressure is applied, they open and spray fuel. The diesel fuel-system must:

1. Deliver the right amount of fuel to meet the operating requirements.

2. Time the opening of the injection nozzles so the fuel enters the engine cylinders at the proper instant. As engine speed increases, fuel injection must start earlier. This gives the fuel enough time to burn and produce pressure on the pistons. Without the advance, the pistons would be over TDC and moving down before the fuel fully ignites. The pistons would keep ahead of the pressure rise. This wastes fuel and power.

3. Deliver the fuel to the cylinders under high pressure. Injection pressure must be high enough to overcome the high compression pressure in the diesel engine. At the end of the compression stroke, *compression pressure may be 500 psi [3447 kPa] or higher.*

➤ 23-7 CLEANING DIESEL FUEL

Diesel fuel must be clean. Water or dirt in the fuel means trouble. Tiny particles can clog the injection nozzles and cause them to fail. Water can rust fuel-pump and injection-nozzle parts.

1. WATER IN DIESEL FUEL Diesel fuel oil absorbs water freely. Many vehicles have a *water detector* located in the fuel tank (Fig. 23-4). Water sinks to the bottom of the tank. Fuel oil floats on top.

When enough water has gathered at the bottom of the tank (1 to 2 1/2 gallons [3.8 to 9.5 L]), the water completes an electric circuit. This turns on a warning light on the instrument panel.

To remove the water, remove the fuel-tank cap. Connect a pump or siphon to the tank fuel-return hose. Pump or siphon until all water is removed and diesel fuel starts

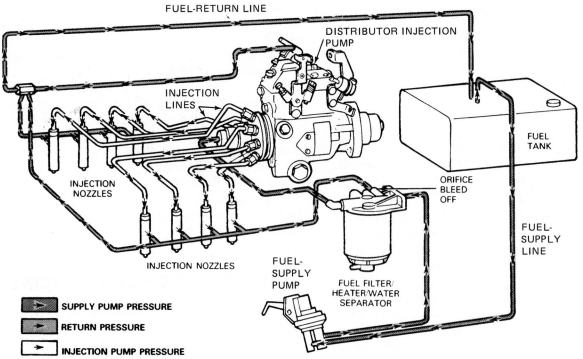

Fig. 23-3 Typical fuel system for an automotive diesel engine. (*Ford Motor Company*)

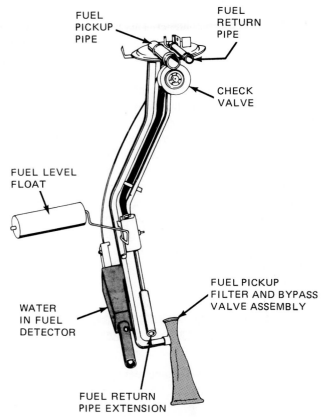

Fig. 23-4 Diesel fuel-guage tank unit, with water-in-fuel detector mounted on the bottom of the fuel pickup tube. (*Buick Division of General Motors Corporation*)

coming out. Reconnect the fuel-return hose and reinstall the fuel tank cap.

Vehicles without an intank water detector usually have a *fuel conditioner* (Figs. 23-3 and 23-5). This is a combination fuel filter, *fuel heater*, and *fuel-water separator*. The fuel flows through and any water settles to the bottom. Drain the water by turning the nut at the bottom of the unit. This opens the drain valve. The fuel heater helps prevent wax from forming in the fuel during cold weather.

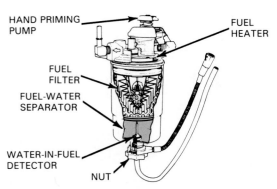

Fig. 23-5 A diesel fuel conditioner, which is a combination fuel heater, fuel filter, water detector, and fuel-water separator. (*Ford Motor Company*)

2. FUEL-PICKUP BYPASS VALVE The *fuel pickup assembly* (Fig. 23-4) includes a *bypass valve*. It allows fuel to pass if the pickup filter becomes plugged with wax during temperatures below about 20°F [−6°C]. This can happen with number 2 diesel fuel (➤23-4). If plugging occurs, the last four gallons [15 L] of fuel in the tank will not be picked up. Keep the fuel tank above 1/4 full to avoid running out of fuel.

DIESEL FUEL-INJECTION SYSTEMS

➤ 23-8 DIESEL FUEL-INJECTION PUMPS

Automotive diesel engines use two types of fuel-injection pumps. One is an inline cam-operated pump. It has a plunger for each engine cylinder. The other is a rotary, distributor-type pump. One or two plungers supply the fuel for all injection nozzles. Following sections describe both types.

➤ 23-9 INLINE-PLUNGER INJECTION PUMP

Figure 23-6 shows an *inline-plunger pump* on a six-cylinder diesel engine. The pump has a *barrel-and-plunger* assembly for each cylinder. An *injection line* or *tube* connects each barrel-and-plunger assembly to an injection nozzle.

The construction of a barrel-and-plunger assembly is shown in Fig. 23-7. Low-pressure fuel from the fuel-supply pump flows through the *inlet port* (Fig. 23-8) into the space above the plunger. The plunger has a roller that rides on a cam on the camshaft. This is like the roller tappets used in some engine valve trains (Fig. 14-25). When the cam lobe comes up under the plunger, the lobe

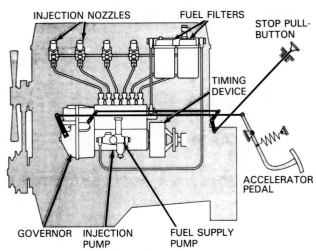

Fig. 23-6 Fuel system for a six-cylinder diesel engine using an inline fuel injection pump. (*Robert Bosch Corporation*)

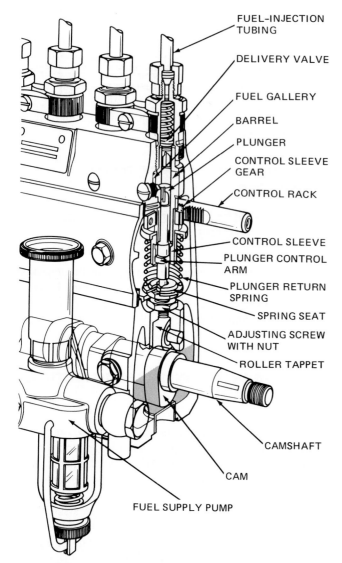

FUEL–INJECTION TUBING

DELIVERY VALVE

FUEL GALLERY

BARREL

PLUNGER

CONTROL SLEEVE GEAR

CONTROL RACK

CONTROL SLEEVE

PLUNGER CONTROL ARM

PLUNGER RETURN SPRING

SPRING SEAT

ADJUSTING SCREW WITH NUT

ROLLER TAPPET

CAMSHAFT

CAM

FUEL SUPPLY PUMP

Fig. 23-7 Construction of an inline-plunger injection pump. (*Robert Bosch Corporation*)

raises the plunger. This applies high pressure on the fuel trapped above the plunger. The fuel is forced through the tube to the injection nozzle in the cylinder where the piston is reaching TDC on the compression stroke. The fuel sprays out and ignites from the heat of compression.

The amount of fuel injected is varied by varying the *effective stroke* of the plunger. This is shown in Fig. 23-8. The control rod connects by linkage through the *governor* (➤23-12) to the accelerator pedal. As the driver depresses the pedal, the linkage causes the control rod to move. This turns the plunger in its barrel. The plunger has a groove and an inclined *helix* machined into it. Turning the plunger for more fuel rotates the helix so a wider section faces the inlet port. This closes the port for a longer time, increasing the effective stroke of the plunger. Fuel delivery begins when the top edge of the plunger closes off the inlet port. Fuel delivery stops when the helix opens the inlet port.

The fuel-injection pump has a speed-advance mechanism. It advances the time of injection as engine speed increases. This gives the fuel the necessary time to ignite, burn, and produce high pressure. Without injection advance (➤23-6), weak power strokes result at higher engine speeds.

➤ ## 23-10 ROTARY-DISTRIBUTOR INJECTION PUMP

Figure 23-3 shows a V-8 engine fuel system using a rotary-distributor injection pump. Figure 23-9 shows an inline six-cylinder engine with a rotary-distributor injection pump. This pump has a rotor that sends fuel to the injection nozzles in the engine cylinders as it rotates. The pump is driven by a pair of bevel gears at half crankshaft speed.

Figure 23-10 shows the distributor pump removed from the engine. Figures 23-11 and 23-12 show how the pump works. It has a rotor (Fig. 23-13) with a pair of cam rollers and plungers. These rollers roll on the inner surface of an internal cam. They move in and out as they roll over the cam lobes. When they move out, they cause the plungers to move out. This increases the size of the internal chamber. Fuel flows into this chamber. Then the rollers meet the cam lobes and push the plungers in. This pressurizes the fuel, forcing it out through an opening in the rotor.

The opening indexes with stationary openings in the outer shell of the pump. There are the same number of these openings as there are cylinders in the engine. An

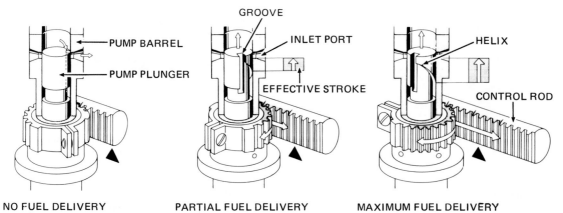

PUMP BARREL

PUMP PLUNGER

GROOVE

INLET PORT

EFFECTIVE STROKE

HELIX

CONTROL ROD

NO FUEL DELIVERY   PARTIAL FUEL DELIVERY   MAXIMUM FUEL DELIVERY

Fig. 23-8 Movement of the toothed control rod turns the inline-pump plungers to vary the amount of fuel injected. (*Robert Bosch Corporation*)

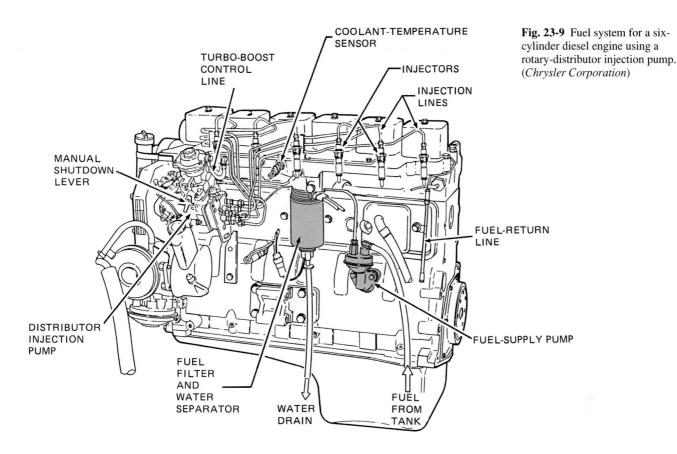

Fig. 23-9 Fuel system for a six-cylinder diesel engine using a rotary-distributor injection pump. (*Chrysler Corporation*)

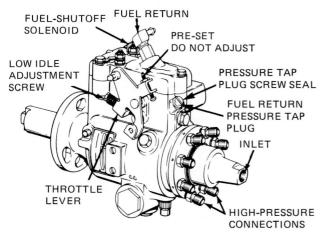

Fig. 23-10 Distributor-type injection pump for a diesel engine. (*Chevrolet Division of General Motors Corporation*)

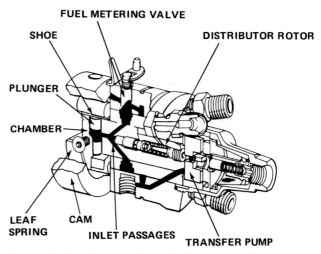

Fig. 23-11 Charging cycle in the distributor pump. The two plungers move apart to cause fuel to enter the chamber. (*Oldsmobile Division of General Motors Corporation*)

injection pipe connects each opening to an injection nozzle in a cylinder. As the rotor turns, its opening indexes with the stationary openings. This sends high-pressure fuel to the injection nozzles in the engine firing order.

➤ 23-11 DISTRIBUTOR-PUMP CONTROLS

The distributor pump has two controls. One controls timing and the other controls the amount of fuel injected. The timing device connects to the internal cam ring. This is the cam on which the rollers roll. As engine speed increases, the cam ring moves ahead. This causes the two

plungers to move out and in earlier, advancing the start of injection (Fig. 23-14). At the same time, the internal governor (➤23-12) regulates the amount of fuel delivered to the cylinders.

➤ 23-12 MECHANICAL GOVERNORS FOR FUEL-INJECTION PUMPS

Moving the accelerator pedal changes the setting of the governor. It then automatically controls the amount of fuel

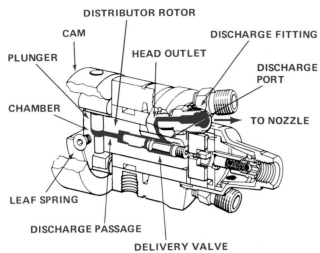

Fig. 23-12 Discharge cycle in the distributor pump. The plungers are moving together, forcing fuel from the chamber, past the delivery valve and through the discharge port. The rotor has turned so that the port in the rotor aligns with the next discharge port. This port is connected through an injection line to the injector in the cylinder in which the piston is approaching TDC on the compression stroke. (*Oldsmobile Division of General Motors Corporation*)

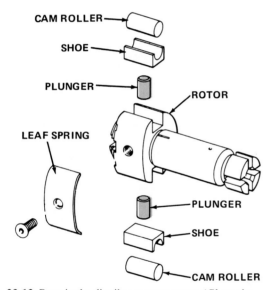

Fig. 23-13 Parts in the distributor-pump rotor. (*Chevrolet Division of General Motors Corporation*)

injected. Without a governor, a diesel engine can stall at low speeds or run so fast it will self-destruct. Automotive diesel engines use a mechanical (centrifugal), pneumatic, or electronically-controlled governor. These are all *variable-speed governors*. They control an engine that runs at varying speeds.

> **NOTE** Engines that run at constant speed, such as a diesel engine that drives an electric generator, use *constant-speed governors.*

A mechanical governor has flyweights that spin with the injection-pump camshaft. The faster they spin, the further out they move. This acts on the plungers and adjusts the fuel delivery.

Figure 23-15 shows an engine with a pneumatic governor. It has a throttle valve in the intake manifold to provide a vacuum signal to the governor. This valve does *not* control airflow into the engine.

A venturi section in the intake manifold connects by a hose to a vacuum chamber in the governor. As the driver changes accelerator-pedal position, the throttle-valve position also changes. This changes the amount of vacuum applied to the diaphragm in the vacuum chamber. The diaphragm moves, repositioning the control rod (Fig. 23-8) in the injection pump. This rotates the plungers to vary the amount of fuel delivered.

Some diesel engines are turbocharged (Fig. 23-9). In these engines, the governor is connected by a tube to the intake manifold. This allows the governor to match fuel delivery with the pressure (the amount of air) in the intake manifold. Air-fuel ratios in a diesel engine range from about 100:1 at idle to about 20:1 under full load. The governor keeps the air-fuel ratio within these limits. An air-fuel ratio richer than 20:1 produces unacceptable smoke in the exhaust.

➤ **23-13 DIESEL ELECTRONIC-CONTROL SYSTEM**

A diesel engine may have an electronic control system (Chap. 10) with an electronic control module (ECM). The ECM may only control the emissions systems, or it may increase the fuel-metering accuracy of the governor. On some engines, the electronic control system completely replaces the mechanical governor. The ECM monitors sensors for engine speed, vehicle speed, throttle position, torque-converter clutch, and other conditions. These inputs are evaluated. Then the ECM calculates the correct amount of fuel to be injected.

Mechanical and pneumatic governors (➤23-12) are relatively slow to act. This may cause the engine to receive the wrong amount of fuel. Then the engine may hesitate or the air-fuel ratio may be too rich, causing smoke in the exhaust gas. Electronic controls act almost instantly to changed conditions. This maintains the proper air-fuel ratio as operating conditions change.

➤ **23-14 INJECTION NOZZLE**

Figures 23-16 and 23-17 show typical injection nozzles. A spring holds the *needle valve* or *nozzle valve* closed until the high *injection pressure* is applied through the injection pipe. This forces the valve off its seat so fuel sprays out into the cylinder. The instant the pressure drops, the spring reseats the valve and fuel injection stops.

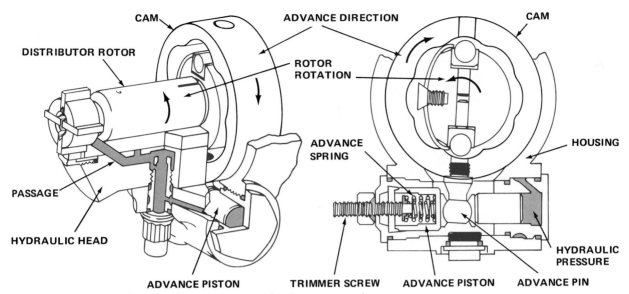

Fig. 23-14 Two views of the distributor-pump automatic advance system that provides automatic advance of injection timing. Hydraulic pressure, which increases with speed, moves the cam ahead. (*Oldsmobile Division of General Motors Corporation*)

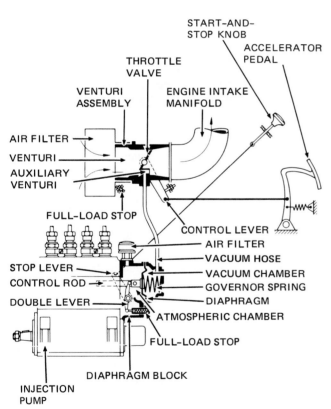

Fig. 23-15 A diesel engine with a pneumatic governor has a throttle valve in the intake manifold to provide a vacuum signal to the governor. (*Robert Bosch Corporation*)

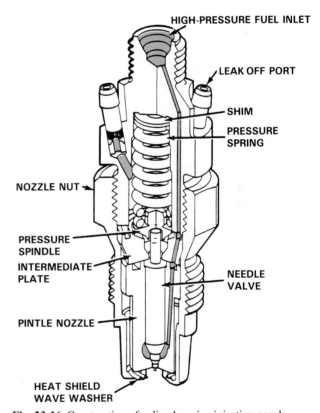

Fig. 23-16 Construction of a diesel-engine injection nozzle. (*Chevrolet Division of General Motors Corporation*)

➤ **23-15 DIRECT AND INDIRECT INJECTION**

Figure 23-1 shows a diesel engine using *direct injection*. The fuel is injected directly into the combustion chamber.

Figure 23-18 shows *indirect injection*. The fuel for each cylinder is injected into a *precombustion chamber* (➤13-11). A glow plug (Fig. 23-19) has a small electric heating element. It heats the air in the precombustion chamber during cold weather to assure easy starting. Instead of glow plugs, some diesel engines have an electronic intake-manifold heater to warm the intake air.

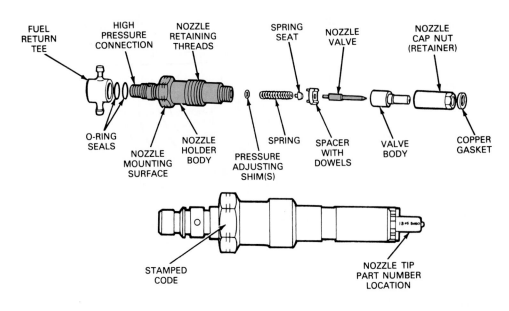

Fig. 23-17 Disassembled diesel-engine injection nozzle. (*Ford Motor Company*)

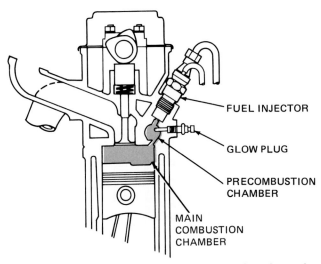

Fig. 23-18 Location of precombustion chamber, glow plug, and fuel injector in a diesel engine with indirect injection. (*Volkswagen of America, Inc.*)

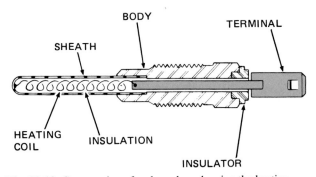

Fig. 23-19 Construction of a glow plug, showing the heating coil. (*General Motors Corporation*)

The fuel ignites in the precombustion chamber and streams out into the main combustion chamber. There the burning fuel mixes with the combustion-chamber air and combustion is completed. A diesel engine always has excess air so combustion is relatively complete.

Diesel engines for trucks and heavy equipment use direct injection (Fig. 23-1). It causes harder starting and rougher and noisier operation. Direct injection is not normally used in passenger-car engines.

DIESEL-ENGINE OPERATION

➤ 23-16 DIESEL STARTING PROCEDURES

Diesel engines require a different starting procedure from gasoline engines. If the diesel engine is cold, the intake air must be preheated before cranking the engine. A heating coil in an electric intake-manifold heater or in a glow plug in each precombustion chamber (Fig. 23-18) supplies the heat.

A typical starting procedure follows. When the engine is cold, turn the ignition key to ON or RUN. This connects the glow plugs to the battery so they quickly heat the precombustion chambers. It also turns on a WAIT light on the instrument panel. After a few seconds, the precombustion chambers are heated sufficiently. The glow plugs and WAIT light turn off.

Press the accelerator pedal halfway down. Turn the ignition key to START. The engine will crank and should start. If it does not start in 15 seconds, turn the ignition key back to ON or RUN. If the WAIT light comes on again, leave the ignition key in ON or RUN. When the light goes off again, try starting once more.

Pumping the accelerator pedal does not help starting a diesel engine. The fuel-injection system has no accelerator pump as in a carburetor.

CAUTION!

Do not use starting aids such as ether, gasoline, or similar material. These can delay starting and may cause engine damage.

➤ 23-17 COOLANT AND FUEL HEATERS

For very cold weather operation in temperatures down to 0°F [−18°C] or below, coolant and fuel heaters (➤23-7) make starting easier. One type of *coolant heater* or *block heater* (Fig. 23-20) has an electrical element that works when plugged into a 115-volt electric outlet. The type of lubricating oil in the engine and the temperature determines how long to use the heater.

The fuel heater is a metal heating element wound around the fuel pipe. The heater may be part of a fuel filter or fuel conditioner (Figs. 23-3 and 23-5). When the ignition key is turned ON, the heater operates if the fuel temperature is so low that wax could form. Warming the fuel reduces the possibility that wax will plug the filters.

➤ 23-18 VACUUM PUMP

The diesel-engine car or truck needs a vacuum source to operate the power brakes and air-conditioning vacuum motors. Many automotive diesel engines have a camshaft-driven *vacuum pump* that supplies this vacuum.

DIESEL ENGINE AND FUEL-INJECTION SERVICE

➤ 23-19 SERVICING DIESEL ENGINES AND FUEL SYSTEMS

Basic servicing procedures on diesel engines are similar to those for spark-ignition engines. Chapters 39 to 41 cover engine service. Figure 23-21 is a diesel fuel-injection system trouble-diagnosis chart. Following sections describe various diesel fuel-system service procedures.

The *transfer pump* or *fuel-supply pump* (Figs. 23-3 and 23-9) is similar to the mechanical fuel pump used with carbureted spark-ignition engines. Chapter 22 covers its diagnosis and testing. Air in the fuel-return line of a diesel

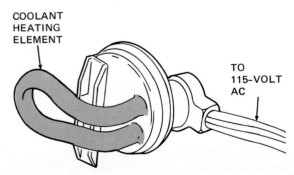

Fig. 23-20 Block heater, which installs in a core-plug hole in the cylinder block. When plugged into a 115-volt electric outlet, the heating element warms the coolant to make the engine easier to start in cold weather. (*Phillips Temro, Inc.*)

engine can be caused by a leak in the line between the pump and the fuel tank. This is the vacuum side of the pump and it will draw in air.

➤ 23-20 SERVICING INJECTION LINES AND FITTINGS

Injection lines in diesel-engine fuel-injection systems are also called *high-pressure fuel lines, injection tubes,* and *injection pipes.* They carry fuel under high pressure from the injection pump to the injection nozzles. Figures 23-3 and 23-9 show the various shapes of injection lines between the injection pump and the nozzles.

When a line requires replacement, always install the line specified by the vehicle manufacturer. Variations from specified length and internal diameter may cause engine troubles. New lines are preformed. Avoid twisting or bending them out of shape during installation.

Careful! Relieve the line pressure and cover the connection with a shop towel before loosening any fitting.

Whenever lines are disconnected, cap the lines, nozzles, and pump fittings. This prevents dirt from entering the fuel system. Cleanliness is very important when working on the diesel fuel system. A particle so small as to be almost invisible can clog an injection nozzle.

➤ 23-21 FUEL-FILTER SERVICE

The fuel filter (Fig. 23-3) is located in the low-pressure fuel line from the fuel tank to the injection pump (➤23-7). The filter element is similar to filters used in engine lubricating systems (Chap. 24). The fuel must pass through the filter element which traps any dirt particles. Replace the filter periodically as recommended by the manufacturer.

➤ 23-22 INJECTION-NOZZLE SERVICE

Never remove an injection nozzle from the engine except for service or replacement. The following indicate injection-nozzle trouble:

1. One or more cylinders knocking.
2. Loss of power.
3. Smoky black exhaust.
4. Engine overheating.
5. Excessive fuel consumption.

One way to check injection nozzles is to run the engine at fast idle. Loosen the connector at each nozzle in turn, one at a time. Wrap a cloth around the connection before you loosen it to keep fuel from spurting out. If loosening the connector causes engine speed to drop, the nozzle is probably working normally. If the engine speed remains

Complaint	Possible Cause	Check or Correction
1. Engine cranks normally but will not start	a. Incorrect or dirty fuel b. No fuel to nozzles or injection pump c. Plugged fuel-return line d. Pump timing off e. Inoperative glow plugs, incorrect starting procedure, or internal engine problems	Flush system—use correct fuel Check for fuel to nozzles Check return line, clean Retime
2. Engine starts but stalls on idle	a. Fuel low in tank b. Incorrect or dirty fuel c. Limited fuel to nozzles or injection pump d. Restricted fuel-return line e. Idle incorrectly set f. Pump timing off g. Injection-pump trouble h. Internal engine problems	Fill tank Flush system—use correct fuel Check for fuel to nozzles and to pump Check return line, clean Reset idle Retime Install new pump
3. Rougle idle, no abnormal noise or smoke	a. Low idle incorrect b. Injection line leaks c. Restricted fuel-return line d. Nozzle trouble e. Fuel-supply-pump problem f. Uneven fuel distribution to nozzles g. Incorrect or dirty fuel	Adjust Fix leaks Clear Check, repair or replace Check, replace if necessary Selectively replace nozzles until condition clears up Flush system—use correct fuel
4. Rough idle with abnormal noise and smoke	a. Injecton-pump timing off b. Nozzle trouble	Retime Check cylinders in sequence to find defective nozzle
5. Idle okay but misfires as throttle opens	a. Plugged fuel filter b. Injection-pump timing off c. Incorrect or dirty fuel	Replace filter Retime Flush system—use correct fuel
6. Loss of power	a. Incorrect or dirty fuel b. Restricted fuel-return line c. Plugged fuel-tank vent d. Restricted fuel supply e. Plugged fuel filter f. Plugged nozzles g. Internal engine problems, loss of compression, compression leaks	Flush system—use correct fuel Clear Clean Check fuel lines, fuel-supply pump, injection pump Replace filter Selectively test nozzles, replace as necessary
7. Noise—"rap" from one or more cylinders	a. Air in fuel system b. Gasoline in fuel system c. Air in high-pressure line d. Nozzle sticking open or with low opening pressure e. Engine problems	Check for cause and correct Replace fuel Bleed system Replace defective nozzle
8. Combustion noise with excessive black smoke	a. Timing off b. Injection-pump trouble c. Nozzle sticking open d. Internal engine problems	Reset Replace pump Clean or replace

Fig. 23-21 Diesel fuel-injection-system trouble-diagnosis chart.

the same, the nozzle is not working properly. Clogged holes are preventing fuel delivery or causing an improper spray pattern (Fig. 23-22).

Some manufacturers recommend a spray test of the detached injection nozzle. This requires a *nozzle tester*, which is a special hydraulic pump and pressure gauge. Attach the nozzle and apply pressure. The fuel should spray in an acceptable pattern (Fig. 23-22) when the specified pressure is reached. Releasing the pressure should stop the spray abruptly without any drip from the nozzle.

CAUTION!

Direct the spray from the nozzle into a suitable container. Do not allow the spray to hit your skin. The pressure is high enough to force fuel oil through the skin. You can be seriously injured because the oil could cause an infection.

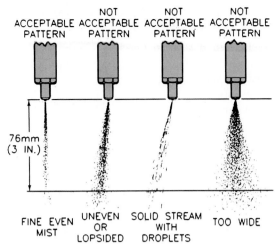

Fig. 23-22 Injection-nozzle spray patterns. (*Ford Motor Company*)

NOT ACCEPTABLE PATTERN NOT ACCEPTABLE PATTERN NOT ACCEPTABLE PATTERN NOT ACCEPTABLE PATTERN

76mm (3 IN.)

FINE EVEN MIST UNEVEN OR LOPSIDED SOLID STREAM WITH DROPLETS TOO WIDE

If the engine misses at all speeds and produces a puff of exhaust smoke each time it misfires, an injection nozzle is probably sticking open. The nozzle can be disassembled and cleaned. Some manufacturers recommend replacing a faulty nozzle. If you disassemble a nozzle, do not damage the tip or enlarge the holes. This can cause leakage and other troubles.

➢ 23-23 INJECTION-PUMP SERVICE

Fuel-injection pumps and fuel lines are installed in a variety of ways. To remove an injection pump, follow the procedure in the vehicle service manual. Rebuilding diesel fuel-injection pumps is not covered in this book. A faulty injection pump is usually exchanged for a new or rebuilt pump. Installation and timing the injection pump are covered in the vehicle service manual.

TRADE TALK

cetane number
compression ignition
direct injection

glow plug
helix
indirect injection

injection lines
injection nozzles
precombustion chamber

water detector

MULTIPLE-CHOICE TEST

Select the **one** *correct, best, or most probable answer to each question.*
You can find the answers in the section indicated at the end of the question.

1. Technician A says the diesel engine compresses air alone on the compression stroke. Technician B says the fuel is ignited by the heat of compression. Who is right? (➢23-2)
   a. A only
   b. B only
   c. both A and B
   d. neither A nor B

2. All the following are true about diesel engines EXCEPT (➢23-3)
   a. no throttle valve
   b. high compression ratio
   c. speed and power controlled by quantity of fuel injected
   d. spark plugs make starting easier

3. Technician A says cetane number is the same as octane rating. Technician B says cetane number is the opposite of octane rating. Who is right? (➢23-5)
   a. A only
   b. B only
   c. both A and B
   d. neither A nor B

4. The distributor injection pump has (➢23-10)
   a. a rotor that sends fuel to the injection nozzles
   b. a barrel-and-plunger assembly for each cylinder
   c. a helix cut in each plunger
   d. a control rod attached to the accelerator pedal

5. All the following are true about governors EXCEPT (➢23-12)
   a. A throttle valve in the air intake indicates a pneumatic governor
   b. Moving the accelerator pedal changes the setting of the governor
   c. Air-fuel ratio at full load is about 20:1
   d. All automotive diesel engines use a constant-speed governor

6. Technician A says with indirect injection the fuel is injected into the combustion chamber just as the piston reaches TDC. Technician B says with indirect injection the fuel is injected into the precombustion chamber. Who is right? (➢23-15)
   a. A only
   b. B only
   c. both A and B
   d. neither A nor B

7. The purpose of the glow plug is to (➤23-15)
   a. control engine idle speed
   b. provide sparks to ignite the compressed air-fuel mixture
   c. warm the fuel
   d. add heat to the precombustion chamber

8. Warming the fuel with a fuel heater reduces the possibility that (➤23-17)
   a. wax in the fuel will plug the filters
   b. the glow plugs will overheat
   c. the coolant will freeze
   d. the engine will start

9. All the following are true about servicing injection lines EXCEPT (➤23-20)
   a. cap all lines to prevent dirt from entering
   b. wrap a shop towel around the connection to absorb leaking fuel
   c. a kinked line can be straightened and reused
   d. new lines are preformed

10. Technician A says a sticking injection nozzle may cause the diesel engine to miss at all speeds. Technician B says an injection nozzle sticking open may cause a puff of smoke each time the engine misfires. Who is right? (➤23-22)
    a. A only
    b. B only
    c. both A and B
    d. neither A nor B

REVIEW QUESTIONS

1. Explain how diesel engines are similar to and different from spark-ignition engines. (➤23-1 to 23-3)

2. Describe the importance of cetane number and how it affects ignition lag. (➤23-5)

3. How does water affect diesel fuel and how is the water removed? (➤23-7)

4. Describe the differences between an inline-plunger injection pump and a distributor pump. (➤23-9 to 23-11)

5. How can the operation of an injection nozzle be checked on a running engine? (➤23-22)

CHAPTER 24

ENGINE LUBRICATING SYSTEMS

After studying this chapter, and with proper instruction and equipment, you should be able to:

- Explain the operation of the engine lubricating system.
- Describe five jobs performed by engine oil.
- Explain the viscosity and service ratings of lubricating oil.
- Describe possible troubles in the lubricating system and their causes and corrections.
- Change the engine oil and oil filter.
- Service the engine oil pump and indicating devices.

➤ 24-1 PURPOSE OF LUBRICATING SYSTEM

The *lubricating system* supplies lubricating oil to all moving parts in the engine. Figure 24-1 shows the lubricating system for a four-cylinder OHC spark-ignition engine. The *oil pump* picks up oil from the *oil pan* (➤13-5). The pump sends the oil through the oil filter and then *galleries* (passages) to the main bearings that support the crankshaft. Some oil flows from the main bearings through oil holes drilled in the crankshaft to the rod bearings. The oil flows through the bearing oil clearance and then is thrown off the moving parts.

At the same time, oil flows through an oil gallery to the cylinder head. There the oil flows through an oil gallery to lubricate the camshaft bearings and valve-train parts. After the oil circulates to all engine parts, it drops back down into the oil pan.

Figure 1-16 shows the lubricating system for a V-type camshaft-in-block spark-ignition engine. Figure 24-2 shows an in-line six-cylinder engine. Oil flows up through the hollow pushrods to lubricate the rocker arms and valve stems. Some of the oil thrown off the connecting-rod bearings lands on the cylinder walls. In a V-type engine, the oil splashes on the cylinder wall of the opposing cylinder in the other cylinder bank. This lubricates the pistons, piston rings, and piston pins.

Many engines have small matching grooves or an *oil-spurt hole* (Figs. 24-1 and 24-3) in each connecting rod. The opening provides additional piston and cylinder-wall

lubrication. A spurt of oil sprays out when the hole in the rod aligns with the crankshaft-journal oil hole once each revolution.

Crankshaft bearing lubrication and bearing oil clearance are described in ➤13-18 and 13-19. Figure 13-18 shows the oil passages drilled in a crankshaft. Figures 13-21 to 13-25 show the engine bearings lubricated by the lubricating system. How the piston rings control the oil thrown on the cylinder walls is described in ➤13-33.

ENGINE OIL

➤ 24-2 PURPOSE OF LUBRICATING OIL

The lubricating oil does several jobs in the engine.

1. *The oil lubricates moving parts to reduce wear.* Clearances between moving parts (for example, bearings and rotating shafts) are filled with oil. The parts move on the layers of oil. This reduces power loss in the engine.
2. *As the oil moves through the engine, the oil picks up heat.* The hot oil drops back down into the cooler oil pan where the oil gives up heat. Therefore, the oil serves as a cooling agent. Some engines have *oil nozzles* that spray oil into the underside of the pistons (Fig. 12-9). This removes some heat from the piston heads so the pistons run cooler.
3. *Oil fills the clearances between bearings and rotating journals.* When heavy loads are suddenly imposed on

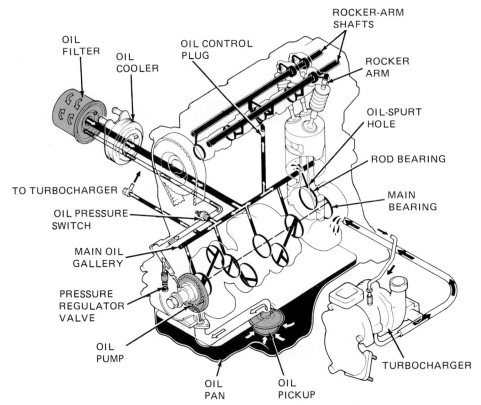

Fig. 24-1 Lubricating system for a four-cylinder OHC spark-ignition engine, which also has a turbocharger and oil cooler. (*Mazda Motors of America, Inc.*)

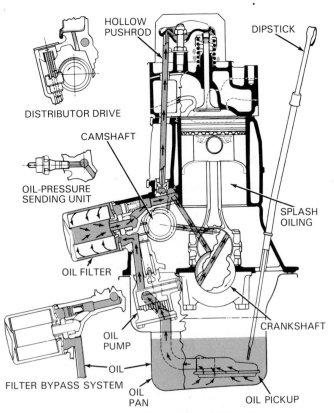

Fig. 24-2 Lubricating system for an inline OHV engine. Arrows show the flow of oil to the moving parts in the engine. (*Buick Division of General Motors Corporation*)

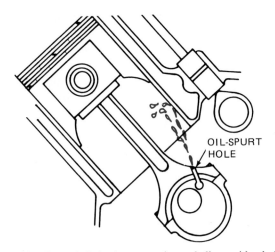

Fig. 24-3 When a hole in the connecting rod aligns with a hole in the crankshaft journal, a spurt of oil sprays onto the cylinder walls to lubricate the piston and rings. (*Ford Motor Company*)

the bearings, the oil helps cushion the shock. This reduces bearing wear.

4. *The oil helps form a gas-tight seal between piston rings and cylinder walls (➤13-29 to 13-33). The oil reduces blowby (➤11-4) in addition to lubricating the pistons and rings.*

5. *The oil acts as a cleaning agent.* The circulating oil picks up particles of dirt and carries them to the oil pan. Larger particles fall to the bottom of the pan. Smaller particles are filtered out by the oil filter (➤24-9).

➤ 24-3 PROPERTIES OF LUBRICATING OIL

The properties needed by an engine lubricating oil include:

1. PROPER VISCOSITY *Viscosity* is a measure of an oil's resistance to flow. A low-viscosity oil is thin and flows easily. A high-viscosity oil is thicker. It flows more slowly.

Engine oil should have the proper viscosity so it flows easily to all moving engine parts. The oil must not be too thin. Low viscosity reduces the ability of the oil to stay in place between moving engine parts. If the oil is too thin (low viscosity), it is forced out from between the moving parts. Rapid wear results.

An oil that is too thick (high viscosity) flows too slowly to engine parts, especially when the engine and oil are cold. This also causes rapid engine wear. The engine runs with insufficient oil when first starting. Also, in cold weather, a high-viscosity oil may be so thick that it prevents normal cranking and starting. A *single-viscosity oil* (defined below) gets thick when cold and thin when hot.

2. VISCOSITY INDEX This is a measure of how much the viscosity of an oil changes with temperature. A single-viscosity oil could be too thick at low temperatures and very thin at high engine temperatures. *Viscosity-index* (VI) *improvers* are added to engine oil so its viscosity stays nearly the same, hot or cold.

3. VISCOSITY NUMBERS There are several grades of single-viscosity oils. They are rated for winter or for other than winter. Winter-grade oils are SAE 0W, SAE 5W, SAE 10W, SAE 15W, SAE 20W, and SAE 25W. The *SAE* stands for the *Society of Automotive Engineers,* which developed the grading system. The W stands for winter. For other than winter use, single-viscosity oil grades are SAE 20, SAE 30, SAE 40, and SAE 50. The higher the number, the thicker the oil.

4. MULTIPLE-VISCOSITY OIL Many engine oils have a viscosity-index improver added. It allows the oil viscosity to remain relatively unchanged, hot or cold. A multiple-viscosity ("multi-viscosity") oil graded SAE 5W-30 has the viscosity of an SAE 5W oil when cold and an SAE 30 oil when hot. Automotive manufacturers recommend multi-viscosity oil for most driving conditions (Fig. 24-4).

5. RESISTANCE TO CARBON FORMATION AND OIL OXIDATION When oil is refined, chemicals are added to fight carbon formation and oxidation. These can occur at the high temperatures inside the engine.

6. CORROSION AND RUST INHIBITORS Additives

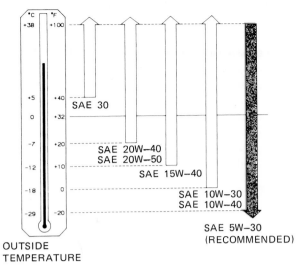

Fig. 24-4 Recommended engine-oil viscosity for different outside temperatures. (*Ford Motor Company*)

are put in the oil to help fight corrosion and rust in the engine. These additives displace water from metal surfaces so oil coats them. The additives also neutralize acids.

7. FOAMING RESISTANCE The churning action of the crankshaft causes the oil to foam or *aerate*. This reduces the lubricating effectiveness of the oil. Foaming can cause the oil to overflow and pass through the crankcase-ventilating system into the intake manifold and air cleaner. The additives help prevent foaming. A baffle in the oil pan (➤13-5) and a *windage tray* between the pan and cylinder block also reduce foaming.

8. DETERGENT-DISPERSANTS These additives are similar in action to soap. They loosen and detach particles of carbon and grit from engine parts. The circulating oil carries the particles to the oil pan.

9. EXTREME-PRESSURE RESISTANCE Additives put into the oil improve the resistance of the oil film to penetration. Engines subject the oil to very high pressures in the bearings and valve train. The *extreme-pressure* (EP) *additives* react chemically with the metal surfaces. The result is a strong, slippery film that resists penetration and being squeezed out.

10. ENERGY-CONSERVING OILS Some oils are *improved* or *energy-conserving* oils. These have special additives (*friction modifiers*) which change some characteristics of the oil. There are two types of modifiers. One is a chemical that dissolves completely in the oil. The other uses powdered *graphite* or *molybdenum* ("moly") held in suspension in the oil. Energy-conserving oils reduce fuel consumption when compared to engine operation with a specified test oil. There are two categories of energy-conserving (EC) engine oils: *EC I* and *EC II*. An oil labeled EC II provides a better fuel-economy improvement than an EC I oil.

11. SYNTHETIC OIL These oils are made by chemical processes and do not necessarily come from petroleum. There are several types. The most common is made from carbon compounds and alcohols. Another is made from coal and crude oil. Synthetic oil tolerates heat better than other oils while producing less sludge (➤24-14) and carbon deposits. The oil companies claim an engine using synthetic oil can safely run longer between oil changes.

➤ 24-4 SERVICE RATINGS OF OIL

Oil is rated by viscosity number (➤24-3) and by its *service rating.* This designation by the American Petroleum Institute (API) indicates the service for which the oil is best suited. There are eight service ratings for spark-ignition lubricating oils: SA, SB, SC, SD, SE, SF, SG, and SH. There are six service ratings for diesel-engine lubricating oils: CA, CB, CC, CD, CE, and CF. The ratings SA through SF are no longer recommended for use in new automotive engines. Figure 24-5 shows the manufacturers' recommendations for using the various spark-ignition (S series) engine oils. Most vehicles on the road today require SG or SH oil.

1. SF OIL This oil was introduced in 1980. It provided more protection against sludge, varnish, wear, oil-screen plugging, and engine deposits than earlier oils. The introduction of SG oil made SF oil outdated. SF oil is no longer widely available.

2. SG OIL This oil was introduced in 1989. It provides better control of engine deposits, oil oxidation, engine wear, and rust and corrosion than SF oil. Any older spark-ignition engine can safely use SG or SH oil.

Note that the service rating is an open-end series. When there is need for oil with additional properties, SI and SJ oils can be produced.

Lubricating oil for diesel engines (C series) must have different properties than oil for spark-ignition engines. The

CA, CB, and CC ratings are obsolete. The CD, CE, and CF ratings indicate oils for severe operating conditions. Use the oil recommended in the owner's manual. The recommended oil may have a *combined rating,* such as *SG/CE* or *SG/CF.* An oil that does not have the recommended combined designation may cause engine damage.

➤ 24-5 OIL-CONTAINER LABELING

The viscosity grade (➤24-3) and service rating (➤24-4) of an oil are different. A high-viscosity oil is not necessarily a "heavy-duty" oil. Viscosity rating refers to the thickness of the oil. This is *not* a measure of heavy-duty quality. An oil with a viscosity rating of SAE 5W-30 will have a service rating of SG or SH, or a combined rating such as SG/CF. Likewise, an oil of any other viscosity grade can have any of the service ratings that are in use.

All oil cans and containers are marked with the API symbol (Fig. 24-6). It tells the type of oil and its viscosity and service ratings. For use in a vehicle, the markings should agree with the recommendations in the owner's manual.

LUBRICATING-SYSTEM COMPONENTS

➤ 24-6 OIL PUMP

Figures 24-7 and 24-8 show two types of oil pumps used in automotive engines. The gear-type pump has a pair of meshing gears. As the gears unmesh, the spaces between the teeth fill with oil from the *pump inlet.* The gears mesh and force the oil out through the *pump outlet.*

The rotor-type oil pump uses an inner rotor and an outer rotor. The inner rotor is driven and drives the outer rotor. As the rotors turn, the spaces between the lobes fill with oil. When the lobes of the inner rotor move into the spaces in the outer rotor, oil is forced out through the pump outlet.

Various arrangements are used to drive the oil pump. In camshaft-in-block engines, the camshaft spiral gear that

Letter Designation	Description	Model Year
SA	Straight mineral oil (non-detergent oil)	Not recommended
SB	Improved non-detergent oil	Not recommended
SC	Meets automobile manufacturers warranty requirements	1967 and prior years
SD	Meets automobile manufacturers warranty requirements	1970 and prior years
SE	Meets automobile manufacturers warranty requirements	1979 and prior years
SF	Meets automobile manufacturers warranty requirements	1988 and prior years
SG	Meets automobile manufacturers warranty requirements	1993 and prior years
SH	Meets automobile manufacturers warranty requirements	Present and prior years

Fig. 24-5 Recommended service ratings of lubricating oils for use in spark-ignition engines.

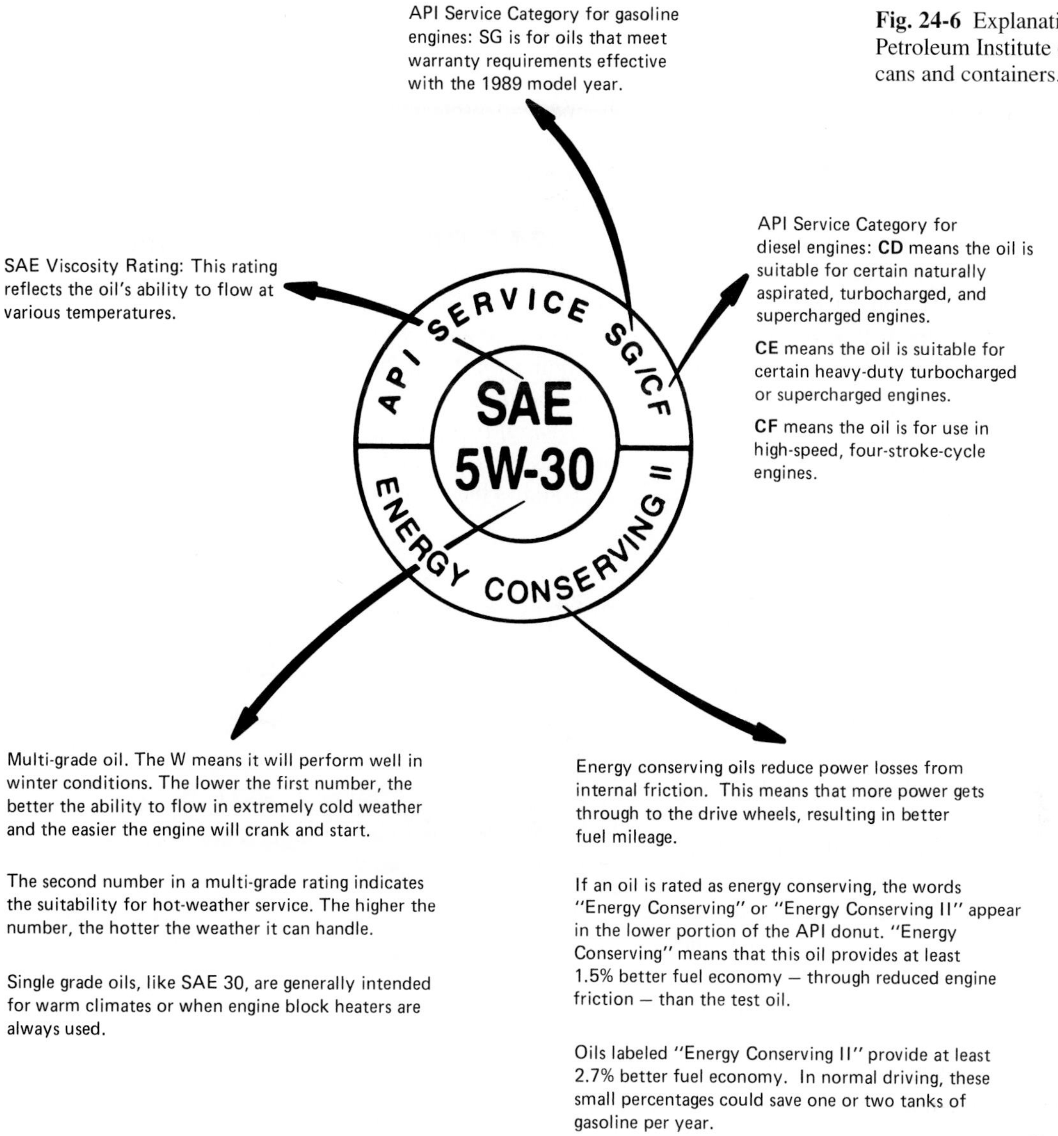

API Service Category for gasoline engines: SG is for oils that meet warranty requirements effective with the 1989 model year.
API Service Category for diesel engines: CD means the oil is suitable for certain naturally aspirated, turbocharged, and supercharged engines.
CE means the oil is suitable for certain heavy-duty turbocharged or supercharged engines.
CF means the oil is for use in high-speed, four-stroke-cycle engines.
SAE Viscosity Rating: This rating reflects the oil's ability to flow at various temperatures.
API SERVICE SG/CF
SAE
5W-30
ENERGY CONSERVING II
Multi-grade oil. The W means it will perform well in winter conditions. The lower the first number, the better the ability to flow in extremely cold weather and the easier the engine will crank and start.
The second number in a multi-grade rating indicates the suitability for hot-weather service. The higher the number, the hotter the weather it can handle.
Single grade oils, like SAE 30, are generally intended for warm climates or when engine block heaters are always used.
Energy conserving oils reduce power losses from internal friction. This means that more power gets through to the drive wheels, resulting in better fuel mileage.
If an oil is rated as energy conserving, the words "Energy Conserving" or "Energy Conserving II" appear in the lower portion of the API donut. "Energy Conserving" means that this oil provides at least 1.5% better fuel economy – through reduced engine friction – than the test oil.
Oils labeled "Energy Conserving II" provide at least 2.7% better fuel economy. In normal driving, these small percentages could save one or two tanks of gasoline per year.

Fig. 24-6 Explanation of the American Petroleum Institute (API) symbol used on oil cans and containers. (*Ford Motor Company*)

PRESSURE-REGULATOR VALVE
DRIVE GEAR
PUMP COVER
SPRING
PIN
DRIVE SHAFT
PUMP BODY
DRIVEN GEAR
PUMP INLET
PICKUP SCREEN

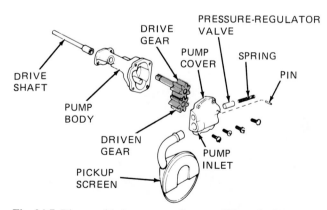

Fig. 24-7 Disassembled gear-type oil pump. (*Chevrolet Division of General Motors Corporation*)

PUMP HOUSING
PRESSURE-RELIEF VALVE
OUTER ROTOR
SPRING
PIN
INNER ROTOR AND SHAFT
ROTOR LOBES
COVER
O RING
PUMP INLET
OIL PICKUP

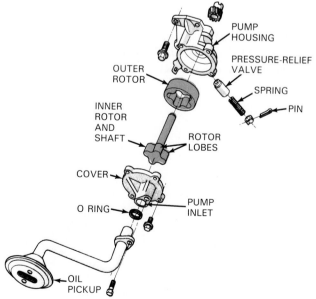

Fig. 24-8 Disassembled rotor-type oil pump. (*Chrysler Corporation*)

drives the ignition distributor usually drives the oil pump (Fig. 12-18). Some engines drive the distributor directly from the end of an overhead camshaft. The oil pump on these engines may be driven by a separate drive shaft (Fig. 12-4) or *jackshaft*. An engine with distributorless ignition

(Chap. 32) may have a *crankshaft-driven oil pump*. Figure 24-1 shows a gear-type oil pump on the front of the crankshaft. Other engines have a crankshaft-driven rotor-type pump.

➤ 24-7 PRESSURE-RELIEF VALVE

To prevent excessive oil pressure, the lubricating system has a *pressure regulator valve* or *relief valve*. It is a spring-loaded ball or plunger (Figs. 24-1 and 24-8). When the pressure reaches the preset value, the ball or plunger compresses the spring. This opens a port through which oil flows back into the oil pan. Enough oil flows past the relief valve to prevent excessive pressure. The oil pump can normally deliver much more oil than the engine requires.

➤ 24-8 OIL COOLER

Some engines use an *oil cooler* (Figs. 1-16 and 24-1). It prevents the oil from getting too hot. In the oil cooler, engine coolant flows past tubes carrying the hot oil. The coolant picks up the excess heat and carries it back to the engine radiator. Outside air passing through the radiator carries away the heat.

Figure 24-9 shows another arrangement that transfers heat to the engine coolant. A hose from the oil filter carries engine oil to an *oil-cooler tube* in the side tank of the radiator. As the oil flows down the tube, the oil loses heat to the coolant. The cooled oil then flows back to the oil filter and to the engine. A similar arrangement cools the fluid in automatic transmissions and transaxles (Chap. 47).

Engines in severe service such as those in taxis and police cars use a radiator-like oil cooler that mounts in front of the engine radiator. The excess heat transfers from the oil to the outside air passing through the oil cooler. A similar system cools automatic-transmission fluid (➤47-18).

➤ 24-9 OIL FILTERS

All automotive engine lubricating systems have an *oil filter* (Fig. 24-1, 24-2, and 24-10). The oil from the pump flows through the filter before reaching the engine bearings. The

filter has a pleated-paper filtering element. It allows the oil to pass through while trapping particles of dirt and carbon.

The filter has a spring-loaded bypass valve (Fig. 24-10). It opens to protect the engine from oil starvation if the filter becomes clogged. Then unfiltered oil bypasses the filter and goes directly to the engine. However, the filter should be changed before this happens (➤24-23).

Some oil filters have an *anti-drainback valve*. It helps prevent oil from draining out of the filter while the engine is off. A full filter supplies oil quickly on starting. This reduces wear and possible damage.

Figures 24-2 and 24-10 show *external* oil filters. They attach to the outside of the engine. Some engines have an *internal* oil filter (Fig. 24-11). It mounts inside the pan and attaches directly to the oil pump. Removing a large *drain plug* allows the filter to be changed.

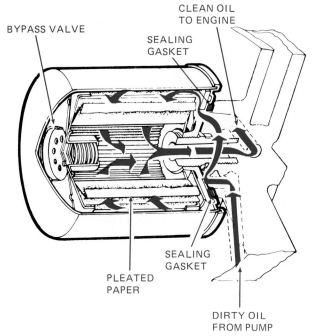

Fig. 24-10 Oil filter, cutaway to show the built-in bypass valve. (*Chrysler Corporation*)

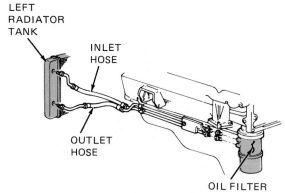

Fig. 24-9 Connections to engine oil cooler, located in the left radiator tank. (*Chevrolet Division of General Motors Corporation*)

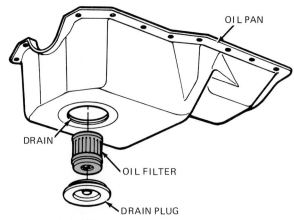

Fig. 24-11 Internal oil filter, which attaches to the oil pump inside the oil pan. (*Pontiac Division of General Motors Corporation*)

LUBRICATING-SYSTEM INDICATORS

➤ 24-10 OIL-PRESSURE INDICATORS

An *oil-pressure indicator* in the instrument panel warns the driver if engine oil pressure is too low. There are four types of oil-pressure indicators.

1. INDICATOR LIGHT The light connects in series with the battery, the ignition switch, and an *oil-pressure switch* on the engine (Fig. 24-12). The oil pressure switch is closed when the engine is not running. When the ignition key is turned to ON, the indicator light glows. As soon as the engine starts, pressure builds up in the lubricating system. This opens the oil-pressure switch and the light goes out. Anytime engine oil pressure falls below a pre-set minimum, the pressure switch closes and the light comes on.

2. ELECTRIC GAUGE Figure 24-13 shows an analog *oil-pressure gauge*. The operation is similar to the fuel gauge. The oil-pressure gauge may be a magnetic gauge or a thermal gauge (➤17-20). In the magnetic oil-pressure gauge shown in Fig. 24-13, the engine unit has a diaphragm connected to a sliding contact. Engine oil pressure pushes the diaphragm up. This moves the sliding contact along the resistance. An increase in oil pressure causes the sliding contact to increase the resistance in the circuit. The amount of current flowing decreases. This allows the right coil to pull the pointer to the right, indicating the increased oil pressure.

3. ELECTRONIC GAUGE Many cars have an electronic instrument cluster (Fig. 17-32). Part of the cluster is an *electronic oil-pressure gauge*. It usually is a bar-graph

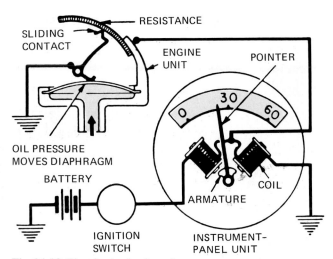

Fig. 24-13 Electric circuit of an oil-pressure gauge.

display made up of a series of segments. The gauge is similar to the electronic fuel-level display (Fig. 17-29). The more segments displayed, the higher the oil pressure. High or low oil pressure causes the bar graph to flash.

4. DIGITAL GAUGE Some cars with an electronic instrument cluster have a *digital oil-pressure gauge*. The number displayed tells the oil pressure in pounds per square inch (psi) or kilopascals [kPa].

➤ 24-11 OIL-LEVEL INDICATORS

An oil-level indicator or *dipstick* is used to measure the crankcase oil level. The dipstick extends down into the oil (Fig. 24-2). To determine the oil level, pull out the dipstick and see how high the oil reaches on the dipstick. Markings usually indicate FULL or ADD OIL. The dipstick tube seals at the top when the dipstick is in place. This prevents unfiltered air from entering the crankcase and crankcase gases from escaping.

Some vehicles have a *low oil-level indicator light*. An *oil-level sensor* (Fig. 24-14) in the oil pan connects to a CHECK OIL LEVEL light in the instrument panel. Turning the ignition key to CRANK or START causes the sensor to check the oil level in the pan. If the oil is not low, the light goes out when the ignition key returns to RUN. If the engine needs a quart [liter] or more of oil, the sensor turns on the CHECK OIL LEVEL light.

➤ 24-12 OIL-CHANGE INDICATOR

The instrument panel of some cars includes an *oil-change indicator light*. The body-control module (BCM) monitors the coolant-temperature sensor, engine-speed sensor, and vehicle-speed sensor. Then the BCM (➤20-13) calculates the remaining useful life of the oil. This is based on the actual driving conditions of the car. When the remaining useful life is zero, the BCM turns on the CHANGE OIL SOON light. Cars with an electronic instrument cluster may display the message CHANGE OIL.

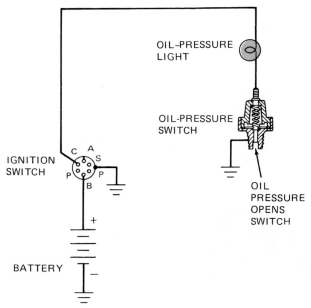

Fig. 24-12 Electric circuit of an oil-pressure indicator light. (*ATW*)

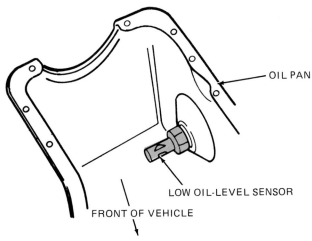

Fig. 24-14 Location of the low-oil-level sensor in the oil pan. (*Ford Motor Company*)

VENTILATION AND CONTAMINATION

➤ 24-13 CRANKCASE VENTILATION

Air must circulate through the crankcase when the engine is running. This removes water, gasoline, and blowby gases from the crankcase. This also helps prevent the formation of *sludge* (➤24-14). In most engines, crankcase ventilation is provided by the *positive-crankcase ventilating* (PCV) system (Chap. 35).

➤ 24-14 SLUDGE FORMATION

Sludge is a thick, creamy, black substance that can form in the engine. It clogs oil screens and lines, preventing oil circulation. The engine then fails from oil starvation.

1. HOW SLUDGE FORMS Water collects in the crankcase in two ways. First, water forms as a byproduct of combustion and enters as blowby (➤11-4). Second, the crankcase ventilating system (Chap. 35) carries air through the crankcase. The moisture in the air condenses on cold engine parts. The crankshaft acts like a big eggbeater, whipping the water and oil into sludge. The black color comes from dirt and carbon.

2. WHY SLUDGE FORMS Water in the crankcase quickly evaporates when the vehicle is driven a long distance each time it starts. The crankcase ventilating system removes the water vapor and no sludge forms. However, sludge forms when the engine operates cold most of the time. For example, sludge forms during home-to-work-to-home driving. This short-trip start-and-stop operation never allows the engine to warm up and reach *normal operating temperature*. The water remains in the oil and forms sludge. Sludge also forms when an engine runs with the cooling-system thermostat (➤25-14)

removed, or with a lower-temperature thermostat than required by the engine.

3. PREVENTING SLUDGE To prevent sludge, the vehicle must be driven long enough to reach normal operating temperature. Then the water in the crankcase vaporizes. This may require trips of 10 miles [16 km] or longer in winter (4 miles [6 km] in summer). Otherwise, change the oil frequently.

➤ 24-15 OTHER AUTOMOTIVE LUBRICANTS

In addition to engine oil, the vehicle needs other lubricants and special fluids. These include automatic-transmission fluid, power-steering fluid, and various other greases listed below.

1. GREASE This is a fluid such as *mineral oil* (made from petroleum) thickened with an agent that makes it a semisolid. The thickening agent may be a metallic soap or nonsoap substance such as clay. Soaps commonly used are lithium, calcium, sodium, aluminum, and barium. Each of these alone or in combination gives the grease special characteristics. Aluminum gives the grease good adhesion. Sodium gives the grease a thick, fibrous appearance.

A good grease must have consistency, stability, oxidation resistance, ability to protect against friction, wear and corrosion, and *feedability*. This is the ability to flow through dispensing equipment.

2. GREASE CLASSIFICATIONS

  a. *Wheel-bearing greases*
  b. *Universal joint greases*
  c. *Chassis greases*
  d. *Extended-lubrication interval (ELI) chassis greases.* These are **lifetime greases** used in joints that are prepacked and sealed. Relubrication normally is not needed for long periods.
  e. *Multipurpose greases* These can be used for chassis, wheel bearings, universal joints, and others. Some ELI greases have multipurpose uses.
  f. *Extreme-pressure (EP) greases* These are suitable for high-load-carrying applications. Some have surface-active additives that bond to the metal and form a barrier that protects if the lubricant film is pierced.
  g. *Other greases* There are special greases for brake-drum mechanisms, speedometer cable, distributor breaker cam, and other special applications.

3. AUTOMATIC-TRANSMISSION AND POWER-STEERING FLUIDS These are compounded to work with specific types and models of automatic transmissions and transaxles, and power-steering systems. Use the specific fluid recommended by the vehicle manufacturer. Automatic-transmission fluid is different from power-steering fluid and cannot be used as a substitute for it on many late-model vehicles.

LUBRICATING-SYSTEM TROUBLE DIAGNOSIS

➤ 24-16 LUBRICATING-SYSTEM TROUBLES

The two most common complaints related to the lubricating system are:

1. Engine uses too much oil (➤24-17).
2. The oil-pressure light or gauge shows low oil pressure (➤24-18).

➤ 24-17 OIL CONSUMPTION

The engine loses oil by burning or by leaking (Fig. 24-15). Three main factors affect oil consumption. These are engine speed, engine wear, and engine sealing.

1. ENGINE SPEED High speed produces high temperature and lower oil viscosity. The oil can more easily get past the piston rings and into the combustion chambers where it burns. High speed also increases the centrifugal force on oil feeding through the crankshaft to the connecting-rod bearings. This throws more oil on the cylinder walls. Also, high speed can cause the oil-control rings to *flutter* or *float*. This allows more oil to get past the rings and reach the combustion chambers. Crankcase-ventilation air passes through the crankcase so fast that some oil flows out as a mist. The PCV system (Chap. 35) carries the mist to the combustion chambers where it burns.

2. ENGINE WEAR As engine parts wear, oil consumption increases. Worn bearings throw more oil on cylinder walls. Worn and tapered cylinders prevent normal action of the oil-control rings. They cannot change size and shape fast enough to scrape off excess oil. More oil gets into the combustion chambers. The oil burns and forms deposits on spark plugs, valves, rings, and pistons. The condition worsens as the piston rings wear and get slightly smaller while the cylinder gets slightly larger. This also reduces the sealing force that the rings apply against the cylinder wall.

Worn intake-valve guides (➤14-9) also increase oil consumption. Oil leaks past the valve stems. The vacuum pulls the oil into the combustion chambers along with the air-fuel mixture every time the intake valves open. Worn exhaust-valve guides also cause high oil consumption. The oil leaks into the exhaust manifold and burns as the hot exhaust gases hit it.

Installation of new valve guides, reaming of guides and installation of valves with oversize stems, and installation of valve-stem oil seals help reduce oil losses (Chap. 39). Also, valve guides can be knurled and reamed to restore proper clearance.

3. ENGINE SEALING Figure 24-15 shows places where oil may leak from an engine. A common cause of oil loss is

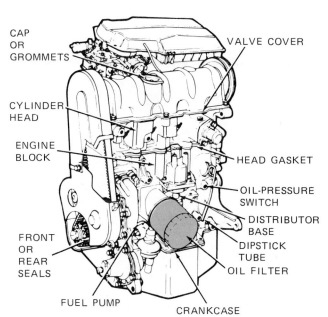

Fig. 24-15 Places where oil may leak from an engine. (*Chrysler Corporation*)

poor sealing. This allows external leaks which may leave spots under the engine of a parked car. The oil can leak from a loose fitting or filter, or from a gasket or seal that fails. Sometimes adding dye to the oil and then shining an ultraviolet light on the leak area will help locate the source.

➤ 24-18 OIL-PRESSURE LIGHT OR GAUGE SHOWS LOW PRESSURE

Sometimes the indicator light flickers or comes on, or the gauge shows low oil pressure. The oil level in the crankcase is probably low. Oil is being picked up only part of the time. The oil pickup (Figs. 24-1 and 24-2) may have fallen off or been pushed up by a bent oil pan. Hitting a curb or other object can bend the oil pan. Another cause could be an oil line clogged by excessive sealant or sludge (➤24-14).

Check for low oil in the oil pan. If there is sufficient oil, the oil-pressure sending unit (➤24-10) may be faulty. Substitute a good unit or install a pressure gauge (Fig. 24-16). Then run the engine to see if the light or gauge reads normally. Noise from the valve lifters and bearings may also warn that oil pressure is low.

If the pressure is actually low, there is probably engine trouble. An engine operating without oil pressure is quickly damaged.

Causes of low oil pressure include:

1. A weak or broken relief-valve spring.
2. A worn oil pump.
3. A broken or cracked oil line.
4. An obstruction in the oil line.

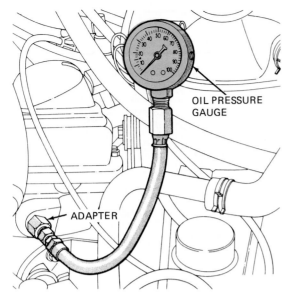

Fig. 24-16 Oil-pressure gauge for measuring oil pressure in a running engine, connected to the engine lubricating system. (*Chrysler Corporation*)

5. Insufficient or thin oil.
6. Worn engine bearings.
7. A leaking oil filter, oil-filter gasket, or oil-pressure sending unit.

Excessive oil pressure may result from:

1. A stuck pressure-relief valve.
2. The wrong spring in the pressure-relief valve.
3. A clogged oil line.
4. Thick oil.

LUBRICATING-SYSTEM SERVICE

➤ 24-19 SERVICING LUBRICATING SYSTEMS

When an engine is rebuilt, the oil pan is removed and cleaned (➤24-24). Oil passages in the crankshaft and cylinder block are cleaned out. Chapter 41 covers these jobs. Following sections describe other lubricating-system services.

➤ 24-20 CHECKING OIL LEVEL

Park the vehicle on a level surface and turn the engine off. Wait a couple minutes for the oil to drain back down into the oil pan.

Withdraw the dipstick (Fig. 24-2) and wipe it clean. Reinsert it and withdraw it again. Note the oil level on the dipstick. The markings on the dipstick indicate if oil should be added.

Note the condition of the oil to determine if it is dirty, thick, or thin. Rub a few drops of oil between your thumb

and fingers to detect particles. Smell the oil to determine if it contains gasoline. If the level is low, add oil. If the oil is contaminated, change it (➤24-21).

➤ 24-21 OIL CHANGES

Change oil when it gets dirty or contaminated. Oil begins to lose its effectiveness the day it is poured into the engine. This loss is largely a result of the depletion or "wearing out" of the additives. The anti-oxidation additive becomes used up, so gum and varnish form. The corrosion and rust inhibitors are gradually used up. This allows corrosion and rust to form.

Engine oil gradually becomes contaminated with carbon that forms in the combustion chamber. Contamination also occurs from fine dust that gets through the air cleaner and metal particles from the engine as it wears. Even though the oil filter removes particles, it does not trap them all.

Automotive manufacturers recommend periodic oil changes. This avoids excessive oil contamination and damaging engine wear. How often the oil should be changed depends primarily on how the vehicle is used. There are normally two recommendations in the maintenance schedule.

Schedule 1 calls for changing engine oil and oil filter every 3000 miles [5000 km] if:

- Most trips in warm weather are less than 4 miles [6 km].
- Most trips in below freezing weather are less than 10 miles [16 km].
- Most trips include extended idling and low speed stop-and-go operation.
- Operating in dusty conditions.
- Towing a trailer

Schedule 2 calls for changing oil every 7500 miles [12,500 km]. Change the oil filter the first oil change and every other time after that. These intervals apply if the vehicle is driven several miles daily and none of the items in Schedule 1 apply.

Many manufacturers recommend SAE 5W-30 oil for spark-ignition engines. Other grades of oil may be used, depending on the temperature in which the car may operate (Fig. 24-4). Always use oil with the viscosity and service rating (Fig. 24-5) specified in the vehicle owner's manual.

➤ 24-22 CHANGING ENGINE OIL

Raise the vehicle on a lift. Place a drain-oil container in position (Fig. 24-17). Then remove the drain plug from the oil pan. After the oil drains, install the plug and lower the vehicle. Add the proper amount of the specified oil. On a cold engine, some recommendations are to disable the ignition or fuel delivery and crank the engine until the oil light goes out. Then start the engine and check for leaks.

Place a new *maintenance sticker* on the vehicle. Write in the odometer reading, the date, and the type of oil used.

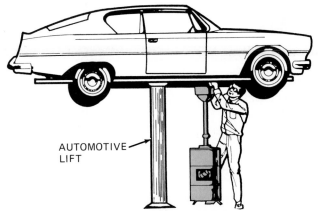

Fig. 24-17 Draining the engine oil. (*ATW*)

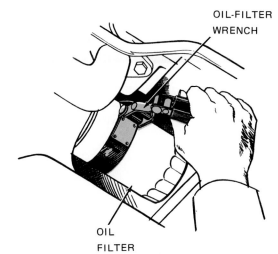

Fig. 24-18 Using an oil-filter wrench to replace an oil filter. (*Lisle Corporation*)

Dispose of the drained engine oil in a legal and environmentally-safe manner. Most shops have a large storage tank that is pumped out periodically by a waste-oil hauler. Do not pour used oil on the ground or down drains and sewers.

➤ 24-23 OIL-FILTER SERVICE

Change the oil filter with every oil change or every other oil change, according to the operating conditions (➤24-21). Most filters are unscrewed and a new filter installed by hand. You may need an *oil-filter wrench* (Fig. 24-18) to loosen the old filter. Clean the filter mount and recess with a clean shop towel. Make sure the old filter sealing gasket (Fig. 24-10) does not remain on the engine. Coat the sealing gasket on the new filter with oil. Then install the new filter. Tighten it until the gasket contacts the filter base on the engine. Then tighten the filter an additional 3/4 to 1 turn. Start the engine and check for leaks.

NOTE Refer to the manufacturer's service manual for procedures on changing the internal oil filter (Fig. 24-11).

Place a new maintenance sticker on the vehicle. Mark the odometer reading, the date, and the oil and filter change on the maintenance sticker.

➤ 24-24 OIL-PAN SERVICE

Whenever the oil pan is removed for engine or oil pump service, clean the pan, oil pickup, and oil pump. Remove all old gasket material from the gasket surfaces on the pan and block. Check the gasket surfaces of a sheet-metal pan for flatness. Overtightened screws raise the metal around the screw holes. This can prevent sealing of the new gasket. Tap the holes lightly with a hammer until the gasket surfaces are flat.

Some gaskets are preformed (➤6-22). Others are formed-in-place from silicone rubber (➤6-24). If using a preformed gasket, be sure to install the gasket "right side up." Align the bolt holes in the gasket and pan. Then install the pan and tighten the bolts to the specified torque.

➤ 24-25 OIL-PUMP SERVICE

Oil pumps (Figs. 24-1 and 24-2) require no service in normal operation. If badly worn, a pump will not maintain pressure. Remove it for service or replacement. Follow the procedures in the manufacturer's service manual.

➤ 24-26 PRESSURE-RELIEF-VALVE SERVICE

Pressure-relief valves (Fig. 24-7 and 24-8) are not adjustable. If the oil pump is not at fault and oil pressure is low, a stronger spring will raise the oil pressure. However, this is not usually recommended. Section 24-18 describes other possible causes of low oil pressure.

➤ 24-27 OIL-PRESSURE INDICATORS

These units normally require no service. Replace a defective engine or instrument-panel unit. A new engine unit can be temporarily substituted for the old unit to determine if it failed. Other diagnosis and service procedures for electronic oil-pressure gauges, oil-level indicator, and oil-change indicator are in the vehicle service manual.

TRADE TALK

crankcase ventilation   multiple-viscosity oil   sludge   viscosity index
detergent-dispersant   oil-change indicator   synthetic oil
dipstick   service rating   viscosity

MULTIPLE-CHOICE TEST

Select the **one** *correct, best, or most probable answer to each question.*
You can find the answers in the section indicated at the end of the question.

1. In addition to lubricating engine parts and acting as a cooling agent, the lubricating oil must (➤24-2)
   a. improve carburetion, aid fuel pump, and seal
   b. increase clearances, cool engine, and seal bearings
   c. cool engine, reduce clearances, and seal
   d. absorb shocks, seal, and clean

2. The two types of oil pumps in automotive engines are (➤24-6)
   a. gear and piston
   b. rotor and piston
   c. gear and rotor
   d. full flow and bypass

3. An oil-pressure indicator may be any of the following EXCEPT a (➤24-10)
   a. dipstick
   b. digital display
   c. light
   d. gauge

4. The only service rating for spark-ignition engine oil for new automobile engines is (➤24-4)
   a. SE
   b. CE
   c. SF
   d. SG

5. A container of oil with the highest API rating for automotive diesel engines is marked (➤24-4)
   a. high sulfur and low viscosity
   b. heavy duty and synthetic
   c. SG/CE or SG/CF
   d. SF/CC or SF/CD

6. The purpose of the pressure-relief valve is to (➤24-7)
   a. ensure minimum pressure
   b. prevent excessive pressure
   c. prevent insufficient lubrication
   d. bypass oil around a clogged filter

7. Most water gets into the crankcase during (➤ 24-14)
   a. high-speed operation
   b. long trips
   c. engine overheating
   d. engine warmup

8. An engine loses oil by (➤24-17)
   a. evaporation
   b. burning in the combustion chamber
   c. condensation
   d. leaking into the transmission

9. Oil can enter the combustion chamber in two ways — around the valve stems and (➤24-17)
   a. past the float-bowl needle
   b. through the exhaust-manifold gaskets
   c. through the intake manifold
   d. past the piston rings

10. Causes of excessive oil consumption can include (➤24-17)
    a. heavy oil and tight bearings
    b. high engine speed and worn engine parts
    c. short trips and cold weather
    d. frequent oil changes and weak valve springs

REVIEW QUESTIONS

1. Describe the properties needed by an engine lubricating oil and the reasons for the additives that are put into it. (➤24-3)

2. Explain the difference between a single-grade oil and a multi-viscosity oil. (➤24-3)

3. How does sludge form in the engine? (➤24-14)

4. What are seven causes of low oil pressure and four causes of high oil pressure? (➤24-18)

5. When should engine oil be changed? (➤24-21)

CHAPTER 25

ENGINE COOLING SYSTEMS

After studying this chapter, you should be able to:

- Describe the purpose and operation of the engine cooling system.
- Explain the difference in coolant flow with the thermostat closed and open.
- Discuss why a fan is needed, the types of fans, and how each is driven.
- Explain the purpose and operation of the two valves in the radiator pressure cap.
- Describe the characteristics and types of antifreeze.

➤ 25-1 HEAT IN THE ENGINE

The burning air-fuel mixture in the engine cylinders may reach 4000°F [2200°C] or higher. This means engine parts get hot. However, cylinder walls must not get hotter than about 500°F [260°C]. Higher temperatures cause lubricating oil to break down and lose its lubricating ability. Other engine parts are also damaged. To prevent overheating, the *cooling system* removes the excess heat (Fig. 15-14). This is about one-third of the heat produced in the combustion chambers by the burning air-fuel mixture.

➤ 25-2 PURPOSE OF COOLING SYSTEM

The cooling system (Figs. 11-23 and 25-1) keeps the engine at its most efficient temperature at all speeds and operating conditions. Burning fuel in the engine produces heat. Some of this heat must be taken away before it damages engine parts. This is one of the three jobs performed by the cooling system. It also helps bring the engine up to *normal operating temperature* as quickly as possible. In addition, the cooling system provides a source of heat for the passenger-compartment *heater-and-air-conditioner* (Chap. 55).

➤ 25-3 OPERATION OF COOLING SYSTEM

The cooling system (Fig. 25-2) uses five basic parts to do its job of controlling engine temperature.

1. WATER JACKETS The cylinder block and cylinder head have internal passages or *water jackets* that surround the cylinder and combustion chamber (Fig. 25-3). Water mixed with antifreeze (the *coolant*) flows through the water jackets, picking up heat. This cools the metal parts and heats the coolant.

2. WATER PUMP An engine-driven *water pump* pushes the hot coolant out of the water jackets and through the radiator.

3. THERMOSTAT A thermostatic valve called a *thermostat* controls coolant flow. When the engine is cold, the thermostat closes to prevent coolant circulation to the radiator. This keeps all heat in the engine so it warms up quickly. The engine produces excessive exhaust emissions of HC and CO when cold. As the engine warms up, the thermostat opens to allow coolant flow through the radiator.

4. RADIATOR The *radiator* is a *heat exchanger* with two sets of passages. One set is for coolant and the other for outside air. In the radiator, the coolant loses heat to the passing air. Then the coolant flows back through the water jackets to pick up heat again. The coolant circulates continuously between the water jackets and the radiator.

5. FAN A *fan* pulls or pushes outside air through the radiator. This improves engine cooling, especially at idle and low speed.

These and other parts continuously work together to control engine temperature and prevent overheating. Following sections describe the construction and operation of the components in the engine cooling system.

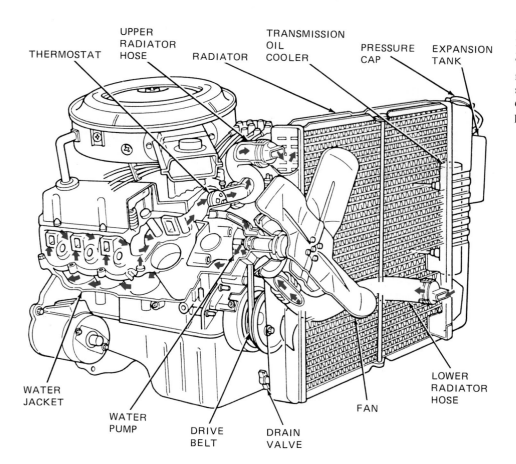

THERMOSTAT · UPPER RADIATOR HOSE · RADIATOR · TRANSMISSION OIL COOLER · PRESSURE CAP · EXPANSION TANK

WATER JACKET · WATER PUMP · DRIVE BELT · DRAIN VALVE · FAN · LOWER RADIATOR HOSE

Fig. 25-1 Cooling system for a longitudinally-mounted engine. This arrangement is typical of rear-wheel-drive vehicles. Arrows show coolant flow with the engine at normal operating temperature. (*Ford Motor Company*)

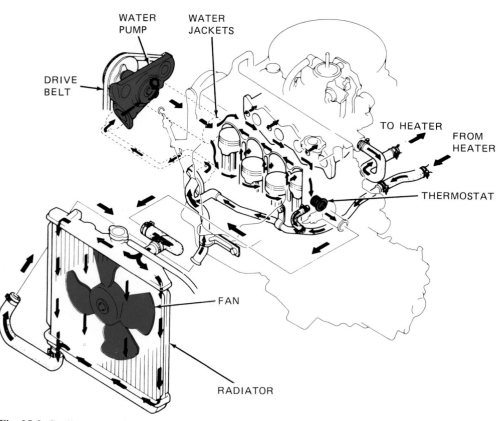

DRIVE BELT · WATER PUMP · WATER JACKETS · TO HEATER · FROM HEATER · THERMOSTAT · FAN · RADIATOR

Fig. 25-2 Cooling system for a transverse engine in a front-wheel-drive vehicle, showing the radiator located on one side of the engine. (*Ford Motor Company*)

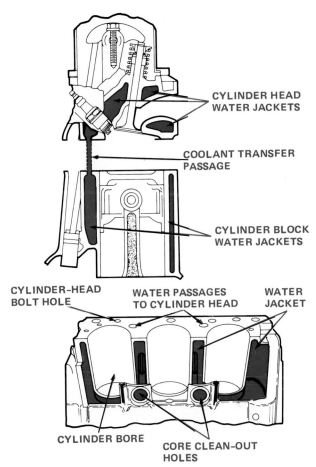

CYLINDER HEAD WATER JACKETS

COOLANT TRANSFER PASSAGE

CYLINDER BLOCK WATER JACKETS

CYLINDER-HEAD BOLT HOLE

WATER PASSAGES TO CYLINDER HEAD

WATER JACKET

CYLINDER BORE

CORE CLEAN-OUT HOLES

Fig. 25-3 Water jackets in cylinder head and block.

COOLING-SYSTEM COMPONENTS

➤ 25-4 WATER JACKETS

The water jackets (Figs. 25-1 and 25-3) are open spaces between the cylinder walls and the outside shell of the block and head. Coolant from the water pump flows first

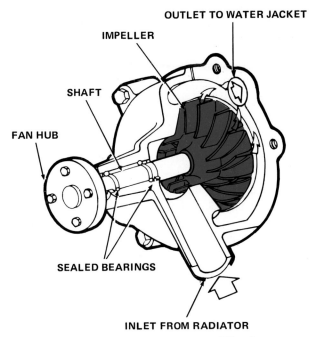

OUTLET TO WATER JACKET

IMPELLER

SHAFT

FAN HUB

SEALED BEARINGS

INLET FROM RADIATOR

Fig. 25-4 Impeller action in the water pump. (*Chrysler Corporation*)

through the block water jackets. Then the coolant flows up through the cylinder-head water jackets and back to the radiator.

➤ 25-5 WATER PUMP

Water pumps are *impeller* pumps (Figs. 25-4 and 25-5). They attach to the front of the engine and are driven by a belt from the crankshaft pulley (Fig. 25-1). The pump circulates as much as 7500 gallons [28,390 L] of coolant an hour. As the impeller rotates, the curved blades draw coolant from the bottom of the radiator. They force the coolant through the pump outlet to the water jackets.

The impeller shaft is supported on sealed bearings which never need lubrication. Seals prevent the coolant from leaking past the bearings. In Fig. 25-1, the water pump is

Fig. 25-5 Disassembled water pump. (*Chrysler Corporation*)

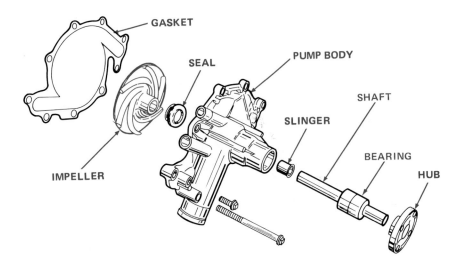

GASKET

SEAL

PUMP BODY

SHAFT

SLINGER

BEARING

HUB

IMPELLER

driven by the *fan belt*. The water pump may also be driven by a single *serpentine belt* that also drives other components (Fig. 25-6). Drive belts are described in ➤25-9. Instead of using a drive belt, the water pump on some engines is gear-driven from the engine crankshaft.

➤ 25-6 ENGINE FAN

The radiator sometimes needs additional airflow through it to prevent the engine from overheating. This usually occurs at idle and slow speed. At higher vehicle speeds, the air rammed through the radiator by the forward motion of the vehicle provides all the cooling that is needed. An *engine fan* or *cooling fan* pulls the additional air through the radiator. The fan may be either a *mechanical fan* or an *electric fan* (➤25-10).

Engines mounted longitudinally in rear-drive vehicles usually have a mechanical fan (Fig. 25-7) that mounts to the water-pump shaft. The fan is made of sheet steel or molded plastic (Fig. 12-14). It has four to seven blades and turns with the water-pump impeller. A *fan shroud* (Fig. 25-8) around the fan directs the airflow. This increases the efficiency of the fan.

➤ 25-7 VARIABLE-SPEED FAN

Many longitudinal engines use a *variable-speed fan* driven through a *fan clutch* (Fig. 25-9). The fan clutch is a temperature-controlled fluid coupling that mounts between the water-pump pulley and the fan (Fig. 12-14). The air passing through the radiator strikes a thermostatic blade or

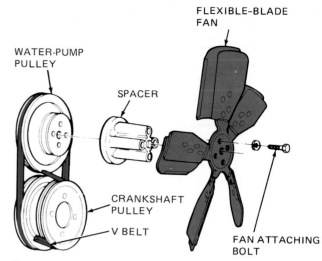

Fig. 25-7 Attachment of the mechanical fan with flexible blades to the spacer that mounts on the water-pump pulley. (*Ford Motor Company*)

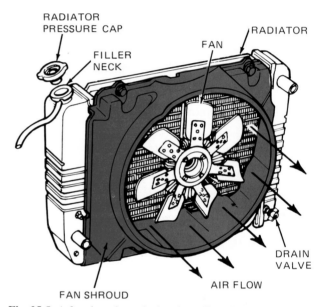

Fig. 25-8 A fan shroud attached to the radiator improves fan performance. (*Chrysler Corporation*)

spring on the front of the clutch. The temperature of the air causes the thermostatic device to bend. This operates a valve that allows *silicone oil* to enter or leave the fluid coupling.

When the engine is cold, the fluid coupling slips so the fan is not driven. This reduces noise and saves engine power. As the engine warms up, the thermostatic device causes more oil to enter the fluid coupling. Then the fan clutch begins to drive the fan.

➤ 25-8 FLEXIBLE-BLADE FAN

Another way to reduce the power needed to drive the fan, and reduce fan noise, is to use *flexible blades* on the fan (Fig. 25-7). In operation, the slant or *pitch* of the blades

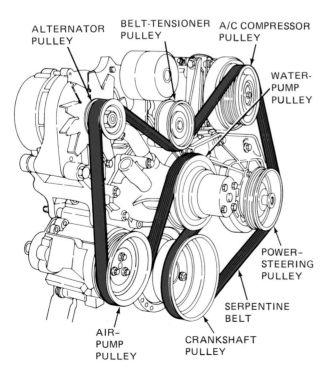

Fig. 25-6 Single serpentine belt that drives the water pump and other engine accessories. (*Pontiac Division of General Motors Corporation*)

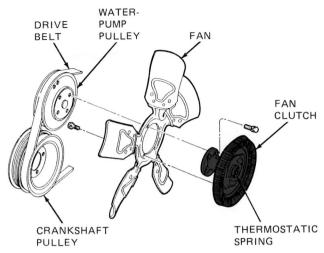

Fig. 25-9 A variable-speed fan driven through a fan clutch that mounts on the water-pump pulley. (*Ford Motor Company*)

decreases as fan speed increases (Fig. 25-10). Centrifugal force flattens the blades so they take a smaller bite of air. This reduces noise and airflow, and the power needed to turn the fan.

CAUTION!

Fan blades can break and fly off. Whenever the engine is running, NEVER stand directly in line with the fan. Keep your hands and tools away from the drive belt and rotating fan.

➤ **25-9 DRIVE BELTS**

A *drive belt* is a continuous loop of reinforced rubber used to transmit power between two shafts. Three types of belts

are used to drive the water pump. These are the *V belt*, the *ribbed belt*, and the *toothed belt*. The V belt (Fig. 25-7) has a V-shaped cross section that wedges into pulley grooves of matching width. Friction between the sides of the belt and the sides of the pulley grooves transmits the power. Power is *not* transmitted through the bottom of the V belt.

The ribbed or serpentine belt (Fig. 25-6) has a series of V-shaped ridges that act like a series of small V belts. The ribs or ridges wedge into matching grooves in the pulleys. Friction between the sides of the small ridges and grooves transmits the power. Power is *not* transmitted through the sides. Some older engines needed four or five V belts to drive all the engine-driven devices. Instead, many newer engines have a single serpentine belt (Fig. 25-6). It can transmit greater power than the V belts.

The toothed belt is described in ➤14-5. A water pump driven by a toothed timing belt has a sprocket (Fig. 14-9) instead of a pulley.

➤ **25-10 ELECTRIC FAN**

Transverse engines in front-drive vehicles usually have an electric fan (Figs. 4-10 and 25-11). An electric motor turns the blades. A *thermostatic switch* turns on the fan only when needed. For example, in one engine, the switch turns on the fan when the coolant reaches 200°F [93°C]. It turns off the fan if the coolant drops below this temperature. On vehicles with air conditioning, turning on the air conditioning bypasses the thermostatic switch. The fan runs all the time when the air conditioner is on. The fan is turned ON and OFF by the electronic control module (ECM) in many vehicles with an electronic engine control system (Fig. 19-26).

Most fans, mechanical and electric, are pull-type fans. They mount behind the radiator and pull air through it.

Fig. 25-10 The blades on a flexible-blade fan change pitch as fan speed increases.

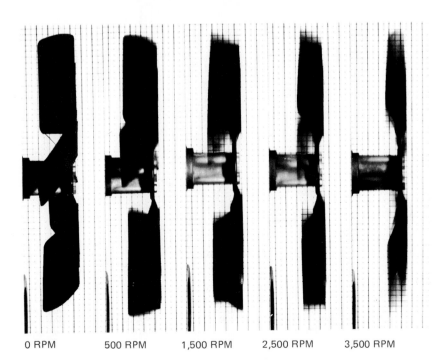

0 RPM   500 RPM   1,500 RPM   2,500 RPM   3,500 RPM

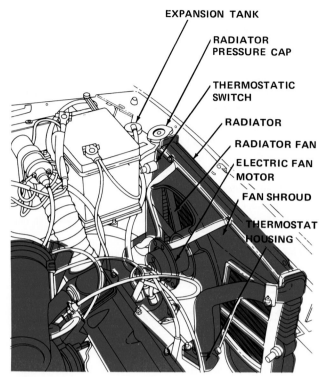

Fig. 25-11 Electric fan, used with a transverse engine. (*Chrysler Corporation*)

➤ 25-11 RADIATOR

The radiator (Figs. 25-2 and 25-13) is a heat exchanger that removes heat from engine coolant passing through it. The heat transfers from the hot coolant to the cooler outside air.

An automotive radiator has three main parts. These are a *radiator core* (Fig. 25-13), and *inlet* and *outlet* tanks. The cores are usually made of aluminum. The tanks may be made of plastic or metal. The core has two sets of passages, a set of *tubes,* and a set of *fins* attached to the tubes. The tubes run from the inlet tank to the outlet tank. Coolant flows through the tubes and air flows between the fins. The hot coolant sends heat through the tubes to the fins. The outside air passing between the fins picks up and carries away the heat. This lowers the temperature of the coolant.

Figures 25-2 and 25-13 show a *down-flow radiator* of *tube-and-fin construction*. The coolant flows from the upper tank down through the tubes to the lower tank. Most

Some cars also have a push-type fan. It mounts in front of the radiator and pushes air through it. Figure 25-12 shows the use of three electric fans on a car with air conditioning. There are two smaller pull fans and a larger push fan.

An electric fan drains less power from the engine and creates less noise than a mechanical fan. Also, there is no fan belt to inspect, adjust, or replace.

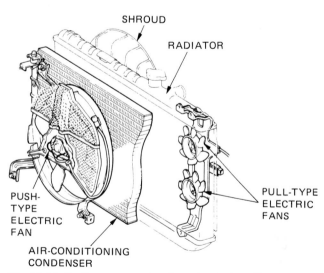

Fig. 25-12 Cooling system using three electric fans. The larger fan pushes air through the air-conditioning condenser and radiator, while the two smaller fans pull air through. (*Toyota Motor Sales, U.S.A., Inc.*)

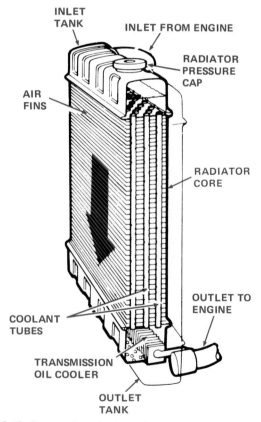

Fig. 25-13 Construction of a down-flow tube-and-fin radiator, which includes a transmission oil cooler. (*Chrysler Corporation*)

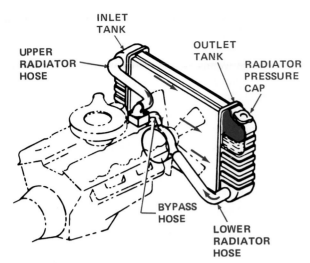

Fig. 25-14 Cooling system using a cross-flow radiator.

cars use a *cross-flow radiator* (Figs. 25-1 and 25-14). The tubes are horizontal so the coolant flows from the inlet tank horizontally to the outlet tank. The cross-flow radiator takes up less space from top to bottom. A car with a cross-flow radiator can have a lower hood line.

A typical radiator in a car with factory-installed air conditioning has seven fins per inch [25.4 mm]. Heavy-duty radiators may have more fins and more rows of tubes. These provide greater cooling capacity to handle additional heat loads such as those caused by the air conditioner or turbocharger.

On vehicles with an automatic transaxle or transmission, the outlet tank has a *transmission oil cooler* (Figs. 25-1 and 25-13). Many radiators have a *drain valve* (Figs. 25-1 and 25-8) in the bottom. Radiators with a *filler neck* (Fig. 25-8) in the top seal the opening with a *radiator pressure cap* (➤25-16).

➤ 25-12 OTHER HEAT EXCHANGERS

Engine coolant is not the only fluid in the car that must have heat removed. Some engines have an *oil cooler* (➤24-8) to control the temperature of the lubricating oil. Most supercharged and turbocharged engines have an *intercooler* (➤18-9). It cools the intake air after it is compressed. Both the oil cooler and the intercooler are types of heat exchangers. Other vehicle systems also use a heat exchanger. These include the automatic transmission (Chap. 47), power steering (Chap. 50), and air conditioner (Chap. 55).

Figure 25-15 shows the heat-exchanger arrangement for a car with a stack of four heat exchangers. An electric push fan at the front helps ensure adequate air through the stack. The *air-conditioner condenser* is next, followed by an air-to-air intercooler. Nearest to the engine is the cooling-system radiator, with the engine oil cooler to one side. An electric pull fan and shroud help provide the needed air flow. Figure 25-16 shows the airflow through the engine compartment. Outside air passes through the heat exchangers, over and around the engine, and exits under the vehicle.

➤ 25-13 EXPANSION TANK

Most cooling systems have a separate plastic reservoir or *expansion tank* (Fig. 25-17). It is partly filled with coolant and connected by an *overflow* or *transfer tube* to the radiator filler neck. As the engine heats up, the coolant expands and flows through the transfer tube into the

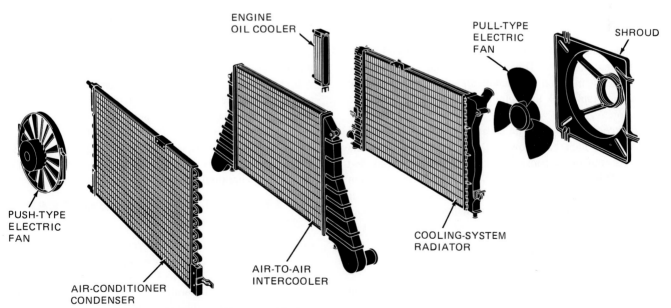

Fig. 25-15 Stack of four heat exchangers used in a car with air conditioning and a turbocharged, intercooled engine. (*Saab Cars USA, Inc.*)

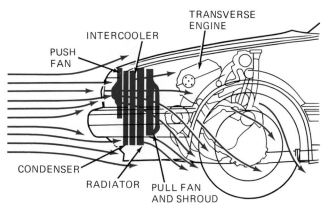

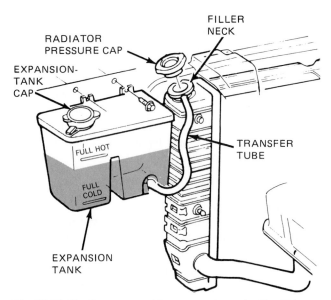

Fig. 25-16 Airflow through the stacked heat exchangers and engine compartment. (*Saab Cars USA, Inc.*)

Fig. 25-17 Cooling system with an expansion tank. (*Ford Motor Company*)

expansion tank. When the engine is turned off and cools, the coolant contracts. This creates a partial vacuum in the cooling system. Then the vacuum siphons coolant from the expansion tank back through the transfer tube and into the radiator.

The cooling system with an expansion tank is a closed system. Coolant can flow back and forth between the radiator and the expansion tank as the engine heats and cools. This keeps the cooling system filled for maximum cooling efficiency. The expansion tank also eliminates air bubbles from the coolant. Coolant without air bubbles can handle more heat.

➤ **25-14 THERMOSTAT**

The thermostat (Figs. 25-1 and 25-18) is a heat-operated valve that regulates coolant temperature. It does this by controlling coolant flow from the engine to the radiator. The thermostat is in the coolant passage between the

cylinder head and the radiator. The valve in the thermostat opens and closes as coolant temperature changes. When the engine is cold, the thermostat closes (Fig. 25-18, left). As the engine warms up, the thermostat opens (Fig. 25-18, right). This prevents or allows coolant flow through the radiator (Fig. 25-19).

By closing the passage to the radiator when the engine is cold, the engine warms up more quickly. Engine heat stays in the engine instead of being carried to the radiator. This shortens warmup time, wastes less fuel, and reduces exhaust emissions. After warmup, the thermostat keeps the engine running at a higher temperature than it would without a thermostat. The higher operating temperature improves engine efficiency and reduces exhaust emissions.

> **NOTE** In some engines, the thermostat is between the lower radiator hose and the engine. This is a *reverse-flow cooling system*. It prevents coolant flow from the radiator to the engine until the thermostat begins to open. Cooling-system operation is the same with the thermostat in either location.

There are several types of automotive thermostats. A heat-sensitive *wax pellet* (Fig. 25-18) operates most thermostats. It expands with increasing temperature to open the valve.

The thermostat opens at a specific temperature or *thermostat rating*. This number is usually stamped on the thermostat. Two common ratings are 185°F [85°C] and 195°F [91°C]. Most thermostats *begin* to open at their rated temperature. They are fully open about 20°F [11°C] higher. For example, a 195°F [91°C] starts to open at that temperature. It is fully open about 215°F [102°C].

➤ **25-15 COOLANT BYPASS PASSAGE**

Most engines have a small *coolant bypass passage* (Figs. 25-14 and 25-18). The bypass may be an external *bypass hose* (Fig. 25-14) on the top of the water pump, or an internal passage. It permits some coolant to circulate within the cylinder block and head when the engine is cold and the thermostat closed. This provides equal warming of the cylinders and prevents hot spots.

Some engines use a *blocking-bypass thermostat*. It has a *bypass valve* that restricts or closes the bypass passage as the thermostat opens after engine warmup. This prevents coolant from continuing to flow through the bypass.

➤ **25-16 RADIATOR PRESSURE CAP**

Cooling systems are sealed and pressurized by a *radiator pressure cap* (Fig. 25-20). Sealing reduces coolant loss from evaporation and allows the use of an expansion tank. Pressurizing raises the boiling temperature of the coolant, thereby increasing cooling efficiency.

At normal atmospheric pressure, water boils at 212°F [100°C]. If air pressure increases, the boiling point also

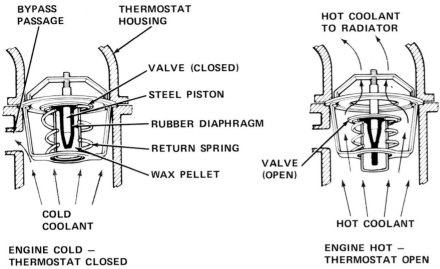

Fig. 25-18 Operation of a wax-pellet type of cooling-system thermostat. (*Chrysler Corporation*)

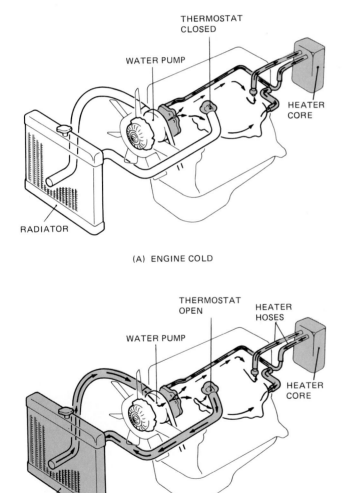

Fig. 25-19 Coolant circulation when the engine is (A) cold and (B) hot. (*Mitsubishi Motor Sales of America, Inc.*)

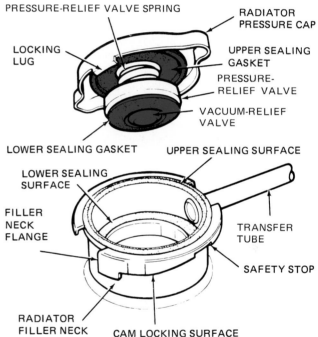

Fig. 25-20 A radiator pressure cap removed from the radiator filler neck. (*Chrysler Corporation*)

increases. For example, if the pressure is raised by 15 psi [103 kPa] over atmospheric pressure, the boiling point is raised to about 260°F [127°C]. Every 1 psi [7 kPa] increase in pressure raises the boiling point of water about 3 1/4°F [1.8°C]. This is the principle on which the pressurized cooling system works.

As the pressure in the cooling system goes up, the boiling point of the coolant goes higher than 212°F [100°C]. There is a greater difference between coolant temperature and outside air temperature. The hotter the coolant, the faster heat moves from the radiator to the cooler passing air. Pressurizing the cooling system also increases water-pump efficiency.

Normal pressure in the cooling system is determined by the vehicle manufacturer. Less than normal pressure allows coolant to be lost and may cause boiling. Too much pressure can damage the radiator and blow off hoses. The radiator cap has a *pressure-relief valve* (Fig. 25-20) to prevent excessive pressure. When the pressure goes too high, it raises the valve. Excess pressure and coolant then escape into the expansion tank (Fig. 25-21, left).

The radiator cap also has a *vacuum-relief valve* (Fig. 25-20). It protects the system from developing a vacuum that could collapse the radiator. When the engine is shut off and begins to cool, the coolant contracts. Cold coolant takes up less space than hot coolant. As the volume of coolant decreases, a vacuum develops in the cooling system. This pulls open the vacuum valve. Coolant from the expansion tank then flows back into the cooling system (Fig. 25-21, right).

The radiator pressure cap must seal tightly if the pressurized cooling system is to work properly. When the cap is put on the filler neck (Fig. 25-20), the locking lugs on the cap fit under the filler-neck flange. The cam locking surface of the flange tightens the cap as it is turned clockwise. This also preloads the pressure-relief valve spring.

CAUTION!

Never attempt to remove the radiator cap from an engine that is near or above its normal operating temperature. Allow the engine to cool before removing the radiator cap. Serious burns or scalding may result if the cap is removed before the engine cools.

Some radiators do not have a filler neck in the top. The pressure cap is in one of the side tanks. To add coolant to this system, remove the cap from the expansion tank.

ANTIFREEZE AND COOLANT

➤ 25-17 ANTIFREEZE

Water freezes at 32°F [0°C]. If only water were used as the coolant, it would freeze if the temperature dropped below 32°F [0°C]. This would stop coolant circulation and the engine would overheat. Water also expands about 9 percent as it freezes. This could crack the cylinder block and head, and split the radiator.

To prevent freezing of the water in the cooling system, *antifreeze* is added to form the coolant. The coolant is the liquid that circulates through the cooling system. It removes waste heat from the engine and delivers the heat through *radiator hose* (Figs. 25-1 and 25-14) to the radiator. This cools the liquid which continuously recirculates through the water jackets, repeating the cooling cycle.

The most commonly used antifreeze is *ethylene glycol.* A mixture of half water and half ethylene glycol is the recommended coolant for year-round use in most cars. The mixture will not freeze above −34°F [−37°C]. That is 34°F below zero. A solution of 70-percent antifreeze will prevent freezing of the coolant at temperatures as low as −84°F [−64°C].

NOTE | A mixture of more than 70-percent antifreeze should not be used. The freeze point gradually goes back up to −9°F [−23°C].

The recommended coolant — the mixture of half water and half antifreeze — performs three basic jobs:

1. It lowers the freezing point of the engine coolant to −34°F [−37°C].
2. It raises the boiling point of the engine coolant to 226°F [108°C]. This makes the coolant less likely to boil away in hot weather.
3. It helps protect the cooling-system metals from deposits and corrosion.

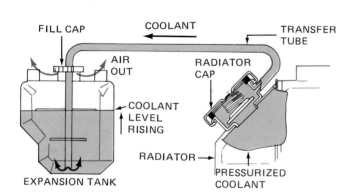

PRESSURE-RELIEF VALVE LIFTED, ALLOWING COOLANT TO FLOW INTO THE EXPANSION TANK

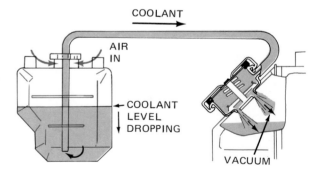

VACUUM-RELIEF VALVE OPEN, ALLOWING COOLANT TO FLOW BACK INTO THE RADIATOR

Fig. 25-21 Operation of the radiator cap under pressure conditions (left) and vacuum conditions (right). With an expansion tank, these actions keep the radiator full. (*Ford Motor Company*)

Antifreeze contains several additives. These include a *corrosion inhibitor* and a *foam inhibitor*. Corrosion or rust can shorten the life of metal parts. It also forms an insulating layer which reduces heat transfer from the metal to the coolant. In engines with severe corrosion, the coolant may be at normal temperature while the cylinders and head are overheating. One reason for having 50-percent antifreeze is to ensure the cooling system contains an adequate amount of corrosion inhibitor.

The foam inhibitor helps prevent the coolant from foaming as it passes through the water pump. Foam contains air bubbles which do not conduct heat as well as the liquid coolant. If the coolant foams excessively, the cooling system becomes less effective. The engine could overheat.

Antifreeze is colored with a *dye* for identification. The color is usually green or blue-green. The dye allows the antifreeze to serve as a leak detector. The distinctive color makes it easier to locate a leak.

Foam and corrosion inhibitors gradually lose their effectiveness. Corrosion occurs and the coolant may become rust colored. Vehicle manufacturers usually recommend changing the coolant every two years. This restores the inhibitors and removes the contaminants in the coolant. Chapter 26 covers the procedure.

➤ 25-18 TYPES OF ANTIFREEZE

There are two types of ethylene-glycol antifreeze, *high silicate* and *low silicate*. This refers to the amount of *silicone silicate inhibitor* added to the ethylene glycol. Most automotive engines use high-silicate antifreeze. It protects aluminum parts. Without this protection, aluminum flakes from the water jackets of an aluminum cylinder head may clog the radiator.

Low-silicate antifreeze is used in diesel or gasoline engines with cast-iron cylinder block and heads. The recommended antifreeze is listed in the vehicle owner's manual.

COOLING-SYSTEM INDICATORS

➤ 25-19 COOLANT-TEMPERATURE INDICATOR

A *coolant-temperature indicator* in the instrument panel warns the driver if the engine coolant temperature goes too high. Excessive temperature usually indicates low coolant or engine trouble. Continued operation could seriously damage the engine. There are four types of coolant-temperature indicators.

1. INDICATOR LIGHT The *temperature-indicator light* is turned on by movement of a thermostatic blade in the *temperature-sending switch* (Fig. 25-22). As the engine coolant and switch heat up, the blade bends. When the

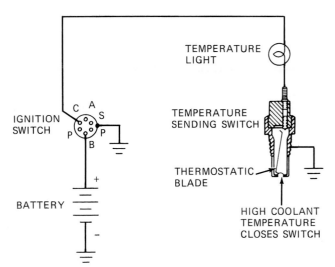

Fig. 25-22 Electric circuit of the coolant temperature-indicator light. (*ATW*)

coolant nears its boiling point, the blade contacts the terminal inside the switch. This completes the circuit and turns on the *temperature light* in the instrument panel.

2. ELECTRIC GAUGE The electric *temperature gauge* is similar to the electric fuel gauge (➤17-20) and the electric oil-pressure gauge (➤24-10). The instrument-panel gauge may be either a magnetic or thermal gauge.

Figure 25-23 shows a *magnetic temperature gauge*. The instrument-panel unit has two coils. The right coil grounds through the *engine sending unit*. It contains a *thermistor* which loses resistance as it heats up. As the sending unit loses resistance, it passes more current. The current flows through the right coil, increasing its magnetism. This pulls the armature and pointer to the right to indicate the increased coolant temperature.

3. ELECTRONIC GAUGE Cars with an electronic instrument cluster may have an *electronic temperature gauge*

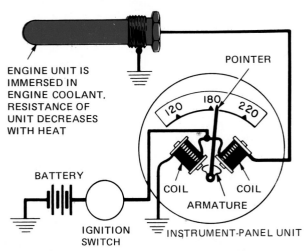

Fig. 25-23 Electric circuit of a magnetic (balancing-coil) temperature gauge.

(Fig. 17-32). A bar-graph display indicates coolant temperature. The more segments that are displayed, the higher the coolant temperature. If the coolant overheats, the *temperature symbol* flashes below the display. Also, a *tone alarm* sounds. This alerts the driver to engine overheating.

4. DIGITAL GAUGE A car with an electronic instrument cluster may have a *digital temperature gauge*. The number displayed tells the coolant temperature in degrees Fahrenheit (F) or Celsius [C].

> ### 25-20 COOLANT-LEVEL INDICATORS

Most expansion tanks (Fig. 25-17) are *translucent* (see-through) plastic. Coolant level is checked by raising the hood and looking at the fluid level in the expansion tank. It should be between the FULL COLD and FULL HOT marks.

Some cars have a *low coolant-level indicator light*. A *coolant-level sensor* (Fig. 25-24) in the expansion tank connects to a LOW COOLANT light in the instrument panel. A small float inside the sensor moves up and down as the coolant level changes. When the coolant gets low, the float closes a switch. This turns on the light in the instrument panel.

Careful! If the LOW COOLANT light is on, check the coolant-temperature indicator. Coolant level may be low in the cooling system causing the engine to overheat.

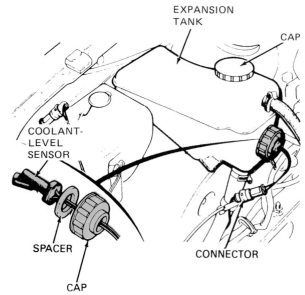

Fig. 25-24 Location of the low-coolant-level sensor in the expansion tank. (*Ford Motor Company*)

TRADE TALK

antifreeze	drive belt	filler neck	thermostat rating
bypass hose	engine sending unit	radiator core	
coolant-level sensor	expansion tank	radiator pressure cap	

MULTIPLE-CHOICE TEST

*Select the **one** correct, best, or most probable answer to each question.*
You can find the answers in the section indicated at the end of the question.

1. The amount of heat produced in the combustion chambers that the cooling system removes from the engine is about (➤25-1)
   a. one-fourth
   b. one-third
   c. half
   d. three-fourths
2. The purpose of the cooling system is to (➤25-2)
   a. prevent the coolant from boiling
   b. prevent the coolant from freezing
   c. keep the engine running as cool as possible
   d. keep the engine running at its most efficient operating temperature

3. The part that rotates to circulate coolant between the radiator and water jackets is the (➤25-5)
   a. impeller
   b. propeller
   c. expeller
   d. bypass valve
4. In normal operation, the coolant in a cross-flow radiator circulates (➤25-11)
   a. from one side to the other
   b. through the bypass
   c. in a circular path in the radiator
   d. between the radiator and the expansion tank

5. The valve in the thermostat is opened and closed by the (➤25-14)
   a. pressure linkage
   b. wax pellet
   c. vacuum linkage
   d. bypass valve
6. The device in the cooling system that raises the boiling point of the coolant is the (➤25-16)
   a. radiator pressure cap
   b. vacuum cap
   c. water jacket
   d. water pump
7. The radiator cap contains two valves. These are the (➤25-16)
   a. pressure valve and bypass valve
   b. atmospheric valve and vacuum valve
   c. pressure valve and vacuum valve
   d. bypass valve and connector valve
8. The most commonly used antifreeze is (➤25-17)
   a. ethyl octane
   b. water
   c. alcohol
   d. ethylene glycol
9. Technician A says the thermostat controls coolant temperature. Technician B says install a thermostat with a lower temperature rating to control engine overheating. Who is right? (➤25-14)
   a. A only
   b. B only
   c. both A and B
   d. neither A nor B
10. What is the main purpose of the coolant bypass passage in the cooling system? (➤25-15)
    a. to reduce pressure at the water-pump outlet
    b. to allow coolant to flow within the engine while the thermostat is closed
    c. to prevent air pockets in the water-pump housing
    d. to prevent collapse of the radiator hose

REVIEW QUESTIONS

1. Explain the differences between a mechanical fan and an electric fan.   (➤25-6 to 25-10)
2. What is a radiator core, and what actions take place in it?   (➤25-11)
3. How does the expansion tank keep the cooling system filled with coolant?   (➤25-13)
4. What is the meaning of the number *195* stamped on a thermostat? What changes occur in the cooling system by replacing it with a thermostat stamped *185*? (➤25-14)
5. Describe the operation of the coolant-temperature light, coolant-temperature gauge, and LOW COOLANT light. (➤25-19 and 25-20)

CHAPTER 26

COOLING-SYSTEM SERVICE

After studying this chapter, and with proper instruction and equipment, you should be able to:

- Diagnose and repair cooling-system troubles.
- Test and adjust antifreeze strength.
- Check and replace the thermostat and water pump.
- Clean, flush, and bleed the cooling system.
- Locate and repair leaks in the cooling system.
- Replace an expansion core plug.

➤ 26-1 WORKING SAFELY ON THE COOLING SYSTEM

There are several safety hazards you must look out for when working on engines and the cooling system.

1. Keep your hands away from the moving fan! The spinning fan blades can mangle your hand and even cut off fingers.
2. Never stand in a direct line with the fan. A fan blade could break off and fly out of the engine compartment. Anyone standing in line with the fan could be seriously injured. Before starting an engine, examine the fan for cracked or loose blades. If you find damage, replace the fan.
3. Electric fans can turn on unexpectedly, especially if the engine is warm. Always disconnect the fan before working in the fan area.
4. Keep your fingers away from the moving belt and pulleys! Your fingers could be pinched and cut off if they are caught between the belt and a pulley.
5. Never attempt to remove the radiator cap from an engine that is near or above its normal operating temperature. Releasing the pressure cap may cause instant boiling of the coolant. You may be scalded and burned by boiling coolant and steam spurting from the radiator filler neck. Allow the engine to cool before removing the radiator cap.
6. Coolant is poisonous! It can cause serious illness or even death if swallowed! Always wash your hands if you get coolant on them.
7. A puddle of drained coolant will poison any pet drinking from it. Coolant is a hazardous material. Dispose of it in a safe and legal manner.
8. Under some conditions, the ethylene glycol in antifreeze is combustible. Do not spill antifreeze on the exhaust manifold or other hot engine parts.
9. If the engine overheats, turn off the engine as soon as it is safe to do so. Continued operation of an overheated engine may cause a fire, the possibility of personal injury, and severe vehicle damage.
10. Never disconnect a hose or attempt to replace any cooling-system part until after the engine cools (➤25-16). Pressure in the system may cause hot coolant to spray out, burning or scalding you.

COOLING-SYSTEM TROUBLE DIAGNOSIS

➤ 26-2 DIAGNOSING COOLING-SYSTEM TROUBLES

Three cooling system complaints are engine overheating, slow warmup, and coolant leaks. The chart in Fig. 26-1 lists these conditions, their possible causes, and the checks or corrections to be made.

➤ 26-3 CAUSES OF COOLANT LOSS

Two indications of coolant leakage are:

1. *System requires frequent addition of coolant.*
2. *Stains at the point of leakage.* Antifreeze has a dye that helps show external leaks.

Condition	Possible Cause	Check or Correction
1. Leak, loss of coolant (➤26-3)	a. Pressure cap and gasket defective	Inspect, wash and pressure test. Replace if cap will not hold pressure.
	b. Leakage	Pressure-test system.
	c. External leakage	Inspect hoses, connections, gaskets, core plugs, drain plugs, oil-cooler lines, water pump, expansion tank and hose, radiator, heater-system components. Repair or replace as required.
	d. Internal leakage	Check head-bolt torque. Disassemble engine as necessary. Check for cracked intake manifold, blown head gasket, cracked head or block.
2. Engine overheats (➤26-4)	a. Low coolant	Fill, check for leakage
	b. Loose belt	Adjust, replace if worn
	c. Pressure cap defective	Test, replace if cannot hold pressure
	d. Radiator or air-conditioner condenser obstructed	Remove bugs, leaves, debris
	e. Thermostat stuck closed	Test, replace if defective
	f. Fan clutch	Replace
	g. Electric fan motor or switch defective	Replace
	h. Ignition faulty	Test, retime if necessary
	i. Coolant flow obstructed	Check water pump, hoses, radiator, block
	j. Exhaust system restricted	Check for restrictions
3. Engine does not reach operating temperature; slow warmup (➤26-5)	a. Open or missing thermostat	Test. Replace or install as necessary

Fig. 26-1 Cooling-system trouble-diagnosis chart.

Coolant leaks are either internal or external. Typical external leaks are from hose or hose connections, the heater core, radiator core, cylinder-block expansion-core plugs, and water-pump shaft.

Internal leaks occur when the coolant leaks into some other part of the engine. They cannot be seen. Having to add coolant frequently and the engine emitting clouds of white exhaust smoke usually indicate an internal leak.

Internal leaks can severely damage the engine. The coolant can contaminate the oil and cause rust. A coolant leak into a cylinder when the engine is stopped could partly fill the cylinder. Then, when the engine is cranked, the upward piston movement could crack the head, block, or piston. Or the connecting rod could bend.

If a cylinder-head or water-pump gasket leaks, replace it. Tighten the bolts to the specified torque. Replace leaking hoses and properly tighten the connections. Repair or replace a leaking radiator.

Cylinder heads may crack or warp, especially aluminum heads. This can result in leaks through the joint between the head and the block. Oil in the coolant indicates leakage from an oil passage or the transmission oil cooler into the cooling system, or a blown head gasket. Pressure testing the cooling system is described in ➤26-11.

➤ 26-4 CAUSES OF ENGINE OVERHEATING

Possible causes of engine overheating include:

1. Low coolant level due to leakage of coolant. Pressure-test the cooling system (➤26-11) and correct the leak (➤26-3).
2. Accumulation of rust and scale which prevents normal circulation of coolant. The system should be flushed (➤26-14).
3. Collapsed hoses which prevent normal coolant circulation. Check the hoses and replace collapsed hoses (➤26-9).
4. Thermostat stuck closed, blocking coolant circulation. If the drive belt is not slipping and the engine overheats without the radiator becoming warm, the thermostat is probably defective. Replace it and retest the system.

NOTE When the thermostat sticks closed, coolant temperature continues to rise until the coolant reaches its boiling point. Then the coolant begins turning to steam. This causes the cooling-system pressure to rise faster than the radiator cap can relieve it (➤25-16). The excessive pressure may rupture or blow off a radiator hose, or loosen a tank seam on the radiator. If this happens and the head gasket is not blown, replace the thermostat.

5. Defective water pump that does not circulate enough coolant. A quick check of the water-pump bearing can be made if a mechanical fan attaches to the water-pump pulley. Remove the drive belt, grasp the fan blades, and try to move the fan in and out (Fig. 26-2). Any movement, or a rough or grinding feeling as the fan is turned, indicates defective water-pump bearings. Bearing failure usually makes the pump noisy. One cause of water-pump bearing failure is an overtight drive belt. Tighten the belt correctly (➤26-13).

Drops of coolant leaking from the water-pump vent hole (Fig. 26-2) indicate a leaky bearing seal. Replace the water pump if it has a defective bearing or seals.

6. A loose or worn drive belt that slips. Then it will not turn the water pump fast enough for normal coolant circulation. Belt service is covered in ➤26-13.
7. *Afterboil.* When the engine is turned off after a long drive, the heat buildup in the engine may cause the coolant to boil.

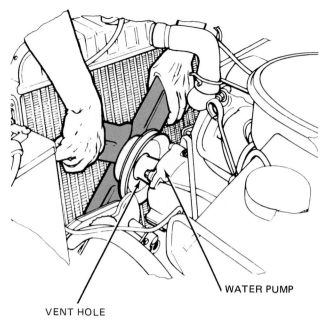

VENT HOLE

WATER PUMP

Fig. 26-2 Checking the water-pump bearing. (*Chrysler Corporation*)

8. Frozen coolant. The combustion chamber heats the coolant around it first. The frozen coolant cannot circulate, so it boils. Freezing of the coolant can crack the head and block, and split the radiator.

> **NOTE** The engine may overheat for reasons unrelated to the cooling system. Possible causes include high-altitude operation, low oil level, engine overload, hot-climate operation, wrong ignition timing, and long periods of slow speed or idling.

➤ 26-5 CAUSES OF SLOW WARMUP

The most likely cause of slow engine warmup is a thermostat stuck open (➤26-8). This allows coolant circulation to the radiator when the engine is cold. The engine has to run longer to warm up. This increases engine wear, sludge formation, and exhaust emissions. The driver's complaint in winter is that it takes too long for the heater to start delivering heat. The problem is less noticeable in summer.

Another possibility is that the thermostat has been removed. If so, replace it. An engine without a thermostat or with a lower-temperature thermostat than specified may run excessively cool. Then the signal from the coolant-temperature sensor (➤19-16) will cause the electronic control module (ECM) to deliver an improper air-fuel mixture to the cylinders. Also, the ECM may not switch to closed-loop operation (➤19-17). This can cause driveability complaints and set trouble codes (➤20-13).

A quick check for a missing or stuck thermostat is to squeeze the upper hose immediately after starting a cold engine (Fig. 26-3). Keep your hand away from the fan! No coolant should be felt flowing through the hose. If coolant flows, the thermostat is open or missing.

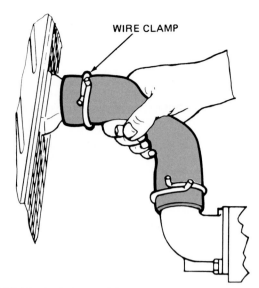

WIRE CLAMP

Fig. 26-3 To check the condition of the radiator hose, squeeze the hose. (*Chrysler Corporation*)

COOLING-SYSTEM CHECKS AND TESTS

➤ 26-6 CHECKING COOLANT LEVEL

Raise the hood and look at the expansion tank (Fig. 25-17) to see if the coolant level is low. If so, mix the proper solution of antifreeze and water in an antifreeze container. Then remove the cap from the expansion tank and fill to the specified level. On a cold engine, fill to the COLD level mark. If the engine is hot, fill to the HOT level mark.

Some vehicles do not have an expansion tank. Others have an expansion tank without a removable cap. The radiator cap must be removed to check coolant level on these cars. To remove the radiator cap, press down and slowly turn the cap back to the safety stop (Fig. 25-20). This releases any pressure. Then further depress and turn the cap until it is free.

> **CAUTION!**
>
> Never remove the radiator cap from a hot engine! Boiling coolant and steam could erupt from the filler neck and scald you. Allow the engine to cool before removing the cap.

Some vehicles may have an aftermarket safety cap on the radiator. The safety cap has a button or lever on top. Pressing the button or raising the lever relieves the pressure in the system. Then the cap can be removed.

On most vehicles, the radiator cap should not be removed except for major service such as flushing the cooling system. The radiator cap should not be removed just to check the coolant level or to add coolant. The expansion tank keeps the cooling system completely filled. Removing the radiator cap may allow the loss of a significant amount of coolant.

However, if a coolant leak is suspected or there is an overheating problem, follow the proper procedure and remove the radiator cap. Check the coolant level in the radiator. As the engine cools, air can be pulled into the cooling system through a leak. Then the heavier coolant from the expansion tank will not flow into the radiator. As a result, the expansion tank may remain full while there is little coolant in the radiator.

➤ 26-7 TESTING ANTIFREEZE STRENGTH

The strength of the antifreeze can be checked with a float hydrometer or a ball hydrometer.

1. FLOAT HYDROMETER This hydrometer (Fig. 26-4A) has a float. Place the end of the rubber tube into the coolant. Then squeeze and release the rubber bulb. This draws coolant up into the hydrometer. The height of the float indicates the strength of the antifreeze. The stronger the antifreeze, the higher the float stem sticks out of the coolant. A thermometer and scale on the hydrometer shows the temperature of the coolant and how low the temperature must go before the coolant would freeze.

2. BALL HYDROMETER This hydrometer (Fig. 26-4B) has four or five balls in a small plastic tube. Coolant is drawn in by squeezing and releasing the bulb. The stronger the solution, the more balls that float.

CAUTION!

Coolant is poisonous! Always wash your hands if you get coolant on them.

Water alone must never be used in engine cooling systems. The temperature-indicator light does not come on until well above the boiling point of water. Plain water could boil while the temperature light remains off. Severe engine damage could occur before the driver realizes the engine is overheating.

➤ 26-8 TESTING THE THERMOSTAT

Different vehicle manufacturers have different thermostat testing procedures. One recommendation is to suspend the thermostat in a solution of coolant (Fig. 26-5). Heat the coolant to 25°F [14°C] above the temperature stamped on the thermostat. The thermostat should open. Then submerge the thermostat in the same solution after it has cooled to 10°F [5.5°C] below the temperature stamped on the thermostat. It should close completely. If the thermostat does not open and close properly, replace it.

On some engines, the scan tool (➤20-14) or diagnostic computer can indicate thermostat opening. With the tester connected and the engine cold, start the engine. Watch the *coolant temperature* display as the engine warms up.

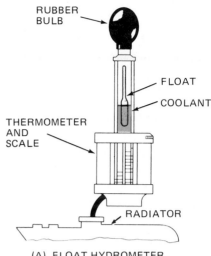

(A) FLOAT HYDROMETER

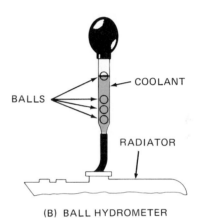

(B) BALL HYDROMETER

Fig. 26-4 Two types of cooling-system hydrometers, used to check the freezing temperature of the coolant.

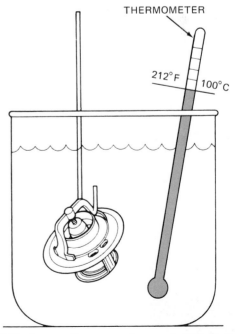

Fig. 26-5 Testing a cooling-system thermostat. Both the thermostat and the thermometer must be suspended so they do not touch the container. (*Ford Motor Company*)

Coolant temperature will rise until the thermostat opens. Then coolant temperature will drop about 10°F [5.5°C] before climbing again. This drop in temperature is caused by the thermostat opening. No temperature drop usually indicates the thermostat is stuck partly open.

➤ 26-9 CHECKING HOSES AND CONNECTIONS

To check a hose, squeeze it (Fig. 26-3). It should not collapse easily. Replace any hose that is soft, hard, rotted, or swollen. Connections must be tight to avoid leaks. Air can be drawn into the cooling system if there are leaks in the hoses or connections between the radiator and water pump.

➤ 26-10 CHECKING FOR EXHAUST-GAS LEAKAGE INTO COOLING SYSTEM

A defective head gasket may allow exhaust gas to leak into the cooling system. This is very damaging. Strong acids can form as the gas unites with the water in the coolant. These acids corrode the radiator and other cooling-system parts.

An *exhaust-gas analyzer* (➤37-9) can be used to check for exhaust-gas leakage into the cooling system. With the radiator cap removed and the engine running, hold the analyzer probe above the open radiator filler neck. Do not put the probe into the coolant! If there is exhaust-gas leakage, the analyzer will detect it.

Another way to check for exhaust-gas leakage into the cooling system is with a Bloc-Chek tester (Fig. 26-6). Install the tester on the radiator filler neck. With the engine running, squeeze and release the bulb. This draws an air sample from the cooling system up through the test fluid.

The test fluid is blue. However, if exhaust gas is leaking into the cooling system, the test fluid turns yellow. If a leak is indicated, the tester can locate the leaking cylinder. Short one spark plug at a time (➤37-11) and retest. When the leaking cylinder is firing, the fluid will be yellow. When non-leaking cylinders only are firing, the fluid will remain blue.

Careful! The procedure of running the engine with spark plugs not firing releases extra HC into the exhaust system. This can damage the catalytic converter if the engine runs too long.

Combustion leaks in the valve areas can cause cracked valve seats and cylinder heads. The leaking gases force the coolant away from the leak area during heavy acceleration. This area gets overheated. Then, when acceleration stops, the diverted coolant rushes back to the overheated area. The sudden cooling can crack the head and valve seat.

➤ 26-11 PRESSURE TESTING THE COOLING SYSTEM

Figure 26-7 shows a *pressure test* of the cooling system. Fill the radiator to about 1/2 inch [13 mm] below the bottom of the filler neck. Then wipe the neck sealing surface and attach the tester. Operate the pump to apply a pressure that does not exceed 3 psi [21 kPa] above the manufacturer's specification. If the pressure holds steady, the system is not leaking. If the pressure drops, there are leaks. Check as explained in ➤26-3.

A further check can be made with the engine warm and running about 3000 rpm. A fluctuating needle on the pressure gauge indicates an exhaust-gas leak. It is probably through the cylinder-head gasket.

If the needle does not fluctuate, accelerate the engine several times. Check for abnormal discharge of fluid or

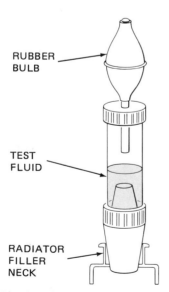

Fig. 26-6 Checking for exhaust-gas leakage into the cooling system with a *Bloc-Chek* tester.

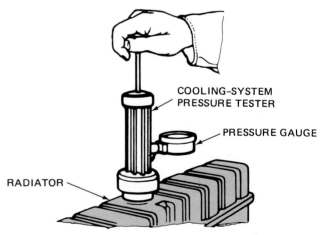

Fig. 26-7 Using a cooling-system pressure tester to check the cooling system for leaks. (*Chrysler Corporation*)

white smoke from the tailpipe. This indicates a cracked block or head, or a leaking head gasket.

➤ 26-12 PRESSURE TESTING THE RADIATOR CAP

Make a pressure test of the radiator cap using the pressure tester (Fig. 26-8). If the cap cannot hold its rated pressure, replace the cap. A defective cap may also allow coolant loss and engine overheating.

➤ 26-13 TESTING THE DRIVE BELT

Check the water-pump drive belt at least once a year for wear and tension. A high-pitched squeal is the typical sound of a loose or slipping belt. It can cause engine overheating and a discharged battery. The water pump will not turn fast enough to maintain coolant circulation. And the alternator turns too slowly to keep the battery charged.

Before checking a belt, make sure the engine is off and will not be cranked. To check a V belt, twist the belt in your fingers. Look for small cracks, grease, glazing, tears, or splits (Fig. 26-9). Replace any belt that shows signs of deterioration.

On vehicles using a set of two V belts, if one is worn and requires replacement, replace both. If you replace only one belt, all the load is on the new belt. It will wear rapidly. When both belts are replaced with a new matched pair, each belt will carry half the load. Use a *belt-tension gauge* (Fig. 26-10) to check and adjust drive-belt tension.

Replace a serpentine belt (➤25-9) if it shows excessive wear, severe glazing, or frayed cords. Small cracks in the back of the belt may be acceptable if no large pieces are missing. When installing the serpentine belt, make sure that all ribs fit into the pulley grooves (Fig. 26-11).

Most serpentine belts have a *belt tensioner* (Fig. 26-12) that maintains proper tension on the belt. To remove or install the belt, compress the tensioner to release tension on the belt. This direction is shown by the arrow in Fig. 26-12.

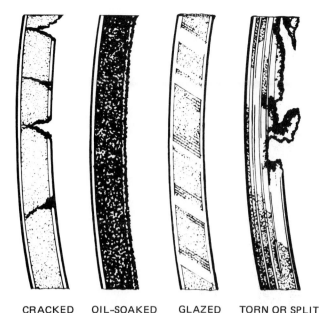

CRACKED   OIL-SOAKED   GLAZED   TORN OR SPLIT

Fig. 26-9 Conditions to look for when inspecting a V belt. (*Chrysler Corporation*)

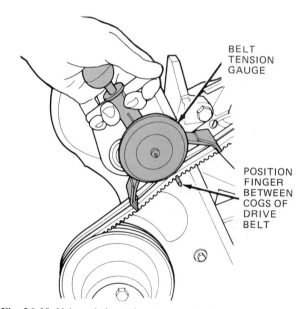

BELT TENSION GAUGE

POSITION FINGER BETWEEN COGS OF DRIVE BELT

Fig. 26-10 Using a belt-tension gauge to check drive-belt tension. (*Ford Motor Company*)

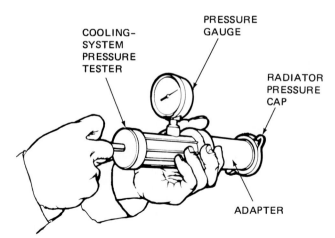

COOLING-SYSTEM PRESSURE TESTER

PRESSURE GAUGE

RADIATOR PRESSURE CAP

ADAPTER

Fig. 26-8 Using the cooling-system pressure tester to check the radiator cap. (*Chrysler Corporation*)

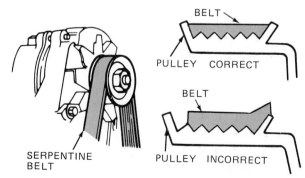

BELT

PULLEY   CORRECT

BELT

SERPENTINE BELT

PULLEY   INCORRECT

Fig. 26-11 When inspecting or installing a serpentine belt, check that all ribs fit into the pulley grooves. (*Ford Motor Company*)

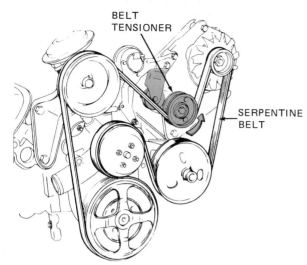

Fig. 26-12 Belt tensioner for a serpentine belt. To remove or install the belt, rotate the tensioner in the direction shown by the arrow. (*Buick Division of General Motors Corporation*)

If the tensioner is out of its operating range, the belt is worn or stretched. Replace the belt.

Sometimes a good belt will slip and squeal even if properly tensioned. A *belt dressing* can be applied to the friction sides of the belt. This may help eliminate noise and increase belt friction. However, some manufacturers recommend not using belt dressing.

COOLING-SYSTEM SERVICE

➤ 26-14 CLEANING THE COOLING SYSTEM

The additives in antifreeze gradually wear out and lose their effectiveness. Drain, flush, and refill the cooling system with fresh water and antifreeze periodically. This removes any contaminants being carried in the old antifreeze and restores the effectiveness of the additives.

Most manufacturers recommend changing antifreeze every one or two years, depending on the vehicle's usage. Others recommend doing it every fall, just before freezing weather sets in. When the coolant takes on a rust color, rust is beginning to form. This indicates the antifreeze needs replacement. It may also indicate the cooling system needs cleaning.

A quick check of the cooling system is made by removing the radiator cap. Then wipe the inside of the filler neck with your finger. If you find oil, grease, rust, or scale, the cooling system needs cleaning. A check of coolant acidity can be made with a digital multimeter (➤27-15). With the multimeter on a low dc-voltage scale, ground one probe to the engine. Insert the other probe into the coolant in the radiator. A reading of 0.4 volt or above indicates the coolant has high acidity. Drain the coolant. Flush and refill the cooling system.

Cleaning the cooling system helps remove rust, scale, grease, oil, and acids formed by exhaust-gas leakage into the coolant. Manufacturers' recommendations vary on how often the cooling system should be cleaned. Chevrolet recommends draining the system and flushing it with water every two years. Then fill the system with fresh coolant of the proper strength for the temperatures in which the vehicle will operate.

Flushing procedures vary. They include the standard flushing method and the fast-flush method. Also, there is the fast-flush-and-fill method which requires a special machine. The standard method is described here.

Drain the cooling system. Remove the thermostat and reinstall the thermostat housing and hose. If you use a cooling-system cleaner, pour it into the radiator. Fill the cooling system with water.

| NOTE | Follow any special instructions on the cleaner container.

Run the engine at fast idle for about 20 minutes, but do not allow the water to boil. Stop the engine and wait for it to cool. Then drain the system.

Use a water hose to put water in the radiator to flush out loosened scale and rust. You can also reverse-flush the radiator and engine water jackets with a *flushing gun* (Figs. 26-13 and 26-14). Continue to flush until the water runs clear. Do not use too much pressure.

After draining the system, install the thermostat and housing and reconnect the hoses. Fill the system with

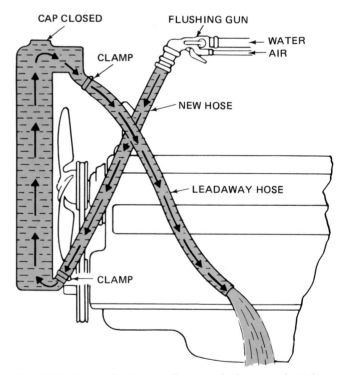

Fig. 26-13 Reverse flushing a radiator. Apply the gun so it sends water to the lower or outlet tank.

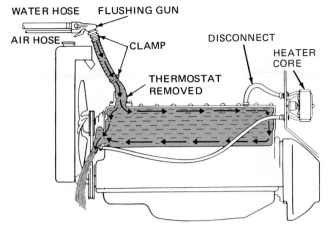

WATER HOSE FLUSHING GUN

AIR HOSE

CLAMP

DISCONNECT

HEATER CORE

THERMOSTAT REMOVED

Fig. 26-14 Reverse flushing the engine water jackets.

coolant of the proper strength for protection against the lowest temperature expected.

➤ 26-15 BLEEDING THE COOLING SYSTEM

When adding new coolant, the cooling system probably will not fill completely. The cold coolant closes the thermostat. This traps air behind the thermostat (Fig. 26-15). On a rear-drive car, start the engine and idle it until the thermostat opens. Then fill the system. To avoid trapping air, fill the block before installing the thermostat.

Some front-drive and mid-engine cars frequently trap air in the cooling system during filling. This happens because the heater core, hoses, and other parts are higher than the radiator cap. When filling the cooling system, note the amount of coolant added. The cooling system may appear full after adding too little coolant. This usually indicates trapped air.

The cooling system may have a *bleed valve* to aid in

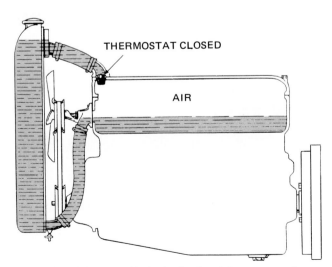

THERMOSTAT CLOSED

AIR

Fig. 26-15 Air is trapped in back of a closed thermostat as the cooling system is filled.

purging the trapped air. If not, raise the front of the car. The radiator cap should be the highest part of the cooling system. Open the heater coolant-control valve (➤55-3). Then fill the cooling system and expansion tank to the proper level.

➤ 26-16 LOCATING AND REPAIRING RADIATOR LEAKS

Radiator leaks often leave telltale marks because of the dye in the antifreeze. Pressure testing can also help locate leaks (➤26-11).

If leaks are found, remove the radiator for repair. Some radiators can be repaired in the shop. Others must be sent to a radiator repair shop. A radiator that has a rotted core or severe leaks or damage is often replaced. The cost of repair may be more than the cost of a new radiator.

➤ 26-17 WATER-PUMP SERVICE

The water pump normally requires no service. The sealed bearings cannot be lubricated. If a water pump develops noise or leaks, replace it. To remove the water pump, drain the cooling system. Detach the hoses from the pump. Remove the drive belt. Remove the attaching bolts and pull the pump straight out.

Check the impeller. In normal operation, impeller blades may wear away due to the abrasive action of sand in the coolant. Blades may rust if the coolant is old and the corrosion inhibitor has lost its effectiveness.

Before installing a new water pump, check the size of the impeller on the new pump against the old pump. If it is a different size, you may have the wrong new pump.

Install the new pump and tighten the bolts to the specified torque. Connect the hoses and install the drive belt. Fill the cooling system. Start the engine and check for leaks.

➤ 26-18 REPLACING EXPANSION-CORE PLUGS

A leaking core plug must be replaced. There are two types of core plugs: *cup* and *expansion* (Fig. 26-16). Special tools are available for removing core plugs. Another way is to put the pointed end of a pry bar against the plug. Tap the bar with a hammer until the point goes through the plug. Then pry the plug out.

Careful! Do not drive the bar in past the plug bore. You could damage the cylinder wall. Do not drive the plug into the water jacket. You could have trouble getting it out. It could block coolant circulation if left in.

After the core plug is out, check the plug bore for rough spots, nicks, or grooves. These could allow the new plug to leak. If necessary, bore out the hole to take the next larger

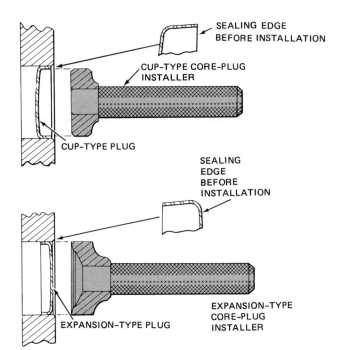

Fig. 26-16 Two types of expansion core plugs and the installation tools required for each. (*Ford Motor Company*)

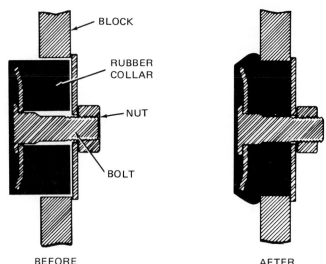

Fig. 26-17 E-Z Seal expansion plug. The plug is inserted into the bore as shown at left. Then, as the nut is tightened, the rubber collar expands, sealing the opening. (*Hunckler Products, Inc.*)

size plug. Coat the new plug with water-resistant sealer before installing it. Figure 26-16 shows how to install two types of core plugs.

1. CUP TYPE Install the cup-type core plug (Fig. 26-16, top) with the flanged-edge out. Use the proper size tool. It must not touch the flange. All driving must be against the internal cup. Drive the plug in until the flange is below the chamfered edge of the hole.

2. EXPANSION TYPE Install the expansion-type core plug (Fig. 26-16, bottom) with the flanged-edge facing inward. The tool does not touch the crowned center of the plug. Instead, the tool drives against the outer part of the plug. Drive the plug in until the center of the crown is below the chamfered edge of the hole.

3. E-Z SEAL EXPANSION PLUG Figure 26-17 shows an expansion plug that has a neoprene rubber collar held between two washers. Select the proper size plug and insert it in the bore. Then use a wrench to tighten the nut on the bolt. This pulls the inner washer inward, expanding the collar to tightly seal the bore (Fig. 26-17, right).

Leaking core plugs are often difficult to replace. Gaining access may require removing the clutch or transmission. On some vehicles, replacing a core plug requires raising or removing the engine. The exhaust manifold, clutch housing, and transmission may also require removal.

TRADE TALK

afterboil	Bloc-Chek tester	hydrometer	safety cap
belt tensioner	external leak	internal leak	
belt-tension gauge	flushing	pressure tester	

MULTIPLE-CHOICE TEST

*Select the **one** correct, best, or most probable answer to each question.*
You can find the answers in the section indicated at the end of the question.

1. Engine troubles directly related to the cooling system include (➤26-2)
   a. hard starting and slow warmup
   b. slow warmup and overheating
   c. slow cranking and warmup
   d. fast idle and slow warmup

2. Accumulations of rust and scale in the engine cooling system cause (➤26-4)
   a. slow warmup
   b. reduced heating capacity
   c. overheating
   d. rough idle

3. If the thermostat sticks closed, the engine will (➤26-4)
   a. warm up slowly
   b. overheat
   c. fail to start
   d. idle roughly

4. If the thermostat sticks open, the engine will (➤26-5)
   a. warm up slowly
   b. overheat
   c. fail to start
   d. idle roughly

5. The strength of the antifreeze solution is checked with a (➤26-7)
   a. micrometer
   b. hydrometer
   c. barometer
   d. thermometer

6. Exhaust-gas leakage into the cooling system is probably caused by a defective (➤26-10)
   a. cylinder-head gasket
   b. exhaust-manifold gasket
   c. water pump
   d. radiator hose

7. Air will be drawn into the cooling system if there are leaks at any point between the (➤26-9)
   a. water pump and jackets
   b. radiator and water pump
   c. thermostat and radiator
   d. radiator cap and bleed valve

8. If the coolant boils when the engine is shut off after a long drive, the condition is known as (➤26-4)
   a. overheating
   b. hard running
   c. clogged radiator
   d. afterboil

9. When reverse flushing the radiator, connect the flushing gun to the (➤26-14)
   a. upper or inlet tank
   b. water-pump inlet
   c. intake manifold
   d. lower or outlet tank

10. When reverse flushing the engine water jackets, connect the flushing gun to the (➤26-14)
    a. upper or inlet tank
    b. lower or outlet tank
    c. thermostat housing
    d. water-pump inlet

REVIEW QUESTIONS

1. List nine safety cautions to follow while working on engine cooling systems.   (➤26-1)
2. What are internal leaks and external leaks, and how does each affect engine operation?   (➤26-3)
3. Describe how to test a thermostat.   (➤26-8)
4. How is the pressure tester used to check the cooling system and the radiator cap?   (➤26-11 and 26-12)
5. Explain how air gets trapped in the cooling system, and how to bleed air out of the system.   (➤26-15)

PART 4

AUTOMOTIVE ELECTRICAL AND ELECTRONIC EQUIPMENT

Part 4 of *Automotive Mechanics* takes up the electrical-electronic system of the automobile. It further expands the discussion of electricity and electronics that began in Chapter 10. Then it explains the battery, starting system, charging system, and electric and electronic ignition systems. The last chapter includes automotive lighting, safety and signaling equipment, and driver information and controls. New developments in the automotive use of computer control, head-up displays, networks, and multiplexing are also described. There are eight chapters in Part 4:

CHAPTER 27

AUTOMOTIVE ELECTRIC AND ELECTRONIC SYSTEMS

After studying this chapter, and with proper instruction and equipment, you should be able to:

- List the functions and components of the automotive electrical system.
- Describe the purpose and uses of a block diagram and a wiring diagram.
- Name the circuit-protection devices, and explain the operation and repair of each.
- Define *series circuits, parallel circuits,* and *series-parallel circuits.*
- Explain the fundamentals of electrical trouble diagnosis.
- Demonstrate the use of jumper wires, test lights, and meters in diagnosing electrical troubles.

➢ 27-1 THE AUTOMOTIVE ELECTRICAL SYSTEM

The automotive electrical system (Fig. 27-1) does several jobs. It *produces* electric energy (electricity) in the alternator. It *stores* electric energy in chemical form in the battery. And it *delivers* electric energy from these sources on demand to any other electrical component in the vehicle.

The electric energy cranks the engine to start it, supplies the sparks that ignite the air-fuel mixture so the engine runs, and keeps the battery charged. These are the jobs performed by the battery, starting, charging, and ignition systems. Other electric and electronic devices and systems on the vehicle include:

a. Electronic engine control systems (➢10-20) and other electronic systems controlled by an electronic control module (ECM) or computer. These may include an electronic automatic transmission or transaxle, power train, brakes, traction control, steering, suspension, air conditioning, and other components that operate under varying conditions.

b. Signaling and accessory systems. These include the lights, horn, instrument-panel indicators, service monitor systems, and other driver information sys-

tems. Also included are the heater and air conditioner, and the radio and tape player.

c. Various motors that operate the seats, windows, door locks, trunk lid, and windshield wipers and washers.

All these components use electric current and voltage. All may be computer-controlled. And all are connected by insulated wires and the ground-return system. Chapter 10 describes basic electricity and the one-wire system. Chapter 19 describes electronic fuel injection and engine-control-system components. Separate chapters cover the battery, starting, charging, and ignition systems. Chapter 34 describes other electric and electronic devices.

ELECTRIC-CIRCUIT COMPONENTS

➢ 27-2 WIRING CIRCUITS

An automotive wiring circuit contains eight basic parts. These are:

1. A source of electric energy, such as the battery or alternator.
2. Conductors, which connect between the source and the other components in the circuit to provide a path for the electric current.

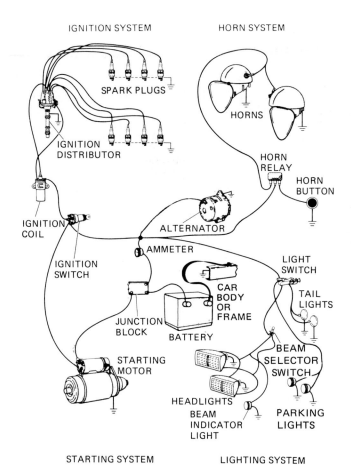

IGNITION SYSTEM   HORN SYSTEM

SPARK PLUGS

IGNITION DISTRIBUTOR

HORNS

HORN RELAY

HORN BUTTON

IGNITION COIL

ALTERNATOR

AMMETER

IGNITION SWITCH

LIGHT SWITCH

CAR BODY OR FRAME

TAIL LIGHTS

JUNCTION BLOCK

BATTERY

STARTING MOTOR

BEAM SELECTOR SWITCH

HEADLIGHTS

BEAM INDICATOR LIGHT

PARKING LIGHTS

STARTING SYSTEM   LIGHTING SYSTEM

Fig. 27-1 Typical automotive electrical system, showing the major electrical units and the connections between them. The symbol ⏚ or ⏚ means ground, or the vehicle body, frame, or engine. By using these metal parts as the return circuit, only half as much wiring is needed.

3. Terminals, at the ends of the conductors (Fig. 27-2), which eliminate the need for soldering together wires and components.

4. A circuit protector, such as a fuse, fusible link, or circuit breaker to open the circuit and stop current flow when overheating caused by excessive current begins to occur.

5. Connectors, such as single connectors which join one pair of terminals, or multiple connectors (Fig. 27-2) that conveniently connect and disconnect two or more pairs of terminals. Connectors usually have a locking tang to prevent separation unless the tang is released.

6. A switch, which opens and closes the circuit to stop and allow current flow.

7. A load, such as the starting motor or headlights. The load is the device in an electric circuit that converts the electric energy from the source into work.

8. Ground, or the return path to the source for the electric current, which is usually the engine or metal chassis parts.

The automotive electrical system in the average car includes about 5000 feet [1524 m] of wire. The size of

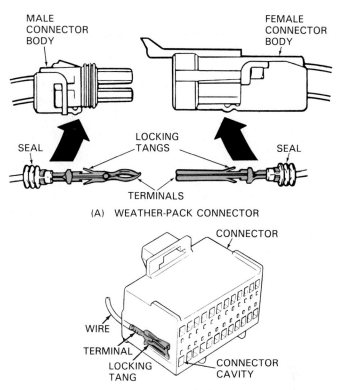

MALE CONNECTOR BODY

FEMALE CONNECTOR BODY

SEAL   LOCKING TANGS   SEAL

TERMINALS

(A) WEATHER-PACK CONNECTOR

CONNECTOR

WIRE

TERMINAL

LOCKING TANG

CONNECTOR CAVITY

(B) MICRO-PACK CONNECTOR

Fig. 27-2 Two types of electrical connectors. Metal terminals attach to the ends of the conductors to make the electrical connection. (*Chevrolet Division of General Motors Corporation*)

each wire (➤10-6) depends on the amount of current it must carry. The greater the current, the larger the wire must be.

Groups of wires are wrapped together with electrical tape or flexible conduit to form a *wiring harness* (Fig. 27-3). Multiple connectors make it easier to remove and install than many separate wires. The color of the insulation identifies each wire in the wiring harness. For example, wires are light green, dark green, blue, red, black, black with white tracer, and so on. The service manuals for each vehicle include special illustrations or *wiring diagrams*. These show the various connections and components, along with the colors of the wires in the circuit.

Figure 27-4 shows the wiring harness and connectors behind the instrument panel. Figure 27-5 shows the wiring harness in the engine compartment. There are other wiring harnesses for the engine and the lights at the front of the car.

➤ **27-3 PRINTED CIRCUITS**

The space behind the instrument panel is limited, and there are many wires and connections (Fig. 27-4). The crowding could cause problems in making all the connections to the gauges and indicators. One solution is to use *printed circuits*.

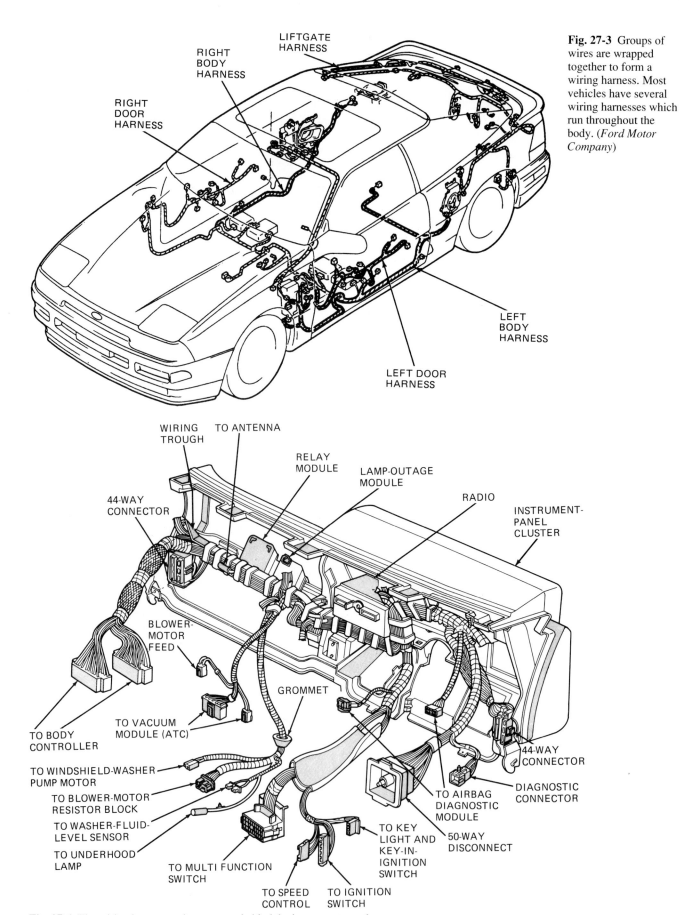

Fig. 27-3 Groups of wires are wrapped together to form a wiring harness. Most vehicles have several wiring harnesses which run throughout the body. (*Ford Motor Company*)

LIFTGATE HARNESS

RIGHT BODY HARNESS

RIGHT DOOR HARNESS

LEFT BODY HARNESS

LEFT DOOR HARNESS

WIRING TROUGH

TO ANTENNA

RELAY MODULE

LAMP-OUTAGE MODULE

RADIO

INSTRUMENT-PANEL CLUSTER

44-WAY CONNECTOR

BLOWER-MOTOR FEED

GROMMET

TO BODY CONTROLLER

TO VACUUM MODULE (ATC)

TO WINDSHIELD-WASHER PUMP MOTOR

TO BLOWER-MOTOR RESISTOR BLOCK

TO WASHER-FLUID-LEVEL SENSOR

TO UNDERHOOD LAMP

TO MULTI FUNCTION SWITCH

TO SPEED CONTROL

TO IGNITION SWITCH

TO KEY LIGHT AND KEY-IN-IGNITION SWITCH

50-WAY DISCONNECT

TO AIRBAG DIAGNOSTIC MODULE

DIAGNOSTIC CONNECTOR

44-WAY CONNECTOR

Fig. 27-4 The wiring harness and connectors behind the instrument panel. (*Chrysler Corporation*)

342

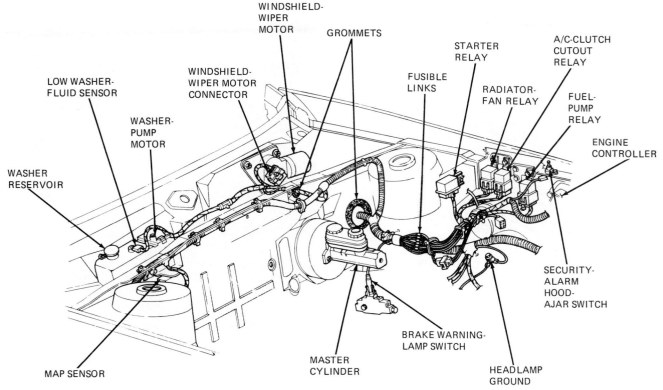

Fig. 27-5 The wiring harness in the engine compartment. (*Chrysler Corporation*)

A printed circuit is a flat piece of insulating material with a series of conducting strips printed on it. Figure 27-6 shows a complete printed circuit for an instrument cluster. When installed behind the instrument cluster, the conducting strips carry current to the various lights and gauges. For example, when the indicator bulbs are installed, the contacts on the bulbs rest on the metallic strips. This completes the circuit.

➤ 27-4 FUSES

Fuses, fusible links, and circuit breakers are *circuit-protection devices*. They open the circuit to protect the electrical and electronic devices if high current starts to

flow. This happens if a short or ground develops. Then the fuse *blows* or the circuit breaker opens.

Figure 27-7 shows an older style *cartridge fuse*. It contains a metal strip connected at the ends to the fuse caps. The fuse is installed in the *fuse block* or *fuse panel* (Fig. 27-8), which is usually in or under the instrument panel. When too much current flows, the center part of the metal strip overheats and melts. This opens the circuit.

Most cars use the newer *blade fuse* (Fig. 27-9). It "plugs in," and is installed and removed easily with your fingers.

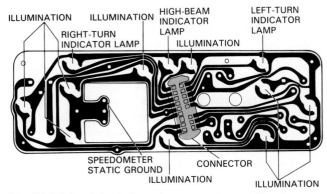

Fig. 27-6 Printed circuit for an instrument cluster. (*Chrysler Corporation*)

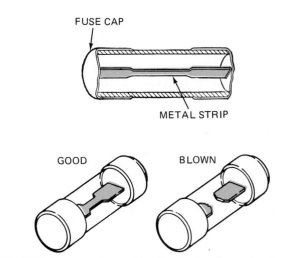

Fig. 27-7 Cutaway of a cartridge fuse (top) and a good and blown fuse (bottom). (*Ford Motor Company*)

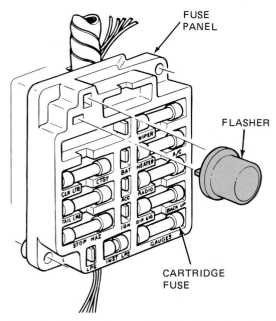

Fig. 27-8 Fuse block, or fuse panel, with cartridge fuses in place. (*Chevrolet Division of General Motors Corporation*)

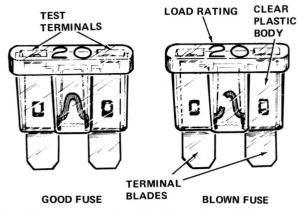

Fig. 27-9 A good and a blown blade fuse. (*General Motors Corporation*)

Fig. 27-10 Location of the blade fuses behind an access cover in the instrument panel. (*Chevrolet Division of General Motors Corporation*)

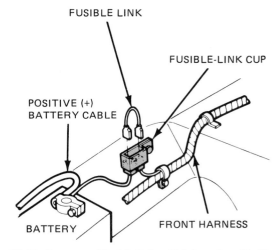

Fig. 27-11 One type of fusible link, which is replaceable like a fuse. (*Ford Motor Company*)

The number on the end of the fuse is its *load rating*. This is the amount of current in amperes that the fuse will carry before it blows. Blade fuses are color-coded by load rating.

Figure 27-10 shows the location of a fuse panel for blade-type fuses. It is behind an access cover on the instrument panel. Extra fuses are stored in the cover. Markings on the inside of the cover show the circuit each fuse protects and the fuse rating. Some vehicles have two fuse panels. One of these may be in the engine compartment.

If a fuse blows, check the circuit to find the cause. After correcting the trouble, install a new fuse.

➤ 27-5 FUSIBLE LINK

A *fusible link* (Fig. 27-11) is a short length of insulated wire connected in series in a circuit. It is usually four gauge sizes smaller than the wire it is protecting. A fusible link may be replaceable like a fuse (Fig. 27-11) or integrated into the wires outside the wiring harness (Fig. 27-5). If excessive current flows, the fusible link melts or *blows*. This protects the circuit and connected electrical or electronic devices from damage. Wiring harnesses have several fusible links. In some vehicles, they are in the feed wires supplying current to all electrical equipment except the starting motor.

A blown fusible link usually discolors the insulation.

Bare wire may be sticking out and the insulation may be bubbled or burned from the heat. Figure 27-12 shows how to repair a blown fusible link.

➤ 27-6 CIRCUIT BREAKER

Circuit breakers protect headlight and sometimes windshield-wiper circuits. One type uses a *bimetal thermostat* (Fig. 27-13). When excessive current flows, the strip heats and bends. This separates the contacts and opens the circuit.

The advantage of this type of circuit breaker is it repeatedly resets itself. When the metal strip cools, it unbends and closes the contacts. If the current is still excessive, the contacts open again. In the headlight circuit, this causes the lights to flash on and off, warning the driver

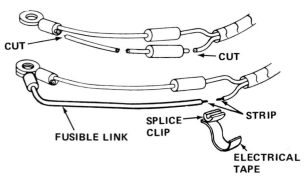

Fig. 27-12 A fusible link that is part of the wiring. To replace this fusible link, cut it out as shown at top. Strip back the insulation. Splice the wires with a splice clip, and solder in the new fusible link. Then tape the splice with a double layer of electrical tape. (*General Motors Corporation*)

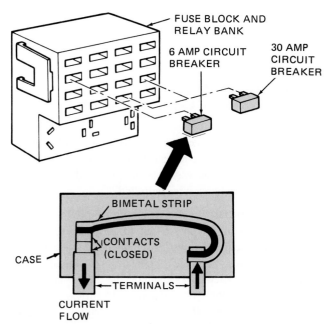

Fig. 27-13 Circuit breaker location and construction. (*Chrysler Corporation*)

of trouble. The flashing lights enable the driver to pull over to the side of the road and stop.

ELECTRICAL SYMBOLS AND WIRING DIAGRAMS

➤ 27-7 ELECTRICAL SYMBOLS

Wiring diagrams use various *symbols* to represent the different devices in the electrical system. Figure 27-14 shows many of these symbols. Some symbols are widely used. Others are seen only occasionally. A symbol may include the basic internal circuit in a device. Others show only the connections to the device.

➤ 27-8 WIRING DIAGRAMS

A wiring diagram (Fig. 27-15) is a drawing or *schematic* that shows the wires, connections, and components in an electric circuit or system. Various electrical symbols (➤27-7) in the wiring diagram represent the components. The correct wiring diagram should show each circuit or system exactly as it is on the car.

An electronic control system may be represented by a *block diagram* (Fig. 27-16). This is a drawing made up of boxes labeled with the circuit or device functions. Lines representing the wiring connect the boxes. The symbol for the major component may be shown in the box. A label *solid state* in the box means the component contains only semiconductors. It has no mechanically-moving parts.

The ECM is usually in the center of the block diagram. The source voltage may be shown as $B+$ which means the battery positive terminal. It is at the top of the diagram. Ground is the connection to the battery negative terminal. It is at the bottom of the diagram. Sensors and inputs are to the left of the ECM. Actuators and outputs are to the right of the ECM. Sensors and actuators may be tested and replaced (➤20-15). Most ECMs are not repairable (➤20-16). One method of testing is to substitute a "known-good assembly" for the ECM (or other device) in the vehicle.

BASIC ELECTRICAL TROUBLE DIAGNOSIS

➤ 27-9 ELECTRICAL TROUBLE DIAGNOSIS

Troubleshooting an electric circuit begins with knowing how the circuit should work. The circuit wiring diagram in the manufacturer's service manual will help you learn this. It serves as a road map to guide you from part to part until you find the trouble. This saves time and may prevent needless damage to other electronic components.

The wiring diagram (Fig. 27-15) does not give the com-

+	POSITIVE	→≻	CONNECTOR
−	NEGATIVE	—→	MALE CONNECTOR
⏚	GROUND	≻|	FEMALE CONNECTOR
—⌒—	FUSE	↓↓↓ YYY	MULTIPLE CONNECTOR
⌒	CIRCUIT BREAKER	—S	DENOTES WIRE CONTINUES ELSEWHERE
—⊢⊢—	CAPACITOR	→≻	SPLICE
Ω	OHMS	◇ J2	SPLICE IDENTIFICATION
—ᴧᴧ—	RESISTOR	◆⌐ ◇⌐	OPTIONAL WIRING WITH / WIRING WITHOUT
—ᴧᴧ—	VARIABLE RESISTOR	—ᴫᴪ—	THERMAL ELEMENT (BIMETAL STRIP)
ᴧᴧᴧᴧ	SERIES RESISTOR	⅄	Y WINDINGS
—ɷɷ—	COIL	△	DELTA WINDINGS
⌒ɷ ⌒ɷɷ	STEPUP COIL	88:88	DIGITAL READOUT
⌐⌐	NORMALLY OPEN CONTACT	⊸ɷɷ⊸	SINGLE-FILAMENT LAMP
⌐⊠	NORMALLY CLOSED CONTACT	⊕	DUAL-FILAMENT LAMP
—•—•—	CLOSED SWITCH	⊕	LIGHT EMITTING DIODE (LED)
—⟋•—	OPEN SWITCH	•—ᴧᴧ—	THERMISTOR
⟟⟟	CLOSED GANGED SWITCH	⊘	GAUGE
⟋⟋	OPEN GANGED SWITCH	TIMER	TIMER
⟋	TWO-POLE SINGLE-THROW SWITCH	⊖○⊖	MOTOR
⎍	PRESSURE SWITCH	⊘	ARMATURE AND BRUSHES
⎍	SOLENOID SWITCH	—•—	DENOTES WIRE GOES THROUGH GROMMET
⎍	MERCURY SWITCH	▣	DENOTES WIRE GOES THROUGH DISCONNECT
—◄—	DIODE OR RECTIFIER	STRG COLUMN	DENOTES WIRE GOES THROUGH STEERING COLUMN CONNECTOR
—◄◄—	BIDIRECTIONAL ZENER DIODE		

Fig. 27-14 Typical symbols used in electrical wiring diagrams. (*Chrysler Corporation*)

ponent locations on the vehicle. Other pages in the electrical-diagnosis section of the service manual provide this information. Also included may be basic system checks for each electrical device, troubleshooting hints, and a separate diagnostic chart for that system. *Harness-connector faces* show the cavity or terminal locations in all multiple connectors, such as the *44-way connector* and the *50-way disconnect* shown in Fig. 27-4.

To use the wiring diagram, begin by tracing the circuit on the diagram and then on the car. Start from the fuse or connector closest to the power source. This is at the top of the wiring diagram in Fig. 27-15. The grounds are shown at the bottom of the diagram. You may see a symbol or abbreviation you do not recognize. If so, find its definition in the *wiring-diagram legend* (Fig. 27-14) or the *abbreviation chart* in the service manual. Abbreviations and symbols are widely used.

➤ 27-10 SERIES AND PARALLEL CIRCUITS

Electric or electronic devices are wired in *series* or in *parallel*. The automotive electrical system uses both types of electric circuits. The way a device is wired determines how it operates and how it is controlled.

1. SERIES CIRCUIT In a series circuit (Fig. 27-17A), the separate parts connect end-to-end to form a single path through which current flows. Components connected this way are in series. Figure 27-17A shows a simple series circuit. If the switch is opened or the bulb burns out, current stops flowing. A disadvantage to series circuits is that every light and other load device requires its own switch and wiring. This is impractical on the vehicle. Too many wires and switches would be needed.

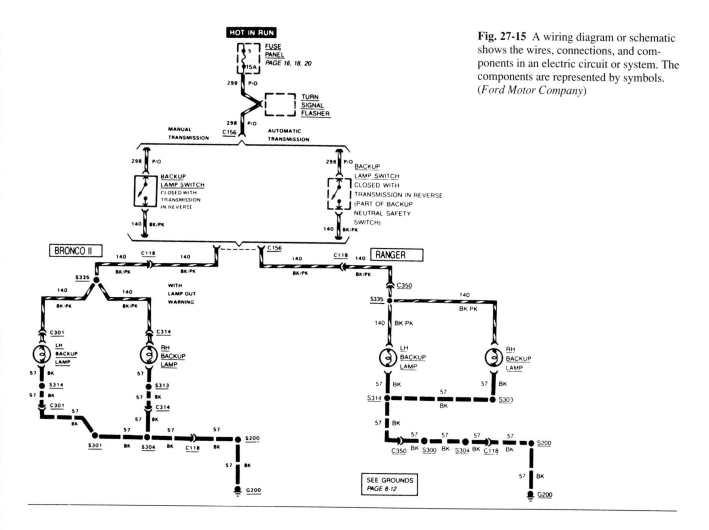

Fig. 27-15 A wiring diagram or schematic shows the wires, connections, and components in an electric circuit or system. The components are represented by symbols. (*Ford Motor Company*)

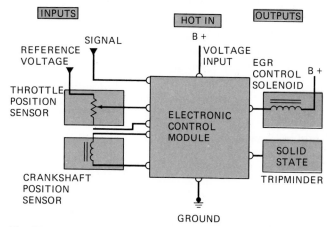

Fig. 27-16 A block diagram made up of boxes labeled with the circuit and device functions. Lines between the boxes represent the wiring that connects the devices. (*Ford Motor Company*)

2. PARALLEL CIRCUIT In a parallel circuit (Fig. 27-17B), two or more loads in separate branches connect to the same power source. A switch in the feed wire will control all branches. However, a switch placed in each branch will turn that load on and off without affecting the others. The feed current divides at the *common point* so

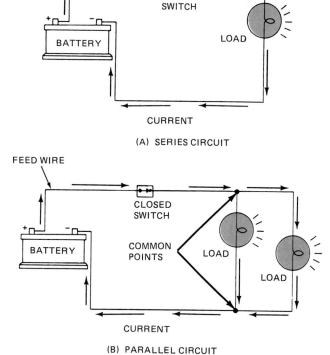

Fig. 27-17 Series and parallel circuits. (*Ford Motor Company*)

347

part of the current flows through each branch. The same voltage is applied to all branches of the parallel circuit.

Compare the simple drawing of a parallel circuit in Fig. 27-17B with the wiring diagram of the *backup lights* in Fig. 27-15. They show basically the same system. The *backup-lamp switch* in Fig. 27-15 is in series in the feed wire. Shifting into reverse closes the switch which sends current through the backup lamps. The right-hand (RH) and left-hand (LH) backup lamps are in parallel with each other. They have a common point for ground. Headlights and taillights are other examples of loads in parallel in the same circuit. All are turned on by the headlight switch, but they operate independently of each other. Vehicles have many parallel circuits.

Some automotive electric circuits are *series-parallel circuits*. These combine both series and parallel circuits. Two or more loads are in parallel, with a load in series in the feed wire. An example is the variable resistor in the headlight switch. Turning the resistor controls the brightness of the instrument-cluster lamps. The resistor is in series in the feed wire and the lamps are in parallel.

| NOTE | Notice in Fig. 27-17 that the arrows show current flow *from* the battery positive terminal through the circuit *to* the negative terminal. The layout of the wiring diagram in Fig. 27-15 shows current flowing down the page, *from* the fuse in the positive or feed wire *to* the negative ground. Electrons flow from negative to positive. However, automotive electrical and electronic equipment is often more easily understood and visualized by following the layout on the car and in the manufacturers' wiring diagrams. This simplification has current flowing from the battery, through the device and ground-return, back to the battery. The operation of a dc circuit is unaffected by the direction of current flow through it. |

27-11 ELECTRIC CIRCUIT PROBLEMS

The three basic electric-circuit problems are the *open circuit*, *short circuit*, and *grounded circuit* (Fig. 27-18). In an open circuit, either the wire has broken or a connection has corroded or loosened. No current flows.

In a short circuit, insulation may have worn through and wires are touching. Then the current takes the short cut instead of following the proper path. High current can flow if the short is across a major feed circuit. This usually blows the fuse or fusible link. Burned out wires and damaged components may result.

In a grounded circuit, the insulation wears through and the bare wire contacts a grounded part of the vehicle. This may be the metal body or engine. A ground often causes a low or discharged battery.

27-12 STATIC-SENSITIVE ELECTRONIC PARTS

Sometimes solid-state electrical parts must be replaced. Proper procedures must be followed or the new part may be damaged or destroyed before installation. When you walk across a carpet and then touch a metal object, a spark may jump from your fingers to the metal. This is *static electricity*. The spark is an *electrostatic discharge* and it can damage solid-state parts.

When you get an electronic part in a package with an *electrostatic discharge* (ESD) *sensitive* (Fig. 27-19) label on it, follow these guidelines:

1. Do not open the package until you are ready to install the part.
2. Do not touch the pins or terminals on the part.
3. Before removing the part from the package, touch the package to a clean metal part of the car, such as the cylinder head. This relieves any difference in static electricity between the package and the vehicle.
4. Always touch a known ground on the car before handling the part. Repeat this touching if you slide across the seat, get up, sit down, or walk. The movement of your body produces an electrostatic charge.

For maximum protection against damage from static

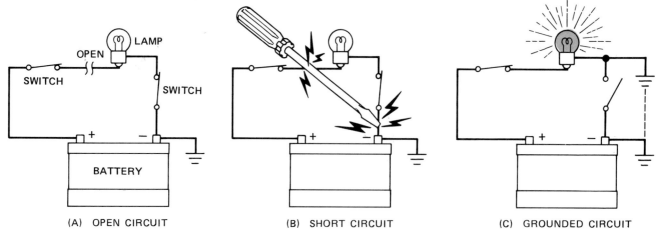

Fig. 27-18 Types of abnormal conditions that can occur in an electric circuit.

(A) OPEN CIRCUIT   (B) SHORT CIRCUIT   (C) GROUNDED CIRCUIT

Fig. 27-19 An *electrostatic discharge sensitive* parts label. The electronic part inside the packaging can be damaged or destroyed if a spark of static electricity occurs while the part is being handled or installed. (*General Motors Corporation*)

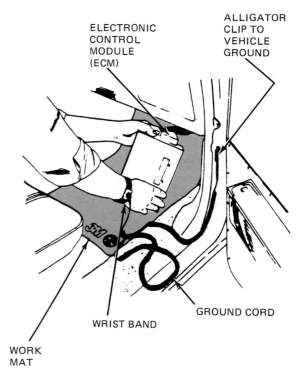

Fig. 27-20 Using a *static protection kit* protects electronic parts against damage from static electricity. (*Ford Motor Company*)

electricity, use a *static protection kit* (Fig. 27-20). It includes:

1. An elastic *wrist band* to drain away any static electricity from the wearer.
2. A flexible *work mat* to drain away any static electricity from an object placed on it.
3. A *ground cord* connected to the wrist band and work mat. Connect the alligator clip on the end of the ground cord to a ground on the vehicle.

Using the static protection kit drains away all static electricity from the technician and the part being handled. This prevents static electricity from damaging electronic modules or other static-sensitive parts.

ELECTRICAL TESTS AND MEASUREMENTS

➤ 27-13 JUMPER WIRE

A *jumper wire* is a length of wire used as a temporary connection between two points in a circuit. It may have alligator clips or various terminals on the ends. Figure 20-10 shows how use of a jumper wire allows testing the electric fuel pump with the engine off. A *fused jumper wire* has a circuit breaker or a fuse-holder and fuse in the wire. If excessive current flows, the circuit-breaker opens or the fuse blows to prevent further damage.

The jumper wire can be used in three ways:

1. To check for poor grounds.
2. To supply current from a known source directly to the load.
3. To bypass a wire or other part of the circuit.

For example, you can use a jumper wire to check a switch that you suspect is defective. Identify the switch terminals. Then turn the switch on. Touch the ends of the jumper wire to the switch terminals for the circuit you are testing. If this causes the circuit or connected electric device to operate, the switch is probably defective.

Careful! Incorrect use of a jumper wire may damage electric and electronic devices. Never bypass the load device in a circuit. Excessive current will flow. The wire will overheat and could cause a fire or burn you. Never use a jumper wire on a solid-state device or printed circuit, unless specified in the manufacturer's service manual. Any sparks that occur may cause high-voltage pulses which damage electronic modules and other devices.

➤ 27-14 TEST LIGHTS

Test lights are used to check circuits or electric components for voltage, continuity, and grounds. There are two types, circuit-powered and self-powered.

1. CIRCUIT-POWERED TEST LIGHT The *12-volt test light* (Fig. 27-21) has a 12-volt bulb connected between a test lead and a probe tip. Connect the alligator clip on the end of the test lead to ground. The bulb lights when the tip contacts a wire or terminal in which voltage is present.

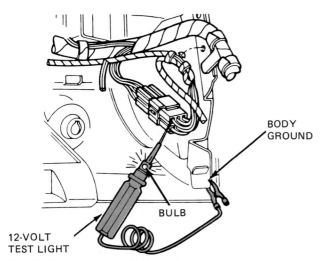

Fig. 27-21 A 12-volt test light is powered by current from the circuit it is testing. (*Ford Motor Company*)

Some test lights have a very small, sharp tip for piercing insulation. After piercing the insulation, cover the hole with electrical tape or silicone-rubber sealant. This prevents water or corrosion from causing a short or other damage.

Careful! Know the circuit you are testing before using a 12-volt test light. The additional current drawn by the test light can damage some electronic devices.

An *electronic circuit tester* (Fig. 27-22) or *digital logic probe* can be safely used on electronic circuits. Small light-emitting diodes (LEDs) glow singly or in combination. This indicates the voltage, the resistance, and the polarity.

2. SELF-POWERED TEST LIGHT The *self-powered test light* (Fig. 27-23) or *continuity tester* has a battery in the

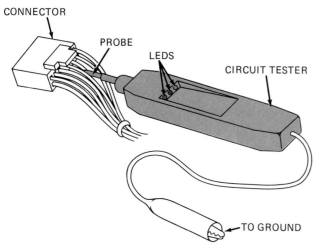

Fig. 27-22 An electronic circuit tester or digital logic probe has small light-emitting diodes (LEDs) that glow singly or in combination to indicate voltage, resistance, or polarity. (*Kent-Moore Automotive Division of SPX Corporation*)

handle. The battery provides the voltage to light the bulb when a complete circuit exists between the test lead and the probe. For example, suppose a wire placed between the probe and the lead causes the bulb to light. This shows the wire is unbroken and has continuity. If the bulb does not light, the wire is open. There is no continuity.

Careful! Never connect a self-powered test light to a live circuit. Always disconnect the battery or isolate any device or lead before checking it. The voltage in the live circuit will burn out the 1.5-volt bulb in the test light. Also, the battery in the test light may damage some electronic devices by applying excessive voltage to them.

➤ 27-15 ELECTRIC METERS

Electrical trouble diagnosis may require you to know the voltage, amperage, and resistance in the circuit. Measuring electricity is described in ➤10-4. This section introduces taking electrical measurements with meters. A *meter* is an instrument that measures and records the quantity or property of something that may be passing through it. Most automotive electrical measurements are made using the *voltmeter, ammeter,* and *ohmmeter* functions of a *multimeter.*

An electric meter or multimeter (Fig. 27-24) has two leads or wires with metal probes or clips on the ends. One

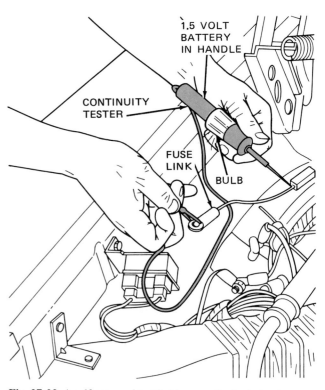

Fig. 27-23 A self-powered test light, or continuity tester, is powered by a small battery in the handle. (*Ford Motor Company*)

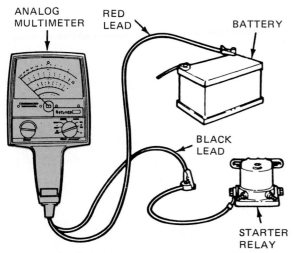

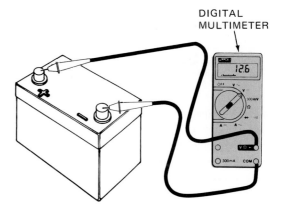

(A) MEASURING VOLTAGE

Fig. 27-24 An analog multimeter, which can be used as a voltmeter, ammeter, or ohmmeter. The movement of the needle or pointer indicates the reading, or measurement. (*Ford Motor Company*)

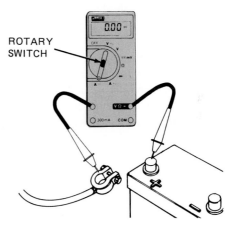

(B) MEASURING AMPERAGE

lead is the *positive lead* and is usually red. The other is the *ground lead* and is usually black. The clips or probes connect the meter to the circuit or device being tested.

On an *analog meter* (Fig. 27-24), the movement of the needle or pointer indicates the reading. The analog meter requires periodic calibration and may damage electronic circuits. However, fluctuating or pulsating readings are more easily followed by watching the swinging of the needle. A *digital meter* (Fig. 27-25) has a number display and should be used on most electronic circuits. Always follow the operating instructions for the meter to avoid damage to the meter or the circuit being tested.

Figure 27-25 shows a digital multimeter measuring voltage, current (amperage), and resistance. The voltmeter measures the voltage between two points. The ammeter measures the amperes of current flowing in a circuit. The ohmmeter measures the resistance (in ohms) of an electrical device or circuit. Turning the rotary switch on the digital multimeter selects the desired function.

> ### 27-16 DISPLAYING ELECTRICAL MEASUREMENTS

Computerized engine analyzers and service-bay diagnostic computers (Fig. 20-23) display information and graphics on a television-like picture tube. This is a *cathode-ray tube* or *CRT*. Many shop CRTs are used as a high-speed voltmeter or *oscilloscope* (Chap. 31). This electrical tester shows the pattern of the rapidly changing voltage in the ignition system. The "scope" also displays voltage patterns or *waveforms* from the alternator, fuel-injection system, and other electrical parts. If the analyzer or computer can be used as a multimeter, the reading in volts, amps, or ohms appears on the screen. The reading may be displayed as numbers or as a varying waveform. The higher the waveform, the higher the voltage.

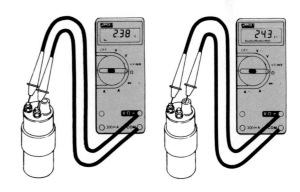

(C) MEASURING RESISTANCE

Fig. 27-25 Taking measurements with a digital multimeter. Turning the rotary switch on the multimeter selects the desired function. (*John Fluke Manufacturing Company, Inc.*)

A *digital storage oscilloscope* accurately displays any incoming voltage signal. This includes the voltage waveforms, pulse widths (Fig. 19-9), and on-off signals from the various sensors and switches on the car. The scope can also store and retrieve patterns to help diagnose intermittent problems. When connected to a computer with

351

a printer attached, a paper printout can be made of the stored waveform.

➤ 27-17 USING OHM'S LAW

Voltage, current, and resistance are all related to one another. A change in one affects the others. This relationship is called *Ohm's Law* (➤10-8). Using Ohm's Law, any value can be determined if the other two values are known. The relationship between current and resistance is *inversely proportional*. This means that when the voltage is constant, reducing the resistance by half causes the current flow to double. For example, doubling the resistance reduces the current flow by half. If the circuit has a voltage of one volt and a resistance of one ohm, a current of one ampere will flow. If the same circuit has a resistance of two ohms, a current of only 0.5 ampere will flow. If the resistance is 0.5 ohm, then current flow will be two amperes.

Sometimes the technician must calculate an unknown electrical measurement when the other two measurements are known. Figure 27-26 is an aid in the use of Ohm's law. Place a finger over the measurement you want to know. Then solve the arithmetic problem shown.

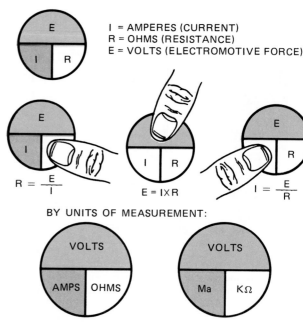

I = AMPERES (CURRENT)
R = OHMS (RESISTANCE)
E = VOLTS (ELECTROMOTIVE FORCE)

$$R = \frac{E}{I} \qquad E = I \times R \qquad I = \frac{E}{R}$$

BY UNITS OF MEASUREMENT:

Fig. 27-26 Ohm's Law states the relationship among current, voltage, and resistance. To use the symbol shown, cover the unit you want to find with your finger. Then solve the arithmetic problem indicated. (*Ford Motor Company*)

TRADE TALK

circuit breaker
digital logic
  probe

electrostatic discharge
  sensitive
fusible link

multimeter
parallel circuit
printed circuit

series circuit
wiring diagram
wiring harness

MULTIPLE-CHOICE TEST

Select the one correct, best, or most probable answer to each question.
You will find the answers in the section indicated at the end of each question.

1. The automotive electrical system does all the following EXCEPT (➤27-1)
   a. produces electric energy in the alternator
   b. stores electric energy in the alternator
   c. stores electric energy in chemical form in the battery
   d. delivers electric energy on demand to other electric components

2. Technician A says the color of the insulation identifies each wire in the wiring harness. Technician B says the color of the insulation identifies the current-carrying capacity of each wire. Who is right? (➤27-2)
   a. A only
   b. B only
   c. both A and B
   d. neither A nor B

3. Technician A says the printed circuit simplifies the wiring behind the instrument panel. Technician B says the printed circuit makes connections to various devices in the instrument cluster. Who is right? (➤27-3)
   a. A only
   b. B only
   c. both A and B
   d. neither A nor B

4. Two types of fuses used in automobiles are (➤27-4)
   a. printed and link
   b. blade and breaker
   c. blade and cartridge
   d. cartridge and breaker

5. The fusible link is (➤27-5)
   a. parallel to the circuit it protects
   b. in series in the circuit it protects
   c. able to reset itself after cooling
   d. made of a bimetal thermostat

6. In an electric circuit, the common point is the place where (➤27-10)
   a. voltage divides
   b. heat is a problem
   c. insulation thickens
   d. feed current divides

7. The three basic electric circuit problems are (➤27-11)
   a. open, closed, grounded
   b. short, long, closed
   c. short, open, closed
   d. short, open, ground

8. A jumper wire may be used in the following ways EXCEPT (➤27-13)
   a. to test a battery
   b. to check for poor grounds
   c. to supply current directly to the load
   d. to bypass a wire or other part of the circuit

9. Technician A says the quickest way to check for voltage in an electronic circuit is to use a 12-volt test light. Technician B says the safest way to check for voltage is to use an electronic circuit tester or digital logic probe. Who is right? (➤27-14)
   a. A only
   b. B only
   c. both A and B
   d. neither A nor B

10. A voltage that is fluctuating or pulsating should be measured with (➤27-15)
   a. a digital voltmeter
   b. a digital multimeter
   c. a test light
   d. an analog voltmeter

REVIEW QUESTIONS

1. List the components of a wiring circuit and describe the job of each.   (➤27-2)

2. Describe how to repair each type of circuit-protection device.   (➤27-4 to 27-6)

3. Explain how the connections to the battery positive terminal and negative terminal are shown on a wiring diagram.   (➤27-8)

4. What precautions do you take when the parts package has an *electrostatic discharge sensitive* label?   (➤27-12)

5. How much current flows through the circuit if the battery voltage is 12.6 and the resistance is 2.38 ohms?   (➤27-15 and 27-17)

CHAPTER 28

AUTOMOTIVE BATTERY: CONSTRUCTION AND SERVICE

After studying this chapter, and with proper instruction and equipment, you should be able to:

- Describe the construction and operation of a lead-acid storage battery.
- Define *reserve capacity* and *cold-cranking rate*.
- Determine the battery state-of-charge and open-circuit voltage.
- Perform a battery-load test and interpret the results.
- Use a battery charger to charge the battery.
- Inspect, clean, and replace the battery and cables.

BATTERY CONSTRUCTION AND OPERATION

➤ 28-1 BATTERY OPERATION

The automotive *battery* (Fig. 28-1) supplies electric current to operate the starting motor and ignition system while starting the engine. It also acts as a voltage stabilizer by supplying current for the lights, radio, and other electrical accessories when the alternator is not handling the load. In addition, the battery supplies a small current to the volatile memory in the electronic control module (ECM) while the ignition key is off (➤10-18).

The battery is an *electrochemical* device. It uses *chemicals* to produce *electricity*. The amount of electricity it can produce is limited. As the chemicals in the battery are depleted, the battery runs down and is *discharged*. It can be *recharged* by supplying it with electric current from the vehicle *alternator* (Chap. 30) or from a *battery charger* (➤28-21). The depleted chemicals are restored to their original condition as the battery becomes recharged.

➤ 28-2 CHEMICALS IN BATTERY

The battery is a *lead-acid storage battery*. The chemicals in it are *sponge lead* (a solid), *lead oxide* (a paste), and *sulfuric acid* (a liquid). These three substances can react chemically to produce a flow of current. The lead oxide and sponge lead are held in *plate grids* to form the positive

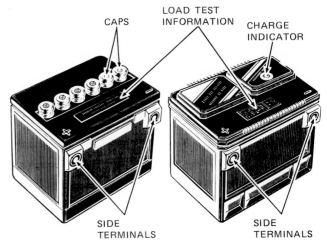

Fig. 28-1 Two types of automotive batteries. Left, caps can be removed to check the battery state of charge and to add water if needed. Right, a maintenance-free battery that requires no additional water. The charge indicator in the top shows the state of charge.

and negative plates (Fig. 28-2). The grids are made of lead with other elements, such as calcium, added.

The sulfuric acid is mixed with water to form the *electrolyte*. This is the liquid in a battery. The electrolyte is about 60 percent water and 40 percent sulfuric acid in a fully-charged battery. As the battery discharges, the electrolyte loses sulfuric acid and becomes mostly water. This allows the weakened electrolyte in a discharged battery to

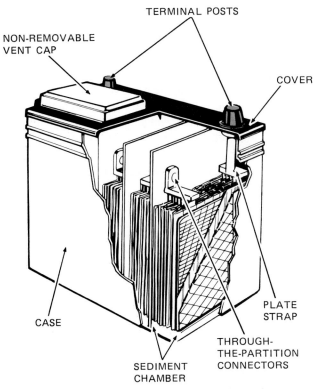

Fig. 28-2 Cutaway 12-volt battery showing its internal construction. (*Ford Motor Company*)

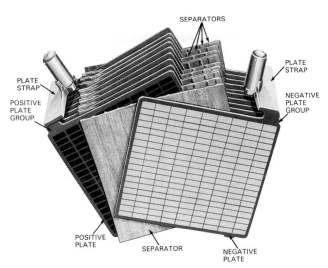

Fig. 28-3 Partly assembled battery element. (*Delco-Remy Division of General Motors Corporation*)

freeze in cold weather. That is why the battery should be kept fully charged during the winter months (➤28-18).

➤ 28-3 BATTERY CONSTRUCTION

The battery case is molded plastic. The plates are welded to plate straps (Fig. 28-3) to form *plate groups*. To make a *battery cell*, a positive plate group fits into a negative plate group. Porous separators are placed between the plates. This prevents positive and negative plates from touching while allowing electrolyte to circulate between the plates.

The assembly of plate groups and separators is an *element*. The elements fit into compartments in the battery case to form cells. Heavy lead connectors attach to the cell terminals and connect the cells in series. A plastic *cover* forms the top of the battery. Some batteries have openings in the cover from which *filler plugs* or *vent caps* (Fig. 28-1) are removed to add water. *Maintenance-free batteries* do not have removable vent caps.

Some batteries are *top-terminal batteries*. They have the two main terminals or posts in the cover (Fig. 28-2). The positive terminal post is larger than the negative terminal post. Other batteries are *side-terminal batteries*. They have the terminals on the side of the battery (Fig. 28-1).

➤ 28-4 CONNECTING CELLS

The 12-volt battery has six cells connected in series. This means the cell voltages add together to produce the battery voltage. Each cell has a voltage of about 2.15 volts at full charge. A fully charged battery has a voltage of about 12.9 volts.

➤ 28-5 BATTERY RATINGS

Two methods of rating batteries are *reserve capacity* and *cold-cranking rate*. An older battery rating is *ampere-hour capacity*. This is the amount of current that a battery can deliver for 20 hours without the temperature-corrected cell voltages dropping below 1.75 volts per cell.

1. RESERVE CAPACITY This is the length of time that a fully charged battery at 80°F [27°C] can deliver 25 amperes. A typical rating is 125 minutes. This indicates the battery can be discharged at 25 amperes for 125 minutes if the alternator is not working.

2. COLD-CRANKING RATE This is a measure of the ability of a battery to crank an engine when the battery is cold. There are two ratings. One is the number of amperes the 12-volt battery can deliver for 30 seconds when it is at 0°F [−18°C] without the battery voltage falling below 7.2 volts. A typical rating for a battery with a reserve capacity of 125 minutes is 430 amperes.

A second cold-cranking rating starts with the battery temperature at −20°F [−29°C]. This rating allows the final voltage to drop to 6 volts. A typical rating for a battery with a reserve capacity of 125 minutes is 320 amperes.

➤ 28-6 BATTERY EFFICIENCY

The ability of a battery to deliver current depends on its *state of charge*, temperature, and discharge rate. A partly discharged battery or a battery at low temperature can deliver less current.

28-7 VARIATIONS IN TERMINAL VOLTAGE

When the battery is being charged, terminal voltage increases with:

a. Increasing charging rate. Voltage must go up to increase the charging rate.

b. Increasing state of charge. It takes a higher voltage to force current through a fully charged battery.

c. Decreasing battery temperature. The lower temperature reduces chemical activity, requiring a higher voltage to maintain the charging rate (➤30-6).

When the battery is being discharged, terminal voltage decreases with:

a. Increasing discharge rate.
b. Decreasing state of charge.
c. Decreasing battery temperature.

BATTERY MAINTENANCE AND SERVICE

28-8 WORKING SAFELY AROUND BATTERIES

Follow the safety cautions listed below when working with batteries, and testing or charging them:

1. The sulfuric acid in the electrolyte is very corrosive. It will eat holes in cloth. It can cause serious burns if it gets on your skin. It can blind you if it gets in your eyes. Wear eye protection when working with, testing, or charging a battery. If you get battery acid on your skin, flush it off at once with water. Continue to flush for 5 minutes. If you get battery acid (electrolyte) in your eyes, flush them with water at once. Then go to the school nurse, a doctor, or hospital emergency room.

2. Gases released from the battery during charging are highly explosive. Ventilate the area. Never allow sparks, an open flame, or burning cigarettes around a battery being charged or a battery that has recently been charging. The flame might cause an explosion or fire and spray you with electrolyte. Even a spark from improperly connecting or disconnecting a battery or battery charger could cause an explosion.

3. Never wear rings, bracelets, watches, or hanging necklaces around batteries. If the metal accidentally shorts the battery, a very high current can flow. You could be seriously burned.

4. A battery that is so discharged that the engine will not crank is a *dead battery.* Starting the engine of a car that has a dead battery by using a charged battery in another car is called *jump starting.* Follow the instructions in Chap. 29. A wrong step can injure you and damage electrical and electronic components.

5. When disconnecting a battery, always disconnect the negative or ground cable first (Fig. 28-4). If you then accidentally ground the insulated terminal or a feed or "hot" wire, it is not a short across the battery.

6. If the battery has vent caps, make sure the vent holes are open before charging. Cover the caps with a damp cloth. Discard the cloth after the battery is charged.

7. Never lean over a charging battery.

8. Do not charge a frozen battery or a maintenance-free battery in which the charge-indicator dot (➤28-19) shows light yellow or clear. The battery could explode!

28-9 BATTERY MAINTENANCE

Battery maintenance includes:

1. Making a visual inspection of the battery.
2. Cleaning the battery top, terminals, and cable clamps.
3. Testing the battery.
4. Charging the battery.

Following sections describe these and other battery services.

28-10 BATTERY VISUAL INSPECTION

Look for signs of electrolyte leakage, cracks in the case or top, missing vent caps, and loose or missing hold-down clamps (Fig. 28-5). On a side-terminal battery, check for loose terminals and leaking electrolyte. Leakage causes white corrosion on the battery tray and surrounding metal.

A cracked cover on a top-terminal battery may result from using the wrong wrench to turn the nut on the cable-clamp bolt. Overtightening the hold-down clamps may

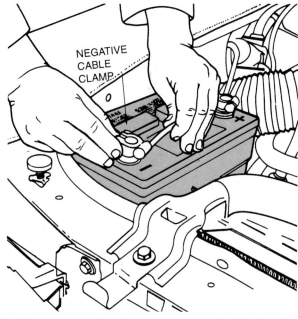

Fig. 28-4 Disconnecting the negative or ground cable from the battery. (*Ford Motor Company*)

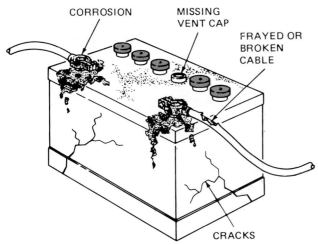

Fig. 28-5 Conditions to look for during a visual inspection of the battery. *(ATW)*

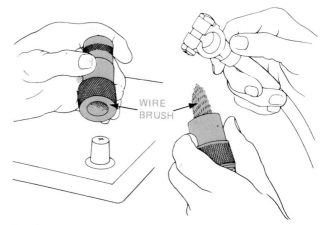

Fig. 28-6 Using a battery-terminal brush to clean the battery terminal posts and clamps. *(ATW)*

crack the battery case. Overtightening the cable bolts in side-terminal batteries may pull the terminal loose.

On vent-cap batteries, remove the vent caps. Check the electrolyte level. Add water if needed.

➤ 28-11 CLEANING THE BATTERY

Top-terminal batteries may corrode around the terminals and clamps. Disconnect the cables and clean the terminals and cable clamps with a *battery-terminal brush* (Fig. 28-6). Brush the battery top with a solution of baking soda and water. After the foaming stops, flush off the battery top with water. To retard corrosion, coat the terminals with anticorrosion compound.

➤ 28-12 BATTERY ADDITIVES

Certain chemical additives are promoted as restoring batteries to good condition when added to the cells. *Never* add chemicals to the battery. This will void the battery warranty and may cause battery failure.

BATTERY TESTING AND TROUBLE DIAGNOSIS

➤ 28-13 ANALYZING BATTERY TROUBLES

Overcharging and *undercharging* are two main causes of battery troubles.

1. OVERCHARGING If a vent-cap battery requires frequent addition of water, it is probably being overcharged. So is a maintenance-free battery that has a low electrolyte level. Overcharging damages the plates and shortens battery life. The exposed plate surfaces may be ruined. Overcharging causes excess heat that can buckle and crumble the plates.

The high voltage that causes overcharging can also damage other electrical and electronic components. For example, high voltage and the resulting high current may damage the ECM. High current may also burn out the filaments in light bulbs. Test the charging system (Chap. 30) when overcharging is suspected.

2. UNDERCHARGING Recharge (➤28-21) a dead or discharged battery. Then try to determine the cause of undercharging. Possible causes include:

a. Charging-system malfunction.
b. Defective connections in charging system.
c. Excessive load demands on battery.
d. Defective battery.
e. Self-discharge resulting from battery sitting idle for long periods.
f. Excessive key-off current drain (➤30-16).

➤ 28-14 TESTING THE BATTERY

Testing determines if the battery:

1. Is in good condition.
2. Needs recharging.
3. Is defective and should be discarded.

Batteries are tested in two ways: for state of charge and for performance. The state of charge of a vent-cap battery is determined with the *hydrometer* (➤28-16). The built-in hydrometer or *charge indicator* in a maintenance-free battery provides this information (➤28-19). An open-circuit voltage test can also be used (➤28-15). The *battery-load test* (➤28-20) indicates if the battery is capable of performing its job.

➤ 28-15 OPEN-CIRCUIT VOLTAGE TEST

Some maintenance-free batteries do not have a charge indicator in the top. To find the state of charge, measure the *open-circuit voltage* (OCV). This test is usually made by measuring terminal voltage with a digital voltmeter (Fig. 27-25A). A battery with an OCV of 12.40 volts or higher is charged enough for load testing (➤28-20). If the voltage is less than 12.40 volts, charge the battery first.

➤ 28-16 HYDROMETER TEST

Two types of hydrometers are the *float* and *ball*. The ball hydrometer is similar to the ball-type coolant hydrometer (Fig. 26-4). Put the rubber tube into the electrolyte. Then squeeze and release the bulb. Electrolyte will be drawn into the tube. If all balls float, the battery is fully charged. If none float, the battery is discharged. The more balls that float, the higher the battery state of charge.

Careful! Do not drip electrolyte on the car or on yourself. Electrolyte will damage the paint and eat holes in your clothes.

The float hydrometer (Fig. 28-7) is used in the same way. It will float in the electrolyte drawn in. Marks on the float stem show the electrolyte *specific gravity*. This indicates the state of charge (Fig. 28-8). The more fully-charged the battery, the higher the float. Figure 28-9 shows the relationship among specific gravity, open-circuit voltage (➤28-15), and state of charge.

➤ 28-17 VARIATIONS IN SPECIFIC GRAVITY

The electrolyte thickens slightly (gains specific gravity) as its temperature goes down. Some hydrometers have a thermometer and a scale to aid in adjusting the reading for temperature. Specific gravity changes four (0.004) points for every 10°F [5.6°C] change in temperature. If the temperature is below 80°F [27°C], subtract points to get the true reading. If higher than 80°F [27°C], add points.

As a battery ages, it begins to wear out and lose specific gravity. Also, some chemical actions in a battery continue when the battery sits idle. This *self-discharge* causes the electrolyte to lose specific gravity. If the hydrometer test shows less than 50 (0.050) points difference between cells, charge the battery. If there is more than a 50-point difference, replace the battery.

➤ 28-18 FREEZING TEMPERATURE OF ELECTROLYTE

The higher the specific gravity, the lower the temperature required to freeze electrolyte (Fig. 28-10). The electrolyte in a discharged battery will freeze slightly below the freezing temperature of water. The electrolyte in a fully charged battery will not freeze until its temperature falls to −95°F [−70°C]. Freezing can ruin the battery. The best protection against freezing is to keep the battery fully charged.

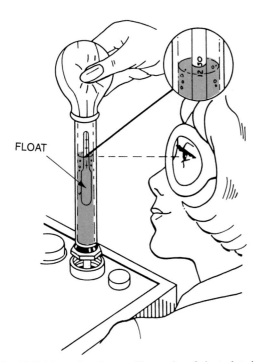

FLOAT

Fig. 28-7 Measuring the specific gravity of electrolyte in a battery cell with a float hydrometer. Reading must be taken at eye level. The higher the float stem sticks out of the electrolyte, the higher the state of charge of that cell.

Specific Gravity	State of Charge
1.265–1.299	Fully charged battery
1.235–1.265	Three-fourths charged
1.205–1.235	One-half charged
1.170–1.205	One-fourth charged
1.140–1.170	Barely operative
1.110–1.140	Completely discharged

Fig. 28-8 Relationship between specific gravity and state of charge.

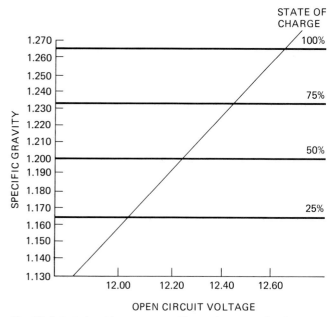

Fig. 28-9 Relationship among specific gravity, open-circuit voltage (OCV), and state of charge. (*Ford Motor Company*)

Specific Gravity	Freezing Temperature Degrees F (C)
1.100	18 [−8.2]
1.160	1 [−17.2]
1.200	−17 [−27.3]
1.220	−31 [−35]
1.260	−75 [−59.4]
1.300	−95 [−70.5]

Fig. 28-10 Specific gravities and freezing temperatures for battery electrolyte.

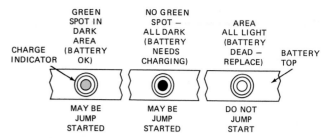

Fig. 28-12 Appearance of the charge indicator under different battery conditions.

➤ **28-19 CHARGE-INDICATOR CONDITION**

The *charge indicator* (Fig. 28-11) is a built-in hydrometer. Its appearance shows the condition and state-of-charge of the battery (Fig. 28-12). If the indicator is light yellow or clear, the electrolyte level is low. Install a new battery.

CAUTION!

If the charge indicator shows light yellow or clear, do not try to charge, load test, or jump start the battery! It could explode!

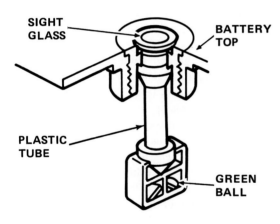

(A) CHARGE-INDICATOR CONSTRUCTION

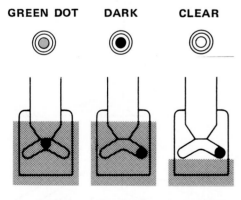

(B) CHARGE-INDICATOR OPERATION

Fig. 28-11 Construction and operation of the built-in hydrometer, or charge indicator. *(ATW)*

➤ **28-20 BATTERY LOAD TEST**

After the battery passes the state-of-charge test, its performance can be checked by making a *battery capacity test* or *battery load test*. This measures terminal voltage while the battery is discharging at a high rate. The load is applied using a tester that includes a voltmeter, an ammeter, and a *carbon-pile* (variable) *resistor* (Fig. 28-13). The manufacturer's specifications or the decal on top of the battery (Fig. 28-1) gives the *cold-cranking amps* (CCA) for the battery. This is used in determining the load to be placed on the battery.

Some manufacturers recommend removing the surface charge by applying a 300-ampere load to the battery for 15 seconds. Wait 15 seconds. Then apply a load equal to *one-half* the cold-cranking amps. After 15 seconds, read the voltage and remove the load. Depending on battery temperature (Fig. 28-14), battery voltage should read 9.6 volts or higher. If the voltage reading is below the minimum, recharge the battery and retest it. A battery that fails the load test a second time is defective.

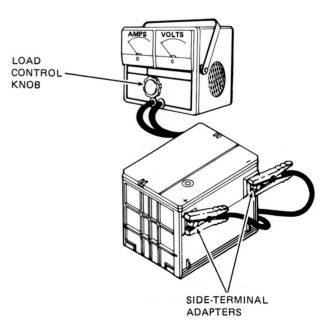

Fig. 28-13 Using a volt-ampere tester with a carbon-pile resistor to make a battery load, or capacity, test. *(Delco-Remy Division of General Motors Corporation)*

Estimated Temperature	Minimum Voltage
70° F (21° C)	9.6
50° F (10° C)	9.4
30° F (0° C)	9.1
15° F (−10° C)	8.8
0° F (−18° C)	8.5
Below 0° F (−18° C)	8.0

Fig. 28-14 Minimum battery voltage related to battery temperature.

> **NOTE** Instead of cold-cranking amps, battery capacity may be given in ampere-hours. Then the test is performed using three times the ampere-hour capacity for the load. The starting motor can also be used to load the battery. Disable the ignition and crank the engine for 15 seconds. Then read the voltmeter and stop cranking. The voltage should be 9.6 volts or higher. This is a *cranking-voltage* or *starter-draw test* (Chap. 29).

When load testing the battery, follow the procedure in the manufacturer's service manual and the tester operating instructions. Some manufacturers recommend removing the cables from the battery. For maintenance-free batteries with charge indicators, first make sure the indicator shows green. If it shows black, recharge the battery before testing it. If the indicator shows light yellow or white, discard the battery.

BATTERY CHARGING AND REPLACEMENT

➤ 28-21 CHARGING BATTERIES

Two methods of battery charging are the *slow charge* and the *quick* or *fast charge*. With slow charging, the battery is given a charge of a few amperes for several hours. A typical fast charge (Fig. 28-15) is a 30-amp charging rate for up to 30 minutes. For further charging, reduce the charging rate to 20 amps or less for up to 3 hours longer.

Charge a maintenance-free battery until the green dot appears (Fig. 28-12). To connect the charger to a side-terminal battery, it may be necessary to install bolts or adapters in the terminal bolt holes (Fig. 28-13).

When charging a battery in a vehicle, disconnect the ground cable from the battery. This protects electrical and electronic components from the high charging voltage.

> **Careful!** Never connect the battery charger backward. The reversed polarity may cause high-current flow which would damage the vehicle electrical equipment.

➤ 28-22 REMOVING AND INSTALLING BATTERY

Connect a *memory holder* (a 9-volt battery and adapter) to the cigarette lighter to keep the volatile memories

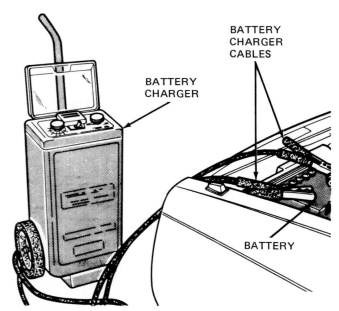

Fig. 28-15 Battery charger connected to battery in a car. Disconnect the negative or ground cable from the battery before connecting the battery-charger cables. (*Chrysler Corporation*)

(➤10-18) alive while the battery is disconnected from the vehicle. Follow the manufacturer's instructions to avoid overloading the 9-volt battery. If a memory holder is not used, write down the radio stations to which the push buttons are preset. All data in this and other volatile memories (➤10-18) will be lost when the battery is disconnected.

Disconnect the ground cable from the battery (Fig. 28-4). To remove a nut-and-bolt cable clamp, use a box wrench or battery pliers (Fig. 28-16). Loosen the clamp bolt. Then pull the clamp from the terminal. Do not use other pliers or an open-end wrench. There is not enough room and they could break the battery cover. If the clamp sticks, use a *battery-clamp puller* (Fig. 28-16). Do not pry the clamp off with a screwdriver or pry bar. You could break the cover. To detach the spring-ring cable clamp, squeeze apart the ends of the rings with pliers.

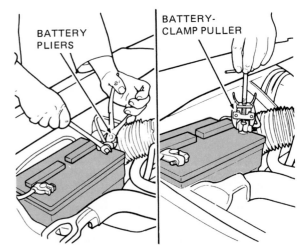

Fig. 28-16 Loosening nut and using battery-clamp puller to remove cable clamp from battery post. (*Ford Motor Company*)

Next, disconnect the insulated cable from the battery. Clean the terminals and cable clamps (Fig. 28-6). Loosen the hold-down clamps and remove the battery. Clean the battery tray and hold-down clamps. If the parts are metal, clean them with a stiff brush and a solution of baking soda and water. Open the water drain holes in the bottom of the tray. After rinsing and drying, paint the tray and other metal parts with *acid-resistant paint*.

When installing the battery, do not reverse the terminal connections. Reconnect the insulated cable first, then the ground cable. Tighten the hold-down clamps. Do not over-tighten. Then reset the radio presets. Follow the procedure to restore data to the ECM and volatile memories.

Careful! Never install a battery backward. The reversed polarity may cause high-current flow which would damage electrical components.

➤ 28-23 CARE OF BATTERIES IN STOCK

Wet batteries are new batteries that are shipped already filled with electrolyte. These batteries periodically require recharging. Do not stack batteries on top of each other without additional support. The weight can collapse the case and the plates in the bottom batteries.

MULTIPLE-CHOICE TEST

Select the **one** *correct, best, or most probable answer to each question.*
You can find the answers in the section indicated at the end of each question.

1. The battery is an electrochemical device. This means the battery (➤28-1)
   a. makes chemicals by electronic means
   b. uses chemicals to provide electricity
   c. has non-chemical plates
   d. does not use an electrolyte
2. The battery performs the following EXCEPT (➤28-1)
   a. supplies current to crank the engine
   b. supplies current when the charging system cannot handle the load
   c. supplies current to the ignition system with the engine off
   d. supplies current to the ECM while the engine is off
3. On a top-terminal battery, the negative terminal post is (➤28-3)
   a. smaller than the positive terminal post
   b. the same size as the positive terminal post
   c. larger than the positive terminal post
   d. none of the above
4. The time in minutes that a fully charged battery at 80°F [27°C] can deliver 25 amperes is the (➤28-5)
   a. charging rate
   b. reserve capacity
   c. cold-cranking rate
   d. ampere-hour rate

5. The number of amperes that the battery can deliver for 30 seconds at 0°F [−18°C] without cell voltages falling below 7.2 volts is called the (➤28-5)
   a. charging rate
   b. reserve capacity
   c. cold-cranking rate
   d. ampere-hour rate
6. To disconnect a battery, first (➤28-8)
   a. remove the vent plugs
   b. disconnect the insulated cable from the battery
   c. disconnect the ground cable from the battery
   d. put the transmission in NEUTRAL
7. Technician A says a battery with an open-circuit voltage of 12.40 or higher can be load tested. Technician B says an OCV of less than 12.40 means the battery must be charged first. Who is right? (➤28-15)
   a. A only
   b. B only
   c. both A and B
   d. neither A nor B

REVIEW QUESTIONS

1. Describe the percentages of water and sulfuric acid that make up the electrolyte at full charge, and how discharging allows it to freeze in cold weather. (➤28-2)
2. Explain how the terminal voltage changes during charging and during discharging. (➤28-7)
3. How are the hydrometer and the digital voltmeter used to check state-of-charge? Explain the meaning of the readings that each provides. (➤28-15 and 28-16)

4. Describe when and how to make a battery load test. (➤28- 20)
5. Discuss the possible causes and troubles from battery overcharging and undercharging. (➤28-13)

CHAPTER 29

STARTING SYSTEM: OPERATION AND SERVICE

After studying this chapter, and with proper instruction and equipment, you should be able to:

- Explain the purpose, construction, and operation of the starting system.
- Describe the construction and operation of the overrunning clutch, and how the pinion is moved in and out of mesh with the ring gear.
- List the three basic starting-system complaints, and the possible causes of each.
- Perform a starting-system diagnosis by making cranking-voltage, voltage-drop, and current-draw tests.
- Remove, service, and install a starting motor.
- Describe the procedure for jump starting.

➢ **29-1 NEED FOR STARTING SYSTEM**

To start the automobile engine, the crankshaft must turn fast enough for air-fuel mixture to enter the cylinders. An electric *starter* or *starting motor* does this job. It converts electrical energy from the battery into mechanical energy that rotates the crankshaft.

The starting system has two separate but related circuits

(Fig. 29-1). One is the low-current *control circuit*. The other is the high-current *motor circuit*. Both operate on battery voltage. When the driver turns the ignition key to START, the control circuit causes heavy contacts to close in a *starter relay* or *solenoid switch*. High current then flows from the battery insulated cable through these contacts to the starting motor. A gear on the starting-motor shaft moves into mesh with the *ring gear* around the engine

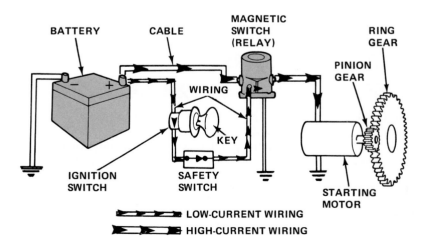

Fig. 29-1 Starting system for the automotive engine. The system has two circuits, a low-current control circuit and a high-current motor circuit. (*Ford Motor Company*)

flywheel or drive plate. As the starting-motor shaft turns, it spins the crankshaft fast enough to start the engine.

The use of a relay or solenoid shortens the distance that heavy-gauge cable must carry the cranking current. The control circuit includes a *safety switch* (Fig. 29-1). It prevents energizing of the relay or solenoid with the automatic transmission or transaxle in gear (➤47-26). In a vehicle with a manual transmission or transaxle (➤42-15), the clutch pedal must be depressed before cranking occurs.

> **NOTE** Some starting systems use both a relay and a solenoid. The relay is in the low-current control circuit. Turning the key to START closes the relay and completes the control circuit to the solenoid. Operation of the starting system is then the same as described below.

➤ 29-2 BASIC MOTOR PRINCIPLES

When current flows through a conductor, a magnetic field builds up around that conductor (Fig. 29-2A). If the conductor is in a magnetic field, as from a horseshoe magnet, the magnetic field exerts a force on the conductor. This is shown in Fig. 29-2B. The cross in the center of the conductor (Fig. 29-2A) indicates the current is flowing away from the reader. This causes the magnetic field due to the current flow to encircle the conductor in a clockwise direction.

In Fig. 29-2B, the circular magnetic field to the left of the conductor is in the same direction as the straight-line magnetic field from the magnet. To the right of the conductor, the circular magnetic field is in the opposite direction. This weakens the field to the right of the conductor. Therefore, the resulting magnetic field distorts around the conductor as shown in Fig. 29-2B.

Magnetic lines of force try to shorten themselves. This causes the bent lines of force in the magnetic-field pattern in Fig. 29-2B to try to straighten out. As they do, they try to push the conductor to the right. The more current flowing, the more the lines of force will be distorted around the conductor. This results in a stronger push on the conductor.

➤ 29-3 STARTING-MOTOR CONSTRUCTION AND OPERATION

Engines are made in various sizes and cylinder arrangements. Similarly, starting motors vary in size and shape. They also vary in construction. For example, most automotive starting motors have used *electromagnets* (➤10-11) to produce the magnetic field. More starting motors now have *permanent magnets* (➤10-10) instead. Later sections describe other differences.

1. STARTING-MOTOR CONSTRUCTION The starting motor has two basic parts: an *armature* and a *field-frame*

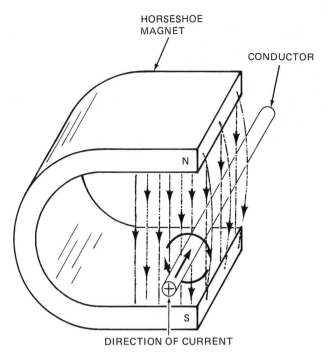

DIRECTION OF CURRENT

(A) ENCIRCLING MAGNETIC FIELD AROUND A CURRENT-CARRYING CONDUCTOR

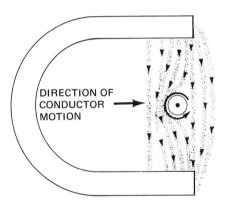

(B) MAGNETIC-FIELD FORCE ACTING ON A CURRENT-CARRYING CONDUCTOR

Fig. 29-2 Principle of the electric motor. (A) When current flows through a conductor, a magnetic field builds up around that conductor. (B) When a current-carrying conductor is in a magnetic field, the magnetic field exerts a force on the conductor by trying to push it out. (ATW)

assembly (Fig. 29-3). The armature is the rotating assembly that includes the main current-carrying conductors. *Field windings* in the *electromagnet starting motor* produce a strong magnetic field when battery current flows through them. In the *permanent-magnet starting motor* strong permanent magnets provide the stationary magnetic field. When current flows, the armature windings and field windings or magnets produce opposing magnetic fields. This forces the armature to rotate and crank the engine.

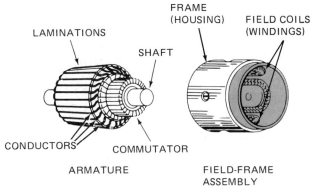

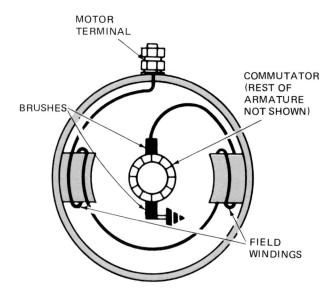

Fig. 29-3 Two major parts of the starting motor, the armature and the field-frame assembly. (*Delco-Remy Division of General Motors Corporation*)

2. STARTING-MOTOR OPERATION Figure 29-4 shows the basic wiring circuit and current flow through an electromagnet starting motor. The current flows in through the large terminal on the starting motor. Then the current flows through the field windings and insulated *brush* to the *commutator*. A brush is a small block of conducting material that rests against the rotating commutator and conducts electric current into and out of the armature.

The commutator (Fig. 29-3) is a ring of copper bars insulated from each other and from the armature shaft. The bars connect to the loops of heavy wire that form the armature windings (Fig. 29-4). When the armature rotates, the insulated brush contacts each bar passing under it. Current then flows through the armature windings and grounded brush, and back to the battery. The armature and field windings are made of heavy copper strips (Fig. 29-5). These have a very low resistance, so a very high current can flow.

Figure 29-4 shows only one armature loop or winding, two field coils and *pole shoes*, and two brushes. The typical starting motor has four field coils and pole shoes, and four brushes. The armature windings are made of many loops of heavy wire. Different wiring circuits and construction are used. However, operation of the electromagnet starting motor is basically the same as shown in Fig. 29-4.

➤ 29-4 STARTING-MOTOR DRIVE

Figure 29-5 shows an electromagnet starting motor with the solenoid mounted on it. The *pinion* gear on the end of the armature shaft meshes with the ring gear on the flywheel or drive plate (Fig. 29-1). A pinion is the smallest gear in a gear set. The ring gear has about 15 times as many teeth as the pinion. This means the armature must rotate 15 times to rotate the ring gear and crankshaft once. When the starting motor operates, the armature spins about 3000 rpm. This rotates the crankshaft about 200 rpm or higher which is fast enough to start the engine.

After the engine starts, crankshaft speed may increase to 3000 rpm or more. If the pinion remains in mesh with the

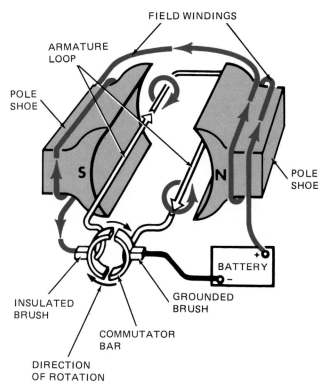

Fig. 29-4 Basic wiring circuit and current flow through an electromagnet starting motor. (*Delco-Remy Division of General Motors Corporation*)

ring gear, the pinion and armature will spin at 45,000 rpm. This is because of the 15 to 1 (15:1) gear ratio. Centrifugal force will pull the commutator bars and windings out of the armature, ruining the starting motor. An overrunning-clutch type of *starting-motor drive* (➤29-5) prevents the armature from overspeeding.

➤ 29-5 OVERRUNNING CLUTCH

The starting motor has an *overrunning clutch* (Fig. 29-5) that transmits torque in one direction and turns freely in the

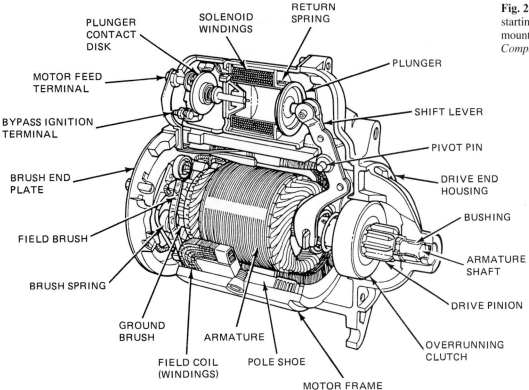

Fig. 29-5 An electromagnet starting motor with the solenoid mounted on it. (*Ford Motor Company*)

Figure labels (Fig. 29-5):
- PLUNGER CONTACT DISK
- MOTOR FEED TERMINAL
- BYPASS IGNITION TERMINAL
- BRUSH END PLATE
- FIELD BRUSH
- BRUSH SPRING
- GROUND BRUSH
- FIELD COIL (WINDINGS)
- ARMATURE
- POLE SHOE
- MOTOR FRAME
- SOLENOID WINDINGS
- RETURN SPRING
- PLUNGER
- SHIFT LEVER
- PIVOT PIN
- DRIVE END HOUSING
- BUSHING
- ARMATURE SHAFT
- DRIVE PINION
- OVERRUNNING CLUTCH

other direction. When the armature turns, the clutch locks and transmits cranking torque to the ring gear. As soon as the engine starts, it spins the pinion faster than the armature is turning. This unlocks the clutch, allowing the pinion to overrun the armature. This prevents damage to the armature from spinning at high speed.

The overrunning clutch (Fig. 29-6) consists of an outer shell and a pinion-and-collar assembly. The outer shell has five steel rollers fitted into five notches. The notches are smaller at one end. When the armature and shell begin to rotate, the rollers roll into the smaller ends of the notches. There, they jam between the shell and the pinion collar.

This forces the pinion to turn with the shell, cranking the engine.

When the engine starts, it drives the pinion faster than the shell and armature. The rollers roll back into the larger ends of the notches. This allows the pinion and collar to spin faster than the shell and armature.

➤ **29-6 OPERATING THE OVERRUNNING CLUTCH**

Figure 29-7 shows how the pinion moves into mesh with the ring-gear teeth. The starting-motor solenoid has a

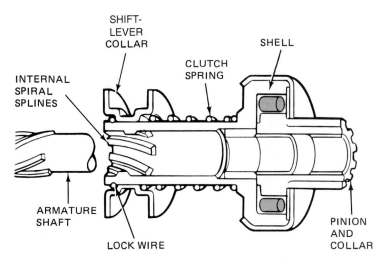

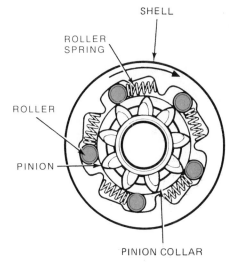

Figure labels (Fig. 29-6):
- INTERNAL SPIRAL SPLINES
- SHIFT-LEVER COLLAR
- CLUTCH SPRING
- SHELL
- ARMATURE SHAFT
- LOCK WIRE
- PINION AND COLLAR

Figure labels (Fig. 29-7 / right diagram):
- SHELL
- ROLLER SPRING
- ROLLER
- PINION
- PINION COLLAR

Fig. 29-6 Construction of an overrunning clutch. (*Delco-Remy Division of General Motors Corporation*)

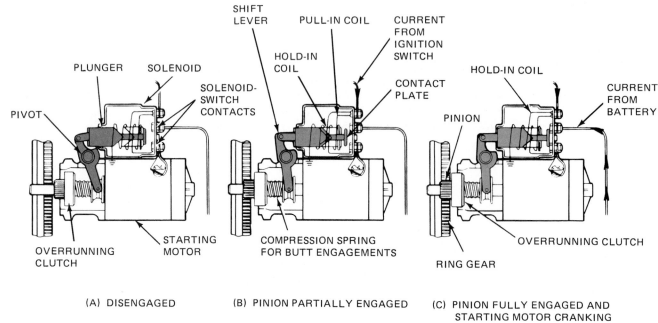

Fig. 29-7 Actions of the solenoid and overrunning clutch as the pinion engages. (*Delco-Remy Division of General Motors Corporation*)

plunger that connects by a *shift lever* to the overrunning clutch. When the driver turns the ignition key to START, current flows to the solenoid (Fig. 29-7B). This creates a magnetic field that pulls the plunger in. The attached shift lever pivots and pushes the pinion into mesh with the ring-gear teeth.

At the same time, pinion movement moves the *contact plate* which closes the contacts in the solenoid switch. This

connects the starting motor to the battery so the armature rotates and cranks the engine (Fig. 29-7C).

The solenoid has two windings, a *hold-in winding* and a *pull-in winding*. Their combined magnetic fields force the pinion into mesh with the ring-gear teeth. Then the pull-in winding is disconnected. This reduces the load on the battery. Less magnetism is required to hold the pinion in mesh than to engage it.

Fig. 29-8 Construction of a movable-pole-shoe starting motor. Ford calls this a "positive engagement" starting motor. (*Ford Motor Company*)

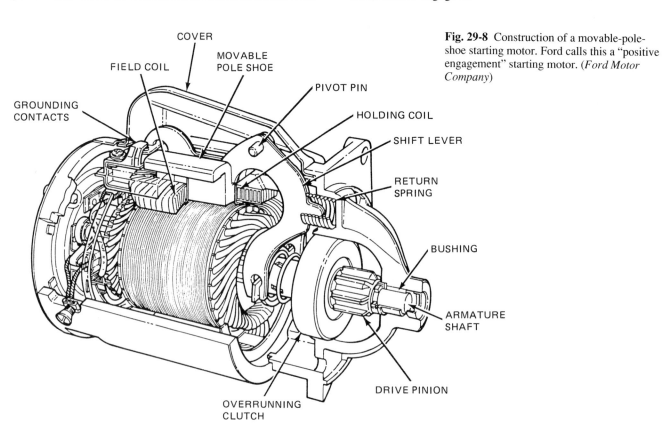

➤ 29-7 MOVABLE-POLE-SHOE STARTING MOTOR

Instead of a solenoid mounted on the starting motor, some cars have a *movable-pole-shoe starting motor* (Fig. 29-8). It uses a movable pole shoe to move the over-running-clutch shift lever. When no current flows to the starting motor, the *return spring* forces the shift lever and over-running clutch back. This raises the movable pole shoe, which is attached to the other end of the shift lever.

The control circuit includes a *magnetic switch* or relay (Fig. 29-1). When the ignition key is turned to START, contacts close in the relay and current flows to the starting motor. The magnetic field from the field coil around the movable-pole shoe pulls it down. As the shoe moves down, the shift lever pivots. This moves the pinion into mesh with the ring-gear teeth.

➤ 29-8 GEAR REDUCTION

To increase cranking torque, many starting motors have internal *gear reduction*. Figure 29-9 shows an electromagnet starting motor with gear reduction. The small pinion gear on the armature shaft drives the larger gear on the clutch shaft. There are two gear reductions. One is the *reduction-gear set* inside the starting motor. The other is the reduction between the overrunning-clutch pinion and the ring-gear teeth. The starting motor shown in Fig. 29-9 provides a gear reduction of 45:1. The armature turns 45 times to turn the crankshaft once. This provides high cranking torque.

A second type of gear reduction uses a *planetary-gear set* (Figs. 29-10 and 29-11) in the starting motor. It provides a gear reduction of about 4.5 to 1. Total gear reduction between the starting-motor armature and crankshaft is about 70 to 1. Many permanent-magnet starting motors (➤29-9) have planetary gears.

➤ 29-9 PERMANENT-MAGNET STARTING MOTORS

Instead of electromagnets (➤29-3), some starting motors use four or six permanent magnets (Fig. 29-11) to provide the stationary magnetic field. This allows permanent-magnet starting motors to be smaller and lighter than similar starting motors with field coils. The electrical energy required to crank an engine is the same for both types of starting motors. Both use magnetism to rotate the armature. The difference is in the source of the magnetism. Most permanent-magnet starting motors have gear reduction (➤29-8).

STARTING-SYSTEM TROUBLE DIAGNOSIS

➤ 29-10 STARTING-SYSTEM TROUBLES

Three basic starting-system complaints are:

1. The engine does not crank.
2. The engine cranks slowly but does not start.

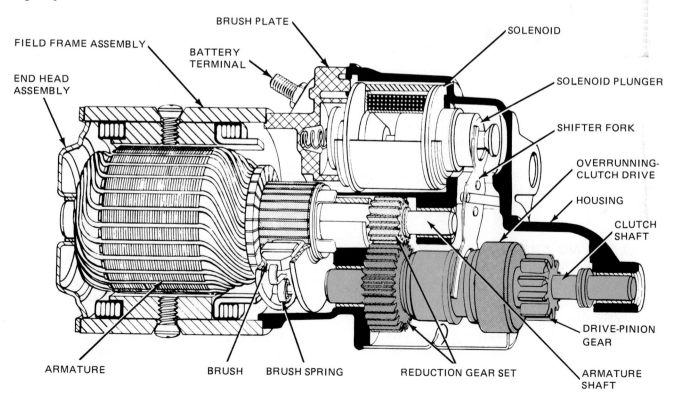

Fig. 29-9 Gear-reduction starting motor with overrunning clutch. (*Chrysler Corporation*)

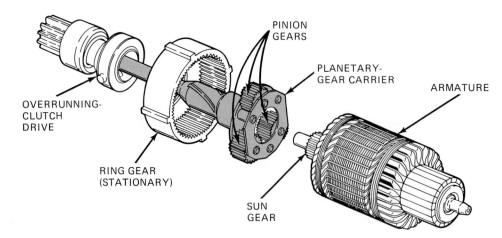

PINION GEARS

PLANETARY-GEAR CARRIER

ARMATURE

OVERRUNNING-CLUTCH DRIVE

RING GEAR (STATIONARY)

SUN GEAR

Fig. 29-10 Internal parts of a permanent-magnet starting motor that uses a planetary gearset for gear reduction. (*Delco-Remy Division of General Motors Corporation*)

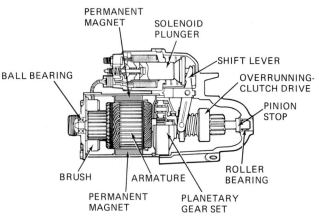

PERMANENT MAGNET

SOLENOID PLUNGER

SHIFT LEVER

OVERRUNNING-CLUTCH DRIVE

BALL BEARING

PINION STOP

ROLLER BEARING

BRUSH   ARMATURE

PERMANENT MAGNET

PLANETARY GEAR SET

Fig. 29-11 Construction of a permanent-magnet starting motor. (*General Motors Corporation*)

3. The engine cranks normally but does not start. This condition is not caused by the starting system. It indicates a problem in the fuel or ignition system, or in the engine.

Other complaints are relay or solenoid chattering, and slow disengagement of the pinion from the ring gear. Turn on the headlights to make a quick check of the starting system. Then watch the headlights (or the inside dome-light) while trying to start the engine. The chart in Fig. 29-12 shows various possible causes of these and other starting-system troubles, and the checks or corrections to make.

➤ 29-11 NO CRANKING, LIGHTS STAY BRIGHT

Current is not getting to the starting motor. Use a voltmeter to check for voltage at the ignition switch and starting-motor terminals with the ignition key turned to START. Battery voltage up to the starting-motor terminal indicates trouble in the starting motor. Trouble is indicated in the relay or solenoid if it has battery voltage but the starting-motor terminal does not.

➤ 29-12 NO CRANKING, LIGHTS DIM HEAVILY

Recharge or replace a discharged battery. The battery is less efficient at low temperatures and engine oil gets thicker. The starting motor cannot always crank the engine with a low battery. These symptoms may also indicate advanced spark timing, excessive starter draw, and loose or dirty connections.

➤ 29-13 NO CRANKING, LIGHTS DIM SLIGHTLY

The drive pinion may not be engaging with the ring gear. If the starting-motor armature spins, then the overrunning clutch is slipping. Also, there may be high resistance or an open circuit in the starting motor.

➤ 29-14 NO CRANKING, LIGHTS GO OUT

There is a poor connection, probably at the battery. Wiggle the cable connections at the battery. If they are tight, make a *voltage-drop test* (➤29-22). If the meter shows voltage, the connection has excessive resistance. Clean the cable clamp and battery terminal. Install and tighten the clamp.

➤ 29-15 NO CRANKING, NO LIGHTS

Either the battery is dead or there is an open in the battery-insulated circuit or ground circuit. Possibilities include a loose connection at the battery, relay, or solenoid. An open fusible link (➤27-5) indicates a short circuit.

➤ 29-16 ENGINE CRANKS SLOWLY BUT DOES NOT START

The battery may be run down or the temperature is very low. A defective starting motor may crank the engine too slowly to start it. Trouble in the engine may prevent normal cranking. Also, the driver may have run the battery down trying to start. See also ➤29-17 below.

Condition	Possible Cause	Check or Correction
1. No cranking, lights stay bright (➤29-11)	a. Open circuit in ignition switch b. Open circuit in starting motor c. Open in control circuit d. Open fusible link	Check switch contacts and connections Check commutator, brushes, and connections Check solenoid or relay, switch, and connections Correct condition causing link to blow; replace link
2. No cranking, lights dim heavily (➤29-12)	a. Trouble in engine b. Battery low c. Very low temperature d. Frozen armature bearings, short in starting motor	Check engine to find trouble Check, recharge, or replace battery Battery must be fully charged, with engine, wiring circuit, and starting motor in good condition Repair starting motor
3. No cranking, lights dim slightly (➤29-13)	a. Faulty or slipping drive b. Excessive resistance or open circuit in starting motor	Replace parts Clean commutator; replace brushes; repair poor connections
4. No cranking, lights go out (➤29-14)	Poor connection, probably at battery	Clean cable clamp and terminal; tighten clamp
5. No cranking, no lights (➤29-15)	a. Battery dead b. Open circuit	Recharge or replace battery Clean and tighten connections; replace wiring
6. Engine cranks slowly but does not start (➤29-16)	a. Battery run down b. Very low temperature c. Starting motor defective d. Undersized battery cables or battery e. Mechanical trouble in engine f. Driver has run battery down trying to start	Check, recharge, or replace battery Battery must be fully charged, with engine, wiring circuit, and starting motor in good condition Test starting motor Install cables or battery of adequate size Check engine See item 7
7. Engine cranks at normal speed but does not start (➤29-17)	a. Ignition system defective b. Fuel system defective c. Air leaks in intake manifold or carburetor d. Engine defective	Make spark test; check timing and ignition system Check fuel pump, line, carburetor or fuel injection system Tighten mounting; replace gasket as needed Check compression, valve timing, etc.
8. Relay or solenoid chatters (➤29-18)	a. Hold-in winding open b. Low battery c. Burned contacts	Replace solenoid Charge battery Replace
9. Pinion disengages slowly after starting (➤29-19)	a. Sticky solenoid plunger b. Overrunning clutch sticks on armature shaft c. Overrunning clutch defective d. Shift-lever return spring weak	Clean and free plunger Clean armature shaft and clutch sleeve Replace clutch Install new spring
10. Unusual noises (➤29-20)	a. High-pitched whine during cranking (before engine fires) b. High-pitched whine after engine fires as key is released c. Loud whoop, buzzing, or siren sound after engine fires but while starter is engaged—sounds like a siren if engine is revved d. Rumble, growl, or knock as starter is coasting to a stop after engine starts	Too much clearance between pinion and ring gear Too little clearance between pinion and ring gear Defective overrunning clutch Bent or unbalanced armature

Fig. 29-12 Starting-system trouble-diagnosis chart.

➤ 29-17 ENGINE CRANKS AT NORMAL SPEED BUT DOES NOT START

When the engine cranks at normal speed, the starting system is okay. The trouble is elsewhere. Item 7 in Fig. 29-12 lists possible causes. Other chapters cover the tests in the *Check or Correction* column.

➤ 29-18 RELAY OR SOLENOID CHATTERS

If this happens when the key is turned to START, the battery is probably low. Charge the battery. The contacts in the relay or solenoid switch may be burned. Replace the relay or the contact plate (Fig. 29-7B). Another cause is a defective solenoid hold-in winding. Replace the solenoid.

➤ 29-19 PINION DISENGAGES SLOWLY AFTER STARTING

Item 9 in Fig. 29-12 lists four possible causes. Also listed are the checks and corrections to make.

➤ 29-20 UNUSUAL NOISES

A high-pitched whine can result if there is too much or too little clearance between the overrunning-clutch pinion and the ring gear. The procedure for adjusting the clearance is in the manufacturer's service manual.

STARTING-SYSTEM TESTING

➤ 29-21 CRANKING-VOLTAGE TEST

The *cranking-voltage test* (Fig. 29-13) measures the voltage available for ignition while the starting motor cranks the engine. If possible, the engine should be at normal operating temperature. Disable the ignition so the engine will not start. Connect a voltmeter across the battery and crank the engine. Note the voltage reading.

If the starting motor cranks normally and the voltmeter reads 9 volts or higher, cranking voltage is normal. Slow cranking with the voltage above 9 volts indicates high resistance in the motor circuit or starting motor. Low cranking speed and low voltage may indicate a discharged battery. If the battery is charged, look for trouble in the starting motor or engine.

➤ 29-22 VOLTAGE-DROP TEST

A *voltage-drop test* (Fig. 29-14) determines if there is excessive resistance across a cable, component, or connection while current flows through it. For example, to check the voltage drop at the battery terminals, disable the

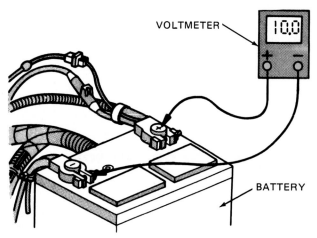

Fig. 29-13 Making a cranking-voltage test by measuring the voltage across the battery terminals while cranking the engine. (*Chrysler Corporation*)

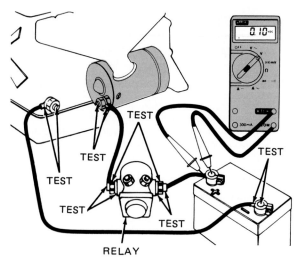

Fig. 29-14 Make a voltage-drop test by cranking the engine and checking for excessive resistance across a connection while current flows through it. (*John Fluke Manufacturing Company, Inc.*)

ignition. Connect the voltmeter leads to the terminal and cable clamp as shown in Fig. 29-14. Then turn the ignition key to START and read the meter. It should show zero. A voltage drop across a connection indicates excessive resistance.

Measure the voltage drop across each cable, component, and connection the same way. Figure 29-15 shows the voltmeter connections to measure voltage drop through the positive battery cable and ground circuit. Typical voltage drop should not exceed 0.2 volts across a wire or cable and 0.3 volts across a switch. Specifications for the car you are testing are in the manufacturer's service manual.

➤ 29-23 CURRENT-DRAW TEST

The *current-draw* or *starter-draw test* (Fig. 10-6) measures the current flow to the starting motor while it cranks the engine. If possible, the engine should be at normal operating temperature. Disable the ignition and connect the ammeter to the battery cable. Figure 10-6 shows the use of a clamp-on type of inductive ammeter. Other ammeters connect in series in the circuit. Follow the operating instructions for the tester you are using. Then turn the ignition key to START and read the current draw.

Specifications vary for starting-motor current draw. A reading of 200 amps is typical for some engines. If the reading is higher than specified, the trouble is in the starting motor or engine. Possible causes of starting-motor trouble include worn armature bushings, a grounded armature, and grounded field coils. Or the engine crankshaft has excessive resistance to turning.

NOTE The procedures above describe using hand-held meters to make cranking-voltage and starter-draw tests. In the shop, the *volt-ampere tester* (Fig. 28-13) or battery-load tester (➤28-20) may be used. Computerized engine analyzers and service-bay

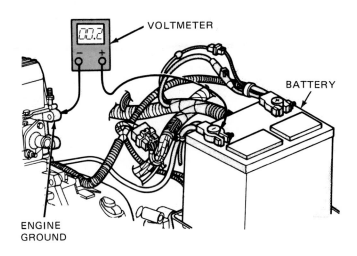

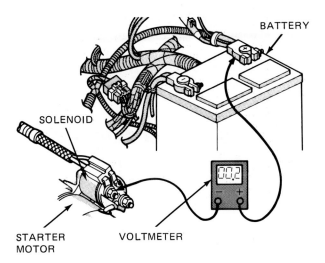

(A) TESTING GROUND-CIRCUIT RESISTANCE

(B) TESTING BATTERY POSITIVE-CABLE RESISTANCE

Fig. 29-15 Measuring voltage drop through the positive battery cable and ground circuit. (*Chrysler Corporation*)

diagnostic computers (Fig. 20-23) also perform these tests. In addition, the computer may measure cranking speed and *amps per cylinder*. This is the change in cranking current as each piston moves through its compression stroke.

➤ 29-24 STARTING-MOTOR BENCH TESTS

Two tests can be made on the starting motor after removing it from the engine. These are the *no-load test* and the *stall test*. The stall test is no longer widely recommended. Follow the procedure in the manufacturer's service manual to make a stall test. Removing the starting motor is described in ➤29-27.

➤ 29-25 NO-LOAD TEST

Figure 29-16 shows the setup to make a no-load test. It requires a voltmeter, ammeter, and carbon pile. Or use the volt-ampere tester. In addition, connect a *remote starter switch* from the large solenoid battery (BAT) terminal to the smaller solenoid (S) terminal.

Hold a *revolution counter* or *rpm indicator* against the end of the armature shaft. Then close the remote starter switch. Note the armature speed (rpm), current, and voltage. These readings will usually be within the range given in the service manual. For more accurate testing, adjust the variable resistor or carbon pile to get the specified voltage. This is usually 10 or 11 volts. Then read the current draw and armature speed.

➤ 29-26 RESULTS OF NO-LOAD TEST

The results of the no-load test (➤29-25) indicate various electrical and mechanical problems in the starting motor.

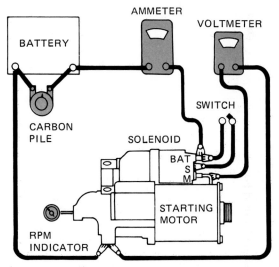

Fig. 29-16 No-load test of starting motor. A remote-starter switch or jumper lead is used to energize the solenoid which then connects the starting motor to the battery. (*Delco-Remy Division of General Motors Corporation*)

1. Rated current draw and speed indicate normal conditions.
2. Low no-load speed and high current draw indicates excessive internal friction or a shorted armature. Excessive friction is due to dirty, tight, or worn bearings, or by the armature dragging on the pole shoes.
3. Failure to operate with a high current draw indicates a grounded terminal or brush assembly, or frozen bearings.
4. Failure to operate with no current draw indicates open brush leads or field circuit, or open armature coils. Other causes include broken brush springs, worn brushes, glazed commutator, or high insulation between the commutator bars.

371

5. Low no-load speed with a low current draw indicates high internal resistance caused by poor connections, defective leads, or a dirty commutator. Item 4 above lists other possible causes.

6. High no-load speed with high current draw indicates shorted fields.

STARTING-MOTOR SERVICE

➤ 29-27 REMOVING AND INSTALLING STARTING MOTOR

To remove the starting motor, disconnect the ground cable from the battery (Fig. 28-4). If necessary, raise the vehicle. Remove any braces, shields, or other parts that may be in the way. Disconnect the wires and cable from the starting motor.

Support the starting motor so it will not fall on you or on the floor. Then remove the starting-motor mounting bolts. Watch for any shims located between the starting motor and its mounting pad. The shims must be reinstalled with the starting motor.

Before installing the starting motor, clean the mounting surfaces on the drive end and on the engine. This ensures good electrical contact. The starting motor is case grounded (➤10-9) through this connection. Then install the starting motor and reconnect the wiring and cable. Start the engine. Follow the procedure to restore data to the ECM and volatile memories. Then check for normal cranking speed and starting-system operation.

➤ 29-28 SERVICING STARTING MOTOR

Many starting motors require no maintenance between major engine repairs or overhaul. However, brushes, bearings, and bushings wear. The solenoid, overrunning clutch, and other parts can fail. A defective starting motor is removed and repaired, or exchanged for a new or rebuilt unit. Follow the procedure in the vehicle service manual.

Permanent magnets in the starting motor increase its useful life or *durability*. Failures caused by shorted or grounded field coils are eliminated. Figure 29-17 shows a disassembled permanent-magnet starting motor with planetary-gear reduction.

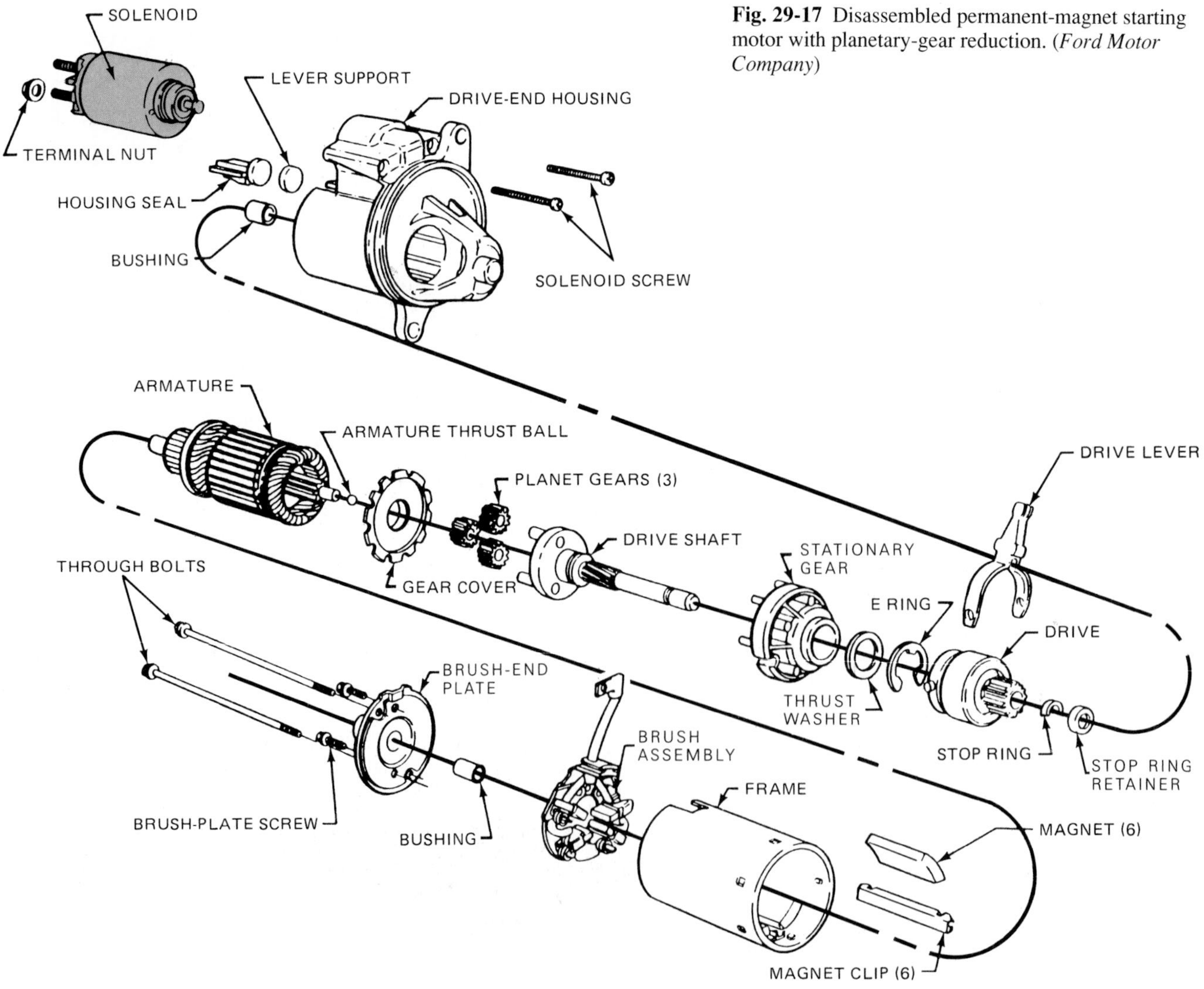

Fig. 29-17 Disassembled permanent-magnet starting motor with planetary-gear reduction. (*Ford Motor Company*)

To disassemble a typical starting motor, remove the solenoid (if used) and the through bolts. Then remove the end frames or housings. Inspect and service the components. Major steps in rebuilding a starting motor include:

1. Replace armature bushings or bearings.
2. Test the armature and field coils (if used).
3. Refinish ("turn down") the commutator.
4. Replace damaged field coils.
5. Replace brushes.
6. Wipe clean or replace overrunning-clutch drive.
7. Replace contacts in solenoid switch.

After completing the tests and inspections, lubricate the shaft splines, bushings, and bearings. Then assemble the starting motor. If required, energize the solenoid and check the *pinion clearance* (Fig. 29-11). This is the clearance between the pinion and the pinion stop when the pinion is in the fully-engaged position (Fig. 29-7C).

➤ 29-29 JUMP STARTING

Jump starting is starting the engine of a vehicle that has a dead battery by using a charged battery, usually in another vehicle. The charged battery is the *booster battery*. Try to avoid jump starting. It is dangerous when performed incorrectly. Sparks may cause a battery explosion. In addition, sparks and improper connections may damage electrical and electronic equipment on the vehicle.

Follow the jump-starting procedure in the vehicle owners manual. Also, follow the safety cautions for working safely around batteries (➤28-8). In addition, observe the safety cautions below when trying to jump start an engine. This will help reduce the chance of injury and damage.

1. Wear eye protection to guard against getting electrolyte in your eyes. If you are not wearing eye protection, *do not try to jump start!*
2. Check the charge indicator on the maintenance-free battery (Fig. 28-12). If it shows light yellow or clear, *do not try to jump start!* The battery could explode!
3. Make the battery connections observing the proper polarity—positive to positive, and negative to negative.

The dead battery could explode if the booster battery is connected backward. Also, damage to the vehicle electrical and electronic equipment can occur.

The jump-starting procedure requires a set of two *jumper cables* (Fig. 29-18). These are lengths of heavy-gauge insulated cable with spring-loaded clamps on the ends. One cable is black. The other is usually red. Adapters may be needed to attach the clamps to a side-terminal battery.

1. Move the vehicle with the charged battery close to the vehicle with the dead battery. Do not allow the vehicles to touch each other.
2. Check that the jumper cables are long enough to reach from battery to battery. Do not allow the jumper-cable clamps to touch the terminals on either battery at this time.
3. Cover the caps of a vent-cap battery with a damp cloth.
4. Set parking brakes in both vehicles. The transmissions or transaxles in both vehicles should be in PARK (automatic) or NEUTRAL (manual).
5. Turn off all lights, switches, and electrical equipment, except the heater blower motor. Turn it on or set the air-conditioning controls to DEFROST. This helps prevent voltage surges from damaging the ECM.
6. On some vehicles with an antilock-braking system (ABS), disable the antilock system (Chap. 53). This may require disconnecting the ABS wiring-harness connector, removing the ABS power relay, or removing the ABS fusible link from near the battery positive terminal. The procedure is in the vehicle owners manual and service manual.
7. Connect one end of the red (positive) jumper cable to the positive (+) terminal of the dead battery (Fig. 29-18). Connect the other end of this jumper cable to the positive terminal of the charged battery.
8. Connect one end of the black (negative) jumper cable to the negative (−) terminal of the charged battery.
9. Connect the other end of the black jumper cable to the engine block or a head bolt at least 18 inches [450 mm] away from the dead battery. Do *not* connect the jumper cable to the negative terminal of the dead battery. This prevents any sparks that occur from causing a battery explosion.

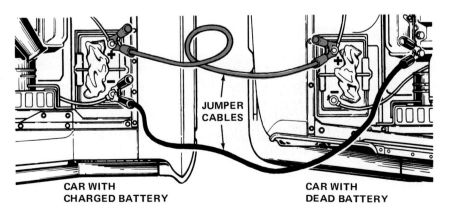

Fig. 29-18 Connections between booster battery and dead battery for jump starting the engine in a vehicle with a dead battery.

JUMPER CABLES

CAR WITH CHARGED BATTERY

CAR WITH DEAD BATTERY

10. Check that the jumper cables are clear of the engine fan and other rotating parts. Start the engine in the vehicle that has the charged battery. Run this engine at fast idle. Start the engine of the vehicle with the dead battery. Do not crank for longer than 30 seconds. If the engine does not start, wait two minutes for the starting motor to cool. Then try again. Prolonged cranking can overheat and damage the starting motor.

11. Disconnect the black jumper cable from the engine block. Then disconnect the other end of this cable. Finally, disconnect the red jumper cable.

12. Safely dispose of the damp cloth used to cover the caps of a vent-cap battery.

Careful! Some high-rate battery chargers or *engine starters* can be used to start cars that have a dead battery. Be sure the equipment is set to 12 volts and negative ground. Do not use a 24-volt setting or charger. The 24 volts can damage the starting motor and other electrical and electronic equipment beyond repair.

MULTIPLE-CHOICE TEST

Select the **one** *correct, best, or most probable answer to each question.*
You can find the answers in the section indicated at the end of each question.

1. Technician A says the starting system includes a low-current control circuit and a high-current motor circuit. Technician B says the starting system includes a relay or solenoid switch and a safety switch. Who is right? (➤29-1)
   a. A only
   b. B only
   c. both A and B
   d. neither A nor B

2. The stationary magnetic field in the starting motor is produced by the (➤29-3)
   a. field windings or permanent magnets
   b. brushes and commutator
   c. armature windings and commutator bars
   d. relay or solenoid

3. To start the engine, the starting motor rotates the crankshaft about (➤29-4)
   a. 3000 rpm
   b. 45,000 rpm
   c. 50 rpm
   d. 200 rpm

4. The overrunning clutch performs all the following EXCEPT (➤29-5)
   a. transmits cranking torque to the engine
   b. damages the armature if it fails to lock
   c. prevents the engine from driving the pinion
   d. acts as a one-way clutch

5. If the headlights go out when the key is turned to START, the cause is probably (➤29-14)
   a. a defective light switch
   b. a dead battery
   c. a loose battery-cable connection
   d. an open starting motor

6. No cranking and no lights when the key is turned to START may be caused by all the following EXCEPT (➤29-15)
   a. burned out light bulbs
   b. an open circuit
   c. a dead battery
   d. an open fusible link

7. If the engine cranks slowly but does not start, a possible cause is (➤29-16)
   a. a discharged battery
   b. low temperature
   c. driver has run-down the battery trying to start
   d. any of the above

REVIEW QUESTIONS

1. Describe the difference in construction between an electromagnet starting motor and a permanent-magnet starting motor.   (➤29-3 and 29-9)

2. Explain two different ways the pinion is moved in and out of mesh with the ring gear.   (➤29-6 and 29-7)

3. Discuss gear reduction and how it affects armature speed and engine cranking speed.   (➤29-8)

4. What is a cranking-voltage test, when should it be made, and what do the results tell the technician? (➤29-21)

5. What is a voltage-drop test and how can it help locate starting-system troubles?   (➤29-22)

CHAPTER 30

CHARGING SYSTEM: OPERATION AND SERVICE

After studying this chapter, and with proper instruction and equipment, you should be able to:

- Describe how voltage is generated and how alternating current is changed to direct current in the alternator.
- Explain how the alternator and the voltage regulator work.
- List four conditions that indicate charging-system trouble and the possible causes of each.
- Perform a charging-system diagnosis by making charging-system output, full-field, and key-off current drain tests.
- Replace the drive belt and an externally-mounted voltage regulator.
- Remove, service, and install the alternator.

➢ 30-1 PURPOSE OF CHARGING SYSTEM

The charging system:

1. Restores to the battery the charge removed to crank the engine.
2. Handles the load of the ignition, lights, radio, and other electrical and electronic equipment while the engine is running.

The charging system includes the alternator with regulator, battery, and connecting wires (Figs. 10-3 and 30-1).

➢ 30-2 ALTERNATOR OPERATION

The *alternator* (Fig. 30-2) converts mechanical energy from the engine into electrical energy. It usually mounts on the side of the engine. The engine crankshaft pulley (Fig. 30-3) drives the alternator through a belt at two to three times crankshaft speed. A *regulator,* usually on or in the alternator, prevents the alternator from producing excessive voltage. Some manufacturers call the alternator a *generator* or *ac generator.*

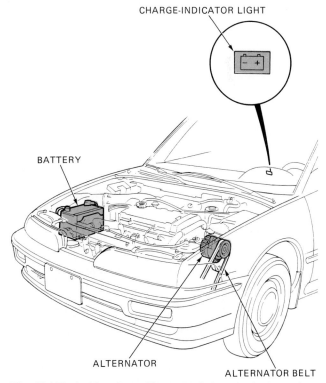

Fig. 30-1 Typical locations of battery and alternator in the engine compartment of a front-wheel-drive car with transverse engine. (*American Honda Motor Company, Inc.*)

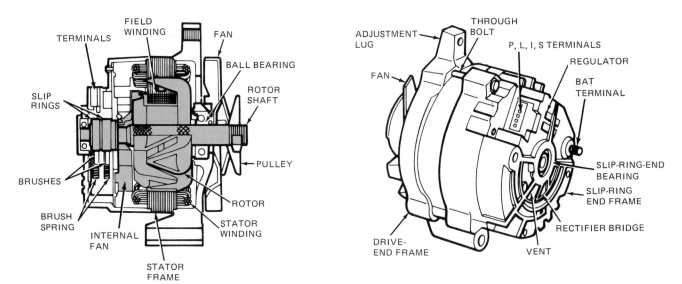

Fig. 30-2 Alternator with built-in rectifier and regulator. (*Cadillac Division of General Motors Corporation*)

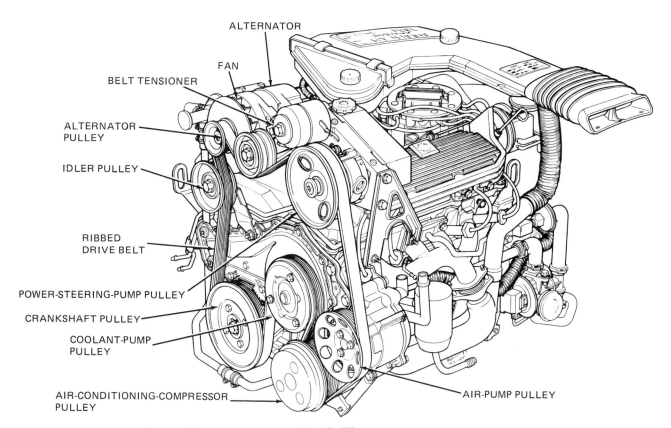

Fig. 30-3 Alternator mounting and drive arrangement on engine. (*Cadillac Division of General Motors Corporation*)

➤ 30-3 ALTERNATOR PRINCIPLES

Moving a bar magnet past a conductor (Fig. 30-4) induces a flow of electrons (electric current) in the conductor. This is how the alternator produces current. Figure 30-5 shows a simple one-loop alternator. The rotating bar magnet supplies a moving magnetic field. As it rotates, the magnetic field passes through the two sides of the stationary loop. At the top, as the south pole moves past the upper side of the loop, current is induced in one direction. Current is induced in the opposite direction when the north pole moves past the upper side of the loop.

A similar condition occurs in the lower side of the loop, but the direction of the induced current is reversed. The

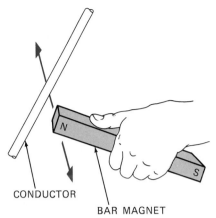

CONDUCTOR

BAR MAGNET

Fig. 30-4 Moving a magnet past a conductor induces a flow of electrons (current) in the conductor. (ATW)

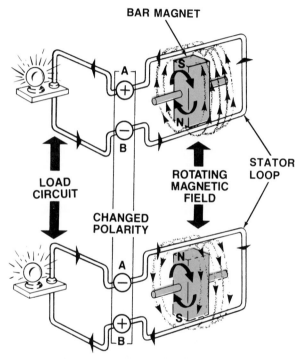

BAR MAGNET

A
+
B
−

LOAD
CIRCUIT

ROTATING
MAGNETIC
FIELD

STATOR
LOOP

CHANGED
POLARITY

A
−
B
+

Fig. 30-5 Simple alternator consisting of a single stationary loop of wire and a rotating bar magnet. The changes in polarity or direction of current flow during one revolution of the magnet are shown at A and B in the top and bottom illustrations. (*General Motors Corporation*)

effect is that an alternating current (ac) flows in the loop. If the current is strong enough, it will light the bulb in the load circuit (Fig. 30-5).

Three conditions will increase the current (number of electrons) moving in the loop:

1. Increasing the strength of the magnetic field.
2. Increasing the speed at which the magnetic field rotates.
3. Increasing the number of loops.

In the alternator, the strength of the magnetic field and the number of loops are increased. Instead of a permanent

magnet, the rotor usually consists of *pole pieces* with a *field coil* or *winding* between them (Fig. 30-6). When current flows through the winding, it becomes an electromagnet (➤10-11). Current flows in and out of the winding through two *brushes* riding on *slip rings*. Each slip ring connects to one end of the winding. The current produces a magnetic field which rotates as the rotor turns. The strength of the magnetic field varies with the amount of current flowing.

The stationary loops or conductors are assembled into a laminated iron frame. The assembly is the *stator* (Fig. 30-7). As the rotating magnetic field cuts through the windings, an alternating current is induced in the stator.

➤ **30-4 RECTIFYING ALTERNATOR CURRENT**

Most automotive electrical equipment requires direct current (dc). Therefore, the ac produced by the alternator must be changed or *rectified* to dc. A set of six diodes forms a six-diode *rectifier* (Fig. 30-8) inside the alternator. A *diode* (➤10-14) is a one-way check valve for electric current (Fig. 10-15). Current can flow through in one direction but not the other.

The loops in the stator are grouped into three sets or legs which form a *delta-connected stator* (Fig. 30-8) or a *Y-connected stator* (Fig. 30-9). The six diodes connect to the three legs to produce a flow of direct current from the *dc output terminal* of the alternator. This is the *BAT terminal* (Fig. 30-2) on most alternators.

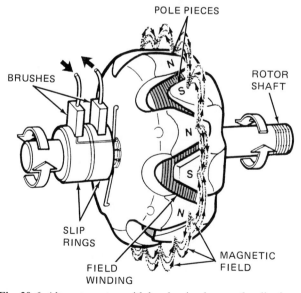

POLE PIECES

BRUSHES

ROTOR
SHAFT

SLIP
RINGS

FIELD
WINDING

MAGNETIC
FIELD

Fig. 30-6 Alternator rotor, with brushes in place on the slip rings to allow current flow through the field windings. The current flow through the windings produces a magnetic field which rotates with the rotor. (*Delco-Remy Division of General Motors Corporation*)

377

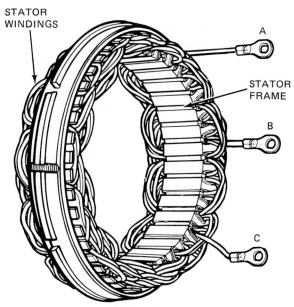

Fig. 30-7 Stator of an alternator. Current is produced in the stator windings as the magnetic field of the rotor turns inside the stator. (*Delco-Remy Division of General Motors Corporation*)

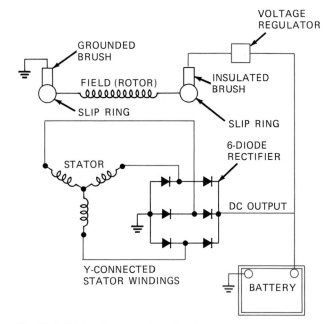

Fig. 30-9 Wiring diagram of the charging system, showing how the regulator controls alternator output by controlling the current flow through the field winding on the rotor. (*ATW*)

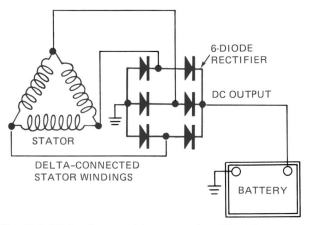

Fig. 30-8 Wiring diagram of the stator and rectifier. The stator has three interconnected windings. The rectifier has six diodes. Two diodes handle each leg of the stator, rectifying the ac produced and changing it to dc.

➤ 30-5 REGULATING THE ALTERNATOR

A *voltage regulator* (Fig. 30-9) prevents the alternator from producing excessive voltage. The regulator limits the current flow through the field winding on the rotor. This controls the strength of the rotating magnetic field. When the voltage starts to go too high, the regulator reduces the current. This weakens the magnetic field and prevents any further rise in voltage.

The alternator does not need a current regulator. The current in the stator produces a magnetic field that creates a *counter-voltage* which limits current output. Load current increases until the alternator reaches its *rated output* (for

example, 100 amps). With the voltage regulator limiting current flow through the field winding, no further increase in speed (➤30-3) can cause more current to flow in the stator. This protects the alternator against overload.

➤ 30-6 ALTERNATOR REGULATOR

Some cars have a separate *electromechanical regulator* that uses relays and contact points. Most charging systems now have a solid-state *electronic regulator*. It is built into the alternator (Fig. 30-2), attached to it, or separately mounted in the engine compartment. Some charging systems do not include a separate regulator. In these *computer-controlled charging systems,* the electronic control module (ECM) regulates the alternator field current.

Rapidly opening and closing the field circuit (Fig. 30-9) controls current flow through the field winding. Some regulators open and close the circuit from 10 to 7000 times a second. The number of cycles per second is the *frequency.* Other regulators operate at a fixed frequency and vary the *duty cycle* (➤21-31). This is the percentage of each ON-OFF cycle that the regulator is ON and allowing current flow.

A typical built-in regulator switches rotor field current on and off at a fixed frequency of 400 cycles per second. At high speed, the ON time could be 10 percent and the OFF time 90 percent. At low speed with a heavy electrical load, the ON time could be 90 percent and the OFF time 10 percent. Varying the ON-OFF time varies the field current to control charging-system voltage.

Many regulators have *temperature-compensation.* The regulator raises the charging voltage in cold weather. A cold battery requires a higher charging rate (➤28-7).

The alternator usually has several terminals (Figs. 30-2 and 30-10). The dc output or BAT terminal connects through the positive battery cable to the battery. Four other terminals are P, L, I (or F), and S. Not all are always used and all may have other names.

The P (*phase*) terminal connects to a single leg or *phase* of the stator winding. The terminal senses the voltage pulses produced in the leg by the rotating magnetic field. The frequency of these pulses is a measure of alternator speed (rpm) and, indirectly, of engine speed. The P terminal may be connected to a tachometer or other device needing a speed signal.

The S (*sense*) terminal connects as closely as possible to the battery positive terminal. It *senses* or measures the voltage across the battery. When the regulator is limiting charging-system voltage, the voltage-regulator setting appears at the S terminal.

The I (*ignition*) or F (*field*) terminal connects directly or through a resistor to the load side of the ignition switch. Both connections are shown in Fig. 30-10. This is the source of current to the positive side of the rotor field coil when the ignition key is ON. The ECM may monitor the voltage at this terminal and set a trouble code for system over voltage (Fig. 20-13) when sensing a defect (➤30-11).

The L terminal, when used, connects to the *charge-indicator light* (➤30-9) on the instrument panel. Both the L and I terminals turn on the regulator and allow field current to flow when the ignition key is ON. Some regulators do not use the L terminal.

Connections to the P, L, I, and S terminals are made through an electrical connector on the end of a wiring harness (Fig. 30-11). Some alternators and regulators have a *ground terminal*. However, most are case grounded (➤10-9). Installing the alternator or regulator in the car completes the ground circuit.

➤ **30-8 ALTERNATOR COOLING**

Automotive alternators have a *fan* behind the drive pulley (Figs. 30-2 and 30-3). Vent holes in both end frames allow the fan to pull ventilating air through the alternator. The cool air enters through the rear or *slip-ring end frame*. The air picks up heat from the rectifier diodes, passes through the alternator, and then exits through openings in the front or *drive-end frame*.

> **NOTE** Diodes can fail from overheating. High current flow through the diodes and high underhood temperatures can contribute to damaging heat buildup.

The alternator in Fig. 30-2 also has an *internal fan*. It pulls air through the slip-ring end frame to help cool the rectifier and the regulator. Some alternators have a duct that carries cool air from the front of the car to the slip-ring

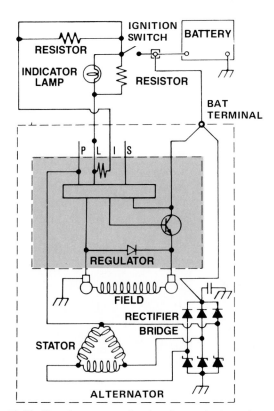

Fig. 30-10 Charging system, showing the terminals on the alternator. A single connector with four terminals attaches to the terminals marked P,L,I, and S. (*Delco-Remy Division of General Motors Corporation*)

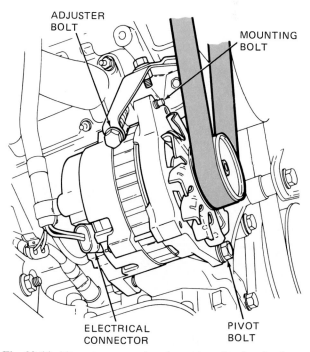

Fig. 30-11 Alternator mounted on the engine, showing the electrical connector from the wiring harness and the adjuster bolt for adjusting drive-belt tension. (*Chrysler Corporation*)

end frame. In some cars, an electric blower motor forces cool air through the duct.

➤ 30-9 INSTRUMENT-PANEL CHARGE INDICATORS

A *charge indicator* in the instrument panel informs the driver about operating conditions in the charging system. There are three types of charge indicators:

1. The *ammeter,* which shows current flow to or from the battery
2. The *voltmeter,* which shows the voltage across the battery, or charging voltage.
3. The *charge-indicator light,* which shows the battery is not charging.

The ammeter (Fig. 30-12) connects in the circuit between the alternator BAT terminal and the battery. Current (except cranking current) flowing to or from the battery flows through the ammeter. This moves the pointer to show the amount and direction of current flow.

The voltmeter measures voltage across the battery. When the engine is not running, this is battery voltage. With the engine running, the voltmeter reads charging-system voltage. Figure 17-32 shows the charging-system voltmeter display in an electronic instrument cluster.

The charge-indicator light (Fig. 30-1) comes on when the key is turned ON. This serves as a bulb test and indicates the alternator is not charging the battery. When the engine starts, the alternator turns fast enough to charge the battery. The indicator light goes out. If the alternator fails to charge the battery, the indicator light comes on and remains on. This alerts the driver to the no-charge condition.

CHARGING-SYSTEM TROUBLE DIAGNOSIS

➤ 30-10 CHARGING-SYSTEM CAUTIONS

The battery is an integral part of the charging system. To work safely around the battery and charging system, follow the cautions in Chaps. 4 and 28. When possible, disconnect the ground cable from the battery while working on the charging system. Additional charging-system cautions are:

1. Never reverse or make wrong connections to the alternator or regulator.
2. Never operate the alternator on open circuit. Excessively high voltage may occur. This can happen if the alternator operates with the wire disconnected from the BAT terminal, or with a cable disconnected from the battery.
3. Never short between or ground any terminals in the charging system, except as required by a safe and proper test procedure.
4. Be careful to avoid the high voltage in a car with an *electrically-heated windshield* (➤55-6). When the driver turns on the heated-windshield control, the voltage in this circuit may reach *30 to 70 volts.* This can injure you. Exercise caution when testing or servicing this charging system. Follow the procedures in the manufacturer's service manual.

➤ 30-11 CHARGING-SYSTEM TROUBLES

Figure 30-13 is a charging-system trouble-diagnosis chart. It lists possible causes of charging-system troubles, and the checks or corrections to make. The following also indicate trouble in the charging system:

a. *Undercharged Battery* Slow cranking is often the first sign of an undercharged battery. The lights may dim excessively during cranking. Another sign is a battery charge indicator (Fig. 28-12) that is all dark or black (instead of green for a charged battery). If the battery charge indicator shows light yellow or clear, replace the battery. It is defective and unsafe to recharge.

b. *Overcharged Battery* Electrolyte may spew from vents of a battery that is being overcharged, and the electrolyte level may be low. Overcharging also causes the lights to flare excessively when engine speed increases. This shortens battery and bulb life, and may damage

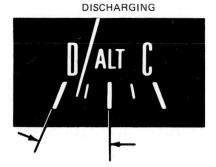

DISCHARGING

BATTERY IS BEING DISCHARGED. ALTERNATOR IS NOT CHARGING OR CAN NOT SUPPLY TOTAL LOAD.

HIGH CHARGING

BATTERY HAS BEEN PARTIALLY DISCHARGED AND ALTERNATOR IS RECHARGING IT.

NORMAL CHARGING

BATTERY CHARGE IS NORMAL. ALTERNATOR IS SUPPLYING TOTAL ELECTRICAL LOAD.

Fig. 30-12 Three charging-system conditions indicated by the ammeter in the instrument panel. (*Ford Motor Company*)

Condition	Possible Cause	Check or Correction
1. Battery does not stay charged—engine starts OK	a. Battery defective b. Loose or worn alternator belt c. Damaged or worn wiring or cables d. Alternator defective e. Regulator defective f. Other electrical system malfunction	Test battery; replace if necessary Adjust or replace belt Repair as required Test and/or replace components as required Test; replace if necessary Check other systems for current draw; service as required
2. Alternator noisy	a. Loose or worn alternator belt b. Bent pulley flanges c. Alternator defective d. Loose alternator mounting	Adjust tension or replace belt Replace pulley Service or replace alternator Tighten
3. Lights or fuses burn out frequently	a. Damaged or worn wiring b. Alternator or regulator defective c. Battery defective	Service as required Test, service, and replace if necessary Test; replace if necessary
4. Charge-indicator light flickers after engine starts or comes on while driving	a. Loose or worn alternator belt b. Alternator defective c. Field-circuit ground defective d. Regulator defective e. Light circuit wiring or connector defective	Adjust tension or replace Service or replace Service or replace wiring or connection Test; replace if necessary Repair as required
5. Charge-indicator light flickers while driving	a. Loose or worn alternator belt b. Loose or improper wiring connections c. Alternator defective d. Regulator defective	Adjust tension or replace belt Service as required Service or replace Test; replace if necessary
6. Charge-indicator gauge or meter shows discharge	a. Loose or worn alternator belt b. Damaged or worn wiring (grounded or open between alternator and battery) c. Field-circuit ground defective d. Alternator defective e. Regulator defective f. Gauge or meter wiring or connections defective g. Damaged or worn gauge or meter h. Other electrical system malfunction	Adjust tension or replace belt Repair or replace wiring Repair or replace wiring Service or replace Test; replace if necessary Service as required Replace Service as required

Fig. 30-13 Charging-system trouble-diagnosis chart.

other electrical parts. The cause of overcharging is usually high alternator voltage. Possible causes are a short or ground in the rotor field winding and a defective regulator.

c. *Abnormal Charge-Indicator Operation* After the engine starts, the charge-indicator light in the instrument panel should turn off. In some cars, the light will flash if the charging voltage is excessively high or low. The instrument-panel ammeter (Fig. 30-12) should show a charging current flowing while the engine is running. The voltmeter should read between 13 and 16 volts. Conditions other than these probably indicate charging-system trouble.

d. *Malfunction-Indicator Light On* System voltage is a continuously monitored input to the ECM (Fig. 19-26). This is the voltage across the battery (*battery voltage* in Figs. 20-18 and 20-19). High charging voltage will not turn on the charge-indicator light in many cars. However, it can cause the ECM to set a trouble code and turn on the CHECK ENGINE light (➤19-20). The code for *system over voltage* may set if the

voltage is higher than 16.9 volts for 50 seconds or longer (➤20-13 and 20-14). The ECM for computer-controlled charging systems can sense and store codes for field-circuit and other charging-system troubles.

CHARGING-SYSTEM TESTING

➤ 30-12 CHECKING THE DRIVE BELT

Check the alternator drive-belt tension and condition before testing the charging system. Figure 26-10 shows the use of a belt-tension gauge. Figures 30-11 and 30-14 show typical belt-tension adjustments.

Figure 26-9 shows conditions to look for when checking V belts. Figure 30-15 shows conditions that occur with ribbed serpentine belts. Minor cracks in the serpentine-belt ribs do not make the belt unusable. Replace any belt that is frayed, torn, worn, or has a chipped rib. Also, replace a belt if it slips or squeals after proper tightening. Do not use belt dressing (➤26-13) on a serpentine belt.

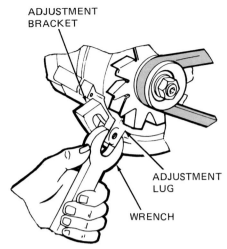

Fig. 30-14 Holding the adjustment lug on the alternator with a wrench to adjust belt tension. (*Ford Motor Company*)

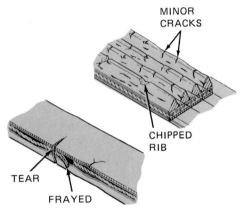

Fig. 30-15 Conditions to look for when making a visual inspection of a ribbed serpentine belt. (*Toyota Motor Sales, U.S.A., Inc.*)

➤ 30-13 CHARGING-SYSTEM TESTING

Below is a procedure for testing Delco Remy CS-series charging systems (Fig. 30-2) on General Motors and other cars. A *charging-system output test* (➤30-14) can also be made on this charging system. Follow the test procedures and specifications in the vehicle service manual.

1. Check the alternator drive belt for tension and wear (➤30-12). Check the condition and routing of the wiring and harness. Terminals and connections should be clean and tight.
2. Check the charge-indicator light as follows:
   a. With the ignition key ON and the engine not running, the light should be on. If not, detach the electrical connector (Fig. 30-11) from the alternator. Ground the lead from the L terminal using a 5-amp *fused jumper wire* (➤27-13). If the light comes on, repair or replace the alternator. If the light remains out, the bulb is burned out. Or the circuit is open between the ignition switch and the fused jumper wire.

b. With the engine running about 2300 rpm, the light should be off. If not, stop the engine. Turn the ignition key ON. Detach the electrical connector from the alternator. If the light goes out, repair or replace the alternator. If the light stays on, check for a grounded L-terminal wire in the wiring harness.
3. If the battery is undercharged or overcharged, detach the electrical connector from the alternator. Turn the ignition key ON but do not start the engine. Identify the I and L terminals in the connector. Either one (or both) of these terminals is the source of battery current for the field winding (➤30-7).

Connect a voltmeter from ground to the L terminal in the connector and then to the I terminal, if used. A zero reading indicates an open circuit between the terminal and the battery. Install the connector in the alternator. Run the engine about 2300 rpm with all electrical accessories off. Measure the voltage across the battery (Fig. 29-13). If it is above 16 volts, repair or replace the alternator.

➤ 30-14 CHARGING-SYSTEM OUTPUT TEST

This test measures the maximum current or *output* that the alternator can produce at a specified voltage. To measure charging-system output, connect an ammeter (➤10-4) at the alternator BAT terminal. Follow the operating instructions for the ammeter you are using. Connect a voltmeter from the BAT terminal to ground. Connect a carbon pile across the battery. In the shop, these connections are usually made by connecting a *volt-ampere tester* (Fig. 30-16) to the battery in the car. Computerized engine analyzers and service-bay diagnostic computers (Fig. 20-23) also perform this test.

Turn on the vehicle lights and electrical accessories. Run the engine about 2300 rpm. Adjust the load-control knob on the tester until the ammeter indicates the maximum amperes from the alternator. If necessary, adjust the load to prevent the voltage from dropping below 13 volts during the test. Then turn the load-control knob OFF.

Careful!   *Some manufacturers allow the voltage to drop to 12 volts during the test. Complete the test within 15 seconds. Applying the load for a longer time may cause rapid overheating and damage.*

If charging-system output is within 15 amperes of the rated output, the charging system is good. On some cars, it is good if the output is within 10 percent of the manufacturer's specifications. These are stamped on the drive-end frame or on a plate attached to some alternators. An alternator marked *15V 60A* means the rated output is 60 amps at 15 volts.

If the output is not within 15 amperes (or 10 percent) of the rated output, the charging system is bad. The stator winding may be shorted or the regulator is defective. Also,

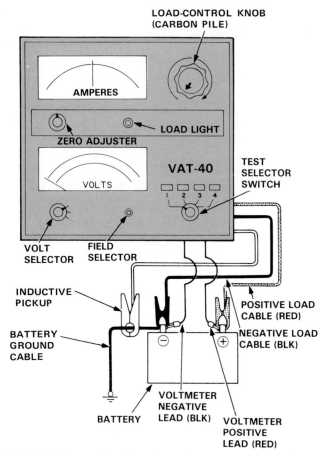

LOAD-CONTROL KNOB
(CARBON PILE)

AMPERES

ZERO ADJUSTER

LOAD LIGHT

VAT-40

VOLTS

TEST
SELECTOR
SWITCH

VOLT
SELECTOR

FIELD
SELECTOR

INDUCTIVE
PICKUP

BATTERY
GROUND
CABLE

POSITIVE LOAD
CABLE (RED)

NEGATIVE LOAD
CABLE (BLK)

BATTERY

VOLTMETER
NEGATIVE
LEAD (BLK)

VOLTMETER
POSITIVE
LEAD (RED)

Fig. 30-16 Connections for using a volt-ampere tester to make a charging-system output test, with the battery in the vehicle. (*American Honda Motor Company, Inc.*)

the fault may be in the wiring or connections. Voltage-drop tests (➤29-22) of the insulated and ground circuits (➤10-9) will locate excessive resistance. An ammeter reading of 0 amps during the output test may indicate an open rotor field winding or circuit.

With the load removed, continue running the engine at the same speed. Watch the voltmeter and ammeter. When the charging current drops below 15 amps, read the voltmeter. This is the voltage-regulator setting.

➤ 30-15 FULL-FIELD TEST

When the charging-system output does not meet specifications, a *full-field test* can be made on some alternators. This test bypasses the voltage regulator and applies full battery voltage to the alternator field circuit. The result is unregulated output from the alternator.

Careful! Follow the recommendations and instructions in the vehicle service manual. Full-fielding is *not recommended* on some alternators (including the Delco Remy CS series) and will damage others. Before starting the procedure, be sure this is a safe and proper test for the alternator being tested.

The regulator is bypassed in various ways. In some Ford charging systems with an external regulator, disconnect the

connector from the regulator. Then install a jumper wire or plug-in type *full-field adapter* between the A and F terminals in the connector. Some alternators have a *test hole* (Fig. 30-17) in the slip-ring end frame. To full-field the alternator, insert a screwdriver into the test hole. Then ground the tab by pressing the screwdriver against the side of the hole. Access to the test hole is often limited by other parts and alternator location.

A typical procedure is to install the jumper wire or full-field adapter with the engine off. Connect a volt-ampere tester (Fig. 30-16) as specified in the tester operating instructions. Start the engine and run it at idle. Adjust engine speed and the load-control knob on the tester until the voltmeter reads 15 volts. Or use a screwdriver to ground the tab (Fig. 30-17) in the alternator. Some volt-ampere testers have a *field lead* and *field-selector switch* (Fig. 30-16) that can be connected to full-field the alternator. With the alternator full-fielded, note the meter readings. Do not allow the voltage to exceed 16 volts during the test. (Some manufacturers allow 18 volts.) Then turn the load-control knob OFF. Stop the engine and remove the jumper wire or adapter.

If alternator output is within the manufacturer's specifications, the regulator probably is defective. If alternator output is not within specifications, repair or replace the alternator.

➤ 30-16 KEY-OFF CURRENT DRAIN

Vehicles with electronic engine controls and other electronic systems have a slight current flow from the battery with the ignition key OFF. This battery drain is the *key-off current drain* (➤10-18) or *ignition off draw* (IOD). It is

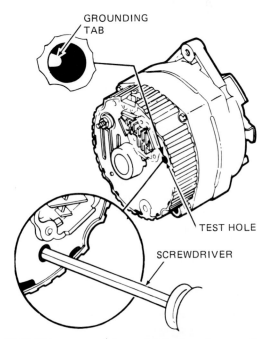

GROUNDING
TAB

TEST HOLE

SCREWDRIVER

Fig. 30-17 Using a screwdriver to full-field an alternator. Insert a screwdriver through the test hole and then press the screwdriver against the end frame while touching the grounding tab. (*Chrysler Corporation*)

also called *parasitic load*. Shorts and grounds may increase the drain from the battery. Also, some electrical devices may fail to shut off. An undercharged or dead battery results. Measure key-off current drain with the ammeter function of a digital multitester (➤27-15).

1. INDUCTIVE AMMETER Turn off the ignition and all electrical loads. Close the car doors and remove the bulb from the underhood light. Follow the tester operating instructions. Clamp the inductive pickup (Fig. 10-6) around either battery cable and any smaller cables leading to the same battery terminal. Read the key-off current drain on the tester.

2. SERIES AMMETER Be sure the current drain is less than the selected ampere range on the tester. Close the car doors and remove the bulb from the underhood light. Follow the tester operating instructions. Do not crank the engine, open a door, or operate any electrical equipment on the car. This could damage the tester or blow the fuse in the tester.

Loosen, but do not disconnect, the cable clamp from the positive battery terminal. Place the tester positive probe on the battery terminal, under the cable clamp. Place the negative probe on the cable clamp. Lift the cable clamp off the battery terminal (Fig. 27-25B). Read current drain on the meter. Then install the cable clamp on the battery terminal.

Compare the reading with the manufacturer's specifications. Most cars should have a key-off current drain of less than 0.050 amps (50 milliamps [mA]). If current drain is excessive, pull the fuses one by one while watching the ammeter. Removing the fuse for the circuit containing the drain will cause the ammeter reading to drop. Sometimes the drain continues after pulling all fuses. Then disconnect the leads one at a time from the starter relay or solenoid. A drop in the ammeter reading indicates the problem circuit.

Careful! One probe must stay in contact with the battery terminal and the other with the cable clamp. If either probe loses contact, the circuit is broken (opened). Some electronic devices may *unlatch* or temporarily disconnect themselves. This will cause an incorrect low reading. Other devices may draw high current when they are reconnected or *repowered*. This could blow the tester fuse or damage the tester.

Current drain may be high for 70 minutes after key-off on some vehicles with air suspension or electronic level control. Then these loads shut off or *time out* and return to their normal key-off condition. On these vehicles, turn the key ON and OFF. Wait 70 minutes to make sure the systems shut off properly before testing for key-off current drain.

CHARGING-SYSTEM SERVICE

➤ 30-17 CHARGING-SYSTEM MAINTENANCE

The charging system does not require periodic maintenance except for drive-belt tension and condition (➤30-

12). Many alternators have an attached or built-in preset regulator and sealed bearings. These are permanently filled with lubricant.

A defective regulator can usually be replaced. Repair or replace a defective alternator. Many shops exchange the old alternator for a new or rebuilt unit.

Check the drive belt at specified intervals. Also, check the alternator mounting bolts (Fig. 30-11) and wiring connections for tightness.

➤ 30-18 REMOVING AND INSTALLING ALTERNATOR

The alternator usually mounts to the engine with two bolts (Fig. 30-11): a *pivot bolt* and a *mounting bolt*. This allows swinging the alternator in (toward the engine) or out to adjust drive-belt tension. An *adjuster bolt* may hold the alternator in position while the other bolts are tightened.

Some alternators mount at the top of the engine and are easily accessible when the hood is open (Fig. 1-8). Others are accessible from under the car (Fig. 30-11). Sometimes the air-conditioning compressor or other parts must be removed or repositioned to reach the alternator. Follow the procedure in the manufacturer's service manual. You may even have to remove the right front wheel, separate the lower ball joint from the lower control arm (Chap. 51), and then remove the drive axle from the transaxle (Chap. 44).

A basic procedure for removing the alternator is to first disconnect the ground cable from the battery. Remove any heat shields, splash shields, and other parts that are in the way. Disconnect the electrical connector and leads from the alternator. Note their connections and routing for proper installation later. Loosen the adjuster bolt, pivot bolt, and mounting bolt. Move the alternator in and remove the belt. Then remove the bolts holding the alternator in place (Fig. 30-18). Remove the alternator. Watch for any spacers or shims used to position the alternator.

To install the alternator, attach the alternator to the mounting bracket with the bolts, washers, and nuts. Be sure any spacers and shims are in place. Install the drive belt and tighten it to the specified tension (➤30-12). Connect the electrical connector, leads, and battery ground

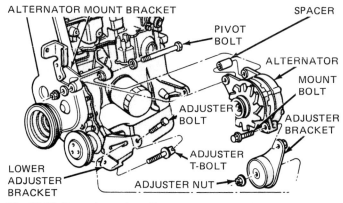

Fig. 30-18 Removing or installing alternator on the engine. (*Chrysler Corporation*)

384

cable. Start the engine. Follow the procedure to restore data to the ECM and volatile memories. Check for normal charging-system operation.

➤ 30-19 ALTERNATOR SERVICE

The drive belt, bearings, brushes, and slip rings cause most alternator problems. These are moving parts that wear with usage. Diodes also fail from heat and shock. When a charging system fails, find and correct any condition that could have caused the failure. Look for damage to the wiring harness, damaged connectors and terminals, and an open fuse or fusible link.

To disassemble most alternators, remove the *through*

bolts (Figs. 30-2 and 30-19) that hold the end frames or housings to the stator frame. Then remove the pulley nut to remove the pulley, fan, and front housing from the rotor shaft. Disassemble the alternator only as far as necessary to complete the service or repair.

After disassembling the alternator, inspect, test, and service the components. Follow the procedures in the manufacturer's service manual. Clean up worn or pitted slip rings with 400-grain polishing cloth, or by turning in a lathe. Test the diodes, stator, and rotor. A typical new brush is about 1/2-inch [13-mm] long. Replace the brushes if worn to half (1/4 inch [6 mm]) or less of new brush length. Then assemble the alternator and install it on the vehicle (➤30-18).

Fig. 30-19 Disassembled alternator, showing the three types of pulleys that may be used–V belt, double V belt, or serpentine belt. (*Chrysler Corporation*)

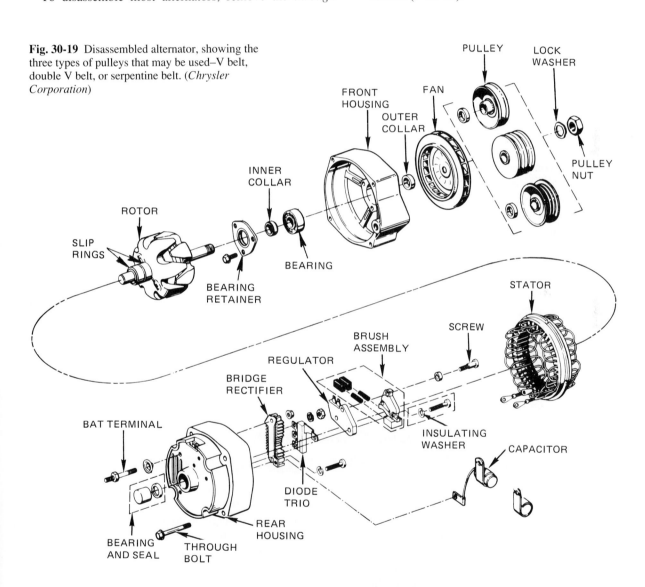

TRADE TALK

alternator	field winding	rotor	voltage regulator
BAT terminal	rated output	stator	
end frame	rectifier	temperature compensation	

MULTIPLE-CHOICE TEST

*Select the **one** correct, best, or most probable answer to each question.*
You can find the answers in the section indicated at the end of the question.

1. The alternator produces an alternating current in its (➤30-3)
   a. rotor field coil
   b. stator windings
   c. regulator
   d. load circuit

2. The purpose of the regulator is to (➤30-5)
   a. prevent the alternator voltage from going too high
   b. allow the alternator to produce a high current
   c. keep alternator speed from going too high
   d. keep alternator voltage high enough to charge the battery

3. All the following are locations for the voltage regulator EXCEPT (➤30-6)
   a. in the engine compartment
   b. in the alternator
   c. on the battery
   d. in the ECM

4. The alternator terminal that connects through cables to charge the battery is the (➤30-7)
   a. L or light terminal
   b. F or field terminal
   c. P or phase terminal
   d. BAT or battery terminal

5. Technician A says the fan behind the alternator drive pulley pushes air into the alternator through holes in the drive-end frame. Technician B says the fan pulls air in through holes in the slip-ring end frame. Who is right? (➤30-8)
   a. A only
   b. B only
   c. both A and B
   d. neither A nor B

6. The engine starts normally but the battery does not stay charged. Any of these could be the cause EXCEPT (➤30-11)
   a. loose alternator drive belt
   b. defective battery
   c. CHECK ENGINE light bulb burned out
   d. damaged wiring

7. All these may indicate overcharging EXCEPT (➤30-11)
   a. a flickering charge-indicator light
   b. a flashing charge-indicator light
   c. a CHECK ENGINE light on
   d. a trouble code stored in the ECM

8. A charging-system output test measures (➤30-14)
   a. unregulated output from the alternator
   b. duty cycle of the current regulator
   c. maximum allowable charging-system voltage
   d. maximum current the alternator can produce

9. The cause of no output from the alternator could be (➤30-14)
   a. an open diode
   b. an open field winding
   c. an open stator winding
   d. all of the above

10. Technician A says to replace the brushes if they are worn to half or less of new brush length. Technician B says to replace the brushes if they are worn to 1/4-inch [6-mm] or less in length. Who is right? (➤30-19)
    a. A only
    b. B only
    c. both A and B
    d. neither A nor B

REVIEW QUESTIONS

1. Describe the construction and operation of the alternator, and how alternating current is changed to direct current.   (➤30-3 and 30-4)

2. Explain how alternator voltage and current output are controlled.   (➤30-5 and 30-6)

3. In the instrument panel, how would the charge-indicator light, ammeter, and voltmeter alert the driver if the drive belt is thrown off?   (➤30-9)

4. What is a full-field test and when can it be performed?   (➤30-15)

5. What is key-off current drain and when should it be measured?   (➤30-16)

CHAPTER 31

CONTACT-POINT IGNITION SYSTEM

After studying this chapter, you should be able to:

- Describe the construction and operation of the contact-point ignition system.
- Define *primary resistance* and *secondary wiring*.
- Locate and identify ignition-system components on various vehicles.
- Explain why centrifugal- and vacuum-advance mechanisms are necessary, and how they work.
- Describe the different types of spark plugs, and explain *heat range* and *reach*.

➤ 31-1 PURPOSE OF IGNITION SYSTEM

The purpose of the *ignition system* (Figs. 11-21 and 31-1) is to ignite the compressed air-fuel mixture in the engine combustion chambers. This should occur at the proper time for combustion to begin (➤16-1). To start combustion, the ignition system delivers an electric spark that jumps a gap at the combustion-chamber ends of the *spark plugs*. The heat from this arc ignites the compressed air-fuel mixture. The mixture burns, creating pressure that pushes the pistons down the cylinders so the engine runs.

The ignition system may be either a *contact-point ignition system* or an *electronic ignition system*. This chapter describes the contact-point ignition system. Chapter 32 covers electronic ignition systems. Ignition-system trouble-diagnosis and service are covered in Chap. 33.

➤ 31-2 COMPONENTS IN CONTACT-POINT IGNITION SYSTEM

The ignition system (Fig. 31-1) includes the battery, ignition switch, ignition coil, ignition distributor (with contact points and condenser), secondary wiring, and spark plugs.

1. IGNITION SWITCH The *ignition switch* (➤31-13) connects the ignition coil to the battery when the ignition key is ON. When the key is turned to START, the starting motor cranks the engine for starting (Chap. 29).

2. IGNITION COIL The *ignition coil* (Fig. 31-2) is a *step-up transformer* that raises the battery voltage to a high voltage that may reach 25,000 volts. In some electronic ignition systems, the voltage may go up to 47,000 volts or higher. The high voltage causes sparks to jump the gap at the spark plugs.

3. IGNITION DISTRIBUTOR The *ignition distributor* (Fig. 31-3) does two jobs. First, it has a set of *contact points* or *breaker points* (Fig. 31-1, lower right) that work as a fast-acting switch. When the points close, current flows through the coil. When the points open, current flow stops and the coil produces a high-voltage surge. A *condenser* connects across the points. It aids in the collapse of the magnetic field and helps reduce arcing that burns away the points.

Second, the distributor distributes the high-voltage surges to the spark plugs in the correct *firing order* (➤12-11). A *coil wire* (Fig. 31-1) delivers the high voltage from the coil to the center terminal of the *distributor cap*. Inside the cap, a *rotor* (Fig. 31-4) is on top of the distributor shaft. In most contact-point distributors, the distributor shaft is driven from the engine camshaft by a pair of spiral gears (Fig. 12-18). The rotor has a metal blade. One end of the blade contacts the center terminal of the distributor cap (Fig. 31-5).

When the rotor turns, the other end passes close to the outer terminals in the distributor cap. These are connected by *spark-plug wires* to the spark plugs. The high-voltage surge jumps the small gap from the rotor blade to the

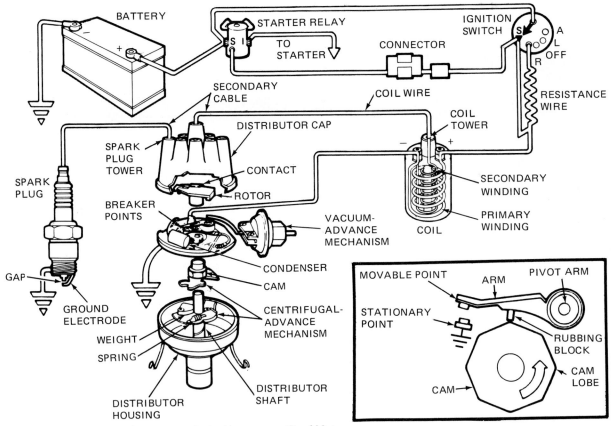

Fig. 31-1 Components in the contact-point ignition system. (*Ford Motor Company*)

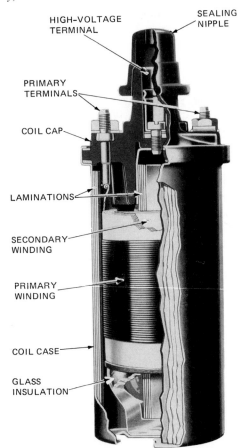

Fig. 31-2 Ignition coil, cutaway to show the windings. (*Delco-Remy Division of General Motors Corporation*)

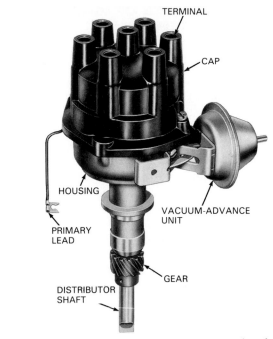

Fig. 31-3 Ignition distributor with vacuum-advance unit and cap. (*Delco-Remy Division of General Motors Corporation*)

terminal. The spark-plug wires carry the high-voltage surge to the spark plug in the cylinder that is ready to fire.

4. SECONDARY IGNITION CABLES The *secondary cables* or *wiring* include the coil wire and the spark-plug wires (Fig. 31-1). These cables connect between the center

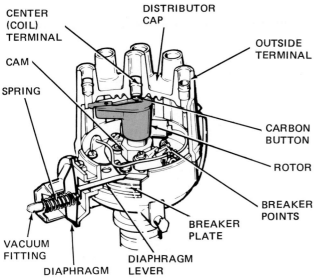

Fig. 31-4 Cutaway ignition distributor and vacuum-advance unit, with rotor and cap in place.

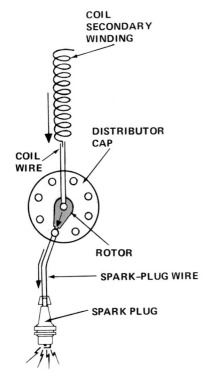

Fig. 31-5 Simplified secondary circuit. The coil secondary winding is connected through the distributor cap, rotor, and wiring to the spark plugs.

of the ignition coil and the distributor cap, and between the distributor cap and the spark plugs. Figure 31-6 compares the construction of an older spark-plug wire with the *resistance cable* now used on all cars. Secondary cables for contact-point ignition systems have a 7 mm (0.276 inch) diameter. Many electronic ignition systems require 8 mm (0.315 inch) cables. The use of a silicone insulating jacket makes these cables larger.

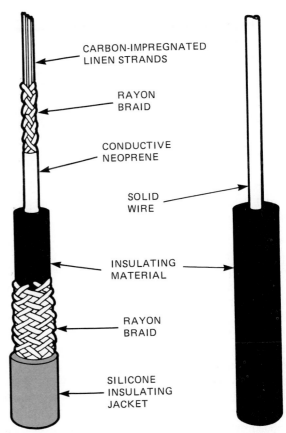

Fig. 31-6 Silicone resistance cable or "spark-plug wire" (left) now used on all vehicles compared with older solid-conductor (right) spark-plug wire. (*AC-Delco Division of General Motors Corporation*)

5. SPARK PLUGS The spark plug (Fig. 31-1) has two solid-metal conductors called *electrodes* positioned to form a gap (➤31-11). The gap is between the insulated center electrode and the ground electrode. The spark jumps the gap to ignite the compressed air-fuel mixture in the engine cylinders.

➤ 31-3 PRODUCING THE SPARK

The ignition system consists of two separate but related circuits: the low-voltage *primary circuit* and the high-voltage *secondary circuit*. The ignition coil (Fig. 31-1) has two windings. The *primary winding* of a few hundred turns of heavy wire is part of the primary circuit. The *secondary winding* of many thousand turns of fine wire is part of the secondary circuit. When the ignition key is ON and the contact points closed, current flows through the primary winding (Fig. 31-7). This produces a magnetic field around the primary windings in the coil (➤10-11).

When the contact points open, current flow stops and the magnetic field collapses. As it collapses, it cuts across the thousands of turns of wire in the coil secondary winding. This produces a voltage in each turn. These add together to produce the high voltage delivered through the secondary circuit to the spark plug (Fig. 31-5).

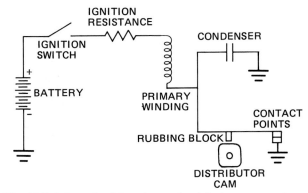

Fig. 31-7 Schematic of the primary circuit in the contact-point ignition system. (*ATW*)

➤ 31-4 CONTACT POINTS

The contact-point set mounts on a *breaker plate* in the distributor (Fig. 31-8). The points are operated by a *breaker cam* on top of the distributor shaft. The cam has the same number of *lobes* as there are cylinders in the engine. As the cam revolves and the points close and open, they act as a mechanical switch to *make* and *break* the primary circuit.

One contact point mounts on the grounded breaker plate and is stationary. The other point mounts on the end of an insulated movable arm (Fig. 31-8). The arm swings back and forth on a pivot as the cam lobes push on the *rubbing block* to open the points. A spring attached to the movable-point arm closes the points.

When the points close, this connects the coil primary winding to the battery. A magnetic field builds up in the coil. As the breaker cam rotates, the next lobe pushes the movable arm away from the stationary contact point. This opens the points and stops the current flow. The magnetic field collapses and a high-voltage surge results. The length of time in degrees of distributor-shaft rotation that the contact points remained closed is the *dwell*. The distance that separates the points when they are fully open is the *gap*. Points are normally adjusted by dwell or gap measurements.

The distributor shaft and cam are driven by the engine camshaft which turns at one-half crankshaft speed. It takes two complete revolutions of the crankshaft to rotate the distributor shaft one complete revolution.

The relationship between piston position and spark-plug firing is *ignition timing* (➤31-7).

➤ 31-5 PRIMARY RESISTANCE

Excessive current flow in the primary circuit causes arcing and burning of the contact points. To prevent this, a resistance is placed between the ignition switch and the coil primary winding (Figs. 31-1 and 31-7). The resistance may be a separate resistor or a special resistance wire. For easier starting, the resistance is bypassed and full battery voltage reaches the coil during cranking. After the engine starts, the resistance reduces coil voltage to 5 to 8 volts.

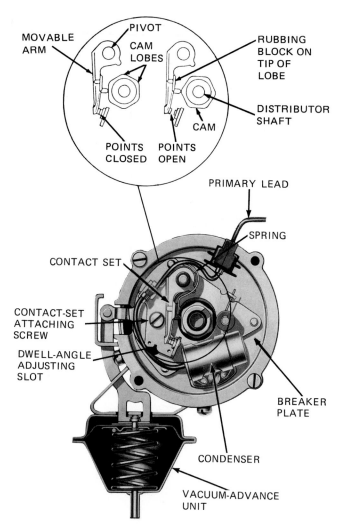

Fig. 31-8 Top view of a contact-point ignition distributor with the cap and rotor removed. Note that the cam has six lobes (for a six-cylinder engine). The drawings at the top show the cam action. When a lobe moves under the rubbing block, the contact arm is moved, separating the points. (*Delco-Remy Division of General Motors Corporation*)

➤ 31-6 SECONDARY VOLTAGE

The high voltages and high rate of change prevent most voltmeters from measuring secondary voltage. Figure 31-9 shows a computerized engine analyzer that includes two cathode-ray tubes (CRTs). The CRT on the left is an *oscilloscope* or *scope* (➤27-16). It can display the primary- and secondary-voltage patterns and the length of time they occur.

Figure 31-10 shows the basic pattern for one spark-plug firing cycle in the secondary circuit. At the left in Fig. 31-10, the points open. This stops the current flow through the coil primary winding. The magnetic field then collapses, causing a sudden high voltage (A to B) in the secondary winding. This is the *firing voltage* that starts the spark jumping the gap at the spark plug. The voltage quickly drops from B to C because it takes less voltage to sustain the spark than it does to start it. The spark continues from C to D, where it stops. This is the *spark line* or

Fig. 31-9 Computerized engine analyzer, with oscilloscope (left) that can display the primary and secondary voltage patterns. (*Sun Electric Corporation*)

burn time. It lasts for about 20 degrees of crankshaft rotation, or 1 to 2 milliseconds (thousandths of a second).

The remaining energy causes voltage ripples or *oscillations* from D to E in Fig. 31-10. However, the voltage is not great enough to restart the spark. At E, the points close and current starts flowing through the coil primary winding. The expanding magnetic lines of force pass through the primary winding, creating a slight alternating voltage in it. This is shown by the dip and small ripples to the right of E in Fig. 31-10.

From E to F in Fig. 31-10 is the *dwell* section. Dwell is the length of time the points are closed and current flows through the primary winding of the coil. Then at F, the points open and the cycle begins again at A as the spark occurs at the spark plug. The whole procedure repeats continuously as long as the engine runs.

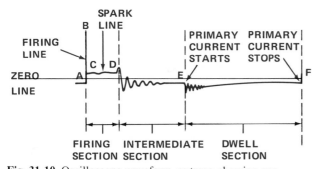

Fig. 31-10 Oscilloscope waveform, or trace, showing one complete spark-plug firing cycle in the secondary circuit. The dwell section is the time period during which current flows through the primary circuit.

➤ 31-7 ADVANCING THE SPARK

When the engine is idling, the spark is timed to reach the spark plug just before the piston reaches TDC on the compression stroke. At higher speeds, the spark must occur earlier. If it does not, the piston will be past TDC and moving down on the power stroke before combustion pressure reaches its maximum. The piston is ahead of the pressure rise which results in a weak power stroke. This wastes much of the energy in the fuel.

To better use the energy in the fuel, the spark takes place earlier as engine speed increases. This *spark advance* causes the mixture to burn producing maximum pressure just as the piston moves through TDC. Most contact-point distributors have two mechanisms to control spark advance. A *centrifugal-advance mechanism* (➤31-8) adjusts the spark based on the engine speed. A *vacuum-advance mechanism* (➤31-9) adjusts the spark based on engine load. On the engine, both work together to provide the proper spark advance for the engine operating conditions.

➤ 31-8 CENTRIFUGAL ADVANCE

The centrifugal-advance mechanism advances the spark by pushing the breaker cam ahead as engine speed increases. Two advance weights, two weight springs, and a cam assembly provide this action. The cam assembly includes the breaker cam and an oval-shaped *advance cam* (Fig. 31-11). At low speed, the springs hold the weights in. As engine speed increases, centrifugal force causes the

391

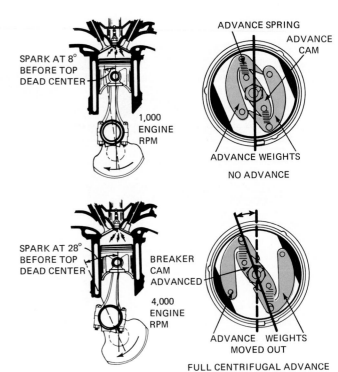

Fig. 31-12 Centrifugal-advance mechanism in no-advance and full-advance positions. In the example shown, the ignition is timed at 8 degrees before TDC on idle. There is no centrifugal advance at 1,000 engine rpm. At 4,000 engine rpm, there is a total of 28 degrees advance (8 degrees original timing plus 20 degrees centrifugal advance).

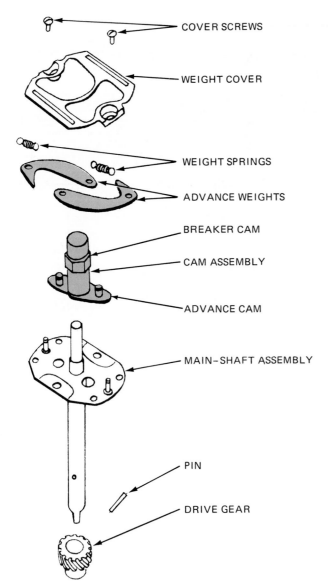

Fig. 31-11 Parts of a centrifugal-advance mechanism for a contact-point ignition distributor.

weights to overcome the spring force and pivot outward (Fig. 31-12). This pushes the cam assembly ahead. The contact points open and close earlier, advancing the spark.

> ## 31-9 VACUUM ADVANCE

When the throttle valve is only partly open, a partial vacuum develops in the intake manifold. Less air-fuel mixture gets into the engine cylinders. Then the fuel burns slower after it is ignited. The spark must be advanced at part throttle to give the mixture more time to burn.

The vacuum-advance mechanism (Figs. 31-8 and 31-13) advances spark timing by shifting the position of the breaker plate. The vacuum-advance unit has a diaphragm linked to the breaker plate. A vacuum passage connects the diaphragm to a port just above the closed throttle valve. When the throttle valve moves past the vacuum port, the

intake-manifold vacuum pulls on the diaphragm. This rotates the breaker plate so the contact points open and close earlier (Fig. 31-14). Any vacuum port above the throttle valve provides *ported vacuum*.

> ## 31-10 COMBINED CENTRIFUGAL AND VACUUM ADVANCE

At any speed above idle, there is some centrifugal advance. Depending on intake-manifold vacuum, there may also be some vacuum advance. The *total advance* curve in Fig. 31-15 shows how the centrifugal and vacuum advance combine. At 40 miles per hour [64 km/h], there are 15 degrees of centrifugal advance. The vacuum advance can produce up to 15 degrees of additional advance at part throttle. The advances shown in Fig. 31-15 combine to produce a maximum advance of 30 (15 + 15) degrees.

When the engine runs at wide-open throttle, intake-manifold vacuum drops to zero. There is no vacuum advance. Normally, the total advance varies between the straight line (centrifugal advance) and the curved line (centrifugal plus vacuum advance) in Fig. 31-15.

> ## 31-11 SPARK PLUGS

The spark plug (Fig. 31-16) has a metal outer shell enclosing a ceramic insulator. Centered in the insulator is the

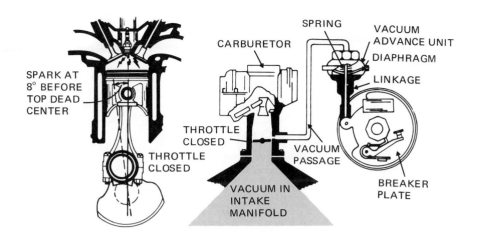

SPARK AT 8° BEFORE TOP DEAD CENTER

CARBURETOR

SPRING

VACUUM ADVANCE UNIT

DIAPHRAGM

LINKAGE

THROTTLE CLOSED

THROTTLE CLOSED

VACUUM PASSAGE

BREAKER PLATE

VACUUM IN INTAKE MANIFOLD

Fig. 31-13 When the throttle valve is closed, there is no vacuum advance. The ported vacuum passage is above the closed throttle valve.

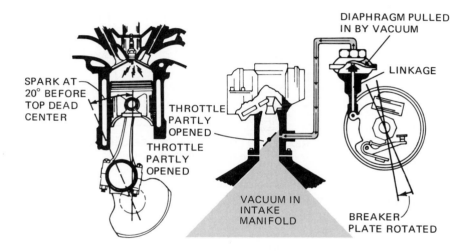

SPARK AT 20° BEFORE TOP DEAD CENTER

DIAPHRAGM PULLED IN BY VACUUM

LINKAGE

THROTTLE PARTLY OPENED

THROTTLE PARTLY OPENED

VACUUM IN INTAKE MANIFOLD

BREAKER PLATE ROTATED

Fig. 31-14 Operation of the vacuum-advance unit. When the throttle valve moves past the port, intake-manifold vacuum is admitted to the vacuum-advance unit on the distributor. The breaker plate then rotates to advance the spark.

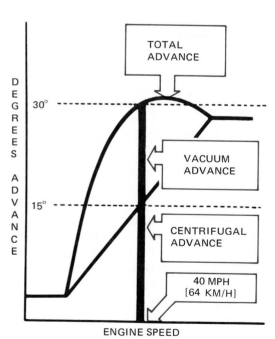

TOTAL ADVANCE

DEGREES ADVANCE

30°

15°

VACUUM ADVANCE

CENTRIFUGAL ADVANCE

40 MPH [64 KM/H]

ENGINE SPEED

Fig. 31-15 Centrifugal and vacuum advance curves for one engine.

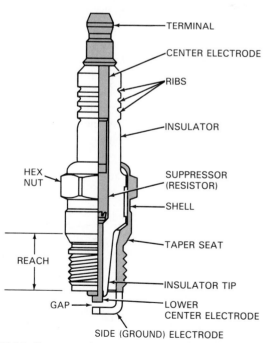

TERMINAL

CENTER ELECTRODE

RIBS

INSULATOR

HEX NUT

SUPPRESSOR (RESISTOR)

SHELL

TAPER SEAT

REACH

INSULATOR TIP

GAP

LOWER CENTER ELECTRODE

SIDE (GROUND) ELECTRODE

Fig. 31-16 Cutaway resistor-type spark plug. The center electrode is insulated. The side electrode is grounded through the engine. (*AC Spark Plug Division of General Motors Corporation*)

center electrode which carries the high-voltage current from the ignition coil. A *ground electrode* attaches to the metal shell and is bent inward to produce the proper spark gap. The gap varies from 0.035 inch [0.9 mm] for contact-point ignition systems to 0.080 inch [2.03 mm] for some electronic ignition systems. The spark jumps from the center electrode to the ground electrode. The wider the gap, the higher the voltage required to jump it.

Spark plugs may have a *suppressor* or resistance built into the center electrode (Fig. 31-16). It reduces television and radio interference (static) caused by the ignition system. Spark plugs may require gaskets when installed to assure a leakproof seal. Many engines use spark plugs with tapered seats which seal without a gasket (Fig. 31-16). Some spark-plug threads are coated with an *antiseize compound* (➤6-14). This makes plug removal easier, especially from aluminum cylinder heads.

Some engines have two spark plugs in each combustion chamber. Both plugs may fire together or one slightly ahead of the other. The additional plugs help reduce exhaust emissions and increase engine power.

Most spark plugs have electrodes made of nickel and chrome alloys that resist corrosion (Fig. 31-16). Some ground and lower center electrodes (Fig. 31-17A) have a copper core. Others also have a thin-wire platinum tip (Fig. 31-17B). These foul and misfire less often, last longer, and have a greater *heat range* (➤31-12) than other plugs.

➤ 31-12 SPARK-PLUG HEAT RANGE AND REACH

Spark plugs are made in different *heat ranges* (Fig. 31-18). The heat range indicates how fast the plug transfers heat from the combustion chamber to the cylinder head. This is primarily determined by the length of the lower insulator. The longer the heat path, the hotter the plug will run. A short path transfers the heat faster so the plug runs cooler.

Sooty deposits accumulate on the firing end of the spark plug if it runs too cold. The end does not get hot enough to burn away the deposits. Then the high-voltage surges short across the deposits instead of jumping the spark-plug gap. A plug that runs too hot burns away the electrodes more

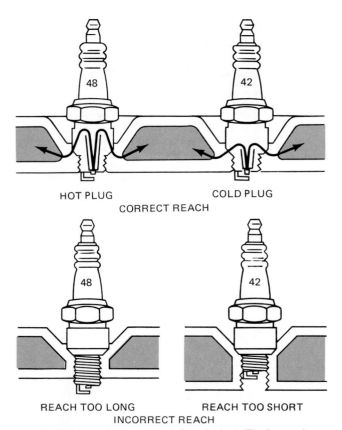

Fig. 31-18 Heat range and reach of spark plugs. The longer the heat path, as indicated by arrows, the hotter the plug runs. (*AC Spark Plug Division of General Motors Corporation*)

rapidly. This can widen the gap so much that the spark cannot jump it and a miss occurs.

Spark-plug reach (Figs. 31-16 and 31-18) is the distance from the shell gasket seat (or top of a tapered seat) to the end of the threads. If the reach is too long, the plug protrudes too far into the combustion chamber. The plug end could interfere with mixture turbulence or be struck by a valve or piston. A plug that does not reach far enough may fail to ignite the mixture properly. The recommended spark plugs for an engine have the correct reach.

➤ 31-13 IGNITION SWITCH

The ignition switch does several jobs. It turns the ignition system on and off. It has a START position for operating the starting motor. It operates the steering-wheel lock, and an audible or light signal if the ignition key is in the ignition lock when a door opens or if seat belts are not buckled. In many vehicles, the electric fuel pump connects to the battery through the ignition switch. Other accessories such as the radio and heater blower motor also receive power through the ignition switch.

In most cars, the ignition key is placed in the *ignition lock* or *lock cylinder* in the steering column (Fig. 31-19). The ignition switch may attach to the lock, or mount farther down the steering column (Fig. 11-21). Turning the

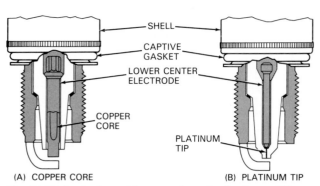

Fig. 31-17 Spark plugs with center electrodes that have a (A) copper core and a (B) platinum tip. (*Robert Bosch Corporation*)

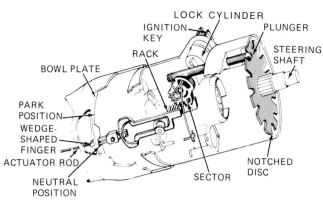

Fig. 31-19 Combination ignition-switch and steering-wheel lock, showing the operating mechanism inside the steering column. (*General Motors Corporation*)

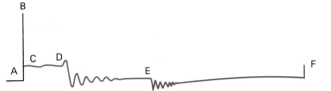

Fig. 31-20 Ignition-system oscilloscope pattern.

ignition key moves an *actuator rod* that operates the ignition switch.

The five positions of the ignition lock are shown in Fig. 31-1. These are ACCESSORY, LOCK, OFF, RUN, and START. Figure 31-19 shows how the ignition lock operates the

steering-wheel lock. The notched disk is splined to the top end of the steering shaft. With the automatic transmission in PARK, the driver turns the key to LOCK. The spring-loaded plunger moves up into a notch in the disc, locking the steering wheel. This also locks the transmission in PARK.

If the key will not move to LOCK, turn the steering wheel until the plunger and a notch align. Then the spring will force the plunger up and the key will turn to LOCK. Turning the key from LOCK to OFF pulls the plunger out of the notch in the disc. This unlocks the steering wheel and the transmission.

TRADE TALK

centrifugal advance	firing order	ignition distributor	vacuum advance
contact points	heat range	ignition timing	
dwell	ignition coil	oscilloscope	

MULTIPLE-CHOICE TEST

*Select the **one** correct, best, or most probable answer to each question.*
You can find the answers in the section indicated at the end of each question.

1. The ignition system performs all the following jobs EXCEPT (➤31-1)
   a. controls the compression pressure
   b. produces the spark that jumps the spark-plug gap
   c. ignites the compressed air-fuel mixture
   d. delivers the spark at the proper time

2. The contact-point distributor has two major jobs (➤31-2)
   a. to advance and retard the spark
   b. to distribute the high-voltage surges and switch the current to the coil on and off
   c. to distribute the battery voltage and switch the current to the spark plugs on and off
   d. to provide centrifugal advance and vacuum advance

3. Technician A says the spark occurs when the contact points open. Technician B says the spark occurs when the coil magnetic field collapses. Who is right? (➤31-3)
   a. A only
   b. B only
   c. both A and B
   d. neither A nor B

4. Technician A says the height of line A-B in Fig. 31-20 shows the voltage required to fire the spark plug. Technician B says line A-B shows that the primary current has been cut off. Who is right? (➤31-6)
   a. A only
   b. B only
   c. both A and B
   d. neither A nor B

5. Technician A says line C-D in Fig. 31-20 shows the length of time the spark jumps the spark-plug gap. Technician B says the height of line C-D shows the voltage required to keep the spark jumping the plug gap. Who is right? (➤31-6)
   a. A only
   b. B only
   c. both A and B
   d. neither A nor B

6. Technician A says line D-E in Fig. 31-20 shows the coil ON time. Technician B says line E-F shows the length of time current flows through the primary winding of the coil. Who is right? (➤31-6)
   a. A only
   b. B only
   c. both A and B
   d. neither A nor B

7. The device that provides spark advance by pushing the breaker cam ahead as engine speed increases is the (➤31-8)
   a. vacuum-advance mechanism
   b. throttle body
   c. primary resistance
   d. centrifugal-advance mechanism

8. Maximum vacuum advance occurs (➤31-9)
   a. at part throttle
   b. only after centrifugal advance reaches maximum
   c. at closed throttle
   d. at wide-open throttle

9. Engines use resistor spark plugs to (➤31-11)
   a. increase secondary voltage
   b. reduce secondary current
   c. make starting easier
   d. reduce television and radio interference

10. The heat range of a spark plug is primarily determined by (➤31-12)
    a. the depth the electrodes enter the combustion chamber
    b. the length of the lower insulator
    c. the number of ribs on the upper insulator
    d. the gap between the electrodes

REVIEW QUESTIONS

1. Describe the basic components in the contact-point ignition system and explain how they operate. (➤31-1 and 31-2)

2. How does the ignition coil produce the high-voltage spark? (➤31-3)

3. When does the engine need additional spark advance and how is it provided? (➤31-7 to 31-9)

4. Explain the difference between spark-plug heat range and spark-plug reach, and how each affects engine operation. (➤31-12)

5. List the five positions of the ignition lock and describe how it locks and unlocks the steering wheel. (➤31-13)

CHAPTER 32

ELECTRONIC IGNITION SYSTEMS

After studying this chapter, you should be able to:

- Explain the differences between contact-point and electronic ignition systems.
- Describe the operation of the pickup-coil sensor, the Hall-effect switch, and photodiodes.
- Describe the similarities and differences between distributor ignition with electronic spark advance and distributorless ignition.
- Define *camshaft sensor* and *crankshaft sensor,* and explain when they are used.
- Explain the operation of the capacitor-discharge ignition system.

➤ 32-1 TYPES OF ELECTRONIC IGNITION SYSTEMS

By the early 1970s, most automotive engines using a contact-point distributor (Chap. 31) could not meet exhaust-emission standards. Federal regulations required the ignition system to operate for 50,000 miles [80,465 km] with little or no maintenance. Contact points cannot do this. They burn and wear during normal operation. This changes the point gap, which changes ignition timing and reduces spark energy. Misfiring and increased exhaust emissions result.

Most 1975 and later automotive engines have an *electronic ignition system* (Fig. 32-1). It does not use contact points. Instead, transistors and other semiconductor devices (Chap. 10) act as an electronic switch that turns the coil primary current on and off.

There are four basic types of electronic ignition systems:

1. Distributor type with mechanical centrifugal and vacuum advance (Figs. 1-19 and 32-2).

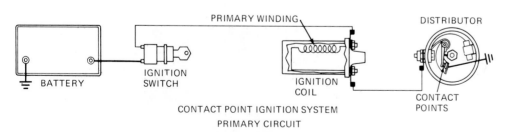

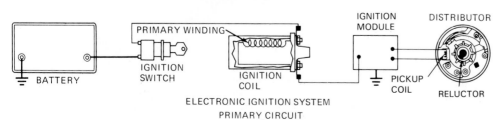

Fig. 32-1 Comparison of the primary circuit of a contact-point ignition system with that of an electronic ignition system.

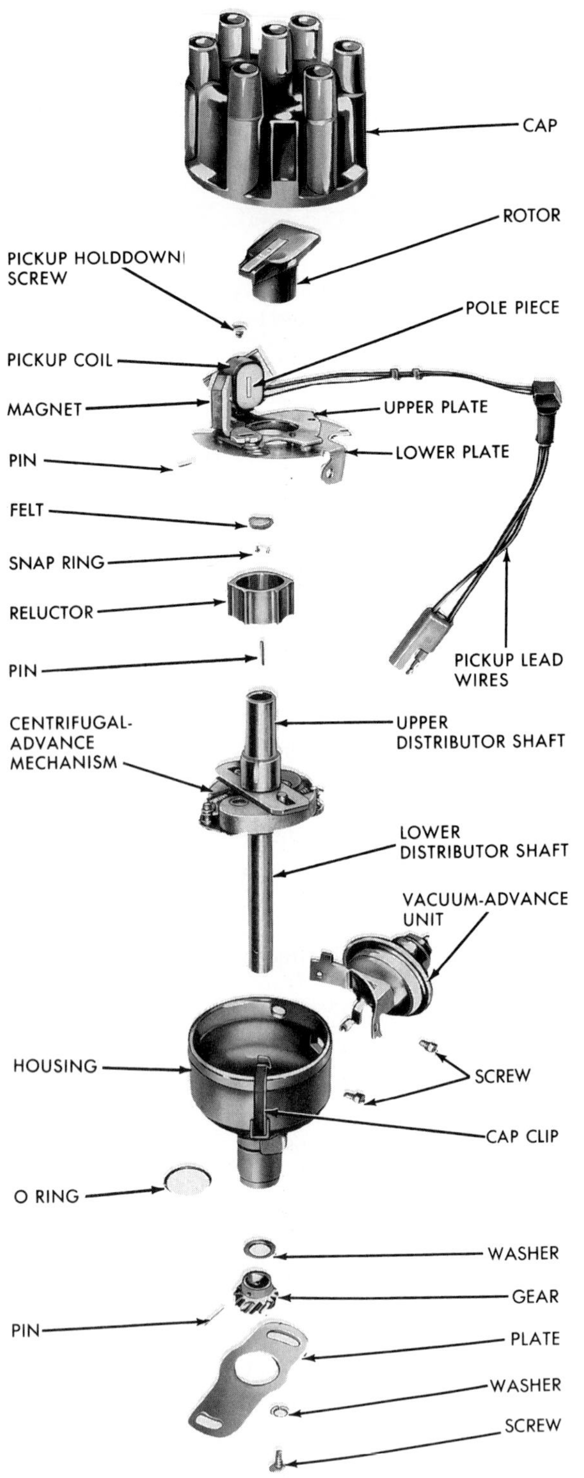

![Disassembled electronic-ignition distributor diagram with labels: CAP, ROTOR, POLE PIECE, PICKUP HOLDDOWN SCREW, PICKUP COIL, MAGNET, PIN, FELT, SNAP RING, RELUCTOR, PIN, UPPER PLATE, LOWER PLATE, PICKUP LEAD WIRES, CENTRIFUGAL-ADVANCE MECHANISM, UPPER DISTRIBUTOR SHAFT, LOWER DISTRIBUTOR SHAFT, VACUUM-ADVANCE UNIT, HOUSING, SCREW, CAP CLIP, O RING, WASHER, GEAR, PIN, PLATE, WASHER, SCREW]

Fig. 32-2 Disassembled electronic-ignition distributor, with mechanical centrifugal and vacuum advances. (*Chrysler Corporation*)

2. Distributor type with electronic spark advance (Figs. 1-27 and 1-28).
3. Distributorless type with multiple ignition coils (Figs. 1-8 and 1-13).
4. Distributorless type with direct capacitor-discharge (CD) ignition for each spark plug (➤32-14).

DISTRIBUTOR WITH MECHANICAL SPARK ADVANCE

➤ 32-2 FUNDAMENTALS OF ELECTRONIC IGNITION

Contact-point and electronic ignition systems are similar in operation and also often in construction. Both distributors (Fig. 32-2) may have centrifugal- and vacuum-advance mechanisms (➤31-8 and 31-9). The major difference is the use of an electronic switch instead of a mechanical switch (contact points) to control the primary current.

Figure 32-1 compares the primary circuits of a basic electronic-ignition system and the contact-point ignition system. The electronic distributor has an *armature* or *reluctor* and a magnetic sensor or *pickup coil* instead of a breaker cam and contact points. Like the breaker cam, the reluctor has the same number of teeth or tips as there are cylinders in the engine. When the reluctor rotates, each tooth creates a voltage pulse in the pickup coil. This signals the *ignition module* to open the primary circuit.

The ignition module may be a separate unit (Fig. 32-1), or mount on or in the distributor. Engines with an electronic-engine-control system (Fig. 19-35) may not have a separate ignition module. The *engine controller* or *electronic control module* (ECM) completely controls the ignition system.

➤ 32-3 PICKUP-COIL VOLTAGE PULSE

The *pickup-coil assembly* consists of a permanent magnet and the pickup coil (Fig. 32-3). The pickup coil is wound around an extension of the mounting bracket called a *pole piece*. The reluctor is made of iron. A small air gap separates the teeth and the pole piece when the distributor shaft rotates.

The pole piece helps the magnet create a magnetic field

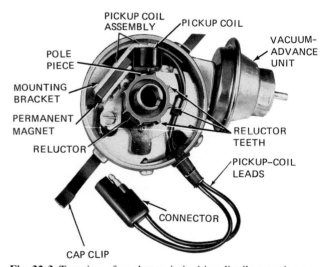

Fig. 32-3 Top view of an electronic-ignition distributor using a pickup coil and mechanical advances, with cap and rotor removed. The reluctor has eight tips for an eight-cylinder engine. (*Chrysler Corporation*)

around the windings in the pickup coil. Each passing reluctor tooth causes the magnetic field to move through the pickup coil, generating a small voltage pulse in it (Fig. 32-4). This voltage pulse signals the ignition module to open the primary circuit. The effect is the same as opening the contact points. The magnetic field in the ignition coil collapses (➤31-6), producing a high-voltage surge. This is carried through the distributor cap, rotor, and wiring to the spark plug in the cylinder that is ready to fire.

After the reluctor tooth moves away from the pole piece, the ignition module closes the primary circuit. This is the same as closing the contact-points. Current flows through the primary winding of the ignition coil, causing the magnetic field to build up in it. The ignition system is now ready to deliver another high-voltage surge.

➤ 32-4 HIGH-ENERGY IGNITION (HEI) SYSTEM

Many electronic ignition systems produce higher secondary voltage (➤31-6) than contact-point ignition. The voltage in these *high-energy ignition* (HEI) systems can reach 47,000 volts or higher. This allows the use of spark plugs with wider gaps. The longer spark can ignite leaner air-fuel ratios. These provide better fuel economy and reduced exhaust emissions.

The secondary circuits are basically the same in both ignition systems. However, the distributor, ignition coil, and secondary wiring are redesigned to handle the higher voltage. Distributor caps are larger with the spark-plug terminals taller and farther apart (Fig. 32-5). This reduces the possibility of arcing between terminals. Arcing can cause

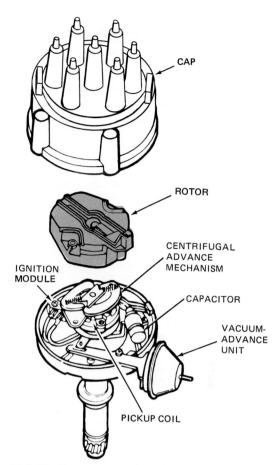

Fig. 32-5 Distributor, rotor, and cap for a high-energy ignition (HEI) system. Note wider distributor and higher, more widely spaced terminals on the cap that reduces arcing between terminals. (*Delco-Remy Division of General Motors Corporation*)

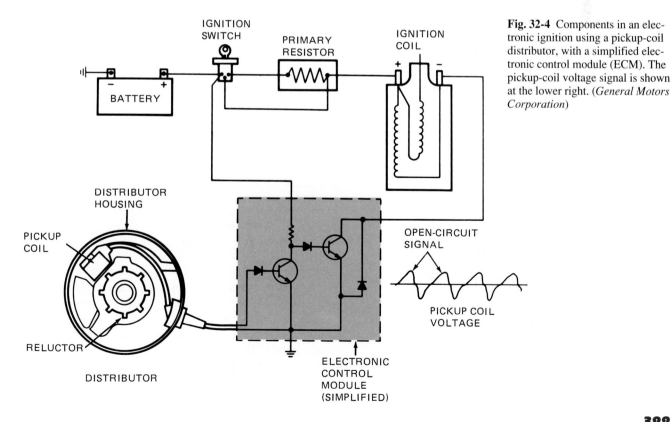

Fig. 32-4 Components in an electronic ignition using a pickup-coil distributor, with a simplified electronic control module (ECM). The pickup-coil voltage signal is shown at the lower right. (*General Motors Corporation*)

engine miss and can damage the cap. The *capacitor* reduces radio interference (static). HEI systems also use the larger 8-mm silicone spark-plug wires and coil wire (Fig. 31-6).

Some General Motors HEI systems for V-type engines mount the ignition coil in the top of the distributor cap (Fig. 32-6). This simplifies ignition wiring. The HEI coil has a different shape and produces a higher voltage than the coil described in Chap. 31. However, its basic operation is the same.

Figure 32-7 is a schematic of the HEI system. Figure 32-8 shows the construction of the magnetic-pickup assembly. The pole piece is a flattened ring with a tooth pointing inward for each cylinder. The reluctor, with matching teeth pointing outward, is called a *timer core*. When the distributor shaft rotates, a voltage pulse is induced in the pickup coil as the timer-core teeth pass the pole-piece teeth.

DISTRIBUTOR WITH ELECTRONIC SPARK ADVANCE

➤ **32-5 ELECTRONIC SPARK ADVANCE**

The electronic ignition systems described above are usually on cars without an electronic-engine-control

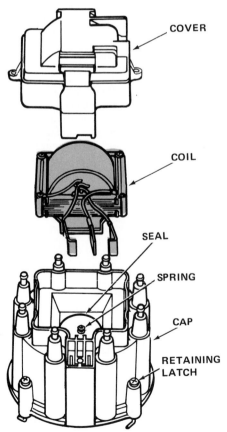

Fig. 32-6 HEI distributor cap for a V-type engine, showing how the ignition coil mounts in the cap. (*Delco-Remy Division of General Motors Corporation*)

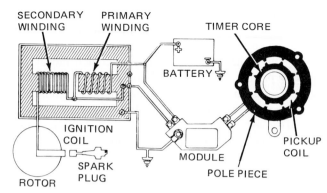

Fig. 32-7 Schematic of an HEI system. The distributor includes the ignition module and pickup coil. (*Ford Motor Company*)

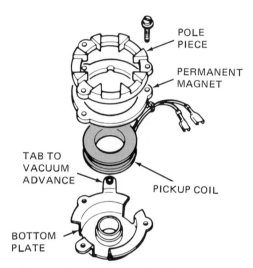

Fig. 32-8 Construction of the magnetic-pickup assembly in an HEI distributor. (*Ford Motor Company*)

system. Cars with an electronic-engine-control system and a distributor usually have *electronic spark advance*. Centrifugal- and vacuum-advance mechanisms are not used. The computer or ECM controls spark advance based on inputs from various sensors (Fig. 19-26). Chapter 19 describes some of these sensors and the operation of the electronic-engine-control system.

NOTE Electronic spark advance affects only the primary circuit of the ignition system. There is no change in the secondary circuit.

Figure 32-9 shows an electronic ignition system using electronic spark advance. The ignition module and the ECM work together to control spark timing. The ignition module mounts on the distributor housing. Inside the distributor, a *profile ignition pickup* or *PIP sensor* (➤32-6) signals the ignition module as each piston nears top dead center (TDC). The ignition module shares this information with the ECM which then computes spark advance. The ECM produces a new signal that Ford calls the *spark output* (SPOUT) signal. It is sent back to the ignition

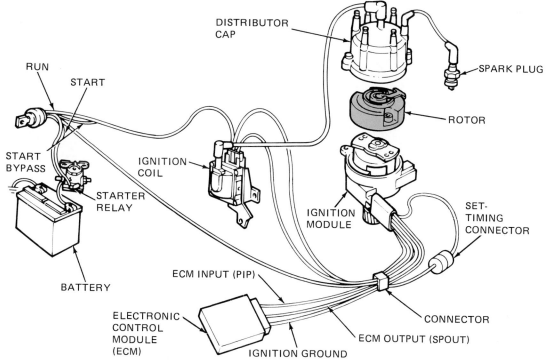

Fig. 32-9 Electronic ignition system with electronic spark advance. (*Ford Motor Company*)

module, which opens the primary circuit at the proper time to fire the spark plug.

Sometimes the ECM or other part fails in the electronic-engine-control system. This may cause the engine to enter its *limp-in* or *limited-operating strategy* (LOS) mode (➤19-20). Then the ignition module uses only the signal from the sensor in the distributor (➤32-3) to open and close the coil primary circuit.

➤ 32-6 HALL-EFFECT SWITCH

Some ignition systems use a *Hall-effect switch* (➤19-18) instead of a pickup coil. The difference is that the pickup coil *generates* a small voltage when a reluctor tooth moves past it. The Hall-effect switch *switches* a supplied voltage on and off with the presence or absence of a magnetic field.

The PIP sensor (➤32-5) in the distributor shown in Fig. 32-9 is a Hall-effect switch. Its on-off voltage pulse tells the ignition module the position of the crankshaft. This signal can also trigger fuel injection (Chap. 19).

The Hall effect occurs when a magnetic field passes through a thin slice of semiconductor material that is carrying an electric current. Then a voltage appears at the edges of the semiconductor. This is the *Hall voltage,* named after its discoverer.

Figure 32-10 shows an ignition distributor using a Hall-effect switch. It has a steel rotor or cup with the same number of *windows* and *shutters* as the engine has cylinders (Fig. 32-11). The shutters are curved to pass through the air gap between the permanent magnet and the *Hall-*

effect sensor. Together, the magnet and sensor make up the Hall-effect switch.

When a shutter is *not* in the air gap (Fig. 32-10A), the magnetic field acts on the Hall-effect sensor (the semiconductor material). It sends a small voltage signal (the Hall voltage) to the ignition module. When a shutter enters the air gap (Fig. 32-10B), the magnetic field is cut off. This turns off the Hall voltage which signals the ignition module to close the primary circuit. The shutter width (Fig. 32-11) can be used to determine dwell, or how long current flows in the primary circuit.

The instant the shutter leaves the air gap (Fig. 32-10A), the Hall voltage reappears. The ECM uses this signal to compute the proper spark advance and then signals the ignition module to open the primary circuit. The resulting high-voltage surge is carried through the secondary circuit to the spark plug.

| NOTE | *Various manufacturers use the Hall-effect switch in different ways. All electronic systems with a Hall-effect switch do not operate exactly as described above. However, all switch a voltage signal on and off.* |

➤ 32-7 HEI DISTRIBUTOR WITH ELECTRONIC SPARK ADVANCE

Figure 32-12 shows an HEI distributor used with electronic spark advance. The distributor is similar to the earlier ver-

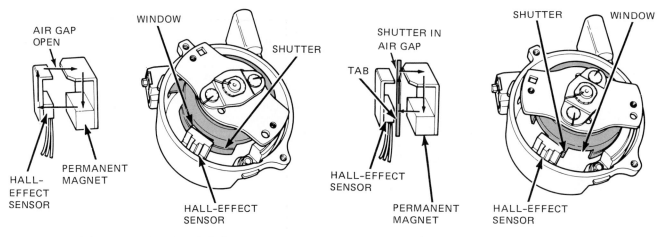

(A) NO SHUTTER IN AIR GAP—
VOLTAGE SIGNAL

(B) SHUTTER IN AIR GAP—
NO VOLTAGE SIGNAL

Fig. 32-10 Ignition distributor using a Hall-effect switch. (A) The window is passing through the air gap. The magnetic field, or flux, from the permanent magnet is imposed on the Hall-effect sensor. (B) The shutter is in the air gap. This cuts off the flux, preventing the magnetic field from acting on the Hall-effect sensor. (*Ford Motor Company*)

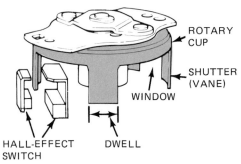

Fig. 32-11 Hall-effect switch. The shutter width determines dwell, or how long current flows in the primary circuit. (*Ford Motor Company*)

sion with mechanical centrifugal- and vacuum-advance mechanisms (Fig. 32-5). *Electronic spark timing* (EST) is controlled by the ECM. It monitors information from various sensors and computes spark advance for best fuel economy, driveability, and minimum exhaust emissions. Then the ECM signals the ignition module (*HEI module* in Fig. 32-13) in the distributor to fire the spark plugs.

Some GM HEI distributors have a Hall-effect switch mounted above the pickup-coil assembly (Fig. 32-14). The pickup coil provides the signal to fire the spark plugs during cranking. The signal from the Hall-effect switch triggers fuel injection and serves as the reference signal to the ECM. This tells the ECM the crankshaft speed and position. After the engine starts, the signal from the Hall-effect switch triggers spark-plug firing.

➤ 32-8 OPTICAL PHOTODIODE DISTRIBUTOR

A *photodiode* or *optical distributor* (Fig. 32-15) uses a light beam to control the primary circuit. *Optical* means pertaining to or using light. A photodiode is a diode that

Fig. 32-12 HEI distributor for a V-8 engine, using electronic spark advance. (*Pontiac Division of General Motors Corporation*)

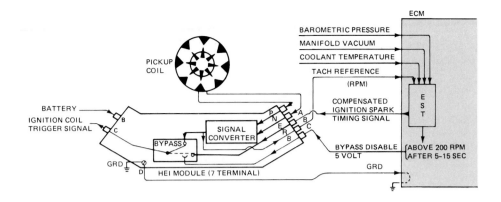

Fig. 32-13 Seven-terminal ignition module, or HEI module, used in the HEI distributor on engines with electronic spark timing. (*Rochester Products Division of General Motors Corporation*)

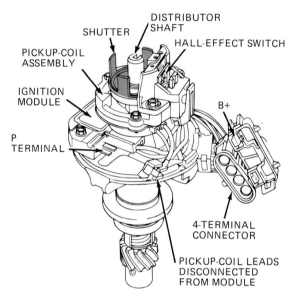

Fig. 32-14 HEI distributor with a Hall-effect switch mounted above the pickup-coil assembly. The pickup coil provides the signal to fire the spark plugs during cranking. (*Chevrolet Division of General Motors Corporation*)

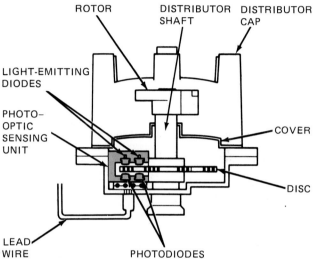

Fig. 32-15 Photodiode, or optical, distributor which uses the on-off action of a light beam to control the primary circuit. (*Chrysler Corporation*)

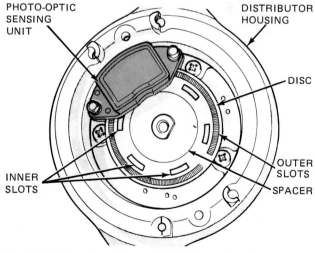

Fig. 32-16 Top view of the optical distributor, showing the slotted disk and photo-optic sensing unit. (*Chrysler Corporation*)

uses the presence or absence of light to switch an applied voltage on and off. In the distributor, a *light-emitting diode* (LED) provides the light beam.

Two LEDs and two photodiodes mount on opposite sides of a slotted disk (Fig. 32-15). The disc rotates with the distributor shaft. When a slot moves under the LED, the light beam strikes the photodiode. It stays turned on until the rotating disc blocks off the light beam. Then the photodiode switches off. This creates an alternating voltage in the photodiode. An integrated circuit in the *photo-optic sensing unit* in the distributor converts the voltage into on-off pulses. These provide engine speed and crank-shaft-position signals directly to the ECM. A separate ignition module is not used. The ECM then uses the signals to control fuel injection, ignition timing, and idle speed.

The timing device in the distributor is a thin disc with two sets of slots in it (Fig. 32-16). Each set of slots produces a voltage signal in one of the photodiodes. The outer or *high-data-rate* slots occur every two degrees of crankshaft rotation. The signal from these slots is used for crankshaft-position sensing and ignition timing at engine speeds up to 1200 rpm.

An inner or *low-data-rate* set of slots has the same number of slots as the engine has cylinders. This signal indicates the top dead center position of each piston and triggers fuel injection. It also is used for ignition timing at engine speeds above 1200 rpm.

403

As in other distributors, the rotor and distributor cap deliver the high-voltage surges from the ignition coil to the spark-plug wires. There is a cover (Fig. 32-15) in the distributor housing below the rotor. This protects the sensing unit from high-voltage damage and the optical system from contamination. On some V-type OHV engines, the optical distributor mounts directly to the camshaft at the front of the engine.

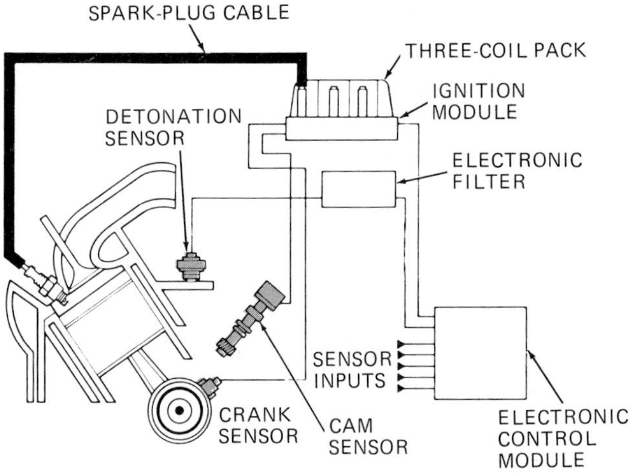

DISTRIBUTORLESS IGNITION WITH MULTIPLE COILS

➤ 32-9 FUNDAMENTALS OF DISTRIBUTORLESS IGNITION

Many engines have a *distributorless ignition system* (Figs. 12-3 and 32-17). This is an electronic ignition system with electronic spark advance, but without a distributor. Sensors signal the position of the crankshaft to the ignition module. It then acts with the ECM to time, trigger, and distribute the high-voltage surges to the spark plugs.

No distributor means fewer moving parts. It also removes the high-voltage rotary switch formed by the distributor cap and rotor. This results in less maintenance and eliminates mechanical adjustments of ignition timing. There is less radio interference and increased spark-timing accuracy.

Fig. 32-17 Distributorless ignition system, which does not have a separate ignition distributor. (*Champion Spark Plug Company*)

Fig. 32-18 A V-6 engine with distributorless ignition system. Note locations of the camshaft sensor and crankshaft sensor. (*Chrysler Corporation*)

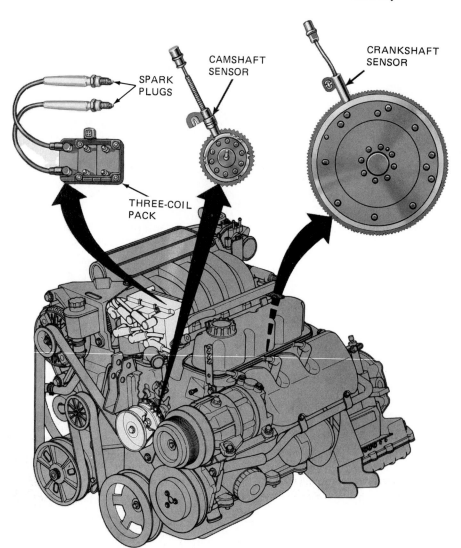

Figure 32-18 shows a V-6 engine with a distributorless ignition system. The system includes the ignition module, a *coil pack* containing three ignition coils, a *crankshaft sensor,* and a *camshaft sensor* (Fig. 32-19). Each ignition coil fires two spark plugs at the same time. One end of each secondary winding connects to a spark plug (Fig.

32-20). The ignition module determines firing sequence and selects the coil to fire. Then the ECM signals the ignition module when to open the primary circuit. The resulting high-voltage surge in the secondary winding causes sparks to jump both spark-plug gaps.

One coil firing two spark plugs at the same time is the *waste-spark method* of spark distribution. It fires the *piston pairs* (➤12-11). These pistons go up and down together. When one of the pistons is ending its compression stroke (Fig. 32-21), the other is ending its exhaust stroke.

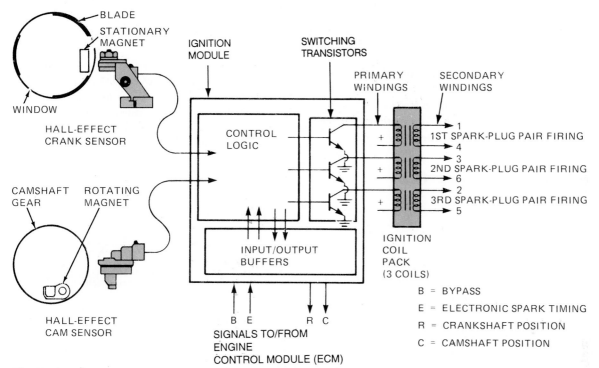

Fig. 32-19 Schematic of distributorless ignition system for a V-6 engine, showing how three ignition coils can fire six spark plugs. (*General Motors Corporation*)

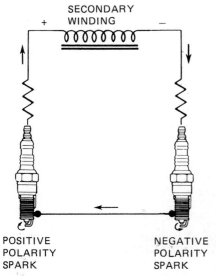

Fig. 32-20 Waste-spark method of spark distribution, showing how the ignition-coil secondary winding can fire two plugs at once. (*Champion Spark Plug Company*)

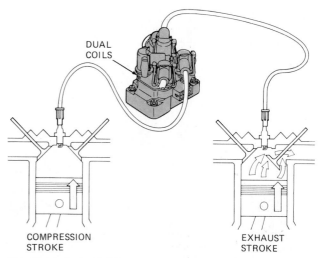

Fig. 32-21 One coil firing two spark plugs in cylinders that are piston pairs. The pistons go up and down together, but on different strokes of the four-stroke cycle. One spark is wasted. (*Ford Motor Company*)

Figure 32-19 shows how three ignition coils can fire six spark plugs. Notice the two ends of the secondary winding for the coil that connects to the spark plugs in cylinders 1 and 4. When cylinder 1 fires at the end of its compression stroke, the spark ignites the air-fuel mixture and the power stroke begins. The spark in cylinder 4 is "wasted." It occurs in the exhaust gas and does nothing. Next, the spark plugs in cylinders 3 and 6 fire, followed by cylinders 2 and 5. This sequence repeats as long as the engine runs.

The spark plug in the cylinder on its exhaust stroke requires very little energy to fire. Much of the exhaust gas has left and the pressure in the cylinder is low. The spark jumps the plug gap easily. This leaves most of the energy in the high-voltage surge for the spark plug in the cylinder on its compression stroke.

Figures 32-17 and 32-18 show the locations of the crankshaft sensor (➢32-11) and the camshaft sensor (➢32-12). The ECM receives the signals from these and other sensors. Then the ECM uses this information to manage the ignition system, and also the fuel system and emission controls.

➢ 32-11 CRANKSHAFT-POSITION SENSOR

The *crankshaft-position sensor* or simply *crank sensor* (Fig. 32-17) reports crankshaft speed and piston position to the ignition module. It must know when the piston in cylinder 1 is nearing TDC on the compression stroke. This is the instant the ignition system must deliver a spark to the spark plug in that cylinder.

Typically, the crank-sensor signal begins at a *timing disc* (Fig. 32-22) or *pulse ring* that rotates with the crankshaft. When a tooth or notch in the disk aligns with the sensor, it produces a voltage pulse. This signal tells the ignition module the crankshaft speed and position.

The crankshaft sensor is either a magnetic pickup-coil (➢32-3) or a Hall-effect switch (➢32-6).

1. PICKUP-COIL CRANKSHAFT SENSOR Figure 32-23 shows the construction of a pickup-coil type of position sensor. The pickup coil is wound around a pole piece that extends from a permanent magnet. Operation is similar to the pickup coil in the electronic distributor (Fig. 32-3). A slotted timing disk or reluctor rotates with the crankshaft (Fig. 32-22). As each slot passes through the magnetic field at the end of the pickup coil, a voltage is induced in it. The higher the engine speed, the higher the induced voltage.

A double notch or *indexing notch* in the reluctor generates a *sync pulse*. This indicates crankshaft position. The ignition module uses the sync pulse to synchronize the coil-firing sequence with the crankshaft position. After the sync pulse, the ignition module counts the passing notches. Then it uses the count to trigger each coil at the proper time. The ECM provides an electronic spark-advance signal to the ignition module as described in ➢32-7.

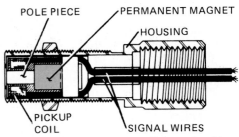

Fig. 32-23 Construction of a pickup-coil type of position sensor. (*Airpax Corporation*)

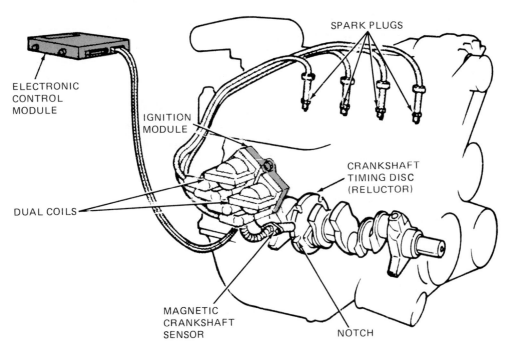

Fig. 32-22 Magnetic crankshaft sensor. Notches in the rotating crankshaft timing disc produce voltage pulses, or signals, which indicate crankshaft speed and position. (*Chevrolet Division of General Motors Corporation*)

2. HALL-EFFECT CRANKSHAFT SENSOR This crank sensor uses a Hall-effect switch to turn on and off a voltage (the *reference voltage*) supplied by the ignition module. The resulting change in the reference voltage provides a series of equal pulses. An *interrupter ring* behind the crankshaft vibration damper (➤13-15) creates the pulses. Equally spaced blades and windows on the ring rotate through the air gap between a permanent magnet and the Hall-effect sensor (Fig. 32-19). This turns the Hall voltage on and off.

Figure 32-24 shows how the Hall-effect switch turns a transistor on and off. When a window passes through the gap between the magnet and the Hall-effect sensor, the magnetic field reaches the sensor. It then produces a voltage that turns on the transistor. This causes a drop in the reference-voltage signal to the ignition module.

When the next blade moves into the air gap, the blade stops the magnetic field from reaching the Hall sensor. Without magnetism, the Hall voltage switches off. This turns off the transistor and restores the high reference-voltage signal to the ignition module.

➤ 32-12 CAMSHAFT-POSITION SENSOR

The *camshaft-position sensor* is also called the *cam sensor* and the *cylinder-identification* (CID) *sensor*. It provides voltage pulses that identify the position of number 1 piston. The sensor is usually a Hall-effect switch (➤32-6).

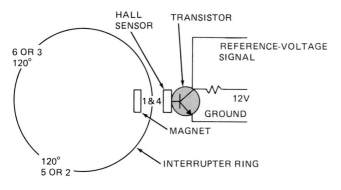

(A) HALL-EFFECT CRANKSHAFT SENSOR

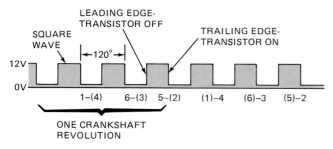

(B) REFERENCE-VOLTAGE SIGNAL

Fig. 32-24 How a Hall-effect switch turns a transistor on and off, which changes the reference-voltage signal. (*General Motors Corporation*)

The ignition module recognizes the cam-sensor signal as the start of each *ignition cycle*. This is the firing of all spark plugs during one complete cycle of engine operation (two crankshaft revolutions).

> **NOTE** Some distributorless ignition systems do not use a cam sensor. The crank sensor (➤32-11) provides the data.

Figure 32-17 shows a distributorless ignition system with the cam sensor mounting in the hole formerly used for the ignition distributor. The cam sensor is driven in the same way — by spiral gears from the camshaft. Figure 32-18 shows another type of cam sensor. Notches in a plate attached to the camshaft sprocket turn a Hall switch on and off. Figure 32-19 shows a Hall sensor which turns on and off as a small magnet mounted on the camshaft gear rotates past.

During two crankshaft revolutions (720 degrees), the crank sensor provides the same number of pulses as the engine has cylinders (Fig. 32-25). The cam sensor provides only one pulse. It identifies the coil to be fired and reestablishes the proper coil-firing sequence in the ignition module.

DISTRIBUTORLESS DIRECT IGNITION

➤ 32-13 DIRECT MULTIPLE-COIL IGNITION

Some engines have a direct ignition system that eliminates spark-plug cables (Fig. 32-26). On a four-cylinder engine, the ignition module and two coils mount under an aluminum cover (Fig. 32-27). Operation is basically the same as the multiple-coil distributorless ignition system described in ➤32-10. However, molded one-piece secondary conductors replace the spark-plug wires.

Cables cause some voltage loss. Without cables, full secondary voltage reaches the spark plugs. Eliminating the

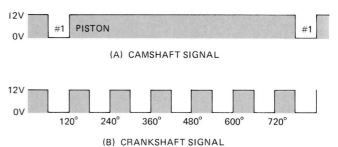

Fig. 32-25 Camshaft-sensor signal related to crankshaft-sensor signal. During two crankshaft revolutions, the crankshaft sensor (B) provides the same number of pulses as the engine has cylinders. The camshaft sensor (A) provides only one pulse. (*General Motors Corporation*)

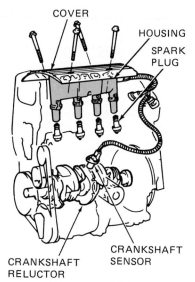

Fig. 32-26 Direct ignition system, which uses no spark-plug cables, on a four-cylinder engine. (*Champion Spark Plug Company*)

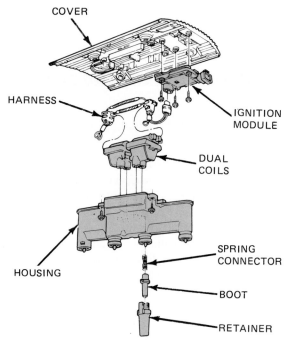

Fig. 32-27 Ignition module and two coils that mount in the housing under the cover of a four-cylinder engine with direct ignition. (*Champion Spark Plug Company*)

cables also reduces maintenance. There are no cables to check and replace.

Similar multiple-coil ignition systems mount a coil directly on each spark plug. This arrangement does not use the waste-spark method. Opening the primary circuit in each coil fires only one spark plug. Other types of ignition systems also use multiple coils (➤32-14).

➤ 32-14 DIRECT CAPACITOR-DISCHARGE IGNITION

The ignition systems described above are all *inductive* ignition systems. They store the primary energy in a coil or *inductor*. A *capacitor-discharge* (CD) ignition system stores the primary energy in a capacitor or condenser. This electrical device can temporarily hold or store a small electric charge.

In a CD ignition system, the spark occurs when a switch or transistor *closes* the primary circuit. Then a charged capacitor discharges through the ignition coil. This produces a high-voltage surge that creates the spark at the spark plug.

Figure 32-28 shows a Saab capacitor-discharge ignition system. It is similar to the direct multiple-coil ignition system (➤32-13). Each spark plug has its own ignition coil and capacitor. The parts fit into an *ignition cartridge* that mounts over the spark plugs (Fig. 32-29). The system delivers a secondary voltage of up to 40,000 volts to the plugs.

The voltage increase is done in two steps. The first step raises battery voltage up to 400 volts. Then the second step increases this voltage up to 40,000 volts.

Battery voltage causes a small current flow through the coil primary winding. When the primary circuit opens, the magnetic field collapses. A voltage of up to 400 volts appears in the primary circuit and charges the capacitor. An ECM controls ignition timing based on signals from a Hall-effect crankshaft sensor (➤32-11). The manifold-

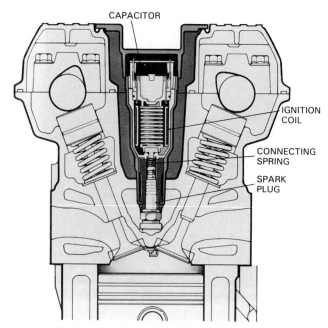

Fig. 32-28 Capacitor-discharge ignition system. Each spark plug has its own ignition coil and capacitor that fit into an ignition cartridge that mounts over the spark plug. (*Saab Cars USA, Inc.*)

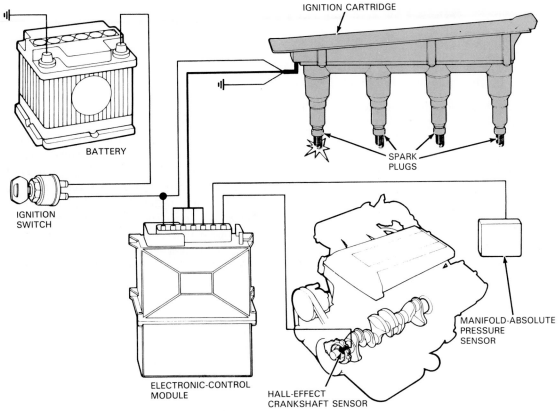

Fig. 32-29 Layout of capacitor-discharge ignition, showing the ignition cartridge. The spark occurs when a switch or transistor closes the primary circuit. This allows the capacitor to discharge through the ignition coil and produce the high-voltage spark. (*Saab Cars USA, Inc.*)

absolute pressure (MAP) sensor provides the ECM with information on engine load (➤19-13). A *detonation* or *knock sensor* (➤18-9) signals when detonation occurs. This indicates the need for less spark advance.

The ECM triggers the proper coil to fire at the proper time. Individual control of the ignition coils allows the ECM to vary ignition timing from cylinder to cylinder. This can be done within the same crankshaft revolution.

Almost instantly after turning the ignition key ON, each spark plug in sequence fires about 50 times. This cleans and dries the spark-plug electrodes to aid starting. If the engine fails to start, all spark plugs together then fire about 1000 times. This occurs after the driver releases the key and again tries to start. When the engine runs at 600 rpm or higher, the ignition system provides only one spark per plug.

TRADE TALK

camshaft sensor	Hall-effect switch	pickup coil	waste spark
crankshaft sensor	ignition module	reluctor	
distributorless ignition system	photodiode	time core	

MULTIPLE-CHOICE TEST

*Select the **one** correct, best, or most probable answer to each question.*
You can find the answers in the section indicated at the end of each question.

1. In the electronic ignition system, the primary circuit is opened and closed by (➤32-2)
   a. a solenoid
   b. contact points
   c. a mechanical switch
   d. an electronic switch

2. Rotation of the reluctor (➤32-3)
   a. moves a magnetic field through the pickup coil
   b. trips the contacts in the distributor
   c. controls secondary voltage
   d. limits vacuum advance

3. Technician A says a Hall-effect switch uses the presence or absence of a magnetic field to switch a supplied voltage on and off. Technician B says the Hall voltage switches on when a steel blade enters the air gap of a Hall-effect switch. Who is right? (➤32-6)
   a. A only
   b. B only
   c. both A and B
   d. neither A nor B

4. Ignition systems with electronic spark advance include an ECM that (➤32-7)
   a. controls engine speed
   b. calculates spark advance
   c. feeds information to a series of sensors
   d. controls centrifugal advance

5. Technician A says a light beam from a photodiode can switch an LED on and off. Technician B says a photodiode uses the presence or absence of light to switch an applied voltage on and off. Who is right? (➤32-8)
   a. A only
   b. B only
   c. both A and B
   d. neither A nor B

6. All the following are true about distributorless ignition EXCEPT (➤32-9 and 32-10)
   a. The ignition module and ECM work together to time, trigger, and distribute the high-voltage surges
   b. There are fewer moving parts, less radio interference, and increased spark-timing accuracy
   c. The waste-spark method fires two plugs, one on the intake stroke and one on the exhaust stroke
   d. Most of the spark energy is used to jump the spark-plug gap in the cylinder on compression

7. After the sync pulse from the crankshaft sensor, the ignition module triggers each coil at the proper time by (➤32-11)
   a. counting the passing notches
   b. checking the reference voltage
   c. referring to the cam sensor
   d. reducing battery voltage

8. Technician A says the cam-sensor signal advances and retards camshaft timing. Technician B says the cam-sensor signal advances and retards ignition timing. Who is right? (➤32-12)
   a. A only
   b. B only
   c. both A and B
   d. neither A nor B

9. All the following are true about the direct multiple-coil ignition shown in Figs. 32-26 and 32-27 EXCEPT (➤32-13)
   a. each coil fires two spark plugs
   b. spark-plug cables are eliminated
   c. closing the primary circuit fires the plugs
   d. only a crankshaft sensor is needed

10. In a capacitor-discharge ignition, the spark occurs when (➤32-14)
    a. a switch or transistor closes the primary circuit
    b. a switch or transistor opens the primary circuit
    c. the capacitor charges with battery voltage
    d. the capacitor charges with 40,000 volts

REVIEW QUESTIONS

1. What is the difference between the ignition module and the electronic-control module (ECM) and the jobs that each performs? (➤32-2 and 32-5)

2. What opens and closes the primary circuit when the engine is in its limp-in or limited-operating strategy (LOS) mode? (➤32-5)

3. How does a Hall-effect switch operate? (➤32-6)

4. What is the waste-spark method of spark distribution, and what effect does it have on spark-plug firing voltage? (➤32-10)

5. Describe the differences in the signals from a cam sensor and a crank sensor. (➤32-11 and 32-12)

CHAPTER 33

IGNITION-SYSTEM DIAGNOSIS AND SERVICE

After studying this chapter, and with proper instruction and equipment, you should be able to:

- List the nine conditions in the ignition-system trouble-diagnosis chart and explain the causes and corrections for each.
- Diagnose ignition-system troubles using the spark tester, oscilloscope, breakout box, and stored trouble codes.
- Inspect and replace the distributor cap, rotor, coil, secondary cables, and spark plugs.
- Check and service the distributor.
- Check and adjust ignition timing.

➤ 33-1 SERVICING IGNITION SYSTEMS

No ignition system is maintenance free. All have parts that deteriorate, wear, and sometimes fail. Various inspections, tests, and services are performed on the ignition system to help prolong normal engine operation. Many of these procedures are the same for both contact-point (Chap. 31) and electronic ignition systems (Fig. 33-1).

When performing ignition-system service, look for the *vehicle emission control information* (VECI) label (Fig. 3-4) in the engine compartment. The VECI label has specifications and tuneup instructions for the engine in the vehicle. The information includes firing order, how to set ignition timing, recommended spark plug, and spark-plug gap.

IGNITION-SYSTEM TROUBLE DIAGNOSIS

➤ 33-2 IGNITION-SYSTEM TROUBLES

For the engine to run, it must have good compression and be properly timed. The cylinders must receive a combustible air-fuel mixture. Then sparks hot enough to ignite

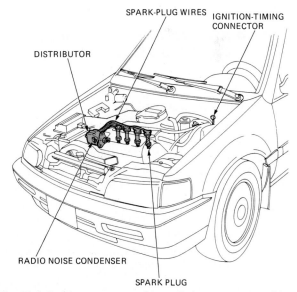

Fig. 33-1 Ignition system on a four-cylinder transverse engine. *(American Honda Motor Company, Inc.)*

the mixture must jump the spark-plug gaps. If any of these conditions is missing, the engine will not start or run properly.

Automotive ignition systems vary in construction, but are similar in basic operation. All have a primary circuit that causes a spark in the secondary circuit. This spark must then be delivered to the correct spark plug at the proper time. These similarities allow the grouping of ignition-system failures into three classes:

1. Loss of energy in the primary circuit.
2. Loss of energy in the secondary circuit.
3. Out of time.

Figure 33-2 is a chart that shows various possible causes of these and other ignition-system troubles. The chart also shows the checks or corrections to make. Refer to the manufacturer's service manual for trouble-diagnosis and service procedures on specific ignition systems. The vehicle diagnostic connector and a scan tool (➤20-13) provide some ignition-system information (Fig. 20-18). However, an oscilloscope, computerized engine analyzer, or service-bay diagnostic computer is usually more helpful in diagnosing ignition-system trouble.

➤ 33-3 ENGINE CRANKS NORMALLY BUT FAILS TO START

Perform a *spark test* (➤33-12) to determine if the ignition system is delivering sparks to the spark plugs. If there is no spark, review the possible causes listed in item 1 in Fig. 33-2. A spark shows that the ignition system is probably okay, although fouled spark plugs or out-of-time ignition could cause the failure to start. However, the most likely cause is no fuel or trouble in the fuel system. The fuel system is not delivering a combustible air-fuel mixture. More possible causes are improper operation of the valves, loss of compression, and other engine conditions.

➤ 33-4 ENGINE BACKFIRES BUT FAILS TO START

A *backfire* is a "pop" or "bang" in the intake manifold or exhaust manifold. It occurs when the spark plug fires while an intake or exhaust valve is open and a combustible mixture is present. Then combustion starts, and noise and flame pop back through the throttle body or exhaust system. Improper ignition timing or *cross-firing* may cause backfire. Cross-firing occurs when the high-voltage surge jumps from its normal path to a nearby terminal or spark-plug cable causing the wrong spark plug to fire. Defective insulation or improper routing of secondary cables allows cross-firing. Also, this can occur if a defective or wet distributor cap or rotor allows high-voltage leakage between terminals.

➤ 33-5 ENGINE RUNS BUT MISSES

A missing cylinder or intermittent misfire jumping from one cylinder to another cannot be located by listening. However, the engine runs roughly and lacks power. When one cylinder misses, the cause could be a defective spark plug or spark-plug cable. The cause could also be a bad

connection or high-voltage arcing across the distributor cap or through the cable insulation. In the engine, a stuck or burned valve or loss of compression resulting from broken piston rings may cause misfiring.

A miss that jumps around may be caused by defects with the ignition module or the *primary trigger* (➤33-13). This includes the breaker cam and contact points, reluctor and pickup coil, shutters and Hall-effect switch, and light-beam and photodiodes (Chap. 32). Other causes include erratic operation of mechanical spark-advance devices and the fuel system delivering a rich or lean mixture. An excessively lean mixture will not fire. An excessively rich mixture can wet or foul spark plugs, causing misfire. The technician normally uses an ignition oscilloscope (➤33-15) to isolate the cause of these problems.

➤ 33-6 ENGINE RUNS BUT BACKFIRES

Improper ignition timing and cross-firing (➤33-4) may cause this condition. Overheated valves or spark plugs, or deposits on the intake valves can cause *preignition* (➤16-8) and backfire. Incorrect air-fuel ratios can cause backfiring. A lean mixture may backfire through the throttle body. A rich mixture or a defective *air-injection system* or *antibackfire valve* (Chap. 36) will cause backfire in the exhaust system.

➤ 33-7 ENGINE OVERHEATS

Loss of coolant through leaks in the cooling system causes most engine overheating. Other causes include a loose or broken fan belt, a defective thermostat, or a defective fan clutch. Engines with an electric fan (➤25-10) may overheat if the thermostatic switch or fan motor fails. Without the fan running, too little air flows through the radiator at low speed to carry away the excess heat. Chapter 26 covers cooling-system trouble diagnosis.

Late ignition or valve timing, lack of engine oil, overloading the engine, or high-speed, high altitude, or hot climate operation can cause engine overheating. Freezing of the coolant causes lack of coolant circulation. This results in local hot spots and boiling. Having no vacuum advance may also cause overheating.

➤ 33-8 ENGINE LACKS POWER

Incorrect ignition timing and any of the conditions in ➤33-5 may cause an engine to lose power. An engine that runs but misses has reduced power. Another cause is a restricted exhaust system which creates excessive back pressure. This prevents normal exhaust flow from the engine so pressure remains in the cylinders. Then a full air-fuel charge cannot enter during the intake stroke. Thick engine oil, the wrong fuel, or excessive rolling resistance can give the impression that the engine lacks power.

Condition	Possible Cause	Check or Correction
1. Engine cranks normally but fails to start (➤33-3)	a. No voltage to ignition system b. Ignition-module lead open, grounded, loose, or corroded c. Primary connections not tight d. Ignition coil open or shorted e. Defective reluctor or pickup coil f. Ignition-module defective g. Defective cap or rotor h. Fuel system faulty i. Engine faulty	Check battery, ignition switch, wiring Repair as needed Clean, seat connectors Test coil, replace if defective Replace Replace Replace See Chaps. 20 and 22 See Chaps. 37 and 38
2. Engine backfires but fails to start (➤33-4)	a. Incorrect timing b. Moisture in cap c. Voltage leak across cap d. Secondary cables not connected in firing order e. Cross-firing between secondary cables	Set timing Dry cap Replace cap Reconnect correctly Replace defective cables
3. Engine runs but misses (➤33-5)	a. Spark plugs fouled or faulty b. Cap or rotor faulty c. Secondary cables defective d. Defective coil e. Bad connections f. High-voltage leak g. Advance mechanisms defective h. Defective fuel system i. Mechanical problems in engine	Clean, regap, or replace Replace Replace Replace Clean, tighten Check cap, rotor, secondary cables Check, repair or replace See Chaps. 20 and 22 Repair
4. Engine runs but backfires (➤33-6)	a. Incorrect timing b. Ignition cross-firing c. Faulty antibackfire valve d. Spark plugs of wrong heat range e. Defective air-injection system f. Engine overheating g. Fuel system not supplying proper air-fuel ratio h. Engine defects such as carbon deposits on valves	Set timing Check cables, cap, rotor for leakage paths Replace Install correct plugs Check system See item 5 See Chaps. 20 and 22 See Chaps. 37 and 38
5. Engine overheats (➤33-7)	a. Late timing b. Lack of coolant or other trouble in cooling system c. Late valve timing or other engine conditions	Set timing See Chap. 26 See Chaps. 37 and 38
6. Engine lacks power (➤33-8)	a. Incorrect timing b. Troubles listed in Item 3 c. Exhaust system restricted d. Thick engine oil e. Wrong fuel f. Excessive rolling resistance g. Engine overheats	Set timing Clear Change, using correct viscosity oil Use correct fuel Check tires, brakes, alignment See item 5
7. Engine pings (spark knock) (➤33-9)	a. Incorrect timing b. Wrong fuel c. Spark plugs of wrong heat range d. Advance mechanism defective e. Carbon buildup in cylinders	Set timing Use correct fuel Install correct plugs Repair or replace Service engine
8. Spark-plugs defective (➤33-10)	a. Cracked insulator b. Plug sooty c. Plug white or gray, with blistered insulator d. Other conditions	Careless installation, install new plug Install hotter plug, correct engine condition Install cooler plug See ➤33-24
9. Engine runs on or diesels (➤33-11)	a. Idle solenoid out of adjustment or fuel shut-off faulty b. Hot spots in combustion chambers c. Engine overheating d. Advanced timing	Adjust or replace Service engine See item 5 Set timing

Fig. 33-2 Ignition-system trouble-diagnosis chart.

➤ **33-9 ENGINE PINGS (SPARK KNOCK)**

Pinging or detonation, also called *spark knock*, may be caused by excessively advanced timing. Other ignition-system causes include faulty advance mechanisms (which allow excessive advance) and spark plugs of the wrong heat range. Some causes are not related to the ignition system, such as fuel with an octane rating too low for the engine. Another is carbon buildup in the combustion chambers. This increases the compression ratio and detonation results. The carbon may get so hot that it glows and causes preignition (➤16-4).

➤ **33-10 SPARK-PLUGS DEFECTIVE**

Spark plugs that run too cold will foul. Plugs that run too hot will wear away rapidly. The plug gap increases due to this eroding effect of the spark combined with the high temperature of the electrodes. Any of these conditions may cause misfiring (➤33-25).

➤ **33-11 ENGINE RUNS ON OR DIESELS**

If the throttle valve does not close completely when the ignition key is turned off, the engine may run on or diesel. Air-fuel mixture gets past the throttle valve and ignites from hot spots in the combustion chambers. This may occur on a carbureted engine because of a defective or improperly adjusted *idle solenoid* (➤22-9).

IGNITION-SYSTEM TESTING

➤ **33-12 SPARK TEST**

When an engine cranks normally but does not start, make a spark test (Fig. 33-3). This quick check of the ignition system determines if high-voltage surges from the coil secondary winding reach the spark plugs.

    Disconnect the spark-plug cable from a spark plug. Insert a metal extender into the terminal at the end of the cable. Using *insulated pliers*, hold the extender about 3/8 inch [10 mm] from the cylinder head or block (Fig. 33-3A). Or attach the cable terminal to a *spark tester* (Fig. 33-3B). Then fasten the tester to a good ground on the engine.

CAUTION!

Hold secondary cables with insulated pliers made of nonconductive material. Do not use metal pliers with insulated handles. The spark in a high-energy ignition system can jump an inch [25.4 mm] or more. It could jump around or through the insulation and give you a dangerous shock. Be sure there is no fuel or fuel vapor near where the spark will occur. The spark could ignite the fuel causing a fire or explosion.

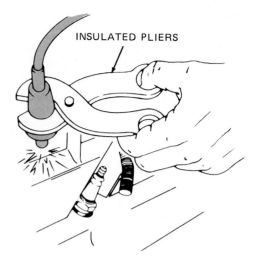

A. SPARK TEST TO GROUND

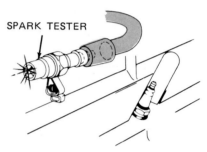

B. USING A SPARK TESTER

Fig. 33-3 Making a spark test (A) using insulated pliers and (B) using a spark tester. *(ATW)*

    Be sure the battery is charged. Crank the engine and watch for sparking across the gap. If blue sparks jump the gap when the engine cranks, the trouble is probably in the fuel system. No sparking indicates trouble in the ignition system. Make a *triggering test* (➤33-13) of the primary circuit. This will show if the primary circuit is opening and closing.

➤ **33-13 TRIGGERING TEST**

All ignition systems have a switch (contact points or electronic) that turns the primary current on and off. This switching action sends pulses of dc current through the coil primary winding. If the primary current does not pulse on and off, the magnetic field in the coil does not build up and collapse. Then no high-voltage surge appears in the secondary circuit.

    When no spark occurs during a spark test (➤33-12), use an *electronic circuit tester* or a *digital logic probe* (➤27-14) to make a triggering test of the primary circuit. Follow the connecting procedure in the manufacturer's operating instructions. Then contact the coil negative terminal or lead with the probe tip. Crank the engine. The *pulse LED* should flash on and off. This shows the triggering of the primary circuit as it switches the primary current on and off. If the LED does not flash, the triggering system is not working.

➤ 33-14 OSCILLOSCOPE PATTERNS

The *oscilloscope* or *scope* (➤31-6) is used to analyze ignition-system operation. The scope patterns show

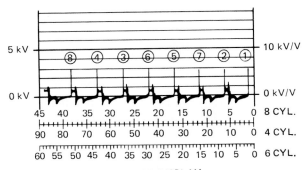

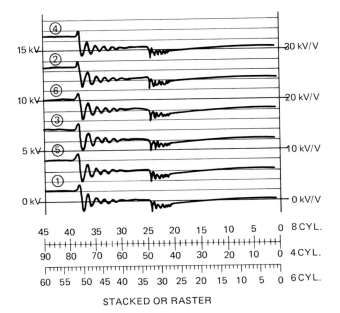

STACKED OR RASTER

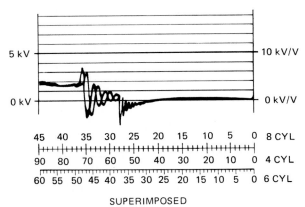

SUPERIMPOSED

Fig. 33-4 Three ways to display ignition secondary voltages for all cylinders in an engine. (*Sun Electric Corporation*)

ignition-system troubles and help pinpoint their causes. Figure 31-10 shows the basic secondary-voltage pattern for one spark-plug firing cycle.

The scope shows other ignition-system patterns which may vary slightly from system to system. These include patterns that show the firing of all spark plugs in the engine (Fig. 33-4). Frequently-used patterns are the *parade* or *display* pattern, the *stacked* or *raster* pattern, and the *superimposed* pattern.

The parade or display pattern (Fig. 33-4, top) shows all plugs firing in a single line. The pattern reads from left to right in the firing order. The firing line for cylinder 1 is on the right. In the stacked or raster pattern (Fig. 33-4, center), each spark-plug firing cycle appears one above the other in the firing order. This allows a comparison among the traces to show any abnormal conditions in one or more cylinders. The superimposed pattern (Fig. 33-4, bottom) places all traces on top of each other. Then the variation among cylinders can be seen.

➤ 33-15 USING THE OSCILLOSCOPE

To display the ignition-system voltage patterns, the scope must have four inputs:

1. Ignition primary circuit.
2. Ground.
3. Ignition secondary circuit.
4. Reference signal to locate start of sequence and trigger retrace.

These connections allow the scope to show voltage patterns from both the primary and secondary circuits.

Figure 33-5 shows how to connect a scope to an engine that has a distributor and a separate coil. The scope

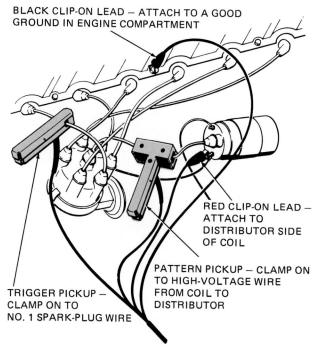

Fig. 33-5 How to connect a scope to an engine that has a distributor and a separate coil.

415

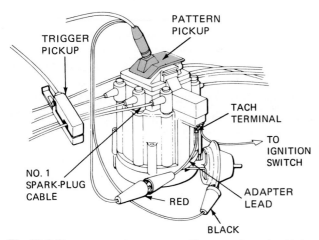

Fig. 33-6 How to connect a scope to a V-type engine using high-energy ignition (HEI) with the coil in the distributor cap. Note the special pattern pickup required. *(Sun Electric Corporation)*

primary leads attach to the coil negative terminal and ground. The *secondary leads* have inductive pickups on the ends. The *pattern pickup* clamps around the coil wire. This picks up the high-voltage pulses in the secondary circuit. The *trigger pickup* clamps around the number 1 spark-plug wire. This pulse is the reference signal to locate the start of the firing order. The pulse for cylinder 1 "triggers retrace" by causing the scope to begin another set of traces. Figure 33-6 shows how to connect the leads to a General Motors HEI distributor with the coil in the cap.

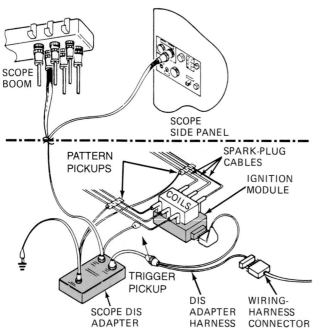

Fig. 33-7 How to connect a scope to an engine with distributorless ignition. Note the adapter installed between the wiring-harness connector and the ignition module. Two secondary leads, or inputs, are needed—one for even-numbered cylinders and one for odd-numbered cylinders. *(General Motors Corporation)*

Some scopes are not made for attachment to distributorless ignition systems (DIS) and direct ignition systems. These systems do not have a high-voltage coil wire and coil primary terminals are not accessible. If connected, the scope may display a pattern. However, the pattern may not accurately show the actions and voltages in the ignition system.

One scope for distributorless ignition systems has two secondary leads (Fig. 33-7). One is for the even-numbered cylinders, the other for the odd-numbered cylinders. Each spark-plug firing becomes a *secondary input* to the pattern pickups on each lead. A *DIS adapter* connects between the wiring-harness connector and the ignition module. This provides the connections to the primary circuit.

➤ 33-16 READING SCOPE PATTERNS

Conditions in the ignition system and in the cylinder affect the oscilloscope pattern. The way it varies from normal indicates where the electrical problem exists. The scope can detect wide or narrow spark-plug gaps, open spark-plug cables, a shorted coil, and improper *dwell*.

Dwell is the length of time current flows in the coil primary winding. In General Motors HEI systems, dwell increases with engine speed and may vary from cylinder to cylinder (Fig. 33-8). In other electronic ignition systems, dwell may increase, decrease, or stay the same as engine speed increases.

The scope also detects engine conditions that change the *firing voltage* (Fig. 33-9). This is the voltage needed to fire the plug. These conditions may alter the length or slope of the *spark line*. Figure 33-10 shows various abnormal secondary patterns. When using a scope, refer to the scope manufacturer's operating instructions. It usually shows several patterns and possible causes for different ignition systems. Knowing the basic ignition patterns and what each section of the pattern represents makes the oscilloscope a valuable tool for isolating engine and ignition problems.

Some scopes display test results as numbers instead of patterns and waveforms. Scopes in computerized engine

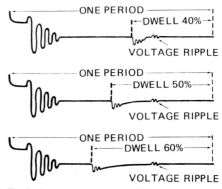

Fig. 33-8 Typical scope patterns for different cylinders in an engine with HEI. *(Oldsmobile Division of General Motors Corporation)*

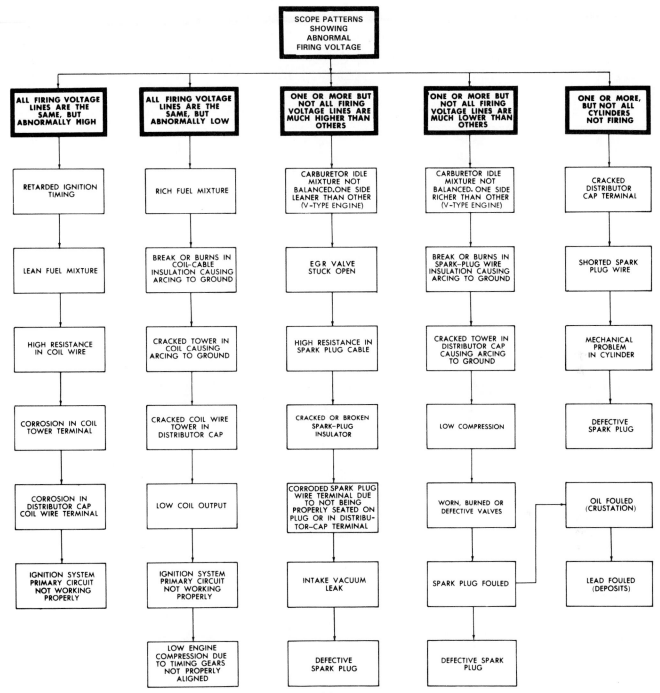

Fig. 33-9 Secondary-circuit trouble-diagnosis chart for abnormal firing voltage. *(Chrysler Corporation)*

analyzers and service-bay diagnostic computers may display both numbers and patterns. Figure 33-11 is a screen or *page* showing spark-plug firing voltages. These are for a V-6 engine with distributorless ignition and three coils. The voltages are given as *kv* or kilovolts (*kilo* means thousand). Firing voltage for cylinder 1 is 10.3 kv or 10,300 volts.

Figure 33-11 also shows engine speed and oil temperature. In addition, the display includes the number of oscillations in the intermediate section (Fig. 31-10) for each coil firing. The *oscillation* reading of "3,3,3"

indicates the normal condition of three oscillations in each of the three coils, read in the order in which the coils fire.

➤ 33-17 STORED IGNITION-SYSTEM TROUBLE CODES

An electronic engine control system has the ability to store trouble codes. However, most of these systems store few codes that indicate trouble in the ignition system. A scan tool may retrieve the code (➤20-13), but may not help further diagnose the problem.

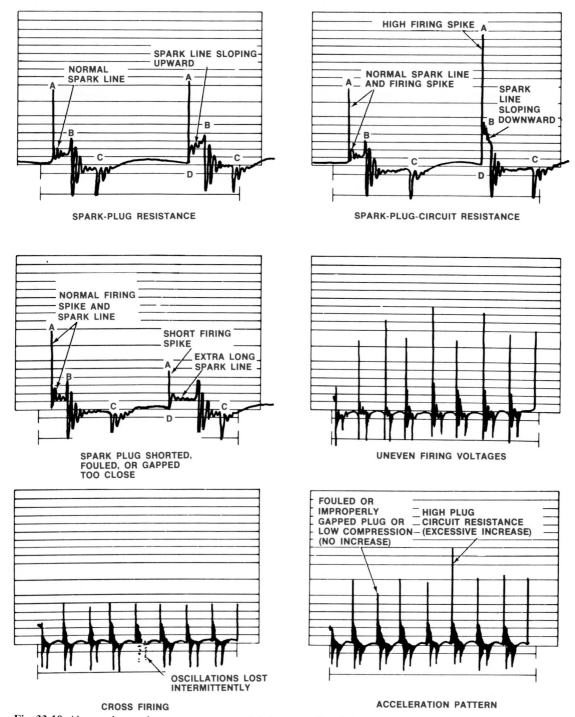

Fig. 33-10 Abnormal secondary scope patterns and their causes. *(Ford Motor Company)*

Figure 20-13 shows the trouble codes that can set in some General Motors cars. Code 42, *electronic spark timing* (EST) *circuit,* is the only code that directly indicates improper operation of the ignition system. A defective ignition module or ECM and open or shorted connections or wiring will set the code. A Code 12, *no distributor reference pulse,* sets in some systems if the Hall-effect switch fails in the distributor (➤32-6).

Typical data that a scan tool or engine analyzer can access through the vehicle diagnostic connector is shown in Fig. 20-18. Only *spark advance* provides information on ignition-system operation. The printout of scan-tool data in Fig. 20-19 also includes *knock retard* and *knock signal.* The printout shows a spark advance (item 15) of seven degrees. The spark advance is reduced by zero degrees of knock retard (item 17). This is because the ECM senses no detonation or knock signal (item 18). Similar data may be supplied by the on-board diagnostic system (➤20-13).

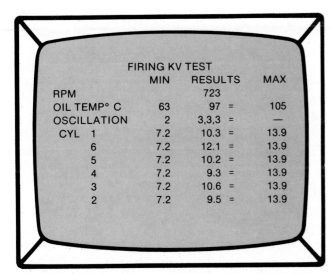

FIRING KV TEST			
	MIN	RESULTS	MAX
RPM		723	
OIL TEMP° C	63	97 =	105
OSCILLATION	2	3,3,3 =	—
CYL 1	7.2	10.3 =	13.9
6	7.2	12.1 =	13.9
5	7.2	10.2 =	13.9
4	7.2	9.3 =	13.9
3	7.2	10.6 =	13.9
2	7.2	9.5 =	13.9

Fig. 33-11 Spark-plug firing voltages displayed digitally on a scope screen. *(Sun Electric Corporation)*

> **NOTE** Other electronic engine control systems can set additional trouble codes. Refer to the vehicle service manual for testing and diagnostic procedures.

➤ **33-18 TESTING WITH A BREAKOUT BOX**

Sometimes tests are needed of difficult to reach parts and circuits in distributorless and direct ignition systems. These tests can be made without needless disassembly by using a *breakout box* (Fig. 33-12). This is an electrical tester that connects in series with the ECM.

Test jacks on the breakout box provide access to every ECM input and output circuit. The test leads of a digital multitester plug into the test jacks. This permits measurement of the voltage, resistance, and continuity of the selected circuit. Piercing insulation on wiring and *back-probing* connectors is avoided. Backprobing is contacting a terminal through the back of a connector (Fig. 27-22). This can push a loose terminal out of the connector, causing possible opens or intermittents.

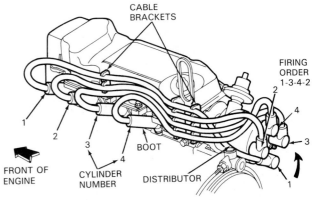

Fig. 33-13 Spark-plug cables should be clean and attached tightly to the distributor-cap or coil terminals and the spark plugs. The cables should be properly positioned in the cable brackets. *(Ford Motor Company)*

Fig. 33-12 Using a breakout box connected in series with the ECM to make electrical tests. This avoids piercing insulation on wires and backprobing connectors. *(Concept Technology, Inc.)*

419

CHECKING IGNITION-SYSTEM COMPONENTS

➤ 33-19 IGNITION-SYSTEM MAINTENANCE

Many parts in the ignition system should be inspected or replaced at the time or mileage given in the vehicle maintenance schedule (➤3-9). These include the spark plugs, spark-plug cables, and distributor cap and rotor (if used).

Make a visual inspection if parts fail or other problems occur in the ignition system. This will locate and identify many troubles and potential troubles.

➤ 33-20 CHECKING SECONDARY WIRING

Secondary cables should be clean and attached tightly to the distributor cap or coils and the spark plugs (Fig. 33-13). Terminals should be fully seated. Loose connections corrode and increase in resistance. Boots should be in good condition and fit tightly on the cap or coils and spark plugs. Loose or punctured boots allow water to enter the towers. Erosion, arc-over, and other ignition problems may result.

To disconnect a cable, grasp the boot, twist and pull at the same time. Do not pull on the cable. Pull on the boot, or use a *spark-plug boot puller*. It has fingers that fit behind the boot. Some Hall-effect distributors have push-in cable terminals that lock in place in the cap (Fig. 33-14). To detach the cables, remove the cap. Use needle-nose pliers to release the terminals.

Clean dirty cables and boots with *waterless hand cleaner* or liquid detergent (soap). Then wipe dry. Examine the boots and cable insulation for brittleness, burns, cracks, and other damage (Fig. 33-15). Bend each cable or wrap it around your finger. Cracks will open and be easily seen. Any of these conditions allows high-voltage leakage and causes engine miss.

Some manufacturers recommend coating the inside of each boot with *silicone grease* before installation. To install new secondary cables or a new cap, replace one cable at a time (Fig. 33-16). Grasp the boot and push the

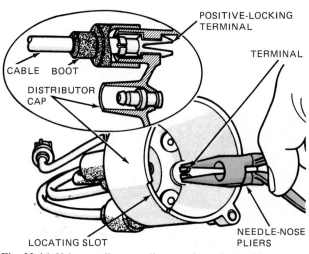

Fig. 33-14 Using needle-nose pliers to release the positive-locking type of push-in terminals on the ends of the spark-plug cables in a Hall-effect distributor cap. *(Chrysler Corporation)*

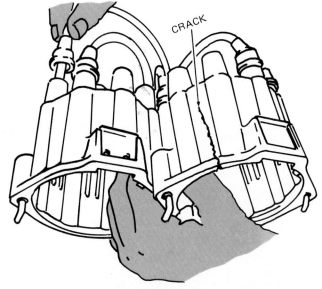

Fig. 33-16 Changing cables from an old cap to a new cap.

  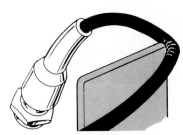

(A) VIBRATION DAMAGE   (B) HEAT DAMAGE   (C) ABRASION DAMAGE

Fig. 33-15 Checking the condition of the boots and insulation on the spark-plug cables. *(Belden Automotive Wire & Cable)*

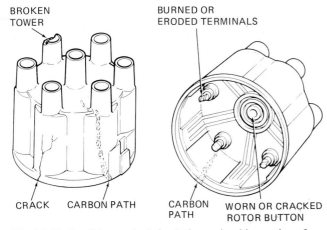

BROKEN TOWER

BURNED OR ERODED TERMINALS

CRACK   CARBON PATH

CARBON PATH

WORN OR CRACKED ROTOR BUTTON

Fig. 33-17 Conditions to look for during a visual inspection of the distributor cap. Discard the cap if any of these conditions is found. *(Chrysler Corporation)*

terminal and boot into the proper tower until the terminal seats. Then position each cable correctly in the cable brackets (Fig. 33-13) and looms. This helps prevent cable damage and cross-firing. Be sure each cable is in its specified position. Improperly positioned cables may allow an induced voltage to affect a nearby sensor or the ECM. This can set trouble codes and cause driveability problems.

➤ 33-21 CHECKING DISTRIBUTOR CAP AND ROTOR

To check the cap and rotor, remove the cap. It is held in place by screws (Fig. 31-3), spring clips (Fig. 32-2), or retaining latches (Fig. 32-6). Examine the cap for cracks, arc-over and carbon paths, cracked and worn rotor button, burned or eroded terminals, and broken cap towers (Fig. 33-17). Clean off light scaling with a knife blade. Heavy scaling requires replacing the cap.

The inside of the cap may be dirty, greasy, or coated with a powdery substance. Disconnect the cables from the cap and wash it with warm water and detergent. Scrub the deposits with a soft brush. Thoroughly rinse the cap and dry with a clean soft cloth.

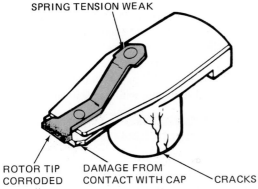

SPRING TENSION WEAK

ROTOR TIP CORRODED   DAMAGE FROM CONTACT WITH CAP   CRACKS

Fig. 33-18 Conditions to look for during a visual inspection of the rotor. Discard the rotor if any of these conditions is found. *(Chrysler Corporation)*

Inspect the rotor for cracks, weak spring tension, signs of contacting the cap, and a burned or corroded tip on the rotor blade (Fig. 33-18). Replace a rotor that has any of these conditions.

When replacing the cap, transfer the spark-plug cables to the new cap or install new cables (➤33-20). Install the cap on the distributor. Be sure the cap is properly positioned and seated. A *locating slot* (Fig. 33-14) or lug in the cap fits a matching section of the distributor housing. If the cap

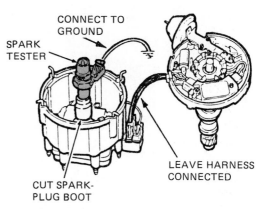

COIL CABLE

(A) SPARK TEST TO GROUND

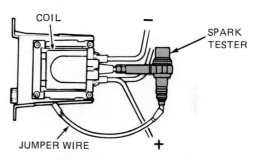

COIL

SPARK TESTER

JUMPER WIRE

(B) SPARK TESTER TO COIL

CONNECT TO GROUND

SPARK TESTER

CUT SPARK-PLUG BOOT

LEAVE HARNESS CONNECTED

(C) SPARK TESTER TO COIL IN CAP

Fig. 33-19 Checking coil operation by making a spark test. (A) Using insulated pliers to hold cable terminal near a ground. (B) Connecting a spark tester to the coil output terminal. (C) Connecting a spark tester to the coil mounted in the distributor cap. *(ATW)*

421

is not seated when the engine cranks, the rotor will hit the cap and probably break.

33-22 TESTING IGNITION COIL

Inspect the coil and coil cable. Wipe away any dirt from the coil tower using a clean cloth and soap and water. Look for cracks, carbon tracking, and arcing and burning of the tower. Replace a coil that has any of these conditions. Check for damage to the boot on the coil end of the secondary cable. Replace the cable if the boot is damaged. Arcing at the tower damages the boot. Placing a damaged boot on a new coil will cause coil failure. Replace the coil cable if it is damaged or shows carbon tracking. Continued use will also cause a new coil to fail.

Coil operation can be checked on the engine by making a spark test (Fig. 33-19). This is similar to the spark test described in ➤33-12. Disconnect the coil wire from the distributor. Insert a metal extender into the terminal. Using insulated pliers, hold the extender about 3/8 inch [10 mm]

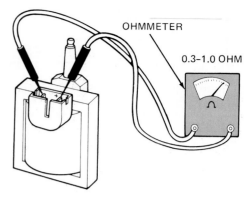

(A) PRIMARY WINDING RESISTANCE TEST

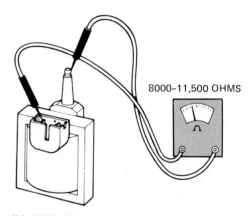

(B) SECONDARY WINDING RESISTANCE TEST

Fig. 33-21 Using an ohmmeter to check primary and secondary resistance of separate ignition coil. Replace the coil if either resistance is not within specifications. *(Ford Motor Company)*

from a good ground. Or attach a spark tester to the coil high-voltage terminal and a jumper wire from the spark tester to ground. Crank the engine and watch for sparking across the gap. If blue sparks jump the gap when the engine cranks, the coil is probably good.

The oscilloscope (➤33-16) shows the operation of the ignition coil or coils (Figs. 33-10 and 33-11). An improperly wired coil or a battery installed backward may cause an upside-down secondary pattern.

To make additional tests of the coil, follow the procedures in the vehicle service manual and the tester-manufacturer's operating instructions. This may include measuring the coil primary and secondary resistance with an ohmmeter (Fig. 27-25C). Figure 33-20 shows how to test the ignition coil mounted in the distributor cap. Figure 33-21 shows testing a separate coil with an ohmmeter. Replace the coil if it is not within specifications.

33-23 CHECKING THE DISTRIBUTOR

No spark during a spark test (➤33-12 and 33-22) may indicate a problem with the primary trigger. It may not be interrupting the current flow in the primary circuit. Or the primary trigger may be working, but the ignition module or

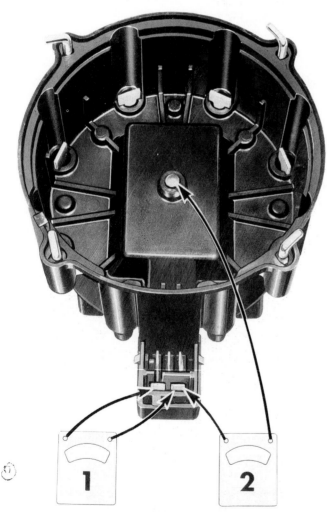

Fig. 33-20 Using an ohmmeter to check primary and secondary resistance of the HEI ignition coil, with coil mounted in distributor cap. *(Cadillac Division of General Motors Corporation)*

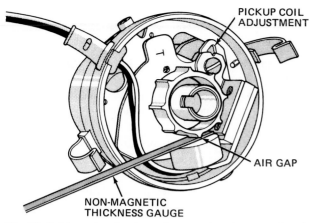

Fig. 33-22 Measuring the air gap between the reluctor tooth and the pickup coil with a nonmagnetic (brass) thickness gauge. *(Chrysler Corporation)*

other part has failed. Follow the procedures and specifications in the vehicle service manual. Typical tests and service procedures are given below.

1. CHECKING THE DISTRIBUTOR DRIVE Remove the distributor cap and verify that the rotor turns as the engine cranks. If not, there is a problem between the camshaft and the distributor drive mechanism (➤14-3). Probably the timing belt or chain has broken, or a sprocket or timing gear has stripped or broken teeth.

2. MEASURING THE AIR GAP Check the air gap between the reluctor tooth and the pickup coil (Fig. 33-22). Use a nonmagnetic (brass) thickness gauge. To set the air gap, loosen the pickup-coil holddown screw. Then insert a 0.008-inch [0.20-mm] nonmagnetic thickness gauge between the reluctor tooth and the pickup coil. Adjust the

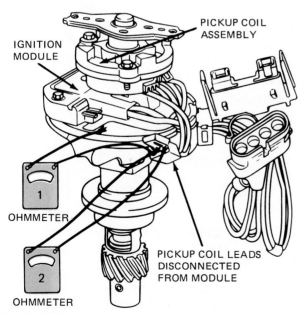

Fig. 33-23 Using an ohmmeter to test the pickup coil in an HEI distributor. *(Chevrolet Division of General Motors Corporation)*

pickup coil so the thickness gauge is snug. Then tighten the holddown screw.

3. TESTING THE PICKUP COIL Use an ohmmeter to measure the pickup-coil resistance (Fig. 33-23) while flexing the leads to check for intermittent opens. On distributors with vacuum advance, this can cause hesitation and stumbling during acceleration. In test 1, the meter should always read infinity. If not, replace the pickup coil. In test 2, the meter should read a steady value that typically is between 500 and 1500 ohms. Replace the pickup coil if the reading varies or is not within specifications.

4. TESTING THE HALL-EFFECT SWITCH To test the Hall-effect switch in General Motors distributors, connect the switch to a battery as shown in Fig. 33-24. Insert a steel thickness gauge or a knife blade in the air gap and allow the blade to rest against the magnet. The voltmeter should read within 0.5 volt of battery voltage. If not, replace the Hall-effect switch.

5. CHECKING THE IGNITION MODULE A test of the ignition module (Fig. 33-23) is to connect a "known good" module to the connectors. Try starting the engine. If the engine does not start, the fault is in the wiring or other part of the system. If the engine starts and runs normally, the original module may be defective. Reconnect the original module and try starting. Failure to start now indicates the module is defective. Apply a coat of silicone grease to the bottom of a new module and the mounting surface of the distributor. This prevents corrosion and helps dissipate heat that could damage the module. Then install the new module.

➤ 33-24 SPARK-PLUG SERVICE

Replace spark plugs at the mileage indicated in the maintenance schedule. Remove plugs for inspection whenever necessary. Look for damage and signs of abnormal conditions in the combustion chamber. Some spark plugs can be cleaned by sandblasting the tip or firing end. Then file and gap the electrodes, and reinstall the plug. However, this procedure is no longer recommended by most vehicle

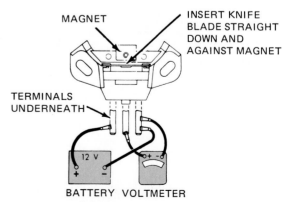

Fig. 33-24 Testing the Hall-effect switch. *(Chevrolet Division of General Motors Corporation)*

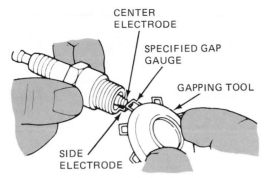

Fig. 33-25 Checking the spark-plug gap. (*Ford Motor Company*)

or spark-plug manufacturers. It may destroy a plug with a palladium or platinum tip (➤31-11), and cause misfiring of others.

To remove the spark plugs, first remove or reposition any part that blocks access to the plugs. If necessary, follow the steps in the spark-plug removal procedure in the vehicle service manual. Disconnect the cables (➤33-20) from the spark plugs. Clean the area around the plugs so dirt will not fall into the cylinders when the plugs are removed. Use the air hose to blow any dirt away from the seat, or loosen the plugs one to two turns. Then reconnect the cables and briefly run the engine. Combustion leakage around the plugs will blow away the dirt.

Use a *spark-plug socket* (➤7-10) to remove the plug and lift it out. Mark each plug as it is removed, or place it in a marked holder. This aids in identifying conditions within each cylinder. Marking also allows reinstalling the plug in the cylinder from which it was removed.

Before installing new or used spark plugs, check and adjust the gap (Fig. 33-25). The VECI label in the engine compartment (Fig. 3-4) gives the proper spark plug and gap. Bend only the side electrode to get the specified gap. The gauge should slip snugly between the tip of the center electrode and the surface of the side electrode. Do not damage the center electrode or insulator while setting the gap.

Apply a thin layer of silicone grease inside the spark-plug boot (➤33-20), if required. Wipe each plug seat in the cylinder head with a clean cloth. If the cylinder-head threads are dirty, clean the threads with a *spark-plug thread chaser and seat-cleaning tool*. Place a new gasket on the spark plug if it uses a replaceable gasket. Put antiseize compound (➤6-14) on the threads of the spark plug before installing it in an aluminum head. Avoid coating the first two threads or using an excessive amount of antiseize compound. This prevents the compound from migrating to the spark-plug electrodes and fouling the plug.

Start the spark plug into the cylinder head by hand. Be careful not to cross-thread the plug. Use a torque wrench to tighten each plug to the specified torque. Then connect the correct cable to the plug. To aid in proper installation, many spark-plug cables are numbered (Fig. 33-26).

➤ 33-25 INSPECTING SPARK-PLUG FIRING ENDS

Figure 33-27 shows several spark-plug conditions and their possible causes. Incorrect installation may also cause

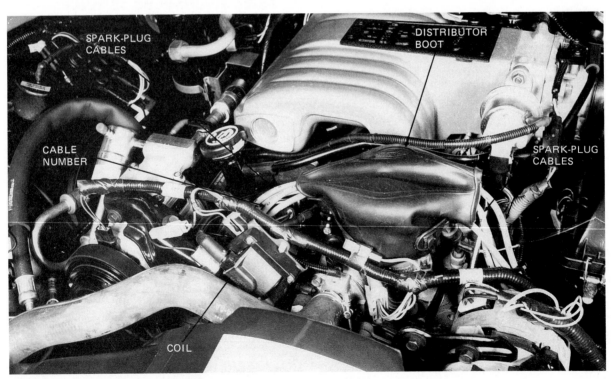

Fig. 33-26 Ignition-system layout in the engine compartment, showing the distributor boot and numbered spark-plug cables. (*ATW*)

NORMAL

Light tan or gray deposits, almost brown with LPG or natural-gas fuel. Yellow or tan deposits may indicate leaded fuel. Slight electrode wear. Plug running at correct temperature in a "healthy" engine.

RECOMMENDATION: Set gap and reinstall. Replace if over recommended mileage.

WORN

Electrodes worn away. This may cause firing voltage to double (even higher on acceleration), poor engine performance, and loss of fuel economy. Plug has served its useful life.

RECOMMENDATION: Set gap and install new plugs.

PREIGNITION

Melting of center electrode, later melting of ground electrode and insulator.

RECOMMENDATION: Check for glowing deposits or hot spots in combustion chamber, poor control of engine heat, crossfiring, spark-plug heat range too high for engine or operating conditions. Set gap and install new plugs.

DETONATION

Insulator nose has cracked and broken away as a result of shock waves from this abnormal combustion.

RECOMMENDATION: Check for faulty EGR valve, lean air-fuel mixture, overadvanced ignition timing, low-octane gasoline. Set gap and install new plugs.

MECHANICAL DAMAGE

Foreign object in combustion chamber or on piston has struck ground electrode, forcing it into center electrode which has bent and broken off insulator nose. Valve overlap may allow object to travel from one cylinder to another.

RECOMMENDATION: Check that no foreign object remains in any cylinder. Make compression test. Set gap and install new plugs.

GAP BRIDGED

Caused by conditions similar to splash fouling. Combustion deposits thrown loose lodge between electrodes, causing short and misfire. Fluffy materials that accumulate on side electrode melt and bridge gap when a sudden heavy load applied to engine.

RECOMMENDATION: Set gap and install new plugs.

CARBON FOULED

Soft, sooty carbon deposits with a dry, black appearance.

RECOMMENDATION: If only one or two plugs fouled, check for sticking valves, cracked distributor cap, bad secondary wiring, malfunctioning fuel injector. If all plugs fouled, check for incorrect spark-plug heat range, rich air-fuel mixture, stuck heat-control valve or choke valve, low secondary voltage, inoperative heated-air system, low cylinder compression. Set gap and install new plugs.

OIL FOULED

Wet, oily coating. Plug shorted by excessive oil entering combustion chamber.

RECOMMENDATION: Check for worn piston rings or cylinder walls, worn valve guides or valve-stem seals, plugged or inoperative PCV system. Set gap and install new plugs.

SPLASHED FOULED

May occur after overdue tuneup. Deposits caused by misfiring and low-power operation break loose when tuneup restores normal combustion temperature. These deposits are then thrown against the hot insulator.

RECOMMENDATION: Set gap and install new plugs.

ASH FOULED

Buildup of deposits primarily from burning of oil and fuel additives during normal combustion. Ash deposits usually nonconductive, but accumulations may cause plug misfire.

RECOMMENDATION: Set gap and install new plugs.

OVERHEATED

Blistered, white or gray insulator nose. Rapid electrode-gap wear.

RECOMMENDATION: Check for overadvanced ignition timing, poor engine cooling, lean air-fuel mixture, leaking intake manifold, spark-plug heat-range too hot. Set gap and install new plugs.

GLAZED

Insulator has shiny conductive coating that may cause misfire at high engine speed. Results from sudden increase in temperature during hard acceleration. Then normal metallic deposits melt before they are shed from the insulator.

RECOMMENDATION: Consider spark plugs with colder heat range. Set gap and install new plugs.

Fig. 33-27 Conditions of spark-plug firing ends and their possible causes. *(Champion Spark Plug Company)*

spark-plug overheating. The plug must be properly tightened to provide a good heat path. Dropping, careless installation, and improper adjustment of the plug gap may crack the insulator.

TIMING THE IGNITION

➤ 33-26 DISTRIBUTOR REMOVAL AND INSTALLATION

Some service procedures require removing the distributor from the engine. Try not to turn the crankshaft while the distributor is out. This simplifies reinstalling the distributor. If the crankshaft turns, the proper relationship (timing) must be reestablished between the distributor rotor and piston position. Most engines *time* on number 1 piston.

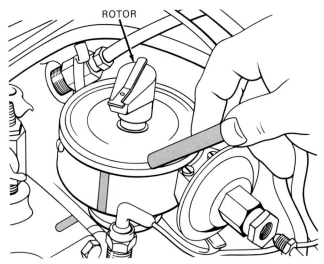

Fig. 33-28 Marking the location of the distributor in the engine. *(ATW)*

NOTE Not all distributors mount vertically. Some mount horizontally and are driven off the end of an overhead camshaft (Fig. 33-13). The basic procedure below covers many distributors. Follow the procedure in the vehicle service manual for other distributors.

1. DISTRIBUTOR REMOVAL Remove the air cleaner or any parts blocking access to the distributor. A water-protective *boot* (Fig. 33-26) may cover the distributor cap and cables. If so, remove it. Disconnect the vacuum line from the distributor vacuum-advance unit, if one is used. Disconnect the primary lead. Remove the distributor cap and move the cap-and-cable assembly to one side. Use a marker or scratch a mark on the distributor housing, under the tip of the rotor (Fig. 33-28). Make another mark on the engine in line with the first mark. These marks locate the position of the distributor to the camshaft. Remove the distributor hold-down bolt and clamp. Lift the distributor from the engine.

2. DISTRIBUTOR INSTALLATION Align the marks on the distributor housing and engine (Fig. 33-28). Check that the base gasket or O-ring seal (Fig. 32-2) is in place on the distributor. Then install the distributor. As a gear-driven distributor seats (Fig. 33-29), the shaft and rotor will turn as the spiral gears mesh. Raise the distributor and turn the rotor back one tooth. Then reinstall the distributor. The rotor should move into the correct position, with the tip and marks in line.

If the distributor does not completely seat, the oil-pump shaft is not engaging. Press down firmly on the distributor housing and bump the engine with the starting motor. Keep your hand clear of the rotor. When the oil-pump shaft aligns, the distributor will drop into place.

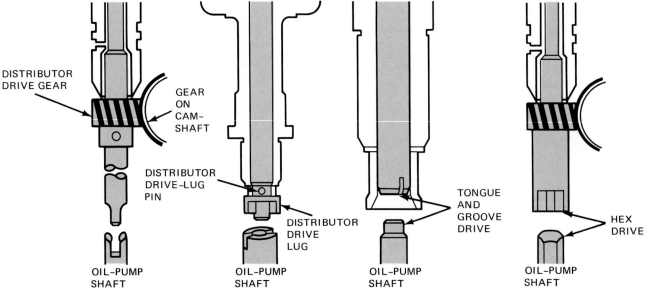

Fig. 33-29 Methods of driving the ignition distributor and oil pump. *(ATW)*

During installation, the distributor must be timed to the engine if the crankshaft has turned while the distributor was out. Locate the firing order and cylinder numbering illustration (Fig. 33-30) for the engine. This is in the vehicle service manual and auto repair manuals. Note the position of the cap latches or screws. Install the distributor in the engine in the same position. Also note the location of the number 1 terminal on the distributor cap. When the number 1 piston is at TDC ending the compression stroke, the rotor tip should point to the number 1 terminal in the cap.

To time the distributor to the engine, remove the number 1 spark plug. Locate the *timing marks* (Fig. 33-31). Most engines have a rotating mark that aligns with a specified stationary mark when ignition timing is correct. The timing

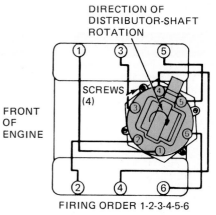

Fig. 33-30 Firing order and cylinder numbering of a V-6 engine, showing proper position and wiring of the distributor cap. (*Chrysler Corporation*)

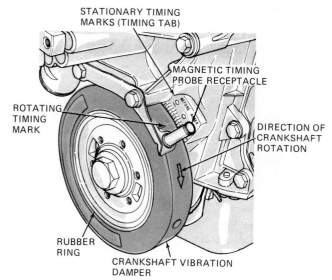

Fig. 33-31 Timing marks and magnetic-timing probe hole on front of an engine. (*Chrysler Corporation*)

marks are usually on the crankshaft vibration damper and the engine front cover. Some are on the flywheel and the housing.

Place a shop towel over your finger and cover the spark-plug hole. Do not allow your finger to enter the spark-plug hole! Crank the engine with the starting motor until you feel compression pressure push against your finger. Continue bumping the engine with the starting motor until the timing marks align. This shows that the number 1 piston is in firing position. Install the distributor, making sure the rotor tip aligns with the cap terminal for the number 1 spark plug.

Install but do not tighten the distributor clamp and bolt. Rotate the distributor until the primary trigger opens the primary circuit. This occurs when:

1. The contact points start to open (Fig. 31-8).
2. The reluctor tip passes alignment with the pole piece (Fig. 32-4).
3. The shutter leaves the air-gap in the Hall-effect switch (Fig. 32-10).
4. The rotating disk interrupts the light beam striking the photodiode (Fig. 32-15).

Hold the cap in its mounting position above the distributor. Check that the rotor tip aligns with the number 1 terminal on the cap. Install the cap. Connect the primary lead. Start the engine and check that the oil light in the instrument panel goes out. If not, stop the engine and check for proper seating of the distributor.

Set the ignition timing (➤33-28). Tighten the holddown bolt. Connect the vacuum hose and install any parts removed.

➤ **33-28 SETTING IGNITION TIMING**

The engine requires two types of ignition timing. One is the *basic* or *initial timing* for starting and idling. This timing is determined by the relationship between piston position and the opening of the primary circuit. The other timing, or *spark advance*, advances and retards the spark from the basic-timing setting, primarily as engine speed and load change. On some distributors, it is mechanically controlled by centrifugal- and vacuum-advance mechanisms (Chap. 31). Other ignition systems have *electronic spark advance*. It is used on many electronic distributors and in all distributorless ignition systems (Chap. 32).

Contact-point distributors should have the timing checked periodically. Always check and adjust the dwell first (➤31-4). As the contact points and rubbing block wear, ignition timing and dwell change. Electronic ignition systems normally do not require periodic timing adjustments once the timing is set.

Adjusting the basic timing so the spark occurs at the correct instant with the engine idling is called *setting the ignition timing*. On most engines with a distributor, this is performed by turning the distributor slightly. Some engines have a distributor that mounts in a fixed position. The timing may be adjusted by installing a different reluctor.

427

Ignition timing is usually not adjustable in a distributorless ignition system.

Check the timing with the engine at normal operating temperature and idling at the specified speed. Eliminate all spark advance—mechanical and electronic—so the engine is running on only basic timing. The low engine speed prevents spark advance from the centrifugal-advance mechanism in the distributor. Removing the vacuum hose from the vacuum-advance unit (Fig. 33-32) disables the vacuum advance. Plug the hose to prevent an air leak into the intake manifold. A golf tee can be used as a plug.

Follow the procedure on the VECI label to disable electronic spark advance. This may include opening a *set-timing connector* (Figs. 32-9 and 33-1) or disconnecting the SPOUT connector. On some General Motors cars, ground the test terminal (B to A) in the diagnostic connector (Fig. 20-14). Chrysler requires disconnecting the coolant-temperature sensor (➤19-16) before checking the timing on some engines.

Turning the distributor in its mounting (Fig. 33-32) adjusts the basic timing. Rotating the distributor in the direction opposite to shaft rotation advances the timing. This opens the primary circuit earlier. Turning the distributor in the same direction as shaft rotation retards the timing. The spark occurs later. Determining when the timing is properly adjusted requires the use of a *timing light* (➤33-29) or a *magnetic timing tester* (➤33-30). Initial timing and spark advance may also be read from a scan tool (Figs. 20-18 and 20-19), computerized engine analyzer, or service-bay diagnostic computer.

➤ **33-29 SETTING TIMING WITH TIMING LIGHT**

You cannot see the rapid periodic alignment of the timing marks in normal light. However, the *stroboscopic* timing light produces instant flashes that match engine speed (Fig. 33-33). This makes the marks appear to stand still. The timing light usually has a set of power leads that connect to the car battery. Another lead with an inductive pickup clamps around the number 1 spark-plug cable. Pressing the trigger causes the light to flash every time the number 1 spark-plug fires.

To adjust the timing, slightly loosen the distributor hold-down clamp bolt (Fig. 33-32). Aim the timing light at the timing marks. Turn the distributor in its mounting. The rotating timing mark will move ahead or back. When the timing is correct, the specified timing marks align. Tighten the distributor clamp bolt (Fig. 33-32). Then recheck the timing to ensure it did not change as the clamp was tightened. Remove the timing light and restore spark-advance operation.

CAUTION!

Keep your hands and the timing-light leads away from the fan and drive belts. Never stand in line with the fan. A blade might fly off and strike you.

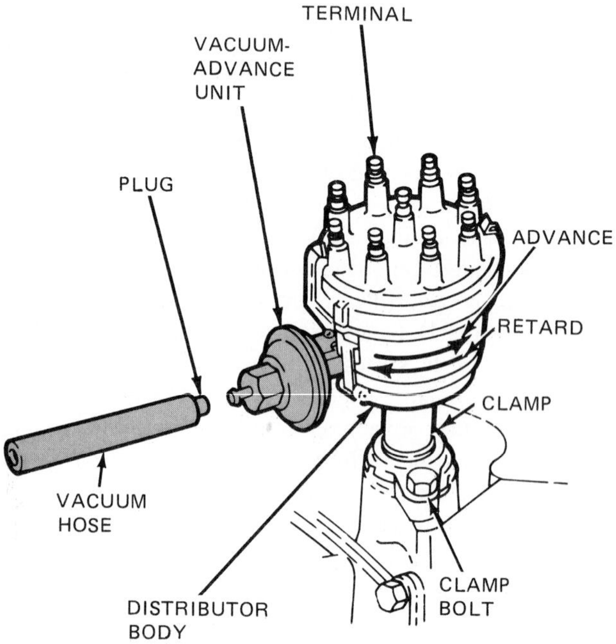

Fig. 33-32 Removing and plugging vacuum hose to distributor before loosening clamp bolt and turning distributor to set ignition timing. (*Ford Motor Company*)

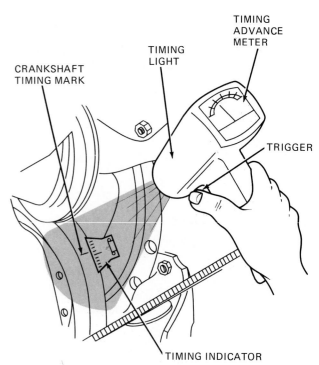

Fig. 33-33 The timing light flashes every time the number 1 spark plug fires.

➤ 33-30 CHECKING TIMING WITH MAGNETIC TIMING TESTER

Engines with a *magnetic timing probe receptacle* (Fig. 33-31) can be timed with a *magnetic timing tester*. This is basically a temporary crankshaft-position sensor (➤32-11).

Connect the tester following the manufacturer's operating instructions. Insert the magnetic probe into the probe hole (Fig. 33-34). As the engine runs, the passage of a slot in the crankshaft vibration damper interrupts a small magnetic field around the probe tip (Fig. 32-23). This signals the position of the number 1 piston to the tester. It then displays the ignition timing. Many computerized engine analyzers and service-bay diagnostic computers use the magnetic-timing probe.

Figure 33-34 shows an analog type of magnetic-timing tester. Movement of the meter pointer shows the ignition timing. Other magnetic timing testers are digital and display the number of degrees. Both types require setting the *offset selector*. This allows the meter to compensate automatically for the various offset angles used by different manufacturers when positioning the probe hole.

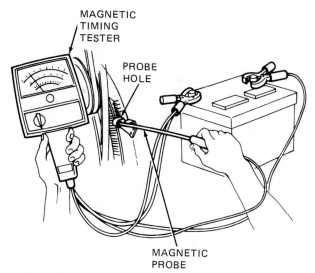

Fig. 33-34 Insert probe for magnetic timing tester into probe hole. *(Ford Motor Company)*

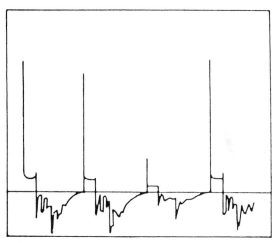

Fig. 33-35 Scope pattern of a four-cylinder engine. *(Ford Motor Company)*

TRADE TALK

backprobing	cross-firing	silicone grease	triggering test
basic timing	ignition timing	spark test	
breakout box	primary trigger	timing marks	

MULTIPLE-CHOICE TEST

Select the **one** *correct, best, or most probable answer to each question.*
You can find the answers in the section indicated at the end of each question.

1. The engine cranks normally but will not start. There is a good spark on the spark test. Technician A says the trouble is probably in the fuel system. Technician B says it probably is in the ignition system. Who is right? (➤33-3)
   a. A only
   b. B only
   c. both A and B
   d. neither A nor B

2. Cross-firing may be caused by all the following EXCEPT (➤33-4)
   a. wet distributor cap or rotor
   b. defective insulation on secondary cables
   c. improper routing of spark-plug cables
   d. a fouled spark plug

3. Detonation or pinging results from (➤33-9)
   a. high idle speed during cold starts
   b. overadvanced ignition timing
   c. high-octane fuel
   d. lowering the compression ratio
4. To determine if the primary circuit is opening and closing, make a (➤33-13)
   a. triggering test with a digital logic probe
   b. spark test at the ends of the spark-plug cables
   c. voltage test at the battery
   d. test of the coil primary-winding resistance
5. The oscilloscope shows dwell increases with engine speed. Technician A says this indicates a faulty pickup coil in a General Motors distributor. Technician B says dwell should remain the same in all ignition systems regardless of engine speed. Who is right? (➤33-16)
   a. A only
   b. B only
   c. both A and B
   d. neither A nor B
6. Figure 33-35 shows the scope pattern of a four-cylinder engine. Technician A says the third cylinder in the firing order may have a fouled spark plug. Technician B says it may have a grounded spark-plug cable. Who is right? (➤33-16)
   a. A only
   b. B only
   c. both A and B
   d. neither A nor B
7. The cables for some Hall-effect distributor caps have push-in terminals that lock in place. To detach these cables (➤33-20)
   a. pull them out by hand with a twisting motion
   b. pull them out with a cable-removing tool
   c. remove the cap and release the terminals with needle-nose pliers
   d. the cables are molded into the cap and cannot be removed

8. In an electronic distributor with vacuum advance, hesitation and stumbling during acceleration may be caused by (➤33-23)
   a. an inoperative vacuum-advance unit
   b. an intermittent open in the pickup-coil leads
   c. an inoperative centrifugal-advance mechanism
   d. a defective electronic control module (ECM)
9. A new spark plug of the proper heat range runs about 2000 miles [3000 km]. Removing the plug shows the lower end of the center electrode melted away. Technician A says the cause is preignition. Technician B says to check for combustion-chamber deposits and cross-firing. Who is right? (➤33-25)
   a. A only
   b. B only
   c. both A and B
   d. neither A nor B
10. When the number 1 piston is at TDC ending the compression stroke, the rotor tip in the distributor should point toward the (➤33-27)
   a. number 1 cylinder in the engine
   b. timing mark on the crankshaft vibration damper
   c. number 1 terminal in the distributor cap
   d. timing tab on the engine front cover

REVIEW QUESTIONS

1. List the three categories of ignition-system failure, and give examples of each. (➤33-2)
2. What is the difference in making a spark test at the plug end of the spark-plug cables and at the coil? (➤33-12 and 33-22)
3. Describe how to perform a triggering test, and explain what it tells you. (➤33-13)
4. Describe how to time the distributor to the engine after the crankshaft has turned while the distributor was out. (➤33-27)
5. Explain how to set the ignition timing using a timing light and a magnetic timing tester. (➤33-28 to 33-30)

CHAPTER 34

LIGHTS, SAFETY AND SIGNALING, AND DRIVER INFORMATION AND CONTROL DEVICES

After studying this chapter, and with proper instruction and equipment, you should be able to:

- Replace headlamps and other lamp bulbs, and check and adjust headlamp aim.
- Diagnose and repair troubles in the horn, vehicle security system, and windshield wipers and washers.
- Service seat belts and air bags.
- Describe analog and electronic instrument panels, and the operation of the speedometer and odometer.
- Explain the operation of the speed-control system, and other electrical and electronic devices.

AUTOMOTIVE LIGHTING

➤ 34-1 AUTOMOTIVE LIGHTS

The automobile uses electric lighting to provide the *illumination* or light needed to safely operate the vehicle. The various lights provide vision and information to the driver, convenience for passengers, and signals and warnings to other drivers and pedestrians.

Figure 34-1 shows the lights used on a typical car.

Wiring harnesses (Figs. 27-3 and 27-4) connect the lights with the battery and alternator. Figure 34-2 shows a typical wiring system for the headlights and taillights. There are switches between the lights and the battery to turn the lights on and off. Other switches dim the lights. Some switches are rotary, some are pushbutton, and some are pull-out. Also, some are automatic, like the automatic headlight dimmer, on-off, and time-delay switches. These are described later. Some cars have a computer-controlled lighting system (➤34-8).

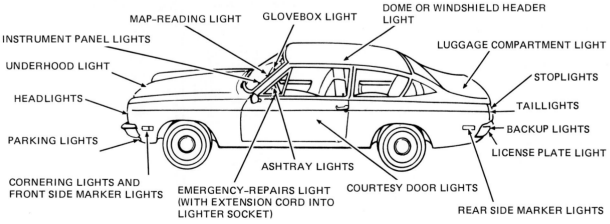

INSTRUMENT PANEL LIGHTS

UNDERHOOD LIGHT

HEADLIGHTS

PARKING LIGHTS

CORNERING LIGHTS AND FRONT SIDE MARKER LIGHTS

MAP-READING LIGHT

GLOVEBOX LIGHT

DOME OR WINDSHIELD HEADER LIGHT

LUGGAGE COMPARTMENT LIGHT

STOPLIGHTS

TAILLIGHTS

BACKUP LIGHTS

LICENSE PLATE LIGHT

ASHTRAY LIGHTS

EMERGENCY-REPAIRS LIGHT (WITH EXTENSION CORD INTO LIGHTER SOCKET)

COURTESY DOOR LIGHTS

REAR SIDE MARKER LIGHTS

Fig. 34-1 Interior and exterior lights on a vehicle. (*Ford Motor Company*)

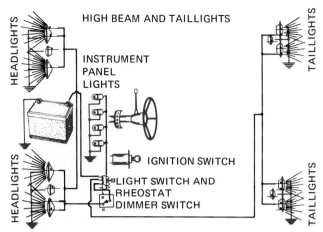

Fig. 34-2 Headlight and taillight wiring circuits, with headlights on high beam.

The outside or *exterior lights* on an automobile include:
1. Two or four *headlamps* (➤34-3) which illuminate the area ahead of the vehicle.
2. *Taillights* to show red at the rear of the vehicle.
3. *Parking lights* to mark the front of a parked vehicle, and to mark the front of the vehicle if a headlamp fails.
4. *License lights* to illuminate the license plate on the rear of the vehicle.
5. *Side-marker lights* on the front and rear sides of the vehicle to indicate its overall length.
6. *Turn-signal lights* (➤34-6) which indicate an intended change in direction by flashing lights on the side toward which the turn will be made.
7. *Backup lights* to illuminate in back of the car when the transmission is shifted into reverse.
8. *Emergency flasher* or *hazard-warning lights* that warn an approaching driver of the presence of a vehicular hazard by flashing all turn-signal lights together.

The inside of the car has a variety of *interior lights*. These include instrument-panel lights, warning and indicator lights, and courtesy and dome lights that turn on when a door opens. Courtesy and dome lights along with glovebox, underhood, and luggage compartment lights are all powered from the fuse panel. They will operate regardless of the position of the ignition key or headlamp switch (➤34-4).

➤ 34-2 LIGHT BULBS

Automotive lighting is provided by various sizes and types of light *bulbs* (Fig. 34-3). When an electric current flows through a fine wire or *filament* in the bulb, the filament gets hot and emits visible light. The bulb may fit into a socket which forms part of a *lamp*.

Some bulbs have two filaments. This allows a single bulb to provide light in two circuits for different purposes. The various bulbs and lighting circuits usually receive power from the fuse panel (➤27-4), ignition switch (➤31-13), or headlamp switch (*light switch* in Fig. 34-2).

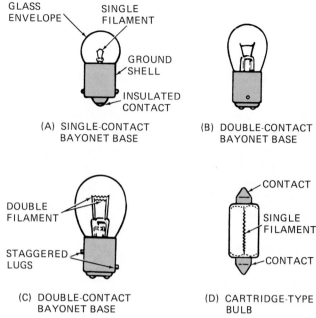

Fig. 34-3 Various sizes and types of light bulbs. *(Ford Motor Company)*

➤ 34-3 HEADLAMPS

The most important lamps for the driver are the headlamps. When switched on, they provide light ahead of the vehicle. Figure 34-4 shows the basic construction of a *sealed-beam headlamp*. The tungsten filament turns white-hot when connected to the battery and gives out light. The light is reflected forward by the curved reflector. Then the light passes through the lens which arranges it in a pattern to light the road ahead. The sealed-beam headlamp is replaced as a unit.

Many vehicles have *halogen* headlamps (Fig. 34-5). These emit a whiter and brighter light than other sealed-beam headlamps. The halogen headlamp has a smaller inner bulb filled with halogen gas which protects the tungsten filament. The outer case is airtight or *hermetically*

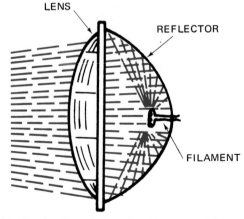

Fig. 34-4 Construction of a tungsten-filament sealed-beam headlamp.

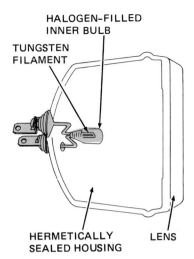

Fig. 34-5 Construction of a halogen sealed-beam headlamp. *(Chrysler Corporation)*

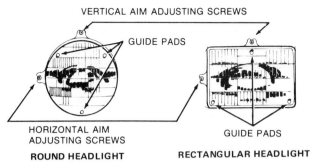

Fig. 34-7 Shapes of round and rectangular headlamps.

sealed. The halogen headlamp shown in Fig. 34-5 is replaced as a unit. Figure 34-6 shows a headlamp with a replaceable dual-filament halogen bulb.

The most widely used headlamps are made in four sizes, two round and two rectangular (Fig. 34-7). The round sizes are 5.75 [146 mm] and 7 inches [178 mm]. The rectangular sizes are 6.5 by 4 inches [165 by 100 mm] and 7.9 by 5.6 inches [200 by 142 mm]. All have the number 1 or 2 molded into the top of the lens. Type 1 has one high-beam filament. Type 2 has two filaments, one for high beam and the other for low beam. The letter H or the word HALOGEN appears on the lens of a halogen headlamp.

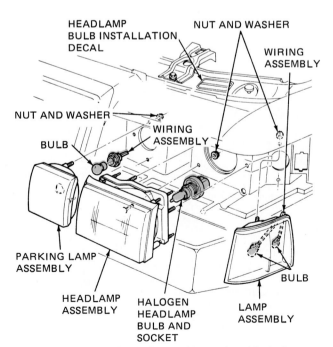

Fig. 34-6 Aerodynamic headlamp with a replaceable dual-filament halogen bulb. *(Ford Motor Company)*

Some cars use smaller rectangular headlamps or aerodynamically-styled *composite headlamps* (Fig. 34-6). These are made of plastic instead of glass and have a replaceable halogen bulb.

The driver selects the beam needed by operating the *beam-selector* or *dimmer switch* (Fig. 34-2). It is either on the floor or on the steering column. Beam selection is made automatically by the *automatic headlamp dimmer* system (➤34-5). A defective dimmer switch, or a corroded or loose dimmer-switch connection, affects both low-beam and both high-beam filaments. The low beams or the high beams may operate normally. However, the other set of filaments may be dim or fail to operate.

A vehicle with four headlamps has two type 1 and two type 2 headlamps. For low-beam driving, one filament in each type 2 headlamp comes on. On high beam, the other filament in the type 2 headlamps comes on along with the single filament in the type 1 headlamps.

➤ **34-4 HEADLAMP SWITCH**

The *headlamp switch* (*light switch* in Fig. 34-2) controls the operation of the headlamps and other exterior and interior lights. It connects directly to the battery and mounts on the instrument panel to the left of the steering wheel. The headlamp switch usually combines a circuit breaker (➤27-6) with a three-position pull switch. It also includes a rotary switch that operates a variable resistor or *rheostat*.

The three positions of the pull switch are OFF, PARK, and HEADLAMPS. Pulling the knob to the first detent or PARK position turns on the parking lights, side-marker lights, and instrument-panel lights. Pulling the knob to the second detent turns on the headlamps. Clockwise rotation of the knob varies the instrument-panel lighting from full bright to dim. Rotating the knob fully counterclockwise turns on the dome light and courtesy lights. Instead of the pull-type headlamp switch, some cars have a three-position *rocker switch* and a rotating thumbwheel on the instrument panel.

The turn-signal (➤34-6) and backup lights (➤27-10) connect to the battery through the ignition switch. They operate independently of the headlamp switch and only when the ignition key is in ON or RUN. Then the turn-signal switch (➤34-6) or *backup-light switch* (➤43-15) must close the circuit (Fig. 27-15).

34-5 AUTOMATIC HEADLAMP CONTROLS

The automatic headlamp dimmer automatically switches the headlamps from high to low beam. This occurs when a *light sensor* senses the headlamps of an approaching vehicle or the taillamps of a vehicle being overtaken. The light sensor triggers a relay that switches beams. When the other car has passed, the system automatically returns the headlamps to high beam. A *sensitivity control* can be set by the driver. This adjusts the light sensor to the surrounding light.

An *automatic on-off headlamp control* turns the headlamps on when it gets dark enough to require light for driving. A light sensor signals the control module when headlamps are needed. The control then switches the headlamps on. This system also includes an adjustable *time-delay turn-off*. The headlamps will stay on for a short time after the ignition key is turned off. This is a convenience when exiting the car at night.

34-6 TURN-SIGNAL LIGHTS

The *turn signals* (Fig. 34-8) permit the driver to signal an intention to turn right or left. The system includes:

1. A lamp at each front and rear corner of the vehicle.
2. A lever-operated *turn-signal switch* in the steering column.
3. A *flasher* (Fig. 27-8), which is an automatic-reset circuit breaker (➤27-6).
4. Left- and right-turn indicator lights in the instrument panel.

The turn-signal lever is moved up for a right turn and down for a left turn. The turn-signal switch then completes the circuits to the proper lamps (Fig. 34-9). Current flows from the battery through the flasher to the lamps. In the flasher, the current passes through a thermostatic blade. The resulting heat causes the thermostatic blade to bend, opening the flasher contacts. The blade quickly cools and the contacts close. This produces a pulsating voltage that causes the turn-signal lights to flash.

After completing the turn, the return movement of the steering wheel automatically cancels the turn signal. The lever moves back to its neutral position, opening the circuit.

A bulb failure or poor ground may cause the turn signals to work in one direction but not the other. If no flashing occurs in either direction, check for a blown fuse or defective flasher.

34-7 FIBER-OPTIC LIGHTING

Some cars have as many as 80 light bulbs. Each bulb can burn out and fail. Some components, such as instrument panels, have many bulbs close together. However, there is little room behind the instrument panel for the bulbs, their sockets, and the connecting wiring. One solution is the use of *printed circuits* (➤27-3). Another is the use of *fiber-optic cables*.

Fiber-optic cables are made of one or more transparent glass or plastic fibers bundled together parallel to one

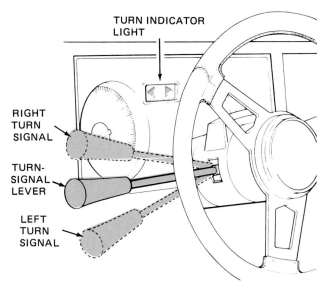

Fig. 34-8 Positions of the turn-signal lever on the steering column, and the turn-indicator light in the instrument panel. *(Chrysler Corporation)*

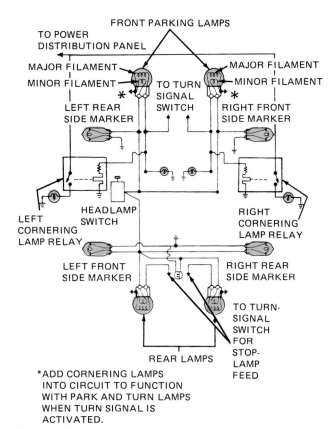

*ADD CORNERING LAMPS INTO CIRCUIT TO FUNCTION WITH PARK AND TURN LAMPS WHEN TURN SIGNAL IS ACTIVATED.

Fig. 34-9 Wiring diagram of the turn signals and other exterior lights. *(Ford Motor Company)*

another. Each cable formed by the fiber or bundle can conduct light, even around bends and corners. As light starts down the fiber, the light keeps reflecting off the internal surfaces of the fiber with little loss. When the light comes out the other end, it is almost as strong as when it entered.

Figure 34-10 shows a fiber-optic *lamp monitor system*. Fiber-optic cables run from the lamps to a lamp monitor on top of each front fender. When the headlamps are on, the lamp monitors show that the lights are working. If a bulb burns out, its monitor also goes out. This warns the driver that the lamp has failed.

Another way to use fiber-optics is to run cables from a central light source to various outlets where light is needed. This allows only one bulb to provide light at many places. Figure 34-11 shows the concept of an automotive *central lighting system*. A special *arc-discharge bulb* provides the light. It is smaller and lasts longer than a halogen bulb. Similar to a fluorescent or neon bulb, there is no filament to burn out. The light appears at each lamp or outlet only when needed. This system would prevent the failure of many individual bulbs.

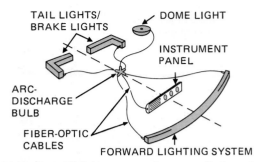

Fig. 34-11 Central lighting system using an arc-discharge bulb. *(General Electric Company)*

> ### 34-8 COMPUTER-CONTROLLED LIGHTING

In most cars, a separate switch controls each lighting circuit. However, an electronic-control module or *lamp module* (Fig. 34-12) can control the complete vehicle lighting system. When the driver operates any switch that controls a lamp circuit, the switch sends an input signal to the lamp module. It then turns the desired lamps on or off. The lamp module provides the intermittent operation of the hazard-warning and turn-signal lamps. No flasher is needed.

In most lighting systems, a switch supplies voltage to lamps that are permanently grounded. With computer-controlled lighting, many circuits operate differently. Voltage is always supplied and a switch or relay provides the lamp ground. The various light switches are grouped on the left side of the steering column in the *left switch pod*.

> ### 34-9 DISTRIBUTED LIGHTING SYSTEM

The *distributed lighting system* is a computer-controlled lighting system (➤34-8) that uses the body-control module (BCM) as the lamp module. The system includes nine solid-state switches or *output switching modules* (OSM), a *serial data line* or *bus*, and the left switch pod (Fig. 34-13). The BCM controls all interior and exterior lighting through the switching modules. Each switching module controls four lamp circuits. Three *jumpers* divide the power feeds into three groups. This prevents a module circuit failure from making all rear or all front lights inoperative.

In addition to controlling and monitoring lamp operation, the system can substitute some lamps for others that have failed (Fig. 34-14). The system includes two extra or *redundant* relays. They automatically provide power to the left headlamp (low beam) and left taillamp if the BCM or the serial data bus fails. Problems in the distributed lighting system cause a LIGHTING FAULT message to display. This also sets a lighting-system trouble code (➤20-13) which is stored in the BCM.

The operation of the distributed lighting system is made possible by *multiplexing* (➤34-21). This is the use of a

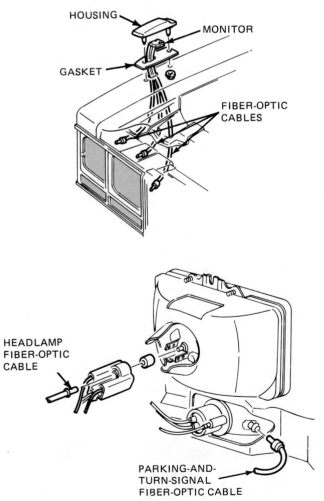

Fig. 34-10 Fiber-optic lamp monitor system. *(Cadillac Division of General Motors Corporation)*

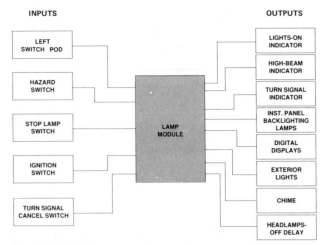

Fig. 34-12 Computer-controlled lighting system. *(Chrysler Corporation)*

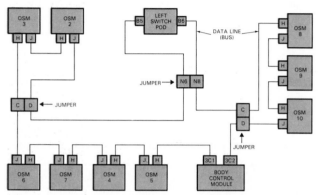

Fig. 34-13 Distributed lighting system using multiplexing, which allows the "serial data bus" to replace many wires. *(Cadillac Division of General Motors Corporation)*

FAILED LAMP	OSM
LOW BEAM, RIGHT	9
LOW BEAM, LEFT	9
HIGH BEAM, RIGHT	8
HIGH BEAM, LEFT	10
TURN SIGNAL, RIGHT FRONT	8
TURN SIGNAL, LEFT FRONT	10
SUBSTITUTE LAMP	OSM
FOG LAMP, RIGHT	8
FOG LAMP, LEFT	10
LOW BEAM, RIGHT	9
LOW BEAM, LEFT	9
PARK LAMP, RIGHT	8
PARK LAMP, LEFT	10

Fig. 34-14 Lamp substitution chart, showing how the distributed lighting system can automatically substitute lamps for others that have failed. *(Cadillac Division of General Motors Corporation)*

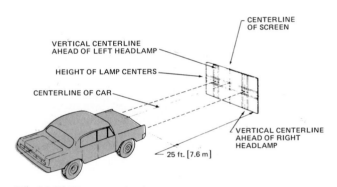

Fig. 34-15 Floor-type headlight aiming screen.

twisted pair of conductors, such as the data bus (Fig. 34-13), to do the job of many wires. A single main-wiring harness simplifies the electrical system. Because of multiplexing, it has fewer connectors which improves reliability.

34-10 HEADLAMP AIMING

Headlamps must be aimed correctly so the driver can see at night and to prevent the blinding of approaching drivers. One method is the use of an *aiming screen* (Fig. 34-15). Park the car on a level floor, 25 feet [7.6 m] from the screen. Then the high beam and low beam can be checked.

Adjust the headlamps to provide the specified pattern. Figure 34-16 shows aiming patterns for round and rectangular sealed-beam headlamps. These are usually adjusted by turning vertical-aim and horizontal-aim adjusting screws (Fig. 34-7). Figure 34-17 shows a *mechanical aimer* for adjusting headlamps. An adapter mounts to the three aiming pads on the headlamp. Then the aimer mounts to the adapter. Some shops have an *optical*

aimer. It does not touch the headlamp. When using a headlamp aimer, follow the manufacturer's operating instructions. Headlamp-aiming patterns and adjustments are in the vehicle service manual.

Some vehicles have aiming devices built into the headlamp assembly. A bubble level indicates the proper height (up-and-down) adjustment as the *vertical aim adjusting screws* (Fig. 34-7) are turned in and out. Other vehicles also have built-in scales and pointers for horizontal (side-to-side) adjustment.

CAUTION!

Halogen bulbs and headlamps get very hot. Do not touch a halogen bulb or lamp while it is on or shortly after it has been turned off. Handle the separately-mounted bulb (Fig. 34-6) carefully. It contains gas under pressure. The bulb may shatter if scratched or dropped. Do not touch the glass envelope. The

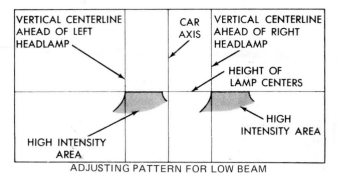

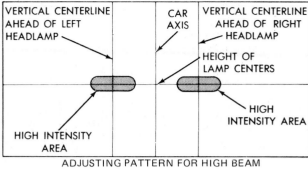

Fig. 34-16 Aiming patterns for round and rectangular sealed-beam headlamps. *(Chrysler Corporation)*

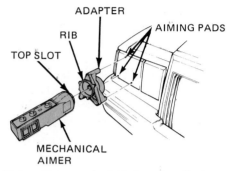

Fig. 34-17 Installing a mechanical aimer for adjusting headlamps. *(Ford Motor Company)*

oil from your skin may damage it. Keep the bulb out of reach of children.

SAFETY AND SIGNALING

➤ 34-11 HORN AND HORN RELAY

Most cars have two *horns* (Figs. 27-1 and 34-18) at the front of the car. Horns are electrically-operated noise-makers used by the driver to provide a loud warning signal. Pressing a *horn button* in the steering wheel or column grounds the circuit connecting the battery to the *horn relay*. This closes contact points in the relay and connects the horns—through the relay—to the battery. The electric current then causes a diaphragm in each horn to vibrate and produce the sound.

When current flows through the coil winding in the horn (Fig. 34-19), the resulting magnetic field pulls the armature toward the pole. The armature attaches to a diaphragm which also moves up. This upward travel then opens the normally-closed contact points and opens the circuit.

As the circuit opens, the magnetic field collapses. The diaphragm and armature "spring back" to their at-rest position. This movement closes the contact points and again completes the circuit. The cycle repeats many times per second to produce the sound, as long as the horn button is depressed. The number of vibrations per second determines the *pitch* of the sound. The greater the number of vibrations, the higher the pitch.

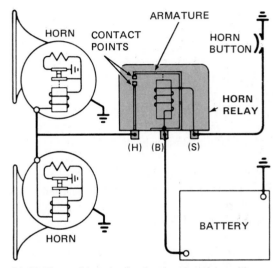

Fig. 34-18 Horn wiring circuit, showing the relay and its connections. *(Delco-Remy Division of General Motors Corporation)*

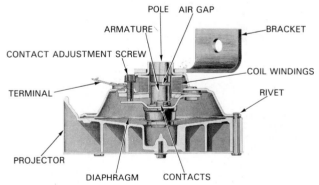

Fig. 34-19 Construction of a horn. *(Delco-Remy Division of General Motors Corporation)*

➤ 34-12 VEHICLE SECURITY SYSTEMS

An *anti-theft* or *security alarm system* (Fig. 34-20) causes the horn to sound and the lights to flash if someone tries to break into the vehicle. There are several different ways to trigger the alarm. Typically, the driver sets the alarm by operating a switch when leaving the vehicle. Then opening

437

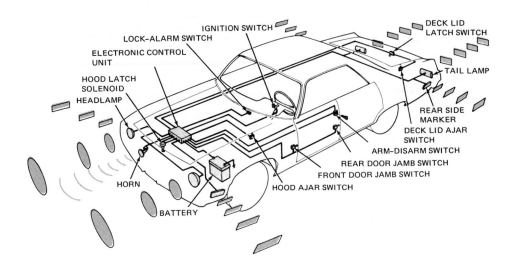

Fig. 34-20 Locations of components in an anti-theft or security alarm system. The circles and rectangles represent the lights that flash when the system is activated. The arcs represent the blowing of the horn. *(Chrysler Corporation)*

or forcing open the hood, trunk, tailgate, or any door triggers the alarm.

Many vehicle security systems include a *starter interrupt*. This prevents starting the engine after any forced entry, even if the ignition switch is bypassed. Figure 34-21 shows a *pass-key* automotive security system. A resistor pellet in the ignition key must match the decoding circuit in the *pass-key module*. Only when the resistance values match will the module energize the starter-enable relay. The module then also signals the electronic control module (ECM) to deliver fuel to the injectors.

> ## 34-13 SEAT BELTS

Seat belts (Fig. 34-22) restrain the vehicle occupants if there is an accident. After entering the car, the driver and passengers each fasten a lap or lap-and-shoulder belt. The belt then helps hold that person in the seat during a collision or rollover. Inertia-sensitive *retractors* (Fig. 34-23) lock the belt in place when an impact occurs.

A *passive restraint* provides protection without requiring any action by the driver or passenger. Two types of passive restraints are air bags (➤34-14) and *motorized seat belts* (Fig. 34-22). These are front-seat shoulder belts

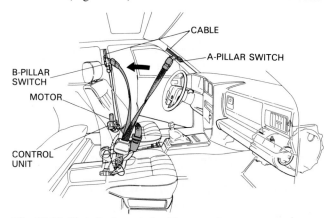

Fig. 34-22 Motorized seat belts. These are front-seat shoulder belts that move into position automatically after closing the door. *(Volkswagen of America, Inc.)*

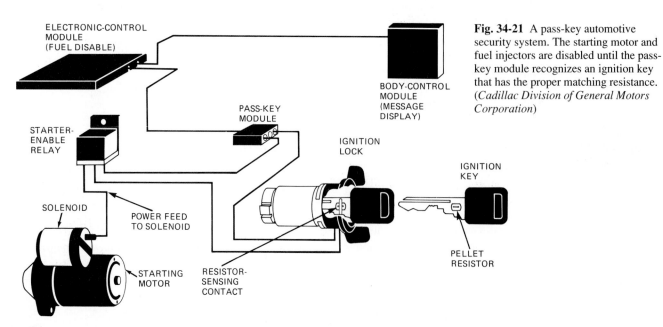

Fig. 34-21 A pass-key automotive security system. The starting motor and fuel injectors are disabled until the pass-key module recognizes an ignition key that has the proper matching resistance. *(Cadillac Division of General Motors Corporation)*

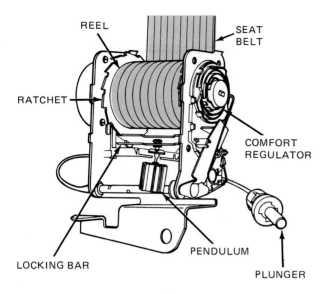

(A) RETRACTOR CONSTRUCTION

Labels: REEL, SEAT BELT, RATCHET, COMFORT REGULATOR, LOCKING BAR, PENDULUM, PLUNGER

RETRACTOR UNLOCKED

Labels: SEAT BELT, BAR, RATCHET MECHANISM, PENDULUM

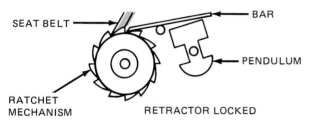

RETRACTOR LOCKED

Labels: SEAT BELT, BAR, PENDULUM, RATCHET MECHANISM

(B) RETRACTOR OPERATION

Fig. 34-23 Construction and operation of inertia-sensitive retractors that lock the belt in place when an impact occurs. (*Ford Motor Company*)

that move into position automatically. After entering the car and closing the door, the driver turns on the ignition key. The electric motor then pulls a cable or tape connected to the belt. The belt travels along a track above the door. When a switch signals the control unit that the belt is in position, the control unit shuts off the motor. The occupants must manually fasten the lap belt.

The belt travels forward and out of the way when the door opens. In some cars with an air bag on only the driver's side, the seat belt for the front-seat passenger automatically tightens in a crash. This provides the passenger with additional protection.

➤ 34-14 AIR BAGS

Air bags (Fig. 34-24) are also called *supplemental inflatable restraints* (SIR). They are balloon-type devices that

inflate automatically to protect the driver (and front-seat passenger in some vehicles) if a front-end crash occurs. The air bag prevents the occupant from being thrown forward and injured by striking the steering wheel or windshield. The seat belt and air bag together provide maximum protection against injury in a collision.

Figure 34-25 shows the components of the air-bag system. When the ignition key is turned on, the *readiness indicator* light should come on for about six seconds. Any

(A) AIR BAG STORED IN CENTER OF STEERING WHEEL.

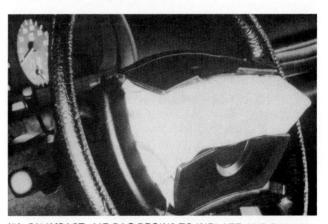

(B) ON IMPACT, AIR BAG BEGINS TO INFLATE AND PUSHES THROUGH STEERING-WHEEL COVER.

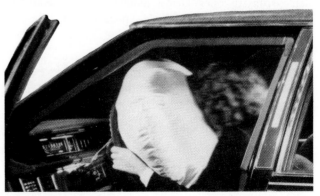

(C) DEPLOYED AIR BAG PREVENTS INJURY FROM STRIKING VEHICLE INTERIOR.

Fig. 34-24 Operation of the driver-side air bag, or supplemental inflatable restraint. (*Motor Vehicle Manufacturers Association*)

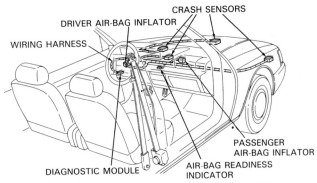

Fig. 34-25 Components of an air-bag system. *(Ford Motor Company)*

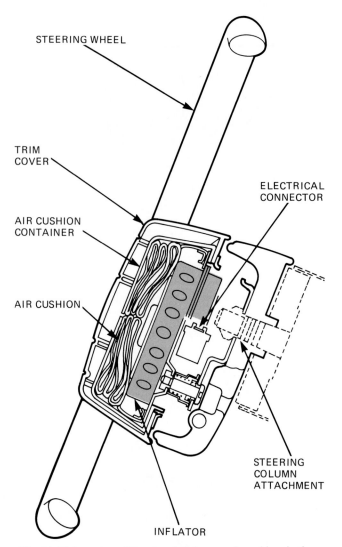

Fig. 34-26 Location of the stored air bag, or air cushion, in the steering wheel. *(Cadillac Division of General Motors Corporation)*

other operation of the light indicates a malfunction. The system is powered directly from the battery. This allows the air bag to inflate with the ignition key in any position, including OFF and LOCK.

If a front-end crash occurs, two of the four sensors must activate to trigger the air bag. This helps prevent a short circuit in a sensor or wiring from causing an unwanted inflation. When the sensors detect a collision, an electric spark below the inflator in the steering-wheel hub ignites a small canister of gas (Fig. 34-26). The gas in turn ignites the propellant (*socium axide*) in the inflator.

The burning propellant creates nitrogen gas. This fills the air bag (*air cushion* in Fig. 34-26) stored above the inflator in the steering-wheel hub. As the bag inflates, it pushes through both the *air-cushion container* and the steering-wheel trim cover (Fig. 34-24B). Deployment time, from impact to full inflation, is about 50 milliseconds (0.050 second) or less. Some systems include a capacitor that will trigger the system if the battery or battery cables are damaged by the impact.

> ## 34-15 AIR-BAG REPLACEMENT

An air bag inflates only once. Then remove the deployed air bag and clean the inside of the vehicle. This is necessary because of the powder emitted as the air bag deploys. Install a new air-bag module. Follow the air-bag service procedures in the vehicle service manual.

CAUTION!

Be careful when working on vehicles with air bags. You could accidentally trigger the system. A deploying air bag could injure you if you are not belted in the normal seated position.

> ## 34-16 WINDSHIELD WIPERS AND WASHERS

Windshield wipers (Fig. 34-27) clean the windshield so the driver can see clearly while driving in rain or snow. The *wiper blades* are moved back and forth by linkage con-

nected to a motor on the firewall in the engine compartment. A switch on the steering column or instrument panel connects the motor to the ignition switch. The motor will run when the ignition key is in the ON or ACC position (➤31-13).

The windshield-wiper switch has at least two or three speeds. Many cars have *intermittent windshield wipers*. These include an adjustable time delay between blade movements. The wiper blades will move across and back, pause, and then repeat the action.

A *windshield washer* is part of the windshield-wiper system. When the driver presses a button, liquid *windshield-washer fluid* squirts on the windshield. This allows the blades to clean more effectively. Some cars have heated windshield-washer nozzles. This prevents ice from clogging the small holes in cold weather.

The rear window in some cars has a similar wiper-and-washer system. Figure 34-28 shows a *headlight wiper-and-washer system*. It works automatically when the windshield washer operates.

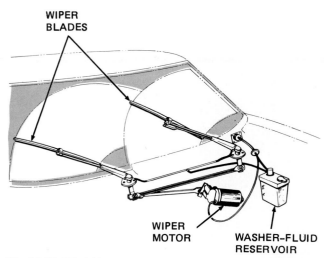

Fig. 34-27 Windshield wiper and washer system. (*Trico Products Corporation*)

Fig. 34-28 Headlight wiper and washer system. (*Saab Cars USA, Inc.*)

DRIVER INFORMATION AND CONTROLS

➤ 34-17 INSTRUMENT PANEL

The *instrument panel* (Fig. 34-29) contains the indicators —gauges, lights, and displays—the driver needs to operate the car. These are usually grouped for easy reading by the driver in an *instrument cluster*. Some driver-operated controls mount on the instrument panel, or above or below it in a *console*. These include the headlamp switch (➤34-4), heating and air-conditioning controls (Chap. 55), and the controls for the radio and tape or compact-disk player.

Automotive instrumentation (➤17-19) may take the form of analog gauges or electronic displays. Analog gauges show the condition being monitored by movement of the pointer on the gauge. Several analog gauges are grouped into an *analog instrument cluster*. In an *electronic instrument cluster,* the various readings and conditions display as numbers or a bar-graph display. Both types of

instrument clusters inform the driver of many conditions including:

1. Vehicle speed (➤34-19).
2. Distance traveled (➤34-19).
3. Engine temperature (➤25-19).
4. Engine oil pressure (➤24-10).
5. Battery charge or discharge (➤30-9).
6. Amount of fuel in fuel tank (➤17-19).

Some cars have a *hybrid instrument cluster* (Fig. 34-29). It includes both analog gauges and electronic displays, along with other indicating devices and warning lights. These may illuminate a symbol or a message such as DOOR AJAR or TAIL LAMP OUT.

➤ 34-18 HEAD-UP DISPLAY

Figure 34-30 shows the driver's view through the windshield of a car with a *head-up display*. Images containing driver information are projected onto the windshield. The information includes displays of vehicle speed, turn-signal indicators, high-beam indicator, and low-fuel warning. These images appear suspended in space near the front bumper (Fig. 34-31). The driver's eyes do not need to move from the road or refocus to view this information.

Only certain information from the instrument panel appears in the head-up display. A warning CHECK GAUGES message appearing on the windshield alerts the driver that a gauge on the instrument panel needs attention. Controls allow adjustment of the head-up display brightness and vertical location in the windshield.

➤ 34-19 SPEEDOMETER AND ODOMETER

A *speedometer* (Fig. 34-32) in the instrument cluster shows the driver how fast the vehicle is moving. Many speedometers are driven from the transmission output shaft by a set of gears. The driven gear fastens to a flexible shaft or *speedometer cable*. It runs from the transmission output shaft to the back of the *speedometer head*.

Inside the speedometer, the cable turns a shaft with a small magnet on it. The rotating magnetic field produces a varying pull on the metal ring surrounding the magnet. A pointer attaches to the metal ring. As the magnetic field spins, it causes the ring to overcome a light spring and swing with the magnetic field. This moves the pointer which then indicates car speed. The faster the car speed, the faster the magnet spins, and the farther the pointer moves.

The *odometer* records the total distance the vehicle has traveled. It is a row of numbers, usually located in the speedometer. The odometer operates by a pair of gears from the speedometer shaft (Fig. 34-32). Its motion is carried through the gears to the mileage or kilometer *number rings*. These turn to show the distance traveled by the vehicle.

Fig. 34-29 Instrument panel using electronic displays and analog gauges. Additional controls are grouped in the steering wheel and center console. (*Chevrolet Division of General Motors Corporation*)

Fig. 34-30 Driver's view through the windshield of a car with a head-up display. (*GM Hughes Electronics Corporation*)

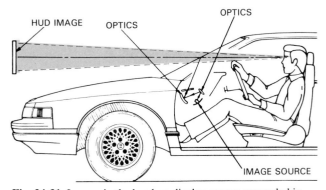

Fig. 34-31 Images in the head-up display appear suspended in space near the front bumper. (*Oldsmobile Division of General Motors Corporation*)

Some vehicles have an electronically-driven speed-ometer and odometer. A *vehicle-speed sensor* (VSS) on the transmission output shaft (➤47-27) sends vehicle speed signals through wiring to the speedometer. This eliminates the speedometer cable. The speed signals operate a small electric stepper motor which turns the odometer number rings. Cars with an electronic instrument cluster have a

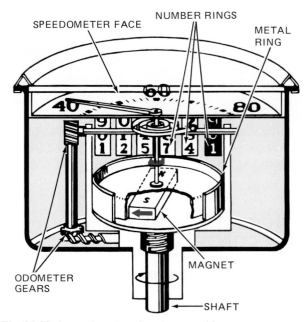

Fig. 34-32 A speedometer-odometer assembly.

digital speedometer and odometer display (Fig. 17-32). When the key is off, the body-control module (BCM) stores the odometer reading. The odometer reading is not lost when the battery is disconnected.

➤ 34-20 SPEED-CONTROL SYSTEM

The *cruise control* or *speed-control system* (Fig. 34-33) helps the vehicle to automatically maintain a speed selected by the driver. When set at any speed above about 25 mph [40 kmph], the driver's foot can be removed from the accelerator pedal. An actuator motor or *vacuum servo*

(Fig. 34-33) then opens and closes the throttle, as needed, to maintain the speed. However, steep grades up or down may cause vehicle speed to vary.

Tapping the clutch or brake pedal operates a switch that disengages the system. Touching the RESUME button or switch causes the vehicle to return to the former speed setting. Depressing the accelerator pedal for passing does not affect the setting. When the pedal is released, the system returns the vehicle to the preset speed. To disengage and turn off the speed-control system, move the OFF-ON switch to OFF.

➤ 34-21 NETWORKS AND MULTIPLEXING

Some cars have several microprocessors (➤10-17) which control the various electronic systems (Fig. 34-34). One way to reduce duplication and wiring is to have these controllers communicate with each other. When this happens, the group of interconnected components and systems becomes a *network.* For example, a sensor is wired to one controller. It then shares the information with all other controllers that require it. The vehicle has fewer sensors, and the amount of wiring and number of connections is greatly reduced.

Figure 34-35 shows how the controllers connect to form a *data bus network.* The "bus" is a single pair of wires that connects in parallel to the controllers. It allows the exchange of information or data between them. This is a *multiplex* system. In a multiplex system, several controllers can send or *broadcast* messages on the same circuit (the bus). Sometimes two or more controllers try to send messages at the same time. To avoid these "data collisions," each message starts with a priority code. The controller with the highest priority then sends its messages first.

Some controllers send and receive messages, some send only, and others receive only. The *engine node* (Figs. 34-35) is a send-only controller. It collects data from the

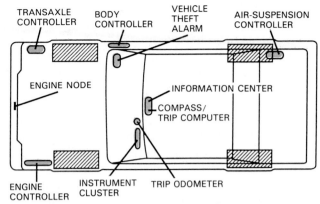

Fig. 34-34 Controllers on a vehicle that can be connected by a data bus into a network. (*Chrysler Corporation*)

sensors and switches in the front of the vehicle. On the vehicle shown in Fig. 34-34, the engine node also contains the compass and outside air-temperature sensor.

➤ 34-22 OTHER ELECTRICAL AND ELECTRONIC DEVICES

The automobile may contain other electrical and electronic devices in addition to those already described. These include *power seats, power windows, heated windshield, voice alert systems, voice command systems, mobile telephones,* and *electronic navigation systems.* Some of these and other electrical and electronic devices are described below.

1. Electric seat adjusters are motors under the seat that operate by push buttons or levers to move the seat forward and back, or up and down. Some also change the inclination and shape, or *contour,* of the seat.
2. The window regulator has a motor in the door that raises or lowers the window as a switch is operated.
3. The voice alert system uses a computerized voice which says "The door is ajar," "The key is in the ignition lock," or "The headlamps are on." These and other messages inform the driver of conditions that need attention.

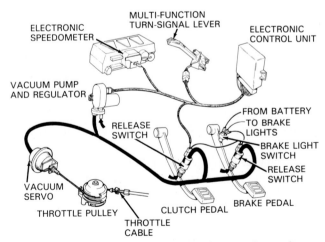

Fig. 34-33 Components in a cruise control, or speed control, system. (*Volvo Cars of North America*)

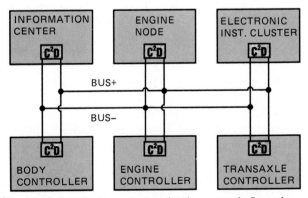

Fig. 34-35 A multiplex system, or data bus network. Several controllers can send, or broadcast, messages on the same circuit (the bus). (*Chrysler Corporation*)

4. The voice command system causes the car to respond in some way to a spoken command. This may be "Tune the radio," "Lower the window," or "Dial a phone number." There are many other voice-command possibilities. One includes using a voice command to unlock the car door and operate the ignition instead of using a key.

5. The *keyless entry system* (Fig. 34-36) has a panel of buttons on the driver-side door. To unlock the door, the buttons must be pressed in the proper order. This code takes the place of the key.

Some keyless entry systems can also be operated from up to 33 feet [10 m] by a small hand-held transmitter. Pushing a button on the transmitter will lock all doors, unlock all doors, or open the trunk. Another button—the PANIC button—acts as a theft deterrent or anti-theft device (➤34-12). Pushing the PANIC button with the ignition off activates the horn and flashes the headlamps.

6. Electronic navigation systems display a map on the instrument panel which shows the location of the vehicle on the road (Fig. 1-31). The location point moves on the map as the vehicle travels on the highway. It also shows the route to the destination. In some systems, a satellite orbiting in space—22,000 miles [35,400 km] above the earth—pinpoints vehicle location.

7. *Radar braking* uses radar to sense how fast a vehicle is closing on the vehicle ahead (Fig. 34-37). The brakes apply automatically to slow the vehicle if necessary to maintain a safe distance. Someday radar braking may be combined with throttle control into *intelligent cruise control*. This could keep traffic moving at a preset speed while radar braking maintains safe intervals between vehicles.

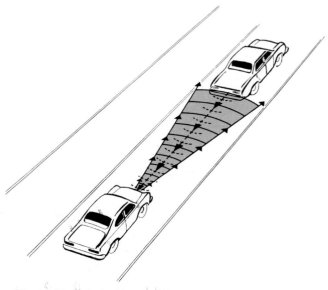

Fig. 34-37 Radar braking, in which the vehicle behind senses how fast the gap between the two vehicles is closing. When the danger point is reached, the system triggers electronic devices that alert the driver and slow the vehicle.

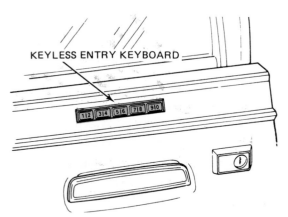

Fig. 34-36 Keyless entry system. Pressing the buttons in the proper order replaces the key. (*Ford Motor Company*)

MULTIPLE-CHOICE TEST

*Select the **one** correct, best, or most probable answer to each question.*
You can find the answers in the section indicated at the end of each question.

1. After replacing a headlamp, the driver complains that the new headlamp is dim. Technician A says a halogen headlamp has been installed in place of a standard headlamp. Technician B says a standard headlamp has been installed in place of a halogen headlamp. Who is right? (➤34-3)
 a. A only
 b. B only
 c. both A and B
 d. neither A nor B

2. Both headlamps are dim in the high-beam position and normal in the low-beam position. Technician A says a shorted headlamp switch could be the cause. Technician B says a loose headlamp ground could be the cause. Who is right? (➤34-3 and 34-4)
 a. A only
 b. B only
 c. both A and B
 d. neither A nor B

3. The headlamp switch controls the vehicle (➤34-4)
   a. instrument-panel lights, parking lights, and head-lamps
   b. turn signals, dome light, and courtesy lights
   c. brake lights, backup lights, and hazard-warning lights
   d. all of the above
4. The turn signals work properly in one direction but not in the other. Which of these is the most probable cause? (➤34-6)
   a. a defective flasher
   b. a defective voltage regulator
   c. a blown turn-signal fuse
   d. a blown bulb or poor ground on the problem side
5. The horns in the circuit shown in Fig. 34-18 only blow when a jumper wire is connected between the B (battery) terminal and the H (horns) terminal of the horn relay. Technician A says a defective horn relay could be the cause. Technician B says a ground in the circuit between the horn relay and the horn button could be the cause. Who is right? (➤34-11)
   a. A only
   b. B only
   c. both A and B
   d. neither A nor B
6. A pass-key automotive security system includes the following EXCEPT (➤34-12)
   a. a starter interrupt that prevents starting even if the ignition switch is bypassed
   b. a resistor pellet in the ignition key that must match the decoding circuit in the pass-key module
   c. a starter-enable relay that prevents fuel delivery to the injectors
   d. a security code that can be entered to provide ignition if the driver forgets or loses the key
7. Triggering of the air bag requires the activation of (➤34-14)
   a. inertia-sensitive retractors
   b. the ignition key
   c. two sensors
   d. motorized seat belts
8. The customer complains that the windshield wipers stop when the ignition key is turned OFF. Technician A says the time-delay is improperly adjusted. Technician B says the wiper motor is wired to the ignition switch and this is normal operation. Who is right? (➤34-16)
   a. A only
   b. B only
   c. both A and B
   d. neither A nor B
9. Technician A says the odometer records the total distance the vehicle has traveled. Technician B says the speedometer reports the miles or kilometers per hour the vehicle is traveling. Who is right? (➤34-19)
   a. A only
   b. B only
   c. both A and B
   d. neither A nor B
10. In the speed-control system, the vacuum servo connects to the (➤34-20)
    a. transmission linkage
    b. throttle linkage
    c. speedometer cable
    d. brake cable

REVIEW QUESTIONS

1. List the various lighting systems on the car and explain how each is powered.   (➤34-1 and 34-4)
2. How can fiber-optic lighting be used on the car? (➤34-7)
3. What is computer-controlled lighting and how does it differ from a distributed lighting system?   (➤34-8 and 34-9)
4. How does a head-up display provide the driver with information?   (➤34-18)
5. Define *network* and *multiplexing,* and explain how they can be used to simplify automotive wiring and connections.   (➤34-21)

PART 5

ENGINE PERFORMANCE AND DRIVEABILITY

Part 5 of *Automotive Mechanics* describes the design changes and devices installed on engines and automobiles that were made to reduce automotive pollution. Following chapters cover servicing emission controls, and engine test equipment and tuneup procedures. These are needed to maintain good engine performance and driveability. The last chapter covers engine trouble diagnosis. Included are the steps to take when there is trouble in the engine or with its performance.

There are four chapters in Part 5:

CHAPTER 35

AUTOMOTIVE EMISSION-CONTROL SYSTEMS

After studying this chapter, you should be able to:

- List the three main air pollutants from the automobile and explain how each is formed.
- Explain the operation of the PCV system and why the crankcase must be ventilated.
- Describe how the evaporative-control system works and the various ways to control it.
- Describe three methods of cleaning the exhaust gas and give examples of each.
- Explain the purpose and operation of the AIR and EGR systems.
- Describe the construction of a three-way catalytic converter and the actions in each section.

AIR POLLUTION

➤ 35-1 AUTOMOTIVE AIR POLLUTION

There are four possible sources of atmospheric pollution from the automobile (Fig. 35-1). Without emission controls, a carburetor and fuel tank emit fuel vapors, the crankcase emits blowby gases and fuel vapor, and the tailpipe emits exhaust gases that contain pollutants. The pollutants are hydrocarbons (HC), carbon monoxide (CO), and nitrogen oxides (NO_x). They are described in ➤16-1.

These air pollutants are harmful to plants and animals, including human beings. They cause *smog*, a word made from *smoke* and *fog*. Smog and other air pollution became so bad that in 1970 Congress amended the Clean Air Act of 1963. The law now requires automotive manufacturers to install emission controls. State and local laws also limit automotive emissions.

Cars that give off excessive amounts of air pollutants may not be allowed on the streets someday. Stronger laws limiting automotive air pollution and mandatory *inspection-and-maintenance* (I/M) programs have been proposed. These laws are part of the government policy that cars must contribute as little as possible to the problem of air pollution.

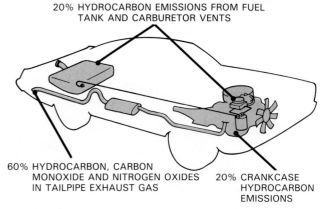

20% HYDROCARBON EMISSIONS FROM FUEL TANK AND CARBURETOR VENTS

60% HYDROCARBON, CARBON MONOXIDE AND NITROGEN OXIDES IN TAILPIPE EXHAUST GAS

20% CRANKCASE HYDROCARBON EMISSIONS

Fig. 35-1 Four possible sources of atmospheric pollution from the automobile. (*Ford Motor Company*)

➤ 35-2 AUTOMOTIVE EMISSION CONTROLS

Figure 35-1 shows the four sources of air pollution from the automobile. Each car now has three major systems for controlling pollutants from these sources:

1. *Positive crankcase ventilation* (PCV). This is a system that sends fresh air through the crankcase to sweep out blowby and fuel vapor. The air then enters the engine

where the pollutants from the crankcase have another chance to burn.

2. *Evaporative emission control.* This is a system that captures any fuel vapors coming from the fuel tank and float bowl (on carbureted engines). It prevents the vapors from escaping into the atmosphere.

3. *Exhaust emission control.* This includes a variety of systems, devices, and strategies. These work together to reduce the pollutants in the exhaust gas emitted from the tailpipe.

Following sections describe various automotive emission controls. Automotive manufacturers may also use other systems for specific engines, and for cars sold in California and high-altitude locations. These are covered in the vehicle service manual.

CONTROLLING CRANKCASE EMISSIONS

➤ 35-3 CRANKCASE VENTILATION

Engines have some blowby (➤11-4). This is mostly unburned gasoline (HC) and some products of combustion that get past the piston rings and into the crankcase. The crankcase ventilation system prevents pressure buildup and oil leaks (➤24-13). In addition, it removes blowby gas to prevent the formation of corrosive acids and sludge (➤24-14).

➤ 35-4 POSITIVE CRANKCASE VENTILATION

Figure 35-2 shows a typical PCV system on a V-type engine. Filtered air from the air cleaner is drawn through the crankcase by intake-manifold vacuum. The air picks up the blowby gas or vapors and carries them to the intake manifold. The vapors then flow through the intake manifold to the combustion chambers. There the unburned fuel burns during normal combustion.

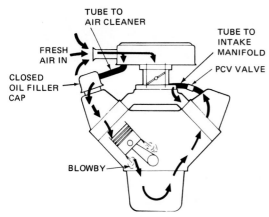

Fig. 35-2 Typical PCV system on a V-type engine. (*Ford Motor Company*)

Too much air flowing through the intake manifold during idling can upset the air-fuel ratio. This can cause poor idling and engine stalling. A fixed-orifice or variable-orifice *flow-control valve* prevents this. Most engines use a *PCV valve* (Fig. 35-3), which has a variable orifice. It allows only a small amount of air to flow through during idle. As engine speed increases, reduced intake-manifold vacuum allows the valve to open further. Then more air flows through. PCV-valve operation is described in Fig. 35-3.

In a worn or defective engine, more blowby may enter the crankcase than can flow through the PCV valve. The excess blowby flows back through the tube to the air cleaner (Fig. 35-2) instead of escaping to the outside air.

CONTROLLING EVAPORATIVE EMISSIONS

➤ 35-5 EVAPORATIVE CONTROL SYSTEMS

The evaporative control system captures the gasoline vapors from the fuel tank and carburetor float bowl and prevents them from escaping into the atmosphere. All 1971 and later carburetor-equipped vehicles have this system. It is called by various names such as *evaporative control system* (ECS), *evaporative emission control* (EEC), *vehicle vapor recovery* (VVR), and *vapor saver system* (VSS). Since fuel injection systems do not have a float bowl, their evaporative control system handles only fuel vapors from the fuel tank.

➤ 35-6 EVAPORATIVE CONTROL SYSTEM FOR CARBURETED ENGINES

Figures 17-1 and 35-4 show an evaporative control system on a car with a carbureted engine. When the engine is shut off, fuel vapors feed from the tank and float bowl into a *carbon* or *charcoal canister* (Fig. 35-5). The activated charcoal in the canister traps or *adsorbs* the fuel vapors. "Adsorb" means the gasoline vapors are trapped by sticking to the outside of the charcoal particles. The vapors are not *a*bsorbed into the particles.

Later, when the engine starts, fresh air flows through the canister and picks up the gasoline vapor. The air then flows into the intake manifold and becomes part of the air-fuel mixture entering the engine cylinders. This action of clearing the trapped fuel vapor from the canister is called *purging*. Running the engine removes or *purges* the vapor from the canister.

The carburetor float bowl has two vents (➤21-5). One connects to the air cleaner and helps compensate for a clogged air cleaner. The other vent connects to the charcoal canister (Fig. 21-6). Various arrangements may control this vent. One uses the accelerator-pump lever to

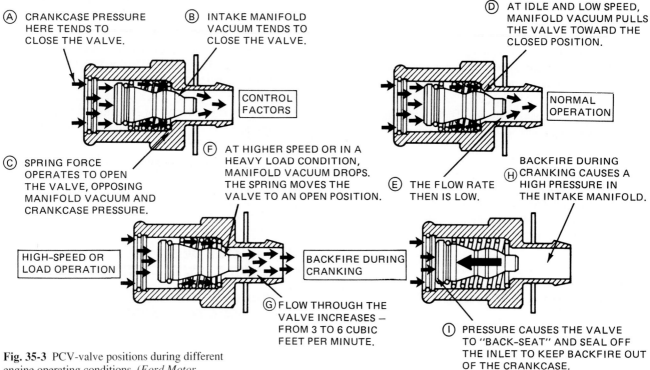

A) CRANKCASE PRESSURE HERE TENDS TO CLOSE THE VALVE.

B) INTAKE MANIFOLD VACUUM TENDS TO CLOSE THE VALVE.

CONTROL FACTORS

C) SPRING FORCE OPERATES TO OPEN THE VALVE, OPPOSING MANIFOLD VACUUM AND CRANKCASE PRESSURE.

D) AT IDLE AND LOW SPEED, MANIFOLD VACUUM PULLS THE VALVE TOWARD THE CLOSED POSITION.

NORMAL OPERATION

F) AT HIGHER SPEED OR IN A HEAVY LOAD CONDITION, MANIFOLD VACUUM DROPS. THE SPRING MOVES THE VALVE TO AN OPEN POSITION.

E) THE FLOW RATE THEN IS LOW.

H) BACKFIRE DURING CRANKING CAUSES A HIGH PRESSURE IN THE INTAKE MANIFOLD.

HIGH-SPEED OR LOAD OPERATION

BACKFIRE DURING CRANKING

G) FLOW THROUGH THE VALVE INCREASES — FROM 3 TO 6 CUBIC FEET PER MINUTE.

I) PRESSURE CAUSES THE VALVE TO "BACK-SEAT" AND SEAL OFF THE INLET TO KEEP BACKFIRE OUT OF THE CRANKCASE.

Fig. 35-3 PCV-valve positions during different engine operating conditions. (*Ford Motor Company*)

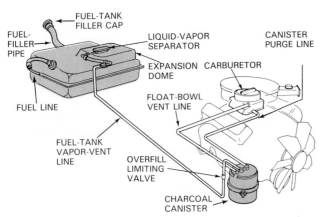

Fig. 35-4 Evaporative emission-control system for a carbureted engine. (*Chrysler Corporation*)

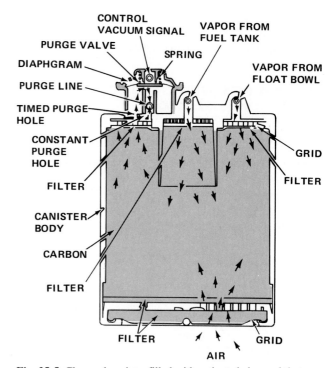

Fig. 35-5 Charcoal canister filled with activated charcoal that adsorbs fuel vapor. (*Pontiac Division of General Motors Corporation*)

open the vent when the engine is off. This allows the vapor to flow to the charcoal canister. Another arrangement uses a solenoid to block the vent when the ignition key is ON.

The canister may have a vacuum-operated *vapor-vent valve* or a *purge valve* (Fig. 35-5). When the engine is idling, the ported vacuum signal (*31-9) provides no vacuum. The spring above the diaphragm extends to hold the purge valve closed. As the throttle valve opens, vacuum raises the diaphragm and opens the purge valve (Fig. 27-5). Some evaporative control systems have the purge valve in the *purge line* (Fig. 35-6). It connects to the throttle body and discharges vapor just above the throttle valve into the intake air. Regardless of how canister purging is controlled, the purpose is to burn the trapped fuel vapor.

➤ 35-7 EVAPORATIVE CONTROL SYSTEM FOR FUEL-INJECTED ENGINES

The fuel-injection system has no float bowl. Therefore, the evaporative control system handles only fuel vapor from

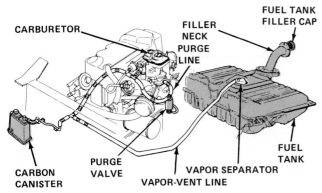

Fig. 35-6 Evaporative control system with a purge valve in the purge line to the carburetor throttle body. (*Ford Motor Company*)

the fuel tank (Figs. 20-1 and 35-7). The canister has two connections. One is the hose from the fuel tank. The other is the purge line to the throttle body. Throttle-body and port-injected engines use similar systems.

Instead of a vacuum-operated purge valve, an electric *canister-purge solenoid* may be used. It mounts on the canister (Fig. 35-8) or in the purge line. The solenoid is normally deenergized. On many engines, the electronic control module (ECM) controls the purge valve or *canister purge* (Fig. 19-26). The ECM opens the purge valve when the engine has reached normal operating temperature and is running above idle. The ECM bases its action on data received from the engine-speed and coolant-temperature sensors (➤19-16 and 19-18).

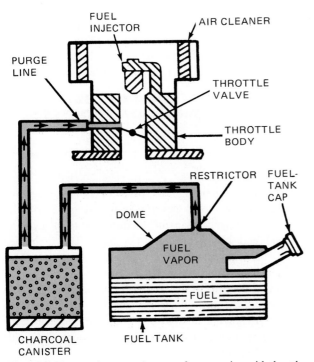

Fig. 35-7 Evaporative control system for an engine with throttle-body injection. The canister has only two connections, one for the fuel tank and one for purging. (*Chevrolet Division of General Motors Corporation*)

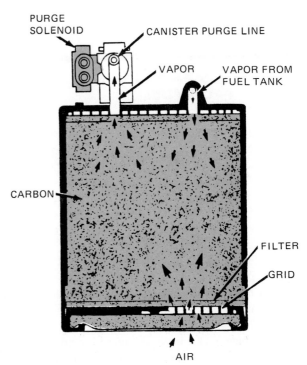

Fig. 35-8 Charcoal canister with a canister-purge solenoid. (*Buick Division of General Motors Corporation*)

When canister-purge should occur, the ECM sends a varying voltage pulse or *pulse-width modulated* (PWM) signal to the purge solenoid. Purge occurs when the solenoid energizes and opens the purge line. This may be for up to 100-percent duty cycle (➤21-31). Minimum purge (100-percent duty cycle) occurs when the solenoid deenergizes and closes the purge line.

Since canister purge is an output from the ECM, the scan tool (➤20-13) can read *purge duty cycle*. This is shown as item 32 on the scan-tool data list in Fig. 20-19. The ECM allows canister purging to occur only after certain conditions are met. This reduces exhaust emissions, and idle and driveability problems.

➤ **35-8 CHARCOAL CANISTERS**

Figure 35-5 shows a charcoal canister used with a four-cylinder engine. It has a purge valve that limits purging during idle. However, it allows full purging during part- to full-throttle operation. In the four-cylinder engine, full purging while idling could upset the air-fuel ratio. The engine might stall because the mixture would become too lean.

During idle, a small amount of purging takes place through a small *constant purge hole* (Fig. 35-5). When the throttle valve opens, it passes a vacuum port in the throttle body. Intake-manifold vacuum then lifts the purge valve off its seat. This opens the purge line that connects to the PCV system. The purge air and fuel vapor flow through the purge line to the PCV system and into the intake manifold. Some canisters have both a vapor-vent valve and a purge valve.

Many canisters are rectangular (Fig. 35-6). Vehicles with big engines may use two canisters. One traps fuel-tank vapors. The other is for carburetor float-bowl vapors.

➤ 35-9 SEPARATING VAPOR FROM FUEL

A vapor-liquid separator prevents liquid gasoline from passing from the tank through the vapor line to the charcoal canister. One type of liquid-vapor separator mounts on top of the tank (Fig. 17-8). The separator is filled with filter material that allows vapor, but not liquid, to pass. Figures 35-6 and 35-9 show a float-type separator that mounts in the tank. If liquid enters, the float goes up and closes the orifice to the canister hose.

Many fuel tanks are domed (Figs. 35-4 and 35-7) and the filler pipe enters slightly below the top of the tank. Either method prevents the tank from filling completely. With the tank completely filled, expansion of the fuel as it warmed up would force fuel out through the tank cap or canister. Some tanks have an internal expansion tank which serves the same purpose. There should be a space equal to 10 percent of the total volume for the gasoline to expand into as it warms up.

CLEANING THE EXHAUST GAS

➤ 35-10 CLEANING THE EXHAUST GAS

Figure 16-1 shows the exhaust-gas pollutants resulting from complete and incomplete combustion. However, combustion in the engine cylinders is never complete. Some unburned gasoline (HC) and carbon monoxide (partly burned gasoline) always remains in the exhaust gas. More of the HC would burn if the combustion temper-

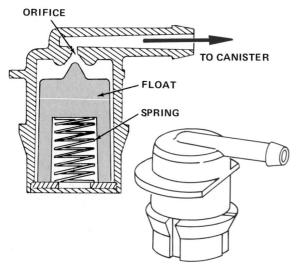

Fig. 35-9 Vapor separator using a float that has an internal spring. (*Ford Motor Company*)

atures were higher, but higher temperatures produce more nitrogen oxides (NO_x).

The four ways to reduce pollutants in the exhaust gas are by:

1. Controlling gasoline quality.
2. Controlling the air-fuel mixture.
3. Controlling the combustion process.
4. Treating the exhaust gas.

Chapter 16 describes automotive fuel and gasoline quality. Following sections describe the other three ways to reduce exhaust emissions.

➤ 35-11 CONTROLLING THE AIR-FUEL MIXTURE

Controlling the air-fuel mixture means:

1. Modifying the fuel system to deliver a leaner air-fuel mixture.
2. Providing faster warmup and quicker choke opening (on carbureted engines)

Feedback carburetors and electronically-controlled fuel injectors work to deliver the ideal stoichiometric air-fuel ratio (➤19-5) to the engine cylinders. Combustion at the stoichiometric ratio produces the minimum exhaust emissions. After the oxygen sensor warms up (➤19-17), it reports to the ECM the amount of oxygen in the exhaust gas. This indicates if the air-fuel mixture is too rich or too lean. The ECM then adjusts the mixture richness.

Faster engine warmup and quicker choke opening reduce exhaust emissions during warmup. Chapter 21 discusses the devices that control the choke and how long the carburetor delivers the rich starting mixture. The thermostatic air cleaner is described in ➤17-10. Chapter 19 covers how the fuel-injection system provides the cold-start mixture and controls the air-fuel ratio during warmup.

➤ 35-12 CONTROLLING THE COMBUSTION PROCESS

Combustion in the engine cylinders is affected by several factors. These include:

1. The air-fuel mixture in the space between the top piston ring, the piston, and the cylinder wall (Fig. 35-10) does not burn. Layers of air-fuel mixture next to the cylinder head and piston head do not burn. This unburned mixture is swept out during exhaust, adding the HC to the exhaust gas.
2. Carbon deposits in the combustion chambers act like a sponge. The carbon absorbs air-fuel mixture during compression and combustion. Then, during exhaust, the lower pressure releases the air-fuel mixture. This adds to the HC in the exhaust gas.
3. Increasing the combustion temperature improves combustion and reduces HC emissions. However, the higher combustion temperature produces more NO_x.

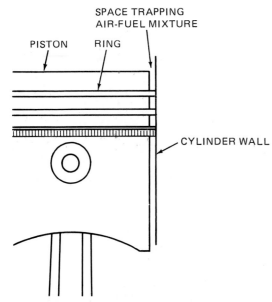

Fig. 35-10 The space above the top ring and between the piston and cylinder wall traps air-fuel mixture that does not burn. (*ATW*)

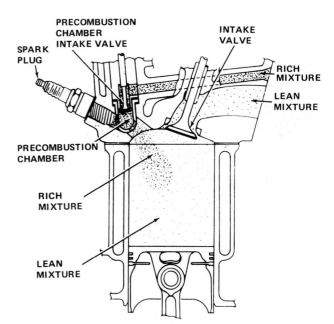

Fig. 35-11 Combustion chamber with precombustion chamber and auxiliary intake valve for a stratified-charge spark-ignition engine. (*American Honda Motor Company, Inc.*)

4. Vacuum advance (➤31-9) in the ignition distributor can cause more NO_x to form. The earlier spark allows a longer time for combustion. Various devices delay or prevent vacuum advance. These include:

   a. A *transmission-controlled spark* (TCS) or *transmission-regulated spark* (TRS) system. It prevents vacuum advance when the transmission is in reverse, neutral, or low forward gears.

   b. A *spark-delay valve* (SDV), which delays vacuum to the vacuum-advance unit during some conditions of vehicle acceleration. Electronic ignition systems provide this type of advance electronically.

➤ 35-13 STRATIFIED-CHARGE COMBUSTION

Stratified means in layers. *Stratified charge* means the air and fuel are not mixed uniformly in the combustion chamber. There are rich layers and lean layers. In the stratified-charge engine, the precombustion chamber fills with a small amount of rich mixture (Fig. 35-11). The spark plug extends into the rich mixture. The main combustion chamber fills with a lean mixture.

When combustion starts, the burning rich mixture streams out of the precombustion chamber and ignites the lean mixture. Since there is so much more lean mixture than rich mixture, the average air-fuel ratio is lean. This provides more complete combustion and reduces exhaust emissions.

High-swirl or turbulence helps mix the rich and lean mixtures. This improves combustion. Different combustion chambers provide stratified charge and turbulence (➤13-10 and 13-11). Some engines have a turbulence-generating pot (TGP) connecting to the combustion

chamber. Others have the precombustion chamber with a small auxiliary intake valve (Fig. 35-11). Another uses an auxiliary intake valve as a jet valve. It opens to admit a jet of air (Figs. 13-13 and 35-12) directly into the combustion chamber. This improves turbulence and combustion.

➤ 35-14 EXHAUST GAS RECIRCULATION

Excessive nitrogen oxides (NO_x) form when peak combustion temperature exceeds 3,500°F [1,927°C]. To lower the combustion temperature, many engines have an *exhaust-gas recirculation* or *EGR system* (Fig. 35-13). It recirculates a small metered amount (typically 6 to 13

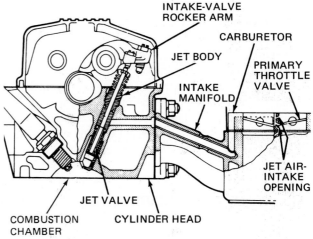

Fig. 35-12 Auxiliary intake valve, or jet valve, that admits additional air into the combustion chamber to improve turbulence and combustion. (*Chrysler Corporation*)

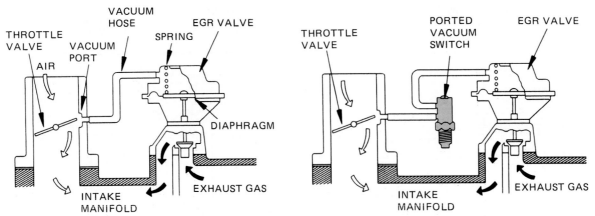

Fig. 35-13 Exhaust-gas recirculation (EGR) systems. Left, EGR valve controlled directly by ported vacuum. Right, EGR valve controlled by the ported vacuum switch which prevents EGR while the engine is cold. (*Chevrolet Division of General Motors Corporation*)

percent) of the inert exhaust gas back into the intake manifold. The cooler exhaust gas absorbs heat from the much hotter combustion process. This reduces peak combustion temperature and lowers the formation of NO_x.

The EGR system (Fig. 35-13) includes a passage between the exhaust manifold and intake manifold. The *EGR valve* opens and closes the passage. Most EGR valves have a spring-loaded diaphragm that forms a vacuum chamber at the top of the valve. The chamber connects by a tube to a vacuum port in the throttle body (Fig. 35-13, left). When there is no vacuum at this port, the spring pushes the diaphragm down and keeps the passage closed. No exhaust gas recirculates. This is the condition during engine idle, when NO_x formation is at a minimum. Also, EGR could stall an idling engine.

As the throttle valve opens, it moves past the vacuum port. Intake-manifold vacuum then acts through the port and pulls the diaphragm up. This opens the valve. Some exhaust gas flows through the valve into the intake manifold. At wide-open throttle, the intake manifold vacuum is low and the EGR valve closes. However, combustion is over more quickly so NO_x has less time to form. No EGR is needed.

Many engines route vacuum to the EGR valve through a *ported vacuum switch* (PVS) or *thermal vacuum switch* (TVS) (Fig. 35-13, right). It prevents EGR until engine temperature reaches 100°F (38°C). The switch mounts in the engine water jacket where it can sense coolant temperature. The switch closes when the engine is cold. This prevents EGR just after a cold engine starts. After the engine warms up so it can tolerate EGR, the switch opens. Vacuum passes through the switch and opens the EGR valve.

> ### 35-15 EGR VALVE WITH BACKPRESSURE SENSOR

This type of EGR valve uses the back-pressure in the exhaust manifold to control exhaust-gas recirculation.

When engine load is light and back pressure is low, the *backpressure sensor* (Fig. 35-14, left) keeps the EGR valve closed. There is no exhaust-gas recirculation. When engine speed and power increase, more exhaust gas flows into the exhaust manifold. Backpressure increases and the EGR valve opens. Then exhaust-gas recirculation begins (Fig. 35-14, right).

Other types of EGR valves control the NO_x emissions of various engines. Some have a second diaphragm to produce increased EGR when the engine is heavily loaded. Others use a modulator system to provide additional control based on car speed. The speed signal may be *venturi vacuum*. This is the weak vacuum in the carburetor venturi that increases with the speed of the airflow through it. A *vacuum amplifier* increases the vacuum enough to operate the EGR valve. A timer and solenoid can delay EGR for a short time after starting a cold engine. This helps prevent stumbling and stalling.

> ### 35-16 ECM-CONTROLLED EGR VALVES

Figure 35-15 shows an EGR system controlled by the ECM. A pressure sensor monitors the exhaust-system pressure. The sensor signals this information to the ECM. The ECM then signals the *electronic vacuum regulator* (EVR) *valve* how much vacuum to apply to the EGR valve. This system accurately controls the amount of exhaust gas recirculated.

Some engines have a *digital EGR valve* (Fig. 35-16) controlled by the ECM. Three solenoids supply EGR to the engine independent of intake-manifold vacuum. Each solenoid controls a different size orifice, which gives seven flow combinations.

The solenoids in the digital EGR valve are normally closed. To open an orifice, the quad driver in the ECM grounds the solenoid coil. This energizes the solenoid, raises the armature, and allows exhaust-gas flow. The response time is about 10 times faster than a vacuum-operated EGR valve.

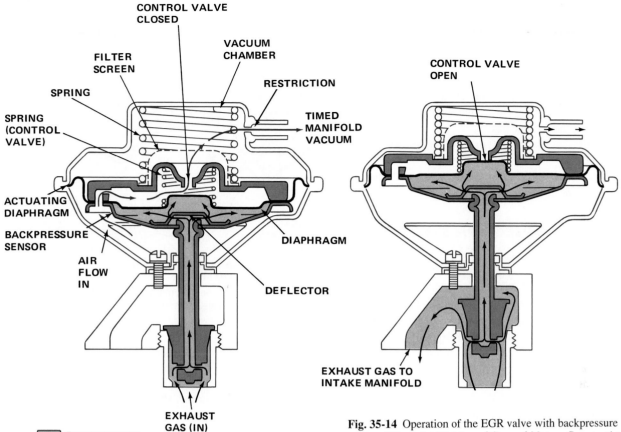

CONTROL VALVE
CLOSED

FILTER SCREEN

VACUUM CHAMBER

RESTRICTION

SPRING

TIMED MANIFOLD VACUUM

SPRING (CONTROL VALVE)

CONTROL VALVE OPEN

ACTUATING DIAPHRAGM

BACKPRESSURE SENSOR

AIR FLOW IN

DIAPHRAGM

DEFLECTOR

EXHAUST GAS (IN)

EXHAUST GAS TO INTAKE MANIFOLD

EXHAUST GAS

Fig. 35-14 Operation of the EGR valve with backpressure sensor. (*Chevrolet Division of General Motors Corporation*)

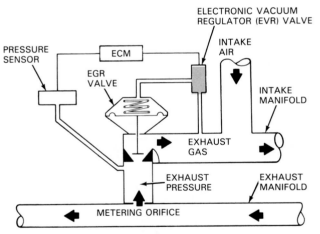

Fig. 35-15 EGR valve controlled by the ECM through the electronic vacuum regulator (EVR) valve. (*Ford Motor Company*)

Figure 19-26 shows *EGR vacuum* as an input to the ECM. Control of *exhaust gas recirculation* is an output from the ECM. Monitoring the *on-off* state of the EGR valve helps the ECM control exhaust emissions. It also provides a signal to the ECM when ignition timing should be retarded to prevent detonation (➤16-4). A scan tool can check the on-off state of each solenoid in a digital EGR valve (Fig. 20-18). These display individually as *EGR1/EGR2/EGR3* ON or OFF. Failure of the EGR system may set one or more trouble codes in the ECM memory (➤20-13).

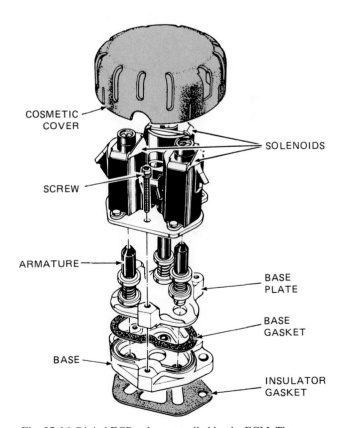

COSMETIC COVER

SOLENOIDS

SCREW

ARMATURE

BASE PLATE

BASE GASKET

BASE

INSULATOR GASKET

Fig. 35-16 Digital EGR valve controlled by the ECM. Three solenoids can supply seven different flows of recirculating exhaust gas. (*Rochester Products Division of General Motors Corporation*)

35-17 TREATING THE EXHAUST GAS

Treating the exhaust gas means that some "cleaning" of the exhaust-gas occurs. It takes place after the exhaust gas leaves the engine cylinders and before it exits the tailpipe and enters the atmosphere. This reduces the amount of HC, CO, and NO_x in the exhaust gas.

The exhaust gas is treated in two ways. One is by injecting fresh air into the exhaust system (➤35-18 and 35-19). The other is by sending the exhaust gas through a *catalytic converter* (➤35-20 and 35-21).

35-18 AIR-INJECTION SYSTEM

The *air-injection* or *AIR system* (Figs. 35-17 and 35-18) reduces HC and CO emissions by injecting fresh air into the exhaust gases after they leave the combustion chamber. The air causes the unburned and partially burned fuel to continue burning. This reduces the amount of these pollutants and helps convert them into carbon dioxide (CO_2) and water. The main parts of an air-injection system are the *air pump*, air switching and control valves, and the one-way check valves.

Figure 35-18 shows the air-injection system on a V-type engine. The air pump is driven by a belt from the crankshaft pulley. When the engine is cold, air is sent to the exhaust manifold (Fig. 35-19). The air enters the manifold through nozzles positioned opposite the exhaust ports. When the air hits the hot exhaust gas coming from the exhaust port, much of the HC and CO changes into H_2O and CO_2.

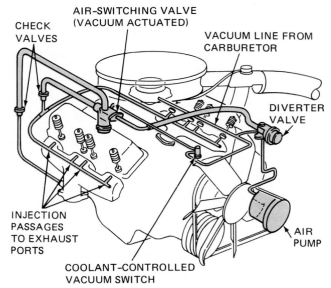

Fig. 35-18 Air-injection system using a belt-driven air pump to deliver air to the exhaust ports. (*Chrysler Corporation*)

When the engine warms up, the ECM switches the air flow to the catalytic converter (Fig. 35-20). There, the air does the same job as in the exhaust manifold. It helps the catalytic converter convert HC and CO into H_2O and CO_2.

After the engine warms up, it gets a leaner mixture. There is less need for air in the exhaust manifold. Also, the oxygen sensor (➤19-17) has warmed up and is now reporting the exhaust-gas oxygen content to the ECM. If extra air was fed into the exhaust manifold, the oxygen sensor would report a high oxygen content. Then the ECM would signal the injectors or carburetor to add more fuel. The result would be a very rich mixture. This is avoided by

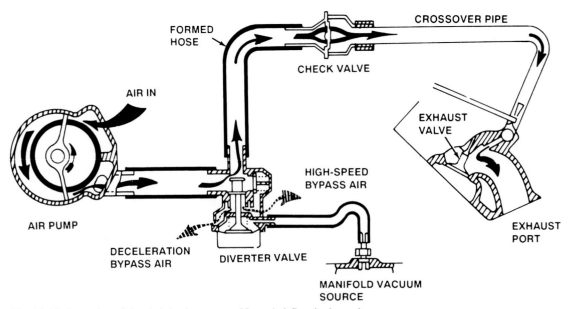

Fig. 35-17 Operation of the air-injection system. Normal airflow is shown by black arrows. Airflow during bypass conditions is shown by the hatched arrows. (*AC-Delco Division of General Motors Corporation*)

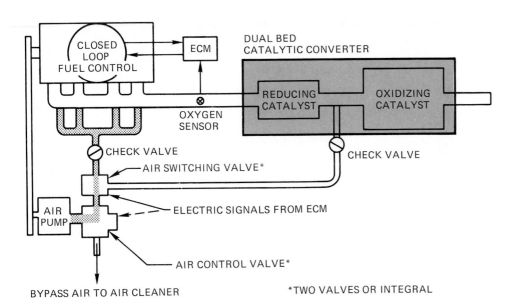

Fig. 35-19 Operation of the air-injection system when the engine is cold. The system sends air from the air pump to the exhaust manifold. (*Chevrolet Division of General Motors Corporation*)

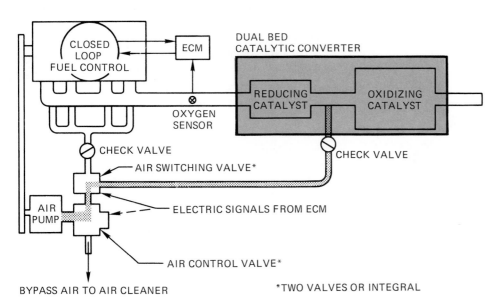

Fig. 35-20 Operation of the air-injection system after engine warmup. The system sends air from the air pump to the catalytic converter. (*Chevrolet Division of General Motors Corporation*)

switching the air flow to the catalytic converter after engine warm up (Fig. 35-20).

The *diverter valve* (Fig. 35-17) prevents backfiring in the exhaust system. This can occur after releasing the accelerator pedal suddenly on a carbureted engine. Some unburned fuel then reaches the exhaust manifold and mixes with the fresh air being injected. Sparks in the hot exhaust gas from the next cylinder that fires ignite the mixture. Backfiring results. To prevent this, the diverter valve diverts the fresh air from the exhaust manifold during deceleration. It dumps the air back into the atmosphere.

Air is also dumped into the atmosphere if:

1. The mixture is too rich as, for example, during deceleration.
2. The ECM recognizes a problem and turns on the CHECK ENGINE light, setting a trouble code.
3. During high engine speed when the air pressure exceeds the setting of the relief valve in the pump.

Check valves are located in the air hose from the pump to the outlets or nozzles (Figs. 35-17 and 35-18). The check valves prevent hot exhaust gases from backing up into the hose and pump.

Most air pumps are driven by the engine accessory drive belt (Fig. 30-3). Some cars have an electric air pump that delivers air to an electric diverter valve. The ECM controls the diverter valve and turns the pump on and off as needed. System operation is basically the same as described above.

➤ **35-19 AIR-ASPIRATOR SYSTEM**

Instead of an air pump, some engines have an *air-aspirator valve* (Figs. 35-21 and 35-22). This is a one-way check valve operated by the vacuum pulses in the exhaust system. The pressure in the exhaust manifold is not uniform. It pulses as the exhaust valves open and close. When exhaust pressure drops below atmospheric pressure, fresh

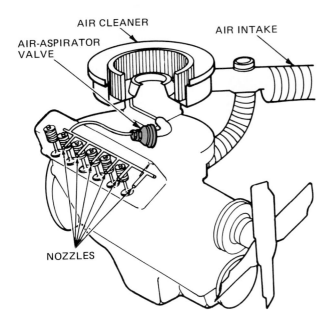

Fig. 35-21 Air-aspirator system which is operated by pulses in the exhaust system. (*Chrysler Corporation*)

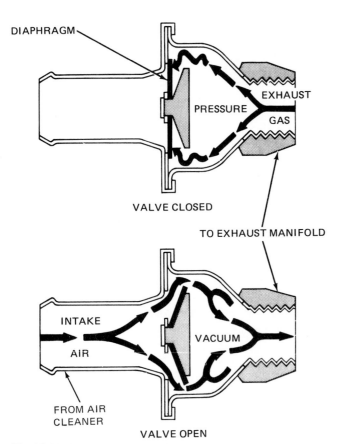

Fig. 35-22 Open and closed positions of the aspirator valve. (*Chrysler Corporation*)

air flows from the air cleaner through the air-aspirator valve to the nozzles in the exhaust manifold. When an exhaust valve opens, the exhaust pressure rises above atmospheric pressure. This closes the air-aspirator valve (Fig. 35-22). The result is similar to a pumping action.

➤ 35-20 CATALYTIC CONVERTER

The catalytic converter (Figs. 17-24 and 35-23) converts harmful pollutants in the exhaust gas into harmless gases. It is located in the exhaust system and all exhaust gas must flow through it. The *catalyst* is a material in the catalytic converter that causes a chemical change without being a part of the chemical reaction. In effect, the catalyst encourages chemicals to react with each other. The result is the exhaust gas leaving the catalytic converter contains less HC, CO, and NO_x than the exhaust gas entering.

A catalytic converter may have two different catalysts. One catalyst treats the HC and CO. The other treats NO_x. The catalyst for HC and CO encourages the HC to unite with oxygen to become H_2O (water) and CO_2 (carbon dioxide). It also encourages the CO to unite with oxygen to become CO_2 or carbon dioxide. This type of converter is an *oxidizing* converter, because it oxidizes the HC and CO. To *oxidize* means to combine with oxygen. The metals platinum and palladium are used as oxidizing catalysts.

The catalyst for the NO_x works differently. It splits the oxygen from the nitrogen. The NO_x becomes harmless nitrogen and oxygen. This type of converter is a *reducing* converter. The metal rhodium reduces the NO_x to nitrogen and oxygen.

Inside the catalytic converter, the exhaust gases pass over a large surface area coated with the catalyst. This surface or *substrate* is either a bed of small beads or pellets, or a ceramic honeycomb (Fig. 35-24). The shape of the converter usually identifies its type. A pellet-type converter is flat. The honeycomb or *monolith* converter is round. Some V-type engines with a dual exhaust system (➤17-14) have two catalytic converters (Fig. 17-25). Other engines may have two catalytic converters in a single exhaust system.

Vehicles with catalytic converters must use unleaded gasoline (➤16-5). Lead in gasoline coats the catalyst and makes it ineffective. For the catalytic converter to be most effective, the air-fuel mixture must have the stoichiometric ratio of 14.7:1 (➤19-5). Small variations in the air-fuel ratio can cause large increases in exhaust emissions.

Most automotive engines have an electronically-

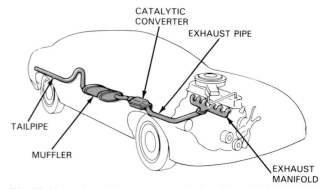

Fig. 35-23 Engine exhaust system, showing the catalytic converter which converts harmful pollutants in the exhaust gas into harmless gases. (*Ford Motor Company*)

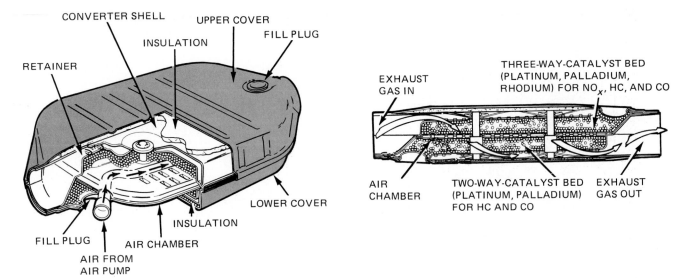

(A) DUAL-BED PELLET-TYPE CATALYTIC CONVERTER

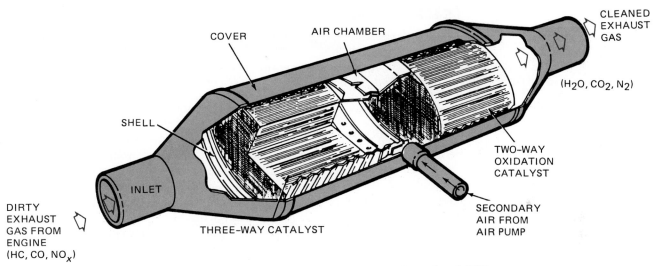

(B) THREE-WAY HONEYCOMB-TYPE CATALYTIC CONVERTER

Fig. 35-24 Types of catalytic converters. (A) Dual-bed pellet type. (B) Three-way honeycomb type. (*Pontiac Division of General Motors Corporation; Ford Motor Company*)

controlled fuel system. It uses electronic fuel injection (Chap. 19) or a feedback carburetor (Chap. 21) to meter fuel. This more accurately maintains the desired air-fuel ratio during most operating conditions.

➤ 35-21 DUAL-BED AND THREE-WAY CATALYTIC CONVERTERS

A *dual-bed catalytic converter* (Fig. 35-24, top) has two pellet beds, one over the other. An air chamber separates the two. The upper bed contains pellets coated with a *three-way catalyst*. This catalyst mainly reduces NO_x to nitrogen and oxygen, but it also oxidizes HC and CO. The lower bed serves as a *two-way catalyst*. It further oxidizes the remaining HC and CO.

When the engine warms up, *secondary air* from the air pump feeds into the air chamber separating the beds (Fig.

21-37). The air helps the oxidizing catalyst convert the HC and CO into carbon dioxide and water. A similar action takes place in the three-way honeycomb catalytic converter (Fig. 35-24, bottom).

| NOTE | Some engines using a three-way catalyst are not supplied with air from an air-injection system. The design of the combustion chamber and electronic control of the fuel system produces cleaner combustion. No extra air is needed. |

When the engine is running, the catalytic converter gets hot. Insulation above it prevents heating the floor pan and warming the passenger compartment. Figure 35-25 shows the *heat shields* around the exhaust manifold and catalytic converter. The heat shields help prevent unwanted heat transfer.

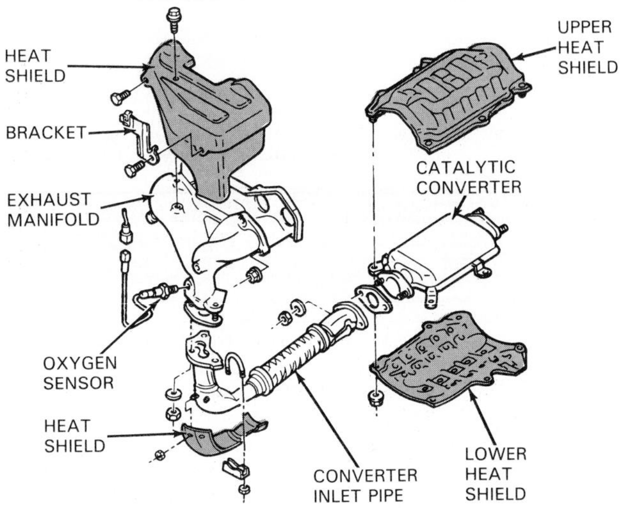

Fig. 35-25 Heat shields around the exhaust manifold and catalytic converter. (*Ford Motor Company*)

Labels in figure:
HEAT SHIELD
BRACKET
EXHAUST MANIFOLD
OXYGEN SENSOR
HEAT SHIELD
CONVERTER INLET PIPE
UPPER HEAT SHIELD
CATALYTIC CONVERTER
LOWER HEAT SHIELD

MULTIPLE-CHOICE TEST

Select the **one** *correct, best, or most probable answer to each question.*
You can find the answers in the section indicated at the end of each question.

1. The three basic pollutants the emission systems control are (➤35-1)
   a. HC, H_2O, and NO_x
   b. CO_2, NO_x, and HC
   c. HC, CO, and NO_x
   d. CO_2, H_2O, and HC

2. The PCV valve does all the following EXCEPT (➤35-4)
   a. allows only a little airflow during engine idle
   b. allows more airflow at higher engine speeds
   c. backseats if a backfire occurs
   d. prevents backfire from occurring

3. Purging of the charcoal canister occurs when (➤35-6)
   a. air from the fuel tank flows through the canister
   b. air from the float bowl flows through the canister
   c. air flows through the canister on its way to the intake manifold
   d. air flows through the canister on its way to the exhaust manifold

4. A vapor-liquid separator in the line between the fuel tank and canister (➤35-9)
   a. allows fuel vapor to flow to the tank
   b. prevents liquid fuel from flowing to the canister
   c. allows the canister to handle liquid fuel
   d. allows the canister to purge itself

5. All the following are ways of cleaning the exhaust gas EXCEPT (➤35-10)
   a. prevent exhaust gas recirculation
   b. control the air-fuel mixture
   c. control the combustion process
   d. treat the exhaust gas

6. Technician A says EGR reduces combustion temperature. Technician B says no exhaust gas recirculates during engine idle. Who is right? (➤35-14)
   a. A only
   b. B only
   c. both A and B
   d. neither A nor B

REVIEW QUESTIONS

1. How does the amount of blowby affect the operation of the PCV valve? (➤35-4)

2. What does *purging* mean, and what controls purging in the evaporative control system? (➤35-5 to 35-7)

3. List four conditions that affect combustion in the engine cylinders and describe how each affects exhaust emissions. (➤35-12)

4. Describe two ways that the ECM can control exhaust-gas recirculation. (➤35-16)

5. Where does the secondary air enter a dual-bed catalytic converter, and why is the additional air needed? (➤35-21)

CHAPTER 36

SERVICING EMISSION-CONTROL SYSTEMS

After studying this chapter, and with proper instruction and equipment, you should be able to:

- Explain why emission-control service is required.
- Diagnose and service PCV and evaporative-control systems.
- Diagnose and service air-injection and EGR systems.
- Diagnose and service the heated-air system and thermostatic air cleaner.
- Diagnose and service the oxygen sensor.
- Diagnose and service catalytic converters.

➤ 36-1 REQUIREMENTS FOR SERVICING EMISSION CONTROLS

Control of emissions from automotive vehicles began with the passage of the *Clean Air Act* of 1963 and its later amendments (➤1-23). As a result, the federal government requires that each vehicle sold in the United States meets the standards of the Clean Air Act.

To enforce compliance, some states and regions require periodic inspection of all motor vehicles. These inspections may include visual and operational checks of all emission-control systems. They may also include a tailpipe check of exhaust-gas emissions.

To ensure that the vehicle continues to run without polluting excessively, automotive manufacturers issue an *emissions warranty* to all new vehicle purchasers. The warranty states that the vehicle will not exceed federal emissions standards during the first 5 years or 50,000 miles [80,467 km] of vehicle service. If it does, the vehicle manufacturer must repair or replace the defective part free of charge. However, the vehicle must be operated and maintained according to the maintenance schedule in the owner's manual. The law also requires that whenever parts are replaced, the new parts must be equal in performance and durability to the original parts.

The vehicle owner is responsible for keeping the vehicle properly maintained for continued emission control. This means all vehicles should be serviced regularly according to the manufacturer's maintenance schedules.

To aid the vehicle owner and service technician, the manufacturer makes detailed information available (➤3-8). This information includes engine identification, the vehicle maintenance schedule (➤3-9), and the service procedures in the owner's manual and the vehicle service

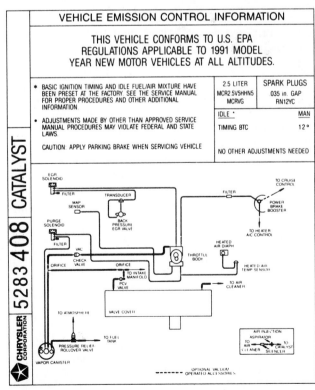

Fig. 36-1 Vehicle emission control information (VECI) label with vacuum-hose routing diagram. (*Chrysler Corporation*)

manual. In addition, the vehicle has a *vehicle emission control information* (VECI) label (Figs. 3-4 and 36-1) in the engine compartment. Follow the instructions on the VECI label when performing any check or service. Other laws impose penalties for modifying or tampering with any emission control system.

> **Careful!** It is against the law to tamper with emission controls on vehicles or vehicle engines. The penalty is a fine of $2500 or more for every vehicle tampered with. Under some conditions, a person found guilty may be imprisoned. When servicing engines and emission controls, do *only* those jobs specified in the manufacturer's service manual. If you remove, disconnect, damage, or render inoperative any emission-control or safety device, you are breaking the law.

➤ 36-2 EMISSION-CONTROL SERVICE

The major emission-control systems that may require service are:

1. Positive-crankcase-ventilation (PCV) system.
2. Evaporative-control system.
3. Air-injection system.
4. Thermostatic air cleaner.
5. Exhaust-gas-recirculation (EGR) system.
6. Catalytic converter.

PCV-SYSTEM SERVICE

➤ 36-3 PCV-SYSTEM TROUBLE DIAGNOSIS

Proper operation of the PCV system usually depends on the PCV valve being free of deposits (Fig. 35-3). With time and mileage, deposits can accumulate in the valve and passages. These can cause several engine troubles. For example, rough idle and frequent stalling may result from a plugged or stuck PCV valve or a clogged PCV air filter. The filter is inside the air cleaner (Fig. 36-2) on many carbureted engines. On fuel-injected engines, the filter may be in the valve cover (Fig. 36-3). Replace a malfunctioning PCV valve or clogged PCV filter.

Vapor flow into the air cleaner and oil in the air cleaner result from *backflow*. Instead of filtered air flowing into the crankcase, crankcase vapors flow into the air cleaner. The cause is a plugged PCV valve or a plugged or leaking condition somewhere in the system. Worn piston rings and cylinder walls also cause backflow. These may allow more blowby than the PCV system can handle. Sludge (➤24-14) or oil dilution in the crankcase can result from a plugged PCV valve or line that prevents normal circulation.

> **NOTE** For a crankcase-ventilating system to work properly, the engine must be warm enough to vaporize the liquid gasoline and water in the crankcase. This may not happen, especially in cold weather, if the vehicle only makes short trips and frequent starts and stops. It may take 10 miles [16 km] or more of driving to vaporize the gasoline and water in the crankcase.

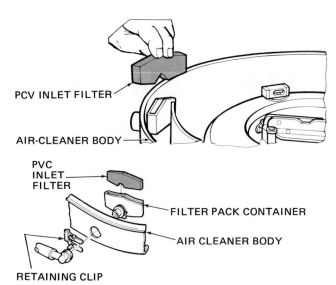

Fig. 36-2 Replacing the PCV filter, or crankcase-air filter, located inside the air-cleaner body. (*Chrysler Corporation*)

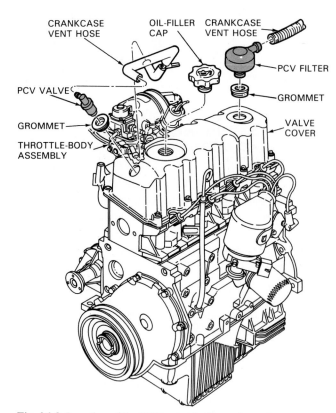

Fig. 36-3 Location of the PCV valve in the engine valve cover. (*Ford Motor Company*)

➤ 36-4 PCV-SYSTEM SERVICE

Replace the PCV valve at regular intervals or whenever it clogs or sticks. Figure 36-3 shows a common location of the PCV valve, in the valve cover. The crankcase vapors flow up to the PCV valve through the internal passages in the engine. These include the passages that allow the valve-train lubricating oil to drain back to the crankcase.

A quick check of the PCV valve is to pull it from its mounting while the engine is warm and idling. You should hear a hissing sound. This indicates the valve and line are not plugged. Shake the valve (Fig. 36-4). You should hear a rattle that indicates the valve is not stuck. Put your thumb over the end of the valve and feel for vacuum (Fig. 36-4). If you feel no vacuum, or if you feel pressure, the system is not working properly. Check the valve, hoses, and connections.

On a non-computer-controlled engine, the *rpm-drop test* can be used to check the PCV system. With the engine warm and idling, connect a tachometer (➤37-3) and note the idle speed. Then pinch the PCV hose closed. Or remove the valve and put your thumb over the end of the valve. Idle speed should drop at least 50 rpm. If it does not, the PCV valve or hose is plugged. Clean the hose and replace the valve.

You can check for crankcase vacuum with the engine idling by removing the oil-filler cap. Hold a piece of stiff paper over the opening. In less than a minute, the crankcase vacuum should pull the paper against the opening.

Figure 36-5 shows a *crankcase-vacuum tester*. It measures the vacuum in the crankcase that should be provided by a properly operating PCV system. If the system fails to pass the test, replace the PCV valve. Clean the hose and tighten the connections.

EVAPORATIVE-CONTROL-SYSTEM SERVICE

➤ 36-5 SERVICING EVAPORATIVE-CONTROL SYSTEMS

These systems require little service. The only periodic service is to replace the filter in the charcoal canister (Fig.

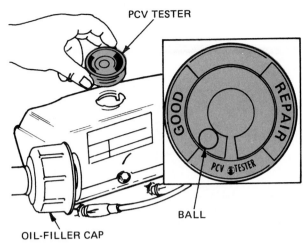

Fig. 36-5 Using a PCV tester to check for crankcase vacuum. (*ATW*)

36-6), if it has one. Most problems in the system can be found by visual inspection or by a strong odor of gasoline.

An *exhaust-gas analyzer* (➤37-9) can find fuel or fuel-vapor leaks (Fig. 36-7). Possible causes of these leaks are:

1. Overfilled fuel tank.
2. Fuel, vapor, or vent line leakage.
3. Wrong or faulty fuel cap.
4. Faulty liquid-vapor separator.
5. Fuel volatility too high.
6. Canister connection loose.

Sometimes a fuel tank collapses. This can occur when a vacuum develops in the tank due to a stuck vacuum-relief valve in the cap (Fig. 17-3). The fuel pump continues to withdraw fuel, increasing the vacuum until the atmospheric pressure bends or crushes the tank.

Excessive pressure buildup in the fuel tank is also possible. It can result from a combination of high temperature and a plugged vent line, liquid-vapor separator, or canister.

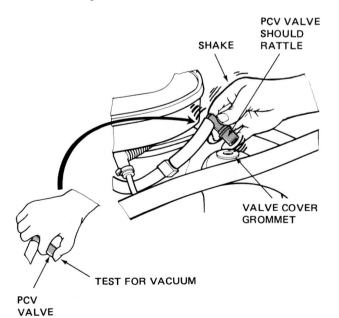

Fig. 36-4 Making a quick check of the PCV valve. (*Chrysler Corporation*)

Fig. 36-6 Replacing the air filter in the charcoal canister.

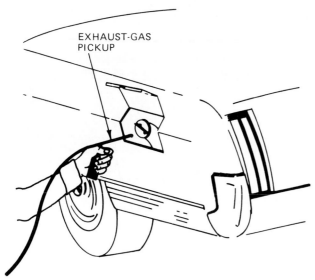

Fig. 36-7 Using the exhaust-gas analyzer to check for fuel vapor leakage from the fuel-tank cap. (*Sun Electric Corporation*)

Poor engine idling can result from faulty connections in the evaporative-control system. Other possible causes are a plugged canister, a vapor-line restrictor missing, or high volatility fuel.

AIR-INJECTION-SYSTEM SERVICE

➤ 36-6 AIR-INJECTION-SYSTEM TROUBLE DIAGNOSIS

The air-injection system injects air into the exhaust manifold when the engine is cold (Fig. 36-8). This helps control exhaust emissions of hydrocarbons (HC) and carbon monoxide (CO). In many vehicles, the system injects air into the catalytic converter after the engine warms up (➤35-18).

Troubles caused by the air-injection system include noise, no air supply, backfire, and high HC and CO levels in the exhaust.

Noise can result from a loose pump drive belt, loose pump mounting, worn pump bearings, or air leaks from the system. The pump is usually not repairable. If damaged, replace it. The belt must be in good condition and adjusted to the proper tension. If the pump is driven by a V-belt, tighten the belt using a *belt-tension adjuster* (Fig. 36-9). Do not pry against the pump housing to tighten the belt. This can damage the pump. If necessary to use a pry bar, pry against the pulley end.

To correct air leaks, tighten the connections. Replace defective tubes and hoses.

High HC and CO emissions could appear in the exhaust with the engine and catalytic converter cold, if no air is reaching the exhaust manifold. This could be due to a defective pump or belt, hose or connection leak, or failure of the diverter or check valve. Replace a defective valve or pump.

A defective diverter valve may cause backfiring. The valve fails to shut off the air supply when high intake-manifold vacuum occurs. A blocked or disconnected vacuum hose also causes backfiring.

➤ 36-7 AIR-INJECTION-SYSTEM SERVICE

The air-injection system requires no routine service except to replace the air filter, if specified in the maintenance

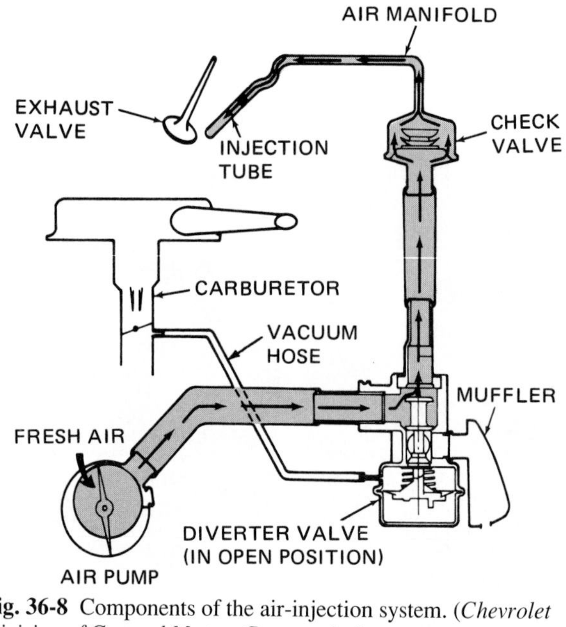

Fig. 36-8 Components of the air-injection system. (*Chevrolet Division of General Motors Corporation*)

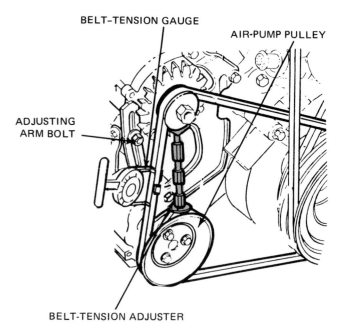

Fig. 36-9 A belt-tension adjuster being used to hold the air pump in place while the adjustment bolts are tightened. (*Ford Motor Company*)

464

schedule. Most air pumps have a centrifugal filter which requires no service.

Check the air-pump drive belt periodically for tension and wear (Fig. 36-9). Replace worn, cracked, or brittle belts (Figs. 26-9 and 30-15) and other defective parts.

HEATED-AIR-SYSTEM SERVICE

➤ 36-8 THERMOSTATIC-AIR-CLEANER SERVICE

The thermostatic air cleaner (Fig. 17-14) has a thermostatically-operated damper or door. When the door is closed, it adds heat from the exhaust manifold to the intake air of a cold engine (➤17-10). Servicing of the air filter is covered in ➤20-18. PCV air-filter service is described in ➤36-3.

A failure in the thermostatic air cleaner usually results in the damper door staying open. The driver probably will not notice anything wrong in warm weather. In cold weather, the driver will notice hesitation, surge, and stalling.

Figure 17-16 shows typical temperatures and positions of the damper door. If the damper does not open properly, check the vacuum motor with a hand vacuum pump (Fig. 36-10). With 9 inches [229 mm] Hg of vacuum applied, the damper should move to the closed HEAT ON position. If it does not, replace the vacuum motor. If it does, replace the temperature sensor.

EXHAUST-GAS-RECIRCULATION-SYSTEM SERVICE

➤ 36-9 EGR-SYSTEM TROUBLE DIAGNOSIS

Too much EGR flow at idle, cruise, or in a cold engine will cause stalling after a cold start or on deceleration. It also causes engine surging while cruising, and a rough idle. Too little or no EGR flow allows combustion temperatures to go too high during acceleration and high-load operation. This can cause spark knock (detonation), engine overheating, and emission-test failure. The exhaust gas will have high HC, CO, and nitrogen oxides (NO_x).

A leaky EGR valve or gasket that allows EGR during idling causes a rough idle and stalling. A defective thermal vacuum switch (TVS) can allow vacuum to operate the EGR valve when it should not. A defective thermal vacuum switch can also cause poor part-throttle performance and poor fuel economy. A sticking or binding EGR valve or deposits in the EGR passages can cause the same problems. Cleaning clogged EGR passages may require removing the intake manifold.

If the engine stalls on deceleration, a restricted vacuum line may be preventing the EGR valve from closing promptly. Detonation at part throttle can be caused by insufficient EGR. This could be due to a clogged or damaged hose, EGR valve, or a defective thermal switch.

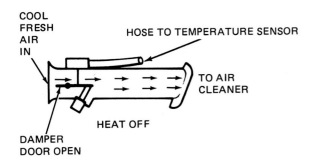

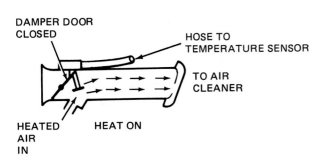

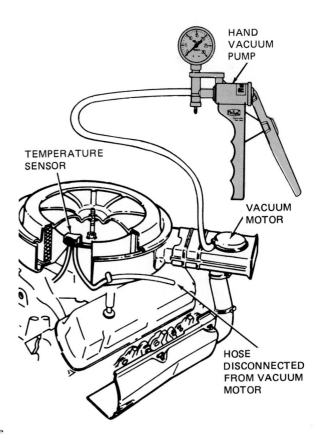

Fig. 36-10 Using a hand vacuum pump to check the vacuum motor in the thermostatic air cleaner. (*Ford Motor Company*)

Failure of the EGR system may set one or more trouble codes (Fig. 20-13) in the electronic control module (ECM). On an engine with a digital EGR valve (Fig. 35-16), a combination of EGR troubles codes indicates an open or shorted solenoid. Other codes indicate only a lack of EGR flow. Additional diagnosis of the system is required to locate the trouble.

➤ 36-10 TESTING THE EGR SYSTEM

To check the thermal vacuum switch, connect a vacuum gauge and a hand vacuum pump as shown in Fig. 36-11. No vacuum should pass through when the engine is cold. Vacuum should pass through after the engine warms up.

There are several types of EGR valves including ported-vacuum (Fig. 35-13), positive backpressure (Fig. 35-14), negative backpressure, and digital (Fig. 35-16). Figure 36-12 shows an *EGR-valve tester* that can test many types of EGR valves after removal from the engine. The tester uses compressed air to create both vacuum and pressure. When using the tester, you can see the movement of the diaphragm or valve stem in the EGR valve.

Many vacuum-operated EGR valves have the stem visible (Figs. 35-14 and 36-13). Check the valve with the engine idling at normal operating temperature. With the transmission in neutral, snap the throttle open to bring engine speed up to about 2000 rpm. The valve stem should move up, indicating the valve is open. If it does not, connect a hand vacuum pump to the EGR valve (Fig. 36-13). Apply vacuum to the EGR valve. It should open. As it opens, the recirculating exhaust gas will cause the engine to idle roughly and perhaps stall. If the EGR valve does not open, it is dirty or defective.

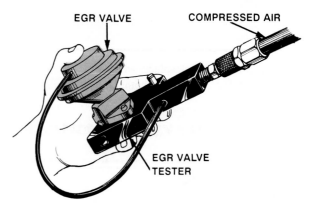

Fig. 36-12 An EGR-valve tester that uses shop compressed air to test many types of EGR valves after removal from the engine. (*Tomco, Inc.*)

To test other EGR valves, follow the procedure in the vehicle service manual.

➤ 36-11 EGR-SYSTEM SERVICE

Some vehicles have a *maintenance reminder light* that comes on at a specified time or mileage. This reminds the driver to have the emissions system checked. Depending on the vehicle, the oxygen sensor, PCV valve, or EGR valve may need service or replacement. An electronic switch or speedometer cable turns on the light.

After performing the service, reset the light. Reset procedures vary. Disconnecting the negative cable from the battery may turn out the electronically-controlled light. Others reset by pressing buttons on the instrument panel. Some cars have a *reset switch*. The proper reset procedure is in the vehicle service manual.

Some manufacturers recommend inspecting the EGR system every 30,000 miles [50,000 km] or 36 months. Many EGR systems do not require periodic inspection. Instead, check the system if trouble develops.

Most EGR service requires replacing the EGR valve, cleaning passages, and installing a new hose. Misrouted vacuum hose causes many complaints about engine

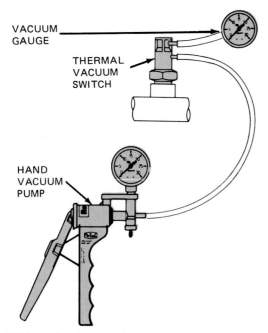

Fig. 36-11 Testing the thermal vacuum switch in the EGR system. (*Ford Motor Company*)

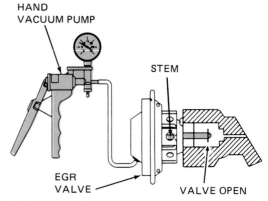

Fig. 36-13 Testing EGR valve operation with a hand vacuum pump. (*Ford Motor Company*)

operation and driveability. The hose-routing diagram is on the VECI label (Fig. 36-1) in the engine compartment.

OXYGEN-SENSOR SERVICE

➤ 36-12 OXYGEN-SENSOR TROUBLE DIAGNOSIS

Vehicles using a three-way catalyst have an oxygen or O_2 sensor (➤19-17) in the exhaust pipe (Fig. 19-24) or exhaust manifold (Fig. 36-14). Periodic replacement of the oxygen sensor may be required. The specified interval ranges from 15,000 to 50,000 miles [24,000 to 80,000 km]. Some cars have an oxygen-sensor light in the instrument panel. It signals when oxygen-sensor replacement is due.

Failure of the oxygen sensor may turn on the CHECK ENGINE light in the instrument panel. Figure 20-13 shows the various trouble codes set in General Motors cars by the oxygen sensor. Low sensor voltage or an open in the oxygen-sensor electrical circuit stores a code 13 in the ECM memory. A lean exhaust sets code 44. A rich exhaust sets code 45. When the CHECK ENGINE light is on, retrieve the trouble codes. Then follow the diagnosis charts in the vehicle service manual to correct the problem.

The scan tool can read oxygen-sensor voltage (Fig. 20-18). It should vary between 100 and 1000 millivolts. Some V-type engines have two oxygen sensors, one in the exhaust manifold for each bank. Item 9 in Fig. 20-19 reads *L.02 R.02*. This shows the scan tool trying to read the out-

put from two oxygen sensors. With no trouble code set, the millivolt readint of *0 124* in item 9 shows the engine has only one oxygen sensor. Its output is 124 millivolts.

The oxygen sensor can fail for several reasons. These include buildup of carbon from a rich air-fuel mixture and lead deposits from the use of leaded gasoline. Other causes are faulty electrical connections and blocking of the reference air to the sensor (Fig. 19-24). Also, fumes from RTV silicone sealant (➤6-25) used as engine gasket material may "poison" or contaminate the sensor.

➤ 36-13 OXYGEN-SENSOR SERVICE

To remove the oxygen sensor, disconnect the negative cable from the battery. If necessary, raise the vehicle for easier access to the sensor. Disconnect the sensor lead from the wiring-harness connector. With an *oxygen-sensor wrench*, remove the oxygen sensor from the exhaust pipe or exhaust manifold (Fig. 36-14). The sensor may be difficult to remove if the engine temperature is *below* 120°F [48°C]. Excessive force may damage the threads in the exhaust manifold or exhaust pipe.

After removal, be careful not to drop or damage the oxygen sensor while handling it. Keep it free of dirt, grease, and other contaminants. If the outside surface of the oxygen sensor is dirty, sometimes cleaning it with a clean cloth will restore proper operation. Never use compressed air or chemical cleaner on an oxygen sensor. Be sure outside air can pass through the openings in the top of the sensor boot. The sensor cannot work without reference air (Fig. 19-24).

Clean the threads in the exhaust manifold or exhaust pipe with the proper size tap, if necessary. Before reinstalling an oxygen sensor, coat the threads with antiseize compound (➤6-14). This makes the sensor easier to remove next time. The threads of a new oxygen sensor are already coated. Install the oxygen sensor and torque it to specifications. Connect the oxygen-sensor lead to the wiring-harness connector (Fig. 36-14). Then install the negative cable on the battery.

CATALYTIC-CONVERTER SERVICE

➤ 36-14 CATALYTIC-CONVERTER TROUBLE DIAGNOSIS

Catalytic-converter troubles are indicated by noise, small particles coming out the tail pipe, and a rotten-egg smell. Other signs are high HC, CO, and NO_x levels in the exhaust gas and power loss due to a restricted catalytic converter.

Noise could be due to loose exhaust-pipe joints, and a loose or missing converter fill plug (on pellet-type converters). Small particles coming out of the tail pipe mean the converter has overheated so the pellet support has

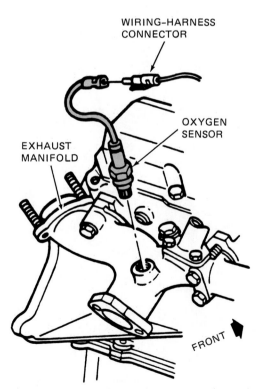

Fig. 36-14 Replacing the oxygen sensor in the exhaust manifold. (*General Motors Corporation*)

warped. Replace a damaged or overheated catalytic converter.

A rotten-egg smell is due to sulfur in the gasoline. The converter combines the sulfur with hydrogen to produce hydrogen sulfide which produces the smell. The driver should try a different brand of gasoline.

A catalytic converter provides almost no sound deadening. Holes in a converter or loose converter-pipe clamps may allow exhaust leakage and noise. But other exhaust-system noise is *not* the fault of the catalytic converter. Mufflers (≻17-17) control exhaust noise on an engine with a catalytic converter.

≻ 36-15 CATALYTIC-CONVERTER SERVICING PRECAUTIONS

Manufacturers recommend the following service precautions for vehicles equipped with a catalytic converter. These precautions help protect the converter from becoming overloaded with gasoline. Feeding the converter a very rich mixture for too long can overheat and ruin it.

1. Avoid prolonged idling, especially fast idling after a cold start.
2. Avoid trying to start a converter-equipped vehicle by pushing or towing. This can load the converter with liquid gasoline.
3. Avoid prolonged cranking with a misfiring or flooded engine.
4. Avoid operating a misfiring engine under heavy load.
5. Never spray or pour liquid engine or carburetor cleaner directly into the carburetor or throttle body.
6. Avoid turning off the ignition with the vehicle in motion and in gear. This overloads the converter with fuel.
7. Use only unleaded gasoline.
8. Do not run out of gasoline while the engine is operating or while driving, especially at high speed.
9. Use only replacement parts that are equivalent to the original-equipment parts (≻36-1). Installing less-than-equivalent parts may be a violation of the Clean Air Act.
10. Do not pump the accelerator to start a hot carbureted engine.
11. Be aware that the converter requires a longer cooling-off period than the muffler.
12. Do not run an engine for more than 30 seconds with more than one spark-plug wire disconnected. The resulting over-rich mixture can damage the converter. Use an oscilloscope (≻33-14) to run the tests.

≻ 36-16 TESTING EXHAUST BACKPRESSURE

The catalytic converter on a properly-maintained engine running only on unleaded gasoline should last the life of the vehicle. However, the converter may become damaged, ineffective, or clogged. Inspect the exhaust system for a dented or collapsed pipe and for heat damage. Make an *exhaust backpressure test* if you suspect a clogged converter or restricted exhaust system.

To check exhaust backpressure, remove the oxygen sensor and install a *backpressure tester* (Fig. 36-15). This is a low-reading pressure gauge similar to the fuel-pump-pressure tester.

NOTE Sometimes the engine may not have an oxygen sensor or the oxygen sensor may be difficult to remove. Then remove the check valve from the air-injection fitting (Fig. 35-18). Using a tapered nipple, connect the backpressure gauge to the check-valve fitting.

With the engine at normal operating temperature and running at 2500 rpm, read the backpressure on the gauge. On some cars, a reading that exceeds 1.25 psi [8.62 kPa] indicates a restricted exhaust system. Other engines may have a higher allowable backpressure. Follow the specifications in the vehicle service manual.

To check for a restricted muffler, disconnect it and repeat the test. No significant change in backpressure points to a restricted converter. When you are sure there is no other cause of excessive backpressure in the exhaust system, replace the catalytic converter.

≻ 36-17 CATALYTIC-CONVERTER SERVICE

The catalytic converter requires no service or maintenance in normal operation. Replace a clogged, damaged, or over-

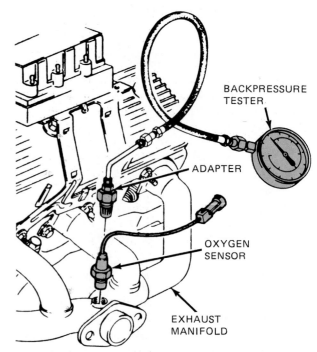

Fig. 36-15 Check exhaust backpressure by removing the oxygen sensor and installing a low-reading pressure gauge, or backpressure tester. (*Buick Division of General Motors Corporation*)

heated converter. Bulging or distortion usually indicates heat damage to the converter. On pellet-type converters, the old pellets can be removed and a fresh charge of pellets installed. This may require special equipment.

No special tools are needed to replace a catalytic converter. Many can be removed by raising the vehicle and disconnecting the converter at the front and rear. Some converters have the exhaust pipe welded to the converter inlet. To remove the converter, cut the pipe. Figure 35-23 shows how one type of converter mounts. Install the new converter with new nuts and bolts.

➢ 36-18 SERVICING CATALYTIC- CONVERTER HEAT SHIELDS

Vehicles with catalytic converters have heat shields (Fig. 35-25) and insulating pads. These protect chassis parts and the passenger-compartment floor from heat damage (➢35-21). Heat shields are installed so air passing rear-ward under the car (the *road draft*) carries away the heat.

Some vehicles require a minimum floor-pan-to-exhaust-system clearance of 5/8 inch [16 mm] at all points while others require more. Any floor covering and insulating pads removed during service must be reinstalled. Restore all parts to their original positions. This is especially important for wiring harnesses, fuel lines, and brake lines.

The lower heat shield (Fig. 35-25) provides added protection against road hazards. It also helps prevent objects from puncturing the converter. Keep rustproofing and undercoating off the heat shields. These coatings reduce the efficiency of the shields in carrying away heat. They also cause strong, objectionable odors.

Check the exhaust system periodically for broken welds, damage, and deterioration. Remove all debris. Replace a missing or torn heat shield. On some vehicles, remove the damaged heat shield by using a chisel to cut through the welds.

TRADE TALK

backflow	emissions-performance	PCV air filter	thermal vacuum switch
backpressure tester	warranty	road draft	thermostatic air cleaner
crankcase-vacuum tester	maintenance-reminder light	rpm-drop test	

MULTIPLE-CHOICE TEST

*Select the **one** correct, best, or most probable answer to each question.*
You can find the answers in the section indicated at the end of each question.

1. The emissions warranty includes all the following EXCEPT (➢36-1)
   a. covers a 5-year period
   b. states the vehicle will not exceed emissions standards
   c. is issued by the vehicle manufacturer
   d. reimburses the owner for vehicle maintenance
2. Technician A says oil in the air cleaner can result from backflow. Technician B says it could be caused by excessive blowby. Who is right? (➢36-3)
   a. A only
   b. B only
   c. both A and B
   d. neither A nor B

3. During the rpm-drop test, the engine speed should (➢36-4)
   a. drop 50 rpm or more
   b. increase 50 rpm or more
   c. not change
   d. drop to 0 as the engine stalls
4. Technician A says the air-injection system helps control exhaust emissions of HC and NO_x. Technician B says the system controls exhaust emissions of NO_x and CO. Who is right? (➢36-6)
   a. A only
   b. B only
   c. both A and B
   d. neither A nor B

5. In the air-injection system, backfiring in the exhaust is prevented by the action of the (➤36-6)
   a. check valve
   b. diverter valve
   c. air pump
   d. thermal vacuum switch

6. Technician A says excessive EGR flow during idle or cold-engine operation can stall the engine. Technician B says it can cause rough idle. Who is right? (➤36-9)
   a. A only
   b. B only
   c. both A and B
   d. neither A nor B

7. No EGR flow can cause all the following EXCEPT (➤36-9)
   a. engine overheating
   b. excessive NO_x in the exhaust gas
   c. detonation
   d. low levels of HC and CO in the exhaust gas

8. Watch the valve stem to check the action of the (➤36-10)
   a. thermal vacuum switch
   b. vacuum-operated EGR valve
   c. digital EGR valve
   d. maintenance-reminder light

9. Catalytic-converter trouble may be indicated by all the following EXCEPT (➤36-14)
   a. small particles coming out the tailpipe
   b. a rotten-egg smell
   c. excessive exhaust noise
   d. a defective oxygen sensor

10. The backpressure in the exhaust system is high. Technician A says this always indicates a clogged catalytic converter. Technician B says to disconnect the muffler and repeat the test. Who is right? (➤36-16)
    a. A only
    b. B only
    c. both A and B
    d. neither A nor B

REVIEW QUESTIONS

1. What is the manufacturer responsible for maintaining and what is the owner responsible for maintaining under the emissions warranty? (➤36-1)
2. What is the penalty for tampering with emission controls on vehicles and vehicle engines? (➤36-1)
3. When should there be a vacuum in the engine crankcase, and how can crankcase vacuum be checked? (➤36-4)
4. How does the thermostatic air cleaner add heat to the intake air, and what happens when this system fails? (➤36-8)
5. What should the minimum floor-pan-to-exhaust-system clearance be to prevent exhaust heat from entering the passenger compartment? (➤36-18)

CHAPTER 37

ENGINE TEST EQUIPMENT AND TUNEUP

After studying this chapter, and with proper instruction and equipment, you should be able to:

- Make cylinder compression and cylinder leakage tests.
- Connect a vacuum gauge and interpret its readings.
- Connect the exhaust-gas analyzer and measure engine exhaust emissions.
- Perform an engine tuneup using an engine analyzer, diagnostic computer, dynamometer, and other available shop equipment.
- Make a car-care inspection during the tuneup and road test.

ENGINE TEST EQUIPMENT

➤ 37-1 ENGINE TESTING

Quick and accurate diagnosis and service of the engine require the use of various test instruments and gauges. These will show if the battery, starting, charging, fuel, ignition, and emissions systems are operating properly. They also indicate the mechanical condition of the engine.

Customer complaints and problems with driveability and engine performance lead the technician to perform *trouble diagnosis* (Chap. 38). Trouble codes and fault messages help the technician with these procedures. However, many driveability complaints and engine troubles do not turn on the CHECK ENGINE light or set a trouble code. The technician then uses a variety of testers to locate the cause of the problem.

Some tests described below are basic tests. They primarily determine if the engine is mechanically sound. This information on non-monitored circuits (➤20-12) and systems is not available from the electronic control module (ECM). Other tests determine if the engine electrical and support systems are operating properly. A dynamometer or road testing checks vehicle performance.

Chapter 26 covers testing procedures for the engine cooling system. Part 3 of this book covers testing of other engine systems. Chapter 27 describes basic testers for electrical-system diagnosis and service. Chapter 28 describes battery testing. Chapter 33 covers ignition testing and use of the oscilloscope and timing light. Chapter 35 describes diagnosis and service of emission-control systems.

Follow the testing procedures in the test-equipment manufacturer's operating instructions. For other tests and test methods, follow the procedures in the vehicle service manual.

➤ 37-2 ENGINE TESTING INSTRUMENTS

Listed below are the engine testing instruments covered in this chapter. Following sections explain how to use them.

1. Tachometer (Fig. 37-1), which measures engine crankshaft speed in *revolutions per minute* or *rpm*.
2. Dwellmeter, which measures duty cycle or how long the ignition-system primary circuit remains closed before it opens again.
3. Cylinder compression tester, which measures the ability of the cylinders to hold compression pressure.
4. Cylinder leakage tester, which locates leaks of compression pressure.
5. Engine vacuum gauge, which measures vacuum in the engine intake manifold.
6. Exhaust-gas or *infrared* analyzer, which measures the amount of certain pollutants and gases in the exhaust gas.
7. Engine analyzer, which combines several testing instruments and may automatically make several tests at once or in sequence.

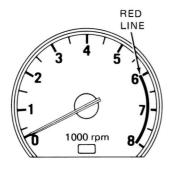

(A) INSTRUMENT-PANEL TACHOMETER

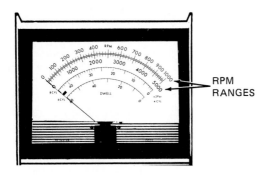

(B) SHOP TACHOMETER (DWELL-TACH)

Fig. 37-1 Instrument-panel and shop tachometers that measure crankshaft speed, or engine rpm.

8. Service-bay diagnostic computer, which performs tests, communicates with the vehicle electronics, stores volumes of service information and specifications, and may be online with the vehicle manufacturer's host computer.
9. Chassis dynamometer, which checks engine and power-train components under operating conditions.

The scan tool (Chap. 20) has become a basic test instrument for many vehicles with an onboard computer. The scan tool provides service information and recalls trouble codes by communicating with the ECM and its memory (Fig. 20-17). Chapter 20 also describes the onboard diagnostic system which acts as a built-in scan tool. Service information and trouble codes display on the vehicle instrument panel.

> ## 37-3 TACHOMETER

The *tachometer* or *tach* (Fig. 37-1) measures engine rpm. The tach may be electric, optical, or magnetic. Figure 37-1A shows an electric tach used in the instrument panel of many vehicles. It counts the electrical pulses in the ignition system and reports the result as engine speed. This tells the driver how fast the engine crankshaft is turning. Then the driver can keep the speed within the allowable range for engine operation. Also, the driver can keep the speed below the *red line*. This marks the maximum allowable engine speed. Operating the engine above this speed may cause failure or reduce its normal life.

Electric or optical tachometers are used in the shop. The electric tachometer (Fig. 37-1B) connects to the ignition primary circuit. The tach counts the number of times per second the primary circuit opens and closes. The optical tachometer has a light beam focused on a rotating part such as the engine crankshaft pulley. The tach counts how many times per second a mark on the pulley passes by.

The magnetic tachometer is usually combined with the magnetic timing tester (➤33-30). It uses a probe inserted in the engine probe hole (Figs. 33-31 and 33-34). The probe reacts to a mark on the crankshaft pulley or to a pulse ring or location indicator on the crankshaft. On an engine with an electronic engine control system (EEC), engine-speed data is available through the diagnostic connector (Figs. 20-18 and 20-19). A scan tool (➤20-13) or a computerized engine analyzer can display the rpm.

> ## 37-4 DWELLMETER

The *dwellmeter* (Fig. 37-2) electrically measures how long the contact points remain closed during each ignition cycle of a contact-point ignition system. The average for all cylinders is then displayed in degrees of distributor-cam rotation. The technician can also use the dwellmeter to set contact-point gap and to check for unwanted dwell variation as engine speed increases. Excessive variation indicates mechanical trouble in the distributor.

In electronic ignition systems, the ECM controls dwell. It is not adjustable. The dwellmeter is used to check the *duty cycle* of the mixture-control solenoid (➤21-32) in a feedback carburetor.

A *dwell-tach meter* (Fig. 37-1B) is a single meter that serves as both a dwellmeter and a tachometer. This is possible because both meters have two leads and require the same connections. Pushing a button or turning a knob on the meter switches the reading from rpm to dwell.

> ## 37-5 CYLINDER COMPRESSION TESTER

The cylinder *compression tester* (Figs. 5-26 and 37-3) measures the ability of the cylinders to hold compression

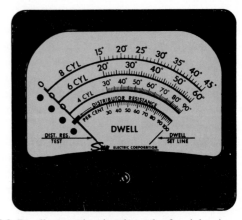

Fig. 37-2 Dwellmeter, showing the scales for eight, six, and four cylinder engines. (*Sun Electric Corporation*)

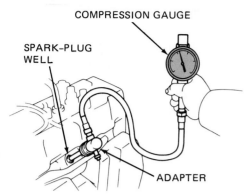

Fig. 37-3 Using a cylinder compression tester. (*Toyota Motor Sales U.S.A., Inc.*)

while the starting motor cranks the engine. The compression tester is a pressure gauge (➤5-21) that measures the amount of pressure, or compression, built up in the cylinder during the compression stroke. How well a cylinder holds compression is an indication of the condition of the piston, piston rings, cylinder wall, valves, and head gasket.

The spark plugs must be removed to use the compression tester. Before removing the spark plugs, be sure the engine is at normal operating temperature and the battery is fully charged. Use compressed air to blow any dirt out of the spark-plug wells. Another way is to disconnect the cables, loosen the spark plugs about one turn, and reconnect the cables. Then start the engine. Run the engine for a few seconds at 1000 rpm. The leaking combustion gases will blow the dirt out of the plug wells.

Remove the spark plugs (➤33-24). Block the throttle wide-open so the maximum amount of air enters the cylinders. Thread the compression-tester adapter into the spark-plug hole of number 1 cylinder (Fig. 37-3). Disable the ignition to prevent coil damage from high-voltage arcing.

> **NOTE** Different steps are necessary to disable various ignition systems. On many engines with a separate ignition coil, disconnect the primary lead from the negative terminal of the coil (Fig. 33-5). Some General Motors engines have high-energy ignition (HEI) with the coil in the cap. Disable these by disconnecting the larger red wire from the distributor (Fig. 33-6). To disable a distributorless ignition system, disconnect the wiring-harness connector between the ECM and the ignition module (Fig. 33-7).

Disable the electric fuel pump (Chap. 20). Operate the starting motor to crank the engine through four compression strokes (eight crankshaft revolutions). The needle on the compression gauge will move around to show the maximum compression pressure in the cylinder. Write down this figure. Then test the other cylinders.

Engine compression readings are usually considered normal if the lowest reading is 75 percent or more of the highest. For example, if one cylinder in an engine has a compression pressure of 120 psi [828 kPa], then

all cylinders should have compression readings of 90 psi [621 kPa] or higher. Typical compression pressures vary among engines and manufacturers. In many General Motors engines, no cylinder should have a compression pressure of less than 100 psi [690 kPa]. Toyota specifies a minimum compression pressure of 142 psi [980 kPa] in some engines. The following section describes interpreting the results of the compression test.

➤ 37-6 RESULTS OF COMPRESSION TEST

The manufacturer's specifications show what the compression pressures should be. If compression is low, there is leakage past the piston rings, valves, or cylinder-head gasket. If the readings vary, *how* they vary may indicate the cause of the problem (Fig. 37-4).

A compression test made as described in ➤37-5 is a *dry* compression test. In a spark-ignition engine, a second or *wet* compression test will help locate the leak. Squirt about 1 tablespoon [15 cc] of engine oil through the spark-plug hole into the cylinder. Recheck the compression.

> **Careful!** Never perform a wet compression test on a diesel engine. The heat of compression (➤23-2) could ignite the oil and damage the compression tester. Also, since the oil is not compressible, it could fill the diesel's smaller combustion chamber and create a hydrostatic lock. This prevents the crankshaft from turning and may damage the engine.

If the compression pressure increases to a more normal value, the low compression probably is due to leakage past worn piston rings. Adding oil helps seal the rings temporarily so the cylinder holds compression better. Other possible causes are a worn piston or cylinder wall, and rings that are broken or stuck in their piston-ring grooves.

Compression Gauge Reading	Probable Engine Condition
Fails to climb during all compression strokes	Valve sticking open
20 PSI [138 kPa] below normal	Faulty rings or valve seating
More than 20 PSI [138 kPa] below normal in two cylinders next to each other	Faulty head gasket
20 PSI [138 kPa] above normal	Excessive carbon buildup in combustion chamber

Fig. 37-4 Compression-gauge readings and the probable engine conditions. (*Ford Motor Company*)

473

If adding oil does not increase compression pressure, the leakage may be past the valves. Possible causes include:

1. Broken valve springs.
2. Incorrect valve adjustment.
3. Sticking valves, valves not seating.
4. Worn or burned valves.
5. Worn or burned valve seats.
6. Worn camshaft lobes.
7. Dished or worn valve lifters.

A *blown head gasket* (➤13-9) also causes a low reading during a wet compression test. The gasket has burned away and compression pressure leaks between the cylinder block and head. Low or no compression in two adjacent cylinders is probably due to a blown head gasket between the two cylinders.

Whatever the cause—rings, pistons, cylinder walls, valves, gasket—the cylinder head must be removed to correct the trouble. The exception is an improper valve adjustment that holds the valves slightly off their seats. Valves are adjusted (Chap. 39) with the cylinder head in place.

➤ 37-7 CYLINDER LEAKAGE TESTER

The *cylinder leakage tester* (Fig. 37-5) checks compression but in a different way. It applies air pressure to the cylinder with the piston at TDC on the compression stroke. In this position, the engine valves are closed. Very little air should escape from the cylinder if the engine is in good condition.

To use the cylinder leakage tester:

1. Remove all spark plugs (➤33-24).
2. Disconnect the air cleaner.
3. Remove the oil-filler cap or dipstick.
4. Remove the radiator cap and fill the radiator to the proper level (Chap. 26).

5. Block the throttle wide-open.
6. Connect the adapter, with the whistle, to the spark-plug hole of number 1 cylinder.
7. Crank the engine until the whistle sounds. This means number 1 piston is moving up on the compression stroke.
8. Continue rotating the crankshaft until the TDC timing marks align (Fig. 33-31).
9. Then disconnect the whistle from the adapter hose and connect the tester.
10. Apply air pressure into the cylinder. Note the gauge reading, which shows the percentage of air leaking from the cylinder. Specifications vary, but a reading of above 20 percent means excessive leakage.
11. Listen at the air intake, tail pipe, and oil-filler hole (Fig. 37-6). If air blows out of an adjoining spark-plug hole, the head gasket is blown between the cylinders. If air bubbles up through the radiator, the trouble is a blown head gasket or a cracked cylinder block or head. Any of these conditions may allow leakage from the cylinder into the cooling system.
12. Check the other cylinders in the same way.

➤ 37-8 ENGINE VACUUM GAUGE

The engine *vacuum gauge* (Figs. 5-27 and 37-7) measures intake-manifold vacuum. The intake-manifold vacuum

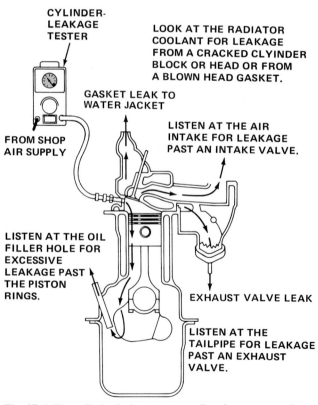

Fig. 37-6 The cylinder-leakage tester applies air pressure to the cylinder through the spark-plug hole with the piston at TDC and the valves closed. Places where air is leaking can then be located. (*Sun Electric Corporation*)

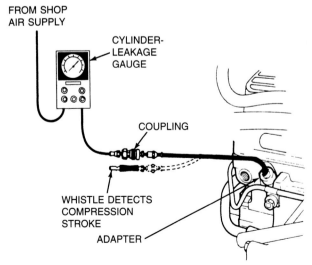

Fig. 37-5 Cylinder-leakage tester. The whistle is used to locate TDC in number 1 cylinder. (*Sun Electric Corporation*)

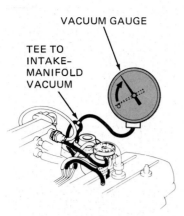

VACUUM GAUGE

TEE TO INTAKE-MANIFOLD VACUUM

Fig. 37-7 Vacuum gauge connected to intake manifold to measure intake-manifold vacuum. (*Toyota Motor Sales U.S.A., Inc.*)

changes with the load on the engine, the position of the throttle valve, and different engine defects. The way the vacuum varies from normal indicates what could be wrong inside the engine. Before making the test, check that all vacuum hoses are properly connected and not leaking. Make a *backpressure test* (➤36-16) if a restricted exhaust system is indicated.

Connect the vacuum gauge to the intake manifold. Start the engine and run it until it reaches normal operating temperature. Then note the vacuum reading at idle and other speeds, as described below. Figure 37-8 shows the meaning of various vacuum-gauge readings. Common vacuum-gauge readings are described below.

1. A steady and fairly high reading on idle indicates normal performance. Specifications vary with different engines. A reading between 17 and 22 inches [432 and 599 mm] of mercury usually indicates normal engine operation. The reading will be lower at higher altitudes because of lower atmospheric pressure. For every 1000 feet [305 m] above sea level, the reading is reduced about 1 inch [25.4 mm] of mercury (Hg).

NOTE *Inches or millimeters of mercury refers to the way the vacuum is measured (➤5-22). There is no mercury in the gauge. The readings compare with the changes that a vacuum would produce on a column of mercury in a barometer. Figure 18-2 shows the relationship among the various measurements of vacuum and pressure.*

2. A steady and low reading on idle indicates late ignition or valve timing, or possibly leakage past the piston rings. This excessive blowby could be due to worn or stuck piston rings, or worn cylinder walls or pistons. Any of these reduces engine power. With less power, the engine does not develop or "pull" as much vacuum.

3. A steady and very low reading on idle indicates an air leak at the intake manifold or throttle body. The leak could be around the throttle shaft. Air leakage into the intake manifold reduces vacuum and engine power. Incorrect timing may also cause this condition.

	READING	DIAGNOSIS
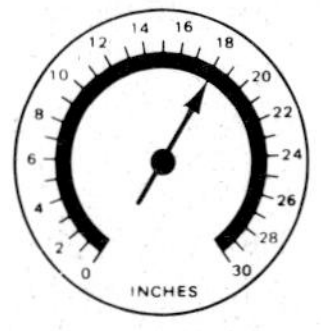 1	Average and steady at 17-22.	Everything is normal.
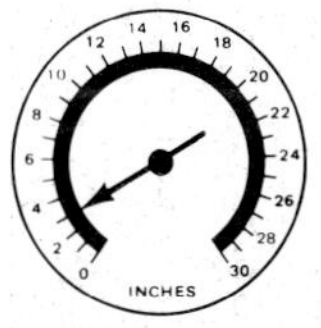 2	Extremely low reading—needle holds steady.	Air leak at the intake manifold or throttle body; incorrect timing.
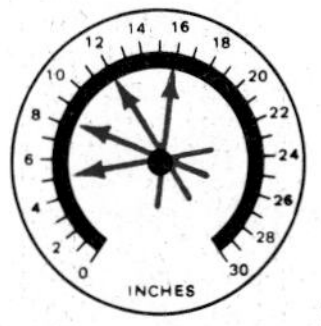 3	Needle fluctuates between high and low reading.	Blown head gasket between two side-by-side cylinders. Check with compression test.
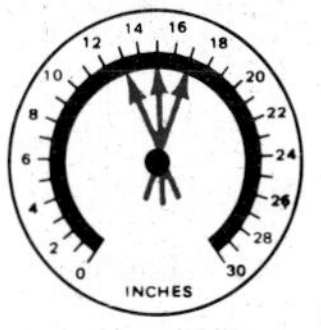 4	Needle fluctuates very slowly, ranging 4 or 5 points	Idle mixture needs adjustment, spark-plug gap too narrow, valves sticking open.
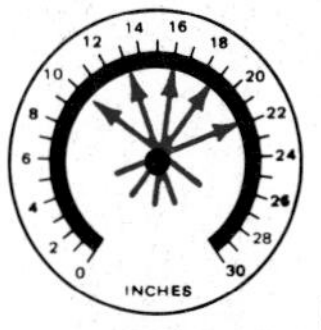 5	Needle fluctuates rapidly at idle—steadies as RPM is increased.	Worn valves guides.
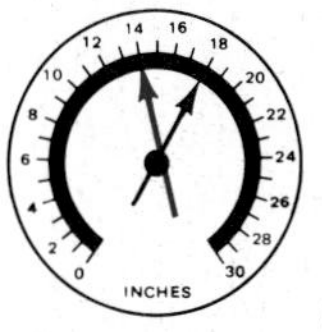 6	Needle drops to low reading, returns to normal, drops back, etc., at a regular interval.	Burned or leaking valve.
 7	Needle drops to zero as engine RPM is increased.	Restricted exhaust system.
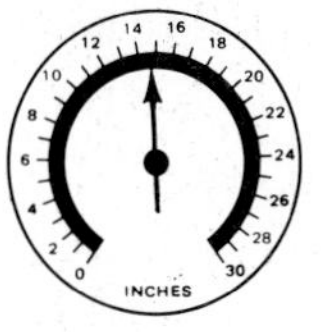 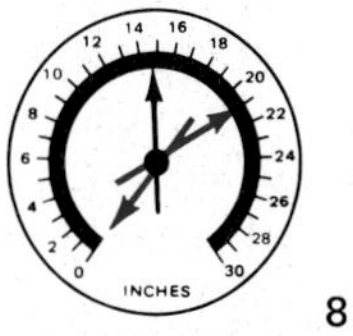 8	Needle holds steady at 12 to 16—drops to 0 and back to about 21 as throttle is opened and released.	Late ignition or valve timing. Leaking piston rings. Check with compression test.

Fig. 37-8 Vacuum-gauge readings and their meanings.

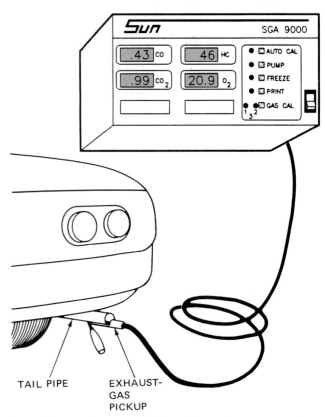

NOTE *Some engines with high-lift cams and longer valve overlap have a lower and more uneven intake-manifold vacuum. Also, some emission-control systems lower intake-manifold vacuum.*

4. A reading that varies rapidly—increasing with engine speed—between 10 and 22 inches [254 and 599 mm] indicates a weak or broken valve spring.

5. A reading that drops back to zero as engine speed increases indicates a restricted exhaust system.

6. Regular dropping back of the needle indicates a valve that is burned or sticking open, or a spark plug not firing.

7. Irregular dropping back of the needle indicates valves that are sticking open only part of the time.

8. Floating motion or slow back-and-forth movement of the needle indicates that the air-fuel mixture is too rich.

On some engines, a vacuum-gauge quick test can be made for loss of compression due to leakage around the piston. This would result from worn piston rings, pistons, or cylinder walls. Race the engine and then quickly release the throttle. The needle should swing around to 23 to 25 inches [584 to 635 mm] as the throttle closes. This indicates good compression. If the needle fails to swing this far, there is compression loss.

Fig. 37-9 Four-gas type of exhaust-gas analyzer connected to tailpipe to test the exhaust gas. (*ATW*)

NOTE *Some V-type engines have a split intake manifold with no passage between the two sections. On these engines, connect the vacuum gauge to each section and note the readings.*

Another test using the vacuum gauge is the *cranking-vacuum test*. With the engine at normal operating temperature, close the throttle valve and plug the PCV line. Disable the ignition and crank the engine. An even cranking vacuum at normal cranking speed indicates the engine is mechanically sound. Unevenness in the needle movement indicates an air leak into one or more cylinders.

➤ 37-9 EXHAUST-GAS ANALYZER

The *exhaust-gas analyzer* (Fig. 37-9) measures the amount of various gases in the exhaust. There are two main types:

1. *Two-gas analyzer* that measures HC and CO.
2. *Four-gas analyzer* that measures HC, CO, O_2, and CO_2.

The purpose of making these measurements is to help determine the condition of the engine, ignition system, fuel system, and emission controls. On a car with a catalytic converter, tail pipe readings made with a two-gas analyzer (Fig. 37-10) are often of little value. Normal action of the catalyst (➤35-20) reduces the HC and CO nearly to zero.

Four-gas analyzers (Fig. 37-9) provide more complete analysis of the tail pipe exhaust gas. Carbon dioxide (CO_2) and oxygen (O_2) in the exhaust gas from the cylinders pass unchanged through the catalytic converter. Measuring

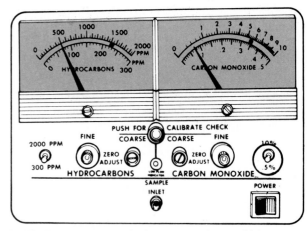

Fig. 37-10 Two-gas type of exhaust-gas analyzer, which measures only hydrocarbons (HC) and carbon monoxide (CO). (*Chrysler Corporation*)

these gases at the tail pipe gives a more complete picture of the air-fuel mixture entering the cylinders and the combustion process.

To use the exhaust-gas analyzer, block off the air flow from the air-injection or air-aspirator system (Chap. 36). This prevents the additional air from affecting the readings. Insert the exhaust-gas pickup or probe into the tail pipe of the car. The probe draws out some of the exhaust gas and carries it through the analyzer. Meters, a display, or a printout show how much of each gas is in the sample of exhaust gas.

An NO$_x$ tester works in almost the same way. It draws exhaust gas from the tailpipe and runs the gas through the analyzer. In the laboratory, the results are reported in *grams per miles* (gpm). Some new exhaust-gas analyzers (*five-gas analyzers*) also measure NO$_x$. These analyzers are being used in emissions testing and automotive-service work.

When testing exhaust emissions, follow the tester-manufacturer's operating instructions. Federal and state laws set maximum limits on the amount of HC and CO in the exhaust gas. Figure 37-11 shows suggested testing specifications. Take the readings with the engine idling at normal operating temperature. Repeat the tests with the engine running at 1500 rpm and 2500 rpm.

> **NOTE** An exhaust-gas analyzer can also be used to check for exhaust-gas leakage into the cooling system (➤26-10). Figure 36-7 shows the exhaust-gas analyzer being used to locate fuel or fuel-vapor leaks (➤36-5).

➤ 37-10 FOUR-GAS ANALYSIS

Figure 19-7 shows the conversion efficiency of the catalytic converter as the air-fuel ratio varies from rich to lean. Combustion at the stoichiometric ratio of 14.7:1 provides maximum conversion efficiency. This minimizes tail pipe emissions of HC, CO, and NO$_x$.

Figure 37-12 shows the relationship among the four gases measured by the four-gas analyzer. Each gas and its readings are described below.

HC READINGS The HC meter reports the amount of hydrocarbons (unburned gasoline) in the exhaust. It reports this as *parts per million* (ppm). A reading of 200 means that every million parts of exhaust gas has 200 parts of HC. The exhaust gas of newer cars has less than 100 ppm of HC. Older vehicles are much higher emitters. Even in good condition they may emit 400 ppm or more.

High HC could result from trouble in the emission controls, or fuel or ignition system. The air-fuel mixture could be rich (or lean so there is misfiring). The ignition system may be out of time or misfiring. An engine with worn rings and cylinders, burned valves, or a blown head gasket emits high levels of HC.

CO READINGS Carbon monoxide is a product of incomplete combustion. The amount of CO is measured as a per-

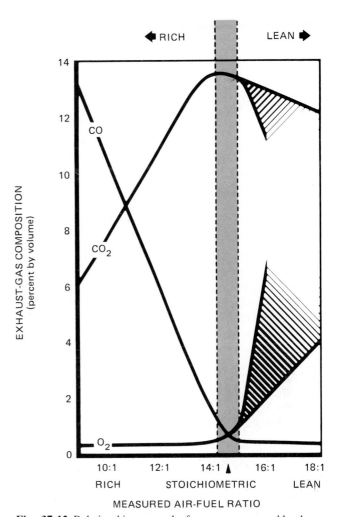

Fig. 37-12 Relationship among the four gases measured by the four-gas analyzer. (*Sun Electric Corporation*)

centage by volume. One percent means that one percent of the exhaust gas is CO. Some automotive engines produce less than 0.5 percent CO. A rich mixture or not enough oxygen to burn the fuel produces excessive CO. Possible causes are misfiring, a restricted air filter, and a leaking fuel injector or carburetor needle-and-seat.

CO$_2$ READINGS Carbon dioxide is a byproduct of combustion that is measured as a percentage by volume. HC must burn to produce CO$_2$. Any change in the air-fuel ratio and the combustion process causes a change in CO$_2$. Normally, CO$_2$ is above eight percent. The highest CO$_2$ reading occurs at about the 14.7:1 stoichiometric air-fuel ratio (Fig. 37-12). The higher the CO$_2$ reading, the more complete the combustion.

O$_2$ READINGS These measure the percentage of oxygen remaining in the exhaust gas after combustion has occurred. The air we breathe is about 21 percent oxygen. At idle, the engine should produce less than three percent O$_2$. If the engine is running richer than 14.7:1, O$_2$ is low. As the air-fuel mixture becomes leaner than 14.7:1, O$_2$ increases. When lean misfire occurs, O$_2$ increases greatly. At the stoichiometric ratio (14.7:1), O$_2$ should about equal CO.

Vehicle Year	HC (ppm) Less Than	CO$_2$ (%) Greater Than	CO (%) Less Than	O$_2$ (%) In the Range of
71–75	400 ppm	8%	3%	.1–5%
76–79	200 ppm	8%	2%	.1–5%
80–	100 ppm	8%	.5%	.1–5%

Fig. 37-11 Suggested test specifications for testing exhaust emissions.

477

➤ 37-11 CYLINDER-BALANCE TEST

The *cylinder-balance test* determines if each cylinder in a running engine produces the same amount of power. Disabling a cylinder should cause a change in engine speed. The change should be about the same for all cylinders.

Connect a tachometer to the engine. Then disable the cylinder. This is done by shorting the spark plug or disconnecting each fuel injector in a port-injected engine (➤20-10). Note the tach reading (Fig. 37-13). Repeat the test on each cylinder. All cylinders are contributing the same amount of power if the rpm drops are the same. Weaker cylinders show less of a rpm change. Shorting or disabling a dead cylinder causes no change in rpm.

On some engines, the ECM can run the cylinder-balance test automatically and store the results. The technician signals the ECM to begin the test. The ECM then turns off the fuel injector to each cylinder and measures engine rpm. This process repeats until testing is completed.

Cylinder-balance testing can also be performed while watching the readings on a four-gas analyzer (➤37-10). This may help diagnose the cause of a cylinder delivering low or no power.

➤ 37-12 ENGINE ANALYZER

An *engine analyzer* (Fig. 37-14) combines several testers, meters, and gauges into a single piece of portable shop equipment. When connected to the vehicle, the analyzer provides quick and accurate testing and diagnosis of various engine and vehicle systems.

Most shop engine analyzers include an oscilloscope (➤33-14). It displays voltage patterns of the ignition

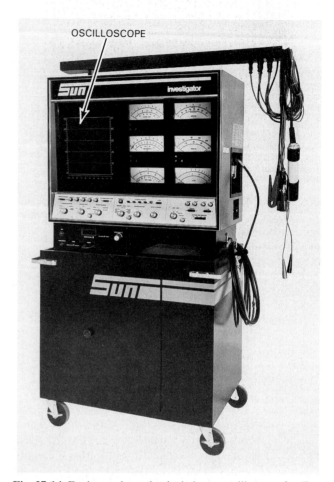

Fig. 37-14 Engine analyzer that includes an oscilloscope for displaying ignition voltages. (*Sun Electric Corporation*)

system, charging system, and electronic fuel injectors. Some computerized analyzers include a second screen (Fig. 37-15). This displays information needed by the technician, such as steps in a test procedure or the test results. The analyzer may have a printer to provide a written report.

➤ 37-13 SERVICE-BAY DIAGNOSTIC COMPUTER

Some new-car dealerships and other service shops have a *service-bay diagnostic computer* (Figs. 20-23 and 37-16). This is a computerized engine-and-exhaust-gas analyzer with additional capabilities (➤20-14). Ideally, the system enables the vehicle to tell the computer what is wrong. Then the system instructs the technician on how to make the needed repairs.

Many of these computers have a touch-sensitive screen. The technician first enters the vehicle identification number (➤3-3). Then the technician answers a series of *yes-no* questions about how the vehicle is equipped. The technician connects the computer to the diagnostic connector on the vehicle. The computer then:

1. Automatically performs the tests.

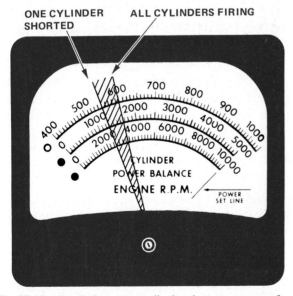

Fig. 37-13 All cylinders are contributing the same amount of power if the tachometer shows that all rpm drops are the same as each cylinder is disabled. (*Sun Electric Corporation*)

Fig. 37-15 Computerized engine analyzer with two scope screens and a printer. (*Sun Electric Corporation*)

Fig. 37-16 A service-bay diagnostic computer with a touch-sensitive screen. (*Buick Division of General Motors Corporation*)

2. Interprets the results.

3. Shows the technician how to correct the faults.

In a dealership, the computer may automatically go *online* every night. This means the computer connects itself through a phone line or satellite link to the vehicle-manufacturer's host computer. The host computer then sends or *downloads* the latest information on:

- Factory product changes.
- Diagnostic and repair techniques.
- Vehicle specifications.
- Service manual information.
- Service bulletin summaries.

During this same connection, the dealership computer sends or *uploads* information fed into it during the day to the host computer. This provides overnight data exchange of the latest service information between the dealer and the manufacturer.

Similar systems are available to independent shops. To provide the capabilities listed above, the computer must store a wide range of service information. This information must be quickly accessible and easily updated. Many computers store data on a compact disc (CD), similar to the audio CD. When new information is needed, the technician replaces the disc (Fig. 37-17).

➤ 37-14 DYNAMOMETER

The *chassis dynamometer* (Fig. 15-13) measures engine power and vehicle speed under various operating con-

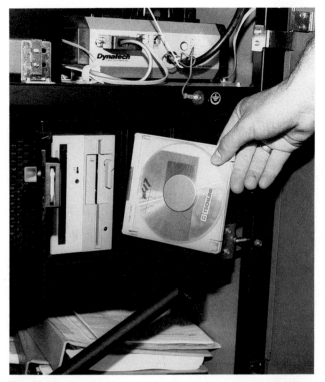

Fig. 37-17 Changing the compact disc to change and update the database in a service-bay diagnostic computer. (*ATW*)

ditions. The vehicle is driven onto two rollers so the drive wheels can spin the rollers. The rollers drive a power absorber which is usually under the floor. The vehicle remains stationary, but the engine and other components operate the same as on a road test. Meters on a console report wheel speed and torque or power.

The power absorber may be a heavy metal flywheel with an *inertia weight* (➤15-5) the same as the weight of the vehicle. Or, the power absorber may be a brake that places a variable load on the rollers. The technician can connect an oscilloscope and a variety of other testers to check the engine under operating conditions. When the vehicle is "driven" on the dynamometer, the test instruments show engine performance while idling, accelerating, cruising, and decelerating. Shift points and other operating conditions of an automatic transmission can also be checked (Chap. 48).

Special dynamometers with two sets of rollers test *all-wheel-drive* vehicles (Chap. 46). Diagnostic dynamometers have sensitive motored rollers that may allow testing of wheel alignment, suspension, steering, and brakes.

ENGINE TUNEUP AND CAR CARE

➤ 37-15 DEFINITION OF A TUNEUP

An engine tuneup restores driveability, power, performance, and economy that have been lost through wear, corrosion, and deterioration of engine parts. These changes take place gradually in many parts through *time and mileage*. This means the parts are affected by normal aging of the vehicle (time) and by normal vehicle operation (mileage).

A tuneup means different things to different people. To some, it means a quick check of the usual engine trouble spots. To others, it means using test instruments to do a complete analysis of the engine and its systems. Then all worn parts are repaired or replaced, and everything is adjusted to specifications.

➤ 37-16 TUNEUP PROCEDURE

An engine tuneup follows a procedure. Many technicians use a printed form supplied by automotive or test-equipment manufacturers (Fig. 37-18). By following the form and checking off the items listed, one by one, the technician avoids overlooking any test in the procedure.

All tuneup forms are not the same. The procedure to follow depends on the vehicle and its engine as well as the shop equipment available. If the shop has an oscilloscope or a dynamometer, use it as part of the tuneup procedure.

In the following section (➤37-17), many steps are given as part of a typical engine-tuneup procedure. Other chapters in this book cover how to perform most of these steps. For more information on each step, refer to the chapter covering that part or system.

SUN SLEUTH ONE/SLEUTH TWO
ENGINE PERFORMANCE TEST REPORT

CUSTOMER NAME_____ PHONE_____ DATE_____
ADDRESS_____ CITY/STATE_____ LICENSE_____
MAKE/YEAR/MODEL_____ MILEAGE_____ MILEAGE SINCE TUNE-UP_____
ENGINE_____ TRANSMISSION--AUTO □ STD □   AIR CONDITIONING--YES □ NO □
CARBURETOR_____ IGNITION TYPE_____ AIR PUMP--YES □ NO □ CONVERTER--YES □ NO □
CUSTOMER COMMENTS_____ TESTED BY_____

TEST MODE	TEST	READ	ENTER SPECIFICATIONS	TEST RESULTS	COMMENTS
ENGINE OFF, KEY OFF	BATTERY VOLTAGE	DIGITAL DISPLAY	VOLTS		
ENGINE OFF, KEY ON	DISTRIBUTOR RESISTANCE *	DIGITAL DISPLAY	VOLTS (MAX)		
CRANKING	COIL OUTPUT *	SCOPE (DISPLAY)	KV (MIN)		
	VACUUM •	VACUUM GAUGE	VACUUM (MIN)		
	DWELL •	DIGITAL DISPLAY	DEG./PERCENT		
	BATTERY VOLTAGE	DIGITAL DISPLAY	VOLTS (MIN)		
RUNNING 2500 RPM (HIGH CRUISE)	ALTERNATOR CONDITION	SCOPE (ALT) RASTER	EVEN RIPPLE		
	DWELL	DIGITAL DISPLAY	DEG./PERCENT		
	TIMING ADVANCE	TIMING LIGHT	DEGREES		
	MANIFOLD VACUUM	VACUUM GAUGE	VACUUM (MIN)		
	HC (HYDROCARBONS) □	HC DIGITAL DISPLAY	PPM		
	CO (CARBON MONOXIDE) □	CO DIGITAL DISPLAY	PERCENT		
	CHARGING VOLTAGE	DIGITAL DISPLAY	VOLTS (MAX)		
RUNNING 1500 RPM (LOW CRUISE)	COIL POLARITY	SCOPE (DISPLAY)	VISUAL		
	SPARK PLUG FIRING VOLTAGE	SCOPE (DISPLAY)	KV		
	MAXIMUM COIL OUTPUT *	SCOPE (DISPLAY)	KV (MIN)		
	SECONDARY INSULATION *	SCOPE (DISPLAY)	VISUAL		
	SECONDARY RESISTANCE	SCOPE (RASTER)	VISUAL		
	COIL — CONDENSER	SCOPE (RASTER)	VISUAL		
	BREAKER POINT CONDITION *	SCOPE (RASTER)	VISUAL		
	CYLINDER TIMING	SCOPE (SUPERIMPOSED)	VISUAL		
	CHARGING VOLTAGE	DIGITAL DISPLAY	VOLTS (MAX)		
	MANIFOLD VACUUM	VACUUM GAUGE	VACUUM (MIN)		
	HC (HYDROCARBONS) □	HC DIGITAL DISPLAY	PPM		
	CO (CARBON MONOXIDE) □	CO DIGITAL DISPLAY	PERCENT		
CYLINDER POWER BALANCE	ENGINE			BASE RPM	BASE VACUUM
	CYLINDER	1	2 3 4 5 6 7 8 9 10 11 12		
	VACUUM CHANGE				
	RPM CHANGE				
SNAP ACCELERATION	SPARK PLUGS UNDER LOAD	SCOPE (DISPLAY)	KV (MAX)		
	ACCELERATOR PUMP ACTION □	CO DIGITAL DISPLAY	PERCENT (MIN)		
RUNNING IDLE	RPM	DIGITAL DISPLAY	RPM		
	DWELL	DIGITAL DISPLAY	DEG./PERCENT		
	INITIAL TIMING	TIMING LIGHT	DEGREES		
	CHARGING VOLTAGE	DIGITAL DISPLAY	VOLTS (MAX)		
	MANIFOLD VACUUM	VACUUM GAUGE	VACUUM (MIN)		
	HC (HYDROCARBONS) □	HC DIGITAL DISPLAY	PPM		
	CO (CARBON MONOXIDE) □	CO DIGITAL DISPLAY	PERCENT		

* This test is not recommended for electronic ignition systems.
• Perform this test under no-start and hard start conditions.
□ For use with the SLEUTH TWO Engine Performance Analyzer.

Fig. 37-18 An engine performance-test report, which may be filled in as part of an engine tuneup. (*Sun Electric Corporation*)

To find other sources and related information, turn to the entry in the index at the back of this book. Refer to the vehicle service manual for details of servicing specific parts and components. Always follow the specifications and procedures listed on the vehicle emission control information (VECI) label in the engine compartment (Fig. 36-1).

➤ 37-17 TYPICAL TUNEUP PROCEDURE

The steps in a typical tuneup procedure are given below. All steps do not apply to all vehicles or to all engines.

1. Test and service the battery and starting motor. If the battery is low or the customer complains that the battery keeps running down, check the charging system. If the battery is defective, install a new battery.
2. Inspect the drive belts. Replace any that are in poor condition. Replace both belts in a two V-belt set. Tighten the belts to the specified tension using a belt-tension gauge.
3. If the engine is cold, operate it for at least 20 minutes at 1500 rpm or until the engine reaches normal operating temperature. Note any problems during warm-up.
4. Connect the engine analyzer or oscilloscope and perform an electrical diagnosis. Check for any abnormal ignition-system condition and the cylinder in which it occurs.
5. Perform a compression test. If necessary, perform a cylinder-leakage test and engine vacuum tests. These provide additional information on engine condition. If mechanical problems are found, tell the owner the engine cannot be tuned satisfactorily until after it is repaired.
6. Remove the spark plugs and inspect the firing ends. Gap and install new spark plugs. If reinstalling the old plugs, first clean, inspect, file, gap, and test them.
7. Inspect the ignition system. Look for the cause of any abnormal conditions seen with the engine analyzer or oscilloscope. Check the condition of the distributor cap, rotor, and primary and secondary wiring. Replace any defective parts. On contact-point ignition systems, clean and adjust (or replace) the contact points. Lubricate the distributor cam. Check the centrifugal and vacuum advance devices. Adjust the ignition timing.
8. Recheck the ignition system with the oscilloscope. Any abnormal condition noted earlier should now be gone.
9. Check the manifold heat-control valve, if used. It should move freely. Lubricate it with heat-control-valve lubricant. Free or replace the valve, if necessary.
10. Test the fuel pump with a fuel-pump tester. Replace the fuel filter. Check the fuel-tank cap, fuel lines, and connections for leakage and damage.
11. Clean or replace the air-cleaner filter. If the engine has a thermostatic air cleaner, check the operation of the vacuum motor.
12. Check the action of the throttle valves. Push the accelerator pedal to the floor to be sure the throttle valves open fully. Check carburetor choke and fast-idle systems, if used. Clean external linkages and check for binding.
13. Inspect all engine vacuum fittings, hoses, and connections. Replace any brittle or cracked hoses.
14. Clean the engine oil-filler cap. Inspect the condition of its gasket or seal.
15. Check the cooling system. If necessary, fill it to the proper level with the specified coolant. Check that the coolant contains the proper amount of antifreeze for adequate freeze protection. Drain and install fresh coolant, if required by the vehicle maintenance schedule.
   Inspect all hoses, connections, radiator, water pump, and fan clutch or electric fan. Pressure-check the cooling system and radiator cap. Squeeze the hoses to check their condition. Replace any defective hoses or other parts.
16. Inspect the PCV system. Check and replace the PCV valve if necessary. Clean or replace the PCV-system air filter if required. Inspect the PCV hoses and connections. Replace any cracked or brittle hoses. Test the system for crankcase vacuum.

17. If the engine has an air-injection pump, replace the pump inlet-air filter, if used. Inspect the system hoses and connections. Replace any brittle or cracked hoses.
18. If the evaporative-control system uses an air filter in the charcoal canister, replace the filter.
19. Check the transmission-controlled spark (TCS) system, if the vehicle is so equipped.
20. Inspect the EGR valve. Clean or replace it, as required. Inspect and clean the EGR discharge port. Test system operation by applying vacuum to the valve with the engine idling. The engine should run rough with vacuum applied, then smooth out with no vacuum.
21. Adjust the engine valves, if necessary. Some manufacturers recommend performing this step first in the tuneup procedure.
22. Adjust the engine idle speed. Check the amount of HC and CO in the exhaust gas. (Checking the HC and CO both before and after a tuneup shows how much the tuneup has reduced these pollutants.) If required, adjust the idle mixture (where possible). Follow the procedure outlined on the VECI label in the engine compartment.
23. If the engine has a turbocharger, check the wastegate operation. Follow the procedure in the vehicle service manual.
24. Tighten the intake-manifold and exhaust-manifold bolts to the specified torque in the proper sequence.
25. Check the maintenance sticker or the lubrication schedule to see if an oil and oil-filter change are due. Also note the schedule for chassis lubrication. Recommend the services due to the vehicle owner.
26. While the car is on the lift, check the exhaust system for leaks. These could admit deadly carbon monoxide (CO) into the passenger compartment. Also look for loose bolts, rust spots, and heat-shield and other under-car damage.
27. Roadtest the car on a dynamometer or on the road. Check for driveability, power, and idling. Any abnormal condition now may require additional checking and service to other parts or systems. Always note any uncorrected abnormal condition on the repair order before returning the car to the customer. If possible, explain the notes on the repair order to the customer. Conditions that affect emissions, fuel economy, reliability, and safety may need immediate attention.

Items 28 to 36 continue below. They are not actually part of the engine tuneup. However, they are important steps in vehicle maintenance or *car care*. Each check can be made quickly during the road test. Other checks outside the vehicle, inside the vehicle, and under the car can also be made. Write a note on the repair order about any abnormal condition found during the road test.

28. Before roadtesting the car, check the tires for specified inflation pressure and for abnormal wear. Abnormal wear could mean suspension trouble and the need for wheel alignment.
29. Check for proper operation of the instrument-panel warning lights, gauges, and information displays.
30. Check the brakes for even and adequate braking.
31. Check the steering system for ease and smoothness of operation. Check for excessive play in the steering system.
32. Check the suspension system for looseness, excessive play, and wear. Check the front-suspension ball joints for excessive wear. Check for loose wheel bearings at the non-driving wheels. Adjust the wheel bearings if necessary.
33. Check the CV joints (Chap. 45) for noise and smooth operation. If a CV-joint boot is torn, check for grit in the grease and for joint wear.
34. Check the operation of the clutch and manual transmission or transaxle. Note the shift timing and shift quality in a vehicle with an automatic transmission or transaxle.
35. Note any unusual noise, vibration, or harshness heard or felt during the road test.
36. Check the headlights and horns to make sure they work. Check all other lights. Replace burned-out bulbs. Check headlight aim, if necessary.

The preceding list of steps for tuneup and car care covers conditions that frequently need service or cause trouble. When performed as a complete procedure, these steps will locate many abnormal conditions that affect driveability and performance. Correcting these conditions will improve vehicle performance and reliability.

TRADE TALK

chassis dynamometer	cylinder-balance test	four-gas analyzer	tuneup
compression tester	cylinder-leakage tester	service-bay diagnostic	wet compression test
cranking-vacuum test	engine vacuum gauge	computer	

MULTIPLE-CHOICE TEST

*Select the **one** correct, best, or most probable answer to each question.*
You can find the answers in the section indicated at the end of each question.

1. When connected to the engine, the tachometer measures (➤37-3)
   a. engine torque
   b. engine rpm
   c. engine compression
   d. engine vacuum

2. After the engine is at normal operating temperature, the first step in using the compression tester is to (➤37-5)
   a. disconnect the battery
   b. adjust engine idle
   c. remove the spark plugs
   d. shift the transmission into low gear

3. The purpose of squirting a small amount of oil through the spark-plug hole when making a compression test is to (➤37-6)
   a. lubricate the piston rings
   b. see if the compression pressure increases
   c. measure manifold vacuum
   d. make it easier to install the spark plugs

4. If squirting engine oil through the spark-plug hole does not increase compression pressure, all the following could be the cause EXCEPT (➤37-6)
   a. leakage past the valves
   b. a broken valve spring
   c. worn camshaft lobe
   d. worn oil-control rings

5. A compression test on an in-line six-cylinder engine shows that cylinders 3 and 4 have readings of 10 psi [69 kPa]. The other cylinders all read between 130 and 135 psi [897 and 932 kPa]. Technician A says this is probably due to a blown head gasket. Technician B says the cause could be improper valve timing. Who is right? (➤37-6)
   a. A only
   b. B only
   c. both A and B
   d. neither A nor B

6. The cylinder leakage tester applies air pressure to the cylinder with the piston (➤37-7)
   a. at TDC with the valves closed
   b. at BDC with the valves closed
   c. starting the compression stroke
   d. at TDC with the valves open

7. A vacuum-gauge needle that swings around to 23 to 25 inches [584 to 635 mm] of mercury after the throttle is quickly opened and released indicates (➤37-8)
   a. stuck valves
   b. low compression
   c. good compression
   d. leaky valves

8. A steady but low vacuum reading with the engine idling indicates that the engine (➤37-8)
   a. is losing power
   b. has a stuck valve
   c. exhaust system is restricted
   d. ignition timing is advanced

9. Technician A says to use tail pipe measurements of HC and CO to check the operation of the catalytic converter. Technician B says tail pipe measurements of O_2 and CO can indicate the air-fuel ratio of the mixture entering the cylinder. Who is right? (➤37-10)
   a. A only
   b. B only
   c. both A and B
   d. neither A nor B

10. A service-bay diagnostic computer may do the following EXCEPT (➤37-13)
    a. automatically perform tests
    b. interpret the results
    c. show how to correct faults
    d. grade the technician's work

REVIEW QUESTIONS

1. What can be learned by making a cylinder-balance test? (➤37-11)
2. Where does a service-bay diagnostic computer get information, and how is this information updated? (➤37-13)
3. What is a chassis dynamometer used for, and what can its use tell the technician? (➤37-14)
4. What is a tuneup and how is it performed? (➤37-15 and 37-16)
5. What record should the technician make of any abnormal condition found during the roadtest? (➤37-17)

CHAPTER 38

ENGINE PERFORMANCE AND DRIVEABILITY DIAGNOSIS

After studying this chapter, and with proper instruction and equipment, you should be able to:

- Describe the checks and corrections for at least six troubles in spark-ignition engines.
- Check the mechanical condition of the engine and the operation of the engine support systems.
- Describe the cause of blue, black, and white exhaust smoke.
- Identify the source of various engine noises.
- Diagnose various troubles in spark-ignition engines.

A PRACTICAL APPROACH TO TROUBLE DIAGNOSIS

➤ 38-1 TROUBLE AND TROUBLE DIAGNOSIS

The engine is a machine. Like any other machine, it wears out through normal use. But during its useful life—between the time it is manufactured and the time it is scrapped—an engine may have a great variety of trouble.

An engine *trouble* is any disturbance or abnormal condition that affects the operation of the engine. The cause of an engine trouble may be in the mechanical parts of the engine itself (the *engine mechanical system*). However, the cause is usually in one or more of the engine-support systems (fuel, lubricating, cooling, and ignition systems), or in other engine-related systems. These include the exhaust, emissions, starting, and electronic engine control (EEC) systems.

Determining the cause of a trouble is *troubleshooting* or *trouble diagnosis*. This is the detective work that answers the question "What is wrong?" Accurately identifying the cause of a trouble is often the most difficult part of the job.

Sometimes the quickest way to locate the cause of a trouble is to make a visual inspection or a simple quick-check of the suspected parts and system. Making a visual inspection of the fuel system is described in ➤20-3. If the cause is not found, then begin following a logical procedure. One way is to follow the steps in the trouble-diagnosis chart in the vehicle service manual. However,

the manual may not have a chart for this trouble. Another way is to use the procedure provided for or built into an engine analyzer or tester (Fig. 38-1).

Fig. 38-1 Locating the cause of a trouble by following the procedure built into the computerized engine analyzer. (*OTC Tool & Equipment Division of SPX Corporation*)

Other chapters in this book describe trouble-diagnosis procedures for the engine-related systems. They also cover the use of scan tools and analyzers, and how to actuate the self-diagnostic system. This chapter primarily covers basic trouble-diagnosis procedures for the engine itself—the engine mechanical system.

> **NOTE** Automotive diesel and spark-ignition engines are similar in construction. Many mechanical conditions or complaints and their possible causes apply to both types of engines. Chapter 23 covers diesel fuel-injection systems.

➤ 38-2 BASIC RULES OF TROUBLE DIAGNOSIS

There are basic rules of trouble diagnosis. In general, they apply to troubles in any automotive part or system. Here are the rules:

1. Know the system. Know the parts, how they work together, and what happens if parts fail to work properly.
2. Learn the *service history* of the system. How old is it? What kind of treatment has it had? Has it been serviced before for the same problem? The answers to these questions may save you a lot of time.
3. Learn the history of the complaint. Did the trouble start all at once, or did it come on gradually? Is it related to other conditions such as an accident or a previous service problem? Does it happen with the engine cold or warm? Accelerating or decelerating?
4. Know the problems. Some happen more often than others.
5. Do not cure the symptom and leave the cause. For example, do not just recharge the battery. Find out what made the battery run down in the first place.
6. Get all information possible from the driver (items 1, 2, 3, and 4). This information may greatly simplify and direct the search for the cause of the trouble.

➤ 38-3 WHAT A SELF-DIAGNOSTIC SYSTEM CANNOT TELL YOU

Most cars with computer-controlled engines have a built-in self-diagnostic system. A scan tool (Fig. 38-2) retrieves any stored trouble codes and fault messages from the computer memory (➤20-13 and 20-14). Using this information helps make trouble diagnosis quicker and more accurate. Also, it can greatly reduce the time required for trouble diagnosis.

However, most trouble codes only indicate a faulty circuit or system. They do not always tell you specifically what has failed or where the failure has occurred. This is because the on-board computer can only monitor the condition or operation of systems and devices connected to it (➤20-12). On many engines, the computer does *not* monitor:

Fig. 38-2 Using the proper cartridge in a scan tool to retrieve stored trouble codes. (*OTC Tool & Equipment Division of SPX Corporation*)

1. Engine mechanical condition.
2. Ignition-system condition.
3. Exhaust-system condition.
4. Basic ignition timing.
5. Hose and tube routing.

When engine trouble diagnosis is necessary, never condemn the electronics until after checking the non-monitored items that can affect driveability. For example, when a cylinder is misfiring, check the spark plug, cable, rotor, distributor cap, compression, and vacuum *before* condemning the ignition module or pickup coil.

DRIVER COMPLAINTS AND ENGINE SYMPTOMS

➤ 38-4 ENGINE TROUBLE-DIAGNOSIS CHART

Most engine troubles are driver complaints that can be grouped under a few basic headings. These symptoms, together with their possible causes and the checks or corrections to be made, are listed in the *Engine Trouble-Diagnosis Chart* (Fig. 38-3). Following sections provide explanations of some of these troubles, and how to find and correct them. Later chapters cover these jobs.

Complaint	Possible Cause	Check or Correction
1. Engine will not crank (➤38-5)	a. Run-down battery	Recharge or replace battery; start engine with jumper battery and cables
	b. Starting-circuit open	Eliminate open; check for dirty or loose connections
	c. Starting-motor jammed	Remove starting motor and repair
	d. Engine jammed	Check and repair engine
	e. Transmission not in *neutral* or *park*	Move shift lever
	f. See also causes listed under item 3; driver may have run down battery trying to start	
2. Engine cranks slowly but will not start (➤38-6)	a. Run-down battery	Recharge or replace battery; start engine with jumper battery and cables
	b. Defective starting motor	Repair or replace
	c. Bad connections in starting circuit	Repair, or clean and tighten
	d. See also causes listed under item 3; driver may have run down battery trying to start	
3. Engine cranks at normal speed but will not start (➤38-7)	a. Defective ignition system	Try spark test, triggering test; check timing, ignition system
	b. Defective fuel system	Repair or replace
	c. Air leak into intake manifold	Tighten connections, replace gasket
	d. Defect in engine	Check compression, leakage
	e. Plugged fuel filter	Replace
	f. Restricted exhaust system	Clear system; replace restricted parts
4. Engine runs but misses in one cylinder (➤38-8)	a. Defective spark plug	Replace
	b. Defective distributor cap, rotor, or cable	Replace
	c. Valve stuck open	Free valve; service engine
	d. Broken valve spring	Replace
	e. Burned valve	Replace; service engine
	f. Bent pushrod	Replace
	g. Flat cam lobe	Replace camshaft
	h. Defective piston or rings	Replace; service cylinder wall
	i. Intake-manifold leaks	Replace gasket; tighten manifold bolts
5. Engine runs but misses in different cylinders (➤38-8)	a. Defective ignition system	Check ignition
	b. Defective fuel system	Check fuel system
	c. Cross-firing plug cables	Replace
	d. Loss of compression	Check compression, leakage
	e. Defective valve action	Service engine
	f. Worn pistons or rings	Replace; service cylinder walls
	g. Overheated engine	Check cooling system
	h. Manifold heat-control valve stuck	Free valve
	i. Restricted exhaust system	Check catalytic converter, muffler, tailpipe; replace restricted parts
6. Engine sluggish, stumbles, lacks power, acceleration, or high-speed performance; hot or cold (➤38-9)	a. Defective ignition	Check ignition
	b. Defective fuel system	Check fuel system
	c. Restricted exhaust system	Check catalytic converter, muffler, tailpipe; replace restricted parts
	d. Loss of compression	Check compression, leakage
	e. Carbon buildup in engine	Service engine
	f. Defective valve action	Check compression, leakage
	g. Excessive rolling resistance	Check for low tires, brakes dragging wheel misalignment
	h. Thick oil	Use specified oil
	i. Wrong or bad fuel	Use correct-octane fuel
	j. Transmission not downshifting, defective torque converter	Check transmission

Fig. 38-3 Engine trouble-diagnosis chart.

Complaint	Possible Cause	Check or Correction
7. Engine lacks power, acceleration, or high-speed performance: hot only (➤38-9)	a. Engine overheats b. Choke stuck c. Manifold heat-control valve stuck d. Vapor lock	Check cooling system Free; repair or replace Free valve Use different fuel, shield fuel line
8. Engine lacks power, acceleration, or high-speed performance: cold only (➤38-9)	a. Choke stuck open b. Manifold heat-control valve stuck open c. Cooling-system thermostat stuck open d. Engine valves stuck open	Free; repair or replace Free valve Replace Service engine
9. Engine overheats (➤38-10)	a. Lack of coolant b. Late ignition timing c. Loose or broken fan belt d. Thermostat stuck closed e. Clogged water jackets or radiator core f. Defective radiator hose g. Defective water pump h. Oil low i. High-altitude, hot-climate operation j. Defective fan clutch k. Valve timing late; timing chain has jumped a tooth l. No vacuum spark advance in any gear	Add coolant; check for leaks Adjust timing Replace; adjust tension Replace Flush and clean Replace Replace Add oil Drive slowly; keep radiator filled Replace Replace Defective vacuum-advance unit
10. Engine idles roughly (➤38-11)	a. Incorrect idle adjustment b. PCV or EGR valve stuck open c. Defective fuel injectors d. See also other causes listed under items 6 to 8	Adjust Replace Replace
11. Engine stalls cold or as it warms up (➤38-12)	a. Choke valve stuck closed or will not close b. Defective fuel system c. Manifold heat-control valve stuck d. Idle solenoid improperly set e. Idle speed low f. PCV or EGR valve stuck open g. Door in thermostatic air cleaner stuck closed h. Misrouted or leaking vacuum hose	Free; service Check fuel system Free valve Adjust Adjust Replace Free; replace vacuum motor Reroute or replace
12. Engine stalls after idling or slow-speed driving (➤38-12)	a. Defective fuel pump b. Engine overheats c. High carburetor float level d. Incorrect idling adjustment e. Faulty PCV or EGR valve f. Idle solenoid improperly set	Replace See item 9 Adjust Adjust Replace Adjust
13. Engine stalls after high-speed driving (➤38-12)	a. Vapor lock b. Carburetor venting or idle-compensator valve defective c. Engine overheats d. PCV or EGR valve stuck open e. Idle solenoid improperly set	Use different fuel; shield fuel line Check and repair or replace See item 9 Replace Adjust

Complaint	Possible Cause	Check or Correction
14. Engine backfires (➤38-13)	a. Ignition timing off	Adjust
	b. Spark plugs of wrong heat range	Install correct plugs
	c. Excessively rich or lean mixture	Check EEC system, oxygen sensor
	d. Engine overheats	See item 9
	e. Carbon in engine	Service engine
	f. Valves hot or stuck	Service engine
	g. High-voltage leakage in coil, distributor cap, rotor	Replace
	h. Inoperative antibackfire valve	Replace
	i. Cross-firing spark-plug cables	Replace
15. Engine run-on or dieseling (➤38-14)	a. Incorrect idle-solenoid adjustment	Adjust
	b. Engine overheats	See item 9
	c. Hot spots in combustion chambers	Check plugs, valves, pistons, cylinders for carbon
	d. Timing advanced	Adjust
16. Excessive HC and CO in exhaust gas (➤38-15)	a. Ignition miss	Check ignition
	b. Incorrect ignition timing	Adjust
	c. Carburetor troubles— see item 20	Check, service carburetor
	d. Faulty air injection	Check pump, hose, electronic control
	f. Defective catalytic converter	Replace
17. Smoky exhaust (➤38-13)		
1. Blue smoke	Excessive oil consumption	See item 18
2. Black smoke	Excessively rich mixture	See item 20
3. White smoke	a. Steam in exhaust	Replace gasket; tighten head bolts to eliminate coolant leakage into combustion chambers
	b. Catalyst burning off fuel residue	Service air-injection system
18. Excessive oil consumption (➤38-16)	a. External leaks	Replace gaskets, seals
	b. Burning oil in combustion chamber	Service engine
	c. High-speed driving	Drive more slowly
	d. Faulty PCV system	Service
19. Low oil pressure (➤38-17)	a. Worn engine bearings	Service engine, replace bearings
	b. Engine overheating	See item 9
	c. Oil dilution or foaming	Replace oil
	d. Lubricating-system troubles	Check oil lines, oil pump, filter, relief valve
20. Excessive fuel consumption (➤38-18)	a. Jackrabbit starts	Drive more reasonably
	b. High-speed driving	Drive more slowly
	c. Short trips	Drive longer distances
	d. Excessive fuel-pump pressure or pump leakage	Replace pump
	e. Choke does not open	Open; repair or replace choke
	f. Clogged air cleaner	Replace filter element
	g. High carburetor float level	Adjust
	h. Stuck or dirty float needle valve	Free and clean
	i. Worn carburetor jets	Service carburetor
	j. Stuck metering rod or power piston	Free and clean
	k. Idle too fast	Adjust
	l. Stuck accelerator-pump check valve	Free, clean
	m. Carburetor leaks	Replace gaskets; tighten screws
	n. Fuel injectors leaking	Replace
	o. Engine misfiring	See items 4 and 5
	p. Automatic transmission slipping or not upshifting	Check transmission
	q. Loss of compression	Check compression, leakage

Complaint	Possible Cause	Check or Correction
	r. Defective valve action	Service engine
	s. Excessive rolling resistance	Check for low tires, dragging brakes, wheel misalignment
	t. Clutch slippage	Adjust, service
21. Engine noises (➤38-19)		
1. Regular clicking	Valve train	Adjust valves; service valve train
2. Ping on load or acceleration	Low-octane fuel, carbon, advanced ignition timing, or causes listed under item 14	Use higher-octane fuel; remove carbon; correct ignition timing
3. Light knock or pound with engine floating	Worn rod bearings or journal; misaligned rod; lack of oil	Service engine
4. Light, metallic double knock, most audible during idle	Worn or loose pin; lack of oil	Service engine
5. Chattering or rattling during acceleration	Worn or broken rings, cylinder walls; low ring tension	Service engine
6. Hollow, muffled bell-like sound (engine cold)	Piston slap due to worn pistons or walls, collapsed piston skirts, misaligned rods, lack of oil	Service engine
7. Dull, metallic knock under load, especially when cold	Regular-worn main bearings, Irregular-worn thrust-bearing knock on clutch engagement or hard acceleration	Service engine
8. Miscellaneous noises	Loosely mounted accessories such as alternator, horn, air pump, etc.	Tighten mounting

➤ 38-5 ENGINE WILL NOT CRANK

If the engine will not crank when starting is attempted, make sure the automatic-transmission selector lever is in Neutral (N) or Park (P). With a manual transmission, depress the clutch pedal while trying to start. Check the battery and cables (Chap. 28).

To help locate the cause, turn on the headlamps and try cranking. There are five possible results. These are described in ➤29-11 to 29-15. If starting-system trouble is indicated, refer to the *Starting-System Trouble-Diagnosis Chart* (Fig. 29-12).

➤ 38-6 ENGINE CRANKS SLOWLY BUT WILL NOT START

The battery is run down, or there may be mechanical trouble in the starting motor or engine. Low temperature reduces the battery cranking ability. Cold weather thickens engine oil, making the engine harder to crank. Also, the driver may have run down the battery trying to start, but some other condition prevented engine starting.

➤ 38-7 ENGINE CRANKS AT NORMAL SPEED BUT WILL NOT START

The trouble is probably in the fuel or ignition system. On a carburetor, the choke valve may not have closed (➤22-8).

If the driver turns the ignition key ON and does not promptly try to start, the electric choke may open fully. Sometimes this can happen if cranking is delayed for 90 seconds or less. Allow the choke to cool and reset. Then try starting again.

A hot carbureted engine may have a choke valve stuck closed. This *floods* the engine because too much fuel is delivered. Open the throttle wide and crank. If the engine does not start, remove the air cleaner. With the ignition off, look down into the carburetor and operate the throttle linkage to open the throttle valve. The accelerator-pump system should deliver a stream of fuel into the venturi (Fig. 22-5). If it does, the fuel system is probably okay. If there is no stream of fuel, fuel is not reaching the carburetor. A defective fuel pump or a clogged fuel line or filter could be the cause. Or the fuel tank may be empty.

CAUTION!

Do not try to start an engine by squirting fuel into the carburetor while cranking. This is *priming* and it is dangerous. A backfire could spray flaming gasoline on you. This could burn you seriously and start a fire.

Check for ignition-system troubles (➤33-2). Make a *spark test* (➤33-12). If there is no spark, make a *triggering test* (➤33-13). If the primary circuit is triggering, the trouble probably is in the secondary circuit. No triggering indicates the trouble probably is in the primary circuit. The pickup coil or ignition module may have failed (➤33-2). A good spark indicates the ignition system is probably okay. However, ignition or valve timing could be off. The timing chain or belt may have "jumped time" or broken. Or there may be other engine problems such as defective valves.

A restricted or collapsed exhaust system causes excessive back pressure (Fig. 38-4). This can prevent normal exhaust and intake so the engine will not start. Also, air leaks into the intake manifold can lean out the mixture so much that it will not ignite. Check the engine with cylinder compression and leakage testers (➤37-5 to 37-7).

➤ 38-8 ENGINE RUNS BUT MISSES

Misfiring or missing causes loss of power and engine roughness. A misfiring cylinder may cause steady pulsations or jerking. It is usually most noticeable as engine load increases and less noticeable at higher engine speeds. The exhaust may have a steady spitting sound at low speeds. It is sometimes difficult to locate the miss. The miss may occur at some speeds but not at other speeds. Also, the miss may skip around. An oscilloscope (➤33-16), exhaust-gas analyzer (➤37-9), engine analyzer (➤37-12), and dynamometer (➤37-14) may help locate the misfiring cylinder and its cause. Misfiring in one cylinder may be due to a fouled or defective spark plug.

Basic tests for locating a misfiring cylinder include making a cylinder-balance test (➤37-11), spark test (➤33-12), and triggering test (➤33-13). Figure 37-13 shows how

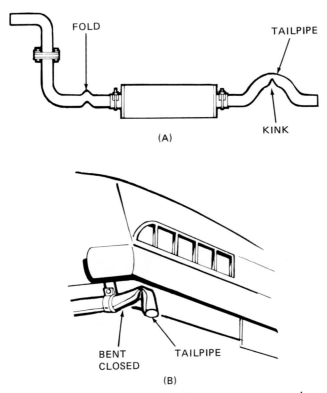

(A)

(B)

Fig. 38-4 A clogged or restricted exhaust system may cause the engine, hot or cold, to lack power. (*Ford Motor Company*)

shorting a cylinder should affect the engine-rpm reading on a tachometer. A clogged fuel injector (➤20-10) may deliver so little fuel that the cylinder misfires. Cleaning fuel injectors (➤20-23) or other fuel-system service may be required.

On a carbureted engine, fuel-system troubles usually do not cause specific cylinders to miss. However, misfiring will occur if air leaks into an intake port through a leaking gasket, porous casting, loose intake manifold, or leaking vacuum hose.

In addition to problems in the fuel or ignition system, loss of engine compression, sticky or damaged valves, an overheated engine, and a restricted exhaust system can cause misfiring. A complete engine diagnosis and tuneup (➤37-17) will locate and eliminate most causes of missing.

➤ 38-9 ENGINE SLUGGISH, STUMBLES, LACKS POWER, ACCELERATION, OR HIGH-SPEED PERFORMANCE

First, find out if the engine lacks power cold, hot, or both cold and hot. Find out if the trouble developed suddenly or if the power gradually fell off over time. An oscilloscope (➤33-16), exhaust-gas analyzer (➤37-9), engine analyzer (➤37-12), and dynamometer (➤37-14) may help locate the misfiring cylinder and its cause.

1. LACKS POWER, HOT OR COLD This could be due to the fuel system feeding an excessively rich or an excessively lean mixture. A lean mixture could be due to a defective fuel pump, clogged fuel line or filter, and air leaks into the intake manifold. A rich mixture could be due to worn carburetor jets or leaking fuel injectors (➤20-10).

On a carbureted engine, a faulty accelerator pump, main-metering system, or power system may be the cause of the trouble (➤22-6). Find out if the engine hesitates or stumbles when the accelerator pedal is depressed, and then runs normally. This indicates the trouble probably is in the accelerator pump. Check pump operation by shutting off the engine and removing the air cleaner. Then operate the throttle linkage to open the throttle valve and watch for fuel discharge (Fig. 22-5).

Many other conditions could be the cause. Incorrect throttle-linkage adjustment could prevent full opening of the throttle valves. The ignition timing may be retarded, or the ignition system may have low secondary voltage or spark plugs of the wrong heat range or reach (➤31-12). The wrong fuel or oil can reduce performance.

Carbon deposits, loss of compression, and defective bearings in the engine can rob power from the engine. Also, a restricted exhaust system (Fig. 38-4) can prevent normal exhaust and intake so the engine lacks performance.

In addition, excessive *rolling resistance* can absorb engine power and hold down acceleration and speed. Causes of excessive rolling resistance include dragging brakes, underinflated tires, misaligned wheels, and excessive friction in the transmission or power train. Also, the automatic transmission may not be downshifting, or the torque converter may be defective.

2. ENGINE LACKS POWER ONLY WHEN HOT The engine may be overheating (➤38-10). The carburetor choke may not be opening. This feeds the engine an excessively rich mixture which burns poorly, causing poor performance. A stuck manifold heat-control valve (Fig. 22-4) overheats the mixture so less gets into the cylinders. Vapor lock may also cause poor engine performance and stalling.

3. ENGINE LACKS POWER ONLY WHEN COLD OR REACHES OPERATING TEMPERATURE TOO SLOWLY The carburetor choke may be stuck open or opening too quickly. The manifold heat-control valve may not close, so too little heat reaches the intake manifold. The cooling system thermostat may be stuck open. Then coolant circulates between the engine and radiator when the engine is cold. This delays engine warmup. Sometimes engine valves stick when cold but become free as the engine warms up. Premature exhaust-gas recirculation, before the engine warms up, will greatly reduce power from a cold engine.

➤ 38-10 ENGINE OVERHEATS

Most overheating (➤26-4) is caused by loss of coolant due to leaks in the cooling system. Other causes include an inoperative electric fan (➤25-10) or a loose or broken fan belt, and a defective water pump. A clogged water jacket or radiator, leaves and trash blocking airflow through the radiator, and a defective radiator hose, thermostat, or fan clutch may cause overheating. Late ignition or valve timing, lack of engine oil, and hot-climate operation also cause engine overheating.

Freezing of the coolant can prevent normal coolant circulation so local hot spots and boiling occur. No ignition vacuum spark advance may cause engine overheating (➤33-7).

NOTE When the vehicle is in slow-moving traffic and the engine begins to overheat, open the windows and turn off the air conditioner. Turn the heater and blower on to maximum. This lightens the load on the engine and takes some of the heat away from it. The passengers may get uncomfortable. However, this may make the difference between radiator boil-over and possibly stalling, or simply a hot engine.

➤ 38-11 ENGINE IDLES ROUGHLY

Rough idle but normal running above idle means the idle speed and mixture may be incorrect. Adjust idle speed, if possible. A carburetor idle mixture may not be adjustable without removing a plug (Fig. 38-5) or partly disassembling the carburetor. A loose or disconnected vacuum hose or a PCV valve (➤36-3) or EGR valve (➤36-9) stuck

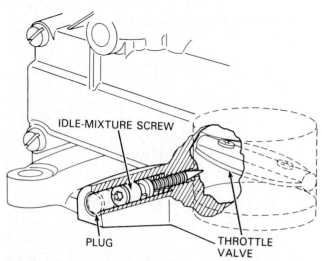

Fig. 38-5 Plug covering the idle-mixture screw in a carburetor throttle body. (*Ford Motor Company*)

open can cause poor idling. Also, see items 6 to 10 in the trouble diagnosis chart (Fig. 38-3).

➤ 38-12 ENGINE STALLS

If the engine starts and then stalls, note when it stalls. It may be before or after the engine warms up, after idling or slow-speed driving, or after full-load or high-speed driving. Stalling can be caused by a sticking PCV valve or improper adjustment of the carburetor idle solenoid (Fig. 22-8).

1. ENGINE STALLS BEFORE WARMING UP This could be due to improper carburetor idle-system adjustments (➤22-10). The choke may not set the linkage on fast idle. Also, stalling could be due to dirt or water in the fuel line or filter, a defective fuel pump, or a plugged fuel-tank cap. In the carburetor, a low float setting, clogged idle system, or carburetor icing could cause stalling.

Some ignition troubles can cause stalling. Ignition troubles that cause stalling often prevent starting. On contact-point systems, burned points and an open primary resistor (➤31-5) can cause stalling. During cranking, the resistor is bypassed. After the engine starts, the current must flow through the resistor. If the resistor is open, the engine will stall as the ignition key returns to RUN. Figure 33-2 is an *Ignition-System Trouble-Diagnosis Chart*.

2. ENGINE STALLS AS IT WARMS UP Sometimes a carburetor choke valve may stick closed (➤22-8). The mixture will then be too rich for a hot engine so the engine stalls. If the manifold-heat-control valve sticks closed (➤21-22), the air-fuel mixture will be too hot and too lean, causing stalling. A low idle-speed setting (➤22-12) can cause stalling as the engine warms up. Overheating (➤26-4) can cause vapor lock and stalling. If the door in the thermostatic air cleaner (➤17-10) sticks closed, the air-fuel mixture will overheat and be too lean. This may stall the engine.

3. ENGINE STALLS AFTER IDLING OR SLOW-SPEED DRIVING A defective mechanical fuel pump (➤22-4) might deliver enough fuel for high speed driving. Then pressure drops too low to deliver fuel when idling or driving slowly.

4. ENGINE STALLS AFTER HIGH-SPEED DRIVING This can occur if enough heat accumulates to cause vapor lock. Correct the condition by shielding the fuel pump and fuel line, or use a less volatile fuel (➤16-3). Overheating may also cause stalling.

➤ 38-13 ENGINE BACKFIRES

Backfiring can result if the anti-backfire valve in the air-injection system is faulty (➤36-6). Late ignition timing or ignition *cross-firing* (➤33-4) can cause backfiring. In addition, backfiring can be due to an excessively rich mixture, overheated engine, hot exhaust valves, or intake valves that stick or seat poorly.

Carbon in the combustion chamber (Fig. 38-6) may get hot enough to ignite the air-fuel mixture as it enters the cylinder. Backfiring results. Carbon also increases the compression ratio and the tendency for detonation and preignition. Spark plugs of the wrong heat range can overheat and cause preignition (➤33-25). Install cooler heat-range spark plugs. If intake valves stick open, combustion may flash back past the throttle valves. Valves ground to a sharp edge (no *margin*), valves that seat poorly, and valves coated with carbon can overheat and cause backfiring. Chapter 39 describes valve troubles and their corrections.

➤ 38-14 ENGINE RUN-ON OR DIESELING

Dieseling is caused by hot spots in the combustion chambers and failure of the throttle valves to close com-

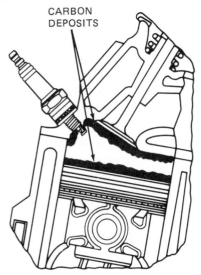

CARBON DEPOSITS

Fig. 38-6 Backfiring may be caused by hot carbon deposits igniting the air-fuel mixture as it enters the combustion chamber. (*Chrysler Corporation*)

pletely. This has been a problem on some carbureted engines. Air gets through so some air-fuel mixture enters the cylinders. Then hot spots ignite the air-fuel mixture and the engine runs with the ignition key OFF.

If the engine diesels, check the idle solenoid (➤22-9). Be sure the engine idle speed is not too high (➤22-12). Correction of hot spots may require spark-plug service (➤33-24). Chapter 39 covers removing the cylinder head for valve service and carbon removal.

OTHER ENGINE TROUBLES

➤ 38-15 EXCESSIVE HC AND CO IN EXHAUST GAS

The exhaust-gas analyzer (➤37-9) detects excessive HC and CO in the exhaust gas. Some causes of high HC and CO readings are described in ➤37-10. Others are described below. HC may be high, CO may be high, or both HC and CO may be high. Each type of reading has a different set of possible causes.

HIGH HC EMISSIONS This can be caused by improper ignition timing, misfiring, crossfiring, and an excessively rich or lean air-fuel mixture. Engine conditions that cause high HC emissions include leaky valves and worn valve guides or lifters. Other possible causes are worn or defective pistons, piston rings, and cylinder walls. In addition, carbon deposits in combustion chambers (Fig. 38-6) may cause high HC emissions. The carbon acts like a sponge, soaking up air-fuel mixture during compression and then releasing it during exhaust.

HIGH CO EMISSIONS High CO readings are often caused by a rich air-fuel mixture. Other causes include a restricted air filter, stuck carburetor choke, and improper idle speed.

HIGH HC AND CO EMISSIONS When both HC and CO are high, possible causes are a restricted PCV system or a heat-control-valve stuck open. Other causes include an inoperative air pump (➤36-6), a stuck door in the thermostatic air cleaner (➤36-8), and an inoperative or removed catalytic converter (➤36-14). Also, excessive fuel in the crankcase oil and the charcoal canister not purging (➤35-6) cause high HC and CO emissions.

➤ 38-16 EXCESSIVE OIL CONSUMPTION

An engine loses oil in three ways (➤24-17). An engine gasket seal may fail, allowing drops of oil to fall on the ground. This is an *external leak*. Excessive blowby or crankcase air flow may carry oil through the PCV system into the combustion chambers to be burned (➤36-3). High-speed driving along with worn intake valve guides (➤14-9) and worn piston oil-control rings (➤13-33) allow oil to pass into the combustion chambers.

Smoky exhaust gas indicates the engine is burning oil, the air-fuel mixture is too rich, or water or coolant has leaked into the combustion chamber. The color of the exhaust gas can tell you which condition exists. If the exhaust gas has a bluish tinge, the engine is burning oil. If the exhaust gas is more black than blue, not all the fuel is burning in the cylinders. The air-fuel mixture is probably too rich. Whitish exhaust smoke while the engine is cold may be considered normal. But after warmup, white smoke may indicate water or coolant has turned to steam in the combustion chamber. The engine may have a cracked cylinder head or a blown head gasket.

➤ 38-17 LOW OIL PRESSURE

This often indicates a worn oil pump or worn engine bearings (➤24-18). The bearings pass so much oil that the oil pump cannot maintain oil pressure. The end bearings will be oil-starved and may fail. Other causes are a weak relief-valve spring (➤24-7), broken or cracked oil line, and a clogged oil line or filter. Oil dilution, foaming, sludge (➤24-14), not enough oil, or oil thinned by overheating will cause low oil pressure.

➤ 38-18 EXCESSIVE FUEL CONSUMPTION

Almost anything from the driver to underinflated tires can cause excessive fuel consumption. A *fuel-mileage tester* and some electronic instrument clusters can accurately measure fuel consumption. The compression test (➤37-5), cylinder-leakage test (➤37-7), and vacuum-gauge tests (➤37-8) will help pinpoint the cause. If the cause is in the fuel system, consider the following:

1. A driver who pumps the accelerator pedal while idling and insists on being the first to get away when the traffic light changes to green will use extra fuel.
2. Short-trip or delivery-service operation means the engine operates on warm-up most of the time. This uses extra fuel.
   These two conditions are due to the type of operation. Changing operating conditions is the only cure. If excessive fuel consumption is not due to these conditions, then consider the following:
3. Carburetor choke not opening or not opening fast enough.
4. Carburetor float level too high. This causes flooding and delivery of too much fuel. The needle valve may be stuck open or not seating fully.
5. Carburetor metering rod or power piston stuck in the full power position, using excessive fuel.
6. Carburetor jets worn. Carburetor should be rebuilt.
7. Fuel-injectors leaking.
8. Fuel-pump pressure too high.
   Conditions outside the fuel system can cause high fuel consumption. These include:
9. Failure in the electronic engine control (EEC) or engine management system. Sensor failures (➤20-15) are

possible. These include the coolant-temperature (➤19-16), engine-speed (➤19-18), MAP (➤19-13), oxygen (➤36-12), and throttle-position sensor (➤19-10). Also, the electronic control module (ECM) and actuators such as solenoids, switches, and valves may fail.
10. Worn engine with loss of compression requires more fuel.
11. Excessive fuel consumption can result from underinflated tires, dragging brakes, slipping clutch, defective automatic transmission, and wheel misalignment.

➤ 38-19 ENGINE NOISES

Some engine noises have little significance. Others indicate serious problems that require prompt attention to prevent major engine damage. You can sometimes tell what is wrong with an engine by listening as it runs. Place the point of a listening rod or automotive stethoscope (Fig. 38-7) on different parts. Then abnormal noises can be more easily detected. Move the point around until you find where the noise is the loudest. This often enables you to identify the source or cause of the noise.

Careful! Keep away from moving drive belts and fans when using a listening rod or stethoscope.

Fig. 38-7 Using an automotive stethoscope to locate the source of engine noise. (*ATW*)

1. VALVE AND TAPPAT NOISE This is a regular clicking noise occurring at half engine speed. It may disappear at higher speeds. The cause is usually excessive valve clearance or a defective hydraulic valve lifter. To check on overhead-valve engines, insert a thickness gauge between the valve stem and the rocker arm (Chap. 39). If this reduces the noise, the cause is excessive clearance. Adjust the clearance. If inserting the thickness gauge does not reduce the noise, it is caused by worn lifter faces or rough cams. Other causes are lifters loose in their bores and weak valve springs. Sometimes lifter noise goes away shortly after the engine starts, or after the engine warms up. To stop this noise, replace the noisy lifters.

2. DETONATION Some spark knock or detonation (➤16-4) may be normal when climbing a hill. However, excessive detonation can damage the engine.

3. CONNECTING-ROD NOISE Connecting-rod noise usually is a light knocking or pounding sound. It is most noticeable when the engine is *floating* (not accelerating or decelerating). A worn bearing or crankpin, misaligned connecting rod, or lack of oil can cause rod noise. To locate the rod, perform a cylinder-balance test (➤37-11) to short out the spark plugs one at a time with the engine running. The noise will be reduced when the cylinder that is responsible is not delivering power.

4. PISTON-PIN NOISE Piston-pin noise is similar to valve and tappet noise. However, piston-pin noise has a unique metallic double knock. It is most noticeable during idle with the spark advanced. Causes include a worn or loose piston pin, a worn bushing, or lack of oil. On some engines, the noise becomes most audible at car speeds of about 30 mph [48 km/h]. On some engines, a check can be made by running the engine at idle and advancing the spark. Then short out the spark plugs as explained in item 3, above. The noise is reduced when the responsible cylinder is not delivering power.

5. PISTON-RING NOISE Piston-ring noise is similar to valve and tappet noise. However, ring noise is loudest during acceleration. Low ring tension, broken or worn rings, or worn cylinder walls can produce the noise. A test can be performed by removing the spark plugs and adding a tablespoon [15 cc] of engine oil to each cylinder. Crank the engine for several revolutions to work the oil down past the rings. Install the spark plugs and start the engine. If the noise is reduced, the rings are probably at fault. Cylinder compression and leakage tests (➤37-5 and 37-7) also may help pinpoint the trouble.

6. PISTON SLAP Piston slap produces a muffled, hollow, bell-like sound. It is caused by the piston rocking back and forth in the cylinder. If piston slap occurs only when the engine is cold, it is not serious. Continuous piston slap means the engine needs service. Causes of piston slap include inadequate oil, worn cylinder walls, worn pistons or collapsed skirts, excessive piston-to-cylinder-wall clearance, or misaligned connecting rods.

7. CRANKSHAFT KNOCK Crankshaft knock is a heavy, dull metallic knock. It is most noticeable when the engine is under heavy load or acceleration, especially when cold. When the noise is regular and more of a rumble, it probably results from worn main bearings. Worn rod bearings produce a more distinct knock. A worn crankshaft thrust bearing (➤13-17) produces a noise that is more irregular and sharp. If unusually bad, the thrust bearing produces a noise each time the clutch (for a manual transmission) is released and engaged.

8. MISCELLANEOUS NOISES Other noises result from loosely mounted accessory parts such as the alternator, starting motor, horn, manifolds, flywheel, crankshaft pulley, and oil pan. Also, the clutch, transmission, drive line, CV joints, and drive axle may develop various noises (➤44-14). Steering and suspension, and other noises and vibrations, are described in (➤51-18).

TRADE TALK

dieseling	flood	rolling resistance	trouble diagnosis
external leak	oil consumption	service history	
floating	priming	trouble	

MULTIPLE-CHOICE TEST

*Select the **one** correct, best, or most probable answer to each question.*
You can find the answers in the section indicated at the end of each question.

1. An engine may crank slowly because of (➤38-6)
   a. vapor lock
   b. a defective water pump
   c. a run-down battery
   d. high compression pressure

2. Failure to start even though the engine cranks normally could be due to a (➤38-7)
   a. run-down battery
   b. defective starting motor
   c. sticking engine valve
   d. defective ignition module or pickup coil

3. Missing in one cylinder may result from (➤38-8)
   a. a clogged exhaust
   b. an overheated engine
   c. vapor lock
   d. a fouled spark plug

4. An engine will lose power (hot or cold) if it has (➤38-9)
   a. air leaks into the intake manifold
   b. automatic choke stuck open
   c. incorrect idle speed
   d. cooling-system thermostat stuck closed

5. Overheating may be caused by all the following EXCEPT (➤38-10)
   a. inoperative electric fan
   b. cooling-system thermostat stuck open
   c. loss of coolant from radiator
   d. late ignition or valve timing

6. Engine stalling after high-speed driving can be caused by (➤38-12)
   a. vapor lock
   b. incorrect ignition timing
   c. worn carburetor jets
   d. defective fuel injectors

7. Technician A says backfiring can be caused by spark plugs of the wrong heat range. Technician B says backfiring can be caused by worn rings. Who is right? (➤38-13)
   a. A only
   b. B only
   c. both A and B
   d. neither A nor B

8. High emissions of both HC and CO may be caused by all the following EXCEPT (➤38-15)
   a. a missing or inoperative catalytic converter
   b. crossfiring
   c. an inoperative air pump
   d. charcoal canister not purging

9. An engine uses too much oil. Technician A says gasket leaks could be the cause. Technician B says burning in the combustion chamber could be the cause. Who is right? (➤38-16)
   a. A only
   b. B only
   c. both A and B
   d. neither A nor B

10. Excessive fuel consumption may be caused by (➤38-18)
    a. low fuel-pump pressure
    b. overinflated tires
    c. coolant-temperature sensor failure
    d. low idle speed

REVIEW QUESTIONS

1. What is a *trouble* and where can it be found in the engine? (➤38-1)
2. Explain what a self-diagnostic system cannot tell you. (➤38-3)
3. List three types of exhaust smoke, and the causes of each. (➤38-16)
4. What does low oil pressure indicate, and what are its causes? (➤38-17)
5. Describe five types of engine noise, and how to locate and correct each. (➤38-19)

PART 6

AUTOMOTIVE ENGINE SERVICE

Part 6 of *Automotive Mechanics* describes servicing operations on automotive engines. Included in Part 6 are servicing procedures on valves and valve trains for camshaft-in-block and overhead-camshaft engines. Also included are servicing procedures on cylinder heads, pistons and related parts, bearings, and crankshafts and cylinder blocks. In each chapter, typical specifications are given for many of the most important engine-service measurements.

There are three chapters in Part 6:

CHAPTER 39

ENGINE SERVICE: CYLINDER HEAD AND VALVE TRAINS

After studying this chapter, and with proper instruction and equipment, you should be able to:

- Describe the causes of various valve troubles.
- Adjust valve clearance on various engines.
- Inspect and recondition cylinder head and valve-train parts.
- Reface valves and refinish valve seats.
- Replace the camshaft and camshaft bearings.
- Perform complete valve service on various engines.

➤ 39-1 CARE AND CLEANLINESS

The major enemy of good engine-service work is dirt. This is because the automobile engine contains many machined, honed, polished, and lapped surfaces. Some of these parts have clearances measured in ten-thousandths of an inch [thousandths of a millimeter]. Clean the engine before any major service work. To prevent damage, cover or remove all electrical and engine-mounted units before *steam-cleaning* the engine.

Inspect each part as you remove and clean it. Following sections describe cleaning specific engine parts. After cleaning and drying each part, apply a light coat of engine oil to the bright metal surfaces. This prevents rusting. Apply a light coat of engine oil to all friction surfaces during assembly. The oil helps provide lubrication and reduce wear during initial engine startup. Instead of oil, a special *assembly lubricant* may be used for engine assembly.

Cleanliness is important when performing any internal engine service. Never leave abrasives or dirt in the engine or on engine parts. Proper cleaning and protection of machined and friction surfaces are part of all engine-repair procedures. This may not be stated in each of the following sections or in the vehicle service manual. However, it is required by the manufacturers as a normal shop practice.

When removing valves or other valve-train parts, keep the parts together. Mark the parts or use special boxes or holders (Fig. 39-1). Place the parts in order as they are removed. Friction surfaces are *wear-mated*. During valve-train assembly, install all parts in the same locations and with the same mating surfaces as when they were removed.

Fig. 39-1 Valve rack for holding valves and related valve-train parts. *(Chevrolet Division of General Motors Corporation)*

Disconnect the cables from the battery before performing any major engine service. This prevents damage to the wiring harness and other electrical or electronic parts. Follow the safety rules in Chap. 4 and the safety cautions in other chapters. This will help you avoid injury, and damage to the vehicle or tools you are using.

➤ 39-2 CYLINDER-HEAD AND VALVE SERVICE

Cylinder-head and valve service includes adjusting valve clearance, installing new valve-seat inserts (where used), and replacing camshaft and camshaft bearings. Other services are:

1. Replacing valve-cover gasket.
2. Replacing timing gears, or timing chain or belt and sprockets.
3. Replacing valve springs or valve-stem oil seals.
4. Replacing valve lifters, cam followers, pushrods, and rocker arms.
5. Replacing cylinder-head gasket.
6. Resurfacing cylinder head.
7. Refacing valves and valve seats.
8. Servicing or replacing valve guides.
9. Crack detection.
10. Crack repair.

Figure 39-2 shows one cylinder head from an overhead-valve V-8 engine. The valve train for one cylinder is disassembled. Some valve service can be done with the engine in the vehicle. This includes valve refacing, which usually requires only removal of the cylinder head. The flat-rate manual (➣3-6) lists the time required to do different cylinder-head and valve services. For example, the Ford flat-rate time to grind the valves on one model of V-6 engine is 7.9 hours.

Some typical specifications for various measurements are given in the following sections. The specifications for the engine you are servicing are in the vehicle service

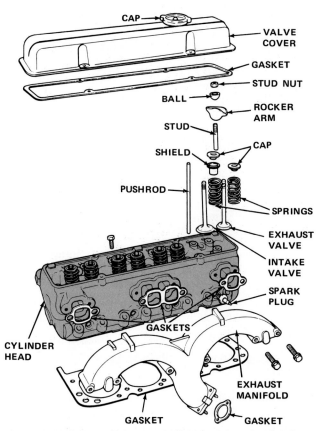

Fig. 39-2 Cylinder head from an OHV V-8 engine, showing the valve train for one cylinder disassembled. (*Chevrolet Division of General Motors Corporation*)

manual, manufacturer's specification books, and auto repair manuals (➣3-4). Figure 3-3 is a page from a Ford *Specification Book* showing the cylinder-head and valve-train specifications for a four-cylinder engine.

VALVE TROUBLE DIAGNOSIS

➣ 39-3 VALVE TROUBLES

Valves must be properly timed. They must operate without lag and seat tightly. On engines with solid valve lifters, valve-train clearance must be checked and adjusted if necessary. Valves that are adjusted too tightly may not close fully after the engine has reached normal operating temperature and the valve-train parts have expanded. Running an engine this way will cause the valves to burn as hot gases blow past the valves during combustion. Valves that have too much clearance open late and close early. This decreases volumetric efficiency (➣15-12). The result is loss of power, poor fuel economy, and high exhaust emissions.

Clearance between the valve stems and valve guides must be correct. Hydraulic valve lifters must operate properly. Figure 39-3 is a *Valve Trouble-Diagnosis Chart*. It lists various valve troubles, their possible causes, and the checks or corrections to be made. Following sections explain these troubles. Other sections describe the required services.

➣ 39-4 VALVE STICKING

Gum or carbon deposits on the valve stem (➣39-9) can cause valves to stick partly open. This occurs because of the excess clearance or wear between the stem and the valve guide. During the intake strokes, oil is pulled through the intake-valve guide into the combustion chamber and burned (Fig. 39-4A). A worn exhaust-valve guide allows oil to enter the exhaust manifold (Fig. 39-4B). Some of the oil striking the valve forms deposits under the head and on the stem (Fig. 39-5D). The deposits may wedge the stem in the guide and hold the valve open.

A bent valve will stick. The bending results from the valve overheating, an off-center valve seat, or a cocked valve spring or retainer. Too little oil also causes valve sticking. Sometimes valves stick when cold and work free as the engine warms up.

➣ 39-5 VALVE BURNING

Burning is usually an exhaust-valve problem (Fig. 39-5B). Poor seating is most often the cause. Valve heat cannot transfer normally to the valve seat. The poor seat allows hot combustion gases to blow by, further heating the valve. An *interference angle* (Fig. 14-16) reduces the chances of valve-seat leakage. However, an interference angle is not always recommended, especially in some smaller engines. Instead, a minimum valve-seat width is specified. A typical specification is 0.043 to 0.067 inch [1.1 to 1.7 mm]. When

Complaint	Possible Cause	Check or Correction
1. Valve sticking (➤39-4)	a. Deposits on valve stem	See item 6
	b. Worn valve guide	Replace
	c. Warped valve stem	Replace valve
	d. Insufficient oil	Service lubricating system; add oil
	e. Cold-engine operation	Valves work free as engine warms up
	f. Overheating valves	See item 2
2. Valve burning (➤39-5)	a. Valve sticking	See item 1
	b. Distorted valve seat	Check cooling system; tighten cylinder-head bolts
	c. Valve-train clearance too small	Adjust
	d. Spring cocked or weak	Replace
	e. Overheated engine	Check cooling system (see Chap. 26)
	f. Lean air-fuel mixture	Service fuel system
	g. Preignition	Clean carbon from engine; use cooler plugs
	h. Detonation	Adjust ignition timing (➤33-28); use higher-octane fuel
	i. Valve-seat leakage	Use an interference angle
	j. Overloaded engine	Reduce load; install heavy-duty valves
	k. Valve-stem stretching from strong spring or overheated engine (see Chap. 26 for causes of overheating)	Use weaker spring; eliminate overheating
	l. Loose valve guide	Replace guide
3. Valve breakage (➤39-6)	a. Valve overheating	See item 2
	b. Detonation	Adjust ignition timing; use higher-octane fuel; clean carbon from engine
	c. Excessive valve-train clearance	Adjust
	d. Seat eccentric to stem	Service
	e. Cocked spring or retainer	Service
	f. Scratches on stem from improper cleaning	Replace valve; avoid scratching stem when cleaning valves
4. Valve-face wear (➤39-7)	a. Excessive valve-train clearance	Adjust
	b. Dirt on face	Check air cleaner
	c. See also causes listed under item 2	
5. Valve-seat recession (➤39-8)	a. Valve face cuts valve seat away	Use coated valves and valve-seat inserts
6. Valve deposits (➤39-9)	a. Gum in fuel (intake)	Use proper fuel
	b. Carbon from rich mixture (intake)	Service fuel system
	c. Worn valve guides	Repair or replace
	d. Carbon from poor combustion (exhaust)	Service fuel system, ignition system, or engine as necessary
	e. Dirty or wrong oil	Service lubricating system, replace oil

Fig. 39-3 Valve trouble-diagnosis chart.

the valve closes, the heat from the valve head transfers from the face through the contact area to the seat. This cools the valve. An excessively narrow contact area results in valve overheating and burning. Since an interference angle reduces contact area, do not grind an interference angle unless specified in the vehicle service manual.

Clogged coolant passages around the valve seats prevent normal coolant circulation and cause hot spots on the valve seats. This can cause seat distortion, poor seating, and overheated valves. Seat distortion also results from improper tightening of the cylinder-head bolts (➤39-28). Other causes include a weak or cocked valve spring and not enough valve-train clearance. They can cause poor

valve seating. A worn valve guide prevents normal seating and can cause the valve to break.

Inspect the valve-stem tips (Fig. 39-6). If the engine uses *valve rotators* (➤14-14), the wear patterns show if the rotator is working. If it is not, local hot spots and valve burning can result.

➤ 39-6 VALVE BREAKAGE

Any condition that causes the valve to overheat may cause it to break. If a valve breaks, it can destroy the engine. An off-center valve seat or cocked valve spring or retainer forces the valve to one side every time it seats. This causes

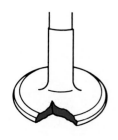

Fig. 39-4 Oil is forced between a worn valve guide and the valve stem by gravity and the difference in air pressure. *(Dana Corporation)*

(A) INTAKE VALVE

(B) EXHAUST VALVE

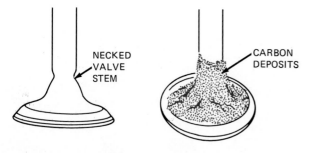

(A) BROKEN VALVE   (B) GUTTERED (BURNED) VALVE

(C) NECKED VALVE STEM   (D) CARBON UNDER HEAD

Fig. 39-5 Various defects on used valves. *(Ford Motor Company)*

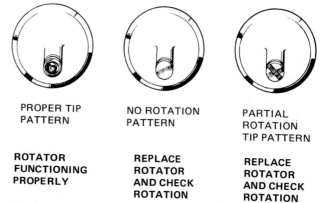

PROPER TIP PATTERN

NO ROTATION PATTERN

PARTIAL ROTATION TIP PATTERN

ROTATOR FUNCTIONING PROPERLY

REPLACE ROTATOR AND CHECK ROTATION

REPLACE ROTATOR AND CHECK ROTATION

Fig. 39-6 Valve-stem-tip wear patterns on valves with valve rotators. *(Oldsmobile Division of General Motors Corporation)*

the valve to seat with a heavy impact. It also causes pounding on the valve tip, resulting in mushrooming of the tip end. Valve-train clearance is kept to a minimum to reduce noise and wear as the valve-train parts hit together to open the valve. Dirt on the valve and seat can also cause rapid wear.

➤ 39-8 VALVE-SEAT RECESSION

This is the gradual wearing away of the seat so it recedes away from the combustion chamber (➤14-6). Valve-train clearance is reduced. With solid lifters or tappets, there can be a complete loss of clearance. In addition, valve-train parts expand as the engine warms up. This also reduces valve-train clearance. If the valve no longer closes completely, the valve and seat will burn.

metal fatigue and breakage. Section 39-20 covers valve-spring inspection.

➤ 39-7 VALVE-FACE WEAR

Excessive valve-train clearance can cause rapid valve-face wear and valve breakage. The excessive clearance causes

Gum in fuel can deposit on the intake valve (Fig. 39-5D). Carbon deposits may form because of a rich mixture or oil passing through a worn valve guide (Fig. 39-4A). Poor combustion due to a defective ignition system, loss of compression, or cold-engine operation results in carbon deposits on the exhaust valves and piston rings. The wrong engine oil or dirty oil can also cause carbon deposits.

In port-injected engines (Chaps. 19 and 20), the fuel injector sprays fuel at the stem and underside of the valve head (Fig. 19-1). Some of the fuel may stick to the valve and form deposits under the head. The deposits may act like a sponge and soak up part of each fuel charge. Then the cylinder receives a lean mixture. Hesitation may result.

| NOTE | Deposits on valves and piston rings may be loosened or removed by chemical additives that can be poured into the engine oil or fuel. Read the instructions on the container to make sure the additive will not damage the catalytic converter. |

ADJUSTING VALVE-TRAIN CLEARANCE

➤ 39-10 VALVE ADJUSTMENTS

The valve-train clearance on engines with solid or mechanical valve lifters (➤14-15) must be adjusted after any cylinder-head or valve service. The vehicle maintenance schedule may also require a *valve adjustment* periodically. This is the same as adjusting *valve clearance* or making a *tappet* or *lash adjustment.* "Lash" means freeplay or clearance.

Engines with hydraulic valve lifters (➤14-16) and lash adjusters (➤14-17) normally require no adjustment of valve-train clearance. The clearance is taken up hydraulically. The hydraulic lifter or lash adjuster also takes care of any small changes in valve-train length.

In any valve train, refinishing the valves and seats reduces valve-train clearance. Too much clearance results from worn valve-train parts. Because exhaust valves run hotter and expand more, exhaust-valve clearance usually is greater than intake-valve clearance. Too much valve clearance causes noise and poor engine performance. Too little valve clearance causes valve and seat burning.

➤ 39-11 ADJUSTING VALVES ON SOLID-LIFTER OHV ENGINES

Figure 39-7 shows how to check and adjust the valve clearance on an overhead-valve (OHV) engine that has solid lifters and shaft-mounted rocker arms. The engine should be off and at normal operating temperature. Disable the ignition and remove the valve cover (Fig. 39-2). Bump the crankshaft with the starting motor until the *heel* (Fig.

11-16) or base circle of the cam is under the valve lifter (Fig. 14-3, right).

Measure the clearance between the valve stem and rocker arm with a thickness gauge (Fig. 39-7). Turn the adjusting screw until the clearance is within the manufacturer's specifications. Tighten the locknut and recheck the clearance.

Figure 39-8 shows how to adjust valve clearance on a stud-mounted rocker arm. Backing out the *stud nut* (Fig. 39-2) increases valve clearance.

| NOTE | Valve clearance or valve lash refers to the freeplay in the valve train while the valve is closed. It is usually measured at the tip end of the valve stem |

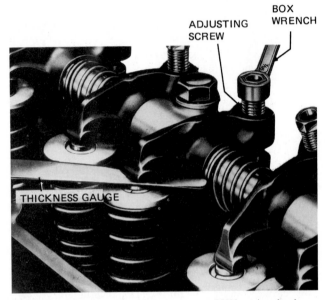

Fig. 39-7 Adjusting valve clearance on an OHV engine that has solid lifters and shaft-mounted rocker arms. (*Ford Motor Company*)

Fig. 39-8 Adjusting valve clearance on an OHV engine with rocker arms mounted on ball studs. Backing out the stud nut increases clearance. (*Chevrolet Division of General Motors Corporation*)

(Fig. 39-8). The gap typically varies from 0.006 to 0.016 inch [0.15 to 0.4 mm]. Valve clearance is not the same as the much smaller *valve-stem-to-guide clearance.* This is the clearance between the valve stem and the valve guide (➤39-21). Stem-to-guide clearance typically varies from 0.0006 to 0.002 inch [0.015 to 0.05 mm].

➤ 39-12 ADJUSTING HYDRAULIC VALVE LIFTERS ON OHV ENGINES

Adjustment of the hydraulic-valve-lifter *initial setting* may be needed after resurfacing the cylinder head or refinishing the valves and seats. This adjustment should properly position the lifter plunger in the center of its travel. Sometimes additional clearance is needed and no adjustment method is provided by the engine manufacturer. Then up to 0.020 inch [0.5 mm] may be ground off the tip end of the valve stem (➤39-23). An excessively high valve stem will bottom the plunger in the lifter.

1. FORD OHV ENGINES To check valve clearance, turn the crankshaft until the lifter is on the base circle of the cam. Use a *tappet collapser* (Fig. 5-9) to force the oil out of the lifter. This bottoms the plunger in the lifter (Fig. 14-26). Check valve clearance with a thickness gauge. Install a longer pushrod if the clearance is excessive. Pushrods are available in various lengths. If the clearance is too small, use a shorter pushrod.

2. PLYMOUTH OHV ENGINES With the valve seated, put the *valve-stem height gauge* over the valve stem (Fig. 39-9). If the height exceeds the specifications, grind up to 0.020 inch [0.5 mm] off the valve-stem tip end (➤39-23).

3. CHEVROLET OHV ENGINES With the valve lifter on the base circle of the cam, back off the stud nut until the pushrod is loose (Fig. 39-10). Slowly turn the adjusting nut down while rotating the pushrod with your fingers. When

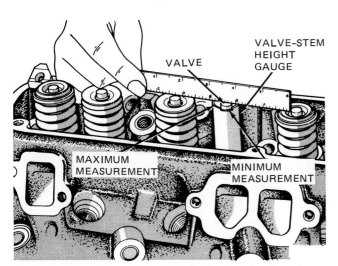

Fig. 39-9 Measuring valve-stem height after inserting the valve in the valve guide. (*Chrysler Corporation*)

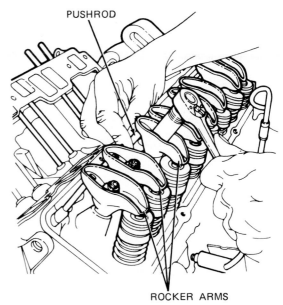

Fig. 39-10 Adjusting the valve rocker-arm-stud nut to properly position the plunger in the hydraulic valve lifter. (*Chevrolet Division of General Motors Corporation*)

the pushrod tightens and will not rotate easily, turn down the adjusting nut one additional full turn. This positions the valve-lifter plunger in the center of its travel.

➤ 39-13 ADJUSTING VALVES ON OHC ENGINES

Overhead-camshaft (OHC) engines use a variety of valve trains to operate the valves (Fig. 14-1). OHC engines with hydraulic tappets (Fig. 14-28) or lash adjusters normally do not require valve adjustments (➤14-16). Various adjusting methods are used with mechanical tappets. On an OHC engine, always check valve-train clearance every time the cylinder head is resurfaced. Cylinder-head resurfacing changes the center-to-center distance between the crankshaft and the camshaft. This then affects valve timing.

Listed below are typical valve-adjusting procedures for various OHC valve trains. Adjustment procedures on other OHC engines may differ. Follow the procedure in the vehicle service manual.

1. SOLID BUCKET TAPPETS Figures 14-4 and 39-11 show double-overhead-camshaft (DOHC) engines with solid bucket tappets (➤14-15). To check valve clearance, rotate the crankshaft until the tappet is loose. Measure the clearance between the *adjusting shim* and the base circle of the cam with a thickness gauge. Change the thickness of the shim to adjust the clearance. To remove the shim, a special spring depressor may be needed to slightly compress the spring. Then remove the shim with special pliers.

2. ADJUSTABLE SHAFT-MOUNTED ROCKER ARMS Figure 39-12 shows the valve train of a four-valve engine. A single overhead camshaft (SOHC) uses adjustable rocker

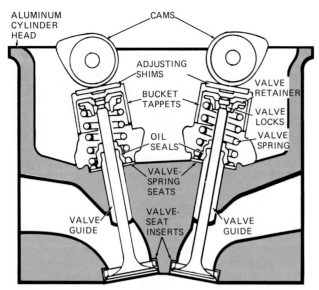

Fig. 39-11 Valve train with bucket tappets, showing location of adjusting shims inside the bucket tappets. *(Chevrolet Division of General Motors Corporation)*

arms (➤14-11) mounted on shafts to operate the valves. To check valve clearance, rotate the crankshaft until the rocker arm is on the base circle of the cam. Measure the clearance between the rocker-arm adjusting screw and the valve stem. If adjustment is necessary, hold the adjusting screw with a screwdriver (Fig. 39-12B). Loosen the locknut and turn the adjusting screw to get the specified

clearance. Then tighten the locknut and recheck the clearance.

3. ADJUSTABLE STUD-MOUNTED ROCKER ARMS Figure 14-20 shows an OHC valve train using a valve lifter and a stud-mounted rocker arm. This arrangement may use solid or hydraulic valve lifters. In engines with solid lifters, adjust the clearance by turning the crankshaft until the lifter is on the base circle of the cam. Measure the clearance between the rocker arm and the valve stem. Adjust the clearance by turning the stud nut.

4. ADJUSTABLE STUD AND FLOATING ROCKER ARM Figures 14-22 and 39-13 show an overhead camshaft that operates the valves through floating rocker arms. The rocker arms float between a hydraulic tappet or stationary stud on one side and the valve stem on the other side. Clearance can be adjusted on engines using the stationary stud. Rotate the crankshaft until the base circle of the cam is over the center of the rocker arm. Measure the clearance between the two with a thickness gauge (Fig. 39-13). Adjust the clearance by loosening the locknut and turning the adjusting screw. Turning the screw in increases clearance. After making the adjustment, tighten the locknut. Then recheck the clearance.

➤ **39-14 JET-VALVE ADJUSTMENT**

Some overhead-camshaft engines use a *jet valve* (Fig. 39-14) or secondary intake valve that admits only air

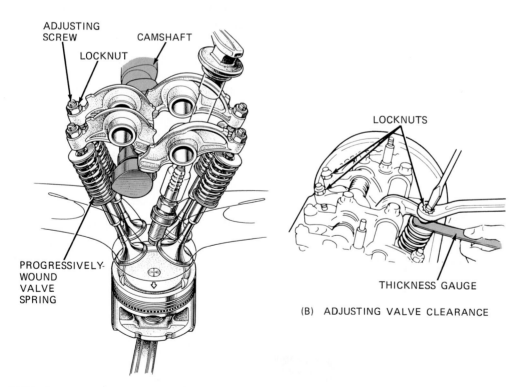

(B) ADJUSTING VALVE CLEARANCE

(A) OVERHEAD CAMSHAFT WITH ADJUSTABLE ROCKER ARMS

Fig. 39-12 OHC-engine valve train using adjustable rocker arms on shafts to operate the valves. *(American Honda Motor Company Inc.)*

Fig. 39-13 Checking valve clearance on an OHC engine using rocker arms. (*Ford Motor Company*)

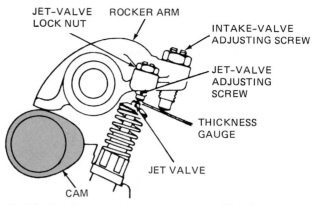

Fig. 39-14 Adjusting the jet-valve clearance. (*Chrysler Corporation*)

(➤13-10). Adjust the jet valve before adjusting the intake valve. Rotate the crankshaft to place the number 1 piston at TDC on the compression stroke. Back off the intake-valve adjusting screw two turns.

Loosen the jet-valve locknut. Back off the jet-valve adjusting screw until a 0.010-inch [0.25 mm] thickness gauge fits loosely between the jet-valve stem and the adjusting screw (Fig. 39-14). Turn the adjusting screw in until it just touches the thickness gauge. Hold the adjusting screw and tighten the locknut. Recheck the clearance. Then adjust the intake valve.

CYLINDER-HEAD AND VALVE-TRAIN SERVICE

➤ 39-15 COMPLETE VALVE SERVICE

The complete valve service includes the following steps.

1. Disconnect the negative cable from the battery.
2. Drain the cooling system and disconnect the upper radiator hose from the engine.
3. Disconnect or remove the air cleaner. Disconnect the throttle linkage, fuel lines, and air and vacuum hoses as necessary to get at the cylinder head. If necessary, mark the hoses for identification.
4. Disconnect the spark-plug cables (➤33-20) and coolant-temperature sensor. (➤19-16)

CAUTION!

Always wear eye protection if it is necessary to move the air-conditioner compressor or other components out of the way. Do not disconnect any air-conditioner connection or hose unless necessary. These hold refrigerant under pressure. Disconnecting them allows refrigerant to escape. This can be dangerous. The escaping refrigerant can freeze anything it

touches, including your hands, face, and eyes. Also, you must then evacuate and recharge the system with refrigerant after the engine work is completed. If disconnecting refrigerant lines is necessary, follow the procedures in Chap. 56.

5. On some in-line engines, the cylinder head can be removed without removing the manifolds. On V-type engines, remove the intake manifold.
6. Remove the valve cover.
7. Remove the stud-mounted rocker arm and pushrods (if used). Place the valve-train parts in order in a rack so they can be reinstalled in their original positions (Fig. 39-1). Inspect and service the valve-train parts, if necessary, as explained later.
8. On shaft-mounted rocker arms, remove the shaft assembly and pushrods, if used.
9. On OHC engines, remove the camshaft. Some OHC engines have the camshaft held in place by camshaft-bearing caps. Remove the cap bolts or stud nuts in several steps.
10. Remove the cylinder-head bolts and cylinder head.

Careful! Never remove a cylinder head from a hot engine The head may warp and become unusable. Wait until the engine is cool.

11. Use a *valve-spring compressor* (Fig. 39-15) and remove the valves and springs from the head. Place the parts in order in a rack (Fig. 39-1). If a valve cannot be pulled out of the valve guide by hand, check for a tip end that is mushroomed or peened over. If this has happened, use a file or small grinding stone to slightly *chamfer* the tip end (Fig. 39-4A). Forcing a valve through the guide will damage or break the guide.

CAUTION!

Some exhaust valves have hollow stems filled with sodium for cooling (➤14-7). Never nick or break a *sodium-cooled valve*

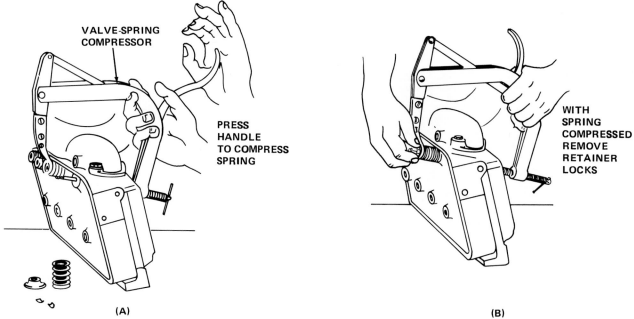

Fig. 39-15 Using a valve-spring compressor. (A) Compressing the spring. (B) Removing the retainer locks.

(Fig. 14-14). Escaping sodium could explode and severely injure you. Discard a sodium-filled valve as hazardous waste (➤4-13).

12. Inspect the valves, valve seats, and valve guides and service as necessary. Later sections describe these steps.
13. After all parts are serviced, install all parts in and on the cylinder head. Then install the head on the engine. Reconnect all disconnected hoses and lines.
14. Check and adjust valve clearance, if necessary.

➤ **39-16 CYLINDER-HEAD SERVICE**

Remove all head bolts, including any that are hidden from view. Lift the cylinder head from the engine. If the head sticks in place, carefully pry it loose. Place the head on *head stands* or in a secure position on the bench. Clean the carbon from the combustion chambers using a motor-driven wire brush (Fig. 39-16). Some technicians leave the valves in place during this operation to protect the valve seats and also to clean the valve heads.

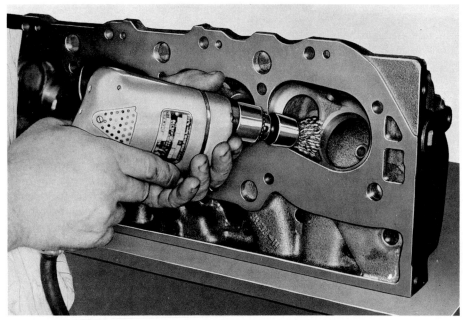

Fig. 39-16 Cleaning combustion chamber and valve ports with a wire brush. *(Chevrolet Division of General Motors Corporation)*

Remove all old gasket material from the cylinder head with a flat scraper or spray gasket remover. *Do not scratch the gasket surface!* Remove dirt and grease from the head and clean it in the solvent tank (➤8-24) or with a spray washer (➤8-25). Be sure the cylinder-head water jackets are clean and free of deposits.

Inspect the combustion chambers, head-gasket and manifold surfaces, and valve guides and ports for traces of leakage or cracks. Many cracks in cylinder heads and other engine parts are not easily seen. If cracks are suspected, check the area using a *crack detector*. One way to check a cast-iron head is with a *magnetic-particle crack detector* (Fig. 39-17). Check an aluminum head with a spray-can kit of *dye penetrant*. Many diesel cylinder heads should be pressure-tested to ensure that water does not leak around the injector tubes.

Check the head for warpage (Fig. 39-18). This includes checking the head-gasket surface, manifold mounting surfaces, and camshaft-bearing bore alignment. In OHC heads, warpage throws the camshaft bearings out of line. Warped heads from OHC engines may require replacement, or heat-straightening and light resurfacing. Warped heads from OHV engines can usually be resurfaced and reinstalled.

Check the valve guides (➤39-21) and valve seats (➤39-24). Clean and service as necessary. Also, check and replace any expansion-core plugs (➤26-18) in the cylinder head.

➤ 39-17 ROCKER-ARM-STUD SERVICE

Check each rocker-arm stud (Fig. 39-2) for looseness. Some studs thread into the head, but many are a press fit. If

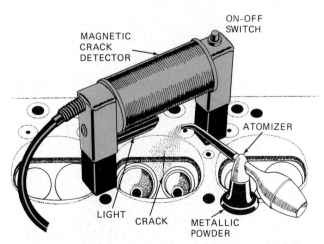

Fig. 39-17 Using a magnetic-particle crack detector to check the cast-iron cylinder head for cracks between the valve seats. (*Gregory Olcott Company*)

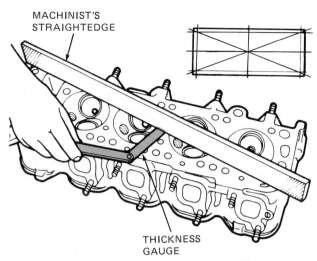

Fig. 39-18 Checking cylinder head for warpage with a straightedge and thickness gauge. (*Chrysler Corporation*)

a stud is loose, replace it. Remove the press-fit stud with a *stud puller*. Then ream the hole and install an oversize stud. Or tap the hole and install a threaded stud. Some rocker-arm studs have an oil hole (Fig. 14-18C). Check that it is open.

➤ 39-18 ROCKER-ARM SERVICE

Inspect the rocker arms (Figs. 39-10 and 39-12) for wear. Check the pushrod end, valve-stem end, pivot hole or shaft bore, bushings or needle bearings, and oil hole (if used). Also check any rocker-arm surfaces that ride on the cams (Figs. 39-12 and 39-13). Replace damaged or worn rocker arms. Some rocker arms with shaft bushings can be *rebushed*. This rocker arm may also have the valve-stem end resurfaced on a valve-refacing machine (➤39-23).

Replace any excessively worn rocker-arm shaft. Check that all oil holes in rocker-arm shafts are open. Many rocker-arms and shafts install with the oil holes in the shaft facing down. If the oil holes face upward, improper lubrication and low oil pressure will result. Be sure the springs and rocker arms are in their original positions when the shafts are attached to the head.

➤ 39-19 PUSHROD SERVICE

Inspect both ends of each pushrod (Figs. 39-2 and 39-10) for wear. Roll the pushrod on a flat surface to check for straightness. Replace a worn or defective pushrod. Some pushrods have one end hardened and marked with a colored stripe or band. Install the hardened end toward the rocker arm.

➤ 39-20 VALVE-SPRING INSPECTION

Inspect each valve spring for cracks or other damage. Then check the valve spring for proper *tension, free length,* and *squareness.* Tension is checked using a *valve-spring tester.* It measures the force required to compress the spring a specified distance. Figure 39-19A shows how to measure free length with a vernier caliper. All springs should be within 1/16 inch [1.6 mm] of the manufacturer's specifications.

Check the spring for squareness by placing the close-coil end against a flat surface such as a *combination square* (Fig. 39-19B). Rotate the spring. Discard the spring if the top coil moves away from the square by more than 1/16 inch [1.6 mm].

Replace valve springs that are weak, too long, too short, or not square. Some manufacturers recommend installing new valve springs during valve service.

➤ 39-21 VALVE-GUIDE SERVICE

The valve guide must be serviced before refinishing the valve seats. Clean the guide with a wire brush or adjustable blade cleaner (Fig. 39-20). Check the amount of valve-guide wear (Fig. 39-4). One way is to insert a good valve in the guide. Then measure the side movement with a dial indicator (Fig. 39-21). Another way is to use a *small-hole gauge* and an outside micrometer (Fig. 5-25).

A worn valve guide requires service or replacement. On

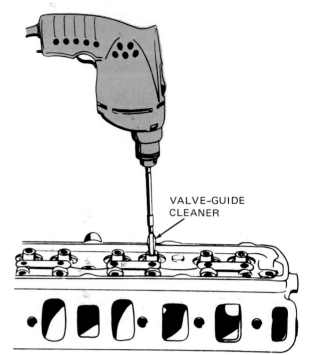

Fig. 39-20 Cleaning the valve guide with a valve-guide cleaner. (*Oldsmobile Division of General Motors Corporation*)

heads with replaceable valve guides (Figs. 39-4A and 39-11), use a driver and drive the worn guide out of the head. Install a new guide. Then use a *reamer* and ream the guide to the proper size. A worn guide can also be reamed oversize and then a new valve with an oversize stem installed.

Service a worn integral valve guide (Fig. 39-4B) by first reaming the guide oversize. Then install a *valve-guide bushing* in the guide. Ream it to the standard valve-guide

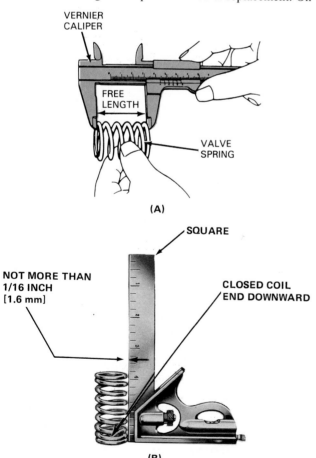

Fig. 39-19 Checking a valve spring. (A) Measuring free length. (B) Checking for squareness. (*Toyota Motor Sales U.S.A., Inc.; Ford Motor Company*)

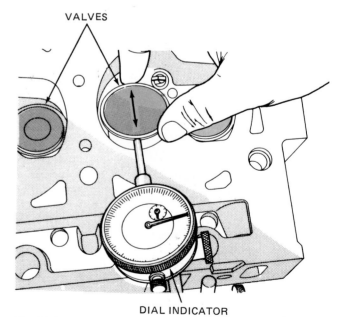

Fig. 39-21 Checking valve-guide wear by using a dial indicator to measure side movement of the valve head. (*Chrysler Corporation*)

diameter. Another service procedure is to *knurl* the guide (Fig. 39-22) by running a *knurling tool* down into the guide. As the tool slowly turns, it pressure-forms a spiral groove in the guide. Remove the knurling tool and ream the guide to the original diameter.

➤ 39-22 VALVE CLEANING AND INSPECTION

When disassembling the cylinder head, remove and inspect each valve. Figure 39-23 shows the areas to be checked. Measure the stem diameter for wear and check for wear of the *lock* or *keeper groove* (Fig. 39-22). Figure 39-5 shows damaged valves that must be discarded. Remove the carbon and deposits from each valve with a wire wheel. *Do not scratch the valve face or valve stem!*

CAUTION!

Wear eye protection when using the wire wheel.

Use fine emery cloth to polish the valve stems, if necessary. Do not remove metal, only the deposits. Refacing the valve removes small pits or burns on the valve face. In many engines, the valve faces are given a thin coat of

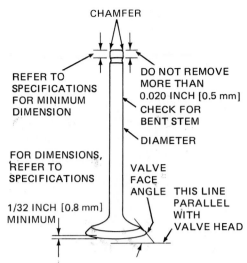

Fig. 39-23 Parts to be checked during inspection of each valve.

aluminum, nickel, or other metal during manufacture. This helps prevent valve-seat recession (➤14-6). Coated valves have a dull, almost rough appearance on their head and face. *Do not lap or reface coated valves!* This removes the protective coating, which shortens valve and seat life.

➤ 39-23 VALVE SERVICE

Valves may be refaced by grinding on a *valve-refacing machine* or by cutting on a *lathe-type valve refacer*.

1. REFACING VALVE-STEM TIPS Figure 39-24 shows a *valve-refacing machine*. Lightly grind the tip ends of the valve stems to remove any roughness (Fig. 39-6). Use the V-block and grinding stone on the right side of the valve refacer (Fig. 39-24). One recommendation is to grind the same amount from the tip that is removed from the valve face. This makes up for the amount that the valve sinks into the seat. Do not remove more than 0.020 inch [0.5 mm] from the valve-stem tip (Fig. 39-23).

After reconditioning the valve-stem tip, inspect the bevel angle or chamfer (Figs. 14-14 and 39-23) on the stem end. The chamfer should be about 1/32 inch [0.8 mm] wide. Restore the chamfer by placing the valve stem in a V block set at a 45-degree angle to the grinding wheel on the valve refacer (Fig. 39-24). Adjust the coolant spray to cover the stem end. Then slowly rotate the valve stem while holding the end against the grinding wheel.

2. REFACING VALVES Set the *chuck* or the grinding wheel on the valve refacer (Fig. 39-24) to grind the valve face at the specified angle. This angle must match the valve-seat angle or be an interference angle of 1/4 to 1 degree less than the seat angle (Fig. 14-16). Place the valve stem in the chuck. When the machine is turned on, both the valve and the grinding wheel rotate. A coolant spray from the coolant nozzle should cover the rotating valve face. This prevents the valve from overheating during grinding. To reface the valve, move the valve face back

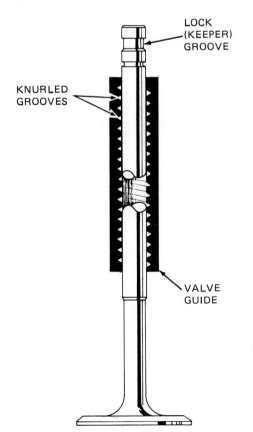

Fig. 39-22 Valve in place in a knurled and reamed valve guide. The valve stem is partly cut away, showing the grooves in the valve guide. (*United Tool Processes*)

COOLANT NOZZLE

CHUCK

Fig. 39-24 A valve-refacing machine. (*Sioux Tools Inc.*)

and forth across the grinding wheel (Fig. 39-25). Follow the valve-refacer operating instructions for specific steps in the procedure.

Figure 39-26 shows a lathe-type valve refacer. Place the valve stem in the *collet* or holder. When the motor is turned on, the valve rotates. To reface the valve, move the cutting tool across the valve face. This generates less heat than grinding, so no coolant spray is required.

Discard a valve if it is ground so much that the margin is lost (Fig. 39-27). The margin must be at least 1/32 inch [0.8 mm]. Lightly reface new valves that have a bright-metal finish. Do not reface valves that have a coated, dull face and head.

> ## 39-24 VALVE-SEAT SERVICE

Valve seats are of two types: integral and insert (➤14-8). Replace a damaged or loose valve-seat insert by using a chisel or puller to remove the old insert. Install a new insert of the proper size. If necessary, chill the new insert to shrink it enough to fit. Then the seat is driven in, peened in place, and refinished.

1. REFINISHING VALVE SEATS Valve seats can be refinished with a motor-driven grinding stone. Carbide-steel cutters turned by hand or with a motor can also be used. With either method, first service the valve guide (➤39-21). The *pilot shaft* for the stone or cutter installs in the valve guide. A dirty guide may cause the pilot shaft to be off center.

The *valve-seat grinder* (Fig. 39-28) rotates a grinding stone of the proper shape on the valve seat. The stone is kept concentric with the valve seat by the pilot installed in the valve guide (Fig. 39-29). After refinishing the seat, measure the seat width (Fig. 39-30) with a steel scale. A typical recommendation is that the seat should be 1/16 inch [1.6 mm] wide (Fig. 39-31) and centered on the valve face.

If the seat is too wide, narrow it to the specified width. Use a 15-degree upper stone and a 60-degree lower stone as necessary to grind away the upper and lower edges of the seat (Fig. 39-31). This narrows the seat *contact line* (Fig. 39-30) on the valve face. If the contact line is too high on the valve face, lower the seat by grinding with the 15-degree stone. If the contact line is too low, use a 60-degree stone to raise the seat.

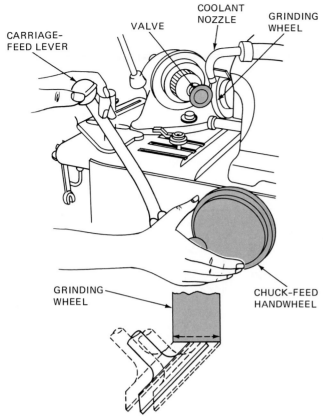

Fig. 39-25 To reface the valve, move the lever to carry the valve face back and forth across the rotating grinding wheel. (*Ford Motor Company*)

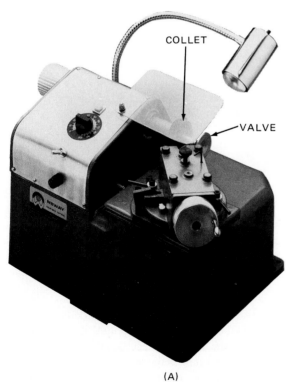

(A)

Fig. 39-26 (A) A lathe-type valve refacer. To reface the valve, the carbide-tipped cutting tool is moved across the valve face (B). (*Neway Manufacturing, Inc.*)

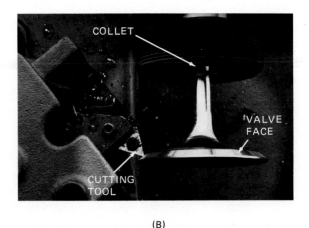

(B)

Fig. 39-26 (cont.)

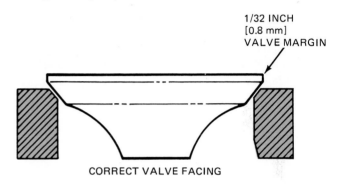

CORRECT VALVE FACING

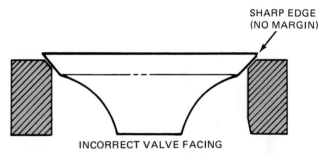

INCORRECT VALVE FACING

Fig. 39-27 Correct and incorrect valve refacing. The valve at the bottom has no margin and would soon burn. (*Chrysler Corporation*)

Figure 39-32 shows the use of a valve-seat cutter. Place the pilot in the valve guide. Then place the cutter on the pilot. As the cutter rotates, it cuts metal from the seat. Different cutters or blades are used to cut different seat angles. They can also narrow the seat and raise or lower it. Some cutters cut all three seat angles at the same time.

2. CHECKING VALVE-SEAT RUNOUT For good valve seating, the valve guide and seat must be concentric. They must have a common center and little or no runout. After servicing the valve guides and seats, check for runout with a *valve-seat runout gauge* (Fig. 39-33). Mount the gauge in the valve guide and place the indicating finger on the valve seat. As the gauge rotates, any runout shows on the dial indicator.

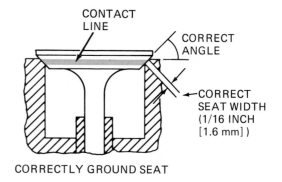

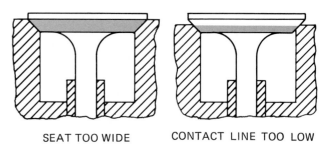

CORRECTLY GROUND SEAT

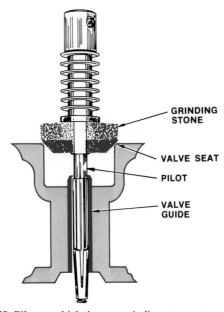

Fig. 39-28 Reconditioning a valve seat with a valve-seat grinder. (*Black & Decker, Inc.*)

SEAT TOO WIDE　　CONTACT LINE TOO LOW

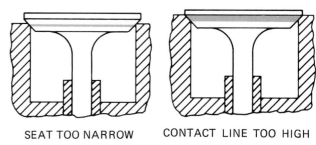

SEAT TOO NARROW　　CONTACT LINE TOO HIGH

Fig. 39-30 Various problems with valve seating that require further cutting and grinding. (*Ford Motor Company*)

Fig. 39-29 Pilot on which the seat-grinding stone rotates. The pilot keeps the stone concentric with the valve guide. (*Black & Decker, Inc.*)

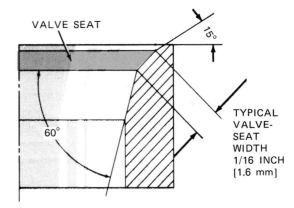

Fig. 39-31 A properly refaced valve seat. (*Chrysler Corporation*)

The seating can also be checked by coating the valve face with Prussian blue or other material. Install the valve and turn it with light force. If the coating appears all around the seat, the seat and guide are concentric. Remove the coating from the valve face and seat. Apply it to the seat. Lightly rotate the valve on the seat. If the coating transfers all the way around the valve face, the valve is not bent. Its face and stem are concentric. This also shows the position and width of the valve-seat contact line on the valve face (Fig. 39-30). The blue should transfer to the center of the valve face. If not, raise or lower the seat as necessary.

Another test of valve seating is to mark lines with a marker or pencil about 1/4 inch [6.35 mm] apart around the valve face. Put the valve in place. Apply light force and turn the valve half a turn to the left and then half a turn to the right. If this removes the marks, the seating is good.

3. CHECKING VALVE-STEM HEIGHT An important step, especially on engines with non-adjustable valve

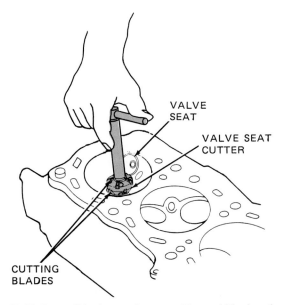

Fig. 39-32 Reconditioning a valve seat with a carbide-tipped valve-seat cutter. (*ATW*)

Fig. 39-33 Checking valve-seat runout. (*Oldsmobile Division of General Motors Corporation*)

trains, is to check *valve-stem height* (Fig. 39-9). A combination of cylinder-head resurfacing along with valve seat and face grinding can cause the valve-stem tip to stick up too far. After cylinder-head installation, the pushrod will then hold the valve slightly open.

After grinding the valves and seats, temporarily slide the valves into the guides and check the stem heights. With the valves seated, turn the head on its side. Use a valve-stem height gauge (➤39-12), or lay a straightedge along the valve-stem tips. Any stem that protrudes much above the

others indicates a problem. Either the valve-stem tip must be reground, the valve seat replaced, or both.

➤ **39-25 CAMSHAFT SERVICE**

Watch the pushrods while the engine idles to locate rough or worn cam lobes in overhead-valve (OHV) engines. A pushrod that turns slowly or does not turn shows that the cam is not rotating the valve lifter (➤14-15). Check the camshaft for alignment and unusual cam wear.

Check camshaft alignment by placing the camshaft on V blocks (Fig. 39-34). Position a dial indicator over each bearing journal. Rotate the camshaft while watching the dial indicator. The runout or *eccentricity* shown on the dial indicator is the amount the camshaft is bent or out of alignment.

Inspect the cams for pitting and wear. Replace the camshaft if a cam is pitted or worn its full width. Install a new camshaft if any cam lobe is excessively worn. Cam-lobe lift can be checked with the camshaft in or out of the engine. A micrometer or the setup shown in Fig. 39-34 can measure lobe lift.

The camshaft bearings may be either one-piece or two-piece *sleeve bearings* (➤13-16) that fit around the camshaft journals. In some engines, the camshaft rotates in *needle bearings*. OHV engines have one-piece camshaft bearings in the cylinder block.

Replace worn or damaged one-piece camshaft bearings using a driver or a threaded installing tool. Oil holes in the new bearings must align with the oil holes in the block or head. With the camshaft in place, measure the camshaft *endplay*. Move the camshaft as far forward and then backward as it will go. Measure the distance with a thickness gauge or a dial indicator.

When installing an overhead camshaft that runs in two-piece bearings, check the bearing clearance (Fig. 39-35). Clean the bearing surfaces and place a strip of Plastigage across each journal. Install the camshaft-bearing caps and tighten to the specified torque. Then remove the caps. Use the measuring scale on the Plastigage package and measure

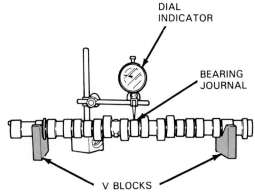

Fig. 39-34 Checking camshaft alignment with a dial indicator. (*Mazda Motors of America, Inc.*)

513

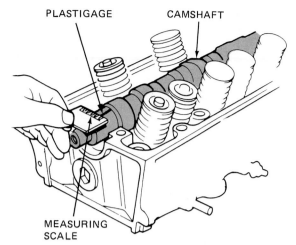

Fig. 39-35 Using Plastigage to measure camshaft-bearing clearance in an OHC engine. (*American Honda Motor Company, Inc.*)

the amount of flattening. The scale will show the bearing clearance.

Always install new valve lifters (➤39-26) or cam followers with a new camshaft. Coat the cams and lifter feet with extreme-pressure (EP) or other specified lubricant. Inspect the camshaft drive belt or *timing belt* (Fig. 39-36). Replace the belt if any defects are found. If the belt is to be reused, mark it to show its normal turning direction before removal. Then reinstall the belt in the same position.

Inspect and replace worn timing gears or sprockets and timing chain. When installing the camshaft drive (➤14-3),

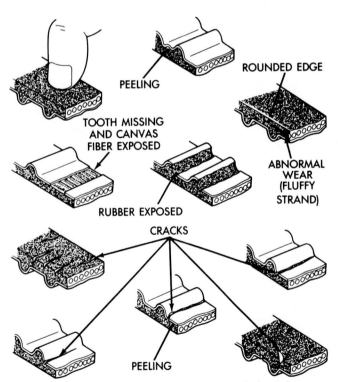

Fig. 39-36 Inspecting the camshaft drive belt, or timing belt. Replace the belt if any of these defects is found. (*Chrysler Corporation*)

align the timing marks on the crankshaft and camshaft gears or sprockets.

➤ 39-26 VALVE-LIFTER SERVICE

In most OHV engines, remove the valve lifters from the pushrod side of the cylinder block. Keep the lifters in order (Fig. 39-1) so they can be reinstalled in their original positions. In some engines, worn lifter bores can be reamed oversize. Then install oversize lifters.

A *leak-down test* can be made on hydraulic valve lifters without removing them from the engine. Insert a thickness gauge between the rocker arm and valve stem. Use a tappet collapser (Fig. 5-9) and note the time it takes the lifter to leak enough oil to seat the valve. As the valve seats, the thickness gauge becomes loose. Install a new lifter if the leak-down time is shorter than specified.

When hydraulic valve lifters are out of the engine, check the lifters in a *leak-down tester* (Fig. 39-37). After filling the lifters with oil, the tester places a standard weight on the lifter. The number of seconds it takes for the lifter to leak down a specified distance is the *lifter leak-down rate*.

Replace a roller lifter if the roller is worn, pitted, or spins roughly or noisily. On the lifter, the foot must be slightly convex and smooth (Fig. 39-38). If it is not, replace the lifter.

CYLINDER-HEAD ASSEMBLY AND INSTALLATION

➤ 39-27 VALVE INSTALLATION

Valve-guide service (➤39-21) and valve-seat service (➤39-24) must be completed before installing the valves

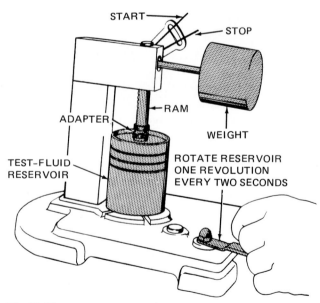

Fig. 39-37 Using a leak-down tester to check the leak-down rate of a hydraulic valve lifter. (*Oldsmobile Division of General Motors Corporation*)

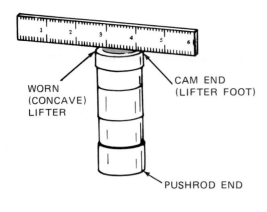

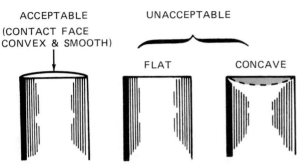

Fig. 39-38 Checking the bottom of the valve lifter for wear. No light should be visible under the straightedge. (*ATW*)

in the cylinder head. Install new valve-stem oil shields (Fig. 39-2) and seals (Fig. 39-11) during head assembly.

The metal removed from the valves and valve seats during refacing may allow the valve stems to stick up higher in the cylinder head. This increases the *valve-spring installed height* (Fig. 39-39) and reduces *valve-spring tension.* To restore normal spring tension, install a *valve*

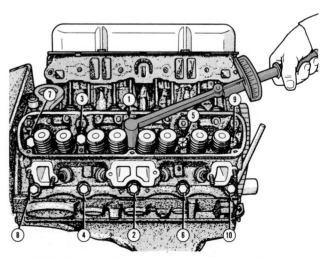

Fig. 39-39 Installing a shim under the valve spring to adjust valve-spring installed height.

spring shim between the spring and the cylinder head. *Do not install a shim that reduces the spring height below the specified minimum!*

Some cast-iron cylinder heads may not need valve-spring shims after valve service (Fig. 39-2). Aluminum heads usually have a *valve-spring seat* (Fig. 39-11) between the valve spring and the cylinder head. The seat prevents the movement of the steel valve spring from wearing away the softer aluminum. Install the shim, if needed, between the seat and the head.

Install *progressively-wound* valve springs (Fig. 39-12A) with the close-spaced coils toward the cylinder head. *Conical* valve springs install with the larger-diameter end toward the head. Sometimes one or two damper springs fit inside the valve spring. The service manual may specify the proper relationship of the damper springs to the valve spring.

After completing all the required steps, install the valve-stem oil seal or shield (Fig. 14-17). Install the valve rotators (➤14-14), if used. Then compress the valve spring (Fig. 39-15) and install the valve retainer and locks. If the valve keepers or locks (Fig. 14-17) are worn, always replace the valve locks in pairs. On OHC engines, install the rocker arms (if used) and the camshaft. Tighten the camshaft-bearing cap bolts to the specified torque. Check the rocker-arm position and install the camshaft seal.

➤ 39-28 CYLINDER-HEAD INSTALLATION

Prepare the block head-gasket surface by removing all old gasket material with a scraper. *Do not gouge the block surface!* Clean any dirt and gasket material from the bolt holes. Head bolts may bottom on the debris and prevent head-to-block sealing. Continued bolt tightening may crack or damage the block.

Fig. 39-40 Sequence for tightening the cylinder-head bolts on a V-8 engine. (*Chrysler Corporation*)

515

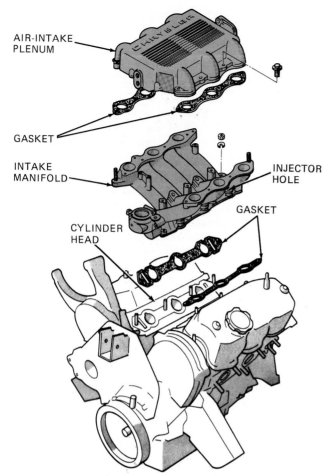

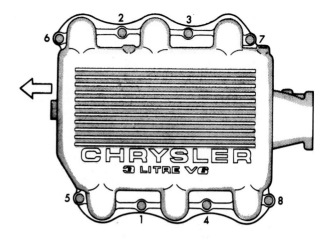

(A) INTAKE-PLENUM TIGHTENING SEQUENCE

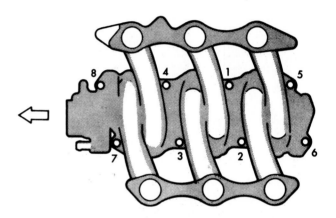

(B) INTAKE-MANIFOLD TIGHTENING SEQUENCE

Fig. 39-42 Sequence for tightening the intake-manifold bolts and intake-plenum bolts on a V-6 engine. (*Chrysler Corporation*)

Fig. 39-41 Check the intake-manifold and intake-plenum for distortion before installing the intake manifold. (*Chrysler Corp.*)

Reinstall all parts removed from the head. Put a new head gasket in place on the block, right side up. If the block does not have *dowel pins* (Fig. 6-25), use two pilot pins set into two bolt holes to insure gasket alignment. Use gasket sealer if specified by the manufacturer. Do not use so much sealer that it seeps into holes and passages.

Lower the head into position. Coat the head bolts with antiseize compound (➤6-14) or sealant (➤6-25), if required. Install the bolts finger tight. Be sure to place the proper bolt in each hole. Some engines have head bolts of different sizes, shapes, and lengths.

Remove the pilot pins and install the bolts in these holes. Using a torque wrench (Fig. 39-40), tighten the bolts in the sequence specified in the vehicle service manual. Tighten each bolt in two or more steps, in sequence.

If the engine uses *torque-to-yield* head bolts (➤6-12), install a new set following the procedure in the vehicle service manual. Typically, the procedure is to tighten each bolt in the proper sequence to a specified initial torque. Then repeat the tightening sequence, turning each bolt through the specified angle. A second sequence of turning each bolt through another specified angle may be required. The use of a *torque-angle gauge* (Fig. 7-12) accurately measures how much the bolt-head turns.

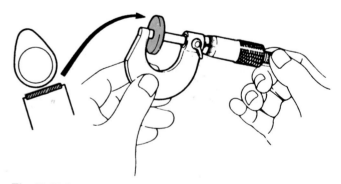

Fig. 39-43 Measuring valve-train parts with a micrometer. (*Toyota Motor Sales U.S.A., Inc.*)

➤ **39-29 INTAKE-MANIFOLD INSTALLATION**

Clean all old gasket material from cylinder-head, intake-manifold, and intake-plenum (if used) mounting surfaces

516

(Fig. 39-41). Check the intake-manifold and intake-plenum mounting surfaces for distortion. Using a straightedge and thickness gauge, check each mounting surface diagonally and across the center (Fig. 39-18, top). Install new gaskets. If the vehicle manufacturer recommends *formed-in-place gaskets* (➤6-24), squeeze a bead of the specified sealant around the areas to be sealed (Fig. 6-28).

Install the intake manifold. Torque the bolts or nuts in sequence to the specified torque. Figure 39-42 shows the tightening sequence for a V-6 engine. On engines with port fuel injection (Chaps. 19 and 20), check that the fuel-injector holes are clean and open.

Coat the fuel-injector O rings with clean engine oil and install the injectors (➤20-26). Then install the fuel rail, fuel lines, hose, and wiring. If the engine has an intake plenum, place the gaskets with their beaded side up on the intake manifold. Install the intake plenum. Tighten the bolts in sequence to the specified torque (Fig. 39-42A).

MULTIPLE-CHOICE TEST

*Select the **one** correct, best, or most probable answer to each question.*
You can find the answers in the section indicated at the end of each question.

1. Technician A says deposits on the valve stem may cause the valve to stick partly open. Technician B says valve-stem deposits usually prevent the valve from opening. Who is right? (➤39-4)
   a. A only
   b. B only
   c. both A and B
   d. neither A nor B
2. Excessive valve-train clearance can cause all the following EXCEPT (➤39-7)
   a. rapid valve-face wear
   b. valve breakage
   c. valve-train noise
   d. valve burning
3. All the following are true EXCEPT (➤39-10)
   a. Refinishing valves and seats reduces valve-train clearance
   b. Worn valve-train parts increase valve-train clearance
   c. Hydraulic valve lifters require periodic adjustment
   d. Exhaust-valve clearance usually is greater than intake-valve clearance
4. In Fig. 39-43, the technician is (➤39-13)
   a. adjusting valve clearance on an OHV engine
   b. measuring camshaft endplay
   c. measuring camshaft-bearing clearance
   d. adjusting valve clearance on an OHC engine

5. To grind an interference angle, grind the valve face at an angle that is (➤39-23)
   a. 1 degree greater than the seat angle
   b. 1 degree less than the seat angle
   c. the same as the seat angle
   d. a right (90-degree) angle
6. After refacing, all but two valves have a 1/32 inch [0.8 mm] margin. One valve has a 1/64 inch [0.4 mm] margin. The other valve has a margin of less than 1/64 inch [0.4 mm]. The technician should (➤39-23)
   a. replace both valves with less than 1/32 inch [0.8 mm] margin
   b. replace the one valve with less than 1/64 inch [0.4 mm] margin
   c. replace all the valves because the margins are too small
   d. reinstall all the valves
7. Technician A says if the contact line on the valve face is too high, grind the seat with a 15-degree stone. Technician B says if the contact line on the valve face is too low, grind the seat with a 60-degree stone. Who is right? (➤39-24)
   a. A only
   b. B only
   c. both A and B
   d. neither A nor B

REVIEW QUESTIONS

1. Explain the importance of care and cleanliness in engine service work.   (➤39-1)
2. What is valve-seat recession and how can it affect the valve train?   (➤39-8)
3. Describe three ways to make the hydraulic-valve lifter *initial setting* on OHV engines.   (➤39-12)
4. Describe four ways to adjust valve clearance on OHC engines.   (➤39-13)
5. What are the steps in installing torque-to-yield head bolts?   (➤39-28)

CHAPTER 40

ENGINE SERVICE: CONNECTING RODS, ROD BEARINGS, PISTONS, AND PISTON RINGS

After studying this chapter, and with proper instruction and equipment, you should be able to:

- Diagnose causes of bearing failure.
- Replace connecting-rod bearings.
- Measure bearing clearance with Plastigage.
- Replace piston rings.
- Replace pistons and piston pins.
- Check for bent or twisted connecting rods.

➤ **40-1 PREPARING TO REMOVE PISTONS AND RINGS**

Pistons and connecting rods are removed from the cylinder block as an assembly (Fig. 40-1). First, remove the cylinder head (Chap. 39). Then check the top of the cylinders for *ring ridges* (Fig. 13-36). These mark the upper limits of ring travel. The rings wear away metal from the cylinder walls. This leaves the ridge, formed by the unworn metal (Chap. 41).

You can feel the ridge with your fingernail (Fig. 40-2). If you try to force the piston out past the ridge, the top ring could jam. This could break the ring or the piston lands (Fig. 40-3).

Remove the ring ridges with a *ring-ridge remover* (Fig. 40-4). Cutting blades on the tool cut off the ridge as the tool is turned. Do not allow the ridge reamer to cut deeper than the ring ridge or cut into the ring-travel area of the cylinder.

CONNECTING-ROD AND ROD-BEARING SERVICE

➤ **40-2 REMOVING PISTON-AND-ROD ASSEMBLIES**

Drain and remove the oil pan (➤24-24). Turn the crankshaft so number 1 piston is near BDC. If the rod and

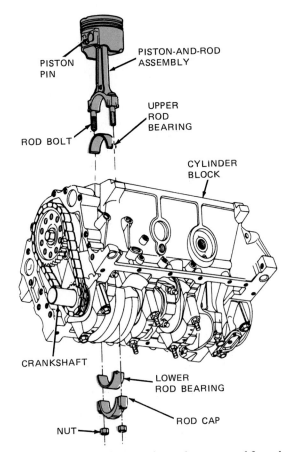

Fig. 40-1 The piston-and-connecting-rod are removed from the block as an assembly. *(Ford Motor Company)*

518

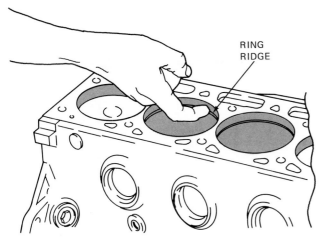

Fig. 40-2 If you can catch your fingernail under the ring ridge, it should be cut away before removing the piston. (*Ford Motor Company*)

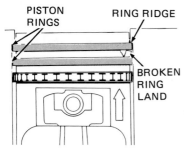

Fig. 40-3 If the ring ridge is not removed, forcing the piston out of the cylinder can break the piston ring lands. (*ATW*)

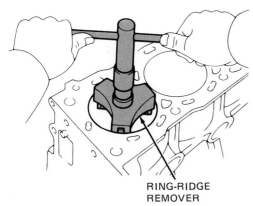

Fig. 40-4 Ring-ridge remover in place. As the tool is turned, cutting blades remove the ring ridge. (*Toyota Motor Sales U.S.A., Inc.*)

cap have no identifying marks, mark a "1" on each. The rod and cap are matched and belong to number 1 cylinder. The marks assure that, if the rod and cap are reused, they will be rematched and go back into number 1 cylinder.

Turn the crankshaft to get at and number the rods and caps of the other cylinders.

Careful! If you mark the rods and caps with a hammer and metal numbering dies or a center punch, be very careful. Heavy blows can distort or break the rods and caps. Also, this may cause the beginning of hairline cracks that will later fracture and break.

Remove the rod bolts and cap. Use rod-bolt *guide sleeves* to keep the bolt threads from scratching the crankshaft journal (Fig. 40-5). Push up the piston-and-rod assembly and remove it from the top of the cylinder (Fig. 40-1). Remove the other assemblies. Put them in order in a numbered piston rack.

Careful! Handle the pistons with care. They are soft aluminum and can easily break, crack, or scratch. This could ruin them.

➤ 40-3 SEPARATING PISTONS AND RODS

Some rods attach to the piston with a *free-floating pin* (Fig. 13-26B). To remove the pin, remove the retainers and slide the pin out. If the pin is a *press fit* (Fig. 13-26A), place the piston-and-rod assembly in a special fixture (Fig. 40-6). Then use the shop press to force out the pin. A *pin press* will also do the job. However, failure to properly support the piston may distort or break it.

➤ 40-4 CHECKING CONNECTING RODS

Clean the connecting rods and caps. Blow out oil holes with compressed air. Examine the condition and wear of the bearings (➤40-5). Check the rods for alignment with a

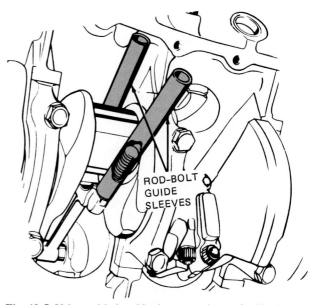

Fig. 40-5 Using rod-bolt guide sleeves or pieces of rubber hose to protect the connecting-rod journals. (*Oldsmobile Division of General Motors Corporation*)

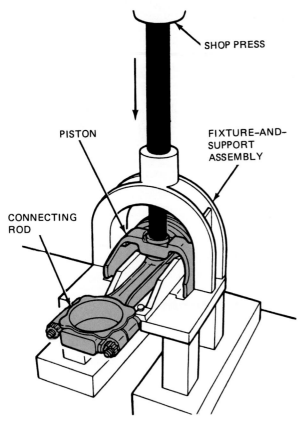

Fig. 40-6 Remove the piston pin by pressing it out of the connecting rod. (*Buick Division of General Motors Corporation*)

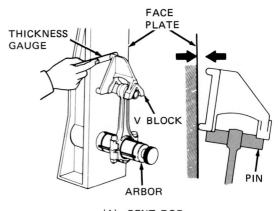

(A) BENT ROD

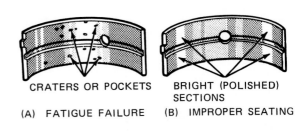

(B) TWISTED ROD

Fig. 40-7 A rod aligner being used to check a connecting rod for bend and twist. (*Toyota Motor Sales U.S.A., Inc.*)

rod aligner (Fig. 40-7). Replace all bent or twisted rods.

Measure the piston-pin bore in the small end of the connecting rods. To prevent piston pin failure, service the bushings or rods if necessary. Replace worn bushings used with free-floating piston pins. Then ream or hone the new bushings to size.

➤ 40-5 INSPECTING CONNECTING-ROD BEARINGS

Examine the condition and wear of each *insert* or bearing half. Figure 40-8 shows various engine-bearing failures. Causes of these failures are described below.

A. FATIGUE FAILURE Repeated excessive loads on a bearing can cause *fatigue failure*. The bearing metal starts to crack and flake out. This leaves craters or pockets in the bearing. As more metal is lost, the remainder carries a greater load and flakes out at a faster rate. Eventually complete bearing failure occurs. Advanced timing and detonation (➤33-9) may cause fatigue failure.

B. IMPROPER SEATING If the bearing is not properly seated in the bore, there will be high spots in the bearing. Figure 40-9 shows what happens when dirt particles are trapped under the bearing. There is too little oil clearance. Also, the air space prevents heat from escaping from the bearing. The combination can cause bearing failure.

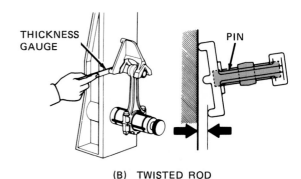

CRATERS OR POCKETS   BRIGHT (POLISHED) SECTIONS

(A) FATIGUE FAILURE   (B) IMPROPER SEATING

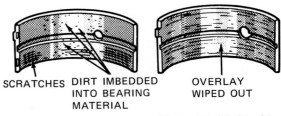

SCRATCHES DIRT IMBEDDED INTO BEARING MATERIAL   OVERLAY WIPED OUT

(C) SCRATCHED BY DIRT   (D) LACK OF OIL OR IMPROPER CLEARANCE

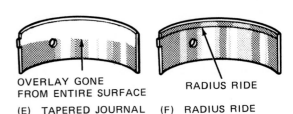

OVERLAY GONE FROM ENTIRE SURFACE   RADIUS RIDE

(E) TAPERED JOURNAL   (F) RADIUS RIDE

Fig. 40-8 Types of engine-bearing failures. The appearance of a bearing usually indicates the cause of its failure. (*Ford Motor Company*)

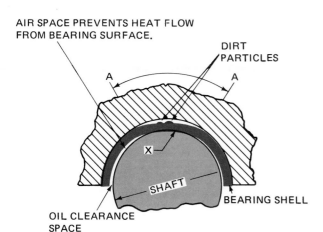

Fig. 40-9 Effect of dirt particles left under the bearing during installation. *(Federal Mogul Corporation)*

C. SCRATCHED BY DIRT If the air and oil filters are not changed regularly, enough dirt can circulate with the oil to scratch the bearings and journals. Bearings overloaded with dirt will fail (Fig. 13-25).

D. LACK OF OIL OR IMPROPER CLEARANCE Lack of oil or improper oil clearance causes the bearing material to be wiped out of the bearing shell. If the friction heat goes high enough, the bearing seizes on the crankshaft and spins in the rod. This "spun bearing" may destroy the rod and the crankshaft. Sometimes the rod welds to the crankshaft journal. Then the engine "throws a rod." The rod breaks and part of it may go through the block. This destroys the engine.

Lack of oil also results from worn bearings which pass more oil than the oil pump can supply. The bearings farthest from the pump are oil-starved and may fail completely. Oil starvation can also result from low oil in the oil pan, clogged oil lines, or a defective oil pump.

E. TAPERED JOURNAL When a crankshaft journal is tapered, the bigger end puts an extra load on that side of both bearing halves. The bearing surface overheats and loses metal until the bearing fails.

F. RADIUS RIDE This is usually the result of an improperly ground crankshaft. The crankshaft cheek is not cut away enough. Then the journal rides on the edge of the bearing. This may lock the crankshaft during engine assembly. If the engine runs, overheating and early bearing failure result. A bent connecting rod causes radius ride on opposite sides of the bearing halves.

➤ 40-6 INSPECTING CONNECTING-ROD JOURNALS

Inspect the crankshaft connecting-rod journals for discoloration, pits, and other damage (Chap. 41). Measure the journals with a micrometer. If they are out of round or tapered more than 0.001 inch [0.025 mm], replace the crankshaft or have it reground. Out-of-round or taper can cause early bearing failure.

PISTON AND RING SERVICE
➤ 40-7 PISTON SERVICE

New piston rings (➤13-29) usually must be installed if the piston is removed from the cylinder after the engine has run. Once the ring break-in coating (➤13-31) and tool marks wear off, the rings will not reseat and seal if they are reinstalled.

Use a *piston-ring expander* (Fig. 40-10) and remove the rings from the pistons. Inspect the pistons for wear, scuff marks, scored skirts, and worn ring grooves. Look for cracks at the ring lands, skirts, pin bosses, and heads. If any pistons are damaged, locate and correct the cause. Discard all damaged pistons.

Scrape the piston-heads clean. Soak the pistons in a parts-cleaning solution that is safe to use on aluminum. Do not use corrosive or caustic solutions. Do not use a wire brush on piston skirts. These could damage the pistons.

> **NOTE** If the pin is too loose in the piston, get a new piston-and-pin set. The pin is prefitted to the piston. Sometimes pistons and rods may be honed or refitted for oversize pins.

Clean out the ring grooves with a ring-groove cleaner or a piece of an old ring. Clean out oil holes or slots in the back of the ring grooves with a drill or small pick.

Measure the diameter of the piston with a micrometer. Measure the diameter of the cylinder (Chap. 41). If the

Fig. 40-10 Using a piston-ring expander to remove or install a compression ring on a piston. *(Dana Corporation)*

clearance is excessive, install a new piston. A typical piston clearance is 0.001 to 0.002 inch [0.025 to 0.05 mm]. Engines with excessively worn or tapered cylinders require *reboring* (Chap. 41). Then install new oversize pistons and rings.

➤ **40-8 PISTON-RING SERVICE**

Piston rings must be fitted to the cylinder and to the ring grooves in the piston (➤13-29). Rings are packaged in sets of graduated sizes to fit various cylinder diameters (➤13-34). Most packages include instructions that describe how to install the rings. Follow these instructions carefully. Install the rings on the piston with the proper side facing up. Piston rings installed upside down may cause excessive oil consumption.

Push a compression ring (➤13-30) from the new ring set down to the bottom of ring travel in the cylinder (Fig. 40-11). Measure the piston-ring *end gap*. Typical end gap is from 0.010 to 0.020 inch [0.25 to 0.51 mm]. If the gap is too small, the ring diameter is too large. A smaller-diameter ring set is needed. Some rings can be filed to get the proper end gap.

If the end gap is within specifications, check the fit of each compression ring in its piston groove (Fig. 40-12). Roll the ring all the way around the groove. If the fit is tight, the groove probably needs cleaning. If the ring is too loose, check the *piston-ring side clearance* or *groove clearance*.

To check ring side clearance, place the ring in the groove. Measure the clearance between the ring and the groove with a thickness gauge. Typical side clearance should be at least 0.001 inch [0.025 mm]. It should not

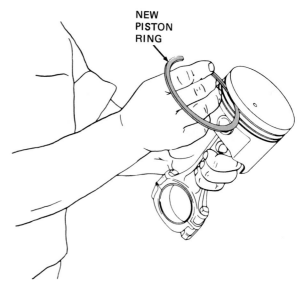

Fig. 40-12 Checking fit of a new compression ring in its ring groove. *(Chevrolet Division of General Motors Corporation)*

exceed 0.004 inch [0.10 mm] for most engines. Side clearance can increase due to the pounding effect of the rings moving up and down in their grooves (➤13-27).

Install the oil rings on the piston (Fig. 40-13). Spiral the oil rings into place. Then install the compression rings with a ring expander (Fig. 40-10). Never try to spiral a compression ring into place. Some are brittle and will break. Others might bend and then stick in the groove. Position the rings so the end gaps have the proper relationship as specified by the manufacturer.

PISTON-AND-ROD ASSEMBLY INSTALLATION

➤ **40-9 INSTALLING CONNECTING-ROD BEARINGS**

Make sure your hands, the workbench, tools, and all engine parts are clean. Do not unwrap the bearings until you are ready to install them. Wipe each bearing half with a clean, lint-free cloth just before installing it.

Put the bearing shells in the cap and rod. If the shells have locking tangs, make sure the tangs enter the notches provided in the cap and rod. Then coat each bearing half with clean engine oil or the specified engine assembly lubricant.

1. **BEARING SPREAD** Bearing shells have *spread* (Fig. 40-14, top). The diameter of the insert is slightly larger than the rod or cap bore. This insures a snug fit when the insert is in place.
2. **BEARING CRUSH** The shells have a little additional height over a full half (Fig. 40-14, bottom). This additional height is crushed down when the cap is installed. This forces the shells to seat firmly in the bores.

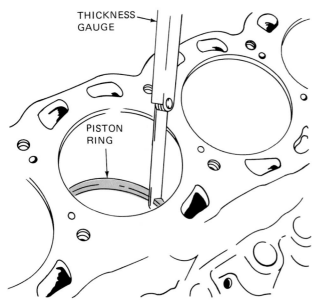

Fig. 40-11 Measure ring gap with the ring at the lower limit of its travel in the cylinder. *(Oldsmobile Division of General Motors Corporation)*

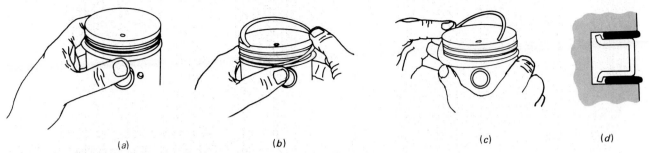

Fig. 40-13 Installation of three-piece oil ring. (A) Place expander-spacer in oil-ring groove with ends of spacer on a solid part of the groove bottom. (B) Hold ends of spacer together, and install steel rail above the spacer. (C) Install other steel rail on lower side of spacer. Be sure ends of spacer are not overlapping. (D) Sectional view of the three parts fitted into groove. *(Dana Corporation)*

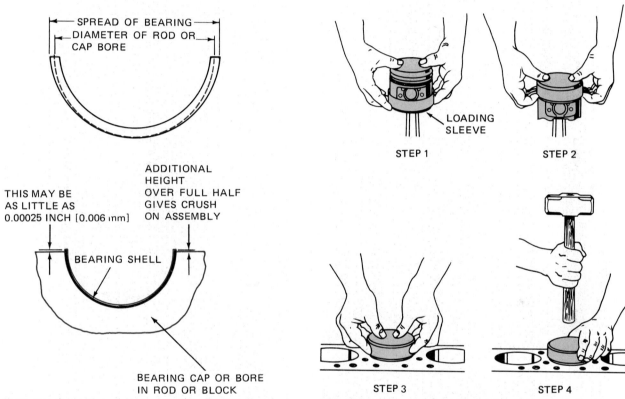

Fig. 40-14 Bearing half, or shell, showing (top) bearing spread and (bottom) bearing crush.

Fig. 40-15 Using a loading sleeve to install a piston-and-rod assembly in a cylinder. *(Chrysler Corporation)*

NOTE Never file off the edges of the bearing shells to remove the crush. Selecting the proper-size bearings ensures they will have the correct crush. These are precision-insert bearings (➤13-16) and should not be tampered with to make them "fit better." This usually leads only to rapid bearing failure.

➤ **40-10 INSTALLING PISTON-AND-ROD ASSEMBLIES**

Dip the pistons in oil. Then compress the rings so they will slide into the cylinders. One method is to use a *piston-ring loading sleeve* (Fig. 40-15). The other is to use a *piston-ring compressor* (Fig. 40-16).

Use guide sleeves to protect the crankpins (Fig. 40-5)

when installing the assemblies. Make sure the pistons and rods are assembled and installed facing in the proper directions. Some pistons have the word "FRONT" stamped on the head. This indicates the piston pin may be offset and the piston may have valve reliefs. These must match the valve locations in the cylinder head. Many pistons have notches to show the proper installed position (Fig. 40-16).

➤ **40-11 CHECKING CONNECTING-ROD BEARING CLEARANCE**

After reattaching the rods to the crankshaft, check the bearing clearance using *Plastigage* (Fig. 40-17). This is a plastic thread used as a measuring tool (➤39-25).

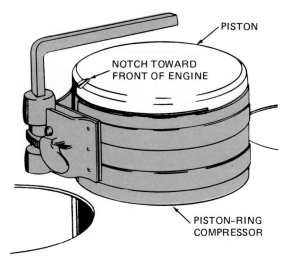

Fig. 40-16 Piston-ring compressor installed on a piston to compress the rings into their grooves in the piston. (*Oldsmobile Division of General Motors Corporation*)

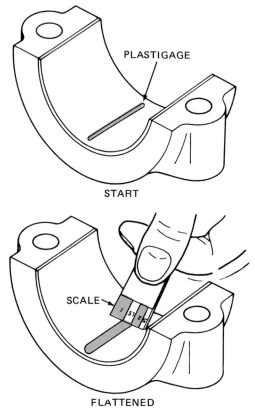

Fig. 40-17 Checking bearing clearance with Plastigage. Top, Plastigage in place before tightening the cap. Bottom, measuring the amount of flattening (or bearing clearance) with the scale on the Plastigage package. (*Chrysler Corporation*)

With the cap off, wipe the oil from the bearing and journal. Lay a strip of Plastigage on the cap bearing. Put the cap in place and tighten the cap nuts to the specified torque. Remove the cap and measure the amount that the Plastigage has flattened. Measure this width with the scale on the Plastigage package. The flatter the Plastigage, the

smaller the clearance. If the clearance is excessive, install undersize bearings.

> **NOTE** Some rod-cap bolts use *torque-to-yield* bolts (➤6-12). These bolts must not be reused. Install the cap with a new set of the proper bolts.

➤ 40-12 CHECKING CONNECTING-ROD SIDE CLEARANCE

With a thickness gauge, measure the connecting-rod side clearance (Fig. 40-18). Too little clearance means a bent or twisted connecting rod (➤40-4).

If rod side clearance is within specifications, complete the installation of the piston-and-rod assemblies. Follow the steps described above for each cylinder. If no additional engine-service work is to be performed, the oil pan can be installed (➤24-24).

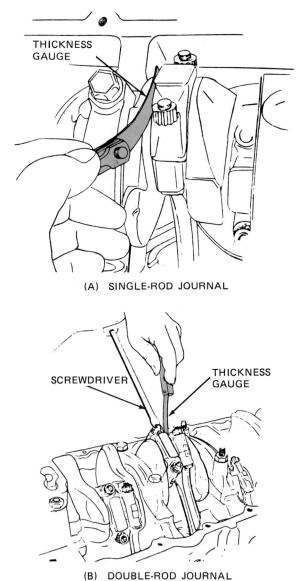

(A) SINGLE-ROD JOURNAL

(B) DOUBLE-ROD JOURNAL

Fig. 40-18 Measuring connecting-rod side clearance. (*Buick Division of General Motors Corporation*)

TRADE TALK

bearing crush

bearing spread

fatigue failure

free-floating pin

insert

piston-ring gap

piston-ring side clearance

Plastigage

ring ridge

spun bearing

MULTIPLE-CHOICE TEST

*Select the **one** correct, best, or most probable answer to each question.*
You can find the answers in the section indicated at the end of each question.

1. Remove the ring ridge before taking the piston out of the cylinder to avoid (➤40-1)
   a. damaging the piston pin
   b. scratching the cylinder wall
   c. breaking the connecting rod
   d. breaking the piston
2. To separate the pistons from the rods, all the following may be used EXCEPT (➤40-3)
   a. a hammer and punch
   b. a fixture and the shop press
   c. a pin press
   d. removing the retainers and sliding the pin out
3. If the bearing overlay is wiped out, the cause is (➤40-5)
   a. fatigue failure
   b. dirt in the oil
   c. radius ride
   d. lack of oil
4. If both bearing halves fail on the same side, the cause is probably (➤40-5)
   a. a bent rod
   b. a tapered journal
   c. lack of oil
   d. heavy loads
5. A typical piston clearance in the cylinder is (➤40-7)
   a. 0.100 inch [2.5 mm]
   b. 0.010 inch [0.25 mm]
   c. 0.001 inch [0.025 mm]
   d. 0.0001 inch [0.0025 mm]

6. If the pin fits too loosely in the piston (➤40-7)
   a. install an undersize pin
   b. install a new piston-and-pin set
   c. ream the piston bore and install a bushing
   d. install new compression rings
7. To check piston-ring end gap, install the ring (➤40-8)
   a. above the ring ridge
   b. in the piston groove
   c. at the bottom of the cylinder
   d. below the ring ridge
8. Install compression rings (➤40-8)
   a. by spiraling them into place
   b. with Plastigage
   c. with a ring expander
   d. as a press fit
9. Piston rings installed upside down may cause (➤40-8)
   a. excessive oil consumption
   b. broken piston lands
   c. rapid cylinder-wall wear
   d. overheating
10. Bearing crush is (➤40-9)
    a. additional spread of the bearing shell
    b. what happens when a bearing fails from lack of oil
    c. the amount the Plastigage flattens
    d. the amount of additional height over a full half

REVIEW QUESTIONS

1. What is the reason for marking the connecting rod and cap before removing the cap?   (➤40-2)
2. What is the difference between a bent connecting rod and a twisted connecting rod?   (➤40-4)
3. Describe five types of bearing failure and possible causes of each.   (➤40-5)

4. How is Plastigage used, and how does it show the bearing clearance?   (➤40-11)
5. Describe how to check connecting-rod side clearance. (➤40-12)

CHAPTER 41

ENGINE SERVICE: CRANKSHAFTS AND CYLINDER BLOCKS

After studying this chapter, and with proper instruction and equipment, you should be able to:

- Remove and install engines.
- Replace engine mounts.
- Replace main bearings.
- Recondition cylinder blocks.
- Hone and bore cylinders.
- Install cylinder liners.

➤ 41-1 ENGINE SHORT BLOCK

When an engine requires major service, it may be cheaper to install a *short block* (Fig. 41-1). This is a new or reconditioned cylinder block assembled with new or usable internal parts. These include pistons, rings, rods, bearings, crankshaft, camshaft (if in block), and timing gears or chain. To complete the engine, the technician adds the water pump, oil pump, oil pan, front cover, cylinder heads, and manifolds. These are usually transferred from the unserviceable engine.

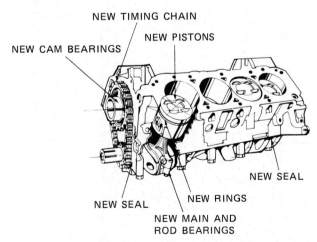

NEW TIMING CHAIN
NEW PISTONS
NEW CAM BEARINGS
NEW SEAL
NEW SEAL
NEW RINGS
NEW MAIN AND ROD BEARINGS

Fig. 41-1 A remanufactured-engine short block, showing the new parts installed in the reconditioned block. (*Ford Motor Company*)

Installing a short block may cost less than the parts and labor for rebuilding an engine. However, when minor service will restore engine operation, making the repair is probably cheaper than installing the short block.

➤ 41-2 ENGINE-MOUNT SERVICE

Broken or damaged engine mounts (➤13-35) and torque struts allow excessive engine movement. This puts extra strain on other mounts and the drive line. It can also prevent normal clutch and transmission operation, and uneven throttle opening.

Replacing an engine mount (Figs. 13-37 to 13-40) usually requires lifting the engine. Then remove the damaged mount and install the new mount. Follow the procedure in the vehicle service manual.

➤ 41-3 ENGINE REMOVAL

Many engine jobs can be done with the engine in the vehicle. Services such as boring cylinders or main-bearing bores require engine removal. The job to be done and the location and position of the engine usually determine if it must be removed.

Some engines are removed with the transmission or transaxle attached (Fig. 41-2). Other engines remove more easily after detaching these units. Some vehicles must be raised on a lift (➤8-21). Then remove the engine or engine-transmission assembly by lowering it from under the vehicle.

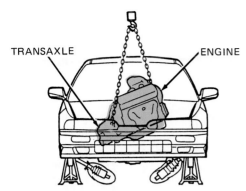

Fig. 41-2 Removing the engine with the transaxle attached. (*American Honda Motor Company, Inc.*)

CAUTION!

To avoid injury or damage when removing or installing the engine, follow the procedure in the vehicle service manual. Wear eye protection and follow all safety rules (Chap. 4). Never place your body in such a position that you would be injured if the engine falls.

CRANKSHAFT SERVICE

➤ 41-4 CRANKSHAFT AND MAIN-BEARING SERVICE

In some engines, main bearings can be replaced without removing the crankshaft. Remove the caps (➤41-5) and inspect the bearings (➤41-6). If the bearings have worn evenly, all that may be required is to check the journals and install new bearings. However, if the main bearings have worn unevenly, remove the crankshaft (➤41-12). Check the crankshaft for worn or damaged journals (➤41-7) and clogged oil passages (Fig. 13-18).

➤ 41-5 REMOVING MAIN-BEARING CAPS

Drain the engine oil and remove the oil pan (➤24-24). Check that the main-bearing caps are marked or numbered. Be sure you can identify the side of the caps which faces the front. Caps must be reinstalled in the same position from which they were removed.

Starting at the front of the engine, remove one main-bearing cap at a time to check the bearing and journal. Some cap nuts or bolts are locked with lock washers or locking tangs. Tangs must be bent back before the nuts or bolts can be removed. If a cap sticks, loosen it by tapping lightly with a plastic hammer.

Careful! Heavy hammering or prying can break the cap. *Align boring* or *honing* of the block may be required to fit a new cap. This is a major machine-shop job. It uses special equipment to rebore or hone the main-bearing bores into alignment.

➤ 41-6 INSPECTING MAIN BEARINGS

Main bearings have the same troubles as rod bearings. Figure 40-8 shows various bearing troubles (➤40-5). If some main bearings are more worn than others, replace all the main bearings. Replacing only one can throw the crankshaft out of alignment. Then it could break or the bearings could fail. When some bearings are more worn than others, the crankshaft may be bent. Check the crankshaft for alignment (➤41-13).

➤ 41-7 CHECKING CRANKSHAFT JOURNALS

Main-bearing journals can be checked with the crankshaft in the block. Use a *crankshaft gauge* (Fig. 41-3) or a crankshaft micrometer. To use the micrometer, first remove the upper bearing shell. If journals are rough or worn, or have excessive taper, ridges, or out-of-round, remove the crankshaft for service. Journals tapered or out of round by more than 0.001 inch [0.025 mm] should be reground. Then install undersize bearings (➤41-10).

➤ 41-8 CHECKING MAIN-BEARING CLEARANCE

This procedure is the same as for checking connecting-rod-bearing clearance (➤40-11). Plastigage is normally used.

➤ 41-9 CHECKING CRANKSHAFT ENDPLAY

Thrust-bearing wear will cause excessive crankshaft endplay. To measure crankshaft endplay, place a dial indicator against the nose of the crankshaft (Fig. 41-4, top).

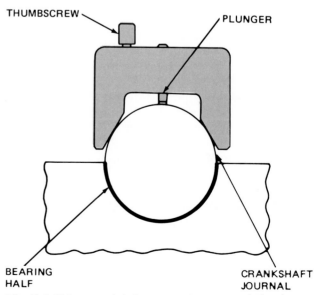

Fig. 41-3 Using a crankshaft gauge to measure a main-bearing journal with the crankshaft in the engine. (*Federal Mogul Corporation*)

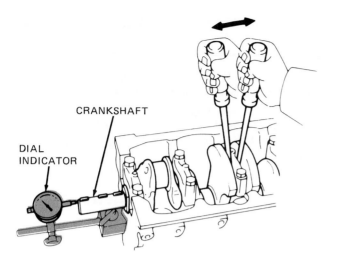

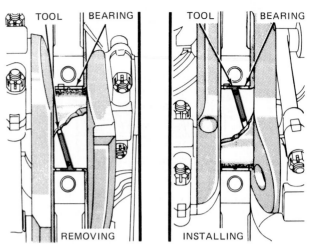

Fig. 41-5 Removal and installation of the upper main-bearing half. The crankshaft journal is partly cutaway, showing the tool inserted in the oil hole in the journal. (*Chrysler Corporation*)

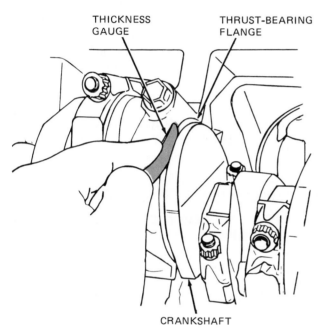

Fig. 41-4 Measuring crankshaft endplay (top) with a dial indicator and (bottom) with a thickness gauge at the thrust bearing. (*Toyota Motor Sales U.S.A., Inc.; Oldsmobile Division of General Motors Corporation*)

Force the crankshaft back and forth with a screwdriver. The dial indicator will show the endplay. Another method is to force the crankshaft as far as it will go in one direction. Then measure the clearance between the crankshaft and the thrust-bearing flange (➤13-17) with a thickness gauge (Fig. 41-4, bottom). The clearance is the endplay.

➤ 41-10 REPLACING MAIN BEARINGS

Main bearings can be replaced, one at a time. Remove the main-bearing cap (➤41-5). Inspect the crankshaft main-bearing journal (➤41-7). If okay, remove the upper half of the main bearing (Fig. 41-5). The tool installs in the oil

hole in the journal. Turn the crankshaft to force out the upper bearing shell.

To install the upper bearing half, coat the inside of the new bearing with oil. Leave the outside dry. Use the tool in the oil hole to force the bearing shell into place. Install the bearing cap and tighten the bolts or nuts to the specified torque. Remove the cap and check the bearing clearance with Plastigage (Fig. 40-17). If okay, reinstall the cap.

> **NOTE** Installing main bearings with the crankshaft in place cannot be done successfully on all engines. The upper bearing shell may not properly seat in the bore.

➤ 41-11 REPLACING THRUST BEARING

The rear main-bearing journal of some crankshafts does not have an oil hole. This prevents use of the tool shown in Fig. 41-5. However, one type of thrust bearing located at the rear main bearing can be removed with pliers (Fig. 41-6). Start the bearing out with a small punch and hammer. Then use pliers with taped jaws to hold the bearing half against the oil slinger. Turn the crankshaft so the bearing rises up out of the bore.

Install the new bearing in the same way. Tap it down in place with a punch and hammer.

➤ 41-12 REMOVING THE CRANKSHAFT

Drain the engine oil. Remove the oil pan (➤24-24) and oil pump (➤24-25). Detach the connecting rods (Chap. 40). Push them up out of the way, but not too far up. If a piston ring gets out of the cylinder, the rod will not pull back down. The cylinder head must be removed. Then a ring

Fig. 41-6 Replacing a rear-main-bearing half with pliers. In this engine, the crankshaft has no oil hole in the rear journal. (*Chevrolet Division of General Motors Corporation*)

compressor (Fig. 40-16) is needed to compress the rings while the piston is pushed down the cylinder.

Remove the crankshaft gear, or sprocket and chain or belt. When removing the crankshaft with the engine in the vehicle, remove the clutch and flywheel (➤42-32) or automatic-transmission drive plate (➤48-19). Support the crankshaft as the main-bearing caps are removed. *The crankshaft is heavy and can cause injury or damage if it falls.*

➤ **41-13 CHECKING THE CRANKSHAFT**

Rotate the crankshaft on V blocks and use a dial indicator to check for alignment (Fig. 41-7). If the crankshaft is bent or out of line, install a new or reground crankshaft.

Inspect the bearing journals for wear, scratches, and other damage. Use a micrometer to check each journal for

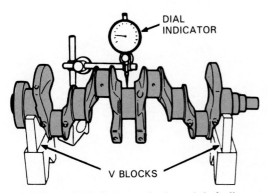

Fig. 41-7 Using a dial indicator to check crankshaft alignment. (*Mazda Motors of America, Inc.*)

wear, taper, and out-of-round. A crankshaft with worn journals can be reground in a *crankshaft lathe*. Use a magnetic-particle crack detector (➤39-16) to check the crankshaft for cracks.

➤ **41-14 CLEANING THE CRANKSHAFT**

To clean the crankshaft completely, remove the oil-gallery plugs from the crankshaft. Some of these plugs may have to be drilled out. Wash the crankshaft in solvent. Use a valve-guide or other long brush to clean the oil passages. Blow out the passages with compressed air. Coat all journals with oil after cleaning.

CYLINDER-BLOCK SERVICE

➤ **41-15 CYLINDER-BLOCK INSPECTION**

Make a visual inspection of the block. Look for cracks and pushed out or missing expansion-core plugs (➤26-18). If cracks are suspected, check the area with a crack detector (➤39-16). Use a magnetic-particle crack detector (Fig. 39-17) on a cast-iron block. On an aluminum block, use a dye penetrant.

Check the condition of the cylinder bores (➤41-17) and the main-bearing bores. Check the alignment of the main-bearing bores by placing a straightedge across them (Fig. 41-8). A 0.0015-inch [0.04-mm] thickness gauge should not slip under the straightedge. If it does, the block is warped. Replace the block or have it align-bored (➤41-5).

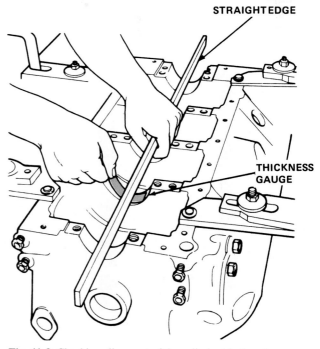

Fig. 41-8 Checking alignment of the cylinder-block main-bearing bores. (*Federal Mogul Corporation*)

529

Put the main-bearing caps in place on the cylinder block. Tighten the bolts to the specified torque. Measure the main-bearing bores for diameter, taper, and out-of-round. Some aluminum blocks may have an increase in bearing-bore diameter. This is caused by steel-backed bearings pounding out the aluminum. If a main-bearing bore is damaged or out of specs, align-bore the block or replace it.

➤ 41-16 CYLINDER-BLOCK CLEANING

If the block is to be reused, remove all old gasket material, pipe plugs, and expansion plugs. This allows cleaning of the oil passages and water jackets. Also remove all identification tags and sensors from the block.

Clean the block in a spray washer or by another suitable method. Allow the block to cool and rinse it with water. Clean out all oil galleries with a brush. Blow out all oil and coolant passages, and threaded holes, with compressed air. If the threads are in poor condition, clean them with a tap (➤7-23) or *thread chaser*. Repair severely damaged threads by installing a thread insert (➤6-15).

➤ 41-17 CYLINDER SERVICE

Cylinders wear the most at the top of the ring travel, where pressures are greatest (Fig. 41-9). Wipe the cylinder walls and inspect them for scores and spotty wear. These show up as dark, unpolished spots. Cylinders with scores or spots require *honing* or *boring* (➤41-18).

Measure the cylinders for wear, taper, and out-of-round (Fig. 41-10). These measurements can be made with an inside micrometer (Fig. 5-11). A telescope gauge or cylinder-bore gauge (Figs. 5-1 and 5-21) and outside

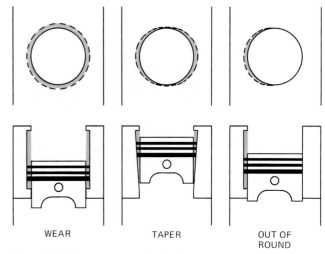

WEAR   TAPER   OUT OF ROUND

Fig. 41-10 Measure each cylinder for wear, taper, and out of round. (*ATW*)

micrometer (Fig. 5-22) can also be used. Many blocks do not require reboring if cylinder taper is 0.006 inch [0.15 mm] or less. Cylinder out-of-round should not exceed 0.002 inch [0.05 mm].

Cylinders with little taper may only need new piston rings. However, the greater the taper, the more difficult it is for the rings to control blowby, oil burning, and exhaust emissions. Recondition cylinders that have excessive taper or out-of-round by honing or boring.

➤ 41-18 REFINISHING CYLINDERS

The cylinder *hone* (Fig. 41-11) has a series of abrasive stones that revolve in the cylinder to remove small

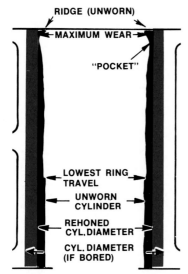

RIDGE (UNWORN)

MAXIMUM WEAR

"POCKET"

LOWEST RING TRAVEL

UNWORN CYLINDER

REHONED CYL. DIAMETER

CYL. DIAMETER (IF BORED)

Fig. 41-9 Taper of an engine cylinder (shown exaggerated). Maximum wear is at the top, just under the ring ridge. Honing the cylinder usually removes less metal than boring, as shown in the illustration. (*Sunnen Products Company*)

Fig. 41-11 Honing a cylinder. (*Sunnen Products Company*)

amounts of metal. One manufacturer recommends honing cylinders if the taper is 0.005 inch [0.13 mm] or less and the out-of-round is 0.003 inch [0.076 mm] or less. If taper or out-of-round is greater, rebore the cylinders.

Proper honing leaves a cross-hatch pattern on the cylinder walls (Fig. 41-12). The hone marks should intersect at about a 60-degree angle. This leaves the surface needed to retain oil and quickly seat new piston rings.

A cylinder that cannot be cleaned or straightened by honing must be bored. Boring uses a *boring bar* which rotates a cutting tool in the cylinder to shave off metal. This increases the cylinder-bore diameter so new oversize pistons and rings (➤13-34) must be installed. Most manufacturers have replacement pistons and rings available in at least two oversizes. Common oversizes are 0.010 inch [0.25 mm] and 0.020 inch [0.50 mm]. Many blocks can be bored even larger. After boring, hone the cylinder to provide the proper cylinder-wall finish.

Some cylinder blocks do not need honing and boring. However, cylinder walls take on a hard, smooth glaze after the engine has been running. The glaze may slow the seating of new piston rings. *Break the glaze* on the cylinder walls before installing the piston-and-ring assemblies (➤40-10). Figure 41-13 shows a brush-type cylinder hone removing the glaze from a cylinder.

➤ 41-19 CLEANING CYLINDERS

After honing or boring, the cylinders must be cleaned. Even slight traces of grit on the cylinder walls can cause rapid ring and piston wear. One procedure is to wipe the cylinder wall with fine crocus cloth. This loosens embedded dirt and knocks off any metal fuzz left by the hone or boring bar. Next, wash the cylinder wall with soapy water and a stiff brush. Then wipe the cylinder with a cloth dampened with light oil. The cloth should come away from the cylinder wall showing no trace of dirt.

Fig. 41-13 Removing the glaze from the cylinder with a brush-type cylinder hone. (*Brush Research Manufacturing Company, Inc.*)

> **NOTE** Do not try to clean the cylinder walls with gasoline or kerosene. Neither of these will remove all the grit from the walls.

➤ 41-20 INSTALLING CYLINDER LINERS

There are two types of cylinder liners: wet and dry (➤13-6). Installing a dry liner may salvage a cracked block, or a block with a damaged or badly worn cylinder (Fig. 41-14). To install a dry liner, bore the cylinder oversize. Press the liner into place. Then bore the liner to the proper size to take the new piston-and-ring set.

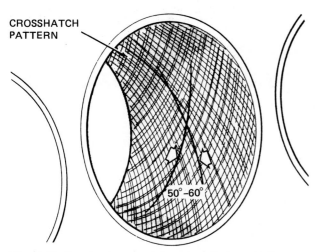

Fig. 41-12 Crosshatch pattern left on the cylinder wall after honing. (*Chrysler Corporation*)

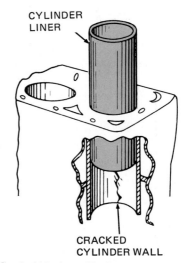

Fig. 41-14 Cracked blocks and badly scored or damaged cylinder bores can sometimes be repaired by installing a cylinder liner, or sleeve. (*Sealed Power Corporation*)

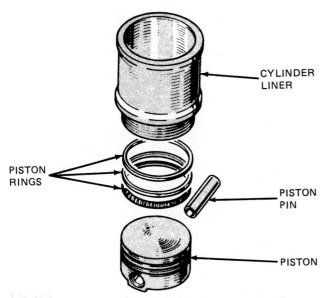

Fig. 41-15 Parts in a cylinder liner kit, used when replacing a wet liner, or sleeve. (*Chrysler Corporation*)

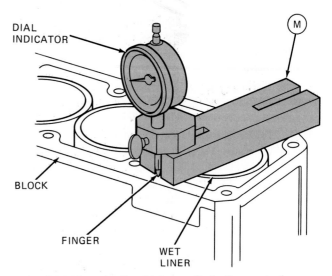

Fig. 41-16 Measuring how high the cylinder liner protrudes above the block surface after installing a wet liner. (*Chrysler Corporation*)

Replace a wet liner using a *cylinder liner kit* (Fig. 41-15). It contains the liner, piston, pin, and rings. The parts are prefitted and matched to ensure the correct clearances. After installing the cylinder and liner seal (Fig. 13-7) in the block, the top of the liner sticks up slightly above the top of the block. This is called *liner protrusion*. Chrysler specifies a 0.002- to 0.005-inch [0.05- to 0.012-mm] liner protrusion on a V-6 engine.

Figure 41-16 shows the use of a dial indicator to measure liner protrusion. Take a second measurement in the position marked *M*. To adjust the amount of protrusion, change the thickness of the liner seal (Fig. 13-7).

➤ 41-21 INSTALLING CYLINDER-BLOCK PLUGS

Install all plugs that were removed so the block could be cleaned (➤41-16). Replacing the expansion-core plugs is described in ➤26-18. Identification tags and sensors removed earlier should also be reattached.

TRADE TALK

align boring	crankshaft lathe	honing	wet liner
boring	cylinder liner kit	liner protrusion	
crankshaft gauge	dry liner	short block	

MULTIPLE-CHOICE TEST

*Select the **one** correct, best, or most probable answer to each question.*
You can find the answers in the section indicated at the end of each question.

1. If a worn main bearing requires replacement, you should replace (➤41-6)
   a. only the damaged main bearing
   b. adjacent connecting-rod bearings
   c. all camshaft bearings
   d. all main bearings

2. Crankshaft journals should be reground if they are tapered or out-of-round by more than (➤41-7)
   a 0.0003 inch [0.0076 mm]
   b. 0.001 inch [0.025 mm]
   c. 0.010 inch [0.25 mm]
   d. 0.030 inch [0.76 mm]

3. Check crankshaft main-bearing journals for (➤41-7)
   a. bend and stretch
   b. taper, ridges, and out-of-round
   c. spots and color
   d. all of the above

4. Technician A says to check main-bearing clearance with Plastigage. Technician B says check main-bearing clearance with a stepped thickness gauge. Who is right? (➤41-8)
   a. A only
   b. B only
   c. both A and B
   d. neither A nor B

5. Thrust-bearing wear will cause excessive (➤41-9)
   a. crankshaft bending
   b. crankshaft vibration
   c. crankshaft endplay
   d. crankshaft speed

6. Main-bearing bores in the cylinder block should be checked for all the following EXCEPT (➤41-15)
   a. alignment
   b. diameter
   c. taper and out-of-round
   d. thread depth

7. Technician A says rebore a cylinder if taper exceeds 0.006 inch [0.15 mm]. Technician B says rebore the cylinder if out-of-round exceeds 0.002 inch [0.05 mm]. Who is right? (➤41-17)
   a. A only
   b. B only
   c. both A and B
   d. neither A nor B

8. Removing the glaze from cylinder walls before installing new piston rings helps avoid (➤41-18)
   a. quick seating of the piston rings
   b. engine overheating
   c. slow seating of the piston rings
   d. excessive friction

9. After boring or honing cylinders, clean and protect the cylinder walls with (➤41-19)
   a. soapy water and light oil
   b. light oil and gasoline
   c. gasoline and kerosene
   d. steam cleaning and air drying

10. When installing wet liners in the cylinder block, adjust the amount of liner protrusion by (➤41-20)
   a. changing the thickness of the head gasket
   b. grinding off the protruding amount
   c. changing the thickness of the liner seal
   d. grinding an equal amount from the cylinder head

REVIEW QUESTIONS

1. When should you consider installing a short block instead of rebuilding an engine? (➤41-1)
2. What problems can be caused by a defective engine mount or torque strut, and how is it replaced? (➤41-2)
3. How should a crankshaft be cleaned and inspected? (➤41-13 and 41-14)
4. Describe the checks and measurements to make when inspecting a cylinder block. (➤41-15)
5. What are the differences between installing dry liners and wet liners? (➤41-20)

PART 7

AUTOMOTIVE DRIVE TRAINS

This part of *Automotive Mechanics* describes automotive drive trains, which carry power from the engine to the vehicle wheels. The drive train consists of a clutch (in some vehicles), transmission (manual or automatic), drive line, and drive axle with the final-drive gearing and differential. In addition to front-wheel and rear-wheel drive, some vehicles have four-wheel drive or all-wheel drive. All these automotive drive trains are described in the following chapters.

There are seven chapters in Part 7:

CHAPTER 42

AUTOMOTIVE CLUTCHES: OPERATION AND SERVICE

After studying this chapter, and with proper instruction and equipment, you should be able to:

- Explain the purpose of the clutch.
- Describe the construction and operation of various automotive clutches.
- Describe the operation of hydraulic clutch linkage.
- Diagnose and correct clutch troubles.
- Service and adjust clutch linkage.
- Remove, inspect, and install a clutch.

CLUTCH CONSTRUCTION AND OPERATION

➤ 42-1 PURPOSE OF THE CLUTCH

The automotive drive train or power train (➤1-11) carries power from the engine to the drive wheels. In vehicles with a *manual transmission* or *manual transaxle* (Chap. 43), the power flows through a *clutch* (Figs. 1-19 and 42-1). This device couples and uncouples the manual transmission or transaxle and the engine. The clutch is usually operated by the driver's foot. Some clutches have a power-assist device to reduce driver effort. Various electronic devices may be used so that the clutch operates automatically (➤42-13).

The clutch is located between the engine flywheel and the transmission or transaxle. Figure 42-1 shows the clutch location in a front-wheel-drive power train. This engine mounts longitudinally. Figure 42-2 shows the clutch location in a front-wheel-drive car with a transversely-mounted engine. Clutch layout in a car with front engine and rear-wheel drive is shown in Fig. 42-3.

Movement of a foot pedal operates the clutch (Figs. 42-3 and 42-4). When the driver pushes the *clutch pedal* down, the clutch disconnects or *disengages* from the engine flywheel. No engine power can flow through to the transmission or transaxle. When the driver releases the clutch pedal, the clutch *engages*. This allows power to flow through.

NOTE To avoid needlessly repeating the phrase *transmission or transaxle,* following references generally are to the *transmission.* This may indicate a separate transmission or the *transmission section* of a manual transaxle. *Transaxle* is used when the reference applies only to a transaxle. Chapter 43 describes manual transmissions and transaxles.

➤ 42-2 FUNCTIONS OF THE CLUTCH

The clutch has four functions:

1. It can be disengaged (clutch pedal down). This allows engine cranking and permits the engine to run freely without delivering power to the transmission.
2. While disengaged (clutch pedal down), it permits the driver to shift the transmission into various gears. This allows the driver to select the proper gear (first, second, third, fourth, fifth, reverse, or neutral) for the operating condition.
3. While engaging (clutch pedal moving up), the clutch slips momentarily. This provides smooth engagement and lessens the shock on gears, shafts, and other drive-train parts. As the engine develops enough torque to overcome the inertia of the vehicle, the drive wheels turn and the vehicle begins to move.
4. When engaged (clutch pedal up), the clutch transmits power from the engine to the transmission. All slipping has stopped.

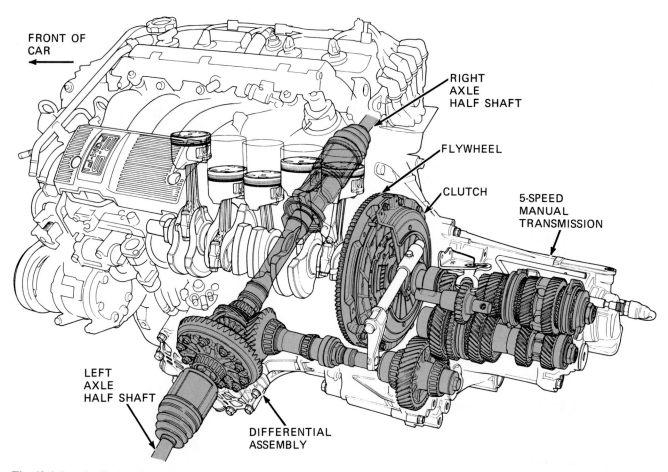

Fig. 42-1 Longitudinal engine with front-wheel drive, showing the clutch and five-speed manual transmission. (*American Honda Motor Company, Inc.*)

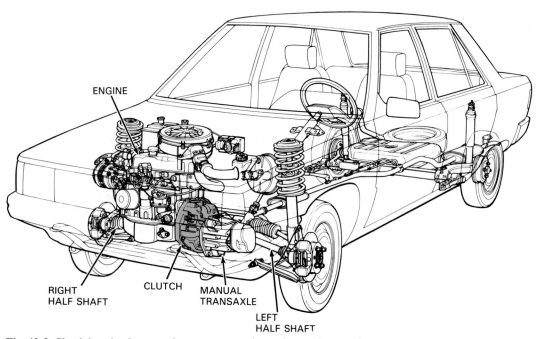

Fig. 42-2 Clutch location between the transverse engine and manual transaxle in a front-wheel-drive car. (*Chrysler Corporation*)

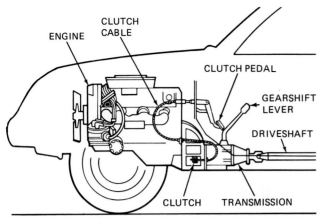

Fig. 42-3 Depressing the foot pedal, or clutch pedal, operates the clutch. (*Ford Motor Company*)

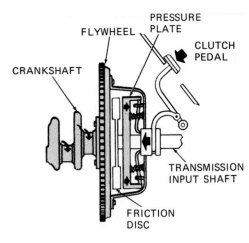

(A) PEDAL DOWN, CLUTCH DISENGAGED

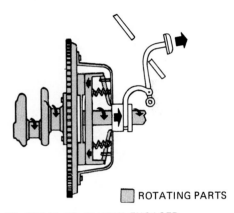

☐ ROTATING PARTS

(B) PEDAL UP, CLUTCH ENGAGED

Fig. 42-4 Operation of the clutch. (A) When the clutch pedal is pushed down, the clutch disengages so no power flows through to the transmission. (B) When the clutch pedal is released, the clutch engages, transmitting power from the crankshaft flywheel to the transmission. (*General Motors Corporation*)

➤ 42-3 STARTING THE ENGINE AND SHIFTING GEARS

The automotive engine cannot start under load. To remove the load, place the *gearshift lever* or *transmission shift lever* (Fig. 42-3) in neutral or disengage the clutch (Fig. 42-4A). Either action disconnects the engine flywheel from the transmission. No power can flow through.

An automotive engine will normally start when cranked at 200 rpm or higher. After the engine starts and with the clutch pedal down, the driver moves the gearshift lever from neutral into first gear. As the driver releases the clutch pedal, spring force in the clutch causes it to engage (Fig. 42-4B). Power flows through the transmission to the drive wheels and the vehicle moves. To increase vehicle speed, the driver then disengages the clutch and shifts the transmission to a higher gear.

➤ 42-4 CLUTCH CONSTRUCTION

The typical clutch consists of three basic parts (Fig. 42-5). These are the engine flywheel (➤11-14), a *friction disc*, and a *pressure plate*. The flywheel and pressure plate are the *drive* or *driving members*. They attach to and rotate with the engine crankshaft (Figs. 42-4 and 42-6). The friction disc is the *driven member* (also called the *driven plate* and *driven disc*). It is about 12 inches [305 mm] or less in diameter and splined to the *clutch shaft* or *transmission input shaft* (Figs. 42-6 and 42-7). Both must turn together, but the friction disc can slide back and forth on the shaft splines.

The pressure plate, with one or more springs, attaches to the *clutch cover* (Fig. 42-6). This *pressure-plate assembly* bolts to the flywheel and rotates with it. Spring force holds the friction disc against the flywheel while the clutch is engaged.

The transmission input shaft has the same centerline as the engine crankshaft (Fig. 42-7). The small end of the input shaft rides in a *pilot bearing* or *bushing* in the end of

the crankshaft. The transmission front bearing or *transmission-input-shaft bearing* supports the other end of the input shaft.

➤ 42-5 CLUTCH OPERATION

Disengaging the clutch (pushing the clutch pedal down) moves the pressure plate away from the friction disc (Fig. 42-4A). Releasing the clutch pedal engages the clutch. Spring force clamps the friction disc between the pressure plate and the flywheel (Fig. 42-4B). Then the friction disc and transmission input shaft turn with the flywheel.

In many clutches, when the driver depresses the clutch pedal (Fig. 42-8), linkage to the *clutch fork* causes it to pivot. The fork pushes against the *release bearing* (➤42-14) or *throwout bearing* (Figs. 42-6 and 42-8). This forces the release bearing inward against *release fingers* or *levers* (described later) in the pressure-plate assembly. These pivot to push the pressure plate away from the friction disc.

538

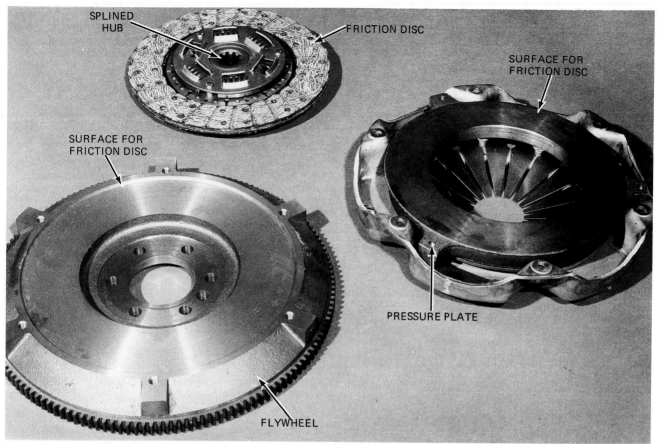

Fig. 42-5 The three basic parts of the clutch: the flywheel, pressure plate, and friction disc. (*Chevrolet Division of General Motors Corporation*)

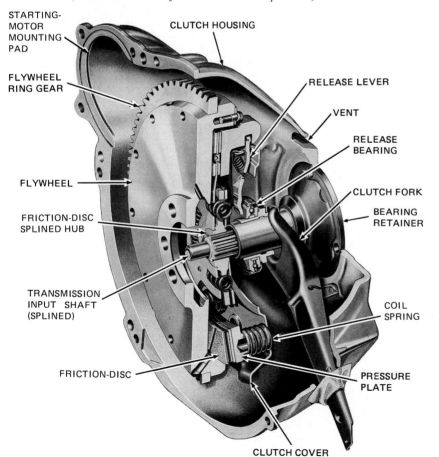

Fig. 42-6 Coil-spring clutch, partly cutaway to show interior construction. (*Ford Motor Company*)

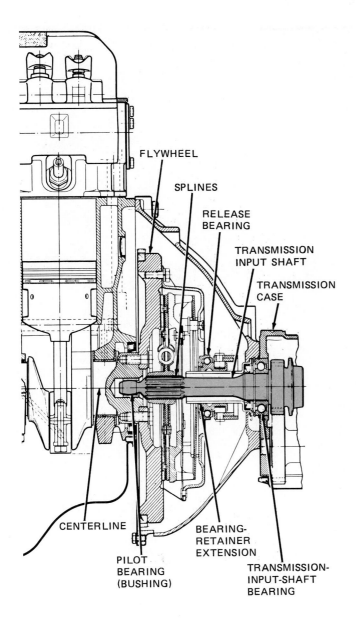

FLYWHEEL

SPLINES

RELEASE
BEARING

TRANSMISSION
INPUT SHAFT

TRANSMISSION
CASE

CENTERLINE

BEARING-
RETAINER
EXTENSION

PILOT
BEARING
(BUSHING)

TRANSMISSION-
INPUT-SHAFT
BEARING

Fig. 42-7 Clutch assembled between engine and transmission. The transmission input shaft has the same centerline as the engine crankshaft. (*Mazda Motor of America, Inc.*)

As the pressure plate moves away from the friction disc, a slight air gap opens between the pressure plate and the friction disc (Fig. 42-8). Another air gap appears between the friction disc and the flywheel. These gaps disengage the clutch so no power flows through it. The typical friction disc travels about 0.060 inch [1.5 mm] as it moves from engaged to disengaged.

➤ 42-6 FRICTION DISC

Figures 42-5 and 42-9 show the friction disc. It has a hub and plate, *cushion springs*, and *dampening springs*. The slightly-waved cushion springs attach to the plate. The friction facings attach to the cushion springs. When the clutch engages, the cushion springs compress slightly to take up the shock of engagement.

The dampening springs or *torsional springs* are heavy coil springs set in a circle around the hub. The hub is driven through these springs. They help reduce the *torsional vibration* (➤13-15) caused by the engine power impulses. This smoothes the power flow to the transmission.

There are grooves on both sides of the friction-disc facings. These grooves prevent the facings from sticking to the flywheel face and pressure plate when the clutch disengages. The grooves break any vacuum that might form and cause the facings to stick. They also help cool the facings.

The facings on many friction discs are made of cotton and asbestos fibers woven or molded together. Then the material is saturated with resins or other binding agents. Copper wire is woven or pressed into the facings of some

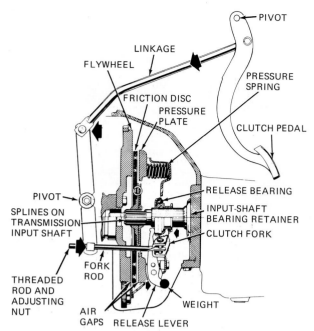

Fig. 42-8 Sectional view of a clutch, showing the linkage to the clutch pedal. (*Buick Division of General Motors Corporation*)

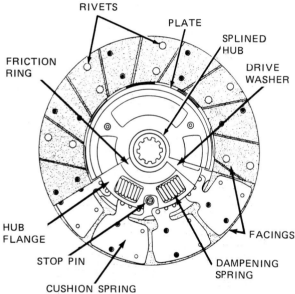

Fig. 42-9 Friction disc, or clutch disc. Facings and drive washer have been partly cutaway to show springs. (*Chevrolet Division of General Motors Corporation*)

friction discs to give them added strength. However, asbestos is a health hazard (➤42-16) and is being replaced with other materials. Some friction discs have ceramic-metallic faces.

➤ 42-7 COIL-SPRING CLUTCH

The clamping force in the pressure-plate assembly is provided by a single *diaphragm spring* (➤42-8) or by several coil springs. These are set in a circle between the

cover and the pressure plate (Figs. 42-8 and 42-10). Depressing the clutch pedal forces the release bearing against the *release levers*. Three are shown in Fig. 42-10. These pivot on eyebolts. Struts then carry the motion to the pressure plate. It moves away from the friction disc (Figs. 42-4A and 42-8), compressing the springs against the clutch cover. This disengages the clutch.

Releasing the clutch pedal allows the coil springs to extend. They again clamp the friction disc between the pressure plate and the flywheel. This engages the clutch (Fig. 42-4B).

The coil springs must be strong enough to prevent clutch slippage. However, the stronger the springs, the harder the driver must push on the clutch pedal. One solution is to use a *semicentrifugal clutch* (Fig. 42-8). It has weights on the ends of the release levers. As speed increases, centrifugal force causes the weights to add to the force of the springs. Figure 42-10 shows another type of semicentrifugal clutch. As speed increases, the rollers move out to increase the clamping force on the friction disc.

➤ 42-8 DIAPHRAGM-SPRING CLUTCH

The diaphragm-spring clutch (Figs. 42-1 and 42-11) is used with most manual transaxles and in many rear-wheel-drive vehicles. A *Belleville spring* or diaphragm spring (Fig. 42-12A) supplies the force that holds the friction disc against the flywheel. The spring has tapered fingers pointing inward from a solid ring. These act as release levers to take up the spring force as the clutch disengages. The diaphragm acts like the bottom of an oil can. After it is pushed inward, it will "spring" back when the applying force is released.

Figure 42-12B shows the clutch engaged. As the driver depresses the clutch pedal, the release bearing pushes against the fingers on the diaphragm spring. This causes the diaphragm to pivot about the inner pivot ring and dish inward. As it does so, the outer section moves in the opposite direction and pushes the pressure plate away from the friction disc. This disengages the clutch (Fig. 42-12C). Spring force varies according to the size and thickness of the diaphragm spring.

Some cars use a diaphragm-spring *pull clutch* (Fig. 42-13). The release bearing has a flange that rides on the inside surface of the diaphragm-spring fingers. Depressing the clutch pedal causes the fork to pull the release bearing and fingers outward. This pulls the pressure plate away from the friction disc and disengages the clutch.

➤ 42-9 DOUBLE-DISC CLUTCH

Sometimes a clutch with greater holding power is needed. When limited space prevents making the clutch larger, then a clutch with two friction discs can be used. Figure 42-14 shows a diaphragm-spring *double-disc clutch*. This provides greater holding force. Double-disk coil-spring clutches are also available. These clutches are used in

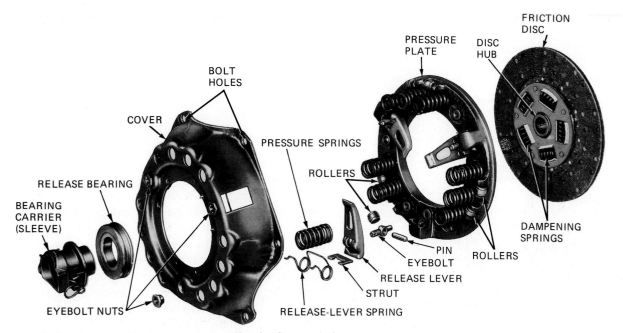

Fig. 42-10 Disassembled coil-spring clutch. (*Chrysler Corporation*)

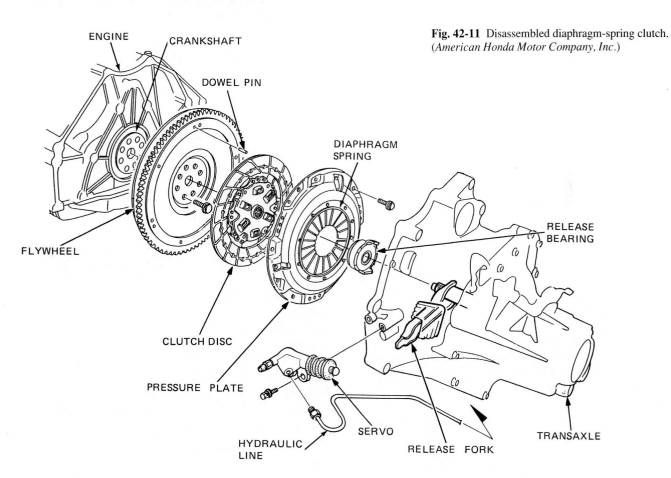

Fig. 42-11 Disassembled diaphragm-spring clutch. (*American Honda Motor Company, Inc.*)

medium and heavy trucks. Use of the second friction disc adds clutch-plate area, thereby providing greater torque-carrying capacity. When the clutch is engaged, each friction disc transmits half of the flywheel torque to the input shaft. These clutches are operated and work in the same way as single-disc clutches.

CLUTCH LINKAGE

➤ 42-10 TYPES OF CLUTCH LINKAGE

The parts that connect the clutch pedal to the release bearing make up the *clutch linkage*. It is either mechanical

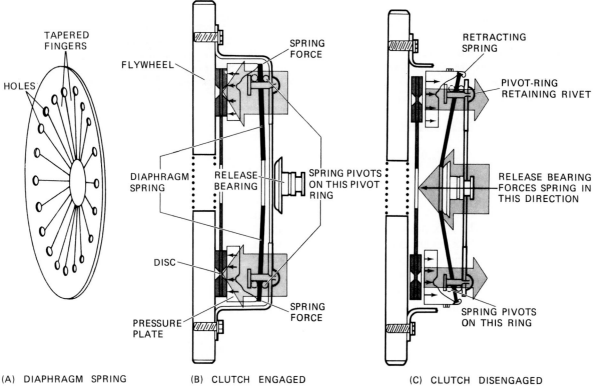

TAPERED FINGERS

HOLES

FLYWHEEL

SPRING FORCE

DIAPHRAGM SPRING

RELEASE BEARING

SPRING PIVOTS ON THIS PIVOT RING

DISC

PRESSURE PLATE

SPRING FORCE

RETRACTING SPRING

PIVOT-RING RETAINING RIVET

RELEASE BEARING FORCES SPRING IN THIS DIRECTION

SPRING PIVOTS ON THIS RING

(A) DIAPHRAGM SPRING

(B) CLUTCH ENGAGED

(C) CLUTCH DISENGAGED

Fig. 42-12 Action of the (A) diaphragm spring with the (B) clutch engaged and (C) clutch disengaged. (*ATW*)

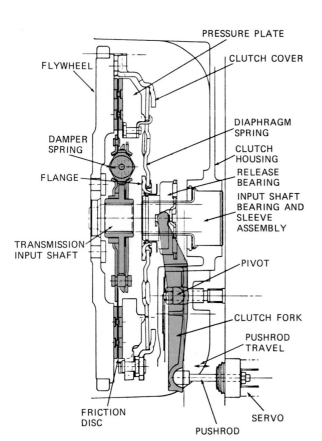

PRESSURE PLATE

CLUTCH COVER

FLYWHEEL

DIAPHRAGM SPRING

CLUTCH HOUSING

RELEASE BEARING

INPUT SHAFT BEARING AND SLEEVE ASSEMBLY

DAMPER SPRING

FLANGE

TRANSMISSION INPUT SHAFT

PIVOT

CLUTCH FORK

PUSHROD TRAVEL

FRICTION DISC

SERVO

PUSHROD

Fig. 42-13 A diaphragm-spring pull clutch, so called because depressing the clutch pedal pulls the release bearing and fingers outward. (*Chevrolet Division of General Motors Corporation*)

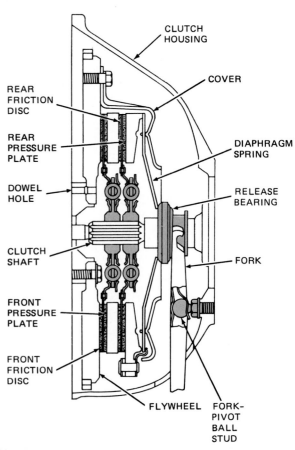

CLUTCH HOUSING

COVER

REAR FRICTION DISC

REAR PRESSURE PLATE

DIAPHRAGM SPRING

DOWEL HOLE

RELEASE BEARING

CLUTCH SHAFT

FORK

FRONT PRESSURE PLATE

FRONT FRICTION DISC

FLYWHEEL

FORK-PIVOT BALL STUD

Fig. 42-14 A diaphragm-spring double-disc clutch using two pressure plates and two friction discs. (*Chevrolet Division of General Motors Corporation*)

543

(rod or cable) or hydraulic. They all convert a light force applied to the clutch pedal into a greatly increased force that moves the release bearing.

Figures 42-4 and 42-8 show rod linkage. It is used on many rear-wheel-drive vehicles. Many front-wheel-drive cars have self-adjusting cable linkage (➤42-11). A variety of vehicles use hydraulic clutch linkage (➤42-12).

➤ 42-11 CABLE CLUTCH LINKAGE

Figures 42-3 and 42-15 show a cable linkage that requires manual adjustment. On many vehicles, it is simpler for the manufacturer to install a cable system than to develop a rod arrangement. The cable operates the release bearing by movement of the clutch fork. The fork passes through a *boot* or *dust cover* that seals the fork opening in the clutch housing. This prevents dirt, dust, and water from entering the clutch through the opening.

Cable linkage may be self adjusting (Fig. 42-16). This eliminates the need for routine clutch adjustment. The cable for the *self-adjusting clutch* attaches to a spring-loaded *quadrant gear*. It attaches to the clutch pedal through a shaft. A toothed *pawl* or pivoted arm at the top of the clutch pedal engages the quadrant-gear teeth. As the clutch pedal is depressed, the pawl rotates the quadrant gear. This pulls the cable and disengages the clutch.

Self-adjustment occurs when the clutch pedal is released. The spring-loaded quadrant gear may continue to rotate slightly after the pedal returns to its stop. If friction-disc wear has occurred, the pawl engages a new tooth on the quadrant gear the next time the pedal is depressed. This adjusts the effective length of the linkage to maintain the proper *freeplay* or *free travel* (➤42-30). The result is correct clutch-pedal height and release-bearing *preload*.

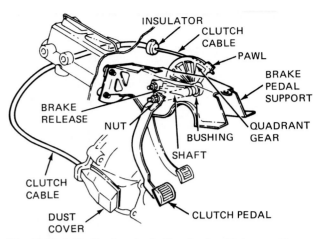

Fig. 42-16 Self-adjusting clutch. The clutch cable has a self-adjusting device that maintains the proper free travel of the clutch pedal. (*Ford Motor Company*)

This is a slight load placed on the bearing before the normal load of disengaging the clutch (➤42-14).

➤ 42-12 HYDRAULIC CLUTCH LINKAGE

Hydraulically-operated clutch linkage (Figs. 42-11 and 42-17) is used when the clutch location makes it difficult to run a rod or cable to it. Hydraulic clutch linkage is also used on high-performance engines. These have strong springs in the pressure-plate assembly and would require high pedal effort.

Operation of the hydraulic-clutch linkage begins when the driver depresses the clutch pedal. This forces a pushrod into the master cylinder (Fig. 42-17). Pressurized fluid is then forced from the master cylinder, through a hydraulic

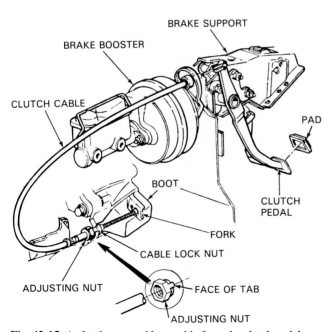

Fig. 42-15 A clutch operated by a cable from the clutch pedal. (*Ford Motor Company*)

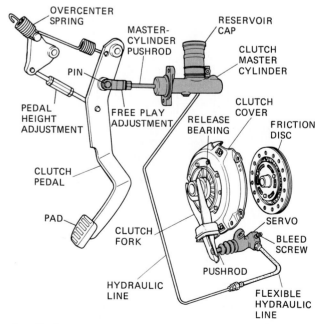

Fig. 42-17 A hydraulically-operated clutch. (*Nissan Motor Corporation*)

544

line, to a *servo* or *slave cylinder*. A servo is a device that converts hydraulic pressure to mechanical movement.

The pressurized fluid then pushes a piston and pushrod out of the servo. The pushrod movement operates the clutch fork and disengages the clutch.

The hydraulic system can be designed so a light force on the clutch pedal produces a heavy force on the clutch fork. This is done by using a small piston in the master cylinder and a large piston in the servo. Chapter 52 on brakes describes how basic hydraulic systems work. Operation of hydraulic clutch linkage is similar to a hydraulic brake system.

Figure 42-18 shows the hydraulic system for a clutch with a *hydraulically-operated release bearing*. No clutch fork is used. The servo and release bearing are included in an assembly that fits on the transmission front-bearing retainer. One end of the servo seats against the front of the transmission case. The release bearing attaches to the bearing carrier on the servo piston at the other end (Fig. 42-19).

When the clutch pedal is depressed, hydraulic fluid flows from the clutch master cylinder to the servo. The fluid pushes the servo piston out of the cylinder. This forces the release bearing against the fingers of the pressure plate and disengages the clutch.

> ## 42-13 ELECTRONICALLY- CONTROLLED CLUTCH

Figure 42-20 shows the layout of an *automatic* or *electronically-controlled clutch*. This is a hydraulically-operated clutch that is electronically controlled. No clutch pedal is needed.

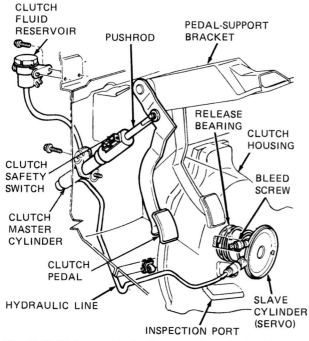

Fig. 42-18 Linkage and hydraulic system for a clutch with a hydraulically-operated release bearing. (*Ford Motor Company*)

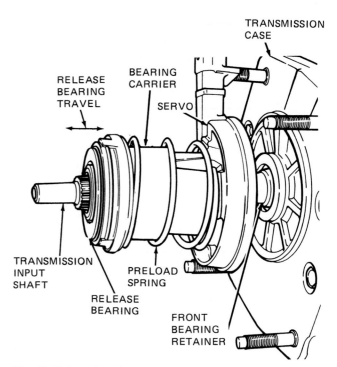

Fig. 42-19 Location of the hydraulically-operated release bearing and servo on the transmission input shaft. (*Ford Motor Company*)

Sensors send information about the operation of the throttle, engine, clutch, and transmission to an electronic control module (ECM). When the driver moves the gearshift lever, the ECM then signals the *hydraulic power pack*. It controls the fluid pressure in the hydraulic cylinder to engage or disengage the clutch. The clutch disengages quickly and remains disengaged until the driver releases the gearshift lever.

There are other types of automatic clutches. They all disengage when the control unit sends the proper signals to an electric, hydraulic, pneumatic, or vacuum actuator. The car may or may not have a clutch pedal.

> ## 42-14 RELEASE BEARING

When the driver depresses the clutch pedal, the clutch linkage (>42-10) moves the release bearing or throwout bearing. The bearing travel pushes or pulls the release levers or fingers inward or outward to disengage the clutch.

The type of clutch linkage determines the type of release bearing. Most are ball bearings, but they vary in construction and operation.

Figures 42-6 and 42-8 show the release bearing used with rod-type clutch linkage. Depressing the clutch pedal forces the release bearing against the release levers. This starts the release bearing rotating. Letting up the clutch pedal moves the release bearing away from the pressure plate. The release bearing must travel far enough so there is some clearance or freeplay between the release levers

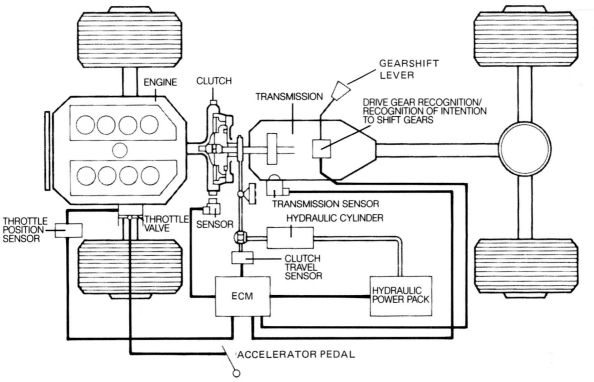

Fig. 42-20 Layout on the car of an electronically-controlled clutch. No clutch pedal is needed. (*LuK, Inc.*)

and the bearing. If not, the bearing continues rotating. Then this type of release bearing will overheat and fail. It may also cause the clutch to slip.

Release bearings used with self-adjusting clutches (cable and hydraulic linkage) are shown in Figs. 42-11 and 42-17. These require a slight preload (➤42-11). The bearing lightly touches the fingers. This causes the bearing to rotate continuously as long as the engine runs. Figures 42-18 and 42-19 show *concentric release bearings* that mount on a bearing carrier attached to the servo piston. These bearings also are preloaded and rotate when the engine runs.

➤ 42-15 CLUTCH SAFETY SWITCH

Many vehicles with a clutch have a *clutch safety switch* or *starter-clutch interlock switch* (Figs. 29-1 and 42-18). It prevents cranking if the clutch is engaged. The clutch pedal must be depressed or the engine will not crank when the ignition key is turned to START (➤29-1). The movement of the clutch pedal closes the safety switch. This completes the electrical circuit to the starting motor.

The clutch safety switch prevents starting with the transmission in gear and the clutch engaged. If this happened, the car might move before the driver is ready.

The clutch safety switch in Fig. 42-18 is a *three-function switch:*

1. It requires the clutch pedal to be depressed before the engine will crank.

2. It disengages the speed-control system (➤34-20) when the clutch pedal is depressed.

3. It sends a fuel-control signal to the ECM in the electronic engine-control system when the clutch pedal is depressed.

CLUTCH TROUBLE DIAGNOSIS

➤ 42-16 CLUTCH TROUBLES

Many different troubles can develop in the clutch, producing various conditions and complaints from the driver. The chart in Fig. 42-21 lists common clutch troubles, their possible causes, and checks or corrections to make. Following sections further explain how to locate and correct clutch troubles. Other clutch troubles and causes are described in the vehicle service manual.

For proper operation of the clutch and transmission, their common centerline (Fig. 42-7) must be maintained. Dowel pins or alignment sleeves on the back of the block maintain the alignment between the block and the clutch housing. However, wear or damage of either the pilot bearing or the transmission-input-shaft bearing may allow the clutch centerline to drop. A variety of clutch and transmission troubles can result. Section 42-26 describes how to check the three bearings in the clutch system. These are the pilot bearing, release bearing, and transmission-input-shaft bearing. Failure of either bearing may cause clutch-system noise.

Complaint	Possible Cause	Check or Correction
1. Clutch slips while engaged (➤42-17)	a. Incorrect clutch-linkage adjustment b. Broken or weak pressure springs c. Binding in clutch linkage d. Broken engine mount e. Worn friction-disc facings f. Grease or oil on disc facings g. Incorrectly adjusted release levers h. Warped friction disc	Adjust Replace pressure-plate assembly Free, adjust, and lubricate Replace Replace disc Replace disc Adjust Replace
2. Clutch chatters or grabs while engaging (➤42-18)	a. Binding in clutch linkage b. Broken engine mount c. Oil or grease on disc facings or glazed or loose facings d. Binding of friction-disc hub on clutch shaft e. Broken disc facings, springs, or pressure plate f. Warped friction disc	Free, adjust, and lubricate Replace Replace disc Clean and lubricate splines; replace defective parts Replace broken parts Replace
3. Clutch spins or drags while disengaged (➤42-19)	a. Incorrect linkage adjustment or operation b. Warped friction disc or pressure plate c. Loose friction-disc facing d. Improper release-lever adjustment e. Friction-disc hub binding on clutch shaft f. Broken engine mount	Adjust, repair or replace Replace defective part Replace disc Adjust Clean and lubricate splines; replace defective parts Replace
4. Clutch noisy while engaged (➤42-20)	a. Friction-disc hub loose on clutch shaft b. Friction-disc dampener springs broken or weak c. Misalignment of engine and transmission	Replace worn parts Replace disc Align
5. Clutch noisy while disengaged (➤42-21)	a. Release bearing worn, binding, or out of lubricant b. Release levers not properly adjusted c. Pilot bearing in crankshaft worn or out of lubricant d. Diaphragm spring worn or damaged	Replace Adjust or replace pressure-plate assembly Lubricate or replace Replace pressure-plate assembly
6. Clutch-pedal pulsates (➤42-22)	a. Engine and transmission not aligned b. Flywheel not seated on crankshaft flange or flywheel bent (also causes engine vibration) c. Clutch housing distorted d. Release levers not evenly adjusted e. Warped pressure plate or friction disc f. Pressure-plate assembly misaligned g. Broken diaphragm spring	Align Seat properly, straighten, replace flywheel Align or replace Adjust or replace pressure-plate assembly Replace Align Replace pressure-plate assembly
7. Rapid friction-disc facing wear (➤42-23)	a. Driver "rides" clutch b. Excessive and incorrect use of clutch c. Cracks in flywheel or pressure-plate face d. Weak or broken pressure springs e. Warped pressure plate or friction disc f. Improper linkage adjustment g. Clutch linkage binding	Keep foot off clutch except when necessary Reduce use Replace Replace pressure-plate assembly Replace defective part Adjust Free, adjust, and lubricate
8. Clutch pedal stiff (➤42-24)	a. Clutch linkage lacks lubricant b. Clutch pedal binds in floor mat c. Misaligned linkage parts d. Overcenter spring out of adjustment e. Bent clutch pedal	Lubricate Free Align Adjust Replace
9. Hydraulic-clutch troubles (➤42-25)	a. Hydraulic clutches can have any of the troubles listed above b. Gear clashing and difficulty shifting into or out of gear	Inspect hydraulic system; check for leakage Inspect hydraulic system; check for leakage

Fig. 42-21 Clutch trouble-diagnosis chart.

Asbestos is used in the facings of many friction discs. However, breathing asbestos dust can cause lung cancer. For this reason, be very careful when working around clutches. *Do not blow the dust out with compressed air*. This dust may contain asbestos fibers. The compressed air would send the fibers into the air around you and you could inhale them. Instead, use a vacuum cleaner with a *High Efficiency Particulate* (HEPA) filter (➤4-6). This filters out the asbestos fibers. Or use damp cloths to wipe out the clutch housing. Dispose of the cloths safely. Then, wash your hands thoroughly to remove any traces of asbestos.

➤ 42-17 CLUTCH SLIPS WHILE ENGAGED

This could be caused by an incorrect linkage adjustment. That could prevent full spring force on the pressure plate and friction disc. Adjust the linkage. It could also be caused by weak pressure springs in the pressure plate and worn or greasy friction-disc facings. Always check the front of the transmission and the engine rear main-bearing oil seal for oil leaks when you service the clutch. Replace the defective parts.

➤ 42-18 CLUTCH CHATTERS OR GRABS WHILE ENGAGING

This is usually due to oil on the disc facings. Loose facings, *heat checks* (small cracks) in the face of the flywheel or pressure plate, broken clutch parts, or binding linkage could also cause the trouble.

➤ 42-19 CLUTCH SPINS OR DRAGS WHILE DISENGAGED

The friction disc spins briefly after the clutch is disengaged. This normal "spin down" is not the same as a *dragging clutch*. When the clutch drags, drivers often complain of *gear clash* while shifting.

Possible causes include linkage out of adjustment, a defective clutch cable, or a leak or failure in the hydraulic system. Other causes include a warped friction disc or pressure plate, or binding of the friction-disc hub on the transmission input shaft. Also, the facings on the friction disc may be loose or torn.

➤ 42-20 CLUTCH NOISY WHILE ENGAGED

Possible causes include broken dampener springs in the friction disc and the disc hub loose on the transmission input shaft. Also, there may be broken parts in the pressure plate or misalignment between the engine and transmission. The engine transmission centerline must be maintained. Otherwise, noise and jumping out of gear may result.

➤ 42-21 CLUTCH NOISY WHILE DISENGAGED

This may be caused by a worn or *dry* (lacking lubricant) release bearing. It makes a grinding or squealing noise as it spins. The pilot bearing or bushing in the end of the crankshaft could be worn or need lubricant. Also, the pressure-plate fingers or release levers could be bent or out of adjustment (Fig. 42-22). Worn *retracting springs* in some diaphragm-spring pressure-plate assemblies also produce noise.

➤ 42-22 CLUTCH PEDAL PULSATES

Clutch-pedal pulsations can be felt when light force is applied to the clutch pedal with the engine running. They may be caused by engine and transmission misalignment. Other causes include a warped or misaligned pressure plate or friction disc, and worn or bent fingers or release levers. A broken diaphragm spring also will cause clutch-pedal pulsations.

➤ 42-23 RAPID FRICTION-DISC FACING WEAR

This can result if the driver "rides" the clutch pedal by resting a foot on it. This partly disengages the clutch so it slips. Misalignment of clutch parts and incorrect linkage adjustment also cause rapid facing wear.

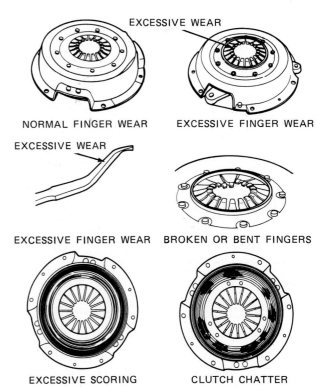

Fig. 42-22 Conditions to look for when making a visual inspection of the pressure-plate assembly. (*Ford Motor Company*)

➤ 42-24 CLUTCH PEDAL STIFF

A clutch pedal that is stiff or hard to depress is probably due to misaligned or binding clutch linkage. The linkage may need adjustment and lubrication, or replacement.

➤ 42-25 HYDRAULIC-CLUTCH TROUBLES

The hydraulic clutch can have any of the troubles described above. In addition, loss of fluid from the hydraulic system may cause gear clash and hard shifting. Fluid loss usually is due to leaks in the master cylinder or servo, or in the hydraulic lines and connections between the two. Loss of fluid prevents normal operation of the hydraulic system (Chap. 52).

➤ 42-26 IDENTIFYING CLUTCH-SYSTEM BEARING NOISE

The pilot bearing or bushing, release bearing, and transmission-input-shaft bearing (Fig. 42-7) can all make noise. To determine which is the source, first be sure there is freeplay in the clutch pedal. Back off the adjustment on self-adjusting linkage until there is freeplay in the pedal.

1. *Checking transmission-input-shaft bearing* Set the parking brake, put the gearshift lever in neutral, and start the engine. Release the clutch pedal if you had to depress it for engine cranking. Any bearing noise you now hear is from a defective transmission-input-shaft bearing (Chap. 44). It is the only bearing turning.
2. *Checking release bearing* Let the engine idle with the gearshift lever in neutral. Depress the clutch pedal to the end of its freeplay. At this point, the fingers or release levers contact the release bearing and it starts spinning. A defective release bearing will begin making noise.
3. *Checking pilot bearing or bushing* With the engine idling and the gearshift lever in neutral, push the clutch pedal to the floor. This disengages the clutch. Any bearing noise that now occurs is from the pilot bearing or bushing.

CLUTCH SERVICE

➤ 42-27 SERVICING THE CLUTCH

Major clutch services include cable replacement, release-bearing and fork replacement, clutch replacement, and flywheel replacement. Vehicles with hydraulic clutch linkage may require rebuilding or replacement of the clutch master cylinder and servo or slave cylinder.

Following sections describe typical procedures for various clutch services. Refer to the vehicle service manual for specifications and procedures on the vehicle you are

servicing. Always follow the safety procedures in ➤42-16 to avoid exposure to asbestos fibers.

➤ 42-28 CLUTCH-LINKAGE ADJUSTMENT

Manual adjustment of the clutch linkage may be required at intervals to compensate for wear of the facings on the friction disc. On some cars, certain points in the linkage or pedal support may require lubrication.

Figures 42-8 and 42-15 show clutch linkage requiring manual adjustment. Adjusting the linkage changes the amount of clutch-pedal freeplay or free travel (➤42-30). To determine if the clutch-linkage needs adjusting, check that:

1. The clutch fully disengages (➤42-29).
2. The clutch has adequate freeplay (➤42-30).

➤ 42-29 CHECKING FOR CLUTCH DISENGAGEMENT

With the engine idling and the brakes firmly applied, hold the clutch pedal about 1/2 inch [13 mm] from the floor. Move the gearshift lever between first and reverse several times. If this can be done smoothly, the clutch is disengaging fully.

If the shifts are hard or gear clash occurs, the clutch is not disengaging. Adjust the linkage. If this does not correct the problem, check for other possible causes. These are listed in the clutch trouble-diagnosis chart (Fig. 42-21) and in the vehicle service manual.

➤ 42-30 CHECKING CLUTCH-PEDAL FREE TRAVEL

Clutch-pedal free travel or freeplay is the distance the pedal moves before the release bearing contacts the pressure-plate fingers or levers. Further pedal movement then requires a noticeably greater force to compress the spring or springs in the pressure plate. Clutch-pedal freeplay may increase or decrease as the friction disc and other parts wear or the cable stretches.

To check pedal freeplay, depress the pedal with your hand. When a greatly increased pedal force is required, you have reached the end of the pedal freeplay. In most cars, clutch-pedal freeplay should be about 1 inch [25 mm].

Improper clutch-pedal freeplay may cause clutch and shifting trouble. Figures 42-8 and 42-15 show manually adjusted clutch linkages. Both have threaded adjustment rods and nuts. Turn the adjusting nut to get the proper freeplay. On some cars with self-adjusting linkage, raising the clutch pedal with your hand causes the linkage to self-adjust. This sets the proper freeplay.

Figure 42-17 shows one type of hydraulic clutch linkage. The *clutch-pedal height* must be checked and adjusted before adjusting the freeplay. Clutch-pedal height

is the distance from the top of the clutch-pedal pad to the floor. Loosening the locknuts and turning the height adjuster raises or lowers the pedal. After clutch-pedal height is correct, adjust the freeplay.

➤ 42-31 BLEEDING CLUTCH HYDRAULIC SYSTEM

Any air trapped in the hydraulic system must be removed by *bleeding* the hydraulic system. Bleeding is a procedure that removes the air, usually by draining part of the fluid. Bleed the system after disconnecting any part or hydraulic line. Also, bleed the system if the fluid level has dropped so low that air could enter the clutch master cylinder.

Clean any dirt and grease from around the reservoir cap (Figs. 42-17 and 42-18). Remove the cap and diaphragm under it. Fill the reservoir to the FULL mark with fresh, new fluid. Use the fluid specified by the vehicle manufacturer. This is usually *DOT 3 brake fluid* (Chap. 52).

Connect one end of a rubber tube to the *bleed screw* in the servo or slave cylinder (Fig. 42-23). Immerse the other end in a half-full container of the specified fluid. Slowly pump the clutch pedal several times. Then have an assistant apply a light force to the clutch pedal. Loosen the bleed screw (Figs. 42-17 and 42-18) until fluid discharges from the tube into the container. Any air bubbles can be seen in the fluid. As the pedal sinks to the floor, close the bleed screw.

Repeat this procedure until no more air bubbles appear in the fluid. Close and tighten the bleed screw. Refill the fluid reservoir, and install the diaphragm and cap.

Careful! Brake fluid quickly softens and dissolves paint. If any brake fluid drips or splashes onto a painted surface, wash it off immediately.

Never reuse fluid that has been bled from the hydraulic system. The fluid may be *aerated* (have air bubbles in it), contain excessive moisture, or be contaminated.

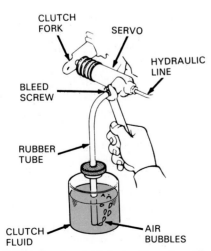

Fig. 42-23 Bleeding the clutch hydraulic system. (*Toyota Motor Sales U.S.A., Inc.*)

➤ 42-32 CLUTCH REMOVAL

Variations in vehicle design and construction make it necessary to use different procedures and tools when removing and installing clutches on various cars. Follow the procedure in the vehicle service manual.

A typical procedure begins with disconnecting the negative cable from the battery. On vehicles with hydraulic clutch linkage, disconnect the clutch master-cylinder pushrod from the clutch pedal (Figs. 42-17 and 42-18). If necessary, disconnect the hydraulic line and remove the slave cylinder. Then remove the transmission or transaxle from the engine (Chap. 44).

Clean the clutch and clutch housing (➤42-16). Examine the clutch cover and flywheel for alignment marks. They may be stamped with an "X" or some similar mark. If not, use a hammer and center punch to mark them. Align these marks during clutch installation. Otherwise, vibration and damage may result.

NOTE Clutch chatter after removal and installation of the engine or clutch housing may be caused by misalignment. Small shims are sometimes used to correct the alignment of the engine to the clutch housing, and the clutch housing to the transmission. These shims can be lost during removal. They must be reinstalled in their original positions during assembly. If the engine and transmission are misaligned, the splines in the hub of the friction disc may wear more at the ends than in the middle.

Install a *clutch aligner* (Fig. 42-24) into the crankshaft pilot bearing or bushing. This prevents slippage and damage to the friction disc. Remove the pressure-plate assembly by loosening the screws that attach the cover to the flywheel. Loosen each screw one turn at a time until the pressure-plate spring force is relieved. Then remove the pressure-plate assembly and friction disc.

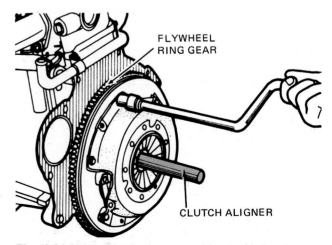

Fig. 42-24 Using a clutch aligner to position the friction disc while removing or installing the pressure-plate assembly. (*Chrysler Corporation*)

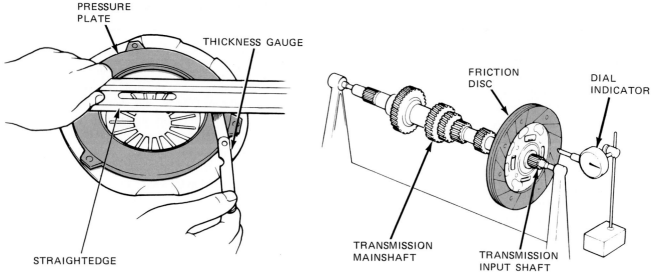

Fig. 42-25 Inspecting clutch parts. (A) Checking the pressure plate for warpage. (B) Checking the runout of the friction disc. (*American Honda Motor Company, Inc.*)

(A) CHECKING PRESSURE-PLATE WARPAGE

(B) CHECKING FRICTION-DISC RUNOUT

➤ 42-33 INSPECTING AND SERVICING CLUTCH PARTS

After removing the clutch, inspect each part following the procedure in the vehicle service manual. Also, inspect the parts of the engine and transmission or transaxle that may affect the clutch. Look for oil leaks from the engine rear-main-bearing oil seal and from the front of the transaxle or transmission. Earlier sections describe when to replace the release bearing, friction disc, and pressure-plate assembly. Figure 42-25 shows how to check the pressure plate for warpage and the friction disc for excessive runout.

1. INSPECTING THE FLYWHEEL Inspect the flywheel ring gear for worn, chipped, or cracked teeth (Fig. 42-24). Inspect the flywheel friction face for uniform appearance and cracks, grooves, heat checks, and uneven wear. If the flywheel has worn unevenly, measure flywheel runout with a dial indicator (Fig. 42-26). If the runout exceeds 0.005 inch [0.13 mm], or if the surface is scored or worn, reface or replace the flywheel. Install a new flywheel if resurfacing removes more than 0.045 inch [1.14 mm] of metal from the flywheel face.

2. INSPECTING THE PILOT BEARING Check the condition and wear of the pilot bearing or bushing in the end of the crankshaft (Figs. 42-7 and 42-26). Turn the inner race of the bearing in its normal direction of rotation with your fingers. Replace the bearing if it is excessively loose, noisy, hard to turn, or fails to turn. If a bushing appears normal, measure its diameter with a small-hole gauge (➤5-20).

➤ 42-34 CLUTCH INSTALLATION

Installation of the clutch is usually the reverse of removal. A typical procedure is to position the friction disc with the

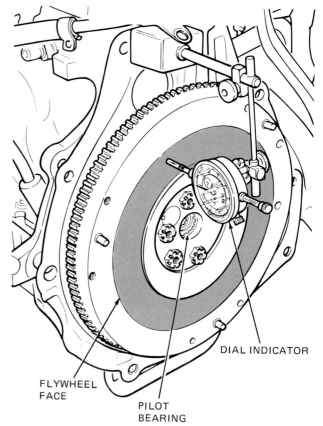

Fig. 42-26 Measuring flywheel runout with a dial indicator. (*Ford Motor Company*)

flywheel side toward the flywheel. Align the "X" or mark on the pressure-plate cover with the similar mark on the flywheel. Hold the pressure plate and friction disc against the flywheel. Install a clutch aligner (Fig. 42-24) in the pilot bearing or bushing. This maintains alignment of the friction disc with the crankshaft centerline.

Install the attaching screws through the holes in the cover. Thread the screws finger-tight into the flywheel. Tighten the screws one turn at a time to take up the pressure-plate spring tension gradually and evenly (Fig. 42-24). Follow the tightening sequence in the vehicle service manual to avoid warping the pressure plate. Then use a torque wrench to tighten the screws to the specified torque.

Lubricate the splines on the transmission-input shaft and the front-bearing-retainer extension. Use multipurpose grease or the specified lubricant. Lubricate and install the release bearing. Remove the clutch aligner. If necessary, install two guide pins in the clutch housing. Then attach the transmission or transaxle to the clutch housing. Install any shims found during removal.

Check that the splines on the input shaft mesh with the splines in the friction-disc hub. Also, check that the end of the input shaft seats in the pilot bearing or bushing. Check for any gap between the transmission or transaxle housing. If the input shaft and housings have seated properly, install the transmission or transaxle attaching bolts (Chap. 44). Attach the clutch linkage and check the clutch-pedal freeplay (➤42-30). Make any adjustments necessary.

If the clutch is self-adjusting, pull up on the clutch pedal until the clicking stops. This indicates the release bearing now has the proper preload. On hydraulic clutch linkage, check the fluid level in the clutch master-cylinder reservoir (➤42-31). Bleed the hydraulic system, if necessary. Refill the reservoir, then check for smooth and full clutch disengagement (➤42-29).

MULTIPLE-CHOICE TEST

Select the **one** *correct, best, or most probable answer to each question.*
You can find the answers in the section indicated at the end of each question.

1. The friction disc is splined to the (➤42-4)
   a. transmission input shaft
   b. pressure plate
   c. flywheel
   d. crankshaft
2. When the clutch pedal is depressed, the release bearing pushes the pressure-plate fingers or levers inward. This causes the pressure plate to move away from the (➤42-5)
   a. release bearing
   b. pressure springs
   c. friction disc
   d. transmission
3. To help reduce the shock of engagement, the friction disc has a series of waved (➤42-6)
   a. cushion pads
   b. facings
   c. cushion springs
   d. discs

4. In the friction disc, torsional vibration is absorbed by the (➤42-6)
   a. cushion bolts
   b. coil springs
   c. waved pads
   d. friction pads
5. In the semicentrifugal clutch, the force of the pressure plate against the friction disc increases with engine speed because of weights located on the (➤42-7)
   a. pressure plate
   b. flywheel
   c. clutch shaft
   d. release levers
6. Clutch dragging is noticeable (➤42-19)
   a. when shifting gears
   b. at road speed
   c. during acceleration
   d. at high speed

REVIEW QUESTIONS

1. What are the advantages of a self-adjusting clutch? (➤42-11)
2. What three functions are performed by the clutch safety switch when the car has an electronic engine control system and a speed-control system? (➤42-15)
3. Describe the procedure to identify clutch-system bearing noise. (➤42-26)

4. When should you bleed the clutch hydraulic system, and what are the steps in the procedure? (➤42-31)
5. What does it mean when you find shims between the transmission and clutch housing during clutch removal? (➤42-32)

CHAPTER 43

MANUAL TRANSMISSIONS AND TRANSAXLES

After studying this chapter, you should be able to:

- Describe the difference between a manual transmission and a manual transaxle.
- Explain the relationship between *gear ratio* and *torque ratio*.
- Explain how shifts are made.
- Describe the operation of synchronizers.
- Define *overdrive* and explain its advantages.
- List and describe the switches and sensors mounted on manual transmissions and transaxles.

TRANSMISSIONS AND TRANSAXLES

➤ 43-1 PURPOSE OF THE TRANSMISSION OR TRANSAXLE

There are three reasons for having a transmission or transaxle in the automotive power train or drive train. The transmission or transaxle can:

1. Provide the torque needed to move the vehicle under a variety of road and load conditions. It does this by changing the gear ratio between the engine crankshaft and vehicle drive wheels.
2. Be shifted into reverse so the vehicle can move backward.
3. Be shifted into neutral for starting the engine and running it without turning the drive wheels.

There are two basic types of transmissions and transaxles: *manual* and *automatic*. Manual transmissions and transaxles are shifted manually, or by hand. Automatic transmissions and transaxles shift automatically, with no help from the driver.

➤ 43-2 DIFFERENCE BETWEEN TRANSMISSIONS AND TRANSAXLES

The *manual transmission* (Figs. 42-1 and 43-1) is an assembly of gears, shafts, and related parts. These are contained in a metal case or housing filled with lubricant

(➤43-16). A manual transmission is used in some front-wheel-drive vehicles (Fig. 42-1) and in front-engine rear-wheel-drive vehicles (Fig. 43-2). It is positioned between the clutch (Chap. 42) and the *driveshaft* (Chap. 45) that carries engine power to the drive wheels. The engine, clutch, transmission, and driveshaft are all in a single line.

The *manual transaxle* (Figs. 42-2 and 43-3) is also an assembly of gears and shafts. It attaches to a front-mounted transverse engine and drives the front wheels (Fig. 43-4). Rear-engine cars use an engine-mounted transaxle to drive the rear wheels. A few front-engine cars drive the rear wheels through a rear-mounted transaxle.

The transaxle includes a *final drive* and a *differential* (*front differential* in Fig. 43-3). These devices are not found in the transmission. The final drive is a set of gears that provides the final speed reduction or *gear ratio* (➤43-4) between the transmission and the drive wheels. The differential permits the drive wheels to rotate at different speeds when the vehicle turns from straight ahead. Both are described in Chap. 45.

Some transaxles include a *viscous coupling* and a *center differential* (Fig. 43-3). These are used in *four-wheel-drive* and *all-wheel-drive* power trains (Chap. 46).

➤ 43-3 MANUAL TRANSMISSIONS AND TRANSAXLES

Older transmissions are three-speed units. They have three forward gear-ratios or *speeds*. These are *first* or *low*, *second*, and *third* or *high*. They also have *reverse* and *neutral*.

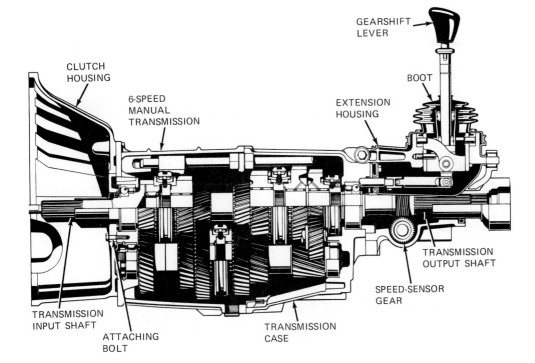

Fig. 43-1 Construction of a six-speed manual transmission. (*ZF of North America, Inc.*)

GEARSHIFT LEVER

CLUTCH HOUSING

6-SPEED MANUAL TRANSMISSION

BOOT

EXTENSION HOUSING

TRANSMISSION OUTPUT SHAFT

SPEED-SENSOR GEAR

TRANSMISSION INPUT SHAFT

ATTACHING BOLT

TRANSMISSION CASE

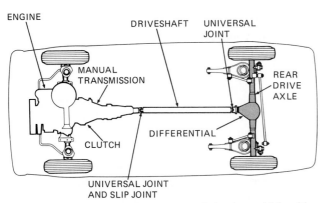

ENGINE

DRIVESHAFT

UNIVERSAL JOINT

MANUAL TRANSMISSION

REAR DRIVE AXLE

DIFFERENTIAL

CLUTCH

UNIVERSAL JOINT AND SLIP JOINT

Fig. 43-2 Location of the manual transmission in a vehicle with front engine and rear-wheel drive. (*Mazda Motors of America, Inc.*)

Four-speed transmissions and transaxles have been widely used. They provide *first, second, third,* and *fourth.* They also have reverse and neutral.

Many transmissions and transaxles are *five speeds* with a fifth forward gear. Fourth gear in some four-speed units and fifth gear in five-speed units is *overdrive*. The output shaft turns faster than, or *overdrives,* the input shaft (Fig. 43-1). This allows a lower engine speed to keep the vehicle moving at its desired road speed. Better fuel economy and reduced engine wear result, with less noise and vibration. Some cars have a six-speed manual transmission (Fig. 43-1) or transaxle. Both fifth gear and sixth gear are overdrive ratios. However, these may not be usable during city driving in heavy traffic.

The different gear ratios are necessary because the engine develops relatively little power at low engine speeds. The engine must be turning at a fairly high speed before it can deliver enough torque to start the vehicle

moving. This means the transmission or transaxle must be in first gear to start out. After the vehicle is moving, progressively higher gears are selected (second, third, fourth, fifth) to suit operating conditions. Usually, the vehicle is in top gear after reaching highway speed.

Moving the *gearshift lever* (Figs. 42-3 and 43-1) makes the shift which changes the gear ratio (➤42-3). In some vehicles, the gearshift lever is on the steering column (➤43-13). In others, it is on the floor or in a *center console* (Fig. 34-29).

GEARS AND GEARING

➤ 43-4 GEARS AND GEAR RATIO

Gears are wheels with teeth that transmit power between shafts (Fig. 43-5). The teeth may be on the edge of the wheel, on the side, or inside (Fig. 43-6). To transmit power, a gear on one shaft is "meshed" with a gear on another shaft. To *mesh* means that the teeth of a gear fit into the spaces between the teeth of another gear. When one gear turns, its teeth then force the other gear to turn. The gear that does the turning is the *driving gear*. The gear that is forced to turn is the *driven gear*.

The relative speed of two meshed gears is determined by the number of teeth in each gear. This is the *gear ratio*. If two meshing gears have the same number of teeth (Fig. 43-5), both will turn at the same speed. When the driven gear has more teeth than the driving gear, the driven gear turns more slowly than the driving gear. For example, if the driving gear has 12 teeth and the driven gear has 24 teeth (Fig. 43-7), the driving gear must turn two times to turn the driven gear once. The gear ratio between the two gears is two to one. This is written as 2:1.

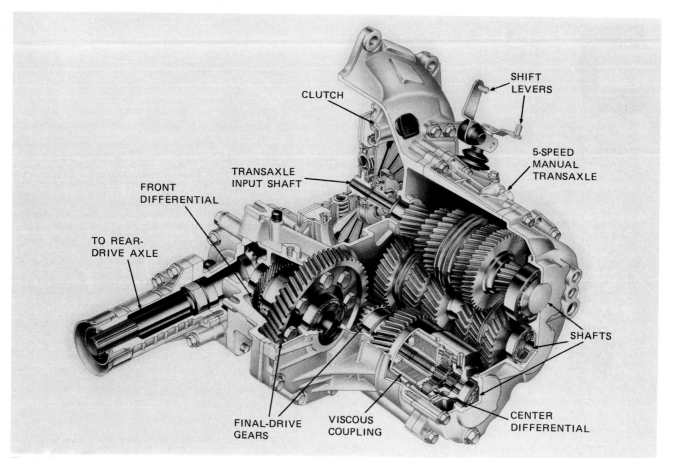

Fig. 43-3 Construction of a five-speed manual transaxle that includes a viscous coupling and a center differential, for use in a vehicle with all-wheel drive, or four-wheel drive. (*Chrysler Corporation*)

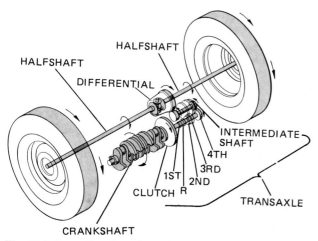

Fig. 43-4 Power flow from the engine crankshaft to the wheels of a vehicle with front-wheel drive. (*Chrysler Corporation*)

If a 12-tooth gear is meshed with a 36-tooth gear, the 12-tooth gear turns three times for every revolution of the 36-tooth gear. The gear ratio is 3:1.

➤ **43-5 GEAR RATIO AND TORQUE**

The gear ratio changes as the number of teeth in the meshing gears change. At the same time, *torque* also changes.

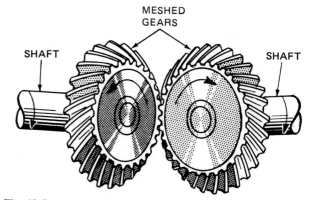

Fig. 43-5 Meshed spiral-bevel gears.

Torque (➤15-4) is a twisting or turning force that may or may not result in motion. It is measured in pound-feet (lb-ft) and Newton-meters [N-m].

To loosen and remove the top from a screw-top jar, you must apply torque to the top (Fig. 15-2). To calculate torque, multiply the applied force times the distance through which the force acts (Fig. 43-8). The torque on a gear is the force on a tooth multiplied by the distance from the tooth to the center of the gear. This distance is the *radius* of a gear or circle.

Two or more meshed gears make a *gearset* or a *gear train*. In a gear system, *speed reduction means torque*

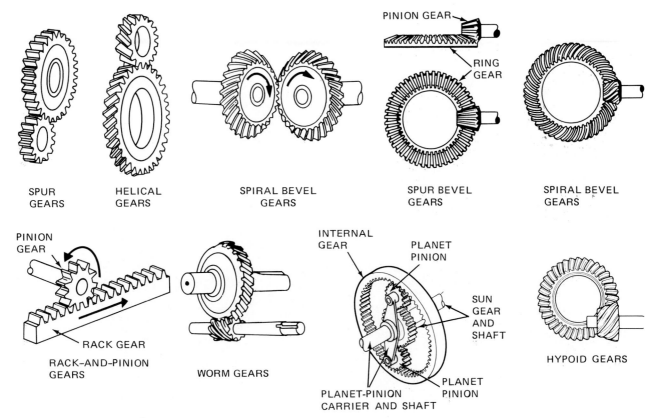

SPUR GEARS   HELICAL GEARS   SPIRAL BEVEL GEARS   SPUR BEVEL GEARS   SPIRAL BEVEL GEARS

RACK-AND-PINION GEARS   WORM GEARS   HYPOID GEARS

Fig. 43-6 Various types of gears.

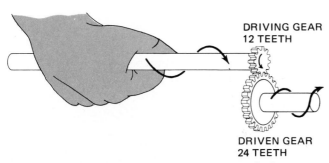

Fig. 43-7 Two revolutions of the small gear are required to turn the large gear once. This is a gear ratio of 2:1.

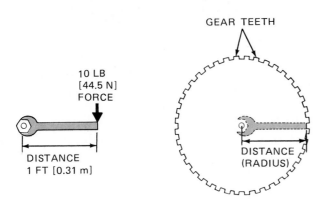

Fig. 43-8 Torque is calculated by multiplying the applied force times the distance through which the force acts. (*Ford Motor Company*)

increase. Also, *speed increase means torque reduction.* An example of torque increase is a car that has a gear reduction of 12:1 from the transmission or transaxle to the drive wheels (Fig. 43-9). The crankshaft turns 12 times to turn the drive wheels once. If the engine is producing a torque of 100 lb-ft [135.6 N-m], then a torque of 1200 lb-ft [1627 N-m] is applied to the drive wheels.

Figure 43-9 shows the radius of the tire is 1 foot [0.31 m]. With the torque acting on the ground at a distance of 1 foot [0.31 m], the force of the tire pushing against the road is 1200 pounds [5338 N].

NOTE Figure 43-9 shows only one tire. The torque is actually split between the *two* drive wheels. Each tire pushes against the road with a force of 600 pounds [2669 N]. Both tires together push with a force of 1200 pounds [5338 N].

MANUAL TRANSMISSIONS

➤ 43-6 MANUAL-TRANSMISSION CONSTRUCTION

Manual transmissions, manual transaxles, and *transfer cases* (Chap. 46) are all various types of *gearboxes*. A gearbox has:

1. Gears that transmit power.

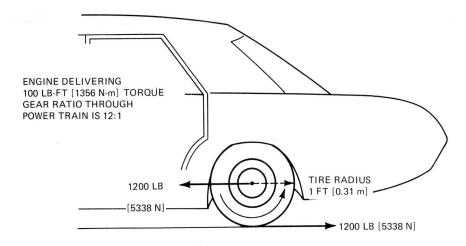

Fig. 43-9 How torque at the drive wheels pushes the vehicle forward. The tire is turned with a torque of 1200 lb-ft [1627 N-m]. Since the tire radius is 1 foot [0.31 m], the push of the tire against the ground is 1200 lb-ft [1627 N-m]. As a result, the vehicle is pushed forward with a force of 1200 pounds [5338 N].

ENGINE DELIVERING
100 LB-FT [1356 N-m] TORQUE
GEAR RATIO THROUGH
POWER TRAIN IS 12:1

1200 LB

[5338 N]

TIRE RADIUS
1 FT [0.31 m]

1200 LB [5338 N]

2. Splined shafts that rotate while other parts slide on them.

3. Bearings that support the shafts and transfer the load to the case or housing.

In a gearbox, the gear teeth and other moving metal parts must not touch. They must be continuously separated by a thin film of lubricant. This prevents excessive wear and early failure. Therefore, a gearbox runs partially filled with a lubricant or *gear oil* (➤43-16). *Oil seals* (➤6-23) prevent loss of lubricant from between the case and the rotating shafts (Fig. 6-27).

The manual transmissions and transaxles in passenger cars have from four to six forward speeds. A few vehicles with three-speed transmissions are still being driven. Many older vehicles and some new ones have four speeds. However, a five-speed transmission or transaxle is used in most cars today. Trucks and buses use bigger transmissions with 4 to 16 forward speeds. Regardless of type, most manual transmissions and transaxles are similar. One difference is the size and heaviness of construction. Another is that transmissions and transaxles with more speeds have more gears and shafts.

Figure 43-10 shows a disassembled five-speed manual transmission with the major parts named. Figure 43-11 shows the assembled gear train of this transmission. It is made as a four-speed (Fig. 43-11A) and, with additional parts, as a five-speed (Fig. 43-11B). The *main-drive gear* or *clutch gear* drives the one-piece *cluster gear* or *countergear.*

In both transmissions, three other helical gears on the countergear are in constant mesh with gears on the output shaft. These output-shaft gears are the *first-speed gear, second-speed gear,* and *third-speed gear.* The gears on the output shaft (except for the reverse gear) mesh with the gears on the countershaft. If the countershaft turns, the gears on the output shaft also turn.

No power flows through if the transmission is in neutral. Then none of the output-shaft gears are locked to it. The gears have bushings or bearings (Fig. 43-10) that permit them to rotate freely on the output shaft. During gear shifting, the gears themselves are not moved. The gears are locked to the shaft by *synchronizer* action (➤43-7). Synchronizers are connecting devices that are splined to the output shaft and rotate with it.

Shift forks fit into grooves in the *synchronizer sleeves* (Fig. 43-10). When the driver moves the gearshift lever, linkage carries the movement to a shift fork. The fork moves the sleeve which then locks the selected gear to the shaft. In Fig. 43-11A, two synchronizers lock gears to the transmission output shaft. The five-speed transmission has an additional synchronizer (*5th synchronizer* in Fig. 43-11B). It locks the *fifth-speed drive gear* to the countergear.

The only gear that actually moves into mesh in Fig. 43-11 and in many other transmissions is the *reverse-idler gear.* It slides on its shaft to engage the reverse gear on the countergear (the spur gear). It also engages reverse gear on the output shaft. This causes the output shaft to turn in the opposite direction of input-shaft rotation.

➤ 43-7 SYNCHRONIZER ACTION

Synchronizers are used in manual transmissions and transaxles to prevent gear clash during gear shifting. These devices ensure that gears and sliding sleeves about to mesh rotate at the same speed. The result is a smooth engagement.

The synchronizer used in the transmission shown in Figs. 43-10 and 43-11 has synchronizing *cones* on the gears and in the *synchronizer rings.* Three *keys* fit into slots in the *synchronizer hub* (Fig. 43-12). The hub is splined to the transmission output shaft. A pair of ring-shaped synchronizer springs apply a slight outward force against the keys.

The synchronizer sleeve (Fig. 43-12) fits over the hub. It has external splines or teeth that mesh with the internal splines or teeth in the sleeve. The keys have raised sections that fit in the *detent groove* in the sleeve. A *detent* is a small depression into which another part moves to provide a locking effect.

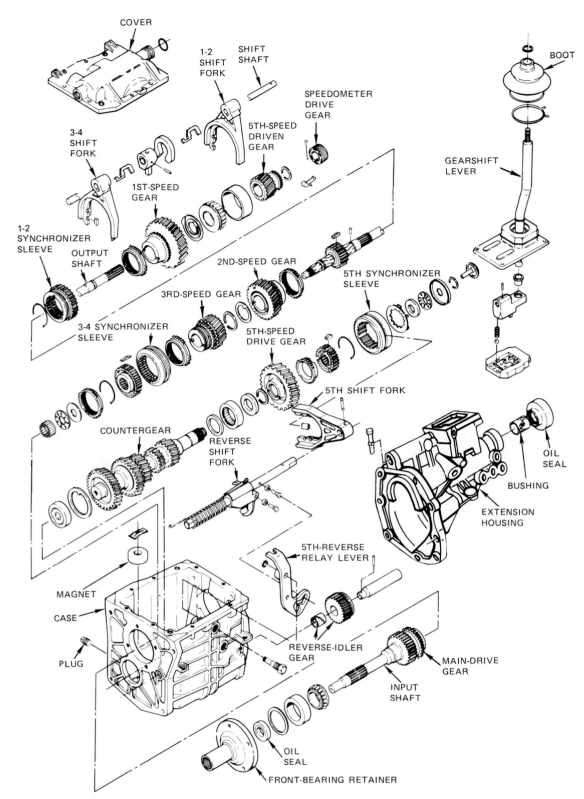

Fig. 43-10 A disassembled five-speed manual transmission with the major parts named. (*Chevrolet Division of General Motors Corporation*)

Synchronization is a three-stage action (Fig. 43-13). To shift the transmission into gear, the synchronizer sleeve is moved toward that gear. The sleeve slides on the hub splines and carries the three keys with it. The keys (Figs. 43-10 and 43-12) butt against the synchronizer ring and push it toward the gear. This brings the cone surface in the ring into contact with the cone surface on the gear (Fig. 43-13B). Friction between the synchronizer ring and the gear brings the two into *synchronous* rotation. They rotate at the same speed.

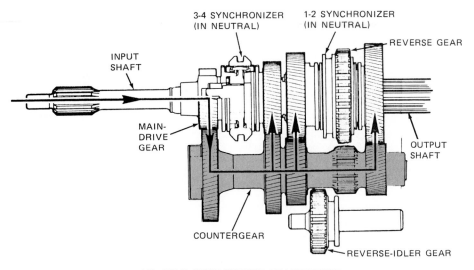

Fig. 43-11 Assembled gear train showing the additional parts needed to make (A) a four-speed manual transmission into a (B) five-speed manual transmission. (*General Motors Corporation*)

3-4 SYNCHRONIZER (IN NEUTRAL)

1-2 SYNCHRONIZER (IN NEUTRAL)

REVERSE GEAR

INPUT SHAFT

MAIN-DRIVE GEAR

OUTPUT SHAFT

COUNTERGEAR

REVERSE-IDLER GEAR

(A) FOUR-SPEED MANUAL TRANSMISSION

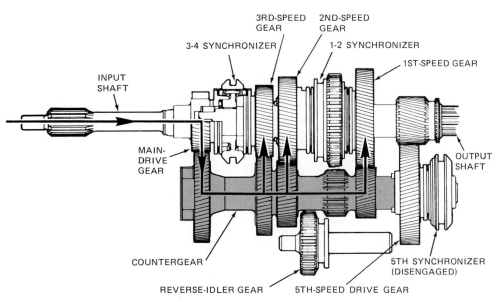

3RD-SPEED GEAR

2ND-SPEED GEAR

3-4 SYNCHRONIZER

1-2 SYNCHRONIZER

1ST-SPEED GEAR

INPUT SHAFT

MAIN-DRIVE GEAR

OUTPUT SHAFT

COUNTERGEAR

5TH SYNCHRONIZER (DISENGAGED)

REVERSE-IDLER GEAR

5TH-SPEED DRIVE GEAR

(B) FIVE-SPEED MANUAL TRANSMISSION

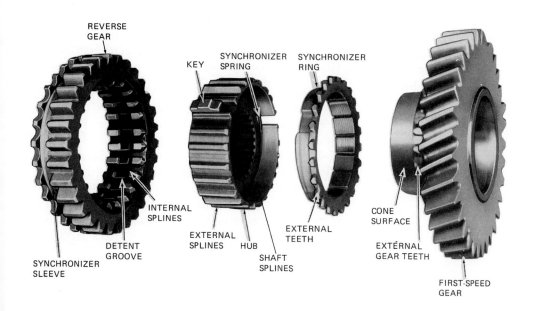

Fig. 43-12 A disassembled synchronizer. (*Chevrolet Division of General Motors Corporation*)

REVERSE GEAR

KEY

SYNCHRONIZER SPRING

SYNCHRONIZER RING

INTERNAL SPLINES

DETENT GROOVE

SYNCHRONIZER SLEEVE

EXTERNAL SPLINES

HUB

SHAFT SPLINES

EXTERNAL TEETH

CONE SURFACE

EXTERNAL GEAR TEETH

FIRST-SPEED GEAR

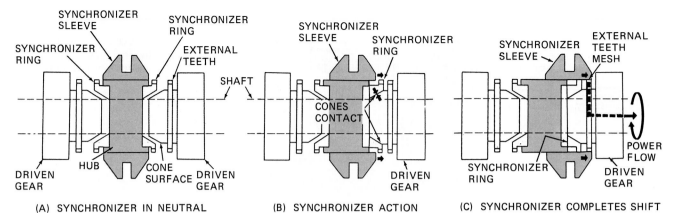

Fig. 43-13 Operation of the synchronizer to engage a gear. (*Deere & Company*)

When the external teeth on the synchronizer ring and on the gear rotate at the same speed, the sleeve slides over them (Fig. 43-13C). This locks the gear to the shaft and completes the shift. Power flows from the gear, through the synchronizer sleeve and hub, to the shaft. Similar actions take place in synchronizers used for other gears. Some transmissions have a synchronizer for reverse.

A transmission that uses synchronizers is a *synchromesh transmission*. The shifts are *synchro*nized and the gears are in constant *mesh*.

➤ **43-8 MANUAL-TRANSMISSION OPERATION**

The actions to obtain each gear in the five-speed manual transmission shown in Figs. 43-10 and 43-11B are described below. Figure 43-14 shows the power-flow through the five-speed transmission for each forward gear and reverse. Power-flow through the four-speed transmission is the same as in the five speed, except for fifth gear.

1. FIRST GEAR (FIG. 43-14A) To shift into first, depress the clutch pedal to disengage the clutch. Move the gearshift lever into the first position. This causes linkage in the transmission to select the first-reverse synchronizer and move its sleeve to the right (Figs. 43-11B and 43-14). The sleeve locks to the first-speed gear. Since the synchronizer-and-sleeve assembly are locked to the output shaft, the first-speed gear drives the output shaft when the clutch is engaged.

In first gear, there is torque multiplication and speed reduction through the transmission. The main-drive gear is smaller than the countergear it drives. This provides gear reduction. There is more gear reduction as the small countergear drives the large first-speed gear. The gear reduction can vary. A typical first-gear ratio is about 4:1. The crankshaft turns four times to turn the output shaft once. There is further gear reduction through the final drive in the rear drive axle (➤45-14).

2. SECOND GEAR (FIG. 43-14B) To shift into second, the first-second synchronizer sleeve moves to the left (Figs. 43-11B and 43-14). The sleeve moves through its center or neutral position, un-locking the first-speed gear and locking the second-speed gear to the output shaft. The second-speed gear, driven by the countergear second gear, now drives the output shaft through the synchronizer sleeve. There is less gear reduction than in first gear because there is less difference in the size of the gears. A typical gear ratio for second gear is about 2.4:1. The input shaft turns 2.4 times to turn the output shaft once.

3. THIRD GEAR (FIG. 43-14C) In third, the first-second synchronizer sleeve moves to its neutral position. The third-fourth synchronizer sleeve moves to the right (Figs. 43-11B and 43-14) so that it meshes with the third-speed gear. The countergear third gear now drives the third-speed gear and the output shaft through the synchronizer. A typical gear reduction in third is about 1.5:1.

4. FOURTH GEAR OR DIRECT DRIVE (FIG. 43-14D) In fourth, the third-fourth synchronizer sleeve moves to the left (Figs. 43-11B and 43-14) so that it meshes with the main-drive gear on the end of the input shaft. The output shaft is now driven by the main-drive gear through the synchronizer. This is *direct drive* and the gear ratio is 1:1.

5. FIFTH GEAR OR OVERDRIVE (FIG. 43-14E) In fifth, both the first-second synchronizer and the third-fourth synchronizer move to neutral. The sleeve on the fifth synchronizer moves forward (Figs. 43-11B and 43-14E). This locks the fifth-speed gear to the countergear. The fifth-speed gear now turns fifth gear which is splined to the output shaft. Overdrive is provided because the fifth-speed gear is larger than the gear it drives. A typical overdrive gear ratio is 0.8:1. The output shaft turns one complete revolution while the countergear turns only 0.8 (a little more than three-quarters) revolution.

6. REVERSE (FIG. 43-14F) In reverse, all synchronizer sleeves are in neutral. The reverse-idler gear slides into

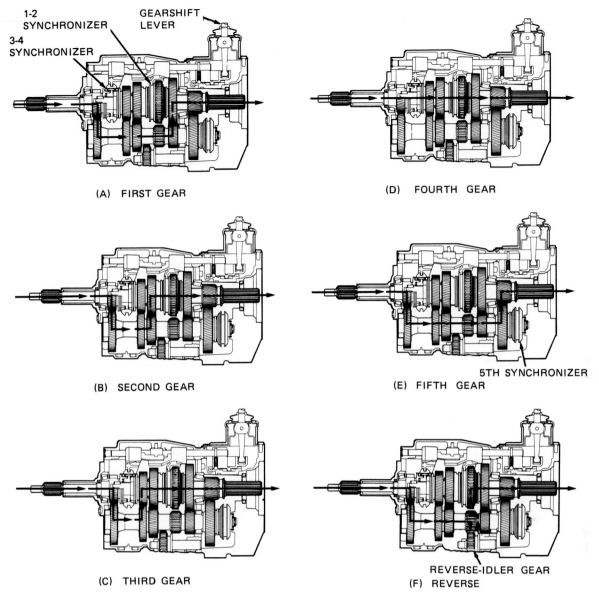

(A) FIRST GEAR

1-2 SYNCHRONIZER

3-4 SYNCHRONIZER

GEARSHIFT LEVER

(D) FOURTH GEAR

(B) SECOND GEAR

(E) FIFTH GEAR

5TH SYNCHRONIZER

(C) THIRD GEAR

(F) REVERSE

REVERSE-IDLER GEAR

Fig. 43-14 Power flow through a five-speed manual transmission for each forward gear and reverse. (*Chrysler Corporation*)

mesh with reverse gear on the countergear and the gear teeth on the first-second synchronizer sleeve. This serves as the reverse gear on the output shaft. The countergear drives the reverse-idler gear and it drives the output shaft through the synchronizer sleeve. The output shaft turns in the reverse direction because of the reverse idler gear. A typical reverse gear ratio is about 3.5:1.

MANUAL TRANSAXLES

➤ 43-9 MANUAL-TRANSAXLE CONSTRUCTION

A manual transaxle combines a manual transmission (*transmission section*) and a drive axle (*differential section*) in a single assembly (Fig. 43-15). Power flow from the engine enters the transmission section through the input shaft. Power leaves the transmission section through a *pinion gear* on the transmission output shaft or mainshaft.

The pinion gear drives the *ring gear* in the differential section. The ring gear sends the power through the differential to the two front-axle *halfshafts* (Fig. 43-4). Then the halfshafts turn the wheels and tires to move the car. The differential allows the front wheels to travel different distances as the vehicle is steered around a curve (➤45-18).

Figure 43-15 shows a four-speed transaxle. The input shaft is part of the countergear or cluster gear. Neutral is obtained when both synchronizers are in their center positions. The four forward gears are obtained the same as in the manual transmission (Fig. 43-11A). Moving the gearshift lever causes the first-second or third-fourth synchronizer sleeve to lock a gear to the mainshaft.

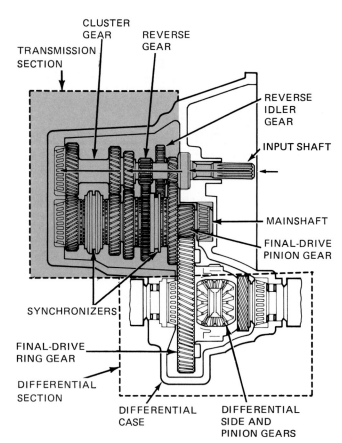

Fig. 43-15 The manual transaxle combines the manual transmission, final-drive gearing, and differential into a single unit. (*Ford Motor Company*)

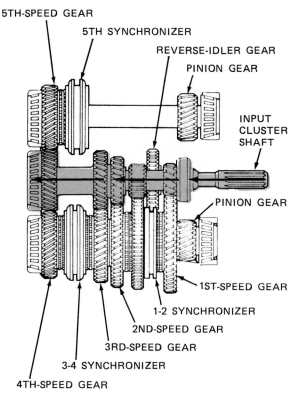

Fig. 43-16 Gears and shafts in the transmission section of a five-speed transaxle. (*Ford Motor Company*)

➤ 43-10 MANUAL-TRANSAXLE OPERATION

The gears and shafts in the *transmission section* of a five-speed transaxle are shown with the case removed in Fig. 43-16. This is basically the same transaxle shown in Fig. 43-15, with the addition of the *fifth-gear shaft assembly.* Operation of both transaxles is the same in all positions except fifth gear.

Figure 43-17 shows the power-flow through each gear position for the five-speed transaxle. In first and second gear, the third-fourth synchronizer sleeve remains in neutral. When the driver moves the gearshift lever to first, the first-second synchronizer sleeve moves forward (Fig. 43-17A). This locks the first-speed gear to the mainshaft. To shift to second, the first-second synchronizer sleeve moves to the rear (Fig. 43-17B). This unlocks the first-speed gear and then locks the second-speed gear to the mainshaft.

When the shift lever moves to third, the first-second synchronizer sleeve moves to neutral. The third-fourth synchronizer sleeve moves forward (Fig. 43-17C). This locks the third-speed gear to the mainshaft. Shifting to fourth unlocks the third-speed gear and moves the synchronizer sleeve to the rear (Fig. 43-17D). Fourth-speed gear is locked to the mainshaft. If the cluster gear and fourth-

speed gear are the same size, this provides direct drive. The gear ratio is 1:1.

Fifth gear is obtained by placing both the first-second and third-fourth synchronizer sleeves in neutral. Fourth gear on the cluster gear is in constant mesh with the fifth-speed gear. When the fifth-synchronizer sleeve moves to the rear (Fig. 43-17E), it locks the fifth-speed gear to its shaft. On the other end of the shaft a pinion gear is in constant mesh with the ring gear. Power flows from fourth gear on the cluster gear, through the fifth-speed gear and shaft. Then the power flows from the pinion on the end of the shaft to the ring gear.

> **NOTE** Both the mainshaft and the fifth-speed-gear shaft have pinion gears in constant mesh with the ring gear. When one shaft drives the ring gear, the other shaft is unlocked and turns freely or *freewheels.*

To get reverse, the first-second and third-fourth synchronizer sleeves move to neutral. The fifth synchronizer is disengaged. The reverse-idler gear moves to the rear (Fig. 43-17F). Its teeth now mesh with the reverse gear on the cluster gear and with the teeth on the 1-2 synchronizer sleeve or *reverse-sliding gear* on the mainshaft. Power flow is from the cluster gear and through the reverse-idler gear which drives the reverse-sliding gear. It reverses the direction of mainshaft rotation. The pinion gear then drives the ring gear in a reverse direction and the car moves backward.

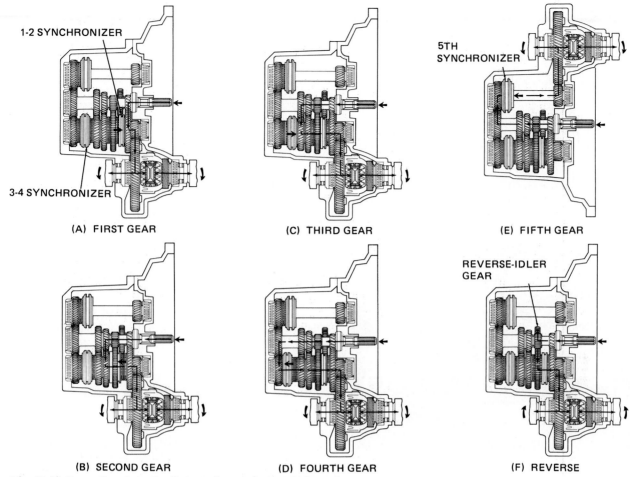

Fig. 43-17 Power flow through a five-speed manual transaxle for each forward gear and reverse. (*Ford Motor Company*)

> ## 43-11 DUAL-RANGE TRANSAXLE

The *dual-range transaxle* (Fig. 43-18) is a four-speed unit. The input shaft has two pinion gears—an *input low gear* and an *input high gear*. These are in constant mesh with matching gears on the countergear. Operation of the *range-selector synchronizer* determines which gear is locked to the input shaft. This results in two speed ranges, the *economy range* and the *power range*.

The transaxle has a total of eight forward speeds. Fourth gear is an overdrive ratio in the economy range. Two shift levers are required. One is the gearshift lever. The other is the *range-selector lever*. Its movement operates the range-selector synchronizer.

> ## 43-12 INTERLOCK DEVICES

Manual transmissions and transaxles use various types of *interlock* devices. The interlock allows only one synchronizer sleeve to move during shifting. If more than one moved, clashing and damage would result.

Figure 43-19 shows one type of interlock in the shift linkage of a five-speed manual transaxle. This interlock is a three-piece mechanism. When the driver moves the gearshift lever to any gear position, only the shift rail for that gear can move. The *interlock shuttles* in the i*nterlock plate* and the *interlock pin* move into notches in the shift rails. This prevents these rails from moving.

GEARSHIFTING AND SHIFT LINKAGE

> ## 43-13 STEERING-COLUMN AND FLOOR-SHIFT LEVERS

Years ago, the automotive manual transmission was a three-speed. The gearshift lever was located on the floor of the driver's compartment, in easy reach of the driver's right hand. The lower end of the lever attached to the shifting mechanism of the transmission. Then the gearshift lever was moved to the steering column, where the lever was more accessible to the driver (Fig. 43-20). This also provided more leg room in the front seat.

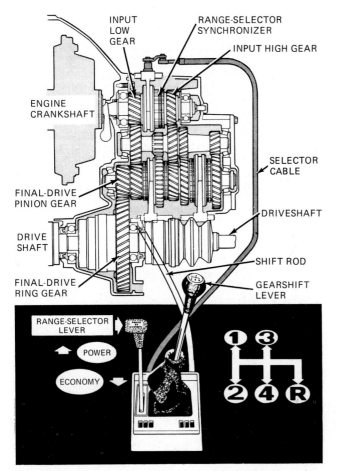

Fig. 43-18 Control levers and linkage for a dual-range transaxle. (*Chrysler Corporation*)

Today, vehicles again use a floor-mounted gearshift lever (Figs. 43-1 and 43-21). Many times it is part of a center console (Fig. 34-29). Figure 43-22 shows typical shift patterns for manual transmissions and transaxles.

➤ 43-14 SHIFT LINKAGE

A variety of linkage arrangements have been used to connect the gearshift lever with the transmission or transaxle. The basic action is the same for all. A shift requires two movements of the gearshift lever. The first movement selects the shift fork and synchronizer for the desired gear. The second movement causes the shift fork to move the synchronizer sleeve. This locks the desired gear to the mainshaft.

Figure 43-20 shows the linkage from a gearshift lever mounted on the steering column to the transmission. Figure 43-21 shows the linkage from a floor-mounted gearshift lever to a four-speed transmission. This arrangement is typical of *external linkage*, which is outside the transmission case. To reduce wear and other problems, most transmissions and transaxles now have *internal linkage* (Figs. 43-1 and 43-14). The shift linkage is enclosed within the transmission or transaxle case.

Figure 43-23 shows the cable linkage for a five-speed transaxle with a floor-mounted gearshift lever. The ends of the cables attach to the shift levers on the transaxle (Fig. 43-3). The *selector cable* selects which shift rail to move. The *shift cable* then moves that shift rail forward or backward.

Fig. 43-19 An interlock in the internal linkage of a five-speed manual transaxle. (*Chrysler Corporation*)

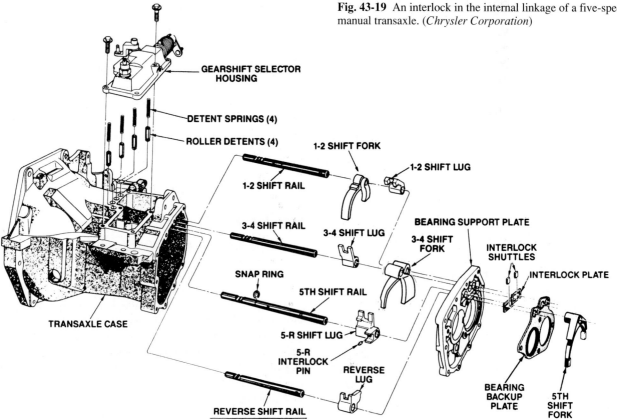

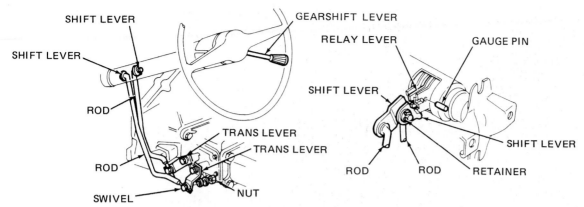

Fig. 43-20 Linkage between the gearshift lever on the steering column and the transmission. (*Chevrolet Division of General Motors Corporation*)

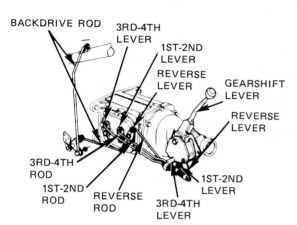

Fig. 43-21 Linkage between the gearshift lever on the floor and the transmission. (*Chevrolet Division of General Motors Corporation*)

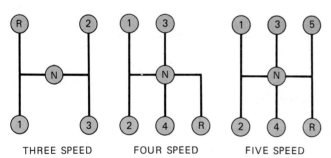

THREE SPEED   FOUR SPEED   FIVE SPEED

Fig. 43-22 Typical shift patterns for three-speed, four-speed, and five-speed manual transmissions and transaxles. (*ATW*)

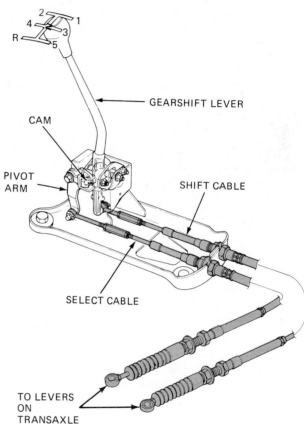

Fig. 43-23 Cable linkage for a five-speed transaxle with a floor-mounted shift lever. (*American Honda Motor Company, Inc.*)

➤ 43-15 SWITCHES AND SENSORS

Various switches and sensors may mount in the transmission or transaxle case (Fig. 43-24). This allows the devices to be operated by movement of the gearshift lever, the linkage, or a shaft. The switch or sensor then controls electrical circuits, or provides gear-position or vehicle-speed information.

1. TRANSMISSION-CONTROLLED SPARK (TCS) SWITCH The TCS system is an emission-control system used on many cars with a vacuum-advance unit on the ignition distributor (➤31-9). The switch is open and prevents vacuum advance in all gears except third in a three-speed or fourth in a four-speed. In these gears, the switch closes and allows vacuum advance. Vacuum advance in other gear positions can increase engine exhaust emissions.

2. BACKUP-LIGHT SWITCH When the ignition key is ON and the gearshift lever is moved to reverse, the linkage closes the *backup-light switch* (Fig. 43-24). This connects the backup lights at the rear of the car (Fig. 34-1) to the battery. The lights illuminate the area behind the car.

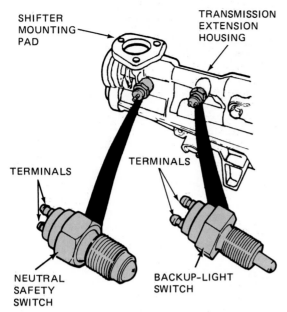

SHIFTER MOUNTING PAD

TRANSMISSION EXTENSION HOUSING

TERMINALS

TERMINALS

NEUTRAL SAFETY SWITCH

BACKUP-LIGHT SWITCH

Fig. 43-24 Neutral-safety switch and backup-light switch that mount in the transmission extension housing. (*Ford Motor Company*)

3. SPEEDOMETER DRIVE On most vehicles, the mechanical speedometer (➤34-19) is driven by a pair of gears in the transmission or transaxle. The *speedometer drive gear* (Fig. 43-10) mounts on the output shaft. The *speedometer driven gear* attaches to the end of the speedometer cable and meshes with the drive gear. The cable connects to the speedometer in the instrument panel.

4. VEHICLE-SPEED SENSOR Many vehicles have an electronic *vehicle-speed sensor* (VSS) in the transmission or transaxle (➤34-19). The speed sensor (Fig. 43-1) measures the speed of shaft rotation. It then sends a signal with this information to the electronic instrument panel and to the electronic control module (ECM). Vehicle speed is an input to the ECM (Fig. 19-26). One type of vehicle-speed sensor is a small electric generator driven by the transmission mainshaft. The higher the voltage generated, the higher the vehicle speed.

5. NEUTRAL-SAFETY SWITCH The starting-system control circuit includes a *safety switch* (➤29-1) or *neutral-safety switch* (Fig. 43-24). On some cars with a manual transmission or transaxle, cranking will not occur unless the gearshift lever is in neutral. This closes the neutral-safety switch and completes the circuit to the starting relay or solenoid (Fig. 29-1).

LUBRICATION

➤ 43-16 GEAR LUBRICANTS

A gear oil (➤43-6) performs five jobs. It must:

1. Lubricate gears and bearings to prevent wear.
2. Reduce friction and power loss.
3. Protect against rust and corrosion.
4. Remove particles from metal surfaces.
5. Help cool bearings and gears.

In addition, the lubricant helps reduce noise from the gearbox.

Most gear oil is a *mineral oil* refined from crude oil. Some gear oil is a manufactured or *synthetic oil*. Chemical additives are mixed with gear oil to improve its load-carrying capacity. This makes an *extreme pressure* (EP) lubricant (➤24-15). Other additives reduce the effects of heat on oil *viscosity* (➤24-3) and prevent foaming, rust, corrosion, and oil-seal damage.

The gear oil used in many cars and trucks is relatively thick and has a viscosity ranging from SAE 75W to SAE 140. Multigrade gear oils, such as SAE 75W-90, are also used. However, some manufacturers specify *synchromesh-transmission fluid* (STF) for manual transmissions and transaxles. Others are filled with *automatic-transmission fluid* (➤47-17).

TRADE TALK

countergear	freewheel	mainshaft	synchronizer
detent	gear ratio	mesh	
direct drive	interlock	overdrive	

MULTIPLE-CHOICE TEST

*Select the **one** correct, best, or most probable answer to each question.*
You can find the answers in the section indicated at the end of each question.

1. Technician A says, in a gearset, speed reduction means torque increase. Technician B says speed increase means torque reduction. Who is right? (➤43-5)
   a. A only
   b. B only
   c. both A and B
   d. neither A nor B

2. A synchronizer does all the following EXCEPT: (➤43-7)
   a. prevents gear clash during shifting
   b. uses friction to make the gear and synchronizer ring rotate at the same speed
   c. locks a gear to the shaft
   d. attaches directly to the shift rail

3. When the gear ratio through the transmission is 1:1, the transmission is in (➤43-8)
   a. overdrive
   b. direct drive
   c. underdrive
   d. neutral

4. Power leaves the transmission section of a manual transaxle through a (➤43-9)
   a. pinion gear
   b. ring gear
   c. cluster gear
   d. countergear

5. Technician A says when a five-speed manual transaxle is in fifth gear, the first-second and third-fourth synchronizer sleeves are in neutral. Technician B says the fifth synchronizer is disengaged. Who is right? (➤43-10)
   a. A only
   b. B only
   c. both A and B
   d. neither A nor B

6. The dual-range transaxle has (➤43-11)
   a. an output shaft with two ring gears
   b. an input shaft with two pinion gears
   c. two countergears
   d. two overdrive ratios

7. The purpose of an interlock device is to (➤43-12)
   a. lock the transmission to prevent theft
   b. complete the electric circuit to the starting motor
   c. prevent locking two gears to the output shaft at the same time
   d. interlock the shift lever to prevent shifting

8. To shift into a gear, the first movement of the gearshift lever (➤43-14)
   a. moves the synchronizer
   b. selects the synchronizer
   c. meshes the gears
   d. moves the synchronizer sleeve

9. Shift linkage enclosed within the transmission or transaxle case is called (➤43-14)
   a. external linkage
   b. floor shift
   c. column shift
   d. internal linkage

10. The speedometer drive gear mounts on the (➤43-15)
    a. input shaft
    b. countergear shaft
    c. output shaft
    d. fifth-gear shaft

REVIEW QUESTIONS

1. Name the basic parts in a gearbox and describe the purpose of each. (➤43-6)
2. What is a "detent" and what does it do in a manual transmission or transaxle? (➤43-7)
3. What are the differences between a four-speed manual transmission and a five-speed manual transmission? (➤43-8)
4. How is reverse obtained in the gear train of a manual transaxle? (➤43-10)
5. Describe the five jobs of a gear oil, and the various types that are used in manual transmissions and transaxles. (➤43-16)

CHAPTER 44

MANUAL TRANSMISSIONS AND TRANSAXLES: DIAGNOSIS AND SERVICE

After studying this chapter, and with proper instruction and equipment, you should be able to:

- Explain how to perform a road test and the reasons for having the customer along.
- List possible transmission and transaxle troubles, and explain the causes of each.
- Diagnose power-train noise in cars with a manual transmission and a manual transaxle.
- Clean and inspect ball and roller bearings.
- Remove, service, and install a manual transaxle and a manual transmission.

➢ 44-1 MANUAL TRANSMISSION AND TRANSAXLE TROUBLE DIAGNOSIS

The type of trouble in a manual transmission or transaxle often indicates its possible cause. Try to determine the cause before attempting any repair (➢3-1). A trouble in the linkage from the gearshift lever to the transmission or transaxle is an *external trouble*. It may be fixed with the transmission or transaxle in the vehicle.

An *internal trouble* inside the transmission or transaxle usually requires removing it from the vehicle. Then the unit is disassembled and the parts inspected for damage and wear. If the repair parts are not available, a new, used, or rebuilt transmission or transaxle may be installed. This may also be done if the estimated cost of repair is higher than the cost of the replacement unit.

Try to *road test* the car with the driver accompanying you (Fig. 44-1). This allows you to verify the driver's complaint and identify the condition the driver wants corrected. Ask about the history of the trouble, the service history of the car, and for copies of previous repair orders. During the road test determine when, where, and how the trouble occurs. Note any related or unusual conditions. Be sure the complaint is not caused by an improperly operating clutch (Chap. 42). If the trouble does not occur while you are

Fig. 44-1 When possible, road test the vehicle with the customer. (*Ford Motor Company*)

operating the vehicle, let the driver show you when the condition occurs.

After repairs are complete, road test the vehicle again. During this *post-repair road test*, the trouble you found on the first road test should no longer exist. The second road test helps prevent shop comebacks later that result from the installation of defective parts or faulty workmanship. It also verifies that you have corrected the condition that concerned the driver.

Careful! Do not road test a vehicle unless you have a valid driver's license *and* your instructor's permission. Then fasten your seat belt and conduct the road test in the area designated by your instructor. Do not exceed the speed limit.

44-2 TYPES OF MANUAL-TRANSMISSSION AND TRANSAXLE TROUBLES

Two types of manual-transmission and transaxle troubles are *noise* and *improper operation*. The cause of either of these may be internal or external (➤44-1). Three general types of noise may come from a manual transmission or transaxle (Fig. 44-2). The type of noise provides information about what is taking place inside the case to make that noise.

The sound of a *periodic clunk* indicates broken gear teeth. A *growl* or *whine* indicates a defective bearing or worn teeth. A defective bearing usually produces a *rough growl* or *grating* noise (➤44-15) rather than a whine, which is more typical of gear noise. *Gear clash* during shifting often indicates a worn or defective synchronizer.

MANUAL-TRANSMISSION TROUBLE DIAGNOSIS

44-3 MANUAL-TRANSMISSION TROUBLES

A complaint of "transmission trouble" may actually be a defective clutch. Check the clutch first (Chap. 42). The procedure for identifying clutch-system bearing noise is described in ➤42-26. If the trouble is in the external shift linkage, the linkage may need lubricating and adjusting or a defective cable replaced.

To determine the cause of other troubles, follow the steps in the manufacturer's service manual and in the *Manual-Transmission Trouble-Diagnosis Chart* (Fig. 44-3). Because of differences among manual transmissions, each possible cause and correction in Fig. 44-3 may not apply to all transmissions. Refer to the trouble-diagnosis charts and procedures in the vehicle service manual.

Explanations of how to locate and correct typical troubles are given in the following sections. Later sections describe procedures for servicing manual transmissions.

CAUTION!

Never go under a vehicle unless you are wearing eye protection—safety glasses or safety goggles. If the vehicle is

---

Noise	Cause
Periodic clunk	Broken teeth
Growl or whine	Defective bearing or worn teeth
Gear clash	Defective synchronizer

Fig. 44-2 Three types of manual-transmission noise and their causes.

raised on a lift, lock the lift (➤4-6, item 7). If the vehicle is raised on a jack (➤8-18), be sure the vehicle is properly supported on safety stands before going under it.

44-4 HARD SHIFTING INTO GEAR

Difficulty in shifting into gear may be caused by improperly adjusted linkage between the gearshift lever and the transmission. This greatly increases the force required to "shift gears." Hard shifting also results if the linkage is bent, jammed, or rusted and in need of lubrication. Other causes include a bent shift fork, a worn or defective synchronizer (Fig. 44-4), a twisted mainshaft, and an improperly adjusted clutch.

44-5 TRANSMISSION STICKS IN GEAR

Conditions that cause difficulty shifting into gear (➤44-4) can also cause the transmission to stick *in* gear. These include improper shift-linkage adjustment and the linkage failing to move freely. Other causes include improper clutch-linkage adjustment and any condition that prevents the clutch from disengaging.

The transmission may stick in gear if the interlock device fails to operate properly and if a synchronizer sleeve does not slide freely on the hub splines. Lack of lubricant in the transmission or use of the wrong lubricant may also cause the transmission to stick in gear.

44-6 TRANSMISSION JUMPS OUT OF GEAR

Improperly adjusted shift linkage may cause the transmission to slip or jump out of gear. Binding or an excessively stiff *boot* (Fig. 43-1) on the gearshift lever may pull it back to neutral from any gear position. To check the boot, squeeze it. If the boot is too stiff, replace it.

Worn splines in the synchronizer sleeve or worn external teeth on the gear (Fig. 43-12) may cause the transmission to jump out of gear. Both the sleeve and the external teeth often wear at the same time. When this condition is found, replace both the sleeve and the gear.

Sometimes the transmission begins jumping out of gear immediately after the clutch or transmission has been serviced or replaced. Check for misalignment between the transmission and the engine. A pulsating clutch pedal (➤42-22) may indicate clutch-housing misalignment (➤42-32). If the clutch housing is out of line, then so is the transmission.

44-7 GEAR CLASH WHEN SHIFTING

A worn or defective synchronizer will cause gear clash during shifting. This may be due to a broken synchronizer

Complaint	Possible Cause	Check or Correction
1. Hard shifting into gear (➤44-4)	a. Shift shaft or interlocks binding	Free
	b. Clutch cable not adjusted properly	Check; adjust or replace
	c. Bent or worn shift fork	Replace
	d. Worn shift shaft	Replace
	e. Gear or synchronizer sleeve tight on shaft or splines	Replace worn parts
	f. Worn synchronizer rings or springs	Replace worn parts
	g. Worn or stripped external teeth on gear	Replace gear
	h. Input shaft or pilot bearing binding	Replace pilot bearing or input shaft
	i. Low lubricant level	Fill to proper level
	j. Improper lubricant used (particularly cold)	Drain and refill with specified lubricant
2. Transmission sticks in gear (➤44-5)	a. Shift shaft or interlock binding	Free
	b. Shift detent sticking	Free
	c. Clutch not disengaging	Repair clutch cable (Chap. 42)
	d. Synchronizer binding	Replace synchronizer
	e. Low lubricant level	Fill to proper level
3. Transmission jumps out of gear (➤44-6)	a. Weak detent spring	Replace
	b. Worn input- or output-shaft bearing	Replace
	c. Worn pilot bearing	Replace
	d. Excessive shaft or gear endplay	Replace worn thrust washer
	e. Worn synchronizer sleeve	Replace synchronizer and gear
	f. Loose or broken input-shaft retainer	Replace
	g. Loose transmission or clutch housing	Tighten attaching bolts
	h. Misaligned transmission	Check alignment
4. Gear clash when shifting (➤44-7)	a. Worn synchronizer	Replace
	b. Clutch dragging	Repair clutch (Chap. 42)
	c. Pilot bearing or input shaft binding	Replace bearing or shaft
	d. High engine idle speed	Adjust
	e. Low lubricant level or improper lubricant	Fill with correct lubricant to proper level
5. Transmission noisy in gear (➤44-8)	a. Defective clutch disc	Replace
	b. Excessive clearance between gear(s) and mainshaft	Replace worn gears or shaft
	c. Worn or defective bearings	Replace
	d. Broken gear tooth	Replace gear
	e. Worn speedometer pinion gear	Replace
	f. Worn synchronizer	Replace
	g. Worn pilot bearing	Replace
	h. Low lubricant level	Fill to proper level
	i. Transmission misaligned	Check alignment
	j. Worn countershaft bearings or thrust washers	Replace worn parts
6. Transmission noisy in neutral (➤44-9)	a. Worn input-shaft bearing	Replace
	b. Broken or worn gear	Replace
7. Transmission noisy in reverse (➤44-10)	a. Reverse-idler gear or shaft bushing worn or damaged	Replace
	b. Reverse gear on mainshaft worn or damaged	Replace
	c. Countergear worn or damaged	Replace
	d. Shift mechanism damaged	Repair, replace defective parts, readjust
8. No power through transmission (➤44-11)	a. Clutch not engaging	Repair clutch
	b. Striped gear teeth	Replace gear
	c. Loose or broken shift fork	Replace
	d. Broken input or output shaft	Replace
9. Transmission oil leaks (➤44-12)	a. Incorrect lubricant or lubricant level too high, causing foaming	Fill with specified lubricant to proper level
	b. Leaking gasket	Replace
	c. Damaged oil seal	Replace
	d. Damaged oil slinger	Replace
	e. Loose fill plug	Tighten
	f. Speedometer pinion seals leaking	Replace seals
	g. Cracked case or extension housing	Replace
	h. Worn extension-housing seal or bushing	Replace

Fig. 44-3 Manual-transmission trouble-diagnosis chart.

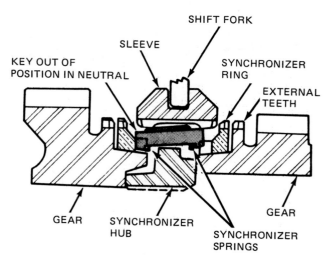

Fig. 44-4 A defective synchronizer, in neutral with the key, or strut, out of position.

spring or a worn cone surface on a synchronizer ring (Fig. 44-5). Gear clash also occurs if the clutch does not fully disengage and if a gear sticks on the mainshaft.

Gear clash may occur if a sudden shift is made to first or to reverse before the gears stop moving. Some transmissions do not have a synchronizer on first or reverse. To shift into either of these positions without gear clash, the driver must wait until the gears stop turning ("spin down"). Then the shift lever can be moved and the gears will mesh without clashing.

A worn or dry pilot bearing or bushing may drag around the input shaft even after the clutch is disengaged. This causes gear clash when shifting, as will incorrect lubricant in the transmission.

➤ 44-8 TRANSMISSION NOISY IN GEAR

Noise while the transmission is in gear could result from any condition in ➤44-7. The noise could also be due to a defective friction disc in the clutch (Chap. 42) or a defec-

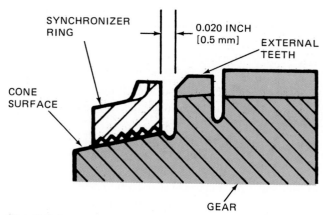

Fig. 44-5 Inspecting synchronizer ring and cone surface for wear. (*Ford Motor Company*)

tive engine vibration damper (➤13-15). Other causes include a worn or dry rear bearing on the transmission output shaft, a loose gear on the output shaft, and worn or damaged gear teeth, synchronizers, or speedometer gears.

Transmission troubles may cause several types of noise (Fig. 44-2). A whining or growling noise may be either steady or intermittent. It can be due to worn, chipped, rough, or cracked gears. As the gears continue to wear, the noise may take on a grinding sound. It will be loudest in the gear position that throws the greatest load on the worn gears.

Bearing trouble often causes a hissing noise that develops into a bumping or thudding sound as the bearing wears. Metallic rattles may be caused by worn or loose parts in the shift linkage, or by gears loose on the shaft splines. Sometimes noise from defective cushion springs in the clutch friction disc or from the engine vibration damper carry into the transmission. Typically, this noise is heard only at certain engine speeds.

While diagnosing transmission noise, listen carefully to determine in which gear position the noise is loudest. This information helps pinpoint the worn or defective parts.

➤ 44-9 TRANSMISSION NOISY IN NEUTRAL

Noise heard with the transmission in neutral and the clutch engaged may be caused by transmission misalignment with the engine. It may also be caused by a defect in any of the parts that are rotating. Possible causes include a worn or dry bearing, a worn gear, a worn or bent countergear, or excessive countergear endplay.

➤ 44-10 TRANSMISSION NOISY IN REVERSE

Noise in reverse is probably due to a damaged or worn reverse-idler gear or bushing, reverse gear on the mainshaft, or countergear. A damaged shift mechanism will also cause noise in reverse.

➤ 44-11 NO POWER THROUGH TRANSMISSION

If no power flows through the transmission when it is in gear and the clutch engaged, the clutch may be slipping (➤42-17). Internal transmission causes include teeth stripped from gears, a broken shift fork or linkage part, splines sheared off, and a broken gear or shaft (Fig. 44-6).

➤ 44-12 TRANSMISSION OIL LEAKS

Figure 44-7 shows various places lubricant may leak from a manual transmission. If the lubricant in the transmission is not the correct type, it may foam excessively. The foam will completely fill the case and then begin to leak out. To prevent foaming, fill the transmission with the specified

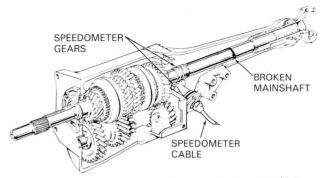

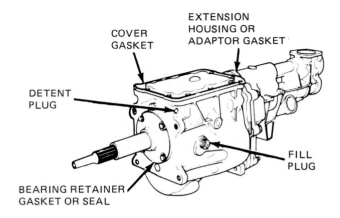

Fig. 44-6 Manual transmission with a broken mainshift which prevents power flow through the transmission. (*Toyota Motor Sales U.S.A., Inc.*)

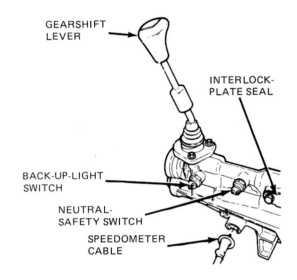

lubricant to the proper level. An overfilled transmission, a loose drain plug or fill plug, and a cracked transmission case or extension housing will also leak oil.

MANUAL-TRANSAXLE TROUBLE DIAGNOSIS

➤ 44-13 MANUAL-TRANSAXLE TROUBLES

The manual transaxle includes a transmission section and a drive-axle or differential section (➤43-2). Diagnosing trouble in the transmission section is similar to trouble-diagnosis of a manual transmission (➤44-3). Take a road test (➤44-1) with the driver, if possible. Find out when the trouble occurs. Then refer to the trouble-diagnosis charts in the vehicle service manual.

Figure 44-8 is a chart that lists various manual-transaxle troubles and their possible causes. The chart can be used as a guide when diagnosing trouble in a manual transaxle and drive train of a front-wheel-drive vehicle. If the trouble is in the transmission section of the transaxle, the *Manual-Transmission Trouble-Diagnosis Chart* (Fig. 44-3) may also be helpful.

➤ 44-14 MANUAL-TRANSAXLE AND DRIVE-TRAIN NOISE

In a front-wheel-drive vehicle, the entire drive train is almost under the driver's feet (Fig. 44-9). This makes any drive-train noise more noticeable than in a rear-wheel-drive vehicle. The noise can vary with vehicle size, type and size of engine, and amount of body insulation.

Noises that sound like they are coming from the drive train may actually be coming from the tires, road surface, wheel bearings, engine, or exhaust system. Transaxle gears may produce some noise during normal operation. If the noise annoys the driver, determine if it is excessive. Listed below are the steps in a typical procedure for identifying the source of manual transaxle and drive-train noise.

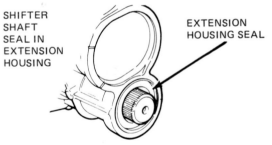

Fig. 44-7 Various places lubricant may leak from a manual transmission. (*Ford Motor Company*)

1. Road test the vehicle by driving it on a smooth, level, paved road. This will reduce tire and road noise to a minimum.
2. Drive the vehicle long enough to warm all lubricants.
3. Note the speed at which the noise occurs and in which gear.
4. Stop the vehicle in a safe area. Shift to neutral and listen for the noise. Then depress the clutch pedal, shift into gear, and listen for the noise.
5. Determine during which of the following driving conditions the noise is most noticeable:

Complaint	Possible Cause
1. Noise is the same in drive or coast	a. Road noise b. Tire noise c. Front-wheel bearing noise d. Incorrect drive-axle angle (standing height)
2. Noise changes on different types of road	a. Road noise b. Tire noise
3. Noise tone lowers as car speed is lowered	Tire noise
4. Noise is produced with engine running, whether vehicle is stopped or moving	a. Engine noise b. Transaxle noise c. Exhaust noise
5. Knock at low speeds	a. Worn CV joint b. Worn side-gear-hub counterbore in differential
6. Noise loudest during turns	Differential-gear noise
7. Clunk on acceleration or deceleration	a. Loose engine or transaxle mounts b. Worn differential pinion shaft in case, or side-gear-hub counterbore in case worn oversize c. Worn or damaged inboard CV joint
8. Clicking noise in turns	Worn or damaged outboard CV joint
9. Vibration	a. Rough wheel bearing b. Damaged drive-axle shaft c. Out-of-round tire d. Tire unbalance e. Worn CV joint f. Incorrect drive-axle angle
10. Transaxle noisy in neutral	Damaged input-shaft bearing
11. Transaxle noisy in gear	a. Damaged or worn output-shaft gear b. Damaged or worn synchronizer
12. Transaxle noisy in reverse	a. Worn or damaged reverse idler gear or idler bushing b. Worn or damaged synchronizer
13. Transaxle noisy in all gears	a. Insufficient lubricant b. Damaged or worn bearings c. Worn or damaged input shaft or output shaft
14. Transaxle jumps out of gear	a. Worn or improperly adjusted linkage b. Transaxle loose on engine c. Shift linkage binds d. Bent or damaged shift cables e. Front-bearing retainer broken or loose f. Dirt between clutch housing and engine g. Stiff gearshift-lever seal or boot
15. Hard shifting into gear	a. Gearshift linkage out of adjustment or needs lubricant b. Clutch not disengaging c. Internal trouble in transaxle
16. Transaxle sticks in gear	a. Gearshift linkage out of adjustment, disconnected, or needs lubricant b. Clutch not disengaging c. Internal trouble in transaxle
17. Gears clash when shifting	a. Incorrect gearshift-linkage adjustment b. Clutch not disengaging c. Clutch linkage needs adjustment d. Internal trouble in transaxle
18. Transaxle oil leaks	a. Drive-axle seals faulty b. Excessive lubricant in transaxle c. Loose or broken front-bearing retainer d. Front-bearing-retainer O ring or lip seal damaged e. Lack of sealant between case and clutch housing or loose clutch housing f. Gearshift-lever seal leaks

Fig. 44-8 Manual-transaxle trouble-diagnosis chart.

a. Driving—light acceleration or heavy pull.

b. Float—constant vehicle speed with light throttle on a level road.

c. Coast—partly or fully closed throttle with transaxle in gear.

d. All of the above.

6. After road testing the vehicle, consider the following:

a. If the noise is the same in drive or coast, it could be due to excessive angle of the drive axles or halfshafts (Fig. 44-9). The front suspension may be binding or the springs may be weak. This could cause the drive-

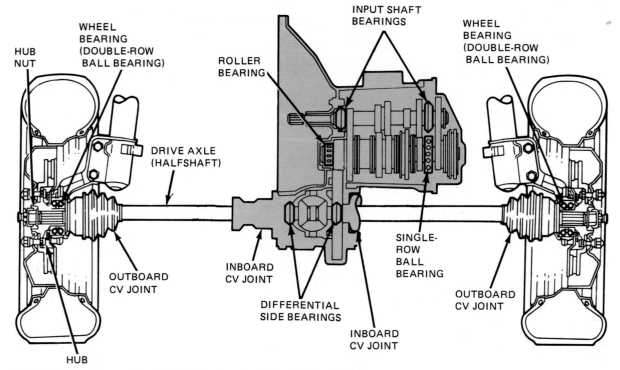

Fig. 44-9 Manual transaxle and drive train for a front-wheel-drive vehicle. (*Chrysler Corporation*)

axle universal joints or *CV joints* (Chap. 45) to be driving through an excessive angle.

b. A knock at low speed could be caused by worn CV joints or by worn counterbores in the side-gear hubs in the differential.

c. A clunk on acceleration or deceleration could be caused by loose engine or transaxle mounts (➤44-16), wear in the differential, and worn or damaged CV joints.

d. Other causes of noise are listed in the *Manual-Transaxle Trouble-Diagnosis Chart* (Fig. 44-8). The noise may occur when the transaxle is shifted into only one of the forward gears (item 11 in Fig. 44-8). Then a possible cause is a defective synchronizer or output-shaft gear for that speed.

e. Bearing noises are described in ➤44-15.

➤ 44-15 BALL- AND ROLLER-BEARING NOISE

Ball- and *roller-bearings* are used to support the shafts in the manual transaxle and drive train (Fig. 44-9). When these bearings become defective, they usually produce a rough growl or grating noise rather than the whine that is typical of gear noise. If transaxle bearing noise is suspected, the transaxle must be removed and disassembled so the bearings can be inspected (➤44-21). Two other bearings that may become noisy are the *differential side bearings* and the *wheel bearings* (Fig. 44-9).

1. DIFFERENTIAL SIDE-BEARING NOISE The differential side bearings are preloaded. Their noise will not lessen or disappear if the vehicle is run with the wheels off the ground. Noise in this area can easily be mistaken for wheel-bearing noise.

Careful! Follow the procedure in the vehicle service manual for running the vehicle with the drive wheels off the ground. If the wheels rotate while hanging, the excessive drive angle may damage the CV joints. Support the vehicle with safety stands placed under the specified lift points.

2. WHEEL-BEARING NOISE A rough wheel bearing produces a vibration or growl which continues when the vehicle is coasting with the transaxle in neutral. The sound from a wheel bearing that is not preloaded should lessen when the vehicle is run with the wheels off the ground. A *brinelled bearing* (➤44-21) causes a knock or click about every two wheel revolutions. The bearing race is brinelled when it has an indentation caused by a ball or roller. To check for brinelling, spin the wheel by hand.

➤ 44-16 DEFECTIVE POWER-TRAIN MOUNT

A defective *engine* or *power-train mount* (➤13-35) may cause a variety of clutch and transaxle troubles. If the mount breaks, the engine-transaxle assembly may move too much. This can prevent clutch disengagement which results in gear clash when shifting. Excess movement can cause the transaxle to jump out of gear. A defective mount may also make noise and transmit engine vibration to the vehicle body.

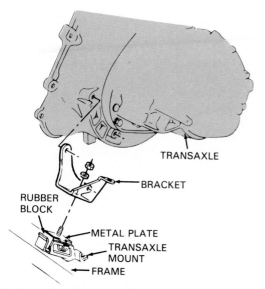

Fig. 44-10 Rubber-block type of manual-transaxle mount. (*Pontiac Division of General Motors Corporation*)

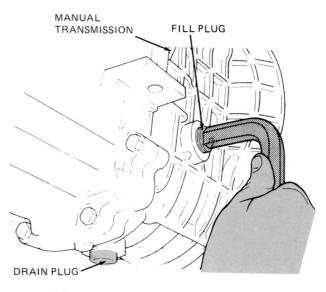

(A) REMOVING/INSTALLING FILL PLUG

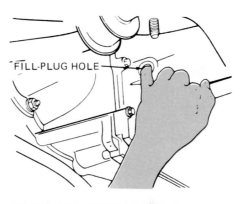

(B) CHECKING LUBRICANT LEVEL

Fig. 44-11 Checking lubricant level in manual transmission. (*General Motors Corporation; Ford Motor Company*)

To check the power-train mounts, raise the engine slightly to remove weight from the mounts and place a slight tension on them. Watch the mounts while raising the engine. Replace a *rubber mount* (Fig. 44-10) if it has cracks in the rubber, rubber separation from a mount metal plate, or a split through the center of the rubber. Replace a *hydraulic mount* (Figs. 13-38 and 13-40A) if it is leaking fluid.

Movement between a mount metal plate and its attaching point indicates loose fasteners. Tighten the nuts or screws to the specified torque.

MANUAL-TRANSMISSION SERVICE

➤ 44-17 MANUAL-TRANSMISSION MAINTENANCE

The manual transmission does not need periodic service or routine maintenance. Transmissions operated by external linkage from the gearshift lever (Figs. 43-20 and 43-21) may require a *shift-linkage adjustment*. Follow the procedure in the vehicle service manual. Typically, this adjustment is made by disconnecting the rods from the levers on the transmission. Then place the gearshift lever and the transmission levers in neutral. Adjust the linkage by turning the threaded pins on the rods until the pins will slip in and then clip into the transmission levers.

An automotive manual transmission holds about three quarts or liters of lubricant. Changing the lubricant is not required unless it becomes contaminated or internal damage occurs in the transmission. Check the lubricant level periodically. A loss of lubricant indicates leakage (➤44-12).

To check the lubricant level in the transmission, park the vehicle on a level surface. Turn the ignition key OFF and

set the parking brake. Clean any dirt and grease from around the fill plug (Fig. 44-11A). Then remove the fill plug using the proper wrench or socket. Check the lubricant level (Fig. 44-11B). It should be even with the bottom of the hole. If low, add the lubricant specified by the vehicle manufacturer. Different transmissions require different lubricants, and some should not be mixed. When the lubricant reaches the proper level, install the fill plug. Tighten it to the specified torque.

➤ 44-18 MANUAL-TRANSMISSION REMOVAL

In most cars, several bolts attach the manual transmission to the clutch housing (Fig. 43-1). A *crossmember* supports the rear of the transmission (Figs. 13-37B and 44-12). The front end of the driveshaft attaches to a universal joint (Chap. 45). A *slip yoke* is part of the universal joint and splined to the transmission output shaft (Fig. 43-2). Shift rods may connect the gearshift lever to the shift levers on the transmission (Figs. 43-20 and 43-21).

Remove the transmission following the procedure in the vehicle service manual. These steps typically include disconnecting the negative cable from the battery and removing the gearshift knob or lever (Fig. 44-7). Raise the vehicle on a lift (➤8-21) and drain the lubricant (Fig. 44-11).

Disconnect the speedometer cable (Fig. 44-6). Then disconnect all wires and electrical connectors attached to sensors and switches in the transmission case, shift cover, and extension housing (Fig. 44-7). If necessary, remove part or all the exhaust system (➤17-14) to allow working room for transmission removal.

Locate or make *index marks* (Fig. 44-12) on the rear-axle yoke and on the driveshaft so it can be reinstalled in the same position. Then disconnect the driveshaft from the rear axle. *Do not allow the universal joint cups and bearings to fall off!* Pull the driveshaft back until the slip yoke slides off the transmission output shaft.

Support the rear of the engine with a support jack or safety stand. Remove the transmission mount and crossmember (Fig. 44-12), if necessary. Remove two upper bolts attaching the transmission to the clutch housing and install *guide pins* in the holes (Fig. 44-13). The guide pins prevent damage to the clutch friction disc as the transmission is removed. Then remove the other bolts. With a helper or using a *transmission jack* (Fig. 44-14), slide the transmission rearward until the input shaft clears the clutch housing. Then lower the transmission and move it out from under the vehicle.

With the transmission out, inspect the condition and tightness of the flywheel and clutch (Chap. 42). Inspect the pilot bearing or bushing in the end of the crankshaft.

GUIDE PINS

Fig. 44-13 Using guide pins during transmission removal or installation to prevent damaging the friction disc. (*Buick Division of General Motors Corporation*)

Perform any services required on the flywheel and clutch before reinstalling the transmission.

➤ 44-19 MANUAL-TRANSMISSION DISASSEMBLY AND CLEANING

Place the transmission in a *holding fixture* (Fig. 44-15) or on the workbench. Follow the procedure in the vehicle

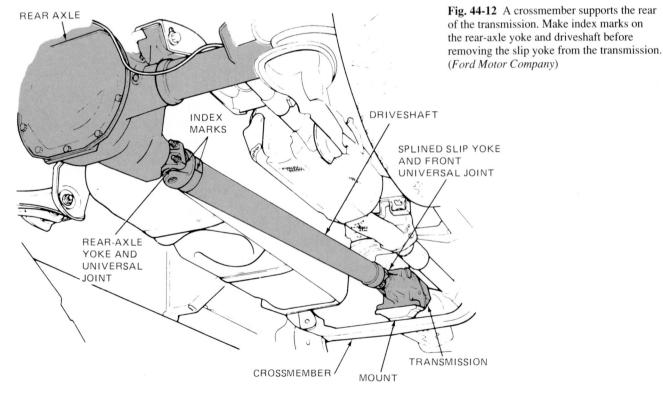

REAR AXLE

INDEX MARKS

DRIVESHAFT

SPLINED SLIP YOKE AND FRONT UNIVERSAL JOINT

REAR-AXLE YOKE AND UNIVERSAL JOINT

CROSSMEMBER

MOUNT

TRANSMISSION

Fig. 44-12 A crossmember supports the rear of the transmission. Make index marks on the rear-axle yoke and driveshaft before removing the slip yoke from the transmission. (*Ford Motor Company*)

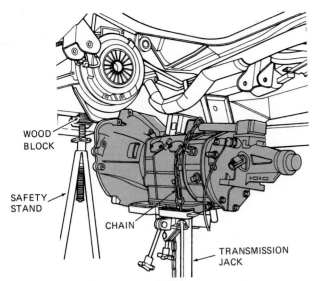

Fig. 44-14 Secure the transmission to the transmission jack. Move the transmission rearward until the input shaft clears the clutch housing and lower the jack. (*Ford Motor Company*)

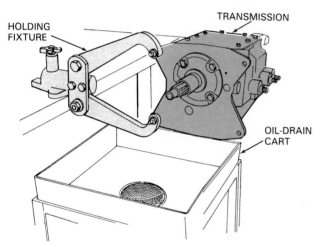

Fig. 44-15 Manual transmission mounted on a holding fixture above an oil-drain cart. (*Ford Motor Company*)

service manual and disassemble the transmission. Figure 43-10 shows a completely disassembled five-speed transmission.

1. CLEANING TRANSMISSION PARTS Wash all transmission parts, except bearings and seals, in solvent. Brush or scrape all dirt from the parts. Do not damage parts with the scraper. Dry each part with compressed air.

CAUTION!

Always wear eye protection—safety glasses, safety goggles, or a face shield—when using compressed air or solvent.

Some transmissions have a magnet at the bottom of the case (Fig. 43-10). Clean the magnet with solvent to remove

any metal particles and dirt. To clean a switch or sensor, wipe it with a clean shop towel. *Never clean switches and sensors in solvent!*

2. CLEANING TRANSMISSION BEARINGS To clean a bearing, rotate it slowly in clean solvent to remove all lubricant. Then hold the bearing assembly stationary so it will not rotate and dry it with compressed air.

Careful! *Never spin a ball or roller bearing with compressed air. Spinning a bearing after the lubricant is removed (a "dry bearing") may damage the bearing. A bearing spinning at high speed may fly apart, injuring you or others.*

As soon as the bearing is dry, lubricate it with transmission lubricant. This prevents microscopic rust from immediately beginning to form on the bearing. Then place each bearing in a clean plastic bag for later inspection.

➤ 44-20 INSPECTING MANUAL-TRANSMISSION PARTS

Inspect the transmission case for cracks and worn or damaged bearing bores and threads. Check the front and back of the case for nicks or burrs that could cause misalignment with the flywheel housing or extension housing. Remove all burrs with a fine file.

Check the condition of the shift levers, shift rails, forks, shafts, and gears. Replace the countergear and any other gear if teeth are worn, broken, chipped, or damaged. Replace the countergear shaft if it is worn, bent, or scored. In some transmissions, the bushings in the reverse gear and reverse-idler gear are not serviced separately. Replace the reverse-idler gear if the bushing is worn. The new gear has a new bushing in it.

Check each synchronizer sleeve for free movement on its hub (Fig. 44-16A). Look for worn or damaged splines. Inspect the teeth on each synchronizer ring (Fig. 44-16B). Replace the synchronizer ring if it has chipped or worn teeth, or marks on the gear face.

Check the amount of synchronizer-ring wear by placing the ring on its gear cone (Fig. 44-16B). With a thickness gauge, measure the clearance between the side faces (Fig. 44-16C). A typical specification is to replace the synchronizer ring or gear if the clearance is less than 0.031 inch [0.8 mm].

Inspect the shift fork and groove in the synchronizer sleeve for wear or damage. Position the shift fork in the synchronizer sleeve. Measure the clearance between the fork and the groove with a thickness gauge (Fig. 44-16D). A typical specification is that the clearance should not exceed 0.031 inch [0.8 mm].

➤ 44-21 INSPECTING BALL AND ROLLER BEARINGS

To inspect a bearing, first clean it as described in ➤44-19. Metal particles clinging to the bearing indicate it has

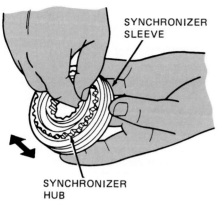

SYNCHRONIZER
SLEEVE

SYNCHRONIZER
HUB

(A) CHECKING HUB AND SLEEVE

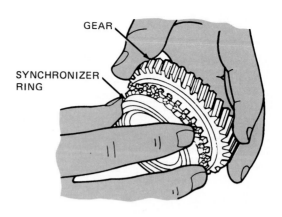

GEAR

SYNCHRONIZER
RING

(B) CHECKING RING WEAR

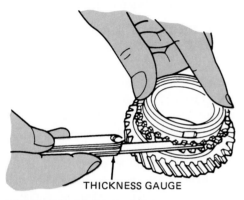

THICKNESS GAUGE

(C) MEASURING RING-TO-GEAR CLEARANCE

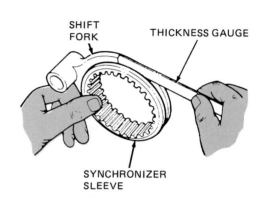

SHIFT
FORK

THICKNESS GAUGE

SYNCHRONIZER
SLEEVE

(D) MEASURING SLEEVE-TO-FORK CLEARANCE

Fig. 44-16 Checking synchronizer for wear and clearance. (*Ford Motor Company*)

become magnetized. Use a *demagnetizer* to remove the magnetism, or replace the bearing.

Figure 44-17 shows various types of roller-bearing failure and the recommended service procedure. Figure 44-18 shows various ball-bearing failures. In addition, inspect for damage or cracks around the snap-ring groove. Also, replace the bearing if the *ball cage* is cracked or deformed. Replace any bearing that is broken, worn, or rough.

If the bearing has no visible damage, give the bearing a *spin test*. Lubricate the bearing races lightly with clean oil. Turn the bearing back and forth slowly to coat the races and balls. Hold the bearing vertically by the inner race. Some vertical movement between the inner and outer races is acceptable.

Spin the outer ring several times by hand, *not with compressed air!* If you notice roughness or vibration, or if the outer ring stops abruptly, reclean the bearing. Then lubricate it and spin it again. Roughness is usually caused by particles of dirt in the bearing. Discard the bearing if it is still rough after cleaning and lubricating it three times.

Hold the bearing horizontally by the inner race with the snap-ring groove up. Spin the outer race several times by

hand. Discard the bearing if it is still rough after cleaning and lubricating it.

➤ 44-22 MANUAL-TRANSMISSION ASSEMBLY

Assemble the manual transmission following the procedure in the vehicle service manual. For proper operation of the clutch and transmission, misalignment or worn transmission parts must not allow the centerline of any shaft or gear to drop. The centerlines must be kept up. Check and adjust shaft and gear endplay during assembly. The preload on some bearings is set using shims.

After assembling the transmission and tightening all bolts to the specified torque, rotate the input shaft. Shift the transmission into neutral and each gear. Check for normal operation in each gearshift-lever position.

➤ 44-23 MANUAL-TRANSMISSION INSTALLATION

Installing a manual transmission is generally the reverse of removal. Clean the faces of the transmission case and fly-

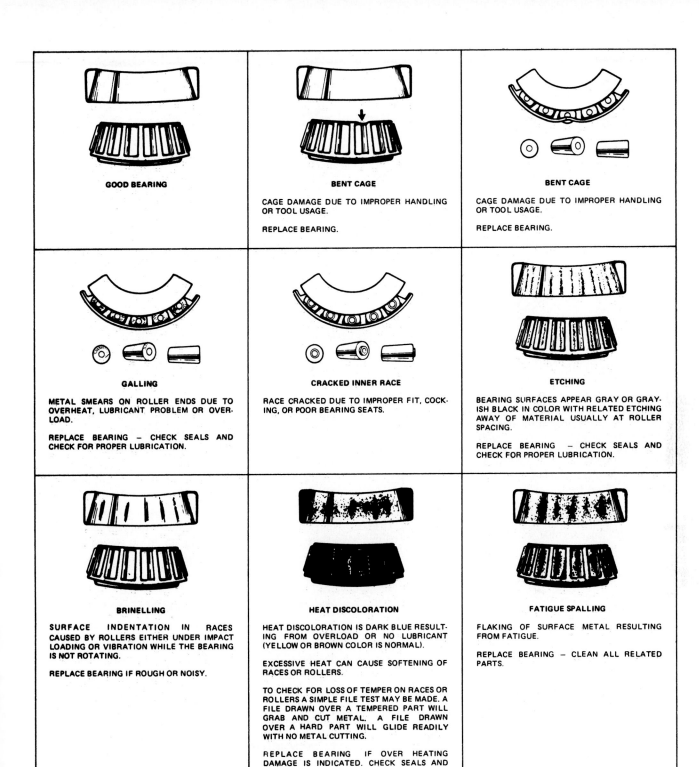

Fig. 44-17 Various types of roller-bearing failure and the recommended service procedure. (*Ford Motor Company*)

wheel housing. Place a small amount of lubricant on the splines of the input shaft. Turn the input shaft so that its splines align with the splines in the friction-disc hub. Install the guide pins in two top bolt holes of the clutch housing (Fig. 44-13).

With a helper or using the transmission jack (Fig. 44-14), lift the transmission and slide it forward into position. If necessary, put the transmission in gear and turn the output shaft until the input-shaft splines align and the transmission seats. Install the attaching bolts. Then remove the guide pins and install the proper bolts. Tighten the bolts to the specified torque.

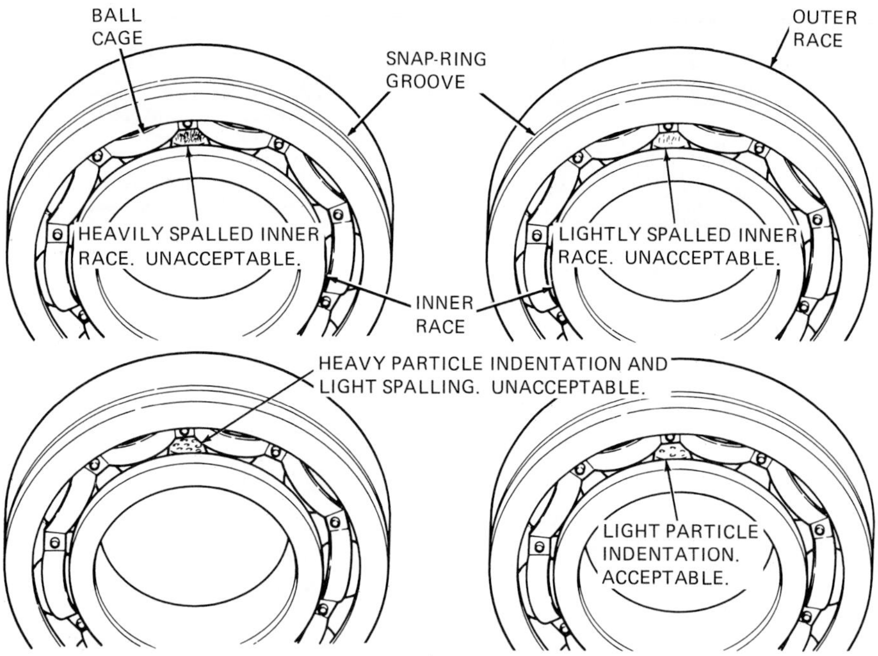

BALL CAGE

SNAP-RING GROOVE

OUTER RACE

Fig. 44-18 Ball-bearing failures. (*Ford Motor Company*)

HEAVILY SPALLED INNER RACE. UNACCEPTABLE.

LIGHTLY SPALLED INNER RACE. UNACCEPTABLE.

INNER RACE

HEAVY PARTICLE INDENTATION AND LIGHT SPALLING. UNACCEPTABLE.

LIGHT PARTICLE INDENTATION. ACCEPTABLE.

Careful! Do not force the transmission if it does not move into place and seat against the flywheel housing. The splines may not be aligned, or dirt, roughness, or transmission trouble may be preventing seating. Installing and tightening the attaching bolts will probably break the transmission case. Move the transmission back or remove it. Then correct the cause of the trouble.

Install the driveshaft, aligning the index marks (Fig. 44-12). This ensures that the driveshaft is in its original position. Use new fasteners, as required. Fill the transmission with the specified lubricant to the proper level (➤44-17). Install the speedometer cable and all other parts and connectors that were removed earlier (➤44-18). Connect and adjust the shift linkage, if necessary. Lower the vehicle to the floor. Depress the clutch pedal and check transmission operation. Then road test the vehicle to check for proper transmission operation in each gear.

MANUAL-TRANSAXLE SERVICE

➤ 44-24 MANUAL-TRANSAXLE MAINTENANCE

The manual transaxle requires no periodic service or routine maintenance. On some vehicles, a shift-linkage adjustment can be made. Follow the procedure in the vehicle service manual.

Manufacturers recommend changing the lubricant in the transaxle only if it becomes contaminated or internal damage occurs in the transaxle. Check the lubricant level periodically. The steps are the same as checking lubricant level in a manual transmission (➤44-17). Some manual transaxles do not have a separate fill plug. A short dipstick serves as the lubricant-level indicator.

Other manual transaxles use the speedometer-driven gear or the vehicle speed sensor as the lubricant-level indicator. To check the lubricant level, remove the speedometer cable from the speedometer-driven gear (Fig. 44-19A) or the wiring harness from the vehicle speed sensor (Fig. 44-19B). Then remove the speed sensor or the driven gear from the transaxle. With a clean shop towel, wipe off the lubricant from the gear or speed sensor. Fully reinsert it in the transaxle. Remove the gear or sensor and check the lubricant level (Fig. 44-20). It should be slightly above the top of the driven gear. If lubricant is needed, add it through the mounting hole for the gear or sensor.

➤ 44-25 MANUAL-TRANSAXLE SERVICE

Several different transaxle designs are used on cars with front-wheel and rear-wheel drive. Various suspension and transaxle installation methods are also used. Follow the procedure in the vehicle service manual to remove, service, and install the manual transaxle you are working on.

1. MANUAL-TRANSAXLE REMOVAL On some vehicles, the engine and transaxle must be removed as an assembly (Fig. 41-2). On others, support the engine and remove the transaxle from below the car. Drain the lubricant first, if required. Figure 44-21 shows the transaxle being lowered to the floor on a floor jack. Notice the use of a hand jack and block to support the engine. This prevents damage to the mounts and other parts.

Careful! Be sure the vehicle and engine are securely supported before removing the transaxle with a floor jack. Chain or clamp the transaxle to the jack. The transaxle must not roll off. This could injure you and damage the transaxle.

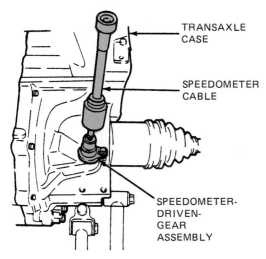

(A) SPEEDOMETER DRIVEN GEAR

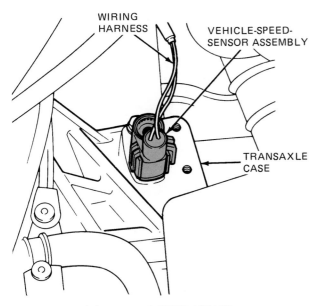

(B) VEHICLE SPEED SENSOR

Fig. 44-19 Checking manual-transaxle lubricant level by (A) removing the speedometer-driven gear or by (B) removing the vehicle-speed sensor. (*Ford Motor Company*)

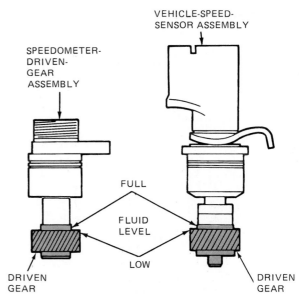

Fig. 44-20 The FULL mark on the driven gear, showing the specified lubricant, or fluid, level. (*Ford Motor Company*)

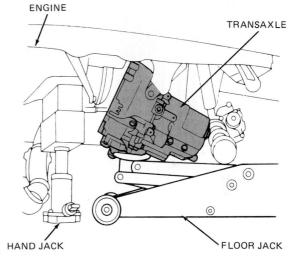

Fig. 44-21 Using a floor jack to lower the transaxle from the vehicle. (*Nissan Motor Corporation*)

Fig. 44-22 Engine support fixture in place to hold engine while transaxle is lowered from under the vehicle on a transmission jack. (*Chrysler Corporation*)

Figure 44-22 shows an *engine-support fixture* in place in the engine compartment. Hooks engage the lift brackets or other engine lift points. Then the vehicle can be raised on a lift and a transmission jack (Fig. 44-14) used to lower the transaxle.

> **CAUTION!**
>
> Follow the instructions when installing the engine-support fixture. It is not intended to support the entire weight of the engine and transaxle. If the fixture slips, the engine could drop and injure you.

2. MANUAL-TRANSAXLE OVERHAUL After removing the transaxle, place it in a holding fixture or on the workbench. Disassemble the transaxle following the pro-

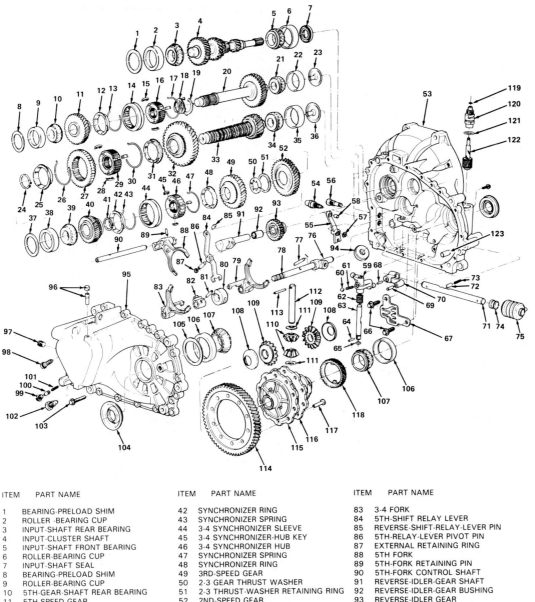

ITEM	PART NAME	ITEM	PART NAME	ITEM	PART NAME
1	BEARING-PRELOAD SHIM	42	SYNCHRONIZER RING	83	3-4 FORK
2	ROLLER -BEARING CUP	43	SYNCHRONIZER SPRING	84	5TH-SHIFT RELAY LEVER
3	INPUT-SHAFT REAR BEARING	44	3-4 SYNCHRONIZER SLEEVE	85	REVERSE-SHIFT-RELAY-LEVER PIN
4	INPUT-CLUSTER SHAFT	45	3-4 SYNCHRONIZER-HUB KEY	86	5TH-RELAY-LEVER PIVOT PIN
5	INPUT-SHAFT FRONT BEARING	46	3-4 SYNCHRONIZER HUB	87	EXTERNAL RETAINING RING
6	ROLLER-BEARING CUP	47	SYNCHRONIZER RING	88	5TH FORK
7	INPUT-SHAFT SEAL	48	SYNCHRONIZER RING	89	5TH-FORK RETAINING PIN
8	BEARING-PRELOAD SHIM	49	3RD-SPEED GEAR	90	5TH-FORK CONTROL SHAFT
9	ROLLER-BEARING CUP	50	2-3 GEAR THRUST WASHER	91	REVERSE-IDLER-GEAR SHAFT
10	5TH-GEAR-SHAFT REAR BEARING	51	2-3 THRUST-WASHER RETAINING RING	92	REVERSE-IDLER-GEAR BUSHING
11	5TH-SPEED GEAR	52	2ND-SPEED GEAR	93	REVERSE-IDLER GEAR
12	SYNCHRONIZER RING	53	CLUTCH HOUSING	94	CASE MAGNET
13	SYNCHRONIZER SPRING	54	BACKUP-LIGHT SWITCH	95	TRANSAXLE CASE
14	5TH-SYNCHRONIZER SLEEVE	55	REVERSE-RELAY LEVER	96	VENT ASSEMBLY
15	5TH-SYNCHRONIZER HUB KEY	56	REVERSE-RELAY-LEVER PIVOT PIN	97	FILL PLUG
16	5TH-SYNCHPONIZER HUB	57	EXTERNAL RETAINING RING	98	REVERSE-SHAFT RETAINING BOLT
17	SYNCHRONIZER SPRING	58	REVERSE-RELAY LEVER PIN	99	DETENT-PLUNGER RETAINING SCREW
18	SYNCHRONIZER RETAINING SPACER	59	SHIFT LEVER	100	SHIFT-SHAFT DETENT PLUNGER
19	SYNCHRONIZER-KEY RETAINER	60	BALL	101	SHIFT-SHAFT DETENT SPRING
20	5TH-GEAR DRIVE SHAFT	61	5TH-REVERSE INHIBITOR SPRING	102	FORK-INTERLOCK-SLEEVE RETAINING PIN
21	5TH-GEAR-SHAFT FRONT BEARING	62	3-4 SHIFT-BIAS SPRING	103	TRANSAXLE-CASE BOLT
22	ROLLER-BEARING CUP	63	SHIFT-LEVER SHAFT	104	LEFT DIFFERENTIAL SEAL
23	5TH-GEAR FUNNEL	64	SHIFT-LEVER PIN	105	DIFFERENTIAL-BEARING-PRELOAD SHIM
24	1-2 SYNCHRONIZER RETAINING RING	65	SHIFT-LEVER-SHAFT SEAL	106	DIFFERENTIAL-BEARING CUP
25	SYNCHRONIZER RING	66	SHIFT-GATE ATTACHING BOLTS	107	DIFFERENTIAL BEARING
26	SYNCHRONIZER SPRING	67	SHIFT-GATE PLATE	108	SIDE-GEAR THRUST WASHER
27	REVERSE-SLIDING GEAR	68	SELECTOR-ARM PIN	109	SIDE GEAR
28	1-2 SYNCHRONIZER-HUB KEY	69	SHIFT-GATE SELECTOR PIN	110	PINION GEARS
29	1-2 SYNCHRONIZER HUB	70	SHIFT-GATE SELECTOR ARM	111	PINION-GEAR THRUST WASHER
30	SYNCHRONIZER SPRING	71	INPUT SHIFT SHAFT	112	PINION-GEAR SHAFT
31	SYNCHRONIZER RING	72	SHIFT-SHAFT DETENT PLUNGER	113	PINION-GEAR-SHAFT RETAINING PIN
32	1ST-SPEED GEAR	73	SHIFT-SHAFT DETENT SPRING	114	FINAL-DRIVE GEAR
33	MAINSHAFT	74	SHIFT-SHAFT SEAL	115	LEFT DIFFERENTIAL CASE
34	MAINSHAFT FRONT BEARING	75	SHIFT-SHAFT BOOT	116	RIGHT DIFFERENTIAL CASE
35	ROLLER-BEARING CUP	76	FORK-CONTROL-SHAFT BLOCK	117	CASE-AND-DRIVE-GEAR ATTACHING
36	MAINSHAFT FUNNEL	77	REVERSE-RELAY-LEVER ACTUATING PIN		RIVET
37	BEARING-PRELOAD SHIM	78	MAIN-SHIFT-FORK CONTROL SHAFT	118	SPEEDOMETER-DRIVE GEAR
38	ROLLER-BEARING CUP	79	1-2 FORK	119	O-RING SEAL
39	MAINSHAFT REAR BEARING	80	FORK-INTERLOCK SLEEVE	120	SPEEDOMETER-GEAR RETAINER
40	4TH-SPEED GEAR	81	SPRING PIN	121	SPEEDOMETER-RETAINER-TO-CASE SEAL
41	3-4 SYNCHRONIZER RETAINING RING	82	FORK-SELECTOR ARM	122	SPEEDOMETER-DRIVEN GEAR
				123	CASE-TO-CLUTCH-HOUSING DOWEL

Fig. 44-23 Disassembled five-speed manual transaxle. (*Ford Motor Company*)

cedure in the vehicle service manual. Cleaning, inspection, and servicing procedures for the manual transaxle are similar to those for a manual transmission (➤44-19 to 44-21).

Figure 44-23 shows a completely disassembled five-speed manual transaxle. The shafts, gears, and power flow in this transaxle are shown in Figs. 43-16 and 43-17. Chapter 45 covers servicing the final drive and differential.

3. MANUAL-TRANSAXLE INSTALLATION Before installing the manual transaxle, check that it works properly.

Shift it into each gear and turn the input shaft. The final-drive ring gear, differential case, and differential side gears should turn.

Fill the transaxle with the specified lubricant to the proper level (➤44-23). Install the speedometer cable and all other parts and connectors that were removed earlier. Connect and adjust the shift linkage, if necessary. Lower the vehicle to the floor. Start the engine and check transaxle operation. Then road test the vehicle to check for proper transaxle operation in each gear.

MULTIPLE-CHOICE TEST

*Select the **one** correct, best, or most probable answer to each question.*
You can find the answers in the section indicated at the end of each question.

1. Hard shifting into gear may be caused by (➤44-4)
   a. a defective synchronizer
   b. an improperly adjusted clutch
   c. a twisted mainshaft
   d. all of the above
2. The transmission may stick in gear because of all the following EXCEPT (➤44-5)
   a. gearshift linkage out of adjustment
   b. clutch not disengaging
   c. stiff gearshift-lever boot
   d. synchronizer sleeve binding
3. Technician A says the transmission may jump out of gear because of worn splines in the synchronizer sleeve. Technician B says the transmission may jump out of gear because of worn external teeth on the gear. Who is right? (➤44-6)
   a. A only
   b. B only
   c. both A and B
   d. neither A nor B
4. Gear clash while shifting could be caused by (➤44-7)
   a. gears loose on the mainshaft
   b. clutch not engaging
   c. broken shift fork
   d. worn synchronizer ring

5. Noise from the transmission in gear could be caused by (➤44-8)
   a. a worn or loose pilot bearing
   b. excessive lubricant
   c. worn or damaged gear teeth
   d. all of the above
6. Noise from the transmission in neutral could be caused by (➤44-9)
   a. clutch not engaging
   b. worn or dry bearings
   c. chipped or broken teeth on mainshaft gears
   d. defective extension-housing seal
7. Noise from the transmission in reverse could be caused by (➤44-10)
   a. worn or damaged reverse idler gear
   b. defective front-bearing retainer
   c. clutch not disengaging
   d. all of the above
8. Transmission oil leaks may be caused by all the following EXCEPT (➤44-12)
   a. jumping out of gear
   b. foaming due to incorrect lubricant
   c. excessive lubricant
   d. damaged or missing oil seals

REVIEW QUESTIONS

1. What is the importance of roadtesting the car with the customer? (➤44-1)
2. Describe how to road test a vehicle to locate manual-transaxle and drive-train noise. (➤44-14)
3. How can you identify differential noise and wheel-bearing noise in a front-wheel-drive vehicle? (➤44-15)

4. Explain how to clean and inspect manual-transmission parts. (➤44-20)
5. Describe how to inspect ball and roller bearings. (➤44-21)

CHAPTER 45

DRIVESHAFTS, UNIVERSAL JOINTS, DIFFERENTIALS, AND DRIVE AXLES

After studying this chapter, and with proper instruction and equipment, you should be able to:

- Describe the various types of universal joints and CV joints, and explain how each works.
- Diagnose, service, and replace a universal joint.
- Diagnose, service, and replace a CV joint.
- Describe the construction and operation of an open differential and a limited-slip differential.
- Diagnose and service an open differential and a limited-slip differential.

➤ 45-1 DRIVE LINES

An automotive *drive line* is an assembly of one or more *driveshafts, universal joints,* and *slip joints*. It transmits torque through varying angles and distances from one shaft to another. Vehicles with front engine and rear-wheel-drive (RWD) have a long *propeller shaft* or driveshaft extending from the transmission to the rear axle (Figs. 44-12 and 45-1). Front-wheel-drive (FWD) vehicles usually have the engine-transaxle assembly mounted transversely. Short driveshafts or *halfshafts* extend from the transaxle to the front wheels (Fig. 44-9).

Various types of driveshafts, universal joints, and slip joints are used to carry engine power from the transmission or transaxle to the wheels. The following sections describe the different drive lines, and their diagnosis and service.

DRIVE LINES FOR REAR-WHEEL DRIVE

➤ 45-2 REAR-WHEEL-DRIVE DRIVE LINES

In a RWD vehicle with front engine, the drive line connects the transmission output shaft to the *rear axle*

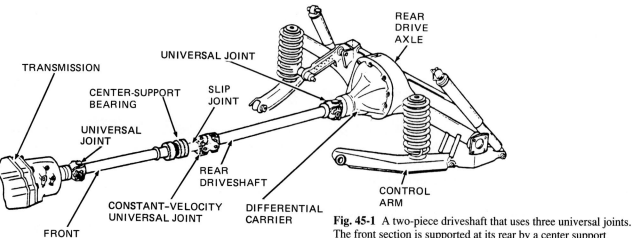

TRANSMISSION

CENTER-SUPPORT BEARING

UNIVERSAL JOINT

SLIP JOINT

UNIVERSAL JOINT

REAR DRIVE AXLE

REAR DRIVESHAFT

CONSTANT-VELOCITY UNIVERSAL JOINT

DIFFERENTIAL CARRIER

CONTROL ARM

FRONT DRIVESHAFT

Fig. 45-1 A two-piece driveshaft that uses three universal joints. The front section is supported at its rear by a center support bearing. (*Buick Division of General Motors Corporation*)

(Figs. 44-12 and 45-1). It contains the *final-drive gears, differential,* and *axle shafts* which drive the rear wheels. Later sections describe these parts.

There are two important facts about drive-line action.

1. The engine and transmission attach to the car body or frame through mounts (➤44-16) that permit little movement.
2. The rear-axle housing (with the rear wheels) moves up and down.

These actions mean that drive-line *length* and drive *angle* must change during normal vehicle operation.

Figure 45-2 shows how up-and-down movement of the wheels causes these changes. At the top, the wheels are up and the drive angle is small. The drive line is at its maximum length. At the bottom, the wheels have moved down to their lowest position. This happens when the wheels drop into a depression in the road. Then the drive angle increases and drive-line length decreases. The shortening occurs because as the rear wheels and axle housing swing down, they also swing forward. The axle housing is attached to the vehicle body or frame by leaf springs or *control arms* (Fig. 45-1). This makes the housing swing in a shorter arc than the drive line.

The drive line includes two kinds of joints: a *slip joint* and *universal joints* (Fig. 45-1). The slip joint takes care of changes in drive-line length. The universal joints on each end of the driveshaft take care of changes in drive angle.

Many driveshafts are made of hollow steel tube. Others are aluminum, or a composite material made of aluminum and carbon fiber. These materials allow the driveshaft to be lighter and quieter than steel tube. There is less vibration and no rusting.

Some long drive lines use two-piece driveshafts (Fig. 45-1). A third universal joint is located between each

section, along with a *center-support bearing.* The front driveshaft attaches to the transmission output shaft and spins in the center-support bearing. This prevents "whipping" of the drive line as it rotates. The rear driveshaft has a slip joint and a universal joint at the front. These allow the rear driveshaft to change length and drive angle.

➤ 45-3 UNIVERSAL JOINTS

A universal joint allows driving torque to be carried through two shafts that are at an angle with each other. Figure 45-3 shows a simple *Cardan universal joint.* It is a double-hinged joint made of two Y-shaped *yokes* and a cross-shaped member or *spider.* One yoke is on the driving shaft, and the other is on the driven shaft. The four arms of the spider or *trunnions* are assembled in needle bearings in the two yokes (Fig. 45-4).

The driving-shaft-and-yoke force the spider to rotate. The other two trunnions of the spider then cause the driven yoke to rotate. When the two shafts are at an angle with each other, the needle bearings permit the yokes to swing around on the trunnions with each revolution.

There are several types of universal joints. The simplest is the spider-and-two-yoke design (Figs. 45-3 and 45-4).

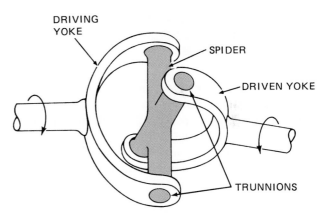

Fig. 45-3 A simple or single Cardan universal joint.

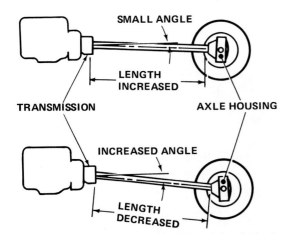

Fig. 45-2 The rear-axle housing, with differential and wheels, moves up and down. As it does, the angle between the transmission output shaft and the driveshaft changes. The length of the driveshaft also changes. The driveshaft shortens as the angle increases because the axle housing moves in a shorter arc than the driveshaft. The center point of the axle-housing arc is the rear-spring hanger or control-arm attachment to the frame.

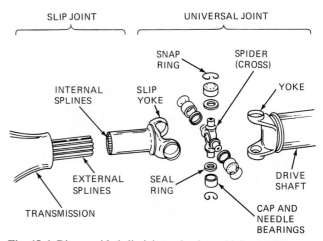

Fig. 45-4 Disassembled slip joint and universal joint. (*ATW*)

However, this is not a *constant-velocity universal joint*. If the two shafts are at an angle, the driven shaft speeds up and slows down slightly, twice per revolution. The greater the angle, the greater the speed varies. This can cause a pulsating load that wears the bearings and gears in the drive axle. Constant-velocity universal joints or *CV joints* eliminate this unwanted speed change.

Figure 45-1 shows a two-piece drive line with the sections connected through a *double-Cardan universal joint* at the center. The double-Cardan joint is one type of constant-velocity universal joint. It basically is two simple universal joints assembled together (Fig. 45-5). They are linked by a centering ball and socket which splits the angle between the two shafts. This cancels any speed variation because the two joints operate at the same angle (half the total). The acceleration of one joint is canceled by the deceleration of the second joint. Later sections describe other types of universal joints.

> ## 45-4 SLIP JOINTS

Figure 45-4 shows a slip joint. It has outside splines on the shaft and matching internal splines in a mating hollow shaft or yoke. When assembled, the splines cause the shafts to rotate together while they can move back and forth. This changes the length of the driveshaft.

> ## 45-5 DRIVESHAFTS FOR INDEPENDENT REAR SUSPENSION

Some cars with front engine and rear drive have *independent rear suspension* (Fig. 45-6). This allows one rear wheel to move up and down without affecting the other. The wheels are driven by short driveshafts or halfshafts with universal joints on each end. Single-Cardan universal joints and tubular shafts are shown in Fig. 45-6. Other

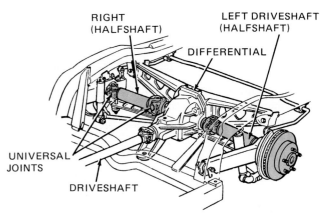

Fig. 45-6 Independent rear suspension using short driveshafts, or halfshafts, with universal joints on each end to drive the rear wheels. (*Chevrolet Division of General Motors Corporation*)

types are used in various rear-drive and front-drive systems (➤45-7 and 45-8).

DRIVE LINES FOR FRONT-WHEEL DRIVE

> ## 45-6 FRONT-WHEEL-DRIVE DRIVE LINES

Front-wheel drive eliminates the long driveshaft needed in rear-drive vehicles. It can also eliminate the long tunnel in the floor pan needed to accommodate the driveshaft. Figure 45-7 shows how the engine-transaxle assembly mounts between the front wheels of a vehicle with front-wheel drive. Power flows from the differential section of the transaxle through halfshafts to the wheels.

Halfshafts may be either solid or tubular, and equal or unequal in length (Fig. 45-8). Some front-wheel-drive cars

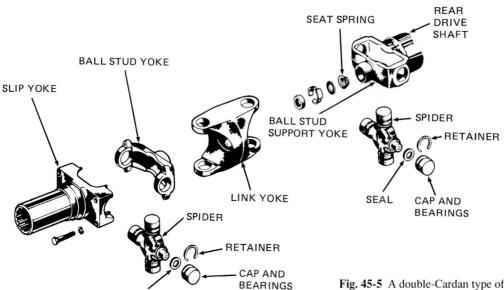

Fig. 45-5 A double-Cardan type of constant-velocity universal joint.

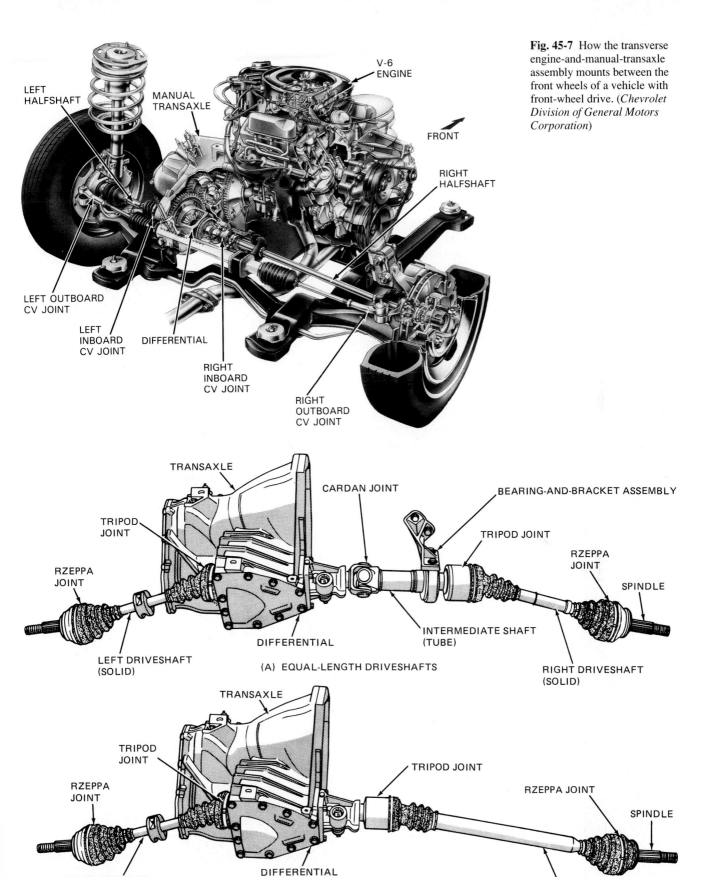

LEFT HALFSHAFT

MANUAL TRANSAXLE

V-6 ENGINE

FRONT

RIGHT HALFSHAFT

LEFT OUTBOARD CV JOINT

LEFT INBOARD CV JOINT

DIFFERENTIAL

RIGHT INBOARD CV JOINT

RIGHT OUTBOARD CV JOINT

Fig. 45-7 How the transverse engine-and-manual-transaxle assembly mounts between the front wheels of a vehicle with front-wheel drive. (*Chevrolet Division of General Motors Corporation*)

TRANSAXLE

CARDAN JOINT

BEARING-AND-BRACKET ASSEMBLY

TRIPOD JOINT

TRIPOD JOINT

RZEPPA JOINT

RZEPPA JOINT

SPINDLE

LEFT DRIVESHAFT (SOLID)

DIFFERENTIAL

INTERMEDIATE SHAFT (TUBE)

RIGHT DRIVESHAFT (SOLID)

(A) EQUAL-LENGTH DRIVESHAFTS

TRANSAXLE

TRIPOD JOINT

TRIPOD JOINT

RZEPPA JOINT

RZEPPA JOINT

SPINDLE

LEFT DRIVESHAFT (SOLID)

DIFFERENTIAL

RIGHT DRIVESHAFT (TUBE)

(B) UNEQUAL-LENGTH DRIVESHAFTS

Fig. 45-8 Front-wheel-drive drive lines use (A) equal-length driveshafts or (B) unequal-length driveshafts. Torque steer is more noticeable with unequal-length driveshafts. (*Chrysler Corporation*)

have noticeable *torque steer*. This is the tendency of cars with unequal-length halfshafts to pull to one side during heavy acceleration. The car pulls toward the side with the longer halfshaft.

The use of an *intermediate shaft* (Fig. 45-8A) allows the use of equal-length driveshafts. This helps equalize the torque to the two front wheels. With equal torque, there is no tendency for torque steer.

Various types of CV joints are used on both ends of the halfshafts. The outer CV joints (➤45-7) are *fixed joints*. They only permit the angle of drive to change. The inner CV joints (➤45-8) are *sliding* or *plunging joints* (Fig. 45-9). They also allow the effective length of each shaft to change as the wheels move up and down, and turn in and out for steering.

CV joints are packed with special grease and covered with a bellows-type rubber *boot* (Figs. 45-7 and 45-8). Clamps seal each end of the boot to the shaft and joint housing. This protects the joint by keeping the grease in, and keeping water and other contaminants out.

➤ 45-7 OUTER CV JOINTS

The most widely-used outer CV joint is the *Rzeppa* (pronounced *Sheppa*) *CV joint*. It can turn the driven shaft at a constant-velocity while running at up to a 40-degree angle. The Rzeppa joint (Figs. 45-8 and 45-10) has six steel balls that move in curved grooves between an inner race and an outer race. A cage holds the balls in position. Torque is

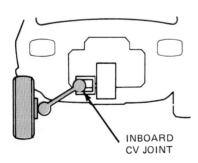

(A) NORMAL SUSPENSION HEIGHT

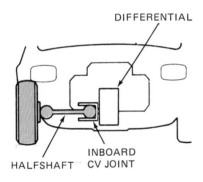

(B) SUSPENSION AND
HALFSHAFT EXTENDED

Fig. 45-9 Sliding, or plunging, action in a constant-velocity (CV) joint as the wheel moves up and down. (*AC-Delco Division of General Motors Corporation*)

588

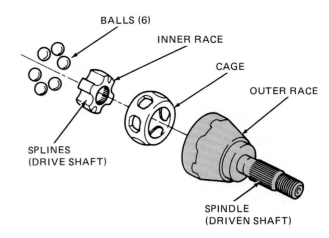

(A) RZEPPA CV-JOINT CONSTRUCTION

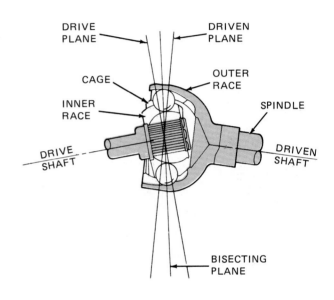

(B) RZEPPA CV-JOINT OPERATION

Fig. 45-10 Construction and operation of a Rzeppa CV joint, widely used as the outer or outboard joint. (*AC-Delco Division of General Motors Corporation*)

transmitted from the inner race, through the balls, to the outer race.

As the Rzeppa joint rotates, the position of the balls changes so they remain in the *bisecting plane* (Fig. 45-10B). The balls split the angle between the drive shaft and the driven shaft. This turns the driven shaft at a constant velocity regardless of the angle of drive.

➤ 45-8 INNER CV JOINTS

The CV joints on the inboard or inner ends of the halfshafts (Figs. 45-7 and 45-8) have less motion than the outer joints. This is because the inner joints do not have to move through the greater angles needed for steering. However, the inner joints are sliding or plunging joints (Fig. 45-9). They move in and out to change the effective length of the halfshaft as the wheels move up and down.

Two types of CV joints are widely used as inner joints. These are the plunging-type Rzeppa or *double-offset CV joint* and the plunging *tripod CV joint.*

1. DOUBLE-OFFSET CV JOINT The right inboard CV joint in Fig. 45-7 is a double-offset joint. The drive shaft or *stub shaft* (Fig. 45-11) fits into a *side gear* in the differential (➤45-13). Splines in the inner race mesh with splines on the inner end of the halfshaft or driven shaft.

Operation of the joint is the same as described for the Rzeppa joint in ➤45-7. However, the outer race is longer and therefore has longer grooves (Fig. 45-11). As the car wheels move up and down, the balls and inner race move back and forth in the grooves. This plunging action changes the effective length of the halfshaft.

2. PLUNGING-TRIPOD CV JOINT The housing or *tulip* (Fig. 45-12) of the plunging-tripod CV joint also has a stub shaft that fits into a differential side gear. Inside the joint, three balls mount on needle bearings which fit over the arms or trunnions of a spider. The spider is splined to the inner end of the halfshaft. The housing has three grooves in which the balls can move back and forth.

Torque is transmitted from the housing, through the balls and spider, to the halfshaft. As the drive-angle changes, the balls move to split the angle between the drive and driven shafts. Up-and-down movement of the wheels causes the balls to move back-and-forth in the grooves. This changes the effective length of the halfshaft.

OTHER DRIVE LINES

➤ 45-9 REAR DRIVE WITH REAR-MOUNTED ENGINE

A few cars have a rear-mounted engine and rear-wheel drive. One layout is similar to the front-engine front-drive arrangement shown in Fig. 45-7. The rear wheels are independently suspended. However, the wheels and the outboard CV joints do not turn through wide angles for steering. Some of these cars have plunging CV joints at both ends of each halfshaft.

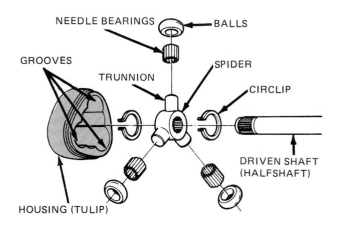

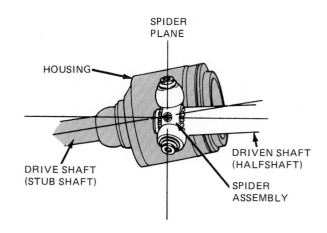

Fig. 45-12 Construction and operation of the inboard tripod CV joint. (*AC-Delco Division of General Motors Corporation*)

➤ 45-10 DRIVE LINES FOR FOUR-WHEEL DRIVE

In four-wheel-drive (4WD) vehicles, the rear-drive arrangement is often like the system described in ➤45-2. The front drive may use Cardan universal joints in an arrangement similar to the independent-rear-suspension system described in ➤45-5. This combination of front-and-rear drive is common in light trucks. Passenger vehicles with *all-wheel drive* (AWD) may use CV joints and halfshafts at both the front (Fig. 45-7) and rear of the vehicle. Chapter 46 covers four-wheel drive.

REAR-DRIVE AXLES

➤ 45-11 TYPES OF AXLES

An *axle* is a theoretical or actual crossbar supporting a vehicle, on which one or more wheels turn. The axle is either a *live axle* or a *dead axle*. A live axle or *drive axle*

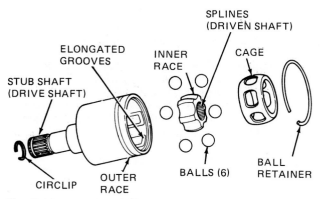

Fig. 45-11 Disassembled double-offset CV joint, used as the inner or inboard joint. (*AC-Delco Division of General Motors Corporation*)

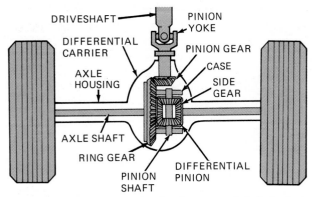

Fig. 45-13 Rear drive axle, showing the gears and shafts in the final drive and differential. (*ATW*)

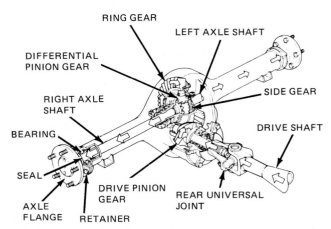

Fig. 45-14 Power flow from the driveshaft through the drive axle to the axle flanges on which the wheels mount. (*Ford Motor Company*)

supports part of the weight of the vehicle and drives the wheels connected to the halfshafts or *axle shafts* (Fig. 45-13). A dead axle or *non-drive axle* carries part of the weight, but does not drive the wheels. A drive axle on which the wheels can pivot for steering is a *steerable drive axle*. It is used on four-wheel-drive trucks (Chap. 46). Most vehicles with front engine and rear drive have a non-steering drive axle or *rear-drive axle*. This is the type shown in Fig. 45-13.

➤ 45-12 FUNCTIONS OF REAR-DRIVE AXLE

The rear-drive axle or *rear axle* is often suspended from the body or frame of the vehicle by leaf springs attached to the axle housing. Vehicles with other types of springs position the rear axle with control arms (Fig. 45-1).

A rear axle performs several functions. These include:

1. Changing the direction of driveshaft rotation by 90 degrees to rotate the axle shafts.
2. Providing a final speed reduction between the driveshaft and the axle shafts through the final-drive gears (➤45-14).
3. Providing differential action (➤45-18) so one wheel can turn at a different speed than the other, if necessary.
4. Providing axle shafts or halfshafts to drive the rear wheels.
5. Acting as a thrust- and torque-reaction member during acceleration and braking (Chap. 52).

➤ 45-13 REAR-AXLE CONSTRUCTION

All other parts of the rear axle are assembled in, or attached to, the *rear-axle housing* (Figs. 45-13 and 45-14). It supports part of the vehicle weight and contains the final-drive gears, differential, axle shafts, and bearings. Shaft seals prevent the gear lubricant from leaking out. The axle shafts are solid shafts, with no universal joints. The wheels attach to mounting flanges on the outer ends of the axle shafts (Fig. 45-14). Splines on the inner ends fit into the differential side gears.

➤ 45-14 FINAL-DRIVE GEARS

The final drive is the gear set that transmits torque received from the transmission output shaft to the differential. The gear set is made up of a smaller driving gear or *pinion gear* and a larger driven gear or *ring gear* (Figs. 45-13 and 45-14). The smaller gear in a gear set is always the pinion gear.

Rear-drive axles use *hypoid gears* (Figs. 43-6 and 45-14). Hypoid gears have teeth cut in a spiral form, with the pinion gear set below the centerline of the ring gear. This lowers the driveshaft, which allows a lower floor pan and driveshaft tunnel. It also allows more teeth to be in contact to carry the load.

The ring gear is three to four times larger than the pinion gear (Fig. 45-14). When the pinion turns the ring gear, it reduces the speed of the axle shafts while increasing the torque applied to them.

The pinion gear connects to the rear end of the driveshaft (Fig. 45-13), and is assembled into the front of the axle housing or *differential carrier*. The ring gear attaches to the *differential case*. The differential side gears are splined to the inner ends of the axle shafts. Rotation of the ring gear rotates the differential case (➤45-18).

> **NOTE** The final-drive gears described above are *bevel* or hypoid gears (Fig. 43-6). They change the direction of power flow by 90 degrees so rotation of the driveshaft rotates the axle shafts (Fig. 45-14). In a transaxle, the final-drive gears are usually *helical gears* (Figs. 43-3 and 43-15). These are used because the pinion gear and ring gear are on parallel shafts. Figure 43-6 shows both types of gears.

➤ 45-15 AXLE RATIO

The ring gear has many more teeth than the pinion gear (Fig. 45-13). This produces a gear reduction through the differential. Depending on vehicle and engine design, passenger-car axle ratios vary from about 2:1 to about 4:1. The ring gear has from two to four times as many teeth as the pinion gear. Therefore, the pinion gear must rotate from two to four times to turn the ring gear once.

The actual gear ratio through a drive axle is the *axle ratio* or *final-drive ratio*. It can be calculated by dividing the number of teeth on the ring gear by the number of teeth on the pinion gear.

➤ 45-16 GEAR-TOOTH NOMENCLATURE

Figure 45-15 shows gear-tooth *nomenclature* (a set of names) for the parts of meshing bevel-gear teeth. The mating teeth to the left show *clearance* and *backlash.* Clearance is the distance between the top of the tooth of one gear and the valley between the adjacent teeth of the mating gear. Backlash is the distance between adjacent meshing teeth in the driving and driven gears. It is the distance one gear can rotate backward before it will cause the other gear to move.

The *heel* is the larger section of the gear tooth (Fig. 45-15) and is farthest from the center of the ring gear. The *toe* is the smaller or inner end of the gear tooth.

DIFFERENTIALS

➤ 45-17 DIFFERENTIAL APPLICATIONS

The differential is a device or gear assembly between two shafts that permits the shafts to turn at different speeds (if necessary) while continuing to transmit torque. It is used in drive axles to allow different rates of wheel rotation on curves.

Differentials are used in:

1. The rear-drive axle of front-engine, rear-wheel-drive vehicles.
2. The transaxles of front-engine, front-wheel-drive and rear-engine, rear-wheel-drive vehicles.
3. The front-drive axle and rear-drive axle of four-wheel-drive vehicles.
4. The *transfer case* (Chap. 46) of some four-wheel-drive vehicles.

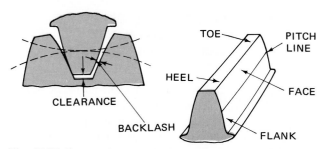

Fig. 45-15 Gear-tooth nomenclature. (*Chrysler Corporation*)

| NOTE | Chapter 46 describes the differentials in four-wheel-drive and all-wheel-drive vehicles. These differentials may be a different type than described below. |

➤ 45-18 DIFFERENTIAL ACTION

Figure 45-16 shows the action of the differential in the rear-drive axle. The vehicle is making a 90-degree or right-angle turn with the inner rear wheel turning on a 20-foot [6.1 m] radius. The inner rear wheel travels about 31 feet [9.5 m]. The outer rear wheel travels about 39 feet [12 m]. The differential permits power-flow to both drive wheels while allowing the wheels to travel different distances during the turn.

Suppose both rear wheels are attached to the ends of a solid shaft. Both wheels would rotate together at the same speed and try to travel the same distance all the time. If the vehicle turned as in Fig. 45-16, each tire would skid an average of 4 feet [1.22 m] during the turn. The tires would wear quickly and the vehicle would be difficult to control. The differential avoids these problems. It allows the outer wheel to turn faster and therefore travel farther than the inner wheel during a turn.

| NOTE | In front-drive vehicles with transverse engine, the differential is part of the transaxle and located between the front wheels (Figs. 43-4 and 43-15). When the vehicle makes a turn, the two front wheels travel different paths and go different distances (Fig. 45-16). |

➤ 45-19 DIFFERENTIAL OPERATION

Figure 45-17 shows the basic parts of a differential. Figure 45-13 shows an assembled differential. When the car is on a straight, level road and both tires have equal *traction,*

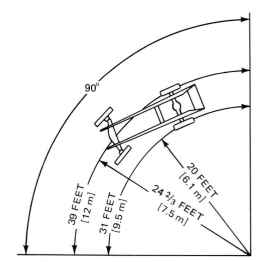

Fig. 45-16 Difference in wheel travel as a rear-wheel-drive vehicle makes a 90-degree turn with the inner wheel turning on a 20-foot [6.1 m] radius.

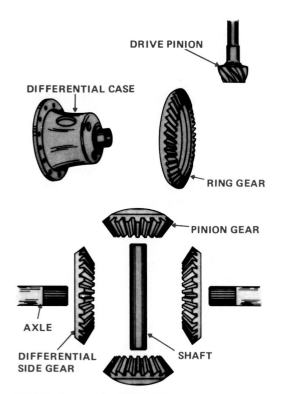

Fig. 45-17 Basic parts of a differential.

there is no differential action. (Traction is the adhesive or pulling friction of a tire on the road.) The ring gear, differential case, differential pinion gears, and differential side gears all turn as a unit. The pinion gears do not rotate on the pinion shaft, but rather turn both side gears and axle shafts at the same speed.

When the vehicle enters a curve, the resistance of the inner tire to turning begins to increase. It now has a shorter distance to travel (Fig. 45-18). The outer tire must travel a greater distance. The differential pinion gears are applying

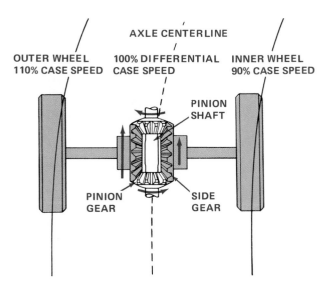

Fig. 45-18 Differential action on turns. (*Chevrolet Division of General Motors Corporation*)

the same torque to each side gear. However, the unequal loads from the tires cause the pinion gears to begin rotating on the pinion shaft. They walk around the slower-turning inner-wheel side gear. This increases the speed of the outer-wheel side gear by the same amount.

Figure 45-18 shows differential action in a typical turn. The differential case speed is 100 percent. The rotating pinion gears carry 90 percent of this speed to the slower-turning inner wheel. The rotating pinion gears carry 110 percent of the speed to the faster-turning outer wheel.

The differential described above is a *standard* or *open differential*. It delivers the same torque to each wheel. If one tire begins to slip and spin, the open differential divides the rotary speed unequally. The tire with good traction slows and stops. This may also stop the vehicle or prevent it from moving.

➤ 45-20 LIMITED-SLIP DIFFERENTIALS

Instead of an open differential, some drive axles have a *limited-slip differential* (Fig. 45-19). It has *clutches* or *cones* in the case. When a wheel spins, the clutches or cones lock the case to the differential side gears. This prevents differential action. Both axles now turn at the same speed.

Each *multiple-disc clutch* (Fig. 45-19) is made of a series of alternating *friction plates* and *steel plates*. The friction plates are splined to the side gear and rotate with it. The steel plates have tangs that fit into the case. When the clutch engages, the plates are forced together. This locks the case to the side gear, and transmits torque to the axle shaft and wheel. Most limited-slip differentials have *preload springs* between the side gears. The spring force pushes outward on the side gears to help provide a quicker locking action.

As the car rounds a curve during normal driving, enough force is released to allow the clutch to slip (Fig. 45-20). This permits the outer wheel to turn faster than the inner wheel.

DRIVESHAFT AND UNIVERSAL-JOINT DIAGNOSIS AND SERVICE

➤ 45-21 DRIVESHAFT AND UNIVERSAL-JOINT TROUBLE DIAGNOSIS

Figure 45-21 is a trouble-diagnosis chart for the drive line in vehicles with front-engine and rear-wheel drive. Complaints such as roughness, vibration, and body boom may not be the fault of the drive line. To determine if the drive line is the cause, connect a tachometer to the engine.

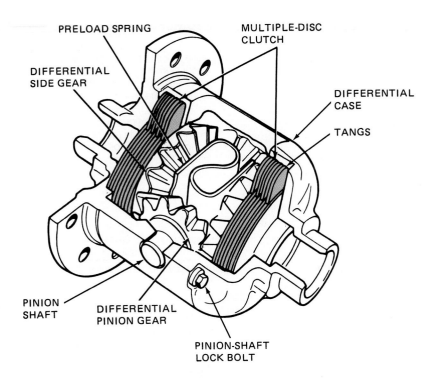

PRELOAD SPRING

MULTIPLE-DISC CLUTCH

DIFFERENTIAL SIDE GEAR

DIFFERENTIAL CASE

TANGS

PINION SHAFT

DIFFERENTIAL PINION GEAR

PINION-SHAFT LOCK BOLT

Fig. 45-19 Limited-slip differential using two multiple-disc clutches. (*Ford Motor Company*)

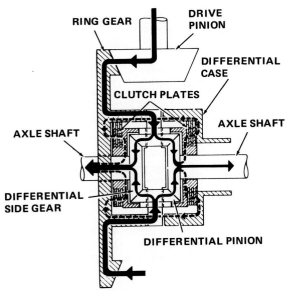

RING GEAR

DRIVE PINION

DIFFERENTIAL CASE

CLUTCH PLATES

AXLE SHAFT

AXLE SHAFT

DIFFERENTIAL SIDE GEAR

DIFFERENTIAL PINION

Fig. 45-20 Power flow through a limited-slip differential when rounding a turn. Heavy arrows show greater speed to the left axle. (*Chrysler Corporation*)

Position the tachometer so you can see it safely while driving. Then road test the vehicle.

During the road test, note the engine speed (rpm) at which the vibration or roughness is most noticeable. Then shift the transmission to a different gear. Drive the vehicle at the same engine speed on the tachometer at which the vibration or roughness occurred before. Note any change in the condition.

If the vibration occurs at the same engine speed regardless of transmission gear, the drive line is probably *not* the cause. However, if the vibration decreases or dis-

appears when the transmission is shifted to a different gear, there may be a problem in the drive line. Check the possible causes listed in the trouble-diagnosis chart (Fig. 45-21).

➤ 45-22 DRIVESHAFT AND UNIVERSAL-JOINT SERVICE

Driveshafts and Cardan universal joints do not require periodic maintenance. Most U joints are lubricated for life during original assembly and cannot be lubricated in the vehicle. A noisy or worn universal joint should be replaced. Follow the procedures in the vehicle service manual. A typical procedure for replacing a single-Cardan universal joint is given below.

Before removing the driveshaft, check for index marks (Fig. 44-12) or mark the position and alignment of the driveshaft and yoke. The driveshaft and universal joints are balanced during original assembly. Aligning the marks during installation will keep the assembly in balance.

After removing the driveshaft (➤44-18), place it on a workbench. Remove the external or internal snap rings (Figs. 45-4 and 45-5) from the bearing caps. If the snap ring is difficult to remove, lightly tap the end of the cap with a hammer. This will relieve the force against the snap ring. Use a press or a vise and push one bearing cap against the spider (Fig. 45-22A). The spider then pushes the other cap out of the yoke. Reposition the driveshaft and remove the remaining cap.

Clean and inspect the seals, snap rings, needle bearings, spider trunnions, and yokes. If any part of a universal joint is broken or damaged, install a new universal joint.

Condition	Possible Cause	Check or Correction
1. Leak at front slip yoke (An occasional drop of lubricant leaking from splined yoke is normal)	a. Rough outside surface on splined yoke	Replace seal if cut by burrs on yoke. Minor burrs can be smoothed by careful use of crocus cloth or honing with a fine stone. Replace yoke if outside surface is very rough or badly burred
	b. Defective transmission rear oil seal	Replace transmission real oil seal. Bring transmission oil up to proper level after correction.
2. Knock in drive line, clunking noise when car is operated under floating condition at 10 mph [16 kmph] in high gear or neutral	a. Worn or damaged universal joints	Replace
	b. Side-gear hub counterbore in differential worn oversize	Replace differential case and/or side gears as required
3. Ping, snap, or click in drive line. Usually occurs on initial load application after transmission has been put in gear either forward or reverse	a. Loose bushing bolts in upper or lower control arm	Tighten bolts to specified torque
	b. Loose companion flange	Remove companion flange, turn 180° from its original position, lubricate splines, and reinstall. Tighten pinion nut to specified torque
4. Roughness, vibration, or body boom at any speed. (Road test using tachometer)	a. Bent or dented driveshaft	Replace
	b. Undercoating on driveshaft	Clean driveshaft
	c. Tire unbalance (30 to 80 [mph] [48 to 129 kmph], not throttle sensitive	Balance or replace
	d. Excessive U-bolt torque	Check and correct to specified torque
	e. Tight universal joints	Hit yokes with a hammer to free. Replace joint if unable to free or if joint feels rough when rotated by hand.
	f. Worn universal joints	Replace
	g. Burrs or gouges on companion flange.	Rework or replace flange. Check snap ring, locating surfaces on flange yoke
	h. Driveshaft or companion flange unbalance	Check for missing balance weights on driveshaft. Remove and reassemble driveshaft to companion flange, 180° from original position
	i. Excessive looseness in slip-yoke splines	Replace necessary parts
	j. Driveshaft runout (50 to 80 mph) [80 to 129 kmph], throttle sensitive	Check driveshaft runout at front and rear. Should be less than specified. If more, rotate shaft 180° and recheck. If still above specifications, replace shaft
5. Roughness at low speeds, light load, (15 to 35 mph) [24 to 56 kmph]	a. U-bolt clamp nuts excessively tight	Check and tighten to specified torque. If torque was excessive or if brinelled pattern on trunnions, replace U joints.
6. Scraping noise	a. Oil slinger, companion flange, or end yoke rubbing on rear-axle carrier	Straighten or replace to remove interference
7. Roughness on heavy acceleration (short duration)	a. Double-Cardan joint ball seats worn	Replace joint
	b. Ball-seat spring broken	Replace
8. Roughness above 35 mph [56 kmph] felt and/or heard	a. Tires unbalanced or worn	Balance or replace

Fig. 45-21 Rear-wheel-drive line trouble-diagnosis chart.

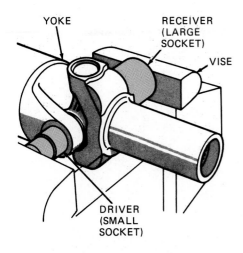

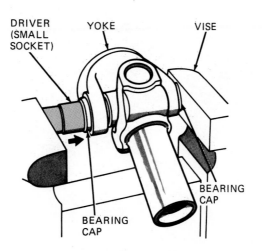

YOKE   RECEIVER (LARGE SOCKET)   VISE   DRIVER (SMALL SOCKET)

DRIVER (SMALL SOCKET)

(A) REMOVING BEARING CAP

DRIVER (SMALL SOCKET)   YOKE   VISE   BEARING CAP   BEARING CAP

(B) INSTALLING BEARING CAP

Fig. 45-22 Using a vise to replace a single Cardan universal joint on the end of a driveshaft. (*Chrysler Corporation*)

If necessary, pack the needle bearings in the caps with the specified grease and fill the grease reservoirs at the end of each trunnion. Put the seals on the spider. Place the bearing caps in the yoke bores and the cross in position. Tap the bearing caps into the yoke far enough to hold the spider in place. Use a press or a vise (Fig. 45-22B) and force the caps in far enough to expose the snap-ring grooves. Install new snap rings. Rotate the yoke and check for full and free movement. If binding occurs, correct the condition before installing the driveshaft.

CV-JOINT AND HALFSHAFT DIAGNOSIS AND SERVICE

➤ 45-23 CV-JOINT AND HALFSHAFT TROUBLE DIAGNOSIS

Unusual noise in the drive line of a front-drive vehicle usually indicates a damaged or worn CV joint. Other conditions in the transaxle, bearings, and tires also create noise. These noises and conditions, along with the possible causes, are listed in the trouble-diagnosis chart in Fig. 44-8. To determine the source of a noise, road test the vehicle. Follow the procedures in ➤44-13 and in the vehicle service manual.

A clicking noise while turning indicates a worn or damaged outer CV joint. A clunk when accelerating or decelerating indicates a worn or damaged inner CV joint. Shudder or vibration during acceleration is also probably caused by defective inner joint. Other possible causes include a bad intermediate-shaft bearing (Fig. 45-8A), outer joint, engine mount, or torque strut (Fig. 13-39). Causes of vibration at highway speed include out-of-balance tires, out-of-round tires or wheels, or an alignment problem.

Vibration or growl may also be caused by a bad wheel bearing. To check the wheel bearing, raise the wheel with a

jack. Place a safety stand under the lower control arm. Then spin the wheel by hand while listening at the hub for bearing noise.

➤ 45-24 CV-JOINT BOOT INSPECTION

The CV-joint boots (Fig. 45-23) deteriorate and may crack or tear during normal use. The boots and outer CV joints fail more frequently than the inner boots and joints. This is because the front wheels move through greater angles for steering. Some manufacturers recommend inspecting the boots every time the engine oil is changed.

Clean the boots and then check for cracks, tears, and grease leakage. The clamps should be in place and tight. If the boot is damaged or leaking, replace it. Continued driving will cause the CV joint to fail due to contamination or loss of lubricant.

➤ 45-25 CV-JOINT AND BOOT SERVICE

Complete boot and CV-joint service requires removing the halfshaft assembly from the car. Follow the procedures in the vehicle service manual. Basic steps in a typical procedure include loosening the front-wheel lug nuts and the hub nut. Raise the vehicle on a lift, supporting the vehicle on the suspension. Remove the lug nuts, wheels, and hub nut.

1. REMOVING THE HALFSHAFT ASSEMBLY Remove the nut holding the lower ball joint to the steering knuckle. Separate the lower ball joint from the knuckle (Fig. 45-24A). Swing the knuckle assembly out and pull the CV joint from the wheel bearing and hub (Fig. 45-24B). Use a *slide-hammer puller* (Fig. 45-24C) and remove the inner CV joint from the transaxle. Support both ends of the halfshaft assembly and remove it from under the vehicle (Fig. 45-24D). Place soft jaws on a vise and clamp the halfshaft in the soft jaws.

Fig. 45-23 Inspecting CV-joint boots and clamps. (*Chrysler Corporation*)

2. INSPECTING THE CV JOINT To inspect the outer CV joint, cut off the boot clamps (Fig. 45-25A) and remove the boot. Rub some of the grease from the CV joint between your fingers (Fig. 45-25B). If the grease feels gritty, the joint probably is damaged. Wipe away the grease and remove the CV joint from the halfshaft. Most are retained by a snap ring or circlip. Force up one side of the cage and inner race, and remove each ball (Fig. 45-25C). Then pivot the cage and inner race so the cage windows align with the lands of the outer race. Lift out the cage and inner race (Fig. 45-25D). Figure 45-10 shows the Rzeppa outer CV joint completely disassembled.

Inspect the cage for cracks and pitting. This allows excess ball movement and causes a clicking sound during turns. Check the inner and outer races for excess wear in the grooves caused by the balls moving back and forth. Shiny areas in the grooves and cage windows are normal. Replace the CV joint only if a part is broken, cracked, severely pitted, or damaged.

3. SERVICING THE HALFSHAFT AND CV JOINTS The CV joints and halfshaft assembly may be serviced in three ways. A *boot kit* includes a new boot and clamps to install if the CV joint is reusable. A defective CV joint is replaced with a *CV-joint kit*. This includes a new joint, boot, and clamps. If there is damage to the halfshaft or both CV joints, a complete *halfshaft assembly* may be installed.

Follow the procedures in the vehicle service manual and the kit instruction sheets to install the new parts. Both the boot kit and the CV-joint kit include a supply of the special grease used in CV joints. Apply the recommended amount of the grease to the joint. Add the remaining grease to the inside of the boot. Then tighten the boot clamps. Installation of the halfshaft assembly is basically the reverse of removal.

DRIVE-AXLE DIAGNOSIS AND SERVICE

➤ 45-26 DRIVE-AXLE TROUBLE DIAGNOSIS

Noise is usually the first sign of trouble in the drive axle or differential. The kind of noise you hear can help you determine what is causing the trouble. Determine if the noise is a hum, a growl, or a knock. Note whether the noise

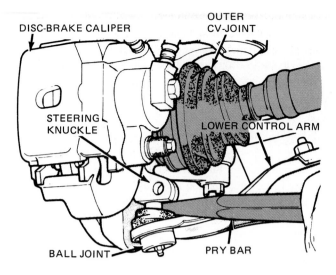

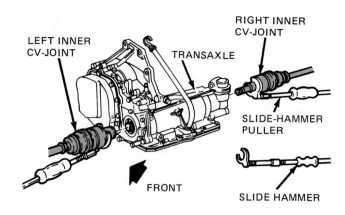

(C) REMOVING INNER CV-JOINTS FROM TRANSAXLE

(A) SEPARATING BALL JOINT FROM STEERING KNUCKLE

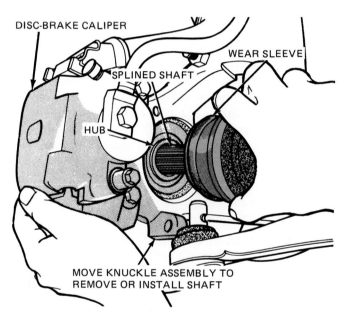

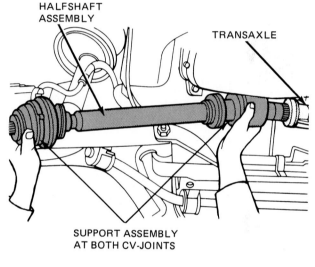

(D) HANDLING HALFSHAFT ASSEMBLY

(B) SEPARATING OUTER CV-JOINT SHAFT FROM HUB

Fig. 45-24 Removing halfshaft assembly with CV joints from vehicle. (*AC-Delco Division of General Motors Corporation*)

is produced when the vehicle runs straight ahead or only on turns. Note whether the noise is louder when the engine is driving the vehicle or when the vehicle is coasting. Ring-and-pinion gear noise usually changes with the load. Pinion-bearing noise changes with vehicle speed and is usually unaffected by load and turns.

It is difficult to diagnose drive-axle and differential noise by running the vehicle in the shop with the wheels raised. Road testing the vehicle (➤44-1) is usually necessary to locate and identify a drive-train noise. Certain operating conditions may be required for the noise to occur. Sometimes the noise can be heard while running the vehicle on a chassis dynamometer (➤37-14).

1. HUMMING A humming noise is often caused by an incorrectly adjusted ring gear and pinion. This prevents proper tooth contact. It can cause rapid tooth wear and early gear failure. The humming noise takes on a growling sound as wear progresses. Follow the procedure in the vehicle service manual to adjust the ring gear and pinion (➤45-30).

2. NOISE ON ACCELERATION Noise that is louder during vehicle acceleration probably means there is heavy contact on the heel (outer) ends of the ring-gear teeth. Noise that is louder when the vehicle is coasting probably means there is heavy toe contact. A loud clunk during

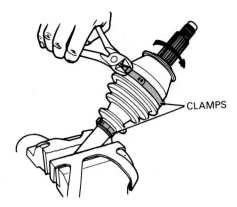

(A) CUTTING BOOT CLAMP

GREASE

(B) CHECKING GREASE FOR GRIT

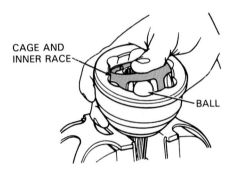

CAGE AND
INNER RACE

BALL

(C) TILTING CAGE AND INNER RACE

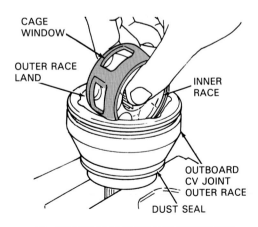

CAGE
WINDOW

OUTER RACE
LAND

INNER
RACE

OUTBOARD
CV JOINT
OUTER RACE

DUST SEAL

(D) LIFTING OUT CAGE AND INNER RACE

Fig. 45-25 Disassembling and inspecting CV joint. (*Ford Motor Company*)

acceleration or deceleration may be caused by excess clearance between an axle shaft and a differential side gear. The noise may also be caused by excessive *ring-gear backlash* (➤45-30) and excess clearance between the pinion gears and side gears in the differential.

3. NOISE ON CURVES If the noise is heard only when the vehicle is going around a curve, the trouble is either a bad axle bearing (Fig. 45-26) or inside the differential. A bad axle bearing usually makes the most noise when it is on the outside of a turn. Then the outside axle bearing is running faster and carrying a greater load than the bearing on the inner axle. Making a turn in the opposite direction will usually reduce or eliminate the noise from a bad axle bearing.

Inside the differential, pinion gears that are tight on the pinion shaft, damaged gears or pinions, too much backlash between the gears, or worn differential-case bearings can cause noise on curves. These are the parts inside the differential that move relative to each other during a turn.

4. TORQUE STEER Different size tires on the wheels of a drive axle can cause torque steer (➤45-6). The vehicle pulls to one side when accelerating.

5. LIMITED-SLIP DIFFERENTIAL PROBLEMS The limited-slip differential requires special lubricant. The wrong lubricant can cause the clutch surfaces to grab. This produces a chattering noise during turns. Correct this condition by draining the lubricant and then adding the specified amount of the proper lubricant.

Use the same type of tire on both wheels of a drive axle with a limited-slip differential. Both tires should have the same pattern, the same air pressure, and the same wear.

➤ **45-27 DRIVE-AXLE AND DIFFERENTIAL SERVICE**

A variety of drive axles are used in rear-drive and four-wheel-drive vehicles. Construction, operation, diagnosis, and service are usually similar. Drive axles are classed as either *removable carrier* (Fig. 45-1) or *integral carrier* (Figs. 44-12 and 45-26). The difference is the way the differential assembly is removed from the axle housing. After disconnecting the driveshaft and removing the axle shafts, the removable-carrier differential comes out the front of the rear-axle housing. The integral-carrier differential is removed from the rear (Fig. 45-26).

Service jobs include replacing axle-shaft bearings and seals, and replacing the drive-pinion seal. Other services include replacing and adjusting the ring-gear and pinion, and overhauling the differential assembly.

➤ **45-28 REPLACING AXLE BEARINGS AND SEALS**

Bearing noise or a lubricant leak may indicate the need for replacing an axle bearing and seal. In a rear axle, each axle

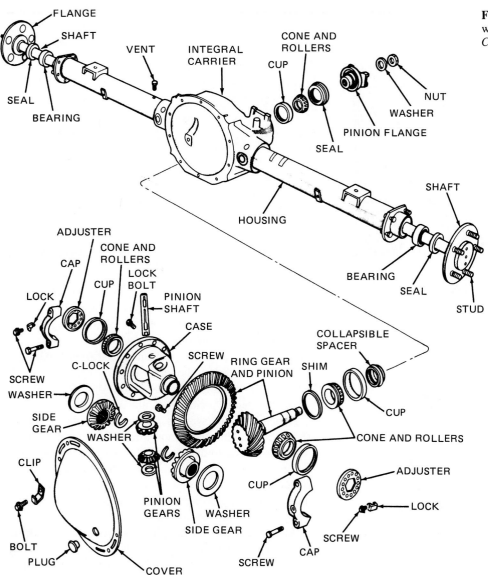

FLANGE

SHAFT

VENT

INTEGRAL CARRIER

CONE AND ROLLERS

CUP

NUT

WASHER

PINION FLANGE

SEAL

SEAL

BEARING

Fig. 45-26 Disassembled drive axle with integral carrier. (*Chrysler Corporation*)

SHAFT

HOUSING

BEARING

SEAL

STUD

ADJUSTER

CAP

CONE AND ROLLERS

LOCK BOLT

LOCK

CUP

PINION SHAFT

CASE

COLLAPSIBLE SPACER

SCREW

C-LOCK

SCREW

RING GEAR AND PINION

SHIM

SCREW

WASHER

SIDE GEAR

CUP

WASHER

CONE AND ROLLERS

CLIP

PINION GEARS

WASHER

SIDE GEAR

CUP

ADJUSTER

LOCK

BOLT

PLUG

COVER

SCREW

CAP

SCREW

shaft is held in place by a *C lock* on the inner end (Fig. 45-26) or a *retainer* on the outer end (Fig. 45-14). The lock or retainer allows the axle shaft to rotate while preventing it from sliding out of the axle housing.

Most integral-carrier rear axles use C locks. To remove the C locks, clean all dirt from the rear cover of the axle housing (Fig. 44-12). Drain the lubricant and remove the rear cover. Remove the pinion-shaft lock bolt and the pinion shaft (Fig. 45-26). Push in on the axle shafts. Remove the C locks from the grooves in the inner ends of the axle shafts, inside the differential case (Fig. 45-27). Then pull the axle shafts out of the axle housing.

Careful! When removing or installing an axle shaft, do not allow the splines on the inner end of the shaft to damage the oil seal. A damaged seal will leak lubricant. Some manufacturers recommend always installing a new seal after removing an axle shaft.

Figure 45-28 shows how to replace the wheel bearing and seal. Using a slide-hammer puller, remove the wheel bearing and seal from the axle housing. With a hammer and the proper installing tools or drivers, install the new wheel bearing and seal. Then lubricate the seal lip to prevent it from being damaged by the rotating axle.

➤ **45-29 REPLACING THE PINION SEAL**

The pinion seal is located at the front end of the differential carrier (Fig. 45-26), ahead of the *front-pinion bearing*. Tightening the pinion nut partially collapses a *collapsible spacer* or *compression sleeve*. This determines the *pinion-bearing preload*. When replacing the pinion seal, the pinion-bearing preload must not be changed.

A typical procedure for replacing the pinion seal begins with raising the vehicle. Locate or make index marks on

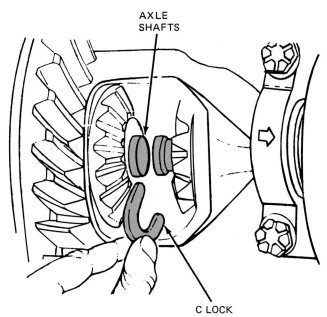

AXLE SHAFTS

C LOCK

Fig. 45-27 Removing or installing C lock in groove at the inner end of the axle shaft, inside the differential case. (*Ford Motor Company*)

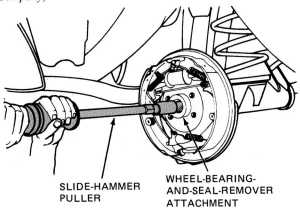

SLIDE-HAMMER PULLER

WHEEL-BEARING-AND-SEAL-REMOVER ATTACHMENT

(A) REMOVING WHEEL BEARING AND SEAL

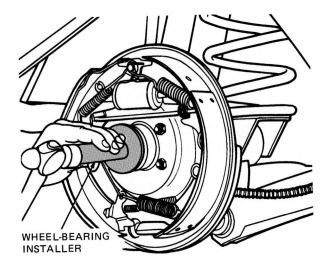

WHEEL-BEARING INSTALLER

(B) INSTALLING WHEEL BEARING AND SEAL

Fig. 45-28 Replacing wheel bearing and seal in a rear drive axle. (*Ford Motor Company*)

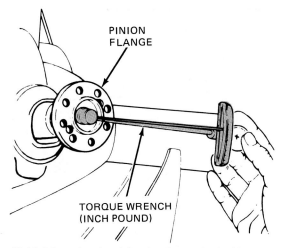

PINION FLANGE

TORQUE WRENCH (INCH POUND)

Fig. 45-29 Measuring the pinion-bearing preload with a torque wrench. (*Ford Motor Company*)

the driveshaft and yoke or pinion flange (Fig. 44-12). Disconnect the driveshaft from the pinion flange, but do not pull the slip yoke off the transmission output shaft. This prevents the transmission lubricant from leaking out. Support the rear of the driveshaft by wiring it to the exhaust pipe or other underbody part. Mark the position of the pinion flange, pinion shaft, and pinion nut.

Attach a torque wrench and socket to the pinion nut (Fig. 45-29). Turn the pinion through several revolutions. Write down the torque required. Then remove the pinion nut, pinion flange, and seal. Inspect the seal surface on the pinion flange. If the surface is grooved or damaged, install a new pinion flange. Remove any burrs in the carrier bore. Then lubricate the seal and install it.

Align the marks on the pinion shaft and pinion flange, and install the pinion flange. Lubricate the washer side of a new nut, and tighten the nut. Rotate the pinion to seat the bearing. Measure the pinion-bearing preload with the torque wrench (Fig. 45-29). Tighten the pinion nut until the original pinion-bearing preload is obtained.

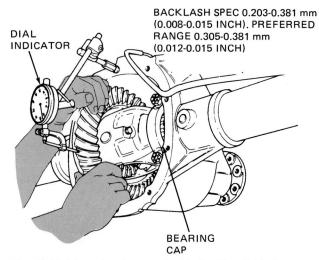

DIAL INDICATOR

BACKLASH SPEC 0.203-0.381 mm (0.008-0.015 INCH). PREFERRED RANGE 0.305-0.381 mm (0.012-0.015 INCH)

BEARING CAP

Fig. 45-30 Measuring ring-gear backlash with a dial indicator. (*Ford Motor Company*)

600

Figure 45-26 shows a completely disassembled rear axle that has an integral carrier and an open differential. To disassemble and service the differential, follow the procedures in the vehicle service manual.

Most differential service is performed by removing the differential assembly from the axle housing, which remains in the vehicle. Inspecting the differential prior to disassembly often provides information about what needs to be done. This information, the customer's complaints, and the road test all help determine the amount of disassembly required.

Before removing the differential, measure pinion-bearing preload (Fig. 45-29) and *ring-gear backlash* (Fig. 45-30). Also, check the *ring-gear tooth contact pattern* (Fig. 45-31). This is done by wiping the lubricant from the carrier and cleaning each tooth on the ring gear. Dip a small brush in a *gear-marking compound* such as Prussian blue. Coat both the drive and coast sides of the ring-gear teeth. Slightly load the ring and pinion gears, and rotate the ring gear one complete revolution in each direction. This leaves a distinct contact pattern on both sides of the ring-gear teeth.

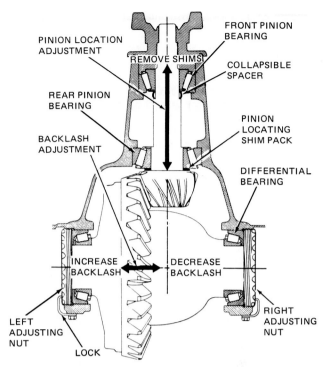

Fig. 45-32 Adjustment procedures to correct gear-tooth contact and backlash on an integral-carrier differential. Shims adjust pinion depth. Adjusting nuts position the ring gear to increase or decrease backlash. (*Ford Motor Company*)

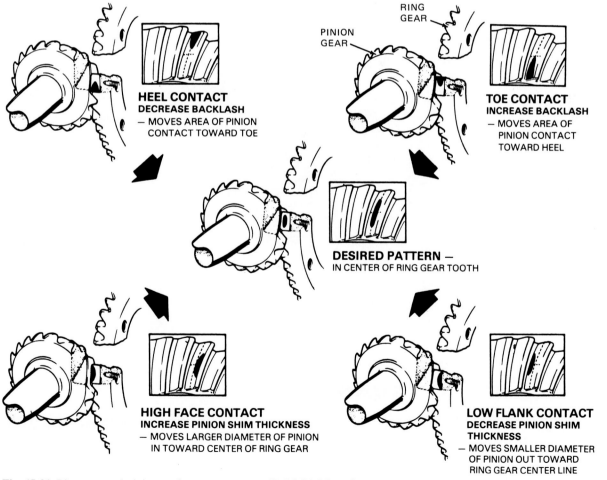

Fig. 45-31 Ring-gear-and-pinion tooth-contact patterns. (*Buick Division of General Motors Corporation*)

Figure 45-32 shows how shims adjust pinion depth and how the adjusting nuts (or shims) position the ring gear. Turning the adjusting nuts or changing the shims increases or decreases ring-gear backlash.

➤ 45-31 SERVICING LIMITED-SLIP DIFFERENTIALS

The operation of a limited-slip differential (➤45-20) can usually be checked without disassembling the rear-drive axle or removing the differential. To check one type of limited-slip differential, turn the ignition key off and place the gearshift lever in PARK. Release the parking brake and raise the vehicle on a lift. Try to rotate each rear wheel. If the wheel will not turn, or if the wheel is very hard to turn, the limited-slip differential is operating properly. If either rear wheel rotates easily, the limited-slip differential is defective.

Figure 45-33 shows a disassembled limited-slip differential. Note the arrangement of the disks in the clutches. Follow the procedures in the vehicle service manual to repair and adjust the limited-slip differential. Drive-pinion position and ring-gear backlash are adjusted the same as in similar open differentials (➤45-30).

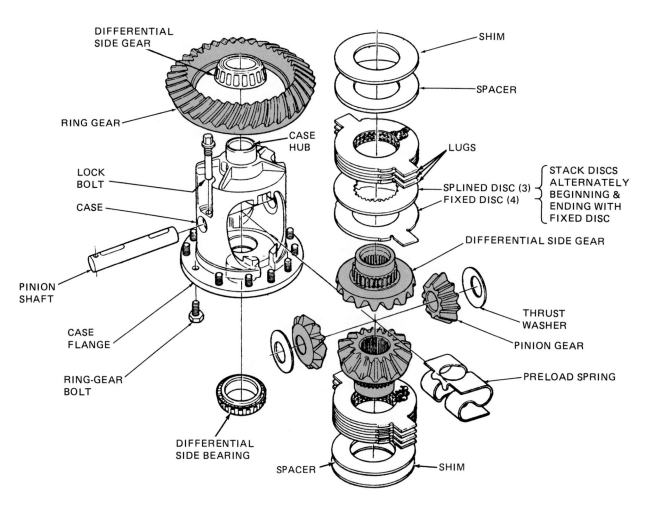

Fig. 45-33 Disassembled limited-slip differential. (*Buick Division of General Motors Corporation*)

TRADE TALK

axle ratio	differential	slip joint	universal joint
collapsible spacer	halfshaft	torque steer	
CV joint	limited-slip differential	traction	

MULTIPLE-CHOICE TEST

*Select the **one** correct, best, or most probable answer to each question.*
You can find the answers in the section indicated at the end of each question.

1. In a rear-wheel-drive vehicle, when the rear wheels move up and down (➤45-2)
   a. the drive line changes length
   b. the angle of drive changes
   c. both a and b
   d. neither a nor b
2. The two types of joints used in the drive line of a rear-wheel-drive vehicle are (➤45-2)
   a. CV joint and universal joint
   b. trunnion joint and slip joint
   c. Rzeppa joint and slide joint
   d. universal joint and slip joint
3. A front-drive car has an intermediate shaft and equal-length halfshafts. Technician A says this helps prevent torque steer during acceleration. Technician B says it helps prevent torque steer during braking. Who is right? (➤45-6)
   a. A only
   b. B only
   c. both A and B
   d. neither A nor B
4. An outboard Rzeppa CV joint has the following EXCEPT (➤45-7)
   a. six steel balls
   b. an inner and outer race
   c. a spider with three arms
   d. a cage
5. In a rear-drive axle, the ring gear is bolted to the (➤45-14)
   a. differential carrier
   b. differential case
   c. drive pinion
   d. axle housing
6. If the rear axle has a 3:1 gear ratio, the pinion gear must turn six times to cause the ring gear to rotate (➤45-15)
   a. one time
   b. two times
   c. three times
   d. four times
7. In a limited-slip differential, when one wheel starts to spin (➤45-20)
   a. all the torque goes to the spinning wheel
   b. the differential side gears become locked to the case
   c. the ring gear is held stationary
   d. the pinion gears are demeshed from the side gears
8. Technician A says the clicking noise in a front-drive vehicle during turns is caused by a worn or damaged outer CV joint. Technician B says a clunk when the front-drive vehicle accelerates or decelerates indicates a worn or damaged inner CV joint. Who is right? (➤45-23)
   a. A only
   b. B only
   c. both A and B
   d. neither A nor B
9. Noise from a rear-drive axle when going around a curve indicates trouble (➤45-26)
   a. inside the differential
   b. caused by a worn ring gear
   c. caused by a worn drive-pinion gear
   d. due to slippage of the clutch
10. A rear-drive axle has a collapsible spacer on the drive pinion. The tightness of the pinion nut determines (➤45-29)
    a. gear-tooth contact pattern
    b. pinion-gear endplay
    c. ring-gear backlash
    d. pinion-bearing preload

REVIEW QUESTIONS

1. What is the difference between a fixed CV joint and a plunging CV joint? (➤45-6)
2. How does a drive axle differ from a dead axle? (➤45-11)
3. Describe the operation of a differential when the vehicle is moving straight ahead and when making a turn. (➤45-19)
4. Explain how to road test a rear-drive car to determine if the drive line is causing roughness and vibration. (➤45-21)
5. What causes a CV-joint boot to crack and tear, and why does the outer boot fail more often than the inner boot? (➤45-24)

CHAPTER 46

FOUR-WHEEL DRIVE, TRANSFER CASES, AND VISCOUS COUPLINGS

After studying this chapter, and with proper instruction and equipment, you should be able to:

- Describe the construction and operation of various types of four-wheel drive and all-wheel drive.
- Explain the operation of single-speed and two-speed transfer cases.
- Discuss the need for viscous couplings and interaxle differentials, and the various ways of locking differentials.
- Diagnose troubles in four-wheel drive, all-wheel drive, and transfer cases.
- Remove, overhaul, and install a transfer case.

➤ 46-1 FOUR-WHEEL DRIVE (4WD)

A vehicle with four-wheel drive (4WD) has a drive train that can send power to all four wheels (Fig. 46-1). This provides maximum traction for off-road driving. It also provides maximum traction when the road surface is slippery, or covered with ice or snow. Some vehicles have a four-wheel-drive system that engages automatically or remains engaged all the time. Other vehicles have a selective arrangement that permits the driver to shift from two-wheel drive to four-wheel drive, and back, according to driving conditions. The instrument panel or console may include an indicator light or display to show when the vehicle is in four-wheel drive.

Many four-wheel-drive vehicles are basically light-duty trucks. They have rear-wheel drive (Chap. 45) with auxiliary front-wheel drive. A two-speed gearbox (➤43-6) or *transfer case* (➤46-3) engages and disengages the front axle, while providing high and low speed ranges. Other vehicles use the front axle as the *main-drive axle*. To get four-wheel drive, the transfer case engages the rear axle which then serves as the *auxiliary-drive axle*. Four-wheel-drive vehicles usually have high ground clearance, oil-pan and underbody protection, and tire treads suitable for off-road use.

➤ 46-2 ALL-WHEEL DRIVE (AWD)

Some passenger vehicles have *all-wheel drive* (AWD). This is a version of four-wheel drive used in vehicles primarily for on-road use. It provides improved traction, especially on slippery or snow-covered road surfaces. A two-speed transfer case is not used, so there is no low range for off-roading. Figure 46-2 shows an AWD car that normally drives both front and rear axles equally. When the wheels on one axle slip, the system automatically transfers torque to the other axle which has better traction.

Other AWD vehicles have front-wheel drive with auxiliary rear-wheel drive, or rear-wheel drive with auxiliary

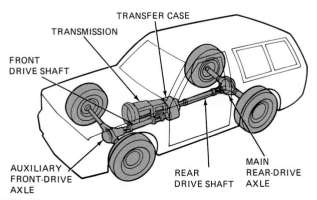

Fig. 46-1 Drive train in a vehicle with four-wheel drive. (*Ford Motor Company*)

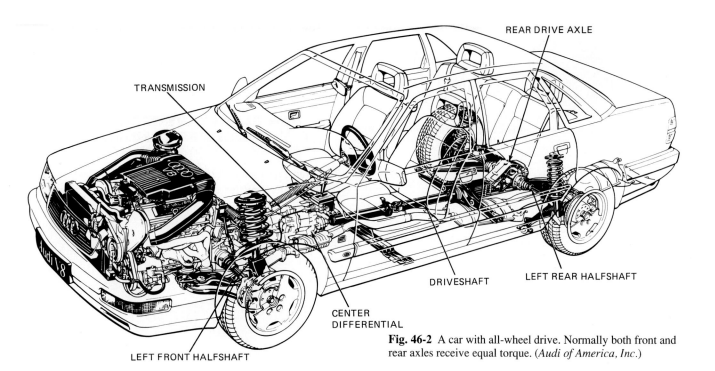

Fig. 46-2 A car with all-wheel drive. Normally both front and rear axles receive equal torque. (*Audi of America, Inc.*)

front-wheel drive. Some AWD vehicles have a single-speed transfer case. Others have the gearing to drive the auxiliary axle built into the transmission or transaxle.

FOUR-WHEEL DRIVE

➤ 46-3 PURPOSE OF THE TRANSFER CASE

The typical transfer case attaches to the rear of the transmission in place of the extension housing (Figs. 46-1 and 46-3). Engine power flows through the transmission output shaft to the transfer-case input shaft. If the vehicle has *part-time* four-wheel drive, the driver selects either two-wheel or four-wheel drive. Gearing in the transfer case then sends power to only the rear axle (two-wheel drive) or to both front and rear axles (four-wheel drive). Some vehicles have *full-time* four-wheel drive. The transfer case remains in four-wheel drive and the front axle engages automatically as soon as the rear wheels begin to spin.

Automotive transfer cases are classified as *single-speed* or *two-speed*. The single-speed transfer case can divide the power and deliver it to either axle or both axles. In addition, the two-speed transfer case has a *low range* and a *high range*. The driver can select either two-wheel drive or four-wheel drive in high range, neutral, or low range with four-wheel drive (Fig. 46-4).

Figure 46-5 shows the power-flow through a two-speed transfer case as the shift lever is moved to the different positions. The four modes of transfer case operation are obtained by moving two sliding gears. These are splined to the transfer-case output shafts for the front and rear axles.

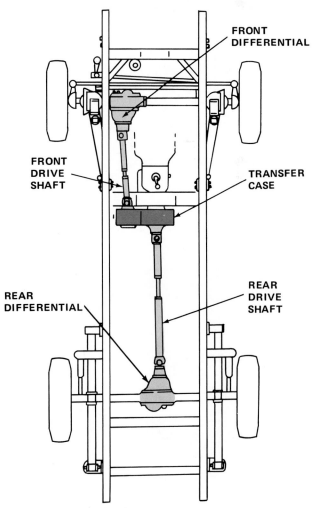

Fig. 46-3 Suspension and drive train for a typical four-wheel-drive vehicle. The transfer case allows the driver to select rear-wheel drive or four-wheel drive. (*Ford Motor Company*)

605

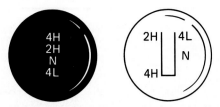

Fig. 46-4 Shift patterns for transfer cases. (*Chrysler Corporation*)

High range in the transfer case provides direct drive, or a gear ratio of 1:1. Low range usually produces a gear reduction of about 2.5:1. This reduces vehicle speed while greatly increasing the low-speed torque available. A single-speed transfer case usually has a 1:1 ratio.

➤ 46-4 PLANETARY-GEAR TRANSFER CASE

All transfer cases do not have spur gears as shown in Fig. 46-5. Many transfer cases use a *planetary gearset* (Fig.

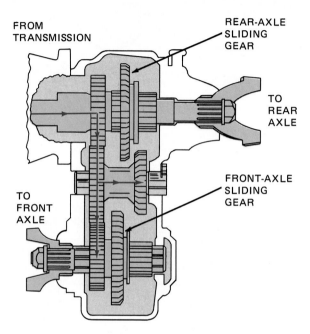

(A) TRANSFER CASE IN NEUTRAL

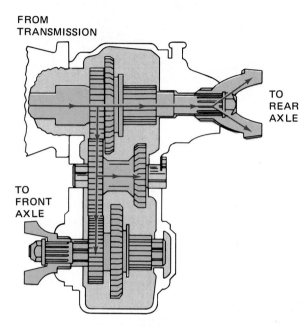

(B) TRANSFER CASE IN TWO-WHEEL DRIVE, HIGH RANGE

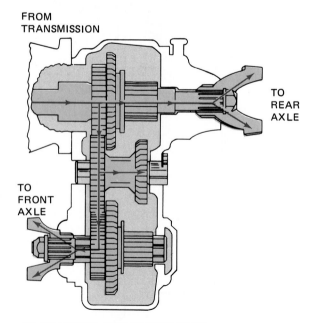

(C) TRANSFER CASE IN FOUR-WHEEL DRIVE, HIGH RANGE

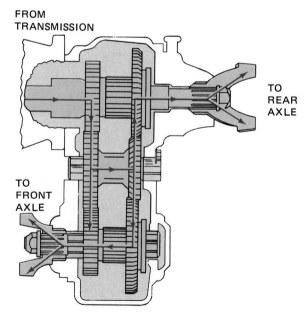

(D) TRANSFER CASE IN FOUR-WHEEL DRIVE, LOW RANGE

Fig. 46-5 Power flow through a two-speed transfer case as the shift lever is moved to the different positions. (*Chrysler Corporation*)

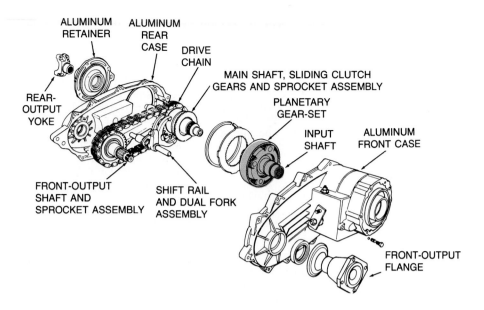

Fig. 46-6 Partly disassembled part-time four-wheel-drive transfer case which uses a planetary gearset to provide gear reduction. (*Chrysler Corporation*)

46-6) to provide gear reduction for low-range operation. A *drive chain* transmits power between the shafts. In two-wheel drive, the internal parts of the transfer case do not rotate. This leaves most of the lubricant undisturbed and reduces power loss caused by dragging gears through it.

An internal oil pump turns with the rear output shaft to maintain lubrication whenever the driveshaft is turning. This improves lubrication and allows towing the vehicle at legal speeds. As long as the rear wheels turn, the oil pump lubricates the bearings in the transfer case. However, if the front wheels have locking hubs, they should be unlocked to avoid unnecessary rotation of drive-train parts.

Figure 46-7 shows the power-flow through the transfer case for each driving range. In neutral, the input shaft turns the planet-pinion gears and the ring gear which spin freely. With this condition, no power flows through the planetary gearset (➤46-5).

➤ 46-5 PLANETARY-GEAR OPERATION

The single planetary gearset shown in Fig. 46-8 is made of three members: a *sun gear,* a *planet-pinion carrier,* and an *internal* or *ring gear.* The sun gear is in the center, on the end of the sun-gear shaft. This is the driving or input gear in Fig. 46-8B. Meshing with the sun gear are three (or four) *planet pinions.* They mount on pins in the planet-pinion carrier. The planet pinions mesh with the internal gear or ring gear. The shaft attached to the planet-pinion carrier is the driven or output shaft (Fig. 46-8B).

The planetary gearset can provide five conditions:

1. Speed increase with torque decrease (overdrive).
2. Speed decrease with torque increase (underdrive or reduction).

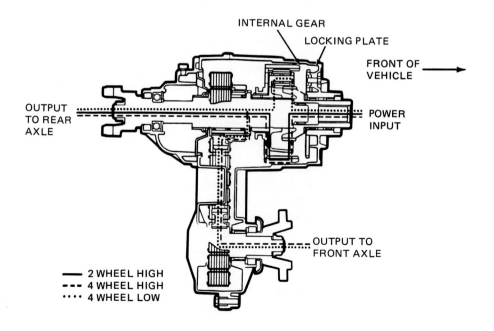

Fig. 46-7 Power flow through the part-time transfer case with planetary gears. (*Chrysler Corporation*)

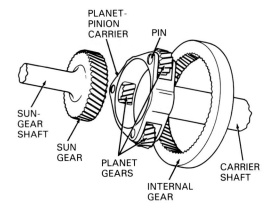

(A) DISASSEMBLED PLANETARY GEARSET

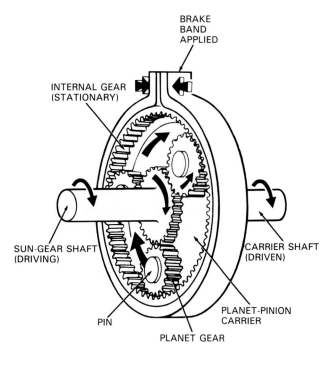

(B) GEAR REDUCTION THROUGH PLANETARY GEARSET

Fig. 46-8 (A) Disassembled planetary gearset. The planet gears rotate on pins that are part of the carrier. (B) Gear reduction through the planetary gearset. With the internal gear held stationary by the applied band, the planet carrier and output shaft turn slower than the sun gear. This provides the transfer case with low range.

3. Direct drive (lockup).
4. Neutral.
5. Reverse.

The two drive conditions used in the transfer case are speed reduction (low range) and direct drive (high range). Direct drive is obtained by locking together any two members of the planetary gearset. Holding the internal gear stationary provides speed reduction (Fig. 46-8B). As the sun gear rotates, it forces the planet pinions to "walk around" the internal gear. This rotates the planet-pinion carrier in the same direction as the sun gear, but more slowly. The carrier shaft is the transfer-case driven shaft or

output shaft. It now turns slower than the input shaft, but with greater torque.

> **NOTE** To illustrate the operation of a planetary gearset, Fig. 46-8 shows the internal gear being held stationary by a *brake band*. However, the planetary-gear transfer case does not use a brake band as a holding device. Moving the selector lever into low range slides the internal gear and planet-pinion carrier forward on its splined shaft (Fig. 46-7). The teeth in the internal gear engage a *locking plate* bolted to the case. This holds the internal gear stationary.

Shifting the transfer case into high range locks the internal gear and planet-pinion carrier together (Fig. 46-7). The complete planetary gearset turns as a unit because the planet pinions cannot rotate on their pins. This provides direct drive. The transfer-case output shaft turns at the same speed as the input shaft.

Other types of transfer cases are also used in four-wheel-drive vehicles. These transfer cases may be shifted manually, or by a vacuum or electric motor (➤46-18). Some transfer cases have differentials and clutches that operate automatically or may be manually locked. Others are computer controlled (➤46-18).

➤ 46-6 AUXILIARY FRONT-DRIVE AXLES

To get four-wheel drive, the driver shifts the transfer case to engage the front axle (Figs. 46-5 and 46-7). In Fig. 46-5C, the *front-axle sliding gear* in the transfer case locks the front-axle driven gear to the front-axle driveshaft. In most transfer cases, the front axle can be engaged or disengaged while the vehicle is moving as long as the front and rear wheels are turning at the same speed. Some transfer cases have synchronizers to make shifting easier (➤43-7). Shifting the transfer case from neutral into gear may require stopping the vehicle and engine.

Power-flow from the yokes on the transfer-case shafts to the drive axles is through tubular driveshafts (Figs. 46-1 and 46-3). Single-Cardan universal joints and slip joints take care of changes in drive angle and driveshaft length (➤45-2).

Figure 46-9 shows the front-drive axle for a four-wheel-drive vehicle. It is similar to the rear-drive axle (➤45-13). The differential and front-axle shafts are carried inside the axle housing. The axle shafts have universal joints at the outer ends. This allows the ends or *spindles* to swing with the steering knuckle for steering. Figure 46-10 shows a front-drive axle with independent front suspension. It has a two-piece axle housing. An additional universal joint in the right-axle shaft allows each wheel to move up and down independently of the other.

➤ 46-7 LOCKING HUBS

In four-wheel-drive vehicles, power flows to one axle—the main-drive axle—all the time. The other axle—or auxiliary-

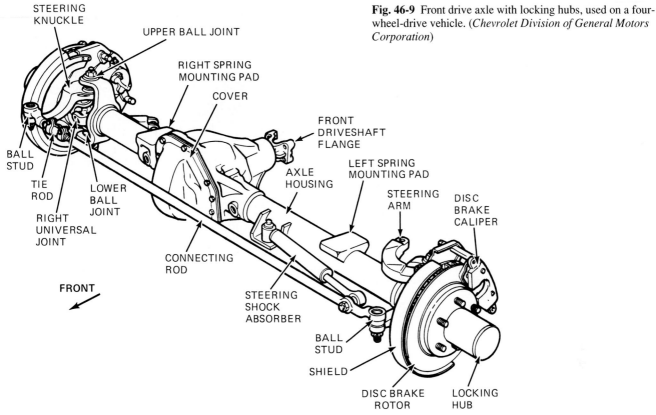

Fig. 46-9 Front drive axle with locking hubs, used on a four-wheel-drive vehicle. (*Chevrolet Division of General Motors Corporation*)

Fig. 46-10 Front drive axle for a four-wheel-drive vehicle with independent front suspension. (*Ford Motor Company*)

drive axle—is engaged by shifting the transfer case. If the wheel hubs are splined directly to the spindles on the outer ends of the axle shafts, shifting the transfer case puts the vehicle in four-wheel drive. However, this type of part-time four-wheel drive is seldom used. In two-wheel drive, the front-axle shafts *back-drive* the ring gear and pinion, and the front-axle driveshaft. Reduced fuel economy and tire life result, along with increased engine and transfer-case wear. One solution is to connect the drive-axle shafts to the drive wheels through *locking hubs* (Figs. 46-11 and 46-12).

1. MANUAL LOCKING HUBS *Manual locking hubs* (Fig. 46-11) are used with part-time four-wheel drive.

They are engaged and disengaged by the driver. To engage the front wheels, the driver stops the vehicle, gets out, and turns the shift knob on each wheel to ENGAGE. This rotates the cam so the spring pushes the sliding gear into mesh with a gear splined to the outer end of the axle shaft. Now, when the driver gets into the vehicle and shifts the transfer case into four-wheel drive, the front wheels drive along with the rear wheels. To disengage the front wheels from the axle shafts, the driver stops the vehicle, gets out, and turns the hubs to DISENGAGE.

2. AUTOMATIC LOCKING HUBS To avoid having to stop the vehicle to engage and disengage the hubs, some vehicles have *automatic locking hubs* (Fig. 46-12). When

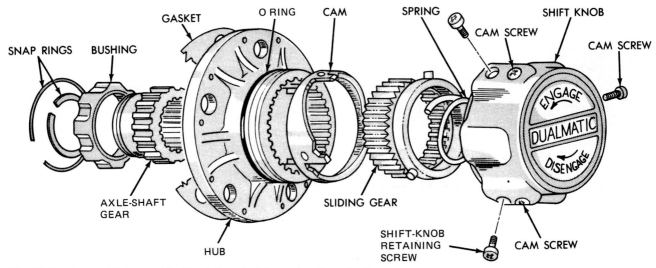

Fig. 46-11 Disassembled manual locking hub used with part-time four-wheel drive. The hubs must be engaged and disengaged manually, or by hand. (*Chrysler Corporation*)

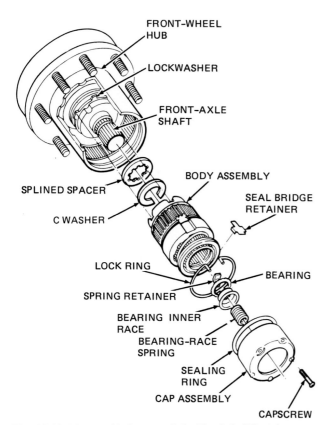

Fig. 46-12 Disassembled automatic locking hub. When the transfer case is in four-wheel drive, the hub locks automatically. (*Ford Motor Company*)

the transfer case is in four-wheel drive, the hubs lock automatically as power flows through the front-wheel axles. To unlock automatic locking hubs, stop the vehicle and shift to two-wheel drive. Then, on some models, drive the vehicle backward for a few feet.

➤ 46-8 FRONT-AXLE DISCONNECT

Instead of locking hubs (➤46-7), some four-wheel-drive vehicles have a *front-axle disconnect* (Fig. 46-13). One front-axle shaft is a two-piece shaft with splines on the ends. When the transfer case is shifted into four-wheel drive, a vacuum motor moves a sleeve which slides over

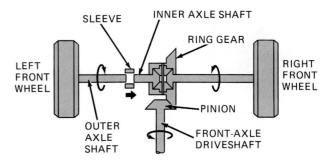

(A) FOUR-WHEEL DRIVE, FRONT AXLE CONNECTED

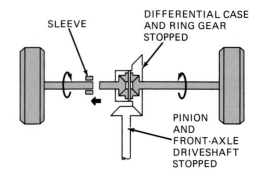

(B) TWO-WHEEL DRIVE, FRONT AXLE DISCONNECTED

Fig. 46-13 Front axle disconnect that uses a vacuum motor to move a sleeve and disconnect the front axle for two-wheel drive. (*Toyota Motor Sales U.S.A., Inc.*)

the splines on the ends of both shafts (Fig. 46-13A). This locks both sections of the shaft together. Operation is now the same as a front-drive axle with the hubs locked (Figs. 46-9 and 46-10).

When the driver shifts the transfer case to two-wheel drive, the vacuum motor moves the sleeve away from the inner section of the axle shaft (Fig. 46-13B). This disconnects the front axle. The ring gear, differential case, and pinion all stop rotating. The front-axle driveshaft and gearing in the transfer case also stop. This relieves the load caused by dragging the front differential and axle shafts. The result is reduced wear and improved fuel economy.

➤ 46-9 WHEEL SPEED AND TRAVEL

The simplest way to get four-wheel drive is to drive both the front and rear axles directly from the transfer case (Fig. 46-3). However, when the vehicle goes around a curve, each wheel must turn at a different speed. The outside wheels on a curve must turn farther and faster than the inside wheels (Fig. 45-16). Also, the front wheels must travel farther and faster than the rear wheels.

Each drive axle has a differential (Chap. 45). It equalizes the difference in speed and distance that the two wheels on that axle will travel. However, this system has no means of equalizing the different distances the front and rear wheels travel on a curve.

For this reason, the front-drive axle in a part-time four-wheel-drive system (➤46-3) should be engaged only when the tires are on a slippery surface. The tires must slip slightly to compensate for the different distances the wheels on the front and rear axles must travel. If the tires cannot slip, a heavy and often damaging load may be placed on the drive train and universal joints.

➤ 46-10 INTERAXLE DIFFERENTIAL

Some four-wheel-drive vehicles have a third differential or *interaxle differential* in the transfer case (Fig. 46-14). This *center differential* compensates for any difference in front-

and rear-wheel travel. It allows the front and rear axles to operate at their own speeds, without forcing wheel slippage during normal driving on dry road surfaces.

However, a simple bevel-gear or *open differential* (➤45-19) in the transfer case has a disadvantage. Suppose the tires on either axle lose traction and begin to spin. Then the transfer-case differential delivers maximum torque to the axle with the minimum traction. As a result, the tires with traction may not receive enough torque to move the vehicle.

To overcome this problem, most full-time transfer cases have some type of *limited-slip differential* (➤45-20). The slip-limiting device may be clutch plates, brake cones, or a *viscous coupling* (➤46-11). All of these divert torque from the axle with the spinning wheels and send it to the axle with the most traction.

➤ 46-11 VISCOUS COUPLING

A viscous coupling (Figs. 46-14 and 46-15) is a type of self-actuated fluid coupling. It can be used in the drive train between the transfer case and the rear axle. If the rear

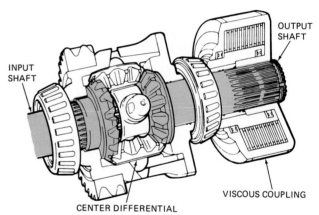

Fig. 46-15 Construction of the center differential and viscous coupling in an all-wheel-drive system. (*Mitsubishi Motor Sales of America, Inc.*)

Fig. 46-14 Layout of a full-time four-wheel-drive system, which has a transfer case with a built-in viscous coupling and center differential. (*Chrysler Corporation*)

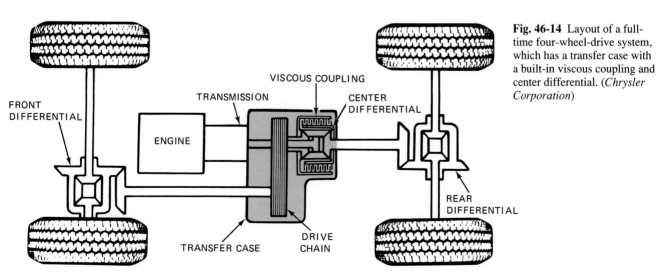

wheels are driving and have normal traction, there is no power flow to the front wheels. When the rear wheels lose traction and turn faster than the front wheels, the viscous coupling locks. The transfer case now sends power to the front wheels. As the rear wheels regain traction and begin turning at the same speed as the front wheels, the viscous coupling unlocks. The vehicle resumes driving only the rear wheels as long as they have normal traction.

The housing of the viscous coupling is attached to and driven by an input shaft (Fig. 46-16). The housing contains a series of thin plates alternately splined to the housing and to the output shaft. The viscous coupling is filled 90 percent with a *silicone fluid* and 10 percent with air. The fluid is very viscous, like a very thick oil. The housing is sealed to prevent leakage and hold the pressure that locks the coupling.

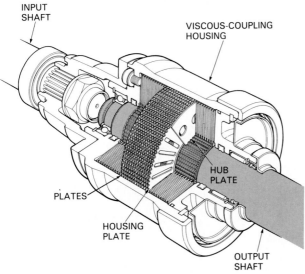

Fig. 46-16 Viscous coupling, cutaway to show the shafts and plates. (*American Honda Motor Company, Inc.*)

When wheel-spin occurs, the two sets of plates spin at greatly different speeds. The friction within the silicone fluid heats it almost instantly. Its temperature can reach 212°F [100°C] in 0.2 second or less. As the heat causes the silicone fluid to expand, the resulting pressure forces the plates to lock together. When the spinning wheels regain traction, the silicone fluid cools and the temperature and pressure drop. This unlocks the viscous coupling.

While the viscous coupling is unlocked, the two sets of plates rotate at about the same speed. Some slippage can take place. This provides differential action that compensates for the different distances the front and rear wheels travel in making turns.

ALL-WHEEL DRIVE

➤ 46-12 ALL-WHEEL-DRIVE SYSTEMS

Various types and arrangements of gears, shafts, universal joints, and differentials are used to provide all-wheel drive (➤46-2). Although similar to four-wheel drive, a vehicle with all-wheel-drive usually does not have a two-speed transfer case and is not designed for off-road use. Many all-wheel-drive vehicles are front-drive with power to the rear wheels only when needed. All-wheel-drive systems may be part-time (➤46-13) or full-time (➤46-14).

➤ 46-13 PART-TIME ALL-WHEEL DRIVE

Figure 46-17 shows a front-drive car with part-time all-wheel drive. It has a single-speed transfer case mounted under the transaxle. The pinion gear for the rear-axle driveshaft is driven from the differential ring gear in the

Fig. 46-17 Part-time all-wheel drive using a single-speed transfer case. The driver-controlled vacuum motor shifts between front-wheel drive and all-wheel drive. (*Ford Motor Company*)

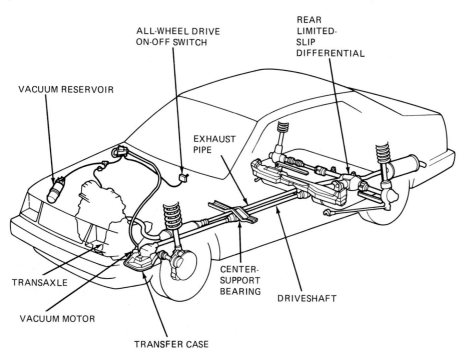

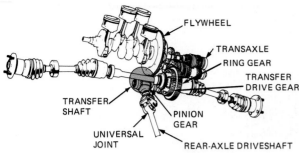

Fig. 46-18 Power train of a front-wheel-drive vehicle with part-time all-wheel drive. No transfer case is used. (*American Honda Motor Company, Inc.*)

transaxle. To get all-wheel drive, the driver moves a switch on the instrument panel. This sends vacuum to a vacuum motor. It moves a sleeve, locking a gear to a shaft and driving the pinion gear for the rear-axle driveshaft.

A similar part-time all-wheel-drive system is shown in Fig. 46-18. To get power to the rear wheels, a *transfer drive gear* next to the ring gear on the front-differential case turns the *transfer-driven gear* (Fig. 46-19). It mounts on a short *transfer shaft*. A bevel gear on the other end of the transfer shaft turns the pinion gear for the rear-axle driveshaft. Movement of the fork moves the sleeve to lock the transfer driven gear to the transfer shaft. This sends power to the rear axle. To disengage four-wheel drive, the sleeve unlocks the transfer shaft from the transfer driven gear.

➤ 46-14 FULL-TIME ALL-WHEEL DRIVE

The use of the viscous coupling to control slippage between two shafts has made possible many different drive

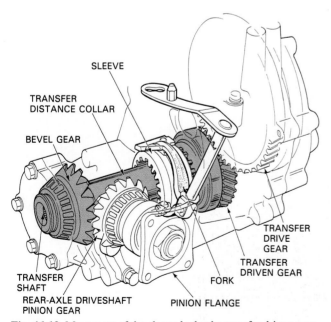

Fig. 46-19 Movement of the sleeve locks the transfer driven gear to the transfer shaft. This sends power to the rear-axle-driveshaft pinion gear for all-wheel drive. (*American Honda Motor Company, Inc.*)

trains. Figure 46-20 shows how the front axle is driven in a car with all-wheel drive. A planetary-gear transfer case (➤46-4) mounts behind a five-speed manual transmission. A viscous coupling (➤46-11) in front of the planetary gearset controls power-flow to the front axle.

During normal driving, the planetary gearset sends about two-thirds of engine torque to the rear wheels and one-third to the front wheels. If the wheels on one axle begin to spin, the viscous coupling locks. This sends the torque to the other axle. Operation of the full-time all-wheel-drive system is automatic.

Figure 43-3 shows a five-speed manual transaxle used in all-wheel-drive vehicles. The arrangement is similar to Figs. 46-19 and 46-20. The center differential and viscous coupling are built into the transaxle.

The drive train for an all-wheel-drive vehicle is shown in Fig. 46-21. The front wheels are normally driven. A viscous coupling connects the two sections of the rear-axle driveshaft. When the front wheels spin, the viscous coupling locks. This sends power to the rear axle.

➤ 46-15 VISCOUS-COUPLING DIFFERENTIALS

Some vehicles have three viscous couplings. One acts as a center differential in the drive line between the front and rear axles (Figs. 43-3 and 46-21). The second is in the front axle where the viscous coupling serves as a limited-slip differential for the front-axle halfshafts. If one front wheel begins to slip, the viscous coupling locks. This locks the two front axle shafts together so both front wheels turn at the same speed.

The third viscous coupling is in the rear axle (Fig. 46-22). There it serves as a limited-slip differential. If one rear wheel loses traction and starts to spin, the viscous coupling locks and both rear-axle shafts turn together.

Some rear axles have twin viscous couplings. The two couplings do three jobs.

1. They split the torque and transfer some of it to the rear wheels if the front wheels lose traction.
2. They serve as the rear differential.
3. They act as a limited-slip differential.

The rear axle does not have a mechanical differential.

➤ 46-16 TORQUE-SENSING DIFFERENTIALS

Differential action may also be provided by a *torque-sensing differential* (Fig. 46-23). It is used as a center differential and as the rear-axle differential in all-wheel-drive systems (Fig. 46-2). The torque-sensing center differential automatically distributes torque evenly (50/50) between the front and rear axles. It has two sets of *worm gears* connected by spur gears. When the wheels on one axle slip, more torque goes to the other axle. This automatically and continuously varies the torque split between the front and rear axles to maximize traction.

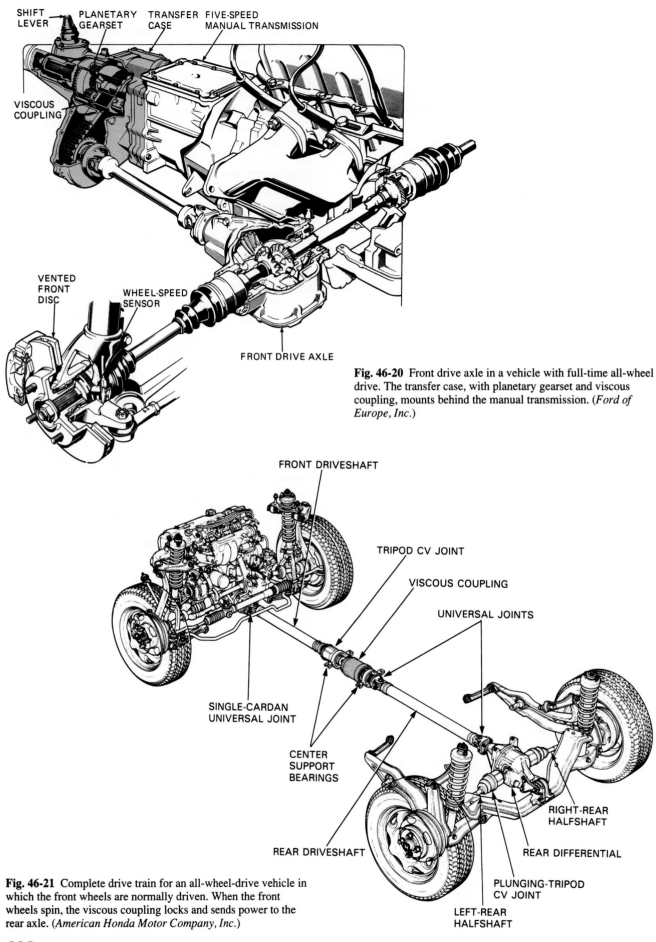

SHIFT LEVER
PLANETARY GEARSET
TRANSFER CASE
FIVE-SPEED MANUAL TRANSMISSION
VISCOUS COUPLING
VENTED FRONT DISC
WHEEL-SPEED SENSOR
FRONT DRIVE AXLE

Fig. 46-20 Front drive axle in a vehicle with full-time all-wheel drive. The transfer case, with planetary gearset and viscous coupling, mounts behind the manual transmission. (*Ford of Europe, Inc.*)

FRONT DRIVESHAFT
TRIPOD CV JOINT
VISCOUS COUPLING
UNIVERSAL JOINTS
SINGLE-CARDAN UNIVERSAL JOINT
CENTER SUPPORT BEARINGS
REAR DRIVESHAFT
LEFT-REAR HALFSHAFT
PLUNGING-TRIPOD CV JOINT
RIGHT-REAR HALFSHAFT
REAR DIFFERENTIAL

Fig. 46-21 Complete drive train for an all-wheel-drive vehicle in which the front wheels are normally driven. When the front wheels spin, the viscous coupling locks and sends power to the rear axle. (*American Honda Motor Company, Inc.*)

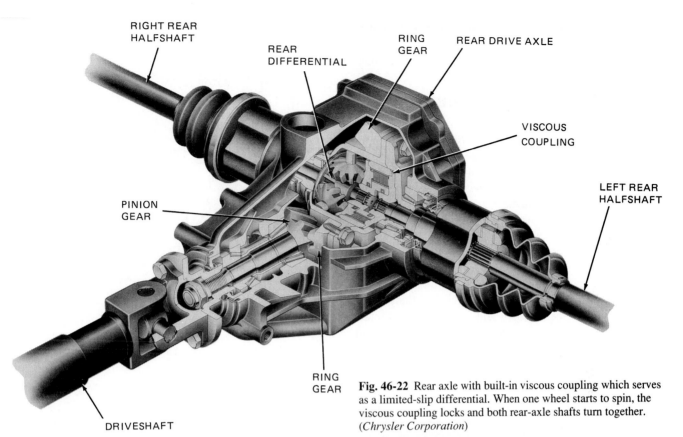

RIGHT REAR
HALFSHAFT

REAR
DIFFERENTIAL

RING
GEAR

REAR DRIVE AXLE

VISCOUS
COUPLING

LEFT REAR
HALFSHAFT

PINION
GEAR

RING
GEAR

DRIVESHAFT

Fig. 46-22 Rear axle with built-in viscous coupling which serves as a limited-slip differential. When one wheel starts to spin, the viscous coupling locks and both rear-axle shafts turn together. (*Chrysler Corporation*)

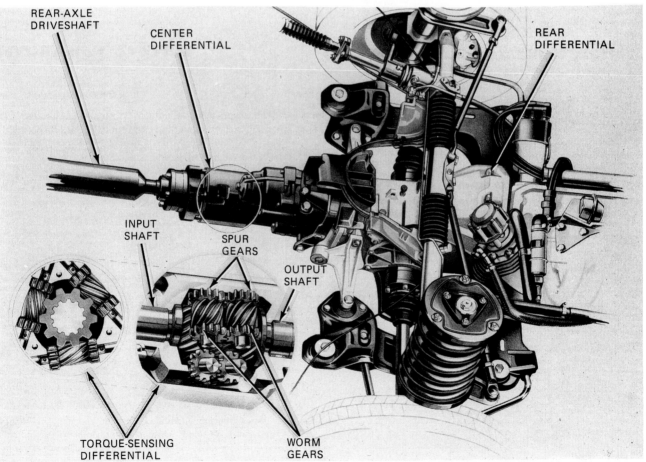

REAR-AXLE
DRIVESHAFT

CENTER
DIFFERENTIAL

REAR
DIFFERENTIAL

INPUT
SHAFT

SPUR
GEARS

OUTPUT
SHAFT

TORQUE-SENSING
DIFFERENTIAL

WORM
GEARS

Fig. 46-23 Torque-sensing center differential that uses two sets of worm gears and spur gears to vary the torque split between the front and rear axles. (*Audi of America, Inc.*)

615

The torque-sensing differential works in the same way when used as the rear-axle differential. Then it varies the torque split between the left and right wheels for maximum traction.

➤ 46-17 LOCKING DIFFERENTIALS

Some differentials can be mechanically locked. This eliminates differential action (➤45-18) and provides maximum traction. Locking a center differential causes both the input shaft and output shaft to rotate at the same speed. Then the same torque is delivered to the driveshafts for the front and rear drive axles.

Figure 46-24 shows a locking arrangement for a rear differential. The locking device is a *dog clutch*. It has a sleeve with projections or teeth that fit into recesses in a mating part. When the driver selects to lock the differential, the dog clutch engages. This locks the right-axle shaft to the differential case. Then the left- and right-axle shafts rotate together. Some vehicles have locks for both the center and rear differentials, or the front and rear differentials. Various combinations are used by different manufacturers.

Careful! The driver should lock a differential only when traction is poor (➤46-9 and 46-10). Excessive tire wear, engine and drive-train damage, and handling problems may result when operating a vehicle with a locked differential on a dry road surface.

➤ 46-18 ELECTRONIC CONTROL OF TRANSFER CASES AND DRIVE TRAINS

Some vehicles that can drive all four wheels have electronic control of the transfer case, axle disconnect, and differential locks. Figure 46-25 shows the layout on the

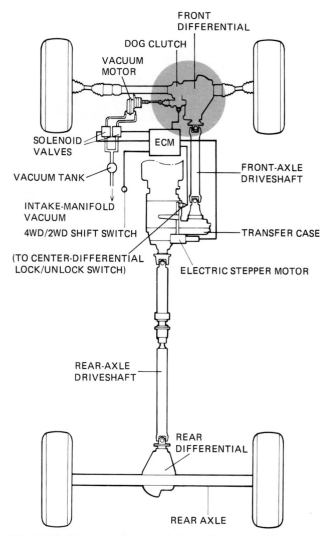

Fig. 46-25 Electronically-controlled transfer case. A driver-operated shift switch signals the ECM for two-wheel drive, four-wheel drive, or four-wheel drive with center-differential lockup. (*Mazda Motors of America, Inc.*)

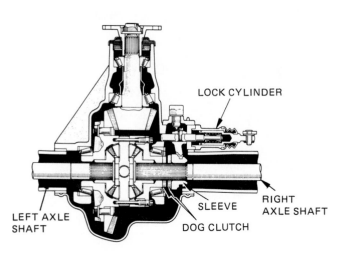

(A) LOCKING REAR DIFFERENTIAL

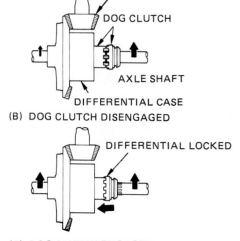

(B) DOG CLUTCH DISENGAGED

(C) DOG CLUTCH ENGAGED

Fig. 46-24 Locking rear differential, engaged and disengaged by operation of a dog clutch. (*Toyota Motor Sales U.S.A., Inc.*)

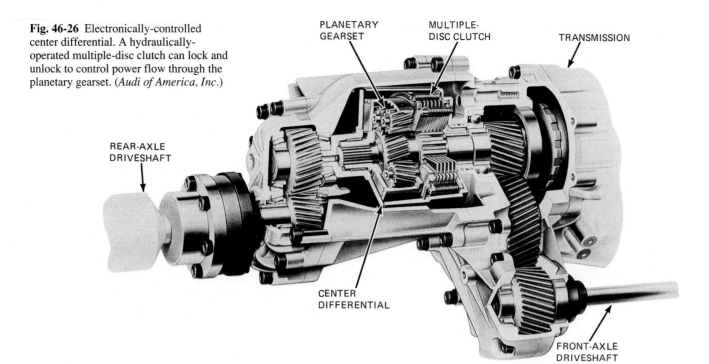

Fig. 46-26 Electronically-controlled center differential. A hydraulically-operated multiple-disc clutch can lock and unlock to control power flow through the planetary gearset. (*Audi of America, Inc.*)

PLANETARY GEARSET

MULTIPLE-DISC CLUTCH

TRANSMISSION

REAR-AXLE DRIVESHAFT

CENTER DIFFERENTIAL

FRONT-AXLE DRIVESHAFT

vehicle of one system. The transfer case is shifted by an electric shift motor or *stepper motor*. This is a motor in which the shaft rotates in short movements such as a quarter or half turn instead of continuously.

Control of the stepper motor is provided by signals from the electronic control module (ECM). This may be the ECM or controller for the transmission or transaxle, and not the ECM for the engine control system. When the driver operates the *4WD/2WD shift switch* (Fig. 46-25), the ECM pulses the stepper motor. Its three positions are:

1. Two-wheel drive.
2. Four-wheel drive.
3. Four-wheel drive with center-differential lockup.

To engage four-wheel drive the ECM signals two *solenoid valves*. These open and close to control intake-manifold vacuum to the vacuum motor for the front-axle disconnect (➤46-8).

Figure 46-26 shows an electronically-controlled center differential. This unit is shown in an all-wheel-drive car in Fig. 46-2. Power flows from the transmission to the planetary-gear center differential. A hydraulically-operated multiple-disc clutch (➤47-15) can lock and unlock to control power flow through the planetary gearset.

During normal driving, the torque is split evenly between the front and rear axles. *Wheel-speed sensors* (Chap. 53) signal the speed of each wheel to the ECM. When one wheel slips and turns faster than the others, signals from the ECM cause hydraulic pressure to increase quickly in the multiple-disc clutch. It then engages and disengages to vary the torque split and send up to 100 percent of the torque to the axle with the best traction.

In some vehicles, the ECM controls a *magnetic clutch* (Chap. 55) in the transfer case. When the front and rear driveshaft speeds vary, the ECM locks and unlocks the

magnetic clutch. This continues until the wheels are turning at the same speed. Then the transfer case resumes its normal condition of sending two-thirds of the torque to the rear axle and one-third to the front axle.

FOUR-WHEEL-DRIVE DIAGNOSIS AND SERVICE

➤ 46-19 TRANSFER-CASE LUBRICATION

Change the transfer-case lubricant at the intervals recommended in the vehicle maintenance schedule. How often depends mostly on the type of vehicle operation. For example, one manufacturer recommends changing the lubricant every 24,000 miles [38,624 km] for normal off-on road work. For heavy-duty work, such as snowplowing or pulling a trailer, change the oil every 12,000 miles [19,312 km]. For severe use, change the oil every 1000 miles [1609 km].

Before draining the transfer case, operate the vehicle in four-wheel drive until the lubricant reaches its normal temperature. Refill the transfer case with the lubricant recommended by the vehicle manufacturer. Using a different lubricant may cause improper operation and customer complaints. Some transfer cases should be filled with engine oil. Others use automatic-transmission fluid (ATF) or gear oil.

➤ 46-20 TRANSFER-CASE TROUBLE DIAGNOSIS

Figure 46-27 is a chart that lists transfer-case complaints, possible causes, and checks or corrections. Typical

Complaint	Possible Cause	Check or Correction
1. Transfer case shifts hard or will not shift	a. Speed too great to permit	Stop to shift, or reduce speed to 2-3 mph [3-4 km/h] before shift
	b. If operated in 4H on dry paved surface, driveline torque may cause hard shifting	Stop, shift transmission to neutral and case to 2H and operate on dry paved surface
	c. External linkage binding	Lubricate, repair, or replace linkage. Tighten loose components
	d. Insufficient or wrong lubricant	Drain and refill with proper amount of specified lubricant
	e. Internal parts binding, worn or damaged	Disassemble unit, replace components as necessary
2. Transfer case noisy in all drive modes	a. Insufficient or wrong lubricant	Drain and refill with proper amount of specified lubricant. If unit still noisy, disassemble and inspect.
3. Noisy engagement	a. Not completely engaged in 4L	Stop vehicle, shift transfer case to neutral, then back to 4L
	b. Linkage loose or binding	Tighten, lubricate, repair
	c. Range fork cracked, binding, or inserts worn	Disassemble unit, repair
	d. Internal gear or lockplate worn or damaged	Disassemble unit, repair
4. Leaking lubricant from vent or shaft seals	a. Case overfilled	Drain to correct level
	b. Vent closed	Clear or replace vent
	c. Seals damaged or incorrectly installed	Replace seals. Seal lip must face interior of case. Seal surfaces must not be nicked or scored. Remove nicks or replace yoke.
5. Abnormal tire wear	a. Extended operation on dry paved surface in 4H	Operate in 2H on paved surface

Fig. 46-27 Transfer-case trouble-diagnosis chart.

troubles with the transfer case include excessive noise, shift lever hard to move, gears slip out of engagement, and leaking lubricant. Many other complaints related to the vacuum- or electric-shift mechanism and the electronic control system are possible. In some vehicles, the ECM has self-diagnostic capability (➤20-16). Follow the diagnosis procedures in the vehicle service manual for the transfer case you are servicing.

CAUTION!

When diagnosing or servicing a vehicle equipped with a center differential and one or more viscous couplings, always raise all tires off the ground. If a tire touches the ground, the viscous coupling may send torque to any wheel that has traction. Then the vehicle would move and could cause an accident or damage.

➤ 46-21 TRANSFER-CASE SERVICE

There are a variety of transfer-case designs and constructions. Refer to the vehicle service manual for information on transfer-case removal, service, and installation. Some transfer cases require a linkage adjustment after installation.

Basic service procedures for transfer cases are similar to

servicing other gearboxes. These procedures are described in Chap. 44 on diagnosis and service of manual transmissions and transaxles. Chapter 48 includes information on diagnosis and service of planetary gearsets, which are used in automatic transmissions and transaxles.

Careful! An electric-shift transfer case does not have NEUTRAL. Disconnect the rear driveshaft before towing a vehicle with this type of transfer case. Severe transmission damage may otherwise occur. The transfer case has positive lubrication, but the transmission does not.

➤ 46-22 SERVICING FOUR-WHEEL AND ALL-WHEEL DRIVE

Many components in a four-wheel-drive or all-wheel-drive system are also other parts of the drive train. Chapter 45 describes the trouble-diagnosis and service of driveshafts, universal joints, differentials, and drive axles. Chapter 20 covers the operation and use of an electronic control system to diagnosis troubles in sensors and the ECM. Wheel-speed sensors are part of the *antilock-braking system* and covered in Chap. 53.

Generally, viscous couplings should not be opened and are not repairable. The coupling contains silicone fluid that is not available to automotive technicians or repair shops. If the viscous coupling is defective, replace it.

TRADE TALK

all-wheel drive
dog clutch
four-wheel drive

front-axle disconnect
interaxle differential
locking differential

locking hubs
torque-sensing differential
transfer case

viscous coupling

MULTIPLE-CHOICE TEST

Select the **one** *correct, best, or most probable answer to each question.*
You can find the answers in the section indicated at the end of each question.

1. Technician A says the purpose of the transfer case is to divide engine torque between the left- and right-drive wheels. Technician B says the two-speed transfer case provides direct drive and overdrive. Who is right? (➤46-3)
   a. A only
   b. B only
   c. both A and B
   d. neither A nor B

2. A planetary gearset includes the following EXCEPT (➤46-5)
   a. a sun gear
   b. an internal or ring gear
   c. a worm gear
   d. a planet-pinion carrier

3. A planetary-gear transfer case is in direct drive when (➤46-5)
   a. two members of the planetary gearset are locked together
   b. a brake band holds the internal gear stationary
   c. the internal gear moves forward to engage a locking plate
   d. four-wheel drive is engaged

4. Locking hubs are used on some front-drive axles to (➤46-7)
   a. improve fuel economy
   b. increase tire life
   c. reduce engine and transfer-case wear
   d. all of the above

5. When a front-axle disconnect is disengaged, the parts that stop rotating include the (➤46-9)
   a. front wheels
   b. front-axle ring gear, differential case, and pinion
   c. front and rear driveshafts
   d. rear-axle shafts

6. The differential that compensates for any difference in travel of the front and rear wheels is the (➤46-10)
   a. center or interaxle differential
   b. front differential
   c. rear differential
   d. locking differential

7. Technician A says a viscous coupling in the transfer case can transfer torque to the front wheels if the rear wheels begin to slip. Technician B says the slippage causes the silicone fluid to expand, creating pressure that locks the plates together. Who is right? (➤46-11)
   a. A only
   b. B only
   c. Both A and B
   d. Neither A nor B

8. A viscous coupling may be used as all the following EXCEPT (➤46-15)
   a. a center differential
   b. a limited-slip differential between the front-axle halfshafts
   c. a limited-slip differential in the rear-drive axle
   d. a plunging CV joint to compensate for changes in halfshaft length

9. A torque-sensing differential varies the torque split between the front and rear axles (➤46-16)
   a. after being mechanically locked
   b. continuously and automatically
   c. according to signals from the ECM
   d. only when the transfer case is in low range

REVIEW QUESTIONS

1. How does a vehicle with four-wheel drive differ from a vehicle with all-wheel drive? (➤46-1 and 46-2)
2. What is the difference between part-time four-wheel drive and full-time four-wheel drive? (➤46-3)
3. Explain why an interaxle differential is needed and the advantages of a viscous coupling over an open bevel-gear differential. (➤46-10)
4. What is a *dog clutch* and how does it work? (➤46-17)
5. What precautions should be taken before towing a vehicle with an electric-shift transfer case? (➤46-21)

CHAPTER 47

AUTOMATIC TRANSMISSIONS AND TRANSAXLES

After studying this chapter, you should be able to:

- Describe the purpose, construction, and operation of the torque converter.
- Explain how a lockup torque converter works.
- Describe planetary-gear construction and operation.
- Explain how bands and clutches control planetary gears.
- Describe the hydraulic control system and how it controls the bands and clutches.
- Discuss electronic shift controls, automatic countershaft transmissions, and continuously-variable transmissions.

> ## 47-1 AUTOMATIC TRANSMISSIONS AND TRANSAXLES

The construction and operation of automatic transmissions and the transmission section in automatic transaxles are similar. Both do the same basic job. They automatically provide several forward gear ratios between the engine crankshaft and the transmission or transaxle output shaft (➤43-1).

Automatic transmissions and transaxles have similar components. Three basic parts include (Fig. 47-1):

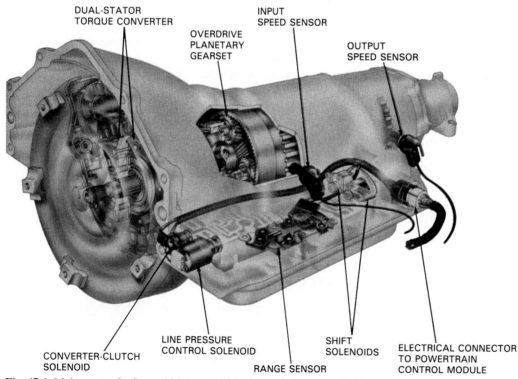

DUAL-STATOR TORQUE CONVERTER

OVERDRIVE PLANETARY GEARSET

INPUT SPEED SENSOR

OUTPUT SPEED SENSOR

CONVERTER-CLUTCH SOLENOID

LINE PRESSURE CONTROL SOLENOID

RANGE SENSOR

SHIFT SOLENOIDS

ELECTRICAL CONNECTOR TO POWERTRAIN CONTROL MODULE

Fig. 47-1 Major parts of a General Motors 4L80-E electronically-controlled four-speed automatic transmission. (*Chevrolet Division of General Motors Corporation*)

1. A *torque converter* that usually has a *lockup clutch* to prevent slippage.
2. A *gear train* that usually has one or more *planetary gearsets*.
3. A *hydraulic system* that may be electronically controlled.

The torque converter connects to the crankshaft (Fig. 47-2) and transmits engine power to the gear train. Hydraulic pressure acting through the *automatic-trans-* *mission fluid* (ATF) in the transmission or transaxle produces the shifts (➤47-17).

➤ 47-2 AUTOMATIC-TRANSMISSION AND TRANSAXLE CONSTRUCTION

In automatic transmissions, the gearing and shifting devices are arranged in a single row along a common centerline (Fig. 47-3). Automatic transaxles have the com-

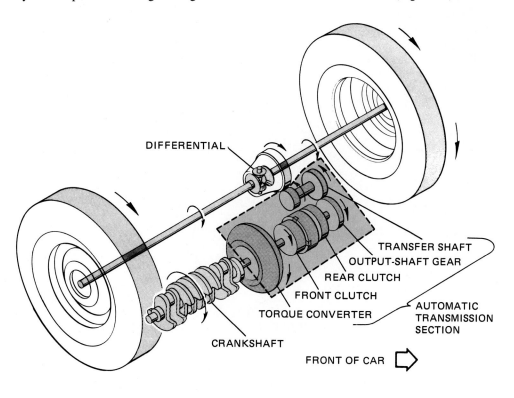

Fig. 47-2 Power flow from the engine crankshaft to the drive wheels for a front-wheel-drive vehicle with automatic transaxle. (*Chrysler Corporation*)

DIFFERENTIAL
TRANSFER SHAFT
OUTPUT-SHAFT GEAR
REAR CLUTCH
FRONT CLUTCH
TORQUE CONVERTER
AUTOMATIC TRANSMISSION SECTION
CRANKSHAFT
FRONT OF CAR

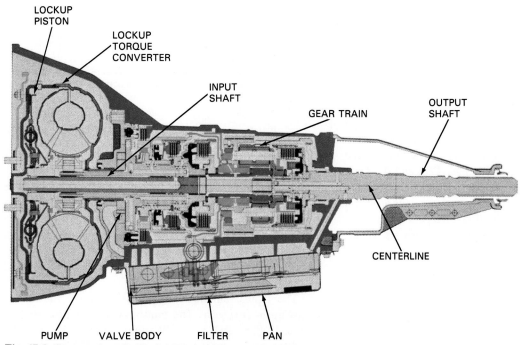

LOCKUP PISTON
LOCKUP TORQUE CONVERTER
INPUT SHAFT
GEAR TRAIN
OUTPUT SHAFT
CENTERLINE
PUMP   VALVE BODY   FILTER   PAN

Fig. 47-3 Construction of a Ford AOD-E electronically-controlled four-speed transmission. (*Ford Motor Company*)

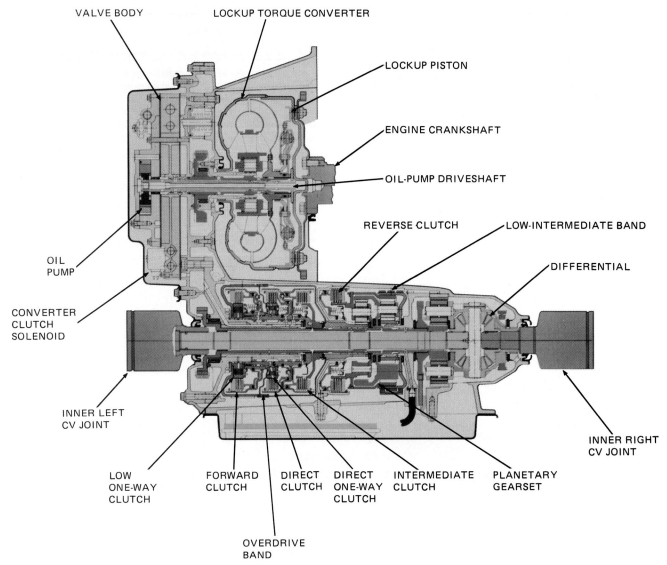

Fig. 47-4 Construction of a Ford AXOD four-speed automatic transaxle, which uses an offset torque converter. (*Ford Motor Company*)

ponents either in a single row (Fig. 47-2) or in two rows with an offset torque converter (Fig. 47-4). The torque converter drives the transmission input shaft through sprockets connected by a drive chain (Fig. 47-5).

The automatic transaxle drives the front wheels through CV joints and halfshafts (Fig. 47-4). These are described in Chap. 45. The drive-axle or differential section of the transaxle contains a differential (Figs. 47-2 and 47-4). It allows the two front wheels to turn at different speeds and to travel different distances when the vehicle goes around a curve. Section 45-18 describes differential action.

Some automatic transmissions and transaxles are similar in construction to manual transmissions and transaxles (Chap. 43). Instead of planetary gears, spur and helical gears attach to two shafts—a mainshaft and a countershaft. These transaxles are described in ➤47-29.

> **NOTE** To avoid needlessly repeating the phrase *transmission or transaxle,* following references generally are to the *transmission.* This may indicate a

separate transmission or the *transmission section* of an automatic transaxle. *Transaxle* is used when the reference applies only to a transaxle.

➤ 47-3 AUTOMATIC-TRANSMISSION OPERATION

The basic operation of an automatic transmission is the same whether for rear-wheel drive, front-wheel drive, or four-wheel drive. Most automatic transmissions have three or four forward speeds. They also have PARK, NEUTRAL, and REVERSE. Fourth speed is usually an overdrive ratio (➤43-3). Some automatic transmissions have five forward speeds with fifth-gear overdrive.

The typical automatic transmission starts the vehicle moving in first gear. The transmission then *upshifts* into second, third, and fourth (if used). These shifts and the locking of the *torque-converter clutch* (TCC) can occur without assistance from the driver. They happen automat-

Fig. 47-5 Offset torque converter driving the transaxle input shaft through sprockets connected by a drive chain. (*Cadillac Division of General Motors Corporation*)

ically as vehicle speed increases and engine load or throttle opening decreases.

To slow and stop the vehicle, the driver releases the accelerator pedal and depresses the brake pedal as needed. The transmission disengages the torque-converter clutch and automatically *downshifts* until it is in first gear when the vehicle stops. A foot-operated clutch (Chap. 42) is not needed. Slippage in the torque converter (➤47-4) allows the engine to idle with the transmission in gear.

TORQUE CONVERTERS

➤ 47-4 TORQUE CONVERTER

The torque converter (Figs. 47-5 and 47-6) is a form of *fluid coupling*. This is a device that uses a fluid (such as automatic-transmission fluid) and vaned rotors to transmit power between shafts. The torque converter is filled with automatic-transmission fluid. When the engine runs, power flows from the crankshaft through the fluid to the transmission input shaft (Fig. 47-3).

Figure 47-6 shows the basic construction and fluid-flow in a torque converter. A *drive plate* attaches to the engine-crankshaft flange. The torque-converter assembly bolts to the drive plate. Inside the fluid-filled circular housing are

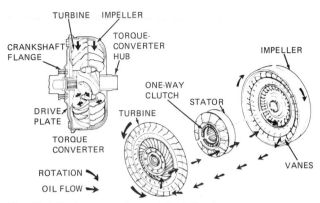

Fig. 47-6 Basic construction and fluid flow in a torque converter as it rotates. (*Ford Motor Company*)

three members. These are the *impeller, turbine,* and *stator.* The impeller is a vaned rotor connected to the drive plate. This is the driving member in the torque converter. It always turns at engine speed. The turbine is a vaned rotor connected to the transmission input shaft. This is the driven member in the torque converter. Unless the torque converter is locked (➤47-7), the turbine normally turns slower than the impeller.

When the engine runs, the fluid between the vanes in the impeller is thrown outward by centrifugal force (Fig. 47-6). The fluid strikes the turbine vanes. This produces a rotating force on the turbine and the transmission input shaft attached to it. The vanes then direct the fluid toward the center of the turbine and back toward the center of the impeller.

➤ 47-5 STATOR

To make the torque converter more efficient, a third member or *sta*tionary reac*tor* called a *stator* is placed between the impeller and turbine (Figs. 47-6 and 47-7). The stator has curved vanes that change the direction of the

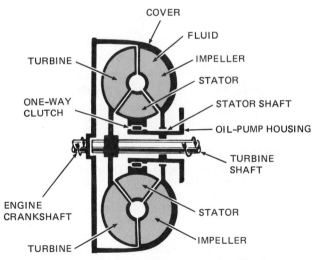

Fig. 47-7 Locations of the impeller, stator, and turbine in a torque converter. (*Chevrolet Division of General Motors Corporation*)

fluid after it leaves the turbine. This causes the fluid to pass through the impeller and then push on the turbine vanes again with a helping force that aids rotation. The result is torque multiplication under certain conditions.

Figure 47-8 shows how the stator works. The fluid circulates continually as long as the engine runs. The continuing push of the fluid on the turbine vanes increases the torque on the turbine. In many torque converters, the torque is more than doubled. For each pound-foot [1.35 N-m] of torque entering the impeller, the turbine delivers more than 2 pound-feet [2.7 N-m] of torque to the transmission input shaft. This is *torque multiplication* (Fig. 47-8C). It is

needed for acceleration and occurs only when the impeller turns faster than the turbine.

Some torque converters have *dual stators* (Fig. 47-1). Their operation is the same as that of the single stator. However, the dual stators provide greater torque multiplication at lower speeds.

➤ 47-6 STATOR ONE-WAY CLUTCH

As the vehicle approaches cruising speed, the turbine begins to "catch up" with the impeller. The speed difference between the impeller and turbine becomes small.

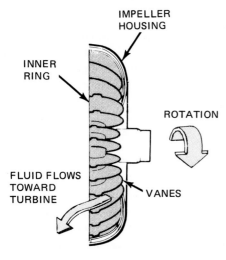

(A) IMPELLER OPERATION

(C) TORQUE MULTIPLICATION

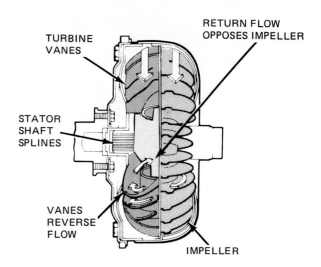

(B) DRIVING THE TURBINE

(D) COUPLING PHASE

Fig. 47-8 Torque-converter action. (A) The impeller sends a flow of oil toward the turbine. (B) The turbine vanes receive the flow and this spins the turbine. The vanes reverse the direction of oil flow and send it back toward the impeller. (C) The stator reverses the flow of the oil into a helping direction and this multiplies the torque. (D) When the turbine speed nears the impeller speed, the oil strikes the backs of the stator vanes, causing the stator to spin forward. This prevents the stator vanes from interfering with the oil flow. (*Ford Motor Company*)

The fluid leaving the turbine is moving at about the same speed as the impeller. This fluid could pass directly into the impeller without stator action. In fact, the stator vanes are now in the way. The fluid is striking the back sides of the stator vanes.

To allow the stator vanes to move out of the way, the stator mounts on a *one-way clutch*. This is a mechanical device that transmits torque in one direction and permits free rotation in the opposite direction (➤43-10). When the speed difference between the impeller and turbine is large, the fluid from the turbine tries to spin the stator backward. This causes the one-way clutch to lock the stator to its shaft (Figs. 47-7 and 47-8C). When the speed difference is small, the clutch unlocks and allows the stator to freewheel (Fig. 47-8D). Two types of one-way clutch are the *roller clutch* and the *sprag clutch*.

1. ROLLER CLUTCH Figure 47-9 shows the construction of a one-way roller clutch. It has a hub, an outer ring or *clutch cam,* and rollers in notches in the cam. The notches are smaller at one end. The rollers have springs behind them. As long as the impeller turns faster than the turbine, the stator is stationary. As the fluid strikes the vanes, it pushes on the stator, trying to turn the stator backward. This causes the rollers to roll into the smaller end of the notches where they jam and lock the stator to the hub. When turbine speed approaches impeller speed, the rollers roll out of the smaller ends of the notches and into the larger ends. There they cannot jam and the stator is able to freewheel.

2. SPRAG CLUTCH *Sprags* are cam-shaped locking elements placed between inner and outer races (Fig. 47-10). The sprags are held in place by two cages and small springs. When stator action is not needed, the outer race unlocks so that the stator spins freely (Fig. 47-10A). When fluid hits the stator vanes and tries to spin the stator backward, the sprags jam between the outer and inner races (Fig. 47-10B). This locks the stator.

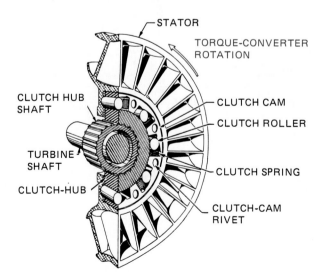

Fig. 47-9 A roller clutch used to support the stator in a torque converter. (*Chrysler Corporation*)

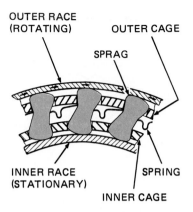

(A) UNLOCKED

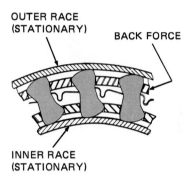

(B) LOCKED

Fig. 47-10 Operation of a sprag clutch.

➤ 47-7 TORQUE-CONVERTER CLUTCH

During normal vehicle operation, the impeller turns faster than the turbine. This difference in speed is *slippage*. It causes a power loss through the torque converter. Most automatic transmissions have a torque-converter clutch (TCC) that can mechanically lock the torque converter to prevent slippage. This improves fuel economy and lowers the temperature of the automatic-transmission fluid.

Figure 47-11 shows a lockup torque converter. As in non-locking torque converters, the impeller attaches to the cover. The turbine attaches to the transmission input shaft. In addition, the lockup torque converter has a *lockup* or *clutch piston* with a lining of friction material. The piston or *plate* attaches to the turbine hub (Fig. 47-12). *Isolator springs* help dampen the shock of engagement as the torque converter locks. They also dampen out the power pulses from the engine while the torque converter is locked (➤42-6).

Figure 47-12 shows the operation of the torque-converter clutch. When the clutch piston is disengaged from the cover (Fig. 47-12B), the piston rotates with the turbine. The torque converter is unlocked. Its operation is the same as described in previous sections. Fluid pressure holds the clutch piston away from the cover.

625

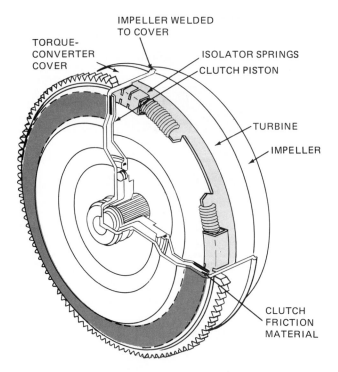

Fig. 47-11 A torque converter with locking clutch. (*Chrysler Corporation*)

Labels: IMPELLER WELDED TO COVER; TORQUE-CONVERTER COVER; ISOLATOR SPRINGS; CLUTCH PISTON; TURBINE; IMPELLER; CLUTCH FRICTION MATERIAL

To get lockup, fluid pressure is applied behind the piston (Fig. 47-12C). This forces the piston against the cover and locks the impeller to the turbine. Power flows from the cover through the piston to the turbine hub which drives the transmission input shaft. The torque converter turns as a unit with no slippage or power loss through it.

➤ **47-8 CONTROLLING THE TORQUE-CONVERTER CLUTCH**

In most vehicles, the *electronic control module* (ECM) controls the torque-converter clutch. Unless conditions are right for lockup, it does not take place.

When the proper conditions exist for lockup, the ECM signals the *converter-clutch solenoid* (Figs. 47-1 and 47-4). It causes fluid pressure to build up on the apply side of the piston. At the same time, fluid escapes from between the piston and the cover. The apply pressure forces the piston against the cover and locks the torque converter.

The torque-converter clutch described above is electronically controlled, but it operates hydraulically. Some torque converters have a centrifugal lockup clutch. Centrifugal force causes it to lock and unlock automatically at preset speeds.

Lockup in some torque converters is provided by a *viscous clutch* controlled by the ECM. The viscous clutch is filled with silicone fluid. It allows a slight slip that eliminates *chuggle*. This is a bucking or jerking condition sometimes noticeable with the torque-converter clutch engaged, especially at low speed.

PLANETARY GEAR TRAINS

➤ **47-9 PLANETARY GEARS**

Most automatic transmissions and transaxles have one or more planetary gearsets (➤46-4). A simple planetary gearset (Fig. 47-13) can provide any of five conditions:

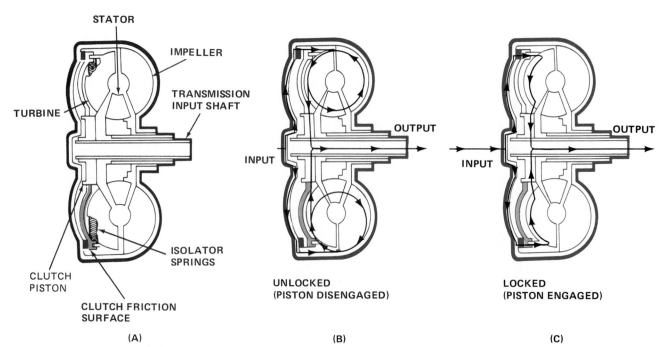

Labels: STATOR; IMPELLER; TRANSMISSION INPUT SHAFT; TURBINE; OUTPUT; INPUT; ISOLATOR SPRINGS; CLUTCH PISTON; CLUTCH FRICTION SURFACE; OUTPUT; INPUT

(A)   (B) UNLOCKED (PISTON DISENGAGED)   (C) LOCKED (PISTON ENGAGED)

Fig. 47-12 Operation of the torque-converter clutch. (*Chrysler Corporation*)

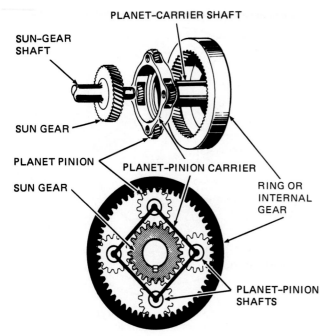

Fig. 47-13 A single planetary gearset.

1. Speed increase with torque decrease (overdrive).
2. Speed decrease with torque increase (underdrive or reduction).
3. Direct drive (input and output shafts turn at the same speed).
4. Reverse direction of rotation (reverse).
5. Neutral (input and output shafts disconnected).

The simple planetary gearset (Fig. 47-13) is made of three members (Fig. 47-13). These are an *internal* or *ring gear*, a *sun gear*, and a *planet-pinion carrier* with two or more *planet pinions*.

➤ 47-10 PLANETARY-GEAR COMBINATIONS

When two gears are in mesh (Fig. 43-5), they will turn in opposite directions. To make them turn in the same direction, put a third gear or *idler gear* between them (Fig. 43-11). The idler gear does no work—it is idle. The idler gear helps provide reverse in manual transmissions and transaxles (Chap. 43).

Another way to get two gears to rotate in the same direction is to use a small external gear inside an internal gear (Fig. 47-14A). Placing another gear in the center and meshed with the external gear creates a simple planetary gearset (Fig. 47-14B).

The center gear is the sun gear because everything rotates around it. The external gears between the sun gear and the internal gear are the planet pinions. They revolve around the sun gear, just as planets revolve around the sun. Figure 47-14B shows two planet pinions. Most planetary gearsets have three or four planet pinions (Fig. 47-13). They rotate on shafts that are part of the planet-pinion carrier (Figs. 46-8 and 47-13).

➤ 47-11 PLANETARY-GEARSET OPERATION

If one member of a planetary gearset is held stationary and another member is turned, there will be either a speed increase, a speed reduction, or reverse. The result depends on which member is held and which member is turned. Figure 47-15 lists the various conditions in a simple planetary gearset. Each condition is described below.

Condition	1	2	3	4	5	6
Internal gear	D	H	T	H	T	D
Carrier	T	T	D	D	H	H
Sun gear	H	D	H	T	D	T
Speed	I	I	L	L	IR	LR

D—Driven (output)   L—Decrease speed
H—Held (stationary)   T—Turned or driving (input)
I—Increase speed

Fig. 47-15 Various conditions possible in the single planetary gearset if one member is held and another is turned.

Fig. 47-14 How internal and external gears can form a simple planetary gearset.

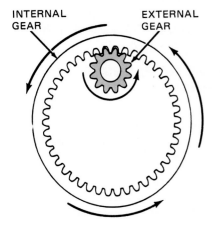

(A) INTERNAL AND EXTERNAL GEARS

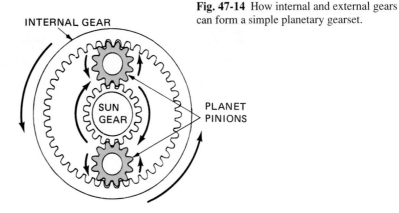

(B) SIMPLE PLANETARY GEARSET

1. SPEED INCREASE 1 An increase in speed results when the sun gear is held stationary and the planet-pinion carrier is turned. As the carrier turns, the planet pinions (which are meshed with the stationary sun gear) rotate on their shafts. Figure 47-16 shows how speed is increased. If the planet-pinion shaft moves 1 foot per second [0.305 m/s], then the tooth meshed with the internal gear is moving at 2 feet per second [0.610 m/s]. This turns the internal gear faster than the carrier. Speed increases. This condition provides fourth-gear overdrive in some automatic transmissions and transaxles.

The gear ratio between the planet-pinion carrier and the internal gear can be altered by changing the sizes of the gears. In Fig. 47-17, the planet-pinion carrier turns 0.7 revolution while turning the internal gear one complete revolution.

2. SPEED INCREASE 2 Another combination is to hold the internal gear stationary and turn the carrier. This drives the sun gear faster than the carrier. The condition is not normally used in automatic transmissions and transaxles.

3. SPEED REDUCTION 1 If the internal gear is turned and the sun gear is held stationary, the planet-pinion carrier turns more slowly than the internal gear. This arrangement can provide second gear.

4. SPEED REDUCTION 2 If the internal gear is held stationary and the sun gear is turned, the carrier is driven at reduced speed. The planet pinions must rotate on their shafts. They must also walk around the internal gear. As the pinions rotate, the carrier also rotates. However, the carrier rotates at a slower speed than the sun gear. This arrangement provides the greatest torque increase. It is often used to get first gear.

5. REVERSE 1 Hold the carrier stationary and turn the internal gear. The planet pinions act as idlers. They drive

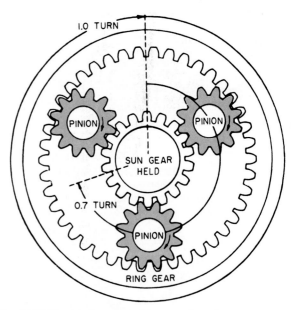

Fig. 47-17 The relative sizes of the gears in a planetary gearset that cause the ring gear to turn once while the planet-pinion carrier makes 0.7 turn. The sun gear is held stationary.

the sun gear in the reverse direction and faster than the internal gear. Since there is no need for a "high-speed" reverse gear, this condition normally is not used to get reverse.

6. REVERSE 2 Hold the carrier stationary and turn the sun gear. The internal gear is then driven in the reverse direction, but slower than the sun gear. This condition provides reverse gear.

7. DIRECT DRIVE If any two members are locked together or driven at the same speed, the planetary gearset acts as a solid shaft. There is no change in speed or direction between the input and output shafts of the gearset. Gear ratio is 1:1. This condition provides third gear or direct drive.

8. NEUTRAL When no clutches are engaged and no bands are applied, no member of the planetary gearset is held. All three members are free. Then no power can be transmitted through the gearset. This is neutral. It removes the load so the engine can be started.

➤ 47-12 TYPES OF PLANETARY GEARSETS

The planetary gearset described above is a simple planetary gearset (Fig. 47-13). Two other types are widely used in automatic transmissions and transaxles. These are:

1. The *Simpson* planetary gearset. It has two separate sets of planet pinions (Fig. 47-18). They revolve around a common sun gear. Each set of planet pinions meshes with its own internal gear.
2. The *Ravigneaux* (pronounced *Raveno*) planetary gearset (Fig. 47-19). It has an internal gear, two sets of planet

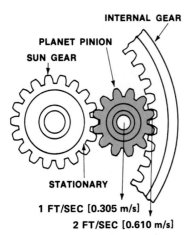

Fig. 47-16 If the sun gear is held stationary and the planet-pinion carrier is turned, the ring gear will turn faster than the carrier. The planet pinion pivots around the stationary teeth. If the center of the pinion shaft is moving at 1 foot per second [0.3 m/s], the tooth opposite the stationary tooth must move at 2 feet per second [0.6 m/s] because it is twice as far away from the stationary tooth as the center of the shaft.

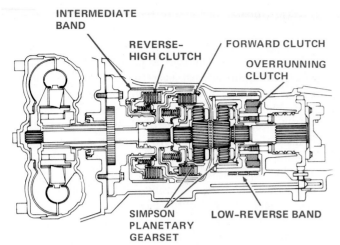

Fig. 47-18 An automatic transmission using a Simpson planetary gearset. (*Ford Motor Company*)

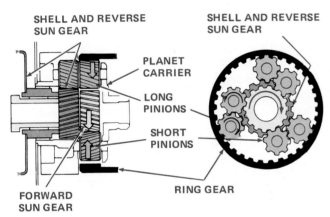

Fig. 47-19 A Ravigneaux, or compound, planetary gearset, using short and long pinions. (*Ford Motor Company*)

pinions (long and short), two sun gears (forward and reverse), and a planet-pinion carrier. This is also called a *compound* planetary gearset. Other compound planetary gear-train arrangements are possible. However, the basic conditions and power flows are similar.

PLANETARY-GEARSET CONTROLS

➤ 47-13 CONTROLLING THE PLANETARY GEARSET

Planetary gearsets are controlled by *bands,* one-way clutches, and *multiple-disc clutches* (➤47-15). The one-way clutch operates automatically to prevent a member from turning backward. Many automatic transmissions have a one-way clutch (*overrunning clutch* in Fig. 47-18) that holds the rear planet carrier stationary in first gear. This clutch operates automatically in the same way as the one-way clutch in the stator (➤47-6). A multiple-disc clutch can engage to drive one member or to hold it sta-

tionary. The multiple-disc clutch can also lock two members together. Then the planetary gearset provides direct drive.

Bands and multiple-disc clutches are operated by springs and fluid pressure. An *oil pump* (Figs. 47-3 and 47-4) driven by the torque-converter cover supplies the fluid pressure. The pump continuously draws fluid through a filter from the pan or *sump*. The pressurized fluid or *line pressure* is delivered to the *valve body* (➤47-25). It then directs the fluid through the proper passages to control the bands and clutches.

➤ 47-14 BAND AND SERVO

Figure 47-20 shows a planetary gearset with two control devices. These are the band and the multiple-disc clutch. The band is a *brake band* that wraps around a metal *clutch drum*. The band is lined with friction material (Fig. 47-21). When the band is *applied*—tightened on the drum—the

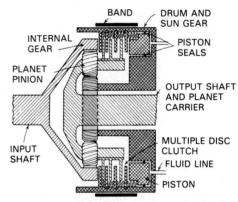

Fig. 47-20 Planetary gearset showing the two hydraulically-operated control devices. One device is a drum and band. The other is a multiple-disc clutch.

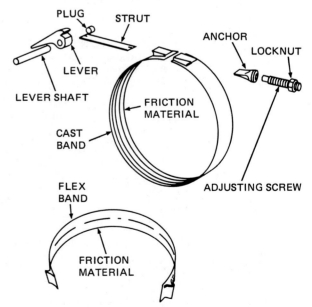

Fig. 47-21 Band with related linkages for an automatic transmission. (*Chrysler Corporation*)

drum and sun gear stop rotating and are held stationary. One end of the band is anchored to the transmission case (Fig. 47-22). The other end is linked to a *servo*. This is a device in a hydraulic system that converts hydraulic pressure to mechanical movement.

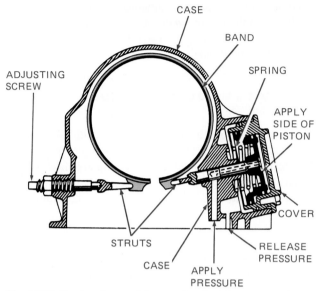

Fig. 47-22 Band and servo (piston and spring) that operates it. (*Ford Motor Company*)

When hydraulic pressure (pressurized fluid) is directed to the *apply side* of the servo piston, the piston is forced to move (Fig. 47-22). It overcomes the *servo spring* and pushes on the strut. This applies the band. With the input shaft driving the internal gear (Fig. 47-20), the planet pinions now walk around the internal gear at reduced speed. This turns the planet carrier and output shaft at reduced speed but with increased torque.

Figure 47-23 shows how this condition provides speed reduction for second gear. The clutch shown is the *forward clutch* in Fig. 47-18. It engages to lock the input shaft to the internal gear. Most transmissions have the forward clutch engaged in all forward gears.

To release the band, the fluid pressure on the apply side of the servo piston is relieved. This allows the servo spring to push the piston back (Fig. 47-22). Fluid pressure is usually redirected from the apply side to the *release side* of the servo piston to assist the spring.

47-15 MULTIPLE-DISC CLUTCH

The multiple-disk clutch is located inside a clutch drum (Figs. 47-23 and 47-24). A series of discs or *clutch plates* fits inside the drum. The plates are alternately *steel plates* and *friction plates*. Steel plates are unlined while friction plates have a lining of friction material on both sides or

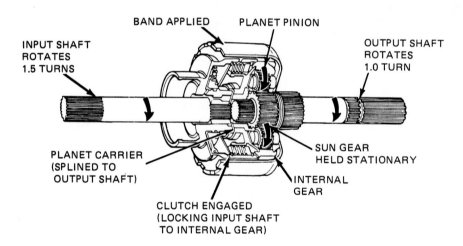

Fig. 47-24 A disassembled multiple-disc clutch. (*Ford Motor Company*)

Fig. 47-23 Power flow through a planetary gearset with the band applied. This provides speed reduction for second gear. (*Ford Motor Company*)

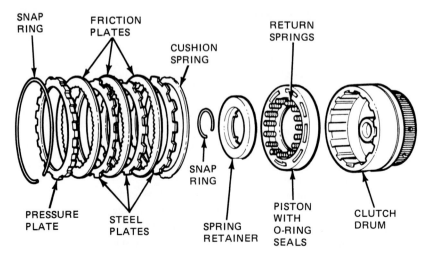

faces. The steel plates are splined to the clutch drum. Friction plates are splined to a hub in the clutch. The drum and hub connect to different members to control the planetary gearset.

Figure 47-25 shows the clutch engaged. Compare this illustration with Fig. 47-20 which shows the same clutch disengaged. In both illustrations, the drum attaches to the sun gear. Splines on the planet carrier serve as the clutch hub.

To engage the clutch, fluid pressure is directed to the apply side of the clutch piston (Figs. 47-24 and 47-25). This forces the piston to move (Figs. 47-24 and 47-25) and push the plates together. The plates lock the sun gear to the planet carrier (Fig. 47-25). The planetary gearset now rotates as a single unit. When fluid pressure is released, the *return springs* help the clutch disengage quickly. Then the two sets of clutch plates rotate independently.

> **NOTE** The bands, clutches, and planetary gearsets in automatic transmissions and transaxles may be arranged in different ways. Their basic function remains the same, however. The band stops the rotation of a drum. The multiple-disc clutch engages to drive one member, lock one member to the case, or lock two members together. Bands and multiple-disc clutches are hydraulic devices. They operate when fluid pressure is applied to them. Some automatic transmissions and transaxles have solenoids (Fig. 47-1) operated by the ECM that control the hydraulic devices (➤47-27).

HYDRAULIC SYSTEM

➤ 47-16 FUNCTIONS OF THE HYDRAULIC SYSTEM

Figure 47-26 shows the complete hydraulic system of a four-speed automatic transmission. The hydraulic system provides the pressurized fluid to operate an automatic transmission or transaxle. The hydraulic system:

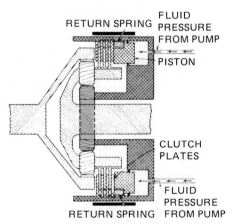

Fig. 47-25 Planetary gearset with clutch engaged. One set of clutch plates is splined to the sun-gear drum. The other set is splined to the planet-pinion carrier. When fluid pressure from the pump acts on the apply side of the clutch piston (as shown by arrows), the clutch plates are forced together. This locks the sun gear to the planet carrier and the planetary gearset rotates as a single unit.

1. Supplies fluid to the torque converter.
2. Directs pressurized fluid to the band servos and multiple-disc clutches.
3. Lubricates the internal parts.
4. Removes heat generated by the torque converter and other moving parts.

These four jobs are possible because the automatic transmission or transaxle is filled with automatic-transmission fluid (ATF). Without the proper amount of fluid, the transmission may not shift and the vehicle may not move. Major components in the hydraulic system include the oil pump (➤47-13), band servos (➤47-14), and multiple-disc clutches (➤47-15). Other major components are the valve body and *governor*. These are described in later sections.

➤ 47-17 AUTOMATIC-TRANSMISSION FLUID

Automatic-transmission fluid is a special lubricant with about the same viscosity as an SAE 20 engine oil (➤24-3). It has several additives such as viscosity-index improvers, oxidation and corrosion inhibitors, extreme-pressure and antifoam agents, detergents, dispersants, friction modifiers, pour-point depressants, and fluidity modifiers. Automatic-transmission fluid is usually dyed red. This makes a leak more easily identifiable by its color.

There are several types of automatic-transmission fluid. Each is compounded to work with certain transmissions. *Dexron-II* is the most widely used. *Type F* is specified for some 1982 and earlier Ford transmissions. *Dexron-IIE* is recommended for use in many electronically-controlled transmissions and transaxles. These use *shift solenoids* (➤47-27) and force motors with small oil-flow passages. For proper operation, the fluid must not thicken excessively in low temperatures. Dexron-IIE maintains the proper viscosity at low temperatures. It can also be used in other automatic transmissions for which Dexron-II is specified.

➤ 47-18 TRANSMISSION-FLUID COOLER

Overheated automatic-transmission fluid can damage the *friction elements* (bands and multiple-disc clutches) in an automatic transmission or transaxle. The heat develops in an unlocked torque converter and in other moving parts.

To prevent the fluid from overheating, automatic transmissions and transaxles have a *transmission-fluid cooler* or *oil cooler* (upper left in Fig. 47-26). It is usually a tube on the bottom or side of the engine radiator (Figs. 25-1 and 25-13). The engine coolant runs at a lower temperature than the automatic-transmission fluid. As the hot transmission fluid flows through the tube, the engine coolant carries away excess heat. *Cooler lines* similar to steel fuel lines carry the transmission fluid between the case and the radiator.

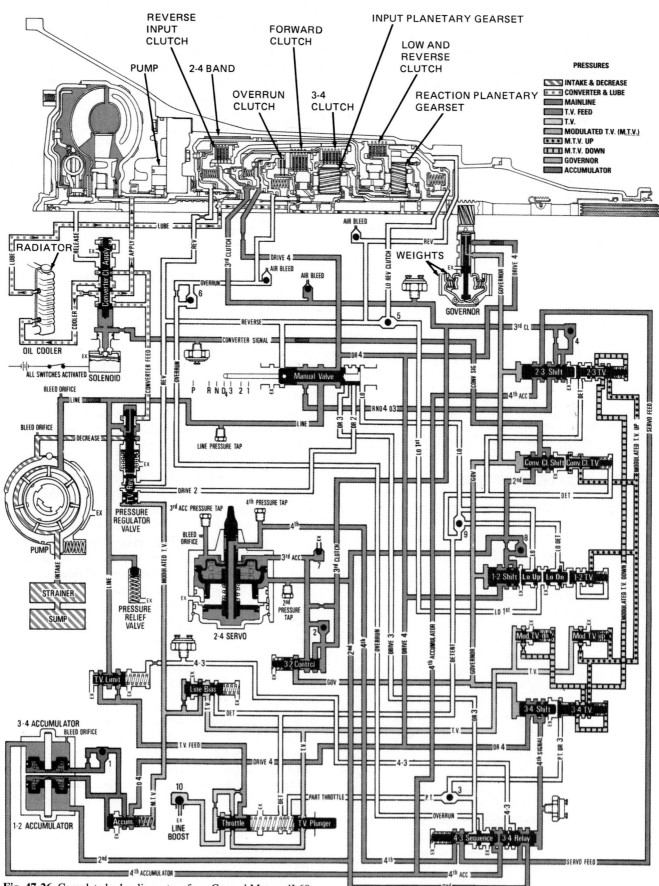

Fig. 47-26 Complete hydraulic system for a General Motors 4L60 (700-R4) hydraulically-controlled four-speed automatic transmission. Conditions shown are with the transmission in overdrive (4th gear) in drive range. (*Hydra-Matic Division of General Motors Corporation*)

632

Some vehicles have an *auxiliary fluid cooler*. This is a small radiator-like heat exchanger. It usually mounts ahead of the radiator and in series with the oil-cooler tube in the radiator. First the hot fluid flows through the oil-cooler tube. Then the fluid flows through the auxiliary fluid cooler. Outside air passing through the fins of the auxiliary fluid cooler carries away additional heat.

➤ 47-19 BASIC HYDRAULIC-CONTROL CIRCUITS

Figure 47-27 shows a simplified hydraulic system for an automatic transmission. A planetary gearset and multiple-disc clutch are in the drum, which has a band around it. The hydraulic system applies and releases the band, and engages and disengages the clutch, as operating conditions require.

To get gear reduction in Fig. 47-27, the band is applied while the clutch is disengaged. A spring in the servo forces the piston to apply the band. This holds the sun gear stationary. When the input shaft turns the internal gear, the planet carrier turns the output shaft at a reduced speed (➤47-11).

To get direct drive in Fig. 47-27, the band is released and the clutch is engaged. Fluid pressure is sent to the release side of the servo piston and the apply side of the clutch piston. As the pistons move, the band releases and the clutch engages. This locks two members together. The planetary gearset turns as a unit to provide direct drive.

An actual automatic transmission or transaxle (Figs. 47-3 and 47-4) has more gears and controls than described above. These enable automatic shifting through the complete driving range.

➤ 47-20 ACCUMULATOR

Sudden application of a band or engagement of a clutch can cause a rough shift. To prevent this, the hydraulic system usually includes an *accumulator* (lower left in Fig. 47-26). It cushions the shock of clutch and servo operation. The result is a smooth but rapid clutch engagement or band application.

The accumulator is basically a fluid chamber that connects to the hydraulic circuit for a band or clutch. The accumulator bore has a spring and piston in it. When a shift is to take place, fluid pressure is directed to one side of the accumulator piston. The fluid acts against the piston which overcomes the spring and travels the length of the bore. Only then can full fluid pressure build up in the clutch or servo. This smoothes the shift.

➤ 47-21 SHIFT TIMING

Controlling the time or point at which each shift occurs is *shift timing*. The controls may be electronic (➤47-27) or hydraulic. Figure 47-1 shows the electronic controls on a four-speed automatic transmission. Figure 47-28 shows a four-speed automatic transmission that has hydraulic controls. Figure 47-26 shows the complete hydraulic system for this transmission.

Shift timing depends primarily on two factors:

1. Vehicle speed.
2. Engine load (or throttle opening).

These two factors—speed and load—produce varying fluid pressures that work against the two ends of the *shift valve* (Fig. 47-27). The valve then moves to produce the shifts.

The shift valve is a *spool valve* inside a bore in the valve body (Figs. 47-27 and 47-28). A spool valve is a metal rod with cutaway sections. It controls fluid-flow in hydraulic circuits. The smaller diameter is the *valve groove*. The larger diameters are the *valve lands*.

Pressure at one end of the shift valve comes from the governor (Fig. 47-27). This is *governor pressure*. Pressure at the other end is *throttle pressure*. It changes as the movement of the driver's foot changes the position of the accelerator pedal. Governor pressure and throttle pressure are the two principal pressures that control shift timing or *shift points*.

➤ 47-22 GOVERNOR PRESSURE

The governor (Figs. 47-26 and 47-27) is a speed-sensitive device that varies hydraulic pressure proportionally to

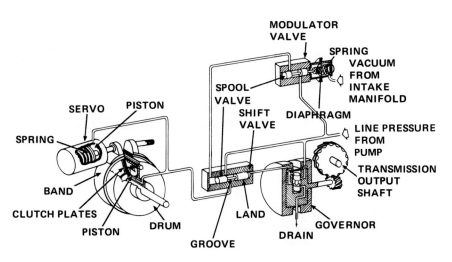

Fig. 47-27 Simplified hydraulic system for an automatic transmission. The hydraulic system applies and releases the band, and engages and disengages the clutch, as operating conditions require.

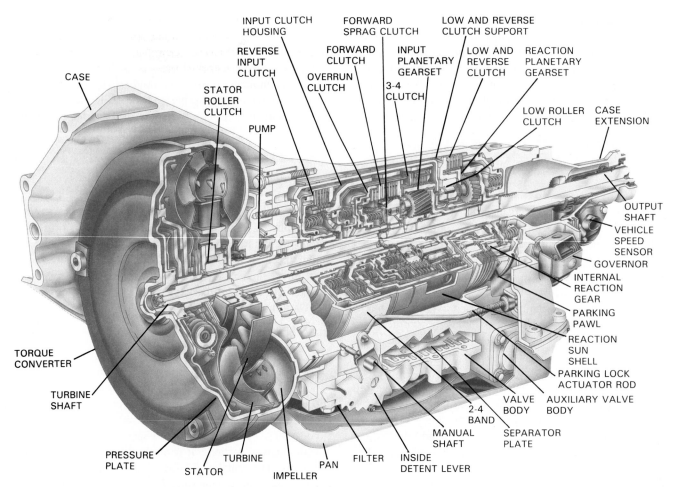

Fig. 47-28 A General Motors 4L60 four-speed automatic transmission, which is hydraulically controlled. (*Oldsmobile Division of General Motors Corporation*)

output-shaft speed. The resulting governor pressure controls gear shifting in relation to vehicle speed. The transmission or transaxle output shaft drives the governor (Fig. 47-28).

The pump sends line pressure (*mainline pressure* in Fig. 47-26) to the governor. When the output shaft is turning slowly, centrifugal force has little affect on the governor *weights* (top right in Fig. 47-26). The governor releases a low pressure to work on one end of the shift valve. As output-shaft and vehicle speed increase, the weights pivot outward. This moves the governor valve which opens farther to increase governor pressure. Figure 47-26 shows governor pressure working on the left end of the *2-3 shift* valve, converter-clutch shift valve, *1-2 shift* valve, and *3-4 shift* valve.

> **47-23 THROTTLE PRESSURE**

Working on the other end of the shift valve is a pressure that changes as the engine throttle position changes. This is throttle pressure or *throttle-valve* (TV) *pressure.* It varies proportionally to the load on the engine. Either mechanical linkage to the accelerator pedal or intake-manifold vacuum provides the signal to the valve body. In Fig. 47-26, movement of the accelerator pedal causes linkage to push

against the *TV plunger.* The resulting throttle pressure acts on the right ends of the shift valves.

In many transmissions, a vacuum-operated *modulator valve* provides the throttle pressure. The simplified hydraulic system in Fig. 47-27 shows the basic operation of the modulator valve or *vacuum modulator.* Line pressure from the pump enters the modulator valve. When high intake-manifold vacuum (➤18-1) acts on the diaphragm in the modulator valve, it pulls a spool valve to the right. This closes the passage and reduces throttle pressure to the left end of the shift valve. Governor pressure now pushes the shift valve to the left. Line pressure passes through the groove in the shift valve. In Fig. 47-27, the pressure releases the band and engages the clutch. This locks the planetary gearset.

> **47-24 CONTROLLING SHIFT TIMING AND QUALITY**

The main reason for varying throttle pressure is to change the shift to meet driving conditions. Each shift should occur at the right time and have the proper quality or *shift feel.* When the vehicle is accelerating, the engine produces high torque. The upshift should take place later (at higher engine speed). Also, higher fluid pressure should be directed to the band and clutches. Without the control provided by the throttle pressure, the shift would be early and the band or clutches could *slip*. This is an unwanted *flaring* or increase in engine speed that results when the torque is greater than a band or clutch can hold.

When the vehicle reaches cruising speed, the engine produces less torque. Throttle pressure decreases as the driver eases up on the accelerator pedal. The shift occurs earlier and the fluid pressure to the bands and clutches is reduced. Otherwise, a *harsh* or *rough shift* occurs. This is an undesirably quick operation of the band or clutch. When the driver wants maximum acceleration, floorboarding the accelerator pedal will force a downshift.

➤ 47-25 HYDRAULIC VALVES AND VALVE BODIES

The metal casting that contains the bores in which most of the hydraulically-operated valves move is the valve body (Fig. 47-28). It is usually in the pan and attaches to the transmission case through a *separator plate*. The valve body contains fluid passages that are opened and closed by movement of the valves. This directs the fluid flow and pressure toward or away from the band servos, clutches, and governor. It also fills the torque converter and operates the torque-converter clutch.

Controlling the shifts is more complicated than described above. Therefore, the valve body contains several multiple-land spool valves in addition to the shift valves (Fig. 47-26). Springs help properly position the valves. The shift valves and springs automatically cause the upshifts and downshifts, as driving conditions require. Other valves help ease the shifts, regulate pressures, and time the downshifts.

The only valve in the valve body directly operated by the driver is the *manual valve* (center in Fig. 47-26). It connects to the gearshift lever or *selector lever* and moves as the driver moves the lever to the gear or range desired. The driver can select P (PARK), R (REVERSE), N (NEUTRAL), D₄ (OVERDRIVE), 3, 2, or 1. Each position moves the manual valve. Then its grooves send fluid to the valves that will produce the desired shift or shifts.

➤ 47-26 STARTING CONTROLS AND SHIFT INTERLOCKS

In a vehicle with an automatic transmission or transaxle, the starting motor should not crank the engine unless the selector lever is in NEUTRAL or PARK (➤29-1). If the engine starts with the transmission in gear, the vehicle would suddenly start to move. This could result in an accident.

Two starting-control systems are widely used. One is the combination *ignition-switch and steering-column lock* (Fig. 31-19). It works with a steering-column-mounted selector lever. The operation of this system is described in ➤31-13. The other arrangement uses a *neutral-safety switch* (Fig. 29-1). It works with either floor shift or column shift (➤29-1).

The neutral-safety switch is open in all positions except PARK and NEUTRAL. If the selector lever is in any other position, the starting motor cannot operate. Moving the selector lever to PARK or NEUTRAL closes the contact points in the neutral-safety switch. Then, turning the ignition key to START causes the starting motor to operate.

Many vehicles have a *shift lock* or *interlock* system. It prevents the driver from moving the selector lever out of PARK unless the brake pedal is depressed. On some vehicles, the brake pedal must also be depressed to move the selector lever out of NEUTRAL. To remove the ignition key, the selector lever must be in PARK. In addition, some cars have *automatic door locks*. All doors automatically lock when the selector lever is moved to DRIVE. The doors automatically unlock when the selector lever is moved to PARK.

ELECTRONIC CONTROL SYSTEM

➤ 47-27 ELECTRONIC SHIFT CONTROLS

Some transmissions and transaxles are electronically controlled. Sensors monitor operating conditions such as vehicle speed, engine load, and coolant temperature. This information is sent to an electronic control module (ECM). The ECM may be a separate *transmission* or *transaxle controller*. Other vehicles have a *powertrain control module* (PCM). It controls both the engine and the transmission or transaxle (Fig. 47-29).

Using information from the various inputs, the ECM determines when (shift timing) and how (shift feel) to make the shift. Signals are sent to electric *shift solenoids* (➤47-28) on the valve body. The solenoids open or close fluid passages. This sends or releases fluid pressure to the band servos and clutches.

Figure 47-1 shows the electronic controls for a four-speed automatic transmission. Similar electronic controls on a four-speed transaxle are shown in Fig. 47-29. Many electronically-controlled transmissions and transaxles have four solenoids. Two are shift solenoids. The third solenoid controls line pressure and eliminates the governor, modulator valve or throttle valve, and related linkage. The signal from the *output sensor* or *vehicle-speed sensor* (Figs. 47-1 and 47-29) takes the place of governor pressure (➤43-15). Another solenoid controls the locking of the torque-converter clutch.

The PCM controls the solenoids based on inputs from the coolant-temperature sensor (➤19-16), throttle-position sensor (➤19-10), manifold-absolute-pressure sensor (➤19-13), and others. These provide the PCM with information about the load on the engine and the power the driver wants. In some vehicles, the PCM retards engine timing and reduces fuel-flow during a shift. As soon as the shift is completed, engine power is restored. This capability also helps the PCM prevent damage to the transmission if it is shifted into gear at high engine speed.

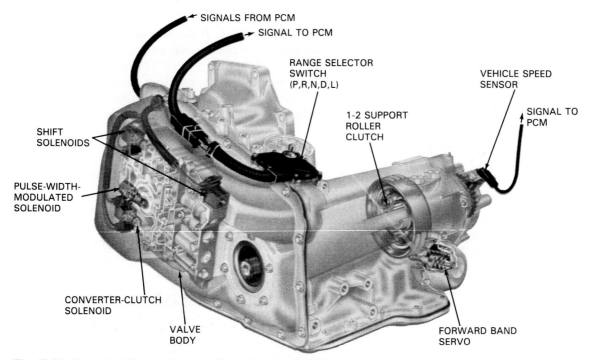

Fig. 47-29 Electronic shift controls on the General Motors 4T60-E four-speed automatic transaxle. The powertrain control module (PCM) controls the upshifts and downshifts, or shift timing. (*Oldsmobile Division of General Motors*)

> ## 47-28 SHIFT SOLENOIDS

The use of two shift solenoids provides four combinations that control the shifts (Fig. 47-30). Each solenoid has a plunger that moves up and down as the ECM turns the solenoid ON and OFF. This causes a valve on the end of the plunger to open and close a port into a fluid passage (Fig. 47-31).

When the ECM turns the solenoid ON, the plunger is pulled up. This opens the port and relieves the fluid pressure that was acting on the shift valve. The shift-valve spring now forces the shift valve to move (Fig. 47-31A). As the shift valve moves, it opens the fluid passage to the proper band servos and clutches to make the shift. The resulting actions are the same as in the hydraulically-controlled transmission described earlier.

When the ECM turns the solenoid OFF (Fig. 47-31B), the solenoid spring forces the plunger down. This closes the port. Fluid pressure now pushes against the shift valve. It

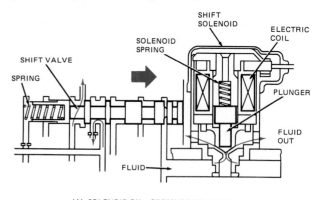

(A) SOLENOID ON – PRESSURE RELEASED

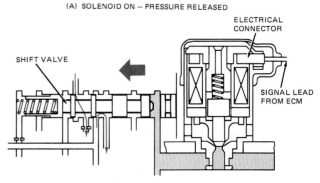

(B) SOLENOID OFF – PRESSURE HELD

Fig. 47-31 Shift-solenoid operation in a Ford 4EAT automatic transaxle, showing how the position of the solenoid plunger (A) releases fluid pressure or (B) holds fluid pressure. (*Ford Motor Company*)

Gear		Solenoid States	
		SS1	SS2
1	M	ON	OFF
	D		
2	M	OFF	OFF
	D		
3		OFF	ON
4		ON	ON
R		ON	OFF
N		ON	OFF
P		ON	OFF

Fig. 47-30 Actions of the two shift solenoids that control the shifts in the Ford AOD-E automatic transmission. Each solenoid can be either ON (energized) or OFF (deenergized). (*Ford Motor Company*)

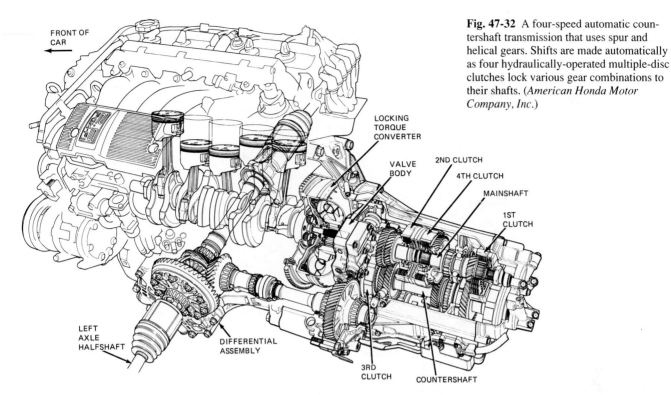

FRONT OF CAR

LOCKING TORQUE CONVERTER

VALVE BODY

2ND CLUTCH

4TH CLUTCH

MAINSHAFT

1ST CLUTCH

LEFT AXLE HALFSHAFT

DIFFERENTIAL ASSEMBLY

3RD CLUTCH

COUNTERSHAFT

Fig. 47-32 A four-speed automatic countershaft transmission that uses spur and helical gears. Shifts are made automatically as four hydraulically-operated multiple-disc clutches lock various gear combinations to their shafts. (*American Honda Motor Company, Inc.*)

overcomes the force of the spring and moves to the left (Fig. 47-31B). This sends fluid pressure from the shift valve through another passage to the proper bands and clutches.

Other upshifts and downshifts are made in the same way. The ECM determines when to make the shift and then signals the proper combination of solenoids. The position of the selector lever and manual valve provides hydraulic control for PARK, NEUTRAL, and REVERSE. Forced downshifts resulting from moving the selector lever may also be hydraulically controlled.

OTHER AUTOMATIC TRANSMISSIONS AND TRANSAXLES

➤ 47-29 AUTOMATIC-SHIFT COUNTERSHAFT TRANSMISSIONS

Some automatic transmissions and transaxles are similar in construction to manual transmissions and transaxles. Instead of planetary gears and a single centerline, two parallel shafts with spur and helical gears are used. The shafts are the *mainshaft* and the *countershaft*. Figure 47-32 shows a four-speed *automatic countershaft transmission*. Compare it with Fig. 42-1 which shows a similar drive train using a five-speed manual transmission.

In the automatic countershaft transmission, the gears on the mainshaft are in constant mesh with the gears on the countershaft. Instead of synchronizers (➤43-7), the transmission has four multiple-disc clutches. Hydraulic pressure operates the clutches (➤47-15). Half of the plates in each

clutch are splined to a gear. The other half are splined to a shaft. When the clutches engage, various gear combinations are locked to their shafts. Power flows from the torque converter, through the mainshaft, to the countershaft which drives the final-drive gearing.

Some countershaft automatic transmissions and transaxles are electronically controlled. The system is basically the same as described in ➤47-27. Four shift solenoids control the torque-converter clutch and gear shifts (➤47-28). An ECM turns the solenoids ON and OFF. To shift gears, the ECM signals the solenoids. The solenoid valves then open and close to send fluid pressure to the proper clutch.

➤ 47-30 CONTINUOUSLY-VARIABLE TRANSMISSIONS

Some small cars have a *continuously-variable transmission* or *transaxle* (CVT). This type of transmission uses a steel belt running in a pair of variable-width pulleys to provide varying gear ratios. Figure 47-33 shows a continuously-variable transaxle. The pulley ratios change with vehicle speed and the load on the engine. This allows the engine to run at a more constant speed and close to its maximum operating efficiency. A hydraulic control system varies the pulley ratio. No torque converter is used.

To get forward motion, the forward clutch locks the sun gear and the planet carrier together. For reverse, the reverse clutch locks the ring gear to the case. This causes the planet pinions to turn the sun gear and output shaft backward. The gear-ratio spread is about the same as provided by a five- or six-speed manual transmission or transaxle. Some continuously-variable transmissions and transaxles are electronically-controlled.

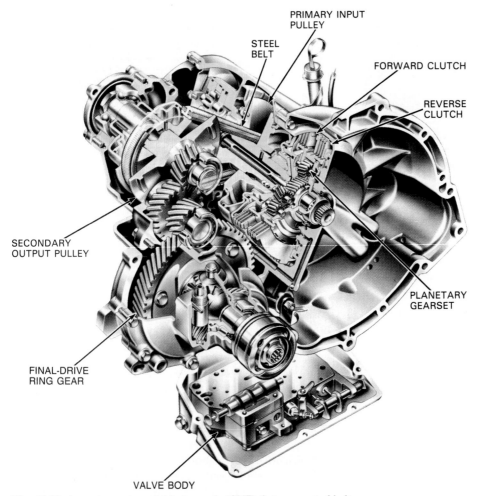

Fig. 47-33 A continuously-variable transaxle (CVT) that uses a steel belt running in a pair of variable-width pulleys to provide varying gear ratios. No torque converter is used. (*Ford of Europe, Inc.*)

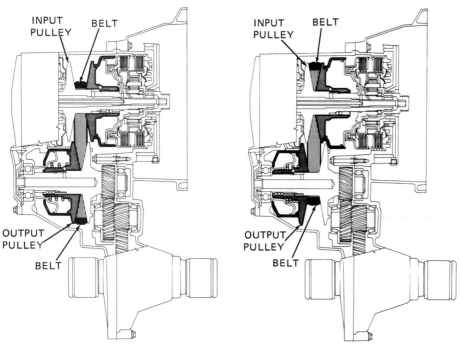

(A) LOW GEAR RATIO   (B) HIGH GEAR RATIO

Fig. 47-34 Operation of the continuously-variable transaxle (CVT), showing how the position of the belt and pulley width varies the gear ratio. The pulley ratios change with vehicle speed and engine load. (*Ford of Europe, Inc.*)

Figure 47-34 shows how the position of the belt and pulley width varies the gear ratio. When the belt is running close to the center of the input pulley and near the outside of the output pulley (Fig. 47-34A), a low ratio is obtained. When the belt runs near the outside of the input pulley and near the center of the output pulley, a high ratio is obtained. Changing the width of the pulley groove determines the position of the belt. A cone-shaped side of one pulley moves in while one side of the other pulley moves out. This changes the width of the pulleys and the resulting gear ratio.

MULTIPLE-CHOICE TEST

*Select the **one** correct, best, or most probable answer to each question.*
You can find the answers in the section indicated at the end of each question.

1. Technician A says all automatic transaxles use planetary gears. Technician B says some automatic transaxles use spur and helical gears instead. Who is right? (➤47-2)
   a. A only
   b. B only
   c. both A and B
   d. neither A nor B
2. The stator begins to turn when (➤47-6)
   a. torque multiplication starts
   b. the turbine turns faster than the impeller
   c. turbine speed approaches impeller speed
   d. the one-way clutch locks
3. When the sun gear is held and the planet carrier is turned, the planetary gearset provides (➤47-11)
   a. speed reduction
   b. speed increase
   c. direct drive
   d. reverse
4. If the internal gear is held and the sun gear turned, the planetary gearset provides (➤47-11)
   a. speed reduction
   b. speed increase
   c. direct drive
   d. reverse
5. The Simpson planetary gearset has all the following EXCEPT (➤47-12)
   a. one sun gear
   b. two sets of planet pinions
   c. two internal gears
   d. long and short planet pinions

6. Technician A says planetary gearsets may be controlled by bands and multiple-disc clutches. Technician B says some automatic transmissions and transaxles have only one-way clutches and multiple-disc clutches. Who is right? (➤47-13)
   a. A only
   b. B only
   c. both A and B
   d. neither A nor B
7. In the automatic transmission, the band is applied by (➤47-14)
   a. a clutch
   b. a drum
   c. an accumulator
   d. a servo
8. Technician A says governor pressure works on one end of the shift valve. Technician B says throttle pressure works on the other end of the shift valve. Who is right? (➤47-21)
   a. A only
   b. B only
   c. both A and B
   d. neither A nor B
9. In an electronic-shift transmission, the plunger in the shift solenoid (➤47-28)
   a. pushes against one end of the shift valve
   b. pulls on the band to release it
   c. pushes against a clutch to engage it
   d. raises to open a fluid passage when turned ON

REVIEW QUESTIONS

1. What two types of one-way clutches are used in automatic transmissions and transaxles, and how do they operate? (➤47-6)
2. What is the difference between a Simpson and a Ravigneaux planetary gearset? (➤47-12)
3. Explain how a band applies and releases, and how a multiple-disc clutch engages and disengages. (➤47-14 and 47-15)

4. List and describe the four jobs performed by the hydraulic system in an automatic transmission. (➤47-16)
5. Define "governor pressure" and "throttle pressure," and explain how they can work together to control shift points. (➤47-22 and 47-23)

CHAPTER 48

AUTOMATIC TRANSMISSIONS AND TRANSAXLES: DIAGNOSIS AND SERVICE

After studying this chapter, and with proper instruction and equipment, you should be able to:

- Check the fluid in automatic transmissions and transaxles, and inspect for fluid leaks.
- Perform a road test and diagnose troubles in various automatic transmissions and transaxles.
- Retrieve trouble codes and diagnose troubles in electronically-shifted automatic transmissions and transaxles.
- Perform pressure tests and stall tests, and interpret the results.
- Perform linkage and band adjustments.
- Rebuild an automatic transmission and transaxle.

➤ **48-1 SERVICING AUTOMATIC TRANSMISSIONS AND TRANSAXLES**

Automatic-transmission and transaxle service can be divided into five parts. These are:

1. Normal maintenance.
2. Trouble diagnosis.
3. On-the-vehicle adjustments and repairs.
4. Resealing.
5. Rebuilding or overhaul.

There are usually several variations of a basic model of transmission or transaxle. This allows the unit to be installed behind engines of various power and in vehicles of different weight. These variations may include *running changes* and *upgrades* made by the manufacturer after the transmission or transaxle enters production. For example, the thickness or height of a part, number of plates in a clutch, or number of splines on a shaft (*spline count*) could change. This means different parts and specifications may be needed to diagnose and service different versions of the same basic transmission or transaxle.

Using the wrong specifications or parts can cause a faulty diagnosis or repair. To avoid these problems, identify the automatic transmission or transaxle in the

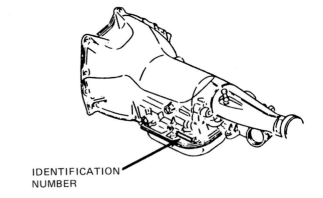

IDENTIFICATION NUMBER

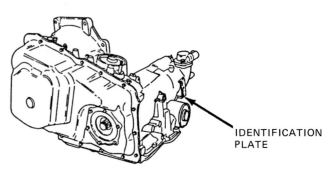

IDENTIFICATION PLATE

Fig. 48-1 The transmission or transaxle identification number, or serial number, is stamped on the case or on a plate attached to the case. (*Buick Division of General Motors Corporation*)

vehicle you are servicing. Most transmissions and transaxles are stamped or have a plate attached (Fig. 48-1) with the serial number or *transmission identification number* (TIN). Other number and letter markings may provide additional information. The meaning of these marks is in the vehicle service manual. Follow the service procedures and specifications recommended by the manufacturer for the transmission or transaxle you are working on.

➤ 48-2 NORMAL MAINTENANCE

Normal maintenance of an automatic transmission or transaxle includes:

1. Checking fluid level, color, and condition.
2. Adding fluid, if necessary.
3. Changing fluid and filter.
4. Checking shift and throttle linkage.
5. Adjusting neutral-safety switch.
6. Adjusting bands, if possible.

The level of the automatic-transmission fluid (ATF) should be checked with every change of engine oil (Fig. 48-2). Many vehicle manufacturers recommend changing the transmission fluid and filter at periodic intervals. The length of the intervals depends on how the vehicle is used. For example, Chevrolet recommends changing the fluid and filter every 100,000 miles [160,000 km] for normal service. For *severe service,* Chevrolet recommends changing the fluid and filter every 15,000 miles [25,000 km]. Severe service includes using the vehicle for trailer towing or as a delivery vehicle, police car, or taxi.

FLUID CHECKS

➤ 48-3 CHECKING FLUID LEVEL AND ADDING FLUID

A check of the fluid level, color, and condition should be made at every change of engine oil. To check the fluid level, drive the vehicle for 15 minutes or until the engine and transmission are at normal operating temperature. Park the vehicle on level ground and firmly apply the parking brake. Let the engine idle. Place the transmission

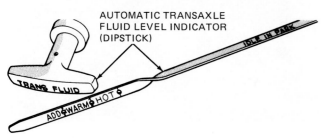

Fig. 48-2 Typical markings on a dipstick for an automatic transmission or transaxle. (*Chrysler Corporation*)

selector lever in PARK (or NEUTRAL if specified by the manufacturer).

Clean any dirt from around the dipstick cap. Pull out the dipstick, wipe it, reinsert it, and pull it out again. Note the fluid level on the dipstick (Fig. 48-2). Touch the fluid on the end of the dipstick to get an indication of fluid temperature. If the fluid feels cool, the fluid level should be on the low side of the dipstick. If the fluid feels warm or hot (too hot to hold), the dipstick level should be on the high side.

Fluid level will vary under normal operating conditions as much as 3/4 inch [19 mm] from cold to hot. For example, as the temperature of the fluid goes from 60°F [16°C] to 180°F [82°C], the level of the fluid may rise as much as 3/4 inch [19 mm]. Some dipsticks are marked to show proper levels at different fluid temperatures.

> **NOTE** On some automatic transaxles, the fluid level goes *down* as temperature increases. The COLD mark on the dipstick is *above* the FULL mark.

If the fluid level is low, add a sufficient amount of the specified fluid to bring the level within the marks for the fluid temperature. Do not overfill an automatic transmission or transaxle. Too much fluid will cause foaming. Foaming fluid cannot operate bands and clutches properly. Then they will slip and probably burn. This could result in a transmission or transaxle that needs an overhaul.

➤ 48-4 CHECKING FLUID COLOR

Automatic-transmission fluid is normally red in color.

1. PINK FLUID This indicates that the fluid cooler in the radiator is leaking. Engine coolant has contaminated the fluid. Repair or replace the fluid cooler, and remove and overhaul the transmission or transaxle. Replace the seals, bands, lined clutch plates, nylon washers, and speedometer and governor gears. Coolant can affect these parts. Clean all other parts and passages. Flush the cooler lines and flush or replace the torque converter.

2. BROWN FLUID ATF may turn dark in normal use. However, contaminated fluid may also have a brown color. If the fluid appears contaminated (➤48-5), drain it (Fig. 48-3). Then remove and inspect the pan (➤48-6). A small amount of metal particles and friction material in the bottom of the pan is normal. Replace the filter (Fig. 48-4) and refill with new fluid. Large pieces of metal or other material indicate excessive wear or failure. The transmission or transaxle should be removed and overhauled. Flush the cooler lines and flush or replace the torque converter.

➤ 48-5 CHECKING FLUID CONDITION

Fluid color (➤48-4) and odor can be checked to determine the condition of the fluid. Look at the color and smell the

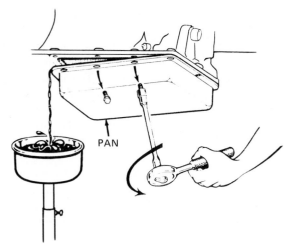

Fig. 48-3 Loosening the pan and draining the automatic-transmission fluid. (*ATW*)

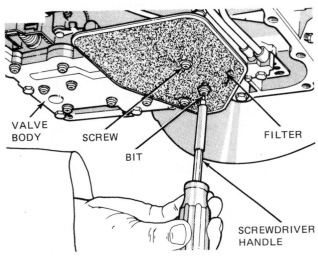

Fig. 48-4 Replacing the fluid filter. (*Chrysler Corporation*)

fluid on the end of the dipstick. If the fluid is brown or black and has a strong burnt odor, bands and clutch plates may have slipped, overheated, and burned. Particles of friction material from the bands and clutch plates have probably circulated through the torque converter, transmission, and fluid cooler. These particles can cause valves in the valve body to stick. This may cause noisy, rough, or

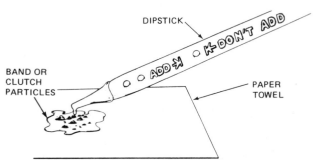

Fig. 48-5 Checking the condition of the fluid in an automatic transmission or transaxle. (*Ford Motor Company*)

642

missed shifts. Slipping may occur because the servos and clutches cannot work properly.

A quick check of fluid condition can be made by placing one or two drops of fluid from the end of the dipstick on a paper towel (Fig. 48-5). As the towel absorbs the fluid, examine the stain for specks or particles. These indicate solid material in the fluid. If the stain spreads and is red to light brown in color, the fluid probably is good. If the stain is dark and remains small, the fluid is *oxidized* and should be changed. Oxidized fluid has combined with oxygen in the air and no longer has its original properties.

➤ 48-6 INSPECTING THE PAN

Gum or varnish on the dipstick, discolored fluid, and particles or specks on the paper towel indicate the sump or pan should be removed and inspected (Fig. 48-6). A small amount of material in the pan is normal. Look for large pieces of metal and large amounts of friction material. These indicate abnormal wear or failure. The unit requires rebuilding or overhaul.

➤ 48-7 CHECKING FOR FLUID LEAKS

When the dipstick shows a low fluid level, look for a fluid leak. Some fluid can be lost through the case vent if the fluid has foamed. To help locate the source of a leak, automatic-transmission fluid is usually dyed red. This makes the leak easier to detect and identify. Another method of leak detection is to use an *ultraviolet leak detector* (➤56-13). If a leak detector is not available, use the following procedure:

1. Clean the suspected area with solvent to remove all traces of fluid.
2. Remove the torque-converter shield, if present, to expose as much of the torque converter as possible.

Fig. 48-6 Inspecting the pan. A small amount of material is normal. Large pieces of metal and large amounts of friction material indicate abnormal wear or failure. (*Chrysler Corporation*)

3. Spray the cleaned area with an aerosol can of white foot powder. This will show the red fluid at the leak points.
4. Start and run the engine at fast idle.
5. If the leak does not appear immediately, recheck the suspected area after the vehicle has been driven normally for one or two days.
6. Repair any leak found by replacing gaskets or seals, tightening attaching bolts, or replacing porous castings.

AUTOMATIC-TRANSMISSION AND TRANSAXLE DIAGNOSIS

➤ 48-8 CAUSES OF FAILURE

Two common causes of automatic-transmission and transaxle trouble are abuse and neglect. Most often these are overloading the unit and not checking the fluid and adding or changing it if necessary.

Overloading may be caused by pulling a trailer, carrying extra weight, long periods of idling in stop-and-go traffic, and racing the engine in gear with the brakes applied. These conditions can overheat the fluid. The heat causes the fluid to deteriorate or oxidize (➤48-5). Gum and varnish form on the dipstick and in the transmission. Valves in the valve body can stick, resulting in slipping bands and clutches.

For mountain driving with a heavy load or trailer, the driver should move the selector lever to the 2 (second) or 1 (first) position. This reduces fluid heating on upgrades of 1/2 mile [0.8 km] or longer. Some vehicles with electronic-shift control have a HOLD button. When the driver presses it, the transmission or transaxle does not shift out of the gear it is in.

Neglect is another cause of damage to an automatic transmission or transaxle. If the vehicle is used in severe service (➤48-2), the fluid and filter should be changed frequently. Any bands should also be adjusted.

Careful! When towing a rear-wheel-drive vehicle with automatic transmission, lift the rear of the vehicle or disconnect the driveshaft. The vehicle can be towed with the rear wheels on the ground and the driveshaft connected for short distances at low speed. However, the transmission is lubricated only when the engine is running. To tow front-wheel-drive vehicles, lift the front end.

➤ 48-9 TROUBLE-DIAGNOSIS PROCEDURES

Most automatic transmissions and transaxles have planetary gearing and are similar in construction and operation. This simplifies basic diagnosis of the mechanical and hydraulic components. Figure 48-7 shows a General Motors 4L80-E electronically-controlled four-speed overdrive transmission. The electronic controls for this unit are shown in Fig. 47-1. Compare these illustrations with Fig. 47-28. It shows the General Motors 4L60

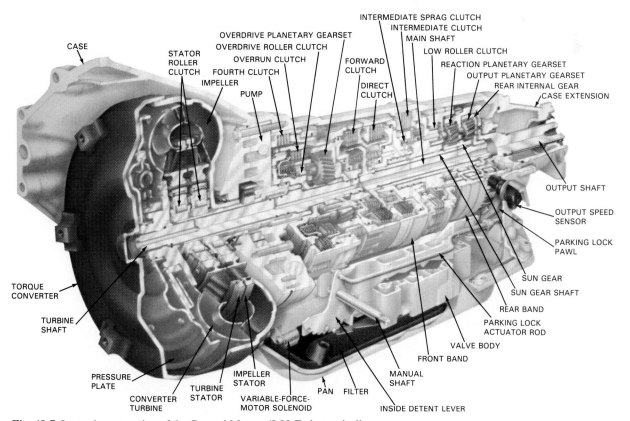

Fig. 48-7 Internal construction of the General Motors 4L80-E electronically-controlled four-speed transmission. (*Chevrolet Division of General Motors Corporation*)

which is a slightly smaller hydraulically-controlled four-speed overdrive transmission.

Figure 48-8 shows a General Motors 4T60-E automatic transaxle. This is also an electronically-controlled four-speed overdrive unit. The electronic controls are shown in Fig. 47-29. *Band-and-clutch application charts* (Fig. 48-9) and trouble-diagnosis procedures for each transmission and transaxle are in the vehicle service manual. It also includes trouble-diagnosis charts that cover many of the most common problems.

Before starting trouble diagnosis, identify the transmission or transaxle in the vehicle (➤48-1). Review the power-flow and the actions of the bands and clutches for each gear. Figure 48-9 shows a typical band and clutch application chart. This is for the Ford AXOD transaxle shown in Fig. 47-4. The transaxle has two bands, four

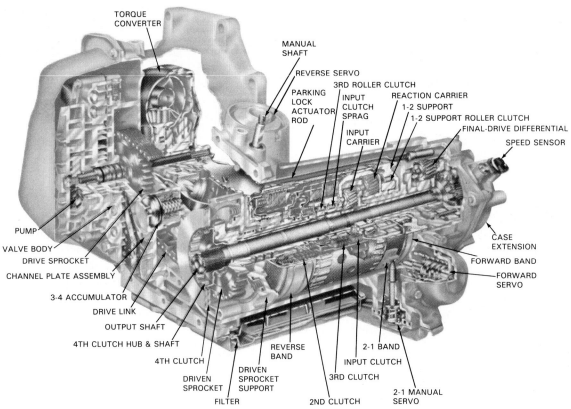

Fig. 48-8 Internal construction of the General Motors 4T60-E electronically-controlled four-speed transaxle. (*Oldsmobile Division of General Motors Corporation*)

Gear	Lo-Int Band	Overdrive Band	Forward Clutch	Intermediate Clutch	Direct Clutch	Reverse Clutch	Low One-Way Clutch	Direct One-Way Clutch
1st Gear (Manual Low)	Applied		Applied		Applied		Applied	Applied
1st Gear (Drive)	Applied		Applied				Applied	
2nd Gear (Drive)	Applied		Applied	Applied			Holding	
3rd Gear (Drive)			Applied	Applied	Applied			
4th Gear (Overdrive)		Applied		Applied	Applied			Holding
Reverse (R)			Applied			Applied	Holding	
Neutral (N)								
Park (P)								

Fig. 48-9 Band and clutch application chart for the Ford AXOD transaxle. (*Ford Motor Company*)

multiple-disc clutches, and two one-way clutches. Knowing the construction and proper operation of the transmission or transaxle will help determine the cause of a trouble.

Study the diagnostic charts and procedures in the vehicle service manual. Then follow the recommended trouble-diagnosis procedure. Any variation could give false readings and damage the unit. All manufacturers do not recommend the same diagnosis and service procedures.

➤ 48-10 NOISE DIAGNOSIS

Various noises may be heard from the powertrain area with the vehicle moving or stopped. The sounds may vary from a high-pitched whistle in all gears to a grinding or rattling sound in only one gear. The first step in noise diagnosis is to determine its source. Chapters 44 and 45 describe how to locate noises in front-wheel-drive and rear-wheel-drive powertrains.

When the noise is from the automatic transmission or transaxle, knowing the power-flow through the gear train will help you determine the parts that are damaged. A noise that occurs in first and second and disappears in third (direct drive) may be caused by damaged teeth in a planetary gearset (Fig. 48-10). No noise is heard in third because the members of the planetary gearset are locked. It rotates as a unit. A noise only in overdrive usually means damage in the planetary gearset for overdrive.

➤ 48-11 ROAD TESTING THE VEHICLE

Figure 48-11 shows a general diagnosis procedure for automatic transmissions and transaxles. All steps do not apply to all transmissions and transaxles. The first five checks are fluid, vacuum, throttle linkage, shift linkage, and engine idle-speed and performance. Perform these checks before the road test. Then perform the road test, if the vehicle is driveable.

The purpose of the road test is to operate the vehicle at various speeds while checking each gear position for slipping or incorrect shifting. Try to have the customer ride along. This allows the technician to identify and verify the customer complaint. Always be aware of how the engine performs. A sluggish or misfiring engine will prevent proper operation of the transmission or transaxle. Engine *flaring* may occur. This is a sudden surge or increase in engine speed before or during a shift. It indicates band or clutch slippage.

During the road test, check the shift points and shift quality under different operating conditions. Note whether the shifts are harsh or spongy. Note the speeds and throttle positions at which the shifts take place. Then compare the results with the specifications in the vehicle service manual.

Upshifts that are very late under light acceleration may be caused by a bad governor (➤47-22). Too much throttle or modulator pressure could also be the cause (➤47-23). If there are problems with engagement or shift feel, recheck and adjust the throttle linkage if necessary. Then make another road test. *Trouble codes* (➤48-12), a *stall test* (➤48-13), or a *pressure test* (➤48-15) may indicate the cause of slipping in all or only certain gears. These checks and tests can often be done in the shop as well as during a road test.

CHIPPED TEETH

Fig. 48-10 Damaged teeth in a gear in a planetary gearset may cause a noise that occurs in first and second gear, and disappears in third, or direct drive. (*ATW*)

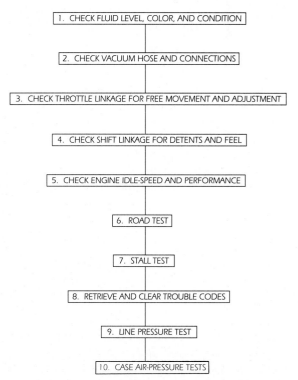

1. CHECK FLUID LEVEL, COLOR, AND CONDITION

2. CHECK VACUUM HOSE AND CONNECTIONS

3. CHECK THROTTLE LINKAGE FOR FREE MOVEMENT AND ADJUSTMENT

4. CHECK SHIFT LINKAGE FOR DETENTS AND FEEL

5. CHECK ENGINE IDLE-SPEED AND PERFORMANCE

6. ROAD TEST

7. STALL TEST

8. RETRIEVE AND CLEAR TROUBLE CODES

9. LINE PRESSURE TEST

10. CASE AIR-PRESSURE TESTS

Fig. 48-11 General diagnosis procedure for automatic transmissions and transaxles. All steps do not apply to all units. (*ATW*)

48-12 CHECKING THE TORQUE-CONVERTER CLUTCH

Check the operation of the torque-converter clutch during the road test. The engine and automatic-transmission fluid must be at normal operating temperature. With the vehicle maintaining a steady speed of about 50 mph [80 kmph], tap the brake pedal with your left foot. Engine speed should increase immediately as the clutch disengages. Continue holding the accelerator pedal in the same position. About five seconds later, engine speed should decrease as the clutch again engages.

If you cannot feel the torque-converter clutch engaging and disengaging, connect a tachometer (➤37-3) or vacuum gauge (➤37-8) to the engine. Then make another road test while watching for changes in engine speed or vacuum. If the torque-converter clutch does not engage, refer to the trouble-diagnosis section in the vehicle service manual.

On many vehicles, a *scan tool* (➤20-13) will show if the electronic-control module (ECM) has signaled for torque-converter clutch engagement (ON) or disengagement (OFF). The scan tool reads the signals sent by the ECM to the *torque-converter-clutch* (TCC) *solenoid* (Fig. 19-26). However, the proper display on the scan tool shows only that the ECM has sent the proper signals. This does not mean that the torque-converter clutch is operating properly. Engine speed should decrease when the scan tool turns ON and increase when the scan tool shows OFF. Some ECMs will store a trouble code if there is a fault in the torque-converter-clutch circuit.

The torque-converter clutch may not engage or it may engage improperly. It is not likely to fail so that it remains engaged, however. This will kill the engine.

48-13 STALL TEST

Some manufacturers recommend performing a stall test as part of the trouble-diagnosis procedure. The stall test determines that the friction elements and one-way clutches are holding. It also checks engine performance. The stall test is performed by firmly applying the service brakes and parking brake, briefly pressing the accelerator pedal to the floor, and reading engine rpm (*stall speed*) on a tachometer (Fig. 48-12).

Careful! To avoid an accident or damage to the transmission or transaxle, follow the steps in the vehicle service manual. Some manufacturers do not recommend the stall test. Others forbid it because of possible damage to the transmission or transaxle.

Before performing a stall test, first determine the minimum and maximum stall speed specified by the manufacturer. For example, Ford specifies a stall speed between 1950 and 2275 rpm for the AXOD transaxle.

To perform the stall test, the engine and automatic-transmission fluid should be at normal operating tem-

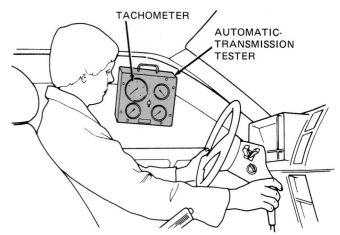

Fig. 48-12 Setup for making a stall test. Be sure the service brakes and parking brake are firmly applied. (*Ford Motor Company*)

perature. Connect a tachometer to the engine. Block the wheels and firmly apply the service brakes and parking brake. *The vehicle must not be allowed to move!* Move the selector lever to each drive range and to REVERSE. In each position, push the accelerator pedal to the floor for not longer than five seconds. Note the engine speed on the tachometer. Then move the selector lever to NEUTRAL and run the engine at fast idle for about one minute. This allows the fluid to cool before making a stall test in the next selector-lever position.

Careful! If the engine rpm exceeds the maximum specified stall speed, release the accelerator pedal immediately. A band or clutch is slipping. Continuing the test may cause greater damage.

The possible results of a stall test are *high, low,* or *OK.* Figure 48-13 is a typical chart showing how slipping bands and clutches, and poor engine performance, affect stall speed. High stall speed indicates a slipping band or clutch. Low stall speed indicates poor engine performance or a slipping one-way clutch in the torque-converter stator (➤47-6).

STALL TEST RESULTS

Selector Position	Stall Speed High (Slip)	Stall Speed Low
D and 3	Planetary one-way clutch	
D, 3, and 1	Forward clutch	
All drive ranges	a. Check throttle-valve adjustment b. Perform line-pressure test	a. Poor engine performance b. Converter stator one-way clutch slipping
R only	Reverse clutch or low-reverse band or servo	

Fig. 48-13 Stall-test diagnosis chart. (*ATW*)

➤ 48-14 ELECTRONIC SHIFT-CONTROL DIAGNOSIS

Many automatic transmissions and transaxles have electronic shift controls (➤47-27). The shifts are made when a *controller* or *powertrain-control module* (PCM) sends signals that switch the *shift solenoids* (➤47-28) on or off (Fig. 48-14). Improper shifting means the technician must determine if the trouble is in the mechanical or hydraulic components, or in the electronic controls. These failures may be:

1. in the computer or PCM.
2. in the wiring and connectors between the PCM and the transmission or transaxle.
3. in the wiring and electronic controls inside the transmission or transaxle.

Figure 48-15 shows the electronic controls in a Ford AXOD-E automatic transaxle. After the road test (➤48-11), use a scan tool or electronic tester to recall any trouble codes (➤20-13). Perform the services required to clear the trouble codes in the engine and then in the transaxle. If a transaxle trouble code resets, follow the procedure in the vehicle service manual to pinpoint and correct the cause.

When no transaxle trouble codes are set and the trouble continues, connect an *electronic-transmission tester* (Fig. 48-16) into the wiring harness between the PCM and the transaxle. The pins in the side electrical connector connect to the shift solenoids (Fig. 48-15). The top connector connects to the *variable-force solenoid* (VFS), *transmission-oil-temperature* (TOT) *solenoid,* and *lockup solenoid* (LUS) for the torque-converter clutch.

Light-emitting diodes (LEDs) on the tester show when each solenoid is on and off. Buttons and switches on the tester can be used to turn each solenoid on and off, and to measure voltages and resistances. The transaxle electronics can be checked with the unit in or out of the vehicle. Follow the procedures and specifications in the vehicle service manual. A pressure gauge (➤48-15) should be connected while performing some tests.

The *turbine-speed sensor* (TSS) and the *vehicle-speed sensor* (VSS) shown in Fig. 48-15 make possible a variety of additional diagnostic tests. For example, the turbine-speed sensor reads the speed of the transaxle *input* shaft. The vehicle-speed sensor reads the speed of the transaxle *output* shaft. In direct drive (1:1), any difference in these speeds indicates slippage in the transaxle. In *underdrive* (gear reduction) or overdrive, the speed difference should be the same as the mechanical gear ratio. Any other reading indicates slippage.

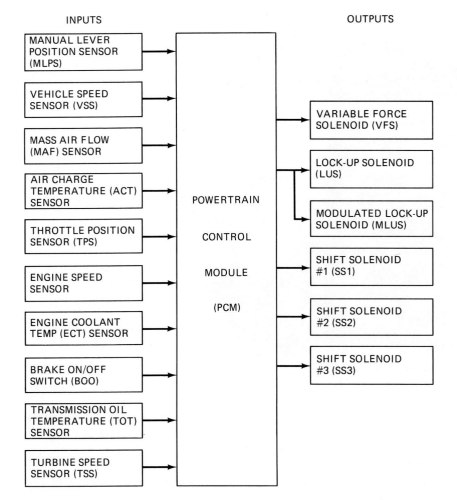

INPUTS — OUTPUTS

Fig. 48-14 Inputs and outputs for the powertrain control module (PCM) of a Ford AXOD-E automatic transaxle. Shifts are made when the PCM switches the shift solenoids ON or OFF. (*Ford Motor Company*)

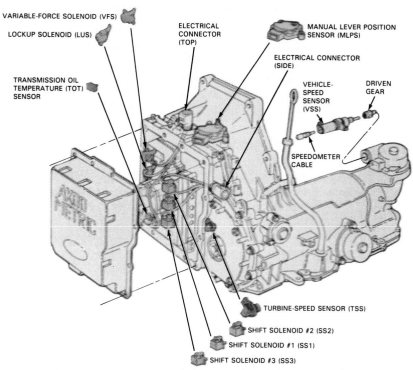

Fig. 48-15 Electronic controls in the Ford AXOD-E automatic transaxle. The terminals or pins in the side electrical connector connect to the shift solenoids. (*Ford Motor Company*)

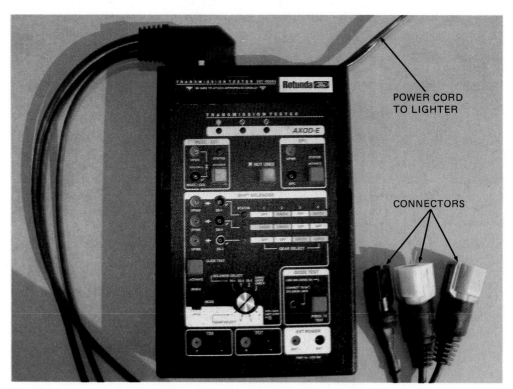

Fig. 48-16 Electronic-transmission tester that connects to the electrical connectors on the top and side of the Ford AXOD-E automatic transaxle. (*ATW*)

➤ 48-15 LINE-PRESSURE TEST

High stall speed in all drive ranges may indicate low line pressure. This can be caused by a worn pump, stuck pressure-regulator valve, or a fluid leak from the pump or valve body. Then the fluid pressure applied to the servos and clutches is not strong enough to prevent slipping. The result is rapid wear and failure of the friction elements, and probably damage to the drum and other hard parts.

Perform a pressure test to check line pressure (➤47-13).

Remove the plug from the line-pressure port in the transmission or transaxle case. Install a pressure gauge (Fig. 48-17) and hose long enough so the gauge can be read from the driver's seat. Firmly apply the service brakes and parking brake, and start the engine. Move the selector lever through each range and record the line pressure in each position.

Figure 48-18 shows the line-pressure specifications for the Ford AXOD automatic transaxle. This transaxle is shown in Fig. 47-4. The pressures are read at idle. Then read the pressures again while making a stall test (➤48-13) at wide-open throttle (WOT). This shows how much throttle pressure raises line pressure as engine load increases. Some manufacturers specify the pressures at certain engine speeds and with a specified vacuum applied to the modulator valve. Follow the test procedure in the vehicle service manual.

Line pressure may be low, high, or within specifications (Fig. 48-19). A sticking modulator valve or throttle valve can cause high pressure. A sticking pressure-regulator valve may cause either high or low pressure. Low pressure only in OD or D can be caused by a fluid leak in the hydraulic circuit for the forward clutch. Low pressure in reverse may be caused by fluid leaking from the hydraulic circuit for the low-and-reverse band.

➤ **48-16 AIR-PRESSURE TESTS**

When line pressure (➤48-15) is within specifications and the vehicle does not move, the cause may be a bad band or clutch. A vehicle with a burned or inoperative forward clutch will move in REVERSE but not in any forward gear. Failure to move in REVERSE can be caused by a bad reverse clutch.

Operation of the bands and multiple-disc clutches can be checked by substituting air pressure for fluid pressure. Drain the fluid from the pan (Fig. 48-3). Then remove the pan, filter, and valve body (Fig. 48-4). Figure 48-20 shows the identification of each case passage on a Chrysler TorqueFlite transaxle. Marked *test plates* bolt to the case to identify each passage (Fig. 48-21).

Using an air nozzle with a tapered rubber tip, apply 30 psi [207 kPa] to the fluid passages for each clutch and servo (Fig. 48-21). Each band and clutch should operate. The sound of a dull thud indicates normal clutch engagement. When air pressure is applied to a servo, its band should tighten.

Air-pressure tests can also locate blocked passages and leaks. However, air tests are sometimes difficult or impossible without removing the unit from the vehicle.

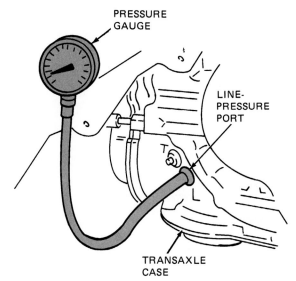

Fig. 48-17 Make a line-pressure test by connecting a pressure gauge to the line-pressure port in the transaxle case. (*Ford Motor Company*)

Range	Idle		WOT Stall	
	kPa	psi	kPa	psi
P, N	558-655	81-95	—	—
R	641-1048	93-152	1669-1924	242-279
Ⓓ, D, 1	558-655	81-95	1089-1262	158-183
L	772-1165	112-169	1089-1262	158-183

Fig. 48-18 Line-pressure specifications for the Ford AXOD automatic transaxle. (*Ford Motor Company*)

Pressure Test Result	Range	Possible Location of Problem	Action to Take
Low	All	Worn pump; fluid leaking from pump, valve body, or transaxle case; pressure-regulator-valve sticking	Disassemble, inspect, repair or replace as required the complete pump or valve body or components.
Low	Ⓓ D	Fluid leaking from hydraulic circuit of forward clutch.	Disassemble, inspect, repair or replace components as required.
Low	R	Fluid leaking from hydraulic circuit of low-and-reverse band	Disassemble, inspect, repair or replace components as required.
High	All	Throttle-valve sticking, throttle-modulator-valve sticking, pressure-regulator-valve sticking	Disassemble, inspect, repair or replace components as required.
Within Specified Limits	All	—	Check throttle pressure.

Fig. 48-19 Pressure-test diagnosis chart. (*Ford Motor Company*)

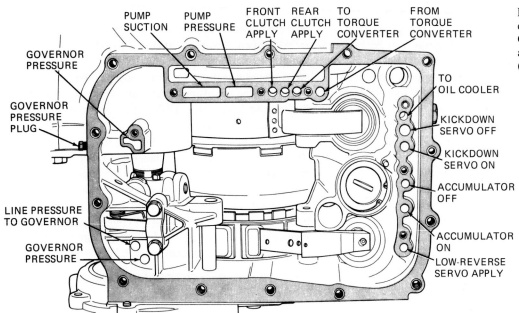

Fig. 48-20 Identification of each case passage in a Chrysler TorqueFlite automatic transaxle. (*Chrysler Corporation*)

PUMP SUCTION
PUMP PRESSURE
FRONT CLUTCH APPLY
REAR CLUTCH APPLY
TO TORQUE CONVERTER
FROM TORQUE CONVERTER
GOVERNOR PRESSURE
GOVERNOR PRESSURE PLUG
LINE PRESSURE TO GOVERNOR
GOVERNOR PRESSURE
TO OIL COOLER
KICKDOWN SERVO OFF
KICKDOWN SERVO ON
ACCUMULATOR OFF
ACCUMULATOR ON
LOW-REVERSE SERVO APPLY

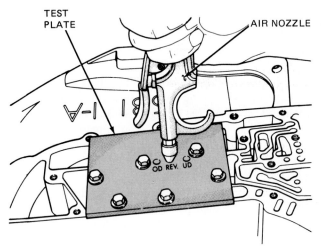

Fig. 48-21 Using a rubber-tipped air nozzle and a marked test plate to make air-pressure tests. (*Chrysler Corporation*)

TEST PLATE
AIR NOZZLE

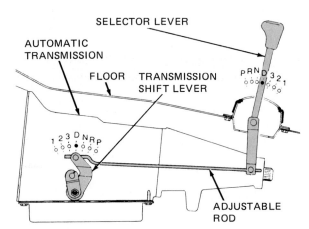

Fig. 48-22 Shift-linkage adjustment on an automatic transmission with a floor-mounted selector lever. (*Ford Motor Company*)

SELECTOR LEVER
AUTOMATIC TRANSMISSION
FLOOR
TRANSMISSION SHIFT LEVER
ADJUSTABLE ROD

AUTOMATIC-TRANSMISSION AND TRANSAXLE SERVICE

➤ 48-17 LINKAGE AND BAND ADJUSTMENTS

There are basically two linkage adjustments. These are the *shift-linkage adjustment* and the *throttle-* or *kickdown-linkage adjustment*. Some bands are also adjustable.

1. SHIFT-LINKAGE ADJUSTMENT When the driver moves the selector lever to any position (Fig. 48-22), the linkage repositions the manual valve in the valve body. An improperly-positioned manual valve may cause delayed upshifts and band and clutch slippage. This can damage the transmission or transaxle. Shift-linkage adjustment pro-

cedures vary. Follow the procedure in the vehicle service manual. In general, adjust the shift rod or cable so the detents for the selector lever match the detents for the shift lever on the transmission or transaxle.

2. THROTTLE- OR KICKDOWN-LINKAGE ADJUSTMENT The throttle or kickdown linkage (Fig. 48-23) causes a downshift if the driver depresses the accelerator pedal to wide-open throttle (within a certain speed range). The adjustment basically is correct if pushing the accelerator pedal to the floor causes a downshift to occur. Some throttle linkage is self-adjusting (➤42-11).

3. BAND ADJUSTMENT Automatic transmissions and transaxles may have one or more bands (Fig. 47-22) that require adjustment. Bands are adjusted by tightening and then loosening the band-adjusting screw a specified number of turns (Fig. 48-24). All bands are not adjustable. Replace the band if it is loose or worn through the lining.

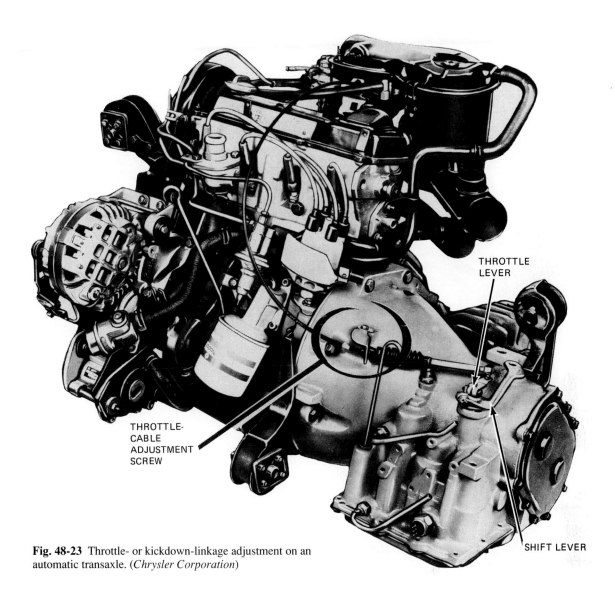

Fig. 48-23 Throttle- or kickdown-linkage adjustment on an automatic transaxle. (*Chrysler Corporation*)

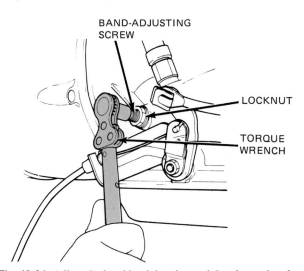

Fig. 48-24 Adjust the band by tightening and then loosening the band-adjusting screw a specified number of turns. (*Ford Motor Company*)

> ## 48-18 IN-VEHICLE REPAIRS

Some repairs can usually be made to an automatic transmission or transaxle without removing the unit from the vehicle. The vehicle service manual describes these jobs. They may include governor, servo, and valve-body service, and installing a new band. However, if the repair does not correct an internal problem, remove the transmission or transaxle from the vehicle.

> ## 48-19 TRANSMISSION AND TRANSAXLE REMOVAL AND INSTALLATION

The removal and installation procedure for automatic transmissions and transaxles varies with different vehicles. In general, here are the parts you may have to disconnect or remove. First, open the hood and disconnect the ground cable from the battery. Then remove or disconnect the following:

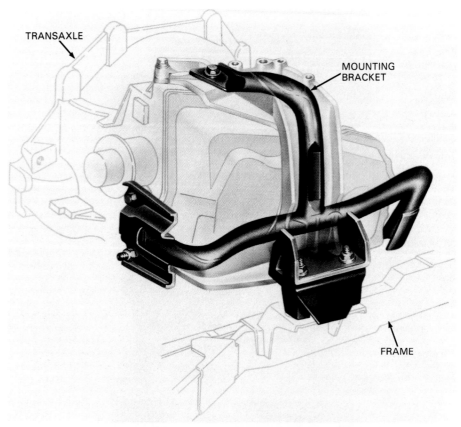

Fig. 48-25 Frame-mounted cradle, or mounting bracket, from which the transaxle must be removed before the unit can be removed from the vehicle. (*Cadillac Division of General Motors Corporation*)

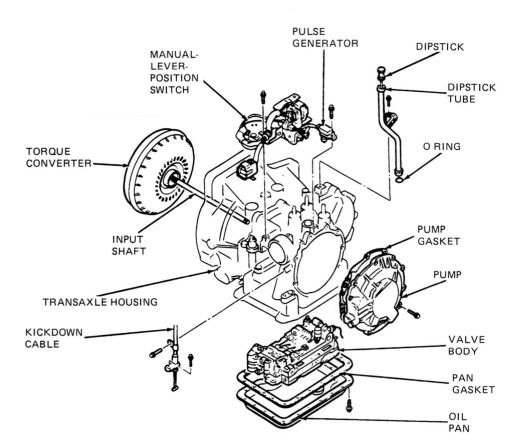

Fig. 48-26 Partially disassembled Ford 4EAT electronically-controlled four-speed automatic transaxle. (*Ford Motor Company*)

- Starting motor.
- Backup-light switch.
- Neutral-safety switch.
- Wiring-harness connectors.
- Vacuum line from modulator valve.
- Cooler lines to fluid cooler.
- Shift linkage.
- Driveshaft or halfshafts.
- Torque-converter driveplate bolts.
- Housing-to-engine bolts.

Some transaxles must be removed from a cradle or mounting bracket (Fig. 48-25). In addition, there may be other items to disconnect or remove. The vehicle service manual covers specific removal procedures. Chapter 44 describes the use of the transmission jack to remove and install transmissions and transaxles.

➤ 48-20 AUTOMATIC-TRANSMISSION OR TRANSAXLE OVERHAUL

Figures 48-26 and 48-27 show the major parts in the disassembly of the Ford 4 EAT electronically-controlled four-speed transaxle. Rebuilding procedures for automatic transmissions and transaxles vary from model to model. Service procedures also vary according to whether the unit is being completely overhauled or only a *single-point repair* is being made. This repair to a single part or failed component should be made only after diagnosis and inspection show that no related parts are worn or damaged.

In the complete overhaul, replace all gaskets, seals, O rings, metal sealing rings, clutch discs, filter, and the modulator valve. Also inspect and replace, if needed, the following:

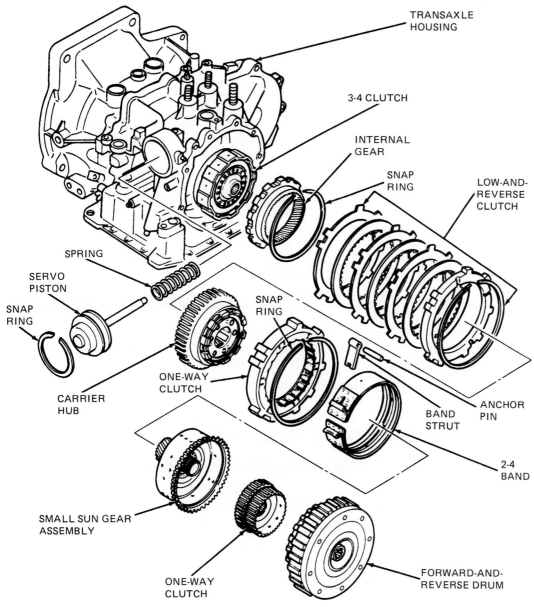

Fig. 48-27 Disassembled gear train of the Ford 4EAT transaxle. (*Ford Motor Company*)

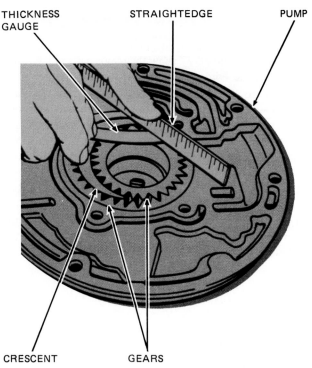

CRESCENT   GEARS

Fig. 48-28 Measuring the clearance between the pump body and gear face. (*Ford Motor Company*)

- Torque converter
- Shafts and splines
- Bushings and bearings
- Pump
- Gears

- Governor
- Linkage

Clean and inspect all other parts after disassembly. This includes the fluid cooler, cooler lines, valve body, governor, clutches, and check balls. Inspect the pump mating surfaces and gear teeth for burrs. Remove minor burrs and scores with crocus cloth. With a straightedge and thickness gauge, measure the clearance between the pump body and the gear face (Fig. 48-28). Replace the pump if it has excessive wear or damage.

Contaminants are a major cause of trouble and comebacks. All deposits, debris, and particles must be removed while cleaning and rebuilding the automatic transmission or transaxle. Clean the parts with a suitable solvent. Then use moisture-free compressed air to blow-dry the parts and clean out the fluid passages. Clean the friction plates, bands, and seals by wiping with a lint-free cloth.

Careful! The torque converter may be cleaned and flushed using a *torque-converter cleaner*. Do not clean the torque converter with solvent!

Soak new friction plates and bands in the proper type of clean automatic-transmission fluid for at least 15 minutes before assembly. Install all of the parts in the overhaul kit, if used. Complete specifications and service procedures for rebuilding an automatic transmission or transaxle are in the vehicle service manual.

TRADE TALK

air-pressure test	kickdown-linkage	oxidized fluid	stall test
band adjustment	adjustment	road test	turbine-speed sensor
flaring	line-pressure test	single-point repair	

MULTIPLE-CHOICE TEST

*Select the **one** correct, best, or most probable answer to each question.*
You can find the answers in the section indicated at the end of each question.

1. Severe service that requires periodic changing of the transmission fluid and filter includes all the following EXCEPT (➤48-2)
   a. taxi service
   b. trailer towing
   c. delivery service
   d. normal driving

2. Pink fluid on the dipstick indicates (➤48-4)
   a. overfilling has caused foaming
   b. oxidized fluid
   c. a leaking radiator fluid cooler
   d. a leaking cooler line

3. Technician A says if the transmission fluid is brown or black and has a strong burnt odor, the clutch plates probably have overheated and burned. Technician B says the bands have overheated and burned. Who is right? (➤48-5)
   a. A only
   b. B only
   c. Both A and B
   d. Neither A nor B
4. Upshifts that are very late under light acceleration may be caused by all the following EXCEPT (➤48-11)
   a. a bad governor
   b. too much throttle pressure
   c. too much modulator pressure
   d. a bad torque-converter clutch
5. Technician A says when diagnosing a transaxle with electronic shift controls, road test the vehicle and clear any trouble codes. Technician B says determine if the trouble is in the PCM or in the transaxle. Who is right? (➤48-14)
   a. A only
   b. B only
   c. Both A and B
   d. Neither A nor B
6. A vehicle with normal line pressure that moves in REVERSE but not in any forward gear may have a (➤48-16)
   a. slipping stator clutch
   b. burned clutch
   c. broken output shaft
   d. stuck governor

7. Technician A says the throttle or kickdown linkage causes the torque-converter clutch to engage. Technician B says the linkage causes the transmission to downshift when the accelerator pedal is pressed to the floor. Who is right? (➤48-17)
   a. A only
   b. B only
   c. Both A and B
   d. Neither A nor B
8. The shift linkage connects between the (➤48-17)
   a. selector lever and manual valve
   b. selector lever and throttle valve
   c. throttle lever and kickdown lever
   d. manual valve and throttle valve
9. Bands are adjusted by (➤48-17)
   a. tightening the adjusting screw a specified number of turns
   b. installing an oversize drum
   c. tightening and then loosening the adjusting screw a specified number of turns
   d. installing an oversize band
10. Before assembling a transmission or transaxle, perform all the following EXCEPT (➤48-20)
   a. soak new friction plates and bands in automatic-transmission fluid
   b. measure the clearance between the pump body and the gear face
   c. clean out all fluid passages
   d. clean the torque converter in the solvent tank

REVIEW QUESTIONS

1. What can checking the fluid color and condition tell you?   (➤48-4 and 48-5)
2. List the steps in the diagnosis procedure for automatic transmissions and transaxles, and describe how to perform each step.   (➤48-11)
3. How do you check the operation of the torque-converter clutch?   (➤48-12)
4. When should case air-pressure tests be made and what can they tell you?   (➤48-16)
5. What are the basic steps in adjusting a band, shift linkage, and throttle- or kickdown linkage?   (➤48-17)

PART 8

AUTOMOTIVE CHASSIS

This part of *Automotive Mechanics* describes the automotive chassis, which includes the suspension, steering, and braking systems. Also included are active suspension, four-wheel steering, anti-lock-braking, traction control, tire-pressure monitoring, and other computerized chassis systems. All these are supported by the wheels and tires, which may have directional, asymmetric tread and be of different sizes for the front and rear. The tires provide the only contact between the vehicle and the road.

There are six chapters in Part 8:

CHAPTER 49

AUTOMOTIVE SUSPENSION SYSTEMS

After studying this chapter, you should be able to:

- Describe the basic types of springs used in automotive vehicles.
- Explain the purpose and operation of shock absorbers, and how air shocks are used in automatic level control.
- Describe the construction and operation of rear-suspension systems using leaf, coil, and torsion-bar springs.
- Describe the construction and operation of front-suspension systems using coil springs, MacPherson struts, leaf springs, and torsion bars.
- Explain electronic-ride control, air suspension, and active suspension, and how each works.

➤ 49-1 PURPOSE OF THE SUSPENSION SYSTEM

The *suspension system* (Fig. 49-1) is located between the wheel axles and the vehicle body or frame. Its purpose is to:

1. Support the weight of the vehicle.
2. Cushion bumps and holes in the road.
3. Maintain traction between the tires and the road.
4. Hold the wheels in alignment.

The suspension system allows the vehicle to travel over rough surfaces with a minimum of up-and-down body movement. It also allows the vehicle to corner with minimum roll or tendency to lose traction between the tires and the road surface. This provides a cushioning action so *road shocks* have a minimal effect on the occupants and load in the vehicle. Road shocks are the actions resulting from the tires moving up and down as they meet bumps or holes in the road.

➤ 49-2 COMPONENTS OF SUSPENSION SYSTEM

The suspension-system components include the *springs* and related parts that support the weight of the vehicle body on the axles and wheels. The springs and the *shock absorbers* (Fig. 49-1) are the two main parts. The springs support the weight of the vehicle and its load, and absorb road shocks. The shock absorbers help control or *dampen* spring action. Without this control, *spring oscillation* occurs. The springs keep the wheels bouncing up and down after they pass bumps or holes. Shock absorbers allow the basic spring movement, but quickly dampen out the unwanted bouncing that follows. These ride control components—springs and shock absorbers—may be mechanically or electronically controlled. Following sections describe both types.

| NOTE | In describing springs and shock absorbers, *jounce* or *compression* is the condition when the wheel moves up. *Rebound* is the condition when the wheel moves down. |

AUTOMOTIVE SPRINGS

➤ 49-3 TYPES OF SPRINGS

Four types of springs are used in automotive suspension systems. These are *coil, leaf, torsion bar,* and *air* (Fig. 49-2).

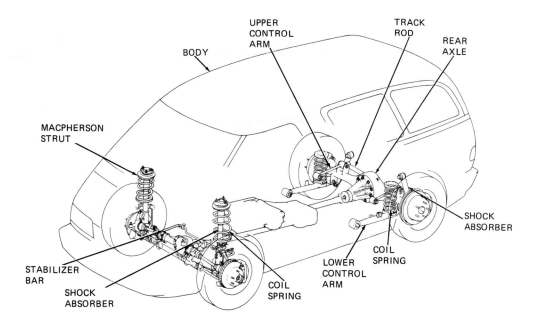

BODY

UPPER
CONTROL
ARM

TRACK
ROD

REAR
AXLE

MACPHERSON
STRUT

STABILIZER
BAR

SHOCK
ABSORBER

COIL
SPRING

LOWER
CONTROL
ARM

COIL
SPRING

SHOCK
ABSORBER

Fig. 49-1 Parts in a vehicle suspension system, using MacPherson struts in front and coil springs in the rear. (*Toyota Motor Sales U.S.A., Inc.*)

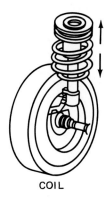

COIL

LEAF

TORSION BAR

AIR

Fig. 49-2 Types of springs used in automotive suspension systems. (*ATW*)

1. COIL SPRING The coil spring is made of a length of round spring-steel rod wound into a coil (Fig. 49-3). Figure 49-1 shows front and rear suspension systems using coil springs. Some coil springs are made from a tapered rod (Fig. 49-3). This gives the spring a variable *spring rate* (➤49-5). As the spring is compressed, its resistance to further compression increases.

2. LEAF SPRING Two types of leaf springs are *single-leaf* and *multileaf springs* (Fig. 49-4). These have several flexible steel plates of graduated length, stacked and held together by clips. In operation, the spring bends to absorb road shocks. The plates bend and slide on each other to permit this action. Single-leaf springs are described in ➤49-13.

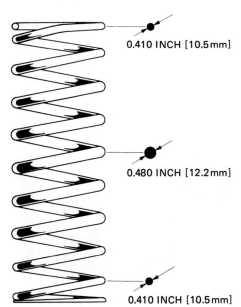

0.410 INCH [10.5 mm]

0.480 INCH [12.2 mm]

0.410 INCH [10.5 mm]

Fig. 49-3 Coil spring made from tapered rod. The rod is larger in diameter at the center of the coil. (*Mazda Motors of America, Inc.*)

659

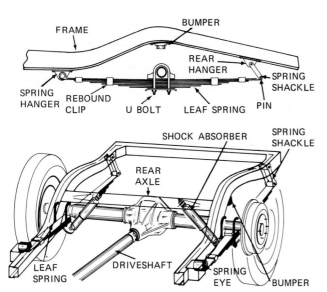

Fig. 49-4 Rear-suspension system using leaf springs, showing how the spring attaches to the frame and axle housing.

3. TORSION BAR The torsion bar is a straight rod of spring steel, rigidly fastened at one end to the vehicle frame or body. The other end attaches to an upper or lower *control arm* (Fig. 49-5). As the control arm swings up and down in response to wheel movement, the torsion bar twists to provide spring action.

4. AIR SPRING The air spring (Fig. 49-6) is a rubber cylinder or *air bag* filled with compressed air. A plastic piston on the lower control arm moves up and down with the lower control arm. This causes the compressed air to provide spring action. If the load in the vehicle changes, a valve at the top of the air bag opens to add or release air. An air compressor connected to the valve keeps the air springs inflated.

➤ **49-4 SPRUNG AND UNSPRUNG WEIGHT**

The total weight of the vehicle includes the *sprung weight* and the *unsprung weight*. The sprung weight is the weight supported by springs. The unsprung weight is the part not

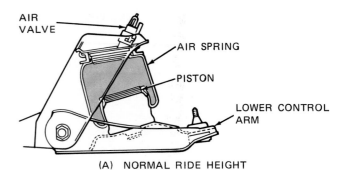

(A) NORMAL RIDE HEIGHT

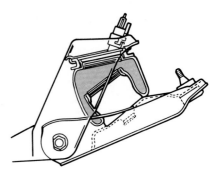

(B) JOUNCE (COMPRESSED)

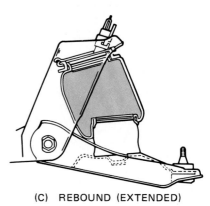

(C) REBOUND (EXTENDED)

Fig. 49-6 Air spring, which is a rubber cylinder or air bag filled with compressed air. (*Ford Motor Company*)

supported by springs. This includes the weight of drive axles, axle shafts, wheels, and tires.

The unsprung weight is kept as low as possible. The roughness of the ride increases as unsprung weight increases. To take an extreme example, suppose the unsprung weight equals the sprung weight. As the unsprung weight moves up and down, due to the wheels meeting road bumps and holes, the sprung weight would move up and down the same amount. For this reason, the unsprung weight should be only a small part of the total weight of the vehicle.

➤ **49-5 SPRING RATE**

The softness or hardness of a spring is its spring rate. This is the load required to move a spring a specified distance. The rate of a spring that compresses uniformly (a *linear-rate spring*) is the weight required to compress it 1 inch

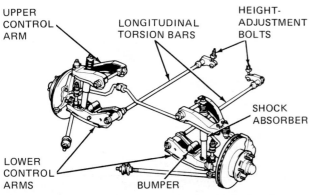

Fig. 49-5 Front-suspension system using longitudinal torsion bars. (*Toyota Motor Sales U.S.A., Inc.*)

[25.4 mm]. If 600 pounds [272 kg] compresses the spring 3 inches [76 mm], then 1200 pounds [544 kg] will compress it 6 inches [152 mm].

Variable-rate springs do not move or *deflect* at a constant or linear rate. The coil spring in Fig. 49-3 is one type of variable-rate spring. Winding the coils from a tapered rod provides the variable rate. The spring rate varies from an initial 72.2 pounds per inch [1.29 kg/mm] to 163.5 pounds per inch [2.92 kg/mm]. Other variable-rate coil springs have the coils closer together at the top than at the bottom, or are wound in a cone or barrel shape.

➤ 49-6 CONTROLLING SPRING ACTION

The ideal spring for automotive suspension absorbs road shock rapidly and then returns to its normal position slowly. This is difficult to attain, however. A very flexible or soft spring allows too much movement. A stiff or hard spring gives too rough a ride. A medium-soft spring and a shock absorber (➤49-7) produce a satisfactory ride. The shock absorber prevents spring *override*. This is excessive and continued spring action after a bump or hole has been passed.

SHOCK ABSORBERS

➤ 49-7 PURPOSE OF SHOCK ABSORBERS

A shock absorber (Figs. 49-1 and 49-7) is a tubular hydraulic device placed near each wheel to control or dampen spring oscillations (➤49-2). One end of the shock absorber attaches to the vehicle body or frame. The other end attaches to a moving suspension part such as the axle hous-

ing or a control arm. Movement of the spring then causes the shock absorber to lengthen and shorten.

The purpose of the hydraulic shock absorber shown in Fig. 49-7 is to dampen spring oscillations. It does not support the weight of the vehicle, nor does it affect vehicle height. Some shock absorbers (described later) can perform these functions.

➤ 49-8 SHOCK-ABSORBER OPERATION

Figure 49-7 shows the construction of a simple shock absorber. It is basically an oil-filled cylinder or tube in which a piston moves up and down. This forces the oil or *hydraulic fluid* in the cylinder to flow through small fluid passages or *orifices* in the piston. The resulting fluid friction limits spring bounce.

A shock absorber may mount separately (Fig. 49-5) or inside a *shock-absorber-and-strut assembly* (Fig. 49-8).

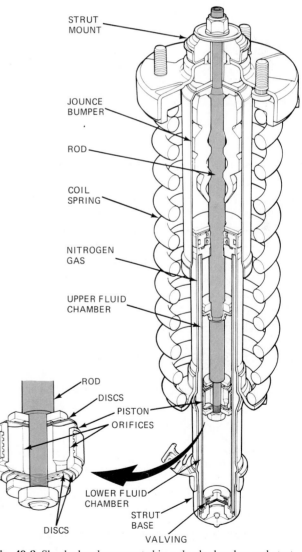

Fig. 49-8 Shock absorber mounted in a shock-absorber-and-strut assembly, with the coil spring. (*American Honda Motor Company, Inc.*)

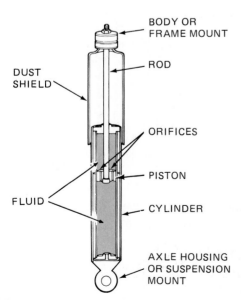

Fig. 49-7 Construction of a simple shock absorber. (*Ford Motor Company*)

Both types work the same way. The piston divides the cylinder into upper and lower fluid chambers. The orifices or holes in the piston are restricted by spring-loaded check valves or disks that deflect under pressure. The more easily the fluid flows through the holes, the softer the ride.

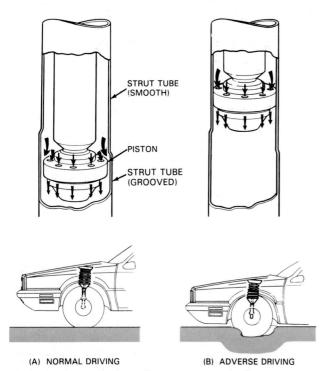

Fig. 49-9 Shock-absorber action in a variable-damping strut. (*Chrysler Corporation*)

Smaller holes have greater restriction and provide a stiffer ride.

Figure 49-9 shows the shock-absorber action in a *variable-damping strut*. During normal driving, grooves in the strut tube allow fluid to pass around the piston. When the wheel suddenly drops into a pothole in the road, the tube extends more than normal. Now the piston is above the grooves. The fluid can pass only through the holes in the piston. This increases the resistance to piston movement and reduces the impact of the suspension against its stops.

➤ 49-9 GAS-FILLED SHOCK ABSORBERS

There is some air above the fluid in the shock absorber. During compression and rebound, the rapid movement of the fluid between the chambers can mix the air with the fluid. Then the fluid foams or *aerates*. When the piston moves through air or foam, it meets little resistance.

One method of reducing foaming is to fill the air space with a pressurized gas such as nitrogen (Fig. 49-8). The gas pressure on the fluid reduces the creation of air bubbles and foaming. Some shock absorbers have a rubber bag or *cell* that contains the gas to prevent mixing.

➤ 49-10 OTHER TYPES OF SHOCK ABSORBER

Various vehicles and suspension systems use different types of shock absorbers. Some shock absorbers can adjust

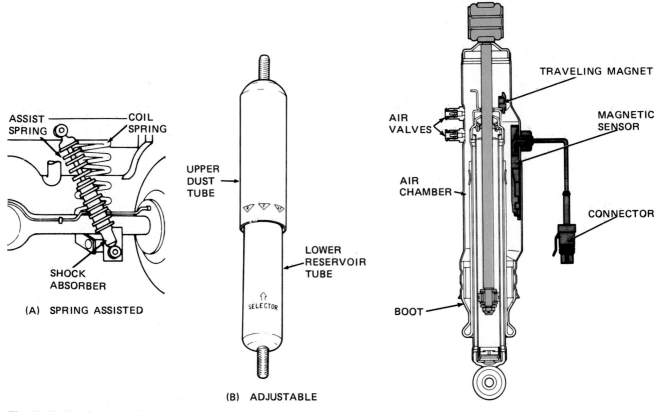

Fig. 49-10 Various types of shock absorbers.

vehicle height. Others can be reset to change vehicle ride and handling. Shock absorbers with additional capabilities include spring-assisted, adjustable, and air.

1. SPRING-ASSISTED SHOCK ABSORBERS Separately-mounted shock absorbers are used with many suspension systems. Some of these shock absorbers have a variable-rate coil spring or *assist spring* attached between the piston rod and the tube (Fig. 49-10A). These *spring-assisted shock absorbers* combine spring action with shock-absorber action. This helps maintain proper vehicle height regardless of load.

2. ADJUSTABLE SHOCK ABSORBERS Some shock absorbers are adjustable, either by hand or electronically. One type of manually-adjusted shock absorber is shown in Fig. 49-10B. It has three positions that can be selected to change the firmness of the shock-absorber action. Turning the upper dust tube one way produces a softer ride. Turning it the other way produces a harder ride. In some cars, the driver can change the shock-absorber setting by moving a switch on the instrument panel. These and other electronic suspension and ride controls are described later.

3. AIR SHOCK ABSORBERS Air shock absorbers have a rubber boot surrounding the shock absorber (Fig. 49-10C). This forms a sealed air chamber which is filled with compressed air. The compressed air increases the load-carrying capacity of the vehicle while maintaining proper rear-end height. Some air shock absorbers are filled through an air valve by attaching a service-station air hose. When the load is removed, enough air should be bled from the shock absorber to lower the vehicle to its normal ride height.

> ## 49-11 AUTOMATIC LEVEL CONTROL

Many vehicles have *automatic level control* or *electronic level control* (Fig. 49-11). The two rear air- shock absorbers are connected by air lines to an air compressor on the vehicle. At least one of the shock absorbers includes a *height sensor* (Figs. 49-10C and 49-11). It signals the electronic control module (ECM) when a load in the rear of the vehicle has caused a change in vehicle height. The ECM then switches on the air compressor to add air to the shock absorbers. Removing the load causes the ECM to open the air valve. This bleeds air from the system.

Some vehicles have electronically-adjusted *air shocks* or *air struts* at all four wheels. These are described in later sections.

REAR SUSPENSION

> ## 49-12 REAR-SUSPENSION SYSTEMS

All four types of springs (leaf, coil, torsion bar, and air) are used in rear suspension systems. On vehicles with *four-wheel steering* (Chap. 50), the rear wheels are supported

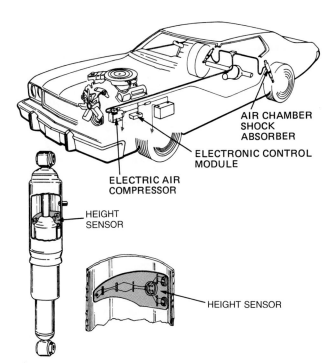

Fig. 49-11 Electronic automatic-level-control system. A height sensor in the shock absorber switches the electric air compressor on and off. (*Monroe Auto Equipment Company*)

so they can swing slightly from side to side. This provides limited rear-wheel steering. Later sections describe electronically-controlled air springs, shocks, and struts in rear-suspension systems.

> ## 49-13 LEAF-SPRING REAR SUSPENSION

Figure 49-4 shows a rear-suspension system using a multi-leaf spring. It attaches by two *U bolts* and is placed either over or under the axle housing. As the spring flexes due to changing loads, the leaves slide on each other as they bend.

A metal cover or *rebound clips* placed along the spring keep the leaves in alignment. They also prevent excessive leaf separation during rebound. The two ends of the longest or *master leaf* are rolled to form *spring eyes* (Figs. 49-4 and 49-12). They attach to the frame by a *spring hanger* at the front and a *spring shackle* at the rear. Figure 49-12 shows a rear-suspension system using single-leaf springs.

1. *Spring hanger* The spring hanger attaches to the vehicle frame (Fig. 49-4). A bolt and rubber bushing attach the spring eye to the hanger (Fig. 49-13). As the spring bends, the spring eye moves back and forth on the bushing. The bushing also dampens vibration from the spring.
2. *Spring shackle* As the spring bends, the distance between the two ends changes. The spring shackle (Figs. 49-12 and 49-13) is a swinging support that allows this change. Rubber bushings permit the shackle to swing back and forth. The bushings also absorb vibration and prevent it from reaching the vehicle body or frame.

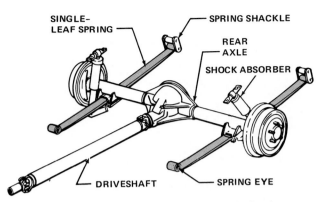

Fig. 49-12 Rear-suspension system using single-leaf springs. (*Chrysler Corporation*)

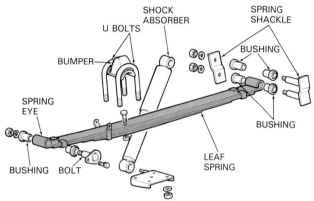

Fig. 49-13 Leaf spring with disassembled spring hanger and spring shackle. (*Chrysler Corporation*)

3. *Single-leaf spring* The single-leaf or *tapered-plate leaf spring* (Fig. 49-12) is made of a single plate. The plate is thick at the center and tapers to the two ends. The single-leaf spring mounts and works the same as the multileaf spring. However, there are no additional leaves to slide on one another.

4. *Transverse leaf spring* Some rear suspension systems use a steel multileaf spring or a fiberglass single-leaf spring mounted transversely (Fig. 49-14). Each wheel is independently suspended by one end of the spring. This provides *independent rear suspension* (IRS). The up-and-down movement of one wheel does not affect the other wheel. If the rear wheels are driven (Fig. 45-6), universal joints in each halfshaft carry the power from the differential to the wheels.

➤ **49-14 COIL-SPRING REAR SUSPENSION (REAR-WHEEL DRIVE)**

On a rear-drive or four-wheel-drive vehicle, the rear suspension must accommodate the driveshaft and rear drive axle. A typical arrangement is shown in Fig. 49-15. The springs are placed between brackets on the vehicle body or frame and *spring seats* on the lower control arms. The control arms allow up-and-down movement of the axle housing, but prevent forward or backward movement. A shock absorber at each wheel controls spring bounce.

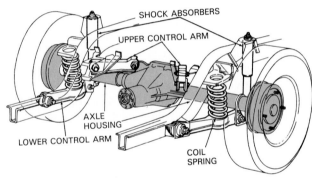

Fig. 49-15 Rear suspension with coil springs placed between brackets on the vehicle frame and spring seats on the lower control arms. (*Ford Motor Company*)

Fig. 49-14 A transverse leaf spring, which provides independent rear suspension. (*Oldsmobile Division of General Motors Corporation*)

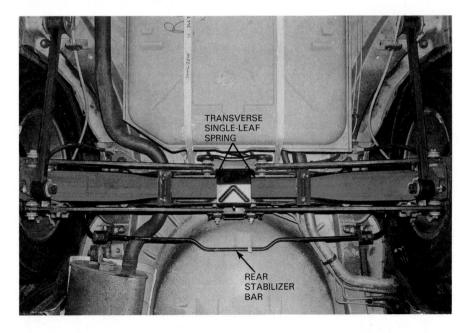

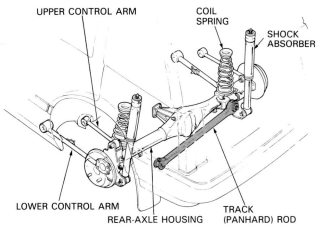

Fig. 49-16 Coil-spring rear suspension used in a four-wheel-drive vehicle. The springs seat on the axle housing. The track rod, or Panhard rod, prevents sideward movement of the axle housing. (*American Honda Motor Company, Inc.*)

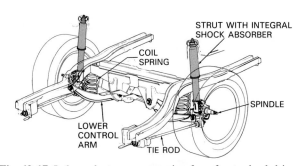

Fig. 49-17 Independent rear suspension for a front-wheel-drive vehicle, using modified MacPherson struts. The coil springs mount on the lower control arm. (*Ford Motor Company*)

Figure 49-16 shows a coil-spring rear suspension in a four-wheel-drive vehicle. The springs seat on the axle housing. Two control arms on each side allow up-and-down movement of the axle housing but prevent forward or backward motion. The *track rod* or *Panhard rod* fastens at one end to the axle housing and at the other end to the vehicle body. This prevents sideward movement of the axle housing.

➤ 49-15 COIL-SPRING REAR SUSPENSION (FRONT-WHEEL DRIVE)

The rear suspension system on a front-drive vehicle does not have to accommodate a drive axle or halfshafts. Figure 49-17 shows a coil-spring rear-suspension system. This is a *modified MacPherson-strut* (➤49-16) design which provides independent rear suspension. The spring mounts on the lower control arm instead of on the strut. The strut, with integral shock absorber, mounts between the body and the spindle. No upper control arm is used.

➤ 49-16 STRUT-TYPE REAR SUSPENSION

A *strut* is a rod or tube that is acted upon by side forces or compression forces. In automotive suspension, the assembly that combines the shock absorber with a coil spring is often called a strut or a *MacPherson strut* (Fig. 49-18). Only a lower control arm is needed. The top of the strut

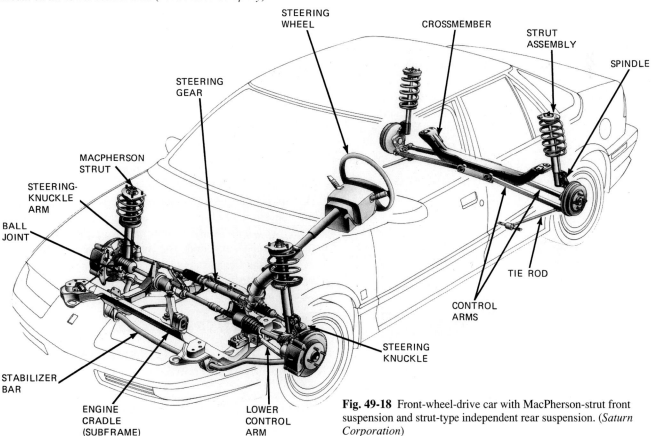

Fig. 49-18 Front-wheel-drive car with MacPherson-strut front suspension and strut-type independent rear suspension. (*Saturn Corporation*)

mounts to the vehicle body. The bottom attaches to the rear-wheel spindle or to the front-wheel steering knuckle. This arrangement simplifies the suspension. Separate mountings are not required for the spring and shock absorber.

➤ 49-17 TORSION-BAR REAR SUSPENSION

Torsion bars may be either longitudinal (Fig. 49-5) or transverse. Figure 49-19 shows a rear suspension using transverse torsion bars. The two *trailing arms* serve as control arms. Spring action is provided by two full-width transverse torsion bars. One end of each torsion bar clamps to a stubby subframe that clamps to the vehicle underbody. The trailing arm clamps to the other end. This causes the torsion bar to twist as the wheel and trailing arm move up and down.

➤ 49-18 REAR-END TORQUE AND SQUAT

In a vehicle with rear-wheel drive, when the rear wheels are being driven, the axle housing tries to rotate in the opposite direction (Fig. 49-20). This is due to *rear-end torque*. In a leaf-spring suspension, the springs absorb the rear-end torque. In other suspensions, control arms absorb the torque.

One effect of rear-end torque is *rear-end squat* during acceleration (Fig. 49-21). When a car accelerates from a standing start, the pinion gear in the axle housing tries to climb the teeth of the ring gear. This causes the pinion and differential carrier to move upward. The result is that the rear springs are pulled downward. Then the rear end of the car moves down or squats. The opposite condition occurs during braking. *Front-end dive* causes the front springs to compress as the front end moves down and the rear end moves up.

Both squat and dive result from *inertia* (➤15-5). Any

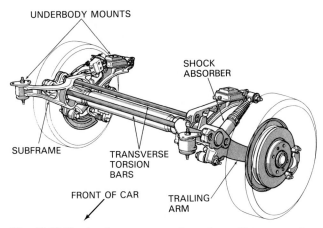

Fig. 49-19 Torsion-bar rear suspension using trailing arms and transverse torsion bars. (*Peugeot Motors of America, Inc.*)

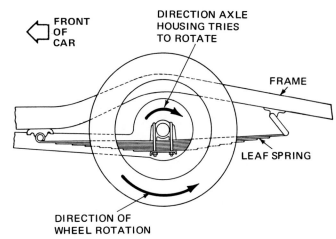

Fig. 49-20 Axle housing tries to rotate in a direction opposite to wheel rotation.

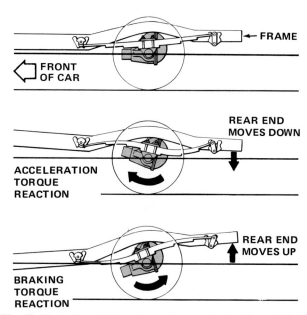

Fig. 49-21 Actions in the spring and rear end when the vehicle is (top) standing, (center) accelerated, and (bottom) braked. (*Ford Motor Company*)

object that is stationary or in motion has inertia. It causes the vehicle to resist the force that starts it moving. Inertia also resists the force that slows or stops the vehicle from moving. Because of inertia, the weight of the vehicle, or its *center of gravity*, shifts to the rear on acceleration and to the front on deceleration. The center of gravity is the point at which the vehicle could be suspended and the weight would balance front and rear, and side to side.

FRONT SUSPENSION

➤ 49-19 FRONT-SUSPENSION SYSTEMS

The front-suspension system must do four jobs:

1. Support the weight of the front end of the vehicle.

2. Absorb road shocks and cushion the passengers and load against those shocks.

3. Provide steering control and wheel alignment.

4. Maintain steering control during severe braking.

All four types of springs—leaf, coil, torsion-bar, and air—are used in front-suspension systems. Figure 49-22 shows a typical front-suspension and steering system. Steering systems are described in Chap. 50. To permit steering, each front *wheel hub* mounts on a *spindle* that is part of a *steering knuckle*. The hub contains the *wheel bearings* through which the spindle passes. The spindle is a short, tapered stationary shaft. It supports the wheel through the wheel bearings and rotating hub. The wheel bearings are ball or roller bearings that minimize friction while allowing the hub and wheel to rotate.

The steering knuckle is supported by a lower control arm that has a *ball joint* (➤49-20) on its outer end. In some front-suspension systems, the steering knuckle is supported by upper and lower control arms with ball joints (Fig. 49-23).

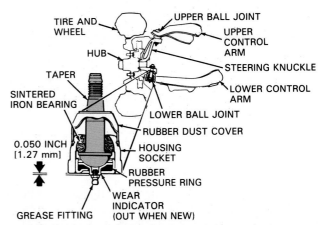

Fig. 49-23 Ball joint, showing how it attaches the steering knuckle to the lower-control arm and how to read the built-in wear indicator. (*Buick Division of General Motors Corporation*)

Fig. 49-22 Typical front-suspension and steering system, with MacPherson struts and power rack-and-pinion steering gear. (*Ford Motor Company*)

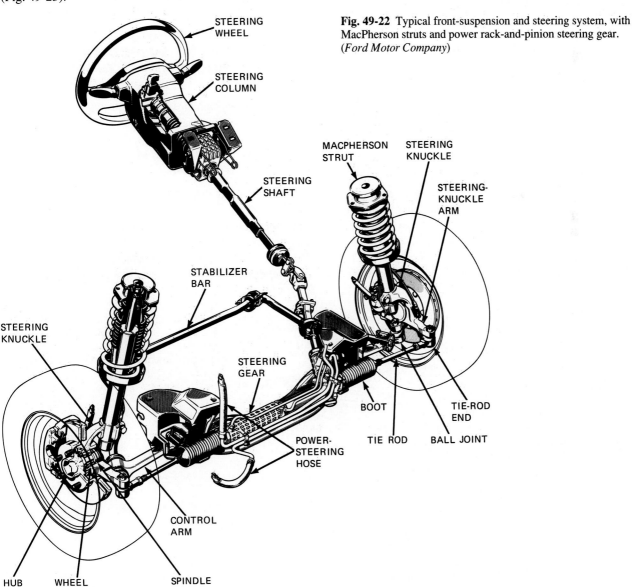

The steering wheel connects to the *steering gear* (Fig. 49-22). When the driver turns the steering wheel, the steering gear moves the *steering linkage*. The *tie rods* then move the *steering-knuckle arms*, which cause the steering knuckles and wheels to swing in and out for steering. This changes the direction of vehicle travel. Many front-suspension systems include a *stabilizer bar* (➤49-21) to help reduce body roll on turns.

➤ **49-20 BALL JOINTS**

The ball joint (Fig. 49-23) is a flexible ball-and-socket that mounts in the outer ends of the front-suspension control arms. It provides a pivoting joint that attaches the steering knuckle to the control arms, which can move only up and down. This allows the steering knuckle and wheel to turn in and out for steering. Figure 49-23 shows a front suspension with upper and lower control arms, and upper and lower ball joints. A MacPherson-strut front suspension uses only a single ball joint (Fig. 49-22). It is in the outer end of each lower control arm.

The ball joint is basically a stud with threads on one end and a ball on the other. The ball seats in a steel socket, with a nylon or sintered-iron bearing between the two. Some ball joints have a spring that applies a force to the ball to take up any play. The ball joint is sealed by a rubber dust cover that keeps out dust and water, and keeps in lubricant. Many ball joints can be lubricated through a grease fitting or removable plug.

➤ **49-21 STABILIZER BAR**

A stabilizer bar helps control *body roll* when cornering or driving on rough or uneven surfaces. The front stabilizer bar (Figs. 49-22 and 49-24) or *sway bar* is a type of torsion bar. It usually connects between the two lower control arms. When the vehicle moves around a curve, the body leans outward. This causes the lower-control arms to move

in opposite directions, twisting the stabilizer bar. However, the stabilizer bar resists being twisted. This stiffens the suspension during turns so less leanout or body roll results.

Stabilizer-bar action may also occur if one tire hits a bump or pothole while the other does not. A stabilizer bar has no affect while the vehicle is traveling straight ahead on a smooth surface. Many rear suspensions include a *rear stabilizer bar* (Fig. 49-14) or *antiroll bar*. Its operation is similar to that described above.

➤ **49-22 TYPES OF
FRONT SUSPENSION**

Many vehicles have a different type of suspension at the front and rear. Most vehicles with front-wheel drive have a MacPherson-strut or similar front-suspension system (Fig. 49-22). Strut-type front suspension is also used on some four-wheel-drive vehicles (Fig. 49-1). Front suspensions on rear-wheel-drive vehicles can be classed as *independent*, *twin I-beam*, and *solid-axle*. Examples of these types are described below.

➤ **49-23 COIL-SPRING
FRONT SUSPENSION
(REAR-WHEEL DRIVE)**

Many automotive vehicles use coil springs in the front suspension. The springs may seat on the lower control arm or on the upper control arm. Coil springs are also used with twin I-beam front axles and in MacPherson-strut front suspension systems (➤49-24).

1. COIL SPRING ON LOWER CONTROL ARM Figure 49-24 shows a coil-spring front suspension using upper and lower control arms of unequal length. This is called a *short-arm/long-arm* (SALA) or *double-wishbone system*. The control arms pivot on the vehicle body or frame. The upper end of the coil spring rests in a pocket in the frame.

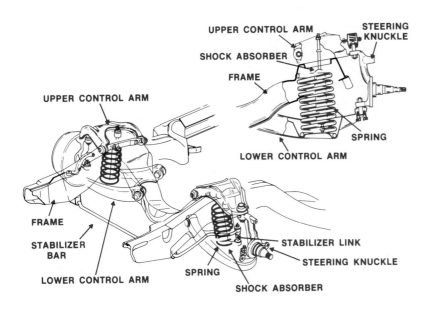

Fig. 49-24 Coil-spring front suspension using upper and lower control arms of unequal length. A stabilizer bar, or sway bar, helps control body roll when cornering and driving on rough surfaces.

The lower end rests on the lower control arm. As the wheel moves up and down, the control arms pivot and the spring shortens or lengthens.

Both control arms in Fig. 49-24 look like a wishbone or the letter "A". They have a single ball joint in the outer ends and two attachment points on the inner ends. The inner ends are supported by rubber bushings. These allow the control arms to move up and down with little resistance. *Rubber bumpers* attached to the frame or control arm prevent metal-to-metal contact when full spring compression occurs. The shock absorber is centered in the spring.

2. COIL SPRING ON UPPER CONTROL ARM In Fig. 49-25, the coil spring sits on top of the upper control arm. The upper end of the spring seats in a *spring tower* that is part of the body sheet metal. As the wheel moves up and down, the control arms move up and down as in Fig. 49-24. The spring is compressed between the upper control arm and the spring tower.

Figure 49-25 shows a *beam-type* lower-control arm. It has only one point of attachment to the frame. When the control arm has only a single pivot point, the suspension system must include a *strut rod* or *brake-reaction rod*. It prevents forward or backward movement of the lower control arm during braking or from road shocks.

| NOTE | There is a *suspension strut rod* (described above) and a strut rod which is the center shaft in a MacPherson strut (➤49-24). Although often called the same, the rods are in different locations and serve different purposes. |

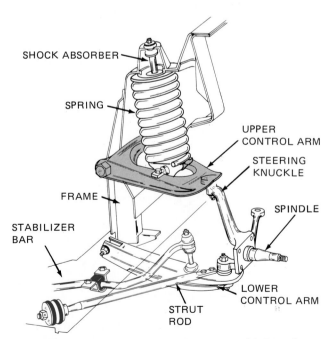

Fig. 49-25 Coil-spring front-suspension system with the spring mounted on the upper control arm. The lower control arm has a single point of attachment to the frame and requires the use of a strut rod, or brake-reaction rod.

A similar type of coil-spring front suspension with upper and lower control arms is shown in Fig. 49-26. The lower arm is the beam type and the upper arm is the A type. The coil spring fits around the shock absorber. The lower end of the shock absorber attaches to the lower control arm. A mount on the upper end attaches to the vehicle body. The lower-control arm is held in position by a *tension strut*. The action is similar to the strut rod in Fig. 49-25.

3. COIL SPRINGS ON TWIN I-BEAM AXLES Ford uses a twin I-beam type of independent front suspension (Fig. 49-27) on many trucks. Each front wheel is supported by a spindle on the end of a separate I-beam axle. A coil spring is between the I beam and a spring seat on the vehicle frame. The other ends of the I beams attach to the vehicle frame through flexible pivots.

As the wheels meet bumps and holes in the road, the I beams pivot up or down. This compresses or expands the springs. The wheel ends of the axles attach to the frame by radius arms. These hold the I beams in position while allowing the wheels and outer ends of the I beams to move up and down.

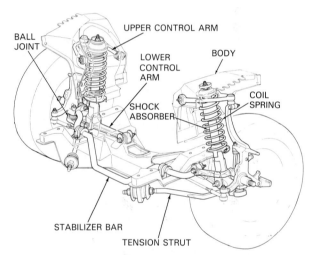

Fig. 49-26 Front suspension using a coil-spring-and-shock-absorber assembly. The upper control arm is the A type. The lower control arm is the beam type and held in position by a tension strut. (*Ford Motor Company*)

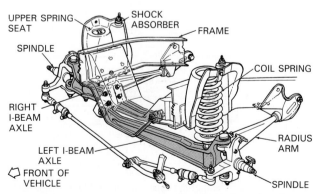

Fig. 49-27 A twin I-beam type of coil-spring independent front suspension, used on trucks. (*Ford Motor Company*)

➤ 49-24 MACPHERSON-STRUT FRONT SUSPENSION

A MacPherson-strut front suspension combines the coil spring and shock absorber into a single assembly (Figs. 49-22 and 49-28). The lower end of the strut connects to the outer end of a beam-type lower control arm. No upper control arm is used. The upper end of the strut attaches to the vehicle body. A bearing (Fig. 49-29) at the top of the strut allows the strut-and-steering-knuckle assembly to turn with the wheels for steering.

The angled arms or ends of an antiroll bar or stabilizer bar (➤49-21) attach to outer ends of the lower control

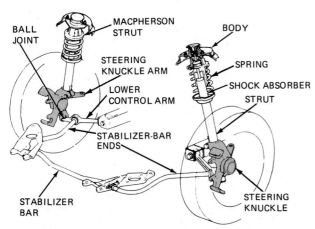

Fig. 49-28 MacPherson-strut front suspension, which uses no upper control arm and a beam-type lower control arm. The stabilizer bar holds the lower control arm in position. (*Ford Motor Company*)

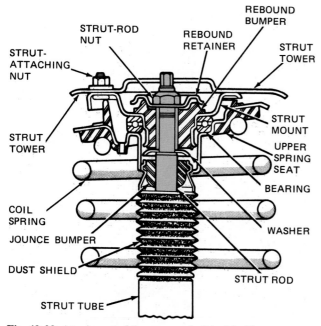

Fig. 49-29 Attachment of the upper end of the MacPherson strut to the vehicle body. The bearing allows the strut to turn with the wheels for steering. (*Chrysler Corporation*)

arms. This allows the stabilizer bar to act like the strut rod in Fig. 49-25 and the tension strut in Fig. 49-26. It holds the lower control arms in position while helping to control the longitudinal loads. The lower end of the strut mounts in the steering knuckle.

A ball joint (➤49-20) attaches the lower end of the steering knuckle to the outer end of the lower control arm (Fig. 49-26). As the tire meets bumps or holes in the road, the wheel and spring move up or down. Turning the steering wheel causes the steering gear to move the steering-knuckle arms in or out. This causes the MacPherson-strut-and-steering-knuckle assembly to pivot in and out for steering.

➤ 49-25 TORSION-BAR FRONT SUSPENSION

Figure 49-5 shows a front suspension system that uses *longitudinal torsion bars*. The rear ends of the torsion bars attach to the vehicle body or frame. The front ends attach to the lower control arms. Pivoting of the control arms twists the torsion bars. This provides the springing effect. Turning the *height-adjustment bolt* on the end of each torsion bar rotates the bar slightly to adjust ride height. Figure 49-30 shows a front suspension using *transverse torsion bars* on a front-engine, rear-wheel-drive vehicle.

➤ 49-26 LEAF-SPRING FRONT SUSPENSION

Some trucks have front leaf springs (Fig. 49-31) and a solid or I-beam front axle. A *kingpin* instead of a ball joint may be used to attach the steering knuckle to the end of the axle. The leaf springs are often placed on top of the axle. This raises the body and chassis for greater ground clearance. As with rear leaf springs (➤49-13), one end of the leaf spring attaches to the body or frame by a spring

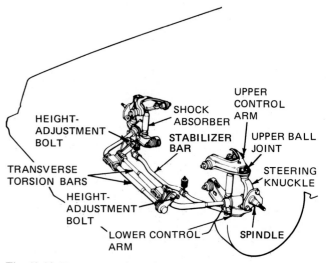

Fig. 49-30 Front suspension using transverse torsion bars, used on vehicles with front-engine and rear-wheel drive. (*Chrysler Corporation*)

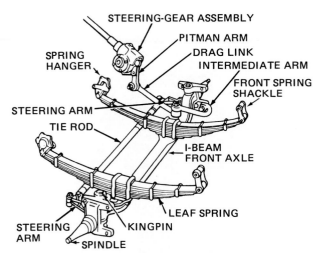

Fig. 49-31 Truck front suspension using a solid I-beam front axle and two leaf springs. (*Ford Motor Company*)

hanger. The other end is attached by a spring shackle. This permits the spring to move back and forth slightly as its effective length changes.

ELECTRONIC SUSPENSION AND RIDE CONTROL

➤ 49-27 ELECTRONIC RIDE CONTROL

Many vehicles have *electronic ride control* or *variable-damping suspension* (Fig. 49-32). The shock absorbers at all four wheels can be electronically adjusted by the driver

for soft, normal, or firm operation. The basic construction of the electronically-adjustable shock absorber is shown on the right in Fig. 49-33. The internal construction of the adjustment mechanism is shown on the left in Fig. 49-33.

When the driver presses the SOFT or FIRM switch (Fig. 49-32), the ECM signals a solenoid or small electric motor in the top of each shock absorber. The motor then rotates slightly, opening or closing various size orifices in the piston. This changes the resistance to fluid-flow within the shock absorber.

The system controls vehicle ride only. It does not control vehicle height. On some cars, a setting allows the shock absorbers to automatically select the proper damping for the road and driving conditions. Similar systems include auxiliary air springs to also control ride height (➤49-11). Various sensors may send the ECM information on vehicle speed, road roughness, and body roll. The ECM then signals the shock absorbers so they adjust to provide the best ride possible under the operating conditions.

➤ 49-28 SONAR-CONTROLLED SHOCK ABSORBERS

Adjustable shock absorbers may be controlled automatically by a *road-surface sensor* (Fig. 49-34). This is a *sonar sensor* that sends out and receives back sound waves to determine short distances. Sonar stands for "sound navigation and ranging." It is used on ships and submarines to detect submerged objects.

The sonar sensor is located at the front of the vehicle. The sensor constantly reads the condition of the road that

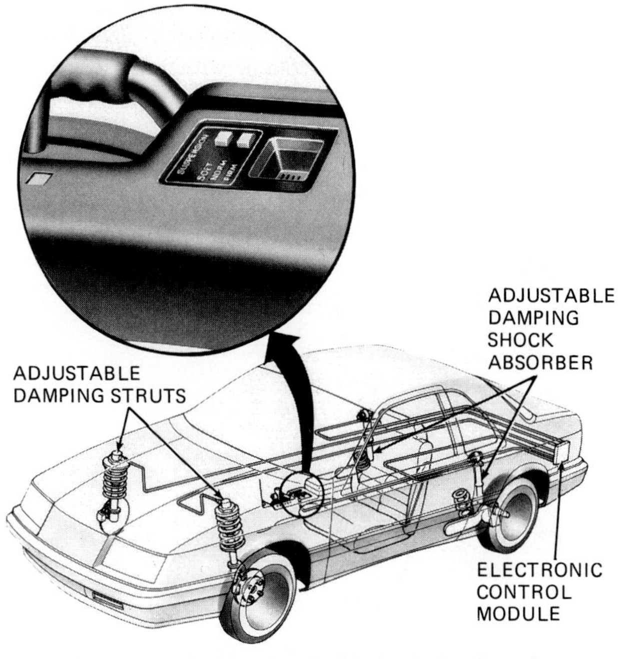

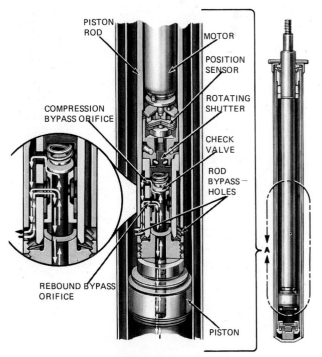

Fig. 49-32 Electronic ride control with shock absorbers that can be electronically adjusted by the driver to provide a soft, normal, or firm ride. (*Chrysler Corporation*)

Fig. 49-33 Construction of an electronically-adjustable shock absorber. (*Chrysler Corporation*)

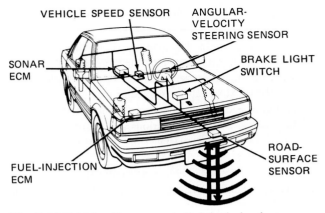

Fig. 49-34 Vehicle with sonar-controlled shock absorbers. (*Nissan Motor Corporation*)

the wheels are about to meet. It does this by sending out short bursts of sound pulses. The length of time it takes for the waves to reach the road and bounce back is fed to the ECM. The time indicates ride height and surface irregularities. Then the ECM adjusts the shock absorbers to provide the best ride and handling.

➤ 49-29 ELECTRONICALLY-CONTROLLED AIR SUSPENSION

The air-suspension system has *air springs* that replace coil springs at all four wheels (Fig. 49-35). The system controls spring rates and provides automatic height and level control. The rear air springs mount ahead of the rear axle on the lower suspension arms. The front air springs are part of the front strut assemblies. These air struts (Fig. 49-36) mount between the vehicle body and the steering knuckle.

An electric air compressor supplies the air pressure that operates the system (Fig. 49-35). An *air dryer* mounted on

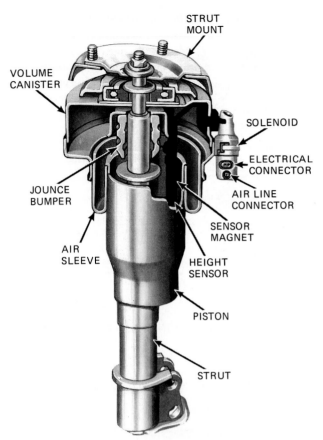

Fig. 49-36 Construction of an air strut, which includes air spring, solenoid, and internal height sensor. (*Chrysler Corporation*)

the compressor removes any moisture from the air. This prevents water—which could damage the system—from entering it. An air line runs from the dryer to each air spring. A solenoid on each air spring opens and closes to control the air pressure and volume within the spring. The

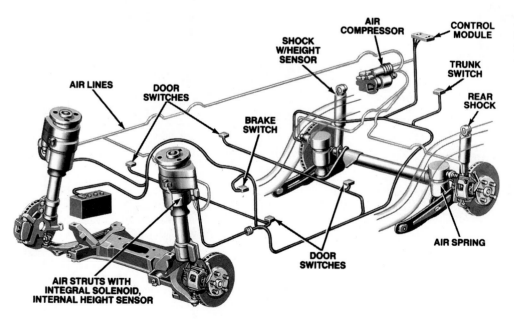

Fig. 49-35 An air-suspension system with air springs at all four wheels. (*Chrysler Corporation*)

control module switches the compressor and the solenoids on and off.

The system includes three height sensors. These are *magnetic sensors* in the front air struts (Fig. 49-33) and in the right-rear shock absorber (Fig. 49-10C). When weight is added to the body, the body settles. The height sensors respond by signaling the control module. It then starts the air compressor and opens the solenoid valves at the air springs. The increased air pressure "pumps up" the air springs. This raises the body back up to its original height or *trim height*. Then the control module turns off the air compressor and closes the solenoid valves.

When the load is removed, the body rises above the trim height. The height sensors signal the control module. It responds by opening the solenoid valves to allow some air to escape from the springs. When the body settles back down to the trim height, the control module closes the solenoid valves.

➤ 49-30 ACTIVE SUSPENSION SYSTEM

Most suspension systems are passive or reactive. For example, a tire hitting a bump or dropping into a hole may not stay in contact with the road surface. The suspension system then reacts by compressing or extending the spring.

These actions affect handling and ride quality, and send shock and vibration to the vehicle body.

Figure 49-37 shows an *active suspension system* that uses *hydraulic actuators* instead of springs and shock absorbers. The hydraulic actuator is a device that converts the hydraulic energy in a pressurized fluid into mechanical

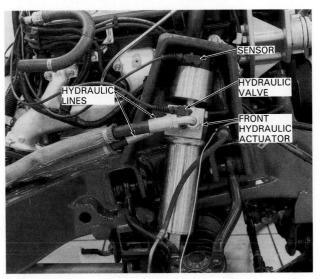

Fig. 49-38 Mounting of the hydraulic actuator at the front wheel of vehicle with an active suspension. (*General Motors Corporation*)

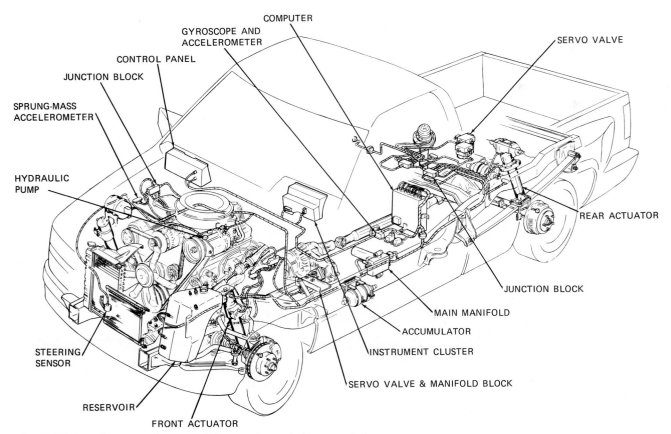

Fig. 49-37 An active suspension system that uses electronically-controlled double-acting hydraulic actuators at each wheel. (*General Motors Corporation*)

motion. The system uses the hydraulic pressure to keep each tire pushing against the road surface with a constant force. This force changes as the tires move up and down. It also changes when the center of gravity shifts during vehicle cornering, and when front-end dive and rear-end squat occur during braking and acceleration.

A sensor in the actuator (Fig. 49-38) signals the computer when the tire force changes. Other sensors on the vehicle signal changes in steering position, acceleration and deceleration, and body stability. An on-board *gyroscope* serves as a *yaw sensor*. It detects any swerving or wandering away from a straight-ahead course.

The computer receives these inputs and then signals the proper *servo valve* (Fig. 49-37). It sends high-pressure hydraulic fluid through a computer-controlled valve in the actuator. The actuator raises or lowers the wheel so the tire maintains the same force against the road. This keeps the vehicle level while providing the best possible ride and handling.

All these actions occur almost instantly, and go unnoticed by the driver. By acting instead of reacting to an irregular road surface, most of the tire-and-wheel movement is absorbed in the suspension system. Little shock and vibration reaches the vehicle body and its occupants.

The hydraulic actuators in Figs. 49-37 and 49-38 are *double-acting*. The hydraulic pressure can force movement both up and down. A hydraulic pump and accumulator maintain high pressure on the actuator fluid. Some vehicles have an active suspension system using *single-acting* actuators. These can push in only one direction. Vehicles with active suspension may also have springs, such as the rear springs shown in Fig. 49-37. These are usually soft and easily overridden by the more powerful actuators. The springs allow the vehicle to be driven if the hydraulic system fails.

MULTIPLE-CHOICE TEST

*Select the **one** correct, best, or most probable answer to each question.*
You can find the answers in the section indicated at the end of each question.

1. As the shock absorber is compressed, fluid passes through the piston orifices and (➤49-8)
   a. out of the dust shield
   b. into the upper part of the cylinder
   c. into the lower part of the cylinder
   d. out of the air or gas chamber
2. Automatic level control takes care of changes in the (➤49-11)
   a. load in the rear of the car
   b. speed of the car
   c. air pressure in the tires
   d. load in the front of the car
3. In the coil-spring rear suspension for a rear-drive vehicle, the axle housing is kept in place by (➤49-14)
   a. U bolts
   b. the stabilizer bar
   c. control arms
   d. the shock absorbers

4. Rear-end squat occurs (➤49-18)
   a. during braking
   b. during acceleration
   c. as the front-end dives
   d. only when the front suspension is defective
5. The steering knuckle attaches to the lower-control arm by a (➤49-20)
   a. kingpin
   b. tension strut
   c. bushing
   d. ball joint
6. A front stabilizer bar is used to (➤49-21)
   a. increase load-carrying capacity
   b. provide a softer ride
   c. stiffen the suspension to control body roll
   d. prevent sideward movement of the axle housing

REVIEW QUESTIONS

1. What is the difference between sprung and unsprung weight, and what effect does unsprung weight have on ride quality? (➤49-4)
2. What advantages are there to variable-rate springs and when are they used? (➤49-5)
3. What is independent rear suspension and how does it affect ride quality? (➤49-13)

4. Explain how electronic ride control changes shock-absorber firmness when the driver presses a switch. (➤49-27)
5. Describe how the hydraulic actuator is controlled and how it operates in an active suspension system. (➤49-30)

CHAPTER 50

AUTOMOTIVE STEERING SYSTEMS

After studying this chapter, you should be able to:

- Explain the purpose, construction, and operation of automotive steering systems.
- Describe the construction and operation of manual and power recirculating-ball steering gears.
- Describe the construction and operation of manual and power rack-and-pinion steering gears.
- Explain the operation of variable-ratio steering, variable-assist power steering, and four-wheel steering.
- Describe the construction and operation of tilt and telescoping steering wheels.
- List and describe the various wheel-alignment angles, including thrust angle and setback.

➤ 50-1 PURPOSE OF THE STEERING SYSTEM

The steering system (Figs. 49-18 and 49-22) allows the driver to control the direction of vehicle travel. This is made possible by linkage that connects the *steering wheel* to the steerable wheels and tires. The steering system may be either *manual* or *power*. When the only energy source for the steering system is the force the driver applies to the steering wheel, the vehicle has *manual steering*. *Power steering* uses a hydraulic pump or electric motor to assist the driver's effort. Most vehicles have power steering to make parking easier.

The basic operation is the same for both manual and power steering. As the driver turns the steering wheel, the movement is carried to the *steering gear* (Fig. 50-1). It changes the rotary motion of the steering wheel into straightline or *linear* motion. The linear motion acts through *steering linkage* or *tie rods* attached to the steering-knuckle arms (➤49-19) or *steering arms*. The steering knuckles then pivot inward or outward on ball joints (➤49- 20). This moves the wheels and tires to the left or right for steering.

MANUAL STEERING

➤ 50-2 STEERING SYSTEM COMPONENTS

The steering system has three major components:

1. The steering wheel and *steering shaft* that transmit the driver's movement to the steering gear.
2. The steering gear that increases the mechanical advantage (➤50-6) while changing the rotary motion of the steering wheel to linear motion.
3. The steering linkage that carries the linear motion to the steering arms.

➤ 50-3 TYPES OF STEERING GEARS

Two types of steering gears are widely used in automotive vehicles. These are the *recirculating-ball steering gear* (Fig. 50-1A) and the *rack-and-pinion steering gear* (Fig. 50-1B). Both steering gears are made in manual and power versions.

A few vehicles have a *worm-and-roller* steering gear. It is similar to the recirculating-ball. Both use a *pitman arm*

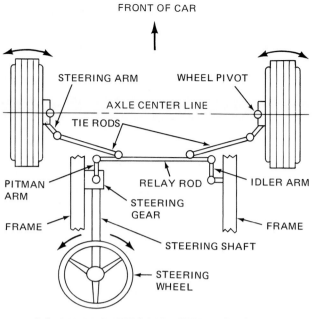

(A) RECIRCULATING-BALL STEERING SYSTEM

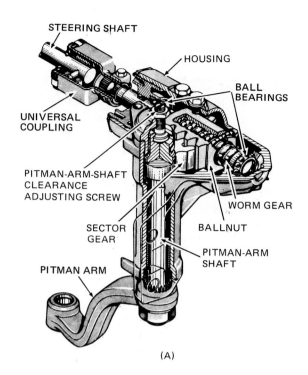

(A)

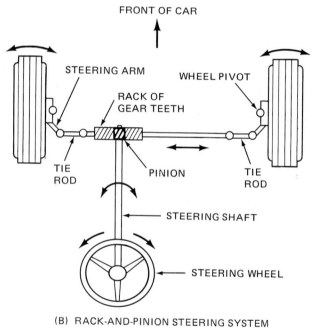

(B) RACK-AND-PINION STEERING SYSTEM

Fig. 50-1 Types of steering systems. *(ATW)*

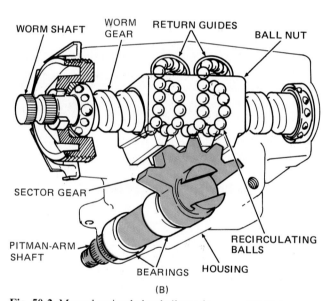

(B)

Fig. 50-2 Manual recirculating-ball steering gear. (A) Cutaway to show construction. (B) Phantom view of nut and recirculating balls. *(Chrysler Corporation; Ford Motor Company)*

and the *parallelogram steering linkage* shown in Fig. 50-1A. The pitman arm connects the steering-gear output shaft to the steering linkage.

➤ 50-4 RECIRCULATING-BALL STEERING GEAR

Trucks and large cars often have a recirculating-ball steering gear (Fig. 50-2). It has a *sector gear* on the inner end of the output shaft. A sector gear is a section of gear teeth from a gear wheel. The output shaft is called the

sector shaft or *pitman-arm shaft*. The teeth on the sector gear mesh with the teeth of a *ball nut*. It rides on the *worm* or *worm gear* that connects to the end of the steering shaft. Balls roll in grooves inside the ball nut and in the worm.

As the steering shaft rotates, the worm forces the balls to roll in the grooves. The balls, as they roll, force the ball nut to move up or down the worm. Movement of the ball nut forces the pitman-arm shaft to turn. This swings the pitman arm (Fig. 50-1A) which forces the steering linkage to pivot the wheels for steering.

The balls are the only contact between the worm and nut. This reduces friction. The balls are *recirculating balls* because they recirculate from one end of the ball nut to the other end during steering. As the balls reach the end of the groove in the ball nut, they enter the *return guides* (Fig. 50-2). The balls then travel back to the other end of the ball nut.

➤ 50-5 RACK-AND-PINION STEERING GEAR

Most smaller and down-sized vehicles use a rack-and-pinion steering gear (Fig. 50-3). It has a *pinion* gear on the end of the steering shaft that meshes with a flat *rack* of gear teeth. Tie rods connect the ends of the rack to the steering arms. As the steering wheel turns, the pinion gear moves the rack to the right or left. This moves the tie rods and steering arms which turn the steering knuckles and wheels inward or outward.

The inner ends of the tie rods have balls which fit into *ball sockets* on the ends of the rack (Fig. 50-3). This allows the outer ends of the tie rods to move up and down with the steering knuckles and wheels. Flexible rubber boots or *bellows* protect the steering gear from dust and water.

Many steering systems have an *intermediate steering shaft* between the steering column and the steering gear (Fig. 50-3). The intermediate shaft has a universal joint at the upper end and a flexible coupling at the lower end. These help prevent road shock and noise from passing up through the steering column to the driver.

➤ 50-6 STEERING RATIO

Mechanical advantage is the ratio of the output force to the input force applied to a mechanical device. With mechanical advantage, a small input force can produce a large output force. In the steering system, the driver applies a relatively small force to the steering wheel. This results in a much larger steering force at the wheels. For example, a 10-pound [44.5-N] force applied to the steering wheel may produce up to 270 pounds [1201 N] or higher at the wheels. This increase is due to the mechanical advantage or *steering ratio* of the steering gear.

Steering ratio is the number of degrees that the steering wheel must turn to pivot the front wheels one degree. In Fig. 50-4, the steering wheel must turn 17.5 degrees to pivot the front wheels 1 degree. The steering ratio is 17.5:1.

Steering ratios vary, depending on the type of vehicle and operation. Typical automotive steering ratios range from about 24:1 with manual steering to 14:1 with power steering. The higher the steering ratio, the easier it is to

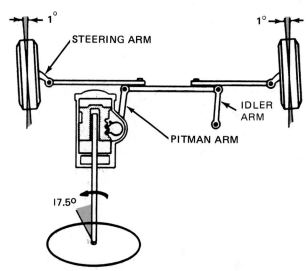

Fig. 50-4 Steering ratio. Turning the steering wheel 17.5 degrees is required to pivot the front wheels 1 degree.

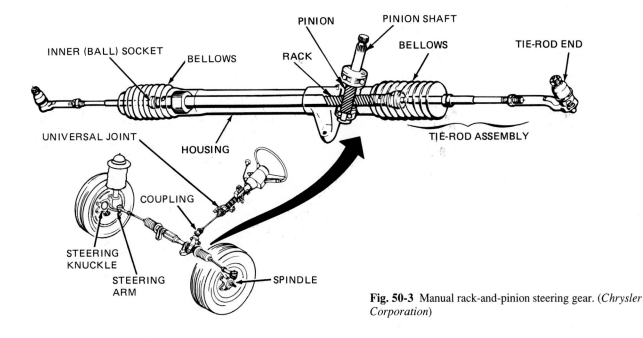

Fig. 50-3 Manual rack-and-pinion steering gear. (*Chrysler Corporation*)

steer. However, the steering wheel must be turned more than with a lower steering ratio. If the steering ratio is 24:1, the driver must turn the steering wheel 24 degrees to pivot the front wheels 1 degree. If the steering ratio is 14:1, the steering wheel must be turned only 14 degrees to pivot the front wheels 1 degree.

Steering ratio is determined by *steering-linkage ratio* and the gear ratio in the steering gear. Steering-linkage ratio for pitman-arm steering gears depends on the relative length of the pitman arm and the steering arm (Fig. 50-4). When the two are the same length, the steering-linkage ratio is 1:1. If the pitman arm is twice as long as the steering arm, the ratio is 1:2. Every degree the pitman arm swings pivots the steering arm and wheels two degrees.

The gear ratio in the pitman-arm steering gear depends on the angle and pitch of the teeth on the worm and sector gears. In the rack-and-pinion steering gear, steering ratio may be determined by the number of teeth on the pinion gear. The fewer the number of teeth, the higher the ratio.

➤ 50-7 VARIABLE-RATIO STEERING

Many steering gears provide *variable-ratio steering*. The steering ratio varies as the steering wheel moves away from straight ahead. A typical change would be from 16:1 to 13:1 (Fig. 50-5). For the first 40 degrees of steering-wheel movement in either direction, the steering ratio is constant. This faster ratio provides good steering control for highway driving. The steering ratio decreases when the steering wheel turns more than 40 degrees (Fig. 50-5). The lower steering ratio helps in city driving during cornering or parking. It reduces the amount the steering wheel must turn for these maneuvers.

The variable ratio is produced by the shape of the gear teeth. In a recirculating-ball steering gear (Fig. 50-6), the center teeth on the sector gear are larger than the outer teeth. When the ball nut has moved far enough to bring the outer teeth into mesh, the effective leverage changes. Further ball nut movement then produces a greater move-

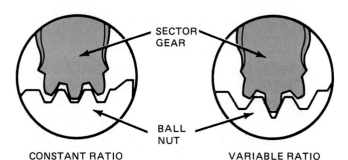

Fig. 50-6 Left, shape of teeth on ball nut and sector gear for constant-ratio steering. Right, shape of teeth for variable-ratio steering. (*Chrysler Corporation*)

ment of the sector gear. In a rack-and-pinion steering gear, the shape of the rack teeth can provide variable-ratio steering.

➤ 50-8 STEERING LINKAGE

The steering linkage connects the steering gear to the front-wheel steering arms (Figs. 50-3 and 50-4). The linkage can be adjusted to produce the proper alignment of the front wheels. Tie-rod ends connect to the steering arms with balls that fit into sockets (Figs. 50-3 and 50-7). These are *ball sockets*. They are smaller but similar in construction to front-suspension ball joints (➤49-20).

In parallelogram steering linkage, the *idler arm* (Figs. 50-1A and 50-4) and other parts connect through rubber bushings. The bushings twist as the parts swing or move. They supply some force to help return the wheels to center after completing a turn. Lubricating these bushings may cause them to slip and wear prematurely.

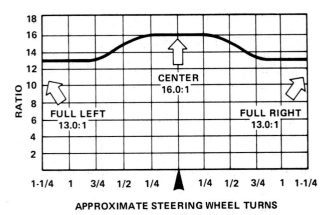

Fig. 50-5 The relationship, or ratio, between steering-wheel turns and movement of the front wheels in right and left turns. (*Chrysler Corporation*)

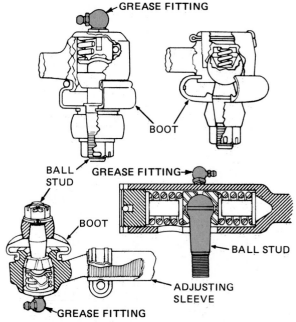

Fig. 50-7 Ball sockets and tie-rod ends. (*Ford Motor Company*)

POWER STEERING

➤ 50-9 POWER STEERING

A vehicle with power steering has an energy source that aids the driver in turning the wheels for steering. Most automotive power-steering systems are hydraulic. A pump supplies high-pressure fluid when the driver turns the steering wheel. This provides most of the required steering effort. Some cars have *electronic power steering* (➤50-14). An electric motor provides the power assist.

➤ 50-10 TYPES OF POWER STEERING

Most power-steering systems are basically a manual steering system with a power booster added. In a *power recirculating-ball steering gear* (Fig. 50-8), the booster is a power cylinder and piston built into the steering gear. This is *integral power steering* because the power booster is integral with the steering gear. Figure 50-9 shows a *power rack-and-pinion steering gear*. It also has a built-in power cylinder and piston. A *linkage-type power steering* (Fig. 50-10) can be attached to manual steering systems that have a pitman-arm steering gear. The power cylinder connects between the vehicle body or frame and the steering linkage to provide the power assist.

All hydraulic power-steering systems work in the same general way. The hydraulic pump pressurizes the fluid. Steering effort applied to the steering wheel causes the *control valve* to open and close fluid passages. These either admit pressurized fluid into the power cylinder, or relieve the pressure. The pressurized fluid causes the piston to move, providing most of the steering effort.

➤ 50-11 POWER-STEERING-SYSTEM COMPONENTS

The power-steering hydraulic system includes a control-valve assembly and a power cylinder. In addition, the system has a hydraulic pump, fluid reservoir, and connecting hoses. The reservoir may be attached to the pump (Figs. 50-9 and 50-10) or separately mounted (Fig. 50-11). A filter may be located in the reservoir or hose to remove dirt and particles from the fluid. Some power-steering systems also have a fluid cooler.

1. POWER-STEERING PUMP The pump usually mounts at the front of the engine and is driven by a belt from the engine crankshaft pulley (Fig. 50-11). The pump can produce high pressure, up to 2000 psi [13,800 kPa] in some systems. Figure 50-12 shows a vane-type power-steering pump. The rotor turns in an oval *cam ring* inside the pump housing. As the rotor turns, the area between the rotor, cam ring, and vanes increases and decreases in size. This forces the pressurized fluid out through the pressure fitting to the pressure hose. Gear and roller-type power-steering pumps are also used. Some pumps are driven by an electric motor instead of the engine.

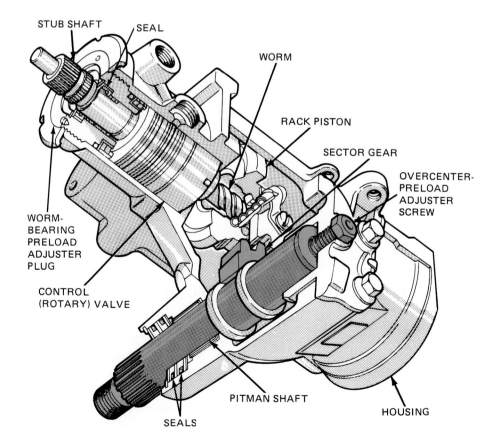

Fig. 50-8 Construction of a power recirculating-ball steering gear. (*Cadillac Division of General Motors Corporation*)

STUB SHAFT   SEAL

WORM

RACK PISTON

SECTOR GEAR

OVERCENTER-PRELOAD ADJUSTER SCREW

WORM-BEARING PRELOAD ADJUSTER PLUG

CONTROL (ROTARY) VALVE

PITMAN SHAFT

SEALS

HOUSING

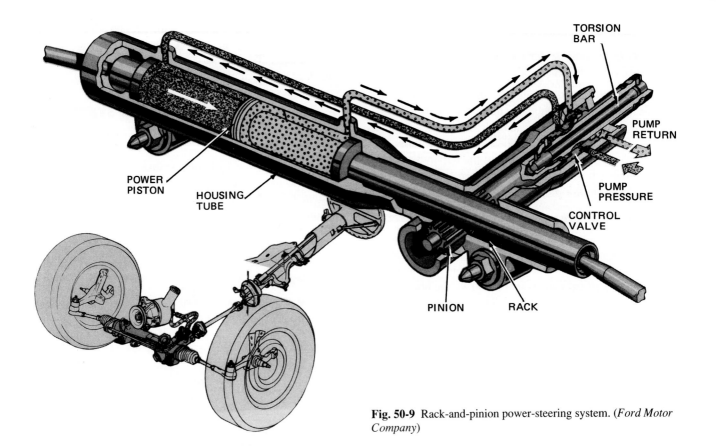

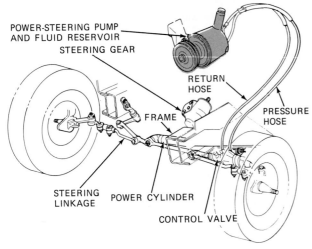

Fig. 50-9 Rack-and-pinion power-steering system. (*Ford Motor Company*)

Fig. 50-10 Linkage-type power-steering system. (*Ford Motor Company*)

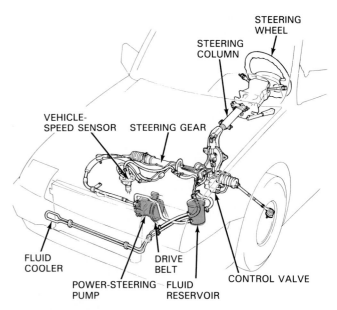

Fig. 50-11 Components in a speed-sensitive rack-and-pinion power steering system that provides variable assist. (*American Honda Motor Company, Inc.*)

2. HOSES AND FITTINGS Most power-steering systems have a *pressure hose* and a *return hose* (Fig. 50-10). The hoses and fittings provide the fluid path between the power-steering pump and the control valve. They are made to take high pressures, temperature extremes, and continual stretching and flexing. The hoses also help reduce noise from pump pulsations.

3. FLUID COOLER Some vehicles with air conditioning and high underhood temperatures have a small *power-steering-fluid cooler* (Fig. 50-11). It prevents excessive

fluid temperature that could damage seals, vanes, and other parts. The fluid cooler may simply be a loop in the tubing (Fig. 50-11) or a small heat exchanger at the front of the vehicle (➤25-12). On some vehicles, the remote-mounted reservoir provides the necessary fluid cooling.

4. POWER-STEERING FLUID Several different hydraulic fluids are used as power-steering fluid. Some man-

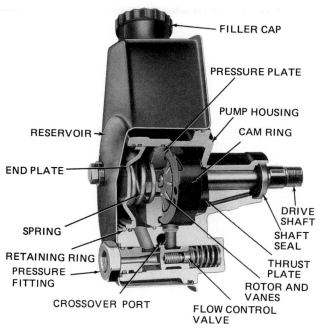

Fig. 50-12 Vane-type power-steering pump. (*Cadillac Division of General Motors Corporation*)

ufacturers specify either type F or Dexron II automatic-transmission fluid (➤47-17). Other manufacturers use a special *power-steering fluid*. It is made to take the high temperatures and pressures. Only the fluid recommended by the vehicle manufacturer should be used in a power-steering system.

5. POWER-STEERING PRESSURE SWITCH Some vehicles have a *power-steering pressure switch* in the pressure line between the pump and the steering gear (➤19-20). The switch signals the engine control module (ECM) to increase engine idle speed when pump pressure or *power-steering load* is high (Fig. 19-26). The switch position (open or closed) can be read through the diagnostic connector (➤20-13) with a scan tool (Fig. 20-18).

➤ 50-12 POWER RECIRCULATING-BALL STEERING GEAR

Figures 50-8 and 50-13 show a General Motors recirculating-ball steering gear. It has an integral power cylinder and piston. The ball nut is part of the power piston.

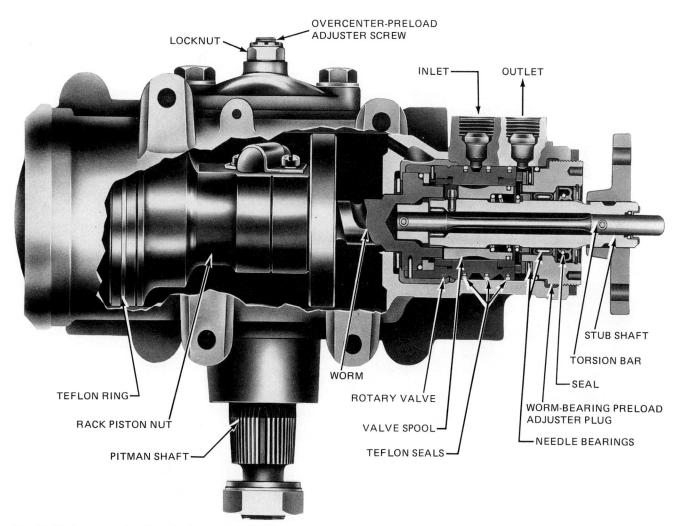

Fig. 50-13 Saginaw recirculating-ball power-steering gear, partly cutaway. (*Pontiac Division of General Motors Corporation*)

681

Applying hydraulic pressure at either end of the piston assists nut and sector-gear movement.

Hydraulic pressure is admitted to one or the other end of the piston by the *rotary valve* (Fig. 50-13). It connects through a torsion bar to the steering shaft. When the steering wheel turns, steering resistance at the front wheels causes the torsion bar to twist. As it twists, it opens the rotary valve. This sends fluid under pressure to one or the other end of the piston (Fig. 50-14). Which end the fluid is sent to depends on the direction the steering wheel turns.

The amount of fluid admitted is determined by the resistance at the vehicle wheels. With greater resistance, the harder the steering wheel must be turned. This twists the torsion bar more which opens the rotary valve more and allows more fluid to enter. The resulting power assist is greater.

The action of other integral recirculating-ball steering gears is similar. Some have a spool valve instead of a rotary valve. As the worm moves, it pivots a *pivot lever*. This moves the spool valve so that pressurized fluid is directed to one end of the power piston.

➤ 50-13 POWER RACK-AND-PINION STEERING GEAR

Figure 50-9 shows fluid-flow in a power rack-and-pinion steering gear. A torsion bar connects to the control valve. When the steering wheel turns, the movement is carried through the torsion bar. The resistance of the front wheels causes the torsion bar to twist. This opens the control valve which sends pressurized fluid to one or the other side of the piston to provide the power assist.

➤ 50-14 VARIABLE-ASSIST POWER STEERING

Some cars have a speed-sensitive, variable-assist power-steering system (Fig. 50-15). Additional parts include a *power-steering controller* (or ECM), *steering-angle sensor*, vehicle-speed sensor (➤34-19), and solenoid valve. The steering-angle sensor measures the rate of

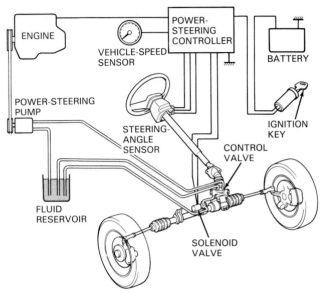

Fig. 50-15 A speed-sensitive, variable-assist, rack-and-pinion power-steering system. (*Ford Motor Company*)

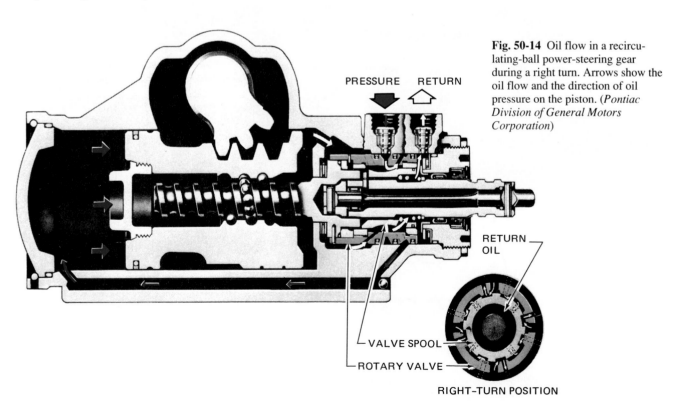

Fig. 50-14 Oil flow in a recirculating-ball power-steering gear during a right turn. Arrows show the oil flow and the direction of oil pressure on the piston. (*Pontiac Division of General Motors Corporation*)

PRESSURE   RETURN

RETURN OIL

VALVE SPOOL

ROTARY VALVE

RIGHT-TURN POSITION

steering-wheel rotation. This information and information from the vehicle-speed sensor are inputs to the controller. The controller determines the amount of power assist needed and sends the proper signals to the solenoid valve. The solenoid valve then acts as an *electronic variable orifice* (EVO). It opens or restricts fluid flow to the steering gear. This varies the power assist, while providing the driver with the same steering feel.

Below about 20 mph [32 kmph], the solenoid valve allows full fluid-flow. This provides full power assist at low speed so only a light steering effort is required for parking. As vehicle speed increases, the solenoid valve reduces fluid-flow to the steering gear. This increases the steering effort and improves road feel. Full assist returns with sudden movement of the steering wheel.

Figure 50-15 shows the solenoid valve on the steering gear. Other systems have the solenoid valve in the power-steering pump. On some cars, setting a switch on the controller increases or decreases steering effort by 10 percent. These cars also have a diagnostic connector from the power-steering controller. An analog voltmeter can retrieve trouble codes through the connector. The trouble codes indicate faults in the system (➢20-14).

Another speed-sensitive rack-and-pinion power-steering system is shown in Fig. 50-11. The vehicle-speed sensor regulates the fluid pressure according to vehicle speed. A steering-angle sensor is not used. Many rack-and-pinion and recirculating-ball power-steering systems have variable assist.

➢ 50-15 ELECTRONIC RACK-AND-PINION POWER STEERING

Some cars have an electronic rack-and-pinion power-steering gear (Fig. 50-16). A fast-acting electric motor inside the rack housing supplies the power assist. The pinion meshes with helical grooves which serve as the rack teeth. A magnet and magnetic sensor on the pinion shaft act as a *torque sensor*. It signals the electronic control

module (ECM) how much torque is being applied and in which direction.

As torque is applied by turning the steering wheel, the magnet moves. The greater the torque and the farther the magnet moves, the stronger the signal to the ECM. The ECM then sends a varying current to the electric motor. The motor is splined to the ball nut. When the motor runs, the ball nut rotates. The rotation causes balls to run through the grooves in the ball nut and the helical grooves in the rack. This applies a force against one end of the rack. The result is that most of the steering effort is supplied by the electric motor.

Electronic power steering does not require a hydraulic pump, hoses, a hydraulic piston on the rack, or a sealed rack housing. In addition, if the driver prefers more or less power assist, it can be changed by resetting a selector switch.

FOUR-WHEEL STEERING

➢ 50-16 PURPOSE OF FOUR-WHEEL STEERING

A variety of military and off-road vehicles have had *four-wheel steering* (4WS) for years. When the front wheels pivot for steering, the rear wheels also pivot and steer the rear end of the vehicle. This improves handling and allows tighter turns.

Some cars have four-wheel steering (Fig. 50-17). It is controlled either mechanically or electronically. The system automatically steers the rear wheels according to the speed of the vehicle and the steering angle of the front wheels. For increased maneuverability at lower speeds, the rear wheels may steer in the opposite direction of the front wheels (Fig. 50-17A). At higher speeds, the rear wheels steer in the same direction as the front wheels (Fig. 50-17B). This provides greater stability during cornering and high-speed lane changes.

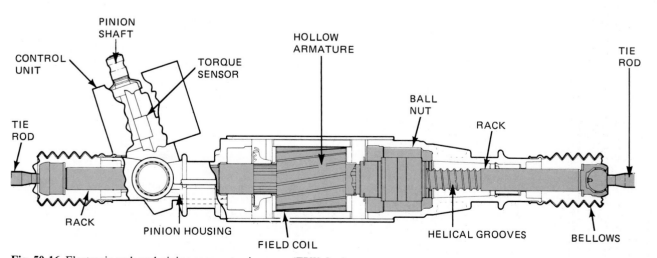

Fig. 50-16 Electronic rack-and-pinion power-steering gear. (*TRW, Inc.*)

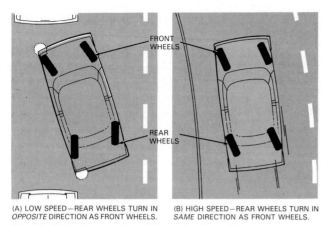

(A) LOW SPEED—REAR WHEELS TURN IN *OPPOSITE* DIRECTION AS FRONT WHEELS.

(B) HIGH SPEED—REAR WHEELS TURN IN *SAME* DIRECTION AS FRONT WHEELS.

Fig. 50-17 Basic operation of four-wheel steering.

➤ 50-17 MECHANICAL FOUR-WHEEL STEERING

Figure 50-18 shows a mechanical four-wheel-steering system. It uses a steering shaft to carry the rotary motion of the steering wheel to the rear steering gear. The rear wheels can swing inward and outward on ball joints similar to those at the front wheels.

During small turns of the steering wheel, as when driving at highway speed, the rear wheels are steered a small amount in the same direction as the front wheels. For example, if the front wheels pivot 8 degrees, the rear wheels pivot in the same direction 1.5 degrees.

When the steering wheel turns a greater amount during low-speed maneuvers, the rear wheels pivot in the opposite direction of the front wheels. For example, if the front wheels pivot 30 degrees, the rear wheels pivot 5 degrees in the opposite direction. The steering shaft to the rear axle operates a mechanism in the rear steering gear that changes the direction in which the rear-wheels pivot.

➤ 50-18 ELECTRONIC FOUR-WHEEL STEERING

Figure 50-19 shows an electronic four-wheel-steering system. The two rear wheels are carried on trailing arms that connect to the rear subframe through flexible *toe-control links*. When the driver turns the steering wheel, the hydraulic pressure applied to the front steering gear acts on the rear control valve. This causes the spool valve to move, directing pressurized fluid from the rear power-steering pump to one side of the piston in the power cylinder. The piston then forces the trailing arms to the right or left. The hydraulic pressure is regulated according to how far and how quickly the driver turns the steering wheel.

Operation of the system when turning left is shown in Fig. 50-19. In this system, the rear wheels always steer in the same direction as the front wheels. The rear-wheel steering angle increases in proportion to velocity, traction, and driver input up to a maximum of 1.5 degrees. The system only activates above 30 mph [48 kmph] and does not operate in reverse.

Other cars use similar systems that are computer-controlled. The trailing arms attach to the subframe which can be moved by the power cylinder. This steers the rear wheels.

Some cars have *electromechanical* four-wheel steering. It varies rear-wheel steering according to front-wheel steering angle and vehicle speed. A shaft from the front

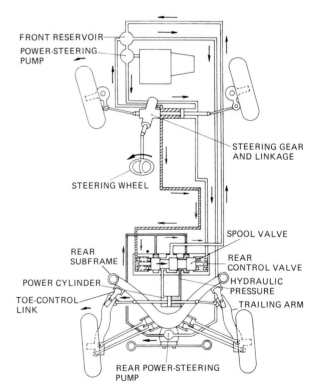

☒ : FRONT-STEERING HYDRAULIC PRESSURE

☰ : REAR-STEERING HYDRAULIC PRESSURE

☰ : RETURN AND SUCTION LINE

Fig. 50-19 Electronic four-wheel steering, showing operation of the system during a left turn. (*Chrysler Corporation*)

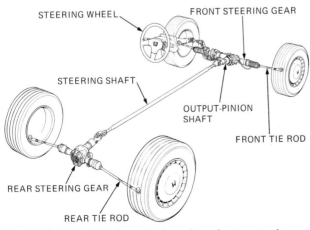

Fig. 50-18 Mechanical four-wheel steering using two steering gears connected by a steering shaft. (*American Honda Motor Company, Inc.*)

steering gear (similar to the *steering shaft* in Fig. 50-18) transmits steering-wheel movement to the rear steering gear. At the same time, the ECM sends control signals to the rear steering gear. At low speed, the rear steering gear turns the rear wheels in a direction opposite of that of the front wheels. At car speeds above 22 mph [35 kmph], the rear wheels steer in the same direction as the front wheels.

STEERING WHEELS AND COLUMNS

➤ 50-19 TILT AND TELESCOPING STEERING WHEELS

The steering wheel attaches to a steering shaft that connects to the steering gear (Fig. 49-22). The *steering column* supports the steering wheel and encloses the steering shaft. Many vehicles have tilting steering wheels (Fig. 50-20). Some tilting steering wheels can also be moved into or out of the steering column. These tilt and telescoping actions make it easier for the driver to get into or out of the vehicle.

Some steering columns can also swing in toward the center of the car to make entry and exit easier. A locking mechanism connects to the transmission selector lever. The steering column is locked in all selector-lever positions except PARK. This prevents the steering column from being accidentally moved while the vehicle is in operation.

➤ 50-20 COLLAPSIBLE STEERING COLUMN

The *collapsible steering column* (Fig. 50-21) protects the driver in a front-end collision. If the driver is thrown forward, the steering column collapses. This cushions the driver and helps reduce the possibility of injury.

Some vehicles also have a *self-aligning steering wheel*. It has an energy-absorbing hub that aligns the steering

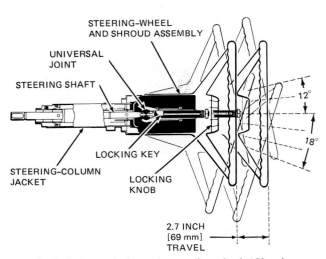

Fig. 50-20 Tilting and telescoping steering wheel. (*Chrysler Corporation*)

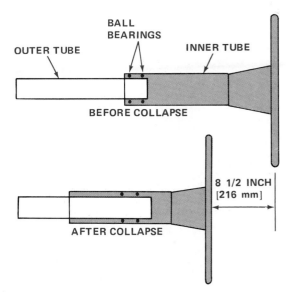

Fig. 50-21 Tube-and-ball type of collapsible steering column. (*General Motors Corporation*)

wheel with the driver's chest during an accident. This spreads the impact forces over the largest possible area of the driver's body. The likelihood and severity of chest and abdominal injuries are reduced.

➤ 50-21 STEERING AND IGNITION LOCK

The ignition lock on the steering column (Fig. 31-19) locks both the ignition switch and the steering wheel. When the ignition key is inserted and turned ON, the steering wheel is freed so the vehicle can be steered. Turning the key to LOCK allows a plunger to enter a notched disk that is splined to the steering shaft (➤31-13). This locks the shaft and prevents movement of the steering wheel.

WHEEL-ALIGNMENT ANGLES

➤ 50-22 FRONT-END GEOMETRY

Front-end geometry or *wheel-alignment angularity* is the relationship of the angles among the front wheels, the front-wheel attaching parts, and the ground. There are six basic factors involved (Fig. 50-22). These are *suspension height, caster, camber, toe, steering-axis inclination* (SAI), and *turning radius*. They affect steering effort, steering stability, ride quality, and tire wear. Other factors that affect wheel alignment include *scrub radius* (➤50-26), *setback* (➤50-31), and *thrust angle* (➤50-32).

➤ 50-23 SUSPENSION HEIGHT

Suspension height is the distance measured from some specific point on the body, frame, or suspension to the ground. If suspension height is not correct, it can affect the

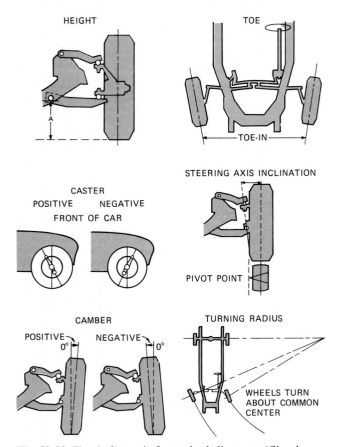

Fig. 50-22 The six factors in front-wheel alignment. (*Chrysler Corporation*)

angles in the steering and suspension systems (the *wheel alignment*). Incorrect height can result from sagging coil or leaf springs, incorrect torsion-bar adjustment, or failure in the air-suspension system.

➤ 50-24 CAMBER

Camber is the inward or outward tilt of a wheel from the vertical when viewed from the front of the vehicle (Fig. 50-22). A wheel that tilts out at the top has *positive* (+) *camber*. If it tilts in, it has *negative* (−) *camber*. The amount of tilt or *camber angle* is measured in degrees.

On many vehicles, the wheel suspension is adjusted to give a slight outward tilt (positive camber). Then when the vehicle is loaded and rolling along the road, the wheels should run straight up and down with *zero camber*. This puts the full width of the tire tread on the road surface. However, average *running camber* of zero seldom occurs. The camber goes negative when the tire hits a bump and moves up. It goes positive when the tire drops into a hole in the road. This action is caused by the unequal-length control arms of the suspension system.

As long as the vehicle rolls on a level road, ideally both front wheels should have the same camber. However, many roads are slightly higher in the center, or *crowned*. Because of the crown, the right wheel runs slightly lower

than the left. This adds a slight amount of positive camber to the right wheel. Also, the vehicle often has only the driver in it. The driver's weight tends to reduce the positive camber of the left front wheel. For these reasons, the left front wheel is often given slightly more (1/4 degree) positive camber. The vehicle will drift or pull in the direction of the wheel with the most positive camber.

During a turn, centrifugal force causes *body roll*. This is the movement of the vehicle body as it leans out toward the outside of the turn. The side forces against the bottom of the tires cause their tops to tilt toward the inside of the turn. In a left turn (Fig. 50-23), the result is positive camber of the left front wheel and negative camber of the right front wheel.

Camber is a *tire wear angle*. Any camber, positive or negative, can cause uneven and rapid tire wear. Tilting the wheel puts more load and wear on one side of the tire tread. Incorrect camber at both wheels can cause hard and unstable steering and wander. Unequal camber can contribute to low-speed shimmy. Sagging springs can change camber. When a rear spring sags, it affects the camber of the diagonally-opposite front wheel. For each one inch [25 mm] of rear-spring sag, the camber of the front wheel can change as much as 3/4 degree.

➤ 50-25 STEERING-AXIS INCLINATION

The *steering axis* is the line around which a front wheel swings for steering. In Fig. 50-24, the steering axis is a line drawn through the centers of the ball joints. The steering knuckle pivots about this line to swing the wheel right or left. On a strut suspension (Fig. 50-24), the steering axis is a line drawn through the center of the upper strut mount and the lower ball joint.

Steering-axis inclination (SAI) is the inward tilt of the steering axis from the vertical as viewed from the front of the vehicle (Fig. 50-24). It is the angle, in degrees, between a vertical line and the steering axis. This inward tilt is desirable for three reasons.

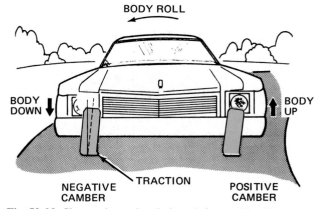

Fig. 50-23 Changes in camber during a left turn. (*Ford Motor Company*)

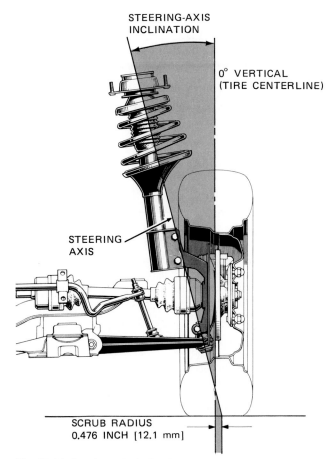

STEERING-AXIS
INCLINATION

0° VERTICAL
(TIRE CENTERLINE)

STEERING
AXIS

SCRUB RADIUS
0.476 INCH [12.1 mm]

Fig. 50-24 Steering-axis inclination, or SAI. (*Mazda Motors of America, Inc.*)

1. It helps steering stability by returning the wheels to straight ahead after a turn is completed. This is called steering-wheel *returnability*.

2. It reduces steering effort, especially if the vehicle is not moving.

3. It reduces tire wear.

SAI also helps keep the front wheels rolling straight ahead. The inward tilt of the steering axis causes the front of the vehicle to raise slightly as the wheels swing away from straight ahead. When a front wheel is rolling straight ahead, the outer end of the spindle is at its highest point. As the steering knuckle pivots away from straight ahead, the outer end of the spindle begins to drop. This is because the spindle and steering knuckle pivot around the steering axis, which is tilted inward.

However, the tire is already in contact with the road and cannot move down any farther. So the steering knuckle, ball joints, suspension, and vehicle body are raised upward. The lift is slight—one inch [25 mm] or less. But it is enough for the weight of the vehicle to help bring the wheels back to straight ahead after completing a turn. This same action provides steering stability. It tends to make the rolling wheels resist any small force that tries to move them away from straight ahead.

Steering-axis inclination is not adjustable. It is designed

into the steering knuckle. If camber can be adjusted to specifications, steering-axis inclination usually is correct. When SAI is not within specifications, the spindle, steering knuckle, ball joints, or other parts are bent or worn. Replace the defective parts.

➤ 50-26 SCRUB RADIUS

Scrub radius or *steering offset* is the distance between the steering axis and the tire contact-area centerline at their intersections with the road surface (Fig. 50-24). If the steering axis intersects the road surface inside the tire centerline, scrub radius is positive. If the point is outside (Fig. 50-24), scrub radius is negative. A *zero scrub radius* means the steering-axis and tire centerline intersect at the road surface.

Scrub radius is not an alignment angle and usually cannot be directly measured. However, it affects steering effort, stability, and returnability. Rear-drive vehicles with unequal-length front-suspension control arms often have positive scrub radius. Front-drive vehicles with MacPherson-strut front suspension usually have negative scrub radius (Fig. 50-24). This tends to turn the front wheels inward as the vehicle moves forward. It also helps maintain directional stability if a tire blows out, and helps maintain straight-line braking if a front-wheel brake grabs or fails. Any unequal forces applied to the steering act inboard of the steering axis.

➤ 50-27 INCLUDED ANGLE

The *included angle* is the camber angle plus the steering-axis-inclination (SAI) angle (Fig. 50-25). It is not an adjustable angle. However, an improper included angle often indicates a bent spindle or strut.

➤ 50-28 CASTER

Caster is the tilt of the steering axis toward the front or rear of the vehicle (Fig. 50-26). If the tilt is toward the

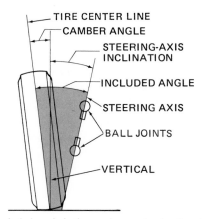

TIRE CENTER LINE

CAMBER ANGLE

STEERING-AXIS
INCLINATION

INCLUDED ANGLE

STEERING AXIS

BALL JOINTS

VERTICAL

Fig. 50-25 Included angle is the camber angle plus the steering-axis-inclination (SAI) angle. Positive camber is shown.

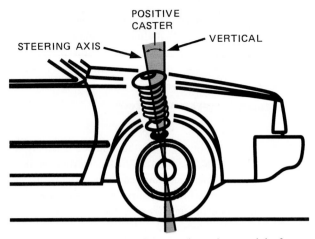

Fig. 50-26 Caster is the tilt of the steering axis toward the front or rear of the vehicle. Positive caster (backward tilt) is shown. (*Chrysler Corporation*)

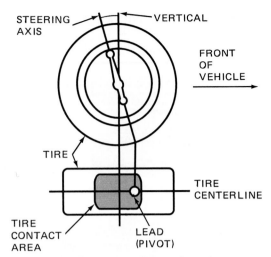

Fig. 50-27 Positive caster causes the steering axis to pass through the road surface ahead of the center of the tire contact area. This causes the steering axis to lead, or pull, the tire and wheel along the road. (*Chrysler Corporation*)

front, the wheel has *negative* (−) *caster*. A rearward tilt provides *positive* (+) *caster* (Fig. 50-26). Caster is measured in degrees.

There are three reasons for using caster:

1. To maintain directional stability and control.
2. To increase steering returnability.
3. To reduce steering effort.

Directional stability is aided by positive caster. It causes the steering axis to pass through the road surface ahead of the center of tire contact with the road (Fig. 50-27). This places the push on the steering axis ahead of the road resistance to the tire. The tire trails behind, as the positive caster causes the steering axis to lead or pull the tire and wheel down the road.

Positive caster tends to keep the wheels pointed straight ahead. It helps overcome any tendency for the vehicle to wander or steer away from straight ahead. However, negative caster makes steering easier. Then only steering-axis inclination needs to be overcome by the driver to steer away from straight ahead.

Vehicles with power steering often have more positive caster than vehicles with manual steering. The positive caster helps overcome the tendency of power steering to hold the front wheels in a turn. The additional positive caster requires greater steering effort. However, the driver does not notice because of the power assist. Positive caster tends to make the front wheels *toe in*. Negative caster tends to make the wheels *toe out*. Toe is described in ➤50-29.

Excessive positive caster may cause increased steering effort, steering-wheel snapback after a turn, low-speed shimmy, and increased road shock in the steering wheel. A decrease of positive caster can result from spring sag (Fig. 50-28). This is one reason to check suspension height.

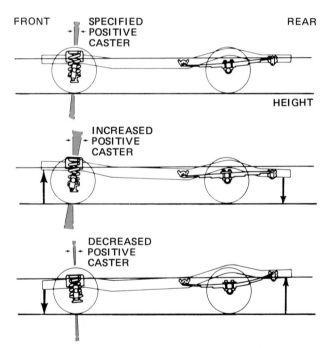

Fig. 50-28 Effect of sagging springs on caster. (*Ford Motor Company*)

➤ **50-29 TOE**

Toe is the measurement of how much the wheels point in or out from the straight-ahead position. The measurement is made in inches, millimeters, or degrees. Ideal *running toe* is zero. This means the wheels are parallel while rolling straight ahead. When the wheels point in, toe is positive (+). The amount the wheels point inward is *toe-in* (Fig. 50-22). If the wheels point out, toe is negative (−). The amount the wheels point out is *toe-out*. *Zero toe* means the wheels run parallel. They are the same distance apart at the front as they are at the rear.

Toe is set with the vehicle standing still. Typically, the front wheels of a rear-drive vehicle are given a slight toe-in of about 1/8 inch [3 mm]. When the vehicle moves forward, road resistance usually causes the front tires to spread apart or toe out. This compresses the steering linkage and takes up any play (Fig. 50-22). As a result, the tires become parallel and roll straight ahead with zero toe. On some front-drive vehicles, the front tires tend to pull in as the vehicle moves forward. These vehicles are often given a small amount of toe-out.

A tire has to move in the direction the vehicle is traveling. Any toe-in or toe-out drags the tire sideways as it rolls. The greater the toe or *toe angle*, the faster the tire wears. Zero toe allows the tires to roll straight ahead, with neither toe-in nor toe-out.

➤ 50-30 TURNING RADIUS

Turning radius is the difference in the angles of the front wheels in a turn (Fig. 50-29). It is also called *toe-out on turns* and *turning angle*. During a turn, the two front wheels travel on concentric circles which have a common center. The inner wheel turns through a greater angle and follows a smaller radius than the outer wheel. This is because the outer wheel must travel a greater distance and make a wider turn than the inner wheel.

In Fig. 50-29, when the inner wheel turns at an angle of 20 degrees, the outer wheel turns 18 degrees. The inner wheel toes out more to reduce tire scrub (scuffing) and wear. This difference in toe-out on turns is achieved by the proper relationship among the steering arms, tie rods, and steering gear (Fig. 50-1). The inner- and outer-wheel angles should not vary more than 1.5 degrees from specifications. If turning radius is not within specifications, check for a bent steering arm or tie rod.

➤ 50-31 SETBACK

Wheel *setback* is the difference in vehicle wheelbase from one side to the other (Fig. 50-30). It occurs when one wheel is behind the other wheel on the same axle. Setback

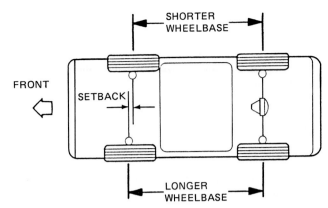

Fig. 50-30 Setback, or difference in vehicle wheelbase from one side to the other. (*Ford Motor Company*)

results from production tolerances during vehicle manufacture and from collision or impact damage. It can also result from improper placement of the engine cradle or subframe (Fig. 49-18). A vehicle will drift or pull toward the side with the shorter wheelbase (Fig. 50-30).

Setback of more than 3/4 inch [19 mm] is excessive. It usually indicates bent parts. Excessive setback also causes the center point of the steering gear to be off. Correct any problem with excessive setback before performing a wheel alignment.

➤ 50-32 THRUST ANGLE

When all four wheels are properly aligned and the steering wheel is centered, the vehicle should travel forward in a straight line. However, if a rear wheel has improper

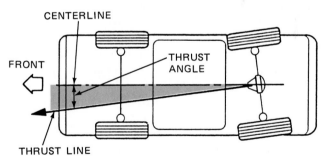

(A) LIVE REAR AXLE

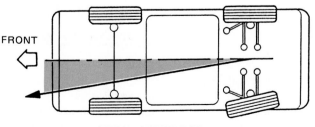

(B) INDEPENDENT REAR SUSPENSION

Fig. 50-31 Thrust angle on a vehicle with (A) a live rear axle and (B) independent rear suspension. (*Ford Motor Company*)

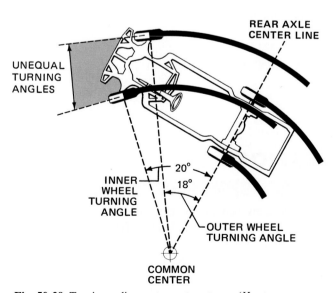

Fig. 50-29 Turning radius, or toe-out-on-turns. (*Hunter Engineering Company*)

alignment or setback (➤50-31), when the vehicle moves forward it may not move straight ahead. The direction of travel is determined by three lines that run the length of the vehicle. These are the *vehicle centerline*, the *geometric centerline*, and the *thrust line*.

The vehicle centerline is a line that passes through the actual center of the vehicle body (Fig. 50-31). This line should be the same as the *geometric centerline* that connects the midpoints of the front wheels and the rear wheels. The *thrust line* is a line from the midpoint between the two rear wheels and the direction the wheels are heading. It determines the direction the vehicle will travel if unaffected by the front wheels.

If the thrust line makes a 90-degree angle with the rear-axle centerline, the thrust line falls on or *coincides* with the vehicle centerline. The vehicle will travel straight ahead. If the thrust line does not coincide with the vehicle centerline, a *thrust angle* is formed between the centerline and the thrust line (Fig. 50-31). The thrust line then represents the path the vehicle will try to take. This condition is also called *tracking*.

The thrust angle affects handling by causing a pull in the direction *away* from the thrust line. In rear-drive vehicles, this may be caused by chassis damage or improper positioning of the rear axle (Fig. 50-31A). Also, independent rear suspensions can have unequal toe adjustments on the rear wheels (Fig. 50-31B). The result can be tire wear similar in appearance to wear caused by improper toe (➤50-29).

MULTIPLE-CHOICE TEST

*Select the **one** correct, best, or most probable answer to each question.*
You can find the answers in the section indicated at the end of each question.

1. Steering ratio is the number of degrees the (➤50-6)
   a. steering wheel must turn to pivot the front wheels one degree
   b. front wheels must turn to turn the rear wheels
   c. outside wheel must pivot to produce a 20-degree pivot of the inside wheel
   d. steering wheel must turn to get full mechanical advantage

2. In an electronic rack-and-pinion steering gear, the power assist is provided by (➤50-15)
   a. a hydraulic pump driven by an electric motor
   b. an engine-driven hydraulic pump
   c. an electric motor that applies force against the pinion
   d. an electric motor that applies force against the rack

3. Technician A says at low speed four-wheel steering causes the rear wheels to pivot in the same direction as the front wheels. Technician B says at high speed the rear wheels pivot in the opposite direction of the front wheels. Who is right? (➤50-16)
   a. A only
   b. B only
   c. both A and B
   d. neither A nor B

4. Camber is (➤50-24)
   a. the outward tilt of the ball joints
   b. caused by sagging springs
   c. the inward or outward tilt of a wheel
   d. the steering-axis inclination

5. Technician A says a line drawn through the centers of the ball joints is the steering axis. Technician B says the inward tilt of the steering axis is the steering-axis inclination. Who is right? (➤50-25)
   a. A only
   b. B only
   c. both A and B
   d. neither A nor B

6. The distance between the steering axis and the tire contact-area centerline at their intersections with the road surface is the (➤50-26)
   a. scrub radius
   b. setback
   c. thrust angle
   d. suspension height

REVIEW QUESTIONS

1. How does power steering differ from manual steering? (➤50-1 and 50-9)
2. What are the advantages of variable-ratio steering and variable-assist power steering? (➤50-7 and 50-14)
3. Explain the purpose of the power-steering pressure switch. (➤50-11)
4. How does bending of the torsion bar in the power-steering rotary or control valve affect the power assist? (➤50-12 and 50-13)
5. List the six basic factors in wheel alignment and describe how each affects steering. (➤50-22 to 50-30)

CHAPTER 51

WHEEL-ALIGNMENT, STEERING, AND SUSPENSION SERVICE

After studying this chapter, and with proper instruction and equipment, you should be able to:

- Diagnose steering and suspension troubles.
- Locate and correct causes of noise, vibration, and harshness.
- Check, adjust, and replace wheel bearings.
- Inspect and replace shock absorbers, ball joints, and MacPherson struts.
- Replace recirculating-ball and rack-and-pinion steering gears.
- Perform front-wheel alignment and four-wheel alignment.

➢ 51-1 STEERING AND SUSPENSION DIAGNOSIS AND SERVICE

The driver may bring the vehicle to the technician because of a variety of steering and suspension troubles. The technician can often determine the cause of the trouble by making a road test and visual inspection (Fig. 51-1). Trouble codes from an electronic control module (ECM) may help in the diagnosis. Some troubles are quickly located and repaired. Others are more difficult. Sometimes an apparent steering problem is actually in the suspension system.

Always turn off the air suspension before raising a vehicle so equipped. Refer to the vehicle service manual for diagnosis and service procedures on electronic steering and electronic suspension systems. Also refer to the vehicle service manual for diagnosis, service, and wheel-alignment procedures on vehicles with four-wheel steering.

The fasteners (Chap. 6) in the steering and suspension systems are vital parts. They affect the proper operation and safety of the vehicle. A fastener failure can cause damage and injury. Reinstall a fastener in the same location from which it was removed. Some fasteners should not be reused. If a fastener needs to be replaced, use the specified replacement. It should have the same part number, or be of equal size or stronger than the original. Use thread-locking compound (➢6-13) where specified. Tighten all fasteners to the specified torque or torque angle (➢7-12).

CAUTION!

Follow all safety cautions in Chap. 4 and in the vehicle service manual during any wheel-alignment, steering, and suspension service. When using a lift, alignment rack, or other shop equipment, always follow the equipment-manufacturer's operating instructions. Raise the vehicle at the specified lift points and support it properly before going under it. Always wear safety glasses or safety goggles. Take care that a tool or part does not fall and injure you or someone nearby. Wheel-alignment, steering, and suspension work is interesting and challenging. But ALWAYS BE CAREFUL!

STEERING-AND-SUSPENSION TROUBLE DIAGNOSIS

➢ 51-2 STEERING AND SUSPENSION TROUBLES

Most steering and suspension troubles fall into one of four groups. These are *hard steering, handling problems, noise,* and *leaks.* Figure 51-2 is a *Steering and Suspension Trouble-Diagnosis Chart.* Following sections further discuss these common conditions. Trouble-diagnosis charts and procedures for specific vehicles are in the vehicle service manual.

➢ 51-3 HARD STEERING

A vehicle has *hard steering* when the driver must exert excessive steering effort to turn the steering wheel. This

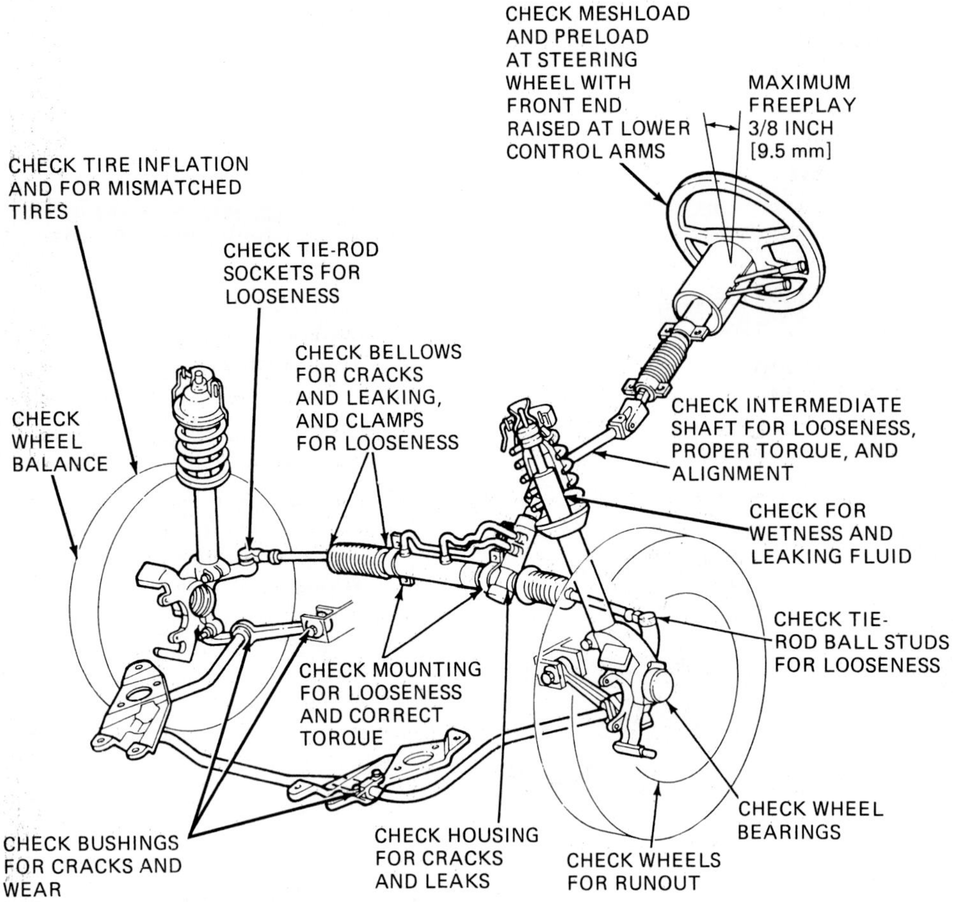

CHECK MESHLOAD AND PRELOAD AT STEERING WHEEL WITH FRONT END RAISED AT LOWER CONTROL ARMS

MAXIMUM FREEPLAY 3/8 INCH [9.5 mm]

CHECK TIRE INFLATION AND FOR MISMATCHED TIRES

CHECK TIE-ROD SOCKETS FOR LOOSENESS

CHECK BELLOWS FOR CRACKS AND LEAKING, AND CLAMPS FOR LOOSENESS

CHECK WHEEL BALANCE

CHECK INTERMEDIATE SHAFT FOR LOOSENESS, PROPER TORQUE, AND ALIGNMENT

CHECK FOR WETNESS AND LEAKING FLUID

CHECK MOUNTING FOR LOOSENESS AND CORRECT TORQUE

CHECK TIE-ROD BALL STUDS FOR LOOSENESS

CHECK BUSHINGS FOR CRACKS AND WEAR

CHECK HOUSING FOR CRACKS AND LEAKS

CHECK WHEELS FOR RUNOUT

CHECK WHEEL BEARINGS

Fig. 51-1 Conditions to look for when making a visual inspection of the steering and suspension. (*Ford Motor Company*)

may be caused by too little clearance in the steering gear (➤51-22) and excessive friction in the steering linkage (➤51-21) or ball joints (➤51-24). Other causes include uneven tire pressure and spring sag. Excessive positive caster (➤50-28) makes the vehicle hard to steer and causes the steering wheel to return too fast.

Sometimes a loss of power assist occurs only while the vehicle is cold or only while cornering and parking. This usually indicates trouble in the control-valve assembly or its sealing. Figure 51-3 shows the control-valve housing on a rack-and-pinion steering gear. The four sealing rings on the control valve have worn grooves in the aluminum housing. This allows fluid leakage which causes *morning sickness,* or no or erratic power assist especially when cold.

A quick check for hard steering is to raise the front end so the tires are off the floor (Fig. 51-1). Start the engine on vehicles with power steering. If the steering wheel turns easily, the steering is not at fault.

➤ 51-4 EXCESSIVE PLAY IN STEERING

Excessive play means there is excessive movement of the steering wheel without corresponding movement of the front wheels. A small amount of freeplay makes steering easier. Too much freeplay reduces the driver's ability to steer accurately and control the vehicle.

Check the amount of freeplay in the steering by placing the steering wheel in the straight-ahead position. Measure the free movement of the steering wheel at the rim (Fig. 51-1). The specification for maximum allowable freeplay is in the vehicle service manual. On the steering system shown in Fig. 51-1, maximum freeplay should not exceed 3/8 inch [9.5 mm]. If the freeplay is excessive, determine if the cause is in the steering column or shaft joints, steering gear, steering linkage, or suspension.

➤ 51-5 WANDER

Wander is the tendency of a vehicle to drift from one side of the road to the other. The driver must continually fight the steering wheel to keep the vehicle traveling in the desired direction. This condition usually results from lost motion somewhere between the steering wheel and the road wheels. In addition to loose steering or suspension, other causes include tire problems, an unevenly loaded or overloaded vehicle, and excessive toe-out.

➤ 51-6 PULLS TO ONE SIDE

Pull is the tendency of the vehicle to drift or pull to one side during normal driving on a level surface. The vehicle pulls toward the side that has the most positive camber (➤50-24) or the least positive caster (➤50-28). Other causes include tire problems, an unevenly loaded or over-

Complaint	Possible Cause	Check or Correction
1. Hard steering (➤51-3)	a. Power steering inoperative	Refer to vehicle service manual
	b. Low or uneven tire pressure	Inflate to correct pressure
	c. Friction in steering gear	Lubricate, adjust, or repair
	d. Friction in steering linkage	Lubricate, adjust, or repair
	e. Friction in ball joints	Lubricate or repair
	f. Excessive positive caster	Align wheels
	g. Body or frame bent or misaligned	Straighten
	h. Spring sag	Replace or adjust
2. Excessive play in steering (➤51-4)	a. Looseness in steering gear	Adjust, replace worn parts
	b. Looseness in linkage	Adjust, replace worn parts
	c. Worn ball joints or steering-knuckle parts	Replace worn parts
	d. Loose wheel bearing	Adjust
3. Wander (➤51-5)	a. Mismatched tires or uneven pressures	Correct
	b. Linkage binding	Adjust, lubricate, replace worn parts
	c. Steering gear binding	Adjust, lubricate, replace worn parts
	d. Excessive toe-out	Align wheels
	e. Looseness in linkage	Adjust, replace worn parts
	f. Looseness in steering gear	Adjust, replace worn parts
	g. Loose ball joints	Replace
	h. Loose leaf springs	Tighten
	i. Unequal load in vehicle	Adjust load
	j. Stabilizer bar ineffective	Tighten or replace
4. Pulls to one side (➤51-6)	a. Uneven tire pressure	Inflate to correct pressure
	b. Uneven caster or camber	Align wheels
	c. Tight wheel bearing	Adjust or replace
	d. Uneven springs (sagging, broken, loose attachment)	Tighten, replace defective parts
	e. Uneven torsion-bar adjustment	Adjust
	f. Brakes dragging	Adjust or repair
5. Pulls to one side while braking (➤51-7)	a. Brakes grab	Adjust, replace brake lining
	b. Uneven tire pressure	Inflate to correct pressure
	c. Incorrect or uneven caster	Align wheels
	d. Causes listed under item 4	
6. Shimmy (➤51-8)	a. Uneven or low tire pressure	Inflate to correct pressure
	b. Loose linkage	Adjust, replace worn parts
	c. Loose ball joints	Replace
	d. Looseness in steering gear	Adjust, replace worn parts
	e. Front springs too soft	Replace, tighten attachment
	f. Incorrect or unequal camber	Align wheels
	g. Irregular tire tread	Replace worn tires, match treads
	h. Wheel imbalance	Balance wheels
7. Tramp (➤51-9)	a. Wheel imbalance	Balance wheels
	b. Excessive wheel runout	Remount tire, straighten or replace wheel
	c. Shock absorbers defective	Replace
	d. Causes listed under item 6	
8. Steering kickback (➤51-10)	a. Tire pressure low or uneven	Inflate to correct pressure
	b. Springs sagging	Replace; adjust torsion bars
	c. Shock absorbers defective	Replace
	d. Looseness in linkage	Adjust, replace worn parts
	e. Looseness in steering gear	Adjust, replace worn parts
9. Poor returnability (➤51-11)	a. Friction in steering	Lubricate, adjust, or repair
	b. Friction in suspension	Lubricate, adjust, or repair
	c. Excessive negative caster	Align wheels
	d. Improper power-steering operation	Clean, repair
10. Tire squeal on turns (➤51-12)	a. Excessive speed	Take curves at slower speed
	b. Low or uneven tire pressure	Inflate to correct pressure
	c. Improper wheel alignment	Align wheels
	d. Worn tires	Replace
11. Improper tire wear (➤51-13)	a. Wear at tread sides from underinflation	Inflate to correct pressure
	b. Wear at tread center from overinflation	Inflate to correct pressure
	c. Wear at one side of tread from excessive camber	Align wheels

Fig. 51-2 Steering and suspension trouble-diagnosis chart.

Continued on next page

Complaint	Possible Cause	Check or Correction
	d. Featheredge wear from excessive toe	Align wheels
	e. Cornering wear from excessive speeds on turns	Take turns at slower speeds
	f. Uneven or scalloped wear	Rotate tires, align wheels, balance wheels, replace worn suspension parts
	g. Rapid wear from speed	Drive more slowly for longer tire life.
12. Suspension topping or bottoming out (➤51-14)	a. Defective spring or shock absorber b. Rubber bumper missing c. Vehicle heavily loaded	Replace Replace Install heavy-duty shock absorbers
13. Excessive Sway on turns (➤51-15)	a. Loose stabilizer bar b. Weak or sagging springs c. Caster incorrect d. Defective shock absorbers	Tighten Repair or replace Align wheels Replace
14. Spring breakage (➤51-16)	a. Overloading b. Leaf spring with loose center or U bolts c. Defective shock absorber d. Tight spring shackle	Avoid overloading Tighten Replace Loosen, replace
15. Improper Suspension Height (➤51-17)	a. Broken leaf spring b. Spring weak c. Defective shock absorber	Replace Replace Replace
16. Noise and Vibration (➤51-18)	a. Loose, worn, or unlubricated steering part b. Loose, worn or unlubricated spring or suspension part c. Power-steering defective d. Tight or dry shock-absorber mounting bushings	Lubricate, tighten, or repair Lubricate, tighten, or repair Repair Lubricate, install properly
17. Harshness or hard ride (➤51-19)	a. Excessive tire pressure b. Defective shock absorbers c. Bent struts d. Excessive friction in spring or suspension	Reduce to correct pressure Replace Replace Lubricate, align parts
18. Leaks (➤51-20)	a. Steering-gear seals worn or damaged b. Power-steering pump overfilled or leaking c. Leaking from power-steering hose, lines, or fittings	Replace Correct fluid level; repair Repair or replace

loaded vehicle, damaged suspension parts, defective power-steering control valve, and brake drag. Improper setback (➤50-31), thrust angle (➤50-32), and wheel alignment also cause pull. A common cause of pull is uneven tire pressure.

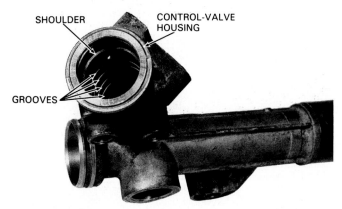

Fig. 51-3 Grooves worn in the rack-and-pinion control-valve housing. (*ATW*)

➤ 51-7 PULLS TO ONE SIDE WHILE BRAKING

Uneven braking or unequal caster may cause the vehicle to swerve or pull to one side when the brakes are applied. A brake will grab if the shoes or pads are soaked with oil or brake fluid, the shoes are improperly positioned, or a piston is stuck in a wheel cylinder or caliper (Chap. 53). Other causes include unequal tire pressure and worn control-arm bushings.

➤ 51-8 SHIMMY

Shimmy is the rapid in-and-out movement or wobble of a front wheel on its steering axis (➤50-25). This causes the front end of the vehicle to shake from side to side. It can result from worn or damaged parts, excessive side-to-side caster difference, and wheel and tire imbalance or runout. With rack-and-pinion steering, possible causes include worn steering-gear mounting bushings and loose rack ball sockets or tie-rod ends.

➤ 51-9 TRAMP

Tramp is the hopping up-and-down of a wheel at higher speeds. This is usually due to wheel and tire imbalance or runout, or a defective strut or shock absorber (➤51-25).

➤ 51-10 STEERING KICKBACK

Steering kickback is the sharp and rapid movement of the steering wheel that results when the front tires meet holes or bumps in the road. Some kickback is normal. If it is excessive, check for uneven tire pressure, sagging springs, defective shock absorbers, and loose steering gear or linkage.

➤ 51-11 POOR RETURNABILITY

Returnability is the tendency of the front wheels to return freely to the straight-ahead position when the driver releases the steering wheel after a turn. Excessive friction or binding in the steering or suspension causes poor returnability. Then the steering wheel returns slowly or the driver may have to return the steering wheel to center. Other causes include the tires and wheel alignment.

➤ 51-12 TIRE SQUEAL ON TURNS

Tire squeal is usually caused by excessive speed on turns. Other causes include low or uneven tire pressure, worn tires, or improper wheel alignment.

➤ 51-13 IMPROPER TIRE WEAR

Various types of abnormal wear occur on tires (Fig. 51-4). The type of wear often indicates its cause. For example, an underinflated tire wears the sides of the tread. An overinflated tire wears the center. Excessive camber (➤50-24) causes one side of the tire tread to wear.

Any running toe (in or out) increases tire wear. This scrapes off rubber and leaves a *feathered edge* on the tread (Fig. 51-4). Excessive *toe-in* wears a feathered edge on the *in*side of the tire tread. Too much *toe-out* causes a feathered edge along the *out*side of the tread. If only one front tire has a feathered edge, check for a bent steering arm. If both front tires have a feathered edge, the front-end has improper toe.

➤ 51-14 SUSPENSION TOPPING OR BOTTOMING OUT

A defective shock absorber may allow the spring to compress and expand too much. Then the suspension hits the rubber bumpers at the top (Figs. 49-4 and 49-5) or bottom of its travel (Fig. 49-29). Check for a weak or broken spring. Install heavy-duty shock absorbers if the suspension tops or bottoms out because of a heavy load.

➤ 51-15 EXCESSIVE SWAY ON TURNS

A broken or loose stabilizer bar will cause excessive sway on turns. The bushings that hold the bar in place may crack or wear (Figs. 49-18 and 51-1). Some stabilizer bars have links that connect the bar to the lower control arms (Fig. 49-24). The links may loosen or break. Other possible causes include weak or sagging springs and defective shock absorbers.

➤ 51-16 SPRING BREAKAGE

A leaf spring can break from overloads, a loose U bolt, or a tight spring shackle. A coil spring or torsion bar can break

CONDITION	RAPID WEAR AT SHOULDERS	RAPID WEAR AT CENTER	WEAR ON ONE SIDE	FEATHERED EDGE	BALD SPOTS	SCALLOPED WEAR
EFFECT						
CAUSE	UNDER-INFLATION OR LACK OF ROTATION	OVERINFLATION OR LACK OF ROTATION	EXCESSIVE CAMBER	INCORRECT TOE	UNBALANCED WHEEL OR TIRE DEFECT	LACK OF ROTATION OF TIRES OR WORN OR OUT-OF ALIGNMENT SUSPENSION
CORRECTION	ADJUST PRESSURE TO SPECIFICATIONS WHEN TIRES ARE COOL. ROTATE TIRES		ADJUST CAMBER TO SPECIFICATIONS	ADJUST TOE TO SPECIFICATIONS	BALANCE WHEELS	ROTATE TIRES AND INSPECT SUSPENSION

Fig. 51-4 Various types of abnormal tire wear. (*Chrysler Corporation*)

because of a defective shock absorber. An air spring may fail to hold air.

➤ 51-17 IMPROPER SUSPENSION HEIGHT

When the front or rear of the vehicle is higher or lower than normal or not level side-to-side, the body has an abnormal *attitude*. Check for heavy or improper loading of the vehicle, spring sag or damage, and improper springs. Measure the suspension height (➤50-23). The side-to-side difference on the vehicle should not exceed 1/2 inch [13 mm]. A greater difference may be caused by sagging springs, a defective automatic level-control system (➤49-11), and an improperly operating air-suspension system (➤49-29). Springs can sag if they are frequently overloaded. A torsion bar can be adjusted to restore normal suspension height.

➤ 51-18 NOISE AND VIBRATION

"Noise" is any unpleasant sound such as booming, buzzing, clunking, humming, tapping, or whistling. Figure 51-5 shows possible causes of *noise, vibration, and harshness* (NVH) in a vehicle with front-wheel drive and unibody construction. Noise often occurs along with vibration and harshness or hard ride (➤51-19).

Knowing the parts involved and the conditions under which the noise develops helps in locating the cause. For example, a buzzing noise is heard when a vehicle with power steering is running at fast idle and the wheels are straight ahead. The noise stops as the wheels are turned. Knowing the operation of the power steering indicates that a sticking pressure control valve could be the cause (➤50-11).

➤ 51-19 HARSHNESS OR HARD RIDE

Harshness (Fig. 51-5) or hard ride is usually caused by the tires or suspension. A hard or rough ride can result from high tire pressure or excessive friction in the suspension.

➤ 51-20 LEAKS

Lubricant will leak from around the rotating shafts in the steering gear if the seals (➤6-23) are worn or damaged (Figs. 50-8 and 50-13). Leaks from the power-steering pump may be caused by overfilling the reservoir, a missing reservoir cap, or failure of the shaft seal (Fig. 50-12). Other causes of power-steering fluid leakage include loose or damaged lines (tube or hose) and fittings, damaged or missing O rings, and leaking rack seals (➤51-22).

INSPECTING STEERING AND SUSPENSION COMPONENTS

➤ 51-21 INSPECTING STEERING LINKAGE

Looseness in the steering linkage can cause wheel shimmy, uneven braking, handling problems, and excessive tire

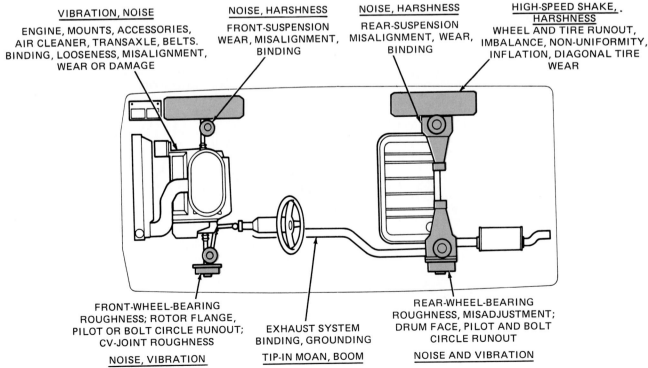

VIBRATION, NOISE
ENGINE, MOUNTS, ACCESSORIES, AIR CLEANER, TRANSAXLE, BELTS. BINDING, LOOSENESS, MISALIGNMENT, WEAR OR DAMAGE

NOISE, HARSHNESS
FRONT-SUSPENSION WEAR, MISALIGNMENT, BINDING

NOISE, HARSHNESS
REAR-SUSPENSION MISALIGNMENT, WEAR, BINDING

HIGH-SPEED SHAKE, HARSHNESS
WHEEL AND TIRE RUNOUT, IMBALANCE, NON-UNIFORMITY, INFLATION, DIAGONAL TIRE WEAR

FRONT-WHEEL-BEARING ROUGHNESS; ROTOR FLANGE, PILOT OR BOLT CIRCLE RUNOUT; CV-JOINT ROUGHNESS
NOISE, VIBRATION

EXHAUST SYSTEM BINDING, GROUNDING
TIP-IN MOAN, BOOM

REAR-WHEEL-BEARING ROUGHNESS, MISADJUSTMENT; DRUM FACE, PILOT AND BOLT CIRCLE RUNOUT
NOISE AND VIBRATION

Fig. 51-5 Possible causes of noise, vibration, and harshness. (*Ford Motor Company*)

wear. To check for loose steering linkage, turn off the *air-suspension switch* (*trunk switch* in Fig. 49-35) on vehicles with air springs. Raise the vehicle until the front tires clear the floor. Start the engine if the vehicle has power steering. Use a *brake-pedal depressor* or have an assistant apply the foot or service brakes (Chap. 52). This eliminates any play caused by loose wheel bearings (➤51-23).

Grasp both tires at the front and push out and then pull in (Fig. 51-6). On vehicles with 16-inch [406 mm] diameter or smaller wheels, the maximum movement at the front or rear of each tire should be 1/4 inch [6.5 mm] or less. Excessive tire movement indicates worn linkage parts such as wear in the tie-rod ends or rack ball sockets (Fig. 51-6). Replace the defective parts and any tie-rod end that has a torn boot (Fig. 50-7). Then align the wheels.

Another method of checking the steering linkage is the *dry-park check*. Park the vehicle on a dry surface with the weight on the wheels. With the engine off and the steering wheel unlocked, watch the various connecting parts (Fig.

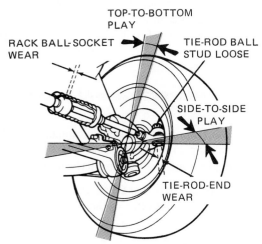

Fig. 51-6 Inspecting steering linkage. (*Ford Motor Company*)

51-6) when the steering wheel is moved. Movement between the tie-rod end and the steering arm indicates a worn tapered-hole in the steering arm or a loose ball-stud in the tie-rod end. Check each tie-rod end and other wear points for excessive looseness, binding, and roughness.

➤ 51-22 CHECKING STEERING GEARS

When there is excessive looseness in the steering, find out if the looseness is in the steering gear. Sometimes a steering-gear adjustment eliminates the looseness. However, an adjustment cannot correct for defective bearings or excessive wear.

1. RECIRCULATING-BALL STEERING GEAR With the wheels on the floor, turn the steering wheel one way and then the other. If excessive steering-wheel movement is required to move the pitman arm, the steering gear is worn or needs adjusting. Two adjustments on the recirculating-ball steering gear are the *worm-bearing preload* and the *overcenter preload* (Figs. 50-8 and 50-13). The worm-bearing preload takes up the worm-shaft endplay. The overcenter preload removes backlash between the worm and the sector gear. These adjustments are usually made on the steering gear after removing it from the vehicle (➤51-28).

2. RACK-AND-PINION STEERING GEAR The rack is supported at two points in the housing. The *rack bushing* (Fig. 51-7) supports the right end. The *rack yoke* supports the left or control-valve end. A spring behind the yoke pushes the rack into the pinion. This rack-to-pinion preload is the *rack-yoke clearance*. It maintains the proper mesh between the pinion and the rack. The rack housing includes an adjuster plug, screw, or shim pack for adjusting rack-yoke clearance.

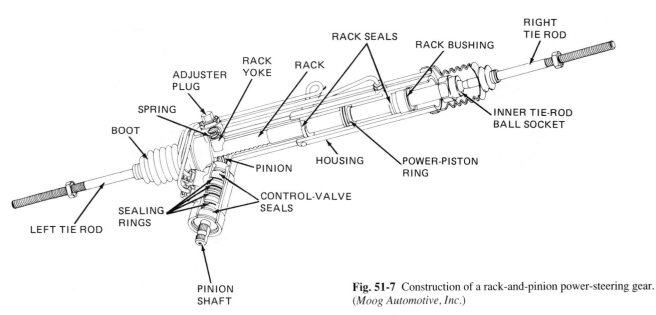

Fig. 51-7 Construction of a rack-and-pinion power-steering gear. (*Moog Automotive, Inc.*)

➤ 51-23 CHECKING WHEEL BEARINGS

Wheel bearings are usually either ball or tapered-roller bearings (➤49-19). These may be adjustable or non-adjustable (Fig. 49-22). The front hubs of rear-drive vehicles and the rear hubs of front-drive vehicles are often supported by two adjustable roller bearings (Fig. 51-8). The *inner bearing* and *outer bearing* mount on the sta-

tionary spindle and should have no preload. Front-drive vehicles have two ball or tapered-roller bearings in each steering knuckle (Fig. 51-9). These bearings are permanently lubricated and are not adjustable.

1. CHECKING ADJUSTABLE WHEEL BEARINGS Turn off the air-suspension switch (*trunk switch* in Fig. 49-35) on vehicles with air springs. Raise the vehicle until the tires clear the ground. Support the vehicle so the ball joints are *loaded*. This means they are carrying the weight of the vehicle. Grasp the tire at the top and bottom (Fig. 51-10) and rock it in and out. If the outer edge of the tire moves more than 1/8 inch [3 mm], have an assistant apply the brakes and rock the tire again. If this eliminates the movement, the wheel bearings are loose.

2. CHECKING NON-ADJUSTABLE WHEEL BEARINGS To check non-adjustable wheel bearings on General Motors and other vehicles, raise the tires off the ground. Remove the wheels and the disc-brake calipers or brake shoes. Install two wheel nuts to hold the drum or disc in place. Mount a dial indicator against the hub. Measure the endplay while pushing in and pulling out on the drum or disc. If the endplay exceeds 0.005 inch [0.13 mm], replace the *hub-and-bearing assembly*. The wheel bearings cannot be replaced separately.

➤ 51-24 INSPECTING BALL JOINTS

Various methods are used to check ball joints. Some have built-in wear indicators. In others, the amount of wear is measured. Replace any ball joint that has a torn boot.

1. WEAR-INDICATING BALL JOINTS Many ball joints have a built-in wear indicator in the cover (Fig. 49-23).

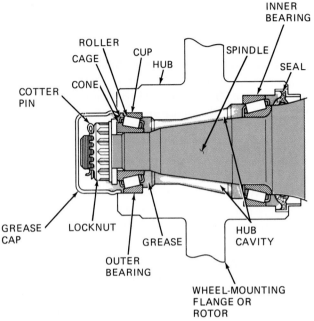

Fig. 51-8 Adjustable wheel bearings in the hub of a non-driving wheel. (*Chrysler Corporation*)

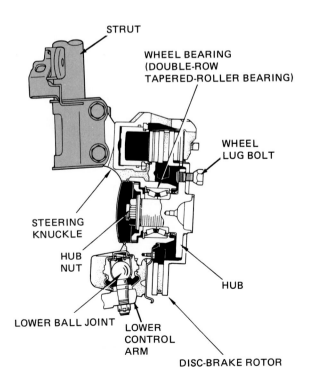

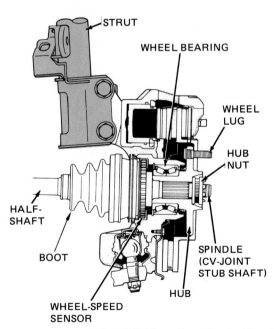

Fig. 51-9 Non-adjustable wheel bearings used with strut suspension. (*Toyota Motor Sales U.S.A., Inc.*)

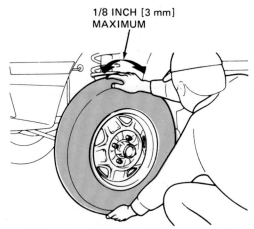

Fig. 51-10 Checking for wear in the ball joints and wheel bearings. (*Mitsubishi Motor Sales of America, Inc.*)

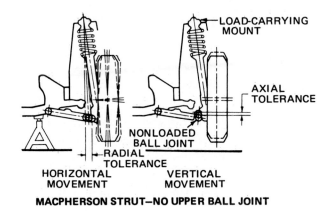

MACPHERSON STRUT—NO UPPER BALL JOINT

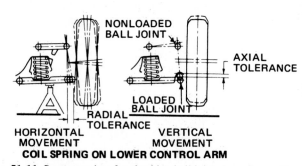

COIL SPRING ON UPPER CONTROL ARM

COIL SPRING ON LOWER CONTROL ARM

Fig. 51-11 Support points for checking ball joints in various coil-spring front-suspension systems. (*Motor Vehicle Manufacturers Association*)

This is a slightly protruding boss into which a grease fitting may be threaded. On a new ball joint, the boss protrudes 0.050 inch [1.27 mm]. It recedes into the cover as the ball joint wears. To check a wear-indicating ball joint, the weight of the vehicle should be on the wheels so the ball joints are loaded. Wipe the grease fitting and boss to remove all dirt and grease. Observe the cover, or scrape a fingernail, steel scale, or screwdriver across it. If the boss is flush with or inside the cover (Fig. 49-23), the ball joint is worn and should be replaced.

A similar check of the lower ball joints is made on Chrysler front-wheel-drive vehicles. However, the wear indicator is that the grease fitting loosens as the ball joint wears. With the weight of the vehicle on the wheels, try to move the grease fitting with your fingers. Replace the ball joint if the grease fitting has any movement.

2. BALL JOINTS WITHOUT WEAR INDICATORS To check ball joints without wear indicators, raise the front end. Support the vehicle at the proper points to remove the load from the ball joints (Fig. 51-11). Attach a dial indicator (➤5-17) to the control arm. Place the dial-indicator plunger against the steering knuckle or pinch-bolt around the ball-joint stud (Fig. 50-24). The dial indicator will show any movement between the ball-joint stud and its socket.

Check vertical movement by lifting the tire and wheel with a pry bar while observing the dial indicator. Some ball joints are preloaded with rubber or springs under compression. They should have very little vertical movement. These ball joints are marked as PRELOADED in specification tables. Check horizontal movement by grasping the top and bottom of the tire (Fig. 51-10) and moving it in and out. More horizontal movement is often allowed because of the ball-joint construction. Some manufacturers do not accept horizontal movement as indicating ball-joint wear. Replace the ball joint if either vertical or horizontal movement exceeds the manufacturer's specifications. Then check the wheel alignment (➤51-33).

➤ **51-25 CHECKING SHOCK ABSORBERS AND STRUT DAMPERS**

One test of shock absorbers and strut dampers is the *bounce test*. Bounce the vehicle at each corner by pushing down and releasing it. The vehicle should return to its original height and stay there. If it continues to bounce up and down, the shock absorber or strut damper is probably defective and should be replaced. Check the shock absorber or strut for wetness and leaking fluid (Fig. 51-1). A shock absorber or strut damper that has lost fluid will not work properly and should be replaced. The units are sealed and fluid cannot be added.

STEERING AND SUSPENSION SERVICE

➤ 51-26 SERVICING STEERING AND SUSPENSION

After inspecting the steering and suspension, correct any defects found before starting a wheel alignment. Follow the procedures in the vehicle service manual. Servicing the steering and suspension includes:

- Removal, installation, and adjustment of tie rods.
- Removal and installation of other steering-linkage parts.
- Removal and installation of steering gears.
- Removal and installation of ball joints and control arms.
- Removal and installation of struts and shock absorbers.
- Removal and installation of wheel hubs.
- Installation and adjustment of wheel bearings.

➤ 51-27 WHEEL-BEARING ADJUSTMENT

Follow the procedure in the vehicle service manual to adjust or replace wheel bearings. Typical recommendations are to inspect and repack adjustable wheel bearings (Fig. 51-8) every 30,000 miles [48,000 km]. To adjust the wheel bearing, raise the vehicle and remove the wheel cover and grease cap. Wipe away excess grease and remove the cotter pin and locknut or *retainer* (Fig. 51-12).

Loosen the adjusting nut three turns. Rock the wheel assembly in and out several times to push the disc-brake pads away from the rotor. While rotating the wheel, tighten the adjusting nut to the specified torque. Then loosen the nut one-half turn. Retighten it to the final specified torque. Install the locknut or retainer with a new cotter pin.

Check that the wheel rotates properly. If the wheel is noisy or rough, inspect and lubricate or replace the bearings. Install the grease cap and wheel cover. Pump the brake pedal several times to restore braking before moving the vehicle.

➤ 51-28 STEERING-GEAR SERVICE

The steering gear should be serviced or replaced if it leaks or does not operate properly. Sometimes adjusting the steering gear will correct excessive looseness (➤51-22).

1. RECIRCULATING-BALL STEERING GEAR The pitman-shaft seals (Fig. 50-8) usually can be replaced with the steering gear in the vehicle. Other services require removing the steering gear. This is done by disconnecting the flexible coupling from the stub shaft (Fig. 50-13). Place a drain pan under the steering gear. Disconnect the power-steering hose from the steering gear and cap the fittings. Remove the nut from the pitman-arm shaft and pull the arm from the shaft. Then remove the bolts that attach the steering gear to the vehicle or frame and remove the steering gear.

Follow these steps in reverse order to install the steering gear. Check that the stub shaft and flexible coupling are properly positioned before tightening the steering-gear attaching bolts. Fill the power-steering reservoir to the proper level with the specified fluid.

Fig. 51-12 A disassembled front-wheel bearing. (*Ford Motor Company*)

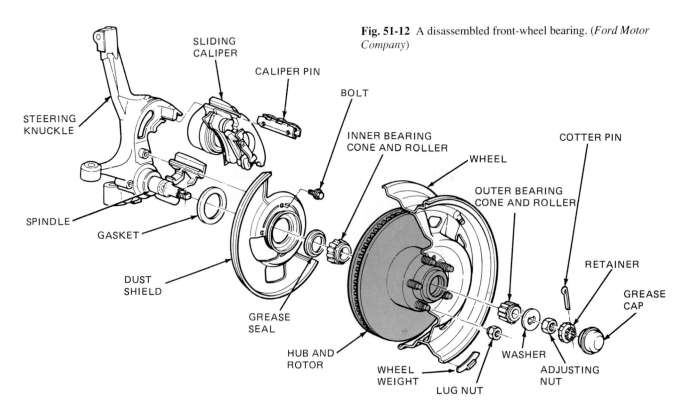

2. RACK-AND-PINION STEERING GEAR The steering-gear bellows or boots and outer tie-rod ends can usually be replaced without removing the unit from the vehicle (Fig. 51-1). Some inner tie-rod ball sockets (Fig. 51-7) can be replaced in the vehicle. However, special tools may be needed to prevent steering-gear damage.

Follow the steps in the vehicle service manual to replace the steering gear. Typical steps include disconnecting the negative cable from the battery and then turning the ignition key ON. Raise the vehicle, support it properly, and remove the front wheels. Place a drain pan under the steering gear. Disconnect the power-steering hose from the steering gear and cap the fittings. Use a puller to separate the tie-rod ends from the steering knuckles (Fig. 51-13).

Remove the pinchbolt connecting the intermediate shaft to the pinion shaft (Fig. 51-14). Then remove the steering-gear mounting bolts and remove the steering gear through

the left wheel opening. To remove the steering gear from some vehicles, support the engine cradle and remove the rear cradle mounting bolts. Lower the cradle four to five inches [102 to 127 mm] to get the necessary clearance. Other vehicles must have the engine raised slightly. Then the steering gear can be removed.

> **NOTE** Two types of replacement rack-and-pinion steering gears are available. These are the *short rack* and the *long rack*. The short rack does not include the rack boots or inner tie-rod ends (ball sockets). These must be installed by the technician.

Compare the old and new steering gears. Sometimes installing a replacement unit requires the use of adapters, rerouting lines and hoses, and relocating switches and wiring. If necessary, install new outer tie-rod ends and locknuts or transfer the parts from the old steering gear. When the unit is ready for installation, reverse the removal procedure and install the steering gear. Use new fasteners where specified. Tighten all fasteners to the specified torque.

If the power-steering fluid could be contaminated, flush out the power-steering pump, lines, and hose with new fluid. Install new O rings and attach the power-steering lines to the steering gear. Avoid damaging the threads in the aluminum housing by cross-threading and over-tightening. Check the fluid level in the power-steering reservoir. With the engine idling, bleed any trapped air from the hydraulic system. One way is to rotate the steering wheel several times from lock to lock. Adjust front-wheel toe (➤51-36). Road test the vehicle to check for proper steering-gear operation. Then inspect for leaks.

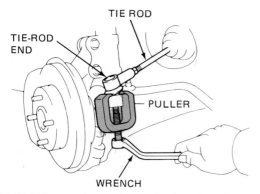

Fig. 51-13 Using a puller to separate the tie-rod end from the steering knuckle. (*Toyota Motor Sales U.S.A., Inc.*)

Fig. 51-14 Removing a rack-and-pinion power-steering gear. (*Mazda Motors of America, Inc.*)

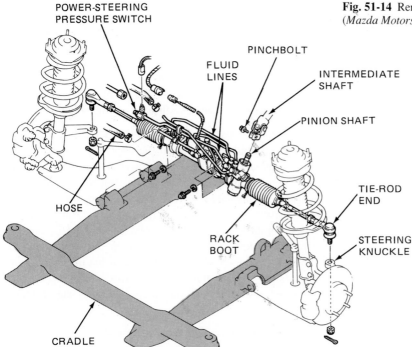

Figure 49-8 shows the shock absorber or damper inside a strut assembly (➤49-8). There are two main types of MacPherson struts: *non-serviceable* and *serviceable*. In a non-serviceable MacPherson strut, the shock absorber cannot be serviced or replaced. The strut is replaced as a complete assembly. A serviceable MacPherson strut has a shock-absorber or *strut cartridge* (Fig. 51-15) that can be replaced. Sometimes this does not require removing the strut from the vehicle.

The coil spring can be replaced on both serviceable and non-serviceable struts. If a bent strut is replaced, the spring can be transferred to the new strut. Follow the procedures in the vehicle service manual when performing any Mac-Pherson-strut service. Be careful not to dent, crush, or bend the strut tube.

1. MACPHERSON-STRUT REMOVAL A typical procedure for removing the strut is to loosen the wheel nuts. Raise the vehicle and remove the wheels. Figure 51-16 shows how to mark the outline of the strut on the steering knuckle and the position of the cam bolt on the strut. Remove the cam bolt, knuckle bolt, and brake-hose mounting bolt. Then remove the strut-attaching nuts (Fig. 51-16) and remove the strut from the vehicle.

2. MACPHERSON-STRUT DISASSEMBLY To disassemble the strut, compress the coil spring with the proper *MacPherson-strut spring compressor* (Fig. 51-17). Some springs have an epoxy-plastic coating and should not be compressed with a hook-type spring compressor. Do not compress the spring so much that the coils contact each other.

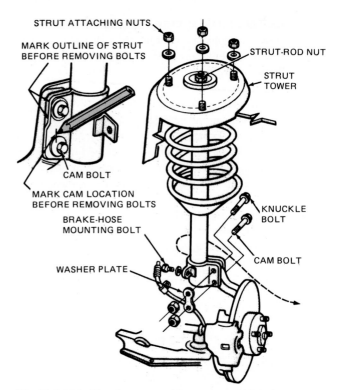

Fig. 51-16 Marking the strut position and cam bolt before removing the strut assembly from the vehicle. (*Chrysler Corporation*)

CAUTION!

Always wear safety glasses or safety goggles while removing and installing a coil spring. If the spring compressor slips while the spring is compressed, the spring could fly out with great force and injure you or anyone nearby. ALWAYS follow the operating instructions for the spring compressor you are using when removing or installing a coil spring.

With the spring compressed, hold the end of the strut rod with a wrench. Remove the strut-rod nut (Figs. 49-29 and 51-16) and strut mount. If both struts are being disassembled, mark the spring RIGHT or LEFT. The springs on the two sides of the vehicle may have different spring rates (➤49-5). Follow the instructions for the spring compressor you are using and remove the coil spring from the strut.

3. MACPHERSON-STRUT INSPECTION Inspect the strut for fluid leaking from the upper end, running down the side, and dripping off the lower end (Fig. 51-1). Slight seepage or dampness between the strut rod and strut-shaft seal is not unusual and does not affect performance.

Inspect the strut mount (Fig. 49-29). Look for severe deterioration of the rubber isolators, cracked or distorted retainers, and bond failure between the rubber and the metal retainers. Check the bearing for binding. Then move the strut rod through its full travel while checking for uneven resistance or "flat spots." Replace any defective parts.

4. MACPHERSON-STRUT ASSEMBLY Follow the procedure in the vehicle service manual to reassemble the

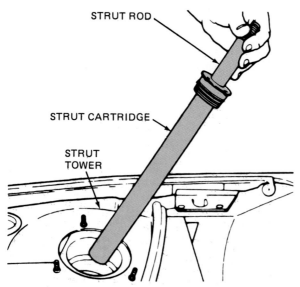

Fig. 51-15 Replaceable strut cartridge, or shock absorber, in a serviceable MacPherson strut. (*Chevrolet Division of General Motors Corporation*)

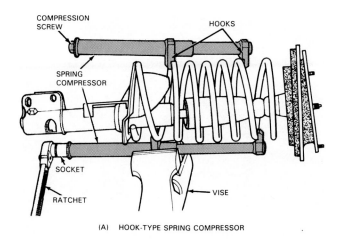

(A) HOOK-TYPE SPRING COMPRESSOR

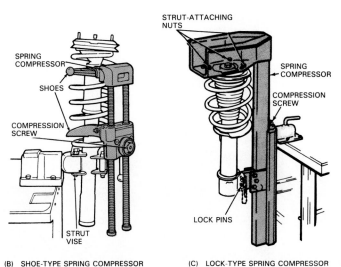

(B) SHOE-TYPE SPRING COMPRESSOR   (C) LOCK-TYPE SPRING COMPRESSOR

Fig. 51-17 Various types of spring compressors used to disassemble the strut. (*ATW*)

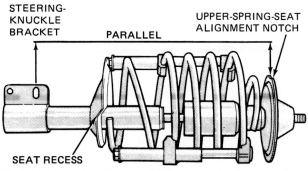

Fig. 51-18 Proper positioning of the spring and spring seats for strut assembly. (*Chrysler Corporation*)

marks (Fig. 51-16). Tighten the bolts as specified and remove the C clamp. Install the wheels. After installing a new strut cartridge, adjust camber (➤51-35) and toe (➤51-36).

WHEEL ALIGNMENT

➤ 51-30 BASICS OF WHEEL ALIGNMENT

The basic purpose of a *wheel alignment* is to restore the vehicle suspension to the original or manufacturer's specifications. It is the proper adjustment of all the interrelated suspension angles affecting the running and steering of the vehicle.

Many types of meters, gauges, and *wheel aligners* are available to measure the alignment angles. Figure 51-19 shows a mechanical *camber-caster gauge* that attaches to the wheel spindle. The angles are read directly from the

strut. Place the compressed spring onto the strut (Fig. 51-18). Install the dust shield, isolator, jounce bumper, spacer (if required), and spring seat onto the top of the strut rod. Check that the ends of the coil spring are properly seated and that the top spring seat is properly aligned. Install the rebound retainer and strut-rod nut (Fig. 51-16). Use special tools, if required, and tighten the strut-rod nut to the specified torque. Then release the coil spring from the spring compressor.

5. MACPHERSON-STRUT INSTALLATION A typical procedure is to install the strut in the strut tower. Tighten the attaching nuts (Fig. 51-16) to the specified torque. Position the top of the steering knuckle into the strut bracket. Install the cam bolt, knuckle bolt, and brake-hose mounting bolt. Align the strut or cam bolt to the mark made during removal.

Place a C clamp on the strut and knuckle. Tighten the clamp only enough to eliminate any looseness between the knuckle and the strut. Check the alignment of the index

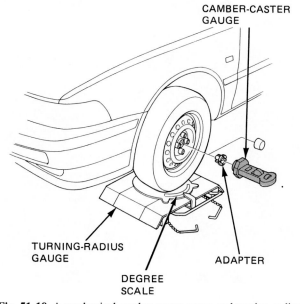

Fig. 51-19 A mechanical camber-caster gauge and turning-radius gauge for measuring wheel-alignment angles. (*American Honda Motor Company, Inc.*)

703

gauge. Some wheel aligners have light beams that display the measurements on a screen in front of the vehicle.

A computerized *four-wheel aligner* simultaneously displays the alignment measurements for all four wheels (Figs. 51-20 and 51-21). It has rim-mounted *heads* or *sensors* on each wheel that feed information to a computer in the console. The specifications, readings, and corrections needed are displayed on meters, screens, or paper printouts. Some computerized wheel aligners provide video instruction on how to make the adjustment or repair.

➤ **51-31 PRE-ALIGNMENT INSPECTION**

Several parts and conditions can affect vehicle steering. These must be checked and corrected before aligning the wheels. Pre-alignment checks include:

- Checking for unusual loads in the vehicle or trunk.
- Checking tire pressure and condition.
- Checking wheel bearings for condition and adjustment.
- Checking wheel and tire balance and runout (Chap. 54).
- Checking ball joints and steering for looseness.
- Checking rear suspension condition.
- Checking front suspension condition.

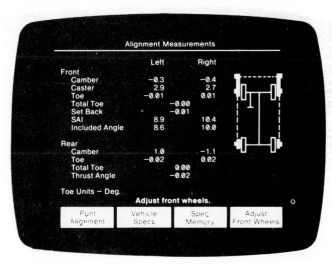

Fig. 51-21 The specifications, readings, and corrections needed can be displayed on the screen of a computerized four-wheel aligner. (*General Motors Corporation*)

Follow the procedures in the vehicle service manual to correct any abnormal condition found. A full tank of fuel and bouncing the front and rear of the vehicle may be recommended before taking the readings. Some vehicles have an adjustable engine cradle or subframe (Fig. 51-14).

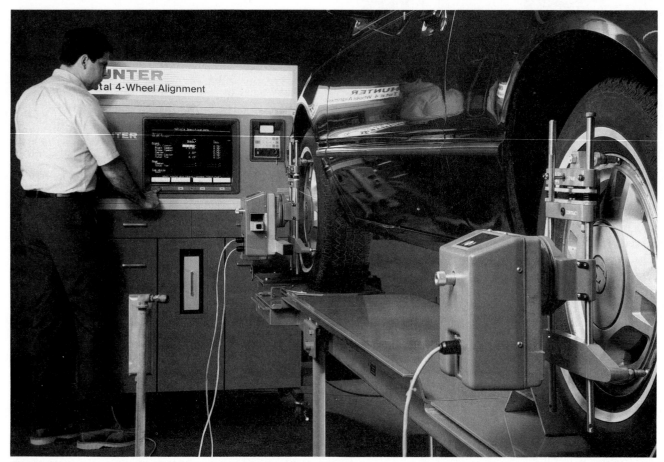

Fig. 51-20 A computerized four-wheel aligner that displays the alignment measurements for all four wheels at the same time. Rim-mounted heads, or sensors, send information to the computer in the console. (*Hunter Engineering Company*)

Check the cradle-to-body alignment before aligning the wheels. The vehicle service manual includes the procedure.

➤ 51-32 FOUR-WHEEL ALIGNMENT

To prevent rear-wheel misalignment causing a drift or pull after alignment of the front wheels, many vehicles should have a *four-wheel alignment* (Fig. 51-20). This is the aligning of the rear wheels and then the front so the vehicle has a common vehicle centerline, geometric centerline, and thrust line (➤50-32). The wheel aligner should measure all four wheels simultaneously (Fig. 51-20) and display the individual toe of each rear wheel (Fig. 51-21). Rear-wheel setback (➤50-31) or unequal rear-wheel toe creates a thrust angle (➤50-32). This causes the vehicle to pull in the opposite direction (➤50-32).

Four-wheel alignment is usually recommended for 1980 and later-model vehicles, and vehicles with front-wheel drive or independent rear suspension. Always align the rear wheels first when performing a four-wheel alignment. Section 51-38 covers typical procedures for aligning the rear wheels.

➤ 51-33 CHECKING FRONT-WHEEL ALIGNMENT ANGLES

The six basic wheel-alignment factors are suspension height (➤51-17), caster, camber, toe, steering-axis inclination, and turning radius. These along with setback and thrust angle are described in Chap. 50. Caster, camber, and toe are the adjustable angles. On some vehicles, only camber and toe—or only toe—can be adjusted. The other angles are not adjustable. Correction is usually made by replacing bent parts.

Figures 51-19 and 51-22 show a mechanical camber-caster gauge being attached to the wheel spindle. This gauge is basically a *level*. The position of a bubble in a

Fig. 51-22 Magnetic camber-caster gauge being attached to the wheel spindle. This gauge also measures steering-axis inclination. (*Snap-on Tools Corporation*)

graduated liquid-filled tube shows horizontal. Another bubble shows the angle the spindle makes in tilting away from horizontal. The following steps describe how to use the gauge to measure camber, caster, steering-axis inclination, and turning radius.

1. *Measuring Camber* The wheels should point straight ahead when the gauge is horizontal. Read camber directly from the bubble in the tube marked CAMBER. Repeat the procedure on the other wheel.
2. *Measuring Caster* Checking caster requires placing the tires on *turning-radius gauges* (Fig. 51-19). Watch the scale on the turning-radius gauge and turn each wheel in 20 degrees. Adjust the gauge until the caster bubble reads zero. Turn the wheel until it is pointing out 20 degrees. Read the caster from the positive or negative side of the caster scale. Repeat the procedure on the other wheel.
3. *Measuring Steering-Axis Inclination* Steering-axis inclination can be read when the caster readings are taken. When the turning-radius gauge shows the wheel points in 20 degrees, zero the bubble in the tube showing steering-axis inclination. This is marked KING-PIN ANGLE in Fig. 51-22. When the wheel is turned out 20 degrees, read the steering-axis inclination.
4. *Measuring Turning Radius* Toe-out on turns or turning radius is checked with a turning-radius gauge under each front tire (Fig. 51-19). Adjust the degree scales to zero. Then turn each wheel in 20 degrees and read the angle shown on the other turning-radius gauge.
5. *Measuring Toe* Toe can be measured with a mechanical *toe gauge* (Fig. 51-23). Measure the distance between the center of the treads at the front of the tires. Then move the toe gauge and measure the distance between the centers at the back of the tires. The difference is *total toe* (Fig. 51-21). Wheel aligners with gauges or sensors on both wheels measure the *individual toe* of each wheel.

When wheel-alignment angles must be adjusted, make the adjustments in the specified order. This is usually caster, camber, and toe. Adjust caster first if it is adjustable. Then adjust camber (if adjustable). Adjust toe last.

➤ 51-34 CASTER AND CAMBER ADJUSTMENTS (SALA SUSPENSION)

There are several methods for adjusting caster and camber on short-arm/long-arm (SALA) suspensions which have unequal-length control arms (➤49-23). These include installing or removing shims, adjusting the cam bolts in the control arms, shifting the control-arm inner shaft, and changing the length of the strut rod.

1. SHIM ADJUSTMENT The shims are located at the upper-control-arm shafts, either outside or inside the frame

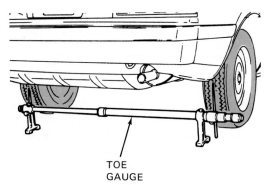

Fig. 51-23 Mechanical toe gauge, used to measure the distance between tire centers at the front and back of the tires. The difference in distances is the total toe. (*Mitsubishi Motor Sales of America, Inc.*)

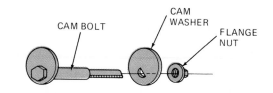

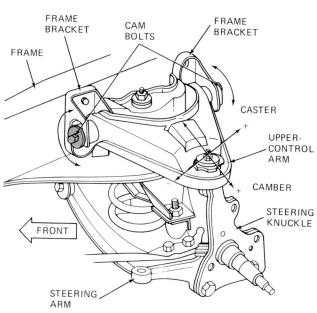

Fig. 51-25 Caster and camber adjustments by turning offset, or eccentric, cam bolts. (*ATW*)

or frame bracket. When the shims are inside the frame bracket (Fig. 51-24), adding shims moves the upper-control arm inward. This reduces positive camber. When the shims are outside the frame bracket, adding shims moves the upper control arm outward. This increases positive camber.

Adding shims at one bolt and removing shims from the other moves the outer end of the upper-control arm forward or backward. This increases or decreases caster (Fig. 51-24).

> **NOTE** Some trucks have an I-beam front axle and leaf springs (Fig. 49-31) instead of upper and lower control arms. Caster is adjusted by installing tapered *caster shims* between the spring and the axle. If the shims are installed backward, the axle will have excessive negative caster. The driver may complain of difficulty in keeping the truck in a straight-ahead position, wander, and pull.

2. CAM-BOLT ADJUSTMENT Figure 51-25 shows one arrangement using offset or eccentric *cam bolts* to adjust caster and camber. The two bushings at the inner end of the upper control arm attach to the frame brackets with two cam bolts. Turning the cam bolts the same amount in the

same direction changes camber. Turning only one cam bolt or turning both cam bolts in opposite directions changes caster. On some vehicles, the cam bolts are in the inner ends of the lower-control arms.

3. PIVOT-SHAFT ADJUSTMENT This arrangement has slots in the frame at the two points where the upper-control-arm *pivot shaft* attaches (Fig. 51-26). Loosening the attaching bolts and moving the pivot shaft in or out changes camber. Moving only one end changes caster.

4. STRUT-ROD ADJUSTMENT Changing the length of the suspension strut rod changes caster (Fig. 49-25). Turning the cam bolt on the inner end of the lower control arm changes camber.

➤ 51-35 CASTER AND CAMBER ADJUSTMENTS (STRUT SUSPENSION)

Many vehicles with MacPherson struts do not have camber and caster adjustments. Others have a cam bolt at the lower end of the struts to adjust camber (Fig. 51-16). Turning the cam bolt moves the top of the wheel in or out. If no camber adjustment is provided, some manufacturers recommend enlarging the bolt holes in the bottom of the strut. On some MacPherson-strut suspensions, caster and camber are

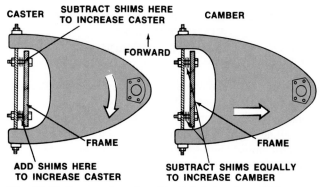

Fig. 51-24 Caster and camber adjustments on some vehicles using shims. (*Chevrolet Division of General Motors Corporation*)

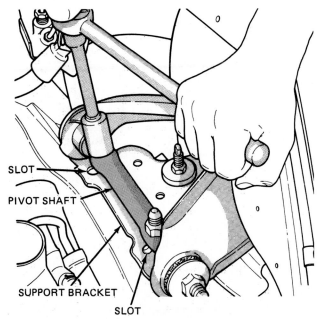

Fig. 51-26 Adjusting caster and camber by shifting the position of the pivot shaft, using slots in the frame. (*Chrysler Corporation*)

adjusted at the upper strut mount (Fig. 51-27). Moving the strut toward the front or rear changes caster. Moving the strut in or out changes camber.

➤ 51-36 TOE ADJUSTMENT

After making caster and camber adjustments, check and adjust toe. Front-wheel toe is measured with the steering-wheel centered and the wheels straight ahead. Figure 51-23 shows a mechanical toe gauge that measures total toe. Its length is adjusted so the pointers are at the centers of the tires. The total toe is the difference in distance between tire centers at the rear and at the front.

To adjust toe, loosen the tie-rod locknuts (Fig. 51-28). Rotate the tie rods until the toe measurement is set to specifications. Do not allow the boots on the ends of the steering gear to twist while making the adjustment. Then tighten the tie-rod locknuts to the specified torque.

➤ 51-37 STEERING-WHEEL CENTERING

When all four wheels are properly aligned and there is no thrust angle, the steering wheel will be centered while the vehicle is moving straight ahead (Fig. 51-29). If not, the steering wheel can be centered by adjusting the tie rods. Adjust the tie rods to steer the front wheels in the same direction the steering wheel is off center. For example, if the steering wheel is off center to the right, adjust the tie rods to make the front wheels steer toward the right.

To make the adjustment, loosen the locknuts and turn both tie rods the same amount in the same direction (Fig. 51-29). On one car, only 1/5-turn of the tie rods moves the steering-wheel rim 0.250 inch [6 mm] or 2 degrees.

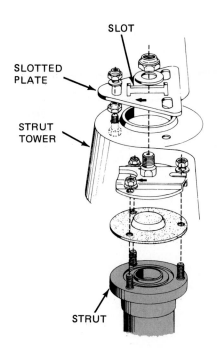

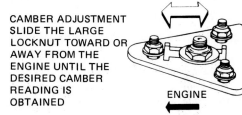

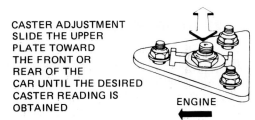

Fig. 51-27 Adjusting caster and camber on a MacPherson strut by repositioning the upper strut mount. (*Moog Automotive, Inc.*)

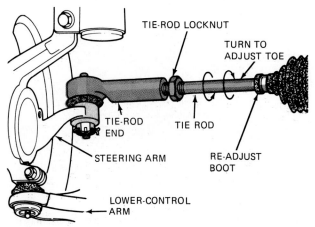

Fig. 51-28 Adjusting toe by changing the length of the tie rod. (*Chrysler Corporation*)

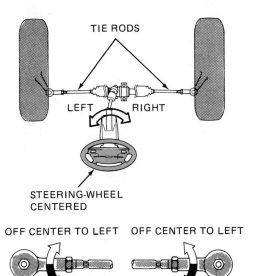

Fig. 51-29 Tie-rod adjustments to center the steering wheel. (*Chrysler Corporation*)

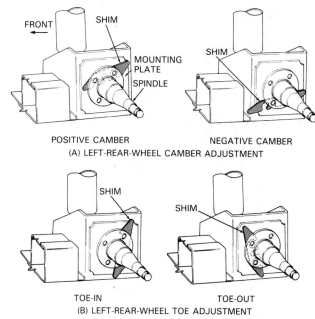

Fig. 51-31 Using shims to adjust rear-wheel camber and toe. Adjustments at the left-rear wheel are shown. (*Chrysler Corporation*)

> ## 51-38 REAR-WHEEL ALIGNMENT

Many front-wheel-drive vehicles have stub axles or spindles on which the rear hubs and wheels mount. Rear-wheel camber and toe may be adjustable. Rear-wheel caster is usually set to zero and is not adjustable. Various methods of adjusting rear-wheel camber and toe are described below. Refer to the vehicle service manual for rear-wheel alignment procedures on specific vehicles.

1. ADJUSTING REAR-WHEEL CAMBER In some vehicles, camber is adjusted by turning a cam bolt in the inner end of the lower-control arm or *spindle-support rod* (Fig. 51-30). On other vehicles, shims placed between the spindle and the mounting plate provide the camber adjustment (Fig. 51-31A).

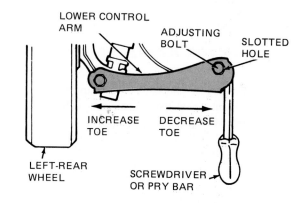

(A) ADJUSTING CONTROL-ARM POSITION

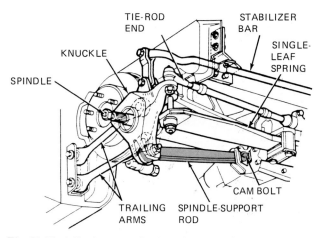

Fig. 51-30 Adjusting rear-wheel camber by turning a cam bolt in the inner end of the lower-control arm, or spindle-support rod. (*Chevrolet Division of General Motors Corporation*)

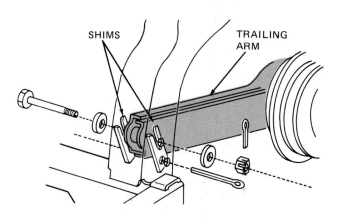

(B) SHIMMING THE TRAILING ARMS

Fig. 51-32 Adjusting rear-wheel toe by (A) adjusting control-arm position and (B) shimming the trailing arms. (*Buick Division of General Motors Corporation; Dana Corportion*)

2. ADJUSTING REAR-WHEEL TOE One method of adjusting rear-wheel toe is a slotted hole in the inner end of the lower-control arm (Fig. 51-32A). This allows changing the position of the control arm by loosening the bolts and prying the control arm in the proper direction. A second method uses shims on the two sides of the rear-suspension trailing arms (Fig. 51-32B). Changing the shim thickness on either side changes the toe. A third method uses shims placed between the stub axle or spindle and mounting plate (Fig. 51-31B). A fourth method uses tie rods that attach to the rear-wheel knuckle (Fig. 51-30). Lengthening or shortening the tie rods changes rear-wheel toe.

➤ 51-39 AFTER-ALIGNMENT PROBLEMS

Sometimes the front wheels are within specifications but the vehicle pulls or drifts. Either wheel setback or improper thrust angle is probably the cause. The problem is avoided by performing a four-wheel alignment and aligning the rear wheels first.

A possible cause of drift or pull after a four-wheel alignment is *tire conicity*. This is the condition when a radial tire is out-of-round because the tire was made with the center belt off-center. One side of the tire is slightly larger in diameter than the other side. The result is that the tire rolls slightly to one side, as does a cone. The condition is more noticeable when the affected tire is mounted on a front wheel.

To locate and correct a tire-conicity problem (or a tire with a different circumference), inflate all tires to the same air pressure. Swap the front wheels and road test the vehicle. If it now pulls in the opposite direction, swap the left-front and left-rear tires. If the pull is gone, the tire now on the left-rear is defective. If the pull still exists, swap the right-front and right-rear tires. If the pull is gone, the tire now on the right-rear is defective. If the vehicle still pulls, the tires are not causing the problem.

TRADE TALK

cam bolt	pull	short rack	wheel alignment
four-wheel alignment	rack yoke	strut cartridge	
individual toe	returnability	total toe	

MULTIPLE-CHOICE TEST

*Select the **one** correct, best, or most probable answer to each question.*
You can find the answers in the section indicated at the end of each question.

1. A right front wheel has too much negative caster. The result will be (➤51-6)
   a. a feathered edge on the inside of the tire tread
   b. a feathered edge on the outside of the tire tread
   c. pulling to the right
   d. pulling to the left

2. A car has no brake problem but pulls to one side during braking. Technician A says the most likely cause is improper toe. Technician B says the most likely cause is worn bushings in a lower-control arm. Who is right? (➤51-7)
   a. A only
   b. B only
   c. both A and B
   d. neither A nor B

3. A car with rack-and-pinion steering has a shimmy. Technician A says improper rack-yoke clearance could be the cause. Technician B says loose rack ball sockets or tie-rod ends could be the cause. Who is right? (➤51-8)
   a. A only
   b. B only
   c. both A and B
   d. neither A nor B

4. A feathered edge on the inside tread of only one front tire may be caused by (➤51-13)
   a. excessive toe-in or a bent steering arm
   b. too much toe-out
   c. a loose wheel bearing
   d. excessive positive caster

5. If a torsion-bar front-suspension system sags, restore proper suspension height by (➤51-17)
   a. replacing the torsion bar
   b. replacing the shock absorber
   c. adjusting the torsion bar
   d. replacing the ball joints
6. A car with power steering has a buzzing noise at fast idle when the wheels are straight ahead. Turning the steering wheel causes the noise to stop. The cause could be (➤51-18)
   a. a defective power-steering pump
   b. worn steering-gear mounting bushings
   c. excessive steering-wheel freeplay
   d. a sticking pressure control valve
7. After replacing the ball joints in a MacPherson-strut front suspension (➤51-24)
   a. compress coil spring
   b. replace the upper strut mount
   c. adjust the wheel bearings
   d. check the wheel alignment

8. Unequal rear-wheel toe (➤51-32)
   a. creates a thrust angle
   b. causes the steering wheel to be off-center
   c. changes caster
   d. affects vehicle suspension height
9. The adjustable wheel-alignment angles are (➤51-33)
   a. steering-axis inclination, caster, and camber
   b. turning radius, setback, and thrust angle
   c. toe, suspension height, and included angle
   d. caster, camber, and toe
10. Methods of adjusting camber on MacPherson struts include all the following EXCEPT (➤51-35)
    a. adding or removing shims
    b. turning a cam bolt
    c. moving the upper strut mount inward or outward
    d. enlarging the strut bolt holes with a file

REVIEW QUESTIONS

1. What is a "dry-park check" and how is it made? (➤51-21)
2. Describe how to check and adjust wheel bearings. (➤51-23 and 51-27)
3. What is a "short rack" and how is it installed? (➤51-28)

4. Explain how to replace a MacPherson strut. (➤51-29)
5. What are the advantages of a four-wheel alignment? (➤51- 32)

CHAPTER 52

AUTOMOTIVE BRAKES

After studying this chapter, you should be able to:

- Describe the construction and operation of the dual braking system.
- List two types of drum brakes and describe their construction and operation.
- List three types of disc brakes and describe their construction and operation.
- Describe the construction and operation of two types of power brakes.
- Explain the purpose and construction of parking brakes.

➤ 52-1 AUTOMOTIVE BRAKES

Figure 52-1 shows the brake system in an automobile. It has two types of brakes:

1. The *service brakes,* operated by a foot pedal, which slow or stop the vehicle.

2. The *parking brakes,* operated by a foot pedal or hand lever, which hold the vehicle stationary when applied.

Most automotive services brakes are *hydraulic brakes.* They operate hydraulically by pressure applied through a liquid. The service or *foundation brakes* on many medium- and heavy-duty trucks and buses are operated by air

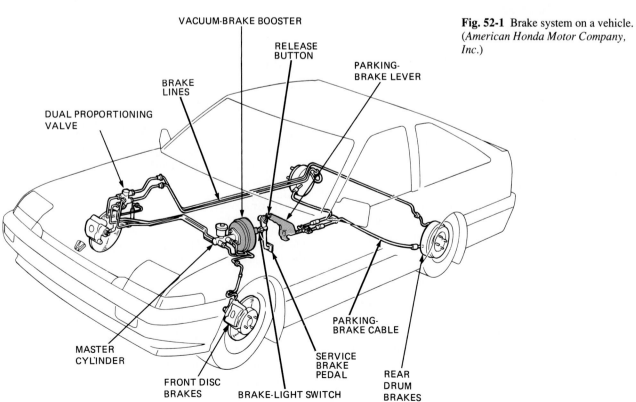

Fig. 52-1 Brake system on a vehicle. (*American Honda Motor Company, Inc.*)

VACUUM-BRAKE BOOSTER

RELEASE BUTTON

PARKING-BRAKE LEVER

BRAKE LINES

DUAL PROPORTIONING VALVE

MASTER CYLINDER

FRONT DISC BRAKES

BRAKE-LIGHT SWITCH

SERVICE BRAKE PEDAL

PARKING-BRAKE CABLE

REAR DRUM BRAKES

pressure (*pneumatic*). These are *air brakes*. Many boat and camping trailers have *electric brakes*. All these braking systems depend on friction (➤52-2) between moving parts and stationary parts for their stopping force.

FRICTION AND BRAKING

➤ 52-2 FRICTION

Friction is the resistance to motion between two objects in contact with each other. It varies with the force applied between the sliding surfaces (the *load*), the roughness of the surfaces, and the material of which the surfaces are made. The amount of friction also depends on whether a fluid, such as oil, is between the surfaces to provide lubrication (Chap. 24).

The three types of friction are *dry, greasy,* and *viscous* (➤15-6). The automotive braking system uses *dry friction* to produce braking action.

➤ 52-3 FRICTION OF REST AND MOTION

More force is required to put an object into motion than is required to keep it moving (Fig. 52-2). In Fig. 52-2, it takes two persons to start the object moving. After it is moving, one person can keep it moving.

The *friction of rest* is greater than the *friction of motion*. These two kinds of friction are *static friction* and *kinetic friction*. *Static* means at rest. *Kinetic* means in motion. Static friction is greater than kinetic friction.

➤ 52-4 FRICTION IN VEHICLE BRAKES

When the brakes are applied by pushing down on the brake pedal, a fluid flows through tubes or *brake lines* (Fig. 52-1) to the brake mechanisms at the wheels. The brake mechanisms apply force on rotating parts so the wheels are slowed or stopped. There are two types of wheel-brake mechanisms (Fig. 52-3), *drum* and *disc*. In the *drum brake* (➤52-11), the fluid pressure pushes lined *brake shoes* against a rotating drum. In the *disc brake,* the fluid pushes lined *brake pads* against a rotating disc.

Friction between the stationary shoes or pads and the rotating drum or disc produces the braking action that slows or stops the wheels. Then friction between the tires and road slows and stops the vehicle.

If the brakes are applied so hard that the wheels lock, the friction between the tires and road is kinetic friction. If the brakes are applied less hard, the wheels continue to rotate. The resulting friction is static friction. Since static friction is greater than kinetic friction (➤52-3), the vehicle stops in a shorter distance if the wheels do not lock. However, the brakes must be applied to the point at which the wheels are almost ready to lock.

FRICTION OF REST (STATIC FRICTION)

FRICTION OF MOTION (KINETIC FRICTION)

Fig. 52-2 Friction of rest is greater than friction of motion. In the example shown, it takes two people to overcome the friction of rest (static friction). But one person can keep the object moving by overcoming the friction of motion (kinetic friction).

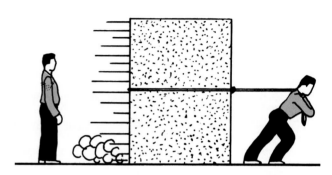

Fig. 52-3 Two types of friction brakes used in automotive vehicles. (*Robert Bosch Corporation*)

That is the principle of the *anti-braking system* (ABS). It prevents wheel lockup and tire skidding during hard breaking. The result is shorter, quicker, and controlled stops. The operation and diagnosis of antilock-braking systems are described in Chap. 53.

HYDRAULICS

➤ 52-5 MEANING OF HYDRAULICS

Hydraulics is the use of a liquid under pressure to transfer force or motion, or to increase an applied force. Pressure on a liquid is called *hydraulic pressure*. It is hydraulic pressure that forces the brake shoes or pads into contact with the rotating drum or disc to produce braking.

➤ 52-6 INCOMPRESSIBILITY OF LIQUIDS

Increasing the pressure on a gas will compress it into a smaller volume (Fig. 52-4). However, increasing the pressure on a liquid will not compress it. The liquid is *incompressible*. This makes it possible to use the pressure on liquids in hydraulic systems to transmit force or motion.

➤ 52-7 TRANSMISSION OF MOTION BY A LIQUID

Figure 52-5 shows two pistons in a cylinder, with a liquid between the pistons. When the *input* or *apply piston* is pushed in 8 inches [203 mm], the *output piston* will be pushed the same distance.

Motion can be sent from one cylinder to another by a tube (Fig. 52-6). As the apply piston moves, it forces pressurized fluid through the tube and into the other cylinder. This forces the output piston to move.

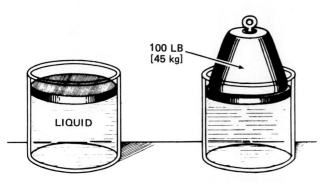

Fig. 52-4 Gas can be compressed when pressure is applied. However, a liquid cannot be compressed.

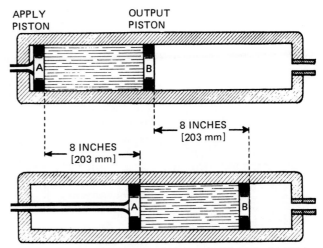

Fig. 52-5 Force and motion can be transmitted by a liquid. When the apply piston is moved 8 inches [203 mm] in the cylinder, the output piston also moves 8 inches [203 mm].

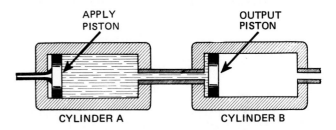

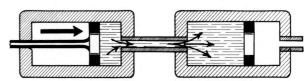

Fig. 52-6 Force and motion can be transmitted through a tube from one cylinder to another by a liquid, or hydraulic pressure.

➤ 52-8 TRANSFERRING FORCE BY A LIQUID

The force that is applied to a liquid is transmitted by the liquid in all directions to every part of the liquid. The piston in Fig. 52-7 has an area of 1 square inch [6.45 cubic centimeters (cc)]. It is applying a force of 100 pounds [445 N]. This is 100 pounds per square inch (psi) [690 kPa]. Note that regardless of position, all gauges in Fig. 52-7 show a pressure of 100 psi.

The size of the piston also determines pressure (Fig. 52-8). In Fig. 52-8B, the piston area is increased to 2 square inches. When the same force of 100 pounds is applied over double the area, the resulting pressure is only 50 psi [345 kPa].

Figure 52-9 shows a hydraulic system with output pistons of different sizes. The bigger the output piston, the greater the output force. For example, in a disc-brake system (➤52-15), an apply force of 100 pounds causes a

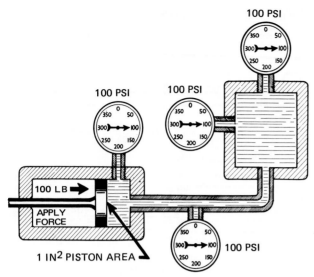

Fig. 52-7 The pressure applied to a liquid is applied equally in all directions. (*Pontiac Division of General Motors Corporation*)

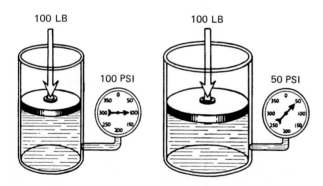

(A) 1 IN² PISTON AREA   (B) 2 IN² PISTON AREA

Fig. 52-8 Pressure in a hydraulic system is determined by dividing the apply force by the area of the apply piston. (*Pontiac Division of General Motors Corporation*)

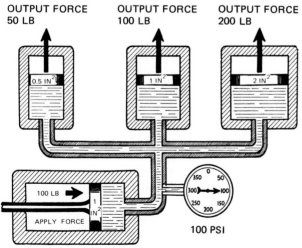

Fig. 52-9 The force applied to the output piston is the pressure in the system (in pounds per square inch) times the area of the output piston (in square inches). (*Pontiac Division of General Motors Corporation*)

smaller-diameter piston in the *master cylinder* (➤52-24) to travel a relatively long distance. The resulting hydraulic pressure then moves a much larger piston in the disc brake a relatively short distance. However, the larger piston has a greatly increased output force.

BRAKES AND BRAKING

➤ 52-9 BRAKE ACTION

The service braking system (Figs. 52-1 and 52-10) includes two basic parts. These are the master cylinder and the drum and disc wheel-brake mechanisms (➤52-4). The master cylinder is a reciprocating-piston pump. It pressurizes the hydraulic system when the driver depresses the brake pedal. This converts the mechanical force from the brake pedal into hydraulic force that applies the brakes at the wheels.

Braking begins at the brake pedal (Fig. 52-10). When the pedal is pushed down, *brake fluid* (➤52-27) is forced from the master cylinder into the lines to the wheel brakes. As hydraulic pressure increases, brake shoes or pads are forced against the rotating drums or discs. The resulting friction slows or stops the wheels and the vehicle.

Figure 52-10 shows the basic service-brake hydraulic system. There are two pistons in the master cylinder. The spaces ahead of the pistons form two pressure chambers. When the pedal is pushed down, the pistons are pushed toward the closed end of the master cylinder. In Fig. 52-10,

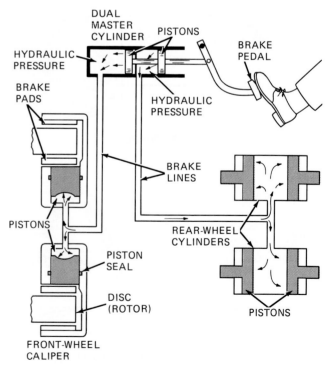

Fig. 52-10 Flow of brake fluid to the calipers at the front and to the wheel cylinder at the rear when the brakes are applied. (*ATW*)

this sends fluid from the front pressure chamber to the front-wheel brakes. Fluid from the rear chamber is sent to the rear-wheel brakes. All four brakes then operate to slow or stop the vehicle. This arrangement using a two-piston *tandem* or *dual master cylinder* is a *dual braking system*.

➤ 52-10 DUAL BRAKING SYSTEM

In a dual braking system, the hydraulic system has a *primary section* and a *secondary section* (Fig. 52-11). The primary section is always closest to the fire wall. However, the dual braking system is hydraulically separated or *split* in different ways. Most vehicles with rear-wheel drive use the *front-rear split* (Figs. 52-10 and 52-11A). Many front-wheel-drive vehicles use the *diagonal split* (Figs. 52-1 and 52-11B).

Splitting the hydraulic system into two sections improves vehicle safety. One section will continue to work and stop the vehicle if the other section leaks and fails. Both sections seldom fail at the same time. In earlier braking systems, there was only one piston in the master cylinder and one hydraulic system. A leak or failure anywhere in the hydraulic system usually meant there were no brakes.

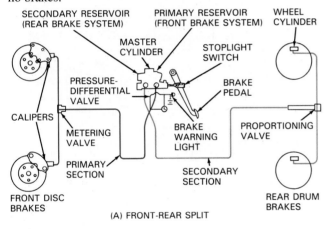

(A) FRONT-REAR SPLIT

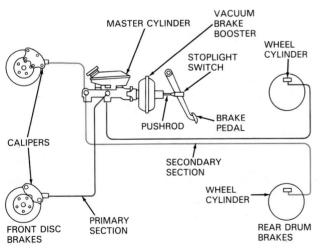

(B) DIAGONAL SPLIT

Fig. 52-11 Two basic types of hydraulically-split braking systems. (*Ford Motor Company*)

DRUM BRAKES

➤ 52-11 DRUM-BRAKE CONSTRUCTION

The drum brake (Fig. 52-12) has a metal *brake drum* that encloses the brake assembly at each wheel. Two curved brake shoes expand outward to slow or stop the drum which rotates with the wheel. The brake assembly attaches to a steering knuckle, axle housing, or strut-spindle assembly. Figure 52-12 shows a drum-brake assembly removed from the rear-wheel spindle on a front-drive car. Older cars and trucks have drum brakes at all four wheels. Newer vehicles using drum brakes have them only in the rear (Fig. 1-26).

> **NOTE** The construction and operation of front drum brakes are the same as rear drum brakes, which are described below. Most vehicles have rear-wheel parking brakes, however (➤52-18). These parts are not included in a front drum brake.

Figure 52-13 shows the parts in typical *leading-trailing* and *duo-servo* drum brakes. The bottoms of the shoes are held apart by *anchor pins* (Fig. 52-13A) attached to the backing plate, or by a floating *adjusting screw* (Fig. 52-13B). The tops of the shoes are held apart by the *wheel cylinder* (➤52-12).

Brake shoes are made of metal (Fig. 52-14). A facing of friction material called *brake lining* is riveted or cemented (*bonded*) to the shoes. The linings are usually made of non-asbestos material such as fiberglass or a semimetallic material that can withstand the heat-producing braking action. Asbestos lining has been used, but is being phased out because of its danger to human health (➤4-6).

➤ 52-12 WHEEL CYLINDER

When the driver depresses the brake pedal, brake fluid flows from a pressure chamber in the master cylinder through brake lines to the *wheel cylinder* (Fig. 52-15). It converts the hydraulic pressure from the master cylinder into mechanical movement. The wheel cylinder has two pistons, with seals or *cups,* and a spring in between. As the pressure increases, the pistons overcome the *brake-shoe return springs* and push the shoes outward into contact with the drum.

In vehicles with four-wheel drum brakes, the front wheel-cylinder pistons are usually larger than the pistons in the rear wheel cylinders. This produces the greater braking force required on the front wheels. Braking transfers more of the vehicle weight to the front wheels.

➤ 52-13 DRUM-BRAKE OPERATION

Figure 52-13 shows two types of drum brakes. The leading-trailing or *non-servo* brake is used on the rear

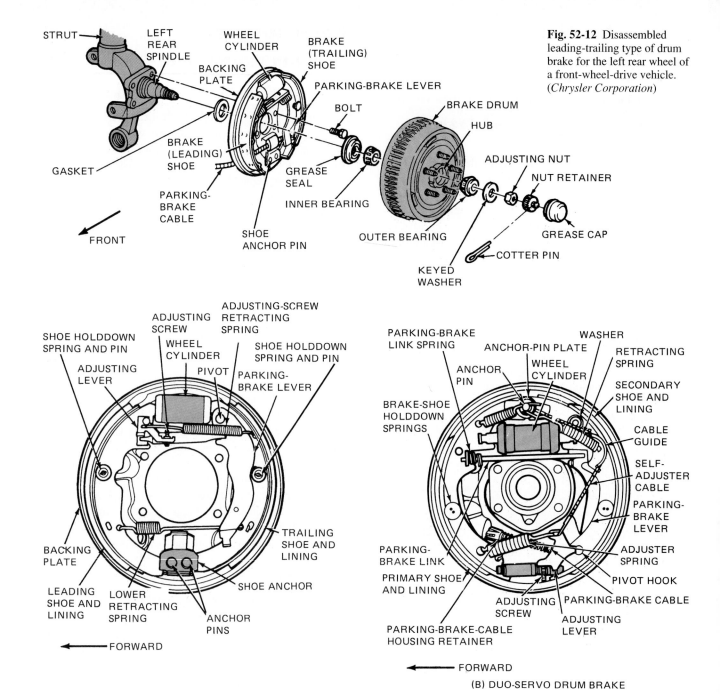

Fig. 52-12 Disassembled leading-trailing type of drum brake for the left rear wheel of a front-wheel-drive vehicle. (*Chrysler Corporation*)

(A) LEADING-TRAILING DRUM BRAKE

(B) DUO-SERVO DRUM BRAKE

Fig. 52-13 Parts in a (A) leading-trailing drum brake compared with (B) a duo-servo drum brake. (*Ford Motor Company*)

wheels of many front-drive vehicles. Rear-drive vehicles usually have duo-servo rear brakes. In a duo-servo brake, the action of one shoe reinforces the action of the other shoe. In a leading-trailing brake, the action of one shoe does not affect the other.

1. LEADING-TRAILING DRUM BRAKE (FIG. 52-13A) The return or *retracting* springs hold both shoes against the wheel cylinder at the top, and against fixed anchor pins at the bottom. Depressing the brake pedal causes the wheel-cylinder pistons to move the tops of the

shoes outward against the drums. Friction between the forward or *leading shoe* and the drum causes the leading shoe to try to rotate with the drum. This *self-energizing* action of the leading shoe forces the bottom of the shoe against the anchor pin. As a result, the leading shoe does most of the braking.

When the rear or *trailing shoe* contacts the drum, drum rotation tries to force the shoe away from the drum. There is no self-energizing action. Therefore, the trailing shoe usually wears less than the leading shoe. The leading and trailing shoes swap jobs when the vehicle is braked while

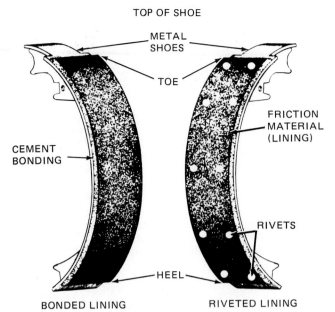

Fig. 52-14 Two methods of attaching the brake lining to the drum-brake shoe. (*Bendix Corporation*)

moving in reverse. This brake is less self-energizing and more dependent on the force supplied by the wheel cylinder than the duo-servo described below.

2. DUO-SERVO DRUM BRAKE (FIG. 52-13B) The tops of the shoes rest against a single anchor pin. The bottoms of the shoes are linked together by a floating adjusting screw. The shoe toward the front of the vehicle is the *primary shoe*. The shoe toward the rear is the *secondary shoe*. The primary shoe normally has shorter lining than the secondary shoe.

When the shoes contact the rotating drum, the friction causes both shoes to try to rotate with the drum. The top of the primary shoe tends to pull into the drum and move

downward. The bottom of the shoe then pushes the adjusting screw rearward. This forces the bottom of the secondary shoe against the drum which moves the secondary shoe upward against the anchor pin. Further drum rotation tends to pull both shoes more tightly into the drum. This further increases the self-energizing action of the secondary shoe.

In a duo-servo brake, the self-energizing action of both shoes make total braking force greater than the amount supplied by the wheel cylinder. The secondary shoe has longer lining because it provides about twice as much braking force as the primary shoe. The functions of each shoe change when braking with the vehicle moving in reverse.

➤ 52-14 DRUM-BRAKE SELF-ADJUSTERS

Most drum brakes self-adjust to compensate for lining wear. This prevents the brake pedal from getting lower and lower during normal use. Two types of *self-adjusters* used on leading-trailing brakes are the *one-shot* (Fig. 52-12) and the *incremental* (Fig. 52-13A). The one-shot makes a single adjustment when the clearance between the lining and drum reaches a preset gap. Then no additional adjustments can be made. The shoes must be replaced and the self-adjuster reset.

Figure 52-13A shows a leading-trailing brake with an incremental adjuster. It moves the shoes outward whenever the gap is large enough to turn the adjusting screw. Adjustment occurs when the vehicle is braked while moving either forward or rearward. As the brake shoes move outward, the *adjusting-screw retracting spring* causes the adjusting lever to pivot upward. If the lining is worn enough, the lever moves above the end of the next tooth on the adjusting wheel. When the brakes are released, the

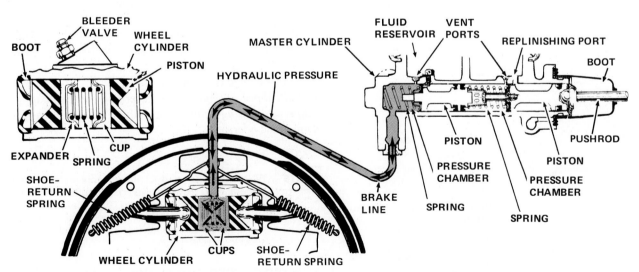

Fig. 52-15 Conditions in the drum-brake system when the brakes are released. Brake fluid leaves the wheel cylinder (upper left) and returns to the master cylinder (upper right), as shown by the arrows. (*Buick Division of General Motors Corporation*)

adjuster lever pivots downward. This turns the tooth. The adjusting screw then lengthens slightly to move the shoes closer to the drum.

Figures 52-13B and 52-16 show an incremental self-adjuster attached to the secondary shoe of a duo-servo brake. An *adjusting lever* attaches to a self-adjuster cable that passes around a *cable guide* and fastens to the anchor pin. The adjustment is made when the vehicle is moving backward and the brakes are applied. Then friction forces the upper end of the primary shoe against the anchor pin. The wheel cylinder forces the upper end of the secondary shoe away from the anchor pin and downward. This causes the cable to pull the adjusting lever upward by pivoting in a hole in the secondary shoe. If the brake linings have worn enough, the lever passes over and engages the end of a new tooth on the adjusting wheel.

When the brakes are released, the *adjuster spring* (Fig. 52-16) pulls the adjusting lever downward. This turns the tooth and slightly lengthens the adjusting screw. The brake shoes move closer to the drum.

| NOTE | Some vehicles have a self-adjuster that works only when the brakes are applied while the vehicle is moving backward. In other vehicles, self-adjustment occurs only when the parking brake is applied. The brakes can get out of adjustment (Chap. 53) if the vehicle is not moved in reverse or if the driver does not set the parking brake. |

DISC BRAKES

➤ 52-15 TYPES OF DISC BRAKES

The disc brake (Fig. 52-17) has a metal disc or *rotor* instead of a drum. It uses a pair of flat, lined shoes or *pads* that are forced against the rotating disc to produce braking. The pads are held in a *caliper* (Figs. 52-17 and 52-18) that straddles the disc. The caliper has one or more pistons,

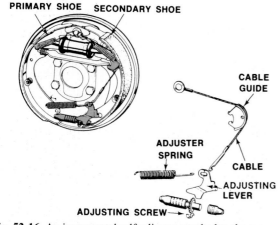

Fig. 52-16 An incremental self-adjuster attached to the secondary shoe of a duo-servo brake. The self-adjuster parts are shown disassembled to the right. (*Bendix Corporation*)

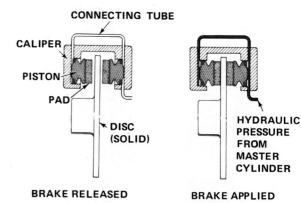

Fig. 52-17 Principle of the disc brake. Left, two brake shoes, or pads, and pistons are positioned on the two sides of a rotating disc. Right, when the brakes are applied, the shoes are forced into frictional contact with the disc, producing the braking action.

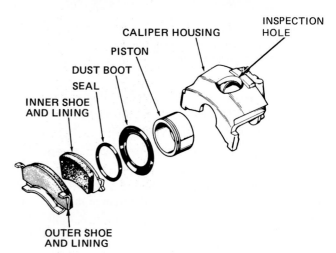

Fig. 52-18 Disassembled sliding caliper, which straddles the disc.

with a seal and dust boot for each. During braking, hydraulic pressure behind each piston in Fig. 52-17 pushes it outward. This forces the pad into contact with the disc. The resulting frictional contact slows and stops the disc and wheel.

There are three types of disc brakes. Figure 52-17 shows a *fixed-caliper* disc brake. The other two are the *floating-caliper* and *sliding-caliper*. Each differs in how the caliper mounts and operates.

| NOTE | All three types of disc brakes work in the same general way. However, vehicle manufacturers have used many variations of each. Typical examples are described below. Refer to the vehicle service manual for information about the brakes on a specific vehicle. |

1. FIXED-CALIPER DISC BRAKE A fixed caliper (Figs. 52-17 and 52-19A) has pistons on both sides of the disc. Some use two pistons, one on each side. Others use four pistons with two on each side. The caliper is rigidly

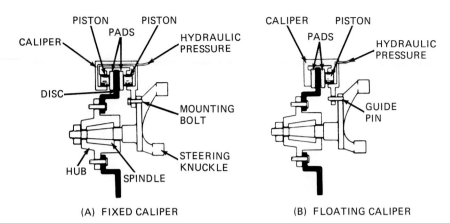

(A) FIXED CALIPER

(B) FLOATING CALIPER

attached to a steering knuckle or other stationary vehicle part. Only the pistons and pads move when the brakes are applied.

2. FLOATING-CALIPER DISC BRAKE A typical floating caliper (Figs. 52-19B and 52-20) has only one piston, located on the inboard side of the disc. The caliper moves or "floats" on rubber bushings on one or two steel *guide pins*. The bushings allow the caliper to move slightly when the brakes are applied. Some floating calipers have two pistons on the inboard side of the disc.

Applying the brakes causes brake fluid to flow into the caliper (Fig. 52-21). This pushes the piston outward so the *inboard shoe* is forced against the disc. At the same time, the pressure pushes against the caliper with an equal and opposite force. This reaction causes the caliper to move slightly on the bushings, bringing the *outboard shoe* into contact with the disc. The two pads clamp the disc to produce the braking action.

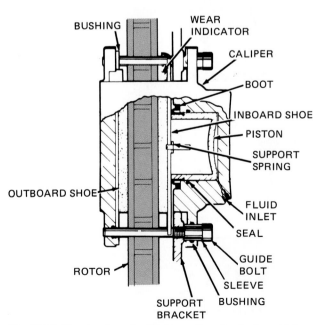

Fig. 52-20 Construction of a floating-caliper disc brake, which uses only one piston. (*Delco Moraine Division of General Motors Corporation*)

3. SLIDING-CALIPER DISC BRAKE Figure 51-12 shows a sliding-caliper disc brake. It is similar to the floating-caliper brake. Both calipers move slightly when the brakes are applied. However, the sliding caliper slides on machined surfaces on the steering-knuckle adapter or anchor plate. No guide pins are used.

➤ **52-16 SELF-ADJUSTMENT OF DISC BRAKES**

Disc brakes are self adjusting for wear. The caliper bore has a groove with a square-cut seal in it (Fig. 52-21). The seals fits tightly around the piston. When the brakes are applied, the piston moves toward the disc (Fig. 52-22). This deflects the seal but it continues to grip the piston. Releasing the brakes allows the seal to relax and return to its original position. This pulls the piston slightly away from the disc. However, the lining may remain in light contact with the disc.

As the lining wears, the piston-travel when the brakes are applied becomes greater than the amount the seal can deflect. The piston then slides outward through the seal and takes a new position. This self-adjustment moves the pad closer to the disc to compensate for lining wear.

The shape of the seal groove in the caliper determines how far the seal travels with the piston. This *seal deflection* determines how far the piston retracts into the caliper bore. Figure 52-22 shows the principle of a *low-drag brake caliper*. The forward edge of the seal groove is cut at an angle. This permits the seal to travel farther with the piston, and to retract the piston farther. With greater *piston retraction*, the lining does not touch the disc while the brakes are released. A *quick-takeup master cylinder* (➤52-26) is needed to quickly move the piston the greater distance when the brakes are applied.

➤ **52-17 DISC-BRAKE WEAR INDICATORS**

Many disc-brake shoes have an audible *wear indicator* on the shoe (Fig. 52-23). When the lining wears so thin that the pad should be replaced, the wear indicator rubs against

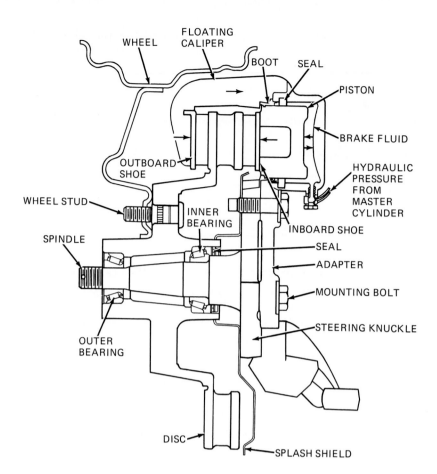

WHEEL

FLOATING
CALIPER

BOOT

SEAL

PISTON

BRAKE FLUID

HYDRAULIC
PRESSURE
FROM
MASTER
CYLINDER

OUTBOARD
SHOE

WHEEL STUD

INNER
BEARING

INBOARD SHOE

SEAL

SPINDLE

ADAPTER

MOUNTING BOLT

STEERING KNUCKLE

OUTER
BEARING

DISC

SPLASH SHIELD

Fig. 52-21 Actions in the floating-caliper disc brake (shown by the arrows) as applying the brakes forces brake fluid into the caliper. (*Chrysler Corporation*)

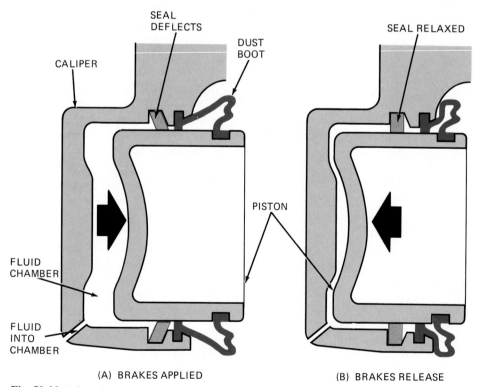

SEAL
DEFLECTS

DUST
BOOT

SEAL RELAXED

CALIPER

PISTON

FLUID
CHAMBER

FLUID
INTO
CHAMBER

(A) BRAKES APPLIED

(B) BRAKES RELEASE

Fig. 52-22 A low-drag brake caliper, showing (A) seal deflection as the brakes are applied and (B) piston retraction as the brakes are released. (*ATW*)

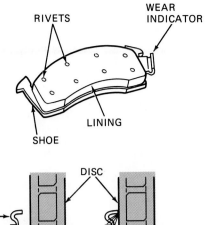

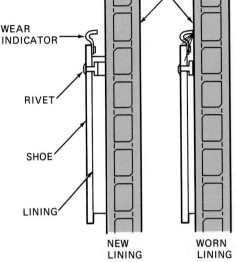

Fig. 52-23 Disc-brake shoe with an audible wear indicator. When the lining, or pad, gets so thin it should be replaced, the wear indicator scrapes the disc and makes a warning noise. (*Chevrolet Division of General Motors Corporation*)

the disc. This makes a loud scraping noise to alert the driver.

PARKING BRAKES

➤ 52-18 TYPES OF PARKING BRAKES

The *parking brake* mechanically applies the rear brakes (or front brakes in some vehicles) to hold the vehicle stationary while it is parked. The parking brake is operated by a hand lever (Fig. 52-1) or by a foot pedal. There are two types of parking brake, *integral* and *independent*.

1. *Integral Parking Brakes* These have parts that are common to both the service brakes and the parking brakes. The arrangements are different for rear drum brakes and rear disc brakes.

a. *Rear drum brake* (Fig. 52-13) A drum brake can be used as a parking brake by attaching a *parking-brake lever* to the rear brake shoe. A *parking-brake link* or *strut* is placed between the two brake shoes. When the *parking-brake cable* is pulled by the hand lever or foot pedal, it causes the parking-brake lever to pivot. The upper end of the lever forces the rear shoe into contact with the drum. At the same time, the section below the pivot forces the link or strut forward. This pushes the front shoe into the drum and applies the parking brake.

b. *Rear disc brake* (Fig. 52-24) This type of caliper has a piston that can be operated either hydraulically or mechanically. A large screw threads into a nut-and-cone assembly that fits inside the piston. When the

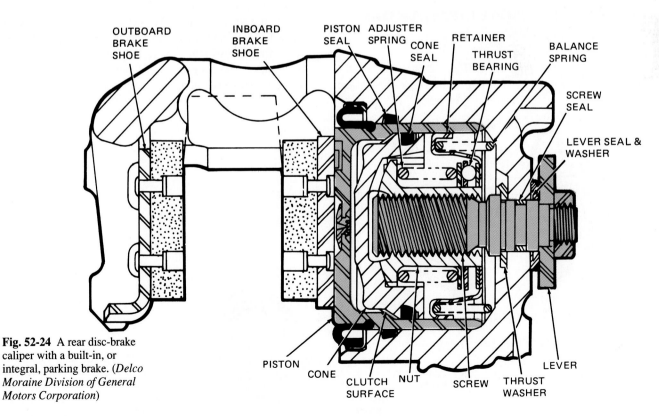

Fig. 52-24 A rear disc-brake caliper with a built-in, or integral, parking brake. (*Delco Moraine Division of General Motors Corporation*)

driver applies the parking brake, the parking-brake cable pulls the lever (Fig. 52-24) which rotates the screw. The nut then pushes the piston out. This forces the shoes into contact with the disc and applies the parking brake.

2. *Independent parking brakes* These share no parts with the service brakes. Figure 52-25 shows one type of drum-type parking brake used with rear-wheel disc brakes. A set of small brake shoes fits into the hub of the disc. The hub surface serves as the brake drum. Another type is the *transmission-mounted parking brake*. It uses a small drum brake mounted on the back of the transmission. The drum attaches to the output shaft.

➤ 52-19 PARKING-BRAKE CONTROLS

The parking-brake hand lever or foot pedal has a ratchet or latching arrangement to hold its position when the parking brake is set. Pushing a *release button* on the hand lever (Fig. 52-1) or pulling a *brake release* handle for the foot pedal releases the parking brake. Some foot pedals automatically release when the engine is running and the transmission is shifted away from PARK or NEUTRAL. This sends intake-manifold vacuum to a vacuum motor that releases the parking brake.

When the ignition key is ON, the instrument panel *brake warning light* (Fig. 17-32) turns on if the parking brake is applied. The light (➤52-20) also illuminates if the parking brake is not fully released.

BRAKE-SYSTEM VALVES

➤ 52-20 PRESSURE-DIFFERENTIAL VALVE

The *pressure-differential valve* (Fig. 52-26) turns on the instrument-panel BRAKE warning light (Figs. 17-32 and

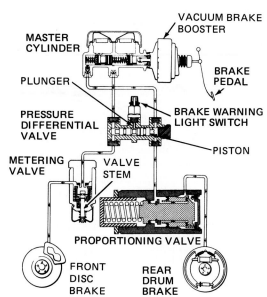

Fig. 52-26 Valves used in the hydraulic system of a vehicle with front-disc and rear-drum brakes. (*Ford Motor Company*)

52-11A) if either section of the hydraulic system loses pressure. The pressure loss on one side of the piston causes it to move toward the side with the lowest pressure. This raises the plunger which closes the switch and turns on the light.

➤ 52-21 METERING VALVE

Many cars with front-disc and rear-drum brakes have a *hold-off valve* or *metering valve* in the line to the front brakes (Figs. 52-11A and 52-26). During light braking, the metering valve prevents the front disc brakes from applying until after the rear brakes start to apply. Disc brakes can act slightly faster than drum brakes. If the front brakes apply first, the weight shift to the front wheels can cause the front end to dip excessively and the rear tires to skid. This condition usually indicates a bad metering valve.

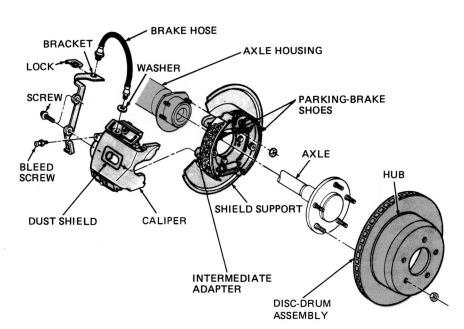

Fig. 52-25 A disassembled sliding-caliper disc brake for a rear wheel. A small independent drum-type parking brake fits into the disc hub. (*Chrysler Corporation*)

Vehicles with four-wheel drum brakes or four-wheel disc brakes may not need a metering valve. Brakes of the same type generally require the same amount of time to apply.

➤ 52-22 PROPORTIONING VALVE

A *proportioning valve* (Figs. 52-1 and 52-26) is used in the rear brake line of some vehicles with front-disc and rear-drum brakes. During hard braking, more vehicle weight transfers to the front wheels. As a result, less braking is needed at the rear wheels. Equal brake pressures could cause the rear wheels to lock and the rear tires to skid.

The proportioning valve has no affect on hydraulic pressure during normal braking. However, hard braking causes the fluid pressure to go above a preset value called the *split point*. The proportioning valve then reduces the amount of pressure increase to the rear drum brakes according to a certain ratio. A vehicle with a diagonally-split hydraulic system (➤52-10) has two proportioning valves, one in each rear-brake section of the hydraulic system. These proportioning valves may be in the master-cylinder outlets (➤52-24) or combined in a separate *dual proportioning valve* (Fig. 52-1).

Some light-duty trucks have a rear-mounted *load-* or *height-sensing proportioning valve* (Fig. 52-27). It adjusts the pressure to the rear brakes according to a change in load or rear body height. When the truck has a light load, a lever partially closes the proportioning valve. This reduces hydraulic pressure to the rear brakes. A heavy load opens the proportioning valve which increases the hydraulic pressure.

Some vehicles with an antilock-braking system (ABS) may not require a proportioning valve. The antilock braking system (Chap. 53) prevents wheel lockup.

➤ 52-23 COMBINATION VALVE

Many vehicles with front-disc and rear-drum brakes use a *combination valve* (Fig. 52-28). It combines the pressure-

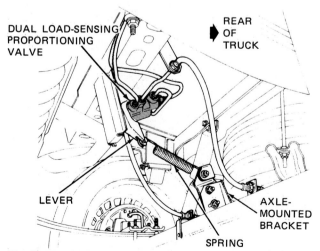

Fig. 52-27 Load-sensing proportioning valve at the rear of a light-duty truck. (*Chrysler Corporation*)

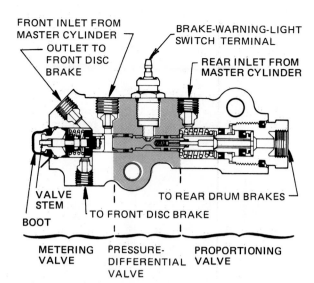

Fig. 52-28 Combination valve with warning-light switch, metering valve, and proportioning valve all in the same assembly. (*Delco Moraine Division of General Motors Corporation*)

differential valve, metering valve, and proportioning valve in a single assembly.

MASTER CYLINDER

➤ 52-24 MASTER-CYLINDER CONSTRUCTION

Figure 52-29 shows an older *integral master cylinder*. It has a single-piece cast-iron body with a dual reservoir. Most vehicles now use a *composite master cylinder* (Fig. 52-30). A separate plastic reservoir attaches to the aluminum body with rubber grommets or seals. Some master cylinders have a built-in *fluid-level sensor* in the reservoirs. The sensor turns on a warning light in the instrument panel when brake fluid is low.

Integral and composite master cylinders work in the same way. Two pistons move back and forth in a common bore (Fig. 52-30). The space in front of each piston serves as a fluid chamber that is kept filled by the reservoir above it. The *primary piston* is closest to the fire wall and directly operated by the pushrod from the brake pedal. The *secondary piston* is ahead of the primary piston.

Two holes in the bottom of each reservoir open into the cylinder bore (Fig. 52-30). The front hole is the *vent port*. The other hole is the *replenishing port*. While the brakes are not applied, fluid flows through the vent ports to fill the high-pressure chamber ahead of each piston. When the piston moves forward as the brakes are applied, the piston pushes the seal or *cup* past the vent port (Fig. 52-31A). This traps the fluid which is forced through the brake lines and hoses. The resulting pressure increase then moves the pistons in the wheel cylinders (Fig. 52-15) and calipers (Fig. 52-19) to apply the brakes at the wheels.

The replenishing port allows fluid from the reservoir to

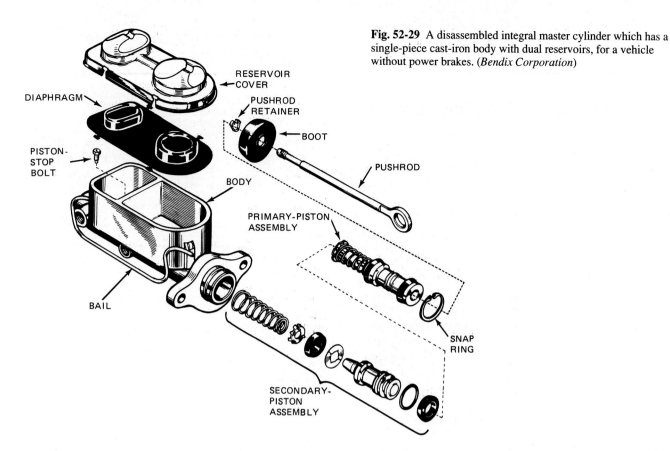

Fig. 52-29 A disassembled integral master cylinder which has a single-piece cast-iron body with dual reservoirs, for a vehicle without power brakes. (*Bendix Corporation*)

RESERVOIR COVER

DIAPHRAGM

PUSHROD RETAINER

BOOT

PUSHROD

PISTON-STOP BOLT

BODY

PRIMARY-PISTON ASSEMBLY

BAIL

SNAP RING

SECONDARY-PISTON ASSEMBLY

fill the low-pressure chamber behind the piston (Fig. 52-31B). When the brakes are released, *return springs* in the master cylinder force the pistons to return to their released positions faster than fluid can flow back to the master cylinder. This tends to create a momentary vacuum.

To prevent a vacuum from forming, fluid flows from the reservoir through the replenishing ports into the low-pressure chamber (Fig. 52-31B). The fluid passes through small holes in the pistons, around the cups, and into the high-pressure chambers. Instead of holes, some pistons have additional piston clearance to allow fluid-flow around the outside of the seal.

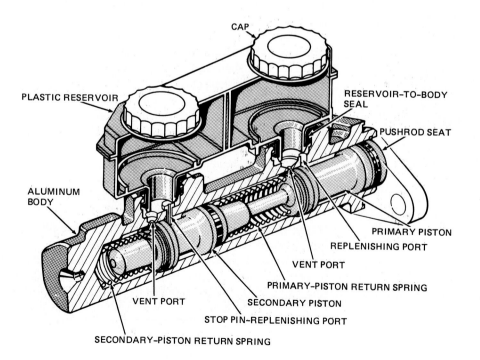

Fig. 52-30 A composite master cylinder, with a separate plastic reservoir that attaches to the aluminum body. (*Chrysler Corporation*)

CAP

PLASTIC RESERVOIR

RESERVOIR-TO-BODY SEAL

PUSHROD SEAT

ALUMINUM BODY

PRIMARY PISTON

REPLENISHING PORT

VENT PORT

PRIMARY-PISTON RETURN SPRING

SECONDARY PISTON

STOP PIN-REPLENISHING PORT

SECONDARY-PISTON RETURN SPRING

VENT PORT

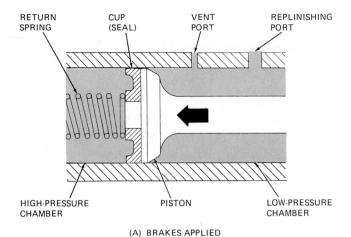

RETURN SPRING   CUP (SEAL)   VENT PORT   REPLENISHING PORT

HIGH-PRESSURE CHAMBER   PISTON   LOW-PRESSURE CHAMBER

(A) BRAKES APPLIED

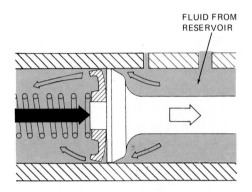

FLUID FROM RESERVOIR

(B) BRAKES RELEASED

Fig. 52-31 Actions of a master-cylinder piston and cup with the (A) brakes applied and (B) brakes released. (*ATW*)

➤ 52-25 RESIDUAL CHECK VALVE

Some master cylinders used mostly with drum brakes have *residual check valves* in the outlets to the wheel cylinders. The check valves close soon after the brake pedal is released. This maintains a slight *residual line pressure* of about 6 to 18 psi [41 to 124 kPa] in the brake lines. The pressure keeps the cups in the wheel cylinders expanded against their bores. This helps prevent brake fluid from leaking out and air from leaking in.

Most master cylinders do not have check valves. *Expanders* (Fig. 52-15) placed in the wheel-cylinder cups do the same job.

➤ 52-26 QUICK-TAKEUP MASTER CYLINDER

Figure 52-32 shows a *quick-takeup master cylinder*. It is used with low-drag brake calipers (➤52-16) to reduce brake drag and improve fuel economy. When the brake pedal is released, the pads are pulled completely away from the disc. This forces a fairly large volume of fluid out of the calipers and back into the master cylinder.

In the quick-takeup master cylinder, the primary piston works in a *step bore* that has two different diameters (Fig. 52-32). Initial movement of the piston forces a large amount of fluid from the low-pressure chamber, past the primary-piston lip seal, and into the primary high pressure chamber. This large amount of fluid quickly applies the

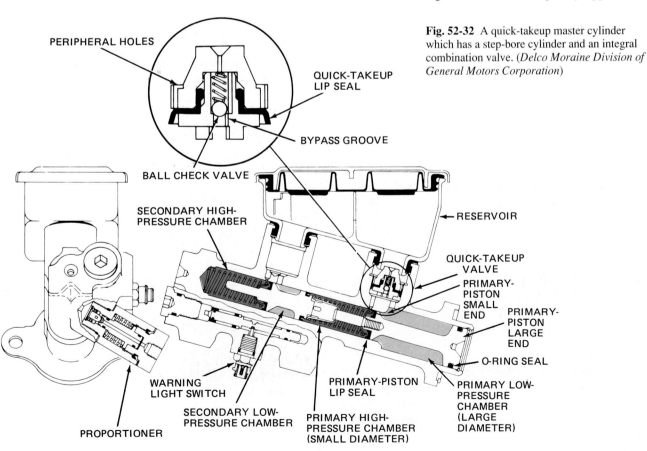

PERIPHERAL HOLES

QUICK-TAKEUP LIP SEAL

BYPASS GROOVE

BALL CHECK VALVE

SECONDARY HIGH-PRESSURE CHAMBER

RESERVOIR

QUICK-TAKEUP VALVE

PRIMARY-PISTON SMALL END

PRIMARY-PISTON LARGE END

O-RING SEAL

PRIMARY LOW-PRESSURE CHAMBER (LARGE DIAMETER)

WARNING LIGHT SWITCH

SECONDARY LOW-PRESSURE CHAMBER

PRIMARY-PISTON LIP SEAL

PRIMARY HIGH-PRESSURE CHAMBER (SMALL DIAMETER)

PROPORTIONER

Fig. 52-32 A quick-takeup master cylinder which has a step-bore cylinder and an integral combination valve. (*Delco Moraine Division of General Motors Corporation*)

brakes connected to the primary section. At the same time, the fluid also forces the secondary piston to travel quickly and apply the brakes connected to the secondary section. All four brakes apply with relatively short travel of the brake pedal.

The quick-takeup master cylinder has a proportioning valve or *proportioner* (Fig. 52-32) in the outlet for each rear wheel. The pressure-differential valve (➤52-20) or brake-warning-light switch is also built into the master cylinder. A separate combination valve is not needed.

➤ **52-27 BRAKE FLUID**

Brake fluid is a chemically-inert hydraulic fluid used to transmit force and motion. It also lubricates the pistons in the master cylinder, wheel cylinders, and calipers. There are three types of brake fluid. These are classified by the Department of Transportation (DOT) as *DOT 3, DOT 4,* and *DOT 5*. This classification must appear on the brake-fluid container.

DOT 3 is most widely used. DOT 4 was developed for disc-brake systems which develop higher temperatures than drum-brake systems. DOT 5 is silicone-based and can take even higher temperatures. However, DOT 5 fluid is incompatible with DOT 3 or 4 fluid and must not be mixed with either of them. New silicone brake fluid can be identified by its purple color. New DOT 3 and 4 fluids have a clear to amber color.

DOT 3 and 4 brake fluids are *hygroscopic*. They will absorb moisture. Moisture in brake fluid lowers its boiling point. Hard and prolonged braking, as when going down a hill, can overheat the brake fluid and cause the moisture to boil. This forms vapor that compresses when the brake pedal is depressed (➤52-6). Then there is little pressure increase in the hydraulic system and braking is lost.

Brake fluid is stored in air-tight containers to protect it from moisture. Master cylinders have flexible diaphragms (Fig. 52-29) or sealed caps that cover the reservoirs. They prevent air from contacting the fluid.

➤ **52-28 BRAKE LINES**

Brake lines are made of steel. Because they are under the floor pan, they may be wrapped with wire armor to protect them from flying debris. The ends are flared in either a *double flare* or an *ISO flare* (Fig. 7-32). The flare (➤7-24) provides maximum protection against leakage. A short flexible brake hose or *flex hose* connects the steel brake lines to the wheel cylinders or calipers (Fig. 52-25).

Another type of end is the *block* or *banjo fitting* (Fig. 52-33). It is used with soft metal washers on each side. A hollow bolt allows fluid to flow from the hose into the caliper.

➤ **52-29 STOPLIGHT SWITCH**

Vehicles driven on the street must have rear *brakelights* or *stoplights* (Fig. 34-1). These illuminate when the driver

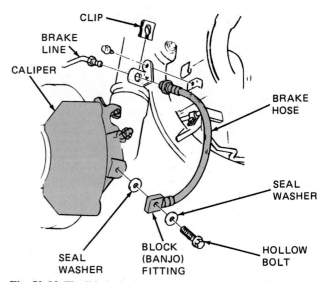

Fig. 52-33 Flexible brake hose connects between the stationary and movable parts of the vehicle. (*Buick Division of General Motors Corporation*)

presses the brake pedal. This alerts drivers following the vehicle that it is slowing or stopping.

Pushing the brake pedal down for braking operates the *brakelight* or *stoplight switch* (Fig. 52-34). This completes the electrical circuit and turns on the rear brake lights until the driver releases the brake pedal. On vehicles with antilock braking (➤53-1), the ABS will not work until the stoplight switch signals that the brake pedal has been depressed.

POWER BRAKES

➤ **52-30 TYPES OF POWER BRAKES**

Most vehicles have power-assisted braking, or *power brakes*. Only a relatively light pedal force is required to slow or stop the vehicle. The assist is provided by either a

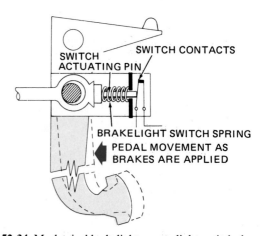

Fig. 52-34 Mechanical brakelight, or stoplight, switch shown closed with the brakes applied. (*Ford Motor Company*)

hydraulic brake booster or a *vacuum brake booster*. Both types allow normal (unassisted) braking if the engine is off or if the booster fails. However, the driver must then push harder on the brake pedal.

➤ 52-31 BASIC VACUUM-BOOSTER OPERATION

Figure 52-1 shows a brake system using a vacuum brake booster. Figure 52-35 shows the basic operation of the unit. It has a cylinder that contains a piston or diaphragm. When the brake pedal is released, the piston is *vacuum-suspended*. It has the same vacuum applied to both sides. The vacuum is supplied by a connection to the engine intake manifold or by a *vacuum pump*.

Depressing the brake pedal causes atmospheric pressure to build up on one side of the piston. This is the right side in Fig. 52-35. The piston then moves to the left, pushing the *master-cylinder pushrod* into the master cylinder. The light force the driver applies to the *brake-pedal pushrod* (Fig. 52-11B) is increased by the "power assist" of the atmospheric pressure.

➤ 52-32 VACUUM BRAKE BOOSTER

Many vehicles use a vacuum brake booster that has a single diaphragm (Fig. 52-36). Depressing the brake pedal causes the brake-pedal pushrod to move the *air valve* away from the *floating-control valve*. Air at atmospheric pressure flows past the valves and into the space between the piston and the *rear housing*. This forces the diaphragm and master-cylinder pushrod toward the master cylinder. As the pistons move into the master cylinder, braking results.

The *reaction disc* to the left of the air valve (Fig. 52-36) gives the driver some braking "feel." A small part of the braking force being applied feeds back through the reaction disc. This feedback is carried through the master-cylinder pushrod and linkage, and is felt by the driver in the brake pedal.

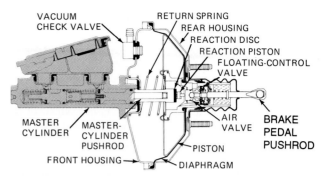

Fig. 52-36 Construction of the vacuum-brake-and-master-cylinder assembly. (*Delco Moraine Division of General Motors Corporation*)

Releasing the brake pedal causes the air valve to move back into contact with the floating-control valve. This reseals the chamber behind the piston-and-diaphragm from atmospheric pressure so the brakes are released. Some vacuum-brake boosters have two diaphragms for additional braking force. These are called *dual-diaphragm* or *tandem* vacuum boosters.

➤ 52-33 HYDRAULIC BRAKE BOOSTER

The hydraulic brake booster mounts on the fire wall, behind the master cylinder (Fig. 52-37). Hydraulic pressure

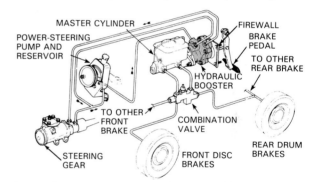

Fig. 52-37 Power brake system using a hydraulic brake booster operated by hydraulic pressure from the power-steering pump. (*Bendix Corporation*)

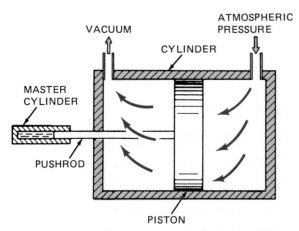

Fig. 52-35 Basic operation of a vacuum brake booster. With vacuum on one side of the piston and atmospheric pressure on the other, the piston moves toward the vacuum side. (*ATW*)

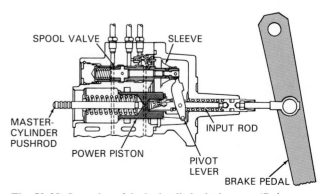

Fig. 52-38 Operation of the hydraulic brake booster. (*Delco Moraine Division of General Motors Corporation*)

supplied by the power-steering pump provides the assist to apply the brakes.

When the engine is running with the brakes released, pump pressure goes to the steering gear. Pushing down on the brake pedal forces the brake-pedal pushrod slightly forward (Fig. 52-38). A pivot arm or lever connects the booster *input rod* to the spool valve. As movement of the brake pedal forces the spool valve forward, this sends additional pump pressure into the space behind the *power piston*. The increased pressure moves the power piston forward (Fig. 52-38). This pushes the master-cylinder pushrod into the master cylinder with a greater force than applied by the driver.

Several other types of hydraulic brake boosters are used. Some include an electrically-driven pump that operates only as needed. This improves fuel economy while providing the pressure needed for braking. A fluid cooler (➤50-11) may be used to prevent fluid overheating.

MULTIPLE-CHOICE TEST

Select the **one** *correct, best, or most probable answer to each question.*
You can find the answers in the section indicated at the end of each question.

1. In a duo-servo brake, the secondary shoe is worn more than the primary shoe. This indicates (➤52-13)
   a. stuck pistons in the wheel cylinder
   b. normal operation
   c. failure of the shoe to self-energize
   d. a defective brake drum
2. On a vehicle with drum brakes, the brake pedal gets lower and lower during normal use. Technician A says the self-adjusters are not working. Technician B says the fluid level in the master cylinder is getting low. Who is right? (➤52-14)
   a. A only
   b. B only
   c. both A and B
   d. neither A nor B
3. Disc brakes self-adjust when the lining wear allows the piston to (➤52-16)
   a. contact the disc
   b. slide outward through the seal
   c. cause seal deflection
   d. reposition the seal groove in the caliper
4. The rear disc brake with an integral parking brake has (➤52-18)
   a. two shoes in a hub-mounted drum brake
   b. a small brake drum mounted on the rear-axle halfshaft
   c. a piston that can be operated hydraulically or mechanically
   d. a separate fluid reservoir for the parking brake

5. Every time the brake pedal is depressed, the instrument-panel BRAKE light illuminates. This indicates (➤52-20)
   a. an improperly-adjusted stoplight switch
   b. low fluid in one section of the hydraulic system
   c. excessive pressure in the hydraulic system
   d. the parking brake is not fully released
6. The front end of a vehicle with front-disc and rear-drum brakes dips excessively when the brakes are applied. This may be caused by a defective (➤52-21)
   a. metering valve
   b. proportioning valve
   c. pressure-differential valve
   d. residual check valve
7. In a master cylinder, the primary piston is the piston that is (➤52-24)
   a. directly operated by the pushrod
   b. nearest the front end of the car
   c. hydraulically operated by the secondary piston
   d. needed only on vehicles with drum brakes
8. The diaphragm under the master-cylinder cover prevents (➤52-27)
   a. brake fluid from spilling out
   b. air from contacting the fluid
   c. a vacuum from forming in the hydraulic system
   d. vapor from forming in the hydraulic system

REVIEW QUESTIONS

1. What is the difference between the friction of rest and the friction of motion, and which provides better braking? (➤52-3)
2. Explain how a hydraulic system uses the incompressibility of a liquid to transfer force and motion. (➤52-5 to 52-8)
3. How does the dual braking system provide an important safety feature? (➤52-10)

4. Describe the basic construction and operation of fixed-caliper, floating-caliper, and sliding-caliper disc brakes. (➤52-15)
5. What are the types and characteristics of brake fluid? (➤52-27)

CHAPTER 53

ANTILOCK BRAKING, TRACTION CONTROL, AND BRAKE DIAGNOSIS AND SERVICE

After studying this chapter, and with proper instruction and equipment, you should be able to:

- Describe the operation of antilock-braking and traction-control systems.
- Diagnose troubles in drum brakes and disc brakes.
- Diagnose troubles in power-brake and antilock-braking systems
- Service drum brakes, disc brakes, master cylinders, and brake lines.
- Flush, fill, and bleed brake hydraulic systems.

ANTILOCK-BRAKING SYSTEMS

➤ 53-1 PURPOSE OF ANTILOCK BRAKING

Tires skid when they slow or *decelerate* faster than the vehicle. One way to help prevent skidding is to keep the brakes from locking. This is the purpose of the *antilock-braking system* (ABS). During normal braking, the antilock-braking system (Fig. 53-1) has no affect on the service brakes. However, during hard or severe braking, the antilock-braking system prevents wheel lockup.

The system allows the brakes to apply until the tires are almost starting to skid. Then the antilock-braking system can vary or *modulate* the hydraulic pressure to the brake at each wheel. This rapid "pumping the brakes" keeps the rate of wheel deceleration below the speed at which the wheels can lock.

➤ 53-2 OPERATION OF THE ANTILOCK-BRAKING SYSTEM

Figure 53-1 shows a vehicle equipped with a vacuum brake booster (➤52-32) and four-wheel antilock brakes. The brake lines from the master cylinder connect to a *hydraulic unit* or *actuator*. Lines from the actuator connect to the wheel brakes. The actuator is controlled by the *ABS control module*.

Wheel-speed sensors (Figs. 53-1 and 53-2) at each wheel continuously send wheel-speed information to the ABS control module. There is no ABS action until the stoplight switch signals the control module that the brake pedal has been depressed. When the control module senses a rapid drop in wheel speed, it signals the actuator to adjust or modulate the brake pressure to that wheel. This prevents wheel lockup.

➤ 53-3 WHEEL-SPEED SENSOR

Figure 53-3 shows typical front- and rear-wheel speed sensors. A toothed ring or *tone ring* rotates with the wheel. The sensor (Fig. 32-23) has a magnetic field around its end. As each tooth passes through the magnetic field, the resulting voltage signal is sent to the ABS control module. The module counts the number of voltage signals per second. This indicates how fast the wheel is turning.

➤ 53-4 ABS HYDRAULIC UNIT

The control module continuously compares the rotary speeds of the four wheels. As long as all are turning at about the same speed, the control module takes no action. When a wheel begins to slow down faster than the other wheels, the control module signals the *ABS relay* (Figs. 53-1 and 53-2) to power the hydraulic unit. One or more solenoids in the hydraulic unit open and close the flow-

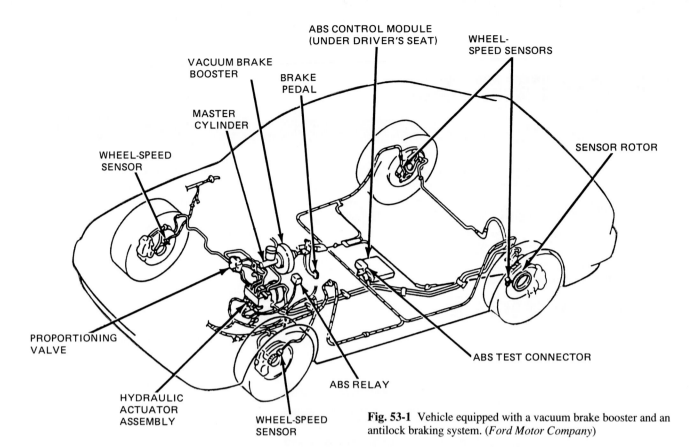

Fig. 53-1 Vehicle equipped with a vacuum brake booster and an antilock braking system. (*Ford Motor Company*)

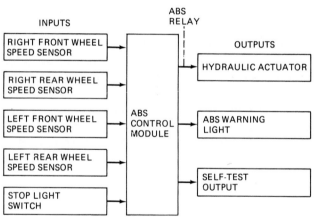

Fig. 53-2 Schematic showing the ABS control module, with inputs and outputs. (*Ford Motor Company*)

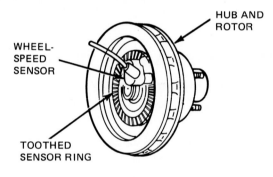

FRONT WHEEL

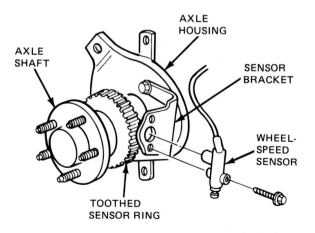

REAR WHEEL

Fig. 53-3 Front and rear wheel-speed sensors. (*Ford Motor Company*)

control valves or *solenoid valves* in the brake lines (Fig. 53-4). The actions of the solenoid valves hold or release the hydraulic pressure to each brake.

Figure 53-4A shows the actions when ABS is not active. Operating the brake pedal causes normal changes in brake pressure at the wheel. Figure 53-4B shows the ABS action when a brake is about to lock. The control module signals the solenoid valve which closes the spring-loaded check ball (right check ball in Fig. 53-4B). This prevents additional fluid from the master cylinder from entering the brake line to the wheel. Hydraulic pressure is held constant. This is the *hold* or *hold-pressure position*.

If the wheel still has a tendency to lock, the antilock-

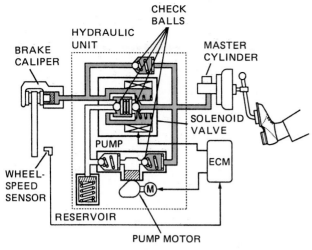

(A) NORMAL BRAKING PRESSURE

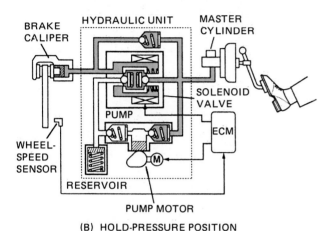

(B) HOLD-PRESSURE POSITION

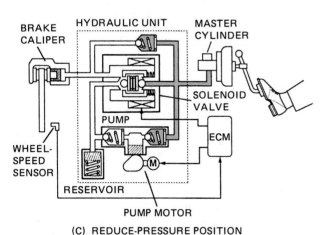

(C) REDUCE-PRESSURE POSITION

Fig. 53-4 Operation of the ABS hydraulic unit and solenoid valves. (*Chrysler Corporation*)

braking system goes to the *reduce* or *reduce-pressure position*. The control module signals the solenoid valve to move the other check ball (left check ball in Fig. 53-4C). This opens a passage that allows fluid to flow from the wheel brake line to the reservoir in the hydraulic unit. The pump motor then sends the fluid from the reservoir back to the master cylinder. The pumping action causes the brake

pedal to *pulsate* (move up and down) slightly during ABS operation.

In some systems, the solenoid valves can also allow a pressure increase. The valves may have separate solenoids or be combined into two- or three-position solenoid valves as shown in Fig. 53-5. In this *3-channel system,* each wheel has a wheel-speed sensor. The front brakes are controlled individually. However, a single *3-position solenoid* controls the pressure to the two rear brakes together. The rear brakes are controlled this way in many antilock-braking systems.

53-5 ABS WITH HYDRAULIC BRAKE BOOSTER

Figure 53-6 shows a vehicle that has the ABS hydraulic unit combined with the master cylinder and a hydraulic brake booster (➤52-33). The hydraulic controls include a valve block with solenoid valves controlled by the ABS control module. An electric pump fills an *accumulator* with pressurized brake fluid. This fluid operates the brakes during normal and antilock braking. The accumulator stores enough pressurized brake fluid for three or four stops if the engine and pump motor are off.

A pressure switch turns the pump motor on and off. If braking exhausts the pressure in the accumulator, the vehicle can be braked normally. However, the driver may have to exert a greater than normal force on the brake pedal.

53-6 REAR-WHEEL ANTILOCK

Many vans and pickup trucks have *rear-wheel antilock* (RWAL). This system (Fig. 53-7) only prevents lockup of the two rear wheels. Instead of separate wheel-speed sensors, the ABS control module uses the signal from the *vehicle-speed sensor* (➤34-19 and 47-27). It reads the rate of rear-wheel deceleration by changes in speed of the transmission-output shaft. Other vehicles with rear-wheel antilock have a single *speed sensor* in the differential carrier (Fig. 53-8). A toothed ring or *exciter ring* mounts next to the ring gear in the rear drive axle. The ABS control module reads rear-wheel speed from how fast the teeth pass the end of the speed sensor.

Figure 53-8 shows the basic layout of a typical rear-wheel antilock system. The hydraulic line from the master cylinder connects to the *dual-solenoid hydraulic valve*. During normal braking, the *isolation valve* is open. The *dump valve* and accumulator are closed. Master-cylinder pressure acts directly on the rear-wheel brakes.

The graph in Fig. 53-9 compares the front and rear brake pressures during heavy braking that causes rear-wheel ABS operation. First the isolation valve closes. This prevents any increase in pressure from reaching the rear brakes. If additional modulation is needed, the control valve briefly opens the dump valve (twice in Fig. 53-9). This relieves the pressure in the rear brakes by allowing fluid to flow from the wheel brake into the accumulator.

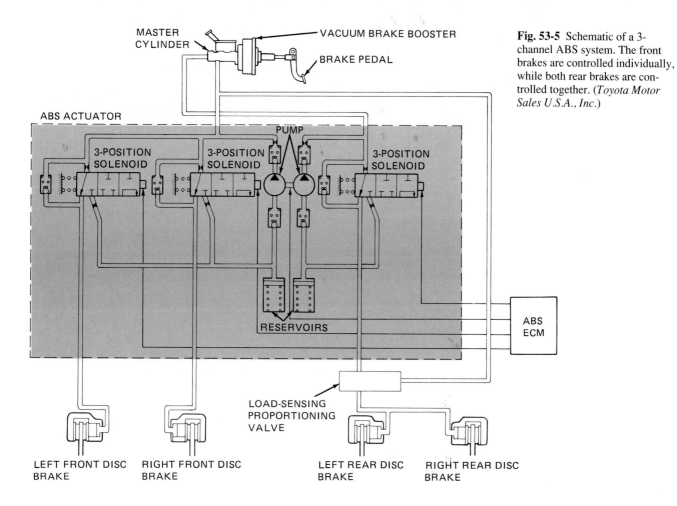

MASTER
CYLINDER

VACUUM BRAKE BOOSTER

BRAKE PEDAL

Fig. 53-5 Schematic of a 3-channel ABS system. The front brakes are controlled individually, while both rear brakes are controlled together. (*Toyota Motor Sales U.S.A., Inc.*)

ABS ACTUATOR

PUMP

3-POSITION SOLENOID

3-POSITION SOLENOID

3-POSITION SOLENOID

ABS ECM

RESERVOIRS

LOAD-SENSING
PROPORTIONING
VALVE

LEFT FRONT DISC BRAKE

RIGHT FRONT DISC BRAKE

LEFT REAR DISC BRAKE

RIGHT REAR DISC BRAKE

ANTILOCK
WARNING
LIGHT

WHEEL-
SPEED
SENSORS

BRAKE
PEDAL

Fig. 53-6 Vehicle that has the ABS hydraulic unit combined with the master cylinder and a hydraulic brake booster. (*Buick Division of General Motors Corporation*)

HYDRAULIC
UNIT

RELAYS

PROPORTIONING
VALVE

ABS CONTROL
MODULE

ACCUMULATOR

WHEEL-SPEED
SENSORS

If the control module senses that the wheels are still about to lock, the dump-valve cycle will repeat. After the control module senses an acceptable wheel speed, the dump valve remains closed. When the driver releases the brake pedal, the isolation valve opens. Any brake fluid in the accumulator flows back into the hydraulic system.

➤ **53-7 FOUR-WHEEL-DRIVE AND ANTILOCK BRAKING**

Some vehicles with ABS do not have antilock braking in four-wheel drive (Chap. 46) or after a limited-slip differential (➤45-20) locks the front wheels together. Engaging

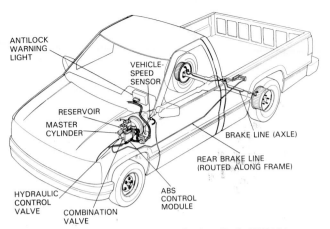

Fig. 53-7 Pickup truck with a rear-wheel antilock (RWAL) system, which only prevents lockup of the rear wheels. (*Chevrolet Division of General Motors Corporation*)

four-wheel drive, or if the differential locks, deactivates the ABS.

Many all-wheel-drive vehicles have an additional input to the ABS control module called a *deceleration sensor* or *G sensor*. It tells the control module if the vehicle is moving or stopped. Suppose the vehicle is on ice and pressing the brake pedal locks all four wheels. The signals from the wheel-speed sensors would indicate that the vehicle has stopped. However, the signal from the deceleration sensor shows the vehicle is still moving.

➤ 53-8 ANTILOCK INDICATOR LIGHT

Many vehicles with an antilock-braking system have a brownish-yellow or amber *ANTILOCK warning light* on the instrument panel. The light illuminates if the ABS control

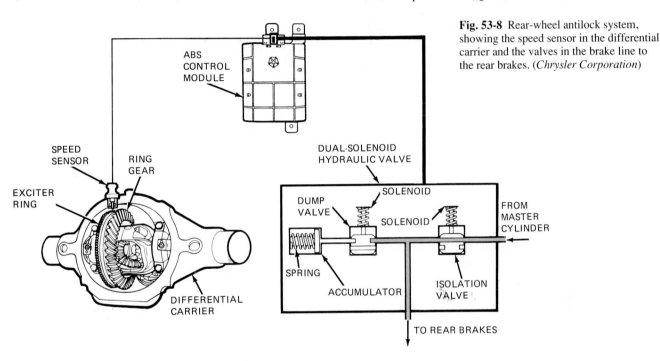

Fig. 53-8 Rear-wheel antilock system, showing the speed sensor in the differential carrier and the valves in the brake line to the rear brakes. (*Chrysler Corporation*)

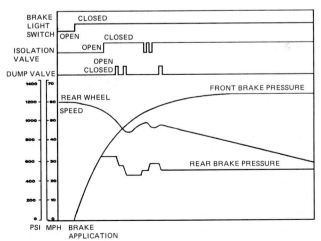

Fig. 53-9 Comparison of the pressures in the front and rear brakes during rear-wheel antilock operation. (*Chrysler Corporation*)

module detects trouble in the antilock-braking system. The light may also turn on to indicate the antilock system is working. Any faults detected by the ABS control module may store a trouble code in its memory (➤20-13).

The fluid reservoir that is part of the hydraulic unit in Fig. 53-6 includes a *low-fluid-level sensor*. If the brake fluid is low, the sensor turns on an instrument-panel warning light or LOW BRAKE FLUID display. The red *brake-warning light* (Fig. 17-32) will glow if there is low pressure in one section of the brake hydraulic system.

TRACTION-CONTROL SYSTEM

➤ 53-9 PURPOSE OF TRACTION CONTROL

Any time a tire is given more torque than it can transfer to the road, the tire loses traction and spins. This usually

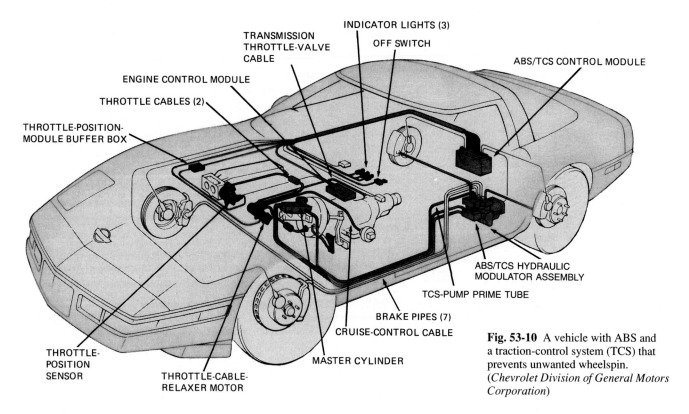

INDICATOR LIGHTS (3)

OFF SWITCH

TRANSMISSION THROTTLE-VALVE CABLE

ENGINE CONTROL MODULE

THROTTLE CABLES (2)

THROTTLE-POSITION-MODULE BUFFER BOX

ABS/TCS CONTROL MODULE

ABS/TCS HYDRAULIC MODULATOR ASSEMBLY

TCS-PUMP PRIME TUBE

BRAKE PIPES (7)

CRUISE-CONTROL CABLE

THROTTLE-POSITION SENSOR

THROTTLE-CABLE-RELAXER MOTOR

MASTER CYLINDER

Fig. 53-10 A vehicle with ABS and a traction-control system (TCS) that prevents unwanted wheelspin. (*Chevrolet Division of General Motors Corporation*)

occurs during acceleration (➤17-11). To prevent unwanted wheelspin, some vehicles with ABS also have a *traction-control system* (TCS). When a wheel is about to spin, the traction-control system (Fig. 53-10) applies the brake at that wheel. This slows the wheel until the chance of wheel spin has passed.

➤ 53-10 OPERATION OF TRACTION-CONTROL SYSTEM

The antilock-braking system and traction-control system share many parts. The wheel-speed sensors report wheel speed to the *ABS/TCS control module* (Fig. 53-10). When a wheel slows so quickly that it is about to skid, the ABS holds or releases the brake pressure at that wheel (➤53-1). If wheel speed increases so quickly that the wheel is about to spin, the TCS applies the brake at that wheel. This slows the wheel and prevents wheel spin.

The TCS can also reduce engine speed and torque if braking alone does not prevent wheelspin. When this is necessary, the ABS/TCS control module signals the engine control module. It then retards the spark and reduces the amount of fuel delivered by the fuel injectors.

DRUM-BRAKE TROUBLE DIAGNOSIS

➤ 53-11 CAUTION FOR WORKING AROUND BRAKE DUST

Some brake linings in drum and disc brakes are made of asbestos. Ingesting asbestos fibers, either by breathing or

swallowing, can cause serious bodily harm. Never use an air nozzle to blow dust off the brakes. Never sand or grind brake linings or clean brake parts with a dry cloth or compressed air.

Instead, clean the parts with an EPA-approved vacuum (Fig. 4-6) that has a *High Efficiency Particulate Air* (HEPA) filter. Another method is to wipe parts with a cloth dampened with water. Dispose of the cloths safely in a special container for hazardous materials (➤4-13). Using dampened cloths or a vacuum with a HEPA filter prevents asbestos fibers from becoming airborne. Always wash your hands after handling dusty brake parts and brake linings.

➤ 53-12 DIAGNOSING DRUM-BRAKE TROUBLES

When the driver depresses the brake pedal, hydraulic pressure forces the brake lining against the drum or discs. The resulting friction and heat cause brake parts to wear. Warning lights and fluid-level and wear indicators help alert the driver to the need for brake service. Improper operation and other driver complaints indicate the need for brake inspection and testing. Correcting a brake problem early helps prevent damage to other parts and possible brake failure.

A complaint of faulty braking should be immediately diagnosed to determine its cause. Figure 53-11 is a drum-brake trouble-diagnosis chart. It also covers brake hydraulic systems. Following sections describe the various complaints, possible causes, and checks or corrections. Later sections describe disc-brake and power-brake trouble diagnosis.

Complaint	Possible Cause	Check or Correction
1. Pedal goes to floor, loss of pedal reserve (➤53-13)	a. Self-adjuster not working b. Bent master-cylinder pushrod c. Linkage or shoes out of adjustment d. Brake linings worn e. Lack of brake fluid f. Air in hydraulic system g. Defective master cylinder	Repair Replace Adjust Replace Add fluid, bleed system Add fluid, bleed system Repair or replace
2. One brake drags (➤53-14)	a. Shoes out of adjustment b. Clogged brake line c. Wheel cylinder defective d. Weak or broken return spring e. Loose wheel bearing	Adjust Clear or replace Repair or replace Replace Adjust or replace
3. All brakes drag (➤53-15)	a. Incorrect linkage adjustment b. Defective master cylinder c. Mineral oil in system	Adjust Repair or replace Replace damaged rubber parts; flush, fill, and bleed system
4. Pulls to one side when braking (➤53-16)	a. Oil on brake linings b. Brake fluid on brake linings c. Brake shoes out of adjustment d. Tires not uniformly inflated e. Brake line clogged f. Defective wheel cylinder g. Brake backing plate loose h. Mismatched linings	Replace linings and oil seals; avoid overlubrication Replace linings; repair or replace wheel cylinder Adjust Adjust tire pressure Clear or replace line Repair or replace Tighten Install matched linings
5. Soft or spongy pedal (➤53-17)	a. Air in hydraulic system b. Brake shoes out of adjustment c. Defective master cylinder d. Loose connections or damaged brake line e. Loss of brake fluid	Add fluid, bleed system Adjust Repair or replace Tighten connection, replace line See item 9, below
6. Poor braking requiring excessive pedal force (➤53-18)	a. Brake linings wet with water b. Shoes out of adjustment c. Brake linings hot d. Brake linings burned e. Brake drum glazed f. Power brake inoperative g. Wheel-cylinder pistons stuck	Allow to dry Adjust Allow to cool Replace Refinish or replace Repair or replace Repair or replace
7. Brakes grab (➤53-19)	a. Shoes out of adjustment b. Wrong linings c. Grease on brake lining d. Oil on brake lining e. Brake fluid on brake lining f. Drums scored g. Backing plate loose h. Power-brake booster defective	Adjust Install correct linings Replace lining; check seals; avoid overlubrication Replace linings; check seals, avoid overlubrication Replace linings; repair or replace wheel cylinders Refinish or replace drums Tighten Repair or replace
8. Noisy brakes (➤53-20)	a. Linings worn b. Shoes warped c. Shoe rivets loose d. Drums worn or rough e. Loose parts	Replace Replace Replace shoe and lining Refinish or replace Tighten
9. Loss of brake fluid (➤53-21)	a. Master cylinder leaks b. Wheel cylinder leaks c. Loose connections, damaged brake line	Repair or replace Repair or replace Tighten connections, replace line
NOTE: After repair, add brake fluid and bleed system.		
10. Brakes do not self-adjust (➤53-22)	a. Adjusting screw stuck b. Adjusting lever does not engage adjusting wheel c. Adjuster incorrectly installed	Free and clean Repair; free or replace adjuster Install correctly
11. Brake warning light comes on while braking (➤53-23)	a. One section of hydraulic system has failed b. Pressure-differential valve defective	Inspect and repair Replace

Fig. 53-11 Drum-brake trouble-diagnosis chart.

➤ 53-13 BRAKE PEDAL GOES TO THE FLOOR

When the brake pedal goes to the floor, there is no *pedal reserve* (Fig. 53-12). This is the distance from the brake pedal to the floor after the brakes are applied. If full pedal travel does not produce adequate braking, a loss of brake fluid may have occurred. One section of the hydraulic system may have failed (both seldom fail at the same time). If only one section is working, greater pedal force is required and the brakes apply only when the pedal is almost to the floor.

Also, the driver may have ignored the brake-warning light, or the light bulb or pressure-differential valve has failed. Other causes of loss of pedal reserve include a bent master-cylinder pushrod, improperly adjusted linkage or brake shoes, worn brake linings, air in the hydraulic system, and a defective master cylinder.

➤ 53-14 ONE BRAKE DRAGS

A brake *drags* when a brake shoe does not move away from the drum as the brakes are released. This could be caused by a piston in the wheel cylinder sticking in its applied position. Other causes include incorrect shoe adjustment, a clogged brake line that does not release pressure from the wheel cylinder, and weak or broken brake-shoe return springs. Also, a loose wheel bearing could permit the wheel to wobble. This could allow the brake drum to contact the brake shoes. When the parking

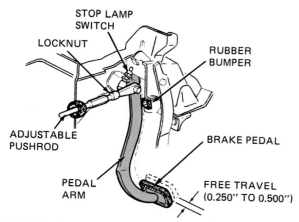

STOP LAMP SWITCH
LOCKNUT
RUBBER BUMPER
ADJUSTABLE PUSHROD
BRAKE PEDAL
PEDAL ARM
FREE TRAVEL (0.250" TO 0.500")

Fig. 53-12 Measuring free travel, or free play, in the brake pedal.

brake is applied overnight, sometimes the brake lining will absorb moisture and stick or freeze to the drum.

➤ 53-15 ALL BRAKES DRAG

All the brakes can drag if the brake pedal does not have enough *free travel* (Fig. 53-12). This is the distance the brake pedal moves before the primary seals on the master-cylinder pistons close the vent ports (➤52-24). Dragging results if the master-cylinder pistons do not fully retract. The vent ports are not opened to relieve the pressure by allowing fluid-flow back into the reservoir. Unless this happens, the hydraulic pressure is trapped in the lines to the wheel cylinders. The shoes cannot retract.

Dragging brakes can also be caused by swollen seals or cups in the master cylinder. This results if oil is added to the system. Oil causes the piston cups to swell. Then they cannot clear the ports and release the pressure. Clogged ports cause the same condition.

Careful! Never put any type of oil in the brake system. It causes rubber parts to swell and break. This could result in complete brake failure.

➤ 53-16 PULLS TO ONE SIDE WHEN BRAKING

If the vehicle pulls to one side when the brakes are applied, there is more braking force on that side. This results from brake lining contaminated with oil or brake fluid, unevenly adjusted shoes, defective wheel cylinders, or clogged brake lines. Any of these can prevent uniform braking at all wheels. A loose brake backing plate and mixing types of brake linings can also cause the vehicle to pull to one side when braking. Other possible causes are improper wheel alignment, a broken spring, and worn control-arm bushings.

In a vehicle with front engine and rear-wheel drive, rear linings can become oil-soaked if the lubricant level in the rear axle is high. The lubricant leaks past the oil seal. In front drum brakes, grease can get on the linings if the wheel bearings are over-lubricated or if the grease seals leak. Wheel cylinders will leak if the cups are defective or if an actuating pin is improperly installed (Fig. 52-15).

Contaminated linings may cause a pull to one side or the other. For example, if oil or brake fluid gets on linings at a left wheel, the linings may tend to grab and cause the vehicle to pull to the left (➤51-7). However, water on the linings at a left wheel may prevent normal friction. Then the vehicle pulls to the right. The direction of pull often depends on the type of lining material and the contaminant.

➤ 53-17 SOFT OR SPONGY PEDAL

Air in the hydraulic system causes a soft or spongy pedal. The air may get in because of a low fluid level in the master cylinder. This permits air to be forced into the system as the pistons move forward during braking. Air is removed by adding brake fluid and bleeding the system (≻53-48).

Plugged air vents in the master-cylinder cap or cover also may cause a vacuum during the return stroke of the pistons. Air then bypasses the primary-piston cup (Fig. 52-29) and enters the system. In addition, some master cylinders have a residual check valve (≻52-25) in the lines to the drum brakes. If the valve leaks and does not maintain a slight pressure in the system, air could leak in around the cups in the wheel cylinder.

➤ 53-18 POOR BRAKING REQUIRING EXCESSIVE PEDAL FORCE

A need for excessive pedal force can be caused by improper brake-shoe adjustment or the wrong brake lining. Another possible cause is *brake fade*. This is a temporary reduction or fading out of braking effectiveness. It occurs when the brake lining overheats from excessively long and hard brake application, as when coming down a hill. Normal braking usually returns after the brakes cool. Fading may also occur after driving through water and getting the linings wet. The water reduces the friction between the lining and the drum. Normal braking usually returns after the linings have dried.

Excessively long braking creates high temperatures that may burn or *char* the braking linings. Then the linings must be replaced. Overheating can also *glaze* the brake drums so they become too smooth for good braking action. Glazed drums must be refinished to remove the glaze. Sometimes normal wear causes drums to glaze, even without excessive overheating.

Failure of the power-brake booster (≻53-35) increases the pedal force needed to produce braking. The power-brake booster must be rebuilt or replaced.

➤ 53-19 BRAKES GRAB

Linings contaminated with grease, oil, or brake fluid tend to grab with light pedal force. These linings must be replaced. Grabbing can also result if the shoes are out of adjustment, if the wrong linings are being used, or if drums are *scored* or rough (Fig. 53-13). A loose brake backing plate can shift as the linings contact the drum and cause grabbing. A defective power-brake booster can also cause grabbing.

➤ 53-20 NOISY BRAKES

Brake noise can result if linings are so worn that the rivets contact the drum, and if the shoes are warped so that contact with the drum is not uniform. Other causes include rivets so loose that they rub on the drum, and a worn or rough drum (Fig. 53-13). Any of these conditions can cause a squeak or squeal when brakes are applied. Also, loose parts, such as the brake backing plate, may rattle.

➤ 53-21 LOSS OF BRAKE FLUID

Leaks result in loss of brake fluid. They can occur from the master cylinder, wheel cylinders (or calipers), lines, and connections (Fig. 53-14). Check the brake lines for secure attachment and check the master-cylinder mounting. The brake lines and attaching nuts must be tight. Brake-line fittings must not show any signs of leakage. After correcting the cause of the leak, add brake fluid and bleed the system (≻53-48).

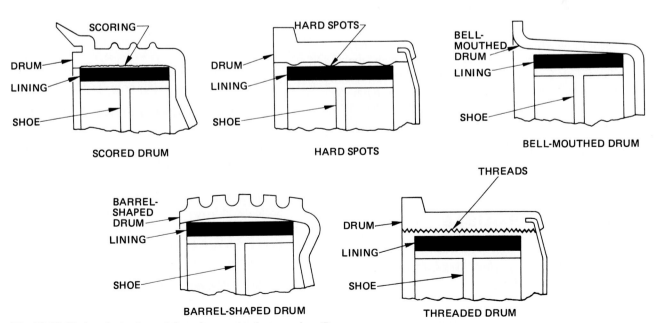

Fig. 53-13 Various brake-drum defects that require drum service. (*Bear Manufacturing Company*)

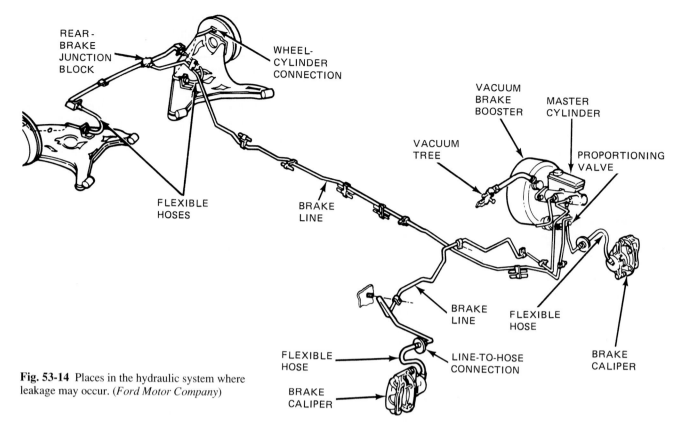

Fig. 53-14 Places in the hydraulic system where leakage may occur. (*Ford Motor Company*)

➤ 53-22 BRAKES DO NOT SELF-ADJUST

If the self-adjuster mechanism is incorrectly installed, the adjusting screw is stuck, or the adjusting lever is not engaging the adjusting wheel (➤52-14), the brakes will not self-adjust. Remove the drum and inspect the brake to find and correct the trouble.

➤ 53-23 BRAKE WARNING LIGHT COMES ON WHILE BRAKING

Illumination of the brake warning light (Fig. 53-10) while braking usually indicates that one section of the hydraulic system has failed. Both sections should be checked so the trouble can be found and corrected. The light may also illuminate because of a defective pressure-differential valve. It may be dangerous to continue to drive the vehicle if the brake warning light comes on while braking. Although the vehicle can be braked, only half the wheel brakes may be working.

DISC-BRAKE TROUBLE DIAGNOSIS

➤ 53-24 DIAGNOSING DISC-BRAKE TROUBLES

Sometimes troubles in disc brakes are similar to troubles in drum brakes. Both braking systems use a brake pedal and linkage, power-brake booster, master cylinder and hydraulic system, and connecting lines and hoses. The diagnosis and service of these common components are basically the same regardless of the type of brake at the wheel. However, the disc brake has fewer parts and is simpler in construction and operation. This makes disc-brake diagnosis and service different from a drum brake.

Vehicles with disc brakes at all four wheels can have some troubles that are not found in four-wheel drum brakes (Fig. 53-11) or front-disc/rear-drum systems. One reason is that many rear disc brakes have an integral parking brake (➤52-18) built into the caliper. Figure 53-15 is a trouble diagnosis chart for front disc and four-wheel disc brake systems. Following sections describe typical complaints, their possible causes, and the checks or corrections to make. Section 53-35 describes power-brake diagnosis.

➤ 53-25 EXCESSIVE PEDAL TRAVEL

Anything that requires excessive movement of the caliper pistons causes excessive pedal travel. For example, a disc brake with excessive runout forces the pistons farther back into their bores when the brakes are released. Then additional pedal travel is required the next time the brakes are applied. Air in the brake lines, low brake fluid, or incorrect brake fluid (with low boiling point) can cause a spongy pedal and excessive pedal travel.

➤ 53-26 PEDAL PULSATIONS

Pulsations felt in the brake pedal are often due to a disc with excessive runout (wobble) or a disc that is out of

Complaint	Possible Cause	Check or Correction
1. Excessive pedal travel (➤53-25)	a. Excessive disc runout	Refinish or replace disc
	b. Air in hydraulic system	Bleed brakes
	c. Low brake fluid	Fill, inspect, repair, and bleed system
	d. Bent shoe and lining or loose insulators	Inspect; replace
	e. Loose wheel bearing	Adjust or replace
	f. Damaged piston seal in caliper	Replace
	g. Power brake inoperative	Repair or replace
	h. Failure of one section of hydraulic system	Inspect and repair. Check brake warning light, if not on.
	i. Caliper parking brake not adjusting	Inspect rear calipers; repair
2. Pedal pulsations (➤53-26)	a. Excessive disc runout (wobble)	Refinish or replace disc
	b. Disc out of parallel (uneven disc thickness)	Refinish or replace disc
	c. Loose wheel bearings	Adjust or replace
	d. Tight caliper slides	Free, repair
	e. Wheel-and-tire vibration	Diagnose vibration
3. Excessive pedal force, grabbing, uneven braking (➤53-27)	a. Power-brake defective	Repair or replace
	b. Brake fluid, oil, grease on lining	Replace
	c. Lining worn	Replace
	d. Wrong lining	Install correct lining
	e. Piston stuck in caliper	Service or replace caliper
	f. Failure of one section of hydraulic system	Inspect and repair. Check brake warning light, if not on.
4. Pulls to one side while braking (➤53-28)	a. Brake fluid, oil, or grease on linings	Replace
	b. Seized caliper	Service
	c. Piston stuck in caliper	Service or replace caliper
	d. Incorrect tire pressure	Adjust
	e. Bent shoe	Replace
	f. Incorrect wheel alignment	Align
	g. Broken rear spring	Replace
	h. Restricted line or hose	Repair or replace
	i. Unmatched linings	Replace
	j. Loose caliper	Tighten
	k. Loose suspension parts	Tighten
5. Brake noise (➤53-29) A. Groan when slowly releasing brakes (creep groan)	a. Typical of some disc brakes	Not detrimental, no action required. Often eliminated when driver increases or decreases brake-pedal force slightly
B. Rattle at low speed	a. Shoe loose on caliper	Clinch shoe tabs to caliper; install new shoes
C. Scraping	a. Mounting bolts too long	Install correct bolts
	b. Disc rubbing caliper	Remove rust or mud from caliper; tighten caliper bolts
	c. Loose wheel bearing	Adjust or replace
	d. Worn lining; wear sensor scraping on disc	Inspect disc; replace lining
	e. Improper assembly	Correct
D. Occasional squeal	a. Typical of many disc brakes	Not detrimental, no action required. Explain to driver that occasional squeal cannot always be eliminated.
E. Frequent or continuous squeal	a. Shoe loose on caliper	Clinch shoe tabs to caliper
	b. Worn or missing parts	Check for damaged or missing antirattle springs, antisqueal shims or insulators, or worn caliper guide pins and bushings
	c. Improper clearance on rear disc brakes	Check clearance between disc and lining
	d. Disc scored or improperly machined	Refinish or replace disc
	e. Antisqueal compound not applied to shoes	Remove and apply antisqueal compound to back of shoes
	f. Glazed linings	Sand linings; inspect disc
	g. Rivets loose in shoe and lining	Replace shoes
6. Brakes fail to release (➤53-30)	a. Power-brake defective	Repair or replace
	b. Brake pedal binding	Free, repair
	c. Master-cylinder pushrod improperly adjusted	Adjust

Fig. 53-15 Disc-brake trouble-diagnosis chart.

Complaint	Possible Cause	Check or Correction
	d. Driver rides pedal	Notify driver
	e. Incorrect stoplight-switch adjustment	Adjust
	f. Caliper piston not retracting	Service or replace
	g. Speed-control switch improperly adjusted	Adjust
	h. Incorrect parking-brake adjustment	Adjust
	i. Restricted pipes, hoses, or banjo bolts	Repair or replace
7. Fluid leaking from caliper (➤53-31)	a. Damaged or worn piston seal b. Scores or corrosion on piston or in caliper bore	Replace Service caliper
8. Front disc brakes grab (rear drum brakes OK) (➤53-32)	a. Defective metering valve b. Incorrect lining c. Improper surface finish on disc	Replace Replace Refinish disc
9. No braking with pedal fully depressed (➤53-33)	a. Piston pushed back in caliper b. Leak in hydraulic system c. Damaged piston seal d. Air in hydraulic system e. Leak past primary cup in master cylinder	Pump brake pedal; check shoe position Repair Replace Add fluid, bleed system Service or replace master cylinder
10. Fluid level low in master cylinder (➤53-34)	a. Leaks b. Worn linings	Repair; add fluid, bleed system Replace
11. Warning light comes on while braking (➤53-23)	a. One section of hydraulic system has failed b. Pressure-differential valve defective	Check both sections; replace Replace
12. Caliper parking brake will not hold vehicle (➤52-18)	a. Improper parking-brake cable adjustment b. Defective rear actuators c. Ineffective rear lining d. Defective parking-brake pedal assembly	Adjust Adjust, repair Inspect, replace Repair
13. Caliper parking brake will not release (➤52-19)	a. Improper cable adjustment b. Vacuum-release system inoperative	Adjust Repair

parallel (uneven thickness). Rotation of the disc pushes the pistons back in their bores. This movement is carried back through the master cylinder to the brake pedal. A loose wheel bearing and tight caliper slides also cause pedal pulsation. In some antilock-braking systems, a pulsating pedal is a normal condition during ABS operation (➤53-4).

➤ 53-27 EXCESSIVE PEDAL FORCE, GRABBING, UNEVEN BRAKING

If excessive pedal force is required for braking, the power brake may be defective. Also, worn, hot, or wet linings need extra force to produce braking. An excessively hard push on the brake pedal may be needed before a caliper with a stuck piston can provide braking.

➤ 53-28 PULLS TO ONE SIDE WHILE BRAKING

Pulling to one side while braking is usually due to uneven braking. Possible causes include a *seized* or non-moving floating-caliper, sliding-caliper, or caliper piston. Other possible causes are brake fluid on the linings, unmatched linings, warped brake shoes, and a restriction in a brake line or hose. Improper wheel alignment, worn control-arm bushings, uneven tire pressures, and a broken or weak suspension spring will also cause the vehicle to pull to one side during braking.

➤ 53-29 BRAKE NOISE

Noise is a common complaint about disc brakes. Some noise such as occasional squealing cannot always be totally eliminated. Inspect the brakes if the driver complains of frequent and continuous noise. A cause of rattle and squeal during braking is a loose brake pad on the caliper. Tightening the shoe tabs against the caliper may eliminate the noise. Sometimes an *antisqueak shim* or *insulator* is installed on the back of the shoe (Fig. 53-16). This prevents vibration between the shoe and the caliper.

Many sets of new brake pads have a container of *antisqueal compound* packaged with the pads. When applied to

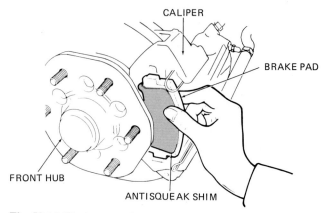

Fig. 53-16 Placing an antisqueak shim, or insulator, between the back of the shoe and the caliper to help reduce noise. (*Chrysler Corporation*)

the back of the shoes, the compound helps dampen the vibrations that are heard as brake squeal. However, a scraping noise when the brakes are applied may be the lining wear sensor (➤52-17) scraping the disc.

➤ 53-30 BRAKES FAIL TO RELEASE

This could result from sticking pedal linkage, a defective power brake, a stuck caliper piston, or the master cylinder not releasing pressure. These conditions cause the linings to ride the disc and get very hot. Even with the brake pedal released, the resulting heat may cause or further increase pressure in the hydraulic system.

To check for pressure in the hydraulic system, open a bleeder valve while the brake pedal is released. If fluid squirts out, this indicates pressure in that section of the hydraulic system. Check the adjustment of the master-cylinder pushrod and the stoplight switch (Fig. 53-12).

Careful! Follow the procedure in the vehicle service manual and ➤53-37 before loosening a bleeder valve on a vehicle with ABS. Then tighten and bleed the hydraulic system (➤53-47 to 53-49) to remove any air that entered through the loosened bleeder valve.

➤ 53-31 FLUID LEAKING FROM CALIPER

A caliper may leak brake fluid because of a damaged or worn piston seal. Leaking is also caused by a rough surface on the piston or in the caliper bore. This may result from scratches, scores, and rust or corrosion.

➤ 53-32 FRONT-DISC BRAKES GRAB

In a vehicle with front-disc and rear-drum brakes, the metering valve (➤52-21) should prevent or hold off front brake application until after the rear-drum brakes apply. Failure of the metering valve may cause the front-disc brakes to grab with light pedal force. Improper lining or disc refinishing will also cause this condition.

➤ 53-33 NO BRAKING WITH PEDAL FULLY DEPRESSED

If the brakes have been serviced, the caliper pistons may have been pushed far back in their bores. A single pedal stroke will not produce braking. After any disc-brake service, pump the brake pedal several times. This moves the pistons into proper position for normal braking.

➤ 53-34 FLUID LEVEL LOW IN MASTER CYLINDER

This can result from leaks or worn linings. As the linings wear, the fluid level goes down in the master-cylinder reservoir. More fluid remains in the calipers (Fig. 53-17).

POWER-BRAKE TROUBLE DIAGNOSIS

➤ 53-35 DIAGNOSING POWER-BRAKE TROUBLES

A quick check of power-brake operation can be made with the booster on the vehicle. With the engine off, pump the brake pedal several times. This uses up any stored vacuum or hydraulic pressure. Then depress the brake pedal and start the engine. If the booster is operating properly, the pedal will fall away or drop slightly. This is a normal condition of power-brake operation.

If the booster is not operating properly, refer to the power-brake trouble-diagnosis chart in the vehicle service manual. Figure 53-18 is a typical chart showing various power-brake troubles and their possible causes and corrections. The vehicle service manual also covers how to repair and replace power-brake boosters.

➤ 53-36 ANTILOCK-BRAKING-SYSTEM TROUBLE DIAGNOSIS

The antilock-braking system is a dual brake system with antilock components added (➤53-2). These include a

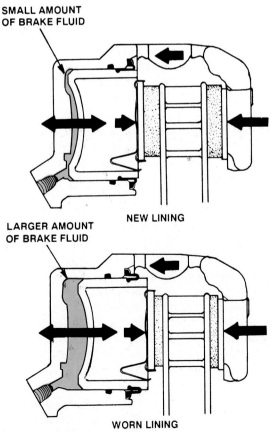

SMALL AMOUNT OF BRAKE FLUID

NEW LINING

LARGER AMOUNT OF BRAKE FLUID

WORN LINING

Fig. 53-17 As disc-brake linings wear, fluid level lowers in the master cylinder. More fluid remains in the calipers. (*Delco Moraine Division of General Motors Corporation*)

Complaint	Possible Cause	Check or Correction
1. Excessive pedal force required (vacuum booster)	a. Defective vacuum check valve b. Hose collapsed c. Vacuum fitting plugged d. Pedal linkage binding e. Air inlet clogged f. Faulty piston seal g. Stuck piston h. Faulty diaphragm i. Causes listed under item 6 in Fig. 53-11 and item 3 in Fig. 53-15	Free or replace Replace Clear, replace Free Clear Replace Clear, replace damaged parts Replace
2. Brakes grab	a. Reaction or "brake feel" mechanism damaged b. Air-vacuum valve sticking c. Causes listed under item 7 in Fig. 53-11 or item 3 in Fig. 53-15	Replace damaged parts Free, replace
3. Pedal goes to floor	a. Hydraulic-plunger seal leaking b. Compensating valve sticking c. Causes listed under item 1 in Fig. 53-11 or item 8 in Fig. 53-15	Replace Replace valve
4. Brakes fail to release	a. Pedal linkage binding b. Faulty check valve c. Compensator port plugged d. Hydraulic plunger seal sticking e. Piston sticking f. Broken return spring g. Causes listed under item 3 in Fig. 53-11 or item 6 in Fig. 53-15	Free Free, replace Clean port Replace seal Lubricate, replace damaged parts Replace
5. Loss of brake fluid	a. Worn or damaged seals in hydraulic section b. Loose line connections c. Causes listed under item 9 in Fig. 53-11 or items 7 and 9 in Fig. 53-15	Replace, fill, bleed Tighten, replace seals

Fig. 53-18 Power-brake trouble-diagnosis chart.

hydraulic or vacuum booster, ABS control module, wheel-speed sensors, and a deceleration sensor (with 4WD or AWD).

A vehicle with ABS can have the same brake-system troubles described above. These are listed in the trouble-diagnosis charts for drum and disc brake systems (Figs. 53-11 and 53-15). An ABS trouble is the failure to prevent wheel lockup. Also, oversize tires on a vehicle can prevent normal ABS operation.

Many vehicles with ABS have two instrument-panel indicator lights, ANTILOCK (amber) and BRAKE (red). A typical starting procedure is that when the ignition key is turned on, the ANTILOCK light should illuminate for three to five seconds. It may stay on for up to 30 seconds while pressure builds in the accumulator.

During cranking, both the BRAKE and the ANTILOCK lights illuminate. After the engine starts, the BRAKE light goes out. The ANTILOCK light remains on for three to five seconds. Both lights should be off at all other times. Any other sequence of light actions may indicate trouble. Refer to the diagnostic procedure in the vehicle service manual.

Some ABS diagnostic procedures require the use of a *breakout box* (➤33-18) and a pressure gauge. The breakout box connects to the ABS wiring-harness connector. The pressure gauge (Fig. 53-19) checks the pressure developed in the hydraulic unit. Other procedures require a scan tool to retrieve trouble codes (➤53-37).

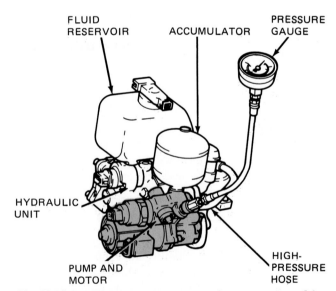

Fig. 53-19 Installing pressure gauge to make pressure tests of the ABS. (*Buick Division of General Motors Corporation*)

➤ 53-37 CHECKING ABS OPERATION

As a first step in ABS diagnosis, perform a visual inspection. Inspect the system for loose connections, faulty master-cylinder operation, abnormal braking action, and leaks. To use the lamp-sequence procedure, turn the ignition OFF for 15 seconds. Then turn the ignition ON and watch the actions of the BRAKE and ANTILOCK lights.

Many ABS control modules store faults or trouble codes in memory (➤10-18). These may be retrieved using a scan tool. The meaning of each trouble code is in the vehicle service manual. Codes can be set for failures of the wheel-speed sensors, vehicle-speed sensor, deceleration sensor, stoplight switch, solenoid valves, relays, and ABS control module.

Sometimes trouble codes result from *driver-induced faults*. These can occur if the vehicle is driven with the parking brake applied or if there is excessive wheelspin. A code indicating a defective control module can be set by improperly connecting and disconnecting the scan tool (➤20-13). This must be done with the ignition key OFF. Any time a fault code appears for the ABS control module, erase the code. Then test the system operation before determining the ABS control module should be replaced.

> **Careful!** Some vehicles have a hydraulic accumulator as part of the antilock-braking system. A very high pressure may exist in the brake lines and hydraulic system. Before performing tests or other brake work on a vehicle with a hydraulic accumulator, first depressurize the accumulator. Follow the procedure in the vehicle service manual. A typical procedure is to turn the ignition key OFF and disconnect the negative cable from the battery. Apply and release the brake pedal with a force of about 50 pounds [222 N] at least 20 times. When the accumulator is depressurized, the brake pedal will have a different feel.

DRUM-BRAKE SERVICE

➤ 53-38 SERVICING DRUM BRAKES

Complaints of faulty braking action should be analyzed to determine the cause. Sometimes all that is necessary is to adjust drum-brake shoes. Other services include:

- Adding brake fluid.
- Flushing the hydraulic system.
- Bleeding the hydraulic system to remove air.
- Repairing or replacing the master cylinder or wheel cylinders.
- Replacing brake linings.
- Refinishing the drums.
- Repairing or replacing the power-brake unit.
- Replacing wheel-speed sensors.

In addition, brake hoses and lines are replaced along with other sensors, switches, and valves. Tube cutting, bending, and flaring are described in ➤7-24.

➤ 53-39 ADJUSTING DRUM BRAKES

Drum brakes without adjusters require periodic adjustment to compensate for lining wear. Self-adjusting drum brakes should require adjustment only after the brakes have been disassembled for service. These services include replacing

brake shoes, and refinishing or replacing the brake drums.

Procedures for adjusting the various types of drum brakes are in the vehicle service manual. Most duo-servo brakes (➤52-11) can be adjusted through a slot or hole in the backing plate (Fig. 53-20). A *brake-shoe adjusting gauge* (Fig. 53-21) can be used to make a preliminary adjustment if the drums are removed. Complete the adjustment by making several alternating reverse and forward stops. If adequate pedal reserve does not build up, the self-adjusters are not working.

➤ 53-40 REPLACING DRUM-BRAKE SHOES

When linings wear, shoes must be replaced. This requires removal of the wheel and brake drum. Then remove the

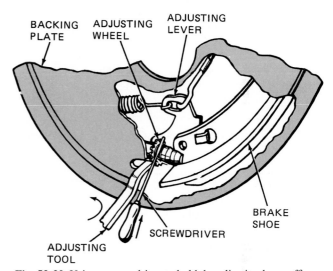

Fig. 53-20 Using a screwdriver to hold the adjusting lever off the adjusting screw so it can be turned with the adjusting tool. (*Bendix Corporation*)

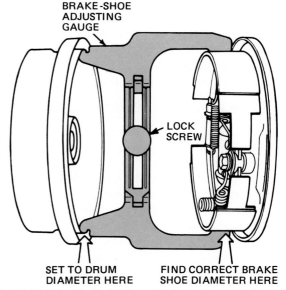

Fig. 53-21 Using the brake-shoe adjusting gauge to set the preliminary clearance between the linings and the drum. (*Ford Motor Company*)

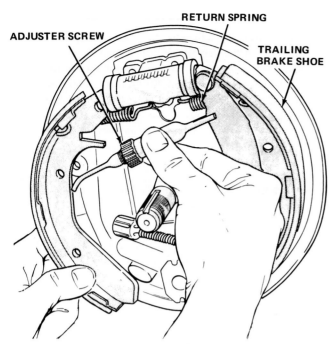

Fig. 53-22 Replacing brake shoes on a rear drum brake. (*Chrysler Corporation*)

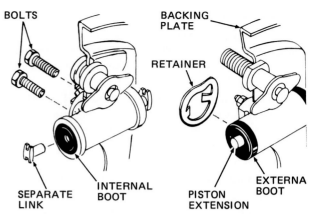

Fig. 53-23 Two methods of attaching the wheel cylinder to the backing plate. (*Delco Moraine Division of General Motors Corporation*)

adjuster screw and worn shoes (Fig. 53-22). Install new shoes.

➤ 53-41 SERVICING BRAKE DRUMS

Service or replace brake drums if they are distorted, cracked, scored, rough, or excessively glazed (Fig. 53-13). Light score marks can be removed with fine emery cloth. Remove all traces of emery. Deeper scores, roughness, or glaze can be removed by turning or grinding the drum on a *brake-drum lathe*. After refinishing, the diameters of the left and right drums on the same axle should be within 0.010 inch [0.24 mm] of each other. If the diameters vary more than this, replace both drums.

Brake drums have a *discard diameter* cast into them. This dimension is the maximum allowable diameter. If the drum must be refinished to a larger diameter, replace it. The drum would be too thin for safe use.

➤ 53-42 WHEEL-CYLINDER SERVICE

Most wheel cylinders can be disassembled and rebuilt on the vehicle. However, many manufacturers recommend removing the wheel cylinder. This makes it easier to properly clean, inspect, and reassemble the wheel cylinder. To remove a wheel cylinder, first remove the wheel and brake drum. Disconnect the brake hose from the wheel cylinder. Take out the attaching bolts or retainer (Fig. 53-23). Plug or tape closed the end of the hose to prevent dirt from entering.

Disassemble the wheel cylinder by pulling off the boots. Push out the pistons, cups, and spring. Clean parts in clean

brake fluid. Dry the parts with the compressed air. Put them on a clean lint-free towel. Blow out the passages in the wheel cylinder with compressed air to make sure they are clear.

Inspect the wheel-cylinder bore for scoring and corrosion. Use crocus cloth to remove light corrosion and stains. Replace the wheel cylinder if this does not clean the bore or if it is pitted or scored. Some wheel cylinders can be honed (Fig. 53-24). However, the bore must not be honed more than 0.003 inch [0.08 mm] larger than its original diameter. If scores do not clean up, replace the wheel cylinder. Also, replace the wheel cylinder if the clearance between the bore and pistons is excessive.

When reassembling the wheel cylinder, lubricate all parts with clean brake fluid. Install all the new parts in the wheel-cylinder repair or rebuild kit when reassembling the wheel cylinder.

Careful! Do not allow any grease or oil to touch the rubber parts or other internal parts in the hydraulic system. Oil or grease will cause the rubber parts to swell. This can lead to brake failure.

➤ 53-43 MASTER-CYLINDER SERVICE

Some master cylinders can be rebuilt. Others should be replaced. The service procedures for cast-iron and composite master cylinders (➤52-24) are similar. However, some master-cylinders have coated bores that should not be honed.

To service the master cylinder, first clean the outside. Then remove the master cylinder from the vehicle. Remove the cover and seal, and pour out any remaining brake fluid. Mount the master cylinder in a vise.

Follow the disassembly instructions in the vehicle service manual. Figure 52-29 shows a disassembled master cylinder. A typical disassembly procedure is to force the primary piston inward and remove the snap ring from the

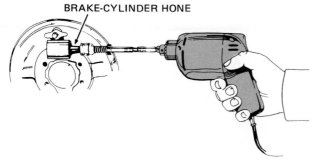

Fig. 53-24 Honing the bore in a wheel cylinder. (*ATW*)

groove in the piston bore. Then remove the primary-piston assembly. Using an air nozzle, apply slight air pressure through the vent port in the secondary reservoir. This will force out the secondary-piston assembly.

Clean all parts in brake fluid or brake-cleaning solvent. Blow dry with compressed air. Replace the master cylinder if the bore is scored, corroded, pitted, or cracked. In master-cylinder bores that can be honed, replace the master cylinder if pits or scores remain after light honing. Assemble the master cylinder following the assembly instructions in the vehicle service manual. Install all the new parts in the master-cylinder repair or rebuild kit.

Bench-bleed the master cylinder before installing it on the vehicle. To do this, install *bleeder tubes* in the outlets (Fig. 53-25). Fill the reservoirs with brake fluid. Then move the pistons back and forth to remove any trapped air. Stop when no more bubbles are visible in the brake fluid.

> **CAUTION!**
>
> Always wear eye protection (safety glasses or safety goggles) when bench-bleeding a master cylinder. Some brake fluid may spray out. Do not hold your face directly above the reservoirs when operating the pistons.

DISC-BRAKE SERVICE

➤ 53-44 SERVICING DISC BRAKES

The brake shoes in fixed calipers usually can be replaced without removing the caliper. With the vehicle on a lift or safety stands, remove the wheel. Remove some fluid from the master-cylinder reservoir (Fig. 53-26). Discard this fluid. Then use slip-joint pliers to push the pistons in. Use two pairs of pliers to pull the shoes out. Removing fluid from the reservoir prevents it from overflowing when the pistons are pushed in.

On the floating and sliding caliper, the wheel and caliper must be removed to replace the shoes. First, remove two-thirds of the fluid from the reservoir (Fig. 53-26). Discard the fluid. Raise the vehicle and remove the wheel. Use a C clamp (Fig. 53-27) and tighten it to force the piston back into its cylinder. Remove the mounting hardware and lift

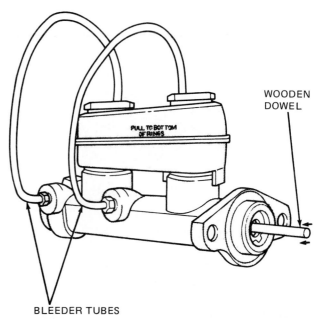

Fig. 53-25 Install bleeder tubes and operate the pistons with a wooden dowel to bench-bleed the master cylinder. (*Chrysler Corporation*)

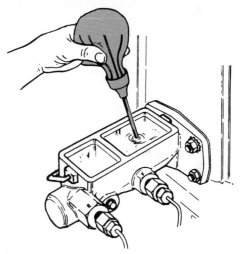

Fig. 53-26 Before performing any disc-brake service, remove about 1/2 to 2/3 of the fluid from the master cylinder. (*ATW*)

off the caliper. Support it with a wire hook so the caliper does not hang from the brake hose. Remove the old shoes. Remove the sleeves and bushings from the caliper. Figure 53-28 shows a disassembled floating caliper.

To install the caliper, first install new sleeves and bushings and the shoes. Make sure the piston is pushed back in its cylinder. Position the caliper over the disc and install the mounting bolts. If necessary, clinch the upper ears of the outboard shoe to hold it in place. The ear should be flat against the caliper.

Add fresh brake fluid to the reservoir. Pump the brake pedal several times to seat the linings against the disc and get a firm pedal. Check and fill the master cylinder if necessary.

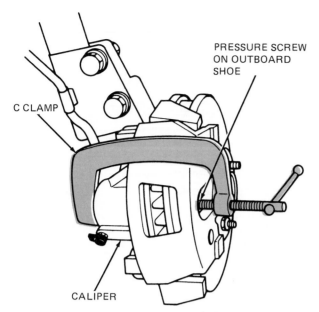

Fig. 53-27 Use a C clamp to force the piston back into the caliper bore. (*Buick Division of General Motors Corporation*)

CAUTION!

Do not try to remove the vehicle until you feel a firm brake pedal.

➤ 53-45 CALIPER SERVICE

If caliper pistons or seals require replacement, remove the caliper from the vehicle. Use a *caliper-piston remover* or compressed air (Fig. 53-29) to remove the piston from the caliper. Clean all parts using alcohol or clean brake fluid and wipe them dry. Clean out all drilled passages and bores.

Inspect the caliper bore for scratches or scoring. Light scratches or corrosion can usually be cleaned out with

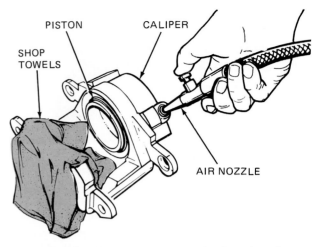

Fig. 53-29 Using air pressure to remove the piston from the caliper. (*Buick Division of General Motors Corporation*)

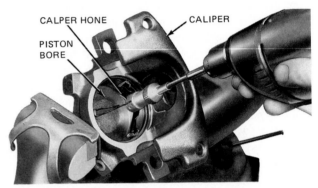

Fig. 53-30 Honing the caliper bore. (*Chrysler Corporation*)

crocus cloth. Bore with light roughness or corrosion can be cleaned with a hone (Fig. 53-30). However, if honing increases the bore diameter more than 0.001 inch [0.025 mm], install a new caliper. Replace any caliper piston that is pitted or scored. Also, replace a metal piston if any of its chrome plating has worn off.

Fig. 53-28 A disassembled floating caliper. (*Buick Division of General Motors Corporation*)

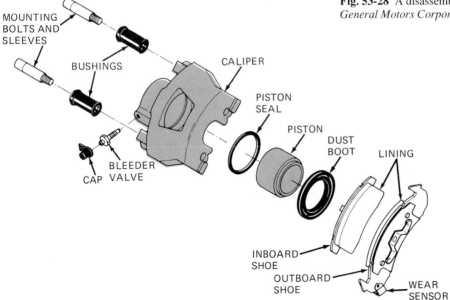

Assemble the caliper by first dipping the new piston seal in clean brake fluid (Fig. 53-28). Install the seal in the groove in the caliper bore. Lubricate the piston with clean brake fluid and install a new dust boot on the piston. Then install the piston in the caliper. Do not unseat or twist the seal. Install the caliper on the vehicle. Check and, if necessary, adjust the wheel bearings.

➤ 53-46 SERVICING BRAKE DISCS

Brake discs require replacement if they become deeply scored or warped. Light scores and grooving are normal

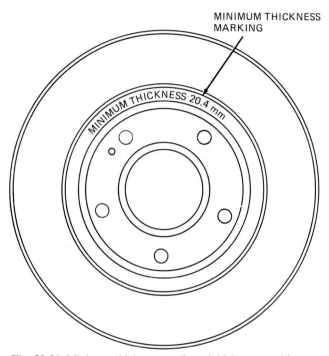

Fig. 53-31 Minimum thickness, or discard thickness, marking on a disc-brake rotor. (*Chrysler Corporation*)

and will not affect braking. Heavier scores require refinishing or replacing the disc. Install a new disc if wear is beyond acceptable limits.

Each brake disc is marked with a *discard thickness* (Fig. 53-31). This is the minimum thickness to which the disc can be refinished. If refinishing would cause the disc thickness to be less than the discard thickness, replace the disc. It would be too thin for safe use.

HYDRAULIC-SYSTEM SERVICE

➤ 53-47 FLUSHING THE NON-ABS HYDRAULIC SYSTEM

Flushing requires removing all of the old brake fluid from the hydraulic system. Some vehicle manufacturers recommend flushing when new parts are installed. The system *must* be flushed if it has been contaminated. Signs of contamination include corroded metal parts and soft or swollen rubber parts. If contamination has occurred, replace all rubber parts before flushing the system.

To flush the system, install a pressure bleeder on the master cylinder (Fig. 53-32). If the system has a metering valve (➤52-21), it must be held in the open position. Bleed the caliper or wheel cylinder farthest from the master cylinder first. Connect a bleeder hose on the bleeder valve. Put the other end of the hose in a transparent container partly filled with clean brake fluid.

A typical bleeding sequence is right rear, left rear, right front, and left front. Open the right-rear bleeder valve about 1 1/2 turns and let fluid drain into the container. Close the valve when the fluid appears clean and clear. Repeat the procedure at each wheel. When flushing is completed, fill the master-cylinder reservoir and bleed the hydraulic system (➤53-48).

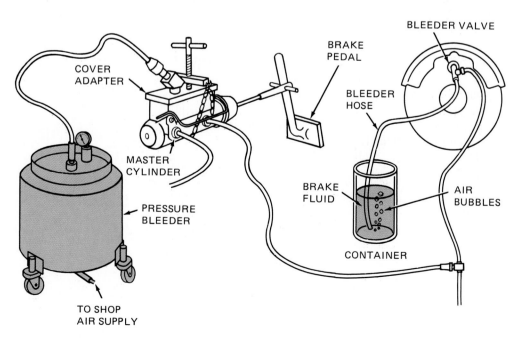

Fig. 53-32 Bleeding the hydraulic system with a pressure bleeder. (*Pontiac Division of General Motors Corporation*)

At least one quart [0.946 L] of brake fluid or *flushing fluid* may be needed to flush the hydraulic system.

➤ 53-48 FILLING AND BLEEDING THE NON-ABS HYDRAULIC SYSTEM

A soft or spongy brake pedal (➤53-17) usually indicates air trapped in the hydraulic system. The system must be bled to remove the air. Bleeding is also required if connections have been loosened or opened during service work. This can allow air to enter the hydraulic system.

Bleeding is similar to flushing (➤53-47). However, watch for air bubbles in the fluid during bleeding. If the master cylinder has a bleeder valve, bleed the master-cylinder first. Continue bleeding at each bleeder valve until the fluid runs out with no air bubbles (Fig. 53-32). During bleeding, make sure the master-cylinder reservoir stays filled. Add fluid as necessary.

➤ 53-49 BLEEDING THE ABS HYDRAULIC SYSTEM

Follow the procedure in the vehicle service manual to bleed the brakes on a vehicle with an antilock-braking system. On some vehicles, the two sections of the hydraulic system are bled in different ways. The front wheels are bled the same way as described in ➤53-48. However, some vehicles with ABS have a hydraulic unit that maintains pressure after the engine and ignition key are OFF. This allows bleeding the rear wheels without using a pressure bleeder.

After connecting the bleeder hose to one rear-wheel bleeder valve, put the lower end of the hose in a container partly filled with clean brake fluid. Then turn the ignition key ON to assure pressure in the hydraulic unit. Slightly depress the brake pedal for at least 10 seconds. When the fluid runs out clear and without bubbles, close the bleeder valve. Then bleed the brake at the other wheel.

MULTIPLE-CHOICE TEST

*Select the **one** correct, best, or most probable answer to each question.*
You can find the answers in the section indicated at the end of each question.

1. The brake pedal goes to the floor. All the following could be the cause EXCEPT (➤53-13)
   a. lack of brake fluid
   b. loose wheel bearing
   c. self-adjusters not working
   d. brake linings worn

2. In a car with front-disc and rear-drum brakes, the brake pedal sinks slowly to the floor while the pedal is depressed at a traffic light. This condition could be caused by (➤53-13)
   a. a leaking cup in the master cylinder
   b. a leaking power-brake booster
   c. a leaking residual check valve
   d. an internal leak in the combination valve

3. A possible cause of all brakes dragging is (➤53-15)
   a. a loose wheel bearing
   b. a piston stuck in a wheel cylinder or caliper
   c. insufficient brake-pedal free travel
   d. insufficient pedal reserve

4. The vehicle pulls to one side when braking. All the following could be the cause EXCEPT (➤53-16)
   a. air in the hydraulic system
   b. oil or brake fluid on linings
   c. shoes out of adjustment
   d. defective wheel cylinder

5. Air can enter the hydraulic system because of (➤53-17)
   a. self-adjusters not working
   b. failure of one section of the hydraulic system
   c. linings contaminated with oil or brake fluid
   d. low fluid level in master cylinder

6. Technician A says brake fade may be caused by brake lining that is overheated or wet. Technician B says failure of the power-brake booster increases the force required on the brake pedal. Who is right? (➤53-18)
   a. A only
   b. B only
   c. both A and B
   d. neither A nor B

7. Excessive pedal travel in a disc-brake system may be caused by all the following EXCEPT (➤53-25)
   a. uneven tire pressure
   b. fluid low in master cylinder
   c. excessive disc runout
   d. loose wheel bearing

CHAPTER 54

TIRES AND WHEELS: CONSTRUCTION AND SERVICE

After studying this chapter, and with proper instruction and equipment, you should be able to:

- Describe the various types of tire construction and tread patterns.
- Explain the size designation and sidewall markings on a tire.
- Inspect tires and wheels, and rotate tires.
- Demount and repair a punctured tire and a leaky wheel.
- Mount tires, and check tire and wheel runout.
- Balance wheels on and off the car.

TIRES AND TUBES

➤ 54-1 PURPOSE OF TIRES

The automotive *chassis* includes the brake, steering, and suspension systems described in earlier chapters. The chassis components that drive the vehicle and support its weight are the *wheels* and *tires* (Fig. 54-1). Only the vehicle tires have contact with the road surface.

Tires have two functions. First, they are air-filled cushions that absorb most of the shocks caused by road irregularities. The tires flex as they meet those irregularities. This reduces the effect of road shocks on the vehicle, passengers, and load. Second, the tires grip the road to provide good traction. This enables the vehicle to accelerate, brake, and make turns without skidding.

➤ 54-2 TYPES OF TIRES

There are two types of tires: *tube* and *tubeless.* Tube tires have an *inner tube* inside the tire (Fig. 54-2). This is a round rubber container that holds the air which supports the vehicle. Both the tube and tire mount on the wheel *rim.* A *tire valve* (➤54-6) is part of the tube and protrudes through the rim. Compressed air is forced through the valve to inflate the tube. The air pressure in the tube then causes the tire to hold its shape.

Tubes are used in some truck and motorcycle tires. Tubes are seldom used in passenger and light-duty vehicles. Most automotive vehicles use tubeless tires (Fig. 54-3). The tire mounts on an airtight rim so air is retained between the flange and the tire bead.

Fig. 54-1 A tire-and-wheel assembly. The tire is the only contact between the vehicle and the road surface. (*Bridgestone Tire*)

➤ 54-3 TIRE CONSTRUCTION

The tire *casings* (Fig. 54-3) for tube and tubeless tires are made in the same way. Layers of cord or *plies* are shaped

749

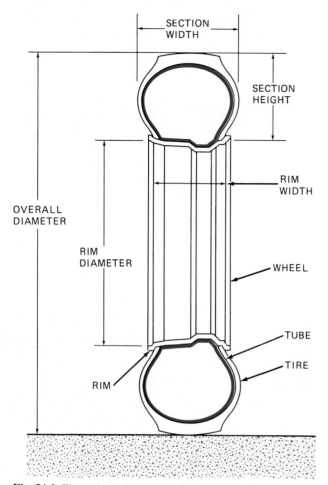

Fig. 54-2 Tire and rim cut away to show the tube. (*ATW*)

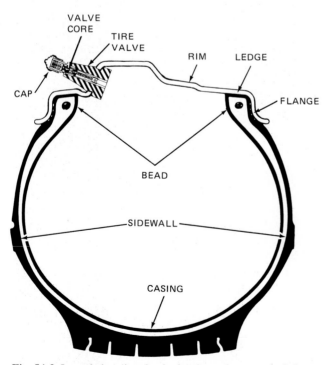

Fig. 54-3 In a tubeless tire, the tire bead rests between the ledges and flanges of the rim to produce an airtight seal. (*ATW*)

on a form and impregnated with rubber. The tire sidewalls and treads are then applied (Fig. 54-4). They are *vulcanized* in place to form the tire. To *vulcanize* means to heat the rubber under pressure. This molds the tire into the desired form.

The number of cord layers or plies varies. Passenger-car tires have 2, 4, or 6 plies. Heavy-duty truck and bus tires may have up to 14 plies. Tires for heavy-duty service, such as earth-moving machinery, may have up to 32 plies.

All tires do not have the same shape or *profile*. The *aspect ratio* or *profile ratio* differs. This is the ratio of a tire's *section height* to *section width* (Fig. 54-5). Three aspect ratios are 80, 70, and 60. The lower the number, the wider the tire appears. A 60-series tire is only 60 percent as high as it is wide.

➤ **54-4 BIAS AND RADIAL PLIES**

Plies can be applied two ways: diagonally or radially (Fig. 54-6). For many years, most tires had diagonal or *bias* plies. These plies crisscross (Fig. 54-6, left). This makes a tire that is strong in all directions because the plies overlap. However, the plies tend to move against each other and produce heat, especially at high speed. Also, the tread tends to close or "squirm" as it meets the road.

Radial tires (Figs. 54-4 and 54-6, right) were brought

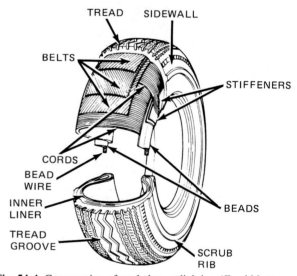

Fig. 54-4 Construction of a tubeless radial tire. (*Ford Motor Company*)

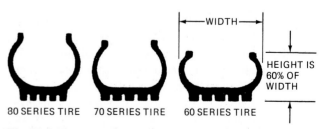

Fig. 54-5 Three aspect ratios of car tires. The lower the number, the wider the tire appears. (*ATW*)

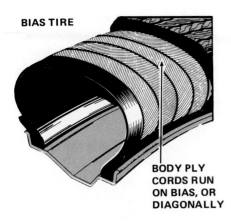
BIAS TIRE

BODY PLY
CORDS RUN
ON BIAS, OR
DIAGONALLY

BODY PLY CORDS RUN ON BIAS FROM
BEAD TO BEAD. BUILT WITH 2 TO 4 PLIES.
CORD ANGLE REVERSED ON EACH PLY.
TREAD IS BONDED DIRECTLY TO TOP PLY.

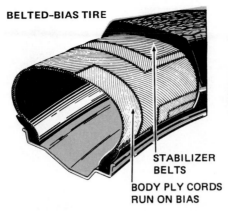
BELTED–BIAS TIRE

STABILIZER
BELTS

BODY PLY CORDS
RUN ON BIAS

STABILIZER BELTS ARE APPLIED DIRECTLY
BENEATH THE TREAD. BODY PLY CORDS
RUN ON BIAS, SIMILAR TO BIAS TIRE
CONSTRUCTION.

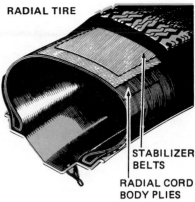
RADIAL TIRE

STABILIZER
BELTS

RADIAL CORD
BODY PLIES

RADIAL PLY CORDS RUN STRAIGHT
FROM BEAD TO BEAD WITH
STABILIZER BELTS APPLIED
DIRECTLY BENEATH THE TREAD.

Fig. 54-6 Three basic tire constructions. (*Firestone Rubber Company*)

out to remedy these problems. In a radial tire, the plies run parallel to each other and vertical to the tire bead. Stabilizer belts are applied over the plies to give strength parallel to the beads. Belts are made of rayon, nylon, fiberglass, or steel mesh.

All new cars and most light-duty vehicles have radial tires. The radial-tire sidewall is more flexible than the bias-ply. Therefore, the radial-tire tread wraps around the edge of the tire to compensate for the flexible sidewall. The result is that the radial tread does not heel up as much when the vehicle rounds a curve (Fig. 54-7). This keeps more of the tread on the road and reduces the tendency of the tire to skid.

The radial tire provides better fuel economy than a bias-ply tire. This is because the radial has less *rolling resistance* and less engine power is required to roll the tire. The radial also wears more slowly. It has less heat buildup and the tread does not squirm as the tire meets the road.

Some bias-ply tires are belted (Fig. 54-6, center). These tires are bias-ply tires to which stabilizer belts have been added under the tread.

➤ **54-5 TIRE TREAD**

The *tread* (Fig. 54-8) is that part of the tire that meets the road. It has a raised pattern molded into it. There are many designs, depending on the intended use of the tire. Many passenger vehicles use *mud-and-snow* tires (Fig. 54-8A). These can be identified by *M+S* or *M&S* molded into the sidewall. They provide quiet running with good traction in mud and snow.

Figure 54-8B shows a mud-and-snow tire used on four-wheel-drive pickup trucks. Its tread pattern is deeper and wider or "more aggressive" than the tread shown in Fig. 54-8A. This provides better mud-and-snow traction with acceptable wear on paved surfaces. The tread compound is also different to resist tearing and chunking.

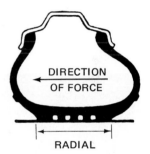

DIRECTION
OF FORCE

BIAS

DIRECTION
OF FORCE

RADIAL

Fig. 54-7 The difference in the amount of tread a bias tire and a radial tire put on the road during a turn.

The treads shown in Figs. 54-8A and 54-8B are *symmetric* and *nondirectional*. "Nondirectional" means the tire can run equally well in either direction. The tire can be installed with either sidewall facing out. Figure 54-8C shows a tire tread that is symmetric and *directional*. The tire must be installed for forward rotation in the direction of an arrow on the sidewall.

Figure 54-8D shows a directional and *asymmetric* sports-car tread used at the rear of the Chevrolet Corvette. "Asymmetric" means the inside half of the tread is not the same as the outside half. The tire is installed on the side of the car marked on the sidewall, and with the specified direction of forward rotation. This tire provides better braking and handling characteristics than a comparable symmetric, nondirectional tire.

Different size tires (➤54-9) are used at the front and rear of the Corvette. As a result, each tire is *position specific*. It can run only in a specified wheel-position on the car.

Other tires are classed as *snow tires, studded tires,* and *off-road tires.* Snow tires have large rubber cleats that cut through snow to improve traction. Studded tires have steel studs that stick out above the tread. These improve traction on ice and snow. However, many states regulate or ban studded tires because of possible damage to the road

(A) MUD-AND-SNOW TREAD-
PASSENGER-CAR TIRE

(B) MUD-AND-SNOW TREAD-
PICKUP-TRUCK TIRE

(C) SYMMETRIC AND DIRECTIONAL TREAD-
SPORTS-CAR TIRE

(D) ASYMMETRIC AND DIRECTIONAL TREAD-
SPORTS-CAR TIRE

Fig. 54-8 Types of tire tread. (*Goodyear Tire & Rubber Company*)

surface. A variety of off-road tires are available. These often have tread patterns using knobs or cleats. Off-road tires usually make noise and wear prematurely when driven on the highway.

Some tires use two different compounds in the tread. One compound is softer than the other for improved traction. In general, the softer the compound, the better the traction. The harder the compound, the longer the tread life.

➤ 54-6 TIRE VALVE

Air is put into the tire or tube through a spring-loaded tire valve or *Schrader valve* (Fig. 54-3). On tube tires, the valve is on the inner tube and sticks out through a hole in the rim. Tubeless tires use a separate tire valve mounted in a hole in the rim.

Spring force and air pressure hold the tire valve in its normally-closed position. A cap is usually threaded over the valve-stem end to protect it from dirt. The cap also helps guard against air leaks. Some tire valves have a non-removable valve core. The core is three-pronged white plastic. A special deflator is required to let air out of the tire.

➤ 54-7 TIRE PRESSURE

The amount of air pressure in the tire depends on the type of tire and how it is used. Passenger-car tires are inflated from about 22 to 36 psi [152 to 248 kPa]. Heavy-duty tires on trucks and buses may be inflated to 100 psi [690 kPa]. The maximum inflation pressure is marked on the tire sidewall (➤54-9). A *tire placard* or *tire information label* (Fig. 54-9) lists the recommended inflation pressure for each tire. This label is usually located on a door edge or door jamb, or inside the glovebox door. The label also lists maximum load and tire size (including spare).

Running the tires at the specified pressure helps provide proper vehicle handling while avoiding premature tire wear (Fig. 51-4). Underinflated tires wear on the outsides of the tread. Also, the tires flex excessively which produces extra

Fig. 54-9 A tire placard, or information label, lists the recommended inflation pressure for each tire on the vehicle. (*Ford Motor Company*)

heat and more rapid wear. Overinflation causes the center of the tread to wear. The tire cannot flex normally and this puts stress on the sidewalls and plies.

➤ 54-8 TIRE-PRESSURE MONITORING

Some vehicles have an electronic *low-tire-pressure warning system* (LTPWS). This system senses or monitors the tire pressures in a moving vehicle. When the pressure drops in a tire, an instrument-panel light illuminates to alert the driver. A *tire-pressure-sensor and transmitter* (Fig. 54-10) mounts inside the tires on each wheel. When the tire pressure falls below 25 psi [172 kPa], the tire-pressure sensor sends a radio signal to the *receiver-control module* in the instrument panel. This turns on the LOW TIRE PRESSURE light.

The receiver-control module also has self-diagnostic capabilities and can store fault codes. If no signal is received from a tire-pressure sensor, the control module turns on a SERVICE LTPWS light. The tire-pressure sensors are *piezoelectric* devices and do not need batteries. In a piezo-electric device, a small voltage appears across a crystal when a pressure is applied. In the tire-pressure sensors, the vibrations produced by the rolling tire generate the voltage. Therefore, the system works only when the vehicle is moving or the tire is being vibrated.

➤ 54-9 TIRE SIZE AND SIDEWALL MARKINGS

Figure 54-11 shows the format for the metric *tire-size designation* found on most tires. Various letters and numbers may appear in each position. Each marking has a special meaning. Figure 54-12 shows the sidewall markings on a

Fig. 54-10 A tire-pressure sensor on the wheel inside the tire, which signals when the tire pressure is low. (*EPIC Technologies, Inc.*)

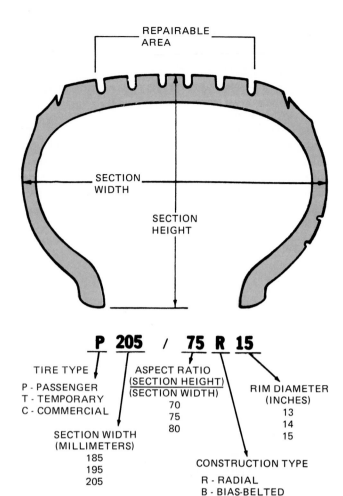

Fig. 54-11 Metric tire-size designations. *(ATW)*

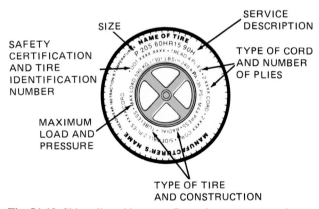

Fig. 54-12 Sidewall markings on a P-metric passenger-car tire. *(Tire Industry Safety Council)*

typical *P-metric* passenger-car tire. The tire size is *P205/60HR15*. *P* stands for passenger (*LT* for light truck). *205* is the tire width in millimeters. *60* is the aspect ratio (➤54-3), or ratio of height to width. *H* is the *speed rating* (➤54-10). *R* means radial (*B* for belted bias, *D* for diagonal bias). *15* is the diameter of the wheel in inches. Wheel diameter is given in inches in all tire-sizing systems.

An example of an older system for designating tire size is *GR78-14*. The *14* means a rim diameter of 14 inches. The *78* indicates the aspect ratio (➤54-3). The *R* means the tire is a radial. "G" indicates the tire is for a standard or full-size car of those years. In addition, *load range B* is also marked on the sidewall. This indicates the allowable load. There are three load ranges for passenger-car tires: *B*, *C*, and *D*. *D* has the highest load-carrying capacity.

> **NOTE** | P-metric tire sizes (Fig. 54-11) do not correspond with the older tire sizes. For example, a P205/75R15 tire is not exactly equal in size and load-carrying capacity to an FR78-15 tire.

➤ 54-10 SPEED-RATED TIRES

An optional letter after the aspect ratio specifies the speed rating of the tire (Fig. 54-13). This helps assure that the tire can operate safely at the rated vehicle speed. The higher the speed rating, the better the tire quality and performance. A tire with a higher speed rating may wear faster than a non-rated or lower speed-rated tire.

Some speed-rated tires carry a *service description* (*90H* in Fig. 54-12) instead of showing the speed symbol in the size designation. The *load index* is 90. The *speed symbol* is H.

When replacing speed-rated tires, the new tires must have the same or higher speed rating. Otherwise, vehicle speed should never exceed that of the tire with the lowest speed rating. A speed-rated tire with a puncture in the tread area may be repaired. The speed rating may no longer apply, however. Also, the speed rating may no longer apply to a tire after it has been *retreaded* (➤54-33).

> **NOTE** | Having speed-rated tires on a vehicle does not mean the vehicle can be safely driven at the maximum speed for which the tires are rated. Bad road and weather conditions, unusual vehicle characteristics, and other factors may make high-speed operation unsafe and unlawful.

➤ 54-11 TIRE GRADING

The Department of Transportation (DOT) requires tire manufacturers to grade their tires for treadwear, traction, and temperature resistance. Numbers and letters indicating these grades are molded into the sidewall (Fig. 54-12). A tire with a *treadwear grade* of 200 should wear twice as long as a tire graded 100, under the same conditions. A *traction grade* of A (the highest grade) indicates the tire should have better ability to stop on wet pavement than a tire graded B or C (the lowest grade). A *temperature grade* of A (the highest grade) indicates the tire should have better resistance to generating heat than a tire graded B or C (the lowest grade).

SPEED SYMBOL	MAXIMUM SPEED
Z	*above 149 mph (240 km/h)
V (No service description)	*above 130 mph (210 km/h)
V (Service description)	149 mph (240 km/h)
H	130 mph (210 km/h)
U	124 mph (200 km/h)
T	118 mph (190 km/h)
S	112 mph (180 km/h)

*Consult tire manufacturer for maximum speed.

Fig. 54-13 Speed ratings of tires. (*Tire Industry Safety Council*)

Fig. 54-14 Sealing action in a self-sealing tire. (*Michelin North America, Inc.*)

Some vehicle manufacturers have a *tire performance criteria* (TPC) specification number molded into the sidewall of original-equipment (OE) tires. This shows the tire meets the vehicle manufacturer's performance standards. These include dimensions, endurance, handling, noise, rolling resistance, and traction. A specific TPC number is usually assigned to each tire size. For example, General Motors assigns *TPC SPEC 1025MS* to a P205/75R14 mud-and-snow tire.

➤ 54-12 SELF-SEALING TIRES

Some vehicles have *puncture-sealing* or *self-sealing tires* (Fig. 54-14). These are tubeless tires with a sealant applied inside the tire. The sealant minimizes air loss if the tread area is punctured by a nail or other object with a diameter of 3/16 inch [4.76 mm] or less.

As the nail penetrates the tire, the sealant coats and sticks to the nail. This reduces the chance of air loss while the nail is in the tire. Removing the nail draws the sealant into the puncture. This seals the hole and prevents air loss.

➤ 54-13 TUBES

Types of rubber used to make tubes include natural rubber and two types of synthetic rubber: *butyl* and *GR-S*. A butyl tube can be identified by a blue stripe. A GR-S tube has a red stripe. Natural rubber is not striped. Three kinds of inner tubes are:

1. *Radial-tire inner tube* A tube used in a radial tire must be rated as a *radial-tire inner tube*. Any other type of tube may fail when installed in a radial tire.
2. *Puncture-sealing tube* This tube has a plastic coating on its inside. The sealant and the sealing action are the same as in self-sealing tires (➤54-12).
3. *Safety tube* This is two tubes in one, one inside the other. If the outer tube fails, the inside tube retains some air pressure.

➤ 54-14 SPARE TIRES

Most vehicles carry a *spare tire*. It is installed if one of the four tires on the vehicle goes flat. In some vehicles, the spare is a regular, full-size tire mounted on the standard wheel. Other vehicles have a temporary *skin-type spare*. This is a lightweight tire with full-size diameter and a thin tread that has limited life. It is used as the spare in some vehicles that have a limited-slip differential (➤45-20).

Figure 54-15 shows two other types of spare tires: the *collapsible spare* and the *compact spare*. Both are also for temporary use only. They are smaller and lighter than a full-size spare and save weight and space. Never include any temporary spare in tire rotation (➤54-21) or use it as a regular tire. All temporary spares have thin tread with limited life. Also, some spare tires may be *non-pneumatic*.

1. COLLAPSIBLE SPARE This space-saving spare (Fig. 54-15A) is installed deflated. Then, before lowering the vehicle, inflate the tire using an aerosol can of pressurized gas called an *inflator*. Follow the instructions on the can. Some vehicles have a small electric air compressor to

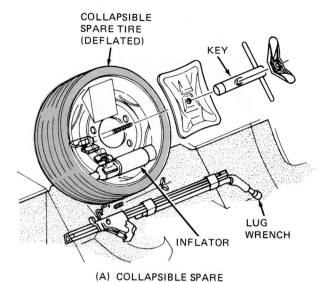

(A) COLLAPSIBLE SPARE

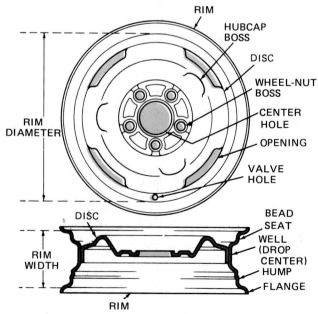

(B) COMPACT SPARE

Fig. 54-15 Two types of temporary spare tires. (*Cadillac Division of General Motors Corporation*)

inflate the tire. The compressor motor is powered by the vehicle battery when plugged into the cigarette-lighter socket. After removal, the collapsible spare can be deflated and stored for use again. Stow a new can of inflator with the collapsible spare.

CAUTION!

Do not drive more than 150 miles [240 km] on the collapsible spare. Vehicle speed must remain below 50 mph [80 kmph]. To exceed these limits risks a blowout.

2. COMPACT SPARE The compact spare (Fig. 54-15B) mounts on its own special wheel (15 × 4, for example). It is stowed inflated to 60 psi [415 kPa]. This gives the vehicle a rough and noisy ride when installed on the car.

The tread will last only about 1000 to 3000 miles [1609 to 4800 km]. Do not exceed 50 miles per hour [80 kmph] when the compact is on the ground.

3. NON-PNEUMATIC SPARE The use of a non-pneumatic or airless spare tire has been approved for passenger cars. The tire may be solid rubber or plastic, or made as part of the wheel. This type of tire is very light. The tire and wheel can be modled from plastic material as a single unit. Speed and mileage restrictions may also apply to the use of a non-penumatic spare.

WHEELS

➤ 54-15 WHEEL CONSTRUCTION

The pressed steel wheel (Fig. 54-16) is widely used. Many vehicles have aluminum wheels (Fig. 54-10). Aluminum is lighter than steel and reduces unsprung weight. This improves the ride because less bouncing is felt. Also, aluminum gets rid of heat faster than steel. Aluminum wheels run cooler and this can improve brake and tire performance.

Some vehicles have molded *composite wheels*. These are made of fiberglass, sheet-molding compound (SMC), and special resins. Composite wheels are lighter than aluminum wheels.

➤ 54-16 WHEEL ATTACHMENT AND WHEEL COVERS

Wheels are usually attached to the brake drum or disc by three to five *wheel nuts* or *lug nuts* (Fig. 51-17). The wheel end of the lug nuts normally has a tapered shape that

Fig. 54-16 Construction of a wheel. (*Chrysler Corporation*)

matches its seat in the wheel. The taper helps tightening the lug nuts to center the wheel.

Hub caps or *wheel covers* fasten by clips to many pressed-steel wheels. *Wheel-cover locks* (Fig. 54-17) provide protection against theft. A special *key wrench* is needed to remove or install the special lock bolt. The key wrench should be stored in the glovebox.

Aluminum wheels often have a *locking lug nut* on each wheel as an antitheft device. A *lug-nut key* is attached to the *lug wrench* (Fig. 54-15A) and stowed with the spare tire. The key has a circular keyway that matches a slot in the lug nut. To remove or install the lug nut, place the key on the lug nut. Then turn the nut with the lug wrench. Do not turn the nut with an impact wrench!

TIRE INSPECTION

➤ 54-17 CAUTIONS FOR SERVICING TIRES

Several cautions must be followed to avoid personal injury and to prevent damage to the wheel and tire.

1. *Matching tire and wheel width* Do not try to install a narrow tire with a high-aspect ratio on a wide rim. For example, a tire with an 80 aspect ratio (Fig. 54-5) must not be installed on a wide rim that requires a 60 tire.
2. *Matching tire and wheel diameter* Do not try to mount a 16-inch tire on a 16.5-inch wheel, or a 15-inch tire on a 15.5-inch wheel. The result could be a deadly explosion when inflating the tire. Check the rim size. It may be stamped near the center of the wheel disc.
3. *Mixing tires* All tires on the vehicle should be the same size, construction (radial or non-radial), and speed rating unless otherwise specified by the vehicle manufacturer. If two radials and two non-radials are on the vehicle, put the radials on the rear. Snow tires should be installed in pairs on the drive axle (either front or rear), or on all four wheels. Never put non-radial (bias or

belted-bias) snow tires on the rear if radials are on the front. Match tire sizes and construction on four-wheel drive vehicles. Tires affect vehicle stability and handling. Mixing tires may cause handling problems.

4. *Respecting compressed air* A terrific force is contained in an inflated tire. An explosion of the tire-and-wheel assembly can result from improper or careless mounting procedures. Never stand over a tire while inflating it. If the tire explodes, the sudden release of compressed air has enough energy to throw a person more than 30 feet [9 m] in the air. People have been seriously injured or killed by exploding tires.
5. *Protecting your eyes* Wear eye protection (safety glasses, safety goggles, or a face shield) when demounting and mounting tires. When deflating a tire, avoid the air stream from the tire valve. The air comes out at high speed and can blow dirt or debris into your eyes.

➤ 54-18 CHECKING TIRE PRESSURE AND INFLATING TIRES

Before checking tire pressure and adding air, know the correct pressure for the tire. The specification is in the owners manual and on the vehicle tire-information label (Fig. 54-9). When the vehicle is carrying a heavy load, pulling a trailer, or driving at sustained highway speed, higher tire pressure may be necessary. Maximum pressure should never exceed the maximum pressure marked on the tire sidewall (Fig. 54-12).

Inflation pressure is given for a cold tire. Pressure increases as tire temperature rises. Highway driving on a hot day can increase the tire pressure from 5 to 7 psi [35 to 48 kPa]. As the tire cools, it loses pressure. Never bleed a hot tire to reduce its pressure. The pressure will then be low when the tire cools. Install the cap on the tire valve after checking pressure or adding air.

➤ 54-19 TIRE INSPECTION

The purpose of inspecting tires is to determine if they are safe for further use. When defects or improper wear patterns are found (Fig. 51-4), inform the driver. Recommend the services that will correct the cause of abnormal wear.

Tires have *tread-wear indicators* or *wear bars* (Fig. 54-18). These are filled-in sections of the tread grooves that will show when the tread has worn down to 1/16 inch [1.6 mm]. A tire with a wear bar showing is worn out and should be replaced. Too little tread remains for continued safe driving. A *tread-depth gauge* can be inserted into the tread grooves to measure tread depth. Some states require a tread depth of at least 1/32 inch [0.8 mm] in any two adjacent grooves at any location on the tire.

Check for bulges in the sidewalls. Bulges mean plies have separated and the tire could fail at any time. Tires with separated or broken plies should be replaced. Remove

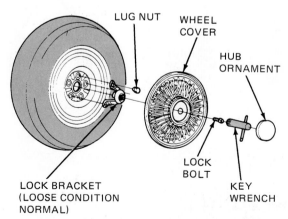

LUG NUT   WHEEL COVER

HUB ORNAMENT

LOCK BOLT   KEY WRENCH

LOCK BRACKET (LOOSE CONDITION NORMAL)

Fig. 54-17 Wheel with locking wheel cover and lock bracket. The special key wrench is needed to remove or install the lock bolt. (*Ford Motor Company*)

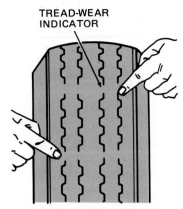

TREAD-WEAR
INDICATOR

Fig. 54-18 A tire tread worn down so much that the tread-wear indicators show.

any stone, pieces of glass, metal, or other objects wedged in the tread. These could work deeper into the tire and cause air loss. Some radial tires may have a slight indentation on the sidewall when the tire is inflated. This is a characteristic of some radial tires and normally does not affect tire performance.

A tire may look okay from the outside and still have internal damage. if you suspect internal damage, remove the tire from the rim. Then inspect the tire from the inside.

TIRE SERVICE

➤ 54-20 REMOVING WHEELS FROM THE VEHICLE

Tire rotation (➤54-21) and other tire and wheel services require removing the wheel from the vehicle. To remove the wheel, first remove the wheel cover or hub cap. This may require a special wrench to remove the locking lug nut (➤54-16) or wheel-cover lock (Fig. 54-17).

If each tire has a position-specific location on the vehicle (➤54-5), mark the position of the wheel to the hub. Aligning the marks helps maintain balance (➤54-28) if the same wheel-and-tire assembly is reinstalled. When using a hand wrench, loosen the wheel nuts before raising the vehicle. On some vehicles, the wheel nuts on the right side have right-hand threads. The nuts on the left side have left-hand threads. This allows the forward rotation of the wheels to tend to tighten the nuts, not loosen them.

Raise the vehicle and support it properly. Remove the wheel nuts. Then remove the wheel from the vehicle.

➤ 54-21 TIRE ROTATION

Some tires wear faster than others on the vehicle. This is because front and rear tires perform different jobs. Also, the type of vehicle and driving habits can cause tires to wear differently. To equalize tire wear, perform a *tire rotation* periodically or when unusual wear occurs. "Tire

rotation" means to switch the wheel-and-tire assemblies from one axle position to another. A typical recommendation is to rotate the tires at 7500 miles [12,000 km] and then every 15,000 miles [24,000 km].

Recommended tire-rotation patterns for rear-wheel drive vehicles are shown in Fig. 54-19. Notice that only the four tires on the vehicle are rotated. This is a *four-tire rotation*. If the vehicle has directional tires of the same size, they can be rotated front to rear (Fig. 54-19, right). Never include a temporary spare in the rotation. It must not be used as a regular tire. Figure 54-20 shows tire-rotation patterns for front-wheel-drive vehicles. A *five-tire rotation*

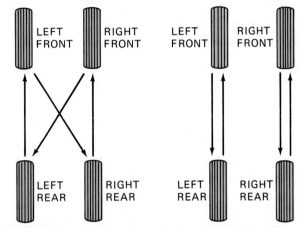

Fig. 54-19 Tire-rotation patterns for rear-wheel-drive vehicles with a temporary, or non-rotatable, spare. (*Buick Division of General Motors Corporation*)

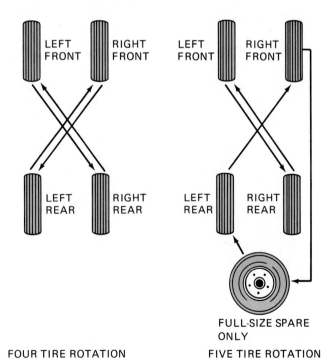

FULL-SIZE SPARE
ONLY

FOUR TIRE ROTATION   FIVE TIRE ROTATION

Fig. 54-20 Tire-rotation patterns for front-wheel-drive vehicles. A five-tire rotation can be made if the vehicle has a regular, full-size spare. (*Ford Motor Company*)

(Fig. 54-20, right) can be made if the vehicle has a regular, full-size spare.

Careful! Before any tire rotation, check that the tires on the vehicle are the same size, construction, and speed rating (➤54-17). Do not rotate tires on vehicles with different size tires on the front and rear. Directional tires must remain on the same side of the vehicle.

Always check tire pressures after rotating tires. Many vehicle manufacturers recommend that the front tires carry a different pressure than the rear tires.

➤ 54-22 DEMOUNTING THE TIRE FROM THE RIM

With the wheel off the vehicle, make a chalk mark or *index mark* across the tire and rim. Then you can reinstall the tire in the same position on the wheel.

To demount the tire, place the tire-and-wheel assembly on a *tire changer* (Fig. 54-21). Remove the valve core (Fig. 54-3) and release the air from the tire. Remove any rim-mounted *wheel weights* (➤54-28). Follow the tire-changer operating instructions to remove the tire from the rim. A typical procedure is to position the *bead breakers* (top and bottom) and loosen both tire beads from the rim flanges.

Lubricate the inside of the wheel and the bead areas with *rubber lubricant*. With the bottom tire bead in the wheel well (Fig. 54-16), place the *tire iron* under the top bead. Push the slot in the tire iron onto the *rotating finger* of the tire changer (Fig. 54-22). Start the tire changer. As the finger rotates, the tire iron removes the top bead from the rim.

Again, lubricate the inside of the wheel along with the well and bead areas. Place the tire iron under the bottom bead and then onto the rotating finger. Hold the side of the tire opposite the tire iron in the wheel well. As the tire iron rotates, the bottom bead is raised up. This frees the tire from the rim.

Fig. 54-21 An air-powered tire changer breaks the bead so the tire can be removed from the wheel. (*Ford Motor Company*)

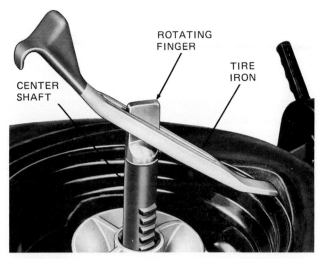

Fig. 54-22 Using the tire changer to lift the upper bead above the rim. The rotating finger rotates, carrying the bead-lifting tool, or tire iron, with it.

➤ 54-23 WHEEL INSPECTION

While the tire is off the wheel, check the wheel for dents and roughness. Do not try to straighten a bent wheel. This could weaken the wheel and cause it to fail later. Clean rust spots from steel wheels with steel wool. Clean aluminum wheels with soap and water. Decorative plastic inserts in wheels can be cleaned using a sponge and soap and water.

File off nicks or burrs. Clean out all filings and dirt. Replace defective tire valves (➤54-24).

➤ 54-24 REPLACING TIRE VALVES

If the tire valve needs replacement, remove it and install a new valve. There are two types: the snap-in type (Fig. 54-3) and the clamp-in type secured with a nut. To remove the snap-in type, cut off the base of the valve. Lubricate the new valve with rubber lubricant. Pull it into place with a *tire-valve installing tool*.

On the clamp-in type, remove the nut and take out the old valve. Install the new valve and tighten the nut securely.

➤ 54-25 MOUNTING THE TIRE ON THE RIM

Position the wheel on the tire changer (Fig. 54-21). Coat the rim and bead with rubber lubricant. When remounting the tire on the same rim, align the chalk marks or index marks made before demounting (➤54-22). Follow the tire-changer operating instructions to mount the tire. Then check the marks. If they are not aligned, reposition the tire.

Slowly inflate the tire. If the beads do not seat and the tire does not hold air, use a *mounting band* to spread the beads. You will usually hear a "pop" as the beads seat on the rim. Then install the valve core and inflate the tire to the recommended pressure. After a tire change or repair, check the wheel-and-tire assembly for balance (➤54-28).

➤ 54-26 INSTALLING THE WHEEL ON THE VEHICLE

Before installing the wheel, use a scraper or wire brush and clean any mud or corrosion from the wheel mounting surfaces. Do not lubricate the wheel studs or wheel nuts with grease or oil! Align any marks made before removal (➤54-20) and install the wheel on the hub. Install the wheel nuts until they are snug. Use the original wheel nuts, or only the same type and size wheel nuts as the originals.

Lower the vehicle. With a torque wrench (Fig. 54-23), tighten the wheel nuts alternately or in the specified sequence to the specified torque. This will prevent bending the wheel, brake drum, or brake rotor. To install a wheel cover (Fig. 54-17), align the *valve-stem extension* with the hole in the wheel cover. Then hit the outside edge of the wheel cover with your hand or tap gently with a rubber mallet until the wheel cover seats completely.

TIRE AND WHEEL BALANCE

➤ 54-27 WHEEL RUNOUT

Wheels that are bent or have excessive *lateral runout* or *radial runout* cause vibration (➤51-18) and balance problems (Fig. 51-5). For example, too much radial runout of the front wheels will cause the front end of the vehicle

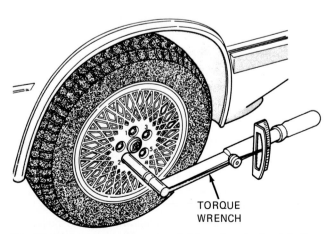

Fig. 54-23 Use a torque wrench and tighten the wheel nuts in the specified sequence to the proper torque. (*Chrysler Corporation*)

to vibrate up and down. Sometimes repositioning the tire on the wheel reduces or eliminates excessive radial runout. A quick check of lateral runout and radial runout can be made using a safety stand (Fig. 54-24).

To measure lateral runout, position a dial indicator or *runout gauge* against the wheel and the scrub rib of the tire as shown in Fig. 54-25A. With the dial indicator in each position, rotate the wheel in both directions. The total indicator reading (➤5-17) shows the amount of lateral runout.

To measure radial turnout, position the dial indicator in

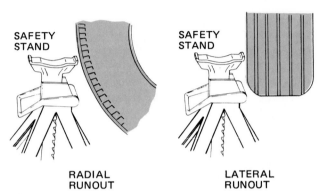

Fig. 54-24 Making a quick check of the radial runout and lateral runout of a tire with a safety stand. (*Ford Motor Company*)

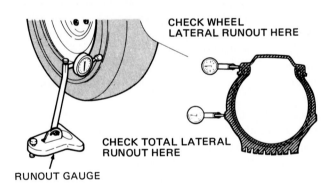

(A) CHECKING LATERAL RUNOUT

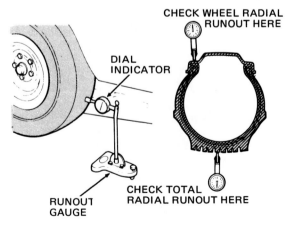

(B) CHECKING RADIAL RUNOUT

Fig. 54-25 Using a dial-indicating runout gauge to measure the wheel and tire (A) lateral runout and (B) radial runout. (*Ford Motor Company*)

the two positions shown in Fig. 54-25B. Rotate the wheel in both directions and note the amount of runout.

> **NOTE** If wheel runout exceeds specifications, the wheel may be bent or the wheel bearing is loose or damaged. Excessive tire runout indicates a worn or damaged tire.

➤ 54-28 WHEEL BALANCE

The wheel-and-tire assembly may be checked for *wheel balance* either on or off the vehicle. There are two types of wheel balance: *static* (at rest) and *dynamic* (in motion). Dynamic balancing is usually the preferred method. A tire and wheel may be in static balance and still have dynamic unbalance. Either static or dynamic unbalance will cause the steering wheel to shake from side to side at higher speeds.

1. STATIC BALANCE This is the equal distribution of weight around the wheel (Fig. 54-26). A wheel that has static unbalance rotates with a bouncing action or wheel *tramp* (➤51-9). Front wheels that have static unbalance may cause the front end to vibrate up and down at most road speeds. This will eventually cause uneven tire wear.

To static balance the wheel, remove it from the vehicle. Place the wheel on a *bubble* or *static balancer* (Fig. 54-27). If the wheel is heavier in one section (unbalanced), the bubble in the center of the balancer will move off center. Balance the wheel by adding *wheel weights* to the rim (Fig. 54-28) until the bubble is centered. Steel wheels and aluminum wheels may require different types of *clip-on weights*. Aluminum wheels may need *adhesive* or *stick-on weights*.

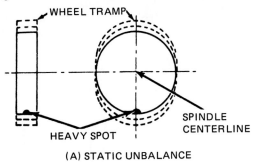

(A) STATIC UNBALANCE

(B) STATIC BALANCE

Fig. 54-26 Static wheel balance. (A) Static unbalance causes wheel tramp. (B) Adding weights restores the equal distribution of weight around the wheel. (*Ford Motor Company*)

Fig. 54-27 Balancing a wheel-and-tire assembly on a bubble, or static, balancer.

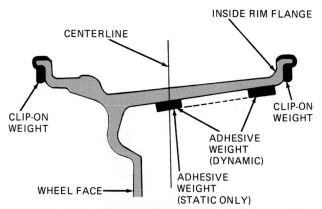

Fig. 54-28 Adding balance weights to the wheel. Clip-on weights may be used on the rim flange. Aluminum wheels may require adhesive, or stick-on, weights. (*Ford Motor Company*)

2. DYNAMIC BALANCE This is the equal distribution of weight on each side of the tire centerline (Fig. 54-29). When the wheel has dynamic balance, there is no tendency for side-to-side movement as the wheel spins. A wheel that has dynamic unbalance may cause wheel *shimmy* (➤51-8).

Dynamic balancing or *spin balancing* is performed with the wheel either on or off the vehicle, depending on the type of *wheel balancer* being used. Inspect the tires (➤54-19). Then balance the wheels following the operating instructions for the balancer. Figure 54-30 shows an off-the-car wheel balancer. Before spinning the wheel, lower the safety hood. It catches any debris or stones thrown out of the tread as the tire spins. The balancer shows where and how much weight is needed to correct the balance.

TIRE AND WHEEL REPAIR

➤ 54-29 TIRE REPAIR

Small holes in tires may be repaired. A rubber plug can be installed with the tire mounted (➤54-30) or demounted

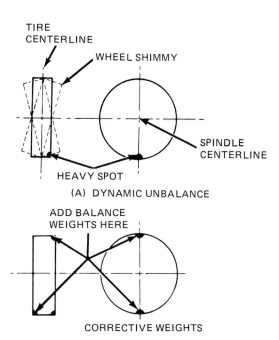

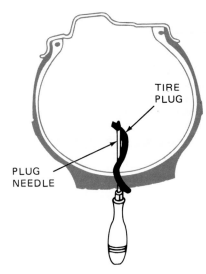

Fig. 54-29 Dynamic wheel balance. (A) Dynamic unbalance causes wheel shimmy. (B) Adding weights restores the equal distribution of weight on each side of the tire centerline. (*Ford Motor Company*)

Fig. 54-31 A plug needle being used to insert a rubber plug into a hole in a tire, making a temporary repair. (*ATW*)

Fig. 54-30 Using an off-the-vehicle wheel balancer to dynamic balance, or spin balance, a wheel after removal from the vehicle. The safety hood must be lowered before spinning the wheel. The balancer shows where and how much weight is needed to correct the balance. (*Hunter Engineering Company*)

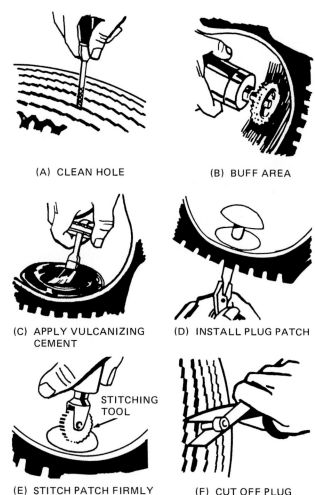

(A) CLEAN HOLE (B) BUFF AREA

(C) APPLY VULCANIZING CEMENT (D) INSTALL PLUG PATCH

(E) STITCH PATCH FIRMLY (F) CUT OFF PLUG

Fig. 54-32 Steps in preparing a tubeless radial tire for repair and installing the plug patch. (*Goodyear Tire & Rubber Company*)

(➤54-31). Installing a plug in a mounted tire is only a temporary repair. It must be replaced with a repair made from inside the tire. Figure 54-11 shows the repairable area of a tire. If the puncture is outside this area, replace the tire.

➤ ### 54-30 TEMPORARY TUBELESS-TIRE REPAIR

Temporary repair of a small puncture in a tubeless tire can be made with the tire mounted on the rim. A *tire plug* (Fig.

762

54-31) installed through the pucture seals it and prevents leakage.

➤ 54-31 TUBELESS-TIRE REPAIR

To repair a small hole in a tubeless tire, remove the puncturing object. Do not try to repair a badly damaged tire. Replace the tire if plies are separated or torn, or have holes in them. Do not try to repair a puncture bigger than 1/4 inch [6 mm]. The patch may not hold.

Remove the tire from the rim. Plug the hole from inside the tire with a head-type *plug patch*. Figure 54-32 shows the steps in preparing the tire and installing the plug patch.

NOTE Do not weld, heat, or peen a steel wheel in an attempt to repair it. If a steel wheel leaks, some manufacturers recommend replacing the wheel.

➤ 54-32 WHEEL REPAIR

Some air leaks around the disc welds (Fig. 54-16) on a steel wheel can be repaired. Clean the area and apply two coats of vulcanizing cement to the inside of the rim. Cement a strip of rubber patching material over the area. Recheck for leaks.

MULTIPLE-CHOICE TEST

*Select the **one** correct, best, or most probable answer to each question.*
You can find the answers in the section indicated at the end of each question.

1. Technician A says the lower the aspect ratio, the wider the tire appears. Technician B says aspect ratio is the ratio of the tire's section height to section width. Who is right? (➤54-3)
   a. A only
   b. B only
   c. both A and B
   d. neither A nor B
2. All the following are true about radial tires EXCEPT (➤54-4)
   a. all plies run parallel to each other
   b. there is less squirm than with bias-ply tires
   c. a belt of steel mesh or other material is applied over the plies
   d. a radial tire has greater rolling resistance than a bias-ply tire
3. Recommended inflation pressures for the front and rear tires on the car are listed in the (➤54-7)
   a. VECI label
   b. tire information label
   c. VIN number
   d. sidewall markings
4. If two radials and two non-radials are on the vehicle, the radials should be (➤54-17)
   a. on the front
   b. on the rear
   c. removed from the vehicle
   d. inflated to a higher pressure

5. When rotating tires, all the following are true EXCEPT (➤54-21)
   a. Do not rotate tires if the front and rear tires are different sizes.
   b. Directional tires must remain on the same side of the car.
   c. Check tire pressures after rotating tires.
   d. Always perform a five-tire rotation.
6. A tire has excessive radial runout. The technician should (➤54-27)
   a. replace the tire
   b. reposition the wheel on the hub
   c. remove the balance weights causing tire distortion
   d. reposition the tire on the wheel
7. A driver says the front end of the car vibrates up and down at most road speeds. Technician A says too much radial runout of the front tires could be the cause. Technician B says static unbalance of the front tires could be the cause. Who is right? (➤54-27 and 54-28)
   a. A only
   b. B only
   c. both A and B
   d. neither A nor B

REVIEW QUESTIONS

1. Describe the different types of tire treads, and the characteristics of asymmetric and directional tires. (➤54-5).
2. Explain the importance of proper inflation pressure, and the operation of the tire-pressure monitoring system. (➤54-7 and 54-8)
3. What is the meaning of each letter and number in the tire-size designation P205/60HR15? (➤54-9)
4. What are the two methods of wheel balancing, and describe the steps in each. (➤54-28)
5. Describe two ways to repair a tubeless tire. (➤54-30 and 54-31)

PART 9

AUTOMOTIVE HEATING AND AIR CONDITIONING

Part 9 of *Automotive Mechanics* describes the ventilating, heating, and air-conditioning systems used in automotive vehicles. Included are explanations of how these systems work and how to diagnose and service them safely—both for the environment and for the technician. Refrigerant 134a is discussed along with how to use the refrigerant-recovery station. Also covered are how to use the scan tool and onboard diagnostics to find air-conditioning troubles more quickly.

There are two chapters in Part 9:

CHAPTER 55 Ventilation, Heating, and Air Conditioning
CHAPTER 56 Heater and Air-Conditioner Service

CHAPTER 55

VENTILATION, HEATING, AND AIR CONDITIONING

After studying this chapter, you should be able to:

- Describe how the passenger compartment is ventilated and heated.
- Explain the operation of the rear-window defogger and the heated windshield.
- Discuss the types of refrigerant and how a refrigeration system works.
- Explain the difference between fixed-displacement and variable-displacement compressors, and how each is controlled.
- Describe the construction and operation of manually-controlled and automatic air-conditioning systems.

VENTILATING AND HEATING

➢ 55-1 VENTILATING THE PASSENGER COMPARTMENT

For health and comfort, some fresh air must pass through the passenger compartment. This replaces the stale and sometimes smoke-filled air inside the vehicle. The process is called *ventilation*. There are two methods: *uncontrolled ventilation* and *controlled ventilation*.

Uncontrolled ventilation occurs when windows are opened. Controlled ventilation is either *ram-air* or *power*. In the ram-air system, opening vents or *ducts* admits air to the passenger compartment. Forward movement then

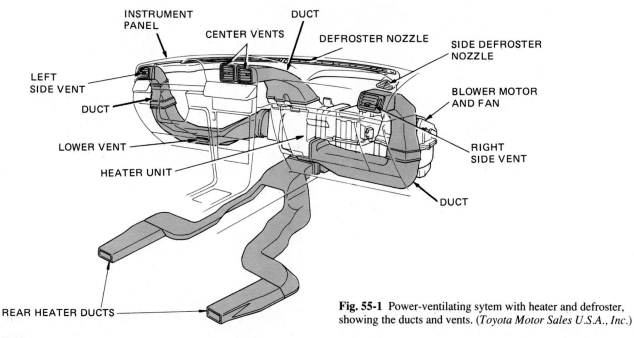

INSTRUMENT PANEL
DUCT
CENTER VENTS
DEFROSTER NOZZLE
SIDE DEFROSTER NOZZLE
LEFT SIDE VENT
DUCT
BLOWER MOTOR AND FAN
LOWER VENT
RIGHT SIDE VENT
HEATER UNIT
DUCT
REAR HEATER DUCTS

Fig. 55-1 Power-ventilating sytem with heater and defroster, showing the ducts and vents. (*Toyota Motor Sales U.S.A., Inc.*)

forces or *rams* air into the vehicle. However, when the vehicle stops or moves slowly, little fresh air enters. This is one reason most vehicles have a *power ventilating system* (Fig. 55-1). An electric *blower motor* and fan provide air circulation regardless of vehicle speed. The blower is also part of the heater (➤55-2) and the air conditioner (➤55-26).

➤ 55-2 PASSENGER-COMPARTMENT HEATER

Vehicles without factory-installed air conditioning (➤55-26) have a passenger-compartment *heater* (Figs. 55-1 and 55-2). Warm air from the heater helps defog or defrost the windshield. On some vehicles, the front side glass may also receive warm air. The *heater housing* (Fig. 55-2) mounts on the engine-compartment firewall. The housing contains a small radiator-like heat exchanger (➤25-12) or *heater core.*

To get heated-air delivery, set the *temperature-control lever* or *knob* (Fig. 55-3) for heat. *Heater hoses* (➤55-3) allow hot coolant from the engine to circulate through the heater core (Fig. 25-19). The heater core then warms the air flowing through it. This air may be recirculated passenger-compartment air, outside air, or a blend of the two. The setting of the *function-control lever* or *knob* controls the source of the air.

➤ 55-3 HEATER CONTROLS

The heater is controlled by the knobs, settings or levers, on a *heater-control panel* (Fig. 55-3). There are usually three basic controls. These are the *function control, temperature control,* and *blower speed.* The function control (➤55-2) determines which outlets discharge the heated air. The temperature control regulates the temperature of the heated air. The blower speed determines how fast the blower fan turns.

Movement of the function and temperature controls operates three doors inside the heater housing (Fig. 55-2). Changing the position of the *temperature door* allows more or less air to pass through the heater core. This controls how much air is heated. The *air door,* or *blend door,* can be moved to allow full air flow, no air flow, or any position in between. This provides *blend air* (Fig. 55-2). Moving the *defroster door* directs heated air onto the inside of the windshield.

The doors are controlled by cables or vacuum motors from the heater-control panel (Fig. 55-3). The function-control lever, or knob, controls the air door and defroster door. Moving the control sends intake-manifold vacuum to vacuum motors. As the vacuum-motor diaphragm moves, an attached arm or lever moves the door to produce the desired result. A cable connects from the temperature-control lever or knob to the temperature door (in Fig. 55-2). Moving the lever, or knob, causes the cable to reposition the door.

Engine coolant may flow continuously through the heater core (Fig. 25-19). This can cause unwanted heat in the passenger compartment. Some vehicles have a vacuum- or cable-operated *heater-* or *coolant-control valve* (Fig. 55-4). The valve is in the *heater inlet hose* that carries coolant from the engine to the heater core. Closing the coolant-control valve prevents coolant flow through the heater core. Sometimes a coolant-control valve will be found installed on a vehicle that did not have one when new.

➤ 55-4 HEATED-AIR DISTRIBUTION

The variable-speed blower motor and fan mount in the heater housing (Figs. 55-1 and 55-2). The position of the *blower-speed switch* (Fig. 55-3) controls the blower speed and resulting air circulation. The blower usually has three to five speeds.

Air from the heater is distributed through instrument-panel and floor outlets to the front-seat occupants. *Rear heater ducts* (Fig. 55-1) may extend under the front seats to deliver heat to the rear-seat passengers. The *defroster nozzle* delivers air to the inside of the windshield. This helps clear fogging of the glass and melts any ice and snow on it. The *side defroster nozzle* delivers air for defogging the front side windows.

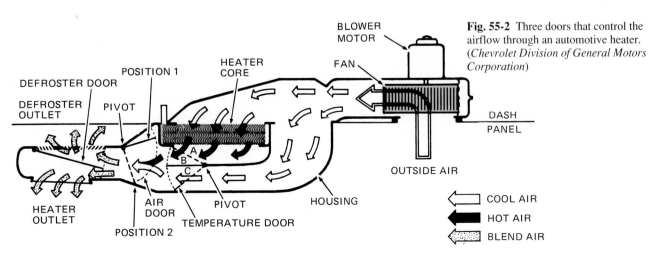

Fig. 55-2 Three doors that control the airflow through an automotive heater. (*Chevrolet Division of General Motors Corporation*)

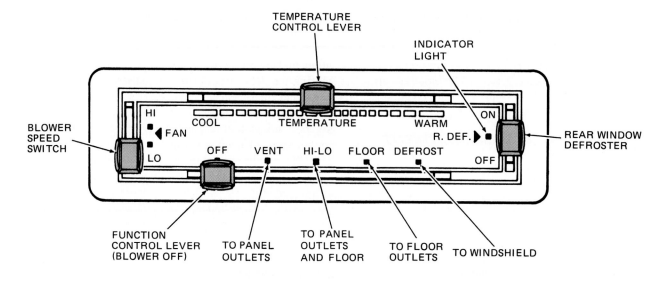

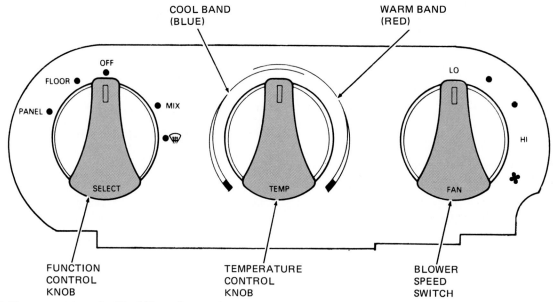

Fig. 55-3 Heater control panels. (*Ford Motor Company*)

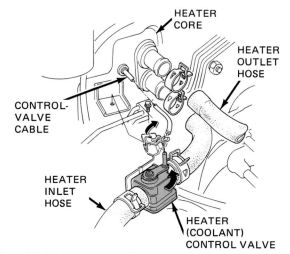

Fig. 55-4 Coolant-control valve in the heater hose. When closed, the valve prevents coolant flow through the heater core. (*American Honda Motor Company, Inc.*)

➤ 55-5 REAR-WINDOW DEFOGGER

Some vehicles have a *heated rear window* or *rear-window defroster* or *defogger* (Fig. 55-5). It heats the rear window to remove or prevent a buildup of fog, ice, or snow. An electric current flows through a grid of resistance wire to provide the heat. The grid is baked onto the inside surface of the rear-window glass.

When the driver switches ON the rear-window defogger (Figs. 55-3 and 55-5), a *defogger relay* closes. This sends current through the grid. It also illuminates an instrument-panel indicator light (Fig. 55-3) and starts a timer. As electric current flows through the grid, the wires get hot and heat the window.

The timer automatically shuts off the rear-window defogger after a preset time. This usually ranges from 10 to 25 minutes. The switch can be turned ON again if the rear window needs additional heat.

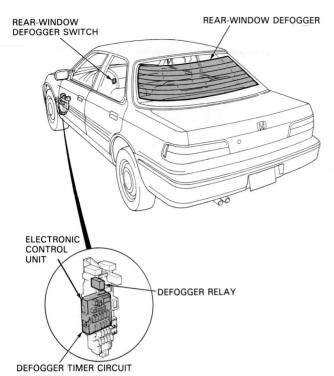

Fig. 55-5 Heated rear window, or rear-window defogger, which uses current flow through a grid of resistance wire to heat the rear window. (*American Honda Motor Company, Inc.*)

➤ 55-6 HEATED WINDSHIELD

Some vehicles have an electrically *heated windshield* (Fig. 55-6). It melts ice and frost three to five times faster than the defroster. The system is similar to the rear-window defogger (➤55-5). However, instead of wires, the windshield heating element is a clear conductive coating. The coating is between the interior and exterior layers of windshield glass.

The driver turns ON the heated windshield by pressing the FRONT DE-ICE switch (Fig. 55-6). The vehicle has a special alternator (Chap. 30). It provides three-phase alternating current (AC) to the *heated-windshield power module*. The power module converts the AC voltage to a

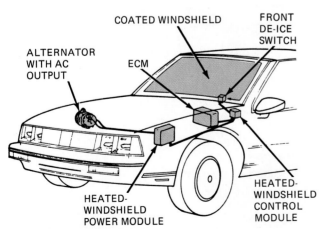

Fig. 55-6 Heated windshield that uses current flow through a clear conductive coating to heat the windshield. (*Cadillac Division of General Motors Corporation*)

higher-voltage direct current (DC). The direct current then flows through the conductive coating which heats the windshield.

The *heated-windshield control module* times the heating cycle. It may vary from 2 to 4 minutes before automatic turn-off occurs. The control module monitors windshield current, DC voltage, and *ambient temperature*. This is the temperature of the outside or surrounding air. The control module also automatically turns off the heated windshield if a problem occurs in the system.

> **CAUTION!**
>
> Be careful to avoid the high voltage in a car with an electrically-heated windshield (➤30-10). When the heated windshild is ON, the voltage in this circuit may reach 30 to 70 volts. This can injure you. Always follow the testing and servicing procedures in the vehicle service manual.

➤ 55-7 SOLAR-POWERED VENTILATION

A *photovoltaic cell* or *solar cell* is a semiconductor device that generates a small dc voltage when exposed to light. Several solar cells can be connected in series or parallel (➤27-10) to provide various outputs. A panel of solar cells on the vehicle roof can run small fan motors or charge the vehicle battery.

1. SOLAR-POWERED VENTILATION Some vehicles have a *solar-powered ventilation* system. When the interior of a parked vehicle gets too hot, an *ambient-temperature sensor* (➤55-6) automatically turns on a small ventilating fan. The output from the solar panels then powers the fan motor. There is no drain on the battery. The fan lowers the inside air temperature by forcing out the hot air and drawing in cooler outside air.

2. SOLAR-POWERED BATTERY CHARGING A parked vehicle does not need ventilating-fan operation on cooler days. Then the output from the solar cells is sent to the vehicle battery. This charges the battery (➤28-21) and keeps it charged even if the vehicle remains parked for a long time.

➤ 55-8 VENTILATION-AIR FILTER

Some vehicles have a *ventilation-air filter* (Fig. 55-7). It filters the outside air entering the passenger compartment. The filter material is fiberglass saturated with a special oil. This removes pollen, dust, and soot before it gets into the passenger compartment. The cleaner air also lessens the buildup of the greasy film that gets on the inside of the windshield. The film reduces visibility, especially in darkness.

Other vehicles have an *activated charcoal filter* or an *electrostatic filter* as part of the heater-air-conditioner (➤55-26). These filters help prevent airborne pollutants and odors from entering the passenger compartment.

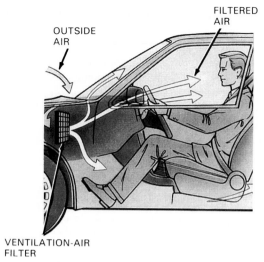

Fig. 55-7 A ventilation-air filter that cleans the air before it enters the passenger compartment. (*Saab Cars USA, Inc.*)

REFRIGERATION AND COOLING

➤ 55-9 REFRIGERATION

Removing heat from a substance such as air makes the air cooler. A mechanical process that removes heat is called *refrigeration*. On the vehicle, the *automotive air conditioner* removes the heat that gets into the passenger compartment (Fig. 55-8). This cools the passenger-compartment air.

The automotive air conditioner is basically a mobile *mechanical vapor-compression refrigeration system*. It provides refrigeration by mechanically compressing a vapor. This occurs after the vapor has absorbed heat from the passenger-compartment air. The heat then transfers through the refrigeration system to the outside air. From there, the heat is carried away from the vehicle.

The refrigeration system in the air conditioner works on three principles. These are *evaporation, condensation,* and *heat transfer.* The following sections describe the principles and parts of the refrigeration system. Later sections describe the construction and operation of automotive air conditioners.

➤ 55-10 EVAPORATION

Evaporation is the change, or conversion, of a liquid into a gas or vapor (Fig. 55-9A). When a liquid evaporates, it takes away heat and cools the adjacent surfaces. Put a little water on the back of your hand. Blow on the water. Your hand will feel cool. As the water evaporates, it takes heat from your hand. A measurement of the quantity of heat is the *British thermal unit* (Btu). One Btu is the quantity of heat necessary to raise the temperature of one pound of water one degree Fahrenheit (1°F).

Two other conditions also affect the evaporation of a liquid. These are temperature and pressure. As temperature goes up, a liquid evaporates more rapidly. When the temperature goes high enough, the liquid *boils*. This means it turns to vapor very quickly.

Pressure also affects evaporation. Figure 55-10 shows a sealed container partly filled with a liquid. The container

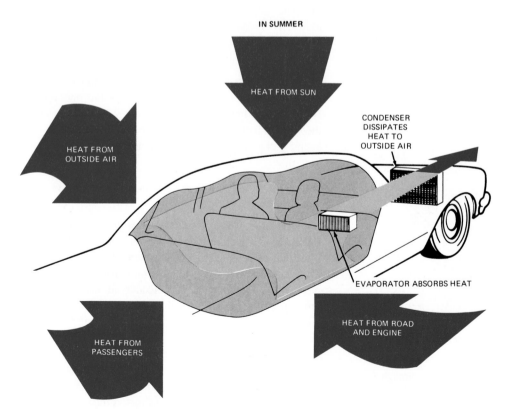

Fig. 55-8 In summer, heat enters the passenger compartment from the sun, the outside air, the road, and the engine. And the passengers themselves produce heat. The evaporator absorbs this heat and carries it to the outside air.

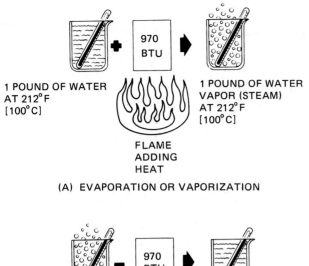

(A) EVAPORATION OR VAPORIZATION

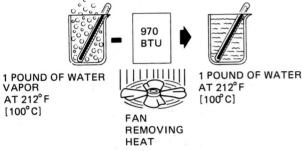

(B) CONDENSATION

Fig. 55-9 How heat causes vaporization or condensation. (A) Adding heat cause evaporation, or vaporization. (B) Removing heat causes condensation. (*Ford Motor Company*)

connects to a pump. When the pump runs, it takes air out of the container. This lowers the pressure which causes the liquid to evaporate more rapidly. The lower the pressure, the more rapidly the liquid evaporates.

➤ 55-11 CONDENSATION

Condensation is the changing of a gas or vapor back into a liquid (Fig. 55-9B). When a vapor cools, it condenses or changes to a liquid. You see this on a glass of ice water. The surrounding air, which contains water vapor, is cooled by being close to the cold glass. Water vapor then condenses as droplets on the outside of the glass.

High pressure on a trapped vapor can also cause it to condense. Suppose the pump in Fig. 55-10 runs backwards and acts as a *compressor* (➤55-19). Pumping air into the container increases its pressure. The vapor then begins to condense. The higher the pressure, the more rapidly the vapor condenses back into a liquid.

➤ 55-12 HEAT TRANSFER

Heat transfer is the movement of heat from one body to another by *conduction, convection,* or *radiation*. Conduction usually means the heat travels through a solid material. Convection usually refers to the transfer of heat by the motion of the heated material. Examples are the movement of engine coolant and heated air. Radiation is the transfer of energy in waves. It includes heat from the sun radiating through the vehicle body and windows (Fig. 55-8).

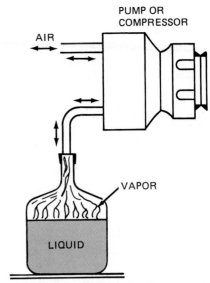

Fig. 55-10 Using a pump to remove the air or vapor from a container. This lowers the pressure and causes the liquid in the container to evaporate more readily. (*ATW*)

Heat travels from a hot object to a cool object. This is the principle of the engine cooling system (Chap. 25). The cooler engine coolant picks up heat as it circulates through the hotter engine. The coolant carries this heat to the radiator. There, the hot coolant gives up heat to the cooler air passing through the radiator.

Cooling the container in Fig. 55-10 creates a similar condition. The cooler the pressurized vapor, the more readily it condenses into a liquid.

➤ 55-13 CHANGE OF STATE

There are three states of matter. These are solid, liquid, and gas or vapor. Solid matter can change to liquid and then to a vapor. A vapor can change to liquid and then to a solid. Each change is a *change of state*. For a change of state to occur, a large quantity of heat must be added to or taken from the changing substance (Fig. 55-9). The liquid in the refrigeration system that undergoes the required changes of state to provide cooling is the *refrigerant* (➤55-16).

➤ 55-14 BASIC REFRIGERATION CYCLE

Figure 55-11 shows the basic refrigeration system in a simplified automotive air conditioner. Notice the four states of the refrigerant during the refrigeration cycle. The refrigerant successively becomes a *high-pressure liquid, low-pressure liquid, low-pressure vapor,* and *high-pressure vapor*. The changes of state occur because of changes in the temperature and pressure of the refrigerant.

Cooling begins at the *evaporator* (Figs. 55-11 and 55-12). This is a small tube-and-fin heat exchanger located in the vehicle passenger compartment (Fig. 55-8). A small amount of liquid refrigerant flows into the evaporator. In a typical refrigeration system (Fig. 55-12), the pressure on the refrigerant is 30 psi [200 kPa]. Its temperature is 32°F

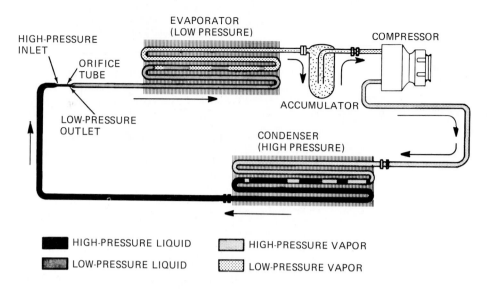

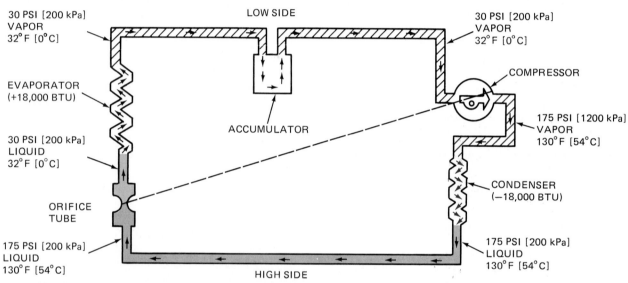

Fig. 55-11 Components in a refrigeration system using an orifice tube and accumulator. Arrows show flow of refrigerant. (*ATW*)

HIGH-PRESSURE INLET

ORIFICE TUBE

EVAPORATOR (LOW PRESSURE)

COMPRESSOR

ACCUMULATOR

LOW-PRESSURE OUTLET

CONDENSER (HIGH PRESSURE)

■ HIGH-PRESSURE LIQUID   ▨ HIGH-PRESSURE VAPOR

▨ LOW-PRESSURE LIQUID   ░ LOW-PRESSURE VAPOR

30 PSI [200 kPa] VAPOR 32°F [0°C]

LOW SIDE

30 PSI [200 kPa] VAPOR 32°F [0°C]

EVAPORATOR (+18,000 BTU)

ACCUMULATOR

COMPRESSOR

30 PSI [200 kPa] LIQUID 32°F [0°C]

175 PSI [1200 kPa] VAPOR 130°F [54°C]

ORIFICE TUBE

CONDENSER (−18,000 BTU)

175 PSI [200 kPa] LIQUID 130°F [54°C]

175 PSI [200 kPa] LIQUID 130°F [54°C]

HIGH SIDE

Fig. 55-12 High side and low side of the refrigeration system, showing typical temperatures and pressures for each component. (*Ford Motor Company*)

[0°C]. As this low-pressure liquid refrigerant enters the evaporator, the refrigerant absorbs heat and vaporizes (➤55-10). This cools the evaporator and the surrounding air (Fig. 55-12).

The low-pressure vapor then flows on through the evaporator and into an *accumulator* (Figs. 55-11 and 55-12). The accumulator traps any liquid refrigerant traveling with the vapor. This prevents the liquid from entering and damaging the compressor, which can only handle refrigerant vapor. The accumulator also usually contains a bag of *desiccant*. This is a drying substance. It adsorbs and removes any water vapor or moisture in the refrigerant.

From the accumulator, the low-pressure vapor flows to the *suction* or *inlet side* of the compressor (Figs. 55-11 and 55-12). The compressor takes in low-pressure refrigerant vapor and pressurizes it to a much higher pressure. Compressing the vapor causes its temperature to go up. In Fig.

55-12, compressing the vapor to 175 psi [1200 kPa] increases its temperature to 130°F [54°C]. The compressor then forces the hot high-pressure vapor out the *discharge* or *outlet side* and into the *condenser* (Fig. 55-11). This is another small tube-and-fin heat exchanger. The condenser mounts in front of the engine radiator (Fig. 55-8).

The temperature of the refrigerant vapor entering the condenser is now hotter than the outside air. The cooler air passing through the condenser carries away heat from the vapor (Fig. 55-12). As the vapor cools, it condenses into a liquid.

The high-pressure liquid leaves the condenser and flows into a refrigerant *flow-control valve* (➤55-15). Figures 55-11 and 55-12 show a system using an *orifice tube*. The orifice tube has a small opening that allows through only a small amount of liquid refrigerant. This lowers the pressure of the liquid refrigerant flowing into the evaporator.

772

Now the basic refrigeration cycle begins to repeat itself. Cooling continues as long as the refrigerant changes from liquid to vapor and then from vapor back into liquid. During this process, the refrigerant carries heat out of the passenger compartment.

➤ 55-15 REFRIGERANT FLOW-CONTROL VALVES

The refrigerant flow-control valve has a small hole, or *orifice,* that restricts the flow of liquid refrigerant. This is necessary because there must be a pressure difference between the condenser and the evaporator. The condenser needs high pressure to condense the refrigerant vapor. The evaporator needs low pressure to vaporize the liquid refrigerant. The compressor and the restriction in the flow-control valve divide the refrigerant system into a *high side* and a *low side* (Fig. 55-12).

Two types of refrigerant flow-control valves are the orifice tube (Fig. 55-11) and the thermostatic *expansion valve* (Fig. 55-13). A receiver is used with the expansion valve instead of an accumulator (➤55-14). The receiver serves as a small reservoir for liquid refrigerant. A screen and desiccant in the receiver filter and adsorb moisture from the refrigerant.

1. ORIFICE TUBE The orifice tube (Fig. 55-12) has a small hole of fixed diameter through which the liquid refrigerant must flow. The hole is a *fixed orifice* because it cannot change size.

2. EXPANSION VALVE The expansion valve (Fig. 55-13) has a *variable orifice.* It changes size as evaporator temperature changes. A *capillary tube* (a tube with a small inside diameter) connects the expansion valve with a *temperature-sensing bulb* (Fig. 55-13). The bulb is placed near the evaporator outlet. A gas in the bulb expands or contracts with changing temperature.

If the evaporator temperature goes too high, the gas expands. It forces the diaphragm in the expansion valve to move down. This opens the valve and admits more liquid refrigerant to the evaporator. Increased cooling results. If the evaporator gets too cold, the gas contracts. Then the spring in the expansion valve pushes the valve up (Fig. 55-13). This closes the valve and reduces the amount of refrigerant entering the evaporator. Less cooling results.

➤ 55-16 REFRIGERANT

The refrigerant is a special substance. It is a liquid at very low temperatures and a vapor at low temperatures. The ideal refrigerant must not be toxic or poisonous, flammable, or explosive. It must be reasonably inert and not damage metal, rubber, or other material it touches. In addition, the refrigerant should not cause environmental damage when released into the atmosphere.

Most automotive air conditioners have used a *chlorofluorocarbon* (CFC) refrigerant that is often referred to by its brand name *Freon.* It is also called *refrigerant-12* or simply *R-12.* However, R-12 is being phased out and replaced by a *hydrofluorocarbon* (HFC) refrigerant called *R-134a.* The release of chlorofluorocarbons such as R-12 into the atmosphere damages the earth's *ozone layer.* This is the protective layer 10 to 30 miles [16 to 48 km] above the earth's surface. The ozone layer shields the earth from the sun's ultraviolet radiation. Hydrofluorocarbons such as R-134a are much less damaging to the ozone layer.

The refrigerants R-12 and R-134a have similar physical properties, but they are not interchangeable. R-12 boils at −22°F [−30°C] at atmospheric pressure. R-134a boils at −15°F [−26°C]. The higher boiling point makes R-134a a slightly less efficient refrigerant than R-12. This lower efficiency requires higher pressures and a greater air flow across the condenser.

R-12 and R-134a require a different *refrigerant oil* (➤55-17) and a different desiccant (➤55-14). However,

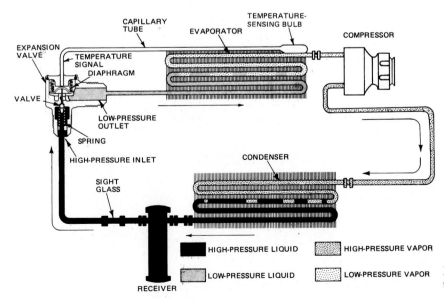

HIGH-PRESSURE LIQUID HIGH-PRESSURE VAPOR
LOW-PRESSURE LIQUID LOW-PRESSURE VAPOR

Fig. 55-13 Refrigeration system using a thermostatic expansion valve.

all refrigerants used in automotive air-conditioning systems must be recovered and recycled (Chap. 56).

NOTE Two thermometers (.9-14) are shown in Fig. 9-9. One is marked in the Fahrenheit (F) scale. The other is marked with the Celsius [C] scale. To convert Fahrenheit temperatures to Celsius, use the formula:

$$C° = 5/9 \ (F° - 32)$$

To convert Celsius temperatures to Fahrenheit, use the formula:

$$F° = 9/5 \ (C°) + 32$$

➤ 55-17 REFRIGERANT OIL

The refrigeration system needs oil to lubricate the compressor and to keep other moving parts and seals lubricated. This lubricating oil is the *refrigerant oil* or *compressor oil*. It is a nonfoaming and highly refined oil. All impurities such as wax, moisture, and sulfur are removed. Some compressors have no way to add oil to them. Oil for compressor lubrication is added to the system during assembly. Then the oil circulates with the refrigerant.

There are different refrigerant oils specified for use with R-12 systems.

An R-134a system uses *polyalkylene glycol* or *PAG oil*. This is a special synthetic lubricant (➤24-3). Never add PAG oil to R-12 systems. Chapter 56 describes when and how to add refrigerant oil.

➤ 55-18 SIGHT GLASS

Some automotive air-conditioning systems have a sight glass (Fig. 55-13). It is usually in the top of the receiver or in the high-pressure liquid line. When the air conditioner runs, the sight glass allows you to see the condition of the refrigerant as it leaves the condenser. For example, gas bubbles (white foam) may indicate loss of refrigerant. Chapter 56 explains more about how to use the sight glass.

COMPRESSORS AND COMPRESSOR CLUTCH

➤ 55-19 TYPES OF AIR-CONDITIONING COMPRESSORS

The compressor (Figs. 55-13 and 55-14) is a pump that compresses refrigerant vapor. This increases its pressure and temperature (➤55-14). The increased pressure forces the refrigerant to circulate through the system. The higher temperature increases the rate of heat transfer through the condenser.

Automotive air conditioners use a variety of compressors. Some are similar to inline and V-type two-cylinder engines (Fig. 12-1). Pistons move up and down in cylin-

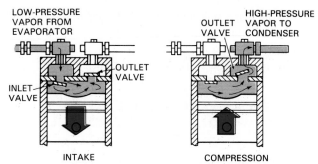

Fig. 55-14 Actions in the compressor. (A) During the intake stroke, the inlet valve opens to allow vapor from the evaporator to flow into the cylinder. (B) During the compression stroke, the inlet valve closes and the outlet valve opens. This forces compressed vapor to flow to the condenser. (*Ford Motor Company*)

ders (Fig. 55-14). Other compressors are round or *rotary compressors* (Fig. 12-5). These may work in different ways. Some have five or six single- or double-ended pistons inside. The pistons are pushed back and forth in cylinders by a *swash plate* or *wobble plate* (Fig. 55-15). Compressors similar to vane-type power-steering pumps (➤50-11) and spiral or scroll-type superchargers (➤18-6) are also used.

Compressors are classified as either *fixed displacement* (➤15-9) or *variable displacement* (➤55-20). Regardless of construction, all compressors perform the same job. They take in low-pressure vapor from the evaporator and send out high-pressure vapor to the condenser (Fig. 55-13).

➤ 55-20 VARIABLE-DISPLACEMENT COMPRESSOR

Figure 55-16 shows a five-cylinder *variable-displacement compressor*. This type of compressor can vary the piston

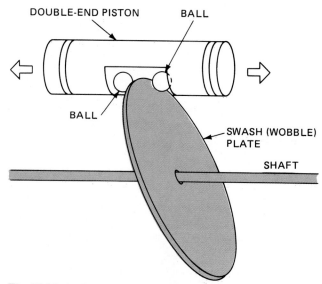

Fig. 55-15 As the swash plate rotates, it causes the double-ended pistons to move back and forth in the cylinder.

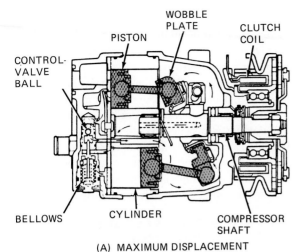

(A) MAXIMUM DISPLACEMENT

(B) MINIMUM DISPLACEMENT

Fig. 55-16 Operation of a five-cylinder variable-displacement compressor. (*Chevrolet Division of General Motors Corporation*)

displacement according to the amount of refrigerant needed. The length of the piston stroke is controlled by a *wobble plate*. It can change angles while the compressor is running. The greater the angle of the wobble plate, the farther the pistons move in their cylinders (Fig. 55-16A). This increases the piston displacement so the piston pumps more refrigerant. Reducing the angle reduces piston travel (Fig. 55-16B). Then each piston stroke pumps less refrigerant. This allows the compressor to run continuously (➤55-22) while only pumping the amount of refrigerant needed.

The wobble-plate angle is controlled by the bellows-operated control valve (Fig. 55-16). The bellows contracts or expands as low-side pressure increases or decreases. This opens or closes the *control-valve ball* to control the pressure in the compressor crankcase. The difference between the low-side pressure and the crankcase pressure determines the wobble-plate position. Maximum displacement (Fig. 55-16A) and maximum cooling occur when the pressures are the same. Minimum displacement (Fig. 55-16B) occurs when high-side pressure is bled into the crankcase.

➤ 55-21 COMPRESSOR CLUTCH

The *compressor clutch* (Figs. 55-16 and 55-17) is a solenoid-type *magnetic clutch* located in the compressor pulley. The clutch engages and disengages so the compressor shaft turns only as needed. When the clutch engages, the compressor runs and cooling takes places. When compressor operation is not needed, the clutch disengages. Then only the pulley turns. The pulley is driven by a belt from the engine crankshaft (Fig. 12-5).

The clutch has a stationary coil (Figs. 55-17 and 55-18) that becomes magnetized when voltage is applied. A *clutch hub* or *armature* attaches to the compressor shaft. When no voltage is applied to the coil, the armature moves forward slightly. This disengages the compressor by opening a slight air gap between the armature and the front face of the pulley (Fig. 55-18A). The pulley mounts on ball bearings so it can rotate freely when the clutch is disengaged.

Applying voltage magnetizes the coil (Fig. 55-18B). This pulls the armature back and locks the pulley to the armature. Now the compressor shaft rotates with the pulley.

➤ 55-22 CYCLING AND NONCYCLING COMPRESSORS

Many automotive air conditioners have a compressor with a *cycling clutch*. It automatically engages and disengages to cycle the compressor on and off (➤55-21). This regulates the temperature of the conditioned air. Clutch cycling is often controlled by evaporator pressure or temperature (➤55-23).

Some compressors run continuously while the engine is running and the air conditioner is ON. These compressors have a *noncycling clutch*. Older systems (➤55-23) may use a *suction-throttling valve* (STV) with a noncycling compressor. Newer vehicles often have a variable-displacement compressor (➤55-20). It runs continuously and varies the amount of refrigerant pumped according to need.

➤ 55-23 CONTROLLING EVAPORATOR ICING

Sometimes the evaporator can get too cold. Then moisture in the air condenses and freezes on the evaporator. This

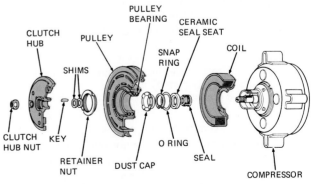

Fig. 55-17 A disassembled magnetic clutch, or compressor clutch. (*Ford Motor Company*)

775

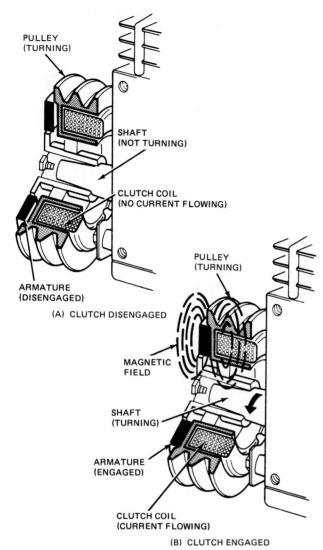

Fig. 55-18 Operation of magnetic clutch. (A) Cutaway of magnetic clutch in the OFF (disengaged) position. (B) Magnetic clutch in the ON (engaged) position. (*Warner Electric Brake and Clutch Company*)

blocks the flow of air and prevents normal cooling. Older systems may use a suction-throttling valve (➤55-22) to control evaporator icing. The valve regulates or "throttles" the flow of refrigerant vapor from the evaporator outlet. Low evaporator-outlet pressure indicates excessive cooling. Then the suction-throttling valve closes off the evaporator outlet so evaporator pressure and temperature go up.

> **NOTE** A variable-displacement compressor (➤55-20) controls the pressure by varying the amount of refrigerant pumped.

Another method of preventing evaporator icing is to turn off the compressor when evaporator-outlet pressure falls too low. Many systems using a cycling-clutch compressor (➤55-22) have a *cycling-clutch pressure switch* (Fig. 55-19) in the accumulator. When the evaporator-outlet pressure is low, the pressure-switch contacts open. This disen-

gages the compressor clutch which stops the compressor. As the evaporator warms up, the increased pressure closes the switch contacts. The compressor clutch engages and the compressor pumps refrigerant.

Instead of a pressure switch, some systems have a *thermostatic switch* in the compressor-clutch circuit. A capillary tube (➤55-15) that senses evaporator temperature operates the thermostatic switch. When the temperature falls to freezing, the switch opens the compressor-clutch circuit. This stops the compressor. After the evaporator temperature goes up, the switch closes. Then the compressor clutch engages and the compressor resumes pumping refrigerant.

➤ 55-24 ELECTRICALLY DRIVEN COMPRESSOR

Some manufacturers have proposed using a compressor driven by an electric motor. The motor is turned on and off as required to maintain the desired temperature. The electric compressor has no drive belts. Therefore, it could be placed anywhere in the vehicle. An electric compressor could also provide air conditioning in an electric vehicle (➤1-28).

➤ 55-25 AIR-CONDITIONER SAFETY DEVICES

Automotive air-conditioning systems have several safety devices to protect the compressor and other parts if something goes wrong. Many of the devices are switches that open the compressor-clutch circuit. Others are valves that relieve pressure. Five safety devices are listed below. In addition, some vehicles have a *wide-open throttle* (WOT) *cutout switch* (➤21-25). It opens the compressor-clutch circuit so more engine power is available to move the vehicle at wide-open throttle.

1. *Ambient-temperature switch* This switch (Fig. 55-20) is in the inlet-air duct. The switch senses the temperature of the outside air entering the system. If the air temperature falls below a preset temperature such as 40°F [4.4°C], the switch opens the compressor-clutch circuit. This prevents the compressor from running. The ambient temperature indicates no air conditioning is needed.

2. *Low-pressure cutoff switch* This switch senses evaporator pressure and disengages the compressor clutch if the pressure drops too low. A very low evaporator pressure usually means the system has lost refrigerant and possibly refrigerant oil (➤55-17). Operating the compressor after an oil loss could damage or destroy the compressor.

3. *High-pressure relief valve* The valve opens if the high-side pressure goes too high. This can happen if the air flow through the condenser gets blocked by leaves or trash. It can also happen as the result of overcharging the system during service (Chap. 56).

4. *High-pressure cutoff switch* The switch is in the compressor outlet. When the discharge pressure goes too

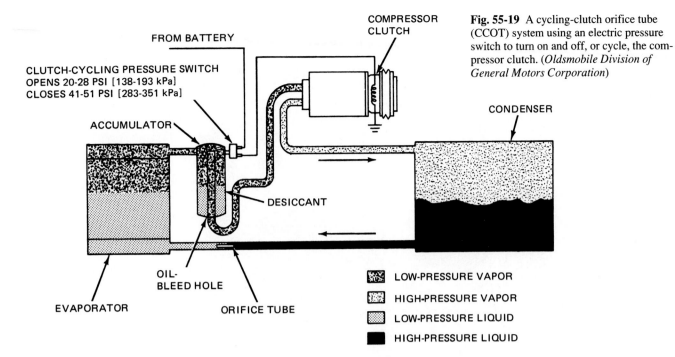

LOW-PRESSURE VAPOR

HIGH-PRESSURE VAPOR

LOW-PRESSURE LIQUID

HIGH-PRESSURE LIQUID

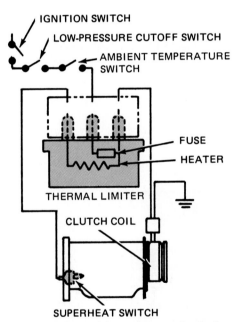

Fig. 55-20 Wiring system of the compressor clutch, showing the safety devices. (*General Motors Corporation*)

high, the switch opens and disengages the compressor clutch. A typical opening pressure is about 430 psi [2967 kPa].

5. *Thermal limiter and superheat switch* The superheat switch (Fig. 55-20) in the end of some compressors is normally open. If the system loses refrigerant, the switch senses the resulting low pressure and high refrigerant temperature. The switch contacts close sending current through the *fuse heater* in the thermal limiter. This melts the fuse and opens the compressor-clutch circuit.

HEATER-AIR-CONDITIONER SYSTEMS

➤ 55-26 AUTOMOTIVE AIR CONDITIONERS

The *automotive air conditioner* (Fig. 55-21) is an accessory system that cleans, cools, dries, and circulates passenger-compartment air. The air conditioner is basically a mobile refrigeration system (➤55-9). It includes an air-delivery system and a temperature-control system. The parts are connected by wiring, hoses, and tubing.

The compressor in the automotive air conditioner is powered by the engine (Fig. 12-5). Running the air conditioner may result in reduced engine performance and fuel economy. In a vehicle with factory-installed air conditioning, the heater (➤55-2) and air conditioner are integrated into a *heater-air-conditioner*. The unit may be manually-controlled (➤55-27) or automatically-controlled (➤55-29).

➤ 55-27 MANUALLY-CONTROLLED AIR CONDITIONERS

Some automotive air conditioners are manually controlled. The driver selects the desired mode by moving a *mode* or *selector lever* (Fig. 55-22). Its position shuts off or allows air delivery through the vents, and controls heater and air-conditioner operation.

Numbers 1 through 7 in Fig. 55-22 show the various positions of the selector lever. The resulting conditions in each position are also described. Moving the temperature *lever* on the control panel controls the *temperature* of the air entering the passenger compartment. Turning the

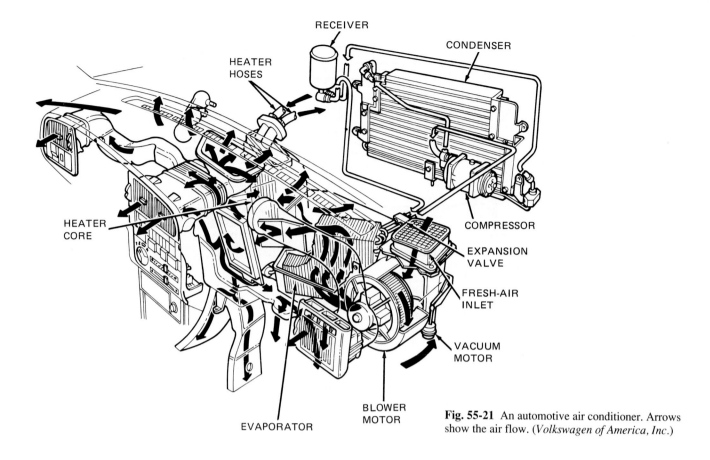

Fig. 55-21 An automotive air conditioner. Arrows show the air flow. (*Volkswagen of America, Inc.*)

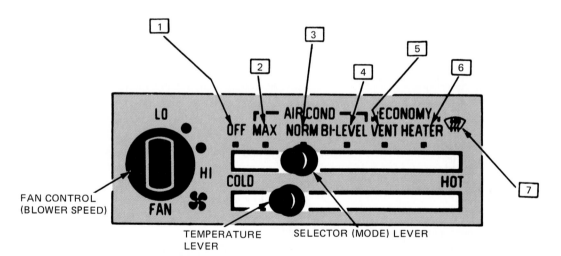

1—NO BLOWER OPERATION WITH MODE LEVER IN OFF POSITION

2—MAXIMUM COOLING WITH THE CONDITIONED AIR DISTRIBUTED THROUGH INSTRUMENT-PANEL OUTLET AND SLIGHT AMOUNT TO FLOOR AT ANY BLOWER SPEED

3—CONDITIONED AIR IS DIRECTED THROUGH INSTRUMENT-PANEL AND FLOOR OUTLETS WITH SOME ALSO TO WINDSHIELD

4—CONDITIONED AIR IS DIRECTED THROUGH INSTRUMENT-PANEL AND FLOOR OUTLETS WITH SOME ALSO TO WINDSHIELD

5—A NON-COMPRESSOR OPERATING POSITION, WITH OUTSIDE AIR DELIVERED THROUGH INSTRUMENT-PANEL OUTLETS

6—A NON-COMPRESSOR OPERATING POSITION WITH OUTSIDE AIR DISTRIBUTED ABOUT 80% TO FLOOR (AND 20% TO WINDSHIELD AND SIDE WINDOWS IN SOME VEHICLES)

7—CONDITIONED AIR DISTRIBUTED ABOUT 80% TO WINDSHIELD AND SIDE WINDOWS, AND 20% TO FLOOR

Fig. 55-22 Control panel for a manually-controlled air conditioner, with explanations of the actions in each selector-lever position. (*Buick Division of General Motors Corporation*)

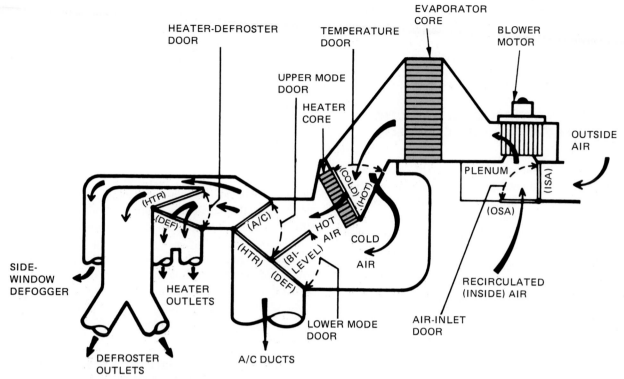

Fig. 55-23 Five doors controlling the airflow through a manually-controlled air conditioner. (*Buick Division of General Motors Corporation*)

blower switch or *fan control* determines the speed of the blower motor.

> ## 55-28 CONDITIONED-AIR DISTRIBUTION

Figure 55-23 shows the airflow through a manually-controlled air conditioner. All air entering or recirculating passes through the evaporator core. The evaporator is kept cold (➤55-14) and the heater core is kept hot (➤55-2). Normally, conditioned air from the air conditioner discharges from the instrument-panel outlets. Heated air discharges from the heater outlets that direct it to the floor.

Five doors control the airflow through the manually-controlled air conditioner in Fig. 55-23. These are:

1. The *air-inlet door* which has two positions. The door can be up for outside air (OSA) or down for inside air (ISA).
2. The *temperature door* which controls the airflow from the evaporator. A cable from the temperature lever on the control panel (Fig. 55-22) operates the door. It can be moved to any position between COLD and HOT (Fig. 55-23). In the COLD position, no cold evaporator air passes through the heater core. In the HOT position, all evaporator air passes through the heater core. Positioning the temperature door anywhere between HOT and COLD produces blend air of the desired temperature.
3. The *upper mode door* which controls the airflow to the A/C ducts or to the heater and defroster outlets. If the upper mode door is up, cold air flows through the A/C ducts into the passenger compartment. If the upper mode door is down, the air flows to the heater and defroster outlets instead.
4. The *lower mode door* which controls the bi-level discharge by moving up or down. *Bi-level* means the air discharges from outlets at two different levels—the instrument panel and the floor. This occurs when the lower mode door closes and the upper mode door opens. At the same time, the *heater-defroster door* must move up.
5. The heater-defroster door which controls whether the air goes to the heater outlets (door up) or to the defroster outlets (door down). The defroster outlets direct the air to the windshield.

All doors in Fig. 55-23 (except the temperature door) are controlled by vacuum motors (Fig. 55-21). A link attached to the vacuum-motor diaphragm connects to the door. Moving the selector lever operates a valve that applies engine intake-manifold vacuum to the diaphragm. This causes the diaphragm to move and open or close the door. Some air conditioners have doors operated by electric motors (➤55- 30).

> ## 55-29 AUTOMATICALLY-CONTROLLED AIR CONDITIONERS

Manually-controlled and automatically-controlled heater-air-conditioner systems are basically the same. The automatic system allows the driver to select automatic control and the desired temperature. The system will then maintain that temperature by providing heat or cooling as required. Many systems also automatically adjust the blower speed. The instrument-panel controls usually allow the driver to override the automatic operation. Then the system operates similar to a manually-controlled system (➤55-27).

➤ **55-30 ELECTRONIC AUTOMATIC TEMPERATURE CONTROL**

In some vehicles, the body-control module (BCM) controls the automatic air conditioner. Other vehicles have a separate air-conditioner control module. Using a microprocessor (➤10-17) allows the system to more accurately maintain the preset temperature. It may also allow the temperature to be adjusted independently for the driver and front-seat passenger. In addition, the system may have separate controls to change the distribution of conditioned air to the rear-seat area. This does not alter airflow to the front seat.

Figure 55-24 shows an *electronic automatic-temperature control* (EATC) *system*. The *EATC control module* receives inputs from six major sources. These are:

1. The *sun-load* or *solar sensor* which is a photovoltaic or solar cell (➤55-7). It mounts on the instrument panel and measures the heat from the sun (Fig. 55-8).
2. The *in-vehicle temperature sensor* that mounts behind the instrument panel and measures the temperature of the air in the passenger compartment.
3. The *ambient-temperature sensor* (➤55-7).
4. The *engine coolant-temperature sensor* (➤19-16).
5. The *clutch-cycling pressure switch* (➤55-23).
6. The *instrument-panel* (IP) settings for mode, temperature, and blower speed (➤55-27).

Using these inputs, the EATC control module determines the correct conditions for the six outputs (Fig. 55-24). These are the four doors, blower motor, and compressor clutch. An electric motor or actuator operates the temperature-blend door. Vacuum motors or actuators operate the other three doors. In addition to controlling the system, the control module can run a self-test and display trouble codes (Fig. 20-20).

Figure 19-26 shows the inputs and outputs in a vehicle with a body-control module (BCM). The BCM receives an *AC REQUEST* signal when the air conditioner is ON. The signal is sent on to the powertrain-control module (ECM or PCM). It then increases idle speed to prevent the compressor load from stalling the engine.

➤ **55-31 AUXILIARY REAR HEATING AND COOLING**

Some vehicles have a large interior space to heat and cool. These vehicles may have an *auxiliary rear heating-and-*

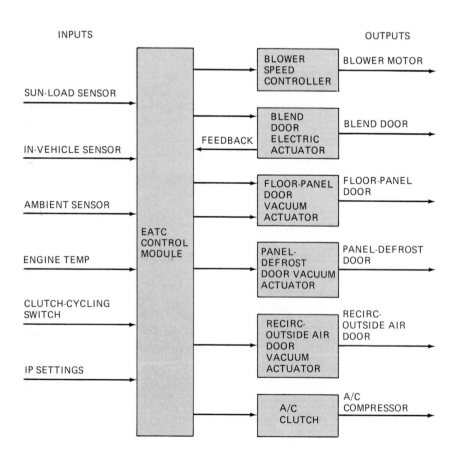

Fig. 55-24 An electronic automatic-temperature-control (EATC) system, showing the EATC control module with inputs and outputs. (*Ford Motor Company*)

INPUTS

OUTPUTS

SUN-LOAD SENSOR

IN-VEHICLE SENSOR

AMBIENT SENSOR

ENGINE TEMP

CLUTCH-CYCLING SWITCH

IP SETTINGS

EATC CONTROL MODULE

FEEDBACK

BLOWER SPEED CONTROLLER — BLOWER MOTOR

BLEND DOOR ELECTRIC ACTUATOR — BLEND DOOR

FLOOR-PANEL DOOR VACUUM ACTUATOR — FLOOR-PANEL DOOR

PANEL-DEFROST DOOR VACUUM ACTUATOR — PANEL-DEFROST DOOR

RECIRC-OUTSIDE AIR DOOR VACUUM ACTUATOR — RECIRC-OUTSIDE AIR DOOR

A/C CLUTCH — A/C COMPRESSOR

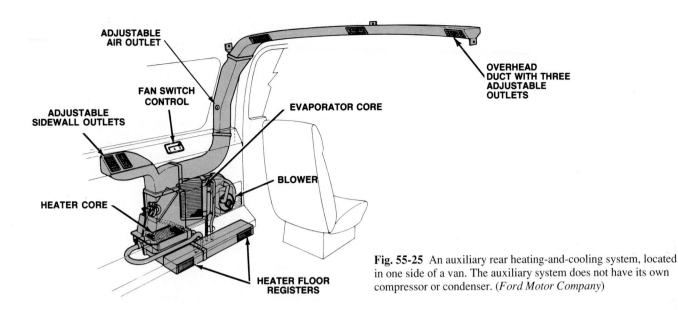

Fig. 55-25 An auxiliary rear heating-and-cooling system, located in one side of a van. The auxiliary system does not have its own compressor or condenser. (*Ford Motor Company*)

cooling system (Fig. 55-25). It keeps the rear passengers more comfortable without disturbing air distribution to the front seat. The auxiliary system may be in the trunk of a car. It may be on the roof or in one side of a van (Fig. 55-25). The system includes a heater core, evaporator core, orifice tube or expansion valve, blower motor and controls, and ducts.

The auxiliary system does not have its own compressor or condenser. Hose and tubing carry the refrigerant between the front of the vehicle and the rear evaporator. Hot engine coolant is also piped to and from the rear heater core.

TRADE TALK

accumulator	expansion valve	R-12	ventilation-air filter
British thermal unit (Btu)	magnetic clutch	R-134a	
desiccant	orifice tube	sun-load sensor	

MULTIPLE-CHOICE TEST

*Select the **one** correct, best, or most probable answer to each question.*
You can find the answers in the section indicated at the end of each question.

1. The power ventilating system circulates air using (➤55-1)
   a. a blower motor and fan
   b. open windows
   c. only ram air
   d. a special compressor
2. The small radiator-like heat exchanger that warms air passing through to the passenger compartment is the (➤55-2)
   a. evaporator
   b. heater core
   c. condenser
   d. defroster

3. All the following are true about the rear-window defogger EXCEPT (➤55-5)
   a. It is heated by an electric current flowing through resistance wire.
   b. It must be turned on by the driver.
   c. It is automatically turned off by a timer.
   d. It cannot be turned on again until after a delay of 10 to 25 minutes.

4. Technician A says when a liquid evaporates, it cools adjacent surfaces. Technician B says heat travels from a hot object to a cool object. Who is right? (➤55-10 and 55-12)
   a. A only
   b. B only
   c. both A and B
   d. neither A nor B

5. The refrigeration system is divided into a high side and a low side by (➤55-15)
   a. the condenser and evaporator
   b. the compressor and the restriction in the orifice tube or expansion valve
   c. the accumulator and receiver
   d. the desiccant and refrigerant

6. Refrigerant-12 (R-12) should not be released into the atmosphere because (➤55-16)
   a. R-12 damages the earth's ozone layer.
   b. R-12 is toxic and poisonous.
   c. R-12 is flammable and explosive.
   d. R-12 is a liquid at high temperatures.

7. Technician A says compressing refrigerant vapor increases its pressure and reduces its temperature. Technician B says compressing refrigerant vapor increases the rate of heat transfer through the condenser. Who is right? (➤55-19)
   a. A only
   b. B only
   c. both A and B
   d. neither A nor B

8. The compressor clutch may be disengaged by all the following EXCEPT (➤55-25)
   a. ambient-temperature switch
   b. low-pressure cutoff switch
   c. high-pressure cutoff switch
   d. high-pressure relief valve

9. The three instrument-panel controls for a manually-controlled air conditioner are (➤55-27)
   a. defogger, defroster, and demisters
   b. rear-window, heated-windshield, and rear-seat controls
   c. mode, temperature, and fan controls
   d. cables, actuators, and vacuum hose

10. Inputs to the EATC control module include the following EXCEPT (➤55-30)
   a. engine speed
   b. sun-load sensor
   c. engine coolant-temperature sensor
   d. clutch-cycling pressure switch

REVIEW QUESTIONS

1. What is a solar-powered ventilation system and how does it work? (➤55-7)
2. Why does the refrigeration system need refrigerant oil circulating with the refrigerant? (➤55-17)
3. Describe the construction and operation of fixed-displacement and variable-displacement compressors. (➤55-19 and 55-20)
4. How is evaporator icing controlled? (➤55-23)
5. List the inputs and outputs, and describe the operation of an electronic automatic-temperature-control system. (➤55-30)

CHAPTER 56

HEATER AND AIR-CONDITIONER SERVICE

After studying this chapter, and with the proper instruction and equipment, you should be able to:

- Diagnose and repair troubles in the heater.
- Make a visual inspection, performance test, and leak test of automotive air conditioners.
- Use pressure gauges, temperatures, and clutch-cycling times to diagnose troubles in the air conditioner.
- Discharge the refrigerant system and recover and recycle the refrigerant.
- Add refrigerant oil, and evacuate and charge the refrigerant system.
- Replace refrigerant hoses, filters, compressors, and other air-conditioner components.

HEATER DIAGNOSIS AND SERVICE

➤ 56-1 HEATER-SYSTEM TROUBLES

Heater problems are usually one of four types. These are

1. Little or no heat.
2. Blower does not work.
3. Coolant leaks.
4. Too much heat.

Figure 56-1 is a heater trouble-diagnosis chart listing these and other heater troubles.

CAUTION!

Follow the safety cautions in Chap. 4 and in ➤26-1 when performing any heater diagnosis or service procedure. The heater hoses and heater core are part of the engine cooling system (Chap. 26). Allow the engine to cool before removing the radiator cap or draining the coolant. Releasing the pressure may cause instant boiling of the coolant. The resulting stream of boiling coolant and steam could scald and burn you. Keep your fingers away from moving belts, pulleys, and electric fans. An electric fan may start running unexpectedly even with the ignition off. Always disconnect the fan-motor electrical connector (Fig. 4-10) before working around an electric fan.

Little or no heat can result from low engine coolant (➤26-6) or insufficient air or coolant circulation. Causes of too little coolant circulation include a misadjusted heater control and an engine cooling-system thermostat that is missing or stuck open (➤26-8). Lack of air circulation may result from an inoperative blower motor. Possible causes are a blown blower-motor fuse, defective blower motor, and bad connections.

Coolant leaks are caused by a leaking heater core, defective hose, or bad connections (➤26-3). Excessive heat can be caused by an open temperature door (➤55-3) or the engine cooling-system thermostat stuck partially closed (➤26-8).

➤ 56-2 TESTING THE VACUUM-CONTROL SYSTEM

A quick check of the vacuum-control system will show if the system operates properly. Move the heater controls to each position or mode. Proper operation of the heater indicates no vacuum leaks and that the vacuum motors are working. A short hissing sound may be normally heard as the mode control moves to each position. Continuous hissing indicates a major vacuum leak. A small vacuum leak may allow normal heater operation with the engine idling. Then during acceleration, unwanted defroster operation may begin.

Complaint	Possible Cause	Check or Correction
1. Little or no heat	a. Insufficient air circulation	Bad blower motor or switch, air leaks from heater housing, misadjusted temperature door or cable, loose carpet obstructing airflow
	b. Coolant hose to heater blocked	Unkink hose, replace defective hose
	c. Air in heater core	Bleed air out
	d. Clogged heater core	Repair or replace core
	e. Bad coolant valve or vacuum motor	Replace
	f. Engine coolant-level low	Add coolant, bleed air out of system, locate and repair leaks
	g. Engine cooling-system thermostat missing or stuck open	Install or replace
2. Blower motor inoperative	a. Blown fuse, bad connections	Repair cause of blown fuse, tighten connections
	b. Motor defective	Replace
	c. Resistor open	Replace
3. Coolant leaks	Check hoses, hose connections, heater core, coolant valve	Repair cause of leak
4. Too much heat	a. Misadjusted temperature-door cable	Adjust
	b. Engine-cooling system thermostat stuck partially closed	Replace
5. Insufficient defrosting	a. Misadjusted defrost-door cable	Adjust
	b. Defrost outlets blocked	Remove obstructions
	c. Any cause of little or no heat	See item 1
6. Inoperative vent door	a. Bad vacuum motor	Replace
	b. Leaky vacuum lines or connections	Repair
	c. Bad control-panel lines or assembly	Repair
7. Controls hard to move	a. Loose or binding control cable	Repair
	b. Sticky door	Free
8. Odors from heater	a. Air leak around blower case	Tighten bolts and check seals and gaskets
	b. Coolant leak from heater core	Repair or replace heater core

Fig. 56-1 Heater trouble-diagnosis chart.

If the quick check indicates improper operation of a door, determine which door is the cause. Then remove the vacuum hose from the vacuum motor for that door. Start the engine and check for vacuum at the end of the hose. If there is no vacuum, the hose may be disconnected, kinked, pinched, or split. Normal vacuum indicates the door may be stuck or the vacuum motor may be defective.

Vacuum-motor operation can also be checked with a hand vacuum pump (Fig. 56-2). Connect the pump to the vacuum motor and apply a vacuum. Some manufacturers specify testing the vacuum-control system using a vacuum of 8 inches [200 mm] of mercury (➤5-22). If the vacuum motor does not work, it is defective or the door is stuck. Replace the vacuum motor or free the stuck door.

➤ **56-3 REPLACING HEATER-SYSTEM COMPONENTS**

A variety of designs and arrangements are used to locate heater-system components. Review the locations and procedures in the vehicle service manual before replacing parts in the heater system.

Figure 56-3 shows how the blower motor and blower wheel (fan) mount in the heater case. Other installations are similar. Many service procedures on the heater are performed from the engine-compartment side of the firewall.

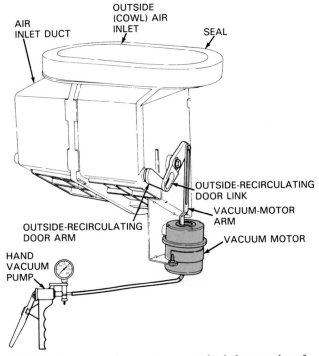

Fig. 56-2 Using a hand vacuum pump to check the operation of an air-door vacuum motor. (*ATW*)

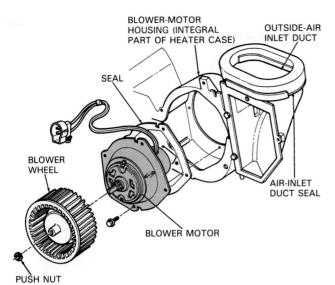

Fig. 56-3 Blower motor and wheel, or fan, installation. (*Ford Motor Company*)

The heater-hose pipes sticking through the firewall (Figs. 55-4 and 55-21) indicate the location of the heater core. To remove the heater core, first drain the cooling system (Chap. 26). Disconnect the heater hoses (Fig. 55-4). Then take off the *access cover* (Fig. 56-4) and other parts necessary to remove the heater core.

AIR-CONDITIONING TROUBLE DIAGNOSIS

➤ 56-4 SAFETY CAUTIONS FOR AIR-CONDITIONING SERVICE

Follow the safety cautions in Chap. 4 when servicing automotive air conditioners. Always wear eye protection when diagnosing or servicing air conditioners (Fig. 56-5). Also, always wear eye protection when handling refrigerant containers and operating refrigerant recovery and recycling equipment. Refrigerant striking your hand or skin can

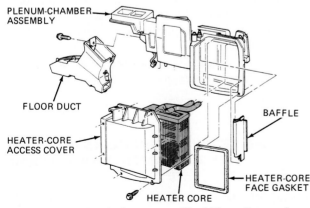

Fig. 56-4 Removing the heater core. (*Ford Motor Company*)

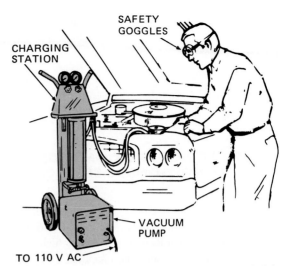

Fig. 56-5 Air-conditioner charging station. Note the technician is wearing safety goggles. (*Ford Motor Company*)

cause *frostbite*. This freezes the flesh which results in permanent damage. Wear gloves or wrap a shop towel around the fitting when you make or break a connection in the refrigerant system.

Refrigerant striking your eyes can blind you. If refrigerant gets in your eyes, immediately flush your eyes for 15 minutes with large quantities of water. Preferably the water should be at room temperature and have very little pressure on it. You can gently pour the water into your eyes from a clean cup or glass. If necessary, place your head under a faucet or over the stream of water from a water fountain (Fig. 4-18). Then get immediate medical attention.

Releasing large amounts of refrigerant in a closed work area can cause death by suffocation. Refrigerant displaces the oxygen in the air. Poisonous phosgene gas is produced if leaking or released refrigerant R-12 comes into contact with a flame. Have adequate ventilation and do not breathe the fumes when using a flame-type *leak detector* (➤56-13).

Always assume the air-conditioner refrigerant system is pressurized and tightly sealed. Never steam-clean, weld, or apply heat to or near any part or line in the air conditioner. Never bake body finishes or use heat around a refrigerant container. Heat can cause excessive pressure buildup. Then a part or container could burst or explode spraying you and anyone nearby with refrigerant.

Never open the high-pressure valve on the gauge set (➤56-12) when the engine is running or while *charging the system* (➤56-18). The high pressure will enter the refrigerant container and cause it to explode. To charge an air-conditioning system while it is running, the refrigerant should be added to the low-side only.

The same safety cautions apply to refrigerant R-134a as to R-12. Follow all local, state, and federal laws that apply to refrigerants and air-conditioner service. Recover, store, and install refrigerants as required by law. Later sections cover these service procedures. Always read and follow the manufacturer's *safety cautions* and the *service cautions* (➤56-5) on the engine-compartment labels and in the vehicle service manual.

(A) FLARE FITTING

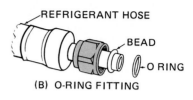

(B) O-RING FITTING

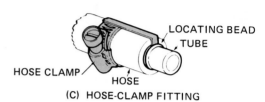

(C) HOSE-CLAMP FITTING

Fig. 56-6 Types of fittings used on refrigerant hose. (*ATW*)

➤ **56-5 SERVICE CAUTIONS FOR AIR-CONDITIONING SERVICE**

Air-conditioning diagnosis and service may be performed safely by following the safety cautions (➤56-4) and service cautions recommended by the vehicle manufacturer. Refrigerants are safe when handled properly and your eyes and skin are protected. Listed below are other air-conditioning service cautions.

1. Disconnect the negative cable from the battery (Fig. 28-4) when servicing air-conditioner components in the engine compartment or behind the instrument panel.

2. Be careful when performing electrical tests that require battery power to operate the system. If further damage is possible, follow the service-manual procedure to isolate the part. Then test it individually.

3. Keep your air-conditioning tools and work area clean. This helps avoid contamination of the refrigeration system during service.

4. Before disconnecting a component in the refrigeration system, clean the outside of the connections.

5. Do not open the refrigeration system or uncap a replacement part unless it is as close as possible to room temperature. This prevents condensation (➤55-11) that forms inside the part when it is cooler than the surrounding air.

6. Never loosen or open a connection before *discharging the system* (➤56-15). Always recover the refrigerant when discharging the system.

7. When loosening a connection, residual or trapped refrigerant may be noticed leaking out. Tighten the connection and repeat the discharge and refrigerant recovery procedure (➤56-15). Refrigerant must not be allowed to escape into the atmosphere.

8. When disconnecting a fitting use a second wrench on the coupling nut (Fig. 7-5). The backup wrench prevents twisting the refrigerant line (Fig. 7-6).

9. Sometimes a refrigerant system has been opened to replace a part or the system has discharged through leakage. Always *completely* discharge the system before *evacuating the system* (➤56-17) and then charging the system (➤56-18). Any refrigerant that enters the *vacuum pump* (➤56-17) during evacuating can damage the pump.

10. Immediately after disconnecting a part from the system, seal the open fittings with a cap or plugs.

11. Do not remove the sealing caps from the ends of a hose or other replacement part until you are ready to install the part.

12. Install a new seal or O ring before connecting an open fitting (Fig. 56-6). Coat the fitting and seal or O ring with the specified refrigerant oil.

13. When installing a refrigerant line or hose, avoid sharp bends. Position the line away from the exhaust system and sharp edges that could chafe or cut the line.

14. Tighten fittings only to the specified torque. Do not overtighten.

15. Refrigerant oil (➤55-17) will absorb moisture from the atmosphere if left uncapped. Do not open a container of refrigerant oil until ready for use. Install the cap immediately after use. Store refrigerant oil only in a clean moisture-free container.

16. When the procedure calls for charging the air conditioner with refrigerant vapor (➤56-18) and while the system is running, never allow liquid refrigerant to enter. Liquid refrigerant can damage the compressor.

17. Do not allow refrigerant to touch bright metal. Refrigerant will tarnish chrome and damage metal and painted surfaces.

18. Never allow gauge-set or service hoses to touch the engine fan or a hot engine exhaust manifold.

➤ **56-6 SERVICE CAUTIONS FOR REFRIGERANT-134A SYSTEMS**

Several differences in servicing and service cautions apply to refrigerant systems using refrigerant R-134a (➤55-16). Most important is that systems using R-12 and those using

R-134a are different systems. R-12 refrigerant and components must be used only in R-12 systems, and R-134a refrigerant and components must be used only in R-134a systems. This includes O rings, hoses, and refrigerant oil. R-134a systems must use a refrigerant oil marked *PAG oil* (➤55-17). PAG oil must not be used in R-12 systems.

Labels in the engine compartment and *R-134a NON-CFC* tags on system components indicate an R-134a system. No markings indicate an R-12 system.

The shop should have two sets of special tools and equipment for air-conditioning service. One set is for R-12 systems and the other for R-134a systems. The separate sets should include the recovery system (➤56-15).

➤ 56-7 ENEMIES OF THE AIR CONDITIONER

Other than mixing R-12 and R-134a parts and refrigerant (➤56-6), the three worst enemies of the air conditioner are

Contaminant	Effects
Moisture	▪ Causes valves to freeze ▪ Forms hydrochloric and hydrofluoric acid ▪ Causes corrosion and rust
Air	▪ Causes high head pressure and high temperatures ▪ Accelerates refrigerant instability ▪ Oxidizes oil and causes varnish ▪ Brings in moisture ▪ Reduces cooling capacity
Dirt	▪ Causes clogged screens and orifices ▪ Provides reactants to cause acids ▪ Abrasive action ▪ Additives hasten breakdown
Alcohol	▪ Attacks zinc and aluminum ▪ Promotes copper plating ▪ Hastens refrigerant breakdown ▪ Serves no useful purpose
Dye	▪ Precipitates out and restricts valves ▪ Results in oil overcharge ▪ Breaks down ▪ Detects only large leaks
Rubber	▪ Deteriorates and clogs system
Metal particles	▪ Clog screens and valves ▪ Gall bearings ▪ Break reed valves ▪ Score moving parts
Incorrect oil	▪ Provides poor lubrication, contains wax, and forms sludge, all of which plug passages and cause valves to stick ▪ Breaks down itself and causes breakdown of refrigerant ▪ Contains additives that break down or cause refrigerant to break down, and some may form butyl rubber ▪ Contains moisture

Fig. 56-7 Various contaminants and the effects of each.

moisture, dirt, and air. They cannot enter a properly operating air conditioner in good condition. However, they can enter if parts deteriorate or damage results from a collision or accident. Also, improper servicing can allow contaminants to enter. Figure 56-7 lists various contaminants and describes how they damage the system.

➤ 56-8 REFRIGERANT-SYSTEM QUICK CHECK

When the refrigeration system is operating normally, the high-pressure side is hot and the low-pressure side is cold (Fig. 55-12). A simple quick check is to touch the hoses and tubing (Fig. 56-8). The high-pressure line from the condenser to the orifice tube should feel warm. The low-pressure line from the orifice tube to the evaporator should feel cold. A line that changes temperature along its length may have an internal restriction. If the compressor runs, little or no difference in temperature between the low-pressure and high-pressure lines indicates low or no refrigerant in the system.

Two conditions help identify whether a refrigerant hose or tube is part of the high side or low side.

1. High-side hose and tubing is often smaller in diameter than the low side.
2. On humid days, water droplets and frost may appear on the low-side hose and tubing.

If the air conditioner is operating improperly, make a visual inspection (➤56-9). Then make a *performance test* (➤56-10). The sight glass (➤55-18), where present, can help diagnose the refrigerant system (Fig. 56-9). Complete diagnosis requires a thermometer, leak detector (➤56-13), and gauge set (➤56-12).

➤ 56-9 AIR-CONDITIONER VISUAL INSPECTION

Many causes of improper air-conditioner operation can be found by visual inspection. These include loose or missing belts, obstructed condenser air passages, loose compressor clutch, and loose or broken compressor mounting brackets. Other improper conditions you can see include disconnected or broken wires and oil from refrigerant leaks (➤56-13). Also, look for conditions in the engine cooling system (➤26-4) that can cause overheating. This slows heat transfer through the condenser (➤55-19).

On systems with electronic automatic temperature control (➤55-30), check for error messages and trouble

Line	Should Feel
Evaporator inlet	Cold
Evaporator outlet	Cold
Low-pressure line	Cold
High-pressure line	Hot

Fig. 56-8 Normal temperatures of air-conditioning hoses and tubing, as they should feel to your hand.

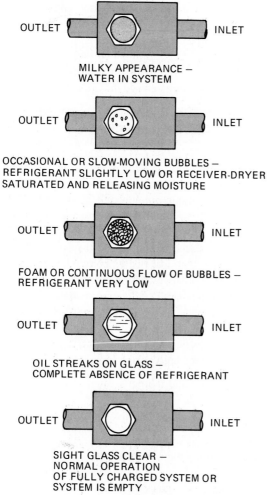

Fig. 56-9 Typical sight-glass indications for various conditions in the refrigerant system. (*Sun Electric Corporation*)

codes during the visual inspection. A scan tool (➤20-13) can be used on many vehicles to display *A/C Request, A/C Clutch, A/C Pressure, Coolant Temperature,* and *Fan* (Fig. 20-18).

Vehicles with an onboard diagnostic system display trouble codes and scan data on the vehicle (➤20-13). For example, some vehicles display *Low A/C Refrigerant* on the instrument panel if the refrigerant charge falls below one-third of normal charge. The information appears on the driver-information center or the air-conditioning control panel (Fig. 20-20). In addition to the display, the low-refrigerant condition causes the control module to store a trouble code and disengage the compressor clutch. Refer to the vehicle service manual for inspection and diagnosis procedures on electronically-controlled air conditioners.

1. REFRIGERANT-SYSTEM INSPECTION The oil in the leaking refrigerant will usually appear as an oily residue at the location of a large leak. Over time, dirt and dust build up in the oil. It then looks like dirty grease. Use a leak detector (➤56-13) and check these spots and the

entire refrigerant system for leaks. Multiple leaks may be found.

Causes of refrigerant leaks include connections with damaged or missing O rings (Fig. 56-6) and the wrong O rings. O rings may look alike but differ in size, shape, and material. Use only the O rings specified by the vehicle manufacturer. Refrigerant may leak from a loose *Schrader-valve core* in a *service valve* (Fig. 56-10) if the valve core is loose or damaged. A *valve cap* missing from a service valve may allow refrigerant to leak out. Without the cap, dirt can enter the service valve. Attaching a *service hose* (Fig. 56-10, lower) to the service valve may then force the dirt into the valve seat. This destroys the seal. If the valve cap is missing, clean the service valve and valve-core surface. Then install a new cap and tighten it finger-tight.

2. ELECTRICAL-SYSTEM INSPECTION During a visual inspection of the air-conditioner electrical system, check for blown fuses and disconnected or damaged wires and connectors. Inspect the clutch, clutch wiring, and clutch-control devices. A sensor or switch can fail. The vehicle service manual has a wiring diagram of the air-conditioner electrical system and the diagnostic procedures to follow.

3. VACUUM-SYSTEM INSPECTION Visual inspection of the vacuum system is similar to inspecting the heater vacuum system (➤56-2). However, the air conditioner has more doors, hoses, and controls. Vacuum-hose routing and diagnostic procedures are in the vehicle service manual.

➤ ## 56-10 AIR-CONDITIONER PERFORMANCE TEST

Make a performance test to check the operation of the air conditioner. The test includes measuring the ambient (outside) air and discharge-air temperatures. Gauges are connected to the system service valves to measure the high-side and low-side pressures (➤56-12). The vehicle

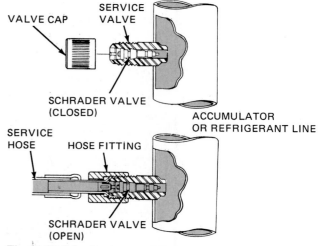

Fig. 56-10 Schrader-type service valves, showing the (top) valve closed and (bottom) valve open with a service hose attached. (*Ford Motor Company*)

should be warmed up and the ambient temperature should be 70°F [21°C] or higher.

Connect a tachometer (➤37-3) to the engine. Connect a gauge set (➤56-11) to the high and low sides of the refrigerant system. Set the mode control for MAX air conditioning (Fig. 55-22) and the temperature control to full cool. Set the blower speed to high. Then start the engine and run it at 1500 rpm.

Place a thermometer in the center outlet of the instrument panel (Fig. 56-11). The thermometer measures the temperature of the cooled *discharge air* entering the passenger compartment. Close the vehicle doors and windows.

On cycling-clutch systems (➤55-22), the compressor clutch may cycle on and off. Some manufacturers specify the *clutch-cycle rate*. This is how many times the clutch cycles on-and-off per minute. When the clutch disengages, the low-side pressure should rise and the high-side pressure should fall.

After 5 minutes, read the discharge-air temperature on the thermometer while the compressor clutch is engaged. Then compare the discharge-air temperature to the chart in the vehicle service manual. Figure 56-12 is a Chrysler chart that relates the temperature and pressure ranges for an air-conditioner performance test. The discharge-air temperature and system pressures should be within the specified range for the ambient temperature.

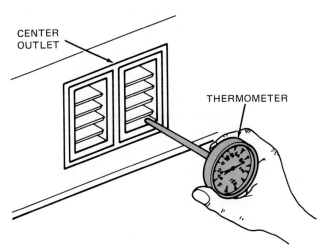

Fig. 56-11 Using a thermometer to measure the temperature of the discharge air. (*ATW*)

If the discharge-air temperature is outside the specified range, refer to the trouble-diagnosis charts in the vehicle service manual. System pressures vary with the temperature and humidity of the outside air. Pressures are higher on hot days than on cooler days. However, the most likely cause of excessive high-side pressure is restricted airflow through the condenser (➤55-25). The compressor clutch may not engage if the system has low or no refrigerant. Rapid cycling of the compressor clutch may indicate low refrigerant. If a refrigerant leak is suspected, check the refrigerant system with a leak detector (➤56-13).

➤ 56-11 USING MANIFOLD-GAUGE SETS AND SERVICE HOSES

A diagnosis of the refrigerant system requires the use of pressure gauges. They must be connected to the high-pressure and low-pressure sides of the system. The gauges are part of a *manifold-gauge set* (Fig. 56-13) or a charging station (Fig. 56-5). This is a wheeled cart that usually combines the manifold-gauge set, container of refrigerant, *charging cylinder,* and vacuum pump (➤56-17) in a single unit. Figure 56-14 shows a portable *service station.* It is similar to the charging station but used with the manifold-gauge set.

Service hoses or *charging hoses* connect the gauges to the service valves on the vehicle refrigerant system (Fig. 56-15). The gauges then measure the pressures while the system is operating. In addition to diagnosis, the manifold-gauge set and charging station are used for discharging (➤56-15), evacuating (➤56-17), and charging (➤56-18) the refrigerant system.

Figure 56-13 shows a manifold-gauge set. The low-pressure gauge is on the left and the high-pressure gauge is on the right. The low-pressure gauge is a *compound gauge.* It measures both pressure and vacuum. The gauge is marked from 0 to 150 pounds per square inch (psi) [0 to 1035 kPa] of pressure. Some gauges are marked from 0 to 100 or 120 psi [0 to 690 or 828 kPa]. The vacuum section of the gauge is marked in inches [millimeters] of mercury (Hg) vacuum from 0 to 30 inches [762 mm]. The scale on the high-pressure gauge ranges from 0 to 500 psi [0 to 3450 kPa]. Other gauges have different markings.

On some gauge sets, the low-pressure gauge housing

Ambient (Outside) Temperature	70°F [21°C]	80°F [26.5°C]	90°F [32°C]	100°F [37.5°C]	110°F [43°C]
Discharge—Air Temperature at Center Instrument-Panel Outlet	35–46°F [2–8°C]	39–50°F [4–10°C]	44–55°F [7–13°C]	50–62°F [10–17°C]	56–70°F [13–21°C]
Compressor Discharge Pressure	140–210 PSI [965–1448 kPa]	180–235 PSI [1240–1620 kPa]	210–270 PSI [1448–1860 kPa]	240–310 PSI [1655–2137 kPa]	280–350 PSI [1930–2413 kPa]
Evaporator Suction Pressure	10–35 PSI [69–241 kPa]	16–38 PSI [110–262 kPa]	20–42 PSI [138–290 kPa]	25–48 PSI [172–331 kPa]	30–55 PSI [207–379 kPa]

Fig. 56-12 Relationship of temperature and pressure ranges for an air-conditioner performance test. (*Chrysler Corporation*)

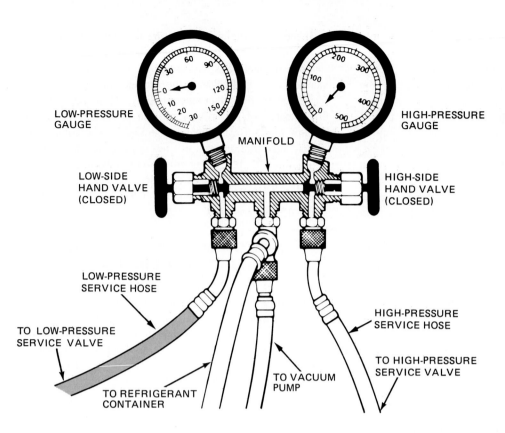

LOW-PRESSURE GAUGE

HIGH-PRESSURE GAUGE

MANIFOLD

LOW-SIDE HAND VALVE (CLOSED)

HIGH-SIDE HAND VALVE (CLOSED)

LOW-PRESSURE SERVICE HOSE

HIGH-PRESSURE SERVICE HOSE

TO LOW-PRESSURE SERVICE VALVE

TO HIGH-PRESSURE SERVICE VALVE

TO REFRIGERANT CONTAINER

TO VACUUM PUMP

Fig. 56-13 Manifold gauge set, showing the low-pressure and high-pressure gauges. The center connection can be connected to the vacuum pump to evacuate the system or to the refrigerant container to charge the system. (*Ford Motor Company*)

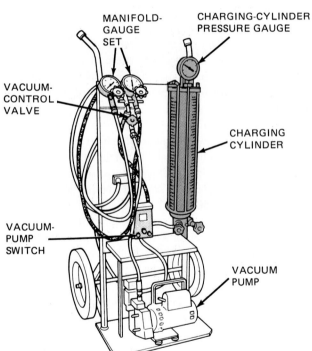

MANIFOLD-GAUGE SET

CHARGING-CYLINDER PRESSURE GAUGE

VACUUM-CONTROL VALVE

CHARGING CYLINDER

VACUUM-PUMP SWITCH

VACUUM PUMP

Fig. 56-14 A portable service station, used with the manifold gauge set. (*Chrysler Corporation*)

and the low-pressure hose are blue. The high-pressure gauge housing and the high-pressure hose are red. Service hoses for R-134a systems may have a black stripe along the hose. Color coding provides quick identification of the hoses and the connections to be made.

The gauges connect to the top of the hollow gauge-set *manifold* (Fig. 56-13). Three hose fittings (low-side,

center, and high-side) extend from the bottom of the manifold. Turning the hand-operated *shutoff valves* or *hand valves* opens and closes each end of the manifold. This allows the center fitting to be used for discharging (➤56-15), evacuating (➤56-17), and charging (➤56-18) the system. Sometimes two hoses connect to the center fitting (Fig. 56-15). Cap any fitting when no hose is attached.

➤ 56-12 CHECKING REFRIGERANT-SYSTEM PRESSURES

The gauge-set manifold is made so the gauges show the pressure in the service hoses even with the hand valves closed (Fig. 56-13). This isolates the gauges from the manifold and keeps them unaffected by it. Opening either hand valve opens the passage between that side of the refrigerant system and the manifold center fitting.

CAUTION!

Always wear safety goggles when connecting or disconnecting the gauge set or working with the refrigerant system. Wear gloves or wrap a shop towel around the fitting when you make or break a connection in the refrigerant system. Never open the high-pressure gauge valve while charging the system. The high pressure will enter the refrigerant container and cause it to explode.

To connect the gauges to the system service valves, follow the steps in the vehicle service manual. Also, follow the gauge-set or charging-station operating instructions.

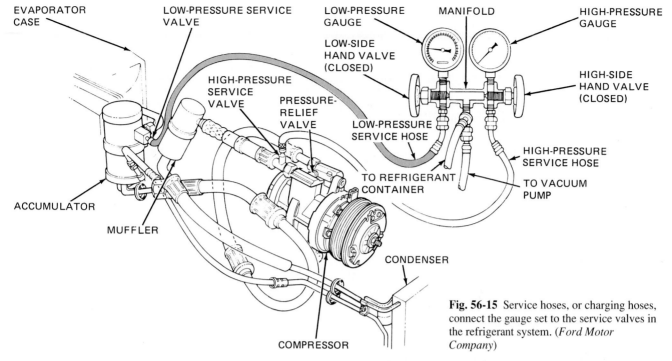

Fig. 56-15 Service hoses, or charging hoses, connect the gauge set to the service valves in the refrigerant system. (*Ford Motor Company*)

There are several sizes and types of service valves. Various adapters and fittings may be needed. Typical procedures for connecting the gauge set and measuring system pressures are described below.

1. With the engine stopped, remove the caps from the system service valves (Fig. 56-10).
2. Close the high-side and low-side valves on the gauge set or charging station. Do this by turning the hand wheels clockwise until the valves seat.
3. Connect the hose fittings to the service valves (Figs. 56-10 and 56-15). Adapters may be required. Some vehicles do not have a low-side service valve. On these, remove the cycling-clutch pressure switch (Fig. 56-16). Install a T adapter on the accumulator fitting. Then connect the low-pressure hose to the adapter. However, first check the vehicle service manual to be sure this is the proper procedure for the vehicle you are servicing. The accumulator fitting must have a Schrader valve (Fig. 56-10) in it.

Careful! Never create adapters that allow gauges and equipment for R-12 systems to be used on R-134a systems, or R-134a gauges and equipment to be used on R-12 systems.

4. Purge the air from the service hoses by loosening the fittings at the gauge set. Loosen the fittings only long enough for the trapped air to escape. Then tighten the fittings.
5. Start the engine and follow the procedures for making a performance test (➤56-10). As soon as the system is stabilized, read the high-side and low-side pressures on the gauges.
6. Compare the pressure readings with the pressures specified for the system you are checking. The chart in

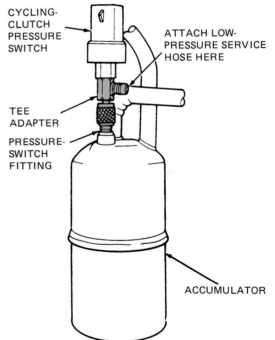

Fig. 56-16 Installing an adapter with a low-pressure hose fitting between the cycling-clutch pressure switch and the accumulator. (*Ford Motor Company*)

Fig. 56-17 shows the normal pressure ranges for various R-12 systems. The amount the pressure differs from specifications indicates the condition of the system.

7. On cycling-clutch systems, note the clutch-cycling time (➤56-10). The chart in Fig. 56-18 lists possible causes if pressures are low or high, or the clutch-cycling time too short or long. For other R-12 and R-134a systems, refer to the vehicle service manual.

791

Ambient (Outside Air) Temperature (°F)	At high-Pressure Test fitting* (psi)	STV, POA, or VIR Systems	Cycling-Clutch System with Expansion Valve and Receiver**	Cycling-Clutch System with Orifice Tube and Accumulator (CCOT)**	CCOT System with Pressure-Cycling Switch	Chrysler Corp. with Evaporator Pressure-Regulator Valve
60	120–170	28–31	7–15	—	—	—
70	150–250	28–31	7–15	24–31	24–31	22–30
80	180–275	28–31	7–15	24–31	24–31	22–37
90	200–310	28–31	7–15	24–32	24–31	25–37
100	230–330	28–35	10–30	24–32	24–36	—
110	270–360	28–38	10–35	24–32	—	—

*Pressures may be slightly higher on very humid days or lower on very dry days.
**Pressure just before clutch disengages (cycles off).

Fig. 56-17 Pressure ranges for normal operation of various R-12 air-conditioning systems. (*AC-Delco Division of General Motors Corporation*)

➤ 56-13 REFRIGERANT LEAK DETECTORS

Low refrigerant can cause compressor damage and abnormal pressures (Fig. 56-18). Refrigerant loss results from hose porosity, seal leakage, and part failures. A refrigerant leak can be located in several ways (Fig. 56-19). These include *liquid leak solution, refrigerant dye, ultraviolet light, electronic detector,* and *flame detector.* Follow the procedures in the vehicle service manual and in the leak-detector operating instructions. The work area must have good ventilation and be free of refrigerant and other fumes. Small traces of contaminated air can affect electronic and flame leak detectors. Some manufacturers do not recommend the use of refrigerant dye (except *tracer dye* used with ultraviolet light) or a flame detector.

1. LIQUID LEAK DETECTOR Large refrigerant leaks can be located with a liquid bubble solution or with soapy water. Brush or squirt it on fittings, hose connections, seals, and other suspected leak areas. Bubbles indicate a leak.

2. REFRIGERANT DYE A small amount of refrigerant dye can be added to the low-pressure side of the system. The dye turns the refrigerant red. Large leaks can then be seen or located by wiping out-of-sight parts with a white cloth or towel.

3. ULTRAVIOLET LIGHT A *leak-tracer dye* can be added to the system using a *tracer-dye injector* and a gauge set (➤56-11). After running the engine and air conditioner for about 10 minutes, shut off the engine. Scan the suspected leak areas with an *ultraviolet light* (Fig. 56-19A). Any dye that has leaked out will glow a bright yellow-green color at the point of leakage.

4. ELECTRONIC DETECTOR An electronic leak detector (Fig. 56-19B) is sensitive and easy to use. Pass the sensing probe slowly over, around, and under all parts and connections. Refrigerant is heavier than air and drops downward toward the floor. The detector has a signal light or a ticking-beeping sound to indicate the presence of refrigerant. When the detector senses a larger amount of escaping refrigerant, the sound becomes more rapid and increasingly shrill.

5. FLAME DETECTOR The flame detector (Fig. 56-19C) is a torch that burns butane or propane. To use the detector, open the gas-control valve and light the flame. Allow it to heat the reactor plate red-hot. Then adjust the flame to 3/8 inch [9.5 mm] above the reactor plate. Move the search hose around and under all connections, seals, and hoses in the system. The color of the flame will vary with the amount of refrigerant passing through the search hose. A blue flame indicates no leak. A yellow-green flame indicates a small leak. A bright blue-purple flame indicates a large leak. The flame detector should be used *only* on R-12 systems.

CAUTION!

Never breathe the fumes or black smoke that is given off by a flame detector if a leak is located. The fumes and smoke contain poisonous gas phosgene. Never use the flame detector where there is combustible vapor, fuel, or dust. The flame could set off an explosion or fire. Use a flame detector only in a well-ventilated area.

AIR-CONDITIONING SERVICE

➤ 56-14 SERVICING THE AIR-CONDITIONING SYSTEM

Basic air-conditioner services include discharging the system and recovering refrigerant (➤56-15), evacuating the system (➤56-17), and charging the system (➤56-18). Other services include adding a partial charge of

NOTE: System test requirements must be met to obtain accurate test readings for evaluation. Refer to the normal refrigerant - system pressure/temperature and the normal clutch - cycle rate and times charts.

HIGH (DISCHARGE) PRESSURE	LOW (SUCTION) PRESSURE	CLUTCH CYCLE TIME			COMPONENT — CAUSES
		RATE	ON	OFF	
HIGH	HIGH				CONDENSER — Inadequate Airflow
HIGH	NORMAL TO HIGH				ENGINE OVERHEATING
NORMAL TO HIGH	NORMAL	CONTINUOUS RUN			REFRIGERANT OVERCHARGE (a) AIR IN REFRIGERANT HUMIDITY OR AMBIENT TEMPERATURE VERY HIGH (b)
NORMAL	HIGH				ORIFICE TUBE — Missing O Rings Leaking or Missing
NORMAL	NORMAL	SLOW OR NO CYCLE	LONG OR CONTINUOUS	NORMAL OR NO CYCLE	MOISTURE IN REFRIGERANT SYSTEM EXCESSIVE REFRIGERANT OIL
NORMAL	LOW	SLOW	LONG	LONG	CLUTCH - CYCLING SWITCH — Low Cutout
NORMAL TO LOW	HIGH	CONTINUOUS RUN			Compressor — Low Performance
NORMAL TO LOW	NORMAL TO HIGH				SUCTION LINE — Partially Restricted or Plugged (c)
NORMAL TO LOW	NORMAL	FAST	SHORT	NORMAL	EVAPORATOR - Low or Restricted Airflow
			SHORT TO VERY SHORT	NORMAL TO LONG	CONDENSER, ORIFICE TUBE, OR LIQUID LINE — Partially Restricted or Plugged
			SHORT TO VERY SHORT	SHORT TO VERY SHORT	LOW REFRIGERANT CHARGE
			SHORT TO VERY SHORT	LONG	EVAPORATOR CORE — Partially Restricted or Plugged
NORMAL TO LOW	LOW	CONTINUOUS RUN			SUCTION LINE — Partially Restricted or Plugged (d) CLUTCH - CYCLING SWITCH — Sticking Closed
ERRATIC OPERATION OR COMPRESSOR NOT RUNNING		—	—	—	CLUTCH - CYCLING SWITCH — Dirty Contacts or Sticking Open POOR CONNECTION AT CLUTCH CONNECTOR OR CLUTCH - CYCLING - SWITCH CONNECTOR ELECTRICAL CIRCUIT ERRATIC — See A/C Electrical Circuit Wiring Diagram

ADDITIONAL POSSIBLE CAUSE - COMPONENTS ASSOCIATED WITH INADEQUATE COMPRESSOR OPERATION

- COMPRESSOR DRIVE BELT — Loose ● COMPRESSOR CLUTCH — Slipping
- CLUTCH COIL Open — Shorted, or Loose Mounting
- CONTROL ASSEMBLY SWITCH — Dirty Contacts or Sticking Open
- CLUTCH WIRING CIRCUIT — High Resistance, Open or Blown Fuse
- COMPRESSOR OPERATION INTERRUPTED BY ELECTRONIC CONTROL MODULE

ADDITIONAL POSSIBLE CAUSE - COMPONENTS ASSOCIATED WITH A DAMAGED COMPRESSOR

- CLUTCH - CYCLING SWITCH - Sticking Closed or Compressor Clutch Seized
- ACCUMULATOR — Refrigerant Oil - Bleed Hole Plugged
- REFRIGERANT LEAKS

(a) Compressor may make noise on initial run. This is slugging condition caused by excessive liquid refrigerant
(b) Compressor clutch may not cycle in ambient temperatures above 80°F [26.6°C] depending on humidity conditions
(c) Low - pressure reading will be normal to high if pressure is taken at accumulator and if restriction is downstream of service valve
(d) Low - pressure reading will be low if pressure is taken near the compressor and restriction is upstream of service valve

Fig. 56-18 Pressure and clutch-cycle-time evaluation chart for an R-12 system with orifice tube and a clutch-cycling pressure switch. (*Ford Motor Company*)

refrigerant, adding refrigerant oil (➤56-16), and replacing parts (➤56-19). Also, the contaminants must be removed from the recovered refrigerant so it is clean enough for reuse (➤56-15).

CAUTION!

Always wear safety goggles when performing any air-conditioning service. Follow the safety cautions in Chap. 4, the safety cautions in ➤56-4, and the service cautions in ➤56-5

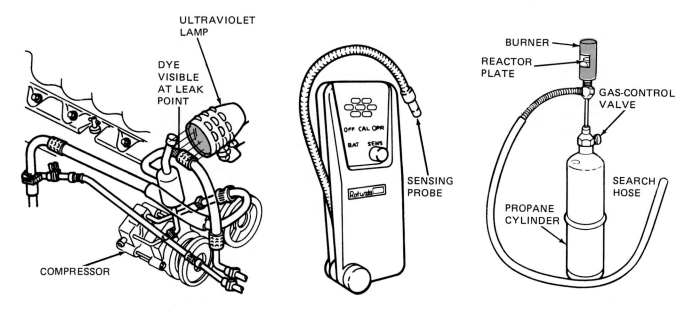

(A) ULTRAVIOLET-LIGHT LEAK DETECTOR (B) ELECTRONIC LEAK DETECTOR (C) FLAME LEAK DETECTOR

Fig. 56-19 Types of refrigerant leak detectors. (*Ford Motor Company*)

and ➤56-6. Also, follow the manufacturer's operating instructions for the equipment being used. Wear gloves or wrap a shop towel around the fitting when you make or break a connection in the refrigerant system. Never open the high-pressure gauge valve when the engine is running or while charging the system. The high pressure will enter the refrigerant container and cause it to explode.

➤ 56-15 DISCHARGING THE SYSTEM AND RECOVERING REFRIGERANT

To properly discharge the vehicle refrigerant system, use a *refrigerant-recovery station* (Fig. 56-20). This is a wheeled cart that includes a pump, a special refrigerant storage container, and a method of removing contaminants from the recovered refrigerant. The recovery station may also be combined with the charging station (➤56-11). Using the recovery station avoids releasing the refrigerant into the atmosphere while discharging the system (➤55-16).

Two types of refrigerant-recovery stations are *single-pass* units and *multi-pass* units. A single-pass unit is described below. Multi-pass units have separate operating modes for recovering refrigerant and for recycling refrigerant. Either method removes the contaminants—moisture, refrigerant oil, and air—from the refrigerant. This makes the refrigerant suitable for reuse.

With the engine not running, connect a charging station or manifold-gauge set to the vehicle refrigerant system (➤56-11). Look for pressure readings on the gauges to be sure there is refrigerant in the system. Do not try to recover refrigerant if there is no pressure in the system.

Connect the hose from the center fitting on the gauge-set manifold to the single-pass refrigerant-recovery station (Fig. 56-20). Follow the equipment manufacturer's operating instructions. These steps may include opening

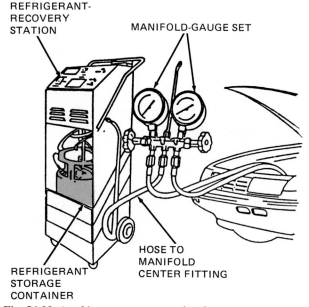

Fig. 56-20 A refrigerant-recovery station that traps, or recovers, the refrigerant when the system is discharged. (*Ford Motor Company*)

both gauge-set valves and turning ON the pump in the recovery station. The pump draws refrigerant from the air conditioner. The refrigerant passes through an oil separator that removes the refrigerant oil. Then the refrigerant flows through a filter-drier that removes moisture and into the refrigerant storage container.

Operate the recovery station until there is a vacuum in the air-conditioner refrigerant system. Then turn off the recovery station and wait for at least five minutes. If pressure appears again in the system, repeat the recovery procedure. All refrigerant is removed when the vacuum remains stable for at least two minutes.

NOTE After recycling refrigerant R-12, the contaminants in the refrigerant should not exceed:
- Moisture—15 parts per million (ppm) by weight.
- Refrigerant oil—4,000 ppm by weight.
- Noncondensable gases (air)—330 ppm by weight.

➤ 56-16 ADDING REFRIGERANT OIL

The proper type and quantity of refrigerant oil (➤55-17) must be added after discharging and service, and before evacuating the system. The oil circulates through the system with the refrigerant. Therefore, the refrigerant and each component have some oil in it when removed.

During discharge and recovery (➤56-15), the oil in the refrigerant is trapped in the recovery-station oil separator. Drain this old oil into a measuring cup. Refrigerant oil is measured by volume (fluid ounces and cubic centimeters [cc] or milliliters [ml]). Add the same amount of new oil to the system. A typical refrigerant system has a total oil charge of about 8 fluid ounces [240 cc].

Refrigerant oil must also be added after replacing the compressor (➤56-22) and other components in the refrigerant system. Refer to the vehicle service manual for specifications on how much oil to add when replacing a component. Figure 56-21 shows the amounts Ford specifies for a system. Pour the oil directly into the component. Tighten all fittings. Then evacuate (➤56-17), charge (➤56-18), and leak-test (➤56-13) the system.

➤ 56-17 EVACUATING THE SYSTEM

When the refrigerant system has been discharged (➤56-15) or a large refrigerant loss has occurred, the system must be *evacuated*. A vacuum pump is connected to the system (Fig. 56-22). This pumps out the air and creates a vacuum that causes any moisture in the system to boil and vaporize. Continued pumping action then removes the moisture-laden vapor.

The vacuum pump connects to the manifold center fitting in Fig. 56-15. The pump can also attach to the manifold high-side fitting (Fig. 56-22). With this arrangement, no connection is made to the system high-side service valve (➤56-18). The drum of refrigerant attaches to the manifold center fitting. A shutoff valve in the top of the drum must remain closed during discharging and evacuating.

Follow the vacuum-pump operating instructions and the procedures in the vehicle service manual. A typical procedure is to make a quick check for leaks after the pump runs for about 10 minutes. Close the gauge-set valves and turn OFF the pump. The vacuum should not drop more than 2 inches [50 mm] in 5 minutes. A greater loss indicates a leak in the system (➤56-13).

If no leak is indicated, continue evacuating the system. At sea level, try to obtain a vacuum of 29.5 inches [750 mm] Hg. Adjust the specification for the change in atmospheric pressure above sea level. For every 1,000 feet increase in altitude of your location, reduce the maximum vacuum reading by 1 inch [25.4 mm] Hg. Evacuate the system for a minimum of 30 minutes after the maximum vacuum reading is reached. Then close the valves and stop the pump. The system is now ready for charging (➤56-18).

➤ 56-18 CHARGING THE SYSTEM

A variety of methods is used for *charging the system*. This means adding the proper amount of clean refrigerant to the air-conditioner refrigerant system. A decal in the engine compartment lists the type and amount of refrigerant needed for a full charge. This information is also in the vehicle service manual. Refrigerant is measured by weight in pounds and ounces [kilograms]. For example, an air conditioner on a large car may require 3 pounds 4 ounces [1.5 kg] of R-12 refrigerant. A van with a rear-mounted auxiliary air conditioner may require more. A small car may take less. To charge an air-conditioning system while it is running, refrigerant vapor should be added to the low-side only.

The charging procedure depends on the type of charging equipment being used and the procedure in the vehicle service manual. The procedure also depends on the size of refrigerant containers available. The basic steps in three charging procedures are described below.

1. CHARGING WITH SMALL CANS At one time, charging with small cans of refrigerant (Fig. 56-23) was widely used. These *one-pound cans* (usually only 14 or 15 ounces) connect to a *refrigerant manifold*. A charging hose connects the refrigerant manifold to the center fitting on the gauge-set manifold. The cans may be placed in a pan of water heated to 125°F [52°C]. This helps the refrigerant vaporize and enter the system more quickly.

Replaced Component ▪ Pour Directly Into Component	Add Oil
Evaporator (Into Vertical-Hold Inlet Pipe)	3 Fluid Ounces (90 cc)
Condenser	1 Fluid Ounce (30 cc)
Accumulator	Old Volume plus 2 Fluid Ounces (60 cc)
Receiver	1 Fluid Ounce (30 cc)
Condenser-and-Receiver Assembly	2 Fluid Ounces (60 cc)
Expansion Valve, Orifice Tube, Hoses	None

Fig. 56-21 Amount of refrigerant oil that should be added to a new air-conditioner component. (*Ford Motor Company*)

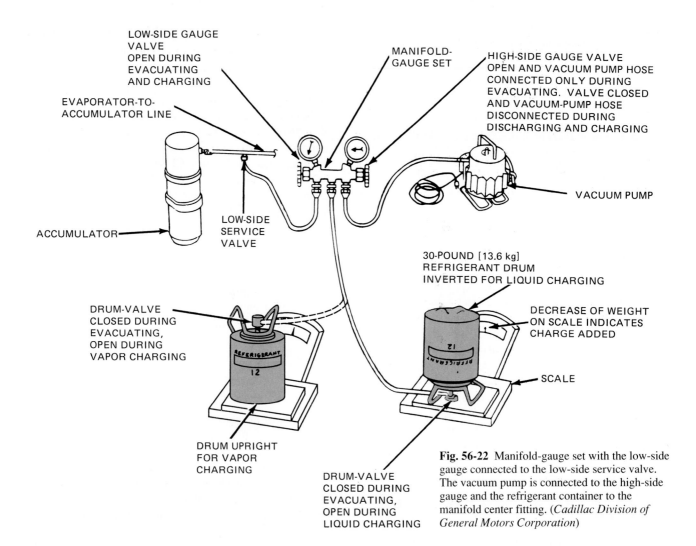

LOW-SIDE GAUGE
VALVE
OPEN DURING
EVACUATING
AND CHARGING

EVAPORATOR-TO-
ACCUMULATOR LINE

MANIFOLD-
GAUGE SET

HIGH-SIDE GAUGE VALVE
OPEN AND VACUUM PUMP HOSE
CONNECTED ONLY DURING
EVACUATING. VALVE CLOSED
AND VACUUM-PUMP HOSE
DISCONNECTED DURING
DISCHARGING AND CHARGING

VACUUM PUMP

ACCUMULATOR

LOW-SIDE
SERVICE
VALVE

30-POUND [13.6 kg]
REFRIGERANT DRUM
INVERTED FOR LIQUID CHARGING

DRUM-VALVE
CLOSED DURING
EVACUATING,
OPEN DURING
VAPOR CHARGING

DECREASE OF WEIGHT
ON SCALE INDICATES
CHARGE ADDED

SCALE

DRUM UPRIGHT
FOR VAPOR
CHARGING

DRUM-VALVE
CLOSED DURING
EVACUATING,
OPEN DURING
LIQUID CHARGING

Fig. 56-22 Manifold-gauge set with the low-side
gauge connected to the low-side service valve.
The vacuum pump is connected to the high-side
gauge and the refrigerant container to the
manifold center fitting. (*Cadillac Division of
General Motors Corporation*)

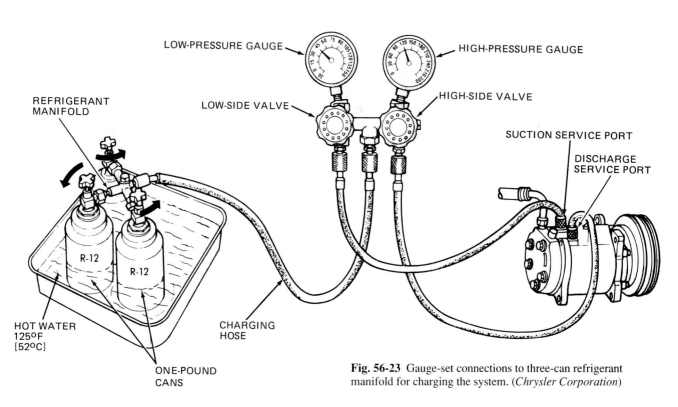

LOW-PRESSURE GAUGE

HIGH-PRESSURE GAUGE

REFRIGERANT
MANIFOLD

LOW-SIDE VALVE

HIGH-SIDE VALVE

SUCTION SERVICE PORT

DISCHARGE
SERVICE PORT

R-12

R-12

HOT WATER
125°F
[52°C]

CHARGING
HOSE

ONE-POUND
CANS

Fig. 56-23 Gauge-set connections to three-can refrigerant
manifold for charging the system. (*Chrysler Corporation*)

tainers, measure the temperature of the water with a thermometer. Never place refrigerant containers in water hotter than 125°F [52°C].

If necessary, purge any trapped air from the charging hose (Fig. 56-23). Do this by loosening the charging-hose fitting at the gauge-set manifold. Slightly open a valve on one small can. Allow only enough refrigerant to flow to force any air from the hose. Then tighten the hose fitting. Close both gauge valves and open all three small-can valves. Start the engine and run it at fast idle. Move the instrument-panel mode control to an air-conditioning positioning (Fig. 55-22). Set the temperature control to full COLD and the blower speed to LOW.

The refrigerant containers in Fig. 56-23 are shown upright. In this position, refrigerant vapor from the top of the cans will flow through the charging hose. Charge the system through the low-side service valve by slowly opening the low-side hand valve on the gauge set. Adjust the valve to prevent excessive pressure by keeping the pressure below 50 psi [345 kPa]. The high-side valve on the gauge set *must* remain closed. When the cans are empty, close the gauge-set valves. Then close the valves on the refrigerant manifold.

Make a performance test (➤56-10). If the system operates properly, disconnect the gauge set. Install the caps on the service valves (Fig. 56-10). If improper pressures or operation results, refer to the air-conditioner trouble-diagnosis section of the vehicle service manual.

2. CHARGING WITH REFRIGERANT DRUM A large container of refrigerant, such as the 30-pound [13.6-kg] drum shown in Fig. 56-22, can be used to charge the system. These containers are often easier to work with because they have a shutoff valve in the top. This helps reduce unwanted loss of refrigerant into the atmosphere. The drum connects to the center fitting of the gauge-set manifold (Fig. 56-22).

Careful! *Some manufacturers recommend performing the entire evacuating and charging procedure through the low side service valve (Fig. 56-22). A hose is not connected to the high-side service valve. Sometimes a mistake is made and the wrong valve accidentally opened. This arrangement prevents high-side pressure from reaching the refrigerant container, charging cylinder, or vacuum pump. Keep the high-side gauge valve closed during discharging and charging.*

Place the drum on a scale (Fig. 56-22) and note the weight before charging begins. Then subtract the weight of the refrigerant charge to be added. Watch the scale during the charging procedure. Close the valves and stop the charging procedure when the scale shows the drum weight has decreased the specified amount.

Charging procedures vary so always check the manufacturer's service manual to make sure you follow the proper procedure. Some procedures include inverting the refrigerant container (Fig. 56-22) and first *liquid charging* with a specified amount of refrigerant. This is done with

the engine off. Then turn the container upright and add the remaining charge by *vapor charging* while the system is operating. Vapor charging is also used to add a partial charge of refrigerant.

3. CHARGING WITH CHARGING CYLINDER The charging station (Fig. 56-5) and the service station (Fig. 56-14) include a drum of refrigerant and a charging cylinder. Markings on the charging cylinder allow it to be filled with the specified amount of liquid refrigerant. This can be done while the system is being evacuated. Separate scales are not needed.

An electric heating element may be part of the charging cylinder. When the heating element is turned on to warm the refrigerant, liquid-charging and vapor-charging take less time. Some charging stations pump a preset quantity of refrigerant into the system and then automatically shutoff. Follow the procedure in the vehicle service manual and the equipment operating instructions when using a charging cylinder or charging station.

REPLACING AIR-CONDITIONER COMPONENTS

➤ 56-19 REMOVING AND INSTALLING PARTS

To replace a part in the refrigerant system, first discharge the system (➤56-15). Replace the part. Add refrigerant oil (➤55-16), if necessary. Then evacuate (➤56-17), charge (➤56-18), and leak-test (➤56-13) the system. The vehicle service manual includes the procedures for removing and installing air-conditioner components. Following sections cover replacing hoses, filters, and compressors.

➤ 56-20 REPLACING REFRIGERANT HOSE

When a refrigerant hose must be replaced, first discharge the refrigerant system (➤56-15). Disconnect the fittings at the ends of the hose. Some hose couplings use flare fittings (Fig. 56-6A). Others seal with O rings (Fig. 56-6B). Hose-clamp fittings (Fig. 56-5C) are also used.

Many refrigerant hoses and lines attach with *spring-lock couplings* (Fig. 56-24). The male fitting has a caged garter spring that expands over the lip of the female fitting when the two fittings are pushed together. This locks the coupling and prevents separation. Two O rings provide the seal to prevent refrigerant leaks. A *spring-lock coupling tool* (Fig. 56-24) must be used to disconnect the coupling.

Careful! *Use only replacement refrigerant hose that is approved for the system you are servicing. Never use heater hose. Never use hose for an R-12 system in an R-134a system, or hose for an R-134a system in an R-12 system.*

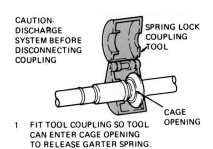

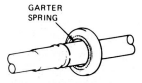

CAUTION-
DISCHARGE
SYSTEM BEFORE
DISCONNECTING
COUPLING

SPRING LOCK
COUPLING
TOOL

1 FIT TOOL COUPLING SO TOOL
CAN ENTER CAGE OPENING
TO RELEASE GARTER SPRING.

CAGE
OPENING

SPRING-LOCK
COUPLING
TOOL

2 PUSH THE TOOL INTO CAGE
OPENING TO RELEASE FEMALE
FITTING FROM GARTER SPRING.
PULL FITTING APART.

FEMALE
FITTING

O RINGS

GARTER
SPRING

MALE
FITTING

CAGE

3 REMOVE TOOL,
SPRING LOCK COUPLING
DISCONNECTED.

(A) DISCONNECTING SPRING-LOCK COUPLING

GARTER
SPRING

3 TO ENSURE COUPLING ENGAGEMENT,
VISUALLY CHECK THAT GARTER SPRING
IS OVER FLARED END OF FEMALE FITTING.

B INSTALL NEW O RINGS. USE
ONLY SPECIFIED O RINGS.

A CLEAN FITTINGS

2
C LUBRICATE
WITH CLEAN
REFRIGERANT
OIL.

D ASSEMBLE FITTING
BY PUSHING TOGETHER
WITH A SLIGHT TWISTING
MOTION.

GARTER
SPRING

1 CHECK FOR MISSING OR DAMAGED
GARTER SPRING. REMOVE DAMAGED
SPRING WITH SMALL HOOKED WIRE.
INSTALL NEW SPRING IF DAMAGED
OR MISSING.

(B) CONNECTING SPRING LOCK COUPLING

Fig. 56-24 Steps in disconnecting and connecting a spring-lock coupling. (*Ford Motor Company*)

➤ 56-21 INSTALLING AND REPLACING REFRIGERANT FILTER

In years past, *flushing the system* removed contaminants such as water, sludge, and metal particles from a compressor failure. The system was discharged and a liquid cleaner or *flushing agent* was forced through the system. This washed out many contaminants that were in lines, hoses, and other parts. However, most flushing used refrigerant R-11 which can no longer be allowed to escape into the atmosphere.

Many air conditioners now have a *refrigerant filter* (Fig. 56-25) in the liquid line between the condenser and the evaporator. The filter contains a screen and filter pad to trap contaminants. Replace or install a refrigerant filter if the orifice tube plugs repeatedly and after a compressor seizes. First discharge and recover the refrigerant. Install the new filter. Then evacuate, charge, and leak-test the system.

➤ 56-22 REPLACING THE COMPRESSOR

The procedure for removing and replacing a compressor varies with the mounting arrangement and the type of compressor. Common procedures include discharging the system and recovering refrigerant, detaching the hoses, and capping or sealing the fittings. Disconnect the electrical connector at the compressor clutch and any other leads and lines to the compressor.

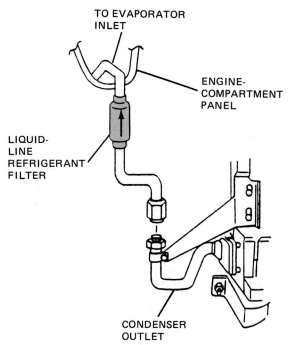

TO EVAPORATOR
INLET

ENGINE-
COMPARTMENT
PANEL

LIQUID-
LINE
REFRIGERANT
FILTER

CONDENSER
OUTLET

Fig. 56-25 Refrigerant filter in liquid line between the condenser and the evaporator. (*Pontiac Division of General Motors Corporation*)

The proper amount of refrigerant oil must remain in the system (➤56-16). After removing the compressor, drain the oil from the compressor into a measuring cup (Fig. 56-26A). Note the amount of oil drained from the old compressor. The new compressor has oil in it. However, all the oil may not be needed in the system.

To prevent an oil overcharge, drain the oil from the new compressor into a clean measuring cup (Fig. 56-26B). Add the same amount of new oil to the new compressor that was drained from the old compressor. Pour the oil into the suction port of the new compressor (Fig. 56-26C). Then install the new compressor.

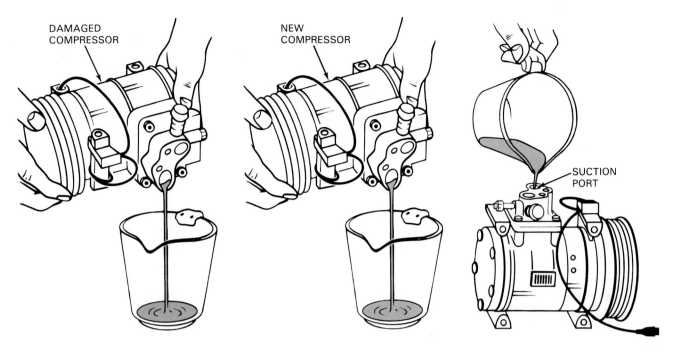

(A) DRAIN OLD COMPRESSOR   (B) DRAIN NEW COMPRESSOR   (C) POUR NEW OIL INTO NEW COMPRESSOR

Fig. 56-26 Adjusting amount of new refrigerant oil in a new compressor. (*ATW*)

TRADE TALK

charge the system	evacuate the system	PAG oil	vapor charging
clutch-cycle rate	leak-test the system	performance test	
discharge the system	liquid charging	spring-lock coupling	

MULTIPLE-CHOICE TEST

*Select the **one** correct, best, or most probable answer to each question.*
You can find the answers in the section indicated at the end of each question.

1. A heater supplies little heat. The blower and engine coolant level are OK. Technician A says a missing or stuck thermostat could be the cause. Technician B says a misadjusted heater control could be the cause. Who is right? (➤56-1)
   a. A only
   b. B only
   c. both A and B
   d. neither A nor B

2. A vacuum-operated door does not work. Technician A says the hose to the vacuum motor is disconnected or leaking. Technician B says the vacuum motor is defective. Who is right? (➤56-2)
   a. A only
   b. B only
   c. both A and B
   d. neither A nor B

3. Three major enemies of the air conditioner are (➤56-7)
   a. gasoline, oil, and electricity
   b. moisture, dirt, and air
   c. cold weather, humid days, and high altitude
   d. warm weather, dry days, and low altitude
4. When you feel a high-pressure line, it should be (➤56-8)
   a. warm
   b. cold
   c. the same temperature as the outside air
   d. the same temperature as the low-pressure line
5. When you feel a low-pressure line, it should be (➤56-8)
   a. warm
   b. cold
   c. the same temperature as the outside air
   d. the same temperature as the high-pressure pipe
6. If the compressor runs, little or no difference in temperature between the low-pressure and the high-pressure lines indicates (➤56-8)
   a. a full refrigerant charge
   b. normal system operation
   c. low or no refrigerant
   d. an overcharge of refrigerant oil
7. The most likely cause of too much high-side pressure is (➤56-10)
   a. restricted refrigerant flow through orifice tube
   b. restricted oil flow through desiccant
   c. restricted airflow through the condenser
   d. restricted airflow through the evaporator
8. A slight vacuum develops in the system at the end of the discharging and recovering procedure. To find out if the system still has pressure, turn off the recovery station and wait at least (➤56-15)
   a. two minutes
   b. five minutes
   c. 20 minutes
   d. 30 minutes
9. To charge an air-conditioning system while it is running, the refrigerant should be added to (➤56-18)
   a. only the high side
   b. only the low side
   c. both high and low sides
   d. neither high nor low sides
10. If the orifice tube plugs repeatedly or the compressor seizes (➤56-21)
   a. flush the system with R-11
   b. flush the system with R-12
   c. check for a refrigerant leak
   d. install or replace the refrigerant filter

REVIEW QUESTIONS

1. What is the most important service caution for R-12 and R-134a systems? (➤56-6)
2. What three systems are included in a visual inspection of the air conditioner, and how is each inspection performed? (➤56-9)
3. Describe how to make a performance test of an air conditioner, and the meaning of the results. (➤56-10)
4. Explain how to check the refrigerant-system pressures, and the conditions indicated by pressures that are too high and too low. (➤56-12)
5. When replacing a compressor, how do you determine the amount of refrigerant oil that should be in the new compressor? (➤56-22)

GLOSSARY

Accelerator pump In the carburetor, a small pump operated by the throttle linkage that momentarily enriches the air-fuel mixture when the accelerator pedal is depressed at low speed.

Accumulator A device that stores fluid in a hydraulic or pneumatic system so the fluid remains available to the system. In air conditioners, it traps liquid refrigerant traveling with the refrigerant vapor. In antilock-braking systems, it provides high-pressure fluid on demand. In automatic transmissions, it cushions the shock of clutch and servo actions.

Actuator In a control system, an output device or transducer that converts electric, hydraulic, or pneumatic energy usually into mechanical motion.

Adiabatic Without loss of heat.

Advance The moving ahead of the ignition spark in relation to piston position; produced electronically or by centrifugal or vacuum devices in accordance with engine speed and intake-manifold vacuum.

Aerobic gasket material Room-temperature-vulcanizing (RTV) silicone rubber that cures only in the presence of air; used on surfaces that flex or vibrate.

Air-aspirator system An exhaust-emission-control system that uses the pulsations in the exhaust system to feed fresh air into the exhaust system.

Air bag A balloon-type passenger-safety device that inflates automatically on vehicle impact.

Air brake A braking system that uses compressed air to supply the force required to apply the brakes.

Air cleaner A device mounted on or connected to the engine air intake for filtering dirt and dust out of the air being drawn into the engine.

Air-fuel ratio The proportions of air and fuel (by weight) supplied to the engine cylinders for combustion.

Air-injection system An exhaust-emission-control system that uses a low-pressure pump to inject fresh air into the exhaust system.

Air-mass metering In some fuel-injection systems, fuel metering controlled primarily by engine speed and the amount of air actually entering the engine.

Air spring In the suspension system, a flexible bag filled with air which compresses to absorb shock.

All-wheel drive (AWD) A type of four-wheel drive, without a two-speed transfer case, used in vehicles that are primarily driven on-road (not off-road).

Alternating current (AC or ac) An electric current that flows first in one direction and then in the other.

Alternator In the vehicle electric system, a device that converts mechanical energy into electric energy for charging the battery and supplying power for the electrical load. Also called an ac generator.

Ammeter An instrument or meter for measuring the rate of current flow in amperes through an electric circuit. In the vehicle instrument panel, the ammeter shows current flow to or from the battery.

Ampere A unit of measure for electric current. One ampere corresponds to a flow of 6.28 x 10^{18} electrons per second.

Ampere-hour capacity A battery rating based on the amperes of current that a battery can deliver for 20 hours, without any temperature-corrected cell voltage falling below 1.75 volts.

Anaerobic sealant A material that cures or hardens only in the absence of air such as when squeezed tightly between two surfaces.

Analog A value or variable that is proportionally analogous, or similar, to changes in an unrelated quantity. For example, a temperature may be represented by a voltage which is its analog.

Analog gauge Any gauge with a pointer or needle.

Antifreeze A chemical, usually ethylene glycol, added to the engine coolant to raise its boiling temperature and lower its freezing temperature.

Antilock brake system A system installed with the service brakes to prevent wheel lockup during braking.

Arcing Name given to the spark that jumps the air gap between two electric conductors, such as the arcing between the brushes and commutator bars in an electromagnetic starting motor.

Armature A part moved by magnetism, or a part moved through a magnetic field to produce current. The rotating assembly that includes the main current-carrying conductors.

Aspect ratio The ratio of tire height to width. The lower the number, the wider the tire.

Atom The smallest unit of an element which usually remains undivided.

Automatic choke A device that positions the choke valve automatically in accordance with engine temperature or time.

Automatic headlamp dimmer Automatically selects the proper headlamp beam (high or low) for the driving conditions.

Automatic level control A suspension system that compensates for variations in vehicle load by maintaining the body at a predetermined height.

Automatic transmission A transmission in which gear ratios are changed automatically instead of by hand as in a manual transmission.

Axle A theoretical or actual crossbar supporting a vehicle on which one or more wheels turn.

Axle ratio In a drive axle, the ratio between the rotational speed (rpm) of the input or drive shaft and that of the output or axle shaft. The gear reduction in the final drive, which may be determined by dividing the number of teeth on the ring gear by the number of teeth on the pinion gear.

Axle shaft A solid or tubular shaft that connects the final drive to the wheels that turn to move the vehicle.

Backfire A pop or bang heard through the air intake or exhaust system.

Backlash In gearing, the clearance between the meshing teeth of two gears.

Ball joint A flexible joint consisting of a ball within a socket, used in steering and suspension systems and valve-train rocker arms.

Band In an automatic transmission, a hydraulically controlled brake band installed around a metal clutch drum that stops or allows drum rotation.

Battery An electrochemical device for storing energy in chemical form so that it can be released as electricity for cranking the engine and powering the electrical load. Also, a group of electric cells connected together.

Battery acid The electrolyte used in a battery; a mixture of sulfuric acid and water.

BDC See Bottom dead center.

Bead That part of the tire which is shaped to fit the rim. The bead is made of steel wires, wrapped and reinforced by the plies of the tire.

Bearing A part that transmits a load to a support and in so doing absorbs most of the friction of moving parts. A bearing is usually replaceable. See Bushing.

Bias-ply tire A tire in which the plies are laid diagonally, crisscrossing one another at an angle of about 30 to 40 degrees.

Bleeding A process by which air is removed from a hydraulic system (brake, cooling, fuel, or power steering), usually by opening a bleed valve and draining part of the fluid or operating the system to work out the air.

Blowby Leakage of compressed air-fuel mixture and burned gases (from combustion) past the piston rings into the crankcase.

Boost pressure The pressure in the intake manifold while the supercharger or turbocharger is operating.

Bottom dead center (BDC) The piston position at the lower limit of its travel in the cylinder, when the cylinder volume is at its maximum.

Brake An energy-conversion device used to slow, stop, or hold a vehicle or mechanism.

Brake drum A metal drum mounted on a vehicle wheel to form the outer shell of the brake; the brake shoes press against the drum to slow or stop drum-and-wheel rotation for braking.

Brake fade A temporary reduction or fading out of braking effectiveness.

Brake fluid A chemically-inert hydraulic fluid used in hydraulic brake systems to transmit force and motion through a closed system of tubing, or brake lines.

Brake horsepower Power available from the engine crankshaft to do work, such as moving the vehicle; bhp = torque X rpm/5252.

Brakelights Lights at the rear of the vehicle which indicate that the brakes are applied. Also called stoplights.

Brake lines The tubes and hoses connecting the master cylinder to the wheel cylinders or calipers in a hydraulic brake system.

Brake lining A high-friction material, in the past often a form of asbestos, attached to the brake shoe by rivets or a bonding process. The lining takes the wear when the shoe is pressed against the brake drum or rotor.

Brake mean effective pressure (BMEP) The pressure which, acting on the top of the piston, would result in a given brake-horsepower output if there were no losses due to friction and driving the engine accessories.

British thermal unit (Btu) A measurement of the quantity of heat. One Btu will raise the temperature of one pound of water one degree Fahrenheit.

Brush A block of conducting substance, such as carbon, which rests against a rotating ring or commutator to form a continuous electric circuit.

BTDC Abbreviation for before top dead center; any position of the piston between bottom dead center and top dead center, on the upward stroke.

Bushing A one-piece sleeve placed in a bore to serve as a bearing surface. See Bearing.

Cables Stranded conductors, usually covered with insulating material, used for connections between electric devices.

Calibrate To determine the correct value of.

Caliper In a disc brake, a housing for pistons and brake shoes, connected to the hydraulic system; holds the brake shoes so that they straddle the disc.

Cam A rotating lobe or eccentric that can be used with a cam follower to change rotary motion to reciprocating motion.

Camber The tilt of the top of the wheel from the vertical; when the tilt is outward, the camber is positive. Also, the angle which a front-wheel spindle makes with the horizontal. A tire-wear angle.

Camshaft A shaft in the engine which has a series of cams for operating the valve mechanisms. It is driven by gears, or by sprockets and a toothed belt or chain from the crankshaft.

Camshaft sensor A magnetic sensor or Hall-effect switch that, as the camshaft rotates, provides the ECM with voltage pulses that identify the position of number 1 piston. Also called camshaft-position sensor.

Carbon (C) A black deposit that is left on engine parts such as pistons, rings, and valves by the combustion of fuel, and which inhibits their action.

Carbon dioxide (CO_2) A colorless, odorless gas that results from complete combustion.

Carbon monoxide (CO) A colorless, odorless, tasteless, poisonous gas which results from incomplete combustion. A pollutant contained in engine exhaust gas.

Carburetor The device in an engine fuel system which mixes fuel with air and supplies the combustible mixture to the intake manifold.

Caster Tilting of the steering axis forward or backward to provide directional steering stability.

Catalyst A material in the catalytic converter that causes a chemical change without being a part of the chemical reaction.

Catalytic converter A mufflerlike device for use in an exhaust system. It converts harmful gases into harmless gases by promoting a chemical reaction between the catalysts and the pollutants.

Center differential A two-position (locked and unlocked) differential located between two drive axles; located in the drive line or transfer case of some four-wheel-drive or all-wheel-drive vehicles. Also called interaxle differential.

Centrifugal advance A rotating-weight mechanism in the ignition distributor that advances and retards ignition timing through the centrifugal force resulting from changes in the rotational speed of the distributor shaft.

Cetane number A measure of the ignition quality of diesel fuel, or how high a temperature is required to ignite it. The lower the cetane number, the higher the temperature required to ignite a diesel fuel.

Charcoal canister A container filled with activated charcoal; used to trap gasoline vapor from the fuel tank and carburetor while the engine is off.

Charge-indicator light Illuminates to indicate the battery is not charging.

Charging rate The amperage flowing from the alternator into the battery.

Check valve A valve that opens to permit the passage of air or fluid in one direction only, or operates to prevent (check) some undesirable action.

Chip One or more integrated circuits manufactured as a very small package capable of performing many functions; may be replaceable or reprogrammable.

Choke In the carburetor, a device that usually operates automatically when starting a cold engine. It "chokes off" the airflow through the air horn, producing a partial vacuum and a richer mixture.

Circuit The complete path of an electric current, including the current source.

Circuit breaker A resettable protective device that opens an electric circuit to prevent damage when the circuit is overheated by excess current flow.

Clearance The space between two moving parts, or between a moving and a stationary part, such as a journal and a bearing. The bearing clearance is filled with lubricating oil when the mechanism is running.

Clearance volume The volume that remains above the piston at TDC.

Clutch A coupling that connects and disconnects a shaft from its drive while the drive mechanism is running. In an automotive power train, the device which engages and disengages the transmission from the engine. In an air-conditioning system, the device that engages and disengages the compressor shaft from its continuously rotating drive-belt pulley.

Clutch pedal A foot-operated pedal that the driver depresses to disconnect the engine from the manual transmission or transaxle.

Clutch shaft In a manual transmission, the input shaft and drive gear. The clutch is assembled on the shaft. The gear drives the countershaft and serves as a pilot for the front end of the mainshaft. External splines on the drive gear are used by the synchronizer sleeve to lock the clutch shaft to the mainshaft for direct drive.

Coil In the automotive ignition system, the transformer used to step up battery voltage (by induction) to the high voltage required to fire the spark plugs.

Cold-cranking rate A battery rating indicating the ability of a battery to crank an engine when the battery is cold.

Combination valve A brake-warning-lamp valve in combination with a proportioning and/or metering valve.

Combustible mixture A mixture that readily burns.

Combustion Burning; fire produced by the proper combination of fuel, heat, and oxygen. In the engine, the rapid burning of air and fuel in the combustion chamber.

Combustion chamber The space

between the top of the piston and the cylinder head, in which the fuel is burned.

Commutator A series of copper bars at one end of a generator or starting-motor armature, electrically insulated from the armature shaft and insulated from one another by mica. The brushes rub against the bars of the commutator, which form a rotating connector between the armature windings and brushes.

Compression Reduction in the volume of a gas by squeezing it into a smaller space. Increasing the pressure reduces the volume and increases the density and temperature of the gas.

Compression-ignition engine An engine operating on the diesel cycle, in which the fuel is injected into the cylinders, where the heat of compression ignites it.

Compression ratio The volume of the cylinder and combustion chamber when the piston is at BDC, divided by the volume when the piston is at TDC. The measure of how much the air-fuel mixture is compressed during the compression stroke.

Compression stroke The piston movement from BDC to TDC immediately following the intake stroke, during which the intake and exhaust valves are closed while the air or air-fuel mixture in the cylinder is compressed.

Compressor The component of an air-conditioning system that compresses refrigerant vapor to increase its pressure and temperature.

Compressor clutch In automotive air conditioners, a magnetic coupling, or solenoid, which engages and disengages to turn the compressor drive shaft as needed. When the clutch is engaged, the compressor is driven and cooling takes place.

Condensation A change of state during which a gas turns to a liquid, usually because of temperature or pressure changes. Also, moisture from the air deposited on a cool surface.

Condenser In the contact-point ignition system, a capacitor connected across the contact points to reduce arcing by providing a storage place for electricity (electrons) as the contact points open. In an air-conditioning system, the radiatorlike heat exchanger in which refrigerant vapor loses heat and returns to the liquid state.

Conductor Any material or substance that allows current or heat to flow easily.

Connecting rod In the engine, the rod that connects the journal on the crankshaft with the piston.

Constant-velocity universal joint Two closely coupled single-Cardan universal joints arranged in such a way that

their acceleration-deceleration effects cancel out. This results in an output-shaft speed that is the same as input-shaft speed, regardless of the angle of drive. See CV joint.

Contact points In the contact-point ignition system, the stationary and the movable points in the distributor which open and close the ignition primary circuit.

Contaminants In an automotive air conditioner, anything other than refrigerant and refrigerant oil in the refrigeration system; includes rust, dirt, moisture, and air.

Control arm A part of the suspension system designed to control wheel movement precisely.

Controller An electronic control module (ECM) or electronic control unit (ECU).

Control system A system in which one or more outputs are forced to change as time progresses. The basic control system has three parts: (1) sensors (inputs) that measure various conditions and send this information to (2) the control unit (system decision maker) which decides how much change, if any, is needed and then signals one or more (3) actuators (outputs) to take the appropriate action.

Coolant The liquid mixture of about 50 percent antifreeze and 50 percent water used to carry heat out of the engine.

Cooling system The system that removes heat from the engine by the forced circulation of air or coolant and thereby prevents engine overheating. In a liquid-cooled engine, the system includes the coolant, water pump, water jackets, radiator, and thermostat.

Coolant-temperature sensor A thermistor that continuously reports engine coolant temperature to the ECM.

Countershaft The shaft in the transmission which is driven by the clutch gear; gears on the countershaft drive gears on the main shaft when the latter are engaged.

Coupling point In a torque converter, the speed at which the oil begins to strike the back faces of the stator vanes; occurs when the turbine and pump speeds reach a ratio of approximately 9:10.

Crankcase The lower part of the engine in which the crankshaft rotates, including the lower section of the cylinder block and the oil pan.

Crankcase emissions Pollution emitted into the atmosphere from any portion of the engine crankcase ventilating or lubricating system.

Crankcase ventilation The circulation of air through the crankcase of a running engine to remove water, blowby, and other vapors; prevents oil

dilution, contamination, sludge formation, and pressure buildup.

Crankshaft A one-piece steel casting or forging that serves as the main rotating member, or shaft, of the engine. The crankshaft has offset journals to which the connecting rods are attached; it converts their up-and-down (reciprocating) motion into circular (rotary) motion.

Crankshaft gear A gear, or sprocket, mounted on the front of the crankshaft, used to drive the camshaft gear, chain, or belt.

Crankshaft sensor A magnetic sensor or Hall-effect switch that, as the crankshaft rotates, provides the ECM with voltage pulses that indicate crankshaft speed and piston position. Also called crankshaft-position sensor.

Cross-fire injection Type of electronic fuel-injection system using two throttle-body-injection assemblies to supply air-fuel mixture through passages that cross over to feed cylinders on the opposite side of the engine.

Curb idle The normal hot-idle speed of an engine.

Current A flow of electrons, measured in amperes.

CV joint Constant-velocity universal joint, in which the speed of the input and output shafts remain the same, regardless of the angle between the shafts. Various types include the Rzeppa, double-offset, and tripod.

Cycle A series of events that repeat themselves. In the automotive engine, the four piston strokes that together produce power.

Cycling-clutch orifice-tube (CCOT) system An air-conditioning system in which a small restriction, or orifice tube, in the refrigerant line acts as the flow-control valve and the compressor clutch is automatically engaged and disengaged (cycling clutch) to prevent evaporator icing.

Cylinder block The basic framework of the engine, in and on which the other engine parts are attached. It includes the engine cylinders and the upper part of the crankcase.

Cylinder head The part of the engine that covers and encloses the cylinders. It contains cooling fins or water jackets and the valves.

Cylinder liner See Cylinder sleeve.

Cylinder sleeve A replaceable sleeve, or liner, set into the cylinder block to form the cylinder bore.

Dashpot A device that controls the rate at which the throttle valve closes.

Defroster The part of the passenger-compartment heater designed to melt frost or ice on the inside or outside of the windshield; includes the required ducts and vents.

Desiccant A drying agent. In a refrigeration system, desiccant is placed in the receiver or accumulator to remove any moisture circulating in the refrigerant.

Detent A small depression in a shaft, rail, or rod into which a pawl or ball drops when the shaft, rail, or rod is moved. This provides a locking effect.

Detonation Commonly referred to as spark knock or ping. In the combustion chamber of a spark-ignition engine, an uncontrolled second explosion (after the spark occurs at the spark plug), with spontaneous combustion of the remaining compressed air-fuel mixture, resulting in a pinging sound.

Diagnosis Answers the question "What is wrong?" or "What caused or is causing the problem?" Also called trouble-diagnosis and troubleshooting.

Diagonal-brake system A dual-brake system with separate hydraulic circuits connecting diagonal wheels together (RF to LR and LF to RR).

Diaphragm A thin dividing sheet or partition which separates an area into compartments; used in mechanical fuel pumps, vacuum pumps, modulator valves, vacuum-advance units, and other devices.

Diesel cycle An engine operating cycle in which air is compressed and then fuel oil is injected into the hot compressed air at the end of the compression stroke. The heat, produced by compression, ignites the fuel oil, eliminating the need for an electric ignition system.

Diesel engine An engine operating on the diesel cycle and burning diesel fuel oil instead of gasoline.

Diesel fuel A light oil sprayed into the cylinders of a diesel engine near the end of the compression stroke.

Dieseling A condition in which a spark-ignition engine continues to run after the ignition is off; caused by carbon deposits or hot spots in the combustion chamber glowing sufficiently to furnish heat for combustion.

Differential A gear assembly between axles that permits one axle to turn at a different speed than the other, while transmitting power to the wheels.

Digital Of or pertaining to information or data processing or transmission in the form of digits; the digital signal has only two states, either ON or OFF (or HIGH or LOW).

Digital meter A meter, usually of high impedance, that provides a numerical display instead of using a pointer or needle.

Dimmer switch A two-position switch operated by the driver to select the high or low headlight beam.

Diode A solid-state electronic device that allows the passage of an electric current in one direction only. Used in the alternator as a rectifier to convert alternating current to direct current for charging the battery.

Direct current (DC or dc) Electric current that flows in one direction only.

Direct drive Condition in a gear set when both the input shaft and the output shaft turn at the same speed, with a ratio of 1:1.

Discard thickness The minimum thickness to which the brake disc can be refinished.

Discharging the system To bleed some or all refrigerant from an air conditioner by opening a valve and allowing the refrigerant to escape into a refrigerant-recovery station.

Disc brake A brake in which brake shoes, in a viselike caliper, grip a revolving disc to stop it.

Displacement In an engine, the total volume of air or air-fuel mixture an engine is theoretically capable of drawing into all cylinders during one operating cycle. Also, the volume swept out by the piston in moving from one end of the cylinder to the other.

Distributor Any device that distributes. In the ignition system, the rotary switch that directs high-voltage surges to the engine cylinders in the proper sequence. See Ignition distributor.

Distributorless ignition system An electronic ignition system without a separate ignition distributor. Sensors signal the position of the crankshaft to the ECM, which then electronically times and triggers the system and controls distribution of the secondary voltages.

Diverter valve In the air-injection system, a valve that diverts air-pump output into the air cleaner or the atmosphere during deceleration; this prevents backfiring and popping in the exhaust system.

Driveability The general operation of a vehicle, usually rated from good to poor; based on characteristics of concern to the average driver, such as smoothness of idle, even acceleration, ease of starting, quick warm-up, and not overheating.

Drive chain A chain that transmits power between shafts.

Drive line An assembly of one or more driveshafts, universal joints, and slip joints that forms the driving connection between the transmission and the drive axle.

Drive pinion A rotating shaft with a small gear on one end that transmits torque to another gear; used in the final-drive gearset in the drive axle. Also called the clutch shaft, in the manual transmission.

Drive shaft An assembly of one or two universal joints connected to a shaft or tube; used to transmit power from the transmission to the drive axle. Also called the propeller shaft.

Drive wheels The wheels that move the vehicle.

Drum brake A brake in which curved brake shoes press against the inner circumference of a metal drum to produce the braking action.

Dual-bed catalytic converter A catalytic converter which combines two bead-type converters (with different catalysts) in a single housing to control HC, CO, and NOx.

Duration The length of time during which something exists or lasts. In the valve train, the length of time the valve is open, measured in degrees of crankshaft rotation.

Dwell In a contact-point distributor, the number of degrees of distributor-cam rotation that the points stay closed before they open again. The length of time the points are closed and current flows through the primary winding of the coil.

Dynamic balance The balance of an object when it is in motion, such as the dynamic balance of a rotating wheel.

Eccentric A disc or offset section (of a shaft, for example) used to convert rotary motion to reciprocating motion. Sometimes called a cam.

Efficiency The ratio between the power of an effect and the power expended to produce the effect; the ratio between an actual result and the theoretically possible result. Comparing the effort exerted with the results obtained.

Electric current A flow of electrons through a conductor such as a copper wire; measured in amperes.

Electric ignition system Supplies the sparks that ignite the compressed air-fuel mixture in the engine cylinders.

Electric system In the automotive vehicle, the system that provides electricity for cranking the engine, firing the spark plugs, charging the battery, and powering the lights and other electric and electronic equipment. Consists, in part, of the battery, starting motor, alternator, regulator, ignition, and the connecting wiring, circuit protection, switches, and other control devices.

Electricity Electric charges and their effects when at rest and in motion; powers most devices on the vehicle.

Element Atoms of one kind grouped together.

Electrode Either terminal of an electric source, through which current enters or leaves. In a spark plug, the spark jumps between two electrodes. The wire passing through the insulator is the center electrode. The small piece of metal welded to the spark-plug shell (and to which the spark jumps) is the side, or ground, electrode.

Electrolyte The liquid mixture of about 40 percent sulfuric acid and 60 percent water, in a fully-charged lead-acid storage battery. The acid enters into chemical reaction with active material in the plates to produce voltage and current.

Electromagnet A coil of wire (usually around an iron core) which produces magnetism as electric current passes through it.

Electromagnetic induction The characteristic of a magnetic field that causes an electric current to be created in a conductor as it passes through the field, or if the field builds and collapses around the conductor.

Electron A negatively charged particle that circles the nucleus of an atom. The flow of electrons is an electric current.

Electronic Of or pertaining to electrons or electronics.

Electronic control module (ECM) The system computer that receives information from sensors and is programmed to operate various systems, circuits, and actuators based on that information. See also Powertrain control module.

Electronic engine control system An engine control or management system that uses various sensors and switches to send or input information (in the form of electrical signals) to the electronic control module. It then computes an output signal that is sent to various actuators, which control the ignition, fuel-injection, and emission-control systems.

Electronic fuel-injection system A system that injects fuel into the engine, and includes an electronic control module to time and meter the fuel flow.

Electronic ignition system An ignition system that uses transistors and other semiconductor devices as an electronic switch to turn the primary current on and off.

Electronic ride control Automatically changes the firmness of the shock absorbers to suit road conditions.

Electronic spark timing (EST) Using the electronic control module to monitor engine load, speed, and coolant temperature, and then electronically provide the proper spark advance for best control of exhaust emissions and fuel economy.

Electronics Electrical assemblies, circuits, and systems that use electronic devices such as transistors and diodes.

Element Any substance made of only one kind of atom.

Emission control Any device or modification added onto or designed into a motor vehicle for the purpose of reducing air-polluting emissions.

End play The distance that a shaft can move forward or backward in its housing or case, as a result of clearance between components.

Energy The capacity or ability to do

work. The most common forms are heat, mechanical, electrical, and chemical. Usually measured in work units of pound-feet [kilogram-meters], but also expressed in heat-energy units of Btus [joules].

Engine A machine that converts heat energy into mechanical energy. A device that burns fuel to produce mechanical power; sometimes referred to as a power plant. Produces power to move the vehicle.

Engine control system Any system (controlled by the driver, automatically, or electronically) that varies engine inputs to obtain the desired engine output.

Engine cradle Stub frame, or subframe, that fastens under the bottom front of the body and to which the engine or engine-transaxle assembly is attached.

Engine efficiency The ratio of the power actually delivered to the power that could be delivered if the engine operated without any power loss.

Engine mounts Flexible rubber or hydraulic insulators through which the engine is bolted to the vehicle body or frame.

Engine power The power available from the crankshaft to do work.

Evacuating the system Using a vacuum pump to pump any air and moisture out of an air-conditioner refrigerant system after discharging the system, or after a large refrigerant loss has occurred.

Evaporation The changing of a liquid into a gas or vapor.

Evaporative control system A system that prevents the escape of fuel vapors from the fuel tank or air cleaner while the engine is off. The vapors are stored in a charcoal canister or in the engine crankcase until the engine is started.

Evaporator The heat exchanger in an air conditioner in which refrigerant changes from a liquid to a gas (evaporates), taking heat from the surrounding air as it does so.

Exhaust emissions Pollutants emitted into the atmosphere through any opening downstream of the exhaust ports of an engine.

Exhaust-gas analyzer A device for measuring the amounts of air pollutants in the exhaust gas of a motor vehicle. Some analyzers used in automotive shops measure HC and CO; others also measure O_2 and CO_2. Exhaust-gas analyzers used in testing laboratories can measure NOx.

Exhaust-gas recirculation (EGR) system An NOx control system that recycles a small part of the inert exhaust gas back through the intake manifold to lower the combustion temperature.

Exhaust manifold A device with

several passages through which exhaust gases leave the engine combustion chambers and enter the exhaust piping system.

Exhaust pipe The pipe connecting the exhaust manifold to the next component in the exhaust system.

Exhaust stroke The piston stroke (from BDC to TDC) immediately following the power stroke, during which the exhaust valve opens so the exhaust gases can escape from the cylinder to the exhaust manifold.

Exhaust system The system that collects the exhaust gases and discharges them into the air. Consists of the exhaust manifold, exhaust pipe, catalytic converter, muffler, tail pipe, and resonator (if used).

Expansion plug A slightly dished plug used to seal core passages in the cylinder block and cylinder head. When driven into place, it is flattened and expanded to fit tightly.

Expansion tank A tank connected by a hose to the filler neck of an engine radiator; the tank provides room for heated coolant to expand and to give off any air that may be trapped in the coolant. Also, a similar device used in some fuel tanks to prevent fuel from spilling out of the tank through expansion.

Expansion valve In an air conditioner, a flow-control valve located between the condenser and evaporator; controls the amount of refrigerant sprayed into the evaporator.

Fan A bladed device in front or behind the radiator to push or pull cooling air through the radiator or around the engine cylinders; may be engine-driven or powered by an electric motor. An air blower such as the fan in the heater and air conditioner.

Fan belt A belt (or belts), driven by the crankshaft, whose primary purpose is to drive the engine fan and water pump.

Feedback carburetor A carburetor with a mixture-control solenoid or vacuum-controlled metering valve; used with an oxygen sensor and an electronic control system to automatically adjust the air-fuel ratio for minimum exhaust emissions.

Field coil A coil, or winding, in a generator or starting motor which produces a magnetic field as current passes through it.

Filter A device through which air, gases, or liquids are passed to remove impurities.

Final drive The final speed-reduction gearing in the power train.

Firing order The order in which the engine cylinders fire, or deliver their power strokes, beginning with number 1 cylinder.

Fixed-caliper disc brake Disc brake using a caliper which is fixed in position and cannot move; the caliper usually has four pistons, two on each side of the disc.

Flasher An automatic-reset circuit breaker used in the directional-signal and hazard-warning circuits.

Fleet Usually five or more vehicles operated by a single owner.

Flex plate On a vehicle with automatic transmission, a light drive plate bolted to the crankshaft, to which the torque converter attaches.

Floating-caliper disc brake Disc brake using a caliper mounted through bushings which permit the caliper to move, or float, when the brakes are applied; there is one large piston in the caliper.

Fluid Any liquid or gas. A substance that can flow.

Flywheel On a vehicle with manual transmission, a heavy metal wheel attached to the engine crankshaft which rotates with it; helps smooth out the power surges from the power strokes and also serves as part of the clutch and cranking system.

Flywheel ring gear A gear, fitted around the flywheel, that is engaged by teeth on the starting-motor drive to crank the engine.

Force Any push or pull exerted on an object; measured in pounds and ounces, or in newtons (N) in the metric system.

Four-stroke cycle The four piston strokes — intake, compression, power, and exhaust — that make up the complete cycle of events in the four-stroke-cycle engine. Also called four-cycle and four-stroke.

Four-wheel drive A vehicle with drive axles at both front and rear, so that all four wheels can be driven; the drive train usually includes a two-speed auxiliary transmission, or transfer case.

Frame In a vehicle with body-and-frame construction, the assembly of metal structural parts and channel sections that supports the engine and body and is supported by the wheels.

Frame angle The angle of a truck frame with the horizontal, which affects caster; can be measured with a bubble protractor at a midpoint between the back of the cab and the centerline of the rear wheel.

Free travel In the hydraulic brake system, the distance the brake pedal moves before the primary seals on the master-cylinder pistons close the vent ports.

Friction The resistance to motion between two bodies in contact with each other.

Friction disc In the clutch, a flat disc, faced on both sides with friction material and splined to the clutch shaft,

positioned between the clutch pressure plate and the engine flywheel. Also called the clutch disc or driven disc.

Friction horsepower The power that an engine uses to overcome the friction of its own internal moving parts.

Front-end geometry The angular relationship between the front wheels, wheel-attaching parts, and vehicle body or frame. Includes camber, caster, steering-axis inclination, toe, and turning radius.

Front-wheel drive A vehicle having its drive wheels located on the front axle.

Fuel Any combustible substance. In a spark-ignition engine, the gasoline or similar fuel is burned and the heat of combustion expands the resulting gases, which force the piston downward to rotate the crankshaft.

Fuel filter A device located in the fuel line that removes dirt and other contaminants from fuel passing through.

Fuel-injection system A system which delivers fuel under pressure into the combustion chamber or into the intake manifold.

Fuel line The pipes or tubes through which fuel flows from the fuel tank to the carburetor or fuel-injection system.

Fuel pump The electrical or mechanical device in the fuel system which forces fuel from the fuel tank to the carburetor or fuel-injection system.

Fuel system In an automobile, the system that delivers the fuel and air to the engine cylinders. Consists of the fuel tank and lines, gauge, fuel pump, carburetor or fuel-injection system, and intake manifold.

Fuse A device that opens an electric circuit when excessive current flows, to protect equipment in the circuit.

Fuse block A boxlike unit or panel that holds the fuses for the various electric circuits in a vehicle.

Fusible link A short length of insulated wire connected in series in a circuit, which melts to open the circuit when excessive current flows.

Gap The air space between two electrodes, as the spark-plug gap or the contact-point gap.

Gas A state of matter in which the matter has neither a definite shape nor a definite volume; air is a mixture of several gases. In an automotive vehicle, the discharge from the tail pipe is called the exhaust gas. Also, gas is a slang expression for the liquid fuel gasoline.

Gasket A thin layer of soft material, such as paper, cork, rubber, copper, synthetic material, or a combination of these, placed between two parts to make a tight seal.

Gasohol An engine fuel made by mixing 10 percent ethyl alcohol with 90

percent unleaded gasoline.

Gasoline A liquid blend of hydrocarbons, obtained from crude oil; used as the fuel in most automobile engines.

Gear lubricant A type of grease or oil designed especially to lubricate gears.

Gear ratio The number of revolutions of a driving gear required to turn a driven gear through one complete revolution. For a pair of gears, the ratio is found by dividing the number of teeth on the driven gear by the number of teeth on the driving gear.

Gears Wheels with meshing teeth that transmit power or turning force between shafts.

Gearshift A linkage-type mechanism by which the gears in an automotive transmission are engaged and disengaged.

Generator A device that converts mechanical energy into electric energy; can produce either ac or dc electricity. An ac generator is often called an alternator.

Glow plug A small electric heater installed in the precombustion chamber of diesel engines to preheat the chamber for easier starting in cold weather.

Governor A device that controls, or governs, another device, usually on the basis of speed or load.

Grease Lubricating oil to which thickening agents have been added.

Ground The return path for current in an electric circuit.

Halfshafts Shafts that connect the transaxle or differential to the drive wheels.

Hall-effect switch Switches a supplied voltage on and off with the presence or absence of a magnetic field.

Halogen headlamp A headlamp with a small inner bulb filled with halogen which surrounds the tungsten filament.

Hazardous waste Any material that could pose danger to human health and the environment after it is discarded.

Headlamp switch Controls the operation of the headlamps and other exterior and interior lights.

Heat of compression Increase of temperature brought about by the compression of air or air-fuel mixture; the source of ignition in a diesel engine.

Heat-control valve In the engine, a thermostatically-operated valve in the exhaust manifold; diverts heat to the intake manifold to warm it before the engine reaches normal operating temperature.

Heater core A small radiatorlike heat exchanger usually mounted on the passenger side of the instrument panel or firewall, through which hot coolant circulates; when heat is needed, air is circulated through the hot heater core.

Heat sink A device for absorbing heat from one medium and transferring it to another. The diodes in alternators are usually mounted in heat sinks which remove heat from the diodes, thereby preventing their overheating and failure.

High-energy ignition (HEI) system An electronic ignition system capable of producing secondary voltages of 35,000 volts or more; may have the ignition coil mounted in the distributor cap.

Horn relay A relay connected between the battery and the horns. Pressing the horn button energizes the relay, which has contact points that then close to connect the horns to the battery.

Horsepower A measure of mechanical power, or the rate at which work is done. One horsepower equals 33,000 ft-lb (foot-pounds) of work per minute, the power necessary to raise 33,000 pounds a distance of one foot in one minute. Roughly the power of one horse.

Hub The center part of a fan, gear, or wheel which is used for attachment to another member.

Hydraulic Of or pertaining to a fluid or liquid.

Hydraulic brake booster A brake booster that uses hydraulic pressure supplied by the power-steering pump, or a separate electrically-driven pump, to assist in applying the brakes.

Hydraulic brakes A braking system that uses hydraulic pressure to force the brake shoes against the brake drums or rotors as the brake pedal is depressed.

Hydraulics The use of a liquid under pressure to transfer force or motion, or to increase an applied force.

Hydraulic pressure Pressure on a liquid.

Hydraulic valve lifter A valve lifter that uses oil pressure from the engine lubricating system to keep the lifter in constant contact with the cam lobe and with the valve stem, pushrod, or rocker arm.

Hydrocarbon (HC) A compound containing only carbon and hydrogen atoms, usually derived from fossil fuels such as petroleum, natural gas, and coal; an agent in the formation of photochemical smog. Gasoline is a blend of liquid hydrocarbons refined from crude oil.

Hydrogen (H) A colorless, odorless, highly flammable gas whose combustion produces water; the simplest and lightest element.

Idler arm In parallelogram steering linkage, a link that supports the tie rod and transmits steering motion to both wheels through the tie-rod ends.

Idle solenoid An electrically-operated plunger used to provide a predetermined throttle setting at idle.

Idle speed The speed, or rpm, at which the engine runs when the accelerator pedal is fully released and there is no load on the engine.

Ignition The action of the spark in starting the burning of the compressed air-fuel mixture in the combustion chamber of a spark-ignition engine. In a diesel engine, the start of the burning of fuel after its temperature has been raised by the heat of compression.

Ignition coil The ignition-system component that acts as a transformer to step up (increase) the battery voltage to many thousands of volts. The high-voltage surge from the coil is transmitted to the spark plug to ignite the compressed air-fuel mixture.

Ignition distributor In distributor ignition systems, the unit that contains the mechanical or electronic switch that closes and opens the primary circuit at the proper time and then distributes the resulting high-voltage surges to the spark plugs.

Ignition module In an electronic ignition system, the electronic control unit that opens and closes the primary circuit; may be a separate unit or a function of the engine electronic control module (ECM).

Ignition resistor A resistance connected into the ignition primary circuit to reduce battery voltage to the coil during engine operation.

Ignition switch The key-operated main power switch that opens and closes the circuit that supplies current to the ignition and other electrical systems.

Ignition system In the spark-ignition engine, the system that furnishes high-voltage sparks to the cylinders, at the proper time, to fire the compressed air-fuel mixture.

Ignition timing The delivery of the spark from the coil to the spark plug at the proper time for the power stroke, relative to the piston position; usually expressed in crankshaft degrees before or after top dead center (TDC) at the end of the compression stroke.

Included angle In the front-suspension system, camber angle plus steering-axis-inclination (SAI) angle.

Induction The action of producing a voltage in a conductor or coil by moving the conductor or coil through a magnetic field, or by moving the field past the conductor or coil.

Inertia The property of an object that causes it to resist any change in its speed or direction of travel.

Inspection Answers the question "Is something wrong?" or "Is there a problem?"

Instrument panel Contains the indicators, gauges, lights, and displays the driver needs to operate the car.

Instrument voltage regulator A thermostatic device that keeps the voltage to instrument-panel gauges at about 5 volts.

Insulation Material that stops the travel of electricity (electric insulation) or heat (heat insulation).

Intake manifold A set of tubes, or casting with several passages, through which air or air-fuel mixture flows from the throttle valves to the intake ports in the cylinder head.

Intake stroke The piston stroke from TDC to BDC immediately following the exhaust stroke, during which the intake valve opens and the cylinder fills with air-fuel mixture from the intake manifold.

Integral Built into, as part of the whole.

Integrated circuit Many very small solid-state devices capable of performing as a complete electronic circuit, usually manufactured as a chip.

Interaxle differential See Center differential.

Intercooler A heat exchanger that cools the air from supercharger or turbocharger before it enters the engine.

Internal gear A gear with teeth pointing inward, toward the hollow center of the gear.

Journal The part of a rotating shaft which turns in a bearing.

Jumper wire A length of wire used as a temporary connection between two points in a circuit.

Jump starting Starting the engine in a vehicle that has a dead battery by connecting a charged battery to the starting system.

Kickdown In automatic transmissions, a system that produces a downshift when the accelerator is pushed down to the floorboard.

Knock A heavy, metallic engine sound that varies with engine speed, usually caused by a loose or worn bearing; name also used for detonation, pinging, and spark knock. See Detonation.

Knuckle A steering knuckle; a front-suspension part that acts as a hinge to support a front wheel and permit it to be turned to steer the vehicle. The knuckle pivots on ball joints or, in trucks and older cars, on kingpins.

Lash The amount of free motion in a gear train, between gears, or in a mechanical assembly, such as the lash in a valve train.

Lead (pronounced "leed") A cable or conductor that carries electric current.

Lead (pronounced "led") A heavy metal; used in lead-acid storage batteries.

Leak detector In air-conditioning service, a device used to locate an opening where refrigerant may escape. Common types include liquid leak solution (soap bubbles), refrigerant dye, ultraviolet light, electronic, and flame.

Light A gas-filled bulb enclosing a wire that glows brightly when an electric current passes through it; a lamp. Also, any visible radiant energy.

Limited-slip differential A differential with cone or multiple-disc clutches (or a viscous coupling) that lock or engage when one wheel spins so that equal power is delivered to both axle shafts. The clutch or coupling allows limited slippage for normal turns. Also called a nonslip differential.

Linkage A hydraulic system or assembly of rods or links, used to transmit motion.

Locking hubs Hubs that can be automatically or manually disengaged so that the normally non-driving drive axle in a four-wheel-drive vehicle can freewheel while the vehicle is in two-wheel drive.

Locking torque converter A torque converter in which the pump can be mechanically locked to the turbine, eliminating any loss through the fluid.

Lubricating system In the engine, the system that supplies engine parts with lubricating oil to prevent contact between any two moving metal surfaces.

Machine work Jobs such as refinishing brake drums, rotors, and engine flywheels, which require the use of machine tools.

MacPherson-strut suspension A suspension system which combines a coil spring and a shock absorber into a single strut assembly using only a beam-type lower control arm. The angled ends, or arms, of a stabilizer bar attach to the outer ends of the lower control arms, holding the arms in position while helping to control the longitudinal loads.

Magnetic clutch A magnetically-operated clutch used to engage and disengage the air-conditioner compressor, and on other devices.

Magnetic field The space around a magnet which is filled by invisible lines of force.

Magnetic lines of force The imaginary lines by which a magnetic field may be visualized.

Magnetic switch A switch with a winding which, when energized by connection to a battery or alternator, causes the switch to open or close a circuit.

Magnetism The ability, either natural or produced by a flow of electric current, to attract iron.

Main bearings In the engine, the bearings that support the crankshaft.

Malfunction An improper or incorrect operation.

Manifold A device with several inlet or outlet passageways through which a gas or liquid is gathered or distributed. See Exhaust manifold, Intake manifold, and Manifold gauge set.

Manifold-absolute pressure (MAP) sensor The sensor that measures the pressure (vacuum) in the intake manifold, and sends this information as a varying voltage signal to the electronic control module (ECM).

Manifold gauge set A high-pressure and a low-pressure gauge mounted as a set on a manifold; used for checking pressures in the air-conditioning refrigerant system.

Manifold pressure The pressure in the intake manifold while the supercharger or turbocharger is providing boost.

Manifold vacuum The vacuum in the intake manifold that develops as a result of the vacuum in the cylinders on their intake strokes.

Manual valve A spool valve in the valve body of an automatic transmission that is manually positioned by the driver through linkage.

Mass air flow The amount of air, by weight, flowing into the engine intake manifold.

Master cylinder The liquid-filled cylinder in the hydraulic braking system or clutch where hydraulic pressure is developed when the driver depresses a foot pedal.

Meshing The mating, or engaging, of the teeth of two gears.

Metering rod and jet In a carburetor, a small movable cone- or step-shaped rod and a jet, used to increase or decrease fuel flow according to engine throttle opening, engine load, or a combination of both.

Metering valve A valve in the disc-brake system that prevents hydraulic pressure to the front brakes until after the rear brakes apply.

Methanol Wood or methyl alcohol.

Microprocessor A small solid-state electronic device that acts as the central processing unit. Switches and sensors provide input information which the microprocessor uses to determine the desired response (if any) and then sends an output signal to an actuator.

Modulator valve On some automatic transmissions, a valve operated by engine intake-manifold vacuum that changes, or modulates, line pressure according to engine load. Also called vacuum modulator.

Molecule The smallest particle into which a substance can be divided and still retain the properties of that substance.

Monitor To keep track of.

Motor A device that converts electrical energy into mechanical energy; for example, the starting motor.

Motor vehicle Any self-propelled vehicle that does not run on rails.

Muffler In the engine exhaust system, a device through which the exhaust gases must pass to reduce noise. In an air-conditioning system, a device to minimize pumping sounds from the compressor.

Multiple-disc clutch A clutch with more than one friction disc; usually there are several driving discs and several driven discs, alternately placed.

Multiple-viscosity oil An engine oil that has a lower viscosity when cold (for easier cranking) and a higher viscosity when hot (to provide adequate engine lubrication) than a single-viscosity oil.

Multipoint injection See Port injection.

Mutual induction The condition in which a voltage is induced in one coil by a changing magnetic field caused by a changing current in another coil. The magnitude of the induced voltage depends on the number of turns in the two coils.

Negative One of the two poles of a magnet, or one of the two terminals of an electrical device. A terminal or electrode that has an excess of electrons, and from which electrons will flow toward a more positive point in a circuit.

Negative terminal The terminal from which electrons flow in a complete electric circuit. On a battery, the negative terminal can be identified as the battery post with the smaller diameter. The minus sign (-) is often used to identify the negative terminal.

Neutral In a transmission, the setting in which all gears are disengaged and the output shaft is disconnected from the input shaft.

Neutral-start switch A switch wired into the ignition switch to prevent engine cranking unless the transmission shift lever is in NEUTRAL.

Nitrogen oxides (NOx) Any chemical compound of nitrogen and oxygen; a basic air pollutant. Automotive exhaust emission levels of nitrogen oxides are limited by law.

Noise Any unpleasant sound such as booming, buzzing, clunking, humming, tapping, or whistling.

North pole The pole from which the lines of force leave a magnet.

Nozzle The opening, or jet, through which fuel or air passes as it is discharged.

Octane rating A measure of the anti-knock properties of a gasoline. The higher the octane rating, the more resistant the gasoline is to spark knock or detonation.

Odometer Records the total distance the vehicle has traveled.

Ohm The unit of electric resistance; it requires 1 volt to force 1 ampere of current through 1 ohm of resistance.

Oil A liquid lubricant usually made from crude oil and used for lubrication between moving parts. In a diesel engine, oil is used for fuel.

Oil clearance The space between the bearing and the shaft rotating within it.

Oil cooler A small radiatorlike heat exchanger that lowers the temperature of oil flowing through it.

Oil filter A filter which removes impurities from the oil passing through it.

Oil-level indicator A dipstick, or an electronic oil-level sensor in the oil pan that turns on a CHECK OIL LEVEL light in the instrument panel if the oil level is low. See Dipstick.

Oil pan The detachable lower part of the engine which encloses the crankcase and acts as an oil reservoir.

Oil-pressure indicator An indicator in the instrument panel that warns the driver if the engine oil pressure is too low. May be an indicator light, an electric analog gauge, an electronic bar-graph or similar display, or a digital number display of the pressure.

Oil pump In the engine lubricating system, the device that forces oil from the oil pan to the moving engine parts.

Open circuit In an electric circuit, a break or opening which prevents the passage of current.

Optical Pertaining to or using light.

Orifice A small opening, or hole, into a cavity.

Orifice tube A restriction that acts as a flow-control valve in the refrigerant line of an air conditioner.

O ring A type of sealing ring, made of a special rubberlike material. When the connection is tightened, the O ring is compressed into a groove to provide the sealing action.

Oscilloscope A high-speed voltmeter that visually displays voltage variations on a television-type picture tube, or cathode-ray tube (CRT).

Output shaft The main shaft of the transmission; the shaft that delivers torque from the transmission to the drive shaft.

Overdrive Transmission gearing that causes the output shaft to overdrive, or turn faster than, the input shaft.

Overhead-camshaft (OHC) engine An engine in which the camshaft is mounted in the cylinder head, instead of in the cylinder block.

Overhead-valve (OHV) engine An engine in which the valves are mounted in the cylinder head above the combustion chamber, instead of in the cylinder block. In this type of engine, the camshaft is in the cylinder block, and the valves are actuated by pushrods.

Overrunning clutch A roller or sprag clutch that transmits torque in only one direction and turns freely in the other; used as the drive mechanism for starting motors and in automatic transmissions.

Overshoot In a heating-and-air-conditioning system with automatic temperature control, the tendency of the system to overshoot the temperature setting and provide excessive heat when set for heating or excessive cooling when set for cooling.

Parallel circuit The electric circuit formed when two or more electric devices have their terminals connected together, positive to positive and negative to negative, so that each may operate independently of the other from the same power source.

Parking brake Mechanically operated brake that is independent of the foot-operated service brakes on the vehicle; set when the vehicle is parked.

Particle A very small piece of metal, dirt, or other impurity which may be contained in the air, fuel, or lubricating oil used in an engine.

Passage A small hole or gallery in an assembly or casting, through which a fluid flows (such as air, coolant, fuel, or oil).

Passive restraint Provides protection without requiring any action by the driver or passenger.

Pawl An arm pivoted so that its free end can fit into a detent, slot, or groove at certain times to hold a part stationary.

PCV valve The valve that controls the flow of crankcase vapors in accordance with ventilation requirements for different engine speeds and loads.

Pedal reserve The distance from the brake pedal to the floor after the brakes are applied.

Photodiode A diode that uses the presence or absence of light to switch an applied voltage on and off.

Photovoltaic cell A semiconductor device that generates a small dc voltage when exposed to light. Also called a solar cell.

Pickup coil In an electronic ignition system, the coil in which voltage is induced by the moving teeth on the reluctor or armature.

Pilot bearing A small bearing, in the center of the output end of the engine crankshaft, which carries the forward end of the clutch shaft.

Ping Engine spark knock or detonation that occurs usually during acceleration. Caused by excessive advance of ignition timing or low-octane fuel.

Pinion gear The smaller of two meshing gears.

Piston A movable part, fitted into a cylinder, which can receive or transmit motion as a result of pressure changes in a fluid. In the engine, the round plug that slides up and down in the cylinder and which, through the connecting rod, forces the crankshaft to rotate.

Piston clearance The distance between the piston skirt and the cylinder wall.

Piston displacement The volume displaced by the piston during one complete stroke, as it moves from BDC to TDC.

Piston engine An internal-combustion engine using reciprocating pistons.

Piston pin The cylindrical or tubular metal piece that attaches the piston to the connecting rod. Also called wrist pin.

Piston rings Rings fitted into grooves in the piston. There are two types: compression rings for sealing the compression pressure in the combustion chamber, and oil rings to scrape excessive oil off the cylinder wall.

Pitman arm On a recirculating-ball steering gear, the arm that connects the steering-gear output shaft to the steering linkage. As the shaft turns, the pitman arm swings back and forth, transferring output-shaft movement into movement of the steering linkage.

Pivot A pin or shaft upon which another part rests or turns.

Planetary-gear system A gear set consisting of a central sun gear surrounded by two or more planet pinions which are, in turn, meshed with a ring (or internal) gear; used in automatic transmissions and transfer cases.

Planet carrier In a planetary-gear system, the carrier or bracket that contains the shafts upon which the planet pinions turn.

Planet pinions In a planetary-gear system, the gears that mesh with, and revolve about, the sun gear; they also mesh with the ring (or internal) gear.

Plastigage A plastic material available in strips of various diameters; used to measure the clearance in crankshaft main bearings and connecting-rod bearings, and in some camshaft bearings.

Plate In a battery, a flat rectangular sheet of spongy lead. Sulfuric acid in the electrolyte chemically reacts with the lead to produce an electric current.

Plies The layers of cord in a tire casing; each of these layers is a ply.

Pneumatic Of or pertaining to air.

Polarity The quality of an electric component or circuit that determines the direction of current flow.

Port In the engine, the passage to the cylinder opened and closed by a valve, and through which gases flow to enter and leave the cylinder.

Port injection A gasoline fuel-injection system with a fuel injector in each intake port which opens to spray fuel into the intake air as it approaches the intake valve. Also called multipoint injection.

Ported vacuum switch (PVS) See

Thermal vacuum switch.

Positive crankcase ventilation (PCV) A crankcase ventilation system that uses intake-manifold vacuum to return crankcase vapors and blowby gases to the intake manifold to be burned, thereby preventing their escape into the atmosphere.

Positive terminal The terminal to which electrons flow in a complete electric circuit. On a top-terminal battery, the positive terminal can be identified as the battery post with the larger diameter; the plus sign (+) is often used to identify the positive terminal.

Post The point at which the cable is connected to the battery.

Potentiometer A three-terminal variable resistor in which the third connection, or wiper, changes the resistance by physically moving up and down the resistor.

Power The rate at which work is done. A common power unit is the horsepower, which is equal to 33,000 ft-lb/min (foot-pounds per minute).

Power brakes A service brake system that uses either a vacuum and atmospheric pressure, or hydraulic pressure, to provide most of the force required for braking.

Powerplant The engine or power source that produces the power to move the vehicle.

Power steering A steering system that uses hydraulic pressure from a pump, or from an electric motor, to multiply the driver's steering force.

Power stroke The piston stroke from TDC to BDC, immediately following the compression stroke, during which the valves are closed and the fuel burns. The expanding compressed gas forces the piston down the cylinder, transmitting power to rotate the crankshaft.

Power train The mechanisms that carry power from the engine crankshaft to the drive wheels; includes the clutch, transmission, drive shaft, differential, and axles.

Powertrain control module (PCM) An electronic module or computer that receives input from various engine and powertrain sensors, and responds by sending output signals to various engine and powertrain controls.

Precombustion chamber In some engines, a separate small combustion chamber where combustion begins.

Preignition Ignition of the air-fuel mixture in the combustion chamber by some unwanted means, before the ignition spark occurs at the spark plug.

Preload In bearings, the amount of load placed on a bearing before actual operating loads are imposed.

Pressure cap A radiator cap with valves which causes the cooling system to operate under pressure at a higher and more efficient temperature.

Pressure-differential valve The valve in a dual-brake system that turns on a warning light if the pressure drops in one part of the hydraulic system.

Pressure plate A spring-loaded metal plate, mounted on and rotating with the flywheel, that holds the friction disc against the flywheel. This keeps the engine and manual transmission coupled.

Pressure regulator A device that operates to prevent excessive pressure from developing. In hydraulic systems, a valve that opens to release oil from a line when the oil pressure reaches a specified maximum.

Pressure-relief valve A valve that opens to relieve excessive pressure.

Pressurize To apply more than atmospheric pressure to a gas or liquid.

Prevailing-torque fasteners Nuts and bolts designed to have a continuous resistance to turning.

Preventive maintenance Work done on a preset schedule.

Primary circuit The low-voltage circuit of the ignition system.

Primary winding The outer winding of relatively heavy wire in an ignition coil.

Printed circuit An electric circuit made by applying a conductive material to an insulating board in a pattern that provides electric circuits between components mounted on or connected to the board.

Propane enrichment Procedure for setting the idle mixture on some vehicles with catalytic converters.

Proportioning valve A valve that reduces pressure to the rear wheels during hard braking.

Pull The tendency of the vehicle to drift or pull to one side during normal driving on a level surface, or when the brakes are applied.

Purge To remove, evacuate, or empty trapped substances from a space.

Purge valve In evaporative-control systems, a valve used on some charcoal canisters to limit the flow of vapor and air to the carburetor during idling.

Quad carburetor A four-barrel carburetor.

Quad driver A semiconductor chip that can operate four separate outputs independently.

Quadrant gear A toothed gear shaped like a quarter circle.

Races The metal rings on which ball or roller bearings rotate.

Rack-and-pinion steering gear A steering gear in which a pinion on the end of the steering shaft meshes with a rack of gear teeth on the major cross-member of the steering linkage.

Rack yoke In a rack-and-pinion steering gear, the yoke-shaped bushing that supports the left, or control-valve, end of the rack. A spring behind the yoke pushes the rack into the pinion to maintain the proper preload, or rack-yoke clearance.

Radial tire A tire in which the plies are placed radially, or perpendicular to the rim, with a circumferential belt on top of them.

Radiator In the engine cooling system, the heat exchanger that removes heat from coolant passing through it; receives hot coolant from the engine and returns the coolant to the engine at a lower temperature.

Ratio Proportion; the relative amounts of two or more substances in a mixture. Usually expressed as a numerical relationship, as in 2:1.

Readout The visual delivery or display of information from an electronic device, circuit, or system.

Rear-end torque The reaction torque that acts on the rear-axle housing when torque is applied to the wheels; tends to turn the axle housing in a direction opposite to wheel rotation.

Receiver In an automotive air-conditioner, a container for holding liquid refrigerant from the condenser.

Recirculating-ball steering gear A steering gear that uses a series of recirculating balls on a worm gear to transfer steering wheel movement to a ball nut. The ball nut meshes with a sector gear and shaft, which moves the attached pitman arm and parallelogram steering linkage.

Rectifier A device that changes alternating current to direct current; in the alternator, a diode.

Refrigerant A substance used to transfer heat in an air conditioner, through a cycle of evaporation and condensation.

Refrigeration Cooling of an object or a substance by removal of heat through mechanical means.

Regulator In the charging system, a device that controls alternator output to prevent excessive voltage.

Reinstall To put back the same part removed.

Relay An electrical device that opens or closes a circuit in response to a voltage signal.

Release bearing In the clutch, the bearing that pushes or pulls the pressure-plate release levers or fingers in or out to disengage the engine from the transmission when the driver depresses the clutch pedal. Also called throwout bearing.

Relief valve A valve that opens when a preset pressure is reached, to relieve or prevent excessive pressure.

Reluctor In an electronic ignition system, a metal armature or rotor (with a series of tips) in the distributor that creates a voltage signal in the pickup coil as each tip passes.

Repair Includes the steps necessary to fix the problem or both the problem and its cause.

Replace To discard the part removed and install a new or different part.

Reserve capacity A battery rating; the number of minutes a battery can deliver a 25-ampere current until the cell voltages drop to 1.75 volts per cell.

Resistance The opposition to a flow of current through a circuit or electrical device; measured in ohms.

Retard To delay the occurrence of the spark in the combustion chamber; the opposite of spark advance.

Returnability The tendency of the front wheels to return freely to the straight-ahead position when the driver releases the steering wheel after a turn.

Return spring A pull-back spring.

Rheostat A variable resistor.

Ring gear In the final drive, a large gear carried by the differential case that meshes with and is driven by the drive pinion, or pinion gear.

Ring ridge The ridge formed at the top of a cylinder as the cylinder wall below is worn away by piston-ring friction.

Rocker arm A pivoted lever that transfers cam or pushrod motion to the valve stem.

Roller tappet A valve lifter with a hardened steel roller on the end riding against the camshaft.

Rotary engine An engine, such as a gas turbine or a Wankel, in which the power is delivered to a spinning rotor.

Rotor A rotating part of a machine, such as an alternator rotor, disc-brake rotor, or Wankel-engine rotor.

Run-on See Dieseling.

Runout Out of round, or wobble.

Schrader valve A spring-loaded valve through which a connection can be made to a tire, tube, or air-conditioner refrigerant system.

Scrub radius The distance between the steering axis and the tire contact-area centerline at their intersections with the road surface. Also called steering offset.

Seal A material, shaped around a shaft, used to close off the operating compartment of the shaft, preventing oil leakage.

Secondary air Air that is pumped to the cylinder-head exhaust ports, exhaust manifold, or catalytic converter to promote the chemical reactions that reduce exhaust-gas pollutants.

Secondary circuit The high-voltage circuit of the ignition system.

Sector gear An arc or section of gear teeth that is not a complete circle, such as the sector gear in the recirculating-ball steering gear.

Segments The bars of a commutator on the armature of a motor or generator.

Self-adjuster A mechanism used on drum brakes that compensates for lining wear by automatically adjusting the shoe-to-drum clearance.

Self-diagnostic system Indicating devices on the vehicle that alert the driver when something is wrong in the system.

Self-induction The inducing of a voltage in a current-carrying coil of wire because the current in that wire is changing.

Semiconductor A material that acts as an insulator under some conditions and as a conductor under other conditions.

Sensor An input device that receives and reacts to a signal, such as a change in voltage, temperature, or pressure, and relays that information (usually as a varying voltage signal) to the electronic control module (ECM).

Series circuit An electric circuit in which the devices are connected end to end, positive terminal to negative terminal. The same current flows through all the devices in the circuit.

Servo A device in a hydraulic system that converts hydraulic pressure to mechanical movement. Consists of a piston that moves in a cylinder as hydraulic pressure acts on it.

Setback The difference in vehicle wheelbase from one side to the other.

Shackle The swinging support by which one end of a leaf spring is attached to the vehicle body or frame.

Shift lever The lever used to change gears in a transmission. Also, the lever on the starting motor which moves the drive pinion into or out of mesh with the teeth in the ring gear around the flywheel or drive plate.

Shift solenoid In an electronically-controlled automatic transmission, a computer-controlled solenoid that opens or closes a fluid passage to a shift valve.

Shift timing In an automatic transmission, controlling when each shift occurs, either electronically or hydraulically.

Shift valve In an automatic transmission, a valve that moves to produce a shift from one gear ratio to another.

Shock absorber A device placed at each vehicle wheel to regulate spring rebound and compression.

Shoe In the brake system, a metal plate that supports the brake lining and absorbs and transmits braking forces.

Short block A new or reconditioned cylinder block assembled with new or usable internal parts.

Short circuit A defect in an electric circuit which permits current to take a short path, or circuit, instead of following the desired path.

Side clearance The clearance between the sides of moving parts when the sides do not serve as load-carrying surfaces.

Sight glass In an automotive air conditioner, a viewing glass or window in the refrigerant line or top of the receiver that allows a visual check of the refrigerant passing from the receiver to the evaporator.

Silicone rubber See Aerobic gasket material.

Single-point injection See Throttle-body injection.

Single-point repair A repair to a single part or failed component that should be made only after diagnosis and inspection show that no related parts are worn or damaged.

Slip joint In the drive train, a variable-length connection that permits the drive shaft to change its effective length.

Slip rings In an alternator, the rings that form rotating connections between the field winding and the brushes.

Solar cell A semiconductor device that generates a small dc voltage when exposed to light. Also called a photovoltaic cell.

Solder A soft metal alloy, or mixture, of tin and lead.

Solenoid An electromechanical device which, when connected to an electrical source such as a battery, produces a mechanical movement.

Solid-state device A device, such as a diode or transistor, that has no moving parts except electrons.

South pole The pole at which magnetic lines of force enter a magnet.

Spark advance See Advance.

Spark-ignition engine An engine operating on the Otto cycle, in which the fuel is ignited by the heat from an electric spark as it jumps the gap at the end of the spark plug.

Spark plug The assembly, which includes a pair of electrodes and an insulator, that provides a spark gap in the engine cylinder.

Spark-plug heat range The distance heat must travel from the center electrode to reach the outer shell of the spark plug and enter the cylinder head.

Spark test A quick check of the ignition system to determine if the high-voltage surges from the coil secondary winding are being delivered to the spark plugs.

Specific gravity The weight per unit volume of a substance as compared with the weight per unit volume of water.

Speedometer A device or display in the instrument panel that shows the driver how fast the vehicle is moving.

Splayed crankpins The slight spreading apart of a connecting-rod journal, or crankpin, in a V-type engine so that each rod has its own crankpin. This reduces vibration in some V-6 engines that have a 90-degree angle between the banks.

Spool valve A spool-shaped valve or rod with indented sections used to control oil flow in automatic transmissions and power-steering gears.

Sprag clutch In automatic transmissions, a one-way clutch using cam-shaped locking elements that can transmit power in one direction, but not in the other.

Spring A device that changes shape under stress or force but returns to its original shape when the stress or force is removed. In the suspension system, the spring absorbs road shocks by flexing and twisting.

Stabilizer bar A transverse-mounted spring-steel bar, usually connected to the lower-control arms, that helps reduce body roll on turns and when driving on rough or uneven surfaces.

Starting motor A small, powerful electric motor that converts electrical energy from the battery into mechanical energy to spin the crankshaft and start the engine.

Starting-motor drive The drive mechanism and gear on the end of the starting-motor armature shaft, used to couple the starting motor to, and disengage it from, the ring-gear teeth.

Static balance The balance of an object while it is not moving.

Stator The stationary member of a machine, such as an electric motor or generator, in or about which a rotor revolves. In an alternator, the part that contains the conductors within which the field rotates. In a torque converter, the third member, or stationary reactor, between the impeller and turbine, which changes the direction of fluid flow and provides torque multiplication under certain conditions.

Steering arm The arm attached to the steering knuckle, and to which the tie-rod end attaches, that turns the knuckle and wheel in and out for steering.

Steering axis The line around which a front wheel swings for steering.

Steering-axis inclination (SAI) The inward tilt of the steering axis from the vertical as viewed from the front of the vehicle.

Steering gear That part of the steering system located at the lower end of the steering shaft; changes the rotary motion of the steering wheel into linear motion of the front wheels for steering.

Steering kickback Sharp and rapid movement of the steering wheel that results when the front tires meet holes or bumps in the road.

Steering knuckle The part that includes the spindle, on which a front wheel is mounted, and which is turned for steering; supported by the wheel and upper and lower ball joints, or a lower ball joint and the upper strut mount.

Steering offset See Scrub radius.

Steering ratio The number of degrees that the steering wheel must be turned to pivot the front wheels one degree.

Steering shaft The shaft extending from the steering wheel to the steering gear; usually enclosed by the steering column.

Steering system The mechanism that enables the driver to control the direction of vehicle travel.

Stoichiometric ratio In a spark-ignition engine, the ideal air-fuel-mixture ratio of 14.7:1 which must be maintained on engines with catalytic converters.

Stratified In layers.

Stratified-charge engine An engine in which the air and fuel are not mixed uniformly in the combustion chamber. The diesel engine is a stratified-charge engine.

Stroke In an engine cylinder, the distance that the piston moves in traveling from BDC to TDC or from TDC to BDC.

Strut A bar that connects the lower control arm to the vehicle body or frame; used with a beam-type lower control arm which has only one point of attachment to the body or frame. Also called a brake-reaction rod.

Subframe An engine cradle that fastens under the bottom front of the body.

Suction pressure In an air conditioner, the pressure at the inlet to the compressor; the compressor intake pressure.

Sulfation The lead sulfate which forms on battery plates as a result of the battery action that produces electric current.

Sulfuric acid See Electrolyte.

Sulfur oxides (SO_2) Acids that can form in small amounts as the result of a reaction between hot exhaust gas and the catalyst in a catalytic converter.

Supercharger A pump that precompresses the air or air-fuel mixture before it enters the engine cylinder for further compression.

Suspension The system of springs and other parts which supports the upper part of a vehicle on its axles and wheels.

Suspension arm In the front suspension, an upper or lower control arm with an inner end that pivots on the body or frame and a ball joint in the outer end that attaches to the steering knuckle.

Suspension height The distance measured from some specific point on the body, frame, or suspension to the ground.

Suspension system Absorbs the shock of the tires and wheels meeting bumps and holes in the road. Includes springs, shock absorbers, and related parts between the wheels and vehicle body or frame.

Sway bar See Stabilizer bar.

Switch A device that opens and closes an electric circuit.

Synchronizer A device in the transmission that synchronizes gears about to be meshed, so that no gear clash will occur.

Synthetic oil An artificial oil that is manufactured, and not a natural mineral oil made from petroleum.

Tampering The removing, disconnecting, damaging, or rendering inoperative any emission-control or safety device on a motor vehicle or motor-vehicle engine.

Temperature indicator A gauge or electronic display that indicates to the driver the temperature of the engine coolant, or a light that comes on if the coolant gets too hot.

Thermal Of or pertaining to heat.

Thermal vacuum switch (TVS) A vacuum-control valve that senses engine-coolant temperature and then opens or closes to control distribution of intake-manifold vacuum. Also called ported vacuum switch (PVS).

Thermistor A temperature-sensitive resistor whose resistance varies with temperature; used as the sensing device in engine coolant-temperature sending units and in air-temperature sensors.

Thermometer An instrument for measuring heat intensity, or temperature.

Thermostat A device for the automatic regulation of temperature; usually contains a temperature-sensitive element that expands or contracts to open or close off the flow of air, a gas, or a liquid.

Thermostatic Temperature-operated, as a switch or valve.

Thermostatic gauge An indicating device (for fuel quantity, oil pressure, engine temperature) that contains a thermostatic blade.

Thermostatic switch In a cycling-clutch air-conditioner, an electric switch that turns the compressor clutch on and off to prevent water from freezing on the evaporator core, and to control the temperature of the air flowing from the evaporator. Used instead of an electric pressure switch.

Three-way catalytic converter A catalytic converter that uses rhodium and other catalysts to limit the amounts of the air pollutants HC, CO, and NOx in the exhaust gas.

Throttle body The air-control device for fuel-injected and carbureted spark-ignition engines. The amount of air that enters is primarily controlled by the position of the throttle valve which opens or closes as the driver presses and releases the accelerator pedal.

Throttle-body injection (TBI) A gasoline fuel-injection system that sprays fuel under pressure into the intake air passing through the throttle body on the intake manifold. Also called single-point injection.

Throttle-position sensor (TPS) A variable-resistance sensor on the throttle body that continuously sends a varying voltage signal, which is proportional to the throttle valve position, to the electronic control module.

Throttle pressure In a hydraulically-operated automatic transmission, the pressure applied to one end of the shift valve which changes as engine throttle-position or intake-manifold vacuum changes. Also called throttle-valve or TV pressure.

Throttle valve In spark-ignition engines, a disc valve in the throttle body that pivots in response to accelerator-pedal position to admit more or less air or air-fuel mixture into the intake manifold, thereby controlling engine speed and power.

Throwout bearing See Release bearing.

Thrust angle The angle formed between the vehicle and geometric centerlines and the thrust line.

Thrust bearing A bearing that absorbs the force, or thrust, parallel to the axis of rotation of a shaft. The bearing supports axial loads while preventing axial movement of a loaded shaft. In the engine, the main bearing that has thrust faces to prevent excessive end play, or forward and backward movement, of the crankshaft. In the clutch, the release bearing is a thrust bearing.

Thrust line A line running the length of the vehicle, from the midpoint between the two rear wheels, that determines the direction the vehicle will travel if unaffected by the front wheels.

Tie rod In the steering system, an adjustable-length rod that, as the steering wheel turns, transfers the steering force and direction from the rack or linkage to the steering arm.

Timing In an engine, delivery of the ignition spark or operation of the valves (in relation to the piston position) for the power stroke. See Ignition timing and Valve timing.

Tire The casing-and-tread assembly (with or without a tube) that is mounted on a vehicle wheel and usually filled with compressed air to transmit braking and tractive forces to the road.

Toe The amount, in inches, millimeters, or degrees, by which the front of a wheel points inward (toe-in) or outward (toe-out).

Top dead center (TDC) The piston position when the piston has reached the upper limit of its travel in the cylinder and the center line of the connecting rod is parallel to the cylinder walls.

Torque Twisting or turning force.

Torque converter In an automatic transmission, a fluid coupling that incorporates a stator to permit a torque increase.

Torque-converter clutch A clutch in the torque converter that can be engaged automatically or electronically to lock the transmission input shaft to the engine crankshaft, eliminating any slippage through the torque converter.

Torque multiplication In a transmission, mechanical advantage gained by using a lower gear or through the action of the vortex flow in the torque converter.

Torsional vibration Rotary vibration that causes a twist-untwist action in a rotating shaft, so that a part of the shaft repeatedly moves ahead or lags behind the remainder of the shaft.

Torsion-bar spring A long, straight bar fastened to the vehicle body or frame at one end and to a control arm at the other. Spring action is produced by a twisting of the bar as the control arm moves up and down.

Tracking Rear wheels following directly behind (in the tracks of) the front wheels.

Traction-control system A system used with an antilock-brake system to prevent unwanted wheelspin during acceleration.

Transaxle A power-transmission device, attached to one end of the engine, that combines the functions of the transmission and the drive axle (final drive and differential) into a single assembly.

Transfer case An auxiliary transmission mounted behind the main transmission. Used to divide engine power and transfer it to both front and rear drive axles, either full time or part time.

Transistor A three-terminal semiconductor device used to control the flow of an electric current; can act as an electric switch, amplifier, or detector.

Transmission A metal case containing an assembly of shafts, gears, and related parts, used to transmit power from the engine to the driveshaft or final drive of an automotive vehicle; provides different gear ratios, as well as neutral and reverse. May be manual, automatic, or continuously-variable.

Tread The part of the tire that contacts the road. It is the thickest part of the tire and has a raised pattern molded into it to provide traction for driving and stopping.

Trigger A device, pulse, or other signal used to release or activate a mechanism, or cause another event.

Trouble Any disturbance or abnormal condition that affects the operation of an engine, machine, circuit, or system.

Trouble diagnosis Determining the cause of a trouble.

Tuneup A procedure for inspecting, testing, and adjusting an engine, and replacing any worn parts, to restore engine performance.

Turbocharger A centrifugal supercharger or air pump, driven by the engine exhaust gas, that forces an additional amount of air or air-fuel mixture into the intake manifold.

Turning radius The difference in the angles of the front wheels in a turn; the inner wheel toes out more. Also called toe-out on turns.

Two-stroke cycle The two piston strokes during which fuel intake, compression, combustion, and exhaust take place in a two-stroke-cycle engine.

Two-wheel drive A vehicle with four wheels and one drive axle, so only two wheels are driven.

Undersize Either an inside or outside diameter that is less than standard size.

Unitized-body construction The frame and body parts are welded together to form a single unit.

Universal joint A connecting joint that allows power to be transmitted between two rotating shafts that are operating at an angle to each other. See Constant-velocity universal joint and CV joint.

Vacuum The absence of air. Negative gauge pressure, or a pressure less than atmospheric pressure.

Vacuum advance The advancing (or retarding) of ignition timing by changes in intake-manifold vacuum, reflecting throttle opening and engine load. Also, a mechanism on the ignition distributor that uses intake-manifold vacuum to advance the timing of the spark to the spark plugs.

Vacuum modulator See Modulator valve.

Vacuum motor A small motor with a spring and diaphragm, usually operated by intake-manifold vacuum; moves a diaphragm-attached lever in response to changes in the applied vacuum.

Vacuum pump A pump used to evacuate a closed system or container by exhausting the air or gases and maintaining a less-than-atmospheric pressure within.

Vacuum switch A switch that closes or opens its contacts in response to changes in the applied vacuum.

Valve A device that can be opened or closed to allow or stop the flow of a liquid or gas. The word preceding "valve" usually designates the type of valve (needle valve) or the function it performs (check valve).

Valve body A casting located in the oil pan, which contains most of the valves for the hydraulic control system of an automatic transmission.

Valve clearance The clearance in the valve train when the valve is closed. The lash, or air gap, that allows for expansion due to heat.

Valve guide In the cylinder head, a cylindrical part or hole in which the valve is assembled and moves up and down.

Valve lifter In OHV engines, the cylindrical part that transmits cam-lobe movement to the pushrod, causing the rocker arm to rock and open the valve. May be fixed-length or adjustable "solid lifters," or oil-pressure operated "hydraulic lifters" which are non-adjustable. See Hydraulic valve lifter.

Valve overlap The number of degrees of crankshaft rotation during which the intake and exhaust valves are open at the same time.

Valve rotator A device often installed in place of the valve-spring retainer, which turns the valve slightly as it opens.

Valve seat The surface against which a valve comes to rest to provide a seal against leakage.

Valve-seat insert A metal ring installed in the cylinder head to act as a valve seat.

Valve spring The coil spring attached to each valve that closes the valve after the cam lobe has rotated past the valve-open position.

Valve tappet See Valve lifter.

Valve timing The timing of the opening and closing of the valves in relation to the piston position.

Valve train The series of parts that open and close the valves by transferring cam-lobe movement to the valves.

Vane A flat, extended surface that is moved around an axis by or in a fluid; used in air pumps, power-steering pumps, water pumps, and turbochargers.

Vane airflow meter In the engine air-induction system, a sensor with a movable vane connected to a variable resistance; calibrated to measure the amount of air flowing into the engine. The resulting varying voltage signal, or output signal, is sent to the ECM.

Vaporization A change of state from liquid to vapor or gas, by evaporation or boiling; a general term including both evaporation and boiling.

Vapor-liquid separator A device in the evaporative emission control system that prevents liquid fuel from traveling to the engine through the charcoal-canister vapor line.

Vapor lock In the fuel system, a condition in which the fuel boils, vaporizing

and forming bubbles that prevent normal fuel delivery to the carburetor or fuel injectors.

Vapor-return line A line from the fuel pump to the fuel tank through which any vapor that has formed in the pump is returned to the tank.

Variable-speed fan An engine fan that will not exceed a predetermined speed or will rotate only as fast as required to prevent engine overheating.

Variable-venturi (VV) carburetor A carburetor in which the size of the venturi changes according to the engine speed and load.

Vehicle identification number The number assigned to each vehicle by its manufacturer.

Ventilation The circulating of fresh air through any space to replace impure air.

Venturi A narrowing restriction in a carburetor through which the air entering the engine must pass.

Venturi vacuum Vacuum in the venturi of a carburetor which increases with the speed of the airflow through it.

Vibration damper A device usually attached to the front end of the crankshaft to reduce the torsional vibration, or twisting action, caused by the cylinder firing impulses. Also called harmonic balancer.

Viscosity The resistance to flow exhibited by a liquid. A thick oil has greater viscosity than a thin oil.

Viscous coupling A type of self-actuated fluid coupling used in the drive train to automatically lock and unlock, transferring power to non-slipping wheels if the normal drive wheels lose traction.

Viscous friction The resistance to motion between layers of liquid.

Voice alert system A type of driver information system in the vehicle which can speak several words or phrases to the driver.

Voice command system A type of interactive control system in which the driver can give certain spoken commands and the vehicle system responds by performing the act or providing the information desired.

Volatility A measure of the ease with which a liquid vaporizes; has a direct relationship to the flammability of a fuel.

Volt The unit of measurement of electrical pressure in an electric circuit; it takes 1 volt to force a current of 1 ampere through a resistance of 1 ohm.

Voltage The force which causes electrons to flow in a conductor. The difference in electrical pressure (or potential) between two points in a circuit.

Voltage regulator A device that prevents excessive alternator or generator voltage by rapidly inserting and remov-

ing a resistance in, or opening and closing, the field circuit.

Voltmeter An instrument or meter for measuring the potential difference (voltage) between different points of an electric circuit. In the vehicle instrument panel, the voltmeter shows the voltage across the battery, or charging voltage.

Volumetric efficiency A measure of how completely the cylinder fills with air-fuel mixture during the intake stroke of a spark-ignition engine.

Wander The tendency of a vehicle to drift from one side of the road to the other.

Wankel engine A rotary engine, usually with two three-lobe rotors, that turn eccentrically in an oval chamber to produce power.

Wastegate A control device on a turbocharger which limits boost pressure, thereby preventing engine and turbocharger damage.

Water jacket The space between the inner and outer shells of the cylinder block or cylinder head, through which coolant circulates.

Water pump In the cooling system, the device that circulates coolant between the engine water jackets and the radiator.

Wear sensor A tab on a disc-brake shoe that causes a squealing sound when the brake pad is worn thin.

Wheel A disc or spokes with a hub (revolving around an axle) at the center and a rim around the outside for mounting the tire.

Wheel alignment A series of tests and adjustments to ensure that the wheels and tires are properly positioned on the vehicle and running with the specified relationship with the road and with each other.

Wheel balancer A device that checks a wheel-and-tire assembly (statically, dynamically, or both) for balance.

Wheelbase The distance between the centerlines of the front and rear axles.

Wheel cylinder In the drum-brake hydraulic system, usually a dual-piston hydraulic cylinder, or servo, mounted on the brake backing plate. Hydraulic pressure from the master cylinder pushes the wheel-cylinder pistons outward, forcing the brake shoes into contact with the brake drum.

Wiring diagram A drawing or schematic that shows the wires, connections, and components in an electric circuit or system.

Wiring harness A group of individually insulated wires, wrapped together to form a neat, easily installed bundle.

Work The moving of an object against an opposing force.

INDEX